P. Harman

P. G. O'NEILL

# JAPANESE NAMES

## A Comprehensive Index by Characters and Readings

JOHN WEATHERHILL, INC.

*New York & Tokyo*

First edition, 1972

Published by John Weatherhill, Inc., 149 Madison Avenue, New York, New York 10016, with editorial offices at 7–6–13 Roppongi, Minato-ku, Tokyo 106, Japan.  Printed in Japan.

LCC Card No. 70–157274 ISBN 0–8348–0060–8

# TABLE OF CONTENTS

# PREFACE

There is no final or complete solution to the problems of reading Japanese names written in Chinese characters. Such characters usually have special name readings which are distinct from the readings of the characters in their ordinary meaningful usages and therefore have to be learned separately. Virtually all these characters have more than one recognized name reading, and may have other unpredictable ones as well; and the difficulty of choosing the appropriate reading for a particular name may be compounded when, as is usually the case, it is written with two or more characters. Then the same combination of characters may have to be read differently according to whether it refers, for example, to a person, a place, or a literary work. Finally, the same characters referring to the very same person or thing should sometimes ideally be read differently according to the situation or context in which they are used.

It is therefore not surprising that, faced with such complexity, the Japanese should regard possible but mistaken readings with equanimity. It is usually only in speech, however, that they have to commit themselves to a particular reading of a name, for, when writing in their own language, they can leave the name in the obscurity of its characters. Japanese names are thus less of a practical problem for the Japanese themselves than they are for most other people who are concerned with Japan.

The present index is intended to help with the problem of reading Japanese names within the limits of what is feasible. It aims to be comprehensive, for example, but cannot in the nature of things hope to be complete. The impossibility of completeness can be realized from the fact that, while 300 Chinese characters with only one reading each could provide nearly 90,000 possible two-character names, this index contains nearly 3,000 different characters used in names. Nearly all of these have two or more name readings each, and many of them can be used alone as single-character names as well as in combinations with other characters.

The index is comprehensive, then, in the sense that it covers a wide range of Japanese names, some 36,000 in all, and is in two parts to provide both the readings of names written in characters and the characters for known names. It has also been designed to reduce the problems of choosing one from a number of possible readings for the same character or characters by 1) giving the names of nearly 7,000 individuals of literary, historical, or artistic importance; 2) identifying the broad category in which every name reading was found so that the appropriate one can be chosen when alternative readings are in different categories; and 3) giving alternative name readings within the same category in a descending order of frequency so that the first reading in each category is normally the most likely one.

Then, too, each character listed is followed by its name readings as a single character and also by its main name readings when used in combination with other characters, again in descending order of frequency. This means that, by combining the first readings given for the various characters of a name, its most likely reading can in many cases be found even if the name is not listed as a separate entry.

The index was thus compiled to provide the certain readings of most of the names likely to be met in normal circumstances, and the most probable readings for others.

The 36,000-odd names covered by each of the two parts are made up as follows: 13,500 surnames; 11,000 personal names; 6,800 literary, historical, and artistic names; 4,400 place names; and 300 Japanese era names *(nengō)*. These names were collected from a variety of sources, but most of them were obtained by taking all the appropriate name entries from the following main sources:

Araki R. (ed.), *Nanori jiten,* Tōkyōdō, 1959
Fujiki, K. (ed.), *Nihonshi shōjiten,* Gakuseisha, 1960
Gillis and P'ai, *Japanese Personal Names,* Peking, 1940
———, *Japanese Surnames,* Peking, 1939
Hisamatsu S. et al. (ed.), *Gendai Nihon bungaku daijiten,* Meiji Shoin, 1965
Ienaga S. et al. (ed.), *Nihonshi,* Iwanami Shōjiten series, 1957
Kataoka R. (ed.), *Nihon bungaku: kindai,* Iwanami Shōjiten series, 1958
*Nihon bunken chizu,* Nitchi Shuppan, 1964
Takaki I. (ed.), *Nihon bungaku: koten,* Iwanami Shōjiten series, 1955

These sources were then supplemented from the Tokyo telephone directory and a list of personal names intended to help parents to choose names for their children, thus trying to ensure that no common surname or personal name had been missed, and from listings of unusual literary, historical, and geographical name readings in a number of reference works, which were also used to decide doubtful or conflicting readings. Such supplementary sources included the following:

*Daijiten,* 26 vols., Heibonsha, 1934–35
*Engeki hyakka daijiten,* 6 vols., Heibonsha, 1962
Fujimura T. (ed.), *Nihon bungaku daijiten,* 8 vols., Shinchōsha, 1952–53
Haga Y., *Nihon jinmei jiten,* Ōkura Shoten, 1914
Koop and Inada, *Japanese Names and How to Read Them,* Eastern Press, 1923, and Routledge and Kegan Paul, 1963
Nakayama Y. (ed.), *Nankun jiten,* Tōkyōdō, 1966
Noma S. (ed.), *Nihon bijutsu jiten,* Tōkyōdō, 1967
Ōrui, N. (ed.), *Sekai jinmei jiten: Tōyō hen,* Tōkyōdō, 1967
Satō N. (ed.), *Sekai chimei jiten: Nihon Tōyō hen,* Tōkyōdō, 1967
Yashiro K. et al (ed.), *Kokushi daijiten,* Yoshikawa Kōbunkan, 1931
Yoshida T. (ed.), *Dainihon chimei jisho,* 7 vols., Fuzanbō, 1911–13

My sincere thanks are due to my wife for invaluable help in the laborious task of sorting, collating, and numbering the entries, and to the staff of John Weatherhill, Inc., under the editorship of Meredith Weatherby, for their care and expertise, which have greatly improved both the content and the presentation of the index.

P. G. O'Neill

*London, 1971*

# EXPLANATORY NOTES

**1. Type of Names.** The reading of a Japanese name written in characters can vary with the context in which it is used. For example, the same two characters are read Kumano as a surname or place name, but Yuya as the name of a medieval courtesan or the Nō play based upon her life. It is necessary, therefore, to distinguish name readings so that the appropriate one can be chosen in each case.

With the exception of era names, which are identified by the first and last years of the period in question, the different types of names are distinguished from each other in this index by the use of an identifying letter or letters in italics. Since many names belong to more than one category, many surnames and place names in particular being identical, this system of identifying readings has allowed such duplications to be combined into single entries without loss of precision, thus reducing the total number of entries in each part of the index to approximately 32,000.

The category of each entry is indicated in the following manner:

**Surnames** are followed by the letter *s*. This group consists mainly of ordinary family names, but it also includes some assumed literary or artistic names to which personal names were normally attached when referring to an individual.

Since a surname is an independent element never modified by other group letters showing literary, historical, or artistic associations, the hyphen used between other letters to show that they refer to separate items (see below under *Literary, historical, and artistic names*) has been omitted after *s*. Thus, *sp* means that the reading was found listed as a surname and, quite separately, as a place name too.

**Personal names** are indicated by the letters *m* and *f*, which show that they are mainly or exclusively male or female respectively.

**Place names** are indicated by the letter *p*. These include all Japanese prefectures, districts, cities, towns, wards, and villages, as well as the main foreign place names likely to be found written in Chinese characters.

The usual spelling of foreign place names has been given in quotation marks after the romanized Japanese version of the name and the appropriate identifying letter or letters, e.g., 'Kafu *p* "Washington." '

In the few cases where the Japanese reading in question is used for both a Japanese and a foreign place, the usual spelling of the foreign name given within quotation marks is enclosed in square brackets. Thus, 'Kantō *p* ["Kwantung"] ' means that Kantō is a Japanese place name and also a foreign place name usually spelled Kwantung.

**Literary, historical, and artistic names** are indicated by the letters *l, h,* and *a,* respectively. When used alone these letters generally signify written works in the case of *l, h,* or *lh,* and art objects in the case of *a*; but they have also been applied to technical terms, movements, organizations, etc., as appropriate. Such entries have been kept within limits by omitting in nearly all cases those which are ordinary meaningful words or phrases and can therefore be found in the standard dictionaries.

In most cases, however, *l, h,* and *a* will be found in combination with other identifying letters, the main letter being given first. Thus *ml* is a male of literary importance, an author, while *lm* (e.g., Hikaru Genji) signifies a "literary male," that is, a male character in a literary work. A hyphen between identifying letters separates distinct elements (except that, as explained above, a hyphen is not given after *s* because this always indicates a separate element). The entry 'Mitsuko *f-l*,' for example, indicates that Mitsuko is a female name and, quite separately, is also of literary importance, being in all probability the title of a literary work.

Most of the entries in this category give both the family and personal names of particular literary, historical, or artistic figures and are therefore followed by *ml, fl, mh, ma, mlh* (a male of both literary and historical importance), etc. Personal names alone are generally followed by such combined group letters only when they can reasonably be taken as exclusive to the persons concerned; that is, when they are assumed names and not ordinary ones likely to be used by other people. Thus, in the case of the writer Natsume Sōseki, his ordinary personal name of Kinnosuke is followed only by *m*, while his assumed literary name of Sōseki is followed by *ml*.

In the names of literary and historical works, the very common final elements *monogatari* 'tale,' *nikki* 'diary,' etc., are omitted unless needed to distinguish the particular entry or unless the full name forms part of a following entry (e.g., *Ise monogatari* followed by *Ise monogatari ketsugishō*).

In the case of the names of non-Japanese persons, the usual spelling has been added in quotation marks, in the same way as for foreign place-names. Thus, 'Kōshi *mlh* "Confucius" ' means that Kōshi is a man of literary and historical importance who is generally known as Confucius.

**Era names** are distinguished by quoting the first and last years of the period to which they refer, e.g., 'Tokuji 1306–08.' (Since the second year of Tokuji was thus 1307, it will be seen that the Western year can be found by adding the year of the era in question to the year *preceding* the first date given.)

Occasionally era dates will be found after an identifying letter, e.g., 'Bunji *m* 1185–90.' This signifies that Bunji is a male name and also the name of the era 1185–90.

The purpose of this system of identification is to show the type of person or thing for which a particular reading is used. The category given will be the most common, and usually the only, application of the reading in question, but the descriptions of the names are not always exhaustive. Some names described only as *s*, for example, may be found also as place names, and vice versa. What the identifying letters show are the categories in which the readings were found within the source material.

In both parts of the index, identifying letters also apply to all following names until a semicolon or the end of the entry is reached. In other words, readings separated by only a comma are of the same type.

For a recapitulation of these identifying letters, see the table on page xvi.

**2. Romanization.** The romanization used is that of the modified Hepburn system as found in Kenkyūsha's *New Japanese-English Dictionary* (1954 ed.) and recommended in the draft proposals of both the U.S. and British Standards institutions. This form of romanization keeps *n* unchanged before other consonants, including *m, b,* or *p* (e.g., Shinbashi rather than Shimbashi), and it uses the macron for long vowels instead of doubling the vowel (e.g., *ō* instead of *oo*). This means that the basic spelling remains unchanged when, as often happens with common place names or in works for the general reader, no indication of long vowels is given. The following list shows alternative spellings according to other systems of romanization in the left-hand columns and the standard equivalents as used in this index on the right:

| | | | | | | | | |
|---|---|---|---|---|---|---|---|---|
| di | = | ji | dzu | = | zu | -mb- | = | -nb- |
| du | = | zu | gw- | = | g- | -mm- | = | -nm- |
| dy- | = | j- | hu | = | fu | -mp- | = | -np- |
| dzi | = | ji | kw- | = | k- | o | = | ō |

| | | | | | | | |
|---|---|---|---|---|---|---|---|
| oh | = ō | | ti | = chi | | wo | = o |
| oo | = ō | | tu | = tsu | | ye | = e |
| si | = shi | | ty- | = ch- | | zi | = ji |
| sy- | = sh- | | wi | = i | | zy- | = j- |

Many of these variants are examples of early forms of romanization, and some name spellings based on them still have a certain amount of currency. They have not been included in the index, but the following are some of the most common of these, listed with their standard equivalents on the right:

| | | | |
|---|---|---|---|
| Idzumo | = Izumo | Noh | = Nō |
| Itoh | = Itō | Ohno | = Ōno |
| Kohno | = Kōno | Satoh | = Satō |
| Kwannon | = Kannon | Uyeno | = Ueno |
| Kwansai | = Kansai | Yedo | = Edo |
| Meidi | = Meiji | Yezo | = Ezo |

Two problems of romanization are particularly intractable, since the pronunciation in these cases often varies from one person to another, or even with the same person at different times. The first of these is the problem of voiced and unvoiced consonants in names (e.g., Osawa/Ozawa, Yanagita/Yanagida, -kama/-gama, -shima/-jima, -hara/-bara/-wara/-ppara, etc.). The principle followed in this index is, in general, to give only the most common reading or, when two or more readings have more or less equal currency, the one with the unmodified consonant, e.g., Kamata rather than Kamada. It should be noted, however, that the sounds liable to this kind of variation (with the alternatives in parentheses) are:

ch (j)
h (b, w, *or* pp)
k (g)
s (z) *except for* sh (j)
t (d) *except for* ts (z)

The second problem is the pronunciation of names with a final vowel written with a separate character and coming immediately after a similar vowel (e.g., Iso-o, Hiro-o, Yu-u, etc.). Some speakers keep the two vowels separate, but often they are pronounced as an unbroken long vowel: Isō, Hirō, Yū, etc. In the index such names have been romanized with double letters, as Isoo, Hiroo, Yuu, etc., but the possibility of the alternative pronunciation and romanization should be borne in mind.

**3. Alternative Name Readings.** The readings given are basically those shown in the standard reference works. Sometimes, however, it has been necessary to add alternative readings because they are in such wide use. In most of these cases, the reference works give the official readings, but because it is difficult to know the correct readings of personal names, for example, and because the convenience of the shorter Sino-Japanese (*on*) readings of characters often leads to names being pronounced according to the *on* readings of the characters, especially in literary, academic, and artistic circles, two or more readings are sometimes found for the same name.

In Part I such alternatives have been separated by an oblique stroke and the more common alternatives have been given first, as usual; e.g., 'Kikuchi Kan/Hiroshi *ml*,' 'Itō Hirobumi/Hakubun *mh*.' In Part II the alternative readings are listed separately according to their alphabetical order.

**4. Forms of Chinese Characters.** The officially recommended forms of Chinese characters have been used for all *tōyō kanji* (Chinese characters in current use) listed in the index, including the 47 recommended for inclusion in the list by the Seventh National Language Commission of Inquiry in December, 1965, and the 31 recommended for omission from the list by the same commission, and for the 92 extra characters approved for use in personal names. All other characters have been used in their full, unsimplified forms as given in Ueda's *Daijiten,* except for just one or two that are virtually never used in their full forms, even in dictionaries, e.g., 餅 has been used in preference to 餠.

The character repetition sign 々 and variant forms of characters, such as 嶋 (for 島) and 閒 (for 間), have been given only when they are used to write the name of a particular person or thing. Thus, Nonomura Sōtatsu is given as 野々村宗達, and Uchida Hyakken as 内田百閒 because 々 and 閒 are regularly used in the names of the individuals in question.

**5. Concerning Part I: From Characters to Readings.** There are approximately 3,050 double-size initial Chinese characters listed in Part I, and they fall into three types: 1) numbered main-entry characters in the approved forms described above; b) numbered old and variant forms of the *tōyō kanji,* with cross-references to the main-entry characters, listed when there is a significant difference between the two forms; and c) a few unnumbered characters listed in possible alternative classification groups, with cross-references to the main entries.

**Main-entry characters.** To make it easier for the index to be used by people without formal Japanese-language training, the use of the traditional radical system of classification is avoided, and the characters are arranged first according to their total stroke count and then according to the way in which constituent elements are put together to form the whole character. This arrangement was developed from the method of grouping parts of characters into left, top, and frame or envelope elements used by Arthur Rose-Innes in his *Beginners' Dictionary of Chinese-Japanese Characters,* and is very similar to that used by Koop and Inada in their *Japanese Names and How to Read Them.**

For those familiar with the name readings of Japanese characters or with the radical system, other means of locating character entries are recommended (see Note 7 below).

Main-entry characters are followed first by their reference number and then, where appropriate, by one of the following small capital letters inside square brackets:

[T] for the 1,850 characters in the original *tōyō kanji* list (except for those coming under [O] below)
[O] for the 31 characters recommended for omission from the list by the National Language Commission of Inquiry in December 1965
[I] for the 47 characters recommended for inclusion in the list by the same Commission
[N] for the 92 extra characters approved for use in proper names only (except for five characters coming under [I] above)

Next come the name readings for the single character where these exist; and finally, within parentheses, come the main component readings of the character (that is, readings used in names only in combination with similar readings of other characters). Whenever there is a choice of name or component reading, the first one listed within a particular group is the most common reading.

* See the introductory sections of this latter work for detailed accounts of the various types of Japanese names and much background information. For a good general account of Japanese names and useful bibliographical advice, see chapters 4 and 5 in Webb's *Research in Japanese Sources: A Guide,* Columbia University Press, 1963.

**Arrangement of name readings.** When there are two or more possible name readings for the same character or characters, the most common one is given first. This is followed by other name readings in the same group, and then by the name readings in the other groups, also as far as possible in a descending order of frequency of use.

**Arrangement of component readings.** The standard Sino-Japanese *(on)* readings are given first in small capitals. They are followed in lower-case type by the other readings for which the character may be found used in names, consisting mainly of the native Japanese *(kun)* readings but including also some variants or corruptions of the *on* readings. The readings are given as far as possible in a descending order of priority.

If the probable reading of a name written with two or more characters is being sought, it will help to remember that *kun* readings are more common in Japanese names as a whole than *on* readings; but this should be checked for each character where possible by comparing the first *on* and *kun* readings listed with the first part of any multi-character names given below the main-entry character in question.

**Multi-character names.** Names written with more than one character appear under the first, main-entry characters, where they are listed according to the number of strokes in the second characters, in ascending order. These numbers are printed beside second characters in names as a guide, where there are large numbers of subentries.

**6. Concerning Part II: From Readings to Characters.** This section is intended to serve primarily as an index to Part I, and the entries in it are arranged in straightforward alphabetical order. There are two main types of entry in this section: full names, listed with an initial upper-case letter, e.g., 'Tanaka'; and component readings, listed in parentheses and with initial lower-case letters, e.g., '(mochi)'.

Where a name can be written in more than one way, the different character versions are arranged first under the various name categories in the order *s, m, f, p, l, h,* and *a* (with each followed by its sub-categories, *sm, sp,* etc.) and within each group according to an ascending order of the number of strokes in the characters. It was not practicable to try to arrange these character versions in any order of frequency but, in the case of surnames at least, the most common way of writing the name can often be seen by looking at the names of individuals with that surname given in following entries. Component readings are also arranged according to an ascending order of the number of strokes in the characters.

A number given after a character entry is the Part I reference number for the initial character of the name. The number is not repeated with every entry but applies to all following entries until a new number occurs.

**7. Finding Readings and Characters.** The characters for the Japanese names listed and for component name readings can be found by simply looking these up in Part II, the alphabetical index. There are, however, three ways of finding in Part I the reading or readings of a name written in characters, the first being recommended as the quickest:

a) If any name reading of the first character is known, look up that reading (or a name beginning with that reading) in Part II, and use the reference number for that character to find the entries listed under it in Part I. For example, if the reading of 池尾 is being sought and it is known that 池 can be read *ike* in names, look for *Ike,* (*ike*), or any entry begining with *Ike* (written 池) in Part II. This will show that names beginning with this character are listed in Part I under main-entry character 251.

b) Find the Part I character number by looking up the character under the traditional radical system in Appendix 1.

c) Find the first character in Part I from its total number of strokes and its character type as explained in Note 8 below, using the columns of characters given in the page margins as a guide. Then, if it is a multiple-character name, look up the second and subsequent characters according to their total strokes.

If the character entry has different readings in more than one category, choose the reading in the category appropriate to the particular context. If there are alternative readings within the same category, the first reading given is the most common one.

**8. Rules for Character Classification.** Characters have been classified from their printed forms throughout, and are divided into ever smaller groups according to:

a) Their total stroke-count.
b) Whether they have a separate *l*efthand element (L-type), *t*op element (T-type), *f*rame element (F-type), or are indivisible *u*nits (U-type). Thus, 得 is 11 L, 字 is 6 T, 病 is 10 F, and 来 is 7 U.
c) The number of strokes in left, top, or frame elements. Thus, 得 is 11 L3, 字 is 6 T3, 病 is 10 F5, and 来 remains 7 U.

These three stages take the classification as far as is needed for the purposes of this index, and most characters can be grouped according to them without difficulty or further explanation; but the following rules will help to make the classification more reliable and consistent.

**Counting of strokes.** The system used here differs in some particulars from the traditional one, again in order to make it possible for persons without formal Japanese-language training to use the index. There are only two rules and one special case:

a) When two lines form an angle at the top right of a character or part of a character without the top line projecting, they are counted as ONE stroke. For example, 九 is 2 strokes, 口 is 3, and 国 is 8; but 文 is 4 strokes because the horizontal line projects beyond the other line forming the angle.
b) All other strokes and all other lines forming distinct angles are counted separately. Thus, 山 is 4 strokes, 母 6, 狂 7, 对 7, and 妥 8; but 乙 is only 1 stroke because at the bottom left the stroke changes direction but does not form a distinct, sharp angle.
c) Old and variant forms of *tōyō kanji* are listed with cross-references to the main entries under the modern forms, with the following exception: *tōyō kanji* with 辶 in their old forms (e.g., 近, 迫) are given only in their modern forms, as 近, 迫, etc., when there is no other difference between the two forms of the characters.

**Classification into character types.** The classification of characters into L, T, F, and U types is decided according to the following principles:

a) L-type and T-type characters: L and T elements are formed either by: 1) the first space, going from left to right or top to bottom respectively, which separates one stroke or more from the rest of the character, e.g., 言 7 T1, 仲 6 L2, 吉 6 T3; or, if there is no space, by 2) the first line through a 'breaking point' where elements of two strokes or more join at only one point, e.g., 寺 is 6 T2, 先 6 T3, and 古 5 T2 (but 白 is 5 U and 里 is 7 U because the top and bottom strokes respectively are only single lines joined to the rest of the character).
Spaces or lines through breaking points may be completely straight or they may bend a little in the middle provided that their extremities form part of what would be roughly the same vertical or horizontal line; e.g., 仏 is 5 L2, 含 7 T3, and 糸 8 T5, but both 多 and 多 are U-type characters because a line dividing their separate elements would clearly be

slanting. (Use common sense rather than a very rigid application of this rule, particularly in the case of a vertical dividing line. One or two elements in some types of print may have a line slanting under them slightly, e.g., 糸 in 統, 絣, 緘, etc., and 臣 in 臥, etc.; or may themselves overhang a little, e.g., 耳 in 取, 耽, 眩, etc. But 糸, 臣, and 耳 are all clearly lefthand elements in these cases, and the characters are therefore classified as L type.)

The top element 亠 (as in 立 5 U, 亦 6 U, and 商 11 F8) is treated like a single stroke for classification purposes; that is, it cannot stand as a separate element unless it is divided from the rest of the character by a space. Thus, 市 is 5 U, but 高 is 10 T2.

b) F-type characters are those in which part of the character is enclosed on two or more sides (e.g., 灰 6 F2, 風 9 F2, 国 8 F3), without joining the surround at more than one point: 日 is therefore 4 U.

Since division through a space takes precedence over division through touching elements, some characters are F-type as a result: 尚, for example, is not 8 T3 but 8 F5.

A short curved stroke rather like an apostrophe (as distinct from a straight line) is not enough to make a framed element. Thus, the stroke at the top right of 戈, etc., forms an indivisible part of that element, and 我 is 7 U and 為 is 9 F5.

When there are two possible framed elements with different numbers of strokes, choose the one with more strokes. Thus, 武 is 8 F4 (the framed elements being the 止 part) and 魁 is 15 F11.

When there are two possible framed elements with the same number of strokes, they cancel each other out and neither is taken as a framed element. Thus, 雨 is 8 U, 坐 7 U, and 爽 13 T8.

c) U-type characters are those which contain no L,T, or F elements.

To sum up, then, in deciding the group to which a character belongs: a) look for a space separating one or more strokes; b) look for a 'breaking point' between parts with two or more strokes each; and c) classify the character as L,T, or F if there is such a space or breaking point, and as U if there is not.

There are inevitably a few characters which would require more detailed rules to place them unquestionably in only one classification group, but there is no need to go to such lengths. Cross-references have been given for most of these characters, and the following remarks will serve as a guide to these borderline cases:

a) Characters which might be either T- or F-type (e.g., 奈, 泰, 尽) have been taken as T-type, since this group comes first in the order of classification.

b) The common radical and lefthand element 忄 (as in 快, 性, etc.) has been classed as L3 rather than as L1, in order to preserve it as a unit and to keep it parallel to 彳 (as in 行), 氵 (as in 流), etc.

c) The characters 水 and 火 are both classed as 4 L2, rather than as 4 L1, since they are best divided by a straight line.

d) In the printed forms of characters, straight 'legs' (as in 只, etc.) are usually separated from the elements above them by a space. Curved legs (as in 兄, etc.), on the other hand, are attached to the top element and therefore indivisible from it. Thus 貝 is classified as 7 T5 and 見 as 7 U.

# ABBREVIATIONS AND SIGNS

*a* = (item of) artistic importance
*f* = female name (or title)
*fa* = female of artistic importance (e.g., actress, dancer, painter)
*fh* = female of historical importance
*fl* = female of literary importance
*f-l* = female name; also item of literary importance
*h* = (item of) historical importance
*ha* = (item of) historical and artistic importance
[I] = a character recommended for inclusion in the *tōyō kanji* list
*l* = (item of) literary importance
*la* = item of literary and artistic importance (e.g., a play, song)
*l-a* = item of literary importance; also item of artistic importance
*lam* = 'literary and artistic male,' i.e., a male character in a literary and artistic work (e.g., a play)
*lf* = 'literary female,' i.e., a female character in a literary work
*lh* = (item of) literary and historical importance
*lm* = 'literary male,' i.e., a male character in a literary work
*m* = male name (or title)
*ma* = male of artistic importance (e.g., actor, painter, swordsmith)
*m-f* = male name; also female name
*mh* = male of historical importance
*ml* = male of literary importance
*mla* = male of literary and artistic importance (e.g., an actor-playwright)
*m-la* = male name; also item of literary and historical importance
*mlh* = male of literary and historical importance
[N] = a character approved for use in names only
[O] = a character recommended for omission from the *tōyō kanji* list
*p* = place name
*ph* = place name of historical importance (e.g., the name of an old province no longer in common use)
*s* = surname (Note: Since a surname is always a separate item, a hyphen is never used immediately after *s*)
*sf* = surname; also female name
*sm* = surname; also male name
*sm-f* = surname; also male name; also female name
*sm-p* = surname; also male name; also place name
*sp* = surname; also place name
[T] = a character in the *tōyō kanji* list not coming under [O] above

* * *

A single initial letter (e.g., H.) indicates the name, or name-element before a hyphen, beginning with that letter in the appropriate name category in the previous entry. (Used in Part I.)

~ indicates a repetition of the corresponding name, or name-element before a hyphen, in the previous entry. (Used in Part II.)

/ separates alternative name readings.

" " mark the usual spelling of a foreign name.

[" "] mark the usual spelling of a foreign name which is also a Japanese name.

Dates following a reading indicate an era name.

# A COMPREHENSIVE INDEX OF JAPANESE NAMES

## Part I. From Characters to Readings

## 1

亅 1 Susumu *m.* (KON)

乙 2 [T] Todomu *m*; Kinoto *p*. (OTSU, ITSU, ICHI, oto, taka, o, tsugi, ki, to, kuni)
$^{3}$川 Otokawa *s*, Otsukawa
$^{4}$女 Otome *f-p*
$^{5}$未平 Kimihei *m*
未生 Tomio *m*
$^{6}$竹 Ottake *s*, Ottachi
州 Otokuni *ml*
吉 Otokichi *m*
$^{7}$男 Otoo *m*, Tsugio
亥正 Otsugase *sp*
$^{9}$津 Ototsu *s*; Otsu *sp*
面 Otome *s*
彦 Otohiko *m*
$^{10}$訓 Otokuni *sp*
骨 Okkotsu *s*, Otobo- ⌊ne
$^{11}$部 Otobe *sp*
黒 Otoguro *s*
魚 Otona *f*
鳥 Tsubame *f*
$^{12}$須 Okisu *s*
$^{13}$葉 Otoba *s* ⌈hata
$^{15}$幡 Otohata *s*, Otsu-
熊 Otokuma *m*
$^{16}$叡 Takatoshi *m*
$^{21}$縄 Takatsuna *m*

一 3 [T] Hajime *m*, Hitoshi, Hajimu, Makoto, Masashi, Osamu, Susumu. (ICHI, ITSU, kazu, hito, moto, katsu, ka, hi, chi, tada, kuni, nobu, hide, hiji, kata, ma)
ノ瀬 Ichinose *s*
の酉 Ichi no tori *l*
の宮 Ichinomiya *p*
$^{2}$二 Kazuji *m*; Hifu *f*
二三 Ijimi *s*, Hiomi, Utakane, Utatane; Isami *m*; Hifumi *f*
二野 Hifuno *f*
十 Kazutō *m*
力 Kazuchika *m*
九 Kazuhisa *m*; Ikku ⌊*ml*
$^{3}$川 Ichikawa *s*
之瀬 Ichinose *s*
三 Ichizō *m* ⌈hiro *m*
口 Imoarai *sp*; Kazu-
大 Ichio *m*
万 Ichimata *s*
万田 Ichimata *s*
丸 Kazumaru *m*, Ichimaru
寸八分 Kamatsuka *s*
寸六分 Kamatsuka *s*
寸木 Masuki *s*
寸法師 Issun-bōshi *l*
$^{4}$心二河白道 Isshin niga byakudō *la*
仁 Kazusane *m*
戸 Ichinohe *sp*
予 Kazumasa *m*
文字 Ichimoji *s*
中節 Itchū-bushi *la*
日宮 Minori *s*
月 Katsuki *m*
円 Hitomaru *s*
方 Hijikata *s*
方井 Ikkatai *sp*
山 Ichiyama *s*, Issan
山一寧 Issan Ichinei
夫 Kazuo *m* ⌊*mlh*
井 Ichinoi *s*
太郎 Ichitarō *m*
木 Hitoki *m*; Ichiki *s*, Ikki, Hitosugi ⌈*a*
木造 Ichiboku-zukuri
尺二寸 Kamanoe *s*
尺八寸 Kamatsuka *s*
尺八分 Kamae *s*
$^{5}$以 Kazuyuki *m*
布 Kazuyoshi *m*
四明 Kazushime *f*
平 Ippei *m*
本松 Ipponmatsu *p*
生 Kazuo *m*, Ichio,
$^{6}$休 Ikkyū *ml* ⌊Issei
休宗純 I. Sōjun *ml*
宇 Ichiu *p*
字 Yōroko *s*
成 Kazushige *m*, Kazuyoshi
西 Kazuaki *m* ⌈*l*
年有半 Ichinen yūhan
色 Isshiki *sp*
$^{7}$位 Kazuhiko *m*
坂 Ichisaka *s*
杉 Ichisugi *s*, Hitosugi
町田 Ichimachida *s*
声 Hitokoe *m*
志 Ichishi *p*
男 Kazuo *m*
谷 Ichitani *s*; Ichinotani *ph*
谷嫩軍記 Ichinotani futaba gunki *la*
条 Ichijō *s*
条重美 I. Shigemi *ml*
条兼良 I. Kanera *ml*
兵卒の銃殺 Ippeisotsu no jūsatsu *l*
尾 Ichio *s*
見 Hitomi *s*
孝 Hidenori *m*
寿子 Kazuko *f* ⌈*la*
角仙人 Ikkaku Sennin
$^{8}$河 Ichikawa *s*
定 Kazusada *m*
英 Kazufusa *m*
忠 Itchū *ma*
秀 Kazuho *m*
迫 Ichinohazama *s*; Ichihasama *p*
夜四歌仙 Ichiya shikasen *l*
$^{9}$保 Ichiho *m*
松 Hitomatsu *s*, Ichi-
城 Ichijō *s* ⌊matsu
治 Motoharu *m*, Ichi-
政 Kazumasa *m* ⌊ji
到 Kazuyuki *s*
品 Ippō *s*
茶 Issa *ml*
音 Kazuo *m*
風迫 Ichinohazama *s*, Ichinohagima
彦 Kazuhiko *m*
省 Kazumi *m*
乗 Ichijō *s*
$^{10}$柳 Ichiyanagi *s*, Hitotsuyanagi, Ichiryū
郎 Ichirō *m*
郎一 Ichiroichi *m*
倉 Ichikura *s*
室 Ichimuro *s*
宮 Ichinomiya *sp*, Ikku; Iku *s*; Kazunomiya *m*; Ichimiya *p*
宮善 Ikuze *s*
馬 Kazuma *m*, Hajime
$^{11}$清 Kazukiyo *m*, Issei
視 Hitomi *m*
啓 Kazutaka *m*
$^{12}$場 Ichiba *s*
敞 Kazuhiro *m*
敬 Kazutoshi *m*
富士 Tanabe *s*
最 Kazumo *s*
森 Ichimori *s*
貫 Kazutsura *m*
番ケ瀬 Ichibagase *s*
筆 Ippitsu *s*
筆庵可候 Ippitsuan Kakō *ml* ⌈suna *l*
$^{13}$握の砂 Ichiaku no
睦 Kazutoki *m*
雄 Kazuo *m*, Kunio
誠 Kazushige *m*
葉 Ichiyō *fl*
豊 Kazutoyo *m*
資 Ichisuke *m*
遍上人 Ippen Shōnin *ml* ⌈ku *l*
遍上人語録 I. S. goro-
$^{14}$個 Kazuhiro *m*
塊 Hitokure *l*
徳 Motonori *m*
種 Kazutane *m*
寧一山 Ichinei Issan
関 Ichinoseki *p* ⌊*mlh*
$^{15}$噌 Issō *s*
衛 Kazue *m*
橋 Hitotsubashi *sp*
瀬 Ichinose *s*

## 2 T1

二 4 [T] Susumu *m*, Tsugi. (NI, JI, futa, kazu, tsugi, tsugu, sa, fu, bu, futatsu)
ツ井 Futatsui *p*
$^{2}$九 Futaku *s*
人 Fuhito *s*
人大名 Futari daimyō *la* ⌈ni *l*
人比丘尼 Ninin biku-
人祇王 Ninin Giō *la*
人袴 Futari-bakama *la*
人静 Futari Shizuka *la*
十一代集 Nijūichidaishū *l*
十二 Jisoji *s*

▼ 亅 乙 一 二 ▲ 乂 几 〆 丁 了 卜 力 刀 又 人

亅 乙 一 二 ▼ 乂 几 〆 丁 了 卜 力 刀 又 人 入 九 ▲ 七 十 八 川 小 三 也 之 于 干

十八宿 Nijūhasshuku l
十九日 Hizume s
十子 Hatako f
十五里 Tsuyuhiji s
十五絃 Nijūgogen l
十冬 Fujikazu m
十世 Hatayo m
十里 Tsuruheiji s
3川 Futagawa s
三 Fumi f
三次 Fumiji m
三郎 Nisaburō m
上 Nikami s, Futagami; Niji p
子 Kazuko f
丈 Nijō p
千石 Jisenseki l
4六新報 Niroku shin-
戸 Ninohe sp ⌊pō l
山 Futayama s
王 Niō sla; Futami m
井 Futai s
木 Futaki sm; Nikki s, Futatsugi
5平 Nihei m
本 Futamoto s
本松 Nihonmatsu sp
6杁 Niiri s
7村 Nimura s, Futamura, Ninomura
谷 Ninotani s
男 Tsugio m
条 Nijō sp ⌈ml
条良基 N. Yoshimoto
条為氏 N. Tameuji ml
見 Futami sp
8国 Nikuni s
9俣 Futamata s
松 Futamatsu s, Ninomatsu ⌈kami
神 Futagami s, Nino-
祐 Kazusuke m
面 Futaomote s
美 Fumi f
10柳 Futatsuyanagi s, Futayanagi
郎 Jirō m
郎丸 Jiromaru m
荒 Futara s
宮 Ninomiya sp
宮尊徳 N. Sontoku mh
11瓶 Nihei s, Nigame
朗 Jirō m
部 Niibe s
12渡 Futawatari s
裕 Kazusuke m
13階堂 Nikaidō s
葉 Futaba sf; Niwa s; Tsuginobu m
葉亭 Fubabatei s
葉亭四迷 F. Shimei ml
16橋 Nihashi s, Futabashi
19藤部 Nitobe s

## —— 2 U ——

乂 5 (GAI, GE, yoshi)

几 6 (KI, yasu)
子 Yasuko f
董 Kitō ml

〆 7 (shime)
子 Shimeko f
治 Shimeharu m

丁 8 [T] Tei s, Yoboro, Yōro, Yorō; Tsuyoshi m. (TEI, CHŌ, yoboro, yorō, yō, yobo)
子 Chōshi s, Yōroko; Yoboroko sm
字 Yōroko s
抹 Denmāku p "Denmark"
野 Yoborono s, Yōno, Yobono, Chōno

了 9 [T] Satoru m, Akira. (RYŌ, aki, sumi, nori)
久 Norihisa m
江 Sumie f
阿 Ryōa ml
雄 Akio m

卜 10 (BOKU, ura, shime)
田 Shimeta s
部 Urabe s ⌈ml
部兼倶 U. Kanetomo
養 Bokuyō ml ⌈l
養狂歌集 B. kyōkashū

力 11 [T] Chikara m, Isao, Tsutomu. (RYOKU, RIKI, o, ka, chika, yoshi, chikara)
人 Chikara m
三 Rikizō m
丸 Rikimaru s
石 Chikaraishi s
造 Rikizō m
蔵 Rikizō m

刀 12 [T] Katana s. (TO, TŌ, katana, tachi, hakashi)
西 Tose s
自 Toji f
自子 Tojiko f
自咩 Tojime f
利 Tori s
佩 Tachihaki s
根 Tone sp
根館 Tonedachi s
禰 Tone s

又 13 [T] Tasuku m. (YŪ, U, mata, suke, yasu)
一郎 Mataichirō m
三郎 Matasaburō m
子 Matako f
夫 Matao m
司 Matashi m
次郎 Matajirō m
吉 Matakichi m
玄 Yasutō m
郎 Matao m, Yasuo
原 Matawara s
野 Matano s
策 Matasaku m
蔵 Matazō m

人 14 [T] Hito m, Hitoshi. (JIN, NIN, hito, to, me, sane, tami, futo, muto)
3上 Hitokami m
丸 Hitomaro m
丸影供 H. eigu l
6吉 Hitoyoshi p
名 Hitona m
7尾 Hitoo s
見 Hitomi s
見東明 H. Tōmei ml
9耶鬼耶 Hito ka oni
首 Musu s ⌊ka l
首川 Hitokabegawa p
11情本 Ninjōbon l
麻呂 Hitomaro m
康 Saneyasu m
12間経 Ningenkyō l
13雄 Tamio m
15磐 Hitowa m
18麿 Hitomaro m
21羅 Hitora s

入 15 [T] Kaeruda s. (NYŪ, iri, iru, shio, nari)
3之波 Shionoha p
4戸野 Iritono s, Nitto-
月 Iritsuki s ⌊no
内島 Iriuchijima s
山 Iriyama s
五郎 Irigorō m
5田 Irita s
矢 Iriya s
6江 Irie s
交 Irimajiri s, Irimaze, Iriai
広瀬 Irihirose p
西 Nissai s ⌈ri a
母屋造 Irimoya-zuku-
7沢 Irizawa s
村 Irimura s
谷 Iritani s
来 Iriki sp
来院 Irikiin s
10倉 Irikura s
屋 Iriya s
11部 Nyūbe s
野 Irino s; Shiono sp
野屋 Nyūnoya s
12善 Nyūzen sp
間 Iruma sp
間川 Irumagawa sl
間野 Irumano s
鹿 Iruka m

九 16 [T] Chikashi m; Ichijiku s. (KU, KYŪ, hisa, kazu, koko, tada, chika)
1一郎 Kuichirō m
2二夫 Kunio m
十九 Tsukumo sm-f-p
十九里 Kujūkuri p
十九院 Tsurushi s
3三子 Kumiko f
万 Tadakatsu m
子 Hisako f
寸五分 Kazuhata s
4戸 Kunohe sp
5石 Sazarashi s
申 Hisanobu m
平 Kuhei m
6仙 Kubutsu s
世戸 Kusenoto l
年坊 Kunenbō s

[7]兵衛 Kyūbee *m*
条 Kujō *s*
条武子 K. Takeko *fl*
条兼実 K. Kanezane *mh*
里 Kuri *s*, Kunori
[9]段 Kudan *p*
度山 Kudoyama *p*
重 Kokonoe *f*; Kujū *p* ⌈*m*
[10]郎右衛門 Kuroemon
竜 Kyūryū / Kūron *p* " Kowloon "
[11]野 Kuno *s*
鬼 Kuki *s*
鬼周造 K. Shūzō *ml*
島 Kushima *s*, Kujima
穂 Kazuo *m*

七 17 [T] (SHICHI, SHITSU, nana, na, kazu)
ヶ浜 Shichigahama *p*
ヶ宿 Shichigashuku *p*
つ面 Nanatsumen *l*
[2]二会 Naniai *p*
二恵 Nanie *f*
十 Nanashige *m*
七五分 Mitsuzuki *s*, Mitsuwata
[3]三五野 Namiino *s*
子 Nanako *f*
寸五分 Kutsuwame *s*, Kutsuwata
夕 Tanabata *s*
[4]戸 Shichinohe *sp*
六 Shichiroku *m*
月代 Natsuyo *f*
山 Nanayama *p*
夫 Nanao *m*
太郎 Shichitarō *m*
五三 Shime *sm-f-p*; Shimekake *s*
五三子 Shimeko *f*
五三介 Shimesuke *m*
五三懸 Shimekake *s*
井 Nanai *s*
[5]加家 Nanakamado *s*
左衛門 Shichizaemon ⌊*m*
田 Shichida *s*
生 Habu *s*
[7]沢 Nanasawa *s*
会 Nanakai *p*
条 Shichijō *s*
尾 Nanao *p*
坐 Nanakura *s*, Nanakuro
見 Nanami *s* ⌈chiri
里 Nanasato *s*, Shi-
[8]宝 Shippō *p-a*
宗 Hichisō *p*
[9]城 Shichijō *s*
珍 Shichichin *s*
美 Shitsumi *sp*
帝 Nananomikado *mh*
要 Kazumasa *m*
重 Nanae *f*
[10]海 Nanaumi *s*
郎 Shichirō *m*
郎平 Shichirobei *m*
家 Nanakama *s*, Nanakamado
[13]塚 Nanatsuka *s*
飯 Nanae *p*
福 Shichifuku *s*
雄 Nanao *m*, Kazuo
[14]種 Saigusa *s*
緒子 Naoko *f*
曜 Shichiyō *l*
騎落 Shichiki-ochi *la*
瀬 Nanase *f*

十 18 [T] Mitsuru *m*, Hisashi; Momoki *s*, Mogiki. (JŪ, SHŪ, tō, to, so, kazu, shige, jitsu, tada, mitsu, tomi, ma, toto, ta- ⌊ri)
[1]一三 Tohimi *m*
一夫 Tochio *m*
一谷 Jūichiya *s*
一谷義三郎 J. Gisaburō *ml*
[2]二月一日 Shiwasuta *s*
二月田 Shiwasuta *s*
二月晦日 Hizume *s*
二仏 Ochiburui *s*, Otsuburui
二仙 Ochiburui *s*, Otsuburui
二里 Tojiri *s* ⌈shi *l*
二段草子 Jūnidan sō-
二神 Ochiburui *s*, Otsuburui, Otsurui, Oppurui
二神島 Ochiburui *s*, Otsuburui, Otsurui
二蔵 Tonizō *m*
九 Tomichika *f*
七夜 Kanō *s*, Kanaki
七夜月 Kanō *s*
八 Tōhachi *m*
八女 Sakari *sp*; Wakairo *s*, Wakaiso
八日 Toyōka *s*
八公 Soyagimi *s*, Soyagin ⌈Sogō
[3]川 Togawa *s*, Togō,
三日 Tomika *m*
三代集 Jūsandaishū *l*
三夜 Jūsan'ya *l*
寸子 Masuko *f*
寸見 Masumi *s*
寸穂 Tosuho *m*, Ma-
[4]六 Isao *m* ⌊suho
六夜 Izayoi *l*
日町 Tōkamachi *p*
文字 Jūmonji *p*
五月 Mochizuki *s*
王 Jūō *p*
太 Jūta *m*
木 Totoki *s*
代 Soshiro *s*
代田 Toshiroda *s*, Toyota, Fushikata, So-
司 Jūji *m* ⌊shiroda
右衛門 Jūemon *m*
市 Toichi *s*, Tōchi
四日 Toyoka *s*
四山 Jūshiyama *p*
四屋 Jūshiya *m*
[6]吉 Kazuyoshi *m*
合 Tōgō *s*, Sogō
字 Jūji *s*, Tsuji
旭 Jikkyoku *m*
[7]余島 Toyoshima *sp*
束 Totsuka *s*
返 Togaeri *s*
返舎一九 Jippensha Ikku *ml* ⌈*ml*
返肇 Togaeri Hajime
[8]河 Sogō *sp*; Togawa *s*
和 Jikka *sp*, Tōwa
和田 Towada *sp*
和田操 T. Misao *ml*
[9]津川 Totsukawa *p*
秋 Toaki *s*
重 Mitsushige *m*
[10]時 Totoki *s*, Toki, Inenuki
訓抄 Jikkunshō / Jikkinshō *l*
郎 Jūrō *m*
[11]島 Toshima *p*
鳥 Totori *s*
問最秘抄 Jūmon saihishō *l*
亀 Sogame *s*
[12]勝 Tokachi *p*
銘 Mitsukata *m*
摩 Tōma *s*

八 19 [T] Wakatsu *m*. (HACHI, ya, wa, kazu, yatsu, hatsu)
ツ橋 Yatsuhashi *s*
[2]九十三 Yakutomi *s*
十 Yaso *m*
十一鱗 Kukuri *s*
十八間 Hatoyama *s*, Hajiyama
十八騎 Todoroki *s*
十川 Yasogawa *s*
十郎 Hachijūrō *m*
十島 Yasoshima *s*
十瀬 Yasose *s*
[3]三 Kazumi *m*
下 Yachige *s*
千代 Yachiyo *p*
千穂 Yachiho *p*
丈 Hachijō *p*
丈部 Yasetsukabe *s*
丈島 Hachijōjima *p*
下田 Yageta *s*
子 Yago *s* ⌈*s*, Yabe
[4]戸 Hachinohe *sp*; Yae
王子 Hachiōji *p*
犬伝 Hakkenden *l*
太 Hachida *s*, Hatsuda, Hatta
日市 Yōkaichi *p*
日市場 Yōkaichiba *p*
月一日 Hozumi *s*
月一日宮 Hozumiya *s*, Hozunomiya
月十五日 Nakaaki *s*
月晦日 Hozumi *s*
月朔日 Hozumi *s*
少女 Yaotome *l*
尺 Yasaka *m*
女 Yame *sp* ⌈*sp*
文字屋 Hachimonjiya
文字屋自笑 H. Jishō *ml* ⌈*ml*
文字屋其笑 H. Kishō *ml*
文字屋其碩 H. Kiseki *ml* ⌈*ml*
文字屋瑞笑 H. Zuishō
木 Yagi *sp*
木八四 Yagiyashi *s*
木下 Yagishita *s*
木田 Yagita *s*
木沢 Yagisawa *s*
木沼 Yaginuma *s*
木秀次 Yagi Hideji *mh*
木重吉 Y. Jūkichi *ml*
木岡 Yagioka *s*
木原 Yagihara *s*

木隆一郎 Yagi Ryūichirō *ml*
木義徳 Y. Yoshinori *ml*
木橋 Yagihashi *s*
山 Hachiyama *s*
方 Happō *s*
[5]代 Yashiro *s*; Yatsushiro *sp*
代集 Hachidaishū *l*
左右 Hachisō *m*
右衛門 Hachiemon *m*
田 Hatta *sp*; Yata *s*, Hachida, Yatsuda
田元夫 Hatta Motoo *ml*
田知紀 H. Tomonori *ml* ⌈*p*
本松 Hachihonmatsu
生 Yabu *s*; Habu *sp*
[6]羽 Yaba *s*
州 Yasu *s*
州仙 Yasunori *m*
次 Hachiji *m*
次郎 Hachijirō *m*
百子 Yaoko *p*
百里 Yaori *m*
百津 Yaotsu *p*
百屋 Yaoya *s* ⌈*la*
百屋お七 Y. O-Shichi
年 Yatose *f*
名 Yana *p*
多 Hatta *s*, Yata, Hachida, Hatsuda; Ha-
[7]坂 Yasaka *sp* ⌊ta *sp*
住 Yasumi *s*
住利雄 Y. Toshio *ml*
村 Yamura *s*
杉 Yasugi *s* ⌈*ml*
杉貞利 Y. Sadatoshi
谷 Yaya *s*, Yatagai
条 Hachijō *s*
尾 Yao *sp-l*; Yatsuo *p*
甫谷 Happōya *s*
束 Yatsuka *sm-p*
里 Yazato *s*
角 Yasumi *s*
角島 Hakashima *s*, Ya-
[8]居 Yako *s* ⌊kata
国分 Yakobu *s*
国生 Yakobu *s*, Yakabu, Yakū, Yakō
国府 Yakobu *s*
武崎 Yabusaki *s*
東 Hattō *p*
並 Yatsunami *s*, Yasonami

[9]信井 Hashii *s*
洲民 Yasumi *m*
相山 Yaeyama *s*
神 Yakami *s*
祐 Yakeshi *s*; Yasuke *p*
美 Yatsumi *f*
巻 Yamaki *s*
重 Yae *f*
重子 Yaeko *f*
重田 Yaeta *s*
重吉 Yaekichi *m*
重沢 Yaezawa *s*
重洲 Yaesu *p*
重垣 Yaegaki *s*
重樫 Yaegashi *s*
重櫛 Yaegushi *s*
[10]郎 Hachirō *m*
郎右衛門 Hachiroemon *m*
郎潟 Hachirōgata *p*
咫子 Yatako *f*
剣 Yatsurugi *s*
竜 Hachiryū *p*
馬 Yauma *s*, Hachi-
[11]峰 Yatsuo *f* ⌊uma
朔 Hozumi *s*
都 Yatsu *s*
島 Yashima *sp-la*
[12]街 Yachimata *p*
隅 Yasumi *s*
椚 Yakunugi *s*
森 Hachimori *sp*
道 Yamichi *s*, Hachidō, Musashi
開 Hachikai *p*
鹿 Yōka *p*
[13]塚 Yatsuka *s*
尋 Yahiro *s*
握 Yatsuka *s*
雲 Yakumo *m-p-l*
雲御抄 Y. mishō *l*
[14]郷 Yasato *p*
[15]潮 Yashio *p*
幡 Yawata *sp*; Yahata *p*, Hachiman
幡平 Hachimantai *p*
幡前 Yawata no mae *l*
幡宮 Hachimangū *p*
幡造 Hachiman-zukuri *a*
幡浜 Yawatahama *p*
箭 Hachiya *m*
[16]橋 Yatsuhashi *sp*, Yabase
頭 Yazu *p*
[17]鍬 Yaguwa *s*
衢 Yachimata *m*

——3 L1——

**川** 20 [T] Kawa *s*. (SEN, kawa)
[2]又 Kawamata *s*
人 Kawahito *s*
[3]之江 Kawanoe *p*
久保 Kawakubo *s*
口 Kawaguchi *sp*
口一郎 K. Ichirō *ml*
口松太郎 K. Matsutarō *ml*
口浩 K. Kō *ml*
上 Kawakami *sp*; Kawaue *p*
上小夜子 K. Sayoko *fl*
上音二郎 K. Otojirō *ma*
上眉山 K. Bizan *ml*
下 Kawashita *s*
[4]元 Kawamoto *s*
戸 Kawado *s*
中 Kawanaka *s*
中島 Kawanakajima *p*
内 Kawauchi *sp*; Sen-
井 Kawai *sp* ⌊dai *p*
手 Kawade *s*
[5]北 Kawakita *sp*
勾 Kawamagari *s*
辺 Kawabe *sp*; Kawanobe *s*; Kawanabe *p*
尻 Kawajiri *sp*; Kawakame *s* ⌈tan *ml*
尻清潭 Kawajiri Sei-
平 Kawahira *s*
本 Kawamoto *sp*
生 Kawaoi *s*
田 Kawada *s*
田順 K. Jun *ml*
[6]地 Kawaji *s*
合 Kawai *s* ⌈*ma*
合玉堂 K. Gyokudō
西 Kawanishi *sp*
名 Kawana *s*
[7]那辺 Kawanabe *s*
村 Kawamura *s*
村花菱 K. Karyō *ml*
谷 Kawatani *s*, Kawa-
廷 Kawatei *s* ⌊dani
里 Kawasato *sp*
見 Kawami *s*
角 Kawazumi *s*, Kawakado
[8]波 Kawanami *s*
枝 Kawaeda *s*
和 Kawawa *s*
東 Kawato *s*

[9]俣 Kawamata *sp*
治 Kawaji *s*
津 Kawazu *s*
城 Kawashiro *s*
畑 Kawabata *s*
枯 Kawakare *s*
松 Kawamatsu *s*
相 Kawasuke *m*, Kawaai; Kawai *s*
面 Kawamo *s*, Kawazura
南 Kawaminami *p*
首 Kawanōbito *s*
前 Kawamae *p*
岸 Kawagishi *s*
[10]浦 Kawaura *s*
柳 Senryū *l*
原 Kawabara *s*, Kawahara; Kawara *sp*
原井 Kawarai *s*
原田 Kawarada *s*
原林 Kawarabayashi *s*
[11]根 Kawane *p*
野 Kawano *s*
野辺 Kawanobe *s*
部 Kawabe *s*
副 Kawazoe *sp*; Kawafuku *s*
副国基 Kawazoe Kunitomo *ml*
浪 Kawanami *s*
添 Kawazoe *s*
島 Kawashima *sp*
島忠之助 K. Chūnosuke *ml*
[12]隅 Kawazumi *s*
場 Kawaba *p*
淵 Kawabuchi *s*
勝 Kawakatsu *s*
棚 Kawatana *p*
崎 Kawasaki *sp*
崎杜外 K. Togai *ml*
崎舎 Kawasakiya *s*
崎長太郎 Kawasaki Chōtarō *ml*
喜田 Kawakita *s*
喜多 Kawakita *s*
森 Kawamori *s*
[13]路 Kawaji *s*
路柳虹 K. Ryūkō *ml*
路聖謨 K. Toshiakira *mh*
[14]越 Kawagoe *sp*
跨 Kawamata *s*
窪 Kawakubo *s*
[15]澄 Kawazumi *s*
幡 Kawabata *s*

端 Kawabata *s*
端千枝 K. Chie *fl*
端玉章 K. Gyokushō *ma*
川端茅舎 K. Bōsha *ml*
端竜子 K. Ryūshi *ma*
端康成 K. Yasunari *ml*
16橋 Kawabashi *s*
鍋 Kawanabe *s*
瀬 Kawase *s*
鰭 Kawabata *s*

小 21 [T] (SHŌ, ko, o, sa, chiisa, sasa)
1一 Koichi *m*
一条 Koichijō *s*
一郎 Koichirō *m*
2十郎 Kojūrō *m*
八重 Kobae *f*
人大 Kotoo *m*
又 Komata *s* ⌈wa *s*
3川 Ogawa *sp*; Koga-
川戸 Okawado *s* ⌈*ml*
川未明 Ogawa Mimei
三郎 Kosaburō *m*
千谷 Ojiya *p*
万 Koman *f*
丸 Komaru *s*
口 Oguchi *s*, Koguchi
口部 Chisakobe *s*
久江 Okue *s*
久保 Kokubo *s*
子 Chiisago *s*
子部 Chisakobe *s*, Chiisakobe ⌈Kohinata
4日向 Kobinata *sp*,
月 Komatsuki *s*
内蔵 Okura *m*
文次 Komonji *s*
方 Ogata *s*
弓 Oyumi *m*
手子 Oteko *f*
手川 Kotegawa *s*
女淵 Onabuchi *s*
天 Oama *sp*
天地 Shōtenchi *l*
木 Ogi *sp*; Kogi *s*
木曾 Ogiso *s*, Kogiso
牛 Koushi *s*
牛田 Kogota *p*
中 Konaka *s*
中川 Konakagawa *s*
中村 Konakamura *s*
中村清矩 K. Kiyonori *ml* ⌈*sp*
山 Koyama *s*; Oyama
山いと子 K. Itoko *fl*
山内 Osanai *s*
山内薫 O. Kaoru *ml*
山田 Oyamada *s*
山正太郎 Koyama Shōtarō *ma*
山祐士 K. Yūshi *ml*
山清 K. Kiyoshi *ml*
山鼎浦 K. Teiho *ml*
井土 Koido *s*
井戸 Koido *s*
井沼 Koinuma *s*
内 Kouchi *s*, Onai
太 Shōta *m*, Shōto
太刀 Kotachi *s*
太郎 Kotarō *m*
五郎 Kogorō *m*
5旧 Oki *s* ⌈ke
仏 Osaragi *s*, Koboto-
代 Koshiro *s*, Kotai, Shōdai
比類巻 Kohirumaki *s*
汀 Obama *s*
永井 Konagai *s*
穴 Koana *s*, Oana
穴隆一 K. Ryūichi *ml*
勾 Komagari *s*
石 Koishi *s*
石川 Koishikawa *sp*
石山 Koishiyama *s*
石原 Koishiwara *p*
布施 Obuse *sp*; Kobuse *s*
右記 Ouki / Shōyūki *lh*
左衛門 Kozaemon *m*
四郎 Koshirō *m*
立 Kodate *s*
矢部 Oyabe *p*
生 Koiku *s*; Komō *p*
市 Koichi *s*
市兵衛 Koichibee *m*
平 Kodaira *sp*; Odaira *s*, Kohira; Obira
平次 Koheiji *m* ⌊*p*
平治 Koheiji *m*
玉 Kodama *s*
用 Koyō *s*
甲 Kokabuto *s*
田 Oda *sp*
田川 Odagawa *s*
田切 Odagiri *s*, Odaki
田切秀雄 Odagiri Hideo *ml*
田中 Odanaka *s*
田木 Odaki *s*
田井 Otai *s*, Odai
田村 Odamura *s*
田垣 Odagaki *s*
田桐 Odagiri *s*
田倉 Odakura *s*
田原 Odawara *sp*
田部 Otabe *s*
田野 Odano *s*
田島 Odajima *s*
田鳥 Odatori *s*
田観螢 Oda Kankei *ml*
田嶽夫 O. Takeo *ml*
6圷 Koakutsu *s*
江 Koe *s*, Oe, Ogō
池 Koike *s*
池堅治 K. Kenji *ml*
竹 Kotake *sp*; Otake *s*, Shinu, Shinō
竹田 Shinoda *s*, Shinuta, Otakeda
竹枝 Sasae *f*
此木 Okonogi *s*
百合 Koyuri *f*, Sayuri
寺 Kodera *s*, Odera
寺融吉 K. Yūkichi *ml*
宅 Koyake *s*; Oyake *sp*
守 Komori *s*
早川 Kobayakawa *s*
早川隆景 K. Takakage *mh*
向 Komukai *s*
向田 Ohinata *s*, Oinata
式部内侍 Koshikibu no Naishi *fl*
辻 Kotsuji *s*
名 Ona *s*
西 Konishi *s* ⌈*mh*
西行長 K. Yukinaga
西惟然 K. Izen *ml*
7作 Kosaku *s*; Ozaku
佐 Kosa *s* ⌊*sp*
佐川 Kosagawa *s*
佐内 Osanai *s*
佐手 Osade *s*
佐佐 Kosaza *p*
佐治 Kosaji *s*
佐野 Osano *s*
住 Osumi *s*
坂 Kosaka *sp*, Osaka
坂井 Kozakai *sp*
阪 Kosaka *s*
沢 Ozawa *s*, Kozawa
沢征爾 O. Seiji *ma*
沢武二 O. Takeji *ml*
沢清 O. Kiyoshi *ml*
沢碧童 O. Hekidō *ml*
沢蘆庵 O. Roan *ml*
村 Komura *s*
村寿太郎 K. Jutarō *mh*
杉 Kosugi *sf*
杉天外 K. Tengai *ml*
杉余子 K. Yoshi *ml*
杉放庵 K. Hōan *ml*
助川 Kosukegawa *s*
助 Odasuku *s*
町 Komachi *sfl*
町谷 Komachiya *s*
豆 Shōzu *p*; Azuki *s*, Ozu ⌈Azusawa *s*
豆沢 Azukisawa *sp*;
豆島 Azukijima *s*, Amejima, Mamejima
谷 Otani *s*, Kotani, Ohase; Ōna *sp*; Otari
谷田 Koyata *s* ⌊*p*
谷津 Koyatsu *s*
谷松 Koyamatsu *s*
谷野 Koyano *s*
余綾 Koyorogi *s*
尾 Obi *s*
花 Kobana *s*, Ohana
安 Koyasu *s*
串 Kogushi *s*, Ogushi
里 Ori *s*
更 Kofuke *s*
亜細亜 Shō-Ajia *p* "Asia Minor"
車梅 Okurume *s*
来川 Kokigawa *s*
角 Osumi *sm*; Otsu-
出 Koide *sp* ⌊nu *m*
出粲 K. Tsubara *ml*
見 Komi *s*, Omi
見川 Omigawa *p*
見戸 Komito *s*
見山 Komiyama *s*, Omiyama
見野 Omino *s*
見濃 Omino *s*
貝 Kokai *s*
8侍従 Kojijū *fl*
彼 Ogano *s*
沼 Konuma *s*, Onuma
波 Sanami *s*; Sasana-
河 Ogawa *s* ⌊mi *f*
河原 Ogawara *s*
泊 Kodomari *p*
泊瀬 Ohase *s*
門 Okado *s*
門勝二 O. Katsuji *ml*
板橋 Koitabashi *s*
坪 Kotsubo *s*
牧 Komaki *sf-p*
牧近江 K. Ōmi *ml*
牧暮潮 K. Bochō *ml*
枝 Koeda *s* ⌈yashi
林 Kobayashi *s*, Oha-

力 刀 又 人 入 九 七 十 八 川 ▼ 小 ▲ 三 也 之 于 千 乃 口 口 巳 巳

力 刀 又 人 入 九 七 十 八 川 ▼ 小 ▲ 三 也 之 于 千 乃 口 口 巳 巳

林一茶 K. Issa *ml*
林古径 K. Kokei *ma*
林多喜二 K. Takiji *ml*
林英夫 K. Hideo *ml*
林秀雄 K. Hideo *ml*
林勇 K. Isamu *ml*
林清親 K. Kiyochika *ma*
林愛雄 K. Yoshio *ml*
知 Ochi *s* ⌈da
和田 Kowada *s*, Owa-
金 Kogane *s*
金井 Koganei *sp*
金井良精 K. Yoshikiyo *mh*
金井喜美子 K. Kimiko *fl*
金沢 Koganesawa *s*
夜 Sayo *f*
夜衣 Sayogoromo *l*
茂田 Komoda *s*
糸 Koito *p*
国 Oguni *sp*
東人 Koazumabito *m*
[9]保方 Obokata *s*
保内 Obonai *s*
俣 Komata *s*, Omata; Obata *p* ⌈Ogi *sp*
城 Koshiro *s*, Kojiro;
狐 Kogitsune *ma*
狭野 Sasano *s*
津 Ozu *s*
治田 Oharida *s*
祖父 Kōji *m*
弥太 Koyata *m*
畑 Obata *s*, Kohata
姉 Koane *f*
柏 Ogashima *s*, Okashima, Kokashima
松 Komatsu *sp*
松沢 Komatsuzawa *s*
松村 Komatsumura *s*
松原 Komatsubara *s*
松屋 Komatsuya *s*
松清 Komatsu Kiyoshi *ml*
松野 Komatsuno *s*
松島 Komatsushima *p*
松崎 Komatsuzaki *s*
祝 Koiwai *s*
南 Kominami *s*
草川 Kogusagawa *s*
岩 Koiwa *s*
岩井 Koiwai *s*
長 Ohase *s*
長井 Konagai *p*
長谷 Ohase *s*, Kohase, Konagaya, Kohasebe ⌈hasebe
長谷部 Ohasebe *s*, Ko-
春 Koharu *s*
泉 Koizumi *s*
泉八雲 K. Yakumo *ml*
泉苳三 K. Tōzō *ml*
泉信三 K. Shinzō *ml*
泉鉄 K. Magane *ml*
巻 Komaki *s*
屎 Okuso *fh*
[10]唄 Kobai *s*
海 Koumi *s*, Kokai; Kōmi *sp*
浦 Koura *s*
浜 Ohama *s*, Kohama; Obama *p*
酒井 Kosakai *s*
酒井不木 K. Fuboku
脇 Kowaki *s* ⌊*ml*
畔 Koaze *s*
袖曾我 Kosode Soga *la* ⌈nagi
柳 Oyanagi *s*, Koya-
柳津 Koyaizu *s*, Oyaizu ⌈izu
柳筒 Koyaizu *s*, Oya-
郡 Kogun *p*, Ogōri
針 Kohari *s*
扇 Koōgi *l* ⌈s
高 Odaka *sp*; Kodaka
室 Komuro *s*
室信夫 K. Shinobu *mh*
室屈山 K. Kutsuzan
宮 Komiya *s* ⌊*ml*
宮山 Komiyama *s*
宮山天香 K. Tenkō *ml*
宮山明敏 K. Akitoshi *ml* ⌈taka *ml*
宮豊隆 Komiya Toyo-
花 Ohana *s*
荷田 Konita *s*
食堂 Sashidō *s*
倉 Ogura *s*, Kogoi; Kokura *p*
倉百人一首 O. hyakunin isshu *l*
華和 Kohanawa *s*
畠 Obata *s*, Kobata, Kobatake, Obatake
竜 Kotatsu *m*
柴 Koshiba *s*
笑 Koemi *f*
栗 Oguri *s*
栗判官 O. Hangan *l*
栗風葉 O. Fūyō *ml*
栗栖 Ogurusu *sp*
隼人 Kohayato *m*
原 Ohara *sp*, Obara; Kohara *s*
屋 Koya *s*
屋貝 Oyakai *s*
連 Komuraji *m*
県 Chiisagata *p*
馬 Kouma *s*, Koma, Ohasama
馬命婦集 Koma / Kouma no Myōbu shū *l*
[11]値賀 Ojika *sp*
添 Osō *s*
清水 Koshimizu *p*
桜 Kozakura *s*
梅 Koume *s*, Konme
峰 Komine *s*
梶 Kokaji *s*
能 Ono *s*
船 Kobune *s*
船井 Kobunai *s*
野 Ono *sp*; Kono *s*
野十三郎 O. Tōzaburō *ml* ⌈chi *fl*
野小町 O. no Koma-
野川 Onokawa *s*
野口 Onoguchi *s*
野上 Onogami *p*
野山 Onoyama *s*
野内 Onouchi *s*
野木 Onoki *s*, Koyagi
野田 Onoda *sp*
野寺 Onodera *s*
野坂 Onozaka *s*
野沢 Onozawa *s*
野村 Onomura *s*
野里 Onozato *s* ⌈*mh*
野妹子 Ono no Imoko
野岡 Onooka *s*
野原 Onohara *s*
野梓 Ono Azusa *mh*
野島 Onojima *s*
野崎 Onozaki *s*
野道風 Ono no Michikaze / Dōfū *mla*
野塚 Onozuka *sp*
野篁 Ono no Takamura *ml*
野蕪子 O. Bushi *ml*
野瀬 Onose *s*
菅 Kosuge *sp*
菊 Kogiku *s*
留 Kotome *f*
笠 Ogasa *sp*
笠原 Ogasawara *sp*
梁川 Koyanagawa *s*
黒 Oguro *s*, Koguro
黒麻呂 Oguromaro *m*
鳥遊 Takanashi *s*
島 Kojima *sp*; Oshima *s* ⌈*ml*
島政二郎 K. Masajirō
島法師 K. Hōshi *ml*
島信夫 K. Nobuo *ml*
島烏水 K. Usui *ml*
島原 Oshimabara *s*
島屋 Oshimaya *s*
島勗 Kojima Tsutomu *ml*
島徳弥 K. Tokuya *ml*
亀 Kokame *s*
[12]湊 Kominato *s*
隅 Osumi *sm*
須 Osu *s*
須戸 Kosudo *p*
須田 Kosuda *s*
堤 Kozutsumi *s*, Kotsutsumi
場 Koba *s*
場瀬 Obase *s* ⌈*ml*
場瀬卓三 O. Takuzō
堺 Kozakai *s*
椋 Ogura *sp*; Oryō *s*
崎 Kozaki *s*, Ozaki
崎弘道 K. Hiromichi
勝 Kokatsu *s* ⌊*ml*
補摩 Ohoma *s*
軽馬 Kokaruma *s*
納 Kona *s*
喜多 Okita *s*
森 Komori *s*
森谷 Komoriya *s*
童子 Kowarawako *m*
貫 Onuki *s*, Konuki
賀野 Ogano *s*
笹 Kozasa *s*, Ozasa
曾根 Kosone *s*, Osone
達 Kotatsu *s*
間 Koma *s*, Omasama
鹿 Kojika *s*; Oshika *sm*
鹿野 Ogano *sp* ⌈*sl*
[13]塩 Koshio *s*; Oshio
塩山 Oshioyama *s*
塚 Kozuka *s*
塙 Kohari *s*
堀 Kobori *s*
堀杏奴 K. Annu *fl*
堀鞆音 K. Tomone / Tomoto *ma*
堀遠州 K. Enshū *ma*
溝 Komizo *s*
滝 Kodaki *s*, Odaki
淵 Obuchi *s*

淵沢 Kobuchizawa *p*
張 Kobari *s*
弾正 Kodanjō *s*
楯 Otate *m*
楠 Ogusu *s*
槌 Kozuchi *s*
郷 Sōgō *s*
路 Shōji *s*; Koji *m*
路頃 Ojigoro *sp*
塞 Oseki *s*
督 Kogō *fl*
園 Osono *s*, Kozono
[14]猿 Kozaru *s*
猿七之助 K. Shichinosuke *la*
槫 Kokure *s* ⌈zui *l*
説神髄 Shōsetsu shin-
管 Kosuge *s* ⌈shi
暮 Kogure *s*, Kogura-
暮政治 Kogure Masaji *ml*
越 Kokoe *s*, Kogoshi, Okoshi
関 Ozeki *s*, Kozeki
関三英 O. San'ei *mh*
[15]幡 Obata *s*, Kohata
槻 Otsuki *s*
諸 Komoro *p*
駒 Kogoma *s*
蔵 Kogura *s*
舞 Komai *s*
熊 Oguma *sp*, Okuma; Kokuma *s* ⌈*ml*
熊秀雄 Oguma Hideo
[16]橋 Kohashi *s*
樽 Otaru *p*
鴨 Okae *s*
館 Kodate *s*
鍛冶 Kokaji *sla*
薬 Kogusuri *s*
薗 Osono *s*
[17]篠 Koshino *f*; Ozasa *s*, Ozase
檜山 Koshiyama *s*
網 Koami *s*
墾田 Obata *s*, Oharida, Konda
霜 Koshimo *f*
[18]藤 Kofuji *s*, Kotō
藤花 Kotōke *s*
[19]小瀬 Kose *s*, Ose
櫃 Kohitsu *s*, Ohitsu; Obitsu *p*
疇 Koaze *s*, Kohata
縮 Kochijimi *s*
鏡 Kokagami *l*
[20]籏 Obata *s*
磯 Koiso *s*
磯国昭 K. Kuniaki *mh*
鷹 Kodaka *s*

—— 3 T1 ——

三 22 [T] (SAN, SHIN, mi, kazu, zō, sabu, so, mitsu, tada, ko, sō, nao, miru)
ヶ日 Mitsukabi *p*
ヶ田 Migata *s*
ヶ島 Migashima *s*
ヶ島葭子 M. Yoshiko *fl*
ツ橋 Mitsuhashi *s*
[2]二 Sōji *m*
二子 Mibuko *f*
十六人集 Sanjūrokuninshū *l*
七全伝南柯夢 Sanshichi zenden Nanka no yume *l*
入 Miru *sp*
刀谷 Mitoya *s*
刀屋 Mitoya *p*
九二 Mikuni *s*
九郎 Sankurō *m*
九娘 Mikura *f*
人片輪 Sannin-gatawa *la*
人吉三廓初買 Sannin Kichizō kuruwa no hatsukai *l*
人法師 S. hōshi *l*
人妻 Sanninzuma *l*
[3]川 Mikawa *p*
三 Mitsuzō *m*
个田 Sangada *s*
之助 Sannosuke *m*
下 Sange *s*
干 Mitate *m*
子 Mitsune *s*
土 Mitsuchi *s*
上 Mikami *s* ⌈*ml*
上於菟吉 M. Otokichi
千年 Michitose *s*
千男 Michio *m*
千代 Michiyo *f*
[4]水 Misui *p*
介 Sansuke *m*
分一 Mibuichi *s*
分一所 Sanbuichisho *s*, Saiisho, Kutsuwata
日月 Mikazuki *p*
山 Miyama *s*; Mitsuyama *la*
五 Mii *sf*; Sago *s*, San-
夫 Mitsuo *m* ⌊go
毛 Mike *s*
手代 Miteshiro *s*
手代人名 M. no Hitona *ml*
文字屋 Sanmojiya *s*
方 Mikata *m-f*
方一方 Kutsuwata *s*
方一新 Kutsuwa *s*, Kutsū
戸 Sannohe *sp*; Mito *s*
戸見 Mitomi *s*
戸部 Mitobe *s*
木 Miki *sp*; Sōki *s*, Miuki; Mitsugi *sm*
木竹二 Miki Takeji *ml*
木清 M. Kiyoshi *ml*
井 Mitsui *s*; Mii *p*
井甲之 M. Kōshi *ml*
井田 Miida *s*
井寺 Miidera *p-la*
井楽 Miiraku *p*
[5]加和 Mikawa *p*
加茂 Mikamo *p*
代吉 Miyokichi *m*
代川 Miyokawa *s*
代実録 Sandai jitsuroku *l*
代集 Sandaishū *l*
石 Mitsuishi *sp*
尻 Migashiri *s*
辺 Minabe *s*
四郎 Sanshirō *m-l*
冊子 Sanzōshi *p*
平 Mihira *s*; Sanpei *m*
玉集 Sangyokushū *l*
半規管喪失 Sanhan kikan sōshitsu *l*
矢 Miya *s*
丘 Mitsuo *m*
本木 Sanbongi *p*
本柱 Sanbon no hashira *la*
田 Mita *s*; Sanda *p*
田川 Mitagawa *p*
田谷 Sandaya *s*
田村 Mitamura *s*
田村鳶魚 M. Engyo *ml*
田澪人 Mita Reijin *ml*
[6]次 Miyoshi *sp*
池 Miike *sp*; Mike *s*
羽 Mitsuha *m*
全 Mittomo *m*
光 Sankō *f*
光子 Mitsuko *f*
吉 Miyoshi *s*; Sankichi *m*
吉屋 Miyoshiya *s*
守 Mimori *sm*; Mikami *s*; Mimoru *m*, Mimore, Tadamori
宅 Miyake *sm-p*
宅川 Miyagawa *s*, Miyakegawa
宅花圃 Miyake Kaho *ml* ⌈*ml*
宅周太郎 M. Shūtarō
宅雪嶺 M. Setsurei *ml*
宅島 Miyakejima *p*
宅観瀾 Miyake Kanran *mh* ⌈dahira
成 Mitsunari *m*, Ta-
[7]阪 Misaka *s*
沢 Misawa *sp*
坂 Misaka *s* ⌈mura
村 Mimura *s*, Mitsu-
杉 Misugi *s*
作 Sansaku *m*
位 Sanmi *mh-fl*
位局 S. no Tsubone *fl*
好 Miyoshi *sp*
好十郎 M. Jūrō *ml*
好松洛 M. Shōraku *ml*
好長慶 M. Chōkei *mh*
好達治 M. Tatsuji *ml*
好豊一郎 M. Toyoichirō *ml*
男 Mitsuo *m*
貝 Migai *s*
芳 Miyoshi *p*
芳野 Miyoshino *s*
谷 Mitani *s*, Miya
谷昭 Mitani Akira *ml*
条 Sanjō *sp*
条西 Sanjōnishi *s*
条西実隆 S. Sanetaka *ml* ⌈*ml*
条西季知 S. Suetomo
条実美 Sanjō Sanetomi *mh*
尾 Mio *s*, Mitsuo
尾木 Mioki *s*
尾谷 Mionoya *s*
角 Misumi *sp*; Kazumi *m*
角寛 M. Kan *ml*
里 Misato *s*
充 Kazumitsu *m*
甫右衛門 Sabuemon *m*
[8]帖和讃 Sanjō wasan *l*
股 Mimata *p*
阿弥 San'ami *ma*

刀 又 人 入 九 七 十 八 川 小 ▼ 三 ▲ 也 之 于 千 乃 口 ロ 巳 已 己

牧 Mimaki *s*
和 Miwa *sp*, Sanwa; Sanna *ml*
河 Mikawa *ph*
河口 Mikawaguchi *s*, Mikkouchi
林 Mibayashi *s*; Mitsumoto *m*
枝 Saigusa *sm*; Saegusa *s*, Miesagusa
枝松 Saegusa *s*
枝部 Saegusa *s*
枝康高 Saigusa Yasutaka *ml*
枝博音 S. Hiroto *ml*
苫 Mitoma *s*
宝名義抄 Sanbō myōgishō *l*
宝絵詞 S. ekotoba *l*
宝類字抄 S. ruijishō *l*
国 Mikuni *sp*
国志演義 Sangokushi engi *l*
国通覧図説 Sangoku tsūran zusetsu *lh*
良坂 Mirasaka *p*
[9]俣 Mitsumata *s*, Minomata
狩 Mikari *sm*
松 Mimatsu *s*
砂 Misuna *m*
政 Kazumasa *m*
段崎 Sandagasaki *s*
依 Miyori *sp*
保 Miho *sp*; Mio *s*
保木 Mioki *s*
保屋 Mioya *s*
津 Mitsu *s*
津川 Mitsugawa *s*
津木 Mitsugi *s*
津木春影 M. Shun'ei *ml*
津沢 Mitsuzawa *s*
神 Mikami *s*
科 Mishina *s*
参岡 Misaoka *s*
春 Miharu *p*
岳 Mitake *sp*
品 Mishina *s*
品蘭渓 M. Rinkei *ml*
宮 Sannomiya *s*
家 Mike *s*, Miyake
草 Mikusa *s*
荘太夫五人嬢 Sanshōdayū gonin musume *l*
岡 Mioka *s*
巻 Mitsumaki *s*
原 Mihara *s*
廻部 Mikurube *s*
省 Kazumi *m*, Sansei
重 Mie *sp*
重郎 Sanjūrō *m*, Mierō
重吉 Miekichi *m*
[10]珠 Mitama *sp*
柳 Mitsuyanagi *s*
浦 Miura *sp*
浦守治 M. Moriharu *ml*
浦朱門 M. Shumon *ml*
浦泰村 M. Yasumura *mh*
浦梅園 M. Baien *mh*
郎 Saburō *m*, Samurō
郎坂 Saisaka *sp*
郎助 Saburosuke *m*
郎兵衛 Saburobee *m*
郎治 Saburōji *m*
倉 Mikura *s*
畠 Mihata *s*
柴 Mishiba *s*
笑 Sanshō *la*
室 Mimuro *s*
室戸 Mimurodo *s*
原 Mihara *sp*
通士 Mitsushi *m*
馬 Sanba *ml*; Mitsuma *m*
[11]陸 Sanriku *p*
渓 Mitani *s*
根 Mine *s*
桝 Mimasu *s*
梓 Sansai *s*
栖 Misu *s*
瓶 Mikame *sp*; Sanbe *p*
船 Mifune *s*
教指帰 Sangō shiiki *l*
野 Mino *sp*; Minu *m*
野宇泥須 Minunounesu *s*
野村 Minomura *s*
笠 Mikasa *sp*
部 Mibe *s*
鬼 Mitsuki *m*
留 Mitome *s*
島 Mishima *sp*
島由紀夫 M. Yukio *ml*
島通庸 M. Michitsune *mh*
島章道 M. Shōdō *ml*
島霜川 M. Sōsen *ml*
[12]隅 Misumi *sp*
須 Misu *s*
崎 Misaki *sp*
朝 Misasa *p*
森 Mitsumori *s*, Mimori
賀尻 Mikajiri *s*, Migashiri
富 Mitomi *sp*
富朽葉 M. Kyūyō *ml*
番叟 Sanbasō *lam*
喜男 Mikio *m*
善 Miyoshi *sp*
善清行 M. no Kiyoyuki *mh*
善康信 M. no Yasunobu *mh*
善康連 M. no Yasutsura *mh*
遊亭 San'yūtei *s*
遊亭円朝 S. Enchō *mla*
間 Mitsuma *s*; Mimap
[13]階屋 Sangaiya *s*
堀 Mibori *s*
塚 Mitsuka *s*
経義疏 Sangyō gisho *l*
滝 Mitaki *s*
淵 Mibuchi *s*, Mitsubuchi
豊 Mitoyo *sp*
觜 Mihashi *s*, Mitsuhashi
雲 Mikumo *sp*
厩 Miumaya *p*, Minmaya
越 Mitsukoshi *s*, Mikoshi
[14]増 Mimasu *s*
郷 Misato *sp*; Sangō *s*
種 Migusa *sm*
嘉喜 Mikaki *m*
統 Mimune *s*
熊 Miguma *s*
幣 Minusa *s*, Miyuki, Minuki
関 Miseki *s*
[15]穂 Miho *s*
穂田 Mihota *sp*
輪 Miwa *sp-la*
輪田 Miwata *s*
輪寿壮 Miwa Jusō *mh*
衛 Mitsue *m*
養基 Miyaki *p*
[16]樹 Miki *sm*
樹雄 Mikio *m*
橋 Mihashi *s*; Mitsuhashi *sp*
橋鷹女 Mitsuhashi Takajo *fl*
厳 Mitsuyoshi *m*
[18]嶽 Mitake *s*
[19]瀬 Mise *s*; Mitsuze *p*
潴 Mitsuma *sp*; Mitsumata *s*
[21]鶴夫 Mitsuo *m*
繩 Minawa *s*
巌 Mitsuyoshi *m*
[22]籟 Sanrai *l*
[24]鷹 Mitaka *sp*

### 3 U

**也** 23 [N] (YA, E, nari, tada, ari, mata)
寸志 Yasushi *m*
有 Yayū *ml*

**之** 24 [N] Itaru *m*. (SHI, no, kore, yuki, yoshi, hide, kuni, tsuna, yori, nobu, hisa)
元 Yoshimoto *m*
布 Yukinobu *m*
貞 Koresada *m*
通 Yukimichi *m*
剛 Yukitaka *m*
勝 Korekatsu *m*

**于** 25 (U, yuki, kiyo)
夫 Kiyoo *m*

**干** 26 [T] (KAN, tate, taku, hi, hosu, moto)
河岸 Hikawagishi *s*, Higashi
城 Tateki *sm*
雄 Tateo *m*, Takuo
潟 Higata *sp*

**乃** 27 [N] Imashi *m*, Osamu. (DAI, NAI, no)
木 Nogi *s*
木子 Nogiko *f*
木希典 Nogi Maresuke *mh*
枝 Noe *f*
武 Nobu *f*
美 Nomi *s*
野 Nono *s*

**囗** 28 Kakō *s*. (I)

**口** 29 [T] (KŌ, KU, kuchi, aki, hiro)
ノ津 Kuchinotsu *p*
人 Kuchūdo *m*, Akikiyo
分田 Kumode *s*, Kumoda, Kubunden
次 Akitsugu *m*
羽 Kuchiba *sp*
和 Kuchiwa *p*
遊 Kuchizusami *l*

巳 30 [N] (SHI, JI, mi)
生子 Miyoko f
代次 Miyoji m
代治 Miyoji m
栄子 Mieko f
野 Mino s
喜男 Mikio m
熊 Mikuma sm

已 31 Owari m. (I, sue)
汶 Imon s

己 32 [T] Komon s. (KO, KI, no, oto)
西 Kose s
斐 Konomi s, Koi
智 Kochi s

夕 33 [T] (SEKI, JAKU, yū, yu)
起子 Yukiko f
張 Yūbari p ⌈shū l
暮遣歌集 Yūgure ika-
輝子 Yukiko f
顔 Yūgao lf-la
霧 Yūgiri lf-fa

寸 34 [T] Hakaru m. (SUN, SON, ki, chika, nori)
土 Sundo l
喜 Suki s

才 35 (SAI, ZAI, tae, toshi, mochi, kata)
一郎 Saiichirō m
木 Saiki s
田 Saida s
伎 Tehito s
光 Taemitsu m
蔵集 Saizōshū l
磨 Saimaro m

丈 36 [T] Hasetsuka s. (JŌ, CHŌ, take, hiro, masu, tomo, hase)
人 Taketo m
巳 Takemi m
夫 Masuo m
太郎 Jōtarō m
平 Jōhei m
次郎 Jōjirō m
草 Jōsō ml
部 Hasebe s, Hasetsukabe
部路 Hasebeji s

凡 37 [T] Ōshi s, Oshi. (HAN, BON, tsune, ōshi, oshi, ō, o, chika) ⌈to m
人 Ōshihito s; Tsune-
川内 Ōshikōchi s
子 Tsuneko f
夫 Tsuneo m
兆 Bonchō ml
河 Ōkawa s, Okkawa
河内 Ōshikōchi s
河内躬恒 Ō. no Mitsune ml
治 Ōji s
部 Obe s, Hobe
海 Oshinumi s, Oshinoumi, Ōshiama

子 38 [T] Shigeru m; Ko s. (SHI, SU, ko, ne, mi, shige, taka, tada, chika, tsugu, toshi, yasu, sane, tane, miru)
ゝ Tadashi m
一 Neichi m
子 Koko s; Shigeko f
子子 Koneko s, Nekoshi
半 Konaka m
生 Yasuo m; Kobi p
地上 Kochigami s, Kochie
母沢 Shimosawa s
母沢寛 S. Kan ml
安 Koyasu s
男 Toshio m
持 Komochi p
建 Kodate s
盗人 Konusubito la
規 Shiki ml

工 39 [T] Tsutomu m, Tsukasa; Takumi sm; Kinunui s. (KŌ, KU, yoshi, tada, ⌊nori)
月 Kutsuki s
匠 Takumi s, Tehito
造 Kinunui s
富 Kudomi s
楽 Kuraku s
藤 Kudō s
藤平助 K. Heisuke mh
藤好美 K. Yoshimi ml

丸 40 [T] Maru s, Wani. (GAN, maru, mari, maro)
[3]川 Marukawa s
之内 Marunouchi p
子 Maruko sf-p; Mariko sf
[4]井 Marui s
毛 Marumo s
女 Marume s
山 Maruyama sp
山作楽 M. Sakura ml
山芳良 M. Yoshimasa ml
山真男 M. Masao ml
山静 M. Shizuka ml
山薫 M. Kaoru ml
[5]田 Maruta s
目 Marume s
本 Marumoto s
[6]地 Maruchi s
[7]作 Marunari m
谷 Maruya s, Marutani
尾 Maruo s
[8]林 Marubayashi s
房 Marufusa m
茂 Marumo s
[9]岡 Maruoka sp
岡九華 M. Kyūka ml
岡明 M. Akira ml
岡桂 M. Katsura ml
[10]屋 Maruya s
[11]野 Maruno s
部 Wanibe s
島 Marushima s
亀 Marugame sp
[12]森 Marumori sp
碆 Marubae s
[16]橋 Marubashi s
橋忠弥 M. Chūya mh
[17]邇 Wani s
[19]瀬布 Maruseppu p

士 41 [T] Osamu m, Tsukasa, Mamoru, Akira. (SHI, JI, o, to, aki, koto, sachi, tada, nori, hito, hiko)
十 Hikotari m
別 Shibetsu p
郎 Shirō m
朗 Shirō ml
清 Kotosuga m
幌 Shihoro p
観 Sachimaro m

土 42 [T] (DO, TO, tsuchi, hiji, hani, tsutsu, tada, nori)
[2]人 Tsuchito m
[3]川 Tsuchikawa s
上 Tsuchigami s; Do-
巳 Tsutsumi m ⌊jō l
子 Tsuchiko s
[4]水 Tsuchimi s
戸 Tsuchido s
山 Tsuchiyama sp
手 Dote s
方 Hijikata s
方定一 H. Teiichi ml
井 Doi s, Tsuchii
井内 Doiuchi s
井晩翠 Doi Bansui ml
[5]公 Dokō s
生 Hanyū s; Habu sp
田 Tsuchida s; Dota sp
田杏村 T. Kyōson ml
田耕平 T. Kōhei ml
本 Tsuchimoto s
[6]江 Tsuchie s
有知 Touchi s
庄 Tonoshō p
気 Toke p
成 Donari p ⌈key"
耳古 Toruko p "Tur-
[7]作 Totsukuri s; Tsuchitsukuri m, Hani- ⌊shi
佐 Tosa sph
佐日記 T. nikki l
佐日記燈 T. n. akashi l
佐山 Tosayama p
佐山田 Tosa Yamada p ⌈mh
佐光信 T. Mitsunobu
佐光長 T. Mitsunaga ma ⌈ma
佐光起 T. Mitsuoki
佐清水 T. Shimizu p
佐房 Tosabō mh
沢 Tsuchizawa s
形 Hijikata s
村 Tsuchimura s
谷 Tsuchiya s
芳 Dohō ml
志田 Toshida s
車 Tsuchiguruma la
[8]門 Tsuchikado s, Domon
岐 Toki sp ⌈ml
岐善麿 T. Zenmaro
肥 Doi s, Dohi; Toi p
肥原 Dohibara s

居 Doi *sp*
居光知 D. Kōchi *ml*
[9]信田 Toshida *s*
持 Tsuchimochi *s*
神 Niwa *s*
[10]浦 Tsuchiura *sp*; Teura *s*
海 Hanami *s*
師 Haji *s*; Hanishi *sfl*
師清二 Haji Seiji *ml*
師部 Hanishibe *s*
師萠 Hajime *m*
倉 Tsuchikura *s*, Tokura
原 Hijiwara *s*
庫 Toko *s*
屋 Tsuchiya *s*
屋文明 T. Bunmei *ml*
屋竹雨 T. Chikuu *ml*
[11]野 Tsuchino *s*
部 Tobe *s*
麻呂 Hijimaro *m*
[12]堅 Hijikata *m*
御 Tsuchigo *s*
御門 Tsuchimikado *mh*
崎 Tozaki *s*
崎田 Tozakida *s*
[15]蔵 Tsuchigura *s*; Dokura *sm*
[16]橋 Tsuchihashi *s*, Dohashi
蜘蛛 Tsuchigumo *la*

**万** 43 [T] Yorozu *m*, Susumu, Tsumoru. (MAN, BAN, kazu, katsu, taka, tsumu, yorozu, yusuru, yoru, yuru)
[1]一郎 Man'ichirō *m*
[2]刀 Makata *s*
[3]三 Manzō *m*
之助 Mannosuke *m*
千代 Machiyo *sf*; Manchiyo *m*
千野 Takema *s*
[4]太郎 Mantarō *m*
木 Maki *s*, Maruki, Yusurugi, Yuruki, Yoruki
[5]代 Mandai *s*, Bandai, Mozu, Mozume; Yorozuyo *f*
代屋 Bandaiya *s*
代集 Mandaishū *l*
司 Manji *m*
石 Mangoku *s*
右衛門 Man'emon *m*
平 Manpei *m*
田 Manda *s*
[6]次郎 Manjirō *m*
字屋 Manjiya *s*
吉 Kazuyoshi *m*
年 Kazutoshi *m*; Mannen *ml*
年艸 Mannensō *l*
年青 Omoto *f*
年馬 Maneba *s*
年場 Maneba *s*
[7]尾 Mao *s*
寿 Manju 1024–28
寿之助 Masunosuke *m*
里小路 Madenokōji *sp*
里小路宣房 M. Nobufusa *mh*
里子 Mariko *f*
里谷 Marigaya *s*
[8]波 Manami *s*
延 Man'en 1860–61
[9]城目 Makime *s*, Manjōme
亭応賀 Mantei Ōga *ml*
治 Manji *m* 1658–61
治郎 Manjirō *m*
[10]栖子 Masuko *f*
華鏡 Kareedosukōpu *l*
屋 Yorozuya *s*
馬 Kazuma *m*
[11]紀之助 Makinosuke *m*
鬼 Nakiri *s*
逸 Man'itsu *m*
[12]場 Manba *p*
場目 Manjōme *s*
朝報 Yorozu chōhō *l*
喜 Maki *s*
[13]葉代匠記 Man'yō daishōki *l*
葉仮名 Man'yōgana *l*
葉考 Man'yōkō *l*
葉集 Man'yōshū *l*
葉集代匠記 M. daishōki *l*
葉集古義 M. kogi *l*
葉集玉の小琴 M. tama no ogoto *l*
葉集抄 M. shō *l*
葉集燈 M. akashi *l*
葉集墨縄 M. suminawa *l*
載狂歌集 Manzai kyōkashū *l*
[14]穀 Takayoshi *m*
[15]蔵 Manzō *m*
衛 Kazue *m*
[17]緑 Banroku *m*

**千** 44 [T] Sen *s*. (SEN, chi, kazu, yuki)
ケ崎 Chigasaki *s*
[2]丁 Senchō *p*
[3]川 Sengawa *s*; Chikawa *m*
之 Kazuyuki *m*, Senshi
万億 Tsumoru *s*, Tsumoi
丈 Chihiro *m*
寸 Yukichika *m*
也 Sen'ya *m*
子 Chine *f*
子部 Chiikobe *s*, Chiisabe, Chiisakobe
千石 Chijiwa *sp*
千和 Chijiwa *s*, Chichiwa
千岩 Chijiiwa *sp*
千輪 Chijiwa *s*, Chichiwa
[4]切木 Chigiriki *l*
方 Chikata *m*
五百番歌合 Sengohyakuban utaawase *l*
夫 Chiburi *sp*; Iburi *s*
木良 Chigira *sp*
太郎 Sentarō *m*
女 Kazuko *f*
手 Senju *fa-la*
手院 Senjuin *s*
[5]仭 Chihiro *m*
代 Chiyo *sf*; Chishiro *s*, Sendai
代川 Chiyogawa *sp*
代三郎 Chiyosaburō *m*
代之助 Chiyonosuke *m*
代女 Chiyojo *fl*
代尼 Chiyoni *fl*
代田 Chiyoda *sp*
代松 Chiyomatsu *sm*
代倉 Chiyogura *s*
代能 Chiyonō *m*
代童子 Chiyodōji *m*
代間 Chiyoma *s*
礼 Kazunori *m*
引 Chibiki *m*
冬 Chifuyu *m*
石 Sengoku *s*
古 Chifuru *m*
田 Senda *s*, Chita
本 Senbon *s*
本松 Senbonmatsu *s*
屯 Chimura *m*
[6]任丸 Sentomaru *m*
羽 Senba *s*
羽鶴 Senbazuru *l*
字文 Senjimon *l*
年 Chitose *p*
年生 Chitose *f*
早 Chihaya *s*
早赤阪 C. Akasaka *p*
曲 Chikuma *p*
[7]住 Senjū *s*
坂 Chisaka *s*
沢 Chisawa *s*
役 Chiburi *s*
役湊 Chiburinominato *s*
村 Chimura *s*
別 Chiwaki *m*
利休 Sen no Rikyū *ma*
足 Senzoku *s*; Chitaru *m*
谷 Chiya *s*
谷子 Chiyako *f*
谷道雄 Chiya Michio *ml*
[8]柄 Chigara *s*
波 Senba *s*
枝 Chieda *m*
明 Chigira *s*
英 Chibusa *m*
苑 Chisono *f*
[9]俣 Chimata *m*
柄 Chigara *s*
弥 Sen'ya *m*
畑 Senhata *p*
秋 Chiaki *s*, Senshū
家 Senge *s*
家元麿 S. Motomaro *ml*
草 Chigusa *s*
首和歌 Senshu waka *l*
岩 Chihaya *s*
栄子 Chieko *f*
春 Chiharu *m*
風 Chikazu *m*
[10]脇 Chiwaki *s*
柳亭 Senryūtei *s*
破屋 Chihaya *s*
剣 Chihaya *m*
倉 Chikura *p*
原 Chihara *s*
屋 Chiya *s*, Chihaya, Hon'ya
馬 Chiba *s*
室 Chimuro *m*
速 Chihaya *s*
[11]振 Chifuri *m*
野 Chino *s*, Senno
鳥 Chidori *sf*
島 Chishima *sp* "Kuriles"
[12]場 Senba *s*
須和 Chisuwa *s*
崎 Senzaki *s*
勝 Chikatsu *s*
尋 Chihiro *m*
萱 Chigaya *s*
賀 Chiga *s*, Senga

賀浦 Chigaura *s*; Chiganoura *p*
[18]幹 Chikara *m*
葉 Chiba *sp*
葉原 Chibahara *s*
葉胤明 Chiba Taneaki *ml*
葉亀雄 C. Kameo *ml*
歳 Chitose *m-p*; Senzai *lam*
装 Senjō *s*, Chizura, Chigira
載集 Senzaishū *l*
厩 Senmaya *p*
[14]種 Chigusa *sp*
種忠顕 C. Tadaaki *mh*
[15]蔭 Chikage *m*
磐 Chihaya *s*
熊 Chikuma *s*
[16]樫 Chikashi *m*
穎 Chikai *m*
綿 Chime *s*
頭 Chikami *s*, Sentō
[20]織 Chiori *m*
麗 Chiyoshi *f*
[21]鶴子 Chizuko *f*
鶴笑 Chizue *f*

**久** 45 [T] Hisashi *m*; Hisa *s*. (KU, KYŪ, hisa, naga, tsune, hiko)
[1]一郎 Hisaichirō *m*
[2]七 Kyūshichi *m*
[3]川 Hisakawa *s*
三郎 Kyūzaburō *m*
下 Kuge *s*, Kumoto, Kusaka
子 Hisako *f*
大 Hisanaga *m*
之浜 Hisanohama *p*
之助 Kyūnosuke *m*
万 Kuma *sp*
万吉 Kumakichi *m*
久利 Kukuri *s*
久野 Kuguno *sp*
[4]仁 Hisato *m*
方 Kuba *s*
山 Hisayama *sp*; Ku-
井 Kui *p* ⌊yama *s*
太郎 Kyūtarō *m*
木村 Kukimura *s*
木 Hisaki *s*
木田 Kukita *s*
木野 Kugino *sp*
五郎 Kyūgorō *m*
[5]代 Kushiro *s*
永 Hisanaga *m*
布白 Kubushiro *s*
田 Hisata *s*
本 Hisamoto *sm*
平 Kyūhei *m*
四郎 Kyūshirō *m*
[6]次 Hisatsugu *m*, Hisaji, Kyūji
次郎 Kyūjirō *m*
地楽 Kuchira *s*
吉 Hisayoshi *sm*; Kyūkichi *m*
光 Hisamitsu *sm*
世 Kuze *sp*
米 Kume *sp*
米川 Kumegawa *s*
米田 Kumeda *s*
米正雄 Kume Masao *ml* ⌈*mh*
米邦武 K. Kunitake
米桂一郎 K. Keiichirō *ma*
米南 Kumenan *p*
米蔵 Kumezō *m*
[7]似美 Kunimi *f*
住 Kuzumi *s*, Hisazumi; Kujū *p*
作 Hisatomo *m*, Kyū-
坂 Kusaka *s* ⌊saku
坂玄瑞 K. Genzui *mh*
村 Hisamura *s*, Kumura
利 Hisatoshi *m*; Kuri *s*
谷 Kutani *sp*
安 Kyūan 1145–51
芳 Kubo *s*, Kubō; Kuba *sp*
志 Kushi *s*
志本 Kushimoto *s*
貝 Kugai *s*
兵衛 Kyūbee *m*
里 Kuri *s*, Saka
我 Kuga *s*, Koga; Kyūga *m*
寿 Kyūju 1154–56
寿弥太 Kusuyata *m*
[8]板 Hisaita *s*
板栄二郎 H. Eijirō *ml*
明 Hisaharu *m*
芽子 Kumeko *f*
宜 Hisayoshi *m*
宗 Hisamune *sm*
居 Hisai *p*
良 Kura *f*
[9]保 Kubo *s*
保より江 K. Yorie *fl*
保川 Kubokawa *s*
保山 Kuboyama *s*
保天随 Kubo Tenzui
保井 Kuboi *s* ⌊*ml*
保木 Kuboki *s*
保内 Kubouchi *s*
保田 Kubota *sp*
保田万太郎 K. Mantarō *ml* ⌈*fl*
保田不二子 K. Fujiko
保田正文 K. Masafumi *ml* ⌈*ml*
保田彦作 K. Hikosaku
保寺 Kubodera *s*
保谷 Kubotani *s*
保栄 Kubo Sakae *ml*
保庭 Kuboniwa *s*
保猪之吉 Kubo Inokichi *ml*
保野 Kubono *s*
保埜 Kubono *s*
保島 Kuboshima *s*
恒 Hisatsune *sm*
津見 Kutsumi *s*
治 Kyūji *m*
治郎 Kyūjirō *m*
柄 Hisamoto *m*
弥 Hisaya *m*
松 Hisamatsu *s*
松潜一 H. Sen'ichi *ml*
美浜 Kumihama *p*
[10]郎 Kurō *m*, Kyūrō; Kuraki *s*
浮 Hisachika *m*
高 Kudaka *s*
家 Kuge *s*, Hisaya
容 Hisanari *m*
原 Kuhara *s*
座 Hisago *s*
連 Hisatsura *m*
連木 Kureko *s*
連松 Kurematsu *s*
馬人 Kumando *m*
[11]後 Kyūgo *s*
域 Hisamura *m*
採 Hisamochi *m*
根崎 Kunezaki *s*
梅 Kume *f*
野 Kuno *s*, Hisano
野豊彦 K. Toyohiko
能 Kunō *s* ⌊*ml*
能木 Kunoki *s*
留 Hisatome *s*
留米 Kurume *p*
留島 Kurushima *s*
埜 Kuno *s*
進 Hisamichi *m*
島 Hisajima *s*, Kujima
[12]須見 Kusumi *s*
須美 Kusumi *s*
順 Hisamoto *m*
隅 Kusumi *s*
接 Hisatsugu *m*
御山 Kumiyama *p*
崎 Kusaki *s*
納 Kunō *s*
富 Hisatomi *sm*
喜 Kuki *sp*
賀 Kuga *sp*
間 Kuma *s*, Hisama
[13]慎 Hisachika *m*
雄 Hisao *m*, Hisakata
幹 Hisatoshi *m*
寛 Hisahiro *m*
茲 Kuji *s*
葛 Hisatsura *m*
[14]徳 Kyūtoku *s*
郷 Hisasato *s*; Kugō *sp*
語 Hisatsugu *m*
静 Hisatsugu *m*
[15]徴 Hisayoshi *m*
雍 Hisayasu *m*
蔵 Kyūzō *m*
[16]積 Kusazumi *s*
継 Hisatsugi *sm*
慈 Kuji *p*
[18]邇 Kuni *s*
邇京 K. no miyako *ph*
邇宮 Kuninomiya *s*
[19]瀬 Kuze *p*

**下** 46 [T] Shimo *p*. (KA, GE, shimo, shita, moto, shi, ji, kuda, ori)
[3]川 Shimokawa *sp*
口 Shimoguchi *s*
[4]仁田 Shimo-nida *p*
水内 Shimo-minochi *p*
方 Shimokata *s*
元 Shimomoto *s*
井 Orii *s*, Shimoi
日佐 Shimōsa *s*
斗 Shimoto *s*
斗女 Shimotome *s*
斗米 Shimotomai *s*
中 Shimonaka *s* ⌈*ml*
中弥三郎 S. Yasaburō
山 Shimoyama *sp*
山田 Shimo-yamada *p*
山佐 Shimoyamasa *s*
毛 Shimoge *p*
毛野 Shimotsukenu *s*, Shimotsukeno
毛野俯見 Shimotsukenufushimi *s*

5石 Oroshi *sp*
司 Gesu *s*
市 Shimoichi *p*
平 Shimodaira *s*
生 Shimonobu *s*
北 Shimo-kita *p* ⌈*p*
北山 Shimo-kitayama
田 Shimoda *sp*; Shitada *p* ⌈ko *flh*
田歌子 Shimoda Uta-
6氷 Shimohi *s*
伊那 Shimo-ina *p*
圷 Shimoakutsu *sp*
江 Shimoe *s*
地 Shimochi *s*
竹 Shimodake *s*
吉 Motoyoshi *m*
耳 Shimoni *s*
世古 Shimoseko *s*
米宮 Amenomiya *s*
舟尾 Shimofunao *s*
7阪 Shimosaka *s*
坂 Shimosaka *sm*
沢 Shimozawa *s*
谷 Shimoya *s*, Shimodani, Shitaya
呂 Gero *p* ⌈*s*, Shimo
条 Shimojō *sp*; Gejō
里 Shimosato *s*
出 Shimoide *s*
村 Shimomura *s*
村千秋 S. Chiaki *ml*
村海南 S. Kainan *ml*
村湖人 S. Kojin *ml*
村観山 S. Kanzan *ma*
8阿久津 Shimoakutsu
枝 Shimoeda *s* ⌊*sp*
京 Shimogyō *p*
河 Shimokawa *s*
河内 Shimokōchi *s*
河辺 Shimokōbe *s*
河辺長流 S. Chōryū *ml* ⌈do *s*
9津 Shimotsu *sp*; Ori-
松 Kudamatsu *sp*
神 Shimotsumiwa *s*
秋 Shimoaki *s*
草 Shitakusa *l*
妻 Shimotsuma *sp*
風 Oroshi *s*
岡 Shimooka *s*
岡蓮杖 S. Renjō *mh*
10高井 Shimo-takai *p*
倉 Shimogura *s*
家 Oroshiya *s*, Watarai, Watakushi
益城 Shimo-mashiki *p*
原 Shimobara *s*
連 Shimotsure *s*
県 Shimo-agata *p*
11振 Shimoburi *s*
船尾 Shimofunao *s*
野 Shimotsuke *fl-ph*; Shimono *s*, Kabata
訳語 Shimōsa *s*
部 Shimobe *sp*
都賀 Shimo-tsuga *p*
笠 Shimogasa *s*
島 Shimojima *s*
閉伊 Shimo-hei *p*
鳥 Shimotori *s*
12曾根 Shimosone *s*
莵上 Shimotsuunakami *s*
道 Shimomichi *s*, Shimotsumichi, Shimotsumi
間 Shimotsuma *s*, Shimoma ⌈*p*
13新川 Shimo-niikawa
蒲刈 Shimo-kamagari
嵐 Oroshi *s* ⌊*p*
14郷 Shimosato *s*; Shimogō *sp*
農 Susogo *s*
関 Shimonoseki *p*
15諏訪 Shimo-suwa *p*
蔵 Shimogura *s*
17総 Shimōsa *ph*, Shimofusa
館 Shimodate *p*
甑 Shimo-koshiki *p*
18濃 Susogo *s*
瀬 Shimose *s* ⌈*mh*
瀬雅允 S. Masachika

**上** 47 [T] Noboru *m*, Takashi, Susumu; Kami *s*; Ue *sp*, Kado. (jō, kami, ue, taka, hozu, masa, uwa, ura, e, hisa, age, aga, kō, kado)
ノ国 Kaminokuni *p*
1一丸 Kamiichimaru *m*
2九一色 Kami-kuishiki *p*
3小阿仁 Kami-koani *p*
三川 Kamimikawa *s*
口 Kamiguchi *s*
之保 Kaminoho *p*
上手 Kamijōzu *s*
上島 Shishima *s*
下 Jōge *p*
子 Urako *f*
士幌 Kami-shihoro *p*
川 Uekawa *s*; Kamikawa *sp*
川井 Kamikawai *s*
久保 Kamikubo *s*
4匂 Katori *s*
五島 Kami-gotō *p*
中 Uenaka *s*, Kaminaka ⌈tsuki *sp*
月 Kamitsuki *s*; Kō-
木 Ueki *s*
水 Kamimizu *s*
水内 Kami-minochi *p*
方 Kamigata *sp*; Uwakata *s*
方武士道 Zeeroku bushidō *l*
山 Kamiyama *sp*; Ueyama *s*
山田 Kami-yamada *p*
山佐 Kamiyamasa *s*
毛 Kamitsuke *s*; Kōtsuke *ph*
毛布 Kamitsukefu *s*
毛野 Kamitsukenu *s*, Kantsukeno
毛野坂本 Kōzukeno-sakamoto *s*
5代 Kamishiro *s*, Jōdai
北 Kamikita *p*
北山 Kami-kitayama *p*
石 Kamiiwa *s*, Kamiishi
石津 Kami-ishizu *p*
勾 Kamimagari *s*
司 Kamitsukasa *s*
司小剣 K. Shōken *ml*
甲 Jōkō *s*
市 Kamiichi *p*
平 Kamihira *s*, Uehira, Uwahira; Kamitaira *p* ⌈moto
本 Uemoto *s*, Kami-
矢作 Kami-yahagi *p*
田 Ueda *sp*; Ageta *s*
田万年 U. Mannen / Kazutoshi *ml*
田広 U. Hiroshi *ml*
田英夫 U. Hideo *ml*
田秋成 U. Akinari *ml*
田敏 U. Bin *ml*
田進 U. Susumu *ml*
田穆 U. Boku *ml*
6伊那 Kami-ina *p*
地 Kamichi *s*, Uechi
竹 Uetake *s*
有智 Kamiuchi *s*; Kōzuchi *sp* ⌈nishi
西 Kaminishi *s*, Ue-
舟尾 Kamifunao *s*
7住 Uwazumi *s*
阪 Kōsaka *s*
抜井見 Kaminukiimi *s*
沢 Kamizawa *s*, Uezawa ⌈ka
坂 Uesaka *s*, Kamisa-
対馬 Kami-tsushima *p*
那賀 Kami-naka *p*
村 Uemura *s*, Kamimura
村松園 U. Shōen *fa*
杉 Uesugi *s*
杉氏憲 U. Ujinori *mh*
杉治憲 U. Harunori *mh* ⌈*mh*
杉重房 U. Shigefusa
杉景勝 U. Kagekatsu *mh* ⌈*mh*
杉慎吉 U. Shinkichi
杉憲実 U. Norizane *mh* ⌈*mh*
杉憲政 U. Norimasa
杉謙信 U. Kenshin *mh*
利 Kamiri *s*, Agari
谷 Uetani *s*, Kamiya
志比 Kami-shihi *p*
条 Kamijō *s*
床 Kamitoko *s*
尾 Ageo *sp*
里 Kamisato *p*
見 Uemi *s*
出 Kamide *s*
8阿久津 Kamiakutsu *s*
牧 Kamimaki *sp*; Kamimoku *p* ⌈numa
沼 Uenuma *s*, Kami-
河 Kamikawa *s*
河内 Kami-kawachi *p*
板 Kamiita *p*
枝 Hozue *sm-f-p*
林 Kanbayashi *s*, Kamibayashi
林暁 Kanbayashi Aka-
房 Jōbō *p* ⌊tsuki *ml*
京 Kamigyō *p*
宝 Kamitakara *s*
9垣 Uegaki *s*
垣内 Kamikōchi *s*
神 Niwa *s*, Hiwa
神吉 Kamikanki *s*
松 Uematsu *s*; Agematsu *sp*

松浦 Kami-matsura *p*; Kamimatsuura *s*
砂 Kamisago *s*
砂川 Kami-sunagawa *p*
保 Uwaho *s*
信 Kaminobu *s*
依知 Kamiichi *s*
津 Kōzu *sp*; Kanzu *s*
津江 Kami-tsue *p*
津浦 Kōtsura *sp*
妻 Kōzuma *s*
泉 Kamiizumi *s*
泉秀信 K. Hidenobu *ml*
岡 Kamioka *s*, Ueoka
10柳 Kamiyanagi *s*, Ueyanagi
郡 Kamigōri *p*
郎 Kōrō *s*
浦 Kamiura *sp*
浮穴 Kami-ukena *p*
海 Shanhai *p-l* "Shanghai"
高井 Kami-takai *p*
高地 Kamikōchi *p*
倉 Uekura *s*, Kamikura
益城 Kami-mashiki *p*
畠 Uehata *s*
宮 Kaminomiya *s*
宮聖徳法王帝説 Jōgū Shōtoku hōōtaisetsu *lh*
屋久 Kami-yaku *p*
県 Kamiagata *sp*; Kamitsuagata *s*
原 Uehara *s*
原勇作 U. Yūsaku *mh*
11峰 Kamimine *sp*
部 Kamibe *s*
都賀 Kami-tsuga *p*
野 Ueno *sp*, Kamino; Agano *s*; Kōzuke *ph*; Uwano *p*
野山 Uenoyama *s*
野壮夫 Ueno Takeo *ml*
野原 Uenohara *sp*
斎原 Kami-saibara *p*
符 Uwabu *s*
基 Takamoto *m*
埜 Ueno *s*
閉伊 Kami-hei *p*
島 Kamijima *s*, Uejima
島鬼貫 K. Onitsura *ml*
12陽 Jōyō *p*
湧別 Kami-yūbetsu *p*
勝 Kamikatsu *sp*
崎 Uesaki *s*
森 Uemori *s*
富良野 Kami-furano *p*
富田 Kami-tonda *p*
道 Kanmichi *s*, Kantsumichi; Jōtō *p*
13塚 Uetsuka *s*
滝 Kōtaki *s*
新川 Kami-niikawa *p*
14郷 Kamisato *s*; Kamigō *p*
領 Kamiryō *s*
遠野 Kamitōno *s*, Uedōno, Kadōno, Kadono, Atano
園 Uezono *s*
関 Kaminoseki *p*; Waseki *s*
16網 Kamiyosami *s*
総 Kazusa *ph*
磯 Kamiiso *p*
鷲 Ōwashi *s*

大 48 [T] Hiroshi *m*, Futoshi, Takashi, Masaru, Takeshi, Yutaka, Hajime; Ō *s*, Ōsumi. (DAI, TAI, ō, o, hiro, naga, moto, tomo, haru, masa, ōi, oi, ōki, ki, futo)
2十女 Otome *f*
刀西 Ōtose *s*
力之助 Dairikinosuke *m*
八木 Ōyagi *s*
八洲学会 Ōyashima gakkai *l*
3口 Ōguchi *sm-p*
子 Hiroko *f*, Tomoko; Daigo *p*
下 Ōshita *s*
下宇陀児 Ō. Udaru *ml*
川 Ōkawa *sp*
川周明 Ō. Shūmei *mh*
川端 Ōkawabata *l*
川原 Ōkawara *s*
川内 Ōkōchi *s*
工 Daiku *s*
工廻 Chakkujaku *s*
工原 Daikuhara *s*
三 Daizō *m*, Futomi
三郎 Daizaburō *m*
三島 Ōmishima *p*
三輪 Ōmiwa *s*
丸 Daimaru *s*
久 Ōhisa *p*
久保 Ōkubo *sp*
久保利通 Ō. Toshimichi *mh*
久保利謙 Ō. Toshiaki *ml*
久保忠保 Ō. Tadayasu *ml*
火 Ōhi *m*
上 Ōkami *s*, Ōue
4仁 Ōhito *sp*
化 Taika 645–50
手 Ōte *sp*
手拓次 Ō. Takuji *ml*
内 Ōuchi *sp*, Ōchi
内兵衛 Ōuchi Hyōe *ml*
内義隆 Ō. Yoshitaka *mh*
内山 Ōuchiyama *sp*
友 Ōtomo *s*
友宗麟 Ō. Sōrin *mh*
友皇子 Ō. no Ōji *mh*
友義鎮 Ō. Yoshishige *mh*
戸 Ōto *sm-p*
元 Ōmoto *s*
分 Ōita *sp*; Ōkita *s*
月 Ōtsuki *sp*; Tsuki *s*
王 Daiō *p*
夫 Haruo *m*; Maetsugimi *s*, Mōchigimi
太郎 Daitarō *m*
方 Ōgata *p*
文字 Daimonji *s*
中 Ōnaka *s*
中川 Ōnakagawa *s*
中臣 Ōnakatomi *s*
中臣能宣 Ō. no Yoshinobu *ml*
中道 Ōnakadō *s*
木 Ōki *sp*
木実 Ō. Minoru *ml*
木惇夫 Ō. Atsuo *ml*
木喬任 Ō. Takatō *mh*
木口 Ōkiguchi *s*
日 Ōhi *s*, Dainichi, Ōgusa
日子 Ōhisu *s*, Ōko
日方 Oikata *s*, Ōhigata, Ōhinata
日佐 Ōosa *s*
日奉 Ōhimatsuri *s*
日南 Ōhinata *s*
井 Ōi *sp*
井川 Ōigawa *p*
井上 Ōinoue *s*
井田 Ōita *s*
井広 Ōi Hiroshi *ml*
井広介 Ōi Hirosuke *ml*
井憲太郎 Ōi Kentarō *mh*
山 Ōyama *sp*; Daisen *p*
山田 Ōyamada *sp*
山定一 Ōyama Teiichi *ml*
山郁夫 Ō. Ikuo *mlh*
山道中栗毛後駿足 Ō. dōchū kurige no shiriuma *l*
山崎 Ōyamazaki *p*
山巌 Ōyama Iwao *mh*
5永 Daiei 1521–28
辺 Ōbe *s*
四郎 Daishirō *m*
目 Ōme *s*
用 Daiyō *s*
兄 Oine *m*
允 Ōmakoto *s*
立 Ōdate *s*
市 Ōichi *sm*; Ōchi *sp*
玉 Ōtama *p*
正 Taishō *mh-p* 1912–26
平 Ōhira *sm-p*; Ōdaira *s*; Taihei *p*
本 Ōmoto *s*
甘 Ōama *s*
丘 Ōoka *sp*
生 Ōbu *s*, Ōmibu; Ōnobu *sp*
矢 Ōya *s*
矢野 Ōyano *sp*
古 Ōko *s*
石 Ōishi *s*
石田 Ōishida *sp*
石橋立 Ōishihashidate *s*
五郎 Daigorō *m*
代 Ōshiro *s*
仏 Osaragi *s*, Ōsaragi; Daibutsu *sa*
仏次郎 O. Jirō *ml*
仏供 Daibuku *s*
仏供養 Daibutsu kuyō *la*
北 Ōkita *s*
田 Ōta *sp*
田川 Ōtagawa *s*
田洋子 Ōta Yōko *fl*
田南畝 Ō. Nanpo *ml*
田代 Ōtajiro *s*
田見 Ōtami *s*
田垣 Ōtagaki *s*
田垣蓮月 Ō. Rengetsu *ml*
田原 Ōtawara *sp*
田黒 Ōtaguro *s*
田税 Ōtachikara *s*
6任 Ōtō *sp*
地 Ōji *s*
竹 Ōtake *sp*
竹新助 Ō. Shinsuke *ml*
池 Ōike *s*

子 工 丸 士 土 万 千 久 下 上 ▼ 大 ▲ 心 刈 切 火 双 水 仂 化 仁 孔

子 工 丸 士 土 万 千 久 下 上 ▼ 大 ▲ 心 刈 切 火 双 水 仂 化 仁 孔

江 Ōe *sp*; Ōmi *sph*
江丸 Ōemaru *ml*
江山 Ōeyama *la*
江田 Ōeda *s*, Oita
江広元 Ōe no Hiromoto *mh*
江匡房 Ōe no Masafusa *ml*
江良太郎 Ōe Ryōtarō *ml*
江健三郎 Ōe Kenzaburō *ml*
江朝綱 Ōe no Asatsuna *ml*
江満雄 Ōe Mitsuo *ml*
羽 Ōba *s*
台 Ōdai *p*
羊 Ōhitsuji *s*
芝 Ōshiba *s*
吉 Ōyoshi *s*
吉郎 Daikichirō *m*
寺 Ōdera *s*
宇陀 Ōuda *p*
宅 Ōyake *sp*; Ōya *s*, Ōyaku
宅世継 Ōyake no Yotsugi *lm*
宅壮一 Ōya Sōichi *ml*
同 Daidō 806–10
弐 Daini *sm*
成 Ōnari *s*; Taisei *p*
辻 Ōtsuji *s*
曲 Ōmagari *sp*, Ōwata
亦 Ōmata *s*
耳 Daini *s*
世古 Ōseko *s*
米 Ōnoki *s*, Ōyagi
名晉我 Daimyō nagusami Soga *l*
多和 Ōtawa *s*, Ōto
多喜 Ōtaki *sp*
西 Ōnishi *sp*
西巨人 Ō. Kyojin *ml*
西克礼 Ō. Yoshinori *ml*
西祝 Ō. Hajime *ml*
西風 Asamaki *s*
[7]阪 Ōsaka *sp*
坂 Ōsaka *ph*
坂屋 Ōsakaya *s*
社 Taisha *p*; Ōyashiro *l*
社造 T.-zukuri *a*
形 Ōgata *s*
町 Ōmachi *sp*
町桂月 Ō. Keigetsu *ml*
利 Ōri *s*
利根 Ōtone *sp*
杉 Ōsugi *s*
杉栄 Ō. Sakae *mlh*
村 Ōmura *sp*
村益次郎 Ō. Masujirō *mh*
村純忠 Ō. Sumitada *mh*
沢 Ōsawa *s*
沢野 Ōsawano *sp*
住 Ōsumi *s*
作 Daisaku *m*
仰 Ōnoki *sp*
伯 Ōku *sp*
伯皇女 Ō. no Himemiko *flh*
佐 Ōsa *sp*
佐和 Ōsawa *p*
伴 Ōtomo *sp*
伴坂上郎女 Ō. no Sakanoe no Iratsume *fl*
伴金村 Ō. no Kanamura *mh*
伴旅人 Ō. no Tabito *ml*
伴家持 Ō. no Yakamochi *ml*
豆 Otō *s*
会 Daie *la*
牟田 Ōmuta *p*
条 Daijō *s*, Ōeda
児 Tako *s*
貝 Ōgai *s*
声 Ōe *s*
志摩 Ōshima *s*
安 Daian *p*
安寺 Daianji *p*
安寺碑文 D. hibun *l*
谷 Ōtani *s*, Ōya
谷木 Ōyagi *s*
谷句仏 Ōtani Kubutsu *ml*
谷津 Ōyazu *s*
谷藤子 Ōtani Fujiko *fl*
谷繞石 Ō. Gyōseki *ml*
串 Ōkushi *s*
出 Ōide *s*
里 Ōsato *sp*
見 Ōmi *s*
更 Ōfuke *s*
臣 Otodo *m*
甫 Daiho *s*
束 Ōtsuka *s*
来目部 Ōkumebe *s*
来皇女 Ōku no Himemiko *flh*
身狭屯倉田部 Ōmusamiyakenotabe *s*
角 Ōsumi *s*
角吹 Haranofuefuki *s*
角集 Ōtsui *s*, Ōtsume, Ōtozumi
[8]供 Ōtomo *s*
作 Ōsaku *s*
阿久 Ōaku *s*
狛 Ōkoma *s*
波 Ōnami *s*
沼 Ōnuma *sp*
河 Ōkawa *s*
河一 Daikaichi *s*
河内 Ōkawachi *sp*, Ōkōchi; Okōchi *s*
河戸 Ōkawato *s*
河平 Ōkobira *s*
河本 Ōkawamoto *s*
河原 Ōkawara *sp*
門 Ōkado *s*, Daimon
股 Ōmata *s*
和 Ōwa *s*
和久 Ōwaku *s*
即 Ōtsuki *s*
坪 Ōtsubo *s*
坪草二郎 Ō. Sōjirō *ml*
炊 Ōi *sm*
炊御門 Ōinomikado *s*, Ōimikado
林 Ōbayashi *s*
枝 Ōeda *s*
邱 Taikyū *p* "Taegu"
私 Ōkisaichi *s*
和 Yamato *sp*; Daiwa *p*, Taiwa
和し美し Y. shi uruwashi *l*
和郡山 Y. Kōriyama *p*
和高田 Y. Takada *p*
和田 Ōwada *s*
和田建樹 Ō. Tateki *ml*
和絵 Yamatoe *a*
房 Ōfusa *s*
幸 Ōsaki *s*, Ōsachi, Daikō, Ōsaka
舎人部 Ōtoneribe *s*, Ōtoribe
金 Ōgane *s*
英 Motofusa *m*
空 Ōzora *s*
典 Taiten *l*
宝 Ōtakara *s*; Daihō 701–04
宝寺 Daihōji *p*
府 Ōbu *p*
迫 Ōhasama *sp*; Ōsako *s*, Ōseko
国 Ōkuni *s*; Nagakuni *m*
国主神 Ōkuninushi no Kami *mh*
国隆正 Ōkuni Takamasa *mh*
武 Ōtake *s*
東 Daitō *p*; Ōhigashi *sp*
[9]保 Ōho *s*
信 Taishin *p*
弥 Ōmi *s*
柿 Ōgaki *sp*
畑 Ōhata *sp*
胡 Ōgo *sp*; Daigo *s*, Taiko
垣 Ōgaki *sp*; Ōgaito *s*
城 Ōki *s*, Ōshiro
松 Ōmatsu *s*
神 Ōkami *s*, Ōmiwa, Ōkane, Ōga
神楮田 Ōmiwashimotoda *s*
神田 Ōkanda *s*
洲 Ōzu *sp*
洋 Ōmi *sm*; Taiyō *p*
派 Ōmata *m*
治 Ōharu *sp*; Daiji 1126–31
洗 Ōarai *p*
津 Ōtsu *sp*
津京 Ōtsu-kyō *ph*
津美 Ōtsumi *s*
政 Ōmasa *s*
草 Ōgusa *s*
星 Ōboshi *s*
前 Ōmae *s*
岩 Ōiwa *s*
長 Daichō *s*
音 Ōto *s*, Ōtachime
栄 Daiei *p*, Taiei
春 Ōharu *s*
春日 Ōkasuga *s*
泉 Ōizumi *sp*
泉黒石 Ō. Kokuseki *ml*
岳 Ōtake *s*
直 Hironao *m*
為 Ōsu *m*
岡 Ōoka *sp*
岡忠相 Ō. Tadasuke *mh*
岡昇平 Ō. Shōhei *ml*
岡政談 Ō. seidan *l*
[10]捌 Ōwake *s*
浜 Ōhama *sp*
脇 Ōwaki *s*
峡 Ōhazama *s*, Ōba
桃 Ōmomo *s*
祓詞後釈 Ōharai no kotoba goshaku *l*
財 Ōtakara *s*
軒 Ōnoki *s*
針 Ōhari *s*
柳 Ōyanagi *s*
柳津 Ōyaizu *s*
悟法 Daigohō *s*
悟法利雄 D. Toshio *ml*
悟法進 D. Susumu *ml*
浦 Ōura *sp*
海 Ōumi *s*; Ōmi *sp*; Ōama *f*
海人 Ōama *mh*
海原 Ōmihara *s*, Ōunabara

高 Ōdaka sp; Ōtaka s
桑 Ōkuwa sp
荒木 Ōaraki s
畠 Ōhata s; Ōbatake sp
倉 Ōkura s
倉桃郎 Ō. Tōrō ml
倉喜八郎 Ō. Kihachi-
宰 Dazai s ⌊rō mh
宰府 Dazaifu ph
宰権帥 Dazai no Gon-no-sotsu mh
家 Ōie s, Ōya, Ōyake
室 Ōmuro s; Nagaie m
宮 Ōmiya sp
宮司 Daiguji s
兼 Ōgane s
栗 Ōguri s
庫 Ōko s
屋 Ōya sp; Ōyake s
庭 Ōba s
庭柯公 Ō. Kakō ml
原 Ōhara sp, Ohara
原富枝 Ō. Tomie fl
原幽学 Ō. Yūgaku mh
原御幸 Ohara gokō la
11倭 Yamato sp ⌈s
猪甘人面 Ōikaihitōmo
瓶猩猩 Taihei shōjō la
後 Daigo s
胐 Ōtsuki s
峰 Ōmine s
蛇 Orochi la
淀 Ōyodo sp
船渡 Ōfunato sp
根 Ōne s
根占 Ōnejime p
野 Ōno sp
野木 Ōnoki s, Ōyagi
野見 Ōnomi p
野林火 Ōno Rinka ml
野洒竹 Ō. Shachiku
野原 Ōnohara p ⌊ml
野誠夫 Ōno Nobuo ml
斎院 Daisaiin fl
斎院御集 D. goshū l
魚 Ōna s ⌈smh
黒 Ōkuro s; Daikoku
黒屋 Daikokuya s
黒連歌 Daikoku renga la ⌈ge l
菩薩峠 Daibosatsu tō-
菅 Ōsuge s, Ōsuga
菊 Ōgiku s
麻 Ōasa s; Ōasha p
達 Ōdate s, Ōdachi
商蛭小島 Ōakinai hiru ga Kojima la

鳥 Ōtori s
鳥造 Ō.-zukuri a
島 Ōshima sp
島如雲 Ō. Joun ma
島博光 Ō. Hiromitsu
雀 Ōsasagi s ⌊ml
12御所 Ōgosho mh
晴日 Ōseijitsu s
脚 Ōshi m
崎 Ōsaki sp
朝 Ōasa sp
隅 Ōsumi sm-ph
陽胡 Ōyako s
納言 Dainagon mh
納言為家集 D. Tame-
塔 Ōtō p ⌊ie shū l
場 Ōba s ⌈rō ml
場白水郎 Ō. Hakusui-
須 Ōsu s
須賀 Ōsuga sp
須賀乙字 Ō. Otsuji ml
須磨 Ōsuma s
湖 Ōgo s
湊 Ōminato sp
湊田名部 Ō. Tanabe p
湯人 Ōyue s
湯坐 Ōyue s
湯座 Ōyuke s
曾根 Ōsone s
富 Ōtomi s
賀 Ōga s
貫 Ōnuki s
笹 Ōzasa s
善 Daizen s
善亮 Daizennosuke s
喜 Ōki s
喜多 Ōkita s
萱 Ōgai s
萱生 Ōkayō s
森 Ōmori sp ⌈mh
森房吉 Ō. Fusayoshi
森義太郎 Ō. Gitarō ml
道 Ōmichi s, Daidō
道寺 Daidōji sp
間 Ōma sp
間間 Ōmama p
鹿 Ōshika sp
鹿卓 Ō. Taku ml
13暗谷 Ōkuradani s
槌 Ōtsuchi sp
煇 Ōteru s
碓 Ōusu m
雄 Daiyū p
辟 Ōsaki s, Ōsake
輔 Daisuke m
飯 Ōi p
滝 Ōtaki sp

溝 Ōmizo s
淵 Ōbuchi s
隈 Ōkuma s; Ōsumi sp
隈言道 Ōkuma Kotomichi ml ⌈mh
隈重信 Ō. Shigenobu
堀 Ōbori s, Ōhori
塩 Ōshio s
塩平八郎 Ō. Heihachirō mh
塚 Ōtsuka s
塚甲山 Ō. Kōzan ml
塚金之助 Ō. Kinnosuke ml
塚保治 Ō. Yasuji ml
塚楠緒子 Ō. Kusuoko
路 Ōji s ⌊fl
豊 Ōtoyo p
歳 Ōtoshi m
義 Ōyoshi m
園 Ōsono s
越 Ōgoe sp; Ōgoshi s
14徳 Daitoku s
徳寺 Daitokuji p
腰 Ōgoshi s
郷 Ōsato sp; Daigō s
給 Ōkyū s, Ogyū
嘉多 Ōkata s
窪 Ōkubo sp
関 Ōzeki s
15儀見 Ōgimi s
潟 Ōgata p
穂 Ōho sp
輝 Ōteru s ⌈be s
蝮壬部 Ōtachihimibu-
調和 Daichōwa l
輪 Ōwa s
輪田 Ōwada sp
輪田泊 Ō.-no-tomari
槻 Ōtsuki s ⌊ph
槻如電 Ō. Joden ml
槻玄沢 Ō. Gentaku mh
槻憲二 Ō. Kenji ml
慧 Hirosato m
磐 Ōiwa s
魯 Tairo ml
紫 Ōshiba s ⌈m
蔵 Ōkura sp; Ōtoshi
蔵永常 Ō. Nagatsune
熊 Ōkuma sp ⌊mh
熊信行 Ō. Nobuyuki ml ⌈ml
熊長次郎 Ō. Chōjirō
16膳 Daizen sm
頭 Ōgashira s, Ōzu
鋸 Ōga sp

鋸屋 Ogaya s
衛 Taisuke m
衡 Ōhira sp ⌈s
網 Ōami sp; Ōyosami
網白里 Ōami Shirasato p
樹 Motoki m; Taiki p
橋 Ōhashi s
橋乙羽 Ō. Otowa ml
橋松平 Ō. Matsuhei ml
橋順蔵 Ō. Junzō mh
築 Ōtsuki s
養徳 Yamato s
17館 Ōdate sp; Ōdachi
翼 Hirosuke m
薩摩 Ōzatsuma s
慈弥 Ōjimi s
18類 Ōrui s
観 Taikan ma
嶺 Ōmine s
藤 Ōfuji s, Daitō
藪 Ōyabu s ⌈mi l
19鏡 Ōgane s; Ōkaga-
鷲 Ōwashi s
韙 Masayoshi m
瀬 Ōse s
瀬戸 Ōseto p
蘇 Ōso s
20鐘 Ōgane s
21磯 Ōiso sp
縄 Ōnawa s
鶴 Ōzuru s
鰐 Ōwani sp
24響 Ōhibiki s
鷹 Ōtaka s

## 4 L1

心 49 [T] (SHIN, mune, kiyo, mi, naka, moto, sane, go, gori)
中二つ腹帯 Shinjū futatsu haraobi la
中天網島 S. ten no Amijima la
中重井筒 S. kasane izutsu la
中宵庚申 S. yoigōshin la
学早染草 Shingaku hayazome-gusa la
敬 Shinkei ml

## 4 L2

刈 50 (KAI, kari)

田 Karita *s*, Kanda; Katta *sp*
込 Karikomi *s*
羽 Kariwa *p*
谷 Kariya *p*
部 Karibe *s*

切 51 [T] (SETSU, kiri, kire)
木 Kiriko *s*
山 Kiriyama *s*
田 Kirita *s*
戸 Kireto *p*
石 Kiriishi *p*
池 Kiriike *s*
河 Kikkawa *s* ⌈ri *a*
妻造 Kirizuma-zuku-

火 52 [T] (KA, hi, ho)
作 Kozukuri *s*
野 Hino *s*
野葦平 H. Ashihei *ml*
撫 Hinozu *s*, Hinade, Honake, Honade

双 53 [T] Narabu *m.* (sō, futa, fu)
三 Futami *p*
木 Namiki *s*
美子 Fumiko *f*
海 Futami *p*
葉 Futaba *s*
蝶蝶曲輪 Futatsu chōchō kuruwa *la*

水 54 [T] Taira *m*; Motori *s.* (SUI, mi, mizu, mina, na, yu, naka, yuku, moto-
[3]川 Mizukawa *s* ⌊ri)
口 Mizuguchi *s*, Mizoguchi; Minakuchi
子 Mizuneko *s* ⌊*sp*
上 Minakami *sp*, Mizukami
上勉 Minakami Tsutomu *ml* ⌈rō *ml*
上滝太郎 M. Takita-
[4]戸 Mito *p*
戸部 Mitobe *s*
元 Mizumoto *s*
分 Mikumari *s*
巴句帖 Suiha kuchō *l*
井 Mizui *s*
太郎 Mizutarō *m*
毛生 Mizumō *s*
木 Mizuki *s*
木京太 M. Kyōta *ml*
木洋子 M. Yōko *fl*
[5]田 Mizuta *s*
主 Minushi *s*, Tonmon, Nuekako
本 Mizumoto *s*
[6]江 Mizue *s*
守 Mizumori *s*; Mimori *m*
守亀之助 M. Kamenosuke *ml*
早 Mizuhaya *s*
[7]沢 Mizusawa *sp*
村 Mizumura *s*
利 Mizukaga *s*
町 Mizumachi *s*
町京子 M. Kyōko *fl*
足 Mizutari *s*
志 Mizushi *s*
谷 Mizutani *s*, Mizunoya ⌈tō *ml*
谷不倒 Mizutani Fu-
谷川 Mizutanigawa *s*, Miyagawa, Mizunoyagawa
尾 Mizuo *sp*; Mizunoo *s*; Mio *sl*
見 Mizumi *s*
出 Mizude *s*
[8]沫集 Minawashū *l*
沼 Mizunuma *s*
明 Suimei *l*
門 Minato *s*
枝 Mizue *f*
取 Motori *s*, Mohitori, Mondori
茎 Mizukuki *s*
府 Suifu *s*
[9]俣 Minamata *p*
津 Mizutsu *s*, Suitsu
垣 Mizugaki *s*
品 Mizushina *s*
荘記 Suisōki *l*
巻 Mizumaki *sp*
岡 Mizuoka *s*
海道 Mizukaidō *p*
郡 Mizugōri *s*
速 Mihaya *s*
原 Mizuhara *s* ⌈*ml*
原秋桜子 M. Shūōshi
[11]掫 Mondori *s* ⌈*la*
掛聟 Mizukake muko
流丸 Tsurumaru *s*
渓 Mizutani *s*
部 Motoribe *s*
野 Mizuno *s*
野仙子 M. Senko *fl*
野広徳 M. Hironori *ml*
野谷 Mizunoya *s*
野忠邦 Mizuno Tadakuni *mh*
野葉舟 M. Yōshū *ml*
島 Mizushima *s*
鳥 Mizutori *s*
崎 Mizusaki *s* ⌈*l*
蛙眼目 Suia ganmoku
登 Mizuto *s*
落 Mizuochi *s*
落露石 M. Roseki *ml*
無子 Minako *f*
無月祓 Minazukibarae *la*
無瀬 Minase *sp-l*
無瀬三吟 M. sangin *l*
道 Minamichi *m*, Mimichi
間 Mizuma *s*
[13]満 Mitsumi *s*
越 Mizukoshi *s*, Mizunoo
[14]溜 Mizutame *s*
窪 Misakubo *p*
澄 Misumi *m*
穂 Mizuho *m*
[16]橋 Mizuhashi *s*
[18]藤 Mizufuji *s*
[19]鏡 Mizu kagami *l*
[20]甕 Mizukame *l*

仂 55 Tsutomu *m*, Hagemu, Masaru. (RYOKU, RIKI)

化 56 [T] (KA, KE, hori) ⌈ga *l*
物會我 Bakemono So-
政 Kasei 1804–29
間 Toga *s*
銀杏 Bakeichō *l*

仁 57 [T] Hitoshi *m*, Masashi, Hiroshi, Yasushi, Hisashi, Tadashi, Shinobu. (NIN, JIN, ni, hito, masa, yoshi, to, kimi, sane, mi, nori, kimu, sato, toyo)
ノ平 Ninohira *s*
[1]一郎 Niichirō *m*
[2]八 Nihachi *s*
[3]三郎 Nisaburō *m*
上 Ninoue *s*
[4]戸田 Nitoda *s*
文 Yoshibumi *m*
王 Niō *smh-la*
井田 Niida *s*
木 Niki *s*, Nikki
木悦子 Niki Etsuko *fl*
礼 Nire *s*; Kimihiro *m*
平 Nihira *s*; Ninbyō 1151–54
田 Nita *s*, Nitta
田原 Nitahara *s*
[6]江 Hitoe *f*
世 Kimiyo *f*
多 Nita *s*
[7]杉 Nisugi *s*, Hitosugi
村 Nimura *s*
安 Nin'an 1166–69
志 Hitoshi *m*
尾 Nio *sp*
見 Nimi *s*
寿 Ninju 851–54; Sanetoshi *m*
[8]和 Ninwa / Ninna 885–89
和寺 Niwaji *s*; Ninnaji *sp*
[9]治 Ninji 1240–43
保 Niho *s*, Nio
信 Yoshinobu *m*
神 Nigami *s*
秋 Nishina *s*
科 Nishina *s*
科芳雄 N. Yoshio *mh*
[10]郎 Nirō *m*
[11]淀 Niyodo *p*
瓶 Nihei *s*
[12]敬 Masahiro *m*
賀保 Nigao *s*; Nika-
道 Yoshine *m* ⌊ho *p*
[13]雄 Hitoo *m*
詮 Yoshiakira *m*
義 Masayoshi *m*, Miyoshi
[14]徳 Nintoku *mh*
[15]監 Masaaki *m*
[18]藤 Nitō *s*
[21]羅山 Nirayama *s*

——4 L3——

孔 58 [T] (KŌ, KU, yoshi, tada, michi, ushi)
一 Yoshikazu *m*
子 Kōshi *mlh* "Confucius"
王 Anao *s* ⌈nie
王部 Amanibe *s*, Ama-

世部 Kusebe *s*
舎農家 Kusanoya *m*
敏 Tadatoshi *m*
雀船 Kujakubune *l*

—— 4 T1 ——

**戸** 59 [T] To *s.* (KO, GO, to, he, be, ie, kado, hiro, mori)
ケ崎 Togasaki *s*
[3]上 Togami *s*
川 Togawa *s*
川幸夫 T. Yukio *ml*
川秋骨 T. Shūkotsu *ml*
川残花 T. Zanka *ml*
丸 Tomaru *s*
口 Toguchi *s*
[4]刈 Tokari *s*
木 Heki *sp*
水 Tomizu *s*
井 Toi *sp*
井田 Toida *s*
山 Toyama *s*
[5]叶 Tokano *s*, Toganō
石 Toishi *s*
辺 Tobe *s*
矢 Toya *s*
田 Toda *sp*; Heta *p*
田茂睡 T. Mosui *ml*
田欽堂 T. Kindō *ml*
[6]次 Hetsugi *sp*
[7]村 Tomura *s*
汲 Tokumi *s*
沢 Tozawa *sp*
坂 Tosaka *s*
坂潤 T. Jun *ml*
谷 Todani *s*, Toya
苅 Togari *s*
出 Toide *sp*
来 Heki *s*, Herai
[8]波 Tonami *s*
河内 Togōchi *p*
枝 Toeda *s*
板 Toita *s*
板康二 T. Yasuji *ml*
所 Todokoro *s*
奈良 Tonara *s*
[9]津 Totsu *s*
畑 Tobata *sp*
松 Tomatsu *s*
前 Tosaki *s*
泉 Toizumi *s*
畔 Tobe *smh-fh*
倉 Togura *sp*
高 Todaka *s*
室 Tomuro *s*
屋 Toya *s*
[11]浪 Tonami *s*
頃 Tokoro *s*
部 Tobe *s*, Kobe
祭 Tomatsuri *s*
島 Toshima *s*
[12]崎 Tosaki *s*, Tozaki
賀崎 Togasaki *s*
鹿里 Togari *s*
[13]塚 Totsuka *sp*
張 Tobari *s*
[14]隠 Togakushi *s*

**元** 60 [T] Hajime *m*, Gen, Hajimu, Tsukasa; Moto *s.* (GEN, GAN, moto, haru, yuki, naga, yoshi, asa, chika, masa)
[1]一 Motoichi *m*
[3]三 Genzō *m*
三郎 Motosaburō *m*
之助 Gennosuke *m*, Motonosuke
久 Motonaga *m*; Genkyū 1204–06
[4]仁 Gennin 1224–25
予 Motoyasu *m*
中 Genchū 1384–92
文 Genbun 1736–41
山 Motoyama *s*
五郎 Motogorō *m*
井 Motoi *s*
太郎 Mototarō *m*
木 Motoki *s*
夫 Motoo *m*
[5]永 Gen'ei 1118–20
田 Motoda *s*
正 Motomasa *m*; Genshō *mh*
生 Motoiki *s*
[6]次郎 Motojirō *m*
圭 Genkei *m*
吉 Motoyoshi *sm*
有 Motoari *m*
[7]信 Motonobu *m*
沢 Motozawa *s*
弘 Motohiro *m*; Genkō 1331–34
村 Motomura *s*
亨 Genkō 1321–24
亨釈書 G. shakusho *lh*
沢 Motozawa *s*
応 Gen'ō 1319–21
尾 Motoo *sm*
臣 Motoomi *m*
[8]明 Genmei *mh*
服曾我 Genbuku Soga *la*
和 Genwa 1615–25
知 Motoaki *m*
京 Motochika *m*
昌 Motoyoshi *m*
良 Motora *s*
良勇次郎 M. Yūjirō *ml*
[9]恒 Mototsune *m*
治 Motoharu *m*; Genji 1864–65
昭 Motoaki *m*
施 Motoharu *m*
貞 Motosada *m*
春 Motoharu *m*
岡 Motooka *s*
[10]祥 Motonaga *m*
造 Motozō *m*
[11]啓 Genkei *m*
島 Motojima *s*
亀 Genki 1570–73
[12]崎 Motozaki *s*
就 Motonari *m*
敬 Genkei *m*
禄 Genroku 1688–1704
禄忠臣蔵 G. chūshingura *la*
森 Motomori *s*
運 Motoyuki *m*
達 Motohiro *m*
[13]源 Motoyoshi *m*
雄 Motoo *m*, Yoshio
経 Genkei *m*
義 Motoyoshi *m*
督 Mototada *m*
照 Mototeru *m*
[14]徳 Gentoku 1329–31
輔 Motosuke *ml*
暦 Genryaku 1184–85
[15]儁 Mototoshi *m*
蕃 Motomitsu *m*
慶 Gangyō 877–85
[16]橋 Motohashi *s*
興 Motooki *m*
[18]藤 Motofuji *s*
簡 Motohiro *m*

—— 4 T2 ——

**方** See 85

**文** See 86

**六** 61 [T] Mutsu *f.* (ROKU, RIKU, mu, mutsu)
ケ所 Rokkasho *p*
[1]一郎 Rokuichirō *m*
[2]二 Rokuji *m*
七八 Munahachi *m*
人 Mutori *s*
人部 Mutobe *s*
十田 Musoda *s*
十谷 Musotani *s*
十里 Tsuihiji *s*
[3]川 Rokugawa *s*
[4]戸 Rokunohe *p*
月一日 Kusaka *s*, Urihari
日 Muika *p*
日市 Muikaichi *p*
[5]平 Mutaka *s*
[6]地蔵 Roku Jizō *la*
合 Kuni *sp*
[7]村 Rokumura *s*
条 Rokujō *sp*
兵衛 Rokubee *m*
車 Mukuruma *s*
角 Rokkaku *s*
[8]波羅 Rokuhara *sph*
所 Rokusho *s*
物 Rokubutsu *s*
国史 Rikkokushi *l*
[9]浦 Mutsuura *s*; Mutsura *p-la*
[10]郎 Rokurō *m*
原 Mutsuhara *s*
造 Rokuzō *m*
[11]野 Rokuno *s*
笠 Mugasa *s*
[12]崎 Mutsuzaki *s*
富 Mutsutomi *m*
鹿 Mutsuga *s*, Rokushika
[13]雄 Mutsuo *sm*
[14]郷 Rokugō *p*
歌仙 Rokkasen *ml-fl*

**予** 62 [T] Atō *m*, Yasushi, Tanoshi. (YO, yasu, masa, a)
子 Yasuko *f*
何人 Anato *m*

**支** 63 [T] Tamotsu *m.* (SHI, KI, naka, moro, hase, yuta)
主 Kisu *s*
那 Shina *p* "China"
考 Shikō *ml*
倉 Hasekura *s*, Hashikura
倉常長 Hasekura Tsunenaga *mh*

化 仁 孔 戸 元 方 文 六 予 支 ▼ 分 父 介 今 日 厄 反 友 斗 勻 匂 弌 火 水 匹 中 ▲ 日 日 円 丹 月 内 片 及 卞 方

**分** 64 [T] (BU, BUN, FUN, chika, wake, waka, kumari)
水 Bunsui *p*
倍 Bunbai *sp*; Bubai *s*
校 Bungyō *sp*
部 Wakebe *s*
銅 Bundō *s*
瀬 Wakese *s*

**父** 65 [T] (FU, chichi, nori)
子鷹 Oyakodaka *l*
代 Chichiyo *m*
鬼 Chichioni *s*

**介** 66 [T] Tasuku *m*, Suke, Katashi. (KAI, KE, suke, aki, yuki, yoshi)
川 Sukegawa *s*
成 Sukenari *m*
寿 Suketoshi *m*
良 Kera *p*

**今** 67 [T] Kon *s*, Ima. (KON, KIN, ima)
[3]小路 Imakōji *s*
川 Imagawa *s*
川了俊 I. Ryōshun *mh*
川仮名目録 I. kana mokuroku *h* ⌈*mh*
川義元 I. Yoshimoto
万 Konman *s*
子 Imako *f*
大路 Imaōji *s*
[4]切 Imagiri *s*
戸 Imado *s*
戸心中 I. shinjū *l*
中 Imanaka *s*
木 Imaki *sfl*
太郎 Imatarō *m*
毛人 Imaebisu *sm*; Imakebito *m*
日子 Kyōko *f*
日出海 Kon Hidemi
井 Imai *s* ⌊*ml*
井田 Imaida *s*
井白楊 Imai Hakuyō *ml*
井邦子 I. Kuniko *fl*
井福治郎 I. Fukujirō
[5]北 Imakita *s* ⌊*ml*
田 Imada *s*; Konda *p*
市 Imaichi *sp*
立 Imadate *sp*
本 Imamoto *s*
[6]江 Imae *s*
吉 Imayoshi *s*
庄 Imajō *sp*
西 Imanishi *s*
成 Imanari *s*
[7]坂 Imasaka *s*
沢 Imazawa *s*
村 Imamura *s*
別 Imabetsu *p*
尾 Imao *s*
里 Imazato *s* ⌈*s*
来才伎 Imakinotebito
[8]枝 Imaeda *s*
林 Imabayashi *s*
出 Imade *s*
出川 Imadegawa *s*
金 Imagane *sp*
官一 Kon Kan'ichi *ml*
昔 Konjaku *l*
奉 Imamatsuri *s*, Imamatsuribe
府 Imafu *s*
居 Imai *s*
武 Imatake *s*
良 Imamairi *s*
東光 Kon Tōkō *ml*
[9]城 Imashiro *s*; Imaki *sm*
津 Imazu *sp*
治 Imabari *sp*
参 Imamairi *l*
春 Konparu *s*
泉 Imaizumi *s*
岡 Imaoka *s*
[10]帰仁 Nakinin *s*
宮 Imamiya *s*
[11]峰 Imamine *s*
剛 Kongō *s*
野 Imano *s*, Konno
野賢三 I. Kenzō *ml*
[12]朝 Kesa *f*
朝美 Kesami *f*
韋倍 Imagunbai *s*
道 Imamichi *s*
[13]堀 Imabori *s*
福 Imafuku *s*
[14]給黎 Imakure *s*, Ima-
様 Imayō *l* ⌊gire
様薩摩歌 I. Satsuma uta *la*
関 Imazeki *s*
[15]熊野 Imagumano *sp*
[16]橋 Imahashi *s*
[18]藤 Imafuji *s*
[19]鏡 Ima kagami *l*
[24]鷹 Imataka *s*

— 4 F —

**曰** See 76

**厄** 68 [T] (YAKU)
巳 Yakumi *s*

**反** 69 [T] (HAN, TAN, sori, modori)
田 Sorita *s*
町 Sorimachi *sp*
保 Tanbo *s*
橋 Modoribashi *s*

**友** 70 [T] (YŪ, U, tomo, suke)
[2]二 Tomoji *m*
[3]之介 Tomonosuke *m*
三 Tomozō *m*
三郎 Tomosaburō *m*
[4]山 Tomoyama *s*
木 Tomoki *s*
[5]礼 Tomonari *m*
四郎 Tomoshirō *m*
永 Tomonaga *s*
田 Tomoda *s*
平 Tomohira *sm*
[6]次郎 Tomojirō *m*
江 Tomoe *s*
吉 Tomokichi *m*
光 Tomomitsu *s*
成 Tomonari *sm*
[7]沢 Tomozawa *s*
安 Tomoyasu *sm*
[8]枝 Tomoeda *s*; Tomoe *f* ⌈shō *ma*
[9]松 Tomomatsu *s*; Yū-
法師 Tomo-hōshi *ma*
治 Tomoji *m*
則 Tomonori *m*
岡 Tomooka *s*
哉 Tomoya *m*
修 Tomoyoshi *m*
[11]悌 Tomoyasu *m*
梅 Yūbai *ml*
野 Tomono *s*
部 Tomobe *sp*
常 Tomotsune *sm*
[12]博 Tomohiro *sm*
随 Tomomichi *m*
禅染 Yūzen-zome *a*
[14]精 Tomokiyo *m*

**斗** 71 [T] Hakaru *m*. (TO, masu, hoshi)
ケ沢 Togezawa *s*
福 Masutomi *m*

**勻** 72 Hitoshi *m*. (KIN, IN)

**匂** 73 Nioi *s*. (nio, niō)
子 Nioko *f*
枝 Nioe *f*
宮 Niōnomiya *l*

**弌** 74 Hajime *m*. (ITSU, ICHI, kazu, ⌊katsu)
子 Kazuko *f*
春 Katsuharu *m*

— 4 U —

**火** See 52

**水** See 54

**匹** See 187

**中** 75 [T] Ataru *m*, Kaname, Tadashi, Nakaba; Naka *sp*; Chū *sm*. (CHŪ, naka, nori, na, yoshi, tada, uchi)
[3]小路 Nakakōji *s*
川 Nakagawa *sp* ⌈*ml*
川一政 N. Kazumasa
川宋淵 N. Sōen *ml*
川淳庵 N. Jun'an *mh*
川喜雲 N. Kiun *ml*
川根 Naka-kawane *p*
三川 Nakamigawa *s*
之口 Nakanokuchi *sp*
之条 Nakanojō *p*
之島 Nakanoshima *sp*
口 Nakaguchi *s*
上 Nakagami *s*
上川 Nakamigawa *s*, Nakagamigawa
上川彦次郎 Nakamigawa Hikojirō *mh*
大兄 Naka no Ōe *mh*
土佐 Naka-tosa *p*
万 Nakama *s*
丸 Nakamaru *s*
大路 Nakaōji *s*
丸子 Nakawaniko *s*
久木 Nakaguki *s*

久喜 Nakaguki *s*
[4]心 Nakago *m*
方 Nakagata *s*
元 Nakamoto *s*
内 Nakauchi *s*
内蝶二 N. Chōji *ml*
山 Nakayama *sp*; Uchiyama *s*
山省三郎 N. Shōzaburō *ml*
山義秀 N. Gishū *ml*
井 Nakai *sp*
井川 Nakaigawa *s*
井竹山 Nakai Chikuzan *mh* ⌈hiko *ml*
井克比古 N. Katsu-
牛馬 Nakagome *s*
[5]代 Nakadai *s*
外経緯伝 Chūgai keiden *l*
北 Nakakita *s*
札内 Naka-satsunai *p*
主 Chūzu *p*
石 Nakaishi *s*
辺路 Naka-heji *p*
込 Nakagome *s*
古雑唱集 Chūko zasshōshū *l*
布利 Nakafuri *s*
央 Chūō *p* ⌈nome
目 Nakame *s*, Naka-
田 Nakata *sp*
田耕治 N. Kōji *ml*
平 Nakahira *s*
巨摩 Naka-koma *p*
本 Nakamoto *s*
矢 Nakaya *s*
平 Nakadaira *s*
[6]仙 Nakasen *p*
伊豆 Naka-izu *p*
次 Nakatsugi *sm*
行 Yoshimichi *m*
江 Nakae *s*
江川 Nakaegawa *s*
江兆民 Nakae Chōmin *mlh*
江藤樹 N. Tōju *mh*
台 Nakadai *s* ⌈kiri
吉 Nakayoshi *s*, Naka-
名生 Nakamyō *s*
辻 Nakatsuji *s*
世 Nakase *s*
米 Chūbei *p* "Central America"
西 Nakanishi *s* ⌈*ml*
西伊之助 N. Inosuke
西悟堂 N. Godō *ml*
西梅花 N. Baika *ml*
[7]沢 Nakazawa *s*
沢道二 N. Dōni *mh*
沢臨川 N. Rinsen *ml*
坂 Nakasaka *s*
沖 Nakaoki *s*
坊 Nakanobō *s*, Nakanbō
杉 Nakasugi *s*
村 Nakamura *sp*
村三郎 N. Saburō *ml*
村不折 N. Fusetsu *mla*
村汀女 N. Teijo *fl*
村白葉 N. Hakuyō *ml*
村正直 N. Masanao *mlh* ⌈*ml*
村正常 N. Masatsune
村正爾 N. Shōji *ml*
村地平 N. Jihei *ml*
村吉蔵 N. Kichizō *ml*
村光夫 N. Mitsuo *ml*
村花痩 N. Kasō *ml*
村武羅夫 N. Burafu *ml*
村柊花 N. Shūka *ml*
村秋香 N. Akika *ml*
村草田男 N. Kusatao *ml*
村星湖 N. Seiko *ml*
村真一郎 N. Shin'ichirō *ml* ⌈*ml*
村憲吉 N. Kenkichi
町 Nakamachi *s*
谷 Nakatani *s*, Nakaya
谷孝雄 Nakatani Takao *ml* ⌈chirō *ml*
谷宇吉郎 Nakaya Uki-
邑 Nakamura *s*
安 Nakayasu *sm*
牟田 Nakamuda *s*
条 Nakajō *sp*; Chūjō *s*
尾 Nakao *s*
出 Nakade *s*
里 Nakazato *sp*
里介山 N. Kaizan *ml*
里恒子 N. Tsuneko *fl*
臣 Nakatomi *s*
臣宅守 N. no Yakamori *ml*
臣寿詞 N. no yogoto *l*
臣鎌足 N. no Kamatari *mh*
臣表 Nakatomiue *s*
出 Nakaide *s*
[8]坪 Nakatsubo *s*
河 Nakagawa *s*
河与一 N. Yoichi *ml*
河内 Naka-kawachi *p*
河幹子 Nakagawa Mikiko *fl*
沼 Nakanuma *s*
林 Nakabayashi *s*
牧 Nakamaki *s*
和 Chūka *p*
金 Nakagane *s*
京 Nakagyō *p*
茎 Nakaguki *s*
東 Nakahigashi *s*; Chūtō *p* "Middle
居 Nakai *s* ⌊East"
[9]俣 Nakamata *s*
城 Nakashiro *s*
津 Nakatsu *sp*; Chūshin *ml*
津川 Nakatsugawa *sp*
津江 Naka-tsue *p*
津軽 Naka-tsugaru *p*
垣 Nakagaki *s*
松 Nakamatsu *s*
神 Nakagami *s*
畑 Nakahata *s*
泉 Nakaizumi *s*
岡 Nakaoka *s* ⌈*mh*
岡慎太郎 N. Shintarō
[10]将 Chūjō *mh*
浦 Nakaura *s*
浜 Nakahama *s*
院 Nakanoin *s*
桐 Nakagiri *s* ⌈*ml*
桐確太郎 N. Kakutarō
郡 Nakagōri *s*
倉 Nakakura *s*
宮 Nakamiya *s*
柴 Nakashiba *s*
庭 Nakaniwa *s*
原 Nakahara *s*; Nakabara *sp* ⌈Chūya *ml*
原中也 Nakahara
原綾子 N. Ayako *fl*
原親能 N. no Chikayoshi *mh*
屋 Nakaya *s*
県 Nakatsuagata *s*
馬 Chūma *s*, Chūman
[11]後 Chūgo *s*
根 Nakane *s*
許 Nakamoto *s*
部 Nakabe *s*
務 Nakatsukasa *sfl-p*
務内侍 N. no Naishi
野 Nakano *sp* ⌊*fl-l*
野三允 N. San'in *ml*
野好夫 N. Yoshio *ml*
野実 N. Minoru *ml*
野重治 N. Shigeharu *ml*
野菊夫 N. Kikuo *ml*
野逍遙 N. Shōyō *ml*
野嘉一 N. Kaichi *ml*
魚沼 Nakauonuma *p*
曾根 Nakasone *s*
埜 Nakano *s*
康 Nakatsune *m*
島 Nakajima *sp*
島河太郎 N. Kawatarō *ml* ⌈*mh*
島信行 N. Nobuyuki
島孤島 N. Kotō *ml*
島哀浪 N. Airō *ml*
島健蔵 N. Kenzō *ml*
島湘煙 N. Shōen *ml*
島斌雄 N. Takeo *ml*
島歌子 N. Utako *fl*
島敦 N. Atsushi *ml*
[12]須 Nakasu *s*
御門 Nakanomikado *s*, Nakamikado
須賀 Nakasuga *s*
崎 Nakazaki *s*
納言 Chūnagon *mh*
勘助 Naka Kansuke
森 Nakamori *s* ⌊*ml*
筋 Nakasuji *s*
富 Nakatomi *sp*
富良野 Naka-furano *p*
道 Nakamichi *sp*; Nakaji *s*
間 Nakama *sp*
[13]堀 Nakabori *s*
塚 Nakatsuka *s*
塚一碧楼 N. Ippekirō
溝 Nakamizo *s* ⌊*ml*
楯 Nakadate *s*
路 Nakaji *s*, Nakamichi ⌈bachi
鉢 Nakabachi *s*, Chū-
新川 Naka-niikawa *p*
新田 Naka-niida *p*
蒲原 Naka-kanbara *p*
園 Nakazono *s*
越 Nakagoe *s*
[14]郷 Nakagō *p*
種子 Naka-tane *p*
頓別 Naka-tonbetsu *p*
静 Nakashizu *s*
[15]標津 Naka-shibetsu
摩 Chūma *s* ⌊*p*
[16]橋 Nakahashi *s*
橋公館 N. Kōkan *l*
橋徳五郎 N. Tokugo-
興 Tadaki *ml* ⌊rō *mh*

反 友 斗 匂 匀 式 火 水 匹 中 ▼ 曰 日 円 丹 月 ▲ 内 片 及 卞 方 文 止 少 山 王

[17]館 Nakadate *s*
[18]藪 Nakayabu *s*
藤 Nakafuji *s*
[19]瀬 Nakase *s*
鏡 Chūkyō *s*
頸城 Naka-kubiki *p*
[21]巌円月 Chūgan Engetsu *mlh*

曰 76 (ETSU, OCHI, nori, wata, o)
佐 Osa *s*
理 Watari *s*
榑崎 Komisaki *s*

日 77 (NICHI, JITSU, hi, aki, ka, haru, hiru)
ノ出 Hinode *p*
の出島 Hinodejima *l*
[1]一 Akikazu *m*
[3]之影 Hinokage *p*
下 Kusaka *s* ⌈geta
下田 Kusakada *s*, Hi-
下部 Kusakabe *s*
[4]戸 Nitto *s*
中 Hinaka *s*
日 Tachigori *s*
内 Utsuhi *s*
月 Tachimori *s*
山 Hiyama *s*
[5]外 Akubi *s*
比 Hibi *s*
比谷 Hibiya *sp*
比野 Hibino *s*
比野士朗 H. Shirō *ml*
永 Hinaga *s*
田 Hita *p* ⌈yuku *s*
立 Hitachi *sp*; Tate-
生 Hinase *sp*
生下 Hiuke *s*
本 Nihon / Nippon *p*; Yamato *s*
本三文オペラ Nihon sanmon opera *l*
本外史 N. gaishi *lh*
本永代蔵 Nippon eitaigura *l*
本国見在書目録 Nihon-koku genzaisho mokuroku *l*
本捕虜志 N. horyoshi *l*
本書紀 N. shoki *l*
本後記 N. kōki *l*
本紀 Nihongi *l*
本霊異記 Nihon reiiki / ryōiki *l*
[6]光 Nikkō *sp-l*
吉 Hiyoshi *sp*; Hie *p*
吉津 Hiezu *p*
吉神社 Hie Jinja *p*
向 Hyūga *ph*; Hinata *sm-p*; Himuka *m*
向野 Hinatano *s*, Higano
名子 Hinako *s*
辻 Hitsuji *s*
色 Hiiro *s*
[7]坂 Hisaka *s*
沖 Hioki *s*
尾 Hio *s*
谷 Hitani *s*
出 Hide *f*; Hiji *p*
出山 Hijiyama *s*
出谷 Hijiya *s*, Hishiya; Hideya *p*
出男 Hideo *m*
出雄 Hideo *m*, Hidenori ⌈ru *m*
出鶴丸 Hidetsuruma-
[8]沼 Hinuma *s*
祀 Himatsuri *s*
和 Hiyori *s*, Hira
和田 Hiwada *sp*
和佐 Hiwasa *sp*
和見 Hiyorimi *m*
英 Hiyoshi *m*
夜 Higurashi *s*, Hitarashi
奔 Hibi *s*
奉 Himatsuri *s*
並知 Hinameshi *mh*
東 Nittō *s*
良麿 Hiramaro *m*
[9]浅 Hiasa *s*
香蚊 Hikaka *m*
前 Hinokuma *s*; Hikuma *sp*
南 Nichinan *p*
南田 Hinata *s*, Hinada
[10]浦 Hiura *s*
柳 Kusayanagi *s*, Ku-
益 Hiiki *s* ⌊sanagi
夏 Hinatsu *s*
夏耿之介 H. Kōnosuke *ml*
高 Hidaka *sp*
高六郎 H. Rokurō *ml*
高只一 H. Tadaichi *ml*
原 Hihara *s*; Nichiha-
[11]能 Hiyoki *s* ⌊ra *p*
根 Hine *s*
根野 Hineno *s*
野 Hino *sp*
野水 Hinomizu *s*
野西 Hinonishi *s*
野島 Hinoshima *s*
野草城 Hino Sōjō *ml*
野富子 H. Tomiko *fh*
野資朝 H. Suketomo
笠 Hikasa *s* ⌊*mh*
進 Nisshin *s*
[13]詰 Hizume *s*
新 Hiyoshi *s*
義 Hiyoshi *s*
照 Akiteru *m*
照雨 Sobae *l*
[14]種 Higusa *s* ⌈na
鼻 Hibana *s*, Kusaha-
暮 Higurashi *s*
暮里 Nippori *p*
蓮 Nichiren *mlh*
置 Heki *sp*, Hioki; Hiki *s*
置川 Hikigawa *p*
置田 Hekida *s*
暦 Nichireki *l*
[16]親 Nisshin *mh*
[18]鎖 Tagusari *s*

円 78 [T] Maru *m*, Madoka; Tsubura *sm*. (EN, maru, mado, mitsu, nobu, kazu, tsubura)
[2]力 Madoka *m*
[4]仁 Ennin *mh*
月 Engetsu *ml*
井 Tsuburai *s*
山 Maruyama *s*
山応挙 M. Ōkyo *ma*
[5]田 Maruta *s*
[6]地 Enchi *s*
地文子 E. Fumiko *fl*
[7]谷 Tsuburaya *s*, Tsumuraya, Kamuroya
[9]城 Enjō *s*
城寺 Enjōji *s*
珍 Enchin *mh*
乗 Enjō *s*
[12]勝寺 Enshōji *s*
裕 Nobuhiro *m*
喜 Mitsuyoshi *m*
覚寺 Enkakuji *p*
覚寺舎利 E. Shari *pa*
[13]満 Hōshō *s*
満井 Emai *s*, Mamai, Hōshō
満井座 Emaiza *a*
満団 Hōshōdan *s*
[14]郷 Mitsusato *m*

丹 79 [O] Akashi *m*, Akira, Makoto; Tan *s*. (TAN, ni, mi, aka)
[2]人 Nyūhito *s* ⌊aka)
[3]下 Tange *s*, Akashita
下左膳 T. Sazen *lm*
[4]山 Tanzan *s*
内 Tannai *s* ⌈*sp*
[5]比 Nii *s*, Taji; Tachii
田 Tanda *s*
生 Nibu *sp*, Nyū; Tanbu *s*, Mibu, Hanyū
生川 Nyūgawa *p*
生谷 Mibunoya *s*
生屋 Mionoya *s*
[6]次郎 Tanjirō *m*
羽 Niwa *sp*, Tanba
羽文雄 N. Fumio *ml*
[7]沢 Tanzawa *s*
児玉 Tankodama *s*
尾 Nio *s*
[8]所 Tanjo *s*
波 Tanba *sp*; Niwa *s*, Taniwa
波山 Tabayama *sp*
波与作待夜の小室節 Tanba Yosaku matsu yo no komurobushi *la*
波瀬 Tanbase *s*
呉 Tango *s*
[9]保 Tanbo *s*
治 Tanji *s*, Tajihi
治比 Tanjihi *s*, Tajihi
南 Tannan *sp*; Tannami *s*
[10]原 Tanbara *p*
[11]後 Tango *sp*
野 Tanno *s*
[12]墀 Tajihi *s*
斐太郎 Niitarō *m*
[15]穂子 Nioko *f*
敷 Nishiki *s*
[16]緑本 Tanrokubon *l*

月 80 [T] Tsuki *m*. (GATSU, GETSU, tsuki, tsugi)
[3]下部 Kasukabe *s*
[4]日 Ochigori *s*
井 Tsukii *s*
[5]本 Tsukimoto *s*
田 Tsukida *s*
[7]形 Tsukigata *sp*
村 Tsukimura *s*
安 Tsukiyasu *s*
見里 Yamanashi *s*

出里 Nudachi *s*
8良 Tsukiyoshi *m*
夜野 Tsukiyono *p*
9草 Tsukikusa *l*
岡 Tsukioka *s*
直 Tsukinao *s*
彦 Tsukihiko *m*
10宮殿 Gekkyūden *la*
11野柄 Tsukinoe *m*
島 Tsukishima *s*
12崎 Tsukizaki *s*
森 Tsukimori *s*
13満 Tsukimaro *m*
15潟 Tsukigata *sp*
輪 Tsukinowa *s*
17館 Tsukidate *sp*
19瀬 Tsukise *sp*; Tsukigase *s*

内 81 [T] (NAI, DAI, uchi, utsu, haru, masa, tada, chika, nobu, mitsu)
ヶ崎 Uchigasaki *s*
3川 Uchikawa *s*
之浦 Utsunoura *sp*
子 Uchiko *sp*
大臣家歌合 Naidaijin-ke utaawase *l*
丸 Uchimaru *sm*
4方 Uchikata *s*
山 Uchiyama *s*
山完造 U. Kanzō *ml*
木 Uchiki *s*, Naiki
5外詣 Uchito mōde *la*
古閑 Uchikoga *s*
本 Uchimoto *s*
生 Nibu *s*
田 Uchida *s*
田百閒 U. Hyakken *ml*
田沾山 U. Senzan *ml*
田康哉 U. Kōsai *mh*
田銀蔵 U. Ginzō *mh*
田魯庵 U. Roan *ml*
6池 Uchiike *s*
芝 Uchishiba *s*
7村 Uchimura *s*
村直也 U. Naoya *ml*
村鑑三 U. Kanzō *mlh*
匠 Takumi *m*
侍 Naishi / Naiji *fh*
沼 Uchinuma *s*
房 Utsubusa *s*
呉 Naiki *s*
9垣 Uchigaki *s*
前 Uchisaki *m*
10記 Naiki *sm*
浦 Uchiura *sp* ⌈umi
海 Utsumi *sp*, Uchi-
海月杖 Utsumi Getsujō *ml*
倉 Uchikura *sm*
原 Uchihara *sp*
11梅 Uchiume *s*
野 Uchino *s*
野倉 Uchinokura *s*
島 Uchijima *s*
12崎 Uchizaki *s*
貴 Naiki *s*
13堀 Uchibori *s*
14郷 Uchigō *sp*; Uchisato *sm* ⌈awase *l*
裏詩歌合 Dairi shika
15蔵 Uchikura *s*, Kura
蔵之助 Kuranosuke *m*
蔵太 Kurata *m*
蔵司 Kuraji *m*
蔵吉 Kurakichi *m*
16膳 Naizen *mh*; Haruyoshi *m*
樹 Uchiki *s*
18藤 Naitō *s*
藤丈草 N. Jōsō *ml*
藤吐天 N. Toten *ml*
藤辰雄 N. Tatsuo *ml*
藤湖南 N. Konan *ml*
藤鳴雪 N. Meisetsu *ml* ⌈*ml*
藤鋠策 N. Shinsaku
藤濯 N. Arō *ml*
麿 Uchimaro *m*, Utsumaro
22灘 Uchinada *p*

片 82 [T] Kata *s*. (HEN, kata)
3上 Katagami *s*
上伸 K. Nobu *ml*
4切 Katagiri *s*
山 Katayama *s*
山広子 K. Hiroko *fl*
山孤村 K. Koson *ml*
山敏彦 K. Toshihiko
山潜 K. Sen *mh* ⌊*ml*
5田 Katada *s*
平 Katahira *sp*
平田 Katahirata *s*
6羽 Kataba *s*
江 Katae *s*
多 Katata *s*
7村 Katamura *s*
貝 Katakai *s*
見 Katami *s*
9品 Katashina *sp*
岡 Kataoka *s*
岡良一 K. Yoshikazu *ml* ⌈*mh*
岡健吉 K. Kenkichi
岡鉄兵 K. Teppei *ml*
10柳 Katayanagi *s*
桐 Katagiri *s* ⌈*mh*
桐且元 K. Katsumoto
桐顕智 K. Akinori *ml*
倉 Katakura *s*
庭 Kataniwa *s*
11根 Katane *s*
野 Katano *s*
寄 Katayori *s*
13淵 Katabuchi *s*
14歌二夜問答 Katauta niya mondō *l*
19瀬 Katase *s*

及 83 [T] Itaru *m*. (KYŪ, GYŪ, chika, shiki, taka, oyo, oyobi)
川 Oyokawa *s*, Oikawa, Obikawa
行 Chikayuki *m*
位 Nozoki *s*
能 Kyūnō *s*
部 Oibe *s*, Oyobibe
淵 Shikibuchi *sm*; Shikinobu *m*

卞 84 Ben *s*, Hen. (BEN, HEN, nori)

方 85 [T] Masashi *m*, Ataru, Tadashi, Tamotsu; Kata *s*. (HŌ, kata, masa, michi, shige, suke, nori, o, mi, taka, tsune, nami, fusa, yasu, yori)
3子 Masako *f*
寸 Michinori *m*
丈記 Hōjōki *l*
4仁 Michihito *m*
升 Masanori *m*
5代 Mozu *s*
正 Katamasa *m*
舟 Masanori *m*; Hakobune *l*
7言 Katatoki *m*
房 Masafusa *m*
波羽 Katabami *s*
波江 Katabami *s*
9城 Hōjō *p*
11副 Masasoe *m*
13雄 Shigeo *m*

文 86 [T] Aya *sf*; Fumi *s*; Fumishi *m*, Hitoshi, Sujime. (BUN, MON, fumi, aya, nori, yuki, ya, mi, aki, tomo, nobu, ito, hisa, fumu, yasu, yoshi)
1一 Bun'ichi *m*
2二 Bunji *m*
七 Bunshichi *m*
3三 Bunzō *m*
三子 Fumiko *f*
三郎 Bunzaburō *m*
之輔 Bunnosuke *m*
子 Ayako *f*, Fumiko
士 Fumiaki *m*
久 Bunkyū 1861–64
4仁 Ayahito *m*
化 Bunka 1804–18
六 Bunroku *m*
六郎 Bunrokurō *m*
中 Bunchū 1372–75
太郎 Buntarō *m*
夫 Fumio *m*
五郎 Bungorō *m*
5代 Fumiyo *f*
永 Bun'ei 1264–75
司 Moji *s*
左衛門 Bunzaemon *m*
平 Bunpei *m*
正 Bunshō 1466–67
正草子 Bunshō-zōshi *l*
6次 Bunji *m*
次郎 Bunjirō *m*
任 Fuminori *m*
吉 Bunkichi *m*
字 Moji *s*
字屋 Mojinoya *s*
成 Fuminari *sm*
7伝 Monden *s*
安 Bun'an 1444–49
男 Fumio *m*
吾 Bungo *m*
呂 Bunro *m*
応 Bun'ō 1260–61
8披 Fumihiro *m*
明 Bunmei 1469–87; Fumiaki *m*
和 Bunwa / Bunna 1352–56
学界 Bungakukai *l*
秀 Fumiho *m*
京 Bunkyō *p*
芸市場 Bungei ichiba *l*
芸倶楽部 B. kurabu *l*
武 Monmu *mh*

武さざれ石 Bunbu sazareishi *l*
武二道万石通 B. nidō mangoku tōshi *l*
9弥 Bun'ya *ma*
炳 Fumiaki *m*
郁 Fumika *f*
政 Bunsei 1818–30
保 Bunpō 1317–19
信 Noriakira *m*
治 Bunji *m* 1185–90
治郎 Bunjirō *m*
彦 Fumihiko *m*, Ayahiko
10珠 Monju *mh*
殊 Monju *mh*
時 Fumitoki *m*
祇 Fumimasa *m*
党 Buntō *l*
室 Fun'ya *s*, Fumiya
屋 Bun'ya *s*, Fun'ya
屋康秀 B. no Yasuhide *ml* ⌈tamaro *mh*
屋綿麻呂 B. no Wa-
華秀麗集 Bunka shūreishū *l*
11峰 Fumitaka *m*
彬 Ayayoshi *m*
規 Ayanori *m*
章 Fumi *f*
章達徳録 Bunshō tattokuroku *l*
亀 Bunki 1501–04
12禄 Bunroku 1592–96
筆眼心抄 Bunpitsu ganshinshō *l*
13雄 Fumio *m*
14徳 Montoku *mh*
徳実録 M. jitsuroku *l*
楼 Bunrō *m* ⌈miaki
郷 Fumisato *m*, Fu-
輔 Bunsuke *m*
暦 Bunryaku 1234–35
15質 Fumitada *m*, Ayami
聡 Ayatoshi *m*
勲 Ayakoto *m*
蔵 Bunzō *m*
16儒 Fubito *m*
壇無駄話 Bundan mudabanashi *l*
18麿 Fumimaro *m*
19鏡秘府論 Bunkyō hifuron *l*

止 87 [T] Todomu *m*, Tomaru. (SHI, tome, tada, moto, to, tomo, oru)
子 Tomeko *f*
文 Motofumi *m*
止呂美 Todoromi *p*
美 Tonomi *s*

少 88 [T] (SHŌ, o, suku, sukuna, masa, mare)
子部 Chiisakobe *s*
女 Otome *l*
弐 Shōni *mh*
老 Ooyu *ml*
年行 Shōnenkō *l*
足 Otari *m*
咋 Okui *m*
草 Igusa *s*
将 Shōshō *mh-fh*
鳥遊 Takanashi *s*
麻呂 Sukunamaro *m*
納言 Shōnagon *mh-fh*
輔 Shō *mh-fl*

山 89 [T] Takashi *m*; Yama *s*. (SAN, SEN, yama, taka, nobu)
ノ内 Yamanouchi *p*
2入 Yamairi *s*
3川 Yamakawa *sp*
川均 Y. Hitoshi *mh*
川菊栄 Y. Kikue *flh*
川登美子 Y. Tomiko *fl*
千代 Yamasendai *s*
久保 Yamakubo *s*
上 Yamakami *s*, Yamanoue, Yamanokami, Yamanoe
上憶良 Yamanoe no Okura *ml*
之口 Yamanoguchi *sp*
之口貘 Y. Baku *ml*
之内 Yamanouchi *s*
之城 Yamanoshiro *s*
下 Yamashita *s*
下秀之助 Y. Hidenosuke *ml*
下陸奥 Y. Mutsu *ml*
口 Yamaguchi *sp*
口波津女 Y. Hatsujo *fl*
口茂吉 Y. Mokichi *ml*
口青邨 Y. Seison *ml*
口誓子 Y. Seishi *ml*
4水長巻 Sansui chōkan
戸 Yamato *s* ⌊*a*
元 Yamamoto *sp* ⌈*ma*
元春挙 Y. Shunkyo
元都星雄 Y. Toseiyū ⌊*ml*
方 Yamagata *sp* ⌊*ml*
井 Yamai *s*, Yamanoi
木 Yamaki *s*
中 Yamanaka *sp*
中峰太郎 Y. Minetarō
片 Yamagata *s* ⌊*ml*
片蟠桃 Y. Bantō *mh*
手 Yamate *sp*; Yamanote *p*
手樹一郎 Yamate Kiichirō *ml*
内 Yamanouchi *s*; Yamauchi *sp*; Sannai *p*
内豊信 Yamanouchi Toyoshige *mh*
内義雄 Y. Yoshio *ml*
5代 Yamashiro *sp*
打 Yamauchi *s*
北 Yamakita *sp*; Sanboku *p*
引 Yamabiki *s*
古志 Yamakoshi *p*
辺 Yamabe *sp*, Yamanobe
石 Yamaishi *s*
田 Yamada *sp* ⌈*mh*
田長政 Y. Nagamasa
田美妙 Y. Bimyō *ml*
田耕筰 Y. Kōsaku *ma*
田清三郎 Y. Seizaburō *ml*
田葩夕 Y. Haseki *ml*
本 Yamamoto *sp*
本土佐掾 Y. Tosanojō *ma* ⌈*ml*
本友一 Y. Tomoichi
本太郎 Y. Tarō *ml*
本正秀 Y. Masahide *ml*
本有三 Y. Yūzō *ml*
本芳翠 Y. Hōsui *ma*
本和夫 Y. Kazuo *ml*
本実彦 Y. Sanehiko *ml* ⌈*ml*
本周五郎 Y. Shūgorō
本宣治 Y. Senji *mh*
本修二 Y. Shūji *ml*
本健吉 Y. Kenkichi *ml*
本達雄 Y. Tatsuo *mh*
本権兵衛 Y. Gonnohyōe *mh*
平 Yamadaira *s*
6地 Yamaji *s*
羽 Yamaba *s*
行 Sankō *l*
江 Yamae *s*
守 Yamamori *sm*
吉 Yamayoshi *s*
成 Yamanari *s*
西 Yamanishi *s*; Sansei *p* "Shansi"
名 Yamana *s*
名氏清 Y. Ujikiyo *mh*
名持豊 Y. Mochitoyo
寺 Yamadera *s* ⌊*mh*
7佐 Yamasa *sp*
住 Yamazumi *s*
坂 Yamasaka *s*
沢 Yamazawa *s*
形 Yamagata *sp*
村 Yamamura *s*
村房次 Y. Fusaji *ml*
村暮鳥 Y. Bochō *ml*
邑 Yamamura *s*
谷 Yamadani *s*, Yamaya, Yatsue; Yamagai *sp*
谷加橋 Yamayakawa *s*
尾 Yamao *s*
角 Yamasumi *s*, Yamakado
我 Yamaga *s*
8河 Yamakawa *s*
門 Yamato *sp*; Yamakado *s*
於 Yamanoe *s*
肩 Yamagata *s*
国 Yamakuni *sp*
武 Sanbu *p* ⌈tung"]
東 Santō *sp* ["Shan-
東京伝 S. Kyōden *ml*
9治 Sanji *m*
科 Yamashina *s*
城 Yamashiro *sph*
城屋 Yamashiroya *s*
畑 Yamahata *s*
南 Sannan *p*
前 Yamasaki *sp*
倉 Yamakura *s*
岸 Yamagishi *s*
岸外史 Y. Gaishi *ml*
岸荷葉 Y. Kayō *ml*
香 Yamaga *sp*
背 Yamashiro *sph*
背大兄 Y. no Ōe *mh*
背部 Yamashirobe *s*
彦 Yamabiko *s*
岡 Yamaoka *sp*
岡元隣 Y. Genrin *ml*
岡荘八 Y. Sōhachi *ml*
岡鉄太郎 Y. Tetsutarō *mh*
10浦 Yamaura *s*

姥 Yamanba / Yamauba *la*
祇 Yamatsumi *s*
脇 Yamawaki *s*
脇東洋 Y. Tōyō *mh*
脇信徳 Y. Shintoku *ml*
高 Yamadaka *s*
脊 Yamashiro *sph*
脊部 Yamashirobe *s*
宮 Sangū *s*, Yamamiya
宮允 S. Makoto *ml*
室 Yamamuro *s*
室軍平 Y. Gunpei *mh*
室静 Y. Shizuka *ml*
家 Yamaga *s*, Yamae, Yamaya, Yamabe, Yanbe
家鳥虫歌 Sanka chōka *l*
家集 Sankashū *l*
原 Yamabara *s*
座 Yamaza *s*
屋 Yamaya *s*
県 Yamagata *sp*
県大弐 Y. Daini *mh*
県有朋 Y. Aritomo *mh*
¹¹猫 Yamaneko *s*
添 Yamazoe *sp*
姫 Yamahime *l*
都 Yamato *sp*
部 Yamabe *sp*
部赤人 Y. no Akahito *ml*
根 Yamane *s*
桜戸 Yamazakurato *m*
桝 Yamamasu *s*
野 Yamano *s*
野井 Yamanoi *s*
野辺 Yamanobe *s*
梨 Yamanashi *sp*
島 Yamashima *s*
¹²須 Yamasu *s*
陰 Yamakage *s*
陰道 San'indō *p*
陽 San'yō *p*
陽道 San'yōdō *p*
椒大夫 Sanshō-dayū *l*
崎 Yamazaki *sp*
崎与次兵衛寿の門松 Y. Yoshibee nebiki no kadomatsu *la*
崎宗鑑 Y. Sōkan *ml*
崎敏夫 Y. Toshio *ml*
崎豊子 Y. Toyoko *fl*
崎紫紅 Y. Shikō *ml*
崎闇斎 Y. Ansai *mh*
森 Yamamori *s*
賀 Yamaga *s*
登 Yamato *s*, Santō
道 Yamamichi *s*, Yamamaji
鹿 Yamaga *sp*
鹿素行 Y. Sokō *mh*
¹³階 Yamashina *s*
極 Yamagiwa *s*
路 Yamaji *s*
路愛山 Y. Aizan *ml*
葉 Yamaba *s*
嵐 Yama-arashi *l*
勢 Yamase *s*
越 Yamagoe *s*
際 Yamagiwa *s*
¹⁴徳 Yamatoku *s*
腰 Yamakoshi *s*
郷 Yamagō *s*
領 Yamaryō *s*
窩血笑記 Sanka kesshōki *l*
¹⁵幡 Yamabata *s*
澄 Yamazumi *s*
¹⁶蔭 Yamakage *s*
¹⁸藤 Santō *s*, Yamafuji
¹⁹瀬 Yamase *s*
²³響集 Kodamashū *l*

王 90 [T] Ō *s*, Kokishi, Konikishi. (ō, kimi, taka, waka, mi, wa)
仁 Wani *mh*
壬 Ikurumi *s*
生 Ikurumi *s*
寺 Ōji *p*
供 Ōtomo *s*
明 Kimiaki *m*
直 Ōchoku *s*
宮西 Okunishi *s*
陽明 Ō Yōmei *mlh* "Wang Yang-ming"
滝 Ōtaki *sp*

五 91 [T] (GO, i, kazu, itsu, izu, sa, yuki)
ヶ瀬 Gogase *p*
¹一 Goichi *m*
一郎 Goichirō *m*
²八夫 Iwao *m*
十 Iso *s*
十川 Isokawa *s*, Isakawa, Ikagawa, Isuzugawa
十子 Ikago *sp*; Irako *s*, Ikashiko
十土 Ikazuchi *s*
十六 Isoroku *m*
十山 Isuyama *s*, Yosuyama
十公 Ikimi *s*
十公野 Izumino *s*; Ijimino *sp*
十羽 Iwane *m*
十字 Ikago *s*
十辻 Ikatsuji *s*
十足 Isotari *m*
十君 Ikimi *s*, Ishimi
十君野 Ikushino *s*
十里 Ikari *s*
十河 Ikagawa *s*, Ikawa
十畑 Ikahata *s*
十迹手 Itode *m*
十彦 Isohiko *m*
十海 Ikari *s*
十馬 Isoma *m*
十部 Isobe *s*
十郎 Irako *s*
十崎 Ikazaki *sp*
十集 Isusaba *s*
十棲 Isozumi *s*, Iozumi, Imazumi, Irazumi
十鈴 Isuzu *m*
十嵐 Igarashi *sp*; Isoarashi *s*
十幡 Isobata *s*, Ikahata
十槻 Itsuki *m*
十槻園 Itsukizono *m*
³三 Izumi *m*
子 Itsuko *f*
大 Godai *m*
大力恋緘 Godairiki koi no fūjime *l*
大院 Godai *s*
⁴戸 Gonohe *sp*
六 Funobori *s*
介 Gosuke *m*
日市 Itsukaichi *p*
山文学 Gozan bungaku *l*
弓 Gokyū *s*
千里 Igimi *s*
月 Satsuki *sm*
月女 Sōtome *s*, Saotome
木 Itsuki *sp*
木雄 Ikio *m*
木田 Gokita *s*
井 Goi *s*, Gonoi
井屋 Goiya *s*
⁵代 Godai *s*
代友厚 G. Tomoatsu *mh*
代院 Godai *s*
四子 Ishiko *f*
本木 Gohongi *s*
⁶百人 Ioto *m*
百川 Imokawa *s*
百子 Ioko *f*
百井 Ioi *s*, Isai
百木 Iogi *s*, Ioki
百木井 Iokii *s*
百木部 Iokibe *s*
百木飄亭 Ioki Hyōtei *ml*
百住 Iosumi *s*, Yusumi
百枝 Ioe *f*
百野 Iono *s*
百旗頭 Iokibe *s*
百棲 Iozumi *s*, Irazumi
百歳 Iorei *s*
百蔵 Ioroi *s*, Iorai
百盤 Iiniwa *s*, Iniwa
百瀬 Iose *s*
百籠 Iorobi *s*, Ioroi
色 Goshiki *p*
色墨 Goshikizumi *l*
辻 Ikatsuji *s*, Ittsuji
⁷位野 Goino *s*
条 Gojō *sp*
返舎 Gohensha *s*
車反故 Gosha hōgo *l*
来 Gorai *s*
⁸明 Gomei *s*, Gomyō
所川原 Goshogawara *p*
和 Itsuwa *p*
味 Gomi *s*
味川 Gomikawa *s*
味川純平 G. Junpei *ml*
味保義 Gomi Yasuyoshi *ml*
味康祐 G. Yasusuke *ml*
味淵 Gomibuchi *s*
⁹城目 Gojōme *p*
松 Itsumatsu *s*
姓田 Goseda *s*
姓田芳柳 G. Hōryū *ma*
泉 Gosen *p*
¹⁰個荘 Gokashō *p*
料 Goryō *s*
郎 Gorō *m*
郎右衛門 Goroemon *m*
郎兵衛 Gorobee *m*
¹¹鬼上 Gokijō *s*
島 Gotō *sp*; Goshima *s*
島茂 Gotō Shigeru *ml*
島美代子 G. Miyoko *fl*
¹²富 Gotomi *s*
間 Gokan *s*
¹³雄 Itsuo *m*, Kazuo
稜郭血書 Goryōkaku kessho *la*
¹⁵艘 Goseki *s*
箇 Goka *p*
器所 Gokiso *s*

月 内 片 及 卞 方 文 止 少 山 ▼ 王 五 ▲ 无 天 不 弓 尺 巴 尹 丑 夬 与

片 及 卞 方 文 止 少 山 王 五 ▼ 无 天 不 弓 尺 巴 尹 丑 夬 与 ▲ 廿 井 夫 太 尤 犬 戈 木 勿 牛

17霞 Goka *p*
18観 Itsumi *m*
藤 Gotō *s*
畿 Goki *p*

无 92 (BU, MU, yori)
邪志 Musashi *s*

天 93 [T] Takashi *m*; Taka *f*; Ama *s*. (TEN, ama, ame, kami, sora) ⌈*l*
うつ浪 Sora utsu nami
に群星 Sora ni muraboshi *l* ⌈*l*
の夕顔 Ten no yūgao
3川 Amakawa *s*
4仁 Tennin 1108–83
水 Tensui *p*
水抄 Tensuishō *l*
元 Tengen 978–83
井 Amai *s*
木 Amaki *s*
方 Amakata *s*
文 Tenmon 1532–55
王 Tennō *p*
王寺 Tennōji *p*
5永 Ten'ei 1110–13
正 Tenshō 1573–92
丙 Amahyō *s*
本 Amamoto *s*
矢 Amaya *s*
田 Amada *sp*
田愚庵 A. Guan *ml*
生 Amō *s*
生目 Amanome *s*
平 Tenpyō 729–49
平宝字 T.-hōji 757–65
平神護 T.-jingo 765–67 ⌈57
平勝宝 T.-shōhō 749–
平感宝 T.-kanpō 749
6休 Tenkyū *s*
羽 Amaha *sp*; Amō *s*
地有情 Tenchi ujō *l*
行 Amayuki *s*
池 Amaike *s*
寺 Amadera *s*
宅 Amanoya *s*
台 Tendai *h*
台大師和讃 T. daishi wasan *l*
7利 Amari *s*
谷 Amadani *s*, Amagaya, Amanoya
安 Ten'an 857–59
児 Amako *s*, Amani
応 Ten'ō 781–82
貝 Amagai *s*
見 Amami *s*
衣紛上野初花 Kumo ni magō Ueno no hatsuhana *la*
8沼 Amanuma *s*
狗 Amainu *sm*
明 Tenmei *s* 1781–89
和 Tenwa / Tenna 1681–84
命 Tenmyō *s*
竺 Tenjiku *sp*
竺徳兵衛韓噺 T. Tokubee ikokubanashi
竺様 T.-yō *a* ⌊*la*
国 Amakuni *sm*
延 Ten'en 973–76
武 Tenmu *mlh*
承 Tenjō 1131–32
9保 Tenpō 1830–44
神林 Tenjinbayashi *s*
城 Amagi *sp* ⌈ma *p*
城湯ヶ島 A. Yugashi-
治 Tenji 1124–26
津 Amatsu *sp*; Tenshin *p* "Tientsin"
津小湊 A. Kominato
栄 Ten'ei *p* ⌊*p*
香 Tenkō *l*
草 Amakusa *splh*
草四郎時貞 A. Shirō Tokisada *mh*
長 Tenchō 824–34
彦 Amabiko *l*
10降言 Amarigoto *l*
海 Amami *s*, Amakai; Tenkai *smh*
狼 Tenrō *l* ⌈nomiya
宮 Amamiya *s*, Ama-
竜 Tenryū *p*
竜寺 Tenryūji *p*
原 Amanohara *sm*
座 Amakura *sm*
11授 Tenju 1375–81
理 Tenri *p*
野 Amano *s*
野谷 Amanoya *s*
野貞祐 Amano Teisuke *ml*
野桃隣 A. Tōrin *ml*
野屋 Amanoya *s*
笠 Amagasa *s*
智 Tenchi *mlh*
12孫 Amahiko *s*
禄 Tenroku 970–73
喜 Tengi 1053–38
童 Tendō *p*
間林 Tenmabayashi *p*
13塩 Teshio *p*
福 Tenpuku 1233–34
鈿女命 Amenouzume-no-mikoto *fh*
鼓 Tenko *la*
満宮 Tenmangū *p*
満宮菜種御供 T. natane no gokū *la*
照大神 Amaterasu Ōmikami *fh*
14語 Amagatari *s*, Amagatarai
徳 Tentoku 957–61
徳歌合 T. utaawase *l*
暦 Tenryaku 947–57
16養 Ten'yō 1144–45
慶 Tengyō 938–47
18藤 Amafuji *s*

不 94 [T] (FU, zu)
2二夫 Fujio *m*
二雄 Fujio *m*
5比等 Fuhito *m*
6羽 Fuwa *s*
同調 Fudōchō *l*
死原 Fushihara *s*
7朽子 Fueko *f*
如帰 Hototogisu *l*
言不語 Iwazu katara-
8波 Fuwa *s* ⌊zu *l*
易流行 Fueki ryūkō *l*
知山 Isayama *s*
知火 Shiranui *p*
9美人 Fumihito *m*
10破 Fuwa *sph-la*
11惜身命 Fushaku shinmyō *l*
動 Fudō *mha-la*
問語 Towazu-gatari *l*
17壊の白珠 Fue no shiratama *l*

弓 95 [T] Yuge *s*. (KYŪ, KU, yu, yumi)
子 Yumiko *f*
4月 Yuzuki *m*
月君 Y. no Kimi *mh*
5矢幡 Yumi Yawata *la*
田 Yumita *s*
9削 Yuge *sp*
削田 Yugeta *s*
11弦 Yuzuru *m*
野 Yumino *s*
12場 Yuba *s*
納持 Yunamochi *s*, Minamochi
13張月 Yumiharizuki *l*
15槻 Yutsuki *f*
18麿 Yumimaro *m*

尺 96 [T] Seki *s*. (SEKI, SHAKU, saku, saka, kane)
土 Sekido *l*
采 Sekie *s*
度 Sakado *s*

巴 97 Tomoe *m-f*. (HA, tomo)
人 Hajin *ml*
山 Tomoeyama *s*
里 Pari *p* "Paris"
波川 Uzumagawa *p-l*
理 Pari *p* "Paris"
絵 Tomoe *f*

尹 98 Tadashi *m*, Makoto; In *s*. (IN, tada, masa, kazu, nobu, kami)
松 Tadamatsu *m*
通 Masamichi *m*
鎮 Tadashige *m*

丑 99 [N] (CHŪ, ushi, hiro)
二 Ushiji *m*
次郎 Ushijirō *m*
徳 Hironori *m*

夬 100 Sadamu *m*. (KAI, KE, KETSU, KECHI, sada, mura)
夫 Sadaaki *m*
介 Sadaaki *m*

与 101 [T] Atae *m*, Atō, Hitoshi. (YO, tomo, yoshi, kumi, ato, nobu, sue, moro)
1一 Yoichi *m* ⌈*m*
一右衛門 Yoichiemon
一郎 Yoichirō *m*
2七 Yoshichi *m*
七郎 Yoshichirō *m*
3三七 Yosashichi *m*
三次 Yosōji *m*
三松 Yosomatsu *m*

三郎 Yosaburō *m*
之 Yoshi *m-f*
[4]五郎 Yogorō *m*
牛富 Yokotomi *s*
[5]左衛門 Yozaemon *m*
市 Yoichi *m*
四吉 Yoshikichi *m*
田 Yoda *s*
田準一 Y. Jun'ichi *ml*
[6]吉郎 Yokichirō *m*
芝 Yoshiba *s*
[7]住 Yosumi *s*
[8]板 Yoita *sp*
志 Yoshi *m*
良 Yora *s*; Nobuyoshi *m*
[9]治 Yoshiharu *m*
美 Atomi *m*
[10]倉 Yogura *s*
[11]清 Tomokiyo *m*
野 Yono *sp*
島 Yoshima *s*
[12]曾房 Yosoo *m*
敬 Tomokata *m*
喜 Yoki *m*
等 Yoto *s*
望都 Yomoichi *m*
[13]雄 Kumio *m*
話情浮名横櫛 Yowa nasake ukina no yokogushi *la*
[15]論 Yoron *p*
[16]謝 Yosa *sp*
謝野 Yosano *s*
謝野礼厳 Y. Reigon *ml*
謝野晶子 Y. Akiko *fl*
謝野鉄幹 Y. Tekkan *ml*
謝野寛 Y. Hiroshi *ml*
謝蕪村 Yosa Buson *ml*

廿 102 (JŪ, tsuzu, tsutsu)
山 Tsutsuyama *s*
日市 Hatsukaichi *p*
日出 Hatsukade *s*
日岩 Hatsukaiwa *s*
屋 Tsuzuya *s*
楽 Tsuzura *s*

井 103 [T] I *s*. (SEI, SHŌ, i, kiyo)
ケ田 Iketa *s*
[3]川 Ikawa *s*; Igawa *sp*
口 Iguchi *s*; Inokuchi *p*
下 Inoshita *s*
下田 Iketa *s*
上 Inoue *s*, Inai
上友一郎 Inoue Tomoichirō *ml*
上日召 I. Nisshō *mh*
上円了 I. Enryō *mh*
上文雄 I. Fumio *ml*
上光晴 I. Mitsuharu *ml*
上良雄 I. Yoshio *ml*
上勇 I. Isamu *ml*
上哲次郎 I. Tetsujirō *mlh*
上通泰 I. Michiyasu *ml*
上康文 I. Kōbun *ml*
上靖 I. Yasushi *ml*
上勤 I. Tsutomu *ml*
上準之助 I. Junnosuke *mh*
上播磨掾 I. Harimanojō *ma*
上毅 I. Kowashi *mh*
上馨 I. Kaoru *mh*
[4]山 Iyama *s*
水 Imizu *s*
元 Imoto *s*
戸 Ido *s*
戸川 Itogawa *s*
戸田 Itoda *s*
内 Iuchi *s*
手 Ide *sp*
[5]代 Ide *s*
石 Iishi *s*, Iseki, Donburi, Doburi
尻 Ijiri *s*, Inoshiri
田 Ida *s*
平 Ihira *s*
本 Imoto *s*, Inomoto
生 Iō *s*
[6]伏 Ibuse *s*
伏鱒二 I. Masuji *ml*
伊 Ii *s*
伊大老の死 Ii Tairō no shi *la*
伊直弼 Ii Naosuke *mh*
合 Iai *s*
[7]坂 Isaka *s*
形 Igata *s*
村 Imura *s*
汲 Ikumi *s*
沢 Izawa *s*
谷 Itani *s*
花 Ibana *s*
芹 Iseri *s*
尾 Io *s*
里 Isato *s*
出 Ide *s*
出井 Izui *s*
出曙覧 Ide no Akemi *ml*
[8]坪 Itsubo *s*
波 Inami *sp*; Iba *s*
門 Ikado *s*, Ito
於 Inoue *s*
東 Itō *s*
[9]狩 Ikari *s*
垣 Igaki *s*
城 Iki *s*
面 Inomo *s*
染 Isome *s*
草 Igusa *s*
泉水 Izumi *m*
岡 Ioka *s*
[10]浦 Iura *s*
桁 Igeta *s*
畔 Iguro *s*
倉 Ikura *s*
原 Ihara *s*; Ibara *sp*
原西鶴 Ihara Saikaku *ml*
[11]深 Ibuka *s*
後 Inoshiri *s*
部 Ibe *s*
野 Ino *s*
野口 Inokuchi *s*
野辺 Inobe *s*
島 Ijima *s*
鳥 Itori *s*
[12]崎 Izaki *s*
蛙抄 Seiashō *l*
筒 Izutsu *sf-la*
筒屋 Izutsuya *s*
[13]塚 Izuka *s*
雲 Igumo *s*
[14]関 Iseki *s*
[15]駒 Ikoma *s*
熊 Ikuma *s*
[16]橋 Ibashi *s*
[18]藤 Itō *s*

夫 104 [T] (FU, o, aki, suke)
木和歌抄 Fuboku wakashō *l*
次郎 Fujirō *m*
馬 Fuma *s*
婦木 Myōtogi *s*
婦善哉 Meoto zenzai *l*

太 105 [T] Futoshi *m*; Ō *s*, Ōno. (TAI, TA, DAI, hiro, moto, futo, taka, to, mi, uzu, ō, shiro, masu)
[1]一 Taichi *m*
一郎 Taichirō *m*
[2]刀川 Tachikawa *s*
刀洗 Tachiarai *p*
刀屋 Tachiya *s*
刀奪 Tachibai *la*
子 Taishi *p*
子屋 Taishiya *s*
介 Tasuke *m*
夫さん Kottai-san *l*
[5]左衛門 Tazaemon *m*
市 Taichi *m*
氏 Hirouji *m*
生子 Tauko *f*
平 Ōdabira *s*
平記 Taiheiki *l*
田 Ōta *sp*
田水穂 Ō. Mizuho *ml*
田玉茗 Ō. Gyokumei *ml*
田青丘 Ō. Seikyū *ml*
田垣 Ōtagaki *s*
田黒 Ōtaguro *s*
田道灌 Ōta Dōkan *mh*
田鴻村 Ō. Kōson *ml*
田麿 Ōtamaro *m*
[6]仲 Tachū *m*
次 Hirotsugu *m*
地 Taiji *p*
吉 Takichi *m*
[7]村 Tamura *s*
安万侶 Ō no Yasumaro *ml*
兵衛 Tahee *m*
茂 Futoshige *m*
[8]良 Tara *p*
[9]首 Futokubi *m*
重 Uzushige *m*
[10]祇 Taigi *ml*
郎 Tarō *m*
郎一 Taroichi *m*
郎三郎 Tarosaburō *m*
郎平 Tarobei *m*
郎館 Tarōdate *s*, Tarōdachi
泰 Motoyasu *m*
秦 Uzumasa *sp*
宰 Dazai *s*
宰府 Dazaifu *ph*
宰治 Dazai Osamu *ml*
宰春台 D. Shundai *mh*
[11]部 Ōbe *s*
虚集 Taikyoshū *l*
[13]雄 Takao *m*
鼓音智勇三略 Taiko no oto chiyū no sanryaku *la*
楽 Taraku *s*
[14]閤記 Taikōki *l*

尤 106 (YŪ, U, moto, motsu)
子 Motoko *f*

无 天 不 弓 尺 巴 尹 丑 夬 与 ▼ 廿 井 夫 太 尤 ▲ 犬 戈 木 勿 牛 午 升 女 爪 壬

**犬** 107 [T] Inu *s.* (KEN, inu)
$^{3}$川 Inugawa *s*
子集 Enokoshū *l*
丸 Inumaru *s*
上 Inugami *sp*
上御田鍬 I. no Mitasuki *mh*
$^{4}$山 Inuyama *sp*
山伏 Inu yamabushi *la*
井 Inui *s*
$^{5}$甘 Inukai *s*
田 Inuta *s*
田川 Inutagawa *m*
田卯 Inuta Shigeru *ml*
$^{6}$伏 Inubuse *s*
江 Inue *s*
$^{7}$阪 Inusaka *s*
坂 Inusaka *s*
村 Inumura *s*
$^{8}$房丸 Inubōmaru *m*
$^{9}$神 Inugami *s*
$^{12}$童 Indō *s*
筑波集 Inu Tsukubashū *l*
$^{13}$塚 Inuzuka *s*
飼 Inukai *sp*
$^{16}$養 Inukai *s*
養健 I. Takeru *ml*
養毅 I. Tsuyoshi *mh*
$^{23}$懸 Inukake *s*

**戈** 108 (KA, hoko, tomo, kata, mochi)
光 Tomomitsu *m*

**木** 109 [T] Iki *s.* (BOKU, MOKU, ki, ko, shige)
ノ内 Kinouchi *s*
$^{1}$一 Kiichi *m*
$^{3}$川 Kigawa *s*
口 Kikuchi *s*
之本 Kinomoto *sp*
之内 Kinouchi *s*
上 Kinoue *s*
工 Kotakumi *s*; Takumi *m*
子 Kigo *s*
下 Kinoshita *s*
下夕爾 K. Yūji *ml*
下利玄 K. Rigen *ml*
下杢太郎 K. Mokutarō *ml*
下尚江 K. Naoe *ml*
下長嘯子 K. Chōshōshi *ml*
下常太郎 K. Tsunetarō *ml*
下順二 K. Junji *ml*
下順庵 K. Jun'an *mh*
々 Kigi *s*
々高太郎 K. Takatarō *ml*
$^{4}$元 Kimoto *s*
戸 Kido *s*, Kigo
戸孝允 Kido Takayoshi *mh*
戸幸一 K. Kōichi *mh*
内 Kiuchi *s*
六駄 Kirokuda *la*
山 Kiyama *s*
山捷平 K. Shōhei *ml*
木 Kigi *s*
$^{5}$付 Kitsuke *s*
古内 Kikonai *p*
辺 Kibe *s*
立 Kidate *s*
目 Kinobe *s*
平 Kihira *s*
本 Kimoto *s*
田 Kita *sp*
田川 Kitagawa *s*
皿 Kisara *s*
$^{6}$次 Kitsugu *s*; Kisuki *p*
江 Kinoe *sp*
全 Kimata *s*
庄 Kinoshō *s*
西 Kinishi *s*
寺 Kodera *s*
名瀬 Kinase *s*
$^{7}$佐貫 Kisanuki *s*
沢 Kisawa *sp*
村 Kimura *s*
村小舟 K. Shōshū *ml*
村卿太 K. Sōta *ml*
村荘八 K. Shōhachi *ml*
村栄 K. Hisashi *mh*
村捨録 K. Suteroku *ml*
村富子 K. Tomiko *fl*
村素衛 K. Motomori *ml*
村毅 K. Ki *ml*
村曙 K. Akebono *fl*
村鷹太郎 K. Yōtarō *ml*
谷 Kitani *s*
呂子 Kiroko *s*
志見 Kishimi *s*
邑 Kimura *s*
尾 Shigeo *s*
里 Kidamari *s*
更津 Kisarazu *p*
$^{8}$使主 Kinoomi *s*
所 Kidokoro *s*
忠 Shigetada *m*
邨 Kimura *s*
$^{9}$俣 Kimata *s*
俣修 K. Osamu *ml*
垣 Kigaki *m*
城 Kijō *sp*; Kishiro *s*
津 Kizu *sp*; Kozu *s*
津谷 Kizutani *s*
祖 Kiso *sp*
畑 Kibata *s*
南 Kinami *s*
$^{10}$倉 Kigura *s*
浦 Kiura *s*
柴 Kishiba *s*
原 Kihara *s*
庭 Koba *s*
造 Kizukuri *sp*; Kozukuri *s*
屋 Kiya *s*
屋之助 Kiyanosuke *m*
屋平 Koyadaira *sp*
$^{11}$船 Kifune *s*
許 Kimoto *s*
野 Kino *s*
野内 Kinouchi *s*
野村 Kinomura *s*
部 Kibe *s*
梨 Kinashi *s*
島 Kishima *s*, Konoshima
島平 Kijimadaira *p*
$^{12}$接 Kitsugi *m*
場 Kiba *s*, Koba
崎 Kizaki *s*
喜代 Shigekiyo *m*
莵 Zuku *m*
登 Kinobori *s*
曾 Kiso *s*
曾川 Kisogawa *sp*
曾岬 Kisosaki *p*
曾義仲 Kiso Yoshinaka *mh*
賀 Kiga *s*
間 Kima *s*
間瀬 Kimase *s*
$^{13}$滝 Kitaki *s*
塚 Kizuka *s*
賊 Tokusa *sla*
越 Kikoshi *s*
$^{14}$幡 Kohata *s*, Kibata
暮 Kigurashi *s*, Kogure
$^{15}$鼠 Kinezumi *s*
$^{16}$魂 Kodama *m*
頭 Kitō *p*
綿 Kowata *s*
綿子 Yūko *f*
$^{17}$檜 Kogure *s*
$^{18}$藤 Kidō *s*
$^{19}$瀬 Kise *s*
蘇 Kiso *s*
蘇穀 K. Koku *ml*

**勿** 110 (KOTSU, BUTSU, na)
巳子 Namiko *f*
来 Nakoso *p*

**牛** 111 [T] (GYŪ, GO, ushi, toshi)
ヶ瀬 Ushigase *s*
$^{2}$九十 Ukuso *s*
$^{3}$久 Ushiku *p*
久保 Ushikubo *s*
丸 Ushimaru *m*
$^{4}$木 Ushiki *s*
円 Ushimaro *s*
山 Ushiyama *s*
$^{5}$込 Ushigome *s*
尼 Ushiama *s*
田 Ushida *s*, Ushima
甘 Ushikai *m*
生 Ushū *m*
$^{7}$沢 Ushizawa *s*
屎 Ubari *s*
尾 Ushio *s*
来 Gorai *s*
$^{9}$津 Ushizu *p*
草 Ushikusa *s*
$^{10}$馬 Gyūba *l*
$^{11}$深 Ushibuka *p*
島 Ushijima *s*
$^{12}$場 Ushiba *s*
窓 Ushimado *p*
奥 Ushioku *s*
$^{13}$堀 Ushibori *p*
塚 Ushizuka *s*
腸 Gochō *s*
越 Ushigoe *s*
$^{14}$窪 Ushikubo *s*
$^{16}$養 Ushikai *m*
$^{17}$糞 Gokoe *s*, Ukuso, Gokoso
$^{18}$麿 Ushimaro *m*

**午** 112 [T] (GO, ma, uma)
介 Umasuke *m*

**升** 113 [T] Noboru *m*, Nobori, Minori, Minoru. (SHŌ, masu, nori, taka, yuki)
田 Masuda *s*
本 Masumoto *s*
屋 Masuya *s*

**女** 114 [T] (JO, NYŌ, NYO, me, ko, taka, yoshi, onna)

²人芸術 Nyonin geijutsu *l*
³川 Onagawa *sp*
大学 Onna daigaku *lh*
⁶光 Yoshimitsu *ma*
⁷男之助 Meonosuke *m*
良 Mera *sp*
郎花 Ominameshi *la*
殺油地獄 Onna-goroshi abura jigoku *la*
屋 Onaya *s*
¹¹部田 Mebuta *s*
鹿 Mega *s*
満別 Memanbetsu *p*
誡扇綺譚 Jokaisen kidan *l*
¹⁴歌舞伎 Onna Kabuki *a*
¹⁷篠 Meshino *s*

爪 115 (sō, tsume)

工 Tsumetakumi *s*, Tsumatakumi, Hatakumi
色の雨 Tsumeiro no ame *l*

壬 116 Akira *m*, Ōi; Mibu *s*. (JIN, NIN, mi, tsugu, mizu, yoshi)
二集 Minishū *l*
八 Miya *f*
子 Mine *f*
士 Yoshihito *m*
夫 Yoshio *m*
太郎 Mizutarō *m*
生 Mibu *sp*
生二位 M. no Nii *ml*
生忠岑 M. no Tadamine *ml*
生川 Mibukawa *s*; Nyūgawa *p*
恵 Mizue *f*

毛 117 [T] (MO, MŌ, BŌ, ke, atsu)
²人 Ebisu *m*
⁴戸 Kedo *s*
内 Monai *s*
⁵穴 Kena *s*
生 Keo *f*
⁷抜 Kenuki *la*
利 Mōri *s*, Mori
利元就 Mōri Motonari *mh*
利敬親 M. Takachika *mh*
利輝元 M. Terumoto *mh*
谷村 Keyamura *s*
呂 Moro *s*
呂山 Moroyama *sp*
呂清春 Moro Kiyoharu *ml*
⁸所 Menjo *s*, Nenjo
牧 Mohira *s*, Momura
受 Menju *s*, Keuke, Menjo, Menjō, Mozu
¹⁰剃 Kezori *s*
馬 Kema *s*, Menma
馬内 Kumanai *s*
¹¹野 Kenu *m*
¹³塚 Mozuka *s*, Kezuka
²³籠 Morō *s*

手 118 [T] Te *s*. (SHU, te, ta, de)
²刀良 Tetora *m*
³川 Tegawa *s*
巾 Hankechi *l*
⁵代木 Teshirogi *s*
末才伎 Tanasuenotebito *s*
白 Teshiro *s*
⁷束 Tezuka *s*
柄 Tegara *s*
柄山 Tegarayama *s*
⁹品 Tejina *s*
¹¹習 Tenarai *l*
島 Teshima *s*
島堵庵 T. Toan *mh*
¹²賀 Tega *s*
¹³播 Tengai *s*
塚 Tezuka *s*
塚富雄 T. Tomio *ml*
越 Tegoshi *s*
¹⁴稲 Teine *p*
結 Tenashi *s*
爾乎葉 Tenioha *l*
²¹綛 Tasuki *s*
²³纏 Tamaki *m*

—5 L1—

旧 119 [T] (KYŪ, KU, GU, furu, hisa, moto, fusa)
井 Furui *s*
事本紀 Kuji hongi *l*

必 120 [T] (HITSU, sada)
佐 Hisa *s*
典 Sadanori *m*

—5 L2—

氷 See 140

加 121 [T] (KA, KE, masu, mata)
³川 Kagawa *s*
子母 Kashimo *sp*
久藤 Kakutō *p*
也 Masuya *m*
⁴孔 Masuyoshi *m*
戸 Kado *s*
内 Kanouchi *s*
山 Kayama *s*
太 Kabuto *s*
⁵加爪 Kagatsume *s*
加江 Kagae *s*
加見 Kagami *s*
加美 Kagami *s*
古 Kako *sp*
古川 Kakogawa *sp*
田 Kata *s*
⁶地 Kachi *s*
地井 Kachii *s*
州 Kashū *p* "California"
西 Kasai *sp*
世 Kase *s*
世田 Kaseda *sp*
名生 Kanō *s*
⁷佐 Kasa *sp*
村 Kamura *s*
男利 Kaori *f*
来 Karai *s*, Kaku
寿子 Kazuko *f*
⁸沼 Kanuma *s*
波山 Kabasan *p*
門 Kamon *s*
舎 Kaya *s*
奈陀 Kanada *p* "Canada"
宜 Kaga *s*
茂 Kamo *sp*
茂物狂 K. monogurui *la*
茂川 Kamogawa *p*
茂宮 Kamonomiya *s*
東 Katō *sp*
⁹保茶 Kabocha *s*
持 Kamochi *s*
津佐 Kazusa *sp*
治 Kaji *s*
治川 Kajikawa *sp*
治木 Kajiki *sp*
治屋 Kajiya *s*
畑 Kabata *s*
計 Kake *sp*
美 Kami *sp*
美山 Kamiyama *s*
¹⁰悦 Kaya *sp*; Kanitsu *s*
倉井 Kakurai *s*
倉井秋を K. Akio *ml*
留田 Karuta *s*
屋 Kaya *s*
¹¹野 Kano *s*
能 Kanō *s*
能作次郎 K. Sakujirō *ml*
部 Kabe *s*
島 Kajima *s*
¹²場山 Kabayama *s*
須 Kasu *s*; Kazo *p*
須屋 Kasuya *s*
納 Kanō *s*
納暁 K. Akatsuki *ml*
賀 Kaga *sp*
賀の千代女 K. no Chiyojo *fl*
賀山 Kagayama *s*
賀谷 Kagaya *s*
賀美 Kagami *s*
登 Kado *s*
曾利 Kasori *s*
集 Kashū *s*, Katsume
¹³勢 Kase *s*
¹⁶頭 Katō *s*
¹⁸藤 Katō *s*
藤一夫 K. Kazuo *ml*
藤千蔭 K. Chikage *ml*
藤木 Katōki *s*
藤介春 Katō Kaishun *ml*
藤友三郎 K. Tomosaburō *mh*
藤弘之 K. Hiroyuki *mlh*
藤周一 K. Shūichi *ml*
藤武雄 K. Takeo *ml*
藤東籬 K. Tōri *ml*
藤咄堂 K. Totsudō *ml*
藤将之 K. Masayuki *ml*
藤高明 K. Takaaki *mh*
藤清正 K. Kiyomasa *mh*
藤朝鳥 K. Chōchō *ml*
藤景正 K. Kagemasa *ma*
藤道夫 K. Michio *ml*
藤楸邨 K. Shūson *ml*
¹⁹瀬 Kase *s*
瀬谷 Kasetani *s*
²¹羅 Kara *ph*

仭 122 Mitsuru *m*. (JIN, NIN, hiro, mitsu)

仍 123 (JŌ, NYŌ, yori, atsu, nao)
久 Yorihisa *m*
敦 Yoriatsu *m*

爪 壬 毛 手 旧 必 氷 加 仮 仍 ▼ 仕 代 付 仗 仏 他 仟 仡 叶 収 以 功 打 比 北 ▲ 外 氺 氿 汀 氾 引 札 主 云 示

仕 124 [T] Tsukasa *m*, Tsukō, Manabu. (SHI, JI)

代 125 [T] Dai *s*. (DAI, TAI, yo, shiro, toshi, nori)
々 Yoyogi *sp*
五郎 Daigorō *m*
代木 Yoyogi *s*
田 Shirota *s*; Daita *p*
主 Shironushi *la*
包 Norikane *m*
長 Toshinaga *m*

付 126 [T] (FU, tomo, tsuke)
知 Tsukechi *p*

仗 127 (JŌ, CHŌ, yori, yoru)
幡 Yorihata *m*

仏 128 [T] Hotoke *f*; Satoru *m*. (BUTSU, FUTSU, hotoke)
木 Hotogi *s*
足石歌 Bussokuseki no uta *l*
法僧 Buppōsō *l*
師 Busshi *la*
原 Hotoke no hara *la*
蘭西 Furansu *p* " France "

他 129 [T] (TA, osa, hito)
戸 Osabe *m*
田 Osada *s*
田日奉部 Osadahimatsuribe *s* ⌈ue *l*
我身之上 Taga mino-

仟 130 Shigeru *m*, Tsukasa. (SEN,
子 Osako *f* ⌊osa)

仡 131 (GITSU, isa)
夫 Isao *m*

——5 L3——

叶 132 Kanō *m*, Kanai. (KYŌ, GYŌ, yasu)
一 Kyōichi *m*
内 Kanouchi *s*

収 133 [T] Osamu *m*, Susumu. (SHŪ, SHU, kazu, mori, sane, naka, nao, nobu, moto, moro)
子 Kazuko *f*
多 Kazuta *sm*
茂 Morishige *m*

以 134 [T] (I, mochi, yuki, tomo, kore, sane, shige, nori)
$^{3}$之 Tomoyuki *m*
久 Yukihisa *m*
$^{4}$仁 Mochihito *m*
仁王 M.-ō *mh*
正 Koremasa *m*
$^{7}$言 Koretoki *m*
良 Mochinaga *m*
良都女 Iratsume *l*
昭 Shigeaki *m*
首一 Ishuichi *s*
$^{10}$修 Yukimasa *m*
悦 Mochiyoshi *m*
$^{11}$紀 Mochinori *m*
$^{14}$節 Iyo *m*
$^{16}$親 Yukichika *m*

功 135 [T] Tsutomu *m*, Isao, Isaoshi. (KŌ, KU, koto, isa, katsu, nari, naru, nori, ō, atsu, kata)
一 Kōichi *m*
力 Kunugi *s*
子 Kotoko *f*
内 Kunugi *s*
男 Norio *m*
阿弥 Kōami *ma*
長 Isanaga *m*
彦 Katsuhiko *m*
康 Kotoyasu *m*

打 136 [T] (DA, uchi, utsu, u)
木 Uchiki *s*
田 Uchida *sp*
矢 Uchiya *s*
宅 Uchida s, Uda
見 Utsumi *s*
越 Uchikoshi *s*, Ugoshi, Uchiichi, Uteichi, Udeshi
聞集 Uchigikishū *l*

比 137 [T] Tasuku *m*. (HI, tomo, taka, chika, hisa, nami,
$^{4}$内 Hinai *sp* ⌊tsune)
勿子 Hinako *f*
$^{5}$布 Pippu *p*
尼縵 Hinekazura *s*
田 Hida *s*
田井 Hidai *s*
$^{6}$企 Hiki *sp* ⌈mh
企能員 H. Yoshikazu
$^{7}$佐 Hisa *s*
和 Hiwa *sp*
$^{8}$良 Hira *s*
良野 Hirano *s*
良麿 Hiramaro *m*
$^{11}$留 Hiru *s*
留間 Hiruma *s*
島 Hitō *p* " Philippines "
$^{12}$喜田 Hikida *s*
登 Hito *m*
等 Hito *m*
婆 Hiba *p*
曾牟 Hisomu *m*
$^{14}$徳 Takanori *m*
嘉 Hika *s*
$^{15}$叡山 Hieizan *p*
叡辻 Heitsuji *s*
$^{20}$護 Higo *s*
$^{21}$羅夫 Hirafu *m*

北 138 [T] Kita *sp*; Kitabashiri *s*. (HOKU, kita, ta)
$^{1}$一輝 Kita Ikki *mh*
九州 Kita-kyūshū *p*
$^{3}$小路 Kitakōji *s*
川 Kitagawa *sp* ⌈ml
川冬彦 K. Fuyuhiko
川辺 Kita-kawabe *p*
口 Kitaguchi *s*
上 Kitakami *sp*
上神 Kitaniwa *s*
久保 Kitakubo *s*
大路 Kitaōji *s*
$^{4}$方 Kitakata *s*; Kita-
井 Kitai *s* ⌊gata *sp*
中 Kitanaka *s*
山 Kitayama *sp*
爪 Kitazume *s*
$^{5}$代 Kitajiro *s*
辺 Kitabe *s*
古賀 Kitakoga *s*
平 Peipin *p* "Peiping"
巨摩 Kita-koma *p*
本 Kitamoto *sp*
田 Kitada *s*
田薄氷 K. Usurai *ml*
白 Kitajiro *s*
白川 Kitashirakawa *sp*
$^{6}$池 Kitaike *s*
宇和 Kita-uwa *p*
馬 Kita-arima *p*
向 Kitamuki *s*, Toki, Tosa
辻 Kitatsuji *s*
多摩 Kita-tama *p*
米 Hokubei *p* "N. America"
$^{7}$佐久 Kita-saku *p*
住 Kitazumi *s*
住敏夫 K. Toshio *ml*
坊 Kitabō *s*
沢 Kitazawa *s*
杜夫 Kita Morio *ml*
村 Kitamura *s* ⌈ml
村小松 K. Komatsu
村山 Kita-murayama *p* ⌈sao *ml*
村寿夫 Kitamura Hi-
村季吟 K. Kigin *ml*
村透谷 K. Tōkoku *ml*
村喜八 K. Kihachi *ml*
会津 Kita-aizu *p*
谷 Kitatani *s*
牟婁 Kita-muro *p*
邑 Kitamura *s*
足立 Kita-adachi *p*
安 Kitayasu *m*
安曇 Kita-azumi *p*
条 Hōjō *sp*; Kitajō *p*
条元一 H. Motokazu *ml*
条氏政 H. Ujimasa *mh*
条氏康 H. Ujiyasu *mh*
条氏綱 H. Ujitsuna *mh*
条早雲 H. Sōun *mh*
条民雄 H. Tamio *ml*
条実時 H. Sanetoki *mh*
条秀司 H. Hideji *ml*
条政子 H. Masako *fh*
条政村 H. Masamura *mh* ⌈mh
条重時 H. Shigetoki
条時行 H. Tokiyuki *mh* ⌈mh
条時政 H. Tokimasa
条時宗 H. Tokimune *mh* ⌈mh
条時房 H. Tokifusa
条時頼 H. Tokiyori *mh* ⌈mh
条高時 H. Takatoki

条泰時 H. Yasutoki *mh*
条誠 H. Makoto *ml*
条義時 H. Yoshitoki *mh*
条顕時 H. Akitoki *mh*
尾 Kitao *s*
里 Kitazato *sm*
里柴三郎 K. Shibasaburō *mh*
見 Kitami *sp* ⌈*fl*
見志保子 K. Shihoko
出 Kitade *s*
$^{8}$河 Kitagawa *s*
河原 Kitagawara *s*
林 Kitabayashi *s*
枝 Hokushi *ml*; Kitae
波多 Kita-hata *p* ⌊*f*
房 Hokubō *p*
京 Pekin *p* "Peking"
茂安 Kita-shigeyasu *p*
居 Kitai *s*
$^{9}$垣 Kitagaki *s*
垣内 Kitagakitō *s*
津軽 Kita-tsugaru *p*
相木 Kita-aiki *p*
相馬 Kita-sōma *p*
松 Kitamatsu *s*
松浦 Kita-matsuura *p*
畑 Kitahata *s*
秋田 Kita-akita *p*
茨城 Kita-ibaraki *p*
風 Kitakaze *s*
岡 Kitaoka *s*
$^{10}$浦 Kitaura *sp*
浜 Kitahama *s*
海部 Kita-amabe *p*
海道 Hokkaidō *p*
脇 Kitawaki *s*
高来 Kita-takaki *p*
桑田 Kita-kuwada *p*
竜 Hokuryū *p*
畠 Kitabatake *s*
畠八穂 K. Yaho *ml*
畠顕家 K. Akiie *mh*
畠親房 K. Chikafusa *ml*
原 Kitahara *s* ⌈*ml*
原白秋 K. Hakushū
原武夫 K. Takeo *ml*
屋 Kitaya *s*
$^{11}$陸道 Hokurikudō *p*
埼玉 Kita-saitama *p*
清水 Kitashimizu *s*
淡 Hokudan *s*
添 Kitazoe *s*
設楽 Kita-shidara *p*
野 Kitano *sp*
野天神縁起 K. Tenjin engi *la* ⌈*p*
部 Kitabe *s*; Hokubu
都留 Kita-tsuru *p*
副 Kitazoe *s*
斎 Hokusai *ma*
魚沼 Kita-uonuma *p*
島 Kitajima *sp*
$^{12}$御牧 Kita-mimaki *p*
崎 Kitazaki *s*
窓 Kitamado *s*
$^{13}$塩原 Kita-shiobara *p*
堀 Kitabori *s*
群馬 Kita-gunma *p*
詰 Kitazume *s*
蒲原 Kita-kanbara *p*
葛城 Kita-katsuragi *p*
葛飾 Kita-katsushika
勢 Hokusei *s* ⌊*p*
園 Kitasono *s*
園克衛 K. Katsue *ml*
$^{14}$郷 Hokugō *sp*; Kitazato *s*, Hongō; Kitagō *p* ⌈*p*
$^{15}$諸県 Kita-morokata
$^{16}$綏 Kitaō *s*
橘 Hokkitsu *p*
橋 Kitahashi *s*
$^{17}$檜山 Kita-hiyama *p*
館 Kitadate *s*
鮮 Hokusen *p* "N. Korea"
$^{18}$藤 Kitafuji *s*

外 139 [T] Todokoro *s*. (GAI, GE, to, soto, tono, hiro, hoka)
$^{3}$川 Sotogawa *s*, Togawa
三郎 Hokasaburō *m*
之助 Hokanosuke *m*
丸 Tomaru *s*
$^{4}$山 Toyama *s*, Sotoyama; Tobi *p*
山ゝ山 Toyama Chūzan *ml*
山正一 T. Masakazu *ml* ⌈*ml*
山卯三郎 T. Usaburō
山座 Tobi-za *a*
$^{5}$立 Hashidate *s*
処 Todokoro *s*
史 Gaishi *m*
$^{6}$次郎 Sotojirō *m*
池 Toike *s*, Tonoike
交官 Tokonori *m*
守 Tomori *m*
$^{7}$村 Tomura *s*, Tonomura, Sotomura
村吏郎 S. Shirō *ml*
村繁 Tonomura Shigeru *ml*
谷 Toya *s*, Todani
出 Hashidate *s*
$^{8}$波 Tonami *s*
所 Todokoro *s*
命婦 Gemyōbu *f*
$^{9}$治 Sotoji *m*
松 Tomatsu *s*
$^{10}$郎売 Uirōuri *la*
美雄 Tomio *m*
栄 Tonoe *f*
岡 Tooka *s*
浦 Tonoura *s* ⌈*p*
海 Sotomi *s*; Sotome
記 Geki *sm*
記座 Gekiza *p*
宮山 Tomiyama *s*
$^{11}$野岡 Tonooka *s*
恵 Tonoe *f*
島 Toshima *s*
$^{12}$崎 Tozaki *s*
雄 Sotoo *m*
園 Hokazono *s*
衛 Tomori *m*
禰子 Toneko *f*

氷 140 [T] Hi *s*. (HYŌ, hi, kiyo)
川 Hikawa *sp*
上 Hikami *sp*
行 Kiyoyuki *m*
見 Himi *p*
車 Higuruma *s*
点 Hyōten *l*
高 Hitaka *s*
室 Himuro *sla*
島 Hyōtō *l*

氻 141 Minoto *m*. (ROKU)

汀 142 Nagisa *f*, Migiwa. (TEI)

氾 143 Hiroshi *m*. (HAN, hiro)
子 Hiroko *f*

———5 L4———

引 144 [T] (IN, hiki, nobu, hisa)
田 Hikida *s*; Hiketa *sp*
佐 Inasa *sp*

札 145 [T] Nusa *s*, Nuki. (SATSU, fuda, sane, nusa)
子 Fudako *f*
場 Fudaba *s*
幌 Sapporo *p*

礼 146 [T] Hiroshi *m*, Masashi. (REI, RAI, nori, hiro, kata, nari, masa, michi, akira, yuki, yoshi, aki, aya, iya, uya)
之助 Reinosuke *m*
文 Rebun *p*
云 Hirohito *m*
本 Norimoto *m*
次郎 Reijirō *m*
吉 Reikichi *m*
助 Reisuke *m*
直 Norinao *m*
重 Hiroshige *m*
記 Raiki *l* "Li Chi"
朝 Hirotomo *m*
弼 Reisuke *m* ⌈*ml*
厳法師 Reigon Hōshi

———5 T1———

主 See 196

云 147 [T] (UN, hito, kore, tomo, oki)

示 148 [T] Shimesu *m*; Shime *f*. (SHI, JI, KI, mi, shime, toki)
元 Tokiyuki *m*

永 149 [T] Nagashi *m*, Hisashi, Naga, Hakaru. (EI, YŌ, naga, nori, tō, tsune, nobu, hisa, hira)
$^{3}$三郎 Eizaburō *m*
川 Nagakawa *s*
万 Eiman 1165–66
久 Eikyū 1113–18; Nagahisa *sm*
久保 Nagakubo *s*
久子 Towako *f*
$^{4}$仁 Einin 1293–99
戸 Nagato *s*, Eito
元 Nagamoto *s*

氿 汀 氾 引 札 礼 主 云 示 永 ▼ 立 市 矛 卉 召 占 古 ▲ 令 公 只 穴 艾 夳 冬 旦 弖 丕

友 Nagatomo s
木 Nagaki s
山 Nagayama s
太郎 Eitarō m
井 Nagai s
井荷風 N. Kafū ml
井竜男 N. Tatsuo ml
5石 Nagaishi s
用 Nagamochi s
正 Eishō 1504–21
平寺 Eiheiji p
田 Nagata s
田青嵐 N. Seiran ml
田耕衣 N. Kōi ml
田鉄山 N. Tetsuzan mh
田衡吉 N. Kōkichi ml
6地 Nagatochi s
江 Nagae s
池 Nagaike s
守 Nagamori m
光 Nagamitsu m
吉 Nagayoshi s; Eikichi m
有 Nagamochi m
7作 Eisaku sm; Nagasaku s
坂 Nagasaka s
沢 Nagasawa s
村 Nagamura s
谷 Nagatani s
安 Nagayasu sm
孚 Eisuke m, Nagasa-
見 Nagami s ⌊ne
8沼 Naganuma s
和 Eiwa 1375–79
享 Eikyō 1426–41
侖 Nagatomo m
延 Eien 987–89
承 Eijō 1046–53
並 Enami s
9保 Eihō 1081–84
持 Nagamochi s
治 Eiji 1141–42
祐 Nagasachi m
松 Nagamatsu s
則 Nagatsune m
岩 Nagaiwa s
長 Nagaosa s; Nagaie m; Eichō 1096–97
妻 Nagatsuma s
岡 Nagaoka s
廻 Nagasako s
10浜 Nagahama s
浦 Nagaura s
祚 Eiso 989–90
倉 Nagakura s
原 Nagahara s
造 Eizō m
11峰 Nagamine s
根 Nagane s
野 Nagano s
留 Nagatome s
盛 Nagamori s
島 Nagashima s
鳥 Nagatori s
12禄 Eiroku 1558–70
富 Nagatomi s
森 Nagamori s
13淵 Nagabuchi s
堀 Nagahori s
塚 Nagatsuka s
滝 Nagataki s
源寺 Eigenji p
福 Nagayoshi m
福門院 Eifuku Mon'in fl
詮 Nagaharu m
楽 Eiraku s
遠子 Towako f
14愷 Nagayasu m
徳 Eitoku 1381–84
暦 Eiryaku 1160–61
15幡 Nagahata s
16緒 Nagao sm
18藤 Nagafuji s
観 Eikan 983–85; Yōkan mh
瀬 Nagase s
瀬清子 N. Kiyoko fl

## 5 T2

立 See 194

市 See 195

矛 150 [T] (BŌ, MU, hoko, take)
雄 Hokoo m

卉 151 Noboru m. (KI)

召 152 [T] (SHŌ, JŌ, meshi, mesu, yoshi, yobu)
子 Meshiko f
田 Meshida ml
波 Shōha ml

占 153 [T] (SEN, shime, ura)
太郎 Shimetarō m
吉 Shimekichi m
冠 Shimukappu p
部 Urabe s

古 154 [T] (KO, KU, furu, hisa, taka)
人大兄 Furuhito no Ōe mh ⌈gawa s
川 Furukawa sp; Ko-
川魁蕾 F. Kairai ml
口 Kokuchi s
子 Furuko f, Hisako; Hisatsugu m
久根 Kokune s
久沢 Kokuzawa s
4仁所 Konisho s
今 Kokon s; Kokin l
今百馬鹿 Kokon hyakubaka l
今和歌六帖 Kokin waka rokujō l
今和歌集 K. wakashū l
今和歌集正義 K. w. seigi l
今著聞集 Kokon chomonjū l
今集 Kokinshū l
今集両度聞書 K. ryōdo kikigaki l
今集注 K. chū l
井 Furui s
井出 Koide s
内 Furuuchi s
山 Furuyama s, Ko-
止 Koto f ⌊yama
木 Furuki s
手屋 Furuteya s
5本 Furumoto s
矢 Furuya s
田 Furuta s, Kota
田土 Kotado s
田島 Kotajima s, Kodashima ⌈bira p
平 Kodaira s; Furu-
市 Furuichi s
立 Kodachi s
史成文 Koshi seibun l
史通 Koshitsū lh
史徴 Koshichō l
6江 Furue s
池 Furuike s, Koike
寺 Kodera s
宇田 Kouda s
在 Furuari s, Kozai
庄 Furushō s
7沢 Furusawa s
坂 Furusaka s
村 Komura s, Furumura
安 Furuyasu s
志 Koshi sp
谷 Furutani s, Furuya, Komoya
谷野 Koyano s
谷綱武 Furuya Tsunatake ml
尾谷 Furuoya s
見 Furumi s
里 Furusato s
寿 Hisatoshi m
来 Furuku s
来風体抄 Korai fūtaishō l ⌈sp
8河 Furukawa s; Koga
性 Furushō s
明地 Komechi s
門 Komon s
林 Kobayashi s, Furubayashi
居 Furui s
東 Kotō s
事記 Kojiki l
事記伝 K. den l
事記燈 K. akashi l
事談 Kojidan l
9俣 Komata s ⌈shiro
城 Kojō s, Furujō, Ko-
松 Furumatsu s
畑 Furuhata s
荘 Furushō s
岳 Kogaku s
泉 Koizumi s
泉千樫 K. Chikashi ml
10郡 Furugōri s
宮 Furumiya s, Komi-
室 Komuro s ⌊ya
家 Furuya s
家榧夫 F. Kayao ml
屋 Furuya s
座 Koza p
座川 Kozagawa p
11野 Furuno s
野生 Konoo s
都 Furuichi s; Koto l
埜 Kono f ⌈jima
島 Furushima s, Ko-
12渡 Furuwatari s, Kowatari; Futto sp
猪之助 Furuinosuke m
崎 Furusaki s
稀春風 Kokishunpū l
森 Furumori s, Ko-
筆 Kohitsu s ⌊mori

衆 Kosu *s*
賀 Koga *sp*
賀春江 K. Harue *ma*
賀精里 K. Seiri *mh*
閑 Kogen *s*, Koga
[13]満 Koma *s*
雅屋 Kogaya *s*
殿 Furudono *p*
[14]郷 Furusato *s*
語拾遺 Kogo shūi *l*
駅 Koeki *l*
越 Furukoshi *s*
関 Kokan *s*, Kozeki
爾 Koko *s*
[16]橋 Furuhashi *s*
館 Furudate *s*
慈悲 Kojihi *m*
[18]藤 Kotō *s*
藤田 Kotōda *s*
[19]瀬 Furuse *s*, Kose

**令** 155 [T] (REI, RYŌ, nori, yoshi, haru, nari)
子 Yoshiko *f*
寿 Yoshinobu *m*
宗 Yoshimune *sm*
家 Yoshiie *m*, Yoshimune
蔵 Reizō *m*

**公** 156 [T] Tadashi *m*, Isao, Tōru, Akira; Kimi *f*. (KŌ, KU, kimi, kin, taka, tomo, masa, hiro, tada, yuki, sato, ō, hito)
[1]一 Tomokazu *m*
[3]三郎 Kimisaburō *m*
子 Kimiko *f*
[4]元 Kinharu *m*
方 Kubō *m*
尹 Kinmasa *m*
文 Kumon *s*
[5]功 Kinnaru *m*
允 Kinchika *m*
正 Kimimasa *m*, Kinnao, Kin'osa
平 Kimihira *sm*; Kōhei *m*, Kimihei
[6]任 Kintō *ml*; Kimihide *m*
行 Naoyuki *m*
光 Masateru *m*
共 Kintomo *m*
名 Kinna *m*
[7]利 Kimisato *m*
条 Kin'eda *m*
男 Kimio *m*
考 Kinnaru *m*
孝 Yukitaka *m*
[8]使 Kuramu *s*
明 Takaaki *m*, Masaaki
門 Kumon *s*
房 Kimifusa *m*
宜 Kinsumi *m*
述 Kinakira *m*
[9]保 Kubo *s*
恪 Kintsumu *m*
城 Kinmura *m*
政 Kinmasa *m*
荘 Kushō *s*
長 Kin'osa *m*
栄 Kinteru *m*
直 Kinnao *m*
[10]修 Kin'osa *m*
威 Kōi *m*
[11]脩 Kin'osa *m*
健 Kintaru *m*
致 Kin'yuki *m*
[12]揖 Kin'osa *m*
暁 Kugyō *mh*
勝 Kinkatsu *m*, Kintō
敬 Kinhaya *m*
董 Kintada *m*
森 Kimimori *s*
望 Kinmochi *m*
遂 Kinkatsu *m*
[13]塚 Kimizuka *s*
張 Takatomo *m*
靖 Hiroyasu *m*
誠 Kinzane *m*, Kinmi
純 Kin'ito *m*
資 Kin'yori *m*
誉 Takayoshi *m*
[14]説 Kinkoto *m*
韶 Kimimasa *m*
[15]毅 Kintake *m*
[16]衡 Kinhira *m*
積 Kintsumu *m*
翰 Kin'oto *m*
維 Kinfusa *m*
燕 Kinnaru *m*
賢 Kimiyoshi *m*
[17]総 Kinmichi *m*
顕 Kin'aki *m*
[18]賓 Kimiyoshi *m*
[19]績 Kin'isa *m*
[20]麗 Kimikazu *m*
[21]彝 Kintsune *m*

—5 T3—

**只** 157 [N] (SHI, SHIN, tada)
八 Tadahachi *m*
木 Tadaki *s*
見 Tadami *sp*
野 Tadano *s*

**穴** 158 [T] (KETSU, ana, kore)
水 Anamizu *sp*
山 Anayama *s*
太 Anō *sp*; Anato *s*, Anaho, Ano, Ana
井 Anai *s*
田 Anata *s*
生 Anō *sp*
吹 Anabuki *p*
沢 Anazawa *s*
原 Anahara *s*
穂部 Anahobe *s*
磯 Anashi *s*

**艾** 159 Yasushi *m*. (GAI, yasu, yoshi)

**太** 160 (TA, TAI, yasu)

**冬** 161 [T] (TŌ, fuyu, kazu, toshi)
二 Fuyuji *m*
三郎 Tōsaburō *m*
木 Fuyuki *s*
夫 Fuyuo *m*
弘 Toshihiro *m*
花帳 Tōkachō *l*
宝 Fuyutomi *m*
青空 Fuyu aozora *l*
柏 Tōhaku *l*
彦 Fuyuhiko *m*
彦集 Fuyuhikoshū *l*
嗣 Fuyutsugu *m*
暦 Tōreki *l*

—5 T4—

**旦** 162 [I] Akira *m*, Tadashi; Asa *s*, Tan. (TAN, DAN, aki, akira, asa)
夫 Asao *m*
来 Awasō *s*

**弖** See 202

**丕** 163 Hajime *m*. (HI, hiro, i)
道 Hiromichi *m*

—5 F1—

**司** 164 [T] Tsukasa *m*, Osamu, Tsutomu. (SHI, SU, mori, kazu, moto)
子 Moriko *f*
氏 Moriuji *m*
辻 Kasatsuji *s*
城 Tsukasagi *m*
亮 Moriaki *m*
直 Kazunao *m*, Motonao
馬 Shiba *s*
馬江漢 S. Kōkan *ma*
馬達等 S. Tatto / Tachito *mh*
馬遷 Shiba Sen *mlh* "Ssu-ma Ch'ien"
馬遼太郎 S. Ryōtarō *ml*

—5 F2—

**可** 165 [T] (KA, yoshi, ari, toki, yoku, yori)
子 Yoshiko *f*
丸 Kamaru *m*
也 Kanari *m*
児 Kaji *s*, Kako; Kani *sp*
寿丙 Kazue *m*
知 Kachi *s*
官 Yoshitaka *m*
恰 Umashi *m*
美 Kami *sp*
重 Arishige *m*
笑子 Emiko *f*
笑記 Kashōki *l*
朗 Yoshiaki *m*
部 Kabe *sp*
都里 Katori *m*
賀 Kayoshi *m*
樹 Yoshiki *m*
薫 Tokishige *m*

**疋** 166 (HIKI, tada)
田 Hikita *s*
和田 Hikiwada *s*
野 Hikino *s*
檀 Hikida *s*

**斥** 167 [T] (SEKI, SHAKU, kata)

**包** See 218

夲 冬 旦 弖 丕 司 可 疋 斥 包 ▼ 匂 左 布 右 石 ▲ 凶 庁 尼 尻 処 込 辺 井 氷 无

匂 168 Magari *s.* (KŌ, KU, magari, maga, sagi)
田 Magata *s*
当 Kōtō *m*
坂 Sagisaka *s*
靫 Magarinoyukei *s*

左 169 [T] Sa *m.* (SA, suke)
[3]口 Sakuchi *s*
也馬 Sayama *m*
[4]今次 Sakuji *s*
文字 Samonji *s*
中 Sachū *m*
中太 Sachūda *s*
[5]司馬 Sajima *m*
右田 Sōda *s* ⌈*ml*
右田喜一郎 S. Kiichirō
右松 Sōmatsu *m*
[6]任 Suketō *m*
吉 Sakichi *m*
吉雄 Sakio *m*
団次 Sadanji *ma*
[7]沢 Aterazawa *s*
近 Sakon *m-fl*
近司 Sakonji *s*
近衛門 Sakoemon *m*
[8]門 Samon *m*
京 Sakyō *p*
[9]治衛 Sajie *m*
柄 Sagara *s*
[10]脇 Sakyō *m*
馬助 Sabanosuke *m*
甚五郎 Hidari Jingorō *ma*
[11]部 Satori *s*
[16]衛 Samori *m*
膳 Sazen *m*

布 170 [T] (FU, HO, nobu, nuno, shiki, tae, yoshi, shiku)
[3]川 Fukawa *s*, Nunokawa
上 Nunogami *s*
子 Nunoko *f*
也布伎 Fuefuki *s*
[5]田 Fuda *s*, Nunoda
目 Nunome *s*
[7]村 Nunomura *s*
忍 Nunoshi *s*, Nunose
[8]良 Mera *p*
[9]津 Futsu *sp*
哇 Hawai *p* "Hawaii"
施 Fuse *sp*
施田 Fuseda *s*
[10]師 Nunoshi *s*
師田 Nunoshita *s*
高 Nobutaka *m*
屋 Nunoya *s*
[11]野 Funo *sp*
部 Fube *sp*
留 Furu *sla*
留川 Furukawa *s*
[12]袋 Hotei *sp*
[13]勢 Fuse *s*

右 171 [T] Tasuku *m*, Migi, Akira. (U, YŪ, suke, migi, taka, aki, kore)
[1]一 Uichi *m*
[3]川 Ukawa *s*
[4]手 Ude *s*
[5]司馬 Ujima *m*
左口 Ubaguchi *sp*
左視 Usami *m*
田 Migita *s* ⌈*ml*
田寅彦 M. Nobuhiko
[6]仲 Sukenaka *m*
[7]弘 Sukehiro *m*
近 Ukon *sm-f*; Oko *s*
近右衛門 Ukon'emon
[8]門 Umon *m* ⌊*m*
門捕物帖 U. torimonochō *l*
京 Ukyō *p*
宗 Takamune *m*
[9]治衛 Ujie *m*
[10]馬四郎 Umashirō *m*
馬允 Umanosuke *m*
馬飼 Umakai *s*, Uba-
[13]働 Udō *s* ⌊kai
[14]遠 Udō *s*
[16]膳 Uzen *m*
橘 Ukichi *m*
衛 Umori *m*
衛門 Uemon *m*
衛門佐 Yomosa *s*
衛門作 Emosaku *m*
衛門尉 Uemonjō *m*

石 172 [T] Seki *s*, Iso, Kazu; Ishi *f.* (SEKI, SHAKU, ishi, iwa, shi, iso, atsu, kata)
[3]川 Ishikawa *sp*
川三四郎 I. Sanshirō *mlh*
川丈山 I. Jōzan *ml*
川千代松 I. Chiyomatsu *mh*
川欣一 I. Kin'ichi *ml*
川桂郎 I. Keirō *ml*
川淳 I. Jun *ml* ⌈*ml*
川啄木 I. Takuboku
川理紀之助 I. Rikinosuke *mh*
川善助 I. Zensuke *ml*
川達三 I. Tatsuzō *ml*
川雅望 I. Masamochi
川巌 I. Iwao *ml* ⌊*ml*
之助 Ishinosuke *m*
下 Ishige *sp*; Ishioroshi *s*
口 Ishikuchi *s* ⌈kina
寸名 Ishikina *fh*, Iwa-
丸 Ishimaru *s*
上 Isonokami *sp*; Ishigami *s*, Ishikami, Ishinokami, Iwakami, Iwanokami
上乙麻呂 Isonokami no Otomaro *ml*
上宅嗣 I. no Yakatsugu *ml*
上玄一郎 I. Gen'ichirō *ml* ⌈to *l*
上私淑言 I. sasamego-
[4]水 Ishimizu *s*
切 Ishikiri *s*
戸 Ishido *s*, Oshito,
手 Ishite *s* ⌊Oshiko
月 Ishitsuki *s*
内 Ishiuchi *s*, Iwauchi
王 Ishiō *s*
无 Iwanasu *s*
毛 Ishige *s*
山 Ishiyama *sp*
山寺縁起絵巻 I.-dera engi emaki *ha*
山徹郎 I. Tetsurō *ml*
井 Ishii *sp*; Iwai *s*
井柏亭 Ishii Hakutei *ma* ⌈rō *ml*
井直三郎 I. Naozabu-
井桃子 I. Momoko *fl*
井菊次郎 I. Kikujirō *mh*
井鶴三 I. Tsuruzō *ml*
井露月 I. Rogetsu *ml*
[5]代 Iwashiro *s*
引 Ishihiki *s*
永 Ishinaga *sp*
占 Iwaura *s*
占井 Ishirai *s*
布 Iwashiki *m*
辺 Isobe *s*
本 Ishimoto *s*
禾 Ishiwa *s*, Isawa
生 Oshiko *s*
生別 Iwanasuwake *s*
田 Ishida *s* ⌈*mh*
田三成 I. Mitsunari
田波郷 I. Hakyō *ml*
田梅巌 I. Baigan *mh*
[6]合 Ishiai *s*
光 Ishimitsu *s*
灰 Ishibai *s*
母田 Ishimoda *s*
母田正 I. Shō *ml*
[7]作 Ishizukuri *s*, Iwatsukuri
沢 Ishizawa *s*
坂 Ishisaka *s*
坂洋次郎 I. Yōjirō *ml*
坂養平 I. Yōhei *ml*
村 Ishimura *s*, Iware
谷 Ishigaya *s*, Ishitani
足 Ishitari *m*, Isotari
志 Iwashi *s*
床 Iwatoko *m*
尾 Ishio *s*
出 Ishide *s*
来 Ishiko *s*, Ishirai, Ishiki
見 Iwami *sp*
見女式 Iwaminojoshiki *l*
[8]河 Ishikawa *s*, Ishiko
附 Ishitsuke *s*
和 Isawa *sp*
和田 Ishiwada *s*
金 Ishigane *s*
居 Ishii *s*
[9]津 Ishizu *s*
垣 Ishigaki *s*
城 Iwaki *sp*
神 Ishigami *s*
祝作 Ishikizukuri *s*
松 Ishimatsu *s*
狩 Ishikari *sp*
狩川 Ishikarigawa *l*
背 Iwase *s*
巻 Ishimaki *s*; Ishinomaki *p*
岡 Ishioka *sp*
飛 Ishitobi *s*
[10]浦 Ishiura *s*
浜 Ishihama *s*
浜金作 I. Kinsaku *ml*
桁 Ishigeta *s*
射 Ishii *s*
倉 Ishikura *s*
栗 Ishikuri *s*, Iwakuri
原 Ishihara *s*
原八束 I. Yatsuka *ml*

原慎太郎 I. Shintarō *ml*
原純 I. Atsushi *ml*
11清水 Iwashimizu *l*
根 Iwane *m*
野 Ishino *s*, Iwano
部 Ishibe *sp*
動 Isurugi *p*
動山 Yusurugi *s*
留 Ishidome *s*
堂 Ishidō *s*
黒 Ishiguro *s*
島 Ishijima *s*
鳥谷 Ishidoriya *p*
亀 Ishigame *s*
12渡 Ishiwatari *s*, Ishiwata
陰 Ishikage *m*
割 Ishiwari *s*
搏 Ishiuchi *s*
場 Ishiba *s*
塔 Ishidō *s*
崎 Ishizaki *s*
賀 Ishiga *s*
曾根 Ishisone *s*
森 Ishimori *s*
森延男 I. Nobuo *ml*
道 Ishimichi *s*
13楠 Shakunage *l*
福 Ishifuku *s*
雄 Iwao *m*
塚 Ishizuka *s*
塚友二 I. Tomoji *ml*
越 Ishikoshi *sp*
14榑 Ishikure *s*, Ishide
榑千亦 Ishikure Chimata *ml*
郷岡 Ishigōoka *s*
関 Ishizeki *s*
15幡 Ishibata *s*
鼎句集 Sekitei kushū *l*
16徹白 Ishidoshiro *s*; Itoshiro *sp*
積 Iwazumi *m*
綿 Ishiwata *s*
橋 Ishibashi *sp*; Shakkyō *la*
橋忍月 I. Ningetsu *ml*
橋辰之助 I. Tatsunosuke *ml*
橋思案 I. Shian *ml*
19館 Ishidate *s*
鍋 Ishinabe *s*
18藤 Ishidō *s*
瀬 Ishise *s*
瀬屋 Ishiseya *s*
21躍 Ishiyaku *s*

—— 5 F3 ——

凶 173 [T] (KYŌ)
徒津田三蔵 Kyōto Tsuda Sanzō *l*

庁 174 [T] Kobanawa *s*. (CHŌ)
鼻 Shibahana *s*, Kobanawa
鼻和 Chōnohanawa *s*

尼 175 [T] (JI, NI, ama, sada, tada, chika)
子 Amako *s*, Amane
崎 Amasaki *s*; Amagasaki *sp*

尻 176 (KŌ, shiri)
岸内 Shirikishinai *p*
高 Shiritaka *s*, Shittaka
掛 Shirikake *s*

処 177 [T] Sadamu *m*. (SHO, SO, sumi, tokoro, fusa, yasu, oki, oru)
之助 Tokoronosuke *m*

込 178 [T] (kome, komi)
山 Komeyama *s*
田 Komeda *s*

辺 179 Hotori *sm*. (HEN, oi)
分 Oiwake *s*
方 Oiwake *s*
見 Henmi *s*

—— 5 F4 ——

井 See 206

—— 5 U ——

氷 See 140

无 180 See 无 92

兄 181 [T] (KEI, KYŌ, e, ani, ne, saki, eda, kore, shige, tada, yoshi)
子 Aniko *m*
国 Ekuni *s*
食下 Ekurashi *m*
部 Kōbe *s*
部坊 Konokonbō *s*
麻呂 Emaro *m*
遠子 Etōko *f*

央 182 [T] Nakaba *sm*; Hisashi *m*, Akira, Hiroshi. (Ō, YŌ, hisa, naka, teru, chika, hiro)
二 Hisaji *m*
子 Teruko *f*, Hiroko
夫 Teruo *m*
江 Hisae *f*
馬 Nakaba *s*

史 183 [T] Fubito *sm*; Chikashi *m*, Sakan. (SHI, chika, fumi, mi, hito, funo)
子 Fumiko *f*
伊 Fumii *f*
侍 Chikashi *m*

甲 184 [T] Yoroi *s*, Kabuto; Masaru *m*; Kinoe *f*. (KŌ, ka, ki, katsu)
3之助 Kinosuke *m*
子七 Kaneshichi *m*
子児 Kineji *m*
子男 Kashio *m*, Kineo
子彦 Kashihiko *m*
子郎 Kashirō *m*, Kōshirō *p*
4山 Kōyama *s*; Kōzan
5代子 Kayoko *f*
可 Kōka *s*
田 Kōda *sp*
6州 Kōshū *p*
州鰍沢報讐 K. Kajikazawa adauchi *l*
地 Kōchi *p*
奴 Kōnu *p*
西 Kōsai *p*, Kōsei
7作客 Kawaratsukurimarōdo *s*
佐 Kōsa *p*
谷 Kōya *s*
8府 Kōfu *p*
府方 Kōfukata *s*
良 Kōra *sp*; Kawara *s*
9南 Kōnan *p*
11峰松 Kanematsu *m*
許母 Kokomo *m*
能 Kōno *s*, Konō
野 Kōno *s*
12賀 Kōga *sp*
賀三郎 K. Saburō *ml*
斐 Kai *sf-ph*
斐庄 Kainoshō *s*
斐根 Kaine *s*
18藤 Kōdō *s*, Kattō, Kabutō

申 185 [T] Shin *sm*; Shigeru *m*. (SHIN, nobu, saru, mi)
二 Nobuji *m*
代 Saruyo *f*
楽 Sarugaku *la*
楽談儀 S. dangi *l*

由 186 [T] Yū *s*. (YŪ, YU, tada, yuki, yoshi, yori)
1一 Yūichi *m*
3三 Yoshikazu *m*
三郎 Yoshisaburō *m*
之 Yoshiyuki *m*
4仁 Yuni *sp*
井 Yui *s*
井正雪 Y. Shōsetsu *mh*
木 Yuki *s*
木尾 Yukio *s*
夫 Yoshio *m*
5比 Yui *sp*
布 Yubu *s*
田 Yoshida *s*
6行 Tadayuki *m*
宇 Yuu *sp*
7扶 Yoshisuke *m*
利 Yuri *sp*
利之助 Yurinosuke *m*
利公正 Yuri Kimimasa *mh*
言 Yoshitoki *m*
豆流 Yuzuru *m*
里子 Yuriko *f*
8佳里の梅 Yukari no ume *l*
岐 Yuki *p*
茅 Yugaya *s*
良 Yura *sp*
良之助 Yuranosuke *m*
9美 Yumi *s*; Yoshimi *m*
10浜 Yuhama *s*
郎 Yoshirō *m*
恭 Yoshitaka *m*
原 Yubara *s*, Yuzuhara
座 Yuza *s*
起 Yuki *s*

[11]後 Yoshinochi *m*
紀夫 Yukio *m*
章 Yoshiaki *m*
路 Yoshimichi *m*
蔵 Yoshizō *m*

**匹** 187 [T] (HIKI, HITSU, atsu, tomo)
他 Hikita *s*
田 Hikida *s*
見 Hikimi *p*
壇 Hikida *s*

**四** 188 [T] (SHI, yo, yotsu, hiro, mochi)
[2]十八朝 Yosonara *s*, Yoinara
十八願 Yoinara *s*
十九員 Tsurushi *s*
十万 Yosuma *s*, Shijima, Shizuma
十四院 Tsurushi *s*
十住 Yosumi *s*, Shiu-
十物 Aimono *s* ⌊chi
十宮 Yosomiya *s*
[3]川 Shisen *p* " Szechwan "
[4]元 Yotsumoto *s*
戸 Shinohe *sp*
分 Shibu *s*
五六 Yogoroku *m*
日 Yokka *s*
日市 Yokkaichi *p*
月 Watanuki *s*
月一日 Watanuki *s*, Watanu, Tsubomi
月朔日 Watanuki *s*
天王 Shitennō *smh*
天王寺 Shitennōji *p*
方 Yomo *sf*; Yokata *s*, Shikata
方子 Yomoko *f*
方四五右衛門 Yomoshigoemon *m*
方田 Yomoda *s*, Shioda ⌈ra *ml*
方赤良 Yomo no Aka-
方男 Yomoo *m*
方治 Shioji *m*
方恵 Yomoe *f*
[5]四 Yoshi *f*
主 Yonushi *s*
本 Yotsumoto *s*
本松 Shihonmatsu *s*
[6]辻 Yotsutsuji *s* ⌈ml
辻善成 Y. Yoshinari

[7]至内 Shishiuchi *s*, Shiuchi, Shikyū
谷 Yotsuya *sp*
谷怪談 Y. kaidan *l*
条 Shijō *sp*
条宮 Shijōnomiya *s*
条宮下野集 S. Shimotsuke-shū *l*
条畷 Shijōnawate *p*
[8]明 Shimei *ml*
[9]亮夫 Shiroo *m*
迷 Shimei *ml*
[10]郎 Shirō *m*
釜 Shikama *s*
倉 Yotsukura *p*
宮 Shinomiya *s*
家 Yotsuya *s*
柴 Shishiba *s*
真田 Shimada *s*
屋 Yotsuya *s*
座一流 Yoza ichiryū *a*
座役者目録 Y. yakusha mokuroku *l*
[12]街道 Yotsukaidō *p*
賀 Shiga *sp*
賀光子 S. Mitsuko *fl*
[17]綱 Yotsuami *m*
瀬 Yotsuse *s*
鏡 Shikyō *l*
纏 Yotsugane *sp*

**田** 189 [T] Den *s*. (DEN, ta, michi, da, tada)
[2]又利 Tatari *s*
人 Tabito *p*
[3]川 Tagawa *sp*
之助 Tanosuke *m*
上 Tanoue *s*; Tagami *sp* ⌈ta, Tage
下 Tanoshita *s*, Tashi-
万川 Tamagawa *sp*
子 Tago *s*; Tatsuko *p*
久保 Takubo *s*
丸 Tamaru *s*
口 Taguchi *s*, Tanokuchi ⌈chi *mlh*
口卯吉 Taguchi Uki-
口掬汀 T. Kikutei *ml*
[4]戸 Tado *s*
方 Tagata *sp*
内 Tauchi *s*, Tanouchi
井 Tai *s*
山 Tayama *s*
山花袋 T. Katai *ml*
中 Tanaka *s*
中丸 Tanakamaru *s*
中千禾夫 Tanaka Chikao *ml*
中王城 T. Ōjō *ml*
中王堂 T. Ōdō *ml*
中冬二 T. Fuyuji *ml*
中正造 T. Shōzō *mh*
中克巳 T. Katsumi *ml*
中英光 T. Hidemitsu *ml*
中保隆 T. Yasutaka *ml*
中貢太郎 T. Kōtarō *ml*
中勝助 T. Katsusuke
中純 T. Jun *ml* ⌊mh
中義一 T. Giichi *mh*
中澄江 T. Sumie *fl*
中館 Tanakadate *s*
中館愛橘 T. Aikitsu
[5]代 Tashiro *sp* ⌊mh
付 Tatsuki *s*
北 Takita *s*
永 Tanaga *s*
公 Tanokimi *s*
令 Tatsukai *s*
布施 Tabuse *sp*
尻 Tajiri *sp*
辺 Tanabe *sp*
辺元 T. Hajime *ml*
辺福麻呂 T. no Sakimaro *ml*
本 Tamoto *s*
田 Tada *s*
平 Tahira *sp*
主 Tanushi *m*
主丸 Tanushimaru *p*
[6]伏 Tabuse *s*
仲 Tanaka *s*
地 Tachi *s*, Taji
光 Tahika *s*
寺 Tadera *s*
老 Tarō *p*
名綱 Tanaami *s*
名部 Tanabe *s*
多民治集 Tadamichi-
母 Tanomo *s* ⌊shū *l*
母神 Tamokami *sp*; Tanokami *s*
母野 Tamono *s*
[7]阪 Tasaka *s*
坂 Tasaka *s*
沢 Tazawa *s*
沢湖 Tazawako *p*
那村 Tanamura *s*
村 Tamura *sp*
村子 Tamurako *f*
村松魚 Tamura Shōgyo *ml*
村俊子 T. Toshiko *fl*
村泰次郎 T. Taijirō *ml*
村隆一 T. Ryōichi *ml*
形 Tagata *s*
町 Tamachi *sp*
谷 Tadani *s*, Taya
安 Tayasu *s* ⌈ml
安宗武 T. Munetake
麦 Tamon *s*
麦俣 Tamonmata *s*
尾 Tao *s*
近 Tachika *s*
寿地 Azechi *s*
[8]使 Tae *s*
附 Tatsuke *s*
河 Tagawa *s*
波 Tanami *s*
波御白 T. Mishiro *ml*
沼 Tanuma *sp* ⌈mh
沼意次 T. Okitsugu
沼意知 T. Okitomo *mh*
所 Tadokoro *s*
林 Tabayashi *s*
知 Tachi *s*
知花 Tachibana *s*
牧 Tamaki *s*
制 Tazei *s*
舎芝居 Inaka shibai *l*
舎源氏 I. Genji *l*
舎館 Inakadate *p*
実 Tajitsu *s*
並木 Tanamiki *s*
[9]保 Tanbo *s*
畑 Tabata *s* ⌈rō *ml*
畑修一郎 T. Shūichi-
面 Tanomo *m*
南 Tanami *s*
草川 Takusagawa *s*
巻 Tamaki *s*
岡 Taoka *s*
岡嶺雲 T. Reiun *ml*
底 Tasoko *p* ⌈p
[10]浦 Taura *s*; Tanoura
桑 Taguwa *s*
倉 Tagura *s*
荷 Tani *s*
宮 Tamiya *s*
宮虎彦 T. Torahiko *ml* ⌈p
原 Tawara *s*; Tahara
原本 Tawaramoto *p*
原屋 Tawaraya *s*
屋 Taya *s*
[11]添 Tazoe *s*
能村 Tanomura *s*
能村竹田 T. Chikuden *mh*
部 Tanabe *s*, Tabe

部井 Tabei *s*
部重治 Tanabe Jūji *ml*
野 Tano *p*
野口 Tanoguchi *s*
野井 Tanoi *s*
野辺 Tanobe *s*
野村 Tanomura *s*
野畑 Tanohata *p*
野倉 Tanokura *s*
野部 Tanobe *s*
盛 Michimori *m*
島 Tajima *sp*
島象二 T. Shōji *ml*
[12]崎 Tazaki *s*
富 Tatomi *sp*
賀 Taga *s*
登 Tanobori *s*
無 Tanashi *p*
鹿 Tajika *s*
[13]淵 Tabuchi *s*
路 Taji *s*, Tamichi, Tōji
楽 Dengaku *a*
[14]窪 Takubo *s*
結 Tayui *s*
[15]幡 Tabata *s*
端 Tabata *s*
熊 Takuma *s*
[16]橋 Tabashi *s*
頭 Tantō *s*, Tagashira
賢 Michikata *m*
[17]総 Tabusa *s*
窳 Takubo *s*
[18]嶋 Tajima *s*
鎖 Tagusari *s*
[21]鶴浜 Tatsuruhama *p*

冊 190 [T] (SATSU, SAKU, nami, fumi, fun)

目 191 [T] Me *m*; Sakan *s*, Sakka. (MOKU, BOKU, me, ma, mi, yori) ⌈gusa *l*
[4]不酔草 Mezamashi-
[5]代 Mete *s*
加田 Mekata *s*
包 Meshiko *s*
[6]色 Meshiko *s*
色部 Meshikobe *s*, Mashikobe
[8]良 Mera *s*
[9]前心後 Mokuzen shingo *l*
[10]時 Metoki *s*
黒 Meguro *sp*
[12]崎 Mesaki *s*
賀 Mega *s*
賀田 Megata *s*
貫 Menuki *s*
貫屋 Menukiya *s*
堅 Mekata *s*
[14]徳 Metoku *s*
[18]鯉部 Meribe *s*

且 192 [O] (SHO, SO, katsu)
子 Katsumi *m*
元 Katsumoto *m*
来 Atsuryū *sp*

用 193 [T] (YŌ, YU, mochi, chika)
土 Yōdo *s*
田 Mochida *s*
随 Mochiyori *m*
徳 Mochiyoshi *m*
瀬 Mochigase *sp*; Mochise *s*, Mochinose

立 194 [T] Tatsu *m*, Tatsuru, Takashi; Tachi *s*, Tate, Ritsu. (RITSU, RYŪ, tatsu, tate, tachi, taka, taru, haru)
[2]入 Tachiiri *s*, Tateiri
[3]川 Tachikawa *sp*; Tategawa *s*, Tatsukawa ⌈bunko *l*
川文庫 Tachikawa
子 Tatsuko *f*
[4]山 Tateyama *sp*
五 Ryūgo *m*
夫 Tateo *m*
木 Tachigi *s*, Tsuiki
[5]石 Tateishi *s*, Tachiishi
田 Tatsuta *sp*; Tachida *s*, Tateda, Tatta
正安国論 Risshō ankokuron *l*
[7]沢 Tachizawa *s*, Tatsuzawa, Tatezawa
花 Tachibana *sp*
花北枝 T. Hokushi *ml*
見 Tatsumi *s*, Tachimi, Tatemi
身 Tatsumi *m*
[8]河 Tachikawa *s*, Tategawa
波 Tatsunami *s*
林 Tatebayashi *s*
[9]松 Tatematsu *s*
科 Tateshina *sp*
岩 Tateiwa *s*, Tachi- ⌊iwa
岡 Tateoka *s*
[10]脇 Tatewaki *s*
家 Tatsuka *s*
原 Tachihara *s*, Tatsuhara, Tatehara
原道造 Tachihara Michizō *ml*
馬 Tatema *s*
[11]野 Tatsuno *s*, Tateno, Tachino
野信之 Tateno Nobuyuki *ml* ⌈jima
島 Tatejima *s*, Tachi-
[13]誠 Tatsuaki *m*
[14]暢 Tatsunaga *m*

市 195 [T] Ichi *s*. (SHI, ichi, chi, machi, naga)
[2]人 Ichindo *m*
[3]川 Ichikawa *sp*
川大門 I. Daimon *p*
川左団次 I. Sadanji *ma* ⌈ma
川団十郎 I. Danjūrō
川房枝 I. Fusae *fh*
川為雄 I. Tameo *ml*
三郎 Ichisaburō *m*
丸 Ichimaru *s*
之瀬 Ichinose *s*
口 Ichiguchi *s*
[4]五郎 Ichigorō *m*
山 Ichiyama *s*
井 Ichii *s*
木 Ichiki *s*
太郎 Ichitarō *m*
毛 Ichike *s*
[5]古 Ichiko *s*
左衛門 Ichizaemon *m*
田 Ichida *s*
正 Ichinokami *s*
[7]沢 Ichisawa *s*
村 Ichimura *s*
兵衛 Ichibee *m*
貝 Ichikai *sp*
来 Ichiki *sp*; Ichiku *s*
[8]河 Ichikawa *s*
征 Ichiyuki *s*, Ichiki
邨 Ichimura *s*
東 Shitō *s* ⌈cago"
[9]俄古 Shikago *p* "Chi-
岡 Ichioka *s* ⌈*sp*
[10]浦 Ichiura *s*; Shiura
師 Ichishi *s*
倉 Ichikura *s*
原 Ichihara *sp*
原豊田 I. Toyota *ml*
[11]野 Ichino *s*
野沢 Ichinosawa *s*
島 Ichijima *sp*
島春城 I. Shunjō *mh*
[12]場 Ichiba *sp*
[13]塚 Ichizuka *s*
路の果 Ichiji no hate *l*
[15]蔵 Ichizō *m*
[16]橋 Ichihashi *s*
[19]瀬 Ichinose *s*, Ichise

主 196 [T] Tsukasa *m*. (SHU, SU, nushi, kazu, mori)
一 Shuichi *m*
子 Kazuko *f*
水 Mondo *m*
田 Nushida *s*
守 Nushimori *m*
信 Morinobu *m*
計 Kazue *m-p*
馬 Kazuma *m*, Shume
税 Chikara *m-p*
殿 Tonomo *sm-p*
膳 Shuzen *m*

卍 197 Manji *l*. (MAN, BAN, manji)
老人 Manji-rōjin *ml*

丙 198 [O] Hinoe *m*. (HEI, HYŌ, e, aki)
子郎 Heishirō *m*

巨 199 [T] (KO, KYO, ō, nao, masa)
田 Ōta *s*
老 Ōoyu *m*
知部 Kochibe *s*
野 Ōno *s*
椋 Ōkura *s*; Ogura *sp*
智 Kochi *s*
曾根 Kosone *s*
曾部 Kosobe *s*
勢 Kose *s* ⌈*ma*
勢金岡 K. no Kanaoka
勢槭田 Kosekakeida *s*, Kosenokashiketa
範 Masanori *m*

丕 See 163

目 且 用 立 市 主 卍 丙 巨 丕 ▼ 互 瓦 弖 平 玉 ▲ 正 井 甘 戊 朮 未 末 本 半 生

互 200 [T] Tagai *s*. (GO)

瓦 201 (GA, kawara)
井 Kawarai *s*
林 Kawarabayashi *s*

弖 202 (te)
良 Tera *s*
秦 Tehata *s*

平 203 [T] Taira *sp*; Hira *s*; Hitoshi *m*, Hakaru, Masaru, Osamu. (HEI, HYŌ, BYŌ, hira, toshi, tsune, naru, taira, sane, taka, nari, mochi, yoshi)
1一 Heiichi *m*
2八 Heihachi *m*
八郎 Heihachirō *m*
3川 Hirakawa *sp*
三郎 Heisaburō *m*
之助 Heinosuke *m*
子 Hirako *sf*; Tairako *f*; Tairai *s*
久 Tairaku *s*
久保 Hirakubo *s*
也 Tsuneya *m*
4元 Hiramoto *s*
戸 Hirado *sp*; Hirato *s*
戸廉吉 Hirato Renkichi *ml*
手 Hirate *s*
中 Heichū *l*
内 Hirauchi *s*; Heinai *m*; Hiranai *p*
方 Hirakata *s*
夫 Hirao *m*
手 Hirade *s*
山 Hirayama *s*
山蘆江 H. Rokō *ml*
太 Heita *m*
太郎 Heitarō *m*
井 Hirai *s*, Tairai
井出 Hiraide *s*
井晩村 Hirai Banson *ml*
木 Hiraki *s*
木二六 H. Niroku *ml*
木白星 H. Hakusei *ml*
5石 Hiraishi *s*
左衛門 Heizaemon *m*
右馬 Heiuma *s*, Heima
右衛門 Heiemon *m*
四郎 Heishirō *m*
目 Hirame *s*
平 Hiradaira *s*
正盛 Taira no Masamori *mh*
本 Hiramoto *s*
氏 Heishi *s*
生 Hirao *sp*; Hirō *s*
生三 Tsunezō *m*
田 Hirata *sp*
田次三郎 H. Jisaburō *ml*
田禿木 H. Tokuboku *ml*
田篤胤 H. Atsutane *ml*
6次郎 Heijirō *m*
吉 Heikichi *m*
光 Hiramitsu *sm*
曲 Heikyoku *la*
7住 Hirazumi *s*
佐 Hirasa *s*
坂 Hirasaka *s*
沢 Hirasawa *s*
沢計七 H. Keishichi *ml*
助 Heisuke *m*
谷 Hiraya *sp*
安 Heian *h*
安京 Heiankyō *ph*
兵衛 Heibee *m*
児玉 Heikodama *s*
尾 Hirao *s*
見 Hirami *s*
出 Hiraide *s*, Hirade
出修 Hiraide Shū *ml*
8沼 Hiranuma *s* *mh*
沼騏一郎 H. Kiichirō
林 Hirabayashi *s*; Hiramori *m*, Narushige
林初之助 H. Hatsunosuke *ml*
林彪吾 H. Hyōgo *ml*
和 Hirawa *s*; Heiwa *p*
取 Hiratori *sp*
定文 Taira no Sadabumi *mh*
宗盛 T. no Munemori *mh*
忠常 T. no Tadatsune *mh*
忠盛 T. no Tadamori *mh*
昇 Hiranori *m*
良 Heira *s*; Hera *sp*
9保 Hirao *s*
治 Heiji *m-l* 1159–60
城 Hiraki *s*
城京 Heijōkyō *ph*
松 Hiramatsu *s*
政子 Taira no Masako *fh*
畑 Hirahata *s*
畑静塔 H. Seitō *ml*
貞文 Taira no Sadabumi *mh*
貞盛 T. no Sadamori *mh*
岩 Hiraiwa *s*
泉 Hiraizumi *sp*
岡 Hiraoka *s*
度繁 Taira no Norishige *mh*
重盛 T. no Shigemori *mh*
10将門 T. no Masakado *mh-l*
高望 T. no Takamochi *mh*
柳 Hirayanagi *s*
秩 Hetsutsu *s*
郡 Hirakuni *s*, Heguri
甕 Hiraka *m*
栗 Heguri *s*, Hirakuri
家 Heike *l-h*
家女護島 H. nyogo no shima *l*
原 Hirabara *s*
11康頼 Taira no Yasuyori *ml*
清盛 T. no Kiyomori *mh-l*
野 Hirano *s*
野万里 H. Banri *ml*
野国臣 H. Kuniomi *mh*
野宣紀 H. Nobunori *ml*
野謙 H. Ken *ml*
部 Hirabe *s*
峯 Hiramine *s*
島 Hirashima *s*
12渡 Hirawatari *s*
富 Hiratomi *s*
森 Hiramori *sm*
賀 Hiraga *sp*
賀元義 H. Motoyoshi *ml*
賀源内 H. Gennai *mlh*
道 Toshimichi *m*
間 Hirama *s*
鹿 Hiraka *sp*
13塚 Hiratsuka *sp*
塚明子 H. Haruko *fh*
福 Hirafuku *s*
福百穂 H. Hyakusui *mla*
群 Heguri *sp*
14徳子 Taira no Tokuko *fh*
16維盛 T. no Koremori *mh*
蔵 Heizō *m*
17壌 Heijō *p* "Pyongyang"
館 Tairadate *p*
厳 Hiraiwa *s*
19櫛 Hirakushi *s*
瀬 Hirase *s*

玉 204 [T] Tama *ma*. (GYOKU, GOKU, tama, kiyo)
ノ浦 Tamanoura *p*
の小琴 Tama no ogoto *l*
の小櫛 T. no ogushi *l*
3川 Tamagawa *sp-l*
之助 Tamanosuke *m*
乃 Tamano *s*
上 Tamagami *s*
子 Tamako *f*
4水 Tamamizu *s*
山 Tamayama *sp*
井 Tamai *s*; Tama no i *la*
木 Tamaki *s*
手 Tamate *s*
5代 Tamashiro *s*
田 Tamada *s*
本 Tamamoto *s*
生 Tamō *s*; Tamanyū *sp*
6江 Tamae *sf*
吉 Tamakichi *m*
有 Tamaari *m*
虫 Tamamushi *sl*
虫厨子 T. no zushi *a*
名 Tamana *sp*
米 Tōmai *sp*
7作 Tamazukuri *s*
汝 Tamana *m*
沢 Tamazawa *s*
村 Tamamura *sp*
利 Tamari *s*
谷 Tamaya *s*
里 Tamari *sp*
8林宴 Gyokurin'en *l*
舎 Tamanoya *s*
東 Gyokutō *p*
9垣 Tamagaki *m*
城 Tamaki *sp*
祖 Tamaoya *s*
松 Tamamatsu *sl*
松操 T. Misao *mh*
岡 Tamaoka *sp*
10陣 Tamaburu *m*
屋 Tamaya *sp*
造 Tamazō *m*; Tamazukuri *p*
11野 Tamano *sp*
島 Tamashima *sp*
島山 Tamashimayama *s*
12湯 Tamayu *p*
勝間 Tamakatsuma *l*
崎 Tamazaki *s*
13楮 Tamakaji *s*, Tamakage
葛 Tamakazura *la*

葉集 Gyokuyōshū l
越 Tamagoe s
[14]腰 Tamakoshi s
箒子 Tamahahaki l
置 Tamaki s, Tama-
[15]穂 Tamaho p ⌊oki
[16]樹 Tamaki m
緒 Tamao m
篋両浦嶼 Tamakushige futari Urashima la
[19]櫛笥 Tamakushige l
藻 Tamamo l
藻集 Tamamoshū l
[20]簪花 Gyokushinka l
[22]鬘 Tamakazura la

正 205 [T] Tadashi m, Tadasu, Masashi, Shō, Akira. (SHŌ, SEI, masa, tada, osa, nao, kimi, sada, taka, yoshi, kami, tsura, nobu) ⌈kazu
[1]一 Shōichi m, Masa-
[2]二 Shōji m
二郎 Shōjirō m
力 Shōriki s
八 Masaya m, Shōhachi ⌈do
人 Masato m, Masan-
[3]三 Shōzō m, Masamitsu
三郎 Shōzaburō m
己 Masaoto m
子 Masako f
大 Masahiro m, Masatomo ⌈shi
士 Masahito m, Masa-
久 Masahisa m ⌈ya
也 Masanari m, Masa-
之 Masayuki m
[4]仁 Tadahito m
化 Shōge s
元 Shōgen 1259–60
戸 Masato sm
中 Shōchū 1324–26; Seichū m
丹 Akira m
方 Masasuke m
五 Shōgo m
五郎 Shōgorō m
夫 Masao m
井 Masai s
午郎 Shōgorō m
月 Mutsuki m
月一日 Ao s
木 Masaki sm ⌈ml
木不如丘 M. Fujokyū
太 Shōta m, Masataka, Masami
太の馬 S. no uma l
太郎 Shōtarō m
文 Masafumi m
[5]外 Masato m
礼 Masanori m
占 Masaura m
令 Masanori m
司 Masamori s
田 Shōda s, Masada, Shida
平 Shōhei 1346–70
白田 Shōhata s
生 Masanari m
史 Masashi m
市 Shōichi m
次 Masatsugu m
次郎 Shōjirō m
行 Masanari m, Masatsura
全 Masatomo m
吉 Shōkichi m
旭 Masaakira m, Masaaki ⌈kō ml
広 Masahiro m; Shō-
式 Masanori m
因 Masayori m, Masayoshi
成 Masashige m
世 Masatoshi m
年 Masatoshi m, Seinen
[7]住 Masazumi s
均 Masahira m
沖 Masaoki m
弘 Masahiro m
村 Masamura sm
妃 Masahime f
好 Masayoshi s
助 Shōsuke m
判 Masachika m
言 Masakoto m
発 Masatoki m
安 Shōan 1299–1302
声 Masana m
孚 Masanobu m
吾 Shōgo m
吾郎 Shōgorō m
児 Masaru m
男 Masao m
応 Shōō 1288–93; Masakazu m
見 Masami m
玄 Shōgen s
寿 Masahisa m, Seiju
孝 Masataka m
甫 Masanami m, Masamoto ⌈sachika
身 Masanobu m, Ma-
臣 Masaomi m
[8]侃 Masaakira m
阿弥 Shōami s
明 Masaaki m, Shōmei, Masateru
肥 Masamitsu m, Masatomo
林 Masabayashi s
和 Shōwa 1312–17
房 Naofusa m
孟 Masamoto m
奐 Masashi m
学 Masaakira m
宗 Masamune sm
宗白鳥 M. Hakuchō
季 Masasue m ⌊ml
辰 Masatoki m
良 Masasuke m
[9]保 Shōhō 1644–48
侶 Masatomo m
信 Masanobu ma
洪 Masahiro m
垣 Masagaki s
恒 Masatsune m
城 Masanari m
治 Shōji m 1199–1201, Masaharu, Masayoshi, Masatsugu
法 Minoru m
法眼蔵 Shōhōgenzō l
柯 Masaeda m
政 Tadamasa m
映 Masateru m
昭 Masaaki m
則 Masanori m
表 Masato m
美 Masami m, Seibi
長 Shōchō 1428–29
栄 Masayoshi m
泉 Masazumi s
岡 Masaoka s
岡子規 M. Shiki ml
直 Masanao m
彦 Masahiko m, Tada-
哉 Masaya m ⌊hiko
[10]修 Masamoto m, Masanao
倚 Masayori m
俊 Masatoshi m
倫 Masamichi m, Masatsune, Masatoshi, Masamoto
祥 Masatada m
師 Masamoro m, Masashi
殷 Masataka m
記 Seiki m
倉院 Shōsōin pa
容 Masakata m
晃 Masaaki m
毘 Masasuke m
真院 Shōshin'in s
益 Masaari m
恭 Masayasu m
造 Shōzō m
[11]脩 Masanaga m
健 Masatate m
得 Masanori m
隆 Masataka m
朗 Akira m
野 Shōno s
訥 Masamori m
致 Masatomo m
敏 Masatoshi m
躬 Masanao m
能 Shōnō s
部家 Shōbuke s
紀 Masatsugu m
剛 Masatake m, Seigō
章 Masaakira m, Masaaki, Masanori
曹 Masatomo m
魚 Masana m
産 Masatada m
彪 Masatora m
[12]博 Masahiro m, Kimihiro
備 Masanari m
陽 Masaharu m, Masaoki
順 Masayori m
嶢 Masataka m
勝 Masakatsu m
董 Seitō m
喬 Masataka m
尊 Shōzon la
奥 Masaoki m
富 Masatomi sm
富汪洋 M. Ōyō ml
達 Masanobu m
道 Masamichi m
鹿 Masaka m
[13]満 Masamitsu m
強 Masatake s
睦 Masayoshi m
雄 Masao m
辞 Masakoto m
路 Masaji m, Masami-
幹 Masami m ⌊chi

鉦 Masakane *m*
純 Masazumi *m*
献 Masatake *m*
凱 Masayoshi *m*
禎 Masatada *m*
福 Masatoshi *m*
誠 Masanari *m*, Masazane, Masasumi
詮 Masanori *sm*
義 Masayoshi *m*
愛 Masayoshi *m*
準 Masatoshi *m*
[14]徳 Masanori *m*; Shōtoku 1711–16
演 Masanobu *m*
弼 Masanori *m*
頌 Masatsugu *m*
銘 Masana *m*
嘉 Shōka 1257–59
節 Yoshimine *m*
愨 Masanao *m*
暦 Shōryaku 990–95
[15]儀 Masanori *m*
鋭 Masatoshi *m*
毅 Masatake *m*, Masatoshi
敷 Masanobu *m*
誼 Masayoshi *m*
論 Masatoki *m*
監 Masami *m*
熊 Shōkuma *m*
遵 Masachika *m*
慶 Shōkei 1332–33
蔵 Shōzō *m*
[16]隣 Masachika *m*
墻 Shōgaki *s*
澂 Masazumi *m*
徹 Masayuki *m*, Masatō; Shōtetsu *ml*
親 Ōgi *sp*; Masachika *m*
親町 Ōgimachi *smh*
親町公和 Ō. Kinkazu *ml*
震 Masanobu *m*
整 Masanari *m*
憑 Masayori *m*
窺 Masachika *m*
憲 Masanori *m*
[17]瞭 Masaakira *m*
謙 Masanobu *m*
[18]鵠 Masanori *m*
鎚 Masatsuchi *m*
燾 Masateru *m*
磨 Osamaro *m*
簡 Masafumi *m*
[20]織 Masaori *m*
[21]纒 Masatsuna *m*

丼 206 Donburi *s*, Toburi. (TAN, TON)

甘 207 [T] (KAN, ama, yoshi, kai)
木 Amagi *p*
名宇 Amanō *s*
味 Amami *s*, Kami
利 Amari *s*
良 Kara *s*
南備 Kannabi *sp*
粕 Amakasu *s*
楽 Kanra *sp*
蔗 Kanja *s*
濃 Amano *s*
糟 Amakasu *s*
縄 Amanawa *s*
露寺 Kanroji *s*

戊 208 Shigeru *m*, Sakaru. (BO, shige)
午集 Bogoshū *l*
申 Shigenobu *m*

朮 209 Okera *m*. (JUTSU, SHUTSU)

未 210 [T] (MI, BI, ima, hitsuji, hide, iya)
子 Hitsujiko *f*
至磨 Mishima *s*

末 211 [T] Hiroshi *m*. (MATSU, MA, sue, tome, hozu)
[3]川 Suekawa *s*
三郎 Shōsaburō *m*
子 Sueko *f*
[4]元 Suemoto *sm*
木 Sueki *s*
[5]永 Suenaga *sm*
田 Sueda *s*
包 Suekane *sm*
[6]次 Suetsugu *sm*, Sueyoshi
次平蔵 Suetsugu Heizō *mh*
吉 Sueyoshi *sm-p*; Suekichi *m*
吉孫左衛門 S. Magozaemon *mh*
広 Suehiro *sm*
広狩 S.-gari *la*
広鉄腸 S. Tetchō *ml*
[7]村 Suemura *s*
弘 Suehiro *sm*
寿 Suehogi *m*
[8]枝 Hozue *f*
延 Suenobu *sm*
武 Suetake *sm*
[9]枯 Uragare *l*
松 Suematsu *s*
松謙澄 S. Kenchō *ml*
貞 Suesada *m*
昆 Suehide *m*
岡 Sueoka *s*
彦 Sueyoshi *m*
[10]高 Suetaka *sm*
兼 Suekane *sm*
盈 Suemitsu *m*
[11]常 Suetsune *sm*
[12]期の眼 Matsugo no me *l*
喜 Sueki *m*
森 Suemori *s*
[13]満留 Tomemaru *m*
雄 Sueo *m*
[14]摘花 Suetsumuhana *l*
[15]耦 Suetomo *m*
蔵 Suezō *m*

本 212 [T] Hajime *m*. (HON, moto, nari)
[2]力 Horiki *s*
[3]川 Hongawa *sp*; Motokawa *s*
川根 Honkawane *p*
[4]戸 Motodo *s*
井 Motoi *s*
山 Motoyama *sp*
山荻舟 M. Tekishū *ml*
木 Motoki *s*
木昌造 M. Shōzō *mh*
[5]目 Honme *s*, Honmoku
田 Honda *s*
田喜代治 H. Kiyoji *ml*
田種竹 H. Shuchiku *ml*
[6]江 Hongō *s*, Motoe
吉 Motoyoshi *sm-p*
因坊 Hon'inbō *sm*
庄 Honjō *sp*
庄陸男 H. Mutsuo *ml*
名 Honna *p*
多 Honda *s*
多光太郎 H. Kōtarō *mh*
多利明 H. Toshiaki *mh*
多秋五 H. Shūgo *ml*
多顕彰 H. Akira *ml*
位田 Hon'iden *s*
沢 Motozawa *s*, Honzawa
村 Honmura *s*
杉 Motosugi *sm*
別 Honbetsu *p*
谷 Motoya *s*
告 Motoori *s*
匠 Honjō *sp*
尾 Motoo *sm*
阿弥 Hon'ami *s*
阿弥光悦 H. Kōetsu *ma*
牧 Honmoku *s*
所 Honjo *s*
居 Motoori *s*
居宣長 M. Norinaga *mlh*
居豊穎 M. Toyokai *ml*
[9]津 Motozu *s*
咲 Honsaki *s*
城 Honjō *sp*
松 Motomatsu *s*
耶馬渓 Hon'yabakei *p*
荘 Honjō *sp*
岡 Motooka *s*
[10]倉 Motokura *s*
宮 Motomiya *sp*; Hongū *p*
原 Motohara *s*
[11]野 Motono *s*
宿 Honshuku *s*
巣 Motosu *p*
堂 Hondō *s*
梨 Motonashi *s*
埜 Motono *sp*
島 Motojima *s*
[12]渡 Hondo *sp*
納 Honnō *sp*
朝二十四孝 Honchō nijūshikō *l*
朝文粋 H. monzui *l*
朝会稽山 H. Kaikeizan *l*
朝書籍目録 H. shoseki mokuroku *l*
朝桜陰比事 H. ōin hiji *l*
朝無題詩 H. mudaishi *l*
朝麗藻 H. reisō *l*
道 Hondō *s*
間 Honma *s*
間久雄 H. Hisao *ml*
間唯一 H. Yuiichi *ml*
[14]郷 Hongō *sp*
[15]儀 Motogi *s*
[16]樹 Motoki *m*
橋 Motohashi *s*
賢 Motokata *m*
蝶 Honchō *s*
[18]藤 Hondō *s*

半 213 [T] Nakaba *m*, Nakarai. (HAN, naka)
²人間 Hanningen *l*
³三郎 Hanzaburō *m*
乃 Hanno *s*
⁴月集 Hangetsushū *l*
太夫 Handayū *ma*
太郎 Hantarō *m*
井 Nakarai *s*
井卜養 N. Bokuyō *ml*
井桃水 N. Tōsui *ml*
⁵布 Han'yū *s*
左衛門 Hanzaemon *m*
四郎 Hanshirō *m*
平 Hanpei *m*
平太 Hanpeida *m*
田 Handa *sp*
田良平 H. Ryōhei *ml*
田義之 H. Yoshiyuki *ml*
⁷沢 Hanzawa *s*
谷 Han'ya *s*, Handani, Hangaya
⁹治 Hanji *m*
草 Nakakusa *s*
¹⁰原 Hanbara *s*
造 Hanzō *m*
¹²間 Hanma *s*
¹⁴蔀 Hajitomi *la*
¹⁶獣神 Hanjūshin *l*
¹⁸藤 Handō *s*

生 214 [T] Ikeru *m*, Umaru, Susumu; Iku *s*, Mibu, Ō. (SEI, SHŌ, iku, iki, nama, ubu, fu, ki, o, ō, mi, oi, bu, taka, nari, i, u, yo, ari, oki, nō, fuyu)
さぬ仲 Nasanu naka *l*
³川 Ikkawa *s*, Namakawa, Narukawa, Oikawa
子 Ikiko *f*, Mine; Seigo *s*
⁴仁 Fumi *f*
水 Shōzu *s*
戸 Ikito *s*
天目 Nabatame *s*
月 Ikutsuki *s*; Ikitsuki *p*
内 Ubuuchi *s*
方 Ubukata *s*
方たつゑ U. Tatsue *fl*
方敏郎 U. Toshirō *ml*
井 Ikui *s*, Namai
石 Ikushi *s*, Ōishi, Oishi
末 Ikusue *s*
玉 Mibu *s*, Ikutama
玉部 Ikutamabe *s*
田 Ikuta *sp*
田万 I. Yorozu *mh*
田川 Ikutagawa *sla*
田目 Namatame *s*
田原 Ikutahara *p*
田長江 Ikuta Chōkō *ml*
田春月 I. Shungetsu *ml*
田敦盛 I. Atsumori *la*
田葵山 I. Kizan *ml*
田蝶介 I. Chōsuke *ml*
⁶地 Ikuji *s*, Oiji
江 Namae *s*
江沢 Namaezawa *s*
池 Ikuchi *s*, Nachi
名 Ikina *p*
⁷沢 Ikuzawa *s*
坂 Ikusaka *s*
形 Ubukata *s*, Ikigata, Ubugata, Ōgata
麦 Namamugi *s*
出 Ikude *s*, Oide
夷 Ikui *s*, Ikuhina
⁸沼 Oinuma *s*
明 Azami *s*
実 Oimi *s*, Oyumi
⁹津 Ikutsu *s*, Namatsu
松 Ikimatsu *s*
松敬三 I. Keizō *ml*
長 Oisaki *s*
¹⁰悦住 Ikezumi *s*
馬 Ikuma *s*
¹¹清 Misumu *f*
野 Ikuno *sp*; Shōno *s*
部 Mibu *s*, Ikube, Obe
都子 Itoko *f*
島 Ikushima *s*
亀 Ikegame *s*
¹³源寺 Shōgenji *s*, Seigenji
越 Ogoshi *s*, Oikoshi, Ikuechi; Ikuo *f*
¹⁴稲 Ikuine *s*, Ikine, Inada
¹⁵駒 Ikoma *sp*
熊 Ikuma *s*
¹⁸幾 Ikushima *s*
¹⁹瀬 Namase *s*
²³懸 Kigake *s*

矢 215 [T] Chikō *m*; Yahagi *s*. (SHI, ya, tada, nao)
ケ崎 Yagasaki *s*
¹一 Yaichi *m*
³口 Yaguchi *s*
巾 Yahaba *p*
乃 Yano *s*
上 Yagami *s*
下 Yashita *s*
土 Yatsuchi *s*
⁴木 Yagi *s*
太郎 Yatarō *m*
内 Yauchi *s*
内原 Yanaihara *s*
内原忠雄 Y. Tadao *ml*
⁵代 Yashiro *s*
代東村 Y. Tōson *ml*
代幸雄 Y. Yukio *ml*
本 Yamoto *p*
田 Yada *s*
田津世子 Y. Tsuseko *fl*
田挿雲 Y. Sōun *ml*
田部 Yatabe *s*
田堀 Yatabori *s*
⁶次 Yatsugi *s*
地 Yaji *s*
守 Yamori *s*
当 Yatō *s*
向 Yakō *s*
⁷作 Yahagi *sp*; Yazukuri *s*
吹 Yabuki *sp*
沢 Yazawa *s*
村 Yamura *s*
花 Yahana *s*
尾板 Yaoita *s*
尾坂 Yaozaka *s*
⁸沼 Yanuma *s*
股 Yamata *s*
板 Yaita *sp*
定 Yasada *s*
延 Yanobe *s*
¹⁰矧 Yahagi *sp*
倉 Yagura *s*
原 Yawara *s*
¹¹掛 Yakake *p*
後 Yago *s*
根 Yane *s*
野 Yano *sp*
野竜渓 Y. Ryūkei *ml*
野峰人 Y. Hōjin *ml*
野島 Yanoshima *s*
部 Yabe *sp*
留 Yadome *s*
祭 Yamatsuri *sp*
島 Yashima *sp*
¹²渡利 Yatori *s*
崎 Yazaki *s*
崎美盛 Y. Yoshimori *ml*
崎弾 Y. Dan *ml*
崎嵯峨の屋 Y. Saganoya *ml*
富 Yatomi *s*
萩 Yahagi *s*
袋 Yamuro *s*
集 Yatsume *s*, Yasu
間 Yazama *s*
¹⁴郷 Yagō *s*
¹⁵幡 Yawata *s*
¹⁶橋 Yabashi *s*; Yabase *sp*
頭 Yatō *s*; Yazu *sp*
鍋 Yanabe *s*

白 216 [T] Shiroshi *m*, Kiyoshi, Akira; Shiro *m-f*; Tsugumo *s*. (HAKU, BYAKU, shiro, shira, kiyo, aki, shi, akira)
³川 Shirakawa *sp*
川渥 S. Atsushi *ml*
三 Akizō *m*
上 Shirakami *s*
子 Shirako *p*; Shiroko *f*
土 Shirato *s*, Shirani
⁴仁 Shirani *s*
水 Shiramizu *s*; Shirōzu *sp*; Hakusui *p*
水郎 Ama *s*
戸 Shiroto *s*
日 Hakujitsu *l*
山 Shirayama *s*; Hakusan *p*
木 Shiroki *s*; Shiraki *sp*
木槿 Shiromukuge *l*
井 Shirai *s*; Shiroi *p*
井健三郎 S. Kenzaburō *ml*
井喬二 S. Kyōji *ml*
⁵石 Shiraishi *s*; Shiroishi *p*; Hakuseki *mlh*
石実三 S. Jitsuzō *ml*
田 Shirota *s*, Hakuta
氏文集 Hakushi monjū *l*
⁶州 Hakushū *p*
江 Shirae *s*
羊宮 Hakuyōkyū *l*
老 Shiraoi *p*
耳義 Berugii *p* "Belgium"
⁷坂 Shirasaka *s*
沢 Shirasawa *sp*
杉 Shirasugi *s*
谷 Shiraya *s*
男川 Shiraogawa *s*
尾 Shirao *s*
里浜 Kujūkuri-no-hama *p*
⁸拍子 Shirabyōshi *fa*
河 Shirakawa *smh-p*
河紀行 S. kikō *l*

平 玉 正 井 甘 戊 朮 未 末 本 ▼ 半 生 矢 白 ▲ 允 包 丘 禾 乎 屯 氏 州 冲 次

甘 戊 朮 未 末 本 半 生 矢 白 ▼ 允 包 丘 禾 乎 屯 氏 州 冲 次 仲 仙 ▲ 伍 伃 仮 伎 休 伏 任 价 伊 巧

居易 Hakkyoi / Haku Kyoi *ml* "Po Chü-i"
金 Shirogane *sm*
夜 Byakuya *l*
$^{9}$洲 Shirasu *s*
津 Shiratsu *s*
神 Shirakami *s* ⌈ka
柄 Shirae *s*, Shiratsu-
松 Shiramatsu *s*
畑 Shirahata *s*
砂 Shirasuna *s*
南風 Shirahae *l*
岩 Shiraiwa *s*
岡 Shiraoka *sp*
$^{10}$浜 Shirahama *sp*
珠 Shiratama *l*
柳 Shirayanagi *s*
柳秀湖 S. Shūko *ml*
倉 Shirakura *s*
馬 Hakuba *p*
馬会 Hakubakai *a*
$^{11}$浪 Shiranami *s*
狼 Hakurō *s*
峰 Shiramine *sp-l*
根 Shirane *sp*; Shirone *p*
桜集 Hakuōshū *l*
菊会 Shiragikukai *l*
島 Shirashima *s*
鳥 Shiratori *sp*, Shirotori ⌈*ml*
鳥省吾 Shirotori Seigo
$^{12}$堤 Shitori *sp*
須 Shirasu *s*
猪 Shirai *s*
崎 Shirasaki *s*
$^{13}$塚 Shiratsuka *s*
鳩 Shirahato *l*
滝 Shirataki *sp*
雄 Shirao *m*
雉 Hakuchi 650–54
路 Hakuro *l*
楽天 Haku Rakuten *ml-la* "Po Lo-tien"
勢 Shirose *s*
$^{14}$旗 Shirahata *s*
樺 Shirakaba *l*
$^{15}$幡 Shirahata *s*
$^{16}$築 Shiratsuki *s*
$^{17}$糠 Shiranuka *p*
輿 Shirakoshi *s*
$^{18}$橿 Kashi *s*
藤 Shirafuji *s*
$^{19}$瀬 Shirase *s*
縫 Shiranui *s*
$^{23}$鬚 Shirahige *la*
$^{24}$鷹 Shirataka *sp*

**允** 217 Makoto *m.* (IN, masa, suke, yoshi, oka, koto, sane, tada, chika, nobu, mitsu, tō, ae)
子 Nobuko *f*
文 Masafumi *m*
明 Yoshiaki *m*
承 Nobutsugu *m*
信 Sukenobu *m*
計 Masakazu *m*
亮 Tadasuke *m*

**包** 218 [T] (HŌ, HYŌ, kane, kata, katsu, shige, sagi)
子 Kaneko *f*
女 Kanetaka *ma*
次 Kanetsugu *m*
坂 Sagisaka *s*
幸 Kaneyoshi *m*
秀 Kanehide *m*
是 Kaneyoshi *m*
高 Kanetaka *m*
真 Kanezane *m*
教 Kanenori *m*
蔵 Kanetoshi *m*

**丘** 219 [T] Oka *s*; Takashi *m.* (KYŪ, KU, o, oka, taka)
人 Obito *m*
子 Okako *f*
谷 Otani *s*
前来目 Okazakikume *s*

**禾** 220 Hide *m*; Hiizu *s.* (KA, WA, ine, nogi, awa)
子 Ineko *f*
田 Awata *s*
麿 Nogimaro *m*

**乎** 221 (KO, GO, O, ka)
古止点 Okoto-ten *l*
佐麿 Osamaro *m*
知人 Ochibito *m*

**屯** 222 Tamuro *m.* (TON, mura, tamuro, mitsu, yori)
倉 Miyake *s*
麿 Tamuromaro *m*

**氏** 223 [T] (SHI, JI, uji, he)
$^{2}$人 Ujindo *m*
$^{4}$心 Ujimune *m*
中 Ujinori *m*
$^{5}$公 Ujikimi *m*
共 Ujitaka *m*
田 Ujita *s*
$^{6}$舟 Ujifune *m*
$^{7}$如 Ujisuke *m*
$^{8}$昉 Ujiakira *m*
命 Ujinori *m*
$^{9}$政 Ujimasa *m*
宥 Ujihiro *m*
彦 Ujiyoshi *m*
$^{10}$家 Ujiie *sp*; Ujie *s*, Ujiya
家信 Ujiie Makoto *ml*
原 Ujihara *s*
$^{13}$鉄 Ujikane *m*
筠 Ujitake *m*
$^{14}$曄 Ujiaki *m*
郷 Ujisato *m*
$^{16}$綏 Ujiyasu *m*
燕 Ujiyoshi *m*
養 Ujikiyo *m*
賢 Ujimasa *m*
$^{19}$識 Ujisato *m*
$^{22}$懿 Ujihisa *m*

## 6 L2

**州** 224 [T] (SHŪ, SHU, SU, kuni)
乂 Kuniyoshi *m*
孝 Kunitaka *m*

**冲** 225 Oki *s*; Tōru *m.* (CHŪ, oki)
子 Okiko *f*

**次** 226 [T] Yadoru *m.* (JI, SHI, tsugu, tsugi, chika, hide, nami)
田 Tsugita *s*
光 Tsugimitsu *m*
信 Tsuginobu *m*
郎 Jirō *m* ⌈*m*
郎左衛門 Jirozaemon
雄 Tsugio *m*, Chikao
義 Tsugiyoshi *m*

**仲** 227 [T] Naka *s*; Nakashi *m.* (CHŪ, naka)
$^{2}$二郎 Nakajirō *m*
$^{3}$小路 Nakakōji *m*
川 Nakagawa *s* ⌈*f*
子 Nakago *s*; Nakako
丸 Nakamaru *s*
$^{4}$太郎 Nakatarō *m*
井 Nakai *s*
山 Nakayama *s*
$^{5}$田 Nakata *s*
本 Nakamoto *s*
目 Nakanome *s*
$^{6}$次郎 Nakajirō *m*
地 Nakaji *s*
光 Nakamitsu *m-la*
西 Nakanishi *s*
多度 Naka-tado *p*
$^{7}$佐 Nakasa *s*
沢 Nakazawa *s*
村 Nakamura *s*
谷 Nakaya *s*, Nakatatani
安 Nakayasu *s*
条 Nakajō *s*
尾 Nakao *s*
寿 Nakatoshi *m*
$^{8}$芸 Nakaki *m*
宗根 Nakasone *s*
$^{9}$俣 Nakamata *s*
治 Nakaji *m*
南 Chūnan *p*
$^{10}$原 Nakahara *s*
$^{11}$野 Nakano *sm-p*
都 Nakahiro *m*
麻呂 Nakamaro *sm*
島 Nakajima *s*
$^{12}$博 Nakahiro *m*
間 Nakama *s*
$^{17}$聴 Nakaakira *m*
$^{18}$麿 Nakamaro *sm*

**仙** 228 [I] Takashi *m*, Yamabito. (SEN, nori, hito, hisa)
$^{3}$太郎 Sentarō *m*
$^{5}$北 Senboku *p*
石 Sengoku *s*
四郎 Senshirō *m*
田 Senda *s*
$^{6}$次郎 Senjirō *m*
台 Sendai *sp*
名 Senna *s*
$^{7}$弘 Norihiro *m*
波 Senba *s*, Sennami
果 Senka *ml*
$^{9}$洞百番歌合 Sentō hyakuban utaawase
南 Sennan *p* ⌊*l*
$^{12}$渡 Sendo *s*
覚 Senkaku *ml*
道 Sendō *s*
$^{16}$頭 Senzu *s*

伍 229 Hitoshi *m*, Atsumu. (GO, itsu, kumi)
子 Kumiko *f*
堂 Godō *s*

伃 230 (YO, yoshi)
子 Yoshiko *f*

仮 231 [T] (KA, ka)
字本末 Kana no motosue *l*
名文章娘節用 Kana majiri musume setsuyō *l*
名手本忠臣蔵 Kanadehon chūshingura *la*
名垣 Kanagaki *s*
名垣魯文 K. Robun *ml*
名草子 Kana-zōshi *l*
名読八犬伝 Kanayomi Hakkenden *l*
谷 Kaya *s*

伎 232 (KI, GI)
芸天 Gigeiten *l*
楽 Kure *s*; Gigaku *a*

休 233 [T] Yasumu *m*, Yasushi. (KYŪ, KU, yasu, yoshi, tane, nobu)
子 Yasuko *f*, Yoshiko
弌 Yoshikazu *m*
広 Yoshishiro *m*

伏 234 [T] (FUKU, BUKU, FŪ, fushi, yasu)
丸 Fukawa *s*
木 Fushiki *s*
代 Fushiyo *f*
見 Fushimi *sma-p*
原 Fushihara *s*
屋 Fuseya *s*
流 Fukuryū *l*
島 Fushijima *s*, Fuseshima

任 235 [T] Tsukasa *m*, Makoto, Takashi, Ataru, Tamotsu, Makashi; Nin *s*. (JIN, NIN, taka, tō, tae, yoshi, tada, nori, hide, to, tane)
子 Takako *f*, Taeko
田 Tōda *s*, Ninden
弘 Takahiro *m*
那 Mimana / Ninna *ph* "Kaya / Karak"
美 Takumi *s*, Tarami
重 Yoshishige *m*

价 236 (KAI, KE, tomo, yoshi)
子 Tomoko *f*

伊 237 [N] (I, yoshi, kore, isa, tada)
ケ崎 Igazaki *s*
[1]一 Tadakazu *m*
[2]十郎 Ijūrō *m*
[3]川 Ikawa *s*
三次 Isōji *m*
三郎 Isaburō *m*
万里 Imari *sp*
大地 Iōji *s*
大知 Iōji *s*
土代丸 Izuchiyomaru *m*
之吉 Inokichi *m*
之助 Inosuke *m*
子 Yoshiko *f*
子志 Isoshi *s*
予 Iyo *m-p*
予三島 I. Mishima *p*
予田 Iyoda *m*
予部 Iyobe *s*
月 Izuki *s*
方 Ikata *p*
文字 Imoji *l*
尹 Koretada *m*
木 Iki *s*
太利 Itari *p* "Italy"
与田 Iyoda *s*
王野 Iōno *s*
王島 Iōshima *p*
井 Ii *s*
井蓉峰 Ii Yōhō *ma*
丹 Itami *sp*
丹三樹彦 I. Mikihiko *ml*
丹屋 Itamiya *s*
[5]比 Ihi *s*
礼 Irei *s*
四郎 Ishirō *m*
田 Ida *s*
本 Imoto *s*
[6]仙 Isen *p*
地知 Ijichi *s*
江 Ie *s*
吉 Iki *s*
気 Ike *s*
舟城 Ifunaki *s*
自牟 Ijimu *s*
自良 Ijira *sp*
[7]佐 Isa *sf-p*
佐山 Isayama *s*
佐野 Isano *s*
坂 Isaka *s*
吹 Ibuki *sp*; Itsuki *s*
吹武彦 Ibuki Takehiko *ml*
沢 Izawa *s*
沢修二 I. Shūji *mh*
形 Igata *s*
那 Ina *sp*
助 Isuke *m*
谷 Itani *s*, Ikoku, Iyoku
志良 Ishira *s*
男 Yoshio *m*
兵衛 Ihee *m*
呂波 Iroha *l*
呂波字類抄 I. jiruishō *l*
豆 Izu *sp*
豆山 Izuyama *s*
豆田 Izuta *s*
豆長岡 Izu Nagaoka *p*
豆屋 Izuya *s*
豆島 Izushima *s*
豆淵 Izubuchi *s*
尾 Io *s*
臣 Iomi *s*, Itomi
何我 Ikaga *s*
[8]阿弥 Iami *sp*
坪 Itsubo *s*
波 Inami *s*
林 Ibayashi *s*
岐 Iki *s*
知郎 Ichirō *m*
金 Isago *s*
具 Igu *sp*
宜我 Ikaga *s*
定 Yoshiyasu *m*
奈 Ina *sp*
奈川 Inagawa *s*
周 Korechika *m*
武 Isamu *m*
良 Ira *s*
良子 Irako *s*
良子清白 I. Suzushiro *ml*
東 Itō *sp*
東巳代治 I. Miyoji *mh*
東月草 I. Gessō *ml*
東玄朴 I. Genboku *mh*
東専三 I. Senzō *ml*
東祐益 I. Sukemasu *mh*
東静雄 I. Shizuo *ml*
[9]保 Iho *s*
津 Itsu *s*
津野 Izuno *s*
神 Ikami *s*
弥頭 Imizu *s*
砂 Isago *s*, Isuka
秋 Izutsu *s*
南 Ina *p*
草 Igusa *s*
美 Koreyoshi *m*
美吉 Imiki *s*
香 Ika *sp*; Ikō *s*, Ikago
香保 Ikaho *p*
[10]従 Iyori *s*
秩 Izutsu *s*
高 Itaka *s*
倉 Ikura *s*
庭 Iba *s*
原 Ihara *s*, Izuhara
原青々園 Ihara Seiseien *ml*
馬 Ima *s*
馬春部 I. Harube *ml*
[11]根 Ine *p*
野 Ino *sp*; Izuno *s*
部 Ibe *s*, Inbe, Korebe
能 Inō *s*, Iyoku
能忠敬 Inō Tadataka *mh*
都 Ito *p*
都国 Itokoku *ph*
都雄 Itsuo *m*
麻 Ima *f*
[12]崎 Izaki *s*
曾保 Isoho *l* "Aesop"
森 Imori *s*
賀 Iga *sp*
集院 Ijūin *sp*
達 Date *sp*; Idate *s*
達宗城 D. Munenari *mh*
達政宗 D. Masamune *mh*
達得夫 D. Tokuo *ml*
達競阿国戯場 D. kurabe Okuni Kabuki *la*
[13]福 Ifuku *s*, Ihoki
勢 Ise *sp*
勢大輔集 I.-dayū shū *l*
勢田 Iseda *s*
勢宗瑞 Ise Sōzui *mh*
勢物語 I. monogatari *l*
勢物語闕疑抄 I. m. ketsugishō *l*
勢品遅部 Isenohonchibe *s*
勢風 Isefū *l*
勢原 Isehara *p*
勢屋 Iseya *s*
勢崎 Isezaki *sp*

[14]雑 Izawa *s*
農 Ino *s*
関 Iseki *s*
[15]統 Itō *s*, Inō ; Koremune *sm*
熊 Ikuma *s*
[16]橋 Ihashi *s*
頭志 Izushi *s*
覩 Ito *s*
賢 Yoshitada *m*
藤 Itō *s*
藤仁斎 I. Jinsai *mlh*
藤永之介 I. Einosuke *ml*
藤左千夫 I. Sachio *ml*
藤若中 I. Jakuchū *ma*
藤東涯 I. Tōgai *mh*
藤信吉 I. Shinkichi *ml*
藤松宇 I. Shōu *ml*
藤野枝 I. Noe *fl*
藤博文 I. Hirobumi / Hakubun *mh*
藤嘉夫 I. Yoshio *ml*
藤銀月 I. Gingetsu *ml*
藤整 I. Sei / Hitoshi ⌊*ml*
[19]瀬地 Isechi *s*
瀬知 Isechi *s*
蘇 Iso *s*
蘇志 Isoshi *s*
[20]織 Iori *m*

——6 L3——

巧 238 [T] Takumi *sm*. (KŌ, KYŌ, tae, ⌊yoshi)
児 Kōji *s*

帆 239 [T] (HAN, ho)
之助 Honosuke *m*
山 Hoyama *s*
足 Hoashi *s*
足万里 H. Banri *mh*

圷 240 Akutsu *sp*; Kutsu *p*.
大野 Akutsu Ōno *p*

地 241 [T] (CHI, JI, tsuchi, kuni, ta- ⌊da)
子 Kuniko *f*
引 Jibiki *s*, Chibiki
主 Jinushi *s*
田 Chida *s*
曳 Jibiki *s*
村 Chimura *s*
倶 Chigu *s*
原 Jihara *s*
獄変 Jigokuhen *l*
霊 Chirei *l*
蔵舞 Jizō-mai *la*

吐 242 (TO, ha)
山 Hayama *sp*
田 Handa *s*, Toda
師 Haji *s*

壮 243 [T] Takeshi *m*, Sakan, Sakari; Take *f*. (sō, SHŌ, take, masa, aki, mori, o)
一 Sōichi *m*
夫 Takeo *m*, Masao
宏 Masahiro *m*
昌 Akimasa *m*
麻呂 Omaro *m*
瞥 Sōbetsu *p*

兆 244 [T] (CHŌ, yoshi, toki)
生 Yoshinari *m*
向 Toki *s*
頼 Tokiyori *m*

行 245 [T] Akira *m*. (KŌ, GYŌ, AN, yuki, michi, tsura, ki, nori, mochi, hira, yasu, taka, nami, name)
[1]一 Kōichi *m*
[2]人 Kōjin *l*
[3]川 Yukigawa *s*, Namikawa
[4]心 Yukikiyo *m*
方 Namegata *sp*; Namikata *s*, Nasukata
山 Yukiyama *s*
五郎 Kōgorō *m*
木 Namiki *s*
夫 Yukio *m* ⌈*s*
[5]田 Gyōda *sp*; Yukida
平 Yukihira *m*
[6]行林 Odoro *s*; Odorobayashi *p*
先 Yukisaki *m* ⌈*ml*
成 Yukinari *m*; Kōzei
[7]沢 Yukizawa *s*
形 Ikinari *s*
芬 Yukihisa *m*
[8]明 Gyōmei *s*, Gyōmyō
欣 Yukiyoshi *m*
武 Yukitake *s*
幸 Miyuki *l*
命 Gyōmei *s*
忠 Yukitada *m*
虎 Michitake *m*
[9]信 Yukinobu *m*
則 Yukinori *m*
為 Yukitame *m*
[10]郎 Yukio *m*
造 Yukinari *m*
[11]基 Gyōki *mh*
[12]尊大僧正集 Gyōson Daisōjō shū *l*
[13]雄 Yukio *m*
歳 Yukitoshi *m*
[14]徳 Gyōtoku *s*
[16]橋 Yukihashi *p*

羽 246 [T] Hamoto *s*, Hanemochi. (U, ha, hane)
ノ浦 Hanoura *p*
[2]二生 Hanyū *s*
入 Hairi *s* ⌈kawa
[3]川 Hagawa *s*, Hane-
[4]切井 Hakii *s*
仁 Hani *s*
仁五郎 H. Gorō *ml*
丹生 Hanyū *s*
山 Hayama *s*
太 Habuto *s*, Hata
毛田 Hageta *s*
[5]石 Haishi *s*
生 Hanyū *sp*; Hagyū *s*, Habu
田 Haneda *sp*; Hata *s*
田井 Hatai *s*
[6]合 Hawai *p*
成 Hanari *s*
曳野 Habikino *p*
[7]佐田 Hasada *s*
佐間 Hasama *s*
住 Hazumi *s*
沢 Hazawa *s*
吹 Habuki *s*
村 Hamura *p*
床 Hayuka *s*
衣 Hagoromo *la*
束 Hatsuka *s*, Hatsukashi
束志 Hatsukashi *s*
[8]咋 Hakui *sp*; Hanemochi *s*, Hamoto
茂 Hamochi *p*; Hanemochi *s*, Hamoto
[9]洲園 Hasuzono *s*
牀 Hayuka *s*
前 Uzen *ph*
[10]倉 Hagura *s*
室 Hamuro *s*
柴 Hashiba *s*
栗 Haguri *s*, Haneguri
原 Habara *s*
[11]深 Habuka *s*
後 Ugo *ph*
根 Hane *s*
根田 Haneda *s*
紅 Ukō *fl*
部 Habe *s* ⌈*s*
黒 Haguro *sp*; Haguri
鳥 Hatori *s*
島 Hashima *sp*
[12]場 Haba *s*
須美 Hasumi *p*
賀 Haga *s*
[13]喰 Hakui *s*
幌 Haboro *p*
淵 Habuchi *s*
[15]衝 Hatsugi *m*
[16]積 Hazumi *m*

竹 247 [T] Takeno *s*; Take *f*. (CHIKU, take, taka)
ノ内 Takenouchi *s*
の里歌 Take no satouta *l*
[2]二郎 Takejirō *m*
入 Takeiri *s*
[3]川 Takegawa *s*
三 Takezō *m*
之下 Takenoshita *s*
之内 Takenouchi *s*
口 Takeguchi *s*
上 Takegami *s*
万 Takema *s*
下 Takeshita *s*, Takenoshita
久 Takehisa *sm*
久夢二 T. Yumeji *ml*
[4]仁 Takani *s*
元 Takemoto *s*
介 Takesuke *m*
友 Taketomo *s*
友藻風 T. Sōfū *ml*
井 Takei *s*
五郎 Takegorō *m*
山 Takeyama *s*
山道雄 T. Michio *ml*
中 Takenaka *s* ⌈*ml*
中久七 T. Kyūshichi
中郁 T. Iku *ml*
内 Takeuchi *s*, Takenouchi
内久一 Takenouchi Hisakazu *ma*

内仁 T. Masashi *ml*
内式部 T. Shikibu *mh*
内好 Takeuchi Yoshimi *ml*
内栖鳳 T. Seihō *ma*
内敏雄 T. Toshio *ml*
内勝太郎 T. Katsutarō *ml*
[5]永 Takenaga *s*
石 Takeishi *s*
市 Takeichi *s*
平 Takehira *s*
本 Takemoto *s* ⌈*ma*
本義太夫 T. Gidayū
生 Takebu *s*, Takō
生島 Chikubushima *p-la*
田 Takeda *sp* ⌈*ml*
田小出雲 T. Koizumo
田出雲 T. Izumo *ml*
[6]州 Takesu *s*
次郎 Takejirō *m*
光 Takemitsu *s*
辻 Taketsuji *s*
[7]坊 Takenobō *s*
沢 Takezawa *s*
村 Takemura *s*
村俊郎 T. Toshio *ml*
谷 Taketani *s*, Takeya
花 Takebana *s*
志 Tsukushi *s*
志田 Takeshita *s*
尾 Takeo *s* ⌈*ml*
尾忠吉 T. Chūkichi
見 Takemi *s*
束 Taketaba *s*
[8]河 Takegawa *s*; Takekawa *sl*
門 Takemo *s*
林 Takebayashi *s*
林抄 Chikurinshō *l*
知 Takechi *s*
取 Taketori *l*
若 Takewaka *s*
居 Takei *s*
迫 Takehazama *s*
良 Chikura *m*
[9]俣 Takemata *s*
垣 Takegaki *s*
城 Takagi *s*
津 Taketsu *s*
治 Takeji *m*
柏会 Chikuhakukai *l*
松 Takematsu *s*
政 Takemasa *s*
前 Takesaki *s*, Take-
岡 Takeoka *s* ⌊mae
廻 Taketaba *s*
[10]脇 Takewaki *s*
倉 Takegura *s*
倉屋 Takeguraya *s*
宮 Takemiya *s*
家 Takeya *s*
柴 Takeshiba *s*
柴其水 T. Kisui *ml*
原 Takehara *sp*
屋 Takeya *s*; Takenoya *sm*
馬 Chikuma *s*
[11]野 Takeno *sp*
部 Takebe *s*
斎 Chikusai *l*
雪 Take no yuki *la*
島 Takeshima *s*
添 Takezoe *s*
[12]崎 Takezaki *s*
崎季長 T. Suenaga *mh*
富 Taketomi *s*
森 Takemori *s*
貫 Takenuki *s*
[13]塚 Takezuka *s*
淵 Takebuchi *s*
雄 Takeo *sm*
葉 Takeba *s*
園 Takezono *s*
越 Takekoshi *s*
越三叉 T. Sansa *ml*
越与三郎 T. Yosaburō *mh*
[14]腰 Takekoshi *s*
蓋 Ofuta *s*
鼻 Takehana *s*
[15]蔵 Takezō *m*
[16]橋 Takehashi *s*

汗 248 [T] Fuzakashi *s*. (KAN)

汎 249 [T] Hiroshi *m*. (HAN, hiro, mina)
子 Minako *f*
秀 Hirohide *m*
慶 Hiroyoshi *m*

汐 250 (SEKI, JAKU, shio, kiyo)
見 Shiomi *s*
明 Shioaki *m*
美 Shiomi *f*
崎 Shiozaki *s*

池 251 [T] Ike *s*. (CHI, ike)
ノ谷 Ikenoya *s*
[3]川 Ikegawa *p*
口 Ikeguchi *s*
之端 Ikenohata *s*
上 Ikegami *s*, Ikenoue
下 Ikenoshita *s*
子 Ikeko *f*
大雅 Ike no Taiga *ma*
[4]戸 Ikedo *s*
井 Ikei *s* ⌈chi
内 Ikeuchi *s*, Ikenou-
内友次郎 Ikenouchi Tomojirō *ml*
山 Ikeyama *s*
[5]永 Ikenaga *s*
穴 Ikeana *s*
尻 Ikejiri *s*, Ikegami
辺 Ikebe *s*, Ikenobe
辺美象 Ikebe Yoshikata *ml*
本 Ikemoto *s*
主 Ikenushi *sm*
田 Ikeda *sp*
田大伍 I. Daigo *ml*
田光政 I. Mitsumasa *mh*
田克巳 I. Katsumi *ml*
田潔 I. Kiyoshi *ml*
[6]守 Ikemori *sm*
西 Ikenishi *s*
[7]坊 Ikenobō *s*
沢 Ikezawa *s*
村 Ikemura *s*
町 Ikemachi *s*
谷 Ikeya *s*, Iketani, Ikegaya, Iketari
谷信三郎 Iketani Shinzaburō *ml*
貝 Ikegai *s*
尾 Ikeo *s*
[9]津 Iketsu *s*
松 Ikematsu *s*
畑 Ikehata *s*
亭記 Chitei no ki *l*
[10]浦 Ikeura *s*
原 Ikehara *s*
[11]添 Ikezoe *s*
後 Ikejiri *s*, Ikenoshiri
野 Ikeno *s*
野谷 Ikenotani *s*
部 Ikebe *s*
皐雨郎 Ike Kōurō *ml*
島 Ikejima *s*
亀 Ikegame *s*
[12]崎 Ikesaki *s*
森 Ikemori *s*
袋 Ikebukuro *sp*
袋清風 I. Kiyokaze *ml*
[13]淵 Ikebuchi *s*
塘集 Chitōshū *l*
越 Ikenokoshi *s*
[15]端 Ikehata *s*

江 252 [T] GŌ *s*. (KŌ, GŌ, e, nobu, kimi, tada)
ノ島 Enoshima *p*
[3]川 Egawa *s*
川坦庵 E. Tan'an *mh*
上 Egami *s*
口 Eguchi *sla*
口渙 E. Kiyoshi *ml*
口榛一 E. Shin'ichi *ml*
之島 Enoshima *la*
之島土産 E. miyage *l*
[4]刈内 Egarinai *s*
戸 Edo *sph*
戸川 Edogawa *sp*
戸川乱歩 E. Ranpo *ml*
戸生艶生樺焼 Edo umare uwaki no kabayaki *l*
戸名所記 E. meishoki *l*
戸作者部類 E. sakusha burui *l*
戸砂子慶曾我 E. sunago kichirei Soga *la*
戸長唄 E. nagauta *a*
戸座 Edoza *l*
戸崎 Edosaki *p*
戸幕府 Edo bakufu *h*
井 Ei *s*
木 Egi *s*
[5]北 Kōhoku *p*
尻 Ejiri *s* ⌈*m*
平 Ehira *s*; Nobuhira
本 Emoto *s*
田 Eda *s*
田島 Etajima *p*
[6]竹 Etake *s*
守 Emori *s*
成 Enari *s*
[7]坂 Esaka *s*
沢 Ezawa *s*
村 Emura *s*
利川 Erikawa *s*
別 Ebetsu *p*
別乙 Ebeotsu *p*
花 Ehana *s*
里口 Eriguchi *s*
角 Esumi *s*
見 Emi *sp*
見水蔭 E. Suiin *ml*
[8]波 Enami *s*

波戸 Ehado *s*
沼 Enuma *sp*; Enu *s*
林 Ebayashi *s*
刺 Esashi *p*
府 Kōfu *p*
迎 Emukae *p*
良 Era *s*
東 Kōtō *p*
$^{9}$津 Gōzu *p*
畑 Ebata *s*
帥集 Gōnosochi-shū *l*
南 Enami *s*; Kōnan *p*
南文三 E. Bunzō *ml*
南亭 Kōnantei *s*
面 Ezura *s*
草 Egusa *s*
香 Kōka *s*, Gōka
乗 Enami *s*
$^{10}$夏 Enatsu *s*
家次第 Kōke shidai *l*
差 Esashi *p*
原 Ebara *s*
原小弥太 E. Koyata *ml*
連 Etsure *s*
馬 Ema *s*
馬修 E. Shū *ml*
$^{11}$添 Ezoe *s*
野 Eno *s*
野財 Enuma *s*
野島 Enoshima *la*
釣子 Ezuriko *p*
部 Enobe *s*
副 Ezoe *s*
黒 Eguro *s* ⌈*la*
島 Ejima *s*; Enoshima
島其礒 E. Kiseki *ml*
島屋 Ejimaya *s*
$^{12}$渡 Eto *s*
崎 Ezaki *s*
森 Emori *s*
間 Ema *s*
間章子 E. Shōko *fl*
$^{13}$塚 Ezuka *s*
$^{15}$幡 Ebata *s*
潮 Kōko *s*
談抄 Gōdanshō *l*
$^{16}$橋 Ebashi *s*
積 Ezumi *s*
頭 Egashira *s*, Etō, Ezu
$^{18}$藤 Etō *s*
藤淳 E. Jun *ml*
藤新平 E. Shinpei *mh*

## 6 L4

**劥** 253 Tsuyoshi *m.* (KŌ, KYŌ)

**此** 254 (SHI, kono, kore)
口 Aza *s*
助 Konosuke *m*
花 Konohana *p*
枝 Konoe *f*
美 Konomi *f*

**朴** 255 [I] Sunao *m*; Boku *s.* (BOKU, e
木 Hōnoki *s* ⌊nao)
次郎 Naojirō *m*
室 Emuro *s*

**奴** 256 [I] (NU, DO)
可 Nuka *s*
田 Nuda *s* ⌈riya
借屋 Nukariya *s*, Ika-
留湯 Nurutō *s*

**列** 257 [T] (RETSU, tsura, shige, toku, nobu)
子 Tsurako *f*
田 Namita *s*
樹 Tsuraki *m*

**刑** 258 [T] Osaka *s.* (KEI, GYŌ, nori)
坂 Osaka *s*
苅 Togawa *s*
事 Osakabe *s*
馬 Keima *s*
部 Osakabe *smh-p*; Osabe *s*, Gyōbu, Okibe, Katabe, Otae
部左衛門 Gyōbuzaemon *m*

**卯** 259 [N] Shigeru *m*, Akira. (BŌ, MYŌ, u, shige)
一 Uichi *m*
三郎 Usaburō *m*
之助 Unosuke *m*
月 Uzuki *s*
木 Uki *s*
外 Shigekado *m*
吉 Ukichi *m*

**印** 260 [T] (IN, aki, shiru, oshi, kane,
$^{4}$木 Uki *s* ⌊oki)
支 Inaki *s*
支部 Inakibe *s*
代 Inashiro *s*
西 Inzai *p*
$^{7}$貝 Isogai *s*
$^{8}$牧 Kanemaki *s*, Inmaki ⌈zumi
具 Igu *s*, Igui, Oshi-
東 Indō *s*
$^{9}$南 Innami *sp*; Innan *s*
巻 Kanemaki *s*
度 Indo *p* "India"
$^{11}$部 Inbe *s*, Isobe
$^{15}$幡 Inba *s*
$^{18}$旛 Inba *p*
藤 Indō *s*
$^{25}$鑰 Innyaku *s*

## 6 L5

**幻** 261 [T] (GEN) ⌈*l*
住庵記 Genjūan no ki

## 6 T1

**亘** 262 Wataru *sm*, Watari; Tan *s*; Motomu *m.* (SEN, nobu, asa). (=宣 919 q.v., but used also for 旦 162 and 亙 317 q.v.)
子 Nobuko *f*
行 Nobuyuki *m*
尾 Asao *s*
理 Watari *sp*

## 6 T2

**旨** 263 [T] Susumu *m.* (SHI, mune, yoshi)
国 Munekuni *m*
武 Munetake *m*
剛 Munetake *m*

**而** 264 (JI, NI, shika, nao, yuki)
慍斎 Jiunsai *ml*

**百** 265 [T] Hagemu *m.* (HYAKU, momo, o, to, mo)
$^{2}$十彦 Todohiko *m*
人一首 Hyakunin isshu *l*
人一首改観抄 H. i. kaikanshō *l*
人一首燈 H. i. akashi *l*
$^{3}$川 Momokawa *s*
三 Hyakuzō *m*
万 Hyakuman *la*
千万億 Tsumoru *s*
千代 Momochiyo *f*
$^{4}$元 Momoto *s*
井 Momoi *s*, Dodoi
木 Momoki *s*
太郎 Hyakutarō *m*
毛 Momoke *s*
$^{5}$石 Momoishi *p*
田 Momota *s*
田宗治 M. Sōji *ml*
目木 Domeki *s*
目鬼 Domeki *s*
$^{6}$江 Momoe *s* ⌈do *sp*
百 Dodo *s*, Sasa; Dō-
百子 Momoko *f*
百山 Momoyama *s*
合 Yuri *sf*
合子 Yuriko *f*
合五郎 Yurigorō *m*
合若大臣 Yuriwaka Daijin *l*
$^{7}$花 Hyakuhana *s*
足 Momotari *sm*; Mukade *s*
足屋 Mukadeya *s*
束 Momozuka *s*
$^{8}$学連環 Hyakugaku renkan *l*
武 Hyakutake *s*
夜 Momoyo *f-l*
$^{9}$津 Momotsu *s*
度 Momoto *m*; Zundo *s*
$^{11}$渓 Momotani *s*
済 Kudara *sph* "Paekche"
済伎 Kudaratebito *s*
済安宿 Kudaraasuka *s*
済河成 Kudara no Kawanari *ma*
済楽 K. gaku *a*
済観音 K. Kannon *a*
島 Momojima *s*
鬼 Momoki *m*; Nakiri *s*
鬼園 Hyakukien *l*
$^{12}$喜 Momoki *m*
$^{19}$瀬 Momose *s*

**去** 266 [T] (KYO, KO, saru, naru)
来 Kyorai *ml*
来川 Isakawa *s*
来抄 Kyoraishō *l*

**圭** 267 [N] Kiyoshi *m.* (KEI, KE, yoshi, tama, kiyo, kado, ka)

三 Keizō *m*
三郎 Keizaburō *m*
介 Keisuke *m*
太 Keita *m*
世子 Kayoko *f*
弘 Yoshihiro *m*
秀 Yoshihide *m*
美 Tamami *f*
雄 Tamao *m*
資 Kiyosuke *m*

寺 268 [T] (JI, tera)
3川 Terakawa *s*
久保 Terakubo *s*
口 Teraguchi *s*
子屋 Terakoya *la-h*
4戸 Terato *s*, Terado
内 Terauchi *s*
井 Terai *sp*
木 Teraki *s*
山 Terayama *s*
5本 Teramoto *s*
田 Terada *s* ⌈*ml*
田寅彦 T. Torahiko
田透 T. Tōru *ml*
西 Teranishi *s*
7坂 Terasaka *s*
沢 Terasawa *s*
村 Teramura *s*
町 Teramachi *s*
谷 Teradani *s*
尾 Terao *s*
尾寿 T. Hisashi *mh*
見 Terami *s*
8泊 Teradomari *p*
門 Terakado *s*
林 Terabayashi *s*
9垣 Teragaki *s*
松 Teramatsu *s*
岡 Teraoka *s*
10脇 Terawaki *s*
師 Terashi *s*
倉 Terakura *s*
家村 Jigemura *s*
原 Terahara *s*
11野 Terano *s*
部 Terabe *s*
島 Terajima *s* ⌈*mh*
島宗則 T. Munenori
12崎 Terazaki *s*
崎広業 T. Kōgyō *ma*
崎浩 T. Hiroshi *ml*
19瀬 Terase *s*

企 269 [T] (KI, moto)
宣 Motonori *m*
救 Kiku *s*
救岳 Kikutake *s*

合 270 [T] Ai *f*. (GŌ, ai, au, kai, haru, yoshi)
川 Aikawa *sp*; Gōkawa *s* ⌈ida
田 Anda *s*, Gōda, Ka-
志 Gōshi *sp*; Awashi *s*, Atsushi, Asshi
津 Gōtsu *s*
巻 Gōkan *l*
浦 Kappo *la*
原 Aibara *s*
渡 Gōto *s*
葉 Aiba *s*
賀 Aiga *s*
歓子 Nemuko *f*
歓垣 Nemugaki *s*

全 271 [T] Tamotsu *m*, Akira; Masa *f*. (ZEN, SEN, masa, tomo, take, mata, mitsu, utsu, haru, yasu)
子 Matako *f*, Haruko
仁 Matahito *m*
田 Matta *s*, Senda
光 Yasumitsu *m*
先 Matsusaki *s*
成 Mitsunari *m*, Utsunari
弘 Masahiro *m*
侊 Masamitsu *m*
亭 Zentei *s*
勝 Takekatsu *m*
雄 Takeo *m*
徳 Takenori *m*

## 6 T3

号 272 [T] Nazuku *m*. (GŌ, KŌ, na)

羊 273 [T] (YŌ)
治郎 Yōjirō *m*

孕 274 (YŌ, harami)
石 Haramiishi *sp*

弁 275 [T] Sonō *m*. (BEN, HAN, sada, wake, naka)
三 Benzō *m*
子 Sadako *f*
千代 Benchiyo *m*
内侍 Ben no Naishi *fl*
官 Bibuga *s*
治郎 Benjirō *m*
道 Sadamichi *m*
蔵 Benzō *m*

台 276 [T] Utena *s*. (TAI, DAI, moto)
北 Taihoku *p* "Tai-
東 Taitō *p* ⌊pei"
記 Taiki *l*
堂 Daidō *s* ⌈wan"
湾 Taiwan *p* "Tai-

各 277 [T] (KAKU, masa, nuka)
田 Nukata *s*
田部 Nukatabe *s*
牟 Kagami *s*
務 Kagami *sp*; Kakumi *s*, Kakumu
務支考 Kagami Shikō *ml*
務原 Kagamigahara *sp*; Kagamihara *s*

吉 278 [T] Hajime *m*. (KICHI, KITSU, yoshi, sachi, tomo, yo)
2人 Yoshito *m*
十 Yoshito *m*
十郎 Kichijūrō *m*
3川 Yoshikawa *sp*; Kikkawa *s*; Yokawa *p* ⌈*ml*
川幸次郎 Y. Kōjirō
川英治 Y. Eiji *ml*
川惟足 Y. Koretaru
三 Kichisa *f* ⌊*mh*
三郎 Kichisaburō *m*
之 Yoshiyuki *m*
之助 Kichinosuke *m*
子 Yoshiko *f*
丸 Yoshimaru *sm*
士 Yoshito *m*, Yoshio; Kishi *s*
4水 Yoshimizu *s*
内 Kichinai *m*
山 Yoshiyama *s*
五郎 Kichigorō *m*
木 Yoshiki *s*
井 Yoshii *sp*
井勇 Y. Isamu *ml*
中 Yoshinaka *s*
5永 Yoshinaga *sm-p*
右衛門 Kichiemon *m*
左衛門 Kichizaemon
本 Yoshimoto *s* ⌊*m*
本隆明 Y. Ryūmei *ml*
田 Yoshida *sp*
田一穂 Y. Issui *ml*
田冬葉 Y. Tōyō *ml*
田正俊 Y. Masatoshi *ml*
田光由 Y. Kōyū *mh*
田定房 Y. Sadafusa *mh*
田茂 Y. Shigeru *mh*
田神道 Y. Shintō *mh*
田松蔭 Y. Shōin *mh*
田兼倶 Y. Kanetomo *mh*
田健一 Y. Ken'ichi *ml*
田精一 Y. Seiichi *ml*
田紘二郎 Y. Genjirō
平 Yoshihira *sm* ⌊*ml*
6仲 Yoshinaka *sm*
次郎 Kichijirō *m*, Yo-
江 Yoshie *s* ⌊shijirō
江喬松 Y. Takamatsu
竹 Yoshitake *s* ⌊*ml*
羽 Yoshiba *s*
行 Yoshiyuki *s*
行淳之介 Y. Junnosuke *ml*
池 Yoshiike *s*
光 Yoshimitsu *s*
広 Yoshihiro *s*
成 Yoshinari *sm*
母 Kichimo *s*
年 Yotoshi *s*
7住 Yoshizumi *s*
阪 Yoshizaka *s*
沢 Yoshizawa *s* ⌈*ml*
沢義則 Y. Yoshinori
孜子 Yoshiko *f*
弘 Yoshihiro *s*
町 Yoshimachi *s*
助 Kichisuke *m*
利 Yoshitoshi *s*, Yotoshi
利支丹文学 Kirishitan bungaku *l*
村 Yoshimura *s*
村寅太郎 Y. Toratarō *mh* ⌈rō *ml*
村鉄太郎 Y. Tetsuta-
亨 Yoshichika *m*
谷 Yoshitani *s*
邑 Yoshikuni *m*
尾 Yoshio *s*
呂 Yoshinaga *m*
兵衛 Kichibee *m*

刑 卯 印 幻 亘 旨 而 百 去 圭 ▼ 寺 企 合 全 号 羊 孕 弁 台 各 吉 ▲ 岳 先 光 当 宅 守 宇 芙 芋 芊

企 合 全 号 羊 孕 弁 台 各 吉 ▼ 兵 先 光 ▲ 当 宅 守 宇 芙 芊 芋 芝 尽 屶

志 Kishi *s*
志部 Kishibe *s*
尾 Yoshio *s*
甫 Yoshinori *m*
見 Yoshimi *sp*
身 Yoshimi *s*
[8]使部 Kishibe *s*
沼 Yoshinuma *s*
河 Yoshikawa *s*
和 Yoshiwa *p*
舎 Kisa *p*
英 Yoshihide *m*
宗 Yoshimune *m*
武 Yoshitake *s*
国 Yoshikuni *s*
固 Yoshikata *m*
事崎 Kitsujisaki *s*
良 Kira *sp*
[9]侯 Kimiko *s*
垣 Yoshigaki *s*
城 Yoshiki *p*
津 Kitsu *s*
弥 Kichiya *m*
弥侯部 Kinekobe *s*, Kimikobe
相 Yoshisuke *m*
柯 Yoshie *f*
松 Yoshimatsu *sp*
品 Yoshinori *m*, Yoshitada
泉 Yoshizumi *s*
臭 Yoshizawa *s*
岡 Yoshioka *sp*
岡禅寺洞 Y. Zenjidō *ml* ⌈miko *s*
彦 Yoshihiko *m*; Ki-
省 Kichishō *m*
[10]修 Yoshinaga *m*
倚 Yoshiyori *m*
浜 Yoshihama *s*
浦 Yoshiura *s*
海 Yoshimi *s*; Yoshi-
祥 Kisshō *m* ⌊umi *p*
祥天 Kichijōten *fh*
師部 Kishibe *s*
郎 Kichirō *m*
郎兵衛 Kichirobee *m*
高 Yoshitaka *s*
倉 Yoshikura *s*
益 Yoshimasu *s*
原 Yoshiwara *sp*
原雀 Y. suzume *a*
造 Kichizō *m*
屋 Yoshiya *s*
屋信子 Y. Nobuko *fl*
兼 Yoshikane *s*
[11]清 Yoshikiyo *s*

祗 Yoshitada *m*
躬 Kimi *s* ⌈nu *s*
野 Yoshino *sp*; Eshi-
野天人 Y. Tennin *la*
野左衛門 Y. Saemon *ml*
野作造 Y. Sakuzō *ml*
野谷 Yoshinotani *p*
野秀雄 Yoshino Hideo *ml*
野拾遺 Y. shūi *l*
野臥城 Y. Gajō *ml*
野鉦二 Y. Shōji *ml*
野静 Y. Shizuka *la*
寅 Yoshinobu *m*.
宿 Yoshiie *m*
峯 Yoshimine *s*
留 Yoshidome *s*
島 Yoshijima *s*, Yoshima
[12]偕 Yoshitomo *m*
備 Kibi *sm-p*
備石无別 Kibiiwanasuwake *s* ⌈kama *l*
備津の釜 Kibitsu no
備品遅 Kibihonji *s*
備真備 Kibi no Makibi *mh*
備麻呂 Kibimaro *m*
場 Yoshiba *s*
崎 Yoshizaki *s*
崎坊 Y.-bō *ph*
報子 Yoshioko *f*
富 Yoshitomi *sp*
森 Yoshimori *s*
賀 Yoshiga *s*
達 Yoshimichi *m*
開 Yoshikai *s*
鹿 Yoshika *s*
[13]塚 Yoshizuka *s*
雄 Yoshio *m*
植 Yoshiue *s*
植庄亮 Y. Shōryō *ml*
葉 Yoshiba *s*
義 Yoshimichi *m*
廉 Yoshikiyo *m*
越 Yoshikoshi *s*
[15]敷 Yoshiki *p*
鋪 Yoshiki *s*
蔵 Kichizō *m*
[16]橋 Yoshihashi *s*
樹 Yoshiki *m*
[17]鴻 Yoshitoki *m*
鍾 Yoshiatsu *m*
[18]藤 Yoshifuji *s*
[19]瀬 Kichise *s*
識 Yoshiki *s*

兵 279 Hisashi *m*. (KI)

先 280 [T] Susumu *m*. (SEN, saki, hiro, yuki)
斗町 Pontochō *p*
光 Sakimitsu *s*
崎 Senzaki *s*

光 281 [T] Mitsuru *m*, Hikaru, Teru, Akira, Sakae, Hiroshi. (KŌ, mitsu, teru, hiro, aki, ari, kanu, kane, ⌊hiko)
[1]一 Kōichi *m*
[3]子 Mitsuko *f-l*; Hiroko *f*; Mitsutaka *m*
寸 Mitsumura *s*
大 Mitsumasa *m*
久 Teruhisa *m*
[4]仁 Kōnin *mh*; Mitsumasa *m*
予 Mitsumasa *m*
山 Mitsuyama *s*, Kōyama
少 Mitsumasa *m*
夫 Mitsuo *m*, Mitsu-
井 Mitsui *s* ⌊suke
太夫 Kōdayū *mh*
太郎 Mitsutarō *m*, Kōtarō
[5]永 Mitsunaga *sm*
田 Mitsuda *s*
正 Mitsumasa *m*
本 Mitsumoto *s*
[6]次 Mitsuji *m*
次郎 Mitsujirō *m*
行 Mitsuyuki *sm*
宅 Mitsutaku *m*
吉 Mitsuyoshi *sm*
広 Mitsuhiro *m*
成 Mitsushige *m*
多 Mitsuna *m*
[7]佐 Mitsusuke *m*
均 Teruo *m*
沢 Mitsuzawa *s*
村 Mitsumura *s*
弘 Mitsuhiro *m*
孚 Mitsuzane *m*, Mitsutada, Mitsutomo
寿 Mitsunaga *m*
孝平 Kōkōhei *s*
[8]明 Kōmyō *fh*; Mitsuaki *m*
林 Kōrin *ma*
和 Mitsuyasu *m*

享 Mitsuyuki *m*
宙 Mitsuoki *m*
秀 Mitsuhide *m*
武 Mitsutake *s*
承 Mitsusuke *s*
[9]法 Mippō *s*
治 Mitsuji *m*
施 Mitsuharu *m*
政 Mitsuosa *m*
秋 Mitsuaki *m*
春 Mitsuharu *m*
栄 Mitsuharu *m*, Mitsunaga
岡 Mitsuoka *s*
圀 Mitsukuni *m*
彦 Teruhiko *m*
[10]俊 Mitsutoshi *m*
悦 Kōetsu *mla*; Mitsunobu *m*
華 Mitsuharu *m*
哲 Kōtetsu *m*
屋 Mitsuie *m*
造 Mitsuzō *m*
威 Mitsutake *m*
[11]淳 Mitsuaki *m*
野 Mitsuno *s*
教 Mitsutaka *m*
副 Mitsusuke *m*
庸 Mitsumochi *m*
彪 Mitsutake *m*
亀 Kōki *m*
[12]傅 Mitsusuke *m*
揚 Teruaki *m*
禄 Mitsutomi *m*
棣 Mitsutomi *m*
[13]源氏 Hikaru Genji
瑗 Teruni *m* ⌊*lm*
雄 Mitsuo *m*
勤 Mitsutoshi *m*
豊 Mitsutoyo *m* ⌈ma
雲 Hiromo *m*; Kōun
[14]増 Mitsumasu *sm*
徳 Mitsue *m*
瑞 Kōzui *m*
榎 Mitsue *f*
暢 Mitsumasa *m*
彰 Mitsuaki *m*
熙 Mitsuhiro *m*, Terusato
[15]蔵 Mitsuzō *m*
遵 Mitsuyori *m*
[16]親 Mitsuyori *m*
[17]慈 Mitsuchika *m*
厳 Kōgon *mlh*
[18]鎮 Mitsushige *m*
藤 Mitsufuji *s*
[20]議 Mitsunori *m*

**当** 282 [T] Tae *m.* (TŌ, masa, tae, tai, matsu)
山 Tōyama *s*
世 Masayo *s*
世下手談義 Imayō heta dangi *l*
別 Tōbetsu *p*
舎 Tōsha *s*
宗 Masamune *sm*
英 Masateru *m*
時 Masatoki *m*
起 Masaoki *m*
麻 Taima *sp*, Tōma; Taema *sla*; Tagima *s*
麻品遅部 Tagimahonjibe *s*
間 Tōma *s*
摩 Tōma *s*

**宅** 283 [T] Taku *s*, Takura. (TAKU, JAKU, ie, yaka, yake, ori)
刀自 Yakatoji *fh*
守 Yakamori *ml*
命 Ienori *m*
部 Yakabe *s*
間 Takuma *s*
嗣 Yakutsugu *m*
磨 Takuma *s*
磨為成 T. no Tamenari *ma*
麿 Takuma *s*

**守** 284 [T] Mamoru *sm-f*; Mamori *sm*; Mori *s*. (SHU, SU, mori, e, ma, more, sane)
$^{1}$一 Moriichi *m*
$^{3}$川 Morikawa *s*
三 Morizō *m*
口 Moriguchi *sp*
之助 Morinosuke *m*
子 Moriko *f*
$^{4}$戸 Morito *s*
元 Morimoto *s*
中 Morinaka *s*
山 Moriyama *sp*
手 Morite *m*
$^{5}$永 Morinaga *s*
田 Morita *s*
本 Morimoto *s*
矢 Moriya *s*
$^{6}$丞 Morisuke *m*
米 Morimitsu *ma*
$^{7}$住 Morizumi *s*
村 Morimura *s*
利 Moritoshi *m*
谷 Moriya *sp*
安 Moriyasu *s*
尾 Morio *s*
$^{8}$門 Sumon *p*
舎 Moriya *m*
武 Moritake *sm*
$^{9}$度 Morito *m*
岡 Morioka *s*
重 Morishige *m*
家 Moriya *s*
$^{10}$真 Morima *m*
屋 Moriya *sm*
$^{11}$脩 Moriosa *m*
峰 Morio *m*
理 Mari *f*
部 Moribe *sm*
$^{12}$随 Shuzui *s*
道 Moriyuki *m*
晨 Moritoki *m*
$^{14}$韶 Moriaki *m*
$^{15}$蔵 Morizō *m*
$^{16}$衛 Morie *m*
$^{18}$藤 Shutō *s*
彝 Moritomo *m*

**宇** 285 [T] (U, uma, taka, noki)
ノ気 Unoke *p*
$^{1}$一 Uichi *m*
$^{3}$川 Ugawa *s*
三郎 Usaburō *m*
之吉 Unokichi *m*
土 Uto *p*
久 Uku *sp*
$^{4}$山 Uyama *s*
夫 Takao *m*
井 Ui *s*
木 Uki *s*
目 Ume *p*
$^{5}$平治 Uheiji *m*
田 Uda *s*
田川 Udagawa *s*
田川文海 U. Bunkai *ml*
田川玄真 U. Genshin *mh*
田川玄随 U. Genzui *mh*
田川榕庵 U. Yōan *mh*
田零雨 Uda Reiu *ml*
$^{6}$合 Umakai *m*, Nokiai
自可 Ujika *s*
多 Uda *smh*
多川 Udagawa *s*
多津 Utazu *p*
多麻呂 Utamaro *m*
$^{7}$佐 Usa *sp*
佐川 Usagawa *s*
佐見 Usami *s*
佐美 Usami *s*
沢 Usawa *s*
豆磨 Uzumaro *m*
$^{8}$泥須 Unesu *s*
陀 Uda *sp*
陀児 Udaru *m*
陀酒部 Udanosakabe *s*
和 Uwa *p*
和川 Uwagawa *s*
和海 Uwaumi *p*
和野 Uwano *s*
和島 Uwajima *p*
知村 Ujimura *s*
奈月 Unazuki *p*
垣 Ugaki *s*
$^{9}$垣一成 U. Kazushige *mh*
治 Uji *sp*
治十帖 U. jūjō *l*
治川 Ujigawa *s*
治田 Ujita *s*
治田原 Uji Tawara *p*
治拾遺 U. shūi *l*
津 Utsu *s*
津木 Utsuki *s*
津保 Utsubo / Utsuho *l*
津宮 Utsunomiya *s*
津野 Utsuno *s*
美 Umi *p*
$^{10}$高 Udaka *s*
$^{11}$根 Une *s*
梶 Ukaji *s*
野 Uno *s*
野千代 U. Chiyo *fl*
野辺 Unobe *s*
野沢 Unozawa *s*
野信夫 Uno Nobuo *ml*
野浩二 U. Kōji *ml*
部 Ube *p*
都 Utsu *s*, Uto
都木 Utsuki *s*
都宮 Utsunomiya *sp*
都野 Utsuno *s*
都野研 U. Ken *ml*
宿 Ushiku *s*
留 Uru *s*
留野 Uruno *s*
島 Unoshima *s*
$^{12}$検 Uken *p*
喜田 Ukita *s*
喜多 Ukita *s*
喜多秀家 U. Hideie *mh*
賀 Uga *s*
賀神 Ukagami *s*
智 Uchi *p*
$^{13}$漢迷 Ukanume *s*
$^{14}$郷 Ugō *s*
$^{15}$鋪 Ushiki *s*
敷 Ushiki *s*
摩 Uma *p*
$^{16}$橋 Uhashi *s*
$^{18}$藤 Utō *s*

**芙** 286 Osamu *m.* (CHI)

**芊** 287 Shigeru *m.* (SEN, shige)
子 Shigeko *f*

**芋** 288 [O] (U, imo)
川 Imokawa *s*
毛 Ikumo *s*
田 Imoda *s*
淵 Imobuchi *s*
瀬 Imose *s*

**芝** 289 Shiba *sp.* (SHI, shiba, shige, shiku, fusa)
$^{3}$川 Shibakawa *sp*
小路 Shibakōji *s*
$^{4}$山 Shibayama *sp*
不器男 Shiba Fukio *ml*
木 Shibaki *s*
木好子 S. Yoshiko *fl*
$^{5}$田 Shibata *s*
本 Shibamoto *s*
生 Shibafu *s*
$^{6}$辻 Shibatsuji *s*
$^{7}$村 Shibamura *s*
$^{8}$金 Shibakin *m*
$^{9}$垣 Shibagaki *s*
亭 Shibatei *s*
$^{10}$原 Shibahara *s*
屋 Shibaya *s*
$^{11}$野 Shibano *s*
$^{12}$崎 Shibazaki *s*
間 Shibama *s*

—— 6 T4 ——

**尽** 290 [T] (JIN)
用而二分狂言 Tsukaihatashite nibu kyōgen *l*

**労** 291 Takashi *m.* (RIKI, RYOKU)

共 292 [T] (KYŌ, GU, tomo, taka)
和 Kyōwa *p*
昌 Tomomasa *m*
重 Tomoshige *m*
福 Tomosachi *m*

交 293 [T] Yoshimi *f.* (KŌ, KYŌ, tomo, kata, michi)
子 Michiko *f*
告 Kōketsu *s*
野 Katano *sp*

光 294 Hikaru *m.* (KŌ, mitsu)
寿 Mitsutoshi *m*

早 295 [T] (SŌ, SA, haya, saki)
[1]乙女 Saotome *s*; Sōtome *sp*
[3]川 Hayakawa *sp*
川幾忠 H. Ikutada *ml*
子 Hayako *f*
[4]水 Hayami *s*
[5]田 Hayata *s*, Sōda; Wasada *sp*
生 Hayanari *s*
[6]竹 Hayatake *s*, Satake
[7]坂 Hayasaka *s*
尾 Sōi *s*, Hayao
見 Hayami *s*
来 Hayakita *p*
[8]苗 Wase *s*; Sanae *f*
苗之助 Sanaenosuke *m*
良 Sōra *s*; Sawara *p*
[9]津 Hayatsu *s*
[10]速 Hayami *s*, Sasoku
馬 Hayama *s*
[11]野 Hayano *s*
船 Hayafune *s*
島 Hayashima *sp*
[12]崎 Hayazaki *s*
[13]雄 Hayao *m*
雲 Hayakumo *s*
[14]歌 Sōka *l*
稲 Wase *f*
稲田 Waseda *p*
[16]蕨 Sawarabi *l*
[18]藤 Hayatō *s*, Hayafuji
[19]瀬 Hayase *s*

## 6 T5

丞 296 [N] Susumu *m.* (JŌ, SHŌ, suke)

氏 297 (TEI, yuki, moto)
良 Tera *s*

## 6 F2

同 298 [T] Hitoshi *m*, Atsumu. (DŌ, atsu, tomo, nobu)
保 Atsuyasu *m*

夙 299 (SHUKU, asa, toshi, haya, tsuto)
子 Asako *f*, Toshiko
夜 Shukuya *m*
興 Toshioki *m*

旭 300 Asahi *sm-f-p*; Akira *m.* (KYOKU, KOKU, akira, teru, aki, asa, asahi)
川 Asahikawa *p*
志 Kyokushi *p*
信 Terunobu *m*
彦 Asahiko *m*

旬 301 [T] Hitoshi *m.* (JUN, toki, tada, masa, hira)
子 Tokiko *f*
江 Tokie *f*
殿実々記 Jun-Den jitsujitsuki *l*

灰 302 [T] (KAI, KE, hai)
野 Haino *s*
野庄平 H. Shōhei *ml*

有 303 [T] Tamotsu *m.* (YŪ, U, ari, tomo, mochi, nao, michi, ri, sumi, tō, nari, aru)
[3]川 Arikawa *sp*
三 Yūzō *m*
久 Tomohisa *m*
也 Naoya *m*
[4]元 Arimoto *s*
山 Ariyama *s*
王 Ariō *s*
井 Arii *s*
木 Ariki *s*
[5]功 Arikoto *m*; Isao *sp*
公 Aritomo *m*
田 Arita *sp*
允 Arisuke *m*
本 Arimoto *s*
本芳水 A. Hōsui *ml*
[6]江 Arie *s*
地 Arichi *s*
竹 Aritake *s*
光 Arimitsu *sm*
吉 Ariyoshi *sm*
吉佐和子 A. Sawako *fl*
在 Arasa *s*
[7]快 Ariyoshi *m*
坂 Arisaka *s*
沢 Arisawa *s*
村 Arimura *s*
言 Ariaya *m*
志太郎 Ushitarō *m*
条 Arieda *m*
尾 Ario *s*
我 Ariga *s*
[8]明 Ariake *sp*
幸郎 Arikōrō *ma*
忠 Tomotada *m*
尚 Aritaka *m*
良 Arikazu *m*
[9]法師 Arihōshi *s*
持 Arimochi *s*
松 Arimatsu *p*
泉 Ariizumi *s*
岡 Arioka *s*
[10]格 Arinori *m*
栖川 Arisugawa *s*
栖川宮熾仁 A.-no-miya Taruhito *mh*
容 Ariosa *m*
家 Ariie *m*; Arie *p*; Ariya *s*, Arake
為男 Uio *m*
原 Ariwara *s*, Arihara
馬 Arima *sp*
馬皇子 A. no Ōji *mh*
馬晴信 A. Harunobu *mh*
馬新七 A. Shinshichi *mh*
馬頼義 A. Yorichika *ml*
[11]野 Arino *s*
動 Udō *s*
梁 Arimune *m*
島 Arishima *s*
島生馬 A. Ikuma *mla*
島武郎 A. Takeo *ml*
[12]渡 Udo *s*
富 Aritomi *s*
森 Arimori *s*
象 Arikata *m*
賀 Ariga *s*, Aruga
賀長雄 Ariga Nagao *ml*
智子 Uchiko *f*
貳 Uni *s*
道 Arimichi *s*
[13]働 Udō *s*
滝 Aritaki *s*
福 Arifuku *s*
漢 Ukan *p*; Uma *s*
路 Ariji *s*
園 Arizono *s*
[16]凞 Arisato *m*
[18]藤 Arifuji *m*
[20]徽 Ariyoshi *m*
[21]磯 Ariso *s*

## 6 F3

后 304 [T] (KŌ, GU, kimi, mi, nochi)
子 Kimiko *f*

瓜 305 (KA, WA, uri)
田 Urita *s*
生 Uryū *s*
生忠夫 U. Tadao *ml*
谷 Uritani *s*
実 Urizane *m*
哇 Jawa *p* "Java"
破 Uriwari *s*
連 Urizura *p*
盗人 Uri nusubito *la*

式 306 [T] (SHIKI, SHOKU, nori, tsune, mochi)
子 Noriko *f*
子内親王 Shikishi Naishinnō *fl*
守 Shikimori *s*
亭三馬 Shikitei Sanba *ml*
胤 Noritane *m*
場 Shikiba *s*
場隆三郎 S. Ryūzaburō *ml*
部 Shikibu *mh-fh*

迅 307 [O] (JIN, toki, haya, toshi)
男 Tokio *m*
彦 Hayahiko *m*
瀬 Hayase *s*

匝 308 (SŌ)
嵯 Sōsa *sp*; Kōsa *s*

回 309 [T] (KAI, mawari)
道 Mawarimichi *s*

団 310 [T] Dan *s*; Madoka *f*. (DAN, TAN, maru, atsu)
々珍聞 Marumaru chinbun *l*
子森 Dangomori *s*
六 Danroku *m*
平 Danpei *m*
琢磨 Dan Takuma *mh*
野 Danno *s*

因 311 [T] Chinami *m*, Yukari. (IN, yori, yoru, yoshi, nami)
子 Yoriko *f*
支 Inaki *s*
香 Yoruka *f*
島 Innoshima *p*
幡 Inaba *ph*
幡堂 Inabadō *l*
藤 Indō *s*

向 312 [T] Mukō *m*; Mukai *s*. (KŌ, muki, muka, hisa, muke, mukai)
$^{3}$子 Hisako *f*
$^{4}$山 Mukōyama *s*, Mukaiyama
日 Mukō *p*
日葵 Higuruma *l*
井 Mukai *s*
井去来 M. Kyorai *ml*
$^{5}$田 Mukōda *s*, Muka-
$^{7}$坊 Mukaibō *s* ⌊da
坂 Sakisaka *s*
$^{8}$東 Mukaihigashi *p*
$^{9}$畑 Mukōbata *s*
$^{10}$原 Mukaihara *p*
高 Mukadaka *sp*
$^{11}$後 Kōgo *s*
野 Kono *s*
宿弥 Mukinosukune *m*
笠 Mugasa *s*
島 Mukaijima *p*

存 313 [T] Tamotsu *m*, Ariya, Yasushi, Susumu. (SON, ZON, masa, ari, naga, sada, tsugi, nobu, akira, yasu, aru)
子 Nagako *f*, Nobuko, Yasuko
久 Nagahisa *m*
男 Tsugio *m*
身 Masamoto *m*
保 Masayasu *m*

在 314 [T] Akira *m*, Mitsuru. (ZAI, SAI, ari, aki, sumi, tō, maki)
$^{3}$川 Arikawa *s*
子 Ariko *f*
$^{5}$田 Arita *s*
$^{7}$村 Arimura *m*
$^{8}$明 Ariake *m*
明亭 Ariaketei *s*
$^{9}$信 Arinobu *sm*
狭田 Arisada *s*
$^{10}$屋 Ariya *m*
原 Ariwara *s*, Arihara
原業平 Arihara / Ariwara no Narihira *ml*
$^{13}$経 Arinori *m*
$^{16}$賢 Akikata *m*
衡 Arihira *m*
$^{18}$藤 Saitō *s*

庄 315 [N] Shō *p*. (SHŌ, sō, masa)
$^{3}$川 Shōgawa *sp*
三郎 Shōzaburō *m*
子 Shōshi *s*
$^{4}$山 Shōyama *s*
内 Shōnai *sp*
五 Masakazu *m*
太郎 Shōtarō *m*
$^{5}$田 Shōda *s*
司 Shōji *s*
$^{7}$兵衛 Shōbee *m*
$^{8}$林 Shōbayashi *s*
和 Shōwa *p* ⌈hara *s*
$^{10}$原 Shōbara *sp*; Shō-
$^{11}$野 Shōno *s*
野潤三 S. Junzō *ml*
$^{15}$蔵 Shōzō *m*

広 316 [T] Hiroshi *m*; Hiro *s*. (KŌ, hiro, o, take, tō, mitsu)
$^{1}$一郎 Hiroichirō *m*
$^{2}$人 Hirondo *m*, Hirome
$^{3}$川 Hirokawa *sp*
大 Hironaga *m*
$^{4}$元 Hiromoto *m*
介 Hirosuke *m*
中 Hironaka *s*
井 Hiroi *s*
木 Hiroki *s*
戈 Hirohoko *m*
山 Hiroyama *s*
太 Hirota *m* ⌈tarō
太郎 Kōtarō *m*, Hiro-
$^{5}$矛 Hirohoko *m*
布 Hirotae *m*
斥 Hirokata *m*
田 Hirota *sp*
田社歌合 H.-sha utaawase *l*
田弘毅 H. Kōki *mh*
$^{6}$次 Hirotsugu *m*
次郎 Hirojirō *m*
江 Hiroe *s*
吉 Hirokichi *m*
弁 Hirowake *m*
守 Hiromori *m* ⌈si"
西 Kanshii *p* "Kwang-
虫 Hiromushi *m*
$^{7}$沢 Hirosawa *s*
助 Hirosuke *m*
谷 Hirotani *s*, Hiroya
志 Hiroshi *m*
尾 Hiroo *mp*
見 Hiromi *p*
$^{8}$沼 Hironuma *s*
国 Hirokuni *m* ⌈m
居 Hiroi *sm*; Hiroyasu
東 Kanton *p* "Canton, Kwangtung"
$^{9}$城 Hiroshige *m*
胖 Hironao *m*
神 Hirokami *p*
畑 Hirohata *s*
松 Hiromatsu *s*
相 Hiromi *m*
津 Hirotsu *s*
津和郎 H. Kazuo *ml*
津柳浪 H. Ryūrō *ml*
岡 Hirooka *s*
重 Hiroshige *ma*
$^{10}$海 Hiroumi *sm*, Hi-
原 Hirohara *s* ⌊rōmi
隆寺 Kōryūji *p*
庭 Hironiwa *sm*
屋 Hiroya *s*
通 Hiromichi *m*
$^{11}$惟 Hirokore *m*
野 Hirono *sp*
部 Hirobe *s*
曹 Hirotomo *m*
啓 Takehiro *ma*
島 Hiroshima *sp*
$^{12}$渡 Hirowatari *s*
崎 Hirosaki *s*
道 Hiromichi *m*
$^{13}$階 Hiroshina *s*
寛 Hirotomo *m*
楽 Hiroyoshi *m*
$^{15}$幡 Hirohata *s*
端 Hirohashi *sm*
蔵 Hirozō *m*
$^{16}$滋 Hiroshige *m*
橋 Hirohashi *s*
綾 Kōryō *p*
$^{19}$瀬 Hirose *sp*
瀬哲士 H. Tesshi *ml*
$^{21}$鰭 Hirohata *s*

—— 6 F4 ——

母 See 326

亙 317 [N] Watari *sm*, Wataru, Watasu; Tōru *m*. (KŌ, ⌊nobu)
理 Watari *s*

危 318 [T] (KI)
寸 Kiso *s*

気 319 [T] (KI, KE, oki)
比庄 Kibinoshō *s*
司 Keiji *m*
仙 Kesen *p*; Kesema *s*, Kemase
仙沼 Kesennuma *p*
作 Keisaku *m*
高 Kitaka *p*
賀 Kiga *s*
賀沢 Kigasawa *s*

辻 320 Tsuji *s*. (tsuji)
$^{3}$川 Tsujikawa *s*
子 Tsujiko *f*
$^{4}$元 Tsujimoto *s*
内 Tsujiuchi *s*
井 Tsujii *s*
$^{5}$田 Tsujita *s*
本 Tsujimoto *s*
$^{7}$沢 Tsujisawa *s*
村 Tsujimura *s*
$^{9}$岡 Tsujioka *s*
$^{10}$原 Tsujihara *s*
馬車 Tsujibasha *l*
$^{11}$野 Tsujino *s*
$^{12}$葩 Gahana *s*
$^{15}$潤 Tsuji Jun *ml*
$^{16}$橋 Tsujibashi *s*

戎 321 Ebisu *s*. (JŪ, ebisu, suke)
野 Ebisuno *s*

## 6 F5

**成** 322 [T] Shigeru *m*, Minoru, Sadamu, Osamu, Hakaru, Akira. (SEI, JŌ, nari, shige, fusa, hira, yoshi, naru, sada, masa, hide, aki, nori, michi)
$^{1}$一郎 Seiichirō *m*
$^{2}$人 Narito *m*
$^{3}$川 Narukawa *s*
之 Nariyuki *m*, Masayuki
子 Shigeko *f*, Naruko, Fusako, Sadako
$^{4}$仁 Fusahito *m*
元 Narimoto *m*
井 Narui *s*
木 Nariki *s*
毛 Narige *s*
$^{5}$田 Narita *sp*
立 Yoshitaka *m*
包 Narikane *m*
允 Shigemitsu *m*, Narimasa
$^{6}$羽 Nariwa *p*
年 Seinen *m*
$^{7}$沢 Narusawa *s*, Narisawa
谷 Naruya *s*
尾 Nario *s*, Narumo
見 Narumi *sm*
$^{8}$和 Narikazu *m*
命 Narinaga *m*
実 Narumi *m*, Shigemi
東 Narutō *p*
$^{9}$相 Nariai *s*, Narai; Shigemi *m*
亮 Masaki *m*
美 Seibi *ml*
$^{10}$海 Narumi *s*
家 Nariie *m*
烈 Naritsura *m*
$^{11}$彬 Nariaki *m*
章 Shigeaya *m*
島 Narushima *s*
島柳北 N. Ryūhoku *ml*
富 Naritomi *s*
尋 Jōjin *mh*
尋阿闍梨母集 J. Ajari Haha no shū *l*
達 Shigemichi *m*
$^{13}$塚 Naritsuka *s*
煥 Nariakira *m*
$^{14}$嘉 Nariyoshi *m*
節 Shigeyoshi *m*
$^{16}$親 Narichika *m*
$^{19}$蹊 Narimichi *m*
瀬 Naruse *s*
瀬仁蔵 N. Jinzō *mh*
瀬無極 N. Mukyoku *ml*

## 6 U

**凸** 323 Takashi *m*. (TOTSU)

**虫** 324 [T] (CHŪ, mushi)
めづる姫君 Mushi mezuru himegimi *l*
生 Mushifu *s*
鹿 Mushika *s*
雄 Mushio *m*
麿 Mushimaro *m*

**亦** 325 [N] (EKI, YAKU, mata)
太郎 Matatarō *m*
助 Matasuke *m*
雄 Matao *m*
野 Matano *s*

**母** 326 [T] (BO, MO)
子叙情 Boshi jojō *l*
末 Bomatsu *s*
台 Motai *s*, Gudai
袋 Motai *s*

**曲** 327 [T] (KYOKU, KOKU, nori, kuma, ma, maga, magari)
$^{4}$山人 Kyokusanjin *ml*
水 Kyokusui *l*
水宴和歌 K.-no-en waka *l*
木 Magariki *s*, Magariki
$^{5}$田 Magata *s*
$^{7}$沢 Magarisawa *s*
$^{9}$垣 Magaki *s*
亭馬琴 Kyokutei Bakin *ml*
直 Mana *s*
直部 Manabe *s*
直瀬 Manase *s*
$^{13}$淵 Magaribuchi *s*
$^{15}$舞 Kusemai *la*
$^{19}$瀬 Magase *s*

**戍** 328 (JU, SHU, mori)
光 Morimitsu *m*

**吏** 329 [T] Tsukasa *m*. (RI, sato, osa)

**弗** 330 (FUTSU)
措 Fusso *s*

**耳** 331 [T] (JI, NI, mi, mimi)
次郎 Mimijirō *m*
名宇 Jinō *s*
底記 Jiteiki *l*
塵集 Nijinshū *l*
瓔珞 Mimi yōraku *l*

**聿** 332 Noboru *m*. (ITSU, ICHI, nobu, kore, yo)
子 Nobuko *f*

**民** 333 [T] Tami *sf*; Mitami *sm*. (MIN, mi, tami, hito, moto)
之助 Taminosuke *m*
平 Minpei *m*
形 Tamigata *s*
谷 Tamiya *s*
使主 Mitaminoomi *s*
彦 Tamihiko *m*
陟 Tamitaka *m*
部 Minbu *m*
輔 Tamisuke *m*
衛 Tamie *m*

**老** 334 [T] Oi *m*. (RŌ, oi, omi, oyu, toshi, fuka)
$^{2}$人 Otona *m*
$^{3}$川 Oikawa *s*
子 Rōshi *mlh* "Lao-tzu"
$^{4}$夫 Otona *m*
$^{5}$田 Oida *s*
$^{6}$江 Oie *f*
名子 Ominako *f*
$^{7}$見 Fukami *s*
$^{8}$武者 Rōmusha *l*
$^{9}$沼 Oinuma *s*
松 Oimatsu *la*
$^{10}$馬 Onma *s*, Onba
$^{11}$麻呂 Oimaro *m*
$^{13}$葉 Wakuraba *l*
$^{15}$鼠堂永機 Rōsodō Eiki *ml*
$^{19}$蘇の森 Oiso no mori *l*

**世** 335 [T] (SE, SEI, yo, tsugi, tsugu, toki, toshi)
$^{4}$仁 Tsuguhito *m*
木 Seki *s*
$^{5}$古 Seko *s*
田 Seta *s*
田谷 Setagaya *p*
$^{6}$吉 Tsugiyoshi *m*; Yoyoshi *l*
$^{7}$谷 Seya *s*
安 Toshiyasu *m*
$^{8}$阿弥 Zeami *mla*
知原 Sechibara *p*
茂 Tsugishige *m*
良 Tokinaga *m*; Sera *s*
良田 Serata *s*
$^{9}$津谷 Setsuya *s*
$^{10}$家真 Seyama *s*
$^{12}$尊寺 Sesonji *s*
間子息気質 Seken musuko katagi *l*
間手代気質 S. tedai katagi *l*
間妾気質 S. tekake katagi *l*
間胸算用 S. munezan'yō *l*
間娘容気 S. musume katagi *l*
$^{13}$誠 Tsuguyoshi *m*
$^{14}$徳 Tsugunori *m*
$^{16}$継 Yotsugi *s*
継曾我 Y. Soga *la*
$^{21}$羅 Sera *sp*
羅西 Seranishi *p*

**西** 336 [T] Nishi *sp*; Sai *s*. (SEI, SAI, nishi, aki, shi)
ケ谷 Nishigaya *s*
$^{2}$八代 Nishi-yashiro *p*
入 Nishiiri *s*
$^{3}$川 Nishikawa *sp*
川光二郎 N. Kōjirō *ml*
川如見 N. Joken *mh*
大寺 Saidaiji *p*; Nishiōji *s*
大条 Nishōeda *s*, Nishioida
大枝 Nishiōeda *s*
大音 Nishimorinai *s*
大路 Nishiōji *s*
口 Nishiguchi *s*
之表 Nishinoomote *p*
土佐 Nishi-tosa *p*
久保 Nishikubo *s*
上 Nishigami *s*

[4]元 Nishimoto *s*
内 Nishiuchi *s*, Nishinouchi
方 Nishikata *p*
文 Kawachinofumi *s*, Kōchinofumi
王母 Seiōbo *la* "Hsi-wang-mu"
五辻 Nishiitsutsuji *s*
井 Nishii *s*
片 Nishikata *s*
木 Nishiki *p*
木戸 Nishikido *s*
山 Nishiyama *sp*
山泊雲 N. Hakuun *ml*
山宗因 N. Sōin *ml*
中 Nishinaka *s*
[5]加茂 Nishi-kamo *s*
代 Nishidai *s*
公談抄 Saikō danshō *l*
四辻 Nishiyotsutsuji *s*
本 Nishimoto *s*
白河 Nishi-shirakawa
目 Nishime *sp* ⌊*p*
目屋 Nishimeya *p*
田 Nishida *sp*
田天香 N. Tenkō *ml*
田幾多郎 N. Kitarō *mlh*
田川 Nishi-tagawa *p*
平 Nishihira *s*
[6]仙北 Nishi-senboku *p*
伊豆 Nishi-izu *p*
池 Nishiike *s*
行 Saigyō *ml*
行桜 S.-zakura *la*
合志 Nishi-gōshi *p*
宇和 Nishi-uwa *p*
吉野 Nishi-yoshino *p*
有 Nishiari *s*
有田 Nishi-arita *p*
有家 Nishi-arie *p*
広 Nishihiro *s*
成 Nishinari *sp*
臼杵 Nishi-usuki *p*
名 Nishina *s*
多摩 Nishi-tama *p*
[7]伯 Saihaku *p*
伯利亜 Shiberia *p* "Siberia"
坂 Nishizaka *s*
沢 Nishizawa *s*
形 Nishikata *s*
村 Nishimura *s* ⌈*p*
村山 Nishi-murayama
村天囚 Nishimura Tenshū *ml*
村茂樹 N. Shigeki *mlh*
村陽吉 N. Yōkichi *ml*
那須野 Nishi-nasuno *p*
谷 Nishitani *sp*; Nishinoya *s*
会津 Nishi-aizu *p*
芳寺 Saihōji *p*
牟田 Nishimuda *s*
牟婁 Nishi-muro *p*
条 Saijō *sp*
条八十 S. Yaso *ml*
尾 Nishio *sp*
貝 Nishigai *s*
来居 Sairaikyo *s*
出 Nishiide *s*
出朝風 N. Chōfū *ml*
角 Nishikado *s*
[8]河 Nishikawa *s*
河原 Nishigawara *s*
泥部 Nishihijirikobe *s*
彼 Seihi *p*
彼杵 Nishi-sonogi *p*
林 Nishibayashi *s*
牧 Nishimaki *s*, Saimoku
邨 Nishimura *s*
京 Nishinokyō *sp*
念 Sainen *s*
宗 Nishimune *s*
周 Nishi Amane *mlh*
居 Nishii *s*
国 Saikoku *sp*
国立志編 S. risshihen *l*
国東 Nishi-kunisaki *p*
武 Seibu *p*
東 Saitō *s*
東三鬼 S. Sanki *ml*
東院 Nishinotoi *s*
[9]保 Nishio *s*
依 Nishiyori *s*
垣 Nishigaki *s*
城 Saijō *s*
洞院 Nishinotōin *sp*, Nishinotoi
浅井 Nishi-asai *p*
津軽 Nishi-tsugaru *p*
洋道中膝栗毛 Seiyō dōchū hizakurige *l*
畑 Nishihata *s*
枇杷島 Nishi-biwajima *p*
松 Nishimatsu *s*
松浦 Nishi-matsuura
神 Nishigami *s* ⌊*p*
祖谷山 Nishi-iya-
面 Nishio *s* ⌊yama *p*
南北 Shinata *m*
茨城 Nishi-ibaraki *p*
巻 Nishimaki *s*
春 Nishiharu *p*
春日井 Nishi-kasugai *p* ⌈*p*
春近 Nishi-haruchika
岡 Nishioka *s*
[10]浦 Nishiura *s* ⌈kai *p*
海 Nishiumi *sp*; Sai-
海枝 Saikachi *sm*
海道 Saikaidō *p*
陣 Nishijin *p*
班牙 Supein *p* "Spain"
桂 Nishi-katsura *p*
脇 Nishiwaki *sp*
脇順三郎 N. Junzaburō *ml*
郡 Nishigōri *s*
高辻 Nishitakatsuji *s*
倉 Nishikura *s*
貢 Saigon *p* "Saigon"
宮 Nishimiya *s*; Nishinomiya *sp*
宮藤朝 Nishinomiya Tōchō *ml*
原 Nishihara *sp*; Sai-
座 Nishiza *s* ⌊hara *s*
馬音内 Nishimonai *s*
[11]淀川 Nishi-yodoga-
淡 Seitan *p* ⌊wa *p*
隆寺 Sairyūji *s*
域 Seiiki *plh* ⌈*p*
桜島 Nishi-sakurajima
根 Nishine *p*
野 Nishino *s* ⌈*ml*
野辰吉 N. Tatsukichi
野入 Nishinoiri *s*
都 Saito *s*
部 Nishibe *s*
紀 Nishiki *p*
翁十百韵 Saiō toppyakuin *l*
垩 Kawachihiji *s*
垩部 Kawachihijibe *s*, Nishihijirikobe
島 Nishijima *s*; Nishinoshima *sp*
島麦南 Nishijima Bakunan *ml*
亀 Nishiki *s*
[12]崎 Nishizaki *s*
勝 Nishikatsu *s*
森 Nishimori *s*
賀 Saiga *s*
粟倉 Nishi-awakura *p*
筑摩 Nishi-chikuma *p*
間 Nishima *s*
[13]堀 Nishibori *s*
塚 Nishizuka *s*
新 Nishiara *s*
蒲原 Nishi-kanbara *p*
園 Nishizono *s*
園寺 Saionji *s*
園寺公望 S. Kinmochi *mh*
[14]暢 Akinobu *m*
漢 Kōchinoaya *s*
漢文 Kawachinoayanofumi *s*
郷 Saigō *sp*; Nishigō *p*
郷隆盛 S. Takamori *mh* ⌈chi *mh*
郷従道 S. Tsugumi-
置賜 Nishi-okitama *p*
[15]潟 Nishigata *s*
諸県 Nishi-morokata *p* ⌈bet"
蔵 Chibetto *p* "Ti-
磐井 Nishi-iwai *p*
[16]興部 Nishi-okoppe *p*
[17]館 Nishidate *s*
[18]藤 Saitō *s*
[19]頸城 Nishi-kubiki *p*
願 Seigen *s*
礪波 Nishi-tonami *p*
[20]織 Nishiori *s*
[21]鶴 Saikaku *ml*
鶴諸国咄 S. shokokubanashi *l* ⌈ge *l*
鶴置土産 S. okimiya-
鶴織留 S. oritome *l*
羅 Sera *s*

## 血 337 [T] (KETSU, KECHI, chi)

沼 Chinuma *s*
脇 Chiwaki *s*
槍九郎 Chiyarikurō *m*
鎗太郎 Chiyaritarō *m*

## 臼 338 (KYŪ, usu)

井 Usui *s*
井大翼 U. Taiyoku *ml*
井吉見 U. Yoshimi *ml*
田 Usuda *sp*
田亜浪 U. Arō *ml*
杵 Usuki *sp*; Usukine
射 Usui *s* ⌊*s*
倉 Usukura *s*

## 舟 339 [T] (SHŪ, SHU, fune, nori)

弗耳聿民老世西血臼舟▼自朱年米弁争色名多▲児冴冷似但佃伸位住伻

[4]戸 Funado s
井 Funai s
木 Funaki s ⌈ml
木重信 F. Shigenobu
山 Funayama s
[5]本 Funamoto s
生 Funyū s
[7]形 Funagata p
見 Funami s
[8]波 Funanami s
[9]津 Funatsu s
岡 Funaoka s
[13]越 Funakoshi s
[16]橋 Funabashi sp
橋聖一 F. Seiichi ml
橋宣賢 F. Nobukata mh

自 340 [T] (JI, SHI, yori, kore, sada, ono)
在丸 Jizaimaru s
助 Onosuke m
見 Jiken s
明 Yoriakira m
国 Yorikuni m
笑 Jishō ml
然居士 Jinen Koji la
鳴鐘 Jimeishō l
綱 Koretsuna m

朱 341 [T] Akemi f; Shu s. (SHU, SU, ake, aya)
子 Ayako f; Shushi mlh "Chu-tzu"
子学 Shushigaku h
門 Shumon l
実 Akemi f
華 Akeha f
馬 Hanba s
鳥 Suchō s ⌈mh
雀 Susaki s; Suzaku
舜水 Shu Shunsui mh
楽 Akera s
楽菅公 A. Kankō ml
欒 Zanboa l

年 342 [T] Minoru m, Susumu. (NEN, toshi, tose, to, kazu, chika)
子 Toshiko f
中行事秘抄 Nenjū gyōji hishō l
立 Toshitatsu m
助 Toshisuke m
美 Toshiharu m
魚 Toshio m
魚麿 Ayumaro m
雄 Kazuo m

米 343 [T] Yone s. (BEI, MAI, yone, kome, mitsu)
[3]川 Yonekawa s
川正夫 Y. Masao ml
子 Yoneko f; Yonago
久保 Yonekubo s ⌊p
丸 Yonemaru s
[4]水津 Yonōzu p
元 Yonemoto s
山 Yoneyama sp; Yonayama s
太郎 Yonetarō m
木 Meki s
井 Yonei s
内 Yonai s
内山 Yonaiyama s, Yonayama
内光政 Yonai Mitsumasa mh
[5]田 Yoneda s, Komeda, Maida
田雄郎 Y. Yūrō ml
市 Yoneichi s
本 Yonemoto s
生 Komefu s
[6]次郎 Yonejirō m
守 Komemori m
吉 Yonekichi m
光 Yonemitsu s
多比 Metabi s, Netami
[7]村 Yonemura s
沢 Yonezawa sp
沢順子 Y. Junko fl
谷 Yoneya s, Kometani, Maiya, Yonetani
里 Yonesato s
[8]林 Yonebayashi s
良 Mera s
[9]持 Yonemochi s, Komechi
津 Yonetsu s, Yonekizu
松 Yonematsu m
岡 Yoneoka s
[10]倉 Yonekura s
原 Yonehara s; Maibara p
屋 Komeya s
造 Yonezō m
[11]野 Meno s, Yoneno
島 Yonejima s
[12]崎 Yonezaki s
集 Yokitsume s
[14]窪 Yonekubo s
[15]蔵 Yonezō m
餅搗 Shitokitsuki s
[16]橋 Yonebashi s
錦 Nishigori s

弁 See 275

争 344 [T] Saka s. (SŌ, saka)
戸 Sakabe s

色 345 [T] (SHOKU, SHIKI, iro, shiko)
川 Irokawa s
子 Iroko f
布知 Shikofuchi m
田 Irota s
主 Ironushi m
竹歌祭文揃 Irotake utazaimon-zoroe l
音論 Shikionron l
部 Irobe s
麻 Shikama p
樹 Iroki m
懺悔 Irozange l

名 346 [T] Nazuku m-f; Akira m; Natori s. (MEI, MYŌ, na, kata, mori, akira)
[3]川 Nagawa sp
子 Nako s
久井 Nakui s
[4]木 Naki s
[5]代 Nashiro m
古屋 Nagoya sp
立 Nadachi p
氏 Shōji s
田 Natta s
田庄 Natashō p
[6]合 Nago s
西 Myōsai sp
[7]見崎 Namizaki s
村 Namura s
足 Nataru m
児形 Nagokata s
児耶 Nagoya s
[8]波 Nanami s
所記 Meishoki l
和 Nawa sp
和長年 N. Nagatoshi mh
取 Natori sp
取川 Natorigawa l
東 Myōtō sp
垂 Natari m
[9]畑 Nahata s
草 Nakusa s
美崎 Namizaki s
[10]倉 Nagura s
栗 Naguri p
[11]執 Natori s
雪 Nayuki s
島 Najima s
理 Natori s
寄 Nayoro p
鳥 Natori m
[12]賀 Naga p
[13]塚 Nazuka s
張 Nabari p
越 Nagoshi s, Nagoe, Nagoya
[14]種 Nagusa s
[19]瀬 Nase p
鏡 Meikyō s
[20]護屋 Nagoya s

多 347 [T] Ōshi sm, Ōno; Ō s, Ōi; Masaru m. (TA, kazu, na, ō, tomi, masa, nao, masaru)
[1]一 Taichi m
[3]川 Tagawa s
之衛門 Tanoemon m
上 Tagami s
子 Kazuko f, Masaruko; Tako s
久 Taku sp
[4]戸 Tado s
内 Tauchi s
木 Taki s
[5]古 Tako s
可 Taka p
尻 Tajiri s
目 Tame s
田 Tada s
田不二 T. Fuji ml
田南嶺 T. Nanrei ml
田裕計 T. Yūkei ml
田爺 T. no Jijii ml
[6]仲 Tachū m
伎 Taki p
米 Tame s
気 Taki sp; Take s
名 Tana s
多 Tada s
多良 Tatara s
多羅 Tatara s
[7]助 Tasuke m, Tasuku

利男 Tario *m*
兵衛 Tahee *m*
[8]門 Ōkado *s*, Tamon
和田 Tawada *s*
岐川 Takigawa *s*
岐川恭 T. Kyō *ml*
芸 Tagi *s*
武保 Tanbo *s*
武峰 Tōnomine *sph*
武峰少将 T. shōshō *l*
良木 Taragi *p*
良見 Tarami *p*
[9]畑 Tabata *s*
胡 Tako *s*
治 Tajihi *s*
治比 Tajihi *s*
治見 Tajimi *sp*
栄 Tomihide *m*
度 Tado *p*
度志 Tadoshi *p*
度津 Tadotsu *sp*
[10]浦 Taura *s*
記 Taki *s*
甚古村 Tajinko-mura *l*
[11]情仏心 Tajō busshin *l*
部 Tabe *s*, Tanabe
野 Tano *sp*
紀 Taki *sp*
島 Tajima *s*
[12]湖 Tako *s*
須久 Tasuku *m*
納 Tanō *s*
賀 Taga *sp*
賀谷 Tagaya *s*
賀城 Tagajō *p*
喜 Taki *s*
喜二 Takiji *m*
喜沢 Takizawa *s*
喜男 Takio *m*
喜蔵 Takizō *m*
喜麿 Takima *m*
[13]勢 Tase *s*
[14]聞 Tamon *m*
槸 Tane *s*
端 Tabata *s*
[15]摩 Tama *p*
磨 Tama *s*
[21]羅尾 Tarao *s*

—— 7 L1–2 ——

児 See 497

冴 348 (KO, GO, sae)
子 Saeko *f*

冷 349 [T] Suzushi *m*. (REI, RYŌ, hiya)
川 Hiyakawa *s*
子洞房 Musukobeya *l*
牟田 Hiyamuda *s*
泉 Reizei *smh*
泉為相 R. Tamesuke *ml*

似 350 [T] Nitori *s*. (JI, SHI, i, ni, nori, ari, are, kata, chika, nise)
内 Nitanai *sp*
鳥 Nitadori *sp*
絵 Nise-e *a*

但 351 [O] (TAN, DAN, tada)
木 Tadaki *sp*
夫 Tadao *m*
次 Tadatsugu *m*
見 Tajimi *m*
東 Tantō *p*
馬 Tajima *ph*
野 Tajino *s*

佃 352 Tsukuda *sm*. (DEN)

伸 353 [T] Noburu *m*, Nobiru, Nobu, Noboru; Shin *sm*. (SHIN, nobu, tada)
子 Nobuko *f-l*; Tadako *f*
次郎 Nobujirō *m*
雄 Nobuo *m*
愛 Nobunaru *m*
顕 Nobuaki *m*

位 354 [T] Takashi *m*. (I, taka, kura, nori, tsura, hiko, hira, mi, tada, nari)
田 Inden *s*
彦 Norihiko *m*

住 355 [T] Sumi *s*. (JU, JŪ, sumi, oki, mochi, yoshi)
[3]川 Sumikawa *s*
[4]友 Sumitomo *s*
山 Sumiyama *s*
井 Sumii *s*
[5]田 Sumita *sp*
用 Sumiyō *p*
[6]江 Suminoe *s*
吉 Sumiyoshi *sp-l*; Suminoe *s*
吉具慶 Sumiyoshi Gukei *ma*
吉造 S.-zukuri *a*
吉詣 S. mōde *la*
[7]谷 Sumitani *s*
[8]英 Sumihide *m*
[11]野 Sumino *s*
[12]道 Suminoto *s*, Sumuji
[13]雄 Sumio *m*
跡 Suminoto *s*

伻 356 Tsukō *m*, Tayori. (HYŌ, suki, sumi, tori)

伽 357 (KA, KYA)
羅 Kyara *s*; Kara *ph* "Kaya / Karak"
羅枕 Kyara makura *l*

体 358 [T] (TAI, TEI, nari, moto, mi)
子 Nariko *f*
仁 Narihito *m*

伝 359 [T] Den *sm*; Tsutō *m*, Tsutae, Tsutomu. (DEN, tsugu, nobu, nori, tada, tsuta, yoshi)
[1]一郎 Den'ichirō *m*
[2]二郎 Denjirō *m*, Tsugujirō
[3]三郎 Denzaburō *m*
[4]五郎 Dengorō *m*
[5]田 Denda *s*
右衛門 Den'emon *m*
平 Denbei *m*
[6]次 Denji *m*, Tadatsugu
[7]作 Densaku *m*
助 Densuke *m*
兵衛 Denbee *m*
[9]法輪 Denpōrin *s*, Teburi
治 Denji *m*
彦 Tsutahiko *m*
[11]教 Dengyō *mh*
[13]義 Nobuyoshi *m*
[14]槌 Tentsuchi *m*
[15]蔵 Denzō *m*

仰 360 [T] Aogu *m*. (KŌ, GYŌ, GŌ, taka, mochi)
木 Aogi *s*, Ōki

伴 361 [T] Ban *s*, Tomo, Tomonai. (BAN, HAN, tomo, suke)
三 Hanzō *m*
久 Sukehisa *m*
田 Banda *s*
平 Banpei *m*
林 Tomobayashi *s*, Banbayashi
信 Tomonobu *m*
信友 Ban Nobutomo *mla*
馬 Banba *s*
野 Tomono *s*, Banno
部 Tomobe *s*
善男 Tomo no Yoshio *mh*

作 362 [T] Tsukuru *m*. (SAKU, SA, nari, tomo, ari, nao, fuka, tsukuri)
[3]三郎 Sakusaburō *m*
之助 Sakunosuke *m*
[4]太郎 Sakutarō *m*
山 Sakuyama *s*
手 Tsukude *p*
木 Sakugi *p*
木綿 Yūtsukuri *s*
[5]田 Sakuda *s*
平 Sakuhei *m*
本 Narimoto *s*, Sakumoto
[6]次 Sakuji *m*
名 Sakuna *s*
[8]並 Sakunami *s*
東 Sakutō *p*
[10]屋 Sakuya *s*
造 Sakuzō *m*
[11]根 Sakune *s*
[12]間 Sakuma *s*
[13]楽 Sakura *m*
楽戸 Sakurado *sm*
楽園 Sakurazono *m*

伯 363 [T] Hakata *s*, Hata, Murako. (HAKU, nori, o, tomo, taka, osa, michi, ho, ku, haka, take)
[3]子 Tomoko *f*
[4]方 Hakata *sp*
太 Hakata *sp*; Hakuta *p*
[6]仙 Hakusen *p*
伎 Hōki *ph*
母ケ酒 Oba ga sake *la*
母捨 Obasute *la*
[7]伯部 Hōkabe *s*

舟 自 朱 年 米 弁 争 色 名 多 ▼ 児 冴 冷 似 但 佃 伸 位 住 伻 伽 体 伝 仰 伴 作 伯 ▲ 佑 佐 状 狂 舛 役 吟 吹 忱 快

位 住 伻 伽 体 伝 仰 伴 作 伯 ▼ 佑 佐 状 狂 舛 役 吟 吹 忱 快 ▲ 阡 防 阪 收 攷 孜 改 攻 技 択

伯壁 Hōkabe *s*
男 Osao *m*
孝 Michitaka *m*
$^{8}$明 Noriaki *m*
岐 Hahaki *s* ⌈lin"
林 Berurin *p* "Ber-
$^{10}$耆 Hōki *ph*
耆原 Hōkiwara *s*
$^{11}$麻呂 Hakamaro *m*

佑 364 Tasuku *m.* (YŪ, U, suke)
山 Sukeyama *p*
貞 Sukesada *m*

佐 365 [T] Tasuku *m.* (SA, suke, yo- ⌊shi)
$^{1}$一 Saichi *m*
$^{2}$八 Sahachi *m*
七 Sashichi *m*
$^{3}$川 Sagawa *sp*
川田 Sakawada *s*
三 Sazō *m*
之治 Sanoharu *m*
上 Sagami *s*
下橋 Sakabashi *s*
土原 Sadowara *sp*
々 Sassa *s*, Sasa
々木 Sasaki *s*
々木小次郎 S. Kojirō *l* ⌈na *ml*
々木弘綱 S. Hirotsu-
々木邦 S. Kuni *ml*
々木孝丸 S. Takamaru *ml* ⌈zō *ml*
々木味津三 S. Mitsu-
々木信綱 S. Nobutsuna *mh* ⌈na *mh-la*
々木高綱 S. Takatsu-
々木基一 S. Kiichi *ml*
々成政 Sassa Narimasa *mh*
々醒雪 S. Seisetsu *ml*
久 Saku *p*
久山 Sakuyama *s*
久間 Sakuma *sp*
久間貞一 S. Teiichi *mh*
久間象山 S. Zōzan *mh*
口 Sakuchi *s*
$^{4}$介 Sakai *s*, Sasuke
分 Saburi *s*, Saori
分利 Saburi *s*
中太 Sachūda *s*
方 Sakata *s*
山 Sayama *sm*
井 Sai *sp*
太 Sada *s*
太郎 Satarō *m*
$^{5}$代 Sade *s*, Sachi
古 Sako *s* ⌈ml
古純一郎 S. Jun'ichirō
左木 Sasaki *s*
左木俊郎 S. Toshirō
田 Sada *sp* ⌊ml
用 Sayo *sp*
本 Samoto *s*
生 Sashō *s*
$^{6}$仲 Sanaka *s*
竹 Satake *s* ⌈hanai
羽内 Sawauchi *s*, Sa-
吉 Sakichi *m*
自努 Sajinu *s*
多 Sata *sp*
多稲子 S. Ineko *fl*
世 Sase *s*; Suketsugi *m*
世山 Saseyama *s*
世保 Sasebo *p*
$^{7}$沢 Sazawa *s*
那河内 Sanagōchi *p*
伝 Yoshinori *m*
伯 Saeki *sp*, Saiki
伯彰一 Saeki Shōichi *ml*
佐 Sassa *sp*, Sasa
佐川 Sasakawa *s*
佐井 Sasai *s*
佐木 Sasaki *s* ⌈ml
佐木茂索 S. Mosaku
佐木信綱 S. Nobutsu-
佐布 Sasō *s* ⌊na *ml*
佐田 Sasada *s*
佐生 Sasō *s*
佐倉 Sasakura *s*
佐原 Sasahara *s*
佐部 Sasabe *s*
佐貴山 Sasakiyama *s*
谷 Sukeya *s*, Satani
呂間 Saroma *s*
尾 Sao *s*
$^{8}$味 Sami *s*
和田 Sawada *p*
波 Sawa *sp*, Saba; Sa-
京 Sakyō *sp* ⌊nami *s*
奈 Sana *s*
奈宜 Sanagu *s*
宗 Sasō *s*
忠 Suketada *m* ⌈ke *s*
武 Suketake *m*; Sata-
良 Sarara *s*, Sara
東 Satō *p*
$^{9}$治 Saji *sp*; Sachi *s*
保 Saho *s*
保田 Sahota *s*
保山 Saoyama *sla*
俣 Samata *s*
香 Saka *s*
$^{10}$海 Sami *s*
柳 Sayanagi *s* ⌈Sōki
脇 Sawaki *s*, Saiki,
倉 Sakura *sp*
倉宗吾 S. Sōgo *mh*
原 Sawara *sp*
怒賀 Sanuga *s*
屋 Saya *sp*
$^{11}$理 Suketaka *m*
都 Sato *s*; Satsu *f*
野 Sano *sp*
野川 Sanokawa *s*
野学 Sano Manabu *ml*
野常民 S. Tsunetami *mh*
鳥 Satori *s*
$^{12}$粧 Sashō *s*
渡 Sado *sp*
渡山 Sadoyama *s*
渡狐 Sado-gitsune *la*
渡島 Sadoshima *sp-l*
善 Saze *s*
賀 Saga *sp*
賀関 Saganoseki *p*
貫 Sanuki *s*
$^{13}$満 Sama *s*
塚 Satsuka *s*
$^{14}$郷 Sagō *s*
$^{16}$橋 Sabashi *s*, Sabase
興 Sukeoki *m*
$^{17}$綱 Sakō *m*
$^{18}$藤 Satō *s*
藤一英 S. Ichiei *ml*
藤佐太郎 S. Satarō *ml*
藤信淵 S. Nobuhiro *mh*
藤春夫 S. Haruo *ml*
藤直方 S. Naokata *mh*
藤紅緑 S. Kōroku *ml*
藤義亮 S. Yoshisuke *ml*
藤義清 S. Norikiyo *ml*
藤惣之助 S. Sōnosuke
雙 Sasō *s* ⌊ml
$^{19}$瀬 Sase *s*
鏡 Sakyō *s*
$^{20}$織 Saori *p*

## 7 L3

状 365A [T] (JŌ, kata, nori)

狂 366 [T] (KYŌ, KŌ, yoshi)
い凧 Kuruidako *l*
句 Kyōku *l*
四郎 Yoshishirō *m*
言 Kyōgen *la*
雲集 Kyōunshū *l*
歌 Kyōka *l*

舛 367 Noboru *m*; Masu *f.* (SEN, SHUN, masu)
水 Masumizu *s*
田 Masuda *s*
本 Masumoto *s*
明 Masuaki *sm*
岡 Masuoka *s*

役 368 [T] Mamoru *m*; Ōse *s.* (EKI, YAKU, yuki, tsura, mata) ⌈mh-p-la
の行者 En-no-gyōja
小角 En no Ozunu *mh*
者口三味線 Yakusha kuchi-jamisen *l*
者論語 Y. rongo *l*
賀 Mataka *s*

吟 369 [T] Akira *m.* (GIN, GON, oto, koe)

吹 370 [T] Suita *s.* (SUI, fuki, fuke, fuku, fu, kaze)
上 Fukiage *sp*
山 Fukiyama *s*
井 Fukii *s*
田 Suita *sp*; Fukita *s*
田順助 S. Junsuke *ml*
負 Fukui *m*; Fukei *s*
野 Fukino *s*
智 Shiuchi *s*
雄 Fukio *m*

忱 371 Makoto *m*, Tadasu. (SHIN, JIN)

快 372 [T] (KAI, yoshi, yasu, haya)
之 Yasuyuki *m*
子 Yoshiko *f*
彦 Yasuhiko *m*
温 Hayaatsu *m*
雄 Yoshio *m*
彰 Yoshitada *m*
慶 Kaikei *ma*

阱 373 (SHŌ, nori)
尚 Noriyori *m*

防 374 [T] (BŌ, fuse)
人 Sakimori *m*
夫 Atato *s*
府 Bōfu *p*

阪 375 (HAN, saka)
口 Sakaguchi *s*
上 Sakanoe *s*, Sakaga-
井 Sakai *s* ⌊gami
井久良伎 S. Kuraki *ml*
本 Sakamoto *s*
本越郎 S. Etsurō *ml*
田 Sakata *s*
谷 Sakatani *s*
庭 Sakaniwa *s*
根 Sakane *s*
部 Sakabe *s*
寄 Sakayori *s*

收 376 See 収 133

攷 377 Tsutomu *m.* (KŌ, nari)

孜 378 Tsutomu *m*, Tadasu. (SHI,
子 Atsuko *f* ⌊atsu)

改 379 [T] (KAI, ara)
井 Kaii *s*
田 Kaida *s*

攻 380 [T] Osamu *m.* (KŌ, KU, yoshi)
質 Yoshimoto *m*

技 381 [T] (KI, GI, aya, waza)
美 Wazayoshi *m*

択 382 [T] Eramu *m.* (TAKU, JAKU,
田 Erita *s* ⌊eri)

扶 383 [T] Tamotsu *m.* (FU, suke, moto)
子 Motoko *f*
信 Sukenobu *m*

桑 Fusō *p*
桑略記 F. ryakuki *l*
桑集 Fusōshū *l*

抜 384 [T] Yahazu *m.* (BATSU, nuki, nuke)
山 Nukiyama *s*
気太首 Nukike no Futokubi *ml*
殻 Nukegara *l*

折 385 [T] (SETSU, SECHI, ori)
[3]下 Orishimo *s*
山 Oriyama *s*
口 Origuchi *s*
口信夫 O. Shinobu *ml*
[4]井 Orii *s*
戸 Orito *s*
[5]本 Orimoto *s*
田 Orita *s*
[8]茂 Orimo *s*
居 Orii *s*
[10]原 Orihara *s*
[11]笠 Origasa *s*
[12]焚く柴の記 Oritaku shiba no ki *lh*
[16]橋 Orihashi *s*

址 386 (SHI, moto)
子 Motoko *f*

均 387 [T] Hitoshi *m.* (KIN, hira, o, nao, tada, nari, masa)
一 Kin'ichi *m*
平 Kinpei *m*
光 Naomitsu *m*

坏 388 (HAI, tsuki)
作 Tsukitsukuri *s*

坊 389 [T] (BŌ) ⌈chimoto
本 Bōnomoto *s*, Ma-
門 Bōmon *s*
城 Bōjō *s*
津 Bōnotsu *p*
野 Bōno *s*

坂 390 [T] Saka *sp*; Ban *s.* (BAN, HAN, saka)
ノ下 Sakanoshita *s*
[2]入 Sakairi *s*
[3]川 Sakagawa *s*
下 Sakashita *sp*
口 Sakaguchi *s*
口安吾 S. Ango *ml*
上 Sakanoue *s*, Sakanoe, Sakaue, Sakagami
上田村麻呂 Sakanoue no Tamuramaro *mh*
上望城 S. no Mochiki *ml* ⌈Iratsume *fl*
上郎女 Sakanoe no
[4]水 Sakamizu *s*
元 Sakamoto *s*
戸 Sakato *sp*; Sakabe *s*
内 Sakauchi *sp*; Bannai *s*
木 Sakaki *s*
牛 Sakaushi *s*
井 Sakai *sp*
井田 Sakaida *s*
爪 Sakazume *s*
[5]北 Sakakita *p*
田 Sakata *sp* ⌈*ml*
田藤十郎 S. Tōjūrō
本 Sakamoto *sp* ⌈*ml*
本四方太 S. Shihōda
本浩 S. Hiroshi *ml*
本竜馬 S. Ryōma *mh*
本紅蓮洞 S. Gurendō *ml*
本雪鳥 S. Setchō *ml*
主 Sakanushi *s*
[6]合部 Sakaabe *s*
西 Sakanishi *s*, Banzai
[7]村 Sakamura *s*
名井 Sakanai *s*
谷 Sakatani *s*
谷部 Sakaibe *s*
尾 Sakao *s*
出 Sakaide *p*
[8]於 Sakanoe *s*
乳 Sakachi *s*
茂 Sakamo *s*, Sakamochi, Sakamoto
東 Bandō *s*
[9]城 Sakaki *p*
祝 Sakahogi *p*
巻 Sakamaki *s*
[10]倉 Sakakura *s*
[11]野 Sakano *s*, Banno
部 Sakabe *s*
寄 Sakaki *s*
梨 Sakanashi *s*
[12]場 Sakaba *s*
崎 Sakazaki *s*
崎紫瀾 S. Shiran *ml*
間 Sakama *s*
[13]雄 Sakao *m*
詰 Sakazume *s*

沚 391 Nagisa *m.* (SHI)

沙 392 (SA, SHA, su, isa, suna) ⌈wa
川 Isagawa *s*, Sunaga-
石集 Shasekishū *l*
田 Isagoda *s*, Masagoda, Masuda
翁 Shaō *ml* "Shakespeare"

汻 393 Migiwa *m.* (KO, KU)

汝 394 (JO, NYO, na)

泛 395 (HAN, hiro)
子 Hiroko *f*

沃 396 (YOKU, nuru)
野 Yokuya *l*

汾 397 (FUN, BUN, kawa, ō, mitsu)
陽 Kawaminami *s*, Kawanami, Kawakita

汶 398 (MON, BUN)
旦 Montan *s*
斯 Monshi *s*

沈 399 [T] Chin *s.* (CHIN, ushi)

沖 400 [T] Fukashi *m.* (CHŪ, oki, na-
山 Okiyama *s* ⌊ka)
田 Okita *s*
村 Okimura *s*
垣 Okigaki *s*
津 Okitsu *s*
美 Okimi *p*
海 Okimi *f*
原 Okihara *s*
野 Okino *s* ⌈rō *ml*
野岩三郎 O. Iwasabu-

沚 沙 汻 汝 泛 沃 汾 汶 沈 沖 ▼ 汪 決 汲 沢 対 社 牡 肝 玖 弘 妃 如 好 形 邢 那 ▲ 邦 杠 朽 材 杙 杖 杜 村 杉 町

島 Okijima *s*

汪 401 Hiroshi *m.* (ō, hiro)
子 Hiroko *f*

決 402 [T] (KETSU, KECHI, sada)
子 Sadako *f*

汲 403 (KYŪ, GYŪ, kumi)
子 Kumiko *f*
田 Kumida *s*
事 Kumiji *m*

沢 404 [T] Sawa *s.* (TAKU, JAKU, sawa, masu)
2二郎 Sawajirō *m*
3口 Sawaguchi *s*
4内 Sawauchi *sp*
山 Sawayama *s*
井 Sawai *s*
木 Sawaki *s*
木欣一 S. Kin'ichi *ml*
中 Sawanaka *s*
5辺 Sawabe *s*
本 Sawamoto *s*
田 Sawada *s* ⌈*ma*
田正二郎 S. Shōjirō
6地 Sawachi *s*
江 Sawae *s*
7村 Sawamura *s*
村田之助 S. Tanosuke *ma-l*
村胡夷 S. Koi *ml*
谷 Sawaya *s*
尾 Sawao *s*
9俣 Sawamata *s*
畑 Sawabatake *s*
宣嘉 Sawa Nobuyoshi *mh*
10浦 Sawaura *s*
柳 Sawayanagi *s*
柳政太郎 S. Masatarō *mh*
畠 Sawabatake *s*
原 Sawabara *s*
屋 Sawaya *s*
11部 Sawabe *s*
野 Sawano *s*
野久雄 S. Hisao *ml*
庵 Takuan *mh*
島 Sawashima *s*
12渡 Sawato *s*
崎 Sawazaki *s*
15潟 Omodaka *s*
16橋 Sawahashi *s*

## 7 L4

対 405 [T] (TAI)
馬 Tsushima *sp*
馬完治 T. Kanji *ml*
間 Taima *s*

社 406 [T] Koso *s*; Yashiro *p.* (SHA, ari, taka, koso)
下 Kosoge *s*
戸 Kosobe *s*
本 Shamoto *s*

牡 407 (BO, BŌ)
丹燈籠 Botan-dōrō *l*
丹平家譚 Natorigusa Heike monogatari *l*
蠣殻 Kakigara *p*

肝 408 [T] (KAN, kimo)
付 Kimotsuki *s*
属 Kimotsuki *sp*
衡 Kimotsuki *s*

玖 409 (KYŪ, KU, tama, ki, hisa)
次 Hisaji *m*
城 Tamaki *m*
珂 Kuga *p*
珠 Kusu *p*

弘 410 [N] Hiroshi *m*, Hiromu, Hirome. (KŌ, KU, hiro, mitsu, o)
1一 Hiroichi *m*
一郎 Hiroichirō *m*
3子 Mitsuko *f*
之 Hiroyuki *m*
4仁 Kōnin 810–24
化 Kōka 1844–48
中 Hironaka *s*
5田 Hirota *s*
6光 Hiromitsu *m*
世 Hirose *sp*
7亨 Hiroaki *m*
邑 Hiromura *m*
安 Kōan 1278–88
玄 Hiroharu *m*
8明 Hiroaki *m*
和 Kōwa 1381–84
矣 Hiroshi *m*
9計 Oke *m* ⌈*ml*
法大師 Kōbō Daishi
治 Kōji 1555–58
前 Hirosaki *p*
長 Kōchō 1261–64
岡 Hirooka *s*
10耿 Hiraaki *m*
訓 Hironori *m*
記 Hirobumi *m*
家 Hiroie *m*
造 Kōzō *s*
馬 Hirome *m*
11渉 Hirosada *m*
視 Hiromi *m*
12逵 Hiromichi *m*
達 Hiroyoshi *m*
道館 Kōdōkan *ph*
13義 Hiroyoshi *m*
14精 Hirokiyo *m*
調 Hirotsugu *m*
毅 Hirotake *m*, Kōki, Hironori, Hiromi, Hirokata
19廬 Hiroyoshi *m*
瀬 Hirose *s*
20徽殿 Kokiden *ph*

妃 411 [T] (HI, hime, ki)
生子 Kiiko *f*

如 412 [T] (JO, NYO, yuki, suke, iku, nao, moto, yoshi)
4月 Kisaragi *f*
6行 Yoshiyuki *m*
9信 Yukinobu *m*
10拙 Josetsu *ma*
11常 Ikutsune *m*
皐 Jokō *ml*
雪 Naoyuki *m*
12道 Yukimichi *m*
13雄 Motoo *m*
意地 Sukeichi *m*
意輪観音 Nyoirin Kannon *fh*
17儡子 Joraishi *ml*
19願 Nyogan *ml*
願法師集 N. Hōshi shū *l*

好 413 [T] Yoshimi *m*, Konomu. (KŌ, yoshi, taka, kono, mi, sumi)
1一 Yoshikazu *m*
3三郎 Kōsaburō *m*
子 Yoshiko *f*
4日 Yoshiharu *s*
5永 Yoshinaga *sm*
示 Yoshimi *s*
古 Yoshihisa *m*
6色一代女 Kōshoku ichidai onna *l*
色一代男 K. i. otoko *l*
色五人女 K. gonin onna *l*
母 Konomo *m*
7見 Yoshimi *s*
佐子 Misako *f*
玄 Yoshinori *m*
孝 Yoshinori *m*
8忠 Yoshitada *m*
9津 Yomizu *m*
祖 Yoshimoto *m*
美 Yoshitomi *m*, Yoshinori
重 Yoshie *f*
10造 Yoshinari *m*
11鳥 Yoshitori *s*
問 Yoshitada *m*
12暁 Yoshiaki *m*
就 Yoshiyuki *m*
間 Yoshima *p*
13経 Takatsune *m*
純 Yoshizumi *m*

形 414 [T] (KEI, GYŌ, kata, nari, yori, sue, are, mi)
山 Katayama *s*
名 Katana *s* ⌈nohara
原 Katahara *s*, Nari-
影抄 Keieishō *l*
舞 Gyōbu *s*

邢 415 (KEI, GYŌ, osaka)
部 Osakabe *s*

那 416 (NA, tomo, fuyu, yasu)
子 Tomoko *f*, Fuyu-
波 Nawa *s* ⌊ko
珂 Naka *sp*
珂川 Nakagawa *p*
珂湊 Naka-minato *p*
倉 Nagura *s*
須 Nasu *sp*
須野 Nasuno *s*
智 Nachi *p*
智勝浦 N. Katsuura *p*
賀 Naka *p*

賀川 Nakagawa *p*
歳 Nasai *m*
覇 Naha *p*

邦 417 [T] Kuni *m.* (HŌ, kuni)
[1]一 Kunikazu *m*
[3]三 Kunizō *m*
子 Kuniko *f*
[4]友 Kunitomo *sm*
太郎 Kunitarō *m*
[5]矛 Kunitake *m*
氏 Kuniuji *m*
[7]寿 Kuninaga *m*
[8]枝 Kunieda *s*
枝完二 K. Kanji *ml*
房 Kuninobu *m*
尚 Kuninao *m*, Kuninari
[9]治郎 Kunijirō *m*
松 Kunimatsu *s*
栄 Kuniyoshi *s*
彦 Kunihiko *m*
彦王 Kuniyoshi-ō *mh*
省 Kunimi *m*
[10]造 Kunizō *m*
[12]敬 Kuniyoshi *m*
[13]雄 Kunio *m*
鼎 Kunitane *m*
[14]輔 Kunisuke *m*

杠 418 Yuzuriha *s*, Akanashi. (KŌ, yuzuri)
葉 Yuzuriha *s*

朽 419 [T] (KYŪ, KU, e, kuchi)
木 Kutsuki *sp*; Kuchiki *s*
折 Tsugisho *s*
網 Kutami *s*, Kuami

材 420 [T] Motoki *m*, Motoshi. (ZAI, SAI, ki, eda)

杙 421 (YOKU, IKU, kui)
瀬 Kuize *s*

杖 422 (JŌ, CHŌ, tsue, ki, mochi)
部 Tsuebe *s*, Hasetsukabe

杜 423 Akanashi *sm*; Yuzuriha *sp*; Mori *s*. (TO, mori)
人 Morito *s*
子春 To Shishun *mlh-l* "Tu Tzu-ch'un"
女 Morime *f*
沢 Hōzawa *s*
若 Kakitsubata *la*
国 Tokoku *ml*
智秦 Echihata *s*

村 424 [T] Mura *sf.* (SON, mura, sue, tsune)
[3]川 Murakawa *s*
士 Suguri *s*
口 Muraguchi *s*
上 Murakami *sp*
上専精 M. Senjō *mh*
上浪六 M. Namiroku *ml*
上鬼城 M. Kijō *ml*
上霽月 M. Seigetsu *ml*
[4]中 Muranaka *s*
木 Muraki *s*
山 Murayama *sp*
山知義 M. Tomoyoshi *ml*
山槐多 M. Kaita *ml*
井 Murai *s*
井長庵 M. Chōan *lm*
井長庵巧破傘 M. C. takumi no yaregasa *la*
井弦斎 M. Gensai *ml*
[5]石 Muraishi *s*
主 Suguri *s*, Muranushi
本 Muramoto *s*
田 Murata *sp*
田春海 M. Harumi *ml*
田珠光 M. Jukō *mh*
田清風 M. Seifū *mh*
[6]地 Muraji *s*, Murachi
西 Muranishi *s*
[7]坂 Murasaka *s*
沢 Murasawa *s*
杉 Murasugi *s*
社 Murakoso *s*
谷 Muratani *s*
尾 Murao *s*
[8]林 Murabayashi *s*
国 Murakuni *s*
雨 Murasame *sf*
[9]侯 Muratoki *m*
垣 Muragaki *s*
治 Muraji *s*
松 Muramatsu *sp*
松正俊 M. Masatoshi *ml*
松定孝 M. Sadataka *ml*
松梢風 M. Shōfū *ml*
松剛 M. Takeshi *ml*
岸 Murakishi *s*
岡 Muraoka *sp*
[10]浦 Muraura *s*
高 Murataka *s*
挙 Murake *s*, Soke
[11]野 Murano *s*
野四郎 M. Shirō *ml*
野次郎 M. Jirō *ml*
島 Murajima *s*
[12]崎 Murazaki *s*
[13]塚 Muratsuka *s*
雲 Murakumo *s*
椿 Muratsubaki *s*
越 Murakoshi *s*
[16]橋 Murahashi *s*
[19]瀬 Murase *s*

杉 425 [I] Sugi *s.* (SAN, sugi)
[3]川 Sugikawa *s*
下 Sugishita *s*
戸 Sugito *p*
[4]中 Suginaka *s*
井 Sugii *s*
木 Sugiki *s*
山 Sugiyama *s*
山丹後掾 S. Tangonojō *ma*
山平助 S. Heisuke *ml*
山杉風 S. Sanpū *ml*
山肥前掾 S. Bizennojō *ma*
山英樹 S. Hideki *ml*
内 Sugiuchi *s*
[5]立 Sugitate *s*
平 Sugihira *s*
本 Sugimoto *s*
生 Sugifu *s*
田 Sugita *s*
田久女 S. Hisajo *fl*
田玄白 S. Genpaku *ml*
田鶴子 S. Tsuruko *fl*
[6]江 Sugie *sf*
[7]坂 Sugisaka *s*
沢 Sugisawa *s*
村 Sugimura *s*
村楚人冠 S. Sojinkan *ml*
谷 Sugitani *s*, Sugiya
[8]林 Sugibayashi *s*
若 Sugiwaka *s*
並 Suginami *p*
[9]妻 Suginome *s*
岡 Sugioka *s*
風 Sanpū *ml*
[10]浦 Sugiura *s*
浦明平 S. Minpei *ml*
浦重剛 S. Shigetake / Jūgō *mlh*
浦翠子 S. Suiko *fl*
原 Sugihara *s*
[11]渓 Sugitani *s*
野 Sugino *s*
島 Sugishima *s*
[12]崎 Sugisaki *s*
森 Sugimori *s*
森久英 S. Hisahide *ml*
森孝次郎 S. Kōjirō *ml*

—7 L5—

町 426 [T] Machi *s.* (CHŌ, machi)
口 Machiguchi *s*
子 Machiko *f*
井 Machii *s*
山 Machiyama *s*
尻 Machijiri *s*
尻子 Machijiriko *f*
田 Machida *p*
田嘉章 M. Kashō *ma*
出 Machide *s*
彦 Machihiko *m*
野 Machino *s*
島 Machijima *s*

初 427 [T] Hajime *m.* (SHO, SO, hatsu, moto)
[3]子 Hatsuko *f*
太郎 Hatsutarō *m*
[4]山 Hatsuyama *s*
山別 Shosanbetsu *p*
山踏 Uiyamafumi *l*
[5]田 Hatsuda *s*, Hatta
[6]次郎 Hatsujirō *m*
[7]沢 Hatsuzawa *s*
谷 Hatsugai *s*
見 Hatsumi *s*
[8]芽 Hatsume *m*
[9]侽 Hatsuo *m*
音 Hatsune *sl*
岡 Hatsuoka *s*
[11]菊 Hatsugiku *f*
雪 Hatsuyuki *la*
島 Hatsushima *s*
[12]鹿 Hajika *s*, Hatsushika
鹿野 Hajikano *sp*; Hatsukano *s*
[16]鴉 Hatsugarasu *l*

杠 朽 材 杙 杖 杜 村 杉 町 初 ▼ 幼 劭 励 助 刢 刹 判 別 利 乱 豆 言 亨 走 克 赤 ▲ 毎 希 甾 発 余 谷 吉 肖 夸 含

[19]瀬 Hatsuse *m*; Hase *p*

**幼** 428 [T] (YŌ, waka, ubu)
方 Ubukata *s*

**劭** 429 Tsutomu *m*. (SHŌ, JŌ)

**励** 430 [T] Tsutomu *m*. (REI)
作 Reisaku *m*

**助** 431 [T] Tasuku *m*. (JO, SHO, ZO, suke, hiro, masu)
[3]川 Sukegawa *s*
千 Sukekazu *m*
[4]六 Sukeroku *la*
太郎 Suketarō *m*
[5]左衛門 Sukezaemon ⌊*m*
市 Sukeichi *m*
[6]休 Sukeyoshi *m*
当 Sukemasa *m*
有 Sukemichi *m*
名 Sukena *m*
[7]弘 Sukehiro *m*
[8]林 Sukemori *m*
受 Suketsugu *m*
[9]映 Sukehide *m*
松 Sukematsu *s*
参 Sukechika *m*
[10]高屋 Suketakaya *s*
盈 Sukemichi *m*
[14]種 Suketane *m*
[16]賢 Suketoshi *m*

**刢** 432 Satoshi *m*. (REI, RYŌ)

**刹** 433 See 初 427

**判** 434 (HAN, sada, chika, naka, yuki)
乃 Hanno *s*
門田 Haneda *s*

**別** 435 [T] (BETSU, waki, waku, nobu)
[3]子山 Besshiyama *p*
[4]木 Bekki *s*
井 Betsui *s*
処 Bessho *s*
[6]当 Bettō *mh*
[7]役 Betsuyaku *s*, Betchaku
[8]所 Bessho *s*
府 Beppu *sp*, Befu
[10]海 Bekkai *p*
宮 Bekku *s* ⌈uchi *s*
[11]倭種 Kotoyamatono-
[12]喜 Bekki *s* ⌈san *l*
[19]願和讃 Betsugan wa-

**利** 436 [T] Toshi *m*, Tōru, Minoru. (RI, toshi, yoshi, sato, to, nori, kaga, kazu, michi, yori, masa)
[1]一 Riichi *m*
[3]川 Toshikawa *s*
三 Toshizō *m*
三郎 Risaburō *m*
上 Toshikami *m*
子 Toshiko *f* ⌈*mh*
[4]仁将軍 Rijin Shōgun
夫 Toshio *m*
井 Kagai *s*
太 Toshimasu *m*
[5]以 Toshimochi *m*
功 Toshikoto *m*
可 Toshiyoshi *m*
尻 Rishiri *p*
生 Rifu *s*
[6]休 Rikyū *ma*
行 Toshihira *m*
吉 Rikichi *m*
光 Toshimitsu *sm*; Kagami *s*
同 Toshiatsu *m*
[7]位 Toshitsura *m*
助 Risuke *m*
初 Toshimoto *m*
亨 Toshinao *m*
克 Toshinari *m*
声 Toshikata *m*
苅 Togari *s*
兵衛 Ribee *m* ⌈akira
見 Toshimi *m*, Toshi-
考 Toshiyasu *m*
寿 Toshihogi *m*
[8]物 Toshitane *m*
和 Toshikazu *m*, Toshiyoshi
制 Toshiyori *m*
定 Toshisada *m*
周 Toshikane *m*
府 Rifu *sp*
[9]治 Yoshiharu *m*
美 Toshiyoshi *m*
彦 Toshihiko *m*
為 Toshinari *m*
[10]家 Toshiie *m*
恭 Toshichika *m*
通 Toshiyuki *m*, Toshimichi
[11]済 Toshitada *m*
理 Toshimasa *m*, Toshitada
躬 Toshimoto *m*
剛 Toshihisa *m*
根 Tone *sp*
根川 Tonegawa *sp*
根子 Toneko *f*
圀 Toshika *m*
島 Toshima *p*
彪 Toshitora *m*, Toshiaya
[12]随 Toshiyuki *m*
温 Toshiyoshi *m*
敬 Toshiyuki *m*
彭 Toshichika *m*
賀 Toga *p*
喜三郎 Rikisaburō *m*
喜太郎 Rikitarō *m*
[13]極 Toshinaka *m*
雄 Toshio *m*, Toshikatsu
幹 Toshitsune *m*
寛 Toshihito *m*
誉 Toshitaka *m*
[14]精 Toshiaki *m*
[15]鋪 Toshiharu *m*
器 Toshikata *m*
[16]賢 Toshikata *m*
[17]謙 Toshinori *m*, Toshikata, Toshiaki
豁 Toshiakira *m*
[20]徽 Toshiyoshi *m*

——7 L6——

**乱** 437 [T] Osamu *m-f*. (RAN)

——7 T1——

**豆** 438 [T] (TŌ, ZU, mame)
田 Mameda *s*

**言** 439 [T] Hogi *s*. (GEN, GON, koto, toki, nobu, nori, aki, aya, toshi, yuki, tomo)
人 Kotondo *m*
夫 Nobuo *m*
同 Kontō *s*
志 Noriyuki *m*
知 Tokisato *m*
忠 Akitada *m*
辰 Tokitatsu *m*
泰 Tokihiro *m*
道 Kotomichi *m*
語同断 Tekurada *s*, Tekura
緒 Tokio *m*
綱 Toshitsuna *m*
縄 Kototsuna *m*
鑒 Kotomi *m*

——7 T2——

**亨** 440 [N] Susumu *m*, Tōru, Akira. (KYŌ, KŌ, michi, yuki, aki, chika, toshi, naga, nao, nari)
子 Michiko *f*
介 Kyōsuke *m*
江 Yukie *f*
吉 Kōkichi *m*
弘 Toshihiro *m*

**走** 441 [T] (SŌ, hashiri, yuki)
井 Hashirii *s*
出 Hashiride *s*
馬燈 Sōmatō *l*
部 Hasebe *s*

**克** 442 [T] Suguru *m*, Katsumi, Katsu, Masaru, Isoshi. (KOKU, katsu, yoshi, tae, nari)
[3]三 Katsumi *m*
巳 Katsumi *m*
子 Katsuko *f*
[4]太郎 Katsutarō *m*
[5]礼 Yoshinori *m*
[7]孝 Yoshitaka *m*
[8]明 Katsuaki *m*
知 Yoshiakira *m*
[9]彦 Katsuhiko *m*
[10]郎 Yoshirō *m*, Yoshi-
修 Yoshinobu *m* ⌊ra
[11]惟 Katsutada *m*
捷 Katsutoshi *m*
[13]禎 Katsusada *m*
[16]衛 Katsue *m*

**赤** 443 [T] Hanyū *m*; Aka *p*. (SEKI, SHAKU, aka, ka, hani, wani)
[2]人 Akahito *m*
[3]川 Akagawa *s*

土 Akahani s, Shakudo
4山 Akayama s
井 Akai s
井川 Akaigawa s
木 Akagi s
木桁平 A. Kōhei *ml*
木格堂 A. Kakudō *ml*
木健介 A. Kensuke *ml*
5司 Akashi s
石 Akaishi s, Akashi
生 Hanyū s
兄 Akae *m*
田 Akada s
平 Akabira *ml*
本 Akahon *l*
6地 Akaji s
池 Akaike s
羽 Akabane *sp*
羽根 Akabane *sp*
光 Shakkō *l*
7佐 Akasa s
阪 Akasaka s
坂 Akasaka *sp*
沢 Akazawa s
尾 Akao s
見 Akami s
見坂 Akamizaka s
8泊 Akadomari *p*
林 Akabayashi s
9津 Akatsu s
垣 Akagaki s
城 Akagi *sp*; Sekijō *sm*
松 Akamatsu s
松則村 A. Norimura *mh*
松満祐 A. Mitsusuke *mh*
星 Akaboshi s
岩 Akaiwa s
岩栄 A. Sakae *ml*
染 Akazome s
染部 Akazome s
染衛門 A. Emon *fl*
岡 Akaoka *p*
彦 Akahiko *m*
10畝 Akaze s
荻 Akaogi s
座 Akaza s
11根 Akane s
野 Akano s
黄男 Kakio *m*
12埴 Akahani s, Akabane
湯 Akayu *p*
須 Akasu s
萩 Akahagi s
崎 Akasaki s
間 Akama s
13碕 Akasaki *p*
塚 Akatsuka s
塩 Akashio s
堀 Akabori *sp*
15蝦夷風説考 Akaezo fūsetsukō *lh*
穂 Akaho s; Akō *p*
穂浪士 Akō rōshi *l*
磐 Akaiwa *p*
16橋 Akabashi s
18藤 Shakudō s
嶺 Akamine s
19禰 Akane s
21鶴 Shakuzuru *sma*
鶴吉成 S. Yoshinari *ma*

**毎** 444 [T] (MAI, BAI, kazu, tsune)
人 Tsuneto *m*
月抄 Maigetsushō *l*
田 Maiden s, Maida
保 Tsuneyasu *m*
治 Tsuneji *m*
高 Maitaka s

**希** 445 [T] (KI, KE, mare)
一 Kiichi *m*
人 Marendo *m*
代 Kidai s
世 Mareyo *m*
男 Mareo *m*
典 Maresuke *m*
雄 Mareo *m*
臘 Girisha *p* " Greece "

**㕣** 446 (KŌ, kin)
定 Kinsada *m*

**兌** 447 Tōru *m*, Satoru, Naoshi, Atsumaru. (DA, TAI, sawa, toki, michi)

**余** 448 [T] Amari s. (YO, ware)
一 Yoichi *m*
川 Yokawa s
四男 Yoshio *m*
田 Yoden s; Aguri *sp*
目 Amarume *sp*
市 Yoichi *p*
奴 Enu s
技 Hakuri s
呉 Yogo *p*
島 Ashima s
郷 Yogō s
語 Yogo s, Jogo
綾 Yurugi s; Yorogi *sp*

**谷** 449 [T] Tani s, Yatsu, Hazama. (KOKU, ya, tani, yatsu, hiro)
3川 Tanikawa s, Tanigawa, Yatsukawa
川俊太郎 Tanikawa Shuntarō *ml*
川徹三 T. Tetsuzō *ml*
口 Taniguchi s, Yaguguchi
下田 Yashimoda s
上 Tanigami s
干城 Tani Tateki *mh*
4元 Tanimoto s
戸 Yato s
中 Yanaka s
内 Taniuchi s, Yachi, Tannai, Yanai
内田 Yachida s
文晁 Tani Bunchō *ma*
山 Taniyama *sp*
五郎 Tanigorō *m*
井 Tanii s, Yatsui, Yasui, Yai
5永 Taninaga s
古田 Yakoda s
古宇 Yakou s
本 Tanimoto s
田 Tanida s; Yata *sp*
田川 Yatagawa s
田貝 Yatagai s
田部 Yatabe *sp*
平 Tanihira s
6地田 Yachida s
行 Tanikō *la*
合 Taniai s
7沢 Tanizawa s, Yazawa
汲 Tanigumi *p*
村 Tanimura s
那 Kokuna s
谷 Yatsuya s, Yatsugaya, Tanigae, Tanigaya
出 Tanide s
貝 Yatsugai s
8河 Tanikawa s, Tanigawa
和原 Yawahara *p*
9津 Tanizu s; Yatsu *sp*
津田 Yatsuda s
治 Yaji s
活東 Tani Kattō *ml*
垣 Tanigaki s
畑 Tanihata s
岸 Tanigishi s
岡 Tanioka s
10時中 Tani Jichū *mh*
脇 Taniwaki s
高 Tanitaka s
原 Tanihara s
11野 Yano s, Tanino
部 Tanibe s
島 Yashima s, Tanishima
12崎 Tanizaki s
崎精二 T. Seiji *ml*
崎潤一郎 T. Jun'ichirō *ml*
森 Tanimori s
13鼎 Tani Kanae *ml*
15蔵 Tanizō *m*
18藤 Tanifuji s
20馨 Tani Kaoru *ml*

## 7 T3

**㫖** 450 See 旨 263

**肖** 451 [T] (SHŌ, ae, are, ayu, sue, taka, nori, yuki)
柏 Shōhaku *ml*
奈 Sena s

**夸** 452 (KO, KU, ya)

**含** 453 [T] (GAN, mochi)
羞草 Nemurigusa *l*

**会** 454 [T] (KAI, E, ai, au, kazu, sada, haru, mochi)
加 Eka s
田 Aida s
合衆 Egōshū *mh*
沢 Aizawa s
沢安 A. Yasushi *mh*
見 Aimi *p*
洲 Aisu s
津 Aizu *sph*
津八一 A. Yaichi *ml*
津坂下 A. Bange *p*
津高田 A. Takada *p*
曾川 Aisogawa s

**牟** 455 (MU, BŌ, moto, masu)
子 Motoko *f*
礼 Mure *sp*
田 Muta s

田口 Mutaguchi *s*
佐 Musa *s*
岐 Mugi *sp*
宜都 Mugetsu *s*
庫 Muku *s*
婁 Muro *p*
義都 Mugetsu *s*

**麦** 456 [T] (BAKU, mugi)
子 Mugiko *f*
水 Bakusui *ml*
生 Mugyū *s*, Mugifu
倉 Mugikura *s*

**条** 457 [T] Koeda *s.* (JŌ, CHŌ, eda, e, naga)
太郎 Jōtarō *m*
野 Jōno *s*
野採菊 J. Saigiku *ml*

**朶** 458 (DA, TA, eda, e)
子 Edako *f*

**呂** 459 [N] Ro *s.* (RO, RYO, tomo, naga, oto, fue)
久 Tomohisa *m*
宋 Ruson *p* "Luzon"
蓮 Roren *l*

**邑** 460 Satoshi *m.* (YŪ, Ō, mura, sato, kuni, sumi)
一 Muraichi *m*
上 Murakami *s*
久 Oku *p*
井 Murai *s*
代 Iishiro *s*
珍 Ōchi *s* ⌈Ōchi *p*
智 Ochi *s*, Okuchi;
楽 Ōaraki *s*; Ōra *p*
治 Ōji *m*

**足** 461 [T] Taruno *s.* (SOKU, ashi, tari, taru, a, nari, mitsu, yuki, tarashi)
[5]代 Ajiro *sp*
尼 Sukune *s*
立 Adachi *sp* ⌈*sp*
[6]羽 Ashiba *s*; Asuwa
守 Ashimori *p*
[7]助 Asuke *sp*
助素一 A. Soichi *ml*
利 Ashikaga *sp*
利成氏 A. Shigeuji *mh*
利持氏 A. Mochiuji *mh*
利政知 A. Masatomo *mh* ⌈*mh*
利直義 A. Tadayoshi
利基氏 A. Motouji *mh*
利尊氏 A. Takauji *mh*
利義尚 A. Yoshihisa *mh* ⌈*mh*
利義持 A. Yoshimochi
利義昭 A. Yoshiaki *mh*
利義政 A. Yoshimasa *mh* ⌈*mh*
利義教 A. Yoshinori
利義満 A. Yoshimitsu *mh*
利義視 A. Yoshimi *mh*
利義詮 A. Yoshiakira *mh* ⌈*mh*
利義輝 A. Yoshiteru
尾 Ashio *p*
尾銅山 A. Dōzan *ph*
[8]和田 Ashiwada *p*
奈 Sukuna *s*
[9]柄 Ashigara *p*
柄上 A.-kami *p*
柄下 A.-shimo *p*
[10]迹 Ashiato *l*
[11]寄 Ashiyoro *p*
[12]達 Adachi *s*
[15]穂 Ashio *s*; Tariho *m*, Taruho

**忌** 462 [T] (KI, imi)
寸 Imiki *s*
町 Itō *s*
部 Inbe *s*
鉄師 Imikanuchi *s*

**忍** 463 [T] Shinobu *m-f*; Oshi *sp*; Oshimi *s*, Oshinumi. (NIN, oshi, shino, tō)
[4]夫 Shinobu *m*
[5]冬 Suikazura *l*
田 Oshida *s*
[7]助 Oshisuke *m*
坂 Osaka *s*
坂部 Osakabe *s*
足 Oshitari *s*, Otari
[8]性 Ninshō *mh*
[9]岡 Shinobugaoka *s*
[10]海 Oshinoumi *s*; Oshimi *sp*
峡 Oshio *s*
[11]野 Oshino *p*
[12]崎 Oshizaki *s*
[13]路 Oshiro *s*
[15]熊 Oshikuma *s*
[16]壁 Osakabe *s*, Oshikabe

**志** 464 [T] Shirusu *m.* (SHI, yuki, sane, mune)
[4]水 Shimizu *s*
内 Shiuchi *s*
方 Shikata *sp*
太 Shida *p*
毛 Shige *s*
[5]比 Shii *s*
比陀 Shihida *s*
布志 Shibushi *p*
立 Shidate *s*, Shidachi
田 Shida *sp*
田野坡 S. Yaba *ml*
田素琴 S. Sokin *ml*
[6]地池 Shichiike *s*
自岐 Shijiki *s*
[7]佐 Shisa *s*
沢 Shizawa *s*
村 Shimura *s*
那 Shina *s*
豆紀 Shizuki *f*
豆機 Shizuhata *s*
我閉 Shikanohe *s*
[8]岐 Shiki *s*
和 Shiwa *p*
知 Shichi *s*
波 Shiwa *s*, Shiba, Shinami
波姫 Shiwahime *p*
免 Shime *p*
茂 Shimori *s*
[9]段 Shidami *s*
紀 Shiki *s*
保 Shio *f*
依 Yukie *f*
津 Shizu *s*
津川 Shizugawa *p*
津野 Shizuno *s*
津梨 Shizuri *s*
津摩 Shizuma *m*
津磨 Shizuma *m*
度 Shido *p*
[10]倉 Shigura *s*
馬 Shima *s*
[11]深村 Shijimimura *s*
野 Shino *s*
[12]朝 Yukitomo *m*
富田 Shibuta *s*
斐 Shibi *s*
筑 Shitsuki *s*, Shizuku
筑忠雄 Shitsuki Tadao *mh*
賀 Shiga *sp-la*
賀直哉 S. Naoya *ml*
賀重昂 S. Shigetaka *mlh*
賀潔 S. Kiyoshi *mh*
賀穴太 Shiganoanaho *s* ⌈shiji
道 Shidō *s*, Shiji, Shi-
[13]雄 Yukio *m*; Shio *p*
純 Yukitō *m*
[15]談 Shidan *s*, Shidami
摩 Shima *sm-p*
[16]頭磨 Shizuma *m*
磨 Shima *s*
[17]濃夫廼舎 Shinobunoya *ml*
[18]鎌 Shikama *s*
藤 Shitō *s*

**声** 465 [T] Nobu *f.* (SEI, SHŌ, na, kata, ato)

**売** 466 [T] (BAI, ME, uri)
木 Urugi *p*
豆紀 Mezuki *s*

**壱** 467 [T] (ICHI, ITSU, kazu, sane, moro)
比韋 Ichihii *s*
礼比 Ichirohi *s*
体比 Ichirohi *s*
岐 Iki *sph*

**宋** 468 Sō *s.* (SŌ, SU, kuni, oki)

**宫** 469 See 穹 948

**宍** 470 (JIKU, NIKU, shishi)
人 Shishūdo *s*, Shishi-
戸 Shishido *s* ⌊do
夫 Shishio *m*
甘 Shishikai *sp*; Shishikō *s*
草 Shishikusa *s*
倉 Shishikura *s*
栗 Shishiguri *s*
粟 Shishizawa *s*; Shizawa *sp*; Shisō *p*

道 Shinji *sp*
喰 Shishikui *p*

完 471 [T] Tamotsu *m*, Mataki, Matashi, Hiroshi, Yutaka; Mitsu *f*. (KAN, GAN, sada, naru, hiro, mitsu, masa, mata, shishi)
二 Kanji *m*
子 Hiroko *f*
戸 Kanto *s*, Shishido
利 Shitori *s*
吾 Kango *m*
孝 Sadataka *m*
治 Kanji *m*
草 Shishigusa *s*
美 Narumi *f*
道 Shishiji *s*
雄 Masao *m*
爾 Kanji *m*
識 Sadanori *m*

安 472 [T] Yasushi *m*; Yasu *sm*. (AN, yasu, sada)
1一郎 Yasuichirō *m*
2八 Anpachi *p*
3川 Yasukawa *s*
三郎 Yasusaburō *m*
口 Hatakuchi *s*, Hatayasu, Hatakasu
之助 Yasunosuke *m*
万 Ama *m*
子 Yasuko *f*
土 Azuchi *p*; Azechi *s*
土桃山 Azuchi Momoyama *h* ⌈*s*
4心院 Ajimi *sp*; Ajimu
元 Angen 1175–77; Yasumoto *s*
中 Yasunaka *s*; Annaka *sp*
王 Yasutaka *m*
五郎 Yasugorō *m*
太郎 Yasutarō *m*
毛 Amo *s*
井 Yasui *s* ⌈*ma*
井曾太郎 Y. Sōtarō
木 Yasugi *s*
木田 Akita *s* ⌈*p*
5代 Yasuyo *s*; Ashiro
礼 Yasumasa *m*
永 An'ei 1772–81; Yasunaga *sm*
古市 Yasufuruichi *p*
旦 Yasuaki *m*, Yasuakira
左衛門 Yasuzaemon *m*
立 Adachi *s*, Anryū
玉 Yasukiyo *m*
本 Yasumoto *s*
生 Anjō *s*
田 Yasuda *sp*
田青風 Y. Seifū *ml*
田章生 Y. Ayao *ml*
田靫彦 Y. Yukihiko
正 Yasumasa *m* ⌊*ma*
6次郎 Yasujirō *m*
江 Yasue *s*
光 Yasumitsu *sm*
吉 Yasukichi *m*; Aki *s*
宅 Ataka *sp-la*; Adaki *s*, Kataka, Yasumi; Yasuori *m*
宅木 Ataki *s*
在 Anzai *s*
成 Yasunari *sm*
成二郎 Y. Jirō *ml*
成貞雄 Y. Sadao *ml*
西 Anzai *s*
西冬衛 A. Fuyue *ml*
7村 Yasumura *s*
但 Yasutada *m*
佐 Asa *p*
佐美 Asami *s*
住 Azumi *s*, Yasuzumi, Anjū ⌈*ml*
住敦 Azumi Atsushi
沢 Anzawa *s*, Yasuza-
形 Agata *s* ⌊wa
谷 Yasutani *s*
究 Yasuzumi *m*
至 Yasuchika *m*
邑 Yasumura *m*
足 Yasutari *sm*
見 Yasumi *s*
寿田 Yasuda *s*
来 Yasugi *p*
8拝 Ae *s*
河内 Yasukōchi *s*
明 Yasuaki *m*
岐 Aki *sp*
和 Anwa 968–70
房 Awa *p*
念 Annen *s*
定 Yasusada *m*
奈木 Anaki *s*
斉 Anzai *s*
努 Anu *s*
典 Yasunori *m*
英 Yasue *f*
芸 Aki *sf-p*; Age *p*
芸凡 Akiōshi *s*
芸津 Akitsu *p*
国寺 Ankokuji *p*
居 Yasui *s*, Ao; Yasuoki *m*
居院 Agui *sml-p*; Akuin *s*, Agoin
武 Yasutake *s*
良沢 Arasawa *s*
良岡 Araoka *s*, Yasu-
東 Andō *s* ⌊raoka
東次男 A. Tsuguo *ml*
9保 Anpo *s*, Abo, Aho
松 Yasumatsu *s*
政 Ansei 1854–66
城 Anjō *sp*
城家の兄弟 Anjōke no kyōdai *l*
治 Yasuharu *m*
治郎 Yasujirō *m*
勅 Ajiki *s*, Achiki, A-
勅城 Ajiki *s* ⌊doki
南 Annan *p* "Annam"
香 Akō *s*
貞 Antei 1227–29
彦 Yasuhiko *m*, Yasuo; Abiko *s*
岡 Yasuoka *s* ⌈*ml*
岡章太郎 Y. Shōtarō
10浦 Yasuura *p*
祥 Anjō *s*
殷 Yasushige *m*
紡 Atogi *s*
紡城 Atogi *s*
倍 Abe *sp*
倍貞任 A. no Sadatō *mh* ⌈*ml*
倍能成 A. Yoshishige
倍晴明 A. no Seimei *mh* ⌈*mh*
倍頼時 A. no Yoritoki
食 Ajiki *sp*; Agui *s*
容 Yasumori *m*
室 Yasumuro *s*
益 Aya *sp*
原 Yasuhara *s*
11後 Yasunochi *m*
族 Yasutsugu *m*
野 Yasuno *s*
都 Yasukuni *m*
部 Abe *s*
部公房 A. Kōbō *ml*
部忠三 A. Chūzō *ml*
部磯雄 A. Isoo *mlh*
宿 Asuka *s*
堂 Andō *s*
斎 Anzai *sml* ⌈*ml*
斎桜磈子 A. Ōkaishi
島 Yasushima *s*, Aji-
閉 Abe *s*, Ae ⌊ma
12順 Yasushige *m*
孫子 Abiko *s*
補 Yasusada *m*
場 Yasuba *s*
堵 Ando *p*
納 Annō *s* ⌈*s*
富 Yasutomi *sp*; Anfu
喜 Yasuyoshi *m*
崇 Yasutaka *m*
間 Anma *s*, Ama, Yasuma
達 Adachi *sp* ⌈*mh*
達泰盛 A. Yasumori
達原 Adachigahara *la*
13喰 Anjiki *s*, Ajiki
塚 Yasuzuka *p*
満 Yasumitsu *sm*
福 Anpuku *s*, Yasukabe, Yasukae, Yasu-
雄 Yasuo *m* ⌊fuku
純 Yasuzumi *m*
誠 Yasumasa *m*
詮院 Azebu *s*
蒜 Anhiru *s*
雲 Yasumo *s*
愚楽鍋 Aguranabe *l*
幕 Amaka *s*, Amari
楽 Anraku *s*
楽城 Araki *s*
楽庵策伝 Anrakuan Sakuden *ml*
14徳 Antoku *mh*
飾 Anjiki *s*
認 Yasumoro *m*
誠 Yasumasa *m*
15蔵 Anzō *s*, Azō
摩 Ama *s*
諦 Ade *sp*
16頭麻呂 Azumaro *m*
歆 Yasuyoshi *m*
積 Azumi *s*; Asaka *sp*
積澹泊 Asaka Tanpaku *mh*
親 Yasuchika *m*
憲 Yasunori *m*
臺 Amaka *s*
17濃 Anō *sp*
濃津 Annotsu *s*
曇 Azumi *sp*; Akumo *s*, Atsumo
曇川 Adogawa *p*
18藤 Andō *s*
藤一郎 A. Ichirō *ml*

忍 志 声 売 壱 宋 宍 宍 完 安 ▼ 芭 芙 芥 芼 芬 芹 苅 芳 花 步 昊 孚 芦 至 杢 杏 李 ▲ 香 告 吾 労 究 辛 邑 男 秃 児

藤広重 A. Hiroshige *ma*
藤昌益 A. Shōeki *mh*
藤信正 A. Nobumasa *mh*
[19]繁 Yasushige *m*
[20]蘇 Aso *sp*
[21]繹 Yasutsugu *m*

芭 473 (BA, HA)
蕉 Bashō *ml*
蕉七部集 B. shichibu-shū *l*

芙 474 (FU, hasu)
代 Hasuyo *f*

芥 475 (KAI, KE, shina, akuta)
川 Akutagawa *sla*
川竜之介 A. Ryūnosuke *ml*

芼 476 (MŌ, HŌ, hiro)
子 Hiroko *f*

芬 477 Kaoru *m.* (FUN, hisa, ka)

芹 478 (KIN, GON, seri)
川 Serikawa *s*
生 Seryū *s*
田 Serita *s*
田鳳車 S. Hōsha *ml*
沢 Serizawa *s*
沢光治良 S. Kōjirō *ml*
草越 Serikoshi *s*
野 Serino *s*

苅 479 (KAI, GAI, GE, kari)
山 Kariyama *s*
田 Kanda *sp*; Karita *s*
田丸 Karitamaru *m*
田麻呂 Karitamaro *m*
込 Karikomi *s*
米 Kariyone *s*
谷 Kariya *s*
部 Karibe *s*
萱 Karukaya *s*
萱道心 K. Dōshin *lm*
萱桑門筑紫轢 K. D. Tsukushi no iezuto *la*

芳 480 [T] Kaoru *m*, Kanbashi, Yoshi. (HŌ, yoshi, ka, michi, fusa, hana, moto)
[2]人 Yoshito *m*
[3]川 Yoshikawa *s*
三郎 Yoshisaburō *m*
子 Yoshiko *f*
久 Yoshihisa *m*
[4]水 Hōsui *m*
井 Yoshii *p*
太郎 Yoshitarō *m*
夫 Yoshio *m*
[5]市 Yoshiichi *m*
生 Michio *m*
[6]次郎 Yoshijirō *m*
名 Yoshina *s*
[7]沢 Yoshizawa *s*
村 Yoshimura *s*
男 Yoshio *m*
[8]林 Yoshibayashi *s*
宜園 Hagizono *s*
武 Yoshitake *m*
[9]香 Hōka *s*
美 Hami *s*
[10]郎 Yoshirō *m*
[11]野 Yoshino *m*
[12]喬 Yoshitaka *m*
賀 Haga *sp*
賀矢一 H. Yaichi *ml*
賀檀 H. Mayumi *ml*
[13]雄 Yoshio *m*
[14]徳 Yoshinori *m*
[15]蔵 Yoshizō *m*
[16]樹 Yoshiki *m*
養 Haya *s*
幾 Yoshichika *m*

花 481 [T] Hana *sf.* (KA, KE, hana, haru)
ケ崎 Hanagasaki *p*
[3]川 Hanakawa *s*
子 Hanako *f*; Hanago *la*
上 Hanaue *s*
[4]水 Hanamizu *s*
井 Hanai *s*
木 Hanagi *s*
月 Kagetsu *la*
月草紙 K. sōshi *l*
山 Hanayama *sp*; Kazan *mlh*
山院 Kazan'in *smlh*
山院長親 K. Nagachika *ml*
[5]矢 Hanaya *p*
生 Hanao *s*
田 Hanada *s*
田比露思 H. Hiroshi *ml*
田清輝 H. Kiyoteru *ml*
本 Hanamoto *s*
[6]守 Hanamori *m*
[7]伝書 Kadensho *l*
坊 Hanabō *s*
沢 Hanazawa *s*
村 Hanamura *s*
形 Hanagata *s*
谷 Hanatani *s*
安 Hanayasu *s*
里 Hanasato *s*
[8]枝 Hanae *f*
房 Hanabusa *s*
[9]咲爺 Hanasakajii *l*
泉 Hanaizumi *p*
香 Hanaka *m*
巻 Hanamaki *p*
岡 Hanaoka *s*
岡謙二 H. Kenji *ml*
[10]柳 Hanayanagi *s*
家 Hanaya *s*
恵 Hanae *f*
屋 Hanaya *s*
笑 Hanae *f*
[11]桜折る少将 Hanazakura oru shōshō *l*
野 Hanano *s*
宴 Hana no en *l*
笠 Hanagasa *s*
島 Hanashima *s*
鳥編 Kachōhen *l*
[12]崎 Hanazaki *s*
散里 Hana chiru sato *l*
間鶯 Kakan'ō *l*
[13]塚 Hanazuka *s*
植 Hanaue *s*
筐 Hanagatami *la*
園 Hanazono *sp*
[14]暦八笑人 Hanagoyomi hasshōjin *l*
[15]輪 Hanawa *sp*
影 Kaei *l*
[17]簇 Hanamure *s*

——7 T4——

步 481A See 步 694

昊 482 Hiroshi *m.* (DAI, TAI)

孚 483 Makoto *m.* (FU, koto, sane, tada, taka, tane, tomo, nobu)
子 Taneko *f*
貞 Nobusada *m*
俊 Takatoshi *m*
麿 Takamaro *m*

芦 484 (RO, ashi, yoshi)
[3]川 Ashigawa *p*
[4]刈 Ashikari *p-l*
[5]北 Ashikita *p*
辺 Ashibe *p*
田 Ashida *sp*
田均 A. Hitoshi *mh*
田恵之助 A. Enosuke *ml*
[7]沢 Ashizawa *s*
別 Ashibetsu *p*
安 Ashiyasu *p*
谷 Ashiya *s*
見 Yoshimi *s*
[9]品 Ashina *sp*
[10]原 Ashiwara *s*; Awara *p*
屋 Ashiya *p*
[11]野 Ashino *s*
[13]葉 Ashiba *s*

至 485 [T] (SHI, yuki, chika, yoshi, nori, michi, mune)
上律 Shijōritsu *l*
子 Yukiko *f*
大 Michitomo *m*
世 Noriyo *f*
弘 Yoshihiro *m*
花道書 Shikadōsho *l*
剛 Shigō *m*
徳 Shitoku 1384–87
鎮 Yoshishige *m*

杢 486 Moku *m.* (moku)
之進 Mokunoshin *m*
網 Mokuami *m*

杏 487 Kyō *s.* (KŌ, KYŌ, anzu)
っ子 Anzukko *l*

李 488 Ri *s.* (RI, momo, sumomo)
子 Momoko *f*
木 Sumomogi *s*
花集 Rikashū *l*
家 Rinoie *s*
陵 Ri Ryō *mh-l* "Li Ling"

**吞** 489 (TON, nomi)
義 Nomiyoshi *m*

**告** 490 [T] Shimesu *m*; Nori *s*. (KOKU, KŌ, tsugu, tsuge)
森 Tsugemori *s*, Kotsumori

**吾** 491 [N] (GO, a, waga, wa, ware, michi)
$^{3}$川 Agawa *p*
$^{5}$北 Gohoku *p*
平 Ahira *p*
$^{6}$全 Waze *s*
$^{7}$助 Gosuke *s*
$^{8}$河 Wakawa *s*, Wagō, Agawa
枝 Wagae *f*
$^{9}$妹 Wagimo *l*
妻 Azuma *sp*; Agatsuma *p*
妻問答 Azuma mondō *l*
妻鏡 A. kagami *lh*
$^{10}$郎 Gorō *m*
$^{11}$笥 Ake *m*
$^{12}$孫 Abiko *s*
孫子 Abiko *s*
$^{15}$髪 Atsura *m*
$^{16}$樹 Aki *f*
$^{23}$鬘 Atsura *m*

—— 7 T5 ——

**労** 491A [T] (RŌ, mori)

**究** 492 [T] Kiwamu *m*. (KYŪ, KU, sata, sumi)

**辛** 493 [T] Kanoto *m*. (SHIN, kara)
夷 Kobushi *l*
島 Karashima *sp*

**皀** 494 Kyū *s*. (KYŪ)
郭 Kyūkaku *s*

**男** 495 [T] (DAN, NAN, o, oto)
也 Otoya *m*
女川 Omegawa *s*
玉 Otama *m*
色大鑑 Nanshoku ōkagami *l*
沢 Ozawa *s*
谷 Odani *s*
足 Otari *s*
波 Onami *f*
壮 Oyuka *s*
梶 Okaji *m*
衾 Obusuma *s*
鹿 Oga *p*

**禿** 496 Kamuro *m*; Kaburu *s*. (TOKU, kamuro)
氏 Kamuroji *s*, Tokushi

**児** 497 [T] Hajime *m*; Chigo *s*. (JI, ko, ru, nori, chigo)
山 Koyama *s*
山敬一 K. Keiichi *ml*
玉 Kodama *sp*
玉花外 K. Kagai *ml*
玉源太郎 K. Gentarō *mh*
谷野 Koyano *s*
馬 Koba *s*
部 Jibe *s*
島 Kojima *sp*
島惟謙 K. Iken *mh*
島喜久雄 K. Kikuo *ml*
湯 Koyu *p*

**貝** 498 [T] (HAI, BAI, kai)
おほひ Kai-ōi *l*
川 Kaikawa *s*
子 Kaiko *f*
田 Kaida *s*
沼 Kainuma *s*
津 Kaizu *s*
原 Kaibara *s*
原益軒 K. Ekiken / Ekken *mh*
島 Kaijima *s*
賀 Kaiga *s*
塚 Kaizuka *sp*
瀬 Kaise *s*

**兵** 499 [T] (HEI, HYŌ, take, hito, mune)
$^{1}$一 Hyōichi *m*
$^{3}$三郎 Hyōsaburō *m*
$^{4}$五郎 Hyōgorō *m*
$^{5}$主 Hyōzu *s*
$^{6}$吉 Hyōkichi *m*
$^{9}$治 Hyōji *m*
$^{10}$俊 Taketoshi *m*
庫 Hyōgo *p*
$^{11}$動 Hyōdō *s*
部 Hyōbu *m*
部卿 H.-kyō *l*
視 Takemi *m*
$^{12}$須 Hyōsu *s*
$^{16}$衛 Hyōe *m-fl*
頭 Hyōdō *s*
$^{18}$藤 Hyōdō *s*

—— 7 F ——

**考** See 540

**孝** See 541

**乕** 500 See 虎 754

**廷** 501 [T] (TEI, naga, taka, tada)

**囲** 501A [T] (I, mori)

**図** 502 [T] Hakaru *m*. (TO, ZU, nori, mitsu)
南 Tonan *m*
師 Zushi *s*

**匠** 503 [T] Takumi *m*. (SHŌ, ZŌ)

**匡** 504 [N] Tadashi *m*, Masashi, Tasuku. (KYŌ, KŌ, masa, tada)
子 Masako *f*
也 Masatada *m*
四郎 Kyōshirō *m*, Tadashirō
房 Masafusa *ml*
徳 Masanori *m*, Tadanori
衛 Masahiro *m*
衡 Masahira *m*

**尾** 505 [T] (BI, o, sue)
$^{3}$川 Ogawa *s*
口 Okuchi *sp*
子 Sueko *f*
上 Onoe *sp*; Ogami *s*
上柴舟 Onoe Saishū *ml*
上菊五郎 O. Kikugorō *ma*
下 Oshita *s*
$^{4}$中 Onaka *s*
方 Ogata *s*
山 Oyama *s*
山篤二郎 O. Tokujirō *ml*
木 Ogi *s*
内 Onai *s*, Ouchi
$^{5}$古 Oko *s*
本 Omoto *s*
田 Oda *s*
$^{6}$池 Oike *s*
辻 Otsuji *s*
竹 Otake *s*
去沢 Osarizawa *p*
宅 Oyake *s*
芝 Oshiba *s*
台 Odai *s*
吉 Suekichi *m*
寺 Odera *s*
西 Bisai *p*
$^{7}$沢 Ozawa *s*
坂 Osaka *s*
佐丸 Osamaru *m*
佐竹 Osatake *s*
佐竹猛 O. Takeo *mlh*
形 Ogata *s*
形光琳 O. Kōrin *ma*
形乾山 O. Kenzan *ma*
形亀之助 O. Kamenosuke *ml*
村 Omura *s*, Onomura
谷 Otani *s*
花 Ohana *s*
花沢 Obanazawa *p*
里 Ozato *s*
見 Omi *s*
身 Omi *s*
$^{8}$林 Obayashi *s*
$^{9}$城 Oshiro *s*
畑 Obata *s*
$^{10}$高 Otaka *s*, Suetaka
原 Ohara *s*
$^{11}$野 Ono *s*
島 Ojima *sp*
$^{12}$崎 Ozaki *s*
崎一雄 O. Kazuo *ml*
崎士郎 O. Shirō *ml*
崎行雄 O. Yukio *mh*
崎孝子 O. Kōko *fl*
崎放哉 O. Hōsai *ml*
崎宏次 O. Hirotsugu *ml*
﨑紅葉 O. Kōyō *ml*
崎喜八 O. Kihachi *ml*
道 Onomichi *p*
$^{13}$張 Owari *ph*
塞 Oseki *s*

芳 花 歩 昊 孚 芦 至 杢 杏 李 ▼ 吞 告 吾 労 究 辛 皀 男 禿 児 貝 兵 考 孝 乕 廷 囲 図 匠 匡 尾 ▲ 近 序 床 応 彣 戒 冏 何 局 君

園 Ozono *s*
[14]関 Ozeki *s*
[17]輿 Okoshi *m*
[18]藤 Bitō *s*
[19]瀬 Ose *s*
瀬敬止 O. Keishi *ml*
[23]鷲 Owase *p*

近 506 [T] Kon *s*, Chika; Chikashi *m*. (KIN, KON, chika)
[4]方 Chikakata *m*
山 Chikayama *s*
木 Chikaki *s*
[5]代詩苑 Kindaishien *l*
田 Chikada *s*
[6]江 Ōmi *sph* ⌈*p*
江八幡 Ō. Hachiman
江県 Ō. agata *l*
江源氏先陣館 Ō. Genji senjin yakata *la*
江聖人 Ō. Seijin *mh*
江脚身 Ōminoashitsumi *s*
世説美少年録 Kinseisetsu bishōnen roku
年諸国咄 Kinnen ⌊*l*
shokoku-banashi *l*
[7]坂 Chikazaka *s*
沢 Chikazawa *s*
来風体抄 Kinrai fūtaishō *l* ⌈East"
[8]東 Kintō *p* "Near
[9]神 Chikami *s*
松 Chikamatsu *sml*
松半二 C. Hanji *ml*
松門左衛門 C. Monzaemon *ml*
松秋江 C. Shūkō *ml*
岡 Chikaoka *s*
[10]俊 Chikatoshi *m*
[11]淡海 Chikatsuōmi *s*
野 Konno *s*
菊 Chikagiku *m*
[12]間 Chikama *s*
路行者 Kinro Gyōja
[13]喰 Konjiki *s* ⌊*ml*
[16]衛 Konoe *sfl*
衛文麿 K. Fumimaro
[18]藤 Kondō *s* ⌊*mh*
藤芳美 K. Yoshimi *ml*
藤芳樹 K. Yoshiki *ml*
藤忠義 K. Tadayoshi *ml*
藤東 K. Azuma *ml*
藤重蔵 K. Jūzō *mh*
藤経一 K. Keiichi *ml*
嶺 Chikane *m*
[19]霧 Chikakiri *m*

序 507 [T] Hisashi *m*. (JO, SHO, tsune, nobu, tsugu)
光 Tsunemitsu *m*
克 Tsunekatsu *m*

床 508 [T] (SHŌ, JŌ, toko, yuka)
井 Tokoi *s*
次 Tokonami *s* ⌈*mh*
次竹二郎 T. Takejirō
波 Tokonami *s*

応 509 [T] (Ō, masa, nori, kazu, taka, nobu)
[3]子 Masako *f*
[4]仁 Ōnin 1467–69
[5]代 Norishiro *m*
永 Ōei 1394–1428
田 Ōta *s*
[7]安 Ōan 1368–75
安新式 Ō. shinshiki *l*
和 Ōwa 961–64
[9]保 Ōhō 1161–63
神 Ōjin *mh-p*
叙 Masanobu *m*
長 Ōchō 1311–12
[11]隆 Masataka *m*
理 Masanori *m*
堂 Ōdō *s*
[12]道 Masatsune *m*
[14]徳 Ōtoku 1084–87
輔 Ōsuke *m*
韶 Masatsugu *m*

彣 510 (BUN, MON, aki, yoshi)

戒 511 [T] (KAI)
三 Kaizō *m*
田 Kaida *s*
重 Kaijū *s*
野 Kaino *s*
能 Kainō *s*
壇院四天王 Kaidan'in shitennō *a*

冏 512 Akira *m*. (KEI, KYŌ, akira)

何 513 [T] Ka *s*. (KA, GA, nani, izu)
丸 Nanimaru *m*
応欽 Ka Ōkin *mh* "Ho Ying-ch'in"
恵 Izue *f*
鹿 Ikaruga *p*

局 514 [T] Tsubone *f*. (KYOKU, GOKU, chika)

君 515 [T] (KUN, kimi, ko, kin, sue, nao, yoshi)
子 Kimiko *f*
仁 Kimihito *m*
手 Kimite *m*
田 Kimita *p*
平 Kunpei *m*
和田 Kimiwada *s*
津 Kimitsu *p*
美 Kimi *f*; Kimiyoshi *m*
家 Ōya *s*
島 Kimishima *s*
袋 Kimibukuro *s*
塚 Kimizuka *s*
雄 Kimio *m*
養 Kiminobu *m*

## 7 U

串 516 (KAN, kushi)
木野 Kushikino *p*
本 Kushimoto *p*
田 Kushida *s* ⌈*ml*
田孫一 K. Magoichi
良 Kushira *p*
原 Kushibara *p*
間 Kushima *p*

里 517 [T] Satomi *m*; Sato *p*. (RI, sato, nori)
川 Satokawa *s*
子 Satoko *f*
内 Satouchi *s*
吉 Satoyoshi *s*
庄 Satoshō *p*
村 Satomura *s*
村欣三 S. Kinzō *ml*
村紹巴 S. Shōha *ml*
見 Satomi *s* ⌈den *l*
見八犬伝 S. hakken-
見弴 S. Ton *ml*
美 Satomi *p*
春 Satoharu *sm*

見 518 [T] (KEN, mi, chika, aki, akira, miru)
[3]子 Miruko *f*
上 Mikami *s*
千 Chikayuki *m*
[4]戸 Mito *s*
山 Miyama *s*
[5]付 Mitsuke *s*
田 Handa *s*
目 Kenmoku *s*
[6]次 Akitsugu *m*
米 Migome *s*
[7]形 Migata *s*
[8]附 Mitsuke *p*
[9]城 Kenjō *s*
参岡 Misaoka *s*
[10]原 Mihara *s*
[11]留 Mitome *s*
[12]崎 Misaki *s*
富 Mitomi *s*
[13]雲 Mikuma *s*

亥 519 [N] (GAI, i, ri)
八 Ihachi *m*
三 Izō *m*, Isamu
子 Ine *s*
太郎 Itarō *m*
久 Iku *f*
六 Iroku *m*
勇夫 Isao *m*

衣 520 [T] E *s*. (I, E, kinu, so, miso)
川 Kinugawa *s*, Koromogawa
江 Kinue *f*
非 Ebi *s*
祝 Ehafuri *s*
枳 Eki *s*
笠 Kinugasa *s*
斐 Ibi *s*, Ebi
揩 Kinuzuri *s*
摺 Kinushiri *s*, Kinu-
箱 Yohomi *s* ⌊zuri
繖 Kinugasa *s*
羅 Yosami *s*

充 521 [T] Mitsuru *m*, Makoto, Takashi. (JŪ, SHŪ, JU, mitsu, michi, mi, atsu)
子 Mitsuko *f*, Atsuko
晤 Mitsuaki *m*
曼 Mitsuhiro *m*
常 Mitsunobu *m*

**玄** 522 [T] Fukashi *m*, Shizuka, Hakaru, Hajime, Hikaru; Gen *sm*. (GEN, haru, kuro, fuka, tō, shizu, tsune, nori, hiro, tora)
[1]一郎 Gen'ichirō *m*
[3]子 Haruko *f*
上 Kurokami *m*, Harumasa, Haruura; Genjō *la*
[4]夫 Fukao *m*
太郎 Gentarō *m*
[6]次 Harutsugu *m*
朴と長英 Genboku to Chōei *la*
広 Haruhiro *m*
[7]玄集 Gengenshū *l*
[8]門 Haruto *m*
明 Haruakira *m*
昉 Genbō *mh*
空 Genkū *ml*
[9]洞 Gendō *ml*
洋社 Gen'yōsha *h*
治 Tsuneharu *m*
[10]海 Genkai *ma-p*
通 Fukamichi *m*
[11]理 Kuromasa *m*
渓 Genkei *m*
[12]御 Gengo *s*
象 Genjō *la*
[15]慧 Gen'e *mh*
[17]綱 Tōtsuna *m*
[21]鶴山房 Genkaku Sanbō *l*

**出** 523 [T] Izuru *m*; Ide *s*. (SHUTSU, SUI, de, izu, ide)
[3]川 Degawa *s*
口 Deguchi *s*
口王仁三郎 D. Wanisaburō *mh* ⌈*mh*
口延佳 D. Nobuyoshi
口直 D. Nao *fh* ⌈*sp*
[4]水 Demizu *s*; Izumi
水川 Demizugawa *p*
井 Dei *s*, Izui, Idei
牛 Deushi *s*
山 Deyama *s*
[5]石 Izuishi *s*; Izushi *sp*
田 Ideta *s*
目 Deme *s*
[6]羽 Dewa *sph*; Izuha *s*
光 Idemitsu *s*
世 Izuyo *f* ⌈kiyo *la*
世景清 Shusse Kage-
[7]村 Demura *s*
見 Izumi *m*
来 Deki *s*
来丸 Dekimaru *m*
来星 Dekiboshi *m*
来島 Dekishima *s*
[10]浦 Deura *s*, Ideura
射 Idei *s*
家 Deie *s*
原 Idehara *s*, Ihara
庭 Dewa *s*, Ideha
[11]隆 Ide Takashi *ml*
野 Izuno *s*, Ideno
島 Dejima / Deshima
[12]温 Deon *s* ⌊*sp*
納 Suinō *s*, Suitō
[13]淵 Debuchi *s*, Izubuchi, Izu
雲 Izumo *sp*
雲阿国 I. no Okuni *fa*
雲国 Izumonokuni *ph*
雲国風土記 I. no fudoki *l*
雲国造神賀詞 I. no miyatsuko no kami yogoto *l*
雲崎 Izumozaki *p*
雲路 Imoji *s*
雲郷 Adakai *s*

**巫** 524 (FU, miko)
学談弊 Fugakudan hei *l* ⌈gi, Kōnai
部 Mikobe *s*, Kanna-

**亜** 525 [T] A *l*. (A, E, tsugi, tsugu)
子 Tsugiko *f*
米利加 Amerika *p* "America"
夫 Tsugio *s*
沙子 Asako *f*
刺比亜 Arabia *p* "Arabia"
周 Tsuguchika *m*
欧堂田善 Aōdō Denzen *ma*
風 Tsugikaze *ma*
彦 Tsuguhiko *m*
細亜 Ajia *p* "Asia"
爾然丁 Aruzenchin *p* "Argentine"

**酉** 526 [N] Minoru *m*. (YŪ, YU, tori,
乙 Torioto *m* ⌊naga)
三 Yūzō *m*, Torizō
子 Toriko *f*
水 Sugai *s*
井 Torii *s*
夫 Torio *m*
雄 Nagao *m*

**臣** 527 [T] Shige *f*; Omi *s*, Onnoko. (SHIN, JIN, omi, tomi, mi, on, shige, mitsu, o)
乙 Omio *f*
江 Omie *f*
直 Tominao *m*

**更** 528 [T] Kawaru *m*. (KŌ, KYŌ, nobu, toku, to, fuke)
子 Nobuko *f*
北 Kōhoku *p*
田 Fukeda *s*
別 Sarabetsu *p*
衣 Kōi *f*; Kisaragi *m*; Watanuki *s*
科 Sarashina *sp*
科紀行 S. kikō *l*
埴 Kōshoku *p*
級 Sarashina *sp*
級日記 S. nikki *l*

**艮** 529 Katashi *m*. (KON, tora, kata, ushi, tada)
雄 Torao *m*

**豕** 530 Inoke *m*. (SHI)

**両** 531 [T] (RYŌ, furu, moro)
角 Morozumi *s*
国 Ryōgoku *p*
津 Ryōtsu *p*
神 Ryōkami *p*

**車** 532 [T] Kuruma *s*, Sha. (SHA, kuru, kuruma, nori)
力 Shariki *p*
田 Kurumada *s*
谷 Shatani *s*
前草 Shazensō *l*
間 Kuruma *s*
僧 Kuruma-sō *la*

**甫** 533 Hajime *m*. (HO, FU, suke, yoshi, nami, moto, nori, mi, kami, masa)
子 Toshiko *f*
冬 Sukefuyu *m*
信 Yoshinobu *m*
美 Namiyoshi *m*
鬼 Hoki *s*
喜山 Hokiyama *s*

**夾** 534 Chikashi *m*. (KYŌ)

**夷** 535 (I, hina, hira, ebisu)
子 Ebisu *mh*
川 Ebisugawa *s*
大黒 Ebisu Daikoku *mh-la*
守 Hinamori *sp*
臣 Hiraomi *m*
毘沙門 Ebisu Bishamon *mh-la*
隅 Isumi *s*
隔 Ishini *s*
麿 Hinamaro *m*

**束** 536 [T] Tsukane *m*, Tsukanu. (SOKU, SHOKU, tsuka, ki,
田 Tsukada *s* ⌊sato)
稲 Tsukane *m*

**求** 537 [T] Motomu *m*. (KYŪ, GU, moto, masa, hide)
己 Motoki *m*
女 Motome *f*
枝 Motoe *f*
周 Masachika *m*
馬 Motome *m*
塚 Motomezuka *la*

**来** 538 [T] Kitaru *m*; Rai *s*. (RAI, ki, ku, ko, na, kuru, yuki)
[5]目 Kume *sm*
正 Kurumasa *s*
生 Kisugi *s*
[6]次 Kitsugu *sp*
[7]住 Kishi *s*
位 Kishū *s*
吹 Kigisu *s*
余 Koromo *s* ⌈chi
[8]河 Kurumi *s*, Kima-
迎和讃 Raigō wasan *l*
[9]城 Raijō *s* ⌈chi
[10]海 Kurumi *s*, Kima-

艮豕両車甫夾夷束求来▼寿考孝坐缶兎我身角協冽佛侃佼侊佰供▲使侑佶侍佳佽佪帖性怜

栖 Kurusu *s*
栖三郎 K. Saburō *mh*
原 Kuruhara *sp*
[11]島 Kurushima *s*
[13]殿 Raiden *la*
[15]熊田 Kumata *s*
[18]臨 Koromo *s*

**寿** 539 [T] Hisashi *m*, Kotobuki, Nagashi, Hiroshi, Tamotsu, Yasushi, Toshinaga. (JU, SHŪ, hisa, naga, yoshi, toshi, hogi, tsune, nobu, hide, kazu, iki)
の門松 Nebiki no kadomatsu *la*
[1]一 Hisaichi *m*, Juichi
[2]乙 Kazuo *m*
人 Hisato *m*; Toshito *m-f*
[3]三郎 Jusaburō *m*
子 Hisako *m*
[4]夫 Ikio *m*
太郎 Toshitarō *m*
[5]永 Juei 1182–85
巨 Hisanao *m*
[6]吉 Jukichi *m*, Hisayoshi
[7]男 Hisao *m*
床 Sudoko *s*
寿木 Suzuki *s*
[8]幸 Toshihide *m*
命 Toshinaga *m*
昌 Nagamasa *m*
[9]津 Suzu *f*
松 Toshimatsu *m*
軌 Hidenori *m*
[10]修 Toshinori *m*
郎 Jurō *m*
格 Toshinori *m*
原 Suhara *s*
[11]都 Suttsu *p*
[12]崎 Susaki *s*
詞 Yogoto *l*
[13]祺 Hisayoshi *m*
雄 Hisao *m*
準 Hisanori *m*
[14]増子 Sumako *f*
[15]摩 Suma *s*
[16]樹 Hisaki *m*
[18]藤 Sudō *s*
[19]瀏 Toshikiyo *m*
[21]纒 Toshitsuna *m*

**考** 540 [T] (KŌ, naru, taka, naka, yasu, tada, chika, toshi, nari, nori, yoshi)

**孝** 541 [T] Takashi *m*, Tsukō. (KŌ, KYŌ, taka, nori, yoshi, michi, yuki, atsu, nari, moto)
[1]一 Kōichi *m*
[2]二 Kōji *m*
[3]子 Kōko *f*
之丞 Kōnojō *m*
之助 Kōnosuke *m*
之亮 Kōnosuke *m*
之輔 Kōnosuke *m*
[4]友 Takatomo *m*
太 Takashiro *m*
太郎 Kōtarō *m*
[5]允 Takayoshi *m*
平 Takahira *s*; Kōhei *m*
四郎 Kōshirō *m*
[6]次 Kōji *m*, Takatsugu
吉 Kōkichi *m*
因 Takayori *m*
[7]作 Kōsaku *m*
[8]明 Kōmei *mh*
弟 Takachika *m*
昌 Takayoshi *m*
季 Norisue *m*
[9]治 Kōji *m*
哉 Kōsai *m*
[10]時 Takatoki *m*
高 Yoshitaka *m*
恭 Takayoshi *m*
[11]徠 Takatome *m*
章 Takanori *m*
[12]順 Takanobu *m*
孫 Takahiko *m*
景 Takakage *m*
道 Takamichi *m*
[13]福 Yoshitomi *m*
雄 Takao *m*
詮 Takanori *m*
幹 Takamiki *m*
経 Kōkyō *l*
[14]徳 Kōtoku *mh*
節 Takatoki *m*
[15]標 Takasue *m-f*
標女 T. no Musume *fl*
蔵 Kōzō *m*
[16]儔 Takatomo *m*
綽 Takayasu *m*
[17]潔 Takakiyo *m*
謙 Kōken *fh*
[18]顕 Takaaki *m*, Noriaki
嶺 Takane *m*

**坐** 542 (SA, ZA, masu, kura, imasu)
間 Kurama *s*

**缶** 543 (FŪ, FU, be)

**兎** 544 See 兔 763

**我** 545 [T] (GA, KA, a, waga)
如古 Kaneko *s*
何 Soga *s*
妻 Azuma *s*, Wagatsuma
彦 Abiko *s*, Gahiko
孫 Abiko *s*
孫子 Abiko *sp*
楽多文庫 Garakuta bunko *l*
謝 Kasha *s*

**身** 546 [T] (SHIN, mi, mu, nobu, chika, moto, tada, yoshi)
人 Myūto *s*, Myūdo, Mutori
人部 Myūtobe *s*, Mitobe
毛 Muge *s*
毛津 Mugetsu *s*
延 Minobu *p-l*
狭 Musa *s*
度部 Mutobe *s*
挾 Musashi *m*

**角** 547 [T] Kaku *s*, Sumi, Tsuno, Tsunu, Roku. (KAKU, sumi, kado, mi, tsuno, tsunu, fusa)
[1]一 Kakuichi *m*
[3]川 Kadokawa *s*
[4]井 Kadoi *s*, Tsunoi
山 Kadoyama *s*
[5]田 Tsunoda *s*, Kadota, Sumida, Kakuda
田川 Sumidagawa *la*
田竹冷 Sumida Chikurei *ml*
田浩々歌客 Kakuda Kōkōkakaku *ml*
本 Kadomoto *s*
[7]折 Tsunoori *s*
村 Tsunomura *s*
谷 Kadotani *s*, Kakuya, Sumiya
尾 Tsunoo *s*
出 Kadode *s*
我 Tsunuga *ph*
[8]和 Tsunowa *s*
国 Kadokuni *m*
[9]南 Sunami *sp*; Suminami *s*
岡 Kakuoka *s*
[10]倉 Sumikura *s*, Suminokura
倉了以 Suminokura Ryōi *mh*
屋 Kadoya *s*, Kakuya, Sumiya
屋七郎兵衛 Kadoya Shichirōbee *mh*
[11]野 Sumino *s*, Kadono
宿禰 Tsununosukune
[12]間 Kadoma *s*
鹿 Tsunuga *s*
[13]張 Kadohari *s*
義 Takayoshi *m*
[17]館 Kakunodate *p*
[18]麿 Sumimaro *m*

## 8 L2

**協** 548 [T] Kanō *m*. (KYŌ, GYŌ, yasu)
中 Yasunaka *m*
和 Kyōwa *p*

**冽** 549 Kiyoshi *m*, Tadashi. (RETSU, kiyo)
子 Kiyoko *f*
泉 Kiyomi *m*

**佛** 550 See 仏 128

**侃** 551 Tadashi *m*, Tsuyoshi, Sunao. (KAN, nao, akira, tada, yasu)
左 Naosuke *m*

**佼** 552 (KŌ, KYŌ, yoshi)

**侊** 553 (KŌ, teru, mitsu)
男 Teruo *m*

**佰** 554 Tsukasa *m*; Momo *f*. (HAKU)

**供** 555 [T] (KYŌ, KU, tomo)
子 Tomoko *f*
愛 Tomonaru *m*

使 556 [T] (SHI)
主 Omi *sm*

侑 557 Atsumu *m*, Susumu. (YŪ, U, yuki)

佶 558 Tadashi *m*. (KITSU, tada, yoshi)

侍 559 [T] (JI, SHI, hito)
従 Jijū *sm*
郎 Jirō *m*

佳 560 [T] Yoshi *m*. (KA, yoshi)
一 Kaichi *m*
人之奇遇 Kajin no kigū *l*
子 Yoshiko *f*
丈 Yoshitake *m*
代子 Kayoko *f*
田 Yoshida *s*
似子 Kaiko *f*
妙 Yoshitō *f*
秧 Kanae *f*
郎 Yoshirō *m*
盛 Kamori *m*

佽 561 (SHI, toshi)
男 Toshio *m*

侚 562 (JUN, SHUN, toshi)
子 Toshiko *f*

——8 L3——

帖 563 (CHŌ, JŌ, sada, tada)
佐 Chōsa *s*

性 564 [T] (SEI, SHŌ, moto, nari)
之 Motoyuki *m*
霊集 Shōryōshū *l*

怜 565 Satoshi *m*. (REI, RYŌ, sato, toki)
子 Satoko *f*

狗 566 (KŌ, KU, inu, koma)
月 Inuzuki *s*, Komatsuki
張子 Inuhariko *l*

狛 567 Koma *sm*. (HAKU, koma)
人 Komōdo *s*
人野 Komōdono *s*
井 Komai *s*
江 Komae *sp*
竪部 Komanochiisakobe *s*

陀 568 (DA)
羅尼 Darani *s*

阿 569 Akutsu *s*. (A, kuma)
$^{2}$刀 Ato *s*
刀田 Atōda *s*
$^{3}$川 Agawa *s*
川弘之 A. Hiroyuki *ml*
三次 Asōji *m*
万 Ama *s*
子島 Akogashima *s*, Akushima
久井 Akui *s*
久比 Agui *p*
久沢 Akusawa *s*
久津 Akutsu *s*
久根 Akune *p*
$^{4}$内 Anouchi *s*
仁 Ani *p*
支奈 Ashina *s*, Akina
介 Asuke *s*
山 Ayama *p*
王丸 Kumawakamaru *m*
尺 Asaka *s*
井 Ai *s*
木 Agi *s*
太肥人 Atakumabito *s*
$^{5}$仏尼 Abutsuni *fl*
礼 Are *m*
比 Ai *s*, Abi
比古 Abiko *s*
比留 Ahiru *s*
古木 Akogi *s*
左古 Asako *s*
由葉 Ayuba *s*
田 Ata *s*, Kumada
$^{6}$竹 Atake *s*
曲 Akuma *s*
多見 Atami *s*
弗利加 Afurika *p* "Africa"
$^{7}$沙丸 Asamaru *m*
形 Agata *s*
那名 Anana *s*
佐井 Asai *s*
佐利 Asari *s*
佐美 Asami *s*
児 Ago *p*
見 Ami *p*
出川 Adegawa *s*
免谷 Ametani *s*
$^{8}$波 Awa *p*, Aba
波之鳴門 Awa no Naruto *l*
波野 Awano *s*
波野青畝 A. Seiho *ml*
知女作法 Achime no waza *l*
知使主 Achi no Omi *mh*
知波 Achiba *s*
知須 Ajisu *p*
国 Okuni *fa*
武 Abu *sp*; Anno *s*
武方 Anno *s*
東 Atō *p*
$^{9}$保 Ao *s*, Abo
治川 Ajikawa *s*
弥陀 Amida *mh*
相 Asō *s*
南 Anan *p*; Anami *s*
直 Ajiki *s*
直岐 Achiki *mh*
祇奈 Akina *s*
$^{10}$耳古 Abiko *s*
射弥 Azami *s*
倍 Abe *s*
倍比羅夫 A. no Hirafu *mh*
倍仲麻呂 A. no Nakamaro *mh*
倍頼時 A. no Yoritoki *mh*
高 Ataka *s*
哲 Atetsu *p*
座上 Azakami *s*
$^{11}$都扇 Atsumi *s*
野 Ano *s*, Aya, Anno
部 Abe *s*
部一族 A. ichizoku *l*
部正弘 A. Masahiro *mh*
部次郎 A. Jirō *ml*
部知二 A. Tomoji *ml*
部信行 A. Nobuyuki *mh*
部真之助 A. Shinnosuke *ml*
部野 Abeno *sp*
部静枝 Abe Shizue *fl*
留多岐 Arutaki *s*
留多岐伯 Arutakii *s*
閉 Abe *sp*; Atoji *s*, Atsuji
閉門人 Abenokadōdo *s*
閉麻呂 Abemaro *m*
閇間人 Abehashihito *s*
島 Ajima *s*
$^{12}$孫 Abiko *s*
曾 Aso *s*
曾谷 Asotani *s*
曾沼 Asonuma *s*
寒 Akan *s*
智 Achi *s*
間 Anma *s*
鹿沼 Akanuma *s*
達 Adachi *s*
$^{13}$蛭 Anhiru *s*
新丸 Kumawakamaru *m*
墓 Abaka *s*, Azumi
$^{14}$漕 Akogi *la*
歌麿 Akamaro *s*
$^{16}$積 Asaka *s*
$^{17}$曇 Azumi *s*
曇比羅夫 A. no Hirafu *mh*
$^{18}$藤 Atō *s*
$^{19}$蘇 Aso *sp*

咋 570 Kui *sm*. (SAKU, SHAKU, kui)
田 Kuita *s*

呼 571 [T] (KO, KA, un, oto, koe, yobu)
子 Yobuko *p*
唹 O *s*, Ō
翁 Un'ō *ma*

味 572 [T] (MI, BI, aji, uma, chika)
戸 Ajito *m*
方 Ajikata *p*
尺 Umasaka *s*
木 Ajiki *s*
村 Mimura *s*
岡 Ajioka *s*
淳 Umasake *s*
酒 Umasake *s*, Misaki
稲 Umashine *ml*

坤 573 Mamoru *m*. (KON, shita)

坦 574 Hiroshi *m*, Hiromu, Taira, Yasushi, Yutaka, Shizuka, Akira; Yasu *f*. (TAN, katsu, hiro, hira)

坪 575 [T] (HYŌ, tsubo)
$^{3}$川 Tsubokawa *s*
上 Tsubogami *s*
$^{4}$山 Tsuboyama *s*
木 Tsuboki *s*

身角協冽佛侃佼侊佰供▼使侑佶侍佳佽侚帖性怜狗狛陀阿咋呼味坤坦坪▲径徂彼往征担披拈抱拜

狗 狛 陀 阿 咋 呼 味 坤 坦 坪 ▼ 径 徂 彼 往 征 担 披 拈 抱 拝 拓 押 泗 泱 泣 注 泊 油 泥 沼 波 河 ▲ 岬 岐 所 門 炊 欣 改 玢 朳 放

井 Tsuboi s ⌈mh
井正五郎 T. Shōgorō
内 Tsubouchi s
内士行 T. Shikō ml
内逍遙 T. Shōyō ml
[5]平 Tsubohira m
田 Tsubota s
田譲治 T. Jōji ml
[7]谷 Tsuboya s
[10]倉 Tsubokura s
[11]野 Tsubono s
野哲久 T. Tekkyū ml

径 576 [T] (KEI, KYŌ, michi)
子 Michiko f

徂 577 (SO, ZO, yuku)
子 Yukuko f
徠 Sorai mlh

彼 578 [T] (HI, nobu, sono, kano)
末 Kanosue s
杵 Sonoki sp; Sōki s
岸過迄 Higan-sugi made l

往 579 [T] (Ō, yuki, hisa, yoshi, nari, mochi)
生要集 Ōjō yōshū lh
生極楽院 Ō. Gokurakuin p
住 Tokozumi s
来 Yukiki m
来物 Ōraimono l
岸 Ōgin s

征 580 [T] Tadasu m, Tadashi. (SEI, SHŌ, yuki, masa, sachi, yuku, so, moto)
之助 Masanosuke m
夫 Masao m, Yukuo
四郎 Seishirō m
矢 Soya s
矢子 Soyako f
矢野 Soyano s
帆 Yukiho m
捷 Yukitoshi m
朗 Sachio s
雄 Yukio s

担 581 [T] Yutaka m. (TAN, SEN, ZEN)

披 582 (HI, hiro, hira)

拈 583 (NEN, DEN)
華微笑 Nenge mishō l

抱 584 [T] (HŌ, mochi)
月 Hōgetsu ml

拝 585 [T] (HAI)
郷 Haigō s

拓 586 [T] Hiraku m, Hiroshi. (TAKU, CHAKU, hiro)
章 Hiroaki m

押 587 [T] (Ō, oshi)
[8]小路 Oshikōji s
川 Oshikawa s
川春浪 O. Shunrō ml
上 Oshiage s
久保 Oshikubo s
[4]木 Oshiki s
水 Oshimizu p
元 Oshimoto s
山 Oshiyama s
切 Oshikiri s
[5]田 Oshida s
本 Oshimoto s
[7]村 Oshimura s
谷 Oshitani s
尾 Oshio s
見 Oshimi s
戻 Oshimodoshi l
[11]野 Oshino s
[20]鐘 Oshikane s

泗 588 (SHI)
水 Shisui p

泱 589 Hiroshi m; Hiro m-f. (Ō, hiro)
夫 Hiroo m

泣 590 [T] (KYŪ, naki)
尼 Nakiama la
菫詩集 Kyūkin shishū l

注 591 [T] (CHŪ, SHU)
連内 Shimeuchi s
連雄 Shimeo m

泊 592 [T] Tomari sp. (HAKU, hatsu)
洎舎 Sadanaminoya ml
橿部 Hatsukashibe s
瀬 Hatsuse sp

油 593 [T] (YU, abura)
小路 Aburanokōji s
川 Yugawa s, Aburakawa
井 Aburai s, Yui
木 Yuki p
田 Yuda s
比 Yui s
谷 Yuya sp; Yutani s, Aburadani
原 Yubara s
屋 Yuya s, Aburaya
糟 Aburakasu l
糟淀川 A. Yodogawa l

泥 594 [I] Nuri s, Hatsukashi. (DEI, ne, doro, nuri)
人形 Doro ningyō l
之助 Doronosuke m
戸 Nurihe s
谷 Hijiya s, Hijinoya
障 Afuri s

沼 595 [T] Numa s. (SHŌ, numa, nu)
[3]上 Numagami s
口 Numaguchi s
子 Numako f
[4]井 Numai s
[5]田 Numata sp
尻 Numajiri s
本 Numamoto s
[7]沢 Numazawa s
尾 Numao s
[8]知 Numachi s
波 Numanami s, Nunami ⌈on ml
波瓊音 Nunami Kei-
垂 Nutari s; Nuttari sp
[9]津 Numazu sp
南 Shōnan p
前 Numasaki s
[10]倉 Numakura s
畠 Numabatake s
[11]浪 Numanami s
野 Numano s
部 Numabe s
島 Numajima s
[12]隅 Numakuma p
崎 Numazaki s
間 Numa s

波 596 [T] Nami f. (HA, nami)
[2]入 Hanyū s
[4]方 Hagata p
木井 Hakii s
太 Hata s
[5]田 Hata sp
田野 Hatano s
平 Naminohira s
白 Hashiro s
[6]伊万世 Haimase s
江 Namie s
多 Hata s
多江 Hatae s
多野 Hatano s
多野完治 H. Kanji ml
[7]佐見 Hasami p
[8]波泊 Hahakabe s, Hōkabe
波伯部 Hahakabe s, Hōkabe, Hahakaga
波泊 Hahakabe s, Hahakaga ⌈Hōkabe
波泊部 Hahakabe s,
[9]重 Namie f
[11]野 Namino sp
部 Habe s
留 Haru f
[12]崎 Hasaki p
斯 Perusha p "Persia"
賀 Haga p ⌈land"
[21]蘭 Porando p "Po-

河 597 [T] (KA, GA, kawa)
[3]子 Kawako f
口 Kawaguchi sp
口湖 K.-ko p
上 Kawakami s ⌈mh
上丈太郎 K. Jōtarō
上肇 K. Hajime mlh
上徹太郎 K. Tetsutarō ml
[4]匂 Kawawa s
手 Kawade s
井 Kawai s
井酔茗 K. Suimei ml
内 Kawachi sp, Kōchi;

Kawauchi *s*; Hanoi *p* "Hanoi"
内山 Kōchiyama *s*
内芳野 Kawachi Yoshino *p*
内長野 K. Nagano *p*
内屋 Kawachiya *l*
[5]北 Kawakita *s*; Kahoku *p*
尻 Kawajiri *s*
辺 Kawabe *sp*
田 Kawada *s*
本 Kawamoto *s*, Kōmoto
[6]池 Kawaji *s*
竹 Kawatake *s* ml
竹新七 K. Shinshichi ml
竹黙阿弥 K. Mokuami *ml* ml
竹繁俊 K. Shigetoshi
合 Kawai *sp*; Tatasu *s*
合曾良 K. Sora *ml*
名 Kawana *s*
曲 Kawakuma *s*, Kawamagari, Kawane; Kawawa *sp*
西 Kawanishi *s*, Kasai
[7]社 Kawayashiro *l*
杉 Kawasugi *s*
杉初子 K. Hatsuko *fl*
村 Kawamura *s*
村瑞軒 K. Zuiken *mh*
村瑞賢 K. Zuiken *mh*
角 Kawazumi *s*
[8]沼 Kawanuma *p*
明り Kawaakari *l*
奈 Kawana *s*
芸 Kawage *p*
居 Kawai *s*
出 Kawade *s*
東 Kawahigashi *sp*; Katō *s*, Kawato
東節 Katō-bushi *a*
東碧梧桐 Kawahigashi Hekigotō *ml*
[9]俣 Kawamata *s*
相 Kawai *s*
津 Kawazu *sp*
治 Kawaji *s*
面 Kōmo *s*, Kawazura
南 Kawaminami *s*, Kawanami; Kanan *p* ["Honan"]
[10]浦 Kawaura *p*
海抄 Kakaishō *l*
郡名 Kawaguna *s*
原 Kawahara *sp*; Kawabara *s*, Kawara
原太郎 Kawara Tarō *l*
原木 Kawaragi *s*
原井 Kawarai *s*
原田 Kawarada *s*
原林 Kawarabayashi *s*
原塚 Kawarazuka *s*
原崎 Kawarazaki *s*
[11]浪 Kawanami *s*
添 Kawazoe *s*
部 Kawabe *s*
副 Kawazoe *s*
野 Kōno *sp*; Kawano *s*
野与一 Kōno Yoichi *ml* mh
野広中 K. Hironaka
野通有 K. Michiari *mh*
野敏鎌 K. Toshigama *mh*
野慎吾 K. Shingo *ml*
盛 Kawamori *s*
盛好蔵 K. Yoshizō *ml*
島 Kawashima *s*
[12]崎 Kawasaki *sp*
喜田 Kawakita *s*
童 Kappa *l*
間 Kawama *s*
[13]路 Kawaji *s*
越 Kawagoe *s*
[14]精 Kayoshi *f*
窪 Kawakubo *s*
[15]端 Kawabata *s*
[17]鍋 Kawanabe *s*
[19]瀬 Kawase *s*
[21]鰭 Kawahire *s*, Kawabata

## 8 L4

**艸** 598 (sō, kusa)
千里 Kusa senri *l*
木虫魚 Sōmokuchūgyo *l*

**岐** 599 [T] Michi *m*; Chimata *s*, Funato. (KI, GI, michi)
阻 Kiso *s*
阜 Gifu *p* mh
神 Funato-no-kami
弥 Kimi *s*
南 Ginan *p*
宿 Kishuku *p*
蘇 Kiso *s*

**所** 600 [T] Tokoro *sm*. (SHO, SO, do, nobu)
古 Ikoma *s*
沢 Tokorozawa *s*
神根 Shoshine *s*
緑の藤波 Yukari no fujinami *l*

**門** 601 [T] Kado *m*, Hiro; Mon *l*. (MON, kado, to, hiro, yuki, kana)
[3]川 Kadokawa *sp*
口 Kadoguchi *s*
[4]井 Kadoi *s*
[5]叶 Toga *s*
司 Moji *sp*; Monji *s*
田 Kadota *s*, Monden
[6]次郎 Monjirō *m*
地 Moji *s*
別 Monbetsu *p*
[8]河 Mokawa *s*
林 Kadobayashi *s*
奈 Monna *s*
居 Kadoi *m*
[9]松 Kadomatsu *s*
前 Monzen *p*
[10]脇 Kadowaki *s*
倉 Kadokura *s*
屋 Kadoya *s*
真 Kadoma *sp*; Monma *s*, Kamato
馬 Kadoma *s*, Monma
[11]野 Kadono *s*
部 Kadobe *s*
[12]勝 Hirokatsu *s*
間 Monma *s*

**炊** 602 [T] (SUI, i, kashi, kashigi, togu)

**欣** 603 [N] Yasushi *m*. (KIN, yoshi)
一 Kin'ichi *m*
子 Yoshiko *f*
永 Yoshinaga *m*
秀 Yoshihide *m*
造 Kinzō *m*

**改** See 379

**玢** 604 Nibu *s*, Chin. (FUN, HIN, chin)

**刱** 605 Hajime *m*. (SHŌ, SŌ)

**放** 606 [T] (HŌ, yuki, kura)
下僧 Hōkazō *la*
生川 Hōjōgawa *la*

**於** 607 Ue *s*, Ōi. (O, U)
田 Oda *sm*
母影 Omokage *l*
金 Okane *s*
国 Okuni *fa*
国歌舞伎 O. Kabuki *a*
保 Oho *s*
染久松色読販 Osome Hisamatsu ukina no yomiuri *la*
庫 Okura *f*
菟 Oto *s*
曾 Oso *s*

**祉** 608 [T] (SHI, KE, tomi, yoshi)

**祈** 609 [T] (KI)
念仏 Kinenbuchi *s*
禱院 Kitōin *p*

**牧** 610 [T] Maki *sp*. (BOKU, MOKU, maki)
[3]口 Makiguchi *s*
[4]水 Bokusui *ml*
戸 Makito *s*
内 Makiuchi *s*
山 Makiyama *s*
[5]田 Makita *s*, Maita
丘 Makioka *p*
[6]西 Makinishi *s*
[7]村 Makimura *s*
[9]岡 Makioka *s*
[10]唄 Makiuta *l*
原 Makihara *s*
[11]野 Makino *s* ml
野信一 M. Shin'ichi
野逸馬 M. Itsuma *ml*
[13]雄 Makio *m*
園 Makizono *sp*
[16]衛 Makie *m*

**物** 611 [T] (BUTSU, MOCHI, MOTSU, mono, tane)
[5]四郎 Monoshirō *m*
江 Monoe *s*
[7]応 Monoō *s*
[9]面 Monomo *m*
草太郎 Monogusa Tarō *l*

11部 Mononobe *s*, Mononofu; Monobe *p*
部守屋 Mononobe no Moriya *mh* ⌈*mh*
部尾輿 M. no Okoshi
12集 Mozume *s*
集女 Mozume *sp*; Mozumime *s*

妍 612 (KEN, GEN, kiyo, kazu, yoshi) ⌈Yoshiko
子 Kiyoko *f*, Kazuko,

妧 613 (GEN, GAN, moto)
香 Motoka *f*

妙 614 [T] Tae *f*. (MYŌ, BYŌ, tae, tō, tayu, tada, yoshi)
竹林話七偏人 Myōchikurin-banashi shichihenjin *l*
光 Taemitsu *m*
見 Yoshimi *s*, Myōken, Myōmi
美 Yoshimi *s*, Taemi
泉 Yoshizumi *s*
高 Myōkō *p*
義 Myōgi *p*

股 615 Mata *s*. (KO, KU, mata)
野 Matano *s*

朋 616 [N] (HŌ, BŌ, tomo)
八 Tomohachi *m*
子 Tomoko *f*
礼 Tomoaya *m*
来 Tomoki *m*
満 Tomomitsu *m*
誠堂喜三二 Hōseidō Kisanji *ml*

肥 617 [T] Yutaka *m*; Kuma *s*. (HI, uma, koe, tomi, tomo, mitsu, kuma)
人 Umahito *m*; Ku- ⌊mahito *s*
田 Hida *s*
田木 Hidaki *s*
田野 Hidano *s*
沼 Koinuma *s*
前 Hizen *ph*
前国 Hizennokuni *ph*
前国風土記 H. no fudoki *l*
後 Higo *sph*
原 Hibara *s*
塚 Kozuka *s*

服 618 [T] Hatori *s*. (FUKU, BUKU, koto, yo, yuki)
巻 Haramaki *s*
部 Hattori *sp*; Hatori *s*
部土芳 Hattori Dohō *ml* ⌈*mh*
部南郭 H. Nankaku
部直人 H. Naoto *ml*
部躬治 H. Motoharu *ml*
部達 H. Tatsu *ml*
部嵐雪 H. Ransetsu *ml*
部嘉香 H. Yoshika *ml*
部撫松 H. Bushō *ml*

昉 619 Akira *m*. (HŌ, aki, akira)

旺 620 Akira *m*. (Ō, akira)

昨 621 Akira *m*. (GO, KU)

昕 622 (KIN, KON, asa)
子 Asako *f*

明 623 [T] Akira *m*, Kiyoshi, Tōru. (MEI, MYŌ, aki, teru, toshi, akira, kuni, haru, hiro, mitsu, ake, aka, yoshi, nori, akaru, akari, akirakei)
る妙 Akaru tae *l*
3三 Mitsuzō *m*
三郎 Meisaburō *m*
子 Teruko *f*; Akirakeiko *fh*
4日香 Asuka *p-l*
月記 Meigetsuki *l*
文 Toshifumi *m*
太郎 Kunitarō *m*
5石 Akashi *sf-p-l*
四 Akirashi *m*
田 Akeda *s*
田川 Akedagawa *s*
氏 Akiuji *m*
6兆 Minchō *ma*
光 Akimitsu *m*
7応 Meiō 1492–1501
8阿弥 Myōami *ml*
林 Akebayashi *s*
和 Meiwa *p* 1764–72
幸 Noritaka *m*
居 Terui *m*
9恒 Akitsune *m*
珍 Myōchin *s*
科 Akashina *p*
軌 Akinori *m*
治 Meiji *mh* 1868–1912; Akiji *m*
治叛臣伝 M. hanshinden *l*
星 Myōjō *sp-l*
10恵 Myōe *mlh*
恵上人歌集 M. Shōnin kashū *l*
祥 Akisachi *m*
珠子 Akemiko *f*
浦 Akera *s*
浜 Akehama *p*
烏 Akegarasu *l*
烏後正夢 A. nochi no masayume *l*
11峰 Akemine *s*
野 Akeno *p*
12渡 Aketo *s*
智 Akechi *sp* ⌈*mh*
智光秀 A. Mitsuhide
13楽 Akera *s*
14徳 Meitoku 1390–94
暦 Meireki 1655–58
16衡 Akihira *ml*
衡往来 Meikō ōrai *l*
親 Haruchika *m*

枌 624 Hegi *s*. (FUN, BUN, nuki, soge, ⌊nire)
田 Nukita *s*
谷 Sogetani *s*

杷 625 (HA, e)
木 Haki *p*

杣 626 Soma *s*. (soma)
子 Somako *f*
山 Somayama *s*
木 Somagi *s*
田 Somada *s*

枕 627 [I] Makura *s*. (CHIN, makura)
物狂 M. monogurui *la*
草子 M. no sōshi *l*
崎 Makurazaki *p*
慈童 Makura Jidō *la*

枅 628 see 桝 1368

杵 629 Kine *s*. (SHO, ki, kine)
杵 Kine *s*
宮 Kinenomiya *s*
屋 Kineya *s*
島 Kishima *p*
筑 Kitsuki *p* ⌈chi
淵 Kibuchi *s*, Kinebu-
雄 Kineo *m*
肄 Kii *s*

枚 630 [T] (MAI, BAI, hira, kazu, fumu)
方 Hirakata *sp*
田 Hirata *sp*
岡 Hiraoka *sp*
野 Hirano *s*

枝 631 (SHI, KI, GI, eda, e, shige)
川 Edagawa *s*
元 Edamoto *s*
木 Edaki *s*
田 Eda *s*
吉 Edayoshi *s*
村 Emura *s*
幸 Esashi *p*
松 Edamatsu *s*
彦 Shigehiko *m*

板 632 [T] (HAN, ita)
4山 Itayama *s*
井 Itai *s*
7坂 Itasaka *s*
沢 Itasawa *s*
谷 Itaya *s*
8門店 Hanmonten *p* "Panmunjon"
取 Itadori *p*
茂 Itamochi *s*
東 Bandō *s*
9津 Itatsu *s*
垣 Itagaki *s*
垣直子 I. Naoko *fl*
垣退助 I. Taisuke *mh*
垣鷹穂 I. Takaho *ml*
10柳 Itayanagi *p*

倉 Itakura *sp* ⌈*mh*
倉重昌 I. Shigemasa
倉勝重 I. Katsushige
荷 Itako *s* ⌊*mh*
原 Itahara *s*
11野 Itano *p*
部岡 Itabeoka *s*
14鼻 Itahana *s*
16橋 Itabashi *sp*

林 633 [T] Hayashi *s*, Rin; Shigeru *m*. (RIN, shige, moto, mori, ki, na, kimi, kimu, toki, fusa, yoshi)
1一 Rin'ichi *m* ⌈*mh*
3子平 Hayashi Shihei
久男 H. Hisao *ml*
4五郎 Ringorō *m*
5古渓 Hayashi Kokei
四郎 Rinshirō *m* ⌊*ml*
田 Hayashida *sp*
平 Rinpei *m*
6次 Moritsugu *m*
次郎 Rinjirō *m*
圭子 Hayashi Keiko *fl*
吉 Rinkichi *m* ⌈*mh*
有造 Hayashi Yūzō
7邑楽 Rin'yūgaku *a*
芙美子 Hayashi Fumi-
出 Hayashide *s* ⌊ko *fl*
8林 Rinbayashi *s*
和 Hayashi Yawara *ml*
房雄 H. Fusao *ml*
述斎 H. Jussai *mh*
9信篤 H. Nobuatsu *mh*
治 Rinji *m*
治郎 Rinjirō *m*
昱 Shigeteru *m*
泉集 Rinsenshū *l*
為 Shigetame *m*
10屋 Hayashiya *s*
原 Hayashibara *s*
原来井 H. Raisei *ml*
11部 Hayashibe *s*
12崎 Hayashizaki *s*
間 Rinkan *l* ⌈*ml*
達夫 Hayashi Tatsuo
14銑十郎 H. Senjūrō
15蔵 Rinzō *m* ⌊*mh*
20甕臣 Hayashi Mikaomi *ml*
21羅山 H. Razan *mhl*

—— 8 L5 ——

壯 634 See 壮 243

的 635 [T] Akira *m*; Ikuha *s*. (TEKI, mato, masa, ikuha)
井 Matoi *s*
屋 Matoya *s*
部 Ikuhabe *s*
場 Matoba *s*

知 636 [T] Satoru *m*, Satoshi. (CHI, tomo, chika, nori, aki, sato, tsugu, akira, oki, toshi, shiri, shiru, shi, kazu, haru)
1一 Tomonobu *m*
2二 Tomokazu *m*
又 Chimata *m*
十 Tomotada *m*
3三 Tomozō *m*
三郎 Tomosaburō *m*
久 Chiku *s*
久平 Chikuhei *m*
也 Tomoya *m*
4内 Shiriuchi *p*
止 Tomotada *m*
夫 Chibu *p*; Chiburi *sp*; Chichiri *s*
5四郎 Tomoshirō *m*
田 Chita *s*
立 Chiryū *p*
6名 China *p*
多 Chita *p*
7言 Chikanobu *m*
至 Tomoyuki *m*
8念 Chinen *s*
9洗 Tomoyoshi *m*
10晄 Tomoaki *m*
哲 Tomoaki *m*
速 Tomohaya *m*, Tomotō
11健 Tomotake *m*
野 Chino *s*
常 Tomotsune *m*
12間 Chima *s*
13福 Tomoyo *m*
強 Tomotake *m*
雄 Tomoo *m*
淵 Tomohiro *m*
満 Norimitsu *m*
義 Tomoyoshi *m*
14暢 Tomonobu *m*
16養 Tomoyasu *m*
17覧 Chiran *p*
18職 Chishiki *s*

私 637 [T] Kisa *s*, Kisai, Kisaichi. (SHI, kisa, ki, tomi)
可多咄 Shikatabanashi *l* ⌈Kiichi *s*
市 Kisaichi *sp*, Kisai;
家集 Shikashū *l*
語 Sasamegoto *l*
撰集 Shisenshū *l*
燭 Shishoku *l*

和 638 [T] Yawara *m*, Yasushi, Wa, Nodoka, Kazu, Hitoshi, Wataru; Kanō *sm*, Yamato, Mikita. (WA, kazu, yasu, yori, tomo, yoshi, toshi, masa, kata, masu, ai, yō, na, chika, katsu, nigi)
1一 Waichi *m*
一郎 Waichirō *m*
2七 Washichi *m*
人 Masando *m*
3三 Yoshikazu *m*
三郎 Wasaburō *m*
子 Kazuko *f*, Tomoko, Masako
久 Waku *s*
久井 Wakui *s*
久田 Wakuta *s*
久兎毛 Wakutomo *s*
4仁 Wani *s*; Katsuhito
介 Wasuke *m* ⌊*m*
夫 Kazuo *m*, Yoshio
木 Waki *sp*
井内 Wainai *s*
井内貞行 W. Sadayu-
井田 Waida *s* ⌊ki *mh*
5外 Kazuto *m*
布刈 Mekari *sla*
布浦 Meura *s*
布麿 Nigitemaro *m*
平 Wahei *m*
正 Yasumasa *m*
氏 Kazuuji *m*
田 Wada *sp*; Mikita *s*, Nigita
田三造 W. Sanzō *ma*
田山 Wadayama *p*
田山蘭 Wada Sanran
田木 Wadaki *s* ⌊*ml*
田合戦女舞鶴 Wada kassen onnamaizuru *la*
田伝 W. Tsutō *ml*
田芳恵 W. Yoshie *ml*
田英作 W. Eisaku *ma*
田垣 Wadagaki *s*
田津 Wadatsu *s*
田義盛 Wada Yoshimori *mh*
田鍋 Watanabe *s*
6地 Wachi *s*
合 Wagō *s*
宇慶 Wauke *s*, Ōki
光 Masamitsu *m*; Wa-
辻 Watsuji *s* ⌊kō *s*
辻哲郎 W. Tetsurō *ml*
気 Wake *sp*; Waki *s*; Yawaki *m*
気広虫 Wake no Hiromushi *fh* ⌈maro *mh*
気清麻呂 W. no Kiyo-
名抄 Wamyōshō *l*
多守 Watamori *m*
多留 Wataru *m*
7作 Wasaku *m*
佐 Wasa *s*
佐二 Wasaji *m*
安部 Waabe *s*
志 Yoriyuki *m*
男 Kazuo *m*
応 Kazumasa *m*
孝 Toshiyuki *m*
束 Watsuka *p*
8知 Wachi *p*
波 Wanami *s*
泊 Wadomari *p*
幸 Kazuyoshi *m*
良 Wara *p*
9貞 Kazusada *m*
育 Kazuyasu *m*
泉 Izumi *sp*
泉が城 I.-ga-jō *l*
泉式部 I. Shikibu *fl*
10珥部 Wanibe *s*
郎 Kazuo *m*
高 Kazutaka *m*
栗 Waguri *s*
宮 Kazunomiya *fh*
家 Kazue *f*
屋 Yamatoya *s*
11島 Washima *p*
12崎 Wasaki *s*
寒 Wassamu *p*
賀 Waga *p*
賀井 Wakai *s*
智 Wachi *s*
達 Wadachi *s*
13誠 Kazunobu *m*
義 Kazuyoshi *m*, Yasuyoshi ⌈shū *l*
漢朗詠集 Wakan rōei-
14徳 Toshinori *m*; Ya-
郷 Wagō *p* ⌊mato *s*

杵 枚 枝 板 林 壯 的 知 私 和 ▼ 社 祀 祁 邪 邯 邱 邨 邵 卦 即 叔 取 劼 劼 効 刺 刷 制 乳 房 毎 斧 卓 幸 ▲ 享 京 金 矣 帚 孟 奇 奄 命 念

銅 Wadō 708–15
歌 Waka *l*
歌九品 W. kuhon *l*
歌月 Wakatsuki *s*
歌山 Wakayama *p*
歌体十種 Wakatai jisshu *l*
歌作者部類 Waka sakusha burui *l*
歌庭訓 W. teikin *l*
歌童蒙抄 W. dōmōshō *l* ⌈shō *l*
歌題林抄 W. dairin-
爾 Wani *s*
15霊 Nigitama *l*
16樽 Wataru *m*
親 Kazuchika *m*
18邇 Wani *s*
邇部 Wanibe *s*
19蘭陀 Oranda *p* "Holland"
22讃 Wasan *l*

社 639 See 社 406

祀 640 (SHI, JI, toshi)
子 Toshiko *f*
夫 Toshio *m*

祁 641 (KI)
答院 Kedōin *p*

邪 642 [T] (JA, YA)
宗門 Jashūmon *l*
馬台国 Yamatai-koku *ph*

邯 643 (KAN)
鄲 Kantan *la*
鄲諸国 K. shokoku *l*

邱 644 Kyū *s.* (KYŪ, oka)
永漢 Kyū Eikan *ml*

邨 645 (SON, SUN, TON, DON, mura)
岡 Muraoka *s*

邵 646 (SHŌ, JŌ, taka)
子 Takako *f*
蔵 Takazō *m*

—8 L6—

卦 647 (KA, KE, KAI)
婁 Keiro *s*

即 648 [T] Chikashi *m*; Tsuku *s.* (SOKU, mitsu, yori, hito, tada, atsu)
子 Mitsuko *f*

叔 649 [T] Hajime *m.* (SHUKU, yoshi)
省 Yoshimi *m*

取 650 [T] (SHU, tori, toru)
手 Torite *p* ⌈s
石 Toroshi *sp*; Tosshi

劼 651 Tsuyoshi *m.* (HI)

劼 652 Tsutomu *m.* (KITSU, KICHI, KATSU)

効 653 [T] Itaru *m*, Susumu. (KŌ, KYŌ, kazu, kata, nari, nori)
子 Kazuko *f*

刺 654 [T] (SHI, SEKI, sashi, sasu)
賀 Sashiga *s*

刷 655 [T] (SATSU, SACHI, kiyo)
雄 Kiyoo *m*

制 656 [T] Osamu *m*, Isamu. (SEI, nori, sada, suke)
子 Sadako *f*

—8 L7—

乳 657 [T] (NYŪ, chi)
戸 Chihe *s*
井 Nyūi *s*, Nioi
乳井 Chichii *s*
部 Mibube *s*

—8 T1—

房 658 [T] (BŌ, HO, fusa, nobu, o)
之助 Fusanosuke *m*
子 Fusako *f*
五郎 Fusagorō *m*
太郎 Fusatarō *m*
次郎 Fusajirō *m*
吉 Fusakichi *m*
俊 Fusatoshi *m*
造 Fusazō *m*
野 Fusano *s*
喜 Nobuyoshi *m*
雄 Fusao *m*

—8 T2—

毎 658A See 毎 444

斧 659 Hajime *m*; Ono *s.* (FU, ono)
田 Onoda *s*
寺 Onodera *s*
馬 Onoma *m* ⌈*l*
琴菊 Yoki koto o kiku

卓 660 [T] Takashi *m*, Makoto, Masaru, Taku. (TAKU, taka, tsuna, tō, mochi)
一 Takuichi *m*
四郎 Takushirō *m*
吉 Takukichi *m*
成 Takashige *m*
哉 Takuya *m*
郎 Takurō *m*
造 Takuzō *m*
淳 Takujun *s*
雄 Takuo *m*
幹 Takamoto *m*
蔵 Takuzō *m*

幸 661 [T] Miyuki *m*; Kō *sm*; Yuki *s.* (KŌ, GYŌ, yuki, yoshi, saki, sachi, taka, hide, sai, tatsu, tomi, tomo, mura)
1一 Kōichi *m*
一郎 Kōichirō *m*
3三 Kōzō *m*
三郎 Saisaburō *m*
之助 Kōnosuke *m*
子 Yukiko *f*, Kōko
久 Yoshihisa *m*
千代 Kōchiyo *m*
丸 Kōmaru *m*
4文 Sachibumi *m*
山 Kōyama *s*
木 Kōboku *l*
手 Satte *p*
太夫 Kōdayū *mh*
太郎 Kōtarō *m*
5四郎 Kōshirō *m*
平 Kōhei *m*
王丸 Kōōmaru *m*
生 Sachio *m*
田 Kōda *sp*
田文 K. Aya *fl*
田露伴 K. Rohan *ml*
6次郎 Kōjirō *m*
守 Yukie *f*
吉 Kōkichi *m*
吉郎 Kōkichirō *m*
母 Kōmo *s*
民 Yukimoto *m*
世 Yukiyo *m-f*
年 Yukitoshi *m*
7佐 Kōsa *m*
村 Kōmura *s*
弘 Sachihiro *sm*
安 Kōan *m*
足 Yukitari *m*
男 Yukio *m*, Sachio, Sakio
8枝 Yukie *f*
宜 Yukiyoshi *m*
若 Kōwaka *sla*
若丸 Kōwakamaru *ma*
辰 Yukitoki *m*
9治郎 Kōjirō *m*
松 Yukimatsu *m*
松丸 Kōmatsumaru *m*
松麿 Kōmatsumaro *m*
前 Kōzen *s*
専 Yukitaka *m*
10高 Yukitaka *m*
11健 Yukiyasu *m*
得 Yoshinari *m*
野 Kōno *s*
堂 Kōdō *s*
堂得知 K. Tokuchi *ml*
島 Kōjima *s*
12景 Yukikage *m*
13殖 Sakitane *m*
雄 Yukio *m*, Sachio, Takao
14徳 Kōtoku *s*
徳秋水 K. Shūsui *mlh*
徳井 Kōtokui *s*
16橘 Kōkitsu *m*
翰 Sachibumi *m*
17謙 Yukikane *m*

享 662 [N] Susumu *m*, Akira. (KYŌ, KŌ, taka, tsura, yuki, michi)
吉 Kōkichi *m*
和 Kyōwa 1801–4
保 Kyōhō 1716–36
禄 Kyōroku 1528–32
徳 Kyōtoku 1452–55

京 663 [T] Takashi *m*, Hiroshi, Osamu; Kyō *s*, Kanadome, Karaguri. (KYŌ, KEI, chika, atsu, ki)
が瀬 Kyōgase *p*
³久保 Kikubo *s*
⁴升屋 Kimasuya *s*
⁵北 Keihoku *p*
田 Kida *s*
⁷伝 Kyōden *ml*
⁹城 Keijō *p* "Seoul"
¹¹猫一斑 Keibyō ippan *l*
都 Kyōto *p*, Miyako
¹²童 Kyō warabe *l*
鹿子 Kyōkanoko *l*
¹³極 Kyōgoku *sp*; Kigoku *s* ⌈*ml*
極杞陽 Kyōgoku Kiyō
極為兼 K. Tamekane *ml* ⌈gokuya
極屋 Kyōgokuya *s*, Ki-

金 664 [T] Kane *m*; Kin *s*, Kon, Kanuchi, Kimu. (KIN, KON, kane, kana, ka)
ケ崎 Kanegasaki *p*
の草鞋 Kin no waraji *l*
²二郎 Kinjirō *m*
³川 Kanekawa *s*
之助 Kinnosuke *m*
万 Konman *s*, Konma
久保 Kanakubo *s*
々先生栄花夢 Kinkin sensei eiga no yume
丸 Kanamaru *s* ⌊*l*
子 Kaneko *s* ⌈*ml*
子元臣 K. Motoomi
子不泣 K. Fukyū *ml*
子光晴 K. Mitsuharu *ml*
子洋文 K. Yōbun *ml*
子筑水 K. Chikusui *ml* ⌈*mh*
子堅太郎 K. Kentarō
子兜太 K. Tōta *ml*
子薫園 K. Kun'en *ml*
⁴戸 Kanedo *s*, Kanae
中子 Kanako *f*
内 Kaneuchi *s*
山 Kanayama *sp*; Kaneyama *p*
木 Kaneki *s*; Kanagi *p*
太 Kanō *s*
太郎 Kintarō *m*
井 Kanai *sp*
井三笑 K. Sanshō *ml*
井田 Kaneida *s*
⁵札 Kinsatsu *la*
古 Kaneko *s*
玉集 Kingyokushū *l*
本 Kanemoto *s*
矢 Kin'ya *m*
生 Kaneo *s*, Kinshō
平 Kanehira *sm*; Kinpei *m*; Kinpira *lm*
平浄瑠璃 Kinpira Jōruri *a*
田 Kanada *sp*; Kaneda *s*; Kanetada *m*
田一 Kindaichi *sp*
田一京助 K. Kyōsuke *ml*
⁶次郎 Kinjirō *m*
仙 Konson *s*
江 Kanae *s*
行 Kaneyuki *sm*
守 Kanemori *sm*
光 Kanemitsu *sm*; Konkō *p*
光明経 Konkōmyōkyō *lh* ⌈nari *sp*
成 Kanenari *s*; Kan-
⁷作 Kanuchi *s*
坂 Kanesaka *s*
村 Kanamura *s*
杉 Kanasugi *s*
沙集 Kinsashū *l*
沢 Kanazawa *sp*; Kanesawa *s*
沢文庫 Kanazawa Bunko *pl* ⌈*ml*
沢種美 K. Tanetomi
安 Kaneyasu *s*
谷 Kanaya *s*, Kanetani
吾 Kingo *sm*
児 Kaneko *s*
尾 Kaneo *s*
出地 Kanaji *s*
甫 Kaneyoshi *m*
⁸門 Kinmon *p* "Quemoy, Golden Gate"
門五三桐 K. gosan no kiri *l*
林 Kanebayashi *s*
枝 Kaneeda *s*
若 Kanawaka *m*
居 Kanei *s*
居田 Kaneida *s*
⁹保 Kaneyasu *s*
津 Kanazu *sp*; Kanetsu *s*
城 Kaneshiro *s*, Kanakusuku, Kanagi
治郎 Kinjirō *m*
神 Konjin *s*
砂郷 Kanasagō *p*
刺 Kanezashi *s*, Kanasasu ⌈Kanemochi
持 Kanaji *s*, Kanachi,
指 Kanezashi *s*
長 Kanenaga *s*
春 Konparu *s* ⌈*mla*
春禅竹 K. Zenchiku
泉 Kaneizumi *s*
巻 Kanemaki *s*
岡 Kanaoka *s*
重 Kaneshige *sm*; Kanae *s*
¹⁰海 Kaneumi *s*
浦 Konoura *p*
高 Kanetaka *s*
屋 Kanaya *sp*
造 Kinzō *m* ⌈hara
原 Kinbara *s*, Kana-
原省吾 Kinbara Seigo
¹¹峰 Kinpō *p* ⌊*ml*
野 Kaneno *s*, Konno,
剛 Kongō *s* ⌊Kinno
剛峰寺 Kongobuji *p*
宿 Kaneie *m*
曾木 Kanesogi *s*
盛 Kanemori *sm*
島 Kanashima *s*, Kaneshima
¹²須 Kisu *s*
勝 Konze *s*
崎 Kanesaki *s*
森 Kanamori *s*
集 Kanatsume *s*
達寿 Kimu Darusu *ml*
道 Kanemichi *m*
¹³塚 Kanetsuka *s*
雄 Kaneo *m*
葉集 Kin'yōshū *l*
¹⁴窪 Kanakubo *s*
閣寺 Kinkakuji *p-l*
¹⁵槐集 Kinkaishū *l*
輪 Kanawa *s*, Konrin
鋳 Kaneto *s*
敷 Kaneshiki *s* ⌈sa
蔵 Kinzō *m*, Kanema-
箱 Kanehako *s*
¹⁶親 Kaneoya *s*
鞍 Kanakura *s*
¹⁷綱 Kanatsuna *s*
¹⁸鷲 Kinga *ml*
²³鑽 Kanasana *s*

—— 8 T3 ——

矣 665 (I, O)

帚 666 (sō, hahaki)
木 Hahakigi *l*
木別注 H. betchū *l*

孟 667 Takeshi *m*, Tsutomu, Hajimu. (MŌ, take, moto, tomo, haru, naga, osa, takeshi) ⌈cius"
子 Mōshi *mlh* "Men-
伯 Takenori *m*
芳 Takeyoshi *m*
郎 Takeshirō *m*
雄 Haruo *m*
懿 Takeyoshi *m*

奇 See 752

奄 668 (EN, hisa)
智 Anchi *s*

侖 669 Rin *f*. (RIN, RON, tomo)

念 670 [T] (NEN, mune) ⌈*a*
仏踊 Nenbutsu odori

命 671 [T] Makoto *m*, Akira; Mikoto *f*. (MEI, MYŌ, nori, nobu, naga, michi, yoshi, toshi, mi, na, ya, kata, mori)
之 Michiyuki *m*
子 Noriko *f*, Nobuko
尾 Meio *s*, Meo
孝 Michitaka *m*
啓 Nagahiro *s* ⌈tone
婦 Myōbu *f*, Hime-

**盲** See 936

**官** 672 [T] (KAN, nori, hiro, taka, kimi, kore, osa)
佳 Hiroyoshi *m*

**宙** 673 [T] Hiroshi *m*. (CHŪ, oki, michi)
子 Michiko *f*
造 Chūzō *m*

**宏** 674 [N] Hiroshi *m*, Kō. (KŌ, hiro, atsu)
平 Kōhei *m*
亘 Hironobu *m*
枝 Hiroe *f*
海 Kōkai *m*
富 Hiroto *m*

**宜** 675 [T] Yoroshi *m*. (GI, yoshi, nobu, masa, yasu, ki, noru, sumi, taka, nari)
仁 Yoshihito *m*
孝 Yoshitaka *m*
保 Kibo *s*
治 Senji *m*
政 Norimasa *m*
彦 Nobuhiko *m*
振 Yoshifuru *m*
野湾 Ginowa *s*
剛 Yoshitaka *m*
雄 Yoshio *m*, Masao
慶 Yasuyoshi *m*

**宝** 676 [T] Takashi *m*; Takara *m-f*. (HŌ, taka, tomi, yoshi, kane, take, tomo, michi)
の槌 Takara no tsuchi *la*
1一 Hōichi *m*
4山 Takarayama *s*
井 Takarai *s*
井其角 T. Kikaku *ml*
5永 Hōei 1704–11
田 Takarada *s*
正 Hōshō *s*
本 Takaramoto *s*
生 Hōshō *s*
7男 Tomio *m*
来 Hōrai *s*
寿 Takatoshi *m*
8性 Hōjō *s*
忠 Yoshitada *m*
物集 Hōbutsushū *l*
9治 Hōji 1247–49
治二年百首 H. ninen hyakushu *l*
栄 Yoshinaga *m*
10珠山 Hōshuyama *p*
11亀 Hōki 770–80
13塚 Takarazuka *p-a*
満 Hōman *s*
飯 Hoi *p*
14徳 Hōtoku 1449–52
暦 Hōreki 1751–64
15蔵院 Hōzōin *s*

**定** 677 [T] Sadamu *m*, Sadame, Mata. (TEI, JŌ, sada, tsura, yasu)
1一 Sadaichi *m*
2二郎 Yasujirō *m*
3之助 Sadanosuke *m*
子 Sadako *f*
4方 Sadakata *sm*
5加 Sadamasu *m*
功 Sadanari *m*, Sadaisa
正 Sadamasa *m*
6次郎 Sadajirō *m*
芝 Sadashige *m*
吉 Teikichi *m*, Sadakichi
7助 Sadasuke *m*
条 Teijō *m*, Sadae
8房 Sadafusa *m*
宗 Sadamoto *m*
忠 Sadanori *m*
武 Sadatake *m*
9信 Sadanobu *m*
治郎 Sadajirō *m*
省 Sadakami *m*
10俊 Sadatoshi *m*
祥 Sadanaga *m*
家 Sadaie *m-ml*; Teika *ml*
兼 Sadakane *m*
11猗 Sadayori *m*
剛 Sadayoshi *m*
逸 Sadatoshi *m*
12順 Sadanori *m*
温 Sadayoshi *m*
琮 Sadamizu *m*
朝 Jōchō *ma*
敬 Sadanori *m*, Sadaaki
13塚 Jōzuka *s*
豊 Sadaatsu *m*
輔 Teisuke *m*
静 Sadakiyo *m*, Sadayasu
豪 Sadakatsu *m*
17謨 Sadakoto *m*
19識 Sadanori *m*

**実** 678 [T] Minoru *m*, Makoto, Sane. (JITSU, sane, mi, mitsu, nori, nao, ma, kore, chika, tsune, miru)
3川 Jitsukawa *s*
万 Sanetsumu *m*
4仁 Mihito *m*
方 Sanekata *ml*; Jitsukata *s*
5用 Sanechika *m*
生 Mishō *l*
6吉 Saneyoshi *sm*
光 Sanemitsu *m*
世 Saneyo *m*
7利 Sanesato *m*
孚 Sanekoto *m*
近 Sanechika *m*
8枝 Saneeda *m*
和 Saneai *m*
宜 Minoru *m*
英 Saneakira *m*
受 Saneshige *m*
9柿 Mikaki *m*
政 Sanemori *m*
美 Sanetomi *m*
栄 Saneharu *m*
岳 Saneoka *m*
10夏 Naonatsu *m*
11隆 Sanetaka *ml*
淳 Saneatsu *m*
敏 Sanetoshi *m*
梁 Saneyane *m*
庸 Sanemochi *m*
12揖 Saneosa *m*
順 Saneaya *m*
勝 Sanetō *m*
程 Minori *m*
朝 Sanetomo *m*
堅 Sanemi *m*
逵 Sanekatsu *m*
13福 Sanetaru *m*
誠 Sanemi *m*
廉 Saneyasu *m*
遠 Sanetō *m*
14徳 Saneatsu *m*
15勲 Saneisa *m*
16曈 Saneaki *m*
穎 Sanehide *m*
頼 Saneyori *m*
17総 Saneosa *m*
20麗 Saneakira *m*

**宗** 679 [T] Takashi *m*, Hajime; Sō *s*. (SHŪ, sō, mune, moto, toki, kazu, toshi, nari, hiro)
2二 Muneji *m*
3三 Sōzō *m*
于 Muneyuki *m*
子 Muneko *f*, Motoko; Munechika *m*
4友 Munetomo *m*
方 Munakata *s*
文 Sōbun *s*
不旱 Sō Fukan *ml*
5功 Muneisa *m*
礼 Muneaki *m*
右馬 Sōma *s*
田 Muneta *s*
平 Sōhei *m*
6吉 Sōkichi *m*
光 Munemitsu *m*
因 Sōin *ml*
在 Muneari *m*
広 Munehiro *m*
7均 Munehira *m*
那 Muneyasu *m*
形 Munakata *s*
弘 Munemitsu *m*
村 Sōmura *s*
判 Munesada *m*
谷 Sōya *p*
志 Sōji *m*
至 Muneyoshi *m*
近 Munechika *sm*
臣 Muneomi *m*
寿 Munenaga *m*
孝 Munemichi *m*
8阿弥 Sōami *ma*
享 Munetaka *m*
茂 Muneshige *m*
忠 Munetada *m*
武 Munetake *m*
良 Munenaga *m*
9城 Munenari *m*, Munesane
治郎 Sōjirō *m*
衍 Munenobu *m*
砌 Sōzei *ml*
軌 Munenori *m*
前 Sōzen *s*
長 Sōchō *ml*
春 Sōshun *ml*
岳 Muneoka *s*, Munaoka, Soga

直 Munenao *m*
岡 Muneoka *s*, Munaoka, Soga
[10]従 Muneyori *m*
祇 Sōgi *ml*
祇終焉記 S. shūen no ki *l*
宮 Sōmiya *s*
恵 Muneyoshi *m*
[11]理 Munemichi *m*, Munetada
梁 Muneyana *m*
啓 Munenori *m*
[12]敬 Munetaka *m*, Muneyoshi
彭 Sōhō *mh*
素 Sōso *s*
尊 Munetaka *mh*
達 Sōtatsu *ma*
[13]睦 Munechika *m*
雄 Muneo *m*
純 Sōjun *ml*
[14]像 Munekata *sp*
憧 Munenori *m*
徳 Munee *m*
[15]論 Shūron *l*
[16]穎 Munehide *m*
輸 Munemoto *m*
薫 Muneshige *m*
賢 Muneyasu *m*
[17]厳 Muneyoshi *m*
[18]贇 Muneyoshi *m*
[21]巌 Muneyoshi *m*
[23]鑑 Sōkan *ml*

**苣** 680 (KYO, GO, chisa)
子 Chisako *f*

**茇** 681 Yadori *m*, Yadoru. (BATSU)

**苑** 682 (EN, ON, sono)
部 Sonobe *s*

**茉** 682A (MATSU, ma)
莉 Mari *f*
理子 Mariko *f*

**芽** 683 [T] (GA, GE, me, mei)
子 Meiko *f*
室 Memuro *p*

**茎** 684 [T] (KEI, KŌ, GYŌ, kuki)
子 Kukiko *f*
崎 Kukisaki *p*

**苗** 685 [T] (MYŌ, BYŌ, nae, mitsu, nari, tane, e)
太郎 Naetarō *m*
代 Myōji *s*, Naeshiro
村 Naemura *s*, Namura, Nawamura
鹿 Nōka *s*

**苫** 686 (SEN, TEN, toma)
小牧 Tomakomai *p*
田 Tomada *sp*; Tomoda *s*
米地 Tomabechi *sp*
前 Tomamae *p*

**苦** 687 [T] (KU, niga)
力頭の表情 Kūriigashira no hyōjō *l*
竹 Nigatake *s*
瓜 Nigauri *s*
林野 Kururino *s*
桃 Nigamomo *s*, Kutō, Kumera

**苓** 687A (REI, RYŌ, fusa)
北 Reihoku *f*

**苞** 688 Shigeru *m*; Shige *f*. (HŌ, HYŌ, moto, suga)
子 Motoko *f*, Sugako

**芸** 689 [T] (GEI, UN, ki, yoshi, gi, saku, nori, masa)
北 Geihoku *p*
西 Geisei *p*
阿弥 Geiami *mla*
林間歩 Geirinkanpo *l*
亭 Untei *plh*
濃 Geino *p*
鑑 Geikan *l*

**茅** 690 Kaya *s*. (BŌ, MYŌ, kaya, chi)
ケ崎 Chigasaki *p*
[3]子 Kayako *f*
[5]代 Chishiro *s*, Chichishiro
[10]原 Kayahara *s*
原華山 K. Kazan *ml*
[11]停 Chinu *s*
根 Chine *s*, Chinone
野 Chino *sp*; Kayano *s*
野雅子 C. Masako *fl*
野蕭々 C. Shōshō *ml*
島 Kayashima *s*
[12]場 Kayaba *p*
渟 Chinu *s*
崎 Chigasaki *p*

**茂** 691 [T] Shigeru *m*, Shigemi. (MO, BŌ, shige, toyo, mochi, yuta, ari, taka, tō, moto, ikashi, shigei)
[2]二 Shigeji *m*
[3]三治 Mosōji *m*
上 Mogami *s*
子 Shigeko *f*, Shigeiko
丸 Ikashimaro *m*
[4]仁 Toyohito *m*, Yutahito
木 Mogi *s*; Motegi *sp*
手木 Motegi *s*
太 Shigeta *m*
太郎 Shigetarō *m*
山 Shigeyama *s*
[5]左衛門 Mozaemon *m*
田 Shigeta *s*
田井 Motai *s*
平 Mohei *m*
氏 Shigeuji *m*
[6]吉 Mokichi *m*
在 Mozai *s*
[7]作 Mosaku *s*
村 Shigemura *s*
呂 Moro *s*
亥 Shigeri *m*
[8]明 Shigeaki *m*
幸 Shigeyuki *m*
茂 Shigemoto *m*
秀 Shigehide *m*
[9]垣 Mogaki *s*
岳 Shigeoka *m*
[10]原 Shigehara *s*; Mobara *p*
庭 Moniwa *s*
[11]済 Shigemasa *m*
野 Shigeno *s*
[12]登 Moto *m*
[13]雄 Shigeo *m*
[14]徳 Shigenori *m*
語 Shigetsugu *m*
[16]憲 Mochinori *m*
橘 Shigekichi *m*
樹 Shigeki *m*, Shigetatsu
薫 Shigeyuki *m*

**若** 692 [T] (JAKU, NYAKU, waka, yori, waku, nao, masa, yoshi)
[3]子 Wakako *f*, Wakuko
[4]水 Wakamizu *sm*
月 Wakatsuki *s*
井 Wakai *s*
木 Wakagi *s*
山 Wakayama *s*
山牧水 W. Bokusui *ml*
山喜志子 W. Kishiko *fl*
[5]代 Wakashiro *s*
比売 Wakahime *f*
田 Wakada *s*
目田 Wakameda *s*
市 Nyakuichi *l*
生 Wakō *s*
[6]江 Wakae *s*
竹 Wakatake *s*
芝 Jakushi *s*
色 Wakairo *s*
[7]杉 Wakasugi *s*
杉慧 W. Kei *ml*
売 Wakume *f*
尾 Wakao *s*
見 Wakami *s*
[8]林 Wakabayashi *s*
林強斎 W. Kyōsai *mh*
命 Wakamikoto *s*, Wakamei
[9]狭 Wakasa *sph*
松 Wakamatsu *sp*
松賤子 W. Shizuko *fl*
草 Wakakusa *p*
泉 Wakaizumi *s*
癸 Wakaki *s*
竿 Wakasa *s*
[10]柳 Wakayanagi *p*
宮 Wakamiya *sp*
帯 Wakatarashi *s*
原 Wakahara *s*
栗 Wakaguri *s*
[11]桜 Wakasa *p*
桜部 Wakasakurabe *s*
部 Wakabe *s*
菜 Wakana *sf-la*
麻呂 Wakamaro *m*
麻績 Wakaomi *s*
島 Wakashima *s*
雀 Wakasagi *m*

茎 苗 苦 苦 苓 苞 芸 茅 茂 若 ▼ 英 歩 杰 奈 炎 沓 昔 青 斉 忞 忢 忽 ▲ 忠 争 采 妥 肯 旻 昊 杲 昇 易

[12]湯座 Wakayue *s*
森 Wakamori *s*
[13]塚 Wakatsuka *s*
園 Wakazono *s*
[14]紫 Wakamurasaki *l*
[15]穂 Wakaho *p*
槻 Wakatsuki *s*
槻礼次郎 W. Reijirō *mh*
[18]藤 Wakafuji *s*

**英** 693 [T] Hanabusa *sm-p*; Hideru *m*, Suguru, Takeshi. (EI, YŌ, hide, fusa, teru, yoshi, aya, tsune, toshi, hana, hira, akira)
[1]一 Eiichi *m*, Yoshikazu
一郎 Eiichirō *m*
一蝶 Hanabusa Itchō *ma*
[2]二 Hideji *m*, Eiji, Hidetsugu
[3]三 Eizō *m*
[4]五 Eigo *m*
五郎 Eigorō *m*, Hidegorō
太 Eda *s*
太郎 Eitarō *m*, Hidetarō
夫 Hideo *m*
[5]田 Aida *p*
[6]光 Toshimitsu *m*
吉 Eikichi *m*, Hidekichi
早 Hidehaya *m*
多 Aita *s*; Agata *sp*
[7]作 Eisaku *m*
男 Hideo *m*
寿 Hidetsune *m*
[8]征 Hideyuki *m*
延 Fusanobu *m*
尚 Ayanaka *m*
[9]保 Ayaho *s*, Aho
草紙 Hanabusa sōshi *l*
美 Fusatomi *m*
泉 Hidemi *m*
為 Hidetame *m*
彦 Hidehiko *m*
[10]真 Terumi *f*
通 Teruyuki *m*
造 Eizō *m*
[11]脩 Hidenaga *m*
斌 Hideaki *m*
敏 Hidetoshi *m*
[12]喆 Eitetsu *m*
賀 Aga *sp*
[13]雄 Hideo *m*, Hidetaka
経 Fusatsune *m*
資 Eishi *m*
[14]肇 Hidekoto *m*
熙 Hidehiro *m*
[15]蔵 Eizō *m*
[16]薫 Hideshige *m*, Terushige, Teruhide
[18]麿 Hidemaru *m*

———8 T4———

**歩** 694 [T] Susumu *m*, Ayumi. (HO, BU)

**杰** 695 See 傑 1827

**奈** 696 [N] (NA, DAI, nani)
[3]川 Nagawa *p*
[4]井江 Naie *p*
[5]古 Nako *s*
半利 Nabari *p*
[7]佐 Nasa *s*
[8]河 Nagawa *s*
良 Nara *sp*
良己知部 Narakochibe *s*
良井 Narai *s*
良尾 Narao *p*
良岡 Naraoka *s*
良原 Narahara *s*
良屋 Naraya *s*
良屋茂左衛門 N. Mozaemon *mh*
良部 Narabe *s*
良崎 Narasaki *s*
良間 Narama *s*
良詣 Nara mōde *la*
良絵本 N. ehon *la*
良橋 Narabashi *s*
良麿 Naramaro *m*
[9]癸 Naki *s*, Naiki
癸私 Nakisaichi *s*
良麿 Nademaro *m*
[10]倉 Nagura *s*
[11]留 Naru *p*
[12]須 Nasu *s*
[13]義 Nagi *p*

**炎** 697 [T] (EN, honoo)
の人 Honoo no hito *la*
昼 Enchū *l*

**沓** 698 (TŌ, kazu)
手鳥孤城落月 Hototogisu kojō no rakugetsu *la*
沢 Kutsuzawa *s*
冠 Kutsukamuri *l*
掛 Kutsukake *s*

**昔** 699 [T] (SEKI, SHAKU, mukashi, tsune, toki, hisa, furu)
米万石通 Mukashigome mangoku tōshi *la*
語丹前風呂 Mukashigatari tanzenburo *l*

**青** 700 [T] (SEI, SHŌ, ao, kiyo, haru)
ケ島 Aogashima *p*
[4]戸 Aoto *s*
丹よし Aoni yoshi *l*
井 Aoi *s*
女子 Aonao *s*
山 Aoyama *sp*
山杉作 A. Sugisaku *ml*
山霞村 A. Kason *ml*
木 Aoki *sp*
木月斗 A. Getto *ml*
木周蔵 A. Shūzō *mh*
木昆陽 A. Kon'yō *mh*
木健作 A. Kensaku *ml*
木繁 A. Shigeru *ma*
[5]田 Aota *s*
本 Aohon *l*
生 Aō *s*
[6]地 Aochi *s*
池 Aoike *s*
江 Aoe *sf*
江舜二郎 A. Shunjirō *ml*
芝 Aoshiba *l*
名端 Aonahata *s*
[7]谷 Aoya *p*
麦 Aomugi *l*
貝 Aogai *s*
玄 Seigen *l*
[8]沼 Aonuma *s*
果の市 Seika no ichi *l*
[9]垣 Aogaki *p-l*
柿 Aogaki *s*
岡 Aooka *s*
[10]海 Ōmi *p*
柳 Aoyagi *s*
柳有美 A. Yūbi *ml*
柳優 A. Yutaka *ml*
[11]砥 Aoto *s*
猪 Aojishi *l*
猫 Aoneko *l*
根 Aone *s*
梅 Ōme *sp*; Aōmi *s*
野 Aono *s*
野季吉 A. Suekichi *ml*
島 Aojima *s*; Chintō / Seitō *p* "Tsingtao"
[12]森 Aomori *p*
鹿 Aoshika *s*
[16]頭巾 Ao-zukin *l*
[17]嶹 Aojima *s*; Chintō / Seitō *p* "Tsingtao"
鞜 Seitō *l*
[18]嶺 Aone *l*
[24]襲 Aosoi *s*

**斉** 701 [I] Hitoshi *m*, Tadashi. (SAI, nari, tada, toki, toshi, kiyo, nao, masa, mune, yoshi)
[3]川 Saigawa *s*
[4]木 Saiki *s*
[5]田 Saida *s*
[6]吉 Saikichi *m*
広 Naritō *m*
名 Tokina *m*
[7]村 Saimura *s*
[8]明 Saimei *fh*
典 Narioki *m*
[9]信 Tadanobu *m*
荘 Naritaka *m*
[10]宮 Saigū *s*
[11]脩 Narinobu *m*
彬 Nariakira *m*
部 Inbe *s*, Imube
斎 Nariyoshi *m*
粛 Naritari *m*
[12]貴 Naritake *m*
賀 Saiga *s*
間 Saima *s*
[13]雄 Toshio *m*
茲 Narishige *m*
徳 Nariyasu *m*
[14]郷 Saigō *s*
[16]衡 Saikō 854–57
[18]藤 Saitō *s*

**忞** 702 Tsutomu *m*. (BIN)

**忢** 703 (GO, sato)
夫 Satoo *m*

**忽** 704 (KOTSU)
那 Kotsuna *s*, Kutsuna
滑谷 Nukariya *s*, Nukaruya

忠 705 [T] Tadashi *m*, Tadasu, Chū, Sunao, Kiyoshi, Atsushi, Hodokosu. (CHŪ, tada, nori, atsu, nari, tsura, jō)
1一 Chūichi *m*
2二 Tadaji *m*
二郎 Chūjirō *m*
人 Tadato *m*
3三 Chūzō *m*
三郎 Chūzaburō *m*
子 Tadako *f*
大 Tadamoto *m*
也 Chūya *m*
4介 Chūsuke *m*
夫 Tadao *m*
文 Tadafumi *m*
内 Tadanai *s*
太 Chūta *m*
与 Tadayoshi *m*
升 Tadatake *m*
5以 Tadazane *m*
礼 Tadanari *m*
用 Tadamochi *m*
丙 Tadaaki *m*
平 Tadahira *m*, Chūhei
休 Tadayoshi *m*
6次 Tadatsugu *m*
次郎 Chūjirō *m*
光 Tadamitsu *m*
当 Tadamasa *m*
存 Tadaakira *m*
民 Tadamoto *m*
7村 Tadamura *s*
作 Chūsaku *m*
位 Tadataka *m*, Tadanori, Tadakura
邦 Tadakuni *m*
言 Tadatoki *m*, Tadanobu
克 Tadatae *m*
安 Tadayasu *m*
志 Chūji *m*
至 Tadayuki *m*
告 Tadatsugu *m*
兵衛 Chūbee *m*
匡 Tadamasa *m*
見 Tadachika *m*; Tadami *s*
寿 Tadahisa *m*
考 Tadanaka *m*
臣 Tadaon *m*
臣水滸伝 Chūshin suikoden *l*
臣金短冊 C. kogane no tanzaku *l*
臣蔵 Chūshingura *la*
8和 Tadayori *m*, Tadatomo
幸 Atsuyuki *m*
岑 Tadamine *ml*
学 Tadanori *m*, Tadasato
英 Tadateru *m*
苗 Tadamitsu *m*
宗 Tadamune *sm*
宝 Tadatake *m*, Tadamichi, Tadatomo
実 Tadamitsu *m*
居 Tadaoki *m*
述 Tadanobu *m*
良 Tadakata *m*
9治 Chūji *m*
治郎 Chūjirō *m*
持 Tadamochi *m*
珍 Tadaharu *m*
秋 Tadaaki *m*
相 Tadami *s*
刻 Tadatoki *m*
俔 Tadami *m*
信 Tadanobu *m*
洪 Tadahiro *m*
亮 Tadaakira *m*
勇 Tadatoshi *m*
沓 Tadakazu *m*
発 Tadaaki *m*
岡 Tadaoka *p*
囿 Tadasono *m*
度 Tadanori *m*
彦 Tadahiko *m*, Tadasato
直 Tadanao *m*, Tadachika
直卿行状記 Tadanaokyō gyōjōki *l*
重 Tadashige *m*
10俊 Tadatoshi *m*
将 Tadamasa *m*
郡 Tadakuni *m*
郎 Tadao *m*
候 Tadayoshi *m*
倫 Tadatomo *m*
容 Tadayasu *m*
晃 Tadateru *m*
毘 Tadayasu *m*
烈 Tadayasu *m*
要 Tadatoshi *m*
恭 Tadayasu *m*, Tadasumi
恵 Tadashige *m*
挙 Tadataka *m*, Tadahira
哲 Tadaakira *m*
威 Tadaakira *m*
通 Tadamichi *ml*
造 Chūzō *m*
11惇 Tadatoshi *m*
祗 Tadamasa *m*
移 Tadayori *m*
能 Tadayasu *m*
敏 Tadayuki *m*
淳 Tadaatsu *m*
済 Tadamasa *m*
常 Tadatsune *m*
宴 Tadayoshi *m*
啓 Tadahira *m*
脩 Tadataka *m*
恕 Tadayuki *m*, Tadamichi, Tadanori
進 Tadayuki *m*
粛 Tadatoshi *m*, Tadamasa
12順 Tadatoshi *m*, Tadamasa, Tadayori, Tadaosa
馮 Tadayori *m*
揚 Tadataka *m*
晴 Tadaharu *m*
勝 Tadakatsu *m*
款 Tadamasa *m*
敬 Tadaatsu *m*, Tadakata
愈 Tadahisa *m*
裕 Tadayasu *m*
禄 Tadayoshi *m*, Tadatoshi
13禎 Tadayoshi *m*
瑗 Tadamitsu *m*
強 Tadatsuyo *m*, Tadaatsu
雄 Tadao *m*
稠 Tadashige *m*
誠 Tadayoshi *m*
幹 Tadamoto *m*
義 Tadayoshi *m*, Tadaaki
寛 Tadatō *m*
意 Tadaoki *m*
豊 Tadamori *m*
雲 Tadakumo *m*
悳 Tadanori *m*
舜 Tadakiyo *m*
愛 Tadayoshi *m*, Tadanaru
廉 Tadayasu *m*
鼎 Tadakane *m*
14徳 Tadaari *m*
韶 Tadateru *m*
穀 Tadayoshi *m*
嘉 Tadahiro *m*
節 Tadatoki *m*
15鋒 Tadasaki *m*
器 Tadakata *m*
賛 Tadasuke *m*
蔵 Chūzō *m*
16徹 Tadayuki *m*
翰 Tadanaka *m*
親 Tadachika *m*
篤 Tadayuki *m*
震 Tadanari *m*
養 Tadayasu *m*
興 Tadaoki *m*
17総 Tadafusa *m*
藎 Tadae *m*
翼 Tadasuke *m*
18顕 Tadateru *m*
類 Chūrui *p*
熹 Tadateru *m*
19鵬 Tadayuki *m*
20籌 Tadakazu *m*
耀 Tadateru *m*
22懿 Tadanao *m*

争 706 See 争 344

采 707 (SAI, une, aya, koto)
子 Ayako *f*, Kotoko
女 Uneme *sf-p*
男 Uneo *m*
野 Saino *s*

妥 708 [T] (DA, TA, yasu)
江 Yasue *f*

肯 709 [T] (KŌ, saki, mune)

旻 710 Akira *m*, Takashi; Min *mh*. (BIN)

昊 711 Hiroshi *m*. (KŌ, GŌ, hiro)

杲 712 Akira *m*, Akashi, Takashi. (KŌ, aki)
雄 Akio *m*

昇 713 [T] Noboru *m*, Susumu; Nobori *sm*. (SHŌ, nori, kami)
一 Shōichi *m*
平 Shōhei *m*
次郎 Shōjirō *m*
曙夢 Nobori Shomu *ml*

**易** 714 [T] Yasushi *m*. (EKI, YAKU, yasu, osa, kane, kanu)
二郎 Yasujirō *m*
次郎 Yasujirō *m*

**昌** 715 [N] Masashi *m*, Masaru, Sakan, Akira, Sakae. (SHŌ, masa, yoshi, aki, masu, suke, yo, atsu, saka)
[1]一 Masuichi *m*
[3]三 Masami *m*
[4]夫 Masao *m*
介 Shōsuke *m*
女 Akiko *f*
[5]司 Shōji *m*
由 Masayori *m*
正 Yoshimasa *m*
生 Masaki *m*
[6]次 Shōji *m*
吉 Shōkichi *m*
[7]作 Shōsaku *m*
弘 Masamitsu *m*
言 Masayuki *m*
谷 Sakaya *s*, Shōya
寿 Masayoshi *m*
甫 Masayoshi *m*
[8]服 Masamoto *m*
英 Masahide *m*, Masatsune
矣 Masao *m*
幸 Masao *m*
昌 Masaaki *m*
[9]信 Akinobu *m*
胖 Masanao *m*
貞 Masatada *m*
岡 Masaoka *s*
[10]倫 Masanori *m*
泰 Shōtai 898–901
耆 Masatoshi *m*
[11]健 Masatake *m*
後 Masanori *m*
康 Masayasu *m*
[12]崎 Sakazaki *s*
裕 Yoshihiro *m*
喬 Masataka *m*
達 Masayoshi *m*
道 Masanori *m*
[13]植 Masatane *m*
猷 Masamichi *m*
[14]碩 Masahiro *m*
[16]蔵 Masayoshi *m*
[16]穆 Masayoshi *m*
綽 Masanobu *m*
熹 Masayoshi *m*
邁 Masayuki *m*
臧 Masayoshi *m*
[18]穫 Masae *f*

—— 8 T5 ——

**帛** 716 (HAKU, kinu)
江 Kinue *f*
世 Kinuyo *f*

**奉** 717 [T] (HŌ, BU, tomo, yoshi, na, uke)
文 Tomoyuki *m*
天 Hoten *p* "Mukden"
永 Yoshinaga *m*
政 Tomomasa *m*
表 Tomoyoshi *m*

**具** 718 [T] (GU, KU, tomo, kane)
下場 Kugetsuka *s*
下塚 Kugetsuka *s*
氏 Tomouji *m*
志 Gushi *s*
国 Tomokuni *m*
視 Tomomi *m*
集 Kaneai *m*
選 Tomonobu *m*
慶 Kaneyasu *m*
瞻 Tomomi *m*

**学** 719 [T] Manabu *m*, Satoru, Akira. (GAKU, michi, taka, sato, akira, take, nori, sane, hisa)
一 Gakuichi *m*
文 Satofumi *m*
夫 Michio *m*
俊 Takatoshi *m*
習院 Gakushūin *p*
説乞丐袋 Gakusetsu kikkaibukuro *l*
館院 Gakkan'in *ph*

**糸** 720 [T] (SHI, ito)
[3]川 Itogawa *s*
之 Itoshi *f*
子 Itoko *f*
久 Itoku *s*
[4]山 Itoyama *s*
井 Itoi *s*
永 Itonaga *s*
田 Itoda *sp*
竹初心集 Itotake / Shichiku shoshinshū *l*
[7]沢 Itozawa *s*
尾 Itoo *s*
[9]治 Itoji *m*
重子 Itoeko *f*
[10]原 Itohara *s*
屋 Itoya *s*
[11]魚川 Itoigawa *p*
島 Itoshima *p*
[12]貫 Itonuki *p*
賀 Itoga *s*

**舎** 721 [T] Yadoru *m*, Yaguri. (SHA, ya, ie, tone)
人 Toneri *sm-p*
人親王 T. Shinnō *mlh*
川 Tonegawa *s*
子 Ieko *s*
利 Shari *la*
利讃歎 S. santan *l*
弟 Shatei *l*
栄 Ieyoshi *m*

**突** 722 [T] (TOTSU, tsuku)
棒船 Tsukubōsen *l*

**空** 723 [T] (KŪ, taka, sora)
也 Kūya / Kōya *mh*
地 Sorachi *s*
知 Sorachi *p*
海 Kūkai *ml*
華集 Kugeshū *l*
閑 Kuga *s*, Koga
蟬 Utsusemi *l*
穂 Akiho *m*

**秊** 724 See 年 342

**季** 725 [T] Minoru *m*. (KI, sue, toki, toshi, hide)
[3]子 Sueko *f*, Toshiko
[6]次 Suetsugu *m*, Tokitsugu
羽 Sueba *s*
吉 Suekichi *m*
[7]吟 Kigin *ml*
[8]宝 Suetaka *m*
良 Sueharu *m*
[9]彦 Tokihiko *m*
[10]家 Sueie *s*
[11]彬 Suehide *m*
[12]備 Sueyoshi *m*
[13]雄 Sueo *m*, Toshio
茲 Sueshige *m*
[14]鳳 Suetaka *m*
[15]誕 Suenobu *m*
熊 Suekuma *m*
[16]興 Sueoki *m*
[21]巌 Sueyoshi *m*

**秀** 726 [T] Shigeru *m*, Hide, Shū, Hideshi, Sakae, Minoru, Hiizu. (SHŪ, SHU, hide, ho, hozu, yoshi, mitsu, hora, sue)
[1]一 Hideichi *m*, Hidekatsu
[3]三 Shūzō *m*
三郎 Hidesaburō *m*
子 Hideko *f*
[4]心 Hidemi *m*
仁 Mitsuhito *m*
円 Hidemaru *m*
文 Hidebumi *m*
[5]夫 Hideo *m*
太郎 Hidetarō *m*
司 Hideji *m*, Hideshi
句傘 Shūku karakasa *l*
央 Hidenaka *m*
用 Hidemochi *m*
[6]次 Hidetsugu *m*
次郎 Hidejirō *m*
兆 Hideyoshi *m*
光 Hidemitsu *m*
守 Hidemori *m*
吉 Hideyoshi *m*, Hidekichi; Hozuma *s*
成 Hidenari *m*
世 Hidetsugu *m*
[7]伯 Hideo *m*, Hideho
完 Hidesada *m*
臣 Hidemitsu *m*
来 Hideki *m*
[8]枝 Hozue *m-f*
幸 Hideyuki *m*
宝 Hidekane *m*
実 Hidesane *m*, Hidemi; Hozumi *sm*
忠 Hidetada *m*
典 Hidetsune *m*
並 Hidenami *m*
延 Hidenobu *m*
武 Hidetake *m*
虎 Hidetora *m*
[9]治 Hideji *m*
松 Hidematsu *m*
秋 Hideaki *m*
発 Hideoki *m*
郎 Yoshio *m*

倉 Hogura *sm*
真 Hozuma *sm*
造 Hidezō *m*
11猪 Hidei *m* ⌈tō *mh*
能 Hidehisa *m*; Hide-
剰 Hidemasu *m*
恕 Hidehiro *m*
進 Hidenobu *m*
康 Hideyasu *m*
島 Hideshima *s*
12復 Hidemata *m*
13煌 Hideteru *m*
雄 Hideo *m*
幹 Hideki *m*, Homiki
聖 Hidesato *m*
16嶠 Hidetaka *m*
樹 Hideki *m*
積 Hozumi *s*
頼 Hideyori *m*
穎 Hidekai *m*
17禧 Hidetomi *m*
18観 Hidemi *m*

——8 T6——

凭 727 (HYŌ, yori, yoru, yoshi, teru)

努 728 [T] Tsutomu *m*. (DO)

竺 729 Chiku *p*. (CHIKU, JIKU)
志 Tsukushi *s*

受 730 [T] (JU, SHŪ, tsugu, shige, osa, uke, uku)
川 Ukegawa *s*
長 Osanaga *m*

阜 731 Tōru *m*. (FU, taka, oka, na, atsu)
子 Okako *f*, Atsuko

卒 732 [T] (SOTSU, taka, hiki)
都婆小町 Sotoba Komachi *la*
塔婆小町 S. K. *la*
渓 Hikitani *s*

典 733 [T] Tsukasa *m*. (TEN, nori, tsune, yoshi, fumi, michi, suke, oki, mori, yori)
子 Tsuneko *f*, Fumiko, Michiko
文 Yoshifumi *m*
夫 Norio *m*
田 Suketada *m*
次 Yoshitsugu *m*
寿 Norihisa *m*
明 Tsuneaki *m*
暁 Tsunetoshi *m*

其 734 (KI, GI, sono, toki, moto)
二 Sonoji *m*
田 Sonoda *s*
由縁鄙廼俤 Sono yukari hina no omokage *l*
吉 Sonokichi *m*
母 Sonomo *m*
角 Kikaku *ml*
阿弥 Kiami *mh*
面影 Sono omokage *l*
笑 Kishō *ml*
雪影 Sono yukikage *l*
磧 Kiseki *ml*

呉 735 [T] Kure *sp*, Go "Wu." (GO, GU, kure, kuni)
子 Kureko *f*
本 Kuremoto *s*
羽 Kureha *p*
床作 Goshōtsukuri *s*
服 Kureha *sf-la*; Kurehara *s*, Kurehatori, Kurehato
茂一 Kure Shigeichi
妹 Kurese *s* ⌊*ml*
陵軒可有 Goryōken Arubeshi *ml*
須 Gosu *s*
漢 Kureaya *s*
葉 Kureha *f*

——8 F1——

直 See 988

——8 F2——

周 736 [T] Makoto *m*, Chikashi, Amane, Hiroshi, Itaru; Shū *s*. (SHŪ, SHU, chika, nori, kane, tada, kata, nari, kanu)
1一 Shūichi *m*
3三 Shūzō *m*
之 Chikayuki *m* ⌈ko
子 Chikako *f*, Kane-
4仁 Katahito *m*
太郎 Shūtarō *m*
5布 Suu *sp*; Sufu *s*
田 Shūda *s*
平 Kanehira *m*
6次郎 Shūjirō *m*
行 Kaneyuki *m*
吉 Suki *p*
西 Susai *s*
7作 Shūsaku *m*
防 Suō *sph* ⌈chi *p*
知 Tadatomo *m*; Shū-
8房 Norifusa *m*
東 Shūtō *sp*
9秋 Chikaaki *m*
亮 Chikaaki *m*
参見 Sumami *s*; Susami *sp* ⌈rishige
重 Chikashige *m*, No-
10桑 Shūsō *p*
11陸 Chikamichi *m*
恕 Chikayuki *m*
13滑平 Sukoppei *m*
15敷 Sufu *s*
蔵 Shūzō *m*
16翰 Chikataka *m*
18藤 Shūtō *s*

——8 F3——

居 737 [T] (KYO, KO, i, oki, sue, ori, yasu, yori, saya)
石 Sueishi *s*
初 Isome *s*
波 Inami *s*
杭 Igui *l*
具 Igu *s*
貞 Isada *m*
野 Ino *s*
勢 Kose *s*

辰 738 [N] Noburu *m*, Tatsu. (SHIN, JIN, tatsu, toki, nobu, yoshi)
3三郎 Tatsusaburō *m*
之助 Tatsunosuke *m*
口 Tatsunokuchi *p*
巳 Tatsumi *s*
巳婦言 T. fugen *l*
4五郎 Tatsugorō *m*
井 Tatsui *s*
夫 Tokio *m*
木 Tatsuki *s*
太郎 Tatsutarō *m*
午 Tatsuma *m*
5四郎 Tatsushirō *m*
由 Nobuyoshi *m*
市 Tatsuichi *s*
6次郎 Tatsujirō *m*
江 Tatsue *s*
吉 Tokiyoshi *m*
7男 Tatsuo *m*
8良 Tatsuo *m*
9治 Tatsuji *m*
弥 Tatsuya *m*
岡 Tatsuoka *s*
10郎 Tatsurō *m*
馬 Tatsuma *sm*; Tatsuuma *s*
11猪 Tatsui *m*
野 Tatsuno *sp*
野隆 T. Yutaka *ml*
13雄 Tatsuo *m*
14爾 Tokishika *m*

延 739 [T] Noburu *m*, En, Susumu, Tadashi; Nobu *p*. (EN, nobu, naga, tō, suke)
3于 Nobuyuki *m*
子 Nobuko *f*
久 Enkyū 1069–74
4元 Engen 1336–40
文 Enbun 1356–61
太郎 Nobutarō *m*
山 Nobeyama *s*
5生 Nobu *s*
6次郎 Enjirō *m*
全 Nobumasa *m*
光 Tōteru *m*
吉 Nobukichi *m*, Enkichi
7応 En'ō 1239–40
8房 Tōfusa *m*
享 Enkyō 1744–48
宝 Enpō 1673–81
9信 Nobusane *m*
秋 Nobutoki *m*
長 Enchō 923–31
香 Nobuka *m*
岡 Nobeoka *p*
10原 Nobehara *s*
12喜 Engi 901–23
喜式 Engishiki *l*
14徳 Entoku 1489–92
暦 Enryaku 782–806
暦寺 Enryakuji *p*
15慶 Engyō / Enkei 1308–11
慶両卿訴陳状 Engyō ryōkyō sochinjō *l*

**府** 740 [T] Atsu *f.* (FU, moto, atsu, kura)
川 Fukawa *s*
子 Motoko *f*
中 Fuchū *p*
役 Kōmata *s* ⌈shima
島 Kōshima *s*, Kōno-

**庚** 741 Kanoe *f.* (KŌ, KYŌ, ka, tsugu, yasu)
子彦 Kanehiko *m*
子郎 Kaneo *m*
午治郎 Kamajirō *m*

**匣** 742 (KŌ, GŌ, kushige)

**医** 743 [T] Osamu *m.* (I)
王野 Iono *s*

**固** 744 [T] Katamu *m*, Katashi. (KO, kata, taka, moto, mi)
山 Katayama *s*

**国** 745 [T] Kuni *s.* (KOKU, kuni, to-
[1]一 Kuniichi *m* ⌊ki)
[2]十 Kunikazu *m*
[3]三 Kunizō *m*
子 Kuniko *f*
士 Kunio *m*
久 Kunihisa *sm*
[4]元 Kunimoto *s*
分 Kokubu *sp*; Kokubun *s*
分一太郎 Kokubun Ichitarō *ml*
分寺 Kokubunji *p*; Kōdera *s* ⌈gai *ml*
分青厓 Kokubu Sei-
友 Kunitomo *sm*
中 Kuninaka *sm*
日出 Kunihide *m*
方 Kunikata *sm*
壬 Kunitsugu *m*
井 Kunii *s*
木田 Kunikida *s*
木田独歩 K. Doppo *ml*
太郎 Kunitarō *m*
[5]司 Kunitsukasa *s*, Ku-
田 Kunida *s* ⌊nishi
立 Kunitachi *p*
正 Kokushō *s*
本 Kunimoto *s*
氏 Kuniuji *m*
[6]行 Kuniyuki *m*
江 Kunie *s*
守 Kunimori *m*
吉 Kuniyoshi *sm*
光 Kunimitsu *s*
広 Kunihiro *sm*
米 Kokumai *s*
多 Kunikazu *m*
[7]佐 Kunisa *s*
沢 Kunisawa *s*
弘 Kunihiro *s*
谷 Kuniya *s*
芳 Kuniyoshi *m*
安 Kuniyasu *sm*
忍 Kunioshi *m*
見 Kunimi *p*
亜 Kunitsugu *m*
臣 Kunimi *m*
寿丸 Kunijumaru *m*
[8]明 Kuniaki *m*
枝 Kunieda *s*
枝史郎 K. Shirō *ml*
定 Kunisada *s*
定忠治 K. Chūji *mh-l*
宗 Kunimune *m*
府 Kokufu *sp*, Kō
府犀東 Kokufu Saitō *ml*
府方 Kofukata *s*
府田 Kofuda *s*
武 Kunitake *sm*
東 Kunisaki *sp*
[9]保 Kuniyasu *sm*
昭 Kuniaki *m*
祝 Kunitoki *m*
姓爺合戦 Kokusen'ya kassen *la*
柱 Kunihashira *m*
松 Kunimatsu *s*
香 Kunika *m*
背宍人 Kuseshishido *s*
栄 Kuniyoshi *m*
岡 Kunioka *s*
彦 Kunihiko *m*
貞 Kunisada *m*
重 Kunishige *sm*
[10]栖 Kuzu *sla*
宰 Kuninomikotomochi *s*
家 Kuniie *sm*
原 Kunihara *s*
造 Kunizō *m*; Kunitsukuri *s*, Kunitsuko
[11]覓 Kunimogi *s*
巣 Kuzu *s*
康 Kuniyasu *m*
島 Kunishima *s*
隆 Tokitaka *m*
[12]順 Kuniyuki *m*
納 Kunitomo *m*
崎 Kunisaki *s*
崎望久太郎 K. Mokutarō *ml*
富 Kunitomi *sm-p*
賀 Kuniyoshi *m*
[13]満 Kunimaro *m*
[14]領 Kokuryō *s*
歌八論 Kokka hachiron *l* ⌈gen *l*
歌八論余言 K. h. yo-
歌八論余言拾遺 K. h. y. shūi *l*
算 Kunikazu *m*
[15]審 Kunishige *m*
蔵 Kunizō *s*
[16]儔 Kunitomo *s*
頼 Kuniyori *m*
維 Kunifusa *m*
[18]顕 Kuniakira *m*
藤 Kunitō *s*

**迎** 746 [T] Mukai *s.* (GEI, GYŌ)
田 Kōda *s*
達 Itate *s*

**迫** 747 [T] Sako *s*; Hasama *p.* (HAKU, sako, seri, tō)
水 Sakomizu *s*, Sakomi
田 Sakoda *s*, Serita
間 Sakoma *s*, Hazama

**述** 748 [T] Noburu *m.* (JUTSU, SHUTSU, nobu, tomo, akira, nori)
子 Nobuko *f*, Tomo-
史 Nobumi *m* ⌊ko
直 Nobunao *m*

———8 F4———

**者** See 769

**迋** 749 (ō, sumi, yuki)

**或** 750 (WAKU, mochi)
水 Wakumizu *s*

**武** 751 [T] Takeshi *m*, Takeru, Isamu; Take *f.* (MU, BU, take, isa, tatsu, fuka, n)
[1]一 Buichi *m*
[2]二 Takeji *m*
人 Takendo *m*
[3]川 Takegawa *s*; Mu-
三 Buzō *m* ⌊kawa *sp*
三郎 Takesaburō *m*
子 Takeko *f*; Takeshi
下 Takeshita *s* ⌊*s*
久 Takehisa *sm*
之 Takeyuki *m*
之助 Takenosuke *m*
士 Takeshi *sm*
[4]元 Takemoto *sm*
内 Takeuchi *s*, Takenouchi, Takechi
夫 Takeo *m*
太郎 Taketarō *m*
山 Takeyama *s*
山英子 T. Hideko *fl*
井 Takei *s*
井昭男 T. Teruo *ml*
中 Takenaka *s*
[5]永 Takenaga *s*
石 Takeishi *s*, Fuishi, Fuseki; Takeshi *sp*
四郎 Takeshirō *m*
甲 Takekatsu *m*
丕 Takehiro *m*
平 Buhei *m*
本 Takemoto *s*
市 Takeichi *s*, Takechi
市瑞山 Takechi Zuizan *mh*
正 Takemasa *m* ⌈*m*
生 Takefu *sp*; Takeo
生水 Mushōzu *sp*
田 Takeda *s*
田交来 T. Kōrai *ml*
田仰天子 T. Gyōtenshi *ml*
田信玄 T. Shingen *mh*
田泰淳 T. Taijun *ml*
田耕雲斎 T. Kōunsai *mh* ⌈*mh*
田勝頼 T. Katsuyori
田鶯塘 T. Ōtō *ml*
田麟太郎 T. Rintarō
末 Takesue *s* ⌊*ml*
[6]次 Takeji *m*
次郎 Takejirō *m*
江 Takee *s*
光 Takemitsu *sm*
吉 Bukichi *m*

辻 Taketsuji *s*
[7]佐 Musa *s*
沢 Takezawa *s*
社 Musa *s*
村 Takemura *s*
谷 Takeya *s*
芳 Takeyoshi *sm*
安 Takeyasu *sm*
志 Takeshi *m*
男 Takeo *m*
兵衛 Buhee *m*
臣 Taketomi *m*
[8]林 Takebayashi *s*; Takeshige *m*
林無想庵 T. Musōan *ml*
知 Takechi *s*
幸 Takeyuki *m*
命 Takemi *m*, Isami
宜部 Mugebe *s*
芸 Muge *p*
定 Takesada *m*
茂 Mumo *s*
居 Takei *s*
東 Mutō *s*
者 Musha *s*
者小路 Mushakōji *s*, Mushanokōji
者小路実篤 Mushanokōji Saneatsu *ml*
[9]信 Takenobu *s*
津 Taketsu *s*
治 Takeji *m*
律 Fukatsu *s*
松 Takematsu *m*
政 Takemasa *m*
則 Takenori *m*
香 Takeka *m*
直夫 Muneo *m*
岡 Takeoka *s*
彦 Takehiko *m*
重 Takeshige *s*
[10]修 Takenobu *m*
将列伝 Bushō retsuden *l*
射 Musa *s*
宮 Takemiya *s*
家義理 Buke giri *l*
要 Takeyasu *m*
原 Takehara *s*
[11]済 Takemasa *m*
敏 Taketoshi *m*
能 Takenori *m*
野 Takeno *s*
野紹鷗 T. Jōō *mh*
部 Takebe *s*, Takerube
紀 Taketoshi *m*
笠 Mukasa *s*
島 Takeshima *s*
島羽衣 T. Hagoromo *ml*
富 Taketomi *s*
[12]森 Takemori *s*
第 Takekuni *m*
智 Takechi *s*
智鉄二 T. Tetsuji *ml*
智麿 Muchimaro *m*
悪 Buaku *la*
曾 Takeso *s*
道伝来記 Budō denraiki *l*
間 Buma *s*
[13]隈 Takekuma *s*
雄 Takeo *sm-p*
幹 Takeki *m*
豊 Taketoyo *p*
義 Muge *s*
[14]郷 Takesato *m*
[15]儀 Mugi *p*
蔵 Musashi *sm-p*
蔵野 Musashino *sp-l*
蔵鐙 Musashiabumi *s*
[16]衛 Bue *s*
整 Takenobu *m*
[18]駿 Taketoshi *m*
藤 Mutō *s*, Takefu

## 8 F5

**奇** 752 [T] (KI, GI, kusu, aya, saku, yori, kushi)
久麿 Kikumaro *m*
男 Kusuo *m*
奇羅 Kikira *s*
弥 Han'ya *m*

**尚** 753 [I] Hisashi *m*, Naoshi, Takashi. (SHŌ, JŌ, nao, hisa, yoshi, taka, yori, naka, nari, masa, sane, mashi, masu)
[1]一 Naoichi *m*
[3]之 Takayuki *m*
士 Naonori *m*
[4]文 Takabumi *m*
[5]目 Takashime *s*
古 Yoshifuru *m*
[6]同 Hisatomo *m*
[7]住 Naozumi *m*
志 Hisayuki *m*, Naomune
男 Yoshio *m*
[8]征 Naoyuki *m*
服 Naokoto *m*
知 Hisaaki *m*
実 Naozane *m*
武 Naotake *m*
[9]信 Naonobu *m*
[10]真 Naozane *m*
[11]敏 Naotoshi *m*
隆 Naotaka *m*
[12]順 Naoyoshi *m*
備 Naomitsu *m*
敬 Hisayuki *m*
経 Hisatsune *m*
[14]徳 Hisanori *m*
[15]監 Naomi *m*

## 8 F6

**虎** 754 [N] Takeshi *m*, Takeki; Tora *f*. (KO, KU, tora, take)
[1]一郎 Toraichirō *m*
[3]三郎 Torasaburō *m*
之介 Toranosuke *m*
之助 Toranosuke *m*
[4]六郎 Torarokurō *m*
五郎 Toragorō *m*
王丸 Toraōmaru *ma*
太 Torata *m*
太郎 Toratarō *m*
[6]次郎 Torajirō *m*
[7]沢 Torazawa *ma*
谷 Toraya *s*
児 Toraji *m*
尾 Torao *s*
[8]明 Toraakira *m*
林 Torabayashi *s*
[9]治 Toraji *m*
岩 Toraiwa *s*
彦 Torahiko *m*
[10]屋 Toraya *s*
[11]清 Torakiyo *m*
姫 Torahime *p*
[13]雄 Torao *m*
[14]関師錬 Kokan Shiren *mlh*

## 8 U

**辰** See 738

**兩** 755 See 両 531

**來** 756 See 来 538

**兒** 757 See 児 497

**兕** 758 (SHI, JI, take)

**雨** 759 [T] (U, ame, ama, furu, same)
月 Ugetsu *l*
山 Ameyama *l*
田 Uda *s*
谷 Amegaya *s*, Amagaya
夜 Amaya *s*
夜記 Amayo no ki *l*
宮 Amemiya *s*
竜 Uryū *p*
森 Amemori *s*, Amenomori
森芳洲 Amenomori Hōshū *mh*

**承** 760 [T] (SHŌ, JŌ, tsugu, tsugi, yoshi, koto, suke, uke)
久 Jōkyū 1219–22
元 Jōgen 1207–11
平 Jōhei 931–38
安 Jōan 1171–75
応 Jōō 1652–55
和 Jōwa 834–48
昭 Tsuguakira *m*
叙 Tsugumitsu *m*
保 Jōhō 1074–77
徳 Jōtoku 1097–99
暦 Jōryaku 1077–81

**垂** 761 [T] Shigeru *m*. (SUI, ZUI, tari, taru, tare)
水 Tarumi *sp*; Tarumizu *p*
井 Tarui *sp*
氷 Taruhi *s*, Nuruhi
枝 Taree *f*
穂 Tariho *m*
麿 Tarimaro *m*

**免** 762 [T] (MEN)
田 Menda *p*
取 Mendori *s*

**兎** 763 Usa *f*. (TO, u)
也 Tonari *m*
太 Uda *s*
毛 Tomō *m*
原 Uhara *s*

**弟** 764 (TEI, oto, chika, kuni, tsugi, futo)
子丸 Deshimaru *s*
子屈 Teshikaga *p*

兩 來 兒 兕 雨 承 垂 免 兎 弟 ▼ 並 夜 良 事 者 果 東 ▲ 偊 俠 俔 俐 俗 侯 侶 俁 依 保

女 Otome *f*
彦 Otohiko *m*
麻呂 Otomaro *m*
稲 Otoine *m*

並 765 [T] Narabu *m*. (MEI, BYŌ, nami, mitsu, mi, name)
川 Namikawa *s*
之 Mitsuo *f*
木 Namiki *sm*
木千柳 N. Senryū *ml*
木五瓶 N. Gohei *ml*
木正三 N. Shōzō *ml*
木宗輔 N. Sōsuke *ml*
枝 Namie *f* ⌈ka
河 Namikawa *s*, Nabi-
岡 Namioka *s*
始 Okihajime *s*
栗 Namikuri *s*
樹 Namiki *sm*
藤 Namifuji *m*

夜 766 [T] (YA, yo, yoru, yasu)
の禰覚 Yo no nezame
久野 Yakuno *p* ⌊*l*
半の寝覚 Yowa no nezame *l*
半楽 Yahanraku *l*
交 Yomaze *s*
宗 Yorumune *m*
討曾我 Youchi Soga *la*
須 Yasu *sp*
詩 Yoshi *m*

良 767 [T] Makoto *sm*; Ryō *m*, Nagashi, Akira, Naoshi, Tsukasa. (RYŌ, yoshi, rō, naga, ro, ra, o, kazu, kata, suke, taka, haru, hisa, hiko, mi, sane, tsugi, fumi)
1一 Ryōichi *m*
2三 Ryōzō *m*
子 Yoshiko *f*, Ryōko, Nagako
之助 Ryōnosuke *m*
士 Ryōshi *m*, Yoshio
4仁 Nagahito *m*
太 Ryōta *m*, Yoshimoto
太郎 Ryōtarō *m*
5平 Ryōhei *m*
夫 Yoshio *m*
6任 Yoshitō *m*
地 Yoshitada *m*
吉 Ryōkichi *m*
弁 Rōben *mh*
成 Yoshinari *m*
世 Yoshitsugu *m*
7佐 Rasa *f*
作 Ryōsaku *m*
助 Ryōsuke *m*
邑 Yoshimura *m*
忍 Ryōnin *mh*
志子 Yoshiko *f*
男 Yoshio *m*
8知 Yoshitomo *m*, Yoshikazu; Rachi *s*
房 Yoshifusa *m*
茂 Yoshishige *m*
岑 Yoshimine *s*
岑安世 Y. no Yasuyo *ml* ⌈shi *ml*
岑玄利 Y. no Haruto-
9治 Ryōji *m*
長 Takanaga *m*
栄 Yoshihiro *m*
10造 Ryōzō *m*
11野 Yoshino *s*
能 Yoshinori *m*
基 Yoshimoto *m*
12勝 Nagakatsu *m*
敬 Yoshiatsu *m*
逸 Ryōitsu *m*
13源 Ryōgen *mh*
祺 Yoshiyasu *m*
経 Yoshitsune *m*
寛 Ryōkan *mlh*
雄 Yoshio *m*
業 Yoshinari *m*
蒸 Yoshitsugu *m*
輔 Ryōsuke *m*
15澄 Yoshisumi *m*
蔵 Ryōzō *m*
18観 Ryōkan *mh*
20馨 Yoshika *m*

事 768 [T] Tsutomu *m*. (JI, SHI, koto, waza)
主 Kotonushi *m*

者 769 [T] (SHA, hito, hisa)
度 Yotto *s*, Itto

果 770 [T] Hatasu *m*, Hatsuru, Masaru, Akira. (KA, hata)
之 Hatashi *m*
安 Hatayasu *m*

東 771 [T] Azuma *sm-p*; Higashi *sp*; Tō *s*; Akira *m*, Hajime, Agari. (TŌ, higashi, haru, hide, moto)
1一 Tōichi *m*
一郎 Tōichirō *m*
2八代 Higashi-yatsushiro *p* ⌈mōdo
人 Azumabito *m*, Azu-
3川 Higashigawa *sp*
三条 Higashisanjō *s*
万 Tōma *s* ⌈ruko
子 Higashiko *f*, Ha-
久世 Higashikuze *s*
久邇 Higashikuni *s*
久邇稔彦 H. Naruhiko *mh*
4与賀 Higashiyoka *p*
文 Yamatonofumi *s*
方 Higashikata *s*
方朔 Tōbō-saku *ml-la* "Tung-fang Shuo"
山 Higashiyama *sp*; Tōyama *s*
山桜荘子 H. sakura sōshi *la*
山殿花五彩幕 H.-dono no sakura no iromaku *la* ⌈shi *sp*
山梨 Higashi-yamana-
山道 Tōsandō *p*
井 Azumai *s*
5加茂 Higashi-kamo *p*
北 Tōhoku *p*; Tōbo-
司 Tōji *s* ⌊ku *la*
田 Higashida *s*, Tsukada
田川 Higashi-tagawa *p*
由利 H.-yuri *p*
市来 H.-ichiki *p*
平 Tōhei *m*
生 Higashinari *s*
白川 Higashi-shiraka-
本 Tōmoto *s* ⌊wa *p*
6伊豆 Higashi-izu *p*
伏見 Higashifushimi *s*
池田 Toita *s*
地 Tōji *s*
地井 Tochii *s*
宇和 Higashi-uwa *p*
吉野 H.-yoshino *p*
庄 Tōjō *p*
成 Higashinari *p*
成瀬 Higashi-naruse *p*
臼杵 H.-usuki *p*
7住吉 H.-sumiyoshi *p*
伯 Tōhaku *p*
坊城 Higashibōjō *s*
村 Higashimura *s*
村山 Higashi-murayama *p*
利尻 H.-rishiri *p*
谷 Higashidani *s*
安居 Higashiango *s*
牟婁 Higashi-muro *p*
条 Tōjō *sp*; Higashijō *s*
条英機 T. Hideki *mh*
児 Tōji *p*
尾 Higashio *s* ⌈*p*
串良 Higashi-kushira
出 Higashide *s*
出雲 Higashi-izumo *p*
里 Tōri *sm*
里山人 T. Sannin *ml*
8彼杵 Higashi-sonogi
門 Tōmon *s* ⌊*p*
和 Tōwa *p*
京 Tōkyō *p*
金 Tōgane *sp*
国東 Higashi-kunisaki *p*
9城 Tōjō *sp*
洲斎写楽 Tōshūsai Sharaku *ma*
洋 Tōyō *p*
浅井 Higashi-asai *p*
津野 H.-tsuno *p*
津軽 H.-tsugaru *p*
神楽 H.-kagura *p*
祖谷山 H.-iyayama *p*
松 Tōmatsu *s*
松山 Higashi-matsuyama *p*
松浦 H.-matsuura *p*
茨城 H.-ibaraki *p*
岸居士 Tōgan Koji *la*
背振 Higashi-sefuri *p*
春日井 H.-kasugai *p*
栄 Tōei *p*
風浦 Kochiura *s*
彦 Haruhiko *m*
10浦 Higashiura *sp*
海 Tōkai *sp*
海一漚集 T. ichiōshū *l*
海散士 T. Sanshi *ml*
海村 Shōjimura *s*
海林 Shōji *s*
海道 Tōkaidō *p*
海道中膝栗毛 Tōkaidōchū hizakurige *l*
海道四谷怪談 Tōkaidō Yotsuya kaidan *la*

海道名所記 T. meishoki *l*
俱知安行 Higashi-kutchan-kō *l*
砺波 H.-tonami *p*
秩父 H.-chichibu *p*
員 Tōin *p*
宮 Tōgū *s*
家 Toke *s*
恩納 Higashionna *s*
原 Higashihara *s*, Tōhara
屋 Azumaya *l*
通 Higashidōri *p*
馬 Tōma *sm*
11淀川 Higashi-yodogawa *p*
流 Tōryū *s*
根 Higashine *p*
能勢 Higashi-nose *p*
野 Higashino *sp*; Tōno *s*
部 Tōbu *p*
常縁 Tō no Tsuneyori *ml*
島 Higashima *s*, Tōjima
鳥取 Higashi-tottori *p*
12陽 Tōyō *p*
粟倉 Higashi-awakura *p*
筑摩 H.-chikuma *p*
遊 Azuma asobi *l*
道 Azumaji *s*
13雄 Hideo *m*
葛飾 Higashi-katsushika *p*
蒲原 H.-kanbara *p*
園 Higashizono *s*
漢 Yamatonoaya *s*
14歌 Azuma uta *l*
郷 Tōgō *sp*
郷平八郎 T. Heihachirō *mh*
置賜 Higashi-okitama *p*
関紀行 Tōkan kikō *l*
15儀 Tōgi *s*
諸県 Higashi-morokata *p*
磐井 H.-iwai *p*
16樹 Tōju *s*
19頸城 Higashi-kubiki *p*
藻琴 H.-mokoto *p*
22灘 H.-nada *p*
24鷹栖 H.-takasu *p*
26籬 Tōri *s*

## —9 L2—

侽 772 (DAN, o)

俠 773 Satoru *m*, Tamotsu. (KYŌ, GYŌ)

俔 774 (KEN, GEN, mi, chika)
子 Chikako *f*

俐 775 (RI, sato)
子 Satoko *f*

俗 776 [T] Narō *m*. (ZOKU, SHOKU, yo, michi)
神道大意 Zoku shintō taii *l*

侯 777 [T] (KŌ, GU, kimi, toki, kinu, yoshi)
子 Kimiko *f*
雄 Kimio *m*, Kinuo

侶 778 (RO, RYO, tomo, kane, kanu)

俣 779 (mata)
代 Matayo *f*
野 Matano *s*

依 780 [T] (I, E, yori, yo)
氏 Yoriuji *m*
永 Yonaga *s*
田 Yoda *sp*; Yorita *s*
田学海 Yoda Gakkai *ml*
田秋圃 Y. Shūho *ml*
光 Yorimitsu *s*
信 Yorinobu *m*
岡 Yorioka *s*
常 Etsune *s*
智秦 Echihata *s*
徹 Yorimichi *m*
綱 Yosami *s*
藤 Yorifuji *s*
羅 Yosara *s*; Yosami *sp*

保 781 [T] Tamotsu *m*, Yasushi, Mamoru. (HO, HŌ, yasu, mori, mochi, o, yori)
1一 Yasuichi *m*
2二 Yasuji *m*
3川 Yasukawa *s*, Hogawa
之助 Yasunosuke *m*
己一 Hōkiichi *m*
土ケ谷 Hodogaya *p*
土田 Hotoda *s*
4刈 Hogari *s*
元 Hōgen *l* 1156–59
戸田 Hotoda *s*
内 Honai *p*
木 Hoki *s*
太郎 Yasutarō *m*
井 Yasui *s*
井算哲 Y. Santetsu *mh*
5立 Hodate *s*
田 Yasuda *s*, Hoda
田与重郎 Y. Yojūrō *ml*
6次郎 Yasujirō *m*
吉 Yasukichi *m*
母 Hobo *s*
7佐 Hosa *s*
住 Hozumi *s*
坂 Hosaka *s*
利 Hori *s*
谷 Hodani *s*; Hōya *p*
安 Hōan 1120–24
志 Hoshi *s*
見 Homi *s*
孝 Yasutaka *m*
考 Yasutaka *m*
臣 Yasuomi *m*
8知名 Hochina *s*
昌 Yasumasa *m*
忠 Yasutada *m*
固 Yasukata *m*
延 Hōen 1135–41; Honobe *s*
9保 Hobo *s*
浄 Yasukiyo *m*
治 Yasuji *m*
津 Hotsu *s*
津美 Hozumi *s*
科 Hoshina *s*
科正之 H. Masayuki *mh*
栄 Yasuhisa *m*
岡 Hooka *s*
10倉 Hokura *s*
高 Yasutaka *s*
高徳蔵 Y. Tokuzō *ml*
恵 Yasutoshi *m*
原 Hobara *p*
馬 Yasuma *m*
11健 Yasutake *m*
康 Moriyasu *m*
12間 Homa *s*
13誠 Yasumasa *m*
義 Yasuyoshi *m*
15羣 Yasukata *m*
選 Yasukazu *m*
16積 Hozumi *s*

信 782 [T] Makoto *m*, Akira; Shin *sm*. (SHIN, nobu, sane, shino, aki, shige, sada, masa, akira, koto, tada, chika, toki, toshi, michi, sakazu)
1一 Nobuichi *m*, Masakazu
一郎 Shin'ichirō *m*
2二 Shinji *m*, Nobuji
十 Nobukazu *m*
3三 Shinzō *m*
之 Nobuyuki *m*
之介 Shinnosuke *m*
子 Nobuko *f*
乃 Shinano *s*, Shinno, Shinō; Shino *lm*
也 Shin'ya *m*, Nobuya
4心 Nobukiyo *m*
元 Nobuharu *m*
介 Nobusuke *m*
木 Nobuki *s*
尹 Nobutada *m*
方 Nobukata *m*
文 Nobufumi *m*
夫 Nobuo *m*; Shinobu *sm-p*
太 Shinta *m*; Shinoda *sp*, Shida
太郎 Shintarō *m*, Nobutarō
友 Nobutomo *ml*
5公 Nobutaka *m*
古 Nobuhisa *m*
可 Nobuyoshi *m*
四郎 Shinshirō *m*
市 Nobumachi *m*
包 Nobukane *m*
田 Shinoda *s*, Shida, Shita
6次 Shinji *m*, Nobutsugu
任 Nobutō *m*
行 Nobuyuki *m*
州 Shinshū *p*
州川中島合戦 S. Kawanakajima kassen *l*
州新 S. Shin *p*
圭 Nobukado *m*
光 Nobumitsu *m*
旭 Nobuakira *m*
民 Nobuhito *m*
7伝 Nobutsugu *m*
沢 Nobusawa *s*
弘 Saneakira *m*
形 Nobukata *m*
好 Nobuyoshi *m*
亨 Nobumichi *m*, Nobunaga

免 兎 弟 並 夜 良 事 者 果 東 ▼ 侽 俠 俔 俐 俗 侯 侶 俣 依 保 信 ▲ 咩 咲 待 衍 律 独 狐 狭 狩 陌

俠 俔 俐 俗 俟 侶 俣 依 保 信 ▼ 咩 咲 待 衍 律 独 狐 狭 狩 陌 垪 坻 垣 城 ▲ 抵 拇 指 拡 持 拾 恪 恰 恒 恢

志 Nobusane *m*
吾 Shingo *m*
枈 Nobue *f*
尾 Nobuo *m*
更 Jinkō *p*
孝 Nobutaka *m*
[8]明 Saneakira *m*
枚 Nobuhira *m*
享 Nobutsura *m*
舎 Nobuie *m*
昊 Nobuhiro *m*
忠 Nobutada *m*
学 Nobumichi *m*
秀 Nobuhide *m*
凭 Nobuyori *m*
阜 Nobutaka *m*
宝 Nobutaka *m*
実 Nobuzane *m*
国 Nobukuni *s*
兕 Nobutake *m*
良 Nobuyoshi *m*, Akira
[9]俣 Shinomata *s*
恒 Nobutsune *m*
映 Nobuaki *m*
弥 Nobuyoshi *m*
祝 Nobutoki *m*, Nobuyoshi
秋 Nobuaki *m*
治 Shinji *m*, Nobuji
治郎 Shinjirō *m*
美 Nobuyoshi *m*
長 Nobunaga *m*
思 Nobukoto *m*
泉 Nobumoto *m*
発 Nobuoki *m*
岡 Nobuoka *s*
厚 Nobuatsu *m*
重 Nobushige *m*
[10]郎 Nobuo *m*
恩 Nobuoki *m*
高 Nobutaka *m*
真 Nobumasa *m*
原 Nobuhara *s*
[11]部 Shinobe *s*
紀 Nobukazu *m*
常 Nobutsune *m*
菫 Sanemori *m*
[12]順 Nobuyuki *m*
陽 Nobuakira *m*
随 Nobuyori *m*
勝 Nobukatsu *m*
景 Sadakage *m*
策 Nobutsuka *m*
堅 Nobutaka *m*
貴 Shigi *s*
貴山 S.-san *p*
達 Nobumichi *m*
[13]淵 Nobuhiro *m*
卿 Nobuaki *m*
雄 Nobuo *m*, Nobuyoshi
稚 Nobuwaka *m*
義 Nobuyoshi *m*
意 Nobumoto *m*, Nobunori, Nobumune
誉 Nobunori *m*
資 Nobusuke *m*
業 Nobunori *m*
愛 Nobusane *m*, Nobunori, Nobuhide
楽 Shiragaki *p*; Shigaraki *sp*
[14]愷 Nobuyasu *m*
徳 Shintoku *ml*
輔 Nobusuke *m*
嘉 Nobuyoshi *m*
睿 Nobusato *m*
節 Nobuyo *m*
[15]徵 Nobuaki *m*
璋 Nobuaki *m*
毅 Shinki *m*
蕃 Nobushige *m*
蔵 Nobukura *m*
[16]篤 Nobuatsu *m*
慶 Nobuyoshi *m*
頻 Nobutsura *m*
綿 Nobutsura *m*
頼 Nobuyori *m*
親 Nobuchika *m*
賢 Nobukata *m*, Nobumasa, Nobutaka
[17]濃 Shinano *sp*
濃田 Shinoda *s*
緝 Nobutsugu *m*
綱 Nobutsuna *m*
謹 Sanemori *m*
[18]顕 Nobuaki *m*
[20]離 Nobutsura *m*
馨 Nobukiyo *m*
[24]霽 Nobuharu *m*

## 9 L3

咩 783 (BI, me)

咲 784 [T] Saku *f*. (sa, saku, saki)
本 Sakimoto *s*
花 Sakihana *s*
良子 Sakurako *f*
美 Sakumi *f*
麻 Sakuma *m*
喜子 Sakiko *f*

待 785 [T] (TAI, DAI, matsu, machi, naga, michi)
乳 Matsuchi *s*

衍 786 Hiroshi *m*. (EN, nobu, hiro, mitsu)
子 Nobuko *f*

律 787 [T] Tadashi *m*, Tadasu. (RITSU, nori, oto)
夫 Norio *m*

独 788 [T] (DOKU, katsu)
言 Hitorigoto *l*
歩 Doppo *ml*
歩吟 Doppogin *l*
逸 Doitsu *p* "Germany"

狐 789 (KO, GO, kitsune)
川 Kitsunegawa *s*
塚 Kitsunezuka *sla*; Kozuka *s*
鍛治 Kitsunekaji *m*

狭 790 [T] (KYŌ, sa)
川 Sagawa *s*
山 Sayama *sp*
手彦 Sadehiko *m*
衣 Sagoromo *l*
狭城山 Sasakiyama *s*
度 Sado *s*
野茅上娘子 Sanu no Chigami no Otome *fl*
間 Hazama *s*

狩 791 [T] (SHU, kari, mori)
小川 Kakogawa *sp*
戸 Karito *s*
太 Kaributo *p*
谷 Kariya *s*
谷棭斎 K. Ekisai *mlh*
野 Kanō *s*, Kano, Karino
野元信 Kanō Motonobu *ma*
野山楽 K. Sanraku *ma*
野永徳 K. Eitoku *ma*
野正信 K. Masanobu *ma*
野芳崖 K. Hōgai *ma*
野探幽 K. Tan'yū *ma*

陌 792 (HAKU, michi)

垪 793 (HEI)
和 Haga *sp*; Hagai *s*

坻 794 (TEI, oka)
子 Okako *f*

垣 795 [I] Kaki *s*. (KAN, GAN, kaki, taka, han)
子 Kakiko *f*
内 Kakiuchi *s*, Kaitō, Kakitsu, Kakito
内松三 Kaitō Matsuzō *ml*
内田 Kakitsuda *s*
外 Kaito *s*
田 Kakida *s*
本 Kakimoto *s*
谷 Han'ya *s*
見 Kakimi *s*, Kakehi

城 796 [T] Shiro *sm-f*; Jō *s*, Tachi, Kitsuki. (JŌ, SEI, ki, nari, shiro, mura, shige, kuni, sane)
[3]川 Shirokawa *p*
上 Kinokami *s*, Shikinokami
口 Shiroguchi *s*
下 Shiroshita *s*
[4]戸 Kido *s*
戸崎 Kidosaki *s*
山 Shiroyama *sp*
内 Shirouchi *s*, Jōuchi
井 Kii *s*
[5]左門 Jō Samon *ml*
辺 Jōhen *p*
丘前来目 Kinookasakinokume *s*
本 Shiromoto *s*
田 Shirota *s*
[8]所 Kidokoro *s*
東 Kitō *sp*; Jōtō *s*
[9]南 Jōnan *p*
[10]倉 Shirokura *s*
[11]野 Jōno *s*
島 Kishima *s*; Jōjima *p*
[12]陽 Jōyō *p*

崎 Shirosaki *s*; Kinosaki *p*
18塚 Shirotsuka *s*
15端 Jōhana *p*
17篠 Kishino *s*
19縵 Shikinokazura *s*

**抵** 797 [T] (TEI, yasu, atsu, yuki)

**拇** 798 Oyayubi *s*. (BO)

**拡** 799 [T] Hiyoshi *m*, Hiromu. (KAKU, hiro)
充 Hiromitsu *m*

**指** 800 [T] (SHI, sashi, yubi, mune)
田 Sashida *s*
吸 Yubisui *s*
弘 Iiho *s*
保 Iio *s*, Isero, Iseho
原 Sashibara *s*
宿 Sashijiku *s*, Yubisuku; Ibusuki *sp*

**持** 801 [T] (JI, CHI, mochi, yoshi)
丸 Mochimaru *s*
木 Mochiki *s*
田 Mochida *s*
地 Mochiji *s*
永 Mochinaga *s*
言 Mochikoto *m*
明院 Jimyōin *s*
長 Mochinaga *m*
是 Chise *s*
統 Jitō *flh*

**拾** 802 [T] Hirō *s*. (SHŪ, JŪ, hiro, tō)
子 Hiroko *f*
菓抄 Shūkashō *l*
菓集 Shūkashū *l*
遺百番歌合 Shūi hyakuban utaawase *l*
遺集 Shūishū *l*
遺愚草 Shūi gusō *l*

**恪** 803 Tsutomu *m*. (KAKU, KYAKU, taka, tsumu)

**恰** 804 Takashi *m*. (KŌ)

**恆** 805 Wataru *m*, Hisashi. (KŌ, GŌ)

**恢** 806 (KAI, KE, hiro)
子 Hiroko *f*

**恂** 807 Makoto *m*, Jun. (JUN, SHUN, nobu)
子 Nobuko *f*

**怡** 808 (I, haru)
子 Haruko *f*
積弘 Isao *f*

**恒** 809 [T] Tsune *m*, Hisashi, Hitoshi, Wataru. (KŌ, GŌ, tsune, hisa, nobu, chika)
2二郎 Tsunejirō *m*
七 Tsuneshichi *m*
3川 Tsunekawa *s*
三 Tsunezō *m*
子 Tsuneko *f*
之 Tsuneyuki *m*
4心 Tsunemi *m*, Tsunemoto
夫 Tsuneo *m*, Hisao
太 Tsuneta *m*
太郎 Tsunetarō *m*
5平 Tsunehei *m*
6次郎 Tsunejirō *m*
吉 Tsuneyoshi *sm*; Tsunekichi *m*
存 Tsuneari *m*
8河 Tsunegawa *s*
明 Tsuneakira *m*
幸 Tsuneyuki *m*
良 Tsunenaga *sm*
9柯 Tsuneeda *m*
松 Tsunematsu *s*
貞 Tsunesada *m*
彦 Hisahiko *m*
10屋 Tsuneya *s*
11清 Tsunekiyo *m*
12富 Tsunetomi *s*
堅 Tsunekata *m*
13雄 Tsuneo *m*
14徳 Tsuneyoshi *m*
18藤 Tsunetō *s*

**洌** 810 Kiyoshi *m*. (RETSU)

**洪** 811 Hiroshi *m*. (KŌ, KU, hiro, ō)

**派** 812 [T] Minamata *s*. (HA, mata)

**洸** 813 Hiroshi *m*, Fukashi, Takeshi. (KŌ, hiro)
江 Hiroe *f*

**洒** 814 (SHA)
落本 Sharebon *l*

**洵** 815 Makoto *m*. (JUN, SHUN, nobu)
盛 Nobumori *m*

**洽** 816 Hiroshi *m*. (KŌ, GŌ, to)
馬 Koma *m*

**洗** 817 [T] (SEN, yoshi, kiyo)
馬 Seba *s*
波 Senba *s*

**洛** 818 (RAKU)
陽 Rakuyō *ph* ["Loyang"]
陽名所集 R. meishoshū *l*
陽田楽記 R. dengakuki *l*

**活** 819 [T] (KATSU, GACHI, iku, ike)
井 Ikei *s*
玉 Ikutama *s*

**洲** 820 (SHŪ, SU, kuni)
子 Kuniko *f*
内 Sunouchi *s*
本 Sumoto *p*
股 Sunomata *s*
流 Sunagashi *s*
崎 Susaki *s*

**洞** 821 [I] Akira *m*. (DŌ, aki, hiro, hora, horo)
下 Horage *s*
口 Horaguchi *s*
戸 Horado *p*
内 Horouchi *s*
院 Tōin *s*
爺 Tōya *s*

**洋** 822 [T] Hiroshi *m*; Nada *s*. (YŌ, hiro, nami, mi, umi, kiyo)
々社談 Yōyōshadan *l*
子 Yōko *f*
之助 Yōnosuke *m*
大 Hiroo *m*, Namio
六 Hiromu *m*
司 Kiyoshi *m*
右 Yōsuke *m*
次郎 Yōjirō *m*

**浄** 823 [T] Kiyoshi *m*. (JŌ, SEI, kiyo, shizu)
三 Kiyomi *m*
上 Kiyokami *s*
土三部経 Jōdo sanbukyō *l*
土真宗 J. Shinshū *h*
土宗 Jōdōshū *h*
夫 Shizuo *m*
吉 Jōkichi *m*
弁 Jōben *ml*
法寺 Jōbōji *p*
岡 Kiyooka *s*
庭 Kiyoniwa *m*
野 Kiyono *m*
鉱 Jōkō *m*
瑠璃 Jōruri *la*

**法** 824 [T] Hakaru *m*, Tsune. (HŌ, nori, kazu, tsune)
子 Noriko *f*
元 Hōga *s*
王帝説 Hōōtaisetsu *l*
夫 Kazuo *m*
木 Noriki *s*
示 Hōshi *s*
安 Hōan *s*
花寺 Hokkeji *s*
茂 Norishige *m*
城寺 Hōjōji *sp*
隆寺 Hōryūji *p*
師人 Hosuto *s*
華経 Hokekyō / Hokkekyō *lh*
華経義疏 H. gisho *l*
貴 Hōki *s*
然 Hōnen *mlh*

洵 治 洗 洛 活 洲 洞 洋 浄 法 ▼ 治 津 浅 拝 岬 牲 施 弥 弨 珊 玲 珍 炳 ▲ 畑 昵 映 昭 胛 胖 肱 胆 姓 姉

**治** 825 [T] Osamu *m*, Tadasu. (JI, CHI, haru, sada, tsugu, nobu, yoshi, zu, tō)
1一郎 Jiichirō *m*
2人 Haruto *m*
3三 Harumitsu *m*
三郎 Jisaburō *m*
之助 Harunosuke *m*
子 Haruko *f*
4五郎 Jigorō *m*
右衛門 Jiemon *m*
田 Haruta *s*
7安 Jian 1021–24
兵衛 Jihee *m*
8承 Jijō *l* 1177–81
国 Harukuni *m*
9保 Harumori *m*
貞 Harusada *m*
10剣 Haruakira *m*
郎 Jirō *m*
郎右衛門 Jiroemon *m*
通 Harumitsu *m*
11胤 Harumi *m*
脩 Harunaga *m*
済 Harusada *m*
祇 Haruyoshi *m*
朗 Jirō *m*
部 Jibu *p*
部太郎 Jibutarō *m*
12策 Jisaku *m*
14輔 Jisuke *m*
暦 Jiryaku / Chiryaku 1065–69

**津** 826 [T] Tsu *sp*. (SHIN, tsu, zu)
ノ宮 Tsunomiya *s*
3川 Tsugawa *sp*
上 Tsugami *s*
下 Tsuge *s*, Tsushita
久井 Tsukui *sp*
久見 Tsukumi *p*
4戸 Tsudo *s*
山 Tsuyama *sp*
井 Tsui *s*
爪 Tsuzume *s*
5打 Tsuuchi *s*
打治兵衛 T. Jihee *ml*
布久 Tsubuku *s*
辺 Tsube *s*
田 Tsuda *sp*
田左右吉 T. Sōkichi *mlh*
田青風 T. Seifū *ml*
田真道 T. Mamichi *ml*
田梅子 T. Umeko *fh*
本 Tsumoto *s*
6江 Tsue *sp*
守 Tsumori *s*
名 Tsuna *p*
曲 Tsumagari *s*
7吹 Tsubuki *s*
阪 Tsusaka *s*
別 Tsubetsu *p*
村 Tsumura *s*
村秀夫 T. Hideo *ml*
村信夫 T. Nobuo *ml*
谷 Tsuya *s*
8和野 Tsuwano *p*
金 Tsugane *s*
奈木 Tsunagi *p*
具 Tsugu *p*
9南 Tsunan *p*
10高 Tsudaka *p*
原 Tsuhara *s*
屋崎 Tsuyazaki *p*
11野 Tsuno *s*
留 Tsuru *s*, Tsudome
島 Tsushima *sp*
12崎 Tsuzaki *s*
軽 Tsugaru *sp-l*
15幡 Tsubata *p*
摩 Tsuma *f*

**浅** 827 [T] (SEN, ZEN, asa)
2七 Asashichi *m*
3川 Asakawa *sp*
口 Asakuchi *p*
子 Asako *sf*
4水 Asami *s*, Asōzu
山 Asayama *s*
木 Asaki *s*
井 Asai *sp*
井十三郎 A. Jūsaburō *ml*
井了意 A. Ryōi *ml*
井忠 A. Chū *ma*
井長政 A. Nagamasa *mh*
5古 Asako *s*
田 Asada *s*
生 Asō *s*
6次 Asaji *m*
次郎 Asajirō *m*
江 Asanae *s*, Asae
羽 Asaba *sp*
7村 Asamura *s*
利 Asari *s*
尾 Asao *s*
見 Asami *s*
見淵 A. Fukashi *ml*
見絅斎 A. Keisai *mh*
8波 Asaba *s*
沼 Asanuma *s*
茅が宿 Asaji ga yado *l*
9科 Asashina *p*
草 Asakusa *sp*
草の灯 A. no hi *l*
草紅団 A. kurenaidan *l*
香 Asaka *s*
岡 Asaoka *s*
彦 Asahiko *m*
10海 Asami *s*
倉 Asakura *s*
原 Asahara *s*
原六朗 A. Rokurō *ml*
11野 Asano *s*
野長政 A. Nagamasa *mh*
野晃 A. Akira *ml*
野梨郷 A. Rikyō *ml*
野総一郎 A. Sōichirō *mh*
黄 Asaki *s*
12場 Asaba *s*
賀 Asaka *s*
間 Asama *s*
間嶽面影草紙 Asamagatake omokagezōshi *l*
13葉 Asaba *s*
15輪 Asawa *s*

## 9 L4

**拝** 828 See 拝 585

**岬** 829 Misaki *m-f-p*. (KŌ)

**牲** 830 (SEI, SHŌ, nie)
川 Niekawa *s*

**施** 831 [T] Hodokosu *m*; Haru *s*. (SHI, SE, haru, nobu, toshi, masu, mochi)
恩 Shion *s*

**弥** 832 [N] Wataru *m*, Watari, Hisashi; Iyo *f*. (MI, BI, ya, hisa, hiro, mitsu, yoshi, iya, masu, mane, yasu)
1一 Yaichi *m*
一郎 Yaichirō *m*
2二郎 Yajirō *m*
八 Yahachi *m*
3三 Yazō *m*, Yasabu
三次 Yasoji *m*
三吉 Yasakichi *m*
三郎 Yasaburō *m*
子 Hisako *f*
之助 Yanosuke *m*
久太 Yakuta *m*
久太郎 Yakutarō *m*
4仁 Iyahito *m*
太郎 Yatarō *m*
永 Yanaga *s*
市 Yaichi *m*
市郎 Yaichirō *m*
5右 Yaishi *s*
生 Yayoi *sp-h*
6吉 Yakichi *m*, Yayoshi
団次 Yadanji *m*
世継 Iyayotsugi *l*
7助 Yasuke *m*
兵衛 Yahee *m*
8陀如来和讃 Mida Nyorai wasan *l*
幸 Yasaki *m*
忠 Mitsutada *m*
9栄 Yasaka *p*
栄太 Yaeta *m*
彦 Yahiko *p*
10郡 Iyakōri *s*
高 Iyataka *m*
11勒 Miroku *mh*
勒菩薩 M. Bosatsu *mh*
12富 Yatomi *sp*
14蔓 Hiroshi *m*
15続 Yatsugi *m*

**弨** 833 (SHŌ, haru, yumi)

**珊** 834 (SAN, sabu)
朗 Saburō *m*

**玲** 835 [N] Akira *m*. (REI, RYŌ, tama)
枝 Tamae *f*

**珍** 836 [T] Chinu *s*. (CHIN, yoshi, haru, uzu, taka, nori, iya)
丸 Medemaru *s*
田 Chinda *s*
次 Takaji *m*
弘 Yoshihiro *m*
彦 Uzuhiko *m*
重 Yoshishige *m*
磧 Chinseki *ml*
頼 Yoshinori *m*
麿 Uzumaro *m*

**炳** 837 (HEI, HYŌ, aki)

**畑** 838 [T] Hata *s*. (hata)
川 Hatagawa *s*
中 Hatanaka *s*
山 Hatayama *s*
井 Hatai *s*
田 Hatada *s*, Kamata
佐 Hatasa *s*
屋 Hataya *s*
野 Hatano *sp*

**昵** 839 Mutsubi *m*, Mutsumi. (JITSU, NICHI, chika)

**映** 840 [T] Akira *m*. (EI, YŌ, aki, teru, akira, mitsu)
子 Teruko *f*

**昭** 841 [T] Akira *m*. (SHŌ, aki, teru, akira, haru, ika)
之 Teruyuki *m*
四 Akiyo *f*
君 Shō Kun *fh-la* "Chao Chün"
和 Shōwa *p* 1926–
房 Akifusa *m*
実 Akizane *m*
英 Terufusa *m*
良 Haruyoshi *m*
訓 Akikuni *m*
島 Akishima *p*
義 Akiyoshi *m*
憲皇太后 Shōken Kōtaigō *flh*

**胛** 842 Kō *s*. (KŌ)

**胖** 843 Yutaka *m*. (HAN, nao, hiro, ō)

**肱** 844 (KŌ, hiji)
川 Hijikawa *p*

**胆** 845 [T] I *s*. (TAN, i)
大小心録 Tandaishō-shin-roku *l*
沢 Isawa *p*
津 Itsu *m*
香瓦 Ikaga *s*
振 Iburi *p*

**姓** 846 [T] (SEI, SHŌ, uji)

**姉** 847 [T] (SHI, ane, e)
川 Anegawa *sp*
小路 Anenokōji *s*
子 Aneko *f*
帯 Anetai *s*
崎 Anesaki *s*
崎嘲風 A. Chōfu *ml*
歯 Aneha *s*

**妹** 848 [T] (MAI, BAI, imo)
子 Imoko *mh*
尾 Senoo *sp*; Seo *s*
背山婦女庭訓 Imoseyama onna teikin *la*
背牛 Imoseushi *p*
島 Seshima *s*

**祢** 849 See 禰 2800

**祖** 850 [T] Hajime *m*. (SO, moto, o-ya, saki, nori, hiro)
父江 Sobue *sp*
母井 Ubai *s*, Ubagai, Sobagai
母江 Ubagae *s*
村 Motomura *m*
泉 Soizumi *s*
師 Soshi *s*
道 Motomichi *m*

**祝** 851 [T] Iwai *sm*; Iwō *m*, Hajime. (SHUKU, SHŪ, SHU, to-ki, nori, yoshi, i, ho)
乃 Tokino *s*
子 Noriko *f*
山 Hafuriyama *s*
太郎 Noritarō *m*
年子 Ineko *f*
部 Hafuribe *s*, Hafuri, ⌊Hōri
詞 Norito *l*
雄 Tokio *m*

**祐** 852 [N] Tasuku *m*. (YŪ, U, suke, sachi, yoshi, chi, ma-su, mura)
[3]之 Sukeyuki *m*
[4]方 Sukenori *m*
六 Yūroku *m*
夫 Yoshio *m* ⌈tarō
太郎 Suketarō *m*, Yū-
[5]丘 Suketaka *m*
[6]吉 Yūkichi *m*
[7]邦 Sukekuni *m*
[8]命 Sukenobu *m*
[9]乗坊 Yūjōbō *s*
相 Suketomo *m*
彦 Sukehiko *m*, Sa-chihiko
[10]泰 Sukehiro *m*
[12]善 Yūzen *l*
[13]殖 Sukemasa *m*
靖 Sukeyasu *m*
[15]慶 Sukenori *m*

**神** 853 [T] Kami *s*, Miwa, Aho; Shin *sm*. (SHIN, JIN, kami, kan, kō, kiyo, ka, ka-mu, shino, taru, miwa)
[1]一 Kōkazu *s*
[3]川 Kamikawa *sp*
三郡 Kamikuni *s*
丸 Kanmaru *s*
久保 Imonokubo *s*
子 Kamiko *s*
子上 Mikogami *s*
子島 Mikoshima *s*
[4]戸 Kōbe *p*, Gōdo, Kōdo, Kando; Kanbe *s*
中 Jinnaka *s*
木 Kamiki *s*
山 Kamiyama *sp*; Kō-yama *s*
山茂夫 Kamiyama Shigeo *ml* ⌈shiro
[5]代 Kōjiro *sp*, Kuma-
代種亮 Kōjiro Tane-suke *ml*
功 Jingū *fh*
永 Kaminaga *s*
石 Jinseki *p*
辺 Kannabe *p*
目 Kōme *sp*
立 Kandachi *s*
主 Kōsu *s*
生 Kannō *m*
田 Kanda *sp*; Kōda *s*
田孝平 Kanda Taka-hira *mlh*
田橋 Kandabashi *sp*
本 Kamimoto *s*
[6]刑部 Kamiutae *s*
奴 Kando *s*, Kami-yakko
吉 Kamiyoshi *s*, Ka-mikichi, Kamiki, Kangi; Kanki *sp*
字日文伝 Shinji hi-fumiden *l*
在 Jinzai *s*
気 Kiyooki *m*
成 Kaminari *s*
去 Kamiki *s*
名帳考 Shinmeichōkō ⌊*l*
西 Jinzai *s*
西清 J. Kiyoshi *ml*
[7]作 Kamisaku *s*
坂 Kamisaka *s*
沢 Kamizawa *s*, Kan-zawa
社 Kansha *s*, Senja, Kamikoso
村 Kamimura *s*
余 Kanamari *s*
谷 Kamiya *s*
谷戸 Kamiyato *s*
志那 Kōshina *s*
足 Kōtari *s*, Kōtani
尾 Kamio *s*, Kannō
近 Kamichika *s*
近市子 K. Ichiko *flh*
見 Kiyoaki *m*
[8]例 Kanrei *s*
河 Miwakawa *s*
波 Jinba *s*, Kannami, Kōnami
明 Jinmei *s* ⌈*a*
明造 Shinmei-zukuri
門 Kando *s*, Kōdo, Gōto ⌈tori
服 Kanhatori *s*, Hat-
林 Kamibayashi *sp*
私 Kansaichi *s*
奈川 Kanagawa *p*
奈子 Kanako *f*
奈垣 Kanagaki *s*
努 Kantsukone *s* ⌈*s*
武 Jinmu *mh*; Kōtake
[9]依田 Miwayoda *s*
保 Jinbo *s*, Kanhō; Jinbō *sp* ⌈tarō *ml*
保光太郎 Jinbo Kō-
津 Kōzu *s*, Kamitsu
津島 Kōzushima *s*
垣 Kamigaki *s*
神廻 Shishiba *s*
南 Kōnai *s*
前 Kanzaki *s*
長 Kaminaga *s*
長倉 Kanakura *s*
泉 Kami-izumi *p*

拜 岬 牲 施 弥 弨 珊 玲 珍 炳 ▼ 畑 昵 映 昭 胛 胖 肱 胆 姓 姉 妹 祢 祖 祝 祐 神 ▲ 柱 柯 柁 柚 柑 枯 栘 柾 柄 柵

皇正統記 Jinnō shōtōki l
岡 Kamioka sp
[10]栖 Kamisu p
郎 Taruo m
宮 Jingū s; Shingū sp
宮司 Jingūji s
宮寺 Jingūji s
息 Kiyooki m
恵内 Kamuenai p
原 Kanbara s ⌈ml
原克重 K. Katsushige
原泰 K. Tai ml
屋 Kamiya s
庭 Kanba s
[11]掃石 Miwahakishi s
野 Kamino s, Kanno, Jinno
符麿 Shinobumaro m
麻加牟陀 Miwamakamuda s
麻績 Kan'omi s
島 Kamijima s
亀 Jinki 724–29
[12]崎 Kanzaki sp; Kōzaki p
崎清 K. Kiyoshi ml
道大意 Shintō taii l
道集 Shintōshū l
[13]意 Kiyooki m
楽 Kagura p-a; Karaki s
楽歌 Kagura uta l
楽歌譜入文 K. u. fuiriaya l
楽師 Kakotoshi s
[14]鳴 Kaminari la
漆 Kaminuri s
郷 Shingō p
稲 Kumashiro sp
農 Kannō s ⌈zumi
墨 Kamizumi s, Kō-
[15]霊矢口渡 Shinrei Yaguchi no watashi l
蔵 Kamikura s
[16]薬師 Kakotoshi s
[17]館 Kodate s, Kotachi
[18]鞭 Kōmuchi s
藤 Kamifuji s, Shin-
[19]瀬 Kamise s ⌊dō
[20]護景雲 Jingo-keiun 767–70
[23]鑒 Kagami s

柱 854 [T] (CHŪ, hashira)

柯 855 (KA, e, eda, kado)
斐 Kai s

柁 856 (TA, DA, kaji)
川 Kajikawa s

柚 857 (YŪ, YU, yuzu)
木 Yuzuki s, Yūnoki
原 Yuzuhara s

柑 858 (KAN, KON)
子 Kōji l
本 Kōjimoto s

枯 859 (KO, KU, kare)
木 Kareki s
山水 Kare-sansui a; Kosensui l

柊 860 (SHU, SHŪ, hiiragi, hiragi, kuki)
屋 Hiragiya s
崎 Kukisaki s

柾 861 Masa f; Masaki m. (ma-
子 Masako f ⌊sa)
木 Masaki s

柄 862 [T] (HEI, HYŌ, e, moto, tsuka, kara, eda, kai,
井 Karai s ⌊kami)
井川柳 K. Senryū ml
本 Emoto s
沢 Karasawa s
原 Ebara s

柵 863 (SAKU, mase, yana)
木 Maseki s
原 Yanahara p
頼 Sakurai s
瀬 Sakurai s

柘 864 Tsuge sp; Tsuku s. (JAKU, SHA, tsuku)
垣 Tsugegaki s
植 Tsumie s, Tsuge
榴 Ishitome sp

栃 865 (tochi)
子 Tochiko f
内 Tochiuchi s, Tochinai
木 Tochigi p
本 Tochimoto s
沢 Tochizawa s
谷 Tochiya s
尾 Tochio p
原 Tochihara s

柏 866 Kashiwa sm-p; Kaya sp. (HAKU, kashiwa, kashi)
[4]山 Kashiyama s
木 Kashiwagi sla; Ka-
井 Kashi s ⌊yaki s
[5]田 Kashiwada s
本 Kashimoto s, Kashiwamoto
[7]村 Kashiwamura s
谷 Kashiwaya s
[10]倉 Kashiwakura s
原 Kashihara sp; Kashiwabara smh; Kaibara p
屋 Kashiwaya s
[11]野 Kashino s
[12]崎 Kashiwazaki p-la
[13]淵 Kashiwabuchi s
[15]熊 Kashiwaguma s

柿 867 (SHI, JI, kaki, kage, katsu)
の本 Kakinomoto l
[4]内 Kakiuchi s
木 Kakinoki p
山 Kakiyama s
山伏 Kaki yamabushi
[5]田 Kakida s ⌊la
本 Kakimoto s, Kakinomoto
本人麻呂 Kakinomoto no Hitomaro ml
本人麻呂朝臣勘文 K. no H. Ason kanmon
[7]沢 Kakizawa s ⌊l
花 Kakihana s
[8]沼 Kakinuma s
[9]岡 Kakioka s
[10]栖 Kakisu s
原 Kakihara s
[11]島 Kakishima s
[12]崎 Kakizaki p
[13]園 Kakizono s
[14]蔭集 Shiinshū l
[16]衛門 Kakiemon m

相 868 [T] Tasuku m. (sō, SHŌ, suke, ai, masa, tomo, au, ō, sa, mi, haru, miru, saga)
[3]川 Aikawa sp
子 Aiko f, Masako
[4]内 Aiuchi s
山 Aiyama s
木 Aiki s
[5]可 Ōka s
田 Aida s
生 Aioi sp
[6]羽 Aiba s
合 Aiau s
[7]沢 Aizawa s
近 Sukechika m
見 Aumi m
[8]阿弥 Sōami ma
知 Ōchi p
宗 Aisō s
武 Sagamu s
良 Sagara sp
[10]浦 Aiura s, Ainoura
原 Aibara s
庭 Aiba s
馬 Sōma sp; Sōba s
馬泰三 S. Taizō ml
馬黒光 S. Kokkō ml
馬御風 S. Gyofū ml
[11]根 Sagane s
島 Aijima s
[12]曾 Aiso s
場 Aiba s
勝 Masakatsu m
崎 Aisaki s ⌈sp
賀 Sōga s, Saga; Ōga
智 Sachi f
[13]淵 Aibuchi s
葉 Aiba s
楽 Sōraku sp, Sagara; Sōra s, Sagaraku
[14]模 Sagami sp-fl
模原 Sagamihara p
模湖 Sagami-ko p
聞 Sōmon l, Aigikoe
[15]槻物部 Namitsukimononobe s
[20]磯 Aiso s, Aiiso

松 869 [T] Matsu sf; Tokiwa m. (SHŌ, matsu, masu)
の落葉 Matsu no ochiba l

の葉 M. no ha *l*
1一郎 Matsuichirō *m*
2人 Matsundo *m*
3川 Matsukawa *sp*
川裁判 M. saiban *l*
三 Matsuzō *m*
三郎 Matsusaburō *m*
口 Matsukuchi *s*
之山 Matsunoyama *p*
之助 Matsunosuke *m*
下 Matsushita *s*
子 Matsuko *f*
久 Matsuhisa *s*
丸 Matsumaru *s*
4元 Matsumoto *sp*
戸 Matsudo *sp*
介 Matsusuke *m*
太郎 Matsutarō *m*
木 Matsuki *s*, Matsunoki
方 Matsukata *s* ⌈*mh*
方正義 M. Masayoshi
山 Matsuyama *sp*
山天狗 M. tengu *la*
山鏡 M. kagami *la*
井 Matsui *s*
井如流 M. Joryū *ml*
井須磨子 M. Sumako *fa*
井田 Matsuida *s*
5代 Matsushiro *p*, Matsudai
永 Matsunaga *sp*
永久秀 M. Hisahide *mh*
永尺五 M. Sekigo *ml*
永貞徳 M. Teitoku *ml*
石 Matsuishi *s*
四郎 Matsushirō *m*
末 Matsusue *s*
生 Matsuu *s*
田 Matsuda *sp* ⌈*ml*
田常憲 M. Tsunenori
本 Matsumoto *p*
本昌夫 M. Masao *ml*
本清張 M. Seichō *ml*
平 Matsudaira *p*
平定信 M. Sadanobu *mh* ⌈na *mh*
平信綱 M. Nobutsu-
平容保 M. Katamori *mh* ⌈*mh*
平康英 M. Yasuhide
平慶永 M. Yoshinaga
6次 Matsuji *m* ⌊*mh*
次郎 Matsujirō *m*
伏 Matsubushi *p*

任 Mattō *sp*, Matsutō
地 Matsuji *s*
江 Matsue *sf-p* ⌈*ml*
江重頼 M. Shigeyori
江維舟 M. Ishū *ml*
竹 Shōchiku *a*
吉 Matsuyoshi *sm*; Matsukichi *m*
虫 Matsumushi *la*
年 Shōnen *m*
7住 Matsuzumi *s*
沢 Matsuzawa *s*
阪 Matsuzaka *p*
坂 Matsuzaka *s*
村 Matsumura *s*
村呉春 M. Goshun *ma*
村英一 M. Eiichi *ml*
村緑 M. Midori *ml*
助 Matsusuke *m*
谷 Matsuya *s*
会 Matsue *s*
尾 Matsuo *sp*; Matsunoo *sla* ⌈shō *ml*
尾芭蕉 Matsuo Ba-
見 Matsumi *s*
角 Matsusumi *s*
寿 Shōju *m*
寿丸 Shōjumaru *m*
8沼 Matsunuma *s*
波 Matsunami *s*
波資之 M. Sukeyuki
枝 Matsueda *s* ⌊*ml*
林 Matsubayashi *s*
金 Matsugane *s*
苗 Matsunae *sm*
茂 Matsushige *p*
居 Matsui *s*
居松翁 M. Shōō *ml*
並 Matsunami *s*
9保 Matsuo *s*
信 Matsunobu *s*
垣 Matsugaki *s*
洛 Shōraku *ml* ⌈*ml*
亭金水 Shōtei Kinsui
南 Matsunami *s*
前 Matsumae *sp*, Matsuzaki; Masaki *p*
風 Matsukaze *sla*
岡 Matsuoka *sp*
岡洋右 M. Yōsuke *mh*
岡映丘 M. Eikyū *ml*
岡貞総 M. Teisō *ml*
岡荒村 M. Kōson *ml*
岡譲 M. Yuzuru *ml*
10浦 Matsuura *sp*, Matsura

浦一 Matsuura Hajime *ml*
浦辰男 M. Tatsuo *ml*
浦宮 Matsura-no-miya *l*
脇 Matsuwaki *s*
脂 Matsuyani *la*
倉 Matsukura *s* ⌈*ml*
倉米吉 M. Yonekichi
室 Matsumuro *s*
家 Matsuka *s*
宮 Matsumiya *s*
宮寒骨 M. Kankotsu *ml*
原 Matsubara *sp*
原地蔵尊 M. Jizōson *ml* ⌈noya
屋 Matsuya *s*, Matsu-
廼家 Matsunoya *s*
廼家露八 M. Rohachi *mh-l*
11浪 Matsunami *s*
根 Matsune *sm* ⌈*ml*
根東洋城 M. Tōyōjō
野 Matsuno *sp*
盛 Matsumori *m*
島 Matsushima *sp*
12崎 Matsuzaki *sp*
崎天民 M. Tenmin
森 Matsumori *s* ⌊*ml*
扉 Shōhi *s*
13塚 Matsuzuka *s*
隈 Matsukuma *s*
義 Matsuyoshi *s*
葉 Matsuba *s*
葉谷 Matsubaya *s*
園 Matsuzono *s*
14農波 Matsu no ha *l*
15影 Matsukage *m*
蔭 Matsukage *s*
16橋 Matsuhashi *s*; Matsubase *p*
17濤 Matsunami *s*
18藤 Matsufuji *s*
19韻 Matsuoto *m*
瀬 Matsuse *s*
瀬青々 M. Seisei *ml*
21縄 Matsunawa *s*
巌 Matsuo *m*
22籟 Shōrai *l*

—— 9 L5 ——

**狀** 870 See 状 365A

**祉** 871 See 祉 608

**歧** 872 (KI, tate)
子 Tateko *f*

**衿** 873 (KIN, KON, eri)
子 Eriko *f*

**段** 874 [T] (DAN, TAN)
野 Danno *s*
嶺 Tamine *sp*

**研** 875 [T] Togi *s*. (KEN, GEN, togi, aki, kiyo, ishi, kishi)
一 Ken'ichi *m*
二 Kenji *m*
川 Togikawa *s*
太郎 Kentarō *m*
橋 Ishibashi *s*

**砂** 876 [T] Isago *m*. (SA, SHA, suna, isa) ⌈kawa *s*
川 Sunagawa *sp*; Isa-
子 Sunako *s*, Masago
土居 Sunadoi *s*
山 Sunayama *s*
永 Sunanaga *s*
田 Sunada *s*
村 Sunamura *s*
押 Sunaoshi *s*
金 Isagane *s*, Sunago,
治 Sunaji *s* ⌊Isago
原 Sawara *p*
塚 Sunazuka *s*
賀 Sunaga *s*
越 Sagoshi *s* ⌈*l*
絵呪縛 Sunae shibari

**科** 877 [T] (KA, shina)
子 Shinako *f*
良 Akira *s*
野 Shinano *l*

**秋** 878 [T] Osamu *m*, Akira. (SHŪ, SHU, aki, toki, toshi)
3子 Akiko *f*
4水嶺 Shūsuirei *la*
元 Akimoto *s*
元不死男 A. Fujio *ml*
元松代 A. Matsuyo *fl*
月 Akizuki *s*
月桂太 A. Keita *ml*

山 Akiyama *sp* ⌈*ml*
山秋紅蓼 A. Shūkōryō
山清 A. Kiyoshi *ml*
[5]永 Akinaga *s*
本 Akimoto *s*
生 Tokio *m*
田 Akita *sp*
田実 A. Minoru *ml*
田雨雀 A. Ujaku *ml*
[6]江 Akie *f*
吉 Akiyoshi *s*
成 Akinari *m*
多 Akita *p*
[7]沢 Akizawa *s*
沢修二 A. Shūji *ml*
谷 Akiya *s*, Akitani
声会 Shūseikai *l*
芳 Shūhō *p*
尾 Akio *s*
里 Akizato *s*
[8]和 Akiwa *s*
忠 Akitada *m*
夜長 Aki no yonaga *l*
良 Akira *s* ⌈kyū *p*
[9]保 Akiho *s*, Akio; A-
津 Akitsu *m*
津麿 Akitsumaro *m*
草 Akigusa *s*
香 Akika *m*
岡 Akioka *s*
[10]時 Akitoki *s*
庭 Akiba *sm*
馬 Akiba *s*
[11]清 Akikiyo *m*
野 Akino *s*
[12]場 Akiba *s*
森 Akimori *s*
賀 Aiga *s*
間 Akima *s*
鹿 Aika *s*
島 Akishima *s*
[13]葉 Akiba *s*
[15]穂 Akiho *sm*; Aiho *p*
[17]篠 Akishino *s* ⌈*l*
篠月清集 A. gesseishū

**胡** 879 (KO, GO, hisa)
子 Ebisu *s*
江 Hisae *f*
保 Hisayasu *m*
桃 Kurumi *sf*
蝶 Kochō *la*

**故** 880 [T] (KO, KU, moto, hisa, furu)
木 Motoki *s*
後 Kogo *s*
混馬鹿集 Kokon bakashū *l* ⌈hana *l*
郷の花 Furusato no

**政** 881 [T] Masashi *m*, Tadashi, Tadasu, Sunao; Tsukasa *s*. (SEI, SHŌ, masa, tada, kiyo, kazu, koto, osa, nori, nari, nobu, yuki)
[1]一 Masakazu *m*, Masaichi
[2]二郎 Masajirō *m*
人 Masato *m*
[3]之助 Masanosuke *m*
之輔 Masanosuke *m*
子 Masako *f*
[4]仁 Kotohito *m*
太郎 Masatarō *m*
五郎 Masagorō *m*
木 Masaki *s*
[5]礼 Masakata *m*
令 Masanori *m*
右衛門 Masaemon *m*
司 Seiji *m*
田 Masada *s*
[6]池 Masaike *s*
次 Masaji *m*
次郎 Masajirō *m*
宇 Masanoki *m*
光 Masamitsu *m*
吉 Masakichi *m*
[7]均 Masahira *m*
弘 Masahiro *m*
助 Masasuke *m*
応 Masanobu *m*
男 Masao *m*
尾市 Masaoichi *m*
近 Masachika *m*
孝 Tadasue *m*
[8]所 Mandokoro *sp-h*
知 Masatomo *m*, Masachika ⌈tomo
和 Masayori *m*, Masa-
宗 Masamune *m*
苗 Masamitsu *m*, Masanari
忠 Masatada *m*
青 Masakiyo *m*
秀 Masahide *m*
周 Kiyochika *m*
国 Masakuni *m*
尚 Masahisa *m*
事要略 Seiji yōryaku *l*
[9]治 Masaji *m*
胖 Masahiro *m*
則 Masanori *m*
参 Masamitsu *m*
岡 Masaoka *s*
彦 Masahiko *m*
[10]倫 Masahito *m*
殷 Masatada *m*
恭 Masatada *m*
家 Masaie *m*
容 Masayoshi *m*
速 Masachika *m*
[11]脩 Masanobu *s*
清 Masakiyo *m*
猪 Masai *m*
敏 Masatoshi *m*
章 Masaaki *m*
常 Masatsune *m*
[12]順 Masayoshi *m*
偏 Masayuki *m*
峻 Masamine *m*
森 Masamori *m*
崇 Masataka *m*
[13]誠 Masanari *m*
業 Masanobu *m*
悳 Masayoshi *m*
[14]輔 Masasuke *m*
暦 Masatoshi *m*
[15]醇 Masaatsu *m*
鋪 Masaharu *m*
[16]環 Masaakira *m*
憲 Masanori *m*
養 Masayoshi *m*, Masakiyo
賢 Masatada *m*
興 Masaoki *m*
[17]優 Masakatsu *m*, Masahiro
[18]叢 Masamura *m*
[19]蘆 Masayoshi *m*
[23]鑑 Masaaki *m*, Masaakira

—— 9 L6 ——

**虻** See 1134

**虹** 882 (KŌ, GU, niji)
子 Nijiko *f*

**帥** 883 [T] Sochi *mh*; Sotsu *f*. (SUI, SHUTSU, sochi, sotsu)
宮敦道 Sochinomiya Atsumichi *mh*

**耐** 884 [T] Tsuyoshi *m*. (TAI, DAI, tō)

**封** 885 [T] (FŪ, HŌ, kane)
子 Kaneko *f*

**[illegible]** 886 See [illegible] 605

**籾** 887 (momi)
井 Momii *s*
山 Momiyama *s*
山梓月 M. Shigetsu *ml*

**郊** 888 [T] (KŌ, KYŌ, sato, hiro, oka)
子 Satoko *f*
美 Satomi *f*

**耶** 889 (YA)
馬渓 Yabakei *p*
麻 Yama *p*

**郁** 890 [N] Kaoru *m*, Takashi. (IKU, ka, aya, fumi)
子 Ikuko *f*
子園 Mubezono *s*; Ikushien *mh*
夫 Ikuo *m*, Ayao
次郎 Ikujirō *m*
芳門院 Ikuhō Mon'in ⌊*fh*
良 Ikuo *m*
彦 Ikuhiko *m*

—— 9 L7 ——

**卽** 891 See 即 648

**軌** 892 [T] (KI, nori)
秀 Norihide *m*

**叙** 893 [T] (JO, nobu, mitsu)
衡 Nobuhira *m*

**訂** 894 [T] Tadasu *m*. (TEI, tada)

**計** 895 [T] Hakaru *m*; Kazue *f*. (KEI, KAI, kazu)
三 Keizō *m*
子 Kazuko *f*
介 Keisuke *m*
夫 Kazuo *m*

束 Totsuka *s*
馬 Kazuma *m*

**勃** 896 (BOTSU, hira, hiro)

**勑** 897 See 勅 898

**勅** 898 [T] (CHOKU, toki, te, de)
丁 Chokutei *s*
子 Tokiko *f*
夫 Tokio *m*
市 Deshi *s*
刺川原 Teshigawara *s*
使河原 Teshigawara *sp*
撰集 Chokusenshū *l*

**荆** 899 Kei *s.* (KEI, KYŌ, ibara)
沢 Ibarasawa *p*
尾 Takarao *s*

**刻** 900 [T] (KOKU, toki)
国 Tokikuni *m*

**到** 901 [T] Itaru *m.* (TŌ, yuki, yoshi)
津 Itōzu *s*

**則** 902 [T] (SOKU, nori, tsune, toki, mitsu)
4心 Norisane *m*
文 Norifumi *m*
6光 Norimitsu *m*
7来 Noriyuki *m*
8宗 Norimune *m*
武 Noritake *s*
9彦 Norihiko *m*
10兼 Norikane *m*
11清 Norikiyo *m*
13雄 Norio *m*
14蓼 Norishige *m*
16録 Noribumi *m*
18瓊 Noriyoshi *m*
麿 Tsunemaro *m*
21耀 Noriteru *m*

——9 L8——

**糺** 903 Tadashi *m,* Tadasu. (KYŪ, KU, tada)
民 Tadatami *m*

——9 T2——

**面** 904 [T] (MEN, BEN, tsura, omo, mo)
川 Omokawa *s*
木 Omoki *s*
西 Menishi *s*
図 Ozu *s*
来 Menrai *s*
河 Omoga *p*
幸 Tsurayuki *m*

**冠** 905 [T] Kan *s,* Kanmuri. (KAN, kabura)
木 Kabuki *s,* Kangi
松次郎 Kanmuri Matsujirō *ml*
城 Kangi *s,* Kaburagi

**軍** 906 [T] Susumu *m.* (GUN, isa, mura, mure)
子 Gunji *s*
司 Gunji *s*
四郎 Gunshirō *m*
平 Gunpei *m*
地 Gunji *s*
雄 Isao *m*

**柔** 907 [T] Yawa *f.* (JŪ, tō, nari, yasu)
子 Nariko *f,* Yasuko

**勇** 908 [T] Isamu *m,* Isami, Isao, Takeshi. (YŪ, toshi, isa, taka, o, sa, haya, yo, soyo)
1一 Yūichi *m*
2人 Hayato *m*
3三 Yūzō *m,* Isami
三郎 Yūsaburō *m*
之助 Yūnosuke *m*
4夫 Toshio *m*
太郎 Yūtarō *m*
山 Isayama *s*
山文継 I. no Fumitsugu *ml*
5礼 Ikure *s*
6吉 Yūkichi *m*
広 Isao *m*
7児 Yūji *m*
作 Yūsaku *m*
8宜 Toshinobu *m*
9治郎 Yūjirō *m*
10記 Isayoshi *m*
11魚 Isao *m*
逸 Takeyasu *m*
15蔵 Yūzō *m*

**亭** 909 [I] Takashi *m.* (TEI)

**兗** 910 Tadashi *m.* (EN)

**亮** 911 [N] Makoto *m,* Akira, Kiyoshi, Tōru. (RYŌ, aki, akira, suke, yoshi, yori, ro, katsu, fusa)
一 Ryōichi *m,* Akikazu
二 Ryōji *m*
三 Ryōzō *m*
太郎 Ryōtarō *m*
夫 Yorio *m*
平 Ryōhei *m*
吉 Ryōkichi *m*
美 Fusami *f*
策 Ryōsaku *m*
道 Akimichi *m*
澄 Sukezumi *m*

**南** 912 [T] Minami *sp.* (NAN, ake, nami, mina, yoshi, minami, na)
3川 Minagawa *s,* Minamikawa
小国 Minami-oguni *p*
小泉村 M.-koizumimura *l*
子 Minamiko *f*
大路 Minamiōji *s*
4山 Minamiyama *s*
山城 Minami-yamashiro *p*
木 Nanboku *s*
木曾 Nagiso *p*
方 Minamikata *p*; Minakata *s*
5外 Nangai *p*
北 Nanboku *ml*
北新話 N. shinwa *l*
巨摩 Minami-koma *p*
白亀 Nabaki *s*
田 Minamida *s*
6伊豆 Minami-izu *p*
江 Nan'e *s*
合 Nangō *s*
光 Nankō *p*
宇和 Minami-uwa *p*
有馬 M.-arima *p*
多摩 M.-tama *p*
7佐久 M.-saku *p*
沢 Minamizawa *s,* Minazawa
那珂 Minami-naka *p*
那須 M.-nasu *p*
村 Minamimura *s*
村山 Minami-murayama *p*
村梅軒 Minamimura Baiken *mh*
会津 Minami-aizu *p*
足柄 M.-ashigara *p*
安曇 M.-azumi *p*
牟婁 M.-muro *p*
谷 Minamidani *s*
条 Nanjō *p*
条文雄 N. Bun'yū *mh*
条範夫 N. Norio *ml*
里 Minasato *s,* Nanri
串山 Minami-kushiyama *p*
出 Minamide *s*
8陀羅 Nadara *m*
杣笑楚満人 Nansenshō Somahito *ml*
知多 Minami-chita *p*
牧 M.-maki *p,* Nanmoku
波 Nanba *sp*
河内 Minami-kawachi *p*
河原 M.-kawara *p*
茅部 M.-kayabe *p*
京 Nankin *p* "Nanking"
国 Nangoku *p*
国太平記 N. taiheiki *l*
9津軽 Minami-tsugaru *p*
城 Nanjō *s*
秋田 Minami-akita *p*
信濃 M.-shinano *p*
保 Nanbo *s*
松浦 Minami-matsuura *p*
相木 M.-aiki *p*
長尾 Minaminagao *s*
岩倉 Minamiiwakura *s*
界 Soji *s*
10浦 Minamiura *s*
海 Nankai *p*
海部 Minami-amabe *p*
海道 Nankaidō *p*
高来 Minami-takaki *p*
桑田 M.-kuwata *p*
荒 Minamiarai *s*
宮 Nangū *s*
家 Nanke *s*
原 Nanbara *s,* Nangen

拁 籾 郊 耶 郁 即 軌 叙 訂 計 ▼ 勃 勑 勅 荆 刻 到 則 糺 面 冠 軍 柔 勇 亭 兗 亮 南 ▲ 奎 表 彖 品 客 宥 宣 単 首 前

紆面冠軍柔勇亭尭亮南▼奎表粂品客宥宣単首前羑美▲荊茘茸茆茆茜苔荏茶茨

原繁 Nanbara Shigeru *ml* ⌈ma *p*
[11]埼玉 Minami-saitama *p*
設楽 M.-shidara *p*
都留 M.-tsuru *p*
淡 Nandan *p*
野 Nōno *s*
部 Nanbu *sp*; Minabe *p* ⌈ml
部修太郎 N. Shūtarō
部川 Minabegawa *p*
留別志 Narubeshi *l*
魚沼 Minami-uonuma *p*
島 Nantō *p* ⌈s
鬼窪 Minamionikubo
[12]博 Minami Hiroshi
陽 Nan'yō *p* ⌊ml
場 Nanba *s*
湖 Nanko *s*
晴 Akeharu *m*; Nansei *s* ⌈no *p*
富良野 Minami-furano *p*
窗集 Nansōshū *l*
[13]幌 Minami-horo *p*
雄 Minao *m* ⌈ml
新二 Minami Shinji
淵 Minabuchi *sp*; Nanbuchi *s*, Inabuchi
淵請安 M. no Shōan *mh* ⌈ragi *p*
葛城 Minami-katsuragi *p*
雲 Nagumo *s*
勢 Nansei *p*
[14]郷 Nangō *sp*
種子 Minami-tane *p*
箕輪 M.-minowa *p*
置場 M.-okitama *p*
関 Nankan *p*
[15]摩 Nama *s*
[17]濃 Nannō *p*
総 Nansō *p*
総里見八犬伝 N. Satomi hakkenden *l*
鮮 Nansen *p* "S. Korea"
[18]嶺 Nanrei *ml*

——9 T3——

奎 913 (KEI, fumi)
吾 Keigo *m*
彦 Fumihiko *m*

表 914 [T] Kozue *m*, Akira; Omote *s*, Ue. (HYŌ, aki, yoshi, to, kinu, o, uwa, suzu, omo)
子 Kinuko *f*
美 Akiyoshi *m*
郷 Omotegō *p*

粂 915 Kume *f*. (kume)
川 Kumegawa *s*
子 Kumeko *f*
田 Kumeda *s*
吉 Kumekichi *m*
枝 Kumee *f*
馬 Kumema *m*
野 Kumeno *sf*

品 916 [T] (HIN, HON, shina, kazu, katsu, tada, nori, hide)
子 Shinako *f*
川 Shinagawa *sp*
川弥二郎 S. Yajirō *mh*
吉 Shinakichi *m*
治 Honji *ph*
遅 Honji *ph*
遅部 Honjibe *s*

客 917 [T] Marōdo *s*. (KAKU, KYAKU, hito, masa)
者評判記 Kyakusha hyōbanki *l*

宥 918 (YŪ, U, hiro, suke)
子 Hiroko *f*

宣 919 [T] Noburu *m*, Shimesu; Sen *sm*. (SEN, nobu, nori, hisa, yoshi, sumi, tsura, fusa, mura)
[1]一 Nobutada *m*
[3]子 Nobuko *f*
[4]夫 Hisao *m*
[6]次 Nobutsugu *m*
[7]男 Nobuo *m*
[8]明 Nobuaki *m*
命 Senmyō *l*
[9]長 Norinaga *m*
[10]家 Nobuie *m*
[12]順 Nobumasa *m*
[13]雄 Yoshio *m*
経 Noritsune *m*
[14]嘉 Nobuyoshi *m*
算 Nobukazu *m*
[16]諭 Norisato *m*
維 Nobutsuna *m*, Nobusumi

単 919A [T] (TAN, ichi, tada)

首 920 [T] Hajime *m*; Obuto *sm*, Obito; Ōto *s*, Ōshi, Ōhito. (SHU, obito, kami, saki)
引 Kubihiki *la*
代 Shudai *s*
名 Obitona *m*
藤 Shudō *s*, Sudō
麿 Obitomaro *m*

前 921 [T] Susumu *m*; Mae *s*. (ZEN, SEN, mae, saki, chika, kuma)
[2]刀 Sakito *s*
[3]川 Maekawa *s* ⌈ml
川佐美雄 M. Samio
口 Maeguchi *s*
子 Sakiko *f*
[4]山 Maeyama *s*
木 Maeki *s*
中 Maenaka *s*
[5]田 Maeda, Maita *s*
田川 Maedagawa *s*
田夕暮 Maeda Yūgure *ml*
田正名 M. Masana *mh*
田玄以 M. Gen'i *mh*
田利家 M. Toshiie *mh*
田河 Maedakō *s*
田河広一郎 M. Hiroichirō *ml* ⌈ml
田林外 Maeda Ringai
田青邨 M. Seison *ma*
田香雪 M. Kōsetsu *ml*
田晁 M. Akira *ml*
田普羅 M. Fura *ml*
田鉄之助 M. Tetsunosuke *ml*
田曙山 M. Shozan *ml*
[6]次 Chikatsugu *m*
光 Sakimitsu *m*
[7]沢 Maezawa *sp*
村 Maemura *s*
[8]波 Maenami *s*, Maeha
[9]津江 Maetsue *p*
畑 Maehata *s*
岡 Maeoka *s*
[10]倉 Maegura *s*
原 Maebara *sp*; Maebaru *p*
[11]野 Maeno *s*
部 Maebe *s*
島 Maejima *s*
島密 M. Hisoka *mh*
[13]雄 Chikao *m*
豊 Sakitoyo *m*
園 Maezono *s*
[16]橋 Maebashi *sp*

羑 922 Susumu *m*. (YŪ, YU, michi)
弘 Michihiro *m*

美 923 [T] Kiyoshi *m*, Umashi; Yoshimi *s*. (MI, BI, yoshi, tomi, haru, uma, umashi, yo, mitsu, hashi)
[3]川 Mikawa *p*
之助 Minosuke *m*
子 Yoshiko *f*, Haruko
土里 Midori *p*
久 Yoshihisa *m*
[4]仁 Yoshinori *m*
方 Mikata *p*
山 Miyama *p*
井 Mii *s*
毛比麿 Mikeimaro *m*
[5]代 Miyo *f*
代子 Miyoko *f*
代蔵 Miyozō *m*
石 Umashi *m*
田 Mita *s*
玉 Mitama *s* ⌈s
甘 Mikamo *sp*; Mikan
[6]帆子 Mihoko *f*
気 Mike *s*
[7]作 Mimasaka *ph*
杉 Misugi *p*
図垣 Mizugaki *s*
図屋 Mizuya *s*
男 Yoshio *m*
里 Misato *p*
臣 Yoshio *m*
[8]和 Miwa *p*
泥 Mine *f*
波留 Miharu *m*
宏 Yoshihiro *m*
努 Mino *s*
奈和集 Minawashū *l*
奈畝 Minase *f*
東 Mitō *p*
並 Minami *p*
[9]保 Miho *p*
保関 Mionoseki *p*
律 Minori *m*
柯 Mie *f*

珍 Yoshiharu *m*
津 Mitsu *s*
津島 Mitsushima *p*
星 Bisei *p*
10唄 Bibai *p*
浦 Miho *s*
浜 Mihama *p*
原 Mihara *p*
座 Miza *s*
馬 Mima *sp*
11陵 Misasagi *p*
野里 Minori *p*
都 Mito *p*
淑 Mitoshi *m*
深 Bifuka *p*
添 Mizoe *s*
章 Yoshiaki *m*
麻 Miasa *p*
亀次郎 Mikijirō *m*
12峻 Yoshitaka *m*
瑛 Biei *p*
喜蔵 Mikizō *m*
智子 Michiko *f*
智太郎 Michitarō *m*
13幌 Bihoro *p*
摸 Yoshinori *m*
雄 Tomio *m*
誠 Yoshiaki *m*
棲 Misumi *s*
楯 Mitate *m*
夢 Miyume *f*
越乃 Miono *m*
14郷 Misato *m-p*
稲 Yoshine *m*, Umashine
静 Yoshizu *m*
15蔭 Yoshikage *m*
16樹 Umiki *m*, Miki, Umaki, Harushige
積 Yoshitsumu *m*
17濃 Mino *p*
濃加茂 M. Kamo *p*
濃風 Minofū *l*
濃部 Minobe *s*
濃輪 Minowa *s*
19禰 Mine *p*
20織 Miori *m*
嚢 Minō *p*; Mikuki *s*

**荊** 923A See 荆 899

**茘** 924 (REI)
支 Nigauri *l*

**茸** 925 (JŌ, NYU, take)
次 Takeji *m*

**茆** 926 (BŌ, MYŌ, shige)
樹 Shigeki *m*

**茽** 927 Shigeru *m*. (CHŪ, shige)
子 Shigeko *f*

**茜** 928 (SEN, akane)
屋 Akaneya *s*
部 Akanabe *s*

**苔** 929 Sunori *s*. (TAI, DAI, koke)
の衣 Koke no koromo *l*
寺 Kokedera *p*

**荏** 930 (JIN, NIN, e)
戸内 Etouchi *s*
原 Ebara *s*
柄 Egara *s*

**茶** 931 [T] (CHA, SA)
山 Sayama *s*
木 Chaki *s*
谷 Chadani *s*, Saya
屋 Chaya *p*
壺 Chatsubo *la*

**茨** 932 (SHI, JI, ibara, ubara)
木 Ibaraki *sp*; Ubaraki *s*
田 Ibata *s*, Ashida, Matsuda, Manda
沢 Ibarasawa *s*
城 Ibaraki *sp*

**荘** 933 [T] Sō *m*, Takashi, Tadashi, Sakō; Shō *s*. (SŌ, SHŌ, taka, masa)
十 Sōjū *m*
川 Shōkawa *p*
子 Takako *f*
内 Sōnai *p*; Shōnai *s*
司 Sōji *s*, Shōji
田 Shōda *s*
行 Masayuki *m*
村 Shōmura *s*
政 Takamasa *m*
原 Shōbara *s*

**草** 934 [T] Kusaka *s*. (SŌ, kusa, shige, kaya)
ケ谷 Kusagaya *s*
3川 Kusagawa *s*
子洗小町 Sōshi-arai Komachi *la*
4刈 Kusakari *s*
双紙 Kusa-zōshi *l*
井地 Kusaichi *s*
5加 Sōka *p*
可 Sōka *s*
生 Kusō *s*
6地 Kusachi *s*
7村 Kusamura *s*
村北星 K. Hokusei *ml*
9津 Kusatsu *p*
10柳 Kusayanagi *s*
11深 Kusabuka *s*
根集 Sōkonshū *l*
野 Kusano *s*
野心平 K. Shinpei *ml*
島 Kusajima *s*
庵集 Sōanshū *l*
12場 Kusaba *s*
間 Kusama *s*
鹿 Kusaka *s*, Kusajika
鹿砥 Kusakado *s*
14郷 Sōgō *s*
15彅 Kusanagi *s*
16薙 Kusanagi *sl*
壁 Kusakabe *s*
23籠 Kusakago *l*

**荒** 935 [T] Ara *s*, Arara, Araragi. (KŌ, ara, ra, arara)
2人 Arando *m*
3川 Arakawa *sp*
三 Arazō *m*
4山 Arayama *s*
井 Arai *s*
木 Araki *s*
木又右衛門 A. Mataemon *mh-l*
木田 Arakida *s*
木田守武 A. Moritake *ml*
木宗太郎 Araki Sōtarō *mh*
木貞夫 A. Sadao *mh*
木巍 A. Takashi *ml*
5正人 Ara Masahito *ml*
本 Aramoto *s*
田 Arata *s*
田井 Aratai *s*
田殖 Aratae *s*
生 Arao *s*
6耳 Aramimi *m*
7沢 Arasawa *s*
助 Arasuke *m*
谷 Araya *s*, Aratani
身 Arami *s*
尾 Arao *sp*
8牧 Aramaki *s*
波 Aranami *s*
波多 Arahata *s*
金 Arakane *s*
居 Arai *s*
9畑 Arahata *s*
畑寒村 A. Kanson *mlh*
城 Araki *s*
垣 Aragaki *s*
垣秀雄 A. Hideo *ml*
巻 Aramaki *s*
岡 Araoka *s*
10浦 Akinoura *s*
荒 Arara *s*
屋 Araya *s*
造 Kōzō *m*
11深 Arabuka *s*
野 Arano *s*, Kōya
島 Arashima *s*
12賀 Araka *s*
15幡 Arahata *s*
16樹 Araki *m*
19瀬 Arase *s*

—— 9 T4 ——

**盲** 936 [T] (MŌ)
安抄 Mōanjō *l*

**革** 937 [T] (KAKU)
新倶楽部 Kakushin kurabu *h*

**枩** 938 See 松 869

**長** 939 [T] Nagashi *m*, Hisashi, Takeshi, Masaru, Tsukasa; Chō *sm*, Osa. (CHŌ, naga, hisa, osa, take, tsune, masa, ie, nobu, masu, michi)
1一 Chōichi *m*, Tsunekazu
2二郎 Chōjirō *m*
十郎 Chōjūrō *m*
人 Hisato *m*
3川 Nagakawa *s*
三郎 Chōzaburō *m*
之 Nagayuki *m*

荏 茶 茨 荘 草 荒 盲 革 枩 長 ▼ 岩 岸 ▲ 岩 昂 昱 昆 星 是 穹 栗 要 奏

万部 Oshamanbe *p*
土呂 Nagadoro *s*
丸 Osamaru *s*
久 Chōkyū 1040–44; Naune *s*
久手 Nagakute *p*
久保 Nagakubo *s*
[4]戸 Nagato *s*
元 Chōgen 1028–37
内 Osanai *sp*
山 Nagayama *s*
井 Nagai *sp*
太郎 Chōtarō *m*
文 Nagabumi *m*
方 Nagakata *m*
与 Nagayo *sp*
与専斎 N. Senzai *mh*
与善郎 N. Yoshirō *ml*
[5]北 Chōboku *s*
礼 Nagamichi *m*
永 Nagae *s*
五郎 Chōgorō *m*
友 Nagatomo *s*
平 Chōhei *m*
本 Nagamoto *s*
生 Naganari *m*, Nagaoki; Chōsei *p*
田 Nagata *sp*; Osada *s*
田秀雄 N. Hideo *ml*
田恒雄 Osada Tsuneo *ml*
田秋濤 O. Shūtō *ml*
田幹彦 Nagata Mikihiko *ml*
[6]次郎 Chōjirō *m*
江 Nagae *s*
合 Nagaai *s*, Nagakai
吉 Nagayoshi *m*
光 Nagamitsu *m*
広 Nagahiro *s*
成 Nagashige *m*
耳国漂流記 Chōjikoku hyōryūki *l*
[7]村 Nagamura *s*
坂 Nagasaka *sp* ⌈su
沙 Nagasuna *s*, Naga-
沢 Nagasawa *s*
沢美津 N. Mitsu *ml*
利 Osari *s*
亨 Chōkyō 1487–89
谷 Hase *sp*; Nagatani *s*, Nagaya
谷川 Hasegawa *sp*
谷川かな女 H. Kanajo *fl*
谷川巳之吉 H. Minokichi *ml*
谷川天渓 H. Tenkei *ml*
谷川四郎 H. Shirō *ml*
谷川伸 H. Shin *ml*
谷川如是閑 H. Nyozekan *ml*
谷川幸延 H. Kōen *ml*
谷川泉 H. Izumi *ml*
谷川時雨 H. Shigure *fl*
谷川素逝 H. Sosei *ml*
谷川等伯 H. Tōhaku *ma*
谷川零余子 H. Reiyoshi *ml* ⌈*ml*
谷川銀作 H. Ginsaku
谷山 Haseyama *sp*
谷見 Hasemi *s*
谷河 Hasegawa *s*
谷部 Hasebe *s*
谷場 Haseba *sp*
谷雄 Haseo *m*
谷健 Hase Ken *ml*
克 Hisakatsu *m*
兵衛 Chōbee *m*
男 Masao *m*
尾 Nagao *sp*
尾景虎 N. Kagetora *mh* ⌈suka
束 Nagatsuka *s*, Nat-
束正家 Nagatsuka Masaie *mh*
[8]沼 Naganuma *sp*
明 Chōmei *ml*
門 Nagato *sp*
岐 Nagaki *s*
和 Chōwa 1012–70; Nagakazu *m*, Nagatoshi
秀 Nagahide *m*
幸 Nagayoshi *m*
命 Chōmei *s*
宗 Osamune *m*, Takemune
孟 Nagatake *m*
岑 Nagamine *s*
季 Tsunesue *m*
良 Nagara *sm*
承 Chōjō 1132–35
[9]保 Chōhō 999–1004
狭 Nagasa *sp*
津 Nagatsu *s*
洲 Nagasu *p*
治 Chōji *m* 1104–06
岫 Nagaana *s*
畑 Nagahata *s*
弥 Tatsuya *m*
松 Nagamatsu *s*
柄 Nagara *sp*
柄川 Nagaragawa *p*
砂 Nagasuna *s*
秋詠藻 Chōshū eisō *l*
亮 Hisakatsu *m*
南 Chōnan *sp*
昱 Nagaakira *m*
育 Naganari *m*
泉 Nagaizumi *p*
岡 Nagaoka *sp* ⌈*mh*
岡半太郎 N. Hantarō
岡京 N.-kyō *ph*
妻 Nagatsuma *s*
[10]唄 Nagauta *a*
浜 Nagahama *sp*
祥 Nagaakira *m*
畝 Naune *sp*
郡 Nagamura *m*
訓 Nagamichi *m*
記 Naganari *m*
倉 Nagakura *s*
宮 Nagamiya *s*
晟 Nagaakira *m*
竜 Chōryū *ml*
挙 Nagataka *m*
原 Nagahara *s*
屋 Nagaya *s*
屋王 N.-ō *mh*
[11]淳 Nagakiyo *m*
流 Nagaru *m*; Chōryū *ml*
峰 Nagamine *s*
根 Nagane *s*
祗 Nagatada *m*
船 Osafune *sp*
船長光 O. Nagamitsu
野 Nagano *sp* ⌊*ma*
野原 Naganohara *p*
部 Osabe *s*
翁 Nagatoshi *m*
著 Nagaakira *m*
盛 Nagamori *m*
康 Nagayasu *m*
庵 Chōan *ml*
島 Nagashima *sp*
順 Nagatoshi *m*
陽 Chōyō *sp*
塩 Nagashio *s*
禄 Chōroku 1457–60
崎 Nagasaki *sp* ⌈*mh*
崎高資 N. Takasuke
曾我部 Chōsokabe *s*
曾我部元親 C. Motochika *mh*
曾根 Nagasone *s*
曾禰 Nagasone *s*
富 Osatomi *s*
森 Nagamori *s*
貴 Nagayoshi *m*
景 Nagakage *m*
[13]卿 Nagaaki *m*
雄 Nagao *sm*; Haseo *m*
詮 Nagatoshi *m*
群 Nagamura *m*
幹 Nagayoshi *m*
猷 Nagakazu *m*
滝 Nagataki *s*
溥 Nagahiro *m*
堀 Nagahori *s*
塚 Nagatsuka *s*
塚節 N. Takashi *ml*
寛 Chōkan 1163–65
[14]徳 Chōtoku 995–99; Naganori *m*
郷 Chōgō *s* ⌈*l*
歌 Nagauta *la*; Chōka
歌撰格 C. senkaku *l*
説 Nagatsugu *m*
諧 Naganori *m*
暦 Chōryaku 1037–40
[15]潤 Osauru *m*
統 Nagamune *s*
監 Nagateru *m*
勲 Nagakoto *m*
蔵 Chōzō *m*
[16]操 Nagamochi *m*
衛 Nagamori *m*
橋 Nagahashi *s*
維 Nagatsuna *m*
壁 Osakabe *s*
[17]孺 Nagachika *m*
縁 Nagayori *sm*
[18]職 Nagamoto *m*
藤 Nagafuji *s*, Chōdō
嬴 Nagamitsu *m*
嶺 Nagamine *s*
[19]瀬 Nagase *s*
[21]縄 Naganawa *s*

岩 940 (CHŌ, taka)

岸 941 [T] Kishi *s*. (GAN, kishi)
[3]川 Kishigawa *s*
上 Kishigami *s*, Kishinoue
下 Kishishita *s*
子 Kishiko *f*
大路 Kishiōji *s*
[4]井 Kishii *s*
[5]本 Kishimoto *sp*
田 Kishida *s*

田吟香 K. Ginkō *mlh*
田国士 K. Kunio *ml*
田俊子 K. Toshiko *fh*
田劉生 K. Ryūsei *mla*
6名 Kishina *s*
7沢 Kishizawa *s*
村 Kishimura *s*
8波 Kishinami *s*
和田 Kishiwada *sp*
11野 Kishino *s*
部 Kishibe *s*

**岩** 942 [T] Iwao *m.* (GAN, iwa, kata, seki, taka)
3川 Iwakawa *s*
三郎 Iwasaburō *m*, Sekisaburō
口 Iwaguchi *s*
子 Iwako *f*
上 Iwagami *s*
上順一 I. Jun'ichi *ml*
下 Iwashita *s*
下俊作 I. Shunsaku *ml*
4切 Iwakiri *s*
戸 Iwato *s*
元 Iwamoto *s*
内 Iwauchi *s*; Iwanai *p*
月 Iwatsuki *s*
山 Iwayama *s*
木 Iwaki *sp*
太 Iwata *m*
手 Iwate *sp*
井 Iwai *sp*
井出 Iwaide *s*
5代 Iwashiro *p*
永 Iwanaga *s*
永胖 I. Yutaka *ml*
田 Iwata *s*
片 Iwakata *s*
立 Iwadate *s*
本 Iwamoto *s*
6次郎 Iwajirō *m*
竹 Iwatake *s*
吉 Iwakichi *m*
成 Iwanari *s*
舟 Iwafune *p*
7沢 Iwasawa *s*
村 Iwamura *sp*
村部 Iwamurabe *s*
佐 Iwasa *s*
佐又兵衛 I. Matabee *ma*
佐東一郎 I. Tōichirō *ml*
坂 Iwasaka *s*
男 Iwao *sm*
谷 Iwaya *s*, Iwatani
谷莫哀 Iwaya Bakuai *ml*
見 Iwami *s*
見沢 Iwamizawa *p*
出 Iwade *sp*
出山 Iwadeyama *p*
尾 Iwao *s*
8附 Iwatsuki *s*
門 Iwakado *s*, Iwato
沼 Iwanuma *sp*
波 Iwanami *s*
波茂雄 I. Shigeo *ml*
国 Iwakuni *sp*
9松 Iwamatsu *s*
政 Iwamasa *s*
津 Iwatsu *s*
浅 Iwasa *s*
治郎 Iwajirō *m*
垣 Iwagaki *s*
城 Iwaki *sp*
城之徳 I. Yukinori *ml*
城準太郎 I. Juntarō *ml*
美 Iwami *p*
泉 Iwaizumi *p*
岡 Iwaoka *s*
垂 Iwataru *s*
重 Iwashige *s*
10脇 Iwawaki *s*
郡 Iwakuri *s*
室 Iwamuro *sp*
倉 Iwakura *sp*
倉具視 I. Tomomi *mh*
倉政治 I. Masaji *ml*
原 Iwahara *sp*; Iwapara *p*
屋 Iwaya *s*
11捲 Genmaku *m*
浪 Iwanami *s*
渓 Iwadani *s*
根 Iwane *sm*
船 Iwafune *p-la*
部 Iwabe *s*
動 Iwarugi *s*, Isurugi
野 Iwano *s*
野泡鳴 I. Hōmei *ml*
堂 Iwadō *s*
島 Iwashima *s*
亀 Iwahisa *m*
12陽 Iwanami *s*
崎 Iwasaki *sp*
崎弥太郎 I. Yatarō *mh*
森 Iwamori *s*
間 Iwama *sp*
13塚 Iwatsuka *s*
楯 Iwadate *s*
淵 Iwabuchi *s*
滝 Iwataki *p*
満 Iwamitsu *s*
雲 Iwakumo *s*
越 Iwakoshi *s*
堀 Iwabori *s*
14窪 Iwakubo *s*
15槻 Iwatsuki *p*
16橋 Iwahashi *s*
17館 Iwadate *s*
18藤 Iwatō *s*, Iwafuji
藤雪夫 Iwatō Yukio *ml*
19瀬 Iwase *sp*
瀬忠震 I. Tadanari *mh*

**昂** 943 Takashi *m*, Noboru, Akira. (KŌ, taka, aki)
式 Takatsune *m*

**昱** 944 (IKU, YOKU, aki, akira)
子 Akiko *f*
太郎 Ikutarō *m*
禧 Ikuyoshi *m*

**昆** 945 Kon *s.* (KON, hide, yasu, hi)
子 Hideko *f*, Yasuko
布 Konbu *s*
沙子 Hisako *f*
野 Konno *s*
解 Komuki *s*, Kongi

**星** 946 [T] Hoshi *s.* (SEI, SHŌ, hoshi, toshi)
3川 Hoshikawa *s*
之助 Hoshinosuke *m*
子 Hoshiko *f*
4戸 Hoshito *s*
山 Hoshiyama *s*
井 Hoshii *s*
5田 Hoshida *s*
6名 Hoshina *s*
7谷 Hoshiya *s*
亨 Hoshi Tōru *mh-la*
沢 Hoshizawa *s*
8舎露玉菊 Hoshi yadoru tsuyu no tamagiku *la*
10郎 Hoshio *m*
倉 Hoshikura *s*
11野 Hoshino *sp*
野天知 H. Tenchi *ml*
野立子 H. Tatsuko *fl*
野麦人 H. Bakujin *ml*
菫派 Seikinha *l*
島 Hoshijima *s*
12港 Shingapōru *p* "Singapore"
落秋風五丈原 Hoshi otsu shūfū gojōgen *l*
14歌 H. no uta *l*

**是** 947 [T] Sunao *m*, Tadashi. (SHI, ZE, kore, yoshi, yuki, tsuna)
1一 Koreichi *m*
3子 Koreko *f*, Yoshiko
4分 Korechika *m*
太 Korehiro *m*, Yoshihiro
5永 Korenaga *s*
公 Korekimi *m*
7沢 Korezawa *s*
我意 Zegai *la*
8枝 Koreeda *s*
9恒 Koretsune *sm*
洞 Koreaki *m*, Yoshiaki
界 Zegai *la*
香 Yoshika *m*
11清 Korekiyo *m*
14彰 Koreaki *m*
15儀 Korenori *m*
16賢 Korekata *m*

**—— 9 T5 ——**

**穹** 948 Takashi *m.* (KYŪ, KU, taka)
子 Takako *f*

**叟** 949 See 更 528

**要** 950 (SEI, masa)
一 Masakazu *m*

**奏** 951 [T] (SŌ, kana)
子 Kanako *f*

**癸** 952 (KI, mizu)
生 Kebu *s*
生川 Kebukawa *s*, Mibukawa

**発** 953 [T] Hiraku *m*, Akira; Okori *s.* (HATSU, HOTSU, oki, akira, aki, shige, chika, toki, nari, nobu, nori)
心和歌集 Hosshin wakashū *l*
心集 Hosshinshū *l*

茨荘草荒盲革杏長岩岸▼岩昂昱昆星是穹叟要奏癸発▲忒岱岳背育妻委香音春

昱 昆 星 是 穹 戛 要 奏 癸 発 ▼ 怤 岱 岳 背 育 妻 委 香 音 春 ▲ 皇 泉 思 界 染 栄 変 帝 皆 専

田 Hotta *s*
地 Hotchi *s*
身 Hatsumi *m*
智 Hotchi *s*

**怤** 954 (FU, yoshi)
子 Yoshiko *f*

**岱** 955 (TAI, DAI)
三 Taizō *m*
明 Taimei *p*

**岳** 956 [T] Takashi *m.* (GAKU, oka, take, taka)
守 Takemori *m*
村 Okamura *s*
男 Takeo *m*
周 Takanori *m*

**背** 957 [T] (HAI, se, shiro, nori)
板 Seita *s*
振 Sefuri *p*
評 Hekobori *s*

**育** 958 [T] (IKU, yasu, nari, suke, naru)
一 Yasukazu *m*
子 Yasuko *f*
作 Ikusaku *m*
英 Yasuhide *m*
郎 Ikurō *m*

**妻** 959 [T] (SAI, SEI, tsuma, me)
子 Tsumako *f*
木 Tsumaki *s*
谷 Tsumatani *s*
我 Mega *s*
沼 Menuma *p*
恋行 Tsumagoiyuki *la*
鳥 Mendori *s*
鹿 Mega *s*
籠 Tsumago *s*

**委** 960 [T] (I, tomo, tsuku, kutsu, moro)
子 Tomoko *f*
文 Shidori *s*

**香** 961 [T] Kaoru *m-f*; Katori *s.* (KŌ, KYŌ, ka, taka, yoshi, kaga)
[3]川 Kagawa *sp*
川進 K. Susumu *ml*
川景柄 K. Kagemoto *ml*
川景樹 K. Kageki *ml*
[4]月 Katsuki *s*, Kōtsuki
山 Kayama *s*, Kaguyama
[5]代 Koshiro *s*
北 Kahoku *p*
田 Kōda *s*
平 Takahira *m*
[6]寺 Kōdera *p*
光 Takamitsu *m*
芝 Kashiba *p*
母 Kōmo *s*
西 Kasai *s*, Kōsai, Kōzei, Konishi
[7]住 Kasumi *p*
坂 Kōsaka *s*
村 Kamura *s*, Kōmura
芳 Niokata *s*
我美 Kagami *p*
[8]取 Katori *sp*; Kandori *s*
取秀真 Katori Hozuma *mla*
宗我部 Kasokabe *s*, Kōsokabe
苗 Kanae *m*
居 Kaori *f*
[9]保留 Kaoru *f*
南 Kōnan *p*
美 Kami *p*; Kagami *sp*
春 Kawara *p*
香地 Kakaji *p*
[10]栖 Kōzumi *s*
[11]野 Kōno *s*
魚音 Ayune *f*
[12]港 Honkon *p* "Hongkong"
曾我部 Kōsokabe *s*
椎 Kashii *s*
焼 Kōyagi *p*
[16]積 Katsumi *s*
[20]織 Kaoru *m*

**音** 962 [T] (ON, IN, oto, ne, o, to, nari)
[2]人 Otondo *m*, Ondo, Otomuto
[3]川 Otogawa *s*
三 Otozō *m*
[4]戸 Ondo *p*
戸瀬戸 O.-no-seto *p*
山 Otoyama *s*
五郎 Otogorō *m*
太 Ō *s*
女 Otome *f*
[5]田 Onda *s*
主 Otonushi *m*
[6]次郎 Otojirō *m*
羽 Otowa *s*
羽屋 Otowaya *s*
吉 Otokichi *m*
[7]那 Otona *f*
別 Onbetsu *p*
更 Otofuke *p*
[8]阿弥 On'ami *ma*
[9]松 Otomatsu *m*
弥 Otoya *m*
治 Otoji *m*
治郎 Otojirō *m*
威子府 Otoineppu *p*
[12]無 Otonashi *s*
[14]輔 Otosuke *m*

**春** 963 [T] Haru *sf*; Kasuga *s*; Hajime *m.* (SHUN, haru, su, ha, azuma, kasu, kazu, toki, atsu)
[1]一 Haruichi *m*
[3]川 Harukawa *s*
小 Haruko *f*
三 Haruzō *m*
子 Haruko *f*
[4]中子 Hanako *f*
及 Haruchika *m*
井 Harui *s*
太郎 Harutarō *m*
木 Haruki *s*
山 Haruyama *s*; Harunobu *m*
山行夫 H. Yukio *ml*
日 Kasuga *sp*; Haruhi *p*; Shunnichi *s*
日井 Kasugai *sp*
日居 Kasugai *p*
日竜神 Kasuga ryūjin *la*
日造 K.-zukuri *a*
日部 Kasugabe *sp*
日権現験記 Kasuga Gongen kenki *la*
[5]田 Haruta *s*
生 Haruo *m*
本 Harumoto *s*
[6]次郎 Harujirō *m*
江 Harue *m-p*
色英対暖語 Shunshoku eitai dango *l*
色辰巳園 Shunshoku tatsumi no sono *l-la*
色恵之花 S. megumi no haha *l*
色梅児誉美 S. umegoyomi *l*
色梅美婦禰 S. ume mibune *l*
光 Harumitsu *m*
夫 Haruo *m*
名 Haruna *s*
[7]告鳥 Harutsugedori *l*
[8]良 Haruhiko *m*
良洲 Karasu *p*
泥 Shundei *l*
門 Haruto *m*
枝 Harue *m-f*; Harueda *s*
定 Tokisada *m*
周 Haruchika *m*
雨 Harusame *l*
[6]信 Harunobu *ma*
秋 Haruaki *s*
秋子 Suzuko *f*
泉 Harumi *m*
栄 Shun'ei *la*
風馬堤曲 Shunpū bateikyoku *l*
彦 Haruhiko *m*
重 Harushige *m*
[10]海 Harumi *m*
恵 Harue *f*
原 Harubara *s*, Suhara, Sunohara, Shunbara
屋妙葩 Shun'oku Myōha *mh*
馬 Kazuma *m*
[11]野 Haruno *p*
部 Kasube *s*; Kasugabe *sp*
魚 Haruna *m*
島 Harushima *s*
[12]琴抄 Shunkinshō *l*
道 Harumichi *s*
遂 Harukata *s*, Kasugata
[13]満 Azumamaro *ml*
殖 Harue *s*
雄 Haruo *m*
路 Haruji *m*
[14]節 Haruyo *m*
[15]澄 Haruzumi *s*
[16]樹 Harushige *m*
燈 Shuntō *l*
[18]麿 Azumamaro *m*
邇 Haruchika *m*
藤 Harufuji *s*, Shundō
[19]繁 Harushige *m*
[21]譲 Harumasa *m*

**皇** 964 [T] Sumeragi *s*. (KŌ, ō, sumera, sube)
子代 Mikoshiro *s*
太后 Kōtaikō *fh*
女和の宮 Kōjo Kazunomiya *l*
甫 Kōho *s*
帝 Kōtei *l*
極 Kōgyoku *fh*

**泉** 965 [T] Izumi *sm-f-p*; Sen *s*, Motoji; Kiyoshi *m*. (SEN, ZEN, izumi, i, izu, mi, moto, zumi, mizo)
[2]二 Motoji *s*
[3]川 Izumikawa *s*
大津 Izumi Ōtsu *p*
[4]水 Sensui *s*
山 Izumiyama *s*
[5]田 Izumida *s*
本 Izumoto *s*
北 Senboku *p*
[7]佐野 Izumi Sano *p*
沢 Izumizawa *s*
谷 Izumiya *s*, Izumitani, Izutani
[9]亭 Izumitei *s*
南 Sennan *s*
[10]原 Izumihara *s*, Izuhara, Motohara
屋 Izumiya *s*
[12]崎 Izumizaki *sp*
[19]鏡花 Izumi Kyōka *ml*

**思** 966 [T] Shida *s*. (SHI, koto, omoi)
草 Omoigusa *l*

**界** 967 [T] Sakai *sp*. (KAI, sakai)
麿 Sakaimaro *m*

**染** 968 [T] (SEN, ZEN, NEN, some)
川 Somekawa *s*
子 Someko *f*
井 Somei *s*
右衛門 Someemon *m*
羽 Shimeha *s*
村 Somemura *s*
谷 Someya *s*, Sometani
谷進 Someya Susumu *ml*
宮 Somemiya *s*
屋 Someya *s*
野 Someno *s*
崎 Somezaki *s*
崎延房 S. Nobufusa *ml*
葉 Oiba *s*

**栄** 969 [T] Sakae *m-f-p*; Shigeru *m*, Sakō, Hisashi. (EI, YŌ, shige, yoshi, saka, hide, naga, haru, masa, teru, hisa, tomo, hiro, taka)
[1]一 Eiichi *m*, Hidekazu
一郎 Eiichirō *m*
[2]八郎 Eihachirō *m*
[3]三郎 Eizaburō *m*
之助 Einosuke *m*
子 Shigeko *f*, Hideko, Nagako, Masako
[4]仁 Yoshihito *m*
介 Eisuke *m*
山 Sakayama *s*
五郎 Eigorō *m*
井 Sakai *s*
夫 Yoshio *m*, Sakao
木 Sakaki *m*
太郎 Eitarō *m*
[5]司 Eiji *m*
右 Masao *m*
四郎 Eishirō *m*
田 Sakata *s*
[6]次 Eiji *m*
次郎 Eijirō *m*
光 Yoshimitsu *m*, Masamitsu
吉 Eikichi *m*
同 Teruatsu *m*
西 Eisai *mh*
[7]作 Eisaku *m*
材 Hideki *m*
助 Eisuke *m*
谷 Sakaedani *s*
花 Eiga *l*
[8]明 Haruaki *m*
[9]信 Naganobu *m*
彦 Shigehiko *m*
[10]帰 Hidemoto *m*
[11]胤 Yoshitsugu *m*
[12]喜 Yoshihisa *m*
量 Masakazu *m*
[15]蔵 Eizō *m*
[16]樹 Shigeki *m*
[17]懐 Hidekane *m*
[18]顕 Hideaki *m*
[21]耀 Hideaki *m*

**——9 T6——**

**変** 970 [T] (HEN)
目伝 Hemeden *l*
通軽井茶話 Hentsū Karuizawa *l*

**帝** 971 [T] (TEI, TAI, mikado, tada)
力 Teiriki *m*

**呰** 972 (SHI, SEI, ata)
女 Atame *f*

**専** 973 [T] Atsushi *m*, Atsumu, Mohara. (SEN, taka, moro)
一郎 Sen'ichirō *m*
之助 Sennosuke *m*
太郎 Sentarō *m*
治 Senji *m*
堯 Morotaka *m*

**巷** 974 (KŌ, sato)
路過程 Kōro katei *l*

**巻** 975 [T] Maki *sp*. (KEN, KAN, maki, maru)
子 Makiko *f*
口 Makiguchi *s*
田 Makita *s*
吉 Kenkichi *m*
島 Makishima *s*
雄 Makio *m*
絹 Makiginu *la*

**卑** 976 [T] (HI)
弥呼 Himiko / Himeko *fh*

**系** 977 [T] Ito *s*. (KEI, ito, tsugi, tsura, toshi)

**参** 978 [T] Mairu *m*. (SAN, SHIN, kazu, michi, mitsu, chika, mi, naka, hoshi)
木 Miki *s*
正 Kazumasa *m*
男 Kazuo *m*
里 Misato *m*
河 Mikawa *s*
和 Sanna *ml*
顕 Michiteru *m*

**奐** 979 Akira *m*. (KAN, akira)

**契** 980 [T] Chigiru *m*. (KEI, KETSU, hisa)
斤 Keikin *s*
沖 Keichū *mlh*

**——9 T7——**

**負** 981 [T] (FU, hi, e, oi, masu)
他 Ōta *s*
嚢者 Fukuroōmono *s*

**貞** 982 [T] Tadashi *m*, Tadasu, Tei, Misao; Sada *s*. (TEI, JŌ, sada, tada, tsuru)
[1]一 Teiichi *m*
一郎 Teiichirō *m*
[2]二 Teiji *m*
二郎 Teijirō *m*
[3]三 Teizō *m*
三郎 Teisaburō *m*
之助 Teinosuke *m*
丈 Sadatake *m*
才 Sadatoshi *m*
子 Sadako *f*
[4]仁 Sadami *m*
元 Jōgen 976–78
方 Sadakata *s*
夫 Sadao *m*
升 Sadamasu *m*
[5]永 Jōei 1232–33
市 Teiichi *m*
央 Sadahisa *m*
允 Sadayoshi *m*
[6]次 Sadatsugu *m*, Teiji
次郎 Teijirō *m*
巧 Sadatae *m*
行 Sadayuki *m*, Sadamochi
光 Sadamitsu *p*
守 Sadamori *m*
吉 Teikichi *m*
成 Sadafusa *m*
老 Sadaoi *m*
[7]作 Sadanari *m*
材 Sadaki *m*
利 Sadanori *m*
亨 Jōkyō 1684–88; Sadanari *m*
応 Jōō 1222–24

[illegible] 岱 岳 背 育 妻 委 香 音 春 ▼ 皇 泉 思 界 染 栄 変 帝 呰 専 巷 巻 卑 系 参 奐 契 負 貞 ▲ 昼 盾 厚 風 岡 南 直 屎 囿 画

専 巻 巻 卑 系 参 奐 契 負 貞 ▼ 昼 盾 厚 風 岡 直 ▲ 屎 囿 画 度 底 追 廻 建 咫 眉

$^{8}$和 Jōwa 1345–50
宗 Sadamune *m*
固 Sadamoto *m*
居 Sadasue *m*
$^{9}$松 Sadamatsu *m*
治 Jōji 1362–68; Teiji *m* ⌈jirō
治郎 Teijirō *m*, Sada-
長 Sadatake *m*
発 Sadaakira *m*
$^{10}$俶 Sadayoshi *m*
祓 Sadakiyo *m*
訓 Sadakuni *m*
哲 Sadayoshi *m*
造 Teizō *m*
$^{11}$朗 Sadao *m*
寄 Sadayori *m*
著 Sadaaki *m*
斎 Sadatoki *m*
盛 Sadamori *s*
啓 Sadanobu *m*
$^{12}$隅 Sadazumi *m*
勝 Sadanori *m*
敬 Sadayuki *m* ⌈ru
喜 Sadaki *m*, Sadaha-
$^{13}$雅 Sadanori *m*
雄 Sadao *m*
幹 Sadatomo *m*, Tadayoshi
意 Sadaoki *m*
載 Sadanori *m*
義 Sadayoshi *m*
$^{14}$徳 Teitoku *ml*
説 Sadatoki *m*
置 Sadaoki *m*
$^{15}$範 Sadanori *m*
慶 Jōkei *mh*
$^{16}$融 Sadatō *m*, Sadaaki
親 Sadachika *m*
$^{17}$懐 Sadakane *m*
謙 Sadayoshi *m*
$^{18}$観 Jōgan 859–77
$^{20}$馨 Sadaka *m*
$^{21}$羅 Sadatsura *m*
$^{22}$懿 Sadayoshi *m*

## 9 T8

**昼** 983 [T] Akira *m*. (CHŪ, hiru, aki, akira)
飯 Hirui *sp*
間 Hiruma *s*

## 9 F2

**盾** 984 [T] (JUN, SHUN, TON, DON, tate)
夫 Tateo *m*

**厚** 985 [T] Atsushi *m-f*; Hiroshi *m*; Atsu *f*. (KŌ, atsu, hiro)
$^{2}$二 Kōji *m*
$^{3}$川 Atsukawa *s*
三 Kōzō *m*
$^{4}$木 Atsugi *sp*
$^{5}$比 Atsutomo *m*
田 Atsuta *p*
生 Atsunari *m*, Atsumi, Atsutaka
生新編 Kōsei shinpen
$^{6}$池 Atsuike *s* ⌊*lh*
吉 Kōkichi *m*
母 Atsumo *s*
$^{7}$沢 Atsuzawa *s*
沢部 Assabu *p*
見 Atsumi *s*
$^{8}$物咲 Atsumonozaki *l*
東 Kōtō *s*
$^{9}$狭 Atsusa *s*; Asa *p*
狭之介 Atsusanosuke
岸 Atsukeshi *p* ⌊*m*
$^{10}$真 Atsuma *p*
$^{13}$誉 Atsutake *s*

**風** 986 [T] (FŪ, FU, kaze, kaza)
$^{3}$土記 Fudoki *l*
土記逸文 F. itsubun *l*
$^{4}$戸 Kazado *s*
斗 Futo *s* ⌈kiku
$^{6}$吉 Kazakiri *s*, Kaza-
早 Kazahaya *s*
$^{7}$花 Kazahana *s*
至 Fushi *s*, Fukeshi
見 Kazami *s* ⌈*ml*
来山人 Fūrai Sanjin
$^{8}$知草 Fuchisō *l*
$^{9}$俗文選 Fūzoku monzen *l*
巻 Kazamaki *s*
巻景次郎 K. Keijirō
岡 Kazaoka *s* ⌊*ml*
$^{10}$連 Fūren *p*
$^{11}$流仏 Fūryūbutsu *l*
流志道軒伝 Fūryū Shidōken-den *l*
流曾我 F. Soga *l*
流微塵蔵 F. mijinzō *l*
流踊 F. odori *a*
流懺法 F. senbō *l*
祭 Kazamatsuri *s*
$^{12}$琴調一節 Fūkin shirabe no hitofushi *l*
間 Kazama *s*
間浦 Kazamaura *p*
$^{13}$雅集 Fūgashū *l*
葉集 Fūyōshū *l*

**岡** 987 Oka *s*. (KŌ, oka)
$^{3}$川 Okagawa *s*
上 Okanoue *s*, Okagami, Okanobori
$^{4}$戸 Okado *s*
元 Okamoto *s*
内 Okauchi *s*
山 Okayama *sp*
井 Okai *s*
太夫 Oka-dayū *l*
$^{5}$永 Okanaga *s*
右衛門 Okaemon *m*
平 Okahira *s*
田 Okada *s* ⌈*fl*
田八千代 O. Yachiyo
田三郎 O. Saburō *ml*
田三郎助 O. Saburōsuke *ma*
田啓介 O. Keisuke *mh*
本 Okamoto *s* ⌈*fl*
本かの子 O. Kanoko
本大無 O. Daimu *ml*
本文弥 O. Bun'ya *ma*
本圭岳 O. Keigaku *ml*
本松浜 O. Shōhin *ml*
本起泉 O. Kisen *ml*
本潤 O. Jun *ml*
本霊華 O. Reika *ml*
本綺堂 O. Kidō *ml*
本癖三酔 O. Hekisansui *ml*
本巌 O. Iwao *ml*
$^{6}$地 Okaji *s*
宅 Okayake *s*, Oiyake
西 Okanishi *s*
$^{7}$沢 Okazawa *s*
沢秀虎 O. Hidetora *ml*
村 Okamura *s*
村柿紅 O. Shikō *ml*
谷 Okaya *sp*; Okatani
安 Okayasu *s* ⌊*s*
芹 Okaseri *s*
尾 Okao *s*
見 Okami *s*
出 Okade *s*
$^{8}$波 Okanami *s*
林 Okabayashi *s*
$^{9}$信 Okanobu *s*
垣 Okagaki *p*
松 Okamatsu *s*
$^{10}$倉 Okakura *s*
倉天心 O. Tenshin *mla* ⌈ru *p*
原 Okahara *s*; Okaha-
庭 Okaniwa *s*
$^{11}$添 Okazoe *s*
根 Okane *s*
野 Okano *s*
野他家夫 O. Takeo *ml*
野知十 O. Chijū *ml*
野直七郎 O. Naoshichirō *ml*
部 Okabe *sp*
埜 Okano *s*
島 Okajima *s* ⌈*ml*
鬼太郎 Oka Onitarō
$^{12}$崎 Okazaki *sp*
崎正宗 O. Masamune *ma* ⌈*ml*
崎清一郎 O. Seiichirō
崎雪声 O. Sessei *ma*
崎義恵 O. Yoshie *ml*
$^{16}$橙里 Oka Tōri *ml*
橋 Okahashi *s*
$^{18}$麿 Okamaro *s*
$^{20}$麓 Oka Fumoto *ml*

**直** 988 [T] Naoshi *m*, Naoki, Tadashi, Tadasu, Sunao, Noburu; Atai *sm*; Atae *s*; Nao *f*. (CHOKU, JIKI, nao, tada, sugu, masa, naga, ma, chika, ne)
$^{1}$一 Naoichi *m*
$^{2}$二郎 Naojirō *m*
入 Naoiri *m-p*
人 Naoto *m*, Naondo, Masahito
$^{3}$川 Naokawa *p*
三 Naozō *m*
三郎 Naosaburō *m*
子 Naoko *f*
上 Nikami *s*
大 Naoki *m*
下 Nōge *s*, Mashimo
$^{4}$心 Naomi *m*
円 Naomitsu *m*
方 Naomasa *m*, Naomichi; Nōgata *sp*
夫 Tadao *m*
井 Naoi *s*
木 Naoki *s* ⌈*ml*
木三十五 N. Sanjūgo
太 Naota *m*
太郎 Naotarō *m*
$^{5}$旧 Naohisa *m*, Nao-
田 Suguta *s* ⌊moto

平 Naohira *m*
矢 Naoya *m*
四郎 Naoshirō *m*
生 Naoki *m*
6次郎 Naojirō *m*
江 Naoe *s*
江津 Naoetsu *p*
吉 Naokichi *m*
交 Naotomo *m*
有 Naomochi *m*
気 Tadaoki *m*
成 Sugunari *m*, Naganari
世 Tadayo *s*
7村 Naomura *s*
助 Naosuke *m*
応 Naotaka *m*
見 Naomi *m*; Nasumi *s*
臣 Naomi *m*
孝 Naotaka *m*
8服 Naokoto *m*
知 Naotoshi *m*
幸 Naohide *m*
秀 Naohide *m*
良 Naoyoshi *m*
9胖 Naohiro *m*
故 Naomoto *m*
計 Naokazu *m*
法 Naonori *m*
治 Naoharu *m*, Naoji
治郎 Naojirō *m*
映 Naomitsu *m*
昭 Naoteru *m*
政 Naomasa *m*
亮 Naosuke *m*, Naoyoshi
柔 Naotō *m*
風 Makaze *m*
彦 Naohiko *m*
哉 Naochika *m*
10浩 Naoharu *m*
桓 Naotaka *m*
称 Naomitsu *m*
俊 Naotoshi *m*
候 Naotoki *m*, Naoyoshi
毘霊 Naobi no mitama *l*
原 Jikihara *s*, Yukihara
馬 Naoma *m*
11陳 Naotsura *m*
砥 Naoto *m*
躬 Naomoto *m*
惇 Naoatsu *m*
惟 Naonobu *m*
康 Naoyoshi *m*
12島 Naoshima *p*
随 Naoyuki *m*
温 Naoatsu *m*, Naoharu
椋 Tadakura *s*
期 Naosane *m*
富 Naohisa *m*
道 Naomichi *m*, Tadaji
13雄 Suguo *m*
幹 Naomi *m*
義 Tadayoshi *m*
廉 Naokiyo *m*
14憧 Naonori *m*
徳 Naonori *m*, Naoe
禔 Naoyoshi *m*
静 Naoyasu *m*
15諒 Naoaki *m*, Naomasa
愈 Naoyasu *m*
熊 Naokuma *m*
蔵 Naozō *m*
16橘 Naokichi *m*
穎 Naotoshi *m*
養 Naonobu *m*, Naokai
19識 Naotsune *m*
21纒 Naotada *m*
彝 Naonori *m*

## 9 F3

**屎** 989 (SHIN, KI, kuso)

**囿** 990 (YŪ, U, sono, aze)

**画** 991 [T] Egaki *s*. (GA, KAKU, egaki)
部 Egakibe *s*

**度** See 1009

**底** 992 [T] Hagemi *s*. (TEI, sada, fuka)

**追** 993 [T] (TSUI, oi)
川 Oikawa *s*
分 Oiwake *p*

**廻** 994 Mawari *s*. (KAI, E, nori)
間 Hazama *s*

**建** 995 [T] Takeru *sm*; Takeshi *m*, Tatsuru. (KEN, KAN, take, tate, tatsu)
3川 Tatekawa *s*
久 Kenkyū 1190–99
4仁 Kennin 1201–04
仁寺 Kenninji *p*
5礼門院 Kenrei Mon'in *fh*
礼門院右京大夫集 K. M. Ukyō-dayū shū *l*
永 Ken'ei 1206–07
石 Tateishi *s*
8武 Kenmu 1334–38
武年間記 K. nenkanki *l*
9城 Tateki *m*
保 Kenpō 1213–19
治 Kenji 1275–78
治新式 K. shinshiki *l*
長 Kenchō 1249–56
長寺 Kenchōji *p*
10桁 Taketa *s*
畠 Tatebatake *s*
通 Tatemichi *m*
11野 Tateno *s*
部 Takebe *sp*; Tatebe *s*, Takerube
部綾足 Takebe no Ayatari *ml*
12陽 Yuya *s*
14徳 Kentoku 1370–72
暦 Kenryaku 1211–13
16樹 Tateki *m*
18顕 Takeaki *m*
麿 Takemaro *m*

## 9 F4

**咫** 996 (SHI, ta, take)

**眉** 997 (BI, mayu)

**南** See 912

**看** 998 [T] Akira *m*. (KAN, mitsu, miru, mi)

**迦** 999 (KA)
具土 Kagu tsuchi *l*

**迢** 1000 (CHŌ, tō, haru)
子 Haruko *f*

**迪** 1001 Susumu *m*, Tadasu. (TEKI, michi, hira, fumi)
一郎 Michiichirō *m*
怜 Michisato *m*

## 9 F5

**圀** 1002 See 国 745

**咸** 1003 (KAN, mina, shige, sane)
子 Minako *f*
陽宮 Kan'yōkyū *la*

**昶** 1004 Akira *m*, Itaru, Sakan, Tōru. (CHŌ, aki, teru, tō, nobu, hisa)
夫 Hisao *m*
光 Nobuteru *m*
彦 Teruhiko *m*
恵 Akie *f*

**為** 1005 [T] (I, tame, nari, yoshi, su, ta, yuki, chi, sada, shige, suke, yori)
3三郎 Tamesaburō *m*
之介 Tamenosuke *m*
子 Tameko *f*
4介 Tamesuke *m*
太郎 Tametarō *m*
5功 Yoshikoto *m*
示 Tami *m*
永 Tamenaga *sm*
永春水 T. Shunsui *ml*
兄 Tamesaki *m*
生 Tameo *m*
氏 Tameuji *ml*
6守 Tamemori *m*
吉 Tamekichi *m*
名 Ina *s*
7我井 Tamegai *s*
8知 Tametsugu *m*
実 Tamenori *m*
奈 Ina *s*
定 Tamesada *m*
学 Tametaka *m*
居 Tameyori *m*
9浄 Tamekiyo *m*
相 Tamesuke *m*
是 Tameyuki *m*
栄 Tameyoshi *m*, Tamehisa
貞 Tamesada *m*
10修 Tamenao *m*
家 Tameie *ml*
恭 Tameyasu *m*, Tamechika
造 Tamezō *m*
兼 Tamekane *m*

契負貞昼盾厚風岡直▼屎囿画度底追廻建咫眉南看迦迢迪圀咸昶為▲哉彦勊度門韭者長省飛

兼和歌抄 T. wakashō *l*
[11]理 Tamemasa *m*, Tamesuke
紀 Tamemoto *m*
逸 Tameyasu *m*
隆 Tameshige *m*
[12]貴 Tameyoshi *m*
善 Tametaru *m*
遂 Tamenaru *m*
[13]暄 Tamenobu *m*
禎 Tametomo *m*
義 Tameyoshi *m*
寛 Tamechika *m*
[14]歌可 Ikaga *s*
適 Tameatsu *m*

——9 F6——

哉 1006 [N] Hajime *m.* (SAI, ya, chika, ei, ka, suke, toshi, kana, ki)
女 Kaname *f*

彦 1007 [N] Hiko *m.* (GEN, hiko, yoshi, o, yasu, sato, hiro)
一 Hikoichi *m*
九郎 Hikokurō *m*
三 Hikozō *m*, Yasuko
三郎 Hikosaburō *m*
士 Hikotada *m*
久保 Hikokubo *s*
石 Hikoishi *m*
正 Yoshimasa *m*
田 Hikoda *s*
次郎 Hikojirō *m*
坂 Hikosaka *s*
助 Hikosuke *m*
兵 Hikohyō *m*
松 Hikomatsu *m*
昴 Hikoaki *m*
家 Hikoya *s*
馬 Hikoma *m*
根 Hikone *sp*
部 Hikobe *s*
衛 Hikoe *m*

——9 F7-8——

勉 1008 Tsutomu *m*, Tsuyoshi.

度 1009 [T[ Wataru *m.* (DO, nori, tada, watara, naga, nobu, michi, moro)
正 Norimasa *m*
会 Watarai *sp*; Watarae *s*
道 Tadamichi *m*
羅 Dora / Tora *ph* "Thailand?"
羅楽 D. / T. gaku *a*

門 1010 (SAN, SEN, kado)

——9 U——

韭 1011 See 韮 1728

者 1012 See 者 769

長 See 939

省 1013 [T] Habuku *m*, Sei, Akira. (SHŌ, SEI, SEN, mi, kami, yoshi, miru)
三 Shōzō *m*, Seizō
三郎 Shōzaburō *m*
市 Shōichi *m*
江 Yoshie *f*
吾 Seigo *m*
輔 Shōsuke *m*
蔵 Shōzō *m*

飛 1014 [T] (HI, tobi, taka)
[4]山 Tobiyama *s*
[5]永 Tobinaga *s*, Hinaga
田 Tobita *s*, Hida
[7]志 Tobishi *s*
来 Hirai *s*
[11]梅千句 Tobiume senku *l*
島 Tobishima *p*; Hishima *s*
鳥 Asuka *sp*
鳥川 A.-gawa *la*
鳥井 Asukai *sp*
鳥井雅経 A. Masatsune *ml*
鳥井雅親 A. Masachika *ml*
鳥寺 Asukadera *p*
鳥清御原宮 Asuka no Kiyomihara-no-miya *ph*
鳥清御原律令 A. no K. ritsuryō *h*
鳥部 Asukabe *s*
[13]塚 Hizuka *s*
弾 Hida *s*
弾瀬 Hidase *s*
雲 Tobikumo *s*; Hiun *l*
越 Tobikoe *l*
[14]鳴 Hita *s*
[15]鋪 Hijiki *s*
[22]騨 Hida *ph*

禹 1015 (U, nobu)
子 Nobuko *f*
昌 Nobumasa *m*

乗 1016 [T] Yotsunoya *s.* (JŌ, SHŌ, nori, shige, aki)
木 Nogi *s*
付 Noritsuke *s*
竹 Noritake *s*
寿 Norikazu *m*
命 Noritoshi *m*
津彦 Noritsuhiko *m*
杉 Norisugi *s*
秩 Noritsune *m*
紀 Noritada *m*
統 Noritsuna *m*
蘊 Norimori *m*

重 1017 [T] Shigeru *m*, Shige, Shigeshi, Atsushi, Kasanu, Omoshi, Katashi; Chō *sm.* (JŪ, CHŌ, JU, shige, e, atsu, kazu, nobu, fusa)
[1]一 Shigekazu *m*
[2]九郎 Chōkurō *m*
[3]之 Shigeyuki *ml*
久 Shigehisa *sm*
[4]仁 Shigesane *m*
元 Shigemoto *sm*
五郎 Jūgorō *m*
太 Shigemoto *m*
太郎 Jūtarō *m*
山 Shigeyama *s*
[5]旧 Shigehisa *m*
功 Shigekatsu *m*
右衛門 Jūemon *m*
田 Shigeta *s*
平 Jūhei *m*
末 Shigesue *sm*
本 Shigemoto *sm*
[6]任 Shigeto *m*
地 Shigeji *s*
行 Shigetsura *m*
次 Shigeji *m*, Shigetsugu
次郎 Jūjirō *m*
吉 Jūkichi *m*
光 Shigemitsu *sm*; Shigeteru *m*
成 Shigenari *m*
老 Shigeoyu *m*
[7]村 Shigemura *s*
助 Jūsuke *m*
近 Shigechika *m*
里 Shigesato *m*
見 Shigemi *s*
臣 Shigeomi *m*
[8]枝 Shigeeda *s*
幸 Shigeyuki *m*
舎 Shigeie *m*
宝 Shigetomi *m*
昌 Shigemasa *m*
忠 Shigetada *m*
迪 Shigemichi *m*
[9]信 Shigenobu *sm-p*
松 Shigematsu *s*, Kasamatsu
政 Shigemasa *m*
昴 Shigetake *m*
音 Shigene *m*
栄 Shigehide *m*
岡 Shigeoka *s*
直 Shigenao *m*
厚 Shigeatsu *m*
彦 Shigehiko *m*
哉 Shigeya *m*
[10]訓 Shigenori *m*
栖 Shigesu *s*
格 Shigenori *m*
容 Shigekata *m*
帯 Shigeyo *m*
要 Shigetoshi *m*
恭 Shigeyuki *m*, Shigenori
原 Shigehara *s*
威 Shigetaka *m*, Shigenori
[11]険 Shigenori *m*
理 Shigemichi *m*
隆 Shigetaka *m*
野 Shigeno *s*
教 Shigemichi *m*
盛 Shigemori *sm-p*; Shigetomi *m*
進 Shigeyuki *m*
[12]陽 Shigeaki *m*
富 Shigetomi *s*
森 Shigemori *s*
喜 Shigeki *m*
量 Kazushige *m*
然 Shigenari *m*
道 Shigemichi *m*
[13]靖 Shigenobu *m*
雄 Shigeo *m*

源 Chōgen *mh*
溥 Shigehiro *m*
茲 Shigekore *m*
廉 Shigekado *m*
遠 Shigetō *m*
[14]徳 Shigenori *m*
[16]隣 Shigechika *m*
樹 Shigeki *m*
親 Shigechika *m*
憙 Shigeyoshi *m*
凞 Shigeteru *m*
憲 Shigetoshi *m*
[17]鴻 Shigehiro *m*
[18]鎌 Shigekane *m*
齢 Shigeyo *m*
巖 Shigesato *m*

—10 L1—

**帰** 1018 [T] (KI, moto, yori, kaeri, ki)
山 Kaeriyama *s*, Kiyama
光 Yorimitsu *m*
厚 Motoatsu *m*
度 Kido *s*

—10 L2—

**虓** 1019 Takeshi *m.* (KŌ, KYŌ)

**凉** 1020 Suzushi *m.* (RYŌ)

**凊** 1021 Suzushi *m.* (SEI, SHŌ)

**凌** 1022 Shinogu *m.* (RYŌ)
雲集 Ryōunshū *l*

**准** 1023 [T] (JUN, SHUN, nori)
子 Noriko *f*

**倞** 1024 Tsuyoshi *m.* (RYŌ, KYŌ)

**倍** 1025 [T] (BAI, masu, yasu)
一 Masuichi *m*
夫 Masuo *m*
男 Yasuo *m*
造 Masuzō *m*

**俶** 1026 Hajime *m.* (SHUKU, yoshi, hide)
子 Yoshiko *f*
男 Yoshio *m*
躬 Yoshimi *m*

**倬** 1027 Akira *m.* (TAKU, aki, tsuna)
男 Akio *m*

**倶** 1028 (KU, tomo, hiro, moro)
利加羅 Kurikara *ph*
志 Tomoshi *m*
知安 Kutchan *p*

**候** 1029 [T] Miyo *f.* (KŌ, KU, toki, yoshi, soro)
兵衛 Sorobee *m*

**倢** 1030 (SHŌ, tsugu)

**倩** 1031 (SEI, SHŌ, yoshi, tsura)
孝 Yoshisue *m*
郎 Yoshirō *m*

**借** 1032 [T] (SHAKU, kari, karu)
屋 Kariya *s*
馬 Karume *s*

**倚** 1033 (KI, I, yori, mochi, kane, kanu)
子 Yoriko *f*
男 Yorio *m*

**倦** 1034 (KEN)
鳥 Kenchō *l*

**俟** 1035 (SHI, JI, KI, GI, machi, matsu)
子 Machiko *f*, Matsuko

**俳** 1036 [T] (HAI)
人蕪村 Haijin Buson *l*
文 Haibun *l*
句 Haiku *l*
星 Haisei *l*
諧 Haikai *l*
諧七部集 H. shichibushū *l*
諧大句数 H. ōkukazu *l*
諧次韻 H. jiin *l*
諧武玉川 H. Mutamagawa *l*
諧亭句楽 Haikaitei kuraku *la*
諧連歌抄 Haikai rengashō *l*
諧馬の糞 H. uma no kuso *l*
諧御傘 H. gozan *l*

**倫** 1037 Hitoshi *m*, Osamu. (RIN, RON, tomo, michi, tsune, nori, toshi, hito, moto, tsugu, shina)
子 Tomoko *f*
方 Tsunekata *m*
太郎 Rintarō *m*
正 Michimasa *m*
明 Michiaki *m*
枝 Norie *f*
治 Tomoharu *m*
彦 Tomohiko *m*
敦 Rondon *p* "London"
敦塔 R.-tō *l*

**修** 1038 Osamu *m*, Shū, Nagashi, Nagaki, Atsumu, Yoshimi. (SHŪ, SHU, osa, naga, hisa, michi, nobu, nao, sane, nori, masa, yoshi, yasu, moto, moro)
[1]一 Shūichi *m*
[2]二 Shūji *m*
[3]三 Shūzō *m*
之 Yoshiyuki *m*
[4]文 Hisafumi *m*
夫 Osao *s*
[6]吉 Shūkichi *m*
[7]男 Nobuo *m*
身 Osami *m*
[9]美 Nagatomi *m*
[10]造 Shūzō *m*
郎 Michirō *m*
[11]理 Shuri *m*
理亮 Shurinosuke *m*
[12]善寺 Shuzenji *p*
道 Nagamichi *m*
[13]禅寺 Shuzenji *la*

**俊** 1039 [T] Suguru *m*, Masaru, Takashi, Masari, Satoshi. (SHUN, toshi, yoshi)
[3]子 Toshiko *f*
士 Toshio *m*
久 Toshihisa *m*, Toshinaga
丸 Toshimaru *m*
[4]六郎 Shunrokurō *m*
太郎 Shuntarō *m*
平 Shunpei *m*
夫 Toshio *m*, Yoshio
[6]次 Toshitsugu *m*
吉 Shunkichi *m*
成 Toshinari *m-ml*; Shunzei *ml*
成女 T. no Musume *fl*
成忠度 Shunzei Tadanori *la*
成卿女集 Toshinari-kyō / Shunzei-kyō no Musume no shū *l*
[7]吾 Shungo *m*
助 Shunsuke *m*
位 Toshihira *m*
作 Shunsaku *m*
完 Toshisada *m*
玄 Toshishizu *m*
寿 Toshihisa *m*
[8]芿 Shunjō *mh*
[9]迪 Toshihira *m*
信 Toshinobu *m*, Toshisane
弥 Toshiya *m*
政 Toshimasa *m*
彦 Toshihiko *m*
[10]将 Toshinobu *m*
郎 Toshirō *m*
恵 Shun'e *ml*
馬 Toshime *m*
[11]章 Toshiaya *m*
基 Toshimoto *m*
[12]順 Toshimune *m*
程 Toshinori *m*
[13]雄 Toshio *m*, Toshitake
寛 Shunkan *mh-la*
義 Toshiyoshi *m*
豊 Toshimori *m*
[15]蔵 Shunzō *m*
[16]親 Toshinaru *m*
頼 Toshiyori *m-ml*; Shunrai *ml*
頼口伝集 T. kudenshū *l*
頼無名抄 T. mumyōshō *l*
頼髄脳 T. zuinō *l*
賢 Toshiyoshi *m*
[17]懋 Toshimasa *m*, Toshiyoshi

—10 L3—

**将** 1040 [T] Susumu *m*, Tasuku,

度 門 韭 者 長 省 飛 禹 乗 重 ▼ 帰 虓 凉 凊 凌 准 倞 倍 俶 倬 倶 候 倢 倩 借 倚 倦 俟 俳 倫 修 俊 将 ▲ 埋 捍 挾 按 唄 咄 唁 徒 徐 従

Tadashi, Tamotsu, Hitoshi. (SHŌ, sō, masa, hata, mochi, nobu, yuki)
之助 Hatanosuke *m*
吉 Shōkichi *m*
志 Masayuki *m*
応 Masanori *m*
門 Masakado *m*
門記 M.-ki / Shōmonki *l*
軍 Ikusanokimi *s*
愛 Masachika *m*
監 Shōkan *m*

埋 1041 [T] (MAI, BAI, ume, uzu)
忠 Umetada *sm*
橋 Uzuhashi *s*

捍 1042 Mamoru *m.* (KAN, mori)

挾 1043 (KYŌ, GYŌ, sashi, mochi)
間 Hasama *sp*

按 1044 (AN)
察 Azechi *sfl-ph*
察使 Azechi *mh*

唄 1045 [I] (BAI, uta)
子 Utako *f*

咄 1046 (TOTSU, hanashi)
本 Hanashibon *l*

唁 1047 Hoki *s*, Negi. (GEN, GON)

徒 1048 [T] (TO, kachi, tada, tomo)
然草 Tsurezuregusa *l*

徐 1049 [T] Jo *s.* (JO, SHO, yasu, yuki)
子 Yasuko *f*
江 Yasue *f*

従 1050 [T] (JŪ, SHŌ, JU, tsugu, yori, shige)
尹 Shigekazu *m*
正 Yorimasa *m*
者 Shitori *s*
者部 Shitoribe *s*
矩 Tsugunori *m*
道 Tsugumichi *m*
徳 Jūtoku *m*

悍 1051 Isamu *m.* (KAN, GAN)

恨 1052 [T] (KON)
の介 Urami no Suke *l*

悟 1053 [T] Satoru *m*, Satoshi, Sato. (GO, sato, nori)
一 Goichi *m*
里 Satori *m*

悦 1054 [O] (ETSU, ECHI, yoshi, nobu)
二郎 Etsujirō *m*
久 Nobuhisa *m*
太郎 Etsutarō *m*
目抄 Etsumokushō *l*
次 Etsuji *m*
耳 Yoshimi *m*
蔵 Etsuzō *m*

院 1055 [T] (IN)
内 Innai *p*
本物 Maruhonmono *a*
相 Innosō *s*

陣 1056 [T] Jin *s.* (JIN, CHIN, buru, tsura)
内 Jinnouchi *s*, Jinnai
野 Jinno *s*

陞 1057 Noboru *m*, Susumu. (SHŌ, nori)

降 1058 [T] (KŌ, GŌ, furi, furu, ri)
矢 Furuya *s*
旗 Furihata *s*
幡 Furihata *s*

除 1059 [T] (JO, CHO, JI, kiyo, saru, noki, yoke, yoki)
村 Yokemura *s*, Yokimura
村吉太郎 Yokimura Yoshitarō *ml*

涉 1060 See 渉 1331

涓 1061 Tōru *m.* (KEN)

涙 1062 [T] (RUI)
痕 Ruikon *l*

浰 1063 Toshi *m.* (RI, toshi)
太 Toshiyasu *m*

浴 1064 [T] Yuami *s*, Ami. (YOKU, yuami, ami, yuki)
永 Yukinaga *s*
部 Yuamibe *s*, Amibe

涌 1065 (YŪ, waki, waku, waka)
子 Wakiko *f*, Wakuko
井 Wakui *s*; Waku i *l*
田 Wakuda *s*
別 Yūbetsu *p*
谷 Wakuya *p*
島 Wakushima *s*
喜 Yūki *s*

酒 1066 [T] Saka *s.* (SHU, saka, sake, mi)
ほがい Sakahogai *l*
[2]人 Sakato *s*, Sakai
[3]川 Sakagawa *s*
上 Sakanoe *s*
[4]介 Sakaji *s*
匂 Sakō *s*
井 Sakai *s*
井田 Sakaida *s*
井田柿右衛門 S. Kakiemon *ma*
井広治 Sakai Hiroji *ml*
井抱一 S. Hōitsu *mla*
[5]本 Sakamoto *s*
匂 Sakawa *sp*; Sakō *s*
田 Sakata *p*
[6]向 Sakamuki *s*, Sakawa, Sakō
西 Susai *s*
[7]作 Sakatoko *s*
君 Sakenokimi *m*
出 Sakade *s*
見 Sakami *s*
[8]居 Sakai *s*
良 Sakara *s*
[9]依 Sakayori *s*
巻 Sakamaki *s*
泉 Sakaizumi *s*
看都 Sakamitsu *s*
[10]酒井 Suzui *s*; Shisui *p*
[11]部 Sakabe *s*
寄 Sakayori *s*
麻呂 Sakamaro *m*
[12]喜男 Mikio *m*
[13]葉 Sakaba *s*
[20]顛童子 Shuten dōji *l*

浦 1067 [T] Ura *s.* (HO, FU, ura, ra)
[3]川 Urakawa *s*
川原 Urakawara *p*
口 Uraguchi *s*
上 Uragami *s*
[4]山 Urayama *s*
井 Urai *s*
木 Uraki *s*
[5]辺 Urabe *s*
田 Urata *s*
本 Uramoto *s*
[6]臼 Urausu *p*
名 Urana *s*
[7]沢 Urasawa *s*
谷 Uraya *s*, Uratani
安 Urayasu *p*
[8]河 Urakawa *p*
和 Urawa *p*
[9]松 Uramatsu *s*
岡 Uraoka *s*
[11]野 Urano *s*
部 Urabe *s*
鬼 Hoki *s*
島 Urashima *s*
島子伝 U.-go no den *l*
[12]崎 Urasaki *s*
[13]幌 Urahoro *p*
[19]瀬 Urase *s*

浩 1068 [N] Hiroshi *m*, Isamu, Yutaka, Ōi, Kiyoshi; Kō *s.* (KŌ, GŌ, hiro, haru)
一郎 Kōichirō *m*
二 Kōji *m*
子 Hiroko *f*
佑 Kōsuke *m*
洋 Hiroumi *sm*, Hirōmi
運 Hiroyuki *m*

浮 1069 [T] (FU, uki, chika)
[5]穴 Ukena *s*
田 Ukita *s* ⌈*ml*
田和民 U. Kazutami
田秀家 U. Hideie *ml*
[6]羽 Ukiha *p*
気 Fuke *s*
名 Ukena *s*
舟 Ukifune *la*
世床 Ukiyo-doko *l*
世草子 U.-zōshi *l*
世風呂 U.-buro *l*
世道中膝栗毛 U. dōchū hizakurige *l*
世絵 U.-e *a*
世親仁形気 U. oyaji katagi *l*
[7]貝 Ukigai *s*
[11]島 Ukishima *s*
[14]標 Bui *la*

浜 1070 [T] Hama *s*. (HIN, hama)
[3]川 Hamagawa *s*
口 Hamaguchi *s*
口雄幸 H. Osachi *mh*
[4]中 Hamanaka *sp*
井 Hamai *s*
[5]北 Hamakita *sp*
辺 Hamabe *s*
田 Hamada *sp* ⌈*ml*
田広介 H. Hirosuke
本 Hamamoto *s*
本浩 H. Hiroshi *ml*
[6]地 Hamaji *s*
池 Hamanoike *s*
成 Hamanari *m*
西 Hamanishi *s*
名 Hamana *sp*
[7]坂 Hamasaka *p*
村 Hamamura *s*
村米蔵 H. Yonezō *ml*
谷 Hamatani *s*, Ha-
尾 Hamao *s* ⌊maya
臣 Hamaomi *m*
[9]松 Hamamatsu *sp*
松納中言 H. Chūnagon *l*
岡 Hamaoka *sp*
[10]高屋 Hamatake *s*, Hamadaki
益 Hamamasu *p*
屋 Hamaya *s*
[11]野 Hamano *s*
部 Hamabe *s*
島 Hamajima *sp*
[12]崎 Hamasaki *sp*
崎玉島 H. Tamashima *p* ⌈*p*
[14]頓別 Hamatonbetsu

海 1071 [T] Ama *s*. (KAI, umi, mi, ama, una)
ノ屋 Uminoya *s*
[2]人 Ama *la* ⌈mo *l*
人の刈藻 A. no karu-
人彦 Amahiko *m*
[3]上 Unagami *s*
上胤平 U. Tanehira
士 Ama *sp-la* ⌊*ml*
士名 Amana *s*
[4]山 Miyama *p*
犬甘 Amanoinukai *s*
犬養 Amainukai *s*
[5]北 Kaihō *s*, Kaihoku
北友松 Kaihō Yūshō
辺 Kaibe *s* ⌊*ma*
田 Umida *s*; Kaita *sp*
平 Umihei *m*
[6]江田 Umieda *s*, Ka-
老 Ebi *s* ⌊ieda
老名 Ebina *sp*
老名弾正 E. Danjō *mh*
老原 Ebihara *s*
老島 Ebijima *s*
老塚 Ebizuka *s*
[7]住 Kaizumi *s*
谷 Kaiya *s*
[8]沼 Kainuma *s*
宝 Kaihō *s* ⌈dan *h*
国兵談 Kaikoku hei-
東 Kaitō *s*
[9]神丸 Kaijinmaru *l*
保 Kaiho *s*, Kaibo
保青陵 Kaiho Seiryō
法保 Kaihō *s* ⌊*mh*
津 Kaizu *sp*
松 Umimatsu *s*
松子 Miruko *f*
南 Kainan *p* [" Hai-
草 Kaisō *p* ⌊nan "]
音 Kaion *ml*
音寺 Kaionji *s*
音寺潮五郎 K. Chōgorō *ml*
[10]祇 Watatsumi *s*
原 Unabara *s*
[11]後 Kaigo *s*
紅 Kaikō *l*
野 Unno *s*, Uchino
野口 Unnokuchi *s*
部 Kaibu *sp*, Amabe, Ama; Kaibe *s*, Amabu
[12]渡 Kaito *s*, Kairo
崎 Kaizaki *s*
賀 Kaiga *s*
道 Kaidō *s*
道記 Kaidōki *l*
[13]塚 Kaizuka *s*
雄 Umio *m*
[14]語 Amagatari *s*
[15]潮音 Kaichōon *l*
[18]藤 Kaidō *s*
[19]瀬 Kaise *s*

## 10 L4

弭 1072 (BI, yasu)
田 Hatta *s*
間 Hazuma *s*

旅 1073 [T] (RYO, RO, tabi, taka, ⌊moro)
人 Tabito *m*
川 Tabigawa *s*
子 Tabiko *f*
順 Ryojun *p* "Port Arthur"

祥 1074 [T] (SHŌ, JŌ, yoshi, sachi, naga, tada, yasu, saka, akira, saki, samu)
三 Yoshikazu *m*
子 Yoshiko *f*
次 Yasutsugu *m*
光 Samumitsu *m*
男 Yoshio *m*
枝 Sakae *f*
哉 Yoshichika *m*
雲 Sakumo *s*, Nagumo
瑞五郎太夫 Shonzui Gorō-tayū *ma*
樹 Yoshiki *m*

班 1075 [T] (HAN, tsura, mi)
女 Hanjo *la*

珉 1076 Tama *f*. (MIN, BIN, tami)
子 Tamiko *f*

珠 1077 [T] Tama *f*. (SHU, tama, mi)
一 Shuichi *m*
洲 Suzu *p*; Suku *s*
流河 Suruga *s*
琉河 Suruga *s*
輝 Tamaki *f*
璣 Tamaki *m*
鶴 Suzu *f*

峡 1078 [T] Hazuma *s*. (KYŌ)

峆 1079 Takashi *m*. (GŌ, KŌ)

岷 1080 (MIN, BIN)
江入楚 Mingō nisso *l*

峠 1081 [T] Tōge *s*. (tōge)
三吉 T. Sankichi *ml*
田 Taoda *s*

胝 1082 Akagari *s*, Akagire. (CHI, SHI)

脇 1083 Waki *sf-p*. (KYŌ, KŌ, waki)
山 Wakiyama *s*
本 Wakimoto *s*
田 Wakida *s*
坂 Wakizaka *s*
沢 Wakizawa *s*
谷 Wakiya *s*
屋 Wakiya *s*
野 Wakino *s*
野沢 Wakinozawa *p*

晄 1084 See 晃 1189

晅 1085 (KEN, KAN, aki)
宣 Akinobu *m*

時 1086 [T] (JI, SHI, toki, yori, yoshi)
[3]川 Tokigawa *s*
三郎 Tokisaburō *m*
之 Yoshiyuki *m*
于 Tokiyuki *m*
万 Tokitsumu *m*
子 Tokiko *f*
[4]友 Tokitomo *s*
山 Tokiyama *s*
[5]田 Tokida *s*
[6]休 Tokiyasu *m*
次郎 Tokijirō *m*
任 Tokitō *s*

除 渉 涓 涙 浰 浴 涌 酒 浦 浩 ▼ 浮 浜 海 弭 旅 祥 班 珉 珠 峡 峆 岷 峠 胝 脇 晄 晅 時 ▲ 妍 姚 姑 姥 姶 始 栢 桟 栩 校

珠 峡 峆 峄 峠 胝 脇 晄 晅 時 ▼ 姸 姚 姞 姥 姶 始 栢 桟 栩 校 栂 株 格 桓 栖 桂 桐 桃 柳 ▲ 竝 袖 矩 眦 畔 砡 砧 破 秧 秝

広 Tokihiro *sm*
存 Tokiari *s*
名 Tokina *m* ⌈koto
[7]言 Tokikoto *m*, Yori-
沢 Tokizawa *s*
[8]枝 Tokieda *s*
枝誠記 T. Motoki *ml*
宗 Tokimune *m*
実 Tokizane *sm*
忠 Tokitada *m*
雨 Shigure *m-f*; Toki-
furu *m* ⌈tsu *l*
雨の炬燵 S. no kota-
雨子 Shigureko *f*
[9]津 Togitsu *p*
岡 Tokioka *s*
直 Tokinao *m*
重 Tokishige *sm*
[10]莘 Tokinaga *m*
原 Tokihara *s*
[11]敏 Tokitoshi *m*
[12]敬 Tokiyoshi *m*
[13]雄 Tokio *m*
[15]蔵 Tokizō *m*
[17]綱 Tokitsuna *m*
懋 Tokishige *m*

妍 1087 See 姸 612

姚 1088 (CHŌ, tao)
子 Taoko *f*

姞 1089 (KITSU, KICHI, yoshi)
子 Yoshiko *f*

姥 1090 (BO, MO, tome, oke, uba)
子 Tomeko *f*
沢 Ubayaki *s*

姶 1091 (Ō, ai)
良 Aira *sp*
罪 Aino *s*

始 1092 [T] Hajime *m.* (SHI, moto, tomo, haru)
男 Motoo *m*
彦 Motohiko *m*
関 Shiseki *s*

栢 1093 See 柏 866

桟 1094 See 棧 1615

栩 1095 Tote *s.* (KO, KU, U, tochi)
木 Tochigi *s*

校 1096 [T] (KŌ, KYŌ, toshi, nari, aze)
条 Menjō *s* ⌈*a*
倉造 Azekura-zukuri

栂 1097 (toga)
井 Togai *s*
坂 Togasaka *s*
野 Togano *s*

株 1098 [T] (SHU, moto, yori)
修 Motonobu *m*
徳 Motonori *m*

格 1099 [T] Tadashi *m*, Tadasu, Kaku, Tsutomu, Kiwame, Itaru. (KAKU, KYAKU, tada, nori, masa)
子 Noriko *f*
文 Tadafumi *m*
安 Tadayasu *m*

桓 1100 Takeshi *m.* (KAN, GAN, take, taka, uji)
千代 Takechiyo *f*
夫 Takeo *m*
武 Kanmu *mh*
武平氏 K. Heishi *h*
虎 Taketora *m*

栖 1101 (SEI, SAI, su, sumi)
千代 Sumichiyo *f*
本 Sumoto *p*
原 Suhara *s*
関 Suseki *s*

桂 1102 [N] Katsura *sm-f-p.* (KEI, KE, katsu, yoshi)
[3]小五郎 Katsura Kogorō *mh*
川 Katsuragawa *s*
川甫周 K. Hoshū *mh*
三 Keizō *m*
之助 Keinosuke *m*
[4]山 Katsurayama *s*
井 Katsurai *s*
夫 Yoshio *m*
太郎 Katsura Tarō *mh*
[5]田 Katsurada *s*
[6]吉 Keikichi *m*
[7]男 Katsuo *m*
[11]野 Katsurano *s*
庵玄樹 Keian Genju
*ml* ⌈*pa*
[20]離宮 Katsura Rikyū

桐 1103 [N] (DŌ, TŌ, kiri, hisa)
ノ谷 Kirinoya *s*
ケ谷 Kirigaya *s*
[1]一葉 Kiri hitoha *la*
[3]子 Kiriko *f*
[4]山 Kiriyama *s*
木 Kiriki *s*
[5]田 Kirita *s*
生 Kiryū *sp*
生織 K. ori *a*
[6]竹 Kiritake *s*
[7]沢 Kirizawa *s*
村 Kirimura *s*
谷 Kiritani *s*, Kiriya, Kirigayatsu
[8]林 Kiribayashi *s*
[10]原 Kirihara *s*
[11]野 Kirino *s*
島 Kirishima *s*
[13]淵 Kiribuchi *s*
[14]壺 Kiritsubo *l*
[18]麿 Kirimaro *m*

桃 1104 [T] Momo *s.* (TŌ, momo)
[3]川 Momokawa *s*
子 Momoko *f*
丸 Momomaru *m*
[4]木 Momoki *s*
山 Momoyama *p*
山譚 M. monogatari *l*
井 Momoi *s*, Momonoi
井直詮 Momonoi Naoakira *ml*
太郎 Momotarō *m*
太郎侍 M.-zamurai *l*
[5]田 Momoda *s*
生 Momō *p*
[7]沢 Momozawa *s*
谷 Momoya *s*, Momotani
李 Momo-sumomo *l*
[9]香 Momoka *f*
[10]配 Momokubari *s*
原 Momohara *s*
[11]麻呂 Momomaro *m*
[13]源集 Tōgenshū *l*
園 Momozono *s*
[16]隣 Tōrin *ml*

柳 1105 [T] Yanagi *s.* (RYŪ, yanagi, yagi, yanai, yana)
[1]一 Ryūichi *m*
[3]川 Yanagawa *sp*
川春葉 Y. Shun'yō *ml*
下 Yanagishita *s*, Yagishita
下亭種員 Ryūkatei Tanekazu *ml*
[4]元 Yanagimoto *s*, Yagimoto
内 Yanagiuchi *s*
山 Yanayama *s*
井 Yanai *sp*
太郎 Ryūtarō *m*
[5]本 Yanagimoto *s*, Yagimoto
生 Yagyū *sp* ⌈*l*
生武芸帖 Y. bugeichō
田 Yanagida *sp*; Yanagita *s* ⌈nio *ml*
田国男 Yanagita Ku-
田泉 Y. Izumi *ml*
[6]多留 Yanagidaru *l*
[7]作 Ryūsaku *m*
沢 Yanagisawa *s*
沢吉保 Y. Yoshiyasu *mh*
沢健 Y. Ken *ml*
町 Yanagimachi *s*
谷 Yanadani *sp*; Yanagiya *s*
[8]沼 Yaginuma *s*
河 Yanagawa *s*
河春三 Y. Shunzō *ml*
宗悦 Yanagi Muneyoshi *ml*
[9]津 Yanaizu *p*
亭 Ryūtei *s* ⌈*ml*
亭種彦 R. Tanehiko
[10]倉 Yanagura *s*
原 Yanagihara *s*
原白蓮 Y. Byakuren *fl*
原極堂 Y. Kyokudō
屋 Yanagiya *s* ⌊*ml*
[11]梧 Ryūgo *m*
島 Yagishima *s*
[13]堀 Yanabori *s*
楽 Yagira *s*, Nadara

園 Yanagizono *sm*
[16]橋 Yanagibashi *s*
橋新詩 Ryūkyō shinshi *l*
樽 Yanagidaru *l*
[19]瀬 Yanase *s*

——10 L5——

竝 1106 See 並 765

袖 1107 Sode *f.* (SHŪ, JU, sode)
ヶ浦 Sodegaura *p*
子 Sodeko *f*
山 Sodeyama *s*
中抄 Shūchūshō *l*
香 Sodeka *f*
岡 Sodeoka *s*
浦 Sodeura *s*
島 Sodeshima *s*
崎 Sodezaki *s*

矩 1108 Tadasu *m,* Tadashi, Kane. (KU, nori, tsune, kane, kado)
夫 Tsuneo *m*
次 Noritsugu *m*
次郎 Tsunejirō *m*
随 Noriyuki *m*
最 Noriyoshi *m*

毗 1109 See 毘 1195

畔 1110 [T] Aze *s.* (HAN, kuro, aze, be)
上 Azegami *s,* Kuroue
田 Kuroda *s*
柳 Kuroyanagi *s,* Azeyanagi, Kuroyagi
高 Azetaka *s*
蒜 Azehiru *s,* Ahiru
蔵 Azekura *s,* Aze

珏 1111 Tadashi *m.* (GYOKU, GOKU)

砧 1112 Kinuta *m-la.* (CHIN, kinu)
子 Kinuko *f*

破 1113 [T] (HA)
切居 Hakii *s*

魔子 Hamako *f*

秧 1114 (ō, nae)

秢 1115 Minoru *m,* Yowai. (REI, RYŌ)

租 1116 [T] Mitsugi *m.* (SO, tsumi, moto)
地 Ochi *s*

秘 1117 [T] (HI)
楽 Higyō *l*

称 1118 [T] (SHŌ, mitsu, yoshi, kami, nori, na, agu)
徳 Shōtoku *fh*

秩 1119 [T] Satoshi *m.* (CHITSU, chichi, tsune)
父 Chichibu *sp*
父別 Chippubetsu *p*
夫 Chichio *m,* Tsuneo

祝 1120 See 祝 851

神 1121 See 神 853

祖 1122 See 祖 850

祐 1123 See 祐 852

祜 1124 (KO, GO, sachi)
子 Sachiko *f*

祓 1125 (FUTSU, HOCHI, kiyo, harai)
川 Haraigawa *s*

祚 1126 (SO, ZO, mura, toshi, sa)
景 Murakage *m*

祇 1127 (GI, KI, SHI, masa, nori, moto, kesa, tsumi)
子 Noriko *f*
文 Masafumi *m*

王 Giō *fa-la*
勝 Kesakatsu *m*
賀 Masanori *m*
園 Gion *sp*

——10 L6——

效 1128 See 効 653

耿 1129 Akira *m.* (KŌ, KYŌ, aki, suke)
子 Akiko *f*

師 1130 [T] Tsukasa *m*; Moro *s.* (SHI, moro, kazu, nori, moto, mitsu)
子 Shishi *s*; Motoko *f*
田 Morota *s*
宅 Moroie *m*
男 Moroo *m,* Norio
垂 Morotaru *m*
宣 Moronobu *ma*
香 Moroka *m*
岡 Morooka *s*
勝 Shikatsu *p*
錬 Shiren *mlh*

耕 1131 [T] Tsutomu *m,* Tagayasu, Osamu; Kō *sm.* (KŌ, KYŌ, yasu)
一 Kōichi *m*
二郎 Kōjirō *m*
三 Kōzō *m*
之介 Kōnosuke *m*
子 Yasuko *f*
太郎 Kōtarō *m*
作 Kōsaku *m*
治人 Kō Haruto *ml*
象 Kōzō *m*
雄 Yasuo *m*
雲 Kōun *ml*
輔 Kōsuke *m*
蔵 Kōzō *m*

粋 1132 [T] (SUI, kiyo, tada)
町甲閭 Suichō kōkei *l*

粉 1133 (FUN, ko)
川 Kogawa *s*
河 Kogawa *p*

虻 1134 (BŌ, abu)
田 Abuta *p*

蚊 1135 [T] (BUN, MON, ka)
相撲 Ka-zumō *la*
野 Kano *s*

航 1136 [T] Wataru *m.* (KŌ, GŌ)

般 1137 [T] (HAN, kazu, tsura)

殺 1138 [T] (SATSU, SETSU)
生石 Sesshōseki *la*
陣師 Tateshi *s*

殷 1139 (IN, taka, shige, tada, tomi, masa, moro)
一 Takaichi *m*
之 Takashi *m*
子 Takako *f*
根 Shigene *m*

——10 L7——

豹 1140 Hadara *m.* (HYŌ)
山 Hyōnosen *p*

配 1141 [T] (HAI, atsu)
子 Atsuko *f*

畝 1142 [O] Une *s.* (HO, BŌ, MO, une, se)
子 Uneko *f*
米 Unebe *s*
尾 Unebi *s,* Uneo
傍 Unebi *s*
傍山 Unebiyama *p*

財 1143 [T] Takara *sm-f.* (ZAI, SAI, takara)
田 Saita *p*
津 Zaitsu *s*
部 Takarabe *sp*
部彪 T. Takeshi *mh*

射 1144 [T] Iri *f.* (SHA, JA, i)
水 Imizu *p*
辻 Inotsuji *s*
兵衛 Ihee *m*
出 Ide *s*

桐 桃 柳 ▼ 竝 袖 矩 毗 畔 珏 砧 破 秧 秢 租 秘 称 秩 祝 神 祖 祐 祜 祓 祚 祇 效 耿 師 耕 粋 粉 虻 蚊 航 般 殺 殷 豹 配 畝 財 射 ▲ 郎 郡 訒

屋 Iya *s*, Iteya
場 Iba *s*
越 Inokoshi *s*

郎 1145 [T] (RŌ, o, ra, iratsuko)

郡 1146 [T] Kōri *s*, Gun. (GUN, KUN, kōri, kuni, sato, tomo)
上 Gujō *sp*; Kujō *s*
戸 Kunito *s*, Gūko, Kōdo
山 Kōriyama *sp*
司 Gunji *s*
孝 Kunitaka *m*
虎彦 Kōri Torahiko *ml*
東 Guntō *s*
昭 Kuniteru *m*
岡 Kōrioka *s*
家 Gūke *s*; Kōge *p*
場 Kōriba *s*
廉 Kunikiyo *m*
領 Kōrinomiyatsuko *s*

訒 1147 Shinobu *f*. (JIN, nobu, kata)

託 1147A [T] (TAKU, yori)
麻 Takuma *sp*
摩 Takuma *s*

訓 1148 [T] (KUN, KIN, kuni, nori, michi, toki, shiri)
三 Tokizō *m*
子 Kuniko *f*
子府 Kunneppu *p*
谷 Kuntani *s*
常 Noritsune *m*
儒麿 Kuzumaro *m*

記 1149 [T] Shirusu *m*. (KI, fumi, nori, toshi, nari, yoshi, fusa)
之 Noriyuki *m*
久 Norihisa *m*
彦 Fumihiko *m*
紀歌謡 Kiki kayō *l*

——10 L8——

勍 1150 Tsuyoshi *m*. (KEI, GYŌ)

剣 1151 [T] Tsutomu *m*. (KEN, haya, akira, tsurugi)
之助 Kennosuke *m*
持 Kenmotsu *s*
淵 Kenbuchi *p*

釗 1152 Tsutomu *m*. (SHŌ, KYŌ, toshi)

釟 1153 (HACHI, shō)
三郎 Hachisaburō *m*
次郎 Shōjirō *m*

釘 1154 (TEI, CHŌ, kugi)
宮 Kugimiya *s*
屋 Kugiya *s*
崎 Kugisaki *s*

針 1155 [T] Hari *f*. (SHIN, hari)
ケ谷 Harigatani *s*
本 Kugimoto *s*
生 Haryū *s*
生一郎 H. Ichirō *ml*
谷 Harigatani *s*
貝 Harigai *s*
金 Harigane *s*
重 Harishige *s*
屋 Hariya *s*
塚 Haritsuka *s*

——10 T1——

扇 1156 [T] (SEN, ōgi, mi)
田 Ōgida *s* ⌈tsu
谷 Ōgiya *s*, Ōgigaya-
迫 Ōgiba *s*, Ōgihaza-
畑 Ōgihata *s* ⌊ma
畑忠雄 Ō. Tadao *ml*

——10 T2——

脅 1157 See 脇 1083

冥 1158 (MEI, MYŌ, kura)
府 Yomi *l*
府山水図 Meifu sansuie *l*
途の飛脚 Meido no hikyaku *l*

食 1159 [T] Mike *s*. (SHOKU, SHIKI, ke, kura, uke, aki, mi-
満 Kema *sm-p* ⌊ke)

釜 1160 (FU, kama)
山 Fuzan *p* "Pusan"
井 Kamai *s*
石 Kamaishi *p*
田 Kamata *s*
次郎 Kamajirō *m*
范 Kamayatsu *s*, Kamayachi
屋 Kamaya *s*
萢 Kamayachi *s*

夏 1161 [T] (KA, GE, natsu)
井 Natsui *s*
木立 Natsu kodachi *l*
山 Natsuyama *s*
山繁樹 N. Shigeki *ml*
目 Natsume *s*
目成美 N. Seibi *ml*
目漱石 N. Sōseki *ml*
足 Nadase *sp*
花 Natsuhana *l*
花少女 Natsubana otome *l*
見 Natsumi *s*
秋 Natsuaki *s*, Nakaba
野 Natsuno *sm*
祭浪花鑑 Natsu-matsuri Naniwa kagami *la*
間 Natsuma *s*
樹 Natsuki *m*

桑 1162 [T] Kuwa *s*. (SŌ, kuwa)
$^{3}$子 Kuwako *f*
$^{4}$山 Kuwayama *s*
木 Kuwaki *s*
木厳翼 K. Gen'yoku
$^{5}$田 Kuwada *s* ⌊ml
本 Kuwamoto *s*
$^{6}$江 Kuwae *s*
名 Kuwana *p*
$^{7}$折 Kōri *sp*
沢 Kuwazawa *s*
村 Kuwamura *s*
谷 Kuwadani *s*
$^{8}$波田 Kuwabata *s*
門 Kuwakado *s*
$^{9}$畑 Kuwabata *s*
岡 Kuwaoka *s*
$^{10}$原 Kuwabara *s*
原武夫 K. Takeo *ml*
原腹赤 K. no Haraaka
屋 Kuwaya *s* ⌊ml
$^{11}$野 Kuwano *s*
島 Kuwajima *s*
$^{12}$港 Sōkō *p* "San Francisco"
$^{15}$絹 Kuwakinu *p*

高 1163 [T] Takashi *m*; Kō *sm*; Taka *s*. (KŌ, taka, ue, take, hodo, takai, akira, su-
$^{2}$力 Kōriki *s* ⌊ke)
$^{3}$川 Takagawa *s*
三 Takasabu *s* ⌈mla
三隆達 T. Ryūtatsu
口 Takaguchi *s*
子 Takako *f*, Takaiko
土 Takatsuchi *s*
千穂 Takachiho *sp*
久 Takahisa *sm*; Takaku *s*
下 Takashita *s*
上 Takagami *s*
$^{4}$戸 Takado *s*
月 Takatsuki *p*
円 Takamado *s*, Takamaro
内 Takauchi *s*
天 Takama *s*
井 Takai *s*
太郎 Takatarō *m*
木 Takagi *sf*, Takaki
木一夫 Takagi Kazuo *ml*
木卓 T. Taku *ml*
木貞治 T. Teiji *mh*
山 Takayama *sp*; Kōyama *p*
山宗砌 T. Sōzei *ml*
山彦九郎 T. Hikokurō *mh*
山毅 T. Tsuyoshi *ml*
山樗牛 T. Chogyū *ml*
中 Takanaka *s*
水 Takamizu *s*
$^{5}$比良 Takahira *s*
司 Takatsukasa *s*
句麗 Kōkuri *ph* "Koguryŏ"
石 Takaishi *p*
左右 Takasō *s*
平 Takahira *s*
玉 Takatama *s*
本 Takamoto *s*, Kō-
丘 Takaoka *s* ⌊moto
市 Takaichi *sp*; Take-

ichi *s*, Takachi, Takechi, Yamato
市黒人 Takechi no Kurohito *ml* ⌈m
市麻呂 Takechimaro
田 Takada *sp*, Takata
田半峰 Takada Hanbō *ml* ⌈ml
田保 Takata Tamotsu
田屋 Takadaya *s*
田屋嘉兵衛 T. Kahee *mh* ⌈p
田馬場 Takadanobaba
田浪吉 Takada Namikichi *ml*
田博厚 T. Hiroatsu *ml*
田瑞穂 T. Mizuho *ml*
田蝶衣 Takata Chōi
6次 Takaji *m* ⌊ml
次郎 Takajirō *m*
任 Takatō *m*
仲 Takanaka *s*
地 Kōchi *s*, Takaji
行 Takayuki *m*
羽 Takaba *s*, Takaha
刑 Takanori *m*
宅 Takaya *s*
光 Takamitsu *ml*
台寺 Kōdaiji *p*
弁 Kōben *mh*
品 Takashina *s*
広 Takahiro *s*
向 Takamuko *s*, Takamuku
向玄理 Takamuko no Kuromaro *mh*
辻 Takatsuji *s*
西 Takanishi *s*
寺 Takadera *s* ⌈ka
7阪 Takasaka *s*, Kōsa-
坂 Takasaka *s*, Kōsaka
沢 Takasawa *s*
沖 Takaoki *s*
沖陽造 T. Yōzō *ml*
杉 Takasugi *s*
杉一郎 T. Ichirō *ml*
杉晋作 T. Shinsaku
弘 Takahiro *m* ⌊mh
村 Takamura *sp*
村光太郎 T. Kōtarō *ml*
村光雲 T. Kōun *ma*
利 Kōri *s*
谷 Takadani *s*, Takaya
発 Takasawa *m*
志 Kōshi *s*, Koshi, Takashi
志壬生 Kōshimibu *s*

枩 Takaeda *m*
芥 Takashina *m*
安 Takayasu *sm*; Kōyasu *p*
安月郊 T. Gekkō *ml*
安国世 T. Kuniyo *ml*
安犬 Kōyasu inu *l*
尾 Takao *sp* ⌈l
尾船字文 T. senjimon
尾野 Takaono *p*
来 Takagi *p*
見 Takami *s*
見順 T. Jun *ml*
見沢 Takamizawa *s*
8沼 Takanuma *s*
波 Takanami *s*
門 Takakado *m*; Oka-
明 Takaaki *m* ⌊do *s*
林 Takabayashi *s*
知 Kōchi *p*
知尾 Takachio *s*
取 Takatori *sp*
孟 Takaosa *m*
武 Kōtake *s*
或 Takamochi *m*
良 Kōra *s*
良城 Takaragi *s*
9信 Takanobu *m*
洲 Takasu *s*
津 Takatsu *s*
城 Takagi *s*, Takashiro; Takajō *p*, Taki
浪 Takanami *s*
垣 Takagaki *s*
弥 Takahisa *m*
畑 Takahata *s*
柿 Takakatsu *m*
砂 Takasago *p-la*
松 Takamatsu *sp*
草 Takakusa *s*
草木 Takakusagi *s*
品 Takakazu *m*
長谷 Takahase *s*
岸 Takagishi *s*
岩 Takaiwa *s*
妻 Takatsuma *s*, Kōtsuma
岳 Takaoka *smh*
栄 Takashige *m*
岡 Takaoka *sp*
10修 Takanaga *m*, Ta-
浦 Takaura *s* ⌊kaosa
浜 Takahama *sp*
浜年尾 T. Toshio *ml*
浜虚子 T. Kyoshi *ml*
時 Takatoki *m*
柳 Takayanagi *sp*

柳重信 T. Shigenobu
矩 Takanori *m* ⌊ml
師直 Kō no Moronao
宮 Takamiya *sp* ⌊mh
荷 Takani *s*
荻 Takahagi *s*
倉 Takakura *s*
倉下 Takakuraji *m*
泰 Takayoshi *m*
畠 Takabatake *s*, Takatsu; Takahata *sp*
畠素之 Takabatake Motoyuki *mlh*
畠藍泉 T. Ransen *ml*
桑 Takakuwa *s*
桑純夫 T. Sumio *ml*
柴 Takashiba *s*
原 Takahara *sp*
座 Takakura *s*; Kōza
屋 Takaya *sp* ⌊p
屋窓秋 T. Sōshū *ml*
11陳 Takayoshi *m*
清水 Takashimizu *p*
規 Takatsuki *p*
峰 Takamine *s*
峰譲吉 T. Jōkichi *mh*
根 Takane *sp*
根沢 Takanezawa *p*
野 Takano *sp*; Kōno *s*; Kōya *p*
野口 Kōyaguchi *p*
野山 Kōya-san *p* ⌈la
野物狂 K. monogurui
野房太郎 Takano Fusatarō *mh*
野長英 T. Chōei *mh*
野素十 T. Sujū *ml*
野聖 Kōya hijiri *l*
野瀬 Takanose *s*
部 Takabe *s*
斎 Takasai *s*
梁 Takahashi *sp*
悠 Takachika *m*
梨 Takanashi *s*
鹿 Takashika *s*
島 Takashima *sp*
島秋帆 T. Shūhan *mh*
鳥 Takatori *s*
12順 Takanobu *m*
場 Takaba *s*
須 Takasu *s*
須梅渓 T. Baikei *ml*
須賀 Takasuka *s*
陰 Takakage *m*
階 Takashina *s*, Takahashi ⌈Sekizen *ml*
階積善 Takashina no

陽 Kōyō *p*
陽院七首歌合 Kayanoin shichishu utaawase *l*
琢 Takaaya *m*
斌 Takayoshi *m*
峻 Takatoshi *m*
崎 Takasaki *sp*
崎正秀 T. Masahide *ml* ⌈ml
崎正風 T. Masakaze
富 Takatomi *sp*
萩 Takahagi *p*
森 Takamori *sp*
達 Takasato *m*
道 Takamichi *m*
遂 Takanaru *m*
間 Takama *s*
13堀 Takabori *s*
塚 Takatsuka *s*
塩 Takashio *s*
塩背山 T. Haizan *ml*
植 Takanao *m*
楊 Takayanagi *s*
楠 Takakusu *s*
楠順次郎 T. Junjirō
雄 Takao *sm* ⌊mh
群 Takamure *s*
群逸枝 T. Itsue *fl*
猷 Takayuki *m*
亶 Takatada *m*
寛 Takanori *m*
遠 Takatō *p* ⌈same
14境 Takaki *s*, Taka-
際 Takagiwa *s*
徳 Takanori *m*
徳院 Kōtokuin *p*
郷 Takasato *p*
精 Takakiyo *m*
15幡 Takahata *s*
標 Takashina *m*
楡 Takayu *s*
聡 Takasato *m*
輪 Takanawa *s*
鉾 Takahoko *s*
幣 Takahei *s*
邁 Takatō *m*
慶 Takayasu *m*
16橋 Takahashi *s*
橋五郎 T. Gorō *ml*
橋由一 T. Yūichi *ma*
橋氏文 T. ujibumi *l*
橋虫麻呂 T. no Mushimaro *ml*
橋阿伝夜叉譚 T. Oden yasha monogatari *l*
橋和巳 T. Kazumi *ml*

釚 釘 針 扇 脅 冥 食 釜 夏 桑 ▼ 高 ▲ 差 倉 貢 員 荒 莘 葱 寅 茹 荅

橋是清 T. Korekiyo *mh* ⌈*mh*
橋景保 T. Kageyasu
橋新吉 T. Shinkichi *ml*
橋禎二 T. Teiji *ml*
橋義孝 T. Yoshitaka
頭 Takatō *s* ⌊*ml*
輸 Takanaka *m*
緒 Takatsugu *m*
維 Takasumi *m*
築 Takatsuki *s*
篠 Takashino *s*
$^{17}$潔 Takakiyo *m*, Takayoshi
濃 Takano *s* ⌈yori
聴 Takaaki *m*, Taka-
謙 Takakata *m*
鍋 Takanabe *p*
鍬 Takakuwa *s*
館 Takadachi *l*
$^{18}$鎌 Takakata *m*
額 Takanuka *s*
藤 Takafuji *s*, Takatō
嶺 Takamine *s*
巖 Takasato *m*
$^{19}$瀬 Takase *s*; Takaze *p* ⌈*ml*
瀬文淵 Takase Bun'en
瀬舟 Takasebune *l*
藪 Takayabu *m*
$^{20}$麗 Koma *sph* "Koguryŏ"; Kōrai *ph* "Koryŏ"; Kōma *s*
麗楽 Koma gaku *a*
$^{23}$鷲 Takawashi *p*
$^{27}$矗 Takanobu *m*

**——10 T3——**

**差** 1164 [T] (SA, sashi, shina, suke)
紙 Sashigami *s*

**倉** 1165 [T] Kura *sm.* (SŌ, SHŌ, kura)
$^{2}$又 Kuramata *s*
$^{3}$上 Kuragami *s*
之助 Kuranosuke *m*
$^{4}$内 Kurauchi *s*
山 Kurayama *s*
井 Kurai *s*
木 Kuraki *s*
方 Kurakata *s*
片 Kurakata *s*
$^{5}$永 Kuranaga *s*
石 Kuraishi *sp*
平 Kurahei *m*
本 Kuramoto *s*
田 Kurata *s*
田百三 K. Momozō / Hyakuzō *ml*
$^{6}$地 Kurachi *s*
光 Kuramitsu *s*
吉 Kurayoshi *m-p*; Kurakichi *m*
成 Kuranari *s*
辻 Kuratsuji *s*
西 Kuranishi *s*
$^{7}$沢 Kurasawa *s*
形 Kuragata *s*
谷 Kuratani *s*, Kuraya
見 Kurami *s*
$^{8}$林 Kurabayashi *s*
知 Kurachi *s*
茂 Kurashige *s*
金 Kurakane *s*
$^{9}$垣 Kuragaki *s*
持 Kuramochi *s*
松 Kuramatsu *m*
科 Kurashina *s*
美 Kurami *f*
品 Kurashina *s*
岳 Kuratake *p*
岡 Kuraoka *s*
彦 Kurahiko *m*
重 Kurashige *s*
$^{10}$員 Kurakazu *s*
$^{11}$掛 Kurakake *s*
野 Kurano *s*
部 Kurabe *s*
島 Kurashima *s*
$^{12}$崎 Kurasaki *s*
梯麿 Kurahashimaro
富 Kuratomi *s* ⌊*m*
賀野 Kuragano *s*
$^{13}$淵 Kurabuchi *p*
塚 Kuratsuka *s*
$^{14}$数 Kurakazu *s*
$^{15}$敷 Kurashiki *p*
$^{16}$橋 Kurahashi *sp*
橋由美子 K. Yumiko *fl*
$^{19}$繁 Kurashige *s*

**貢** 1166 [T] Mitsugi *m-f*; Susumu *m.* (KŌ, KU, tsugu)

**員** 1167 [T] (IN, kazu, sada)
弁 Inabe *sp*
昆 Kazuyasu *m*
従 Kazuyori *m*
恵 Kazutoshi *m*
馬 Kazuma *m*
規 Kazunori *m*
種 Kazufusa *m*
維 Kazutada *m*

**荒** See 935

**莘** 1168 (SHIN, naga, shige)

**荵** 1169 Shinobu *f.* (NIN)

**荑** 1170 (I, TEI, DAI, hae)

**茹** 1171 Kayane *m.* (JO, NYO, tsura)

**莟** 1172 Tsubomi *f.* (GAN)

**茁** 1173 (SATSU, SACHI, setsu)
子 Setsuko *f*

**莅** 1174 (RI, nozoki) ⌈ki
戸 Nozokido *s*, Nozo-

**莫** 1175 Sadamu *m.* (BAKU, MAKU, sata, toshi, naka, ana)
太 Anaho *s*
田 Aita *s*
位 Makui *s*
保 Anaho *s*

**荻** 1176 Ogi *sp.* (TEKI, ogi)
子 Ogiko *f*
久保 Ogikubo *s*
山 Ogiyama *s*
田 Ogita *s*
生 Ogyū *s*
生徂徠 O. Sorai *mlh*
江 Ogie *sf*
村 Ogimura *s*
谷 Ogiya *s*
沼 Oginuma *s*
原 Ogiwara *s* ⌈*ml*
原井泉水 O. Seisensui
原重秀 O. Shigehide
野 Ogino *s* ⌊*mh*
島 Ogishima *s*
須 Ogisu *s*
窪 Ogikubo *p*

**宖** 1177 Hiroshi *m.* (KŌ)

**宲** 1178 Minoru *m.* (HŌ, HATSU)

**宵** 1179 [I] (SHŌ, yoi)
子 Shōko *f*

**宰** 1180 [T] Osamu *m*, Tsukasa. (SAI, tada, suzu, kami)
子 Suzuko *f*
光 Tadamitsu *m*

**害** 1181 [T] (GAI, shishi)
人 Shishihito *s*
人部 Shishihitobe *s*

**容** 1182 [T] Hiroshi *m*, Iruru. (YŌ, YU, kata, yasu, mori, hiro, yoshi, osa, nari, masa)
大 Kataharu *m*
甲枝 Yukie *f*
住 Kataoki *m*
保 Katamori *m*
度 Yasunori *m*
盛 Hiromori *m*
衆 Katahiro *m*
頌 Katanobu *m*

**室** 1183 [T] Muro *s.* (SHITSU, SHICHI, muro, ya, ie)
$^{3}$川 Murokawa *s*
$^{4}$戸 Muroto *p*
井 Muroi *s*
木 Muroki *s*
内 Murouchi *s*
山 Muroyama *s*
$^{5}$田 Murota *s*
生 Murō *sp*
生犀星 M. Saisei *ml*
$^{6}$伏 Murobushi *s*
伏高信 M. Kōshin *ml*
$^{7}$住 Murozumi *s*
沢 Murozawa *s*
町 Muromachi *sph*
町時代小歌集 M. jidai koutashū *l* ⌈tani
谷 Muroya *s*, Muro-
君 Murogimi *l*

寿詞 Muro hogi no kotoba *l*
[8]枝 Muroe *f*
[9]岡 Murooka *s*
[10]原 Murohara *s*
屋 Muroya *sm*
[11]根 Murone *p*
[12]崎 Murozaki *s*
賀 Muroga *s* ⌈*mh*
[13]鳩巣 Muro Kyūsō
越 Murokoshi *s*
[16]橋 Murohashi *s*
積 Murozumi *s*
積徂春 M. Soshun *ml*
[20]蘭 Muroran *p*

宮 1184 [T] Miya *sp*. (GŪ, KYŪ, KU, miya, taka, ie)
[2]入 Miyairi *s*
[3]川 Miyagawa *sp*
口 Miyaguchi *s*
下 Miyashita *s*
久保 Miyakubo *s*
之城 Miyanojō *p*
子 Miyako *sf*
[4]戸 Miyato *s*
元 Miyamoto *s*
中 Miyanaka *s*
木 Miyagi *s*
井 Miyai *s* ⌈nai *m*
内 Miyauchi *sp*; Ku-
内寒弥 M. Kan'ya *ml*
内卿 Kunaikyō *fl*
山 Miyayama *s*
[5]代 Miyashiro *sp*
北 Miyakita *s*
永 Miyanaga *s*
司 Miyaji *s*
石 Miyaishi *s*
処 Miyako *s*
辺 Miyabe *s*, Miyana-
古 Miyako *sp* ⌊be
古路 Miyakoji *s*
田 Miyata *sp*
氏 Miyauji *s*
本 Miyamoto *s* ⌈*fl*
本百合子 M. Yuriko
本武蔵 M. Musashi *ml*
本顕治 M. Kenji *ml*
[6]行 Takayuki *m*
地 Miyachi *sm*; Miyaji *s* ⌈ku *ml*
地嘉六 Miyaji Karo-
守 Miyamori *sp*
吉 Miyakichi *m*
寺 Miyadera *s*
庄 Miyanoshō *s*
成 Miyanari *s*
西 Miyanishi *s*
[7]坂 Miyazaka *s*
沢 Miyazawa *s*
沢賢治 M. Kenji *ml*
村 Miyamura *s*
谷 Miyadani *s*
尾 Miyao *s*
里 Miyazato *s*
[8]所 Miyadokoro *s*
林 Miyabayashi *s*
和田 Miyawada *s*
居 Miyai *s*
武 Miyatake *s*
武外骨 M. Tobone *ml*
武寒々 M. Kankan *ml*
[9]垣 Miyagaki *s*
津 Miyazu *sp*
治 Miyaji *s*
城 Miyagi *sp*; Miyashiro *s* ⌈*ma*
城道雄 Miyagi Michio
城謙一 M. Ken'ichi *ml*
柊二 Miya Shōji *ml*
松 Miyamatsu *s*
首 Miyaji *s*
前 Miyamae *s*
長 Miyanaga *s*
岡 Miyaoka *s*
重 Miyashige *s*
[10]脇 Miyawaki *s*
原 Miyabara *sp*
[11]後 Miyajiri *s*
根 Miyane *s*
野 Miyano *s*
部 Miyabe *s*
麻呂 Miyamaro *m*
島 Miyajima *sp*
島新三郎 M. Shinzaburō *ml*
島資夫 M. Sukeo *ml*
[12]崎 Miyazaki *sp*
崎三昧 M. Sanmai *ml*
崎安貞 M. Yasusada *mh* ⌈shi *ml*
崎湖処子 M. Kosho-
崎夢柳 M. Muryū *ml*
森 Miyamori *s*
道 Miyamichi *s*, Miyaji
道之 Miyajino *s*
[13]塚 Miyazuka *s*
越 Miyakoshi *s*
路 Miyaji *s*
園 Miyazono *s*
[14]腰 Miyakoshi *s*
窪 Miyakubo *sp*
[16]継 Miyatsugu *s*
薗 Miyazono *s*
[18]藤 Miyafuji *s*
[19]瀬 Miyase *s*

家 1185 [T] Yaka *s*. (KA, KE, ie, e, o, ya, yaka, yake)
[2]人部 Yakehitobe *s*
入 Ieiri *s*
[4]仁 Yakahito *m*
介 Iesuke *m*
中 Ienaka *s*
内 Kenouchi *s*
尹 Ienobu *m*
木 Ieki *s*
[5]永 Ienaga *sm*
永三郎 I. Saburō *ml*
田 Ieda *s*
正 Iemasa *m*
[6]守 Kemori *s*
存 Iesada *m*
[7]村 Iemura *s*
寿多 Yasuda *s*
[8]門 Iekado *m*
所 Iedokoro *s*, Kasho
宜 Soki *s*
茂 Iemochi *m*
斉 Ienari *m*
良 Ienaga *m*
[9]垣 Yagaki *s*
持 Yakamochi *ml*
治 Iesada *m*
城 Ieki *s*, Yagi
[10]祥 Iesaki *m*
隆 Ietaka *ml*
原 Iehara *s*, Ehara
屋 Ieya *s*
[11]船 Iefune *m*
康 Ieyasu *m*
島 Iejima *sp*; Yashima
亀 Yakame *s* ⌊*s*
[12]須多 Yasuda *s*
崎 Iezaki *s*
納 Yanō *s*
富 Yatomi *s*
喜 Yagi *s*
達 Iesato *m*

—10 T4—

炭 1186 [T] Sumi *s*. (TAN, sumi)
太祇 Sumi Taigi *ml*
宮 Tannomiya *s*
俵 Sumidawara *l*
塵 Gasu *la*

晟 1187 Akira *m*. (SEI, JŪ, teru, masa, akira)
千世 Masachiyo *m*
子 Teruko *f*

晁 1188 Akira *m*; Chō *sm*. (CHŪ, aki, asa)
子 Asako *f*
沢 Kurumizawa *s*
雄 Akio *m*

晃 1189 [N] Akira *m*, Hikaru, Kō. (KŌ, aki, teru, mitsu, kira)
之 Kirayuki *m*
夫 Akio *m*
司 Mitsushi *m*
央 Teruo *m*
年 Terutoshi *m*
弘 Mitsuhiro *m*
昇 Akinori *m*
治 Kōji *m*

—10 T5—

衷 1190 [T] Tadashi *m*. (CHŪ, tada, atsu, yoshi)
子 Atsuko *f*

党 1191 [T] Akira *m*. (TŌ, tomo, masu, akira) ⌈*l*
生活者 Tōseikatsusha

帯 1192 [T] (TAI, yo, obi, tarashi)
刀 Tatewaki *sm*; Obinata *s*
士 Tarashiko *s*
子 Obiko *f*, Tarashi-
王 Tarashiko *s* ⌊ko
壬 Tachishiro *s*
包 Obikane *s*
広 Obihiro *p*
谷 Obiya *s*
金 Obikane *s*

哥 1193 (KA, uta)
子 Utako *f*

哿 1194 Kanari *s*. (KA, yoshi)
彦 Yoshihiko *m*

毘 1195 (HI, BI, hide, yasu, teru, suke, tomo, nobu, masa)
次 Terutsugu *m*
沙門 Bishamon *mh*
信 Hidenobu *m*

皆 1196 [T] (KAI, KEI, mina, mi, tomo, michi)
川 Minagawa *s*
山 Minayama *s*
木 Minaki *s*
吉 Minayoshi *s*, Minakiri ⌈Sōu *ml*
吉爽雨 Minayoshi
河 Minaka *s*
良 Miyoshi *f*
彦 Minahiko *m*
野 Minano *p*
藤 Kaidō *s*
瀬 Minase *p*

皐 1197 Susumu *m*, Takashi. (KŌ, GŌ, taka)
月 Satsuki *f*

畠 1198 Hata *s*. (hatake, hata)
中 Hatanaka *s*
山 Hatakeyama *s*
山政長 H. Masanaga *mh* ⌈*mh*
山重忠 H. Shigetada
山義就 H. Yoshinari
田 Hatakeda *s* ⌊*mh*
野 Hatakeno *s*

竜 1199 [I] Shigemi *m*, Tōru, Megumu; Tatsu *s*, Ryū, Ryō. (RYŪ, RYŌ, RYU, tatsu, kimi, tō)
ケ岳 Ryūgadake *p*
ケ崎 Ryūgasaki *p*
$^{1}$一 Ryūichi *m*
$^{3}$三 Ryūzō *m*
三郎 Tatsusaburō *m*, Ryūzaburō
之介 Ryūnosuke *m*
之助 Ryūnosuke *m*
土会 Ryūdokai *l*
$^{4}$水 Tatsumi *m*
山 Tatsuyama *sp*; Ryōsen *s*
王 Tatsuō *ma*; Ryūō *p*
太郎 Ryūtarō *m*
木 Tatsuki *s*
$^{5}$北 Ryūhoku *p*
田 Tatsuta *la*
平 Ryūhei *m*
$^{6}$吉 Ryūkichi *m*
$^{7}$沢 Tatsuzawa *s*
安寺 Ryōanji *p*
花 Ryūge *s*
見 Ryūgen *s*, Ryōgen
$^{8}$居 Tatsui *s*
虎 Ryōko *l*
$^{9}$洋 Ryūyō *p*
胆寺雄 Ryūtanji Yū *ml*
神 Ryūjin *p*
泉 Ryūsen *s*
岡 Tatsuoka *s*
$^{10}$海 Tatsumi *m*
造寺 Ryūzōji *s*
馬 Tatsuma *m*, Ryū-
起 Tatsuoki *s* ⌊ma
$^{11}$涎香 Ryūzenkō *l*
蛇 Tatsuhebi *s*
野 Tatsuno *sp*
盛 Kimimori *m*
麻呂 Tatsumaro *m*
$^{12}$崎 Ryūzaki *s*
$^{13}$雄 Tatsuo *m*
$^{14}$郷 Tatsugō *p*
種 Tatsutane *m*
$^{15}$蔵 Ryūzō *m*

盈 1200 Mitsuru *m*. (EI, YŌ, michi, mitsu, ari, tsuchi, tsu-
子 Mitsuko *f* ⌊ne)
比 Michitomo *m*
良 Mitsuyoshi *m*
進 Michinobu *m*

益 1201 [T] Masu *m*, Susumu, Eki. (EKI, YAKU, masu, mashi, ari, nori, mi, mata, mitsu)
$^{2}$人 Masuhito *m*
$^{3}$川 Masukawa *s*
三郎 Masusaburō *m*
子 Mashiko *sp*; Masuko *sf*
$^{4}$戸 Masuto *s*
井 Masui *s*
太郎 Masutarō *m*
$^{5}$以 Masutomo *m*
甲 Yakawa *s*
立 Masutachi *m*
田 Masuda *sp*; Mashida *p* ⌈sada *mh*
田時貞 Masuda Toki-
$^{6}$次郎 Masujirō *m*
広 Masuhiro *m*
$^{7}$位 Masui *s*
材 Masuki *m*
寿子 Masuko *f*
$^{9}$城 Masuki *s*; Mashi-
津 Mashizu *s* ⌊ki *p*
荒 Masura *m*
$^{10}$軒 Ekiken / Ekken
$^{11}$得 Masue *m* ⌊*mh*
$^{12}$富 Masutomi *s*
$^{16}$頭 Mashizu *s*, Masuzu, Masugami

秦 1202 Hata *s*. (SHIN, JIN, hata, masa)
川 Hatagawa *s*
井手 Hataide *s*
皮 Toneriko *l*
佐八郎 Hata Sahachirō *mh*
荘 Hatashō *p*
党 Shinnotō *s* ⌈*p*
野 Hatano *s*; Hadano
豊吉 Hata Toyokichi
誦 Hatasumi *m* ⌊*ml*

泰 1203 [T] Yasushi *m*, Hiroshi, Yutaka, Tōru, Akira; Tai *p* "Thailand". (TAI, hiro, yasu, yoshi)
$^{2}$二 Taiji *m*
$^{3}$三 Taizō *m* ⌈*la*
$^{4}$山府君 Taizanbukun
$^{5}$代 Yasushiro *m*
令 Yasunori *m*
右 Hiroaki *sm*
平 Yasuhira *m*
$^{6}$次郎 Taijirō *m*
光 Yoshimitsu *m*
吉 Taikichi *m*
$^{7}$作 Taisaku *m*
甫 Taisuke *m*
$^{8}$祉 Yasutomi *m*
阜 Yasuoka *sp*
国 Taikoku *p* "Thai-
良 Taira *m* ⌊land"
$^{9}$治 Taiji *m*
彦 Yasuhiko *m*
$^{11}$敏 Yasuharu *m*
啓 Yasuhiro *m*
$^{12}$舒 Yasunobu *m*
$^{13}$経 Yasutsune *m*, Yasunori
義 Yasuyoshi *m*
舜 Yasukiyo *m*
業 Yasunari *m*
$^{16}$儔 Yasutoshi *m*
賢 Yasumasa *m*, Yasukata *m*

—— 10 T6 ——

契 1204 Kiyoshi *m*. (KETSU)

恭 1205 [O] Yasushi *m*, Takashi, Tadashi. (KYŌ, KU, yasu, yuki, taka, chika, yoshi, tada, uya, sumi, tsuka, nori, mitsu)
一 Yukikazu *m*
二 Kyōji *m*
三 Kyōzō *m*
子 Uyako *f*
仁 Kuni *sp*
仁京 Kuni-kyō *ph*
介 Kyōsuke *m*
太郎 Kyōtarō *m*
兄 Tsukae *m*
平 Kyōhei *m*
行 Yasunori *m*
光 Yukimitsu *m*
助 Kyōsuke *m*
彦 Yasuhiko *m*, Taka-
雄 Yasuo *m* ⌊hiko
輔 Kyōsuke *m*
慶 Takayoshi *m*

拳 1206 Tsutomu *m*, Takashi. (KEN, GEN)

挙 1207 [T] (KYO, KO, taka, shige, tatsu, hira, age)
白集 Kyohakushū *l*
母 Koromo *p*, Agemo
周 Takachika *m*
直 Shigenao *m*
雄 Tatsuo *m*

笈 1208 Oi *l*. (KYŪ, oi)
の小文 Oi no kobumi / obumi *l*
川 Oikawa *s*
田 Oida *s*
沼 Oinuma *s*

笑 1209 [T] (SHŌ, e, emi)
子 Emiko *f*
顔 Egao *f*

烝 1210 Susumu *m*, Atsushi. (SHŌ, toshi)

烈 1211 [T] Takeshi *m*, Isao. (RETSU, take, yasu, tsura, yoshi, tsuyo)
女 Yoshime *f*
男 Takeo *m*
資 Takesuke *m*

脊 1212 (SEKI, se)
許 Hekobori *s*

骨 1213 [T] (KOTSU, hone)
皮 Honekawa *la*

耆 1214 (KI, GI, SHI, toshi)
長 Toshinaga *m*

晋 1215 [N] Susumu *m*, Susumi, Shin. (SHIN, SEN, kuni, aki, yuki)
次郎 Shinjirō *m*
匡 Yukimasa *m*

書 1216 [T] Fumi *s*. (SHO, fumi, nobu, nori, hisa, fumu, fun)
上 Kakiage *s*
主 Fuminushi *m*
持 Fumimochi *m*
紀 Shoki *l*

姿 1217 [T] (SHI, shina, kata, taka)
三四郎 Sugata Sanshirō *l*
子 Shinako *f*

要 1218 [T] Kaname *m*, Motomu. (YŌ, toshi, yasu, me, shino)
人 Kanando *m*, Kaname
三郎 Yōzaburō *m*
造 Yōzō *m*
蔵 Yōzō *m*
範 Toshinori *m*

栗 1219 Kuri *f*. (RITSU, kuri, kuru)
の本 Kurinomoto *l*
[2]又 Kurimata *s*
[3]川 Kurikawa *s*
[4]井 Kurii *s*
太 Kurita *p*
山 Kuriyama *sp*
山理一 K. Riichi *ml*
山潜鋒 K. Senpō *mh*
木 Kuriki *s*
[5]田 Kurita *s*
本 Kurimoto *s*
本鋤雲 K. Joun *ml*
生 Kuryū *s*, Kurio
生純夫 Kuryū Sumio *ml*
[7]沢 Kurisawa *p*
谷 Kuriya *s*, Kuritani
花生 Tsuyuo *m*
花落 Tsuyuri *s*, Tsuyu
[8]股 Kurimata *s*
林 Kuribayashi *s*
林一石路 K. Issekiro *ml*
板 Kuriita *s*
辰 Kurihara *s*
東 Rittō *p*
[9]城 Kuriki *s*
岩 Kuriiwa *s*
岡 Kurioka *s*
[10]栖 Kurusu *s*
原 Kurihara *sp*
原潔子 K. Kiyoko *fl*
[11]野 Kurino *sp*
島 Kurishima *s*
崎 Kurisaki *s*
椋 Kurusu *s*
焼 Kuriyaki *l*
殻谷 Kurikaradani *s*
間 Kuruma *s*
[13]隈 Kurikuma *m*
塚 Kurizuka *s*
源 Kurimoto *p*
[15]駒 Kurikoma *p*
[16]橋 Kurihashi *p*
[19]瀬 Kurise *s*

栞 1220 Shiori *f*. (KAN)

柴 1221 Shiba *s*. (SHI, SAI, ZE, shiba, shige)
[3]三郎 Shibasaburō *s*
子 Shibako *f*
[4]内 Shibanai *s*
山 Shibayama *s*
井 Shibai *s*
[5]本 Shibamoto *s*
生田 Shibōta *s*
生田稔 S. Minoru *ml*
田 Shibata *sp*
田天馬 S. Tenma *ml*
田白葉女 S. Hakuyōjo *fl*
田是真 S. Zeshin *ma*
田勝家 S. Katsuie *mh*
田鳩翁 S. Kyūō *mh*
田錬三郎 S. Renzaburō *ml*
[8]沼 Shibanuma *s*
[9]岡 Shibaoka *s*
[10]宮 Shibamiya *s*
原 Shibahara *s*
[11]野 Shibano *s*
野栗山 S. Ritsuzan *mh*
[12]崎 Shibazaki *s*
[16]橋 Shibahashi *s*

怒 1222 [T] (NU, DO)
借屋 Nukariya *s*
留湯 Nuruya *s*

恋 1223 [T] (REN, koi)
川 Koikawa *s*
川春町 K. Harumachi *mh*
女房染分手綱 Koi nyōbō somewake tazuna *la*
衣 Koigoromo *l*
重荷 Koi no omoni *la*
飛脚大和往来 Koibikyaku Yamato ōrai *la*

息 1224 [T] Yasu *f*; Oki *s*. (SOKU, oki, iki, ki)
津 Kitsu *s*
長 Okinaga *sp*
郷 Okisato *sp*

恩 1225 [T[ Megumi *m*. (ON, oki)
田 Onda *s*, Okida
地 Onchi *s*
地孝四郎 O. Kōshirō *ml*
智 Onchi *s*

恵 1226 [T] Megumi *m*, Satoshi. (KEI, E, yoshi, shige, toshi, aya, yasu, sato)
[2]二 Keiji *m*
[3]三 Keizō *m*
三郎 Keizaburō *m*
之輔 Shigenosuke *m*
[4]介 Keisuke *m*
心僧都 Eshin Sōzu *mh*
仁 Ayahito *m*
文 Yoshifumi *m*
尺 Esaku *m*
太郎 Keitarō *m*
[6]江 Yoshie *f*
[7]那 Ena *p*
弘 Yoshihiro *m*, Keikō
[8]武 En *f*
良 Era *s*
[9]美 Emi *sf*
美子 Emiko *f*
美押勝 Emi no Oshikatsu *mh*
[10]庭 Eniwa *p*
[11]教 Yasumichi *m*
[12]敬 Yoshihiro *m*
[13]寛 Ayahiro *m*
[18]藤 Etō *s*

## 10 T7

哲 1227 [T] Satoru *m*, Satoshi, Akira; Tetsu *m-f*. (TETSU, aki, nori, sato, yoshi, akira)
一郎 Tetsuichirō *m*
二 Tetsuji *m*
三 Tetsuzō *m*
太郎 Tetsutarō *m*
夫 Tetsuo *m*, Satoo
史 Tetsushi *m*
四郎 Tetsushirō *m*
次郎 Tetsujirō *m*
西 Tessei *p*
多 Tetta *p*
哉 Norichika *m*
浩 Akihiro *m*
郎 Tetsurō *m*
造 Tetsuzō *m*
致 Noriyoshi *m*

真 1228 [T] Makoto *m*, Shin, Tadashi; Maki *s*. (SHIN, sane, ma, mi, masa, mana, sada, sana, tada, chika, maki, masu,

栗 栞 柴 怒 恋 息 恩 恵 哲 真 ▼ 逕 隼 原 函 屋 途 逆 造 ▲ 退 速 連 通 庨 庬 席 庫 庭 座

nao, mata)
[1]一 Shin'ichi *m*
一郎 Shin'ichirō *m*
[2]人 Makoto *sm*; Matto *sp*
人部 Mahitobe *s*
[3]川 Magawa *s*
三 Shinzō *m*
子 Saneko *f*
大 Mahiro *m*
也 Shin'ya *m*
上 Magami *s*
下 Mashita *s*, Mashimo
下飛泉 Mashimo Hisen *ml*
[4]仁田 Manita *s*
心 Manaka *m*
元 Masamoto *m*
六郎 Shinrokurō *m*
中 Manaka *s*
五郎 Shingorō *m*
弓 Mayumi *sm*
巳 Manami *m*
夫 Chikao *m*
山 Mayama *s*, Miyama
山青果 Mayama Seika *ml*
木 Maki *s*
木柱 Makibashira *l*
[5]辺 Manabe *s*
田 Sanada *sp*
正 Shinsei *p*
玉 Matama *p*
平 Shinpei *m*
[6]行 Sanemichi *m*
光 Sadamitsu *m*
吉 Shinkichi *m*
曲抄 Shinkyokushō *l*
虫 Mamushi *m*
舟 Mafune *m*
[7]佐子 Masako *f*
坂 Masaka *s*
村 Mamura *s*
形 Makata *s*
杉 Masugi *s*
杉静枝 M. Shizue *fl*
如 Shinnyo *mh-la*
利子 Mariko *sf*
志野 Mashino *s*
吾 Shingo *s*
男 Sanao *m*, Masuo
貝 Shinkai *s*
言 Makoto *s*
言宗 Shingonshū *h*
臣 Maomi *m*
[8]門 Makado *sm*
知子 Machiko *f-l*
幸 Masaki *sm-f-p*; Miyuki *m*
金 Magane *m*
宗 Mamune *f*
秀 Mahora *m*
[9]信 Sanenobu *m*
狩 Makkari *p*
神 Magami *s*
神田 Makanda *s*
珠庵過去帳 Shinjuan kakochō *l*
砂 Masago *s*
砂野 Masano *s*
砂園 Masazono *s*
柄 Makara *s*
柱 Mihashira *m*
前 Masaki *m*
長 Mitake *m*
泉 Maizumi *s*
岡 Maoka *p*
風 Makaze *m*
[10]脇 Mawaki *s*
畔 Makuro *m*
記 Matoshi *m*
室川 Mamurokawa *s*
家 Maie *s*
恵美 Maemi *f*
柴 Mashiba *s*
真田 Mamada *s*
庭 Maniwa *p*
[11]流 Managare *s*, Maryū
清 Makiyo *m*, Masumi, Masuga
清水 Mashimizu *s*
梶 Makaji *m*
理子 Mariko *f*
船 Mafune *s*; Mifune *m*
船豊 M. Yutaka *ml*
野 Mano *sp*; Matono *s*
野守 Manomori *m*
野麿 Manomaro *m*
部 Manabe *s*
常 Masatsune *m*
庸 Saneyasu *m*
透 Masuki *m*
島 Majima *sm*, Mashima
[12]備 Mabi *p*; Makibi *m*
揖 Makaji *m*
崎 Masaki *s*, Magasaki
棹 Masao *m*
敵 Masataka *m*
喜雄 Makio *m*
森 Sanemori *m*
景累ケ淵 Shinkei kasanegafuchi *la*
琴 Makoto *m*
善美 Masami *f*
達 Masato *m*
道 Shindō *s*
[13]淵 Mabuchi *mlh*; Mabechi *m*
塩 Mashio *s*
楫 Makaji *m*
楯 Matate *m*, Matachi
雄 Masao *m*
鉄 Magane *m*
鈴 Masuzu *m*
葛 Makuzu *m*
義 Sadayoshi *m*
[14]猿 Masaru *m*
榛 Mahari *m*
郷 Sanezato *m*
稗 Shinnen *m*
奪 Shinbai *l*
節 Sanetake *m*
[15]潮 Mashio *m*
澄 Sanezumi *m*, Masumi
瑤 Matama *m*
鋤 Masuki *m*
鋒田 Masakida *s*
[16]壁 Makabe *sp*
橋 Mahashi *s*
継 Kureki *s*
賢木 Masakaki *l*
[17]鍋 Manabe *s*
[18]観 Shinkan *ml*
藤 Shindō *s*
[21]鶴 Manatsuru *m-p*
[23]鷲 Mawashi *m*

—10 T8—

逕 1229 (KEI, KYŌ, nao, michi)
子 Naoko *f*, Michiko

隼 1230 Hayashi *m*; Hayabusa *s*. (JUN, SHUN, haya, toshi)
人 Hayato *sm-p*; Haito *s*
之 Hayayuki *m*
子 Hayako *f*
太 Hayata *s*
太郎 Hayatarō *m*

—10 F2—

原 1231 [T] Hara *sp*; Hajime *m*. (GEN, GAN, moto, hara, oka)
[3]川 Harakawa *s*
三郎 Hara Saburō *ml*
口 Haraguchi *s*
子 Harako *sf*
子公平 H. Kōhei *ml*
[4]月舟 Hara Gesshū *ml*
山 Harayama *s*
木 Haragi *s*
[5]石鼎 Hara Sekitei *ml*
田 Harada *s*
田実 H. Minoru *ml*
田浜人 H. Hinjin *ml*
田康子 H. Yasuko *fl*
田孫七郎 H. Magoshichirō *mh*
田義人 H. Yoshito *ml*
田種茅 H. Taneji *ml*
[6]地 Haraji *s*
民喜 Hara Tamiki *ml*
[7]沢 Harazawa *s*
村 Haramura *s*
町 Haranomachi *p*
見 Harami *m*
[8]阿佐緒 Hara Asao *fl*
抱一庵 H. Hōitsuan *ml*
坦山 H. Tanzan *mh*
[9]南 Motonami *m*, Motoyoshi
[11]野 Harano *s*
島 Harashima *s*
[12]崎 Harazaki *s*
[13]越 Harakoshi *s*
[15]澄 Motozumi *m*
[16]橋 Harahashi *s*

—10 F3—

函 1232 Susumu *m*. (KAN, hako)
南 Kannami *p*
館 Hakodate *p*

屋 1233 [T] (OKU, ya, ie)
子 Ieko *f*
久 Yaku *p*
代 Yashiro *s*
島 Yashima *la*
富 Yatomi *s*
敷 Yashiki *s*
瀬 Yase *s*

途 1234 [T] (TO, michi, tō)
子 Michiko *f*

逆 1235 [T] (GYAKU, GEKI, saka)
井 Sakai *s*
矛 Sakahoko *l*
田 Sakata *s*

造 1236 [T] Itaru *m*. (zō, sō, nari)

次 Zōji *m*
酒 Miki *m*

**退** 1236A [T] (TAI, noki)
二郎 Taijirō *m*
助 Taisuke *m*
蔵 Taizō *m*

**速** 1237 [T] Hayami *sm*; Hayashi *m*. (SOKU, haya, chika, tō, tsugi, mesu)
人 Hayato *m-f*
水 Hayami *sm*
見 Hayami *sm-p*

**連** 1238 [T] Muraji *sp*; Tsura *s*, Yasu. (REN, tsura, muraji, tsugi, masa, yasu)
一郎 Ren'ichirō *m*
三 Renzō *m*
子 Tsurako *f*; Murajiko *m*
山 Tsureyama *s*
英 Tsurahide *m*
理秘抄 Renri hishō *l*
陽春 Murajiyasu *m*
歌 Renga *l*
歌比況集 R. hikyōshū *l*
歌本式 R. honshiki *l*
歌至宝抄 R. shihōshō *l*
歌盗人 R. nusubito *la*
歌新式 R. shinshiki *l*
歌新式今案 R. s. kon'an *l*

**通** 1239 [T] Tōru *m*, Hiraku. (TSŪ, michi, yuki, mitsu, tō, nao)
3小町 Kayoi Komachi *la*
久 Michitsune *m*
也 Michiya *m*
4円 Tsūen *la*
5生 Michiu *m*
6次 Michitsugu *m*
任 Michitaka *m*
同 Michinobu *m*
7伯 Michitake *m*
孝 Michitaka *m*
言総籬 Tsūgen sōmagaki *l*
8枝 Michieda *m*
武 Michitatsu *m*
9津 Tsuzu *s*
亮 Michiakira *m*
10候 Michitoki *m*
俊 Michitoshi *m*
晃 Michiaki *m*
泰 Michiyasu *m*
11済 Michinari *m*
庸 Michiyasu *m*
12陽 Michiharu *m*
勝 Michikatsu *m*
敬 Michitaka *m*
富 Michitoyo *m*
貫 Michitsura *m*
13誠 Michitomo *m*
16積 Michitsumu *m*
憲 Michinori *m*
禧 Michitomi *m*
19簡 Michihiro *m*

**庨** 1240 Takashi *m*. (KŌ, KYŌ)

**庬** 1241 Hiroshi *m*. (BŌ, MŌ)

**席** 1242 [T] (SEKI, JAKU, suke, nobu, yasu, yori)
田 Mushiroda *s*

**庫** 1243 [T] (KO, KU, kura)
之助 Kuranosuke *m*
吉 Kurakichi *m*
治 Kuraji *m*

**庭** 1244 [T] (TEI, niwa, ba, nao)
木 Niwaki *s*
山 Niwayama *s*
田 Niwata *s*
苔 Niwagoke *l*
訓往来 Teikin ōrai *l*
野 Niwano *s*

**座** 1245 [T] (SA, ZA, e, kura, oki)
田 Zada *s*, Saida
光寺 Zakōji *s*
亀 Zakame *s*
間 Zama *p*

**唐** 1246 [T] Kara *l*. (TŌ, kara)
2人 Karōdo *s*
3川 Karakawa *s*
大和尚東征伝 Tōdaiwajō tōseiden *l*
土 Morokoshi *sp*; Morokuni *s*
4木 Karaki *s*
木田 Karakida *s*
木順三 Karaki Junzō *ml*
牛 Karaushi *s*
7沢 Karasawa *s*
衣 Karakoromo *s*
来三和 Tōrai Sanna *ml*
8物 Karamono *s*
物語 Kara monogatari *l*
和 Tōwa *s*
金 Karakane *s*
9津 Karatsu *sp*
松 Karamatsu *s*
10桑 Karakuwa *p*
原 Tōhara *s*
11船 Tōsen *la*
12渡 Karawatari *s*
崎 Karasaki *s*
14様建築 Kara-yō kenchiku *a*
15端 Karahata *s*
16橋 Karahashi *s*
燎 Niwabi *l*
18鎌 Karakama *s*

## 10 F4

**氣** 1247 See 気 319

**翅** 1248 (SHI, KI, GI, nobu, suke)

**迹** 1249 Ato *s*. (SEKI, SHAKU, to)
見 Tomi *s*

## 10 F5

**病** 1250 [T] (BYŌ)
牀六尺 Byōshō rokushaku *l*

**威** 1251 [T] Takeshi *m*, Takeru. (I, take, taka, tsuyo, toshi, nari, nori, akira)
子 Takeko *f*
士 Takeshi *m*
仁 Takehito *m*
知 Takechi *m*
勇治 Isaharu *m*
海衛 Ikaiei *p* "Weihaiwei"
儀 Nariyoshi *m*

**県** 1252 [T] Agata *sp*. (KEN, GEN, agata, sato, mura, tō)
犬養 Agatainukai *s*
犬養人上 A. no Hitokami *ml*
主 Agatanushi *s*
主前利 Agatanushisakito *s*
守 Agatamori *m*
居 Agatai *m*
直 Agatanoatae *s*
造 Agatanomiyatsuko *s*
麿 Agatamaro *m*

## 10 F6

**虔** 1253 Masashi *m*. (KEN, GEN)

**栽** 1254 [T] Ueru *m*. (SAI, tane)
正 Tanemasa *m*

**彧** 1255 (IKU, OKU, aya)
子 Ayako *f*
雄 Ayao *m*

**烏** 1256 (U, O, E, karasu)
丸 Karasumaru *sp*; Karasuma *p*
丸光広 K. Mitsuhiro *ml*
山 Karasuyama *p*
天 Eten *s*
那 Una *s*
金 Karasugane *l*
胡跛 Okoe *s*
帽子 Eboshi *s*
帽子折 E.-ori *la*
賀陽 Ugayo *s*, Ugaya
麿 Karasumaro *m*

**馬** 1257 Takeshi *m*; Uma *s*. (BA, ME, uma, ma, muma)
2刀沢 Matezawa *s*
入 Magumi *s*
3上 Maue *s*
子 Umako *f*
工 Umamikui *s*, Isara
5加 Makuwa *s*, Makuwari
込 Magome *sp*
目 Mame *s*
次郎 Umajirō *m*

哲 真 巠 隼 原 函 屋 途 逆 造 ▼ 退 速 連 通 庨 庬 席 庫 庭 座 唐 氣 翅 迹 病 威 県 虔 栽 彧 烏 馬 ▲ 咼 荷 尅 赳 起 勉 哥 亜 乗 華

翅迹病威県虔栽彧烏馬▼扃荷尅赳起勉哥亞乘華甚兼▲胤條假停偏偂修偵倦値

[7]杉 Umasugi *s*, Masugi, Basugi
来 Maki *s*, Maku; Marai *p* "Malay"
来田 Makida *s*; Makuta *sm*
[9]神屋 Mamiya *s*
被 Makinu *s*
面 Bamen *s*
[10]屋原 Umayahara *s*, Mayahara
[11]酔木 Ashibi *l*
島 Umashima *s*, Mashima, Majima
[12]場 Baba *s*
場孤蝶 B. Kochō *ml*
場辰猪 B. Tatsui *mh*
御檝 Umamikui *s*
渡 Mawatari *s*, Mōtari, Mōtai
琴 Bakin *ml*
達 Batatsu *s*
鹿 Mega *s*
[13]喰田 Mabata *s*, Babata
淵 Mabuchi *sm*; Mabechi *m*
越 Magoshi *s*, Umagoe
路 Umaji *p*
[14]関 Bakan *ph*
[15]澄 Masumi *s*
[16]頭 Batō *p*
養 Umakai *m*
[19]瀬 Maze *p*
[23]籠 Magome *s*

## 10 F7

扃 1258 Akira *m*. (KŌ, KYŌ, akira)

荷 1259 [T] Kada *s*. (KA, GA, mochi)
兮 Kakei *ml*
田 Kada *s*
田在満 K. no Arimaro *ml*
田春満 K. no Azumamaro *ml*
見 Hasumi *s*
風 Kafū *ml*

尅 1260 (KOKU, katsu)

赳 1261 Takeshi *m*. (KYŪ, KU, take)
夫 Takeo *m*
城 Takeki *m*

起 1262 [T] Okosu *m*; Tatsu *f*; Okoshi *s*. (KI, oki, kazu, tatsu, yuki)
賢 Okikata *m*

## 10 F8

勉 1263 [T] Tsutomu *m*, Masaru. (BEN, katsu, masu)

## 10 U

哥 See 1193

亞 1264 See 亜 525

乘 1265 See 乗 1016

華 1266 [T] (KA, GE, hana, haru, ha)
子 Hanako *f*
山院 Kazan'in *s*
夷通商考 Kai tsūshōkō *h*
府 Kafu *p* "Washington"
岡 Hanaoka *s*
頂 Kachō *s*
厳 Kegon *p-l*

甚 1267 [I] (JIN, SHIN, yasu, shige, tane, tō, fuka)
一 Jin'ichi *m*
一郎 Jin'ichirō *m*
七 Jinshichi *m*
三郎 Jinzaburō *m*
五郎 Jingorō *m*
夫 Yasuo *m*
太郎 Jintarō *m*
与茂 Jin'yomo *m*
目 Jinmoku *s*, Hadame
目寺 Jimokuji *p*
吾 Jingo *m*

兼 1268 [T] Kane *s*. (KEN, kane, tomo, kazu, kata, kanu)
[1]一 Ken'ichi *m*
[2]二 Kenji *m*
乙 Kaneoto *m*
入 Kanenari *m*
人 Kaneto *m*
[3]三郎 Kanesaburō *m*
之 Kanehide *m*
上 Kanetaka *m*
下 Kanemoto *m*
子 Kaneko *sf*
大 Kanehiro *m*
[4]心 Kanekiyo *m*
仁 Kanehito *m*, Tomohito
戸 Kanehiro *m*
分 Kanewaka *m*
日 Kaneaki *m*
及 Kanechika *m*
山 Kaneyama *sp*; Kanetaka *m*
井 Kanekiyo *m*
女 Kanetaka *ma*
太 Kanemoto *m*
太郎 Kanetarō *m*
[5]仍 Kaneyori *m*
付 Kanetomo *m*
代 Kaneyo *m*
外 Kanehiro *m*
公 Kanetomo *m*
令 Kaneyoshi *m*
古 Kanefuru *m*, Kanehisa
田 Kaneda *s*
平 Kanehira *s*
玉 Kanekiyo *m*
正 Kanemasa *m*
本 Kanemoto *s*
氏 Kaneuji *m*
白 Kanekiyo *m*
生 Kanenari *m*
[6]州 Kanekuni *m*
仙 Kanehito *m*
列 Kanetsura *m*
宅 Kaneie *m*
吉 Kanekichi *m*
同 Kanetomo *m*
在 Kaneari *m*
曲 Kanenori *m*
自 Kaneyori *m*
[7]位 Kanetaka *m*
住 Kanezumi *m*
伝 Kaneyoshi *m*
体 Kanemoto *m*
伴 Kanetomo *m*
伯 Kanetaka *m*
作 Kanenari *m*
坂 Kanesaka *s*
村 Kanemura *s*
杜 Kanemori *m*
好 Kenkō *ml*
言 Kanenobu *m*
足 Kanetari *m*
安 Kaneyasu *sm*
花 Kanehana *m*
床 Kaneyuka *m*
充 Kanemitsu *m*
孝 Kanetaka *m*
角 Kanezumi *m*
[8]明 Kaneakira *m*
知 Kanetomo *m*
房 Kanefusa *m*; Kenbō *s*
舎 Kaneie *m*
実 Kanesane *m*
宝 Kaneyoshi *m*
宏 Kanehiro *m*
英 Kanefusa *m*
若 Kanewaka *m*
青 Kaneharu *m*
奉 Kanetomo *m*
辰 Kanetoki *m*
武 Kanetake *m*
並 Kanenami *m*
[9]信 Kanenobu *m*
持 Kanemochi *m*
洞 Kaneaki *m*
待 Kanemachi *m*
施 Kanenobu *m*
姓 Kaneuji *s*
松 Kanematsu *s*
相 Kanesuke *m*
研 Kanekiyo *m*
刻 Kanetoki *m*
計 Kanekazu *m*
前 Kanesaki *m*
香 Kaneka *m*
廻 Kanenori *m*
重 Kaneshige *sm*
[10]倫 Kanetomo *m*
涌 Kanewaka *m*
従 Kanetsugu *m*
師 Kanemoro *m*
高 Kanetaka *s*
家 Kaneie *m*
員 Kanekazu *m*, Kanesada
屋 Kaneie *m*
馬 Kanemuma *m*
[11]惟 Kanetada *m*
陸 Kanemichi *m*
流 Kaneharu *m*, Kanetomo
得 Kanenari *m*
教 Kanenori *m*
常 Kanetsune *sm*
常清佐 K. Kiyosuke *ml*
[12]備 Kanetomo *m*
順 Kaneyori *m*
梢 Kanetaka *m*
敬 Kanetaka *m*

崇 Kanetaka *m*
等 Kanetomo *m*
集 Kanechika *m*
奥 Kaneoki *m*
遠 Kanemichi *m*
[13]源 Kanemoto *m*
福 Kanetomi *m*
植 Kanetane *m*
純 Kanesumi *m*
[14]像 Kanekata *m*
輔 Kanesuke *m*
銅 Kanekane *m*
裏 Kaneura *m*
節 Kanefushi *m*
熙 Kanehiro *m*
聞 Kanehiro *m*
関 Kanemori *m*
[15]誼 Kaneyoshi *m*
[16]衡 Kanehira *m*
続 Kanetsugu *m*
毅 Kanetake *m*
魄 Kaneai *m*
積 Kanetsune *m*
頭 Kanetō *s*
[20]護 Kanemori *m*
離 Kaneaki *m*
籌 Kanekoto *m*

### 11 L1

**胤** 1269 [N] Tsuzuki *m*. (IN, tane, tsugu, kazu, mi, tsugi)
昌 Tanesuke *m*
信 Tanenobu *m*
勇 Taneo *m*
貞 Tanesada *m*
禄 Taneyoshi *m*, Tanesachi
雄 Kazuo *m*
継 Kazutsugu *m*

### 11 L2

**條** 1270 See 条 457

**假** 1271 See 仮 231

**停** 1272 [T] Todomu *m*. (TEI)

**偏** 1273 [T] (HEN, yuki, tsura, tomo)

**偂** 1274 Susumu *m*. (SEN)

**修** 1275 (GAN, GEN, nise)
紫田舎源氏 Nise Murasaki inaka Genji *l*

**偵** 1276 [I] (TEI)
次 Teiji *m*

**偆** 1277 (SHUN, tomi)
子 Tomiko *f*

**値** 1278 [T] (CHI, ne)
賀 Chiga *s*

**俾** 1279 (HI, masa, masu, yasu)
加 Hika *s*

**俵** 1280 [T] Tawara *s*. (HYŌ, tawara)
山 Tawarayama *s*
木 Tawaragi *s*
谷 Tawaraya *s*
屋 Tawaraya *s*
屋宗達 T. Sōtatsu *ma*

**脩** 1281 Osamu *m*. (SHŪ, SHU, naga, nobu, osa, haru, sane, suke, nao)
夫 Nobuo *m*
広 Nagahiro *m*
孝 Naganori *m*
胤 Nobutane *m*

**健** 1282 [T] Ken *m*, Takeshi, Takeru, Tsuyoshi, Masaru, Kiyoshi. (KEN, take, tate, tsuyo, tatsu, taru, yasu, katsu, toshi, kiyo)
[1]一 Ken'ichi *m*
一郎 Ken'ichirō *m*
[2]二 Kenji *m*
二郎 Kenjirō *m*
人 Chikarahito *s*
[3]三 Kenzō *m*
三郎 Kenzaburō *m*
[4]介 Kensuke *m*
夫 Takeo *m*, Tatsuo
太郎 Kentarō *m*
[5]田 Takeda *s*
[6]次 Kenji *m*
次郎 Kenjirō *m*
吉 Kenkichi *m*
[7]作 Kensaku *m*
助 Kensuke *m*
志 Tsuyoshi *m*
吾 Kengo *m*
児 Takeru *m*
[9]治 Kenji *m*
治郎 Kenjirō *m*
[10]郎 Toshio *m*
軍 Takemiya *s*
彦 Takehiko *m*
晋 Katsuaki *m*
[11]康 Takeyasu *m*
[15]蔵 Kenzō *m*
[16]樹 Takeki *m*

**倭** 1283 Yamato *sm*, Shitori; Shizu *sf*; Hitori *s*, Mitori. (WA, I, shizu, yasu, masa, kazu, yamato)
子 Masako *f*
夫 Shizuo *m*, Kazuo
文 Shitori *sm*; Shizu *sf*
文子 Shizuko *f*
代 Yasuyo *f*
市 Waichi *m*
江 Shizue *f*
奴国 Wanona-no-kuni *ph*
名類聚鈔 Wamyō ruijūshō *l*
彦 Shizuhiko *m*
麻呂 Yamatomaro *m*
絵 Yamato-e *a*
蔵 Yasuzō *m*
鍛師 Yamatokanuchi *s*

### 11 L3

**唱** 1284 [T] Tonō *m*. (SHŌ, uta)

**啄** 1285 (TAKU)
二 Takuji *m*
木 Takuboku *ml*
治 Takuji *m*

**唯** 1286 [T] Tada *s*. (I, YUI, tada)
一 Tadaichi *m*, Tadakazu, Tadakatsu
人 Tadando *m*
心房集 Yuishinbōshū *l*
井 Tadai *s*
有 Yuyū *s*
男 Tadao *m*
雄 Tadao *m*
糊 Tadanori *m*

**悃** 1287 Isamu *m*, Hatasu. (KA)

**悴** 1287A (kase)
田 Kaseda *s*

**惇** 1288 Atsushi *m*, Makoto, Sunao. (JIN, SHUN, atsu, toshi)
氏 Atsuuji *m*
信 Atsunobu *m*
郎 Toshio *m*

**悌** 1289 [N] Yasushi *m*, Yoshi. (TEI, yasu, yoshi, tomo)
二郎 Teijirō *m*
三 Teizō *m*
三郎 Teisaburō *m*
夫 Tomoo *m*
次 Teiji *m*
吉 Teikichi *m*
成 Yasunari *m*

**惟** 1290 Tamotsu *m*. (I, YUI, kore, tada, nobu, yoshi, ari)
[1]一 Tadaichi *m*
[4]戸 Koredo *s*
[6]任 Koretō *s*
[7]住 Korezumi *s*
条 Koreeda *m*
[8]明 Koreakira *m*
宗 Koremune *sm*
忠 Koretada *m*
[9]前 Korechika *m*
[10]俊 Tadatoshi *m*
高 Yoshitaka *m*
恵 Yoshie *f*
[11]斌 Koreakira *m*
規 Nobunori *m*, Nobunari
紀 Koretada *m*
粛 Koretada *m*
[12]然 Izen *ml*
[13]詳 Koremitsu *m*
[14]精 Koreyoshi *m*, Koreshige
[15]雍 Koreyasu *m*
[16]親 Korechika *m*
幾 Korechika *m*

健 倭 唱 啄 唯 倮 悴 惇 悌 惟 ▼ 域 培 埼 埒 埃 堆 從 徠 術 得 後 猗 猊 狼 猫 猛 猪 陛 険 陟 陵 陳 陸 ▲ 隆 採 授 探 排 捧 掃 振 掛 推

**域** 1290A [T] (IKI, kuni, mura)

**培** 1291 [T] (BAI, masu)
子 Masuko *f*

**埼** 1292 (KI, sai)
玉 Saitama *p*

**埒** 1293 Osamu *m.* (SŌ, SHŌ)

**埃** 1294 (AI)
及 Ejiputo *p* "Egypt"

**堆** 1295 (TSUI, TAI, taka, nobu, oka)
朱 Tsuishu *sm*
朱屋 Tsuishuya *s*
橋 Uzuhashi *s*

**從** 1296 See 從 1050

**徠** 1297 (RAI, tone)

**術** 1298 [T] Yasushi *m*, Tedate. (JUTSU, yasu, michi)
太 Yasuta *m*

**得** 1299 [T] (TOKU, nari, e, u, ari, nori, yasu)
一 Narikazu *m*
三 Tokuzō *m*
三郎 Tokusaburō *m*
四郎 Tokushirō *m*
平 Tokuhira *sm*
地 Tokuji *s*
江 Tokue *s*
志恵 Ushie *f*
恒 Tokutsune *sm*
美子 Emiko *f*
重 Tokue *s*
馬 Tokuma *m*
能 Tokunō *sl*
道 Noriyori *m*
純 Toku *s*
撫 Uruppu *p*

**後** 1300 [T] Ushirogu *s*, Shitori. (GO, KŌ, nochi, nori, shitsu, shizu, shiri, ushiro, chika, mochi)
$^{3}$川 Shizukawa *sp*
小松 Gokomatsu *mh*
三条 Gosanjō *mh*
上 Gokami *s*
$^{4}$水尾 Gomizunoo *mlh*
月 Shitsuki *p*; Shiritsuki *s*
$^{5}$白河 Goshirakawa *mlh*
生 Nochinari *m*
$^{7}$村上 Gomurakami *mh*
町 Gochō *s*
志 Shiribeshi *p*
$^{8}$河 Shizukawa *s*
拈 Osama *s*
$^{9}$拾遺集 Goshūishū *l*
城 Shitsuki *m*
神 Gokō *s*
$^{10}$宮 Ushiromiya *s*, Ushiroku, Atomiya
$^{11}$深草 Gofukakusa *mh*
部 Shitoribe *s*
部高 Kōbukō *s*
鳥羽院 Gotobain *mlh*
鳥羽院宮内卿 G. Kunaikyō *fl*
亀山 Gokameyama *mh*
$^{12}$陽成 Goyōzei *mh*
間 Gokan *s*
開榛名梅ケ香 Okurezaki haruna no umegaka *la*
閑 Gokan *s*
$^{13}$漢書 Gokanjo *lh* "Hou-Han shu"
$^{14}$嵯峨 Gosaga *mh*
関 Goseki *s*
$^{15}$撰集 Gosenshū *l*
$^{16}$醍院 Godaiin *s*, Godai
醍醐 Godaigo *mh*
$^{18}$藤 Gotō *s*
藤田 Gotōta *s*
藤末雄 Gotō Sueo *ml*
藤宙外 G. Chūgai *mh*
藤祐乗 G. Yūjō *ma*
藤象二郎 G. Shōjirō *mh*
藤新平 G. Shinpei *mh*

**猗** 1301 (I, shige, yori)
夫 Shigeo *m*

**猊** 1302 (GEI, shishi, oi)
倉 Shishikura *s*

**狼** 1303 (RŌ, ōkami, oi)
之助 Ōkaminosuke *m*
坂 Oisaka *s*

**猫** 1304 (MYŌ, neko)
又 Nekomata *s*
丸 Nekomaru *s*
屋 Nekoya *s*

**猛** 1305 [T] Takeshi *m*, Takeru, Takeki, Takeo, Isamu. (MŌ, take, taka)
昌 Takemasa *m*
省 Takemi *m*
猪 Takei *m*
雄 Takeo *m*

**猪** 1306 [N] I *s*, Ino, Inoshishi. (CHO, i, ino, shishi)
$^{1}$一郎 Iichirō *m*
$^{2}$又 Inomata *s*
$^{3}$川 Inokawa *s*
口 Iguchi *s*, Inokuchi
之吉 Inokichi *m*
子 Inoko *s*
$^{4}$山 Inoyama *s*
木 Iki *s*
爪 Izume *s*
$^{5}$田 Ida *s*
甘 Ikai *s*
$^{6}$名 Ina *s*
名川 Inagawa *p*
名部 Inabe *s*
$^{7}$坂 Isaka *s*
村 Imura *s*
尾 Inoo *s*
$^{8}$使 Itsukai *s*
股 Inomata *s*
幸 Isachi *f*
苗代 Inawashiro *sp*
奈部 Inabe *s*
$^{9}$俣 Inomata *s*
狩 Ikari *s*
岡 Ioka *s*
$^{10}$家 Inoie *s*
原 Ihara *s*, Inohara
$^{11}$野 Ino *s*
野口 Inokuchi *s*
野毛 Inoge *s*
野謙二 Ino Kenji *ml*
$^{12}$間 Inoma *s*
$^{13}$隈 Inokuma *s*
越 Inokoshi *s*
$^{14}$腰 Inokoshi *s*
鼻 Inohana *s*
$^{15}$飼 Ikai *s*
熊 Inokuma *s*
$^{16}$橋 Inohashi *s*
養 Ikai *s*
$^{19}$瀬 Inose *s*

**陛** 1307 [T] Noboru *m*. (HEI, BAI, yori, nori)

**険** 1308 [T] (KEN, nori, taka)

**陟** 1309 Noboru *m.* (CHOKU, taka)
章 Takanori *m*

**陵** 1310 [T] Misasaki *s*. (RYŌ, taka, oka, sasaki)
戸 Sasakibe *s*
辺 Sasakibe *s*

**陳** 1311 [T] Noburu *m*; Chin *sm*. (CHIN, JIN, nobu, yoshi, kata, tsura, nori, hisa)
子 Nobuko *f*
内 Jinnouchi *s*
外郎 Uirō *s*
令 Nobuharu *m*
光 Katamitsu *m*
雄 Nobuo *m*

**陸** 1312 [T] Atsushi *m*, Takashi, Hitoshi, Kuga *s*. (RIKU, michi, mutsu, mu, atsu, kuga)
$^{3}$川 Rikukawa *s*
口 Mukuchi *s*
$^{4}$中 Rikuchū *ph*
井 Kugai *s*
$^{5}$田 Rikuda *s*, Kugata
$^{7}$別 Rikubetsu *p*
臣 Mutsuomi *m*
$^{8}$良 Michiyoshi *m*
$^{9}$前 Rikuzen *ph*
前高田 R. Takada *p*
長 Michinaga *m*
$^{10}$郎 Rikurō *m*
原 Rikuhara *s*
$^{12}$奥 Mutsu *sp*

奥子 Mutsuko *f*
奥宗光 Mutsu Munemitsu *mh*
奥話記 M. waki *l*
13雄 Mutsuo *m*
路 Mutsuro *s*
16羯南 Kuga Katsunan *mlh*

**隆** 1313 [T] Takashi *sm*; Yutaka *m.* (RYŪ, RYU, taka, shige, o, toki, naga, mori, oki)
1一 Ryūichi *m*
一郎 Ryūichirō *m*
2二 Ryūji *m*
3三 Ryūzō *m*
4文 Takatomo *m*
夫 Takao *m*
太郎 Ryūtarō *m*
5平 Takahira *m*, Takatoshi
正 Takamasa *m*
生 Takaari *m*
6次 Ryūji *m*
任 Takatō *m*
光 Takamitsu *m*
吉 Ryūkichi *m*, Takatomi
成 Takahide *m*
7玄 Takahiro *m*
声 Takana *m*
考 Takanaru *m*
孝 Takayoshi *m*
来 Tsuburai *s*
8門 Takato *m*
定 Takayasu *m*
孟 Takanaga *m*
英 Takahide *m*
季 Takasue *m*
国 Takakuni *ml*
良 Takahisa *m*
9信 Takanobu *m*
抵 Takayasu *m*
律 Takanori *m*
祐 Takasachi *m*
研 Takaaki *m*
育 Takayasu *m*
10俊 Takatoshi *m*
師 Takakazu *m*
造 Ryūzō *m*
束 Takayoshi *m*
11術 Takamichi *m*
章 Takatoshi *m*
盛 Takamori *m*
12備 Takatomo *m*
彭 Takamichi *m*
董 Takanao *m*
量 Takasato *m*
崇 Takashi *m*
達 Ryūtatsu *mla*
道 Takamasa *m*
13純 Takaito *m*
意 Takaosa *m*
督 Takamasa *m*
遠 Takatō *m*
業 Takanobu *m*
14精 Takasumi *m*
韶 Takatsugu *m*
聚 Takatsumu *m*
15璉 Takateru *m*
慰 Takanori *m*
16賢 Takamasu *m*
興 Takaoki *m*
17禧 Takayoshi *m*
謌 Takauta *m*

**採** 1314 [T] (SAI, mochi)

**授** 1315 [T] Sazuku *m.* (JU, SHŪ)

**探** 1316 [T] (TAN)
題 Tandai *l*

**排** 1317 [T] (HAI, oshi)
蘆小船 Ashiwake obune *l*

**捧** 1318 Sasage *s.* (HŌ, taka, kata, mochi)
泰 Takayasu *m*

**掃** 1319 [T] Kanimori *s.* (SŌ, kani)
守 Kanimori *s*, Kamori
部 Kanimori *s*, Kanbe; Kamon *sm*

**振** 1320 [T] (SHIN, furu, furi, toshi, nobu)
分髪 Furiwakegami *l*
田 Furuta *p*
武 Toshitake *m*

**掛** 1321 [T] (KE, kake)
川 Kakegawa *p*
札 Kakefuda *s*
合 Kakeya *p*
橋 Kakehashi *s*

**推** 1322 [T] (SUI, oshi)
川 Oshikawa *s*
古 Suiko *fh*
名 Oshina *s*

**捷** 1323 Katsu *m-f*; Satoshi *m*, Suguru, Masaru. (SHŌ, katsu, toshi, kachi, haya)
世 Katsuyo *f*
男 Kachio *m*
房 Toshifusa *m*
郎 Hayao *m*

**捨** 1324 [T] Sute *f.* (SHA, sute, ie, eda)
二 Suteji *m*
六 Iemutsu *m*
次郎 Sutejirō *m*
吉 Sutekichi *m*
造 Sutezō *m*
菊 Sutegiku *f*
鍋 Sutenabe *f*

**海** 1324A See 海 1071

**涙** 1325 See 涙 1062

**淺** 1326 See 浅 827

**淨** 1327 See 浄 823

**淇** 1328 Migiwa *m.* (KI, GI)

**浚** 1329 Fukashi *m.* (SHUN, fuka)

**涼** 1330 [T] (RYŌ, suke)
朝 Suketomo *m*

**渓** 1330A [I] Tani *s.* (KEI, tani)
中 Taninaka *s*

**渉** 1331 [T] Wataru *m.* (SHŌ, JŌ, sada, tada, taka)
子 Tadako *f*

**流** 1332 [T] (RYŪ, RU, haru, tomo, shika, nagare, naga)
水 Nagami *s*
山 Nagareyama *p*
石 Sasuga *s*
宣 Tomonobu *m*
綱 Harutsuna *m*

**淀** 1333 Yodo *p.* (TEN, yodo)
川 Yodogawa *p-l*
川油糟 Y. aburakasu *l*
江 Yodoe *p-l*
君 Yodogimi *fh*
屋 Yodoya *s*
屋辰五郎 Y. Tatsugorō *mh*
野 Yodono *s*
野隆三 Y. Ryūzō *ml*

**渋** 1334 [T] (SHŪ, shibu)
川 Shibukawa *sp*
川玄耳 S. Genji *ml*
川春海 S. Shunkai *mh*
川驍 S. Gyō *ml*
井 Shibui *s*
木 Shibuki *s*
右衛門 Shibuemon *m*
江 Shibue *s*
江抽斎 S. Chūsai *mh-l*
沢 Shibusawa *s*
沢栄一 S. Eiichi *mh*
谷 Shibuya *sp*; Shibutani *s*, Shibue
谷定輔 Shibuya Sadasuke *ml*
河 Shibukawa *s*

**淑** 1335 [T] Kiyoshi *m*, Yoshi, Fukashi. (SHUKU, yoshi, toshi, kiyo, sumi, yo, sue, hide)
人 Yoshito *m*
子 Yoshiko *f*, Toshiko, Kiyoko, Sumiko
允 Yoshioka *m*
成 Yoshinari *m*
郎 Toshio *m*
望 Yoshimochi *m*

**済** 1336 [T] Wataru *m*, Watari, Watasu, Tōru, Satoru, I-

猫 猛 猪 陸 険 陟 陵 陳 陸 ▼ 隆 採 授 探 排 捧 掃 振 掛 推 捷 捨 海 涙 淺 淨 淇 浚 涼 渓 渉 流 淀 渋 淑 済 ▲ 淳 添 浪 淡 深 清 族 炫 弦

淇 浚 涼 渓 渉 流 淀 渋 淑 済 ▼ 淳 添 浪 淡 深 清 ▲ 族 炫 弦 朏 胸 視 規 峨 峰 旱

tsuki. (SEI, SAI, nari, masa, sumi, tada, naru, masu, yasu, yoshi, sada, o, kata, wata)
子 Nariko *f*
夫 Masuo *m*
治 Seiji *m*
時 Yasutoki *m*
陽 Watayō *s*

淳 1337 [N] Jun *m*, Sunao, Atsushi, Kiyoshi, Tadashi, Makoto. (JUN, SHUN, atsu, kiyo, suna, toshi, aki, yoshi)
一郎 Jun'ichirō *m*
之助 Junnosuke *m*
子 Atsuko *f*
夫 Sunao *m*
秀 Yoshihide *m*
国 Atsukuni *m*
治 Junji *m*
浩 Kiyohiro *m*
高 Toshitaka *m*
教 Atsunori *m*

添 1338 [T] (TEN, soe)
上 Soekami *p*
子 Soeko *f*
田 Soeda *sp*
野 Soeno *s*
御杖 Soenomitsue *s*

浪 1339 [T] (RŌ, nami)
川 Namikawa *s*
子 Namiko *f*
平 Namihei *s*
江 Namie *f-p*
合 Namiai *sp*
花 Rōka *ml*
花停 Nanbatei *s*
貝 Namikai *m*
秀 Namihide *m*
貞 Namisada *m*
岡 Namioka *p*
速 Naniwa *p*
野 Namino *s*
雄 Namio *m*
越 Nagoshi *s*

淡 1340 [T] Awashi *m*, Awaji. (TAN, ⌊awa, ō)
川 Ōkawa *s*
近 Awachika *s*
河 Akawa *s*, Arakawa, Aikawa, Agō, Awa- ⌊ka
相 Awai *s*
海 Ōmi *sm*
海三船 Ō. no Mifune
屋 Awajiya *s* ⌊*ml*
理 Awamaro *m*
島 Awashima *s* ⌈*ml*
島寒月 A. Kangetsu
路 Awaji *m-p*
輪 Tannowa *s*, Tan- ⌊nori
瀬 Awase *s*

深 1341 [T] Fukashi *m*. (SHIN, fuka, mi, tō)
8川 Fukagawa *sp*
4水 Fukami *s*
日 Fukehi *s*
山 Fukayama *s*, Miya- ⌊ma
井 Fukai *s*
木 Fukaki *s*
5目 Fukame *s*
田 Fukada *sp*; Fukuda *s* ⌈*ml*
田久弥 Fukada Kyūya
田康算 F. Yasukazu
6江 Fukae *sm-p* ⌊*ml*
7作 Fukasaku *s*, Mitsukuri
沢 Fukazawa *s*
沢七郎 F. Shichirō *ml*
坂 Fukazaka *s*
町 Fukamachi *s*
谷 Fukaya *sp*; Fukagai
安 Fukayasu *p* ⌊*s*
尾 Fukao *s*
尾正治の手記 F. Shōji no shuki *l* ⌈*fl*
尾須磨子 F. Sumako
見 Fukami *s*
8和 Fukawa *s*
9洲 Fukasu *s*
津 Fukatsu *s*
柄 Fukae *s*
草 Fukakusa *s*
10浦 Fukaura *p*
海 Fukami *s*, Fukai
栖 Fukasu *s*, Misu
原 Fukabara *s*
11野 Fukano *s*
巣 Fukasu *s*
雪 Miyuki *f*
12間内 Fukamauchi *s*
13淵 Fukasu *s*
溝 Fukamizo *s*, Fuka- ⌊utsu
堀 Fukabori *s*
14翠 Midori *f*
16養父 Fukayabu *m*
17覧 Fukami *m*
19瀬 Fukase *s*
瀬基寛 F. Motohiro *ml*

清 1342 [T] Kiyoshi *m*; Suga *f*; Sei *sm*; Sumeri *s*. (SEI, SHŌ, SHIN, kiyo, suga, sumi, sumu)
1一 Seiichi *m*
一郎 Seiichirō *m*
2二 Seiji *m*
七 Seishichi *m*
人 Kiyohito *m*, Kiyondo
8川 Kiyokawa *sp*
三郎 Seizaburō *m*
之助 Seinosuke *m*
子 Kiyoko *f*
久 Kiyohisa *sm*
4心 Kiyomune *m*
水 Shimizu *sp*, Kiyomizu ; Kiyomi *m*
水千代 S. Chiyo *fl*
水寺 Kiyomizu-dera *p*
水谷 Shimizudani *s*
水信 Shimizu Shin *ml*
水浜臣 S. Hamaomi *ml*
水清玄誓約桜 Kiyomizu Seigen chikai no sakura *la*
水基吉 Shimizu Motoyoshi *ml*
水幾太郎 S. Ikutarō *ml*
元 Kiyomoto *sm-a*
内路 Seinaiji *p*
少納言 Sei Shōnagon *fl* ⌈ma
山 Kiyoyama *s*, Seiya-
夫 Sugao *m*, Kiyoo
太郎 Seitarō *m*
方 Kiyokata *m*
5永 Kiyonaga *s*
公 Kiyokimi *m*
右衛門 Seiemon *m*
左 Kiyosuke *m*
四郎 Seishirō *m*
田 Kiyota *s*, Seita
正 Kiyomasa *m*
生 Kiyō *m*
本 Kiyomoto *s*
6州 Kiyosu *ph*
次 Kiyotsugu *m*
次郎 Seijirō *m*
江 Kiyoe *s*
行 Kiyoyasu *m*
先 Kiyosaki *m*
成 Kiyonari *sm*
7住 Kiyosumi *s*
作 Seisaku *m*
沢 Kiyozawa *sp*
沢満之 K. Manshi *ml*
村 Kiyomura *s*
足 Kiyotari *m*
安 Kiyoyasu *m*
兵衛 Seibee *m*
兵衛と瓢簞 S. to hyō-
里 Kiyosato *p* ⌊tan *l*
見 Kiyomi *sm-p*; Kiyoaki *m*, Seiken
玄 Kiyoharu *m*
臣 Sugaomi *m*
身 Kiyomi *m*
8河 Kiyokawa *s*
枚 Kiyokazu *m*
和 Seiwa *mh-p*
和井 Segai *sp*
房 Kiyofusa *m*
芽 Kiyome *m*
岑 Kiyomine *s*
秀 Kiyohide *m*
武 Kiyotake *p*
尚 Kiyohisa *m*
9信 Kiyonobu *m*
恪 Kiyotaka *m*
洲 Kiyosu *p*
治 Seiji *m*, Kiyoharu
治湯講釈 Seijiyu kō-
砂 Seisa *m* ⌊shaku *l*
科 Kiyoshina *s*
勇 Kiyotake *m*
品 Kiyohide *m*
宣 Kiyonobu *m*
長 Kiyonaga *m*
音 Kiyone *p*
岡 Kiyooka *s*
風 Seifū *s*
彦 Kiyohiko *m*
哉 Kiyoka *m*
10倍 Kiyomasu *m*
修 Kiyonaga *m*
従 Kiyotsugu *m*
海 Kiyomi *sm*
浦 Kiyoura *s*
浦奎吾 K. Keigo *mh*
格 Kiyotada *m*
貢 Kiyotsugu *m*
宮 Kiyomiya *s*, Seimiya ⌈Seige
家 Kiyoie *sm* ; Seika *s*,
原 Kiyohara *s*

原元輔 K. no Motosuke *ml*
原武則 K. Takenori *mh*
原宣賢 K. Nobukata *mh*
原深養父 K. no Fukayabu *ml*
[11]健 Kiyotake *m*
隆 Kiyotaka *m*
猛 Kiyotaka *m*
深 Kiyomi *m*
族 Kiyotsugu *m*
野 Kiyono *s*, Seino
剛 Kiyokata *m*
晏 Kiyoharu *m*
盛 Kiyomori *m*
庸 Kiyonori *m*
馬 Seima *m*, Kiyome
島 Kiyojima *s*
[12]須美 Kiyosumi *s*
温 Kiyoharu *m*
湖 Seiko *m*
就 Kiyonari *m*
閑寺 Seikanji *s*
[13]満 Kiyomitsu *m*
湍 Kiyose *s*
源 Kiyomoto *s*
塚 Kiyozuka *s*
棲 Kiyosumi *s*
張 Kiyoharu *m*
雄 Sumio *m*
意 Kiyonori *m*
義 Kiyoshi *m*
[14]徳 Kiyonori *m*
種 Kiyokazu *m*
輔 Kiyosuke *ml*
豪 Kiyohide *m*, Kiyokata
[15]澄 Kiyosumi *s*
輝 Kiyoteru *m*
輪 Kiyowa *f*
談松の調 Seidan matsu no shirabe *l*
談峰初花 S. -mine no hatsuhana *l*
蔵 Seizō *m*
[16]親 Kiyochika *m*
[17]綱 Kiyotsuna *m*
[18]藤 Seitō *s*, Kiyofuji
[19]瀬 Kiyose *sp*
額 Kiyonuka *s*
[22]曦 Kiyoteru *m*

## ——11 L4——

**族** 1343 [T] Yakara *m.* (ZOKU, SOKU, tsugu, tsugi, eda)

**炫** 1344 (GEN, KEN, aki)
隆 Akitaka *m*

**弦** 1345 [T] (GEN, KEN, tsuru, o, ito, fusa)
一郎 Gen'ichiro *m*
木 Tsuruki *s*
男 Tsuruo *m*
巻 Tsurumaki *s*
彦 Tsuruhiko *m*
孫 Tsuruhiko *m*

**朏** 1346 Mikazuki *s.* (KOTSU, KOCHI)

**胸** 1347 [T] (KYŌ, KU, mune)
刺 Musashi *sp*
治 Muneharu *m*

**視** 1348 [T] (SHI, JI, mi, nori)
之 Noriyuki *m*
秧 Minae *m*

**規** 1349 [T] Tadashi *m*, Tadasu. (KI, nori, tada, nari, chika, moto)
矩 Noritsune *m*, Motonori; Kiku *s*
矩次 Kikuji *m*
清 Norikiyo *m*

**峨** 1350 (GA)
山 Gazan *s*

**峰** 1351 [T] Mine *sp*; Takashi *m.* (HŌ, FU, mine, o, ne, taka)
[1]一郎 Mineichirō *m*
[3]三郎 Minesaburō *m*
子 Mineko *f*
[4]元 Minemoto *s*
山 Mineyama *p*
[5]本 Minemoto *s*
田 Mineta *s*
[7]村 Minemura *s*
尾 Mineo *sf*
[9]松 Minematsu *s*
岸 Minegishi *s*
重 Mineshige *m*
[10]浦 Mineura *s*
浜 Minehama *p*
[11]島 Mineshima *s*
[12]崎 Minezaki *s*

**旱** 1352 Noboru *m.* (KAN, GEN)

**晤** 1353 (GO, aki)

**昢** 1354 (HOTSU, HOCHI, hide)
夫 Hideo *m*

**晧** 1355 Akira *m.* (KŌ, GŌ, aki, tsugu)
之 Akiyuki *m*
章 Tsuguaki *m*

**娥** 1356 Kao *f.* (GA)

**姨** 1357 (I, oba)
捨 Obasute *la*

**姫** 1358 [T] (KI, I, hime)
子 Himeko *f*
戸 Himedo *p*
田 Himeda *s*
野 Himeno *s*
島 Himeshima *sp*
路 Himeji *p*

**球** 1359 [T] (KYŪ, GU, tama)
二 Tamaji *m*
子 Tamako *f*
恵 Tamae *f*
磨 Kuma *p*

**現** 1360 [T] (GEN, KEN, mi, ari)
在七面 Genzai shichimen *la*
在忠度 G. Tadanori *la*
在鵺 G. nue *la*
爾也娑婆 Geniya saba *l*
影 Gen'ei *s*

**理** 1361 [T] Osamu *m*, Tadashi, Tadasu, Sadamu; Michi *f.* (RI, michi, masa, tada, toshi, nori, suke, maro, taka, yoshi, aya, osa)
一郎 Riichirō *m*
二 Toshiji *m*
上 Rinoue *s*
文 Masafumi *m*
夫 Michio *m*
正 Michimasa *m*
作 Risaku *m*
里有楽 Ririura *l*
使 Masatsugu *m*
泰 Masayasu *m*

**梢** 1362 Kozue *m-f.* (SHŌ, taka, sue)

**椛** 1363 Sometimes used mistakenly for 樺 2103 q.v.

**栲** 1364 (KŌ, taku)

**梧** 1365 (GO, kiri)
一 Goichi *m*

**梓** 1366 Azusa *m.* (SHIN, azusa)
川 Azusagawa *p*
神子 Azusa miko *l*

**梛** 1367 (NA, nagi)
男 Nagio *m*
野 Nagino *s*

**桝** 1368 (masu)
子 Masuko *f*
田 Masuda *s*
本 Masumoto *s*
伊 Masui *m*
谷 Masutani *s*

**桶** 1369 (TŌ, TSU, oke)
川 Okegawa *p*
田 Okeda *s*
谷 Oketani *s*
狭間 Okehazama *p*
師 Tsushi *s*

**彬** 1370 Akira *m*, Yoshi, Shigeshi; Aki *f.* (HIN, aki, yoshi, hide, aya, mori)

江 Yoshie *f*
光 Akimitsu *m*
男 Ayao *m*

梶 1371 Kaji *s.* (BI, kaji)
ヶ谷 Kajigaya *s*
川 Kajikawa *s*
山 Kajiyama *s*
木 Kajiki *s*
井 Kajii *s* ⌈*ml*
井基次郎 K. Motojirō
田 Kajita *s*
本 Kajimoto *s*
成 Kajinari *m*
村 Kajimura *s*
谷 Kajiya *s*, Kajitani
浦 Kajiura *s* ⌈*ml*
浦正之 K. Masayuki
原 Kajiwara *s* ⌈*mh*
原景時 K. Kagetoki
野 Kajino *s*
島 Kajishima *s*
塚 Kajitsuka *s*
間 Kajima *s*

根 1372 [T] (KON, ne, moto)
ノ井 Nenoi *s*
3上 Neagari *p*
子 Netsuko *s*
4元 Nemoto *s*
木 Motoki *s*
井 Nei *s*, Nenoi
5石 Neishi *s*
立 Nedate *s*
田 Konda *s*, Neda
本 Nemoto *s*
6羽 Neba *p*
7村 Nemura *s*
尾 Neo *sp*
来 Negoro *sp*
8府川 Nebukawa *s*
東 Kondō *s*
津 Nezu *s*
津権現裏 N. Gongen ura *l* ⌈*sa l*
南志具佐 Nenashigu-
岸 Negishi *s*
長 Nenaga *m*
10室 Nemuro *p*
11麻呂 Nemaro *m*
12橋 Nebashi *s*

桜 1373 [T] Sakura *sm-f-p.* (Ō, sakura)
3川 Sakuragawa *sp-la*
4内 Sakurauchi *s*, Ōuchi
山 Sakurayama *s*
木 Sakuragi *sp*
井 Sakurai *sp*
井天壇 S. Tendan *ml*
井忠温 S. Chūon *ml*
井駅 S. no eki *l*
井錠二 S. Jōji *mh*
5田 Sakurada *s*
田左交 S. Sakō *ml*
田百衛 S. Momoe *ml*
田治助 S. Jisuke *ml*
本 Sakuramoto *s*
6江 Sakurae *p*
7沢 Sakurazawa *s*
町 Sakuramachi *s*
8林 Sakurabayashi *s*
9岡 Sakuraoka *s*
庭 Sakuraba *s*
11根 Sakurane *s*
姫全伝曙草紙 Sakurahime zenden akebono-zōshi *l*
島 Sakurajima *sp-l*
12間 Sakurama *s*, Sakuraba

梅 1374 [T] Ume *sla.* (BAI, ume, me)
ヶ島 Umegashima *p*
3川 Umegawa *s*
小路 Umekōji *s*, Umenokōji
上 Umegami *s*
干 Umeboshi *s*, Hoya
子 Umeko *f*
4戸 Umedo *s*
山 Umeyama *s*
木 Umeki *s*
太郎 Umetarō *m*
5北 Umekita *s*
四郎 Umeshirō *m*
本 Umemoto *s*
本克巳 U. Katsumi *ml*
田 Umeda *sp*
田晴夫 U. Haruo *ml*
田雲浜 U. Unpin *mh*
6地 Umeji *s*, Umechi
吉 Umekichi *m*
辻 Umetsuji *s*
多田 Umetada *s*
7沢 Umezawa *s*
村 Umemura *s*
谷 Umetani *s*
男 Umeo *m*
8沼 Umenuma *s*
門 Umenoto *s*
枝 Umegae *l*
林 Umebayashi *s*
若 Umewaka *s*
忠 Umetada *s*
雨小袖昔八丈 Tsuyu kosode mukashi hachijō *la*
9津 Umezu *s* ⌈*ml*
亭金鵞 Baitei Kinga
家 Umegae *s*
岡 Umeoka *sf*
10浦 Umeura *s*
宮 Umemiya *s*
原 Umehara *s* ⌈*ml*
原北明 U. Hokumei
原竜三郎 U. Ryūsaburō *ma*
屋 Umeya *s*
11渓 Umetani *s*
根 Umene *s*
野 Umeno *s*
島 Umejima *s*
12崎 Umezaki *s*
崎春生 U. Haruo *ml*
森 Umemori *s*
13雄 Umeo *m*
鉢 Umebachi *s*
園 Umezono *sm*
14壺 Umetsubo *f*
暮里 Umebori *s*
暦 Umegoyomi *l*
謙次郎 Ume Kenjirō
巌 Baigan *ml* ⌊*mh*

## 11 L5

皎 1375 Akira *m.* (KŌ, KYŌ, aki)

眠 1376 [T] (MIN, nemuri)
狂四郎 Nemuri Kyōshirō *m*

務 1377 [T] Tsutomu *m.* (MU, BU, kane, chika, naka, tsuyo, michi)
子 Chikako *f*
本 Kanemoto *m*
台 Mutai *s*

移 1378 [T] Wataru *m.* (I, SHI, yori, nobu, ya, yoki)
竹 Ichiku *ml*

祥 1379 See 祥 1074

祇 1380 (SHI, tada, masa, yoshi, masu, yasu)
文 Masafumi *m*

畦 1381 (KEI, aze, une)
森 Unemori *s*
籠 Azekura *s*

畤 1382 (SHI, SHICHI, JI, aze)
籠 Azekura *s*, Azemuro

研 1383 See 研 875

硎 1384 Toki *s.* (KEI, GYŌ)

硈 1385 Katashi *m.* (KATSU, KACHI)

砥 1386 (SHI, TEI, TAI, to)
川 Togawa *s*
上 Togami *s*
用 Tomochi *p*
部 Tobe *p*
鹿 Toga *s*

## 11 L6

蛇 1387 (JA, hebi)
口 Hebiguchi *s*
性の婬 Jasei no in *l*
柳 Jayanagi *l*
塚 Hebizuka *s*

瓶 1388 (HEI, BIN, kame)
子 Heishi *s*
尻 Kameshiri *s*, Mikajiri

粒 1389 [T] (RYŪ, tsubu)
良 Tsubura *s*

粕 1390 (HAKU, kasu)

川 Kasugawa *sp*
谷 Kasuya *s*
屋 Kasuya *p*

船 1391 [T] (SEN, ZEN, fune, funa)
3子 Funako *f*
4水 Funamizu *s*
戸 Funado *s*
戸川 Funatogawa *s*
戸部 Funatobe *s*
井 Funai *sp*
木 Funagi *s*
山 Funayama *s*
山馨 F. Kaoru *ml*
5引 Funahiki *p*
田 Funada *s*
本 Funamoto *s*
生 Funyū *s*
6江 Funae *s*
弁慶 Funa-Benkei *la*
7坂 Funasaka *s*
9津 Funatsu *s*
岡 Funaoka *p*
10倉 Funakura *s*
12場 Funaba *s*
渡 Funado *s*
崎 Funazaki *s*
13越 Funakoshi *sp*
15穂 Funaho *p*
16橋 Funabashi *sp-la*

## ——11 L7——

斜 1392 [T] (SHA)
里 Shari *p*

朔 1393 Hajime *m.* (SAKU, kita, mo- ⌊to)
郎 Kitarō *m*

朗 1394 [T] Akira *m*, Hogara. (RŌ, aki, akira, sae, o, toki)
子 Saeko *f*
詠 Rōei *l*
徹 Akimichi *m*

釈 1395 [T] (SEKI, SHAKU, toki)
日本紀 Shaku Nihongi *l* ⌈kurube
迦如来 Nigume *s*, Ni-
迦牟尼仏 Nikurube *s*, Mikurube, Nikurōbe, Nigurome
迢空 Shaku Chōkū *ml*

躬 1396 (KYŪ, KU, mi, moto, nao, chika, miru)
仁 Mihito *m*
行 Motoyuki *m*
和 Kuwa *s*
恒 Mitsune *m*
治 Motoharu *m*
則 Minori *m*
弦 Mitsuru *m*
澄 Misumi *m*

能 1397 [T] Chikara *m*; Nō *la.* (NŌ, no, yoshi, yasu, nori, hisa, michi, yoki, taka, mu- ⌊ne, tō)
3川 Nogawa *s*
5代 Noshiro *p*
生 Nou *s*
6任 Noto *s*
光 Yasumitsu *m*
有 Yoshiari *m*
因 Nōin *ml* ⌈shū *l*
因法師集 N. Hōshi
因歌枕 N. utamakura ⌊*l*
世 Nose *s*
7作書 Nōsakusho *l*
沢 Nosawa *s*
村 Nomura *s*
見 Nomi *s*
8阿弥 Nōami *ma*
9津 Nozu *s*
宣 Yoshinobu *ml*
美 Nomi *sp*
10恵 Yokie *m*
11都 Noto *p*
島 Nojima *s*
12登 Noto *p*
登川 Notogawa *p*
登屋 Notoya *s*
登島 Notojima *p*
運 Yoshikazu *m*
達 Yoshisato *m*, Michitada
13雄 Yoshio *m*
楽 Nōgaku *la*
義 Nogi *p*
勢 Nose *sp*
19瀬 Nose *s*

野 1398 [T] (YA, no, hiro, nu, tō, nao)
1一色 Noishiki *s*
2七里 Noshichiri *s*
3川 Nogawa *s*
三 Yazō *s*
上 Nogami *sp*
上弥生子 N. Yaeko *fl*
上豊一郎 N. Toyoichirō *ml*
口 Noguchi *s*; Hiroaki *m* ⌈*ml*
口米次郎 N. Yonejirō
口英世 N. Hideyo *mh*
口雨情 N. Ujō *ml*
口寧斎 N. Neisai *ml*
々口 Nonoguchi *s*
々口立圃 N. Ryūho *ml*
々村 Nonomura *s*
々村仁清 N. Ninsei *ma* ⌈*ma*
々村宗達 N. Sōtatsu
4元 Nomoto *s*
分 Nowaki *l* ⌈*ml*
水 Nomizu *s*; Yasui
中 Nonaka *s*
内 Nouchi *s*
火 Nobi *l*
山 Noyama *s*
井 Noi *s*
木 Nogi *sp*
与 Noyo *s*, Noyori
5扒 Noiri *s*
北 Nokita *s*
尻 Nojiri *sp*
尻湖 Nojiriko *p*
辺 Nobe *s*
辺田 Nobeta *s*
辺地 Nobeji *sp*
市 Noichi *p*
本 Nomoto *s*
矢 Noya *s*
生司 Nōsu *s*
田 Noda *sp*
田川 Nodagawa *p*
平 Nohira *s*
末 Nozue *s*
6州良 Yasura *m*
地 Nochi *s*
百合 Noyuri *f*
守 Nomori *la*
寺 Nodera *s*
世渓 Nosedani *s*
老 Tokoro *s*
老山 Tokoroyama *s*
母崎 Nomozaki *p*
7坂 Nozaka *s*, Nosaka
沢 Nozawa *sp*
村 Nomura *sp*
村吉三郎 N. Kichisaburō *mh*
村吉哉 N. Yoshiya *ml*
村朱鱗洞 N. Shurindō *ml*
村泊月 N. Hakugetsu *ml*
村胡堂 N. Kodō *ml*
村隈畔 N. Waihan *ml*
谷 Nodani *s*
安 Noyasu *s*
苅家 Nokariya *s*
条 Nojō *s*, Nozashi
足 Notari *m*
呂 Noro *s*
呂元丈 N. Genjō *mh*
呂松 Noromatsu *s*
里 Nozato *s*
出 Node *s*
見 Nomi *s*
見山 Nomiyama *s*
見山朱鳥 N. Asuka *ml*
8波 Nonami *s*
坡 Yaba *ml*
於 Nonoe *s*
林 Nobayashi *s*
宝 Nomi *s*
迫川 Nosegawa *sp*
9依 Noyori *s*
城 Noshiro *s*
畑 Nohata *s*, Nobata
洲 Yasu *sp*
津 Notsu *sp*; Nozu *s*
津原 Notsuhara *p*
長瀬 Nonagase *s*
栄 Nosaka *p* ⌈kō *l*
10晒紀行 Nozarashi ki-
郎虫 Yarō mushi *l*
宮 Nomiya *s*; Nonomiya *sla*
原 Nohara *s*
馬 Noma *s*
11根 None *s*
野口 Nonoguchi *s*
野山 Nonoyama *s*
野市 Nonoichi *p*
野村 Nonomura *s*
野垣 Nonogaki *s*
野宮 Nonomiya *s*
部 Yabe *s*
副 Nozoe *s*
島 Nojima *s*
12崎 Nozaki *s*
崎左文 N. Sabun *ml*
萩 Nohagi *s*
賀 Noga *s*
雁 Nokari *m*
間 Noma *s*
間宏 N. Hiroshi *ml*
間清治 N. Seiji *ml*
間口 Nomaguchi *s*
13満 Nomitsu *s*

粕船斜朔朗釈躬能野▼訥訢設訳許敍敕救致教敏尉乾彫彩鈔釧釣郭部都執紈糾紅紀▲勔剩剝副剛眞翁巢奇

溝 Nomizo *s*
塚 Nozuka *s*
堀 Nobori *s*
路 Noji *s*
$^{14}$際 Nogiwa *s*
$^{19}$瀬 Nose *s*

訥 1399 (TOTSU, mori)

訢 1400 Makoto *m.* (KIN, KON, yoshi)

設 1401 [T] (SETSU, nobu, oki)
楽 Shidara *sp*

訳 1402 (YAKU, EKI, tsugu, wake)
樋 Wakehi *s*

許 1403 [T] (KYO, KO, moto, yuku)
子 Motoko *f*
六 Kyoroku *ml*
西部 Kosebe *s*
曾部 Kosobe *s*
斐 Kohi *s*, Konomi,
勢 Kose *s* ⌊Koi

敍 1404 See 叙 893

敕 1405 (CHOKU, tada, toki)
介 Tadasuke *m*

救 1406 [T] Tasuke *m.* (KYŪ, KU, suke, nari, hira, yasu)
仁郷 Kunigo *s*
世観音 Guze Kannon
済 Gusai *ml* ⌊*a*

致 1407 [T] Itasu *m*, Itaru. (CHI, tomo, yoshi, nori, mune, yuki, oki)
也 Munenari *m*
公 Yoshitada *m*
行 Yoshiyuki *m*
美 Noriyoshi *m*
陳 Yoshinobu *m*
寛 Tomohiro *m*

教 1408 [T] Oshie *m.* (KYŪ, KŌ, nori, michi, kazu, taka, yuki, ko, nari)
子 Noriko *f*
用 Norimochi *m*
成 Yukinari *m*
邦 Norikuni *m*
来石 Kyōraishi *s*
尚 Noritaka *m*
訓雑長持 Kyōkunzō nagamochi *l*
翅 Norinobu *m*
馬 Kazuma *m*
兼 Norikane *m*

敏 1409 [T] Satoshi *m*, Bin, Toshi, Hayashi, Haya, Minu. (BIN, MIN, toshi, to, haru, sato, haya, yuki)
$^{1}$一 Bin'ichi *m*
$^{8}$之 Satoshi *m*
子 Toshiko *f*
$^{5}$功 Toshikatsu *m*
四郎 Toshirō *m*
且 Toshikatsu *m*
$^{6}$行 Toshiyuki *m*, Toshitsura
$^{7}$男 Toshio *m*
$^{8}$明 Toshiaki *m*
昉 Toshiakira *m*
事 Toshiwaza *m*
$^{9}$保 Haruyasu *m*
彦 Toshihiko *m*
$^{10}$般 Toshikazu *m*
郎 Toshio *m*, Toshirō
馬 Toshima *s*
$^{21}$鎌 Togama *m*

## 11 L8

尉 1410 [T] (I, UTSU, UCHI, jō, yasu)
一 Jōichi *m*
女 Yasujo *f*
功 Yasuko *f*

乾 1411 [T] Tsutomu *m*, Susumu, Takeshi; Inui *s.* (KAN, KEN, kimi, fu)
元 Kengen 1302–03
山 Kenzan *ma*
雄 Kimio *m*
漆像 Kanshitsu-zō *a*

彫 1412 [T] (CHŪ, hori)
物屋 Horimonoya *s*

彩 1413 [T] Aya *f.* (SAI, tami)
世 Tamiyo *f*

鈔 1414 Kiyoshi *m.* (SHŌ)

釧 1415 Tamaki *m*; Kushiro *s.* (SEN, kushi)
路 Kushiro *p*

釣 1416 [I] (CHŌ, tsuru, tsuri)
子 Tsuruko *f*
狐 Tsurigitsune *la*
船 Tsuribune *s*

郭 1417 [T] (KAKU, hiro)
子 Hiroko *f*

部 1418 [T] (BU, HO, be, he, moto, ki-
曲 Kakibe *s* ⌊tsu)
坂 Hesaka *s*
将 Tamuronoosa *s*

都 1419 [T] Miyako *sm-f.* (TO, TSU, kuni, miyako, ichi, sato, hiro)
$^{2}$刀 Tsuto *s*
$^{3}$万 Tsuma *p*
子 Satoko *f*
丸 Tomaru *s*
$^{4}$太夫一中 Miyakodayū Itchū *ma*
木 Takagi *s*
$^{5}$生 Tsuki *f*
甲 Togō *s*, Tokō
氏文集 Toshi bunshū
$^{6}$竹 Tsudake *s* ⌊*l*
江 Kunie *f*
守 Tsumori *s*
吉 Tokichi *m*
$^{7}$住 Tsuzumi *s*
岐沙羅柵 Tsukisaranoki *s*
所 Todokoro *s*
祁 Tsuge *p*
$^{8}$努 Tsuno *s*
並 Tsunami *s*
良香 Miyako no Yoshika *ml*
$^{9}$城 Miyakonojō *s*, Miyashiro
治 Kuniharu *m*; Toji
南 Tonan *p* ⌊*s*
$^{10}$倉 Tokura *s*
$^{11}$野井 Tsunoi *s*
都美 Tsuzumi *sf*
留 Tsuru *sp*
島 Miyakojima *p*
鳥 Tsutori *s*
$^{12}$崎 Tsuzaki *s*
富 Tsutomi *s*
賀 Tsuga *sp*; Toga *s*
賀夫 Tsugao *m*
賀庭鐘 Tsuga Teishō
筑 Tsuzuki *s* ⌊*ml*
$^{13}$路 Tsuji *s*; Miyako-
$^{14}$窪 Tsukubo *p* ⌊ji *p*
$^{16}$操 Tosao *f*
築 Tsuzuki *s*
築省吾 T. Shōgo *ml*
幾川 Tokigawa *p*
$^{17}$濃 Tsuno *sp*

執 1420 (SHITSU, SHŪ, SHU, mori,
子 Moriko *f* ⌊tori)
行 Shugyō *s*, Shikkō

紈 1421 (GAN, kinu)
子 Kinuko *f*

糾 1422 [T] Tadasu *m*, Tadashi, (KYŪ, KU, tada)
夫 Tadao *m*
明 Tadaaki *m*

紅 1423 [T] Kurenai *s.* (KŌ, GU, momi, aka, iro, kure, beni)
子 Momiko *f*
毛 Kōmo *s*
白 Irimazari *s*
谷 Beniya *s*
林 Kurebayashi *s*
良 Akara *f*
草 Inutade *s*
梅 Kōbai *l*
葉 Momiji *f*; Kōyō *ml*
葉狩 M.-gari *l*
葉賀 M. no ga *l*
露 Kōro *s*

紀 1424 [T] Ki *s*, Kii, Kino; Osamu *m*, Tadashi, Shi-

rusu, Hajime, Kaname. (KI, toshi, tada, nori, kazu, moto, yoshi, tsugu, aki, tsuna, osa, koto, sumi)
[1]一 Kiichi *m*
[3]三 Toshikazu *m*
子 Kazuko *f*
久 Toshihisa *m*
[4]元 Akimoto *m* ⌈*ml*
友則 Ki no Tomonori
[5]文 Toshifumi *m*
[6]平 Kihira *s*
伊 Kii *sp*
伊国屋 Kinokuniya *s*
伊国屋文左衛門 K. Bunzaemon *mh*
光 Norimitsu *m*, Motomitsu
成 Norishige *m*
[7]男 Tadao *m*, Yoshio
辛梶 Kinokarakaji *s*
[8]和 Kiwa *p*
宝 Kihō *p*
季 Osasue *m*
国造 Kinokunizō *s*
[9]長谷雄 Ki no Haseo
貞 Norisada *m* ⌊*ml*
[10]酒人 Kinosakahito *s*
海音 Ki no Kaion *ml*
時文 Ki no Tokibumi *ml*
[11]淑望 Ki no Yoshimochi *ml*
[12]貫之 Ki no Tsurayuki *ml*
[13]雄 Tsunao *m*
勢 Kisei *p*
[18]藤 Kitō *s*

**——11 L9——**

**勔** 1425 Tsutomu *m*. (BEN, MEN)

**剰** 1426 [T] (JŌ, SHŌ, masu, nori)

**剝** 1427 (HAKU, muki)
野老 Mukitokoro *l*

**副** 1428 [T] (FUKU, HOKU, suke, sue, soe, tsugi, masu)
田 Soeda *s*, Soyota
安 Sukeyasu *m*
武 Soemu *m*
島 Soejima *s*
島種臣 S. Taneomi *mh*
隆 Suetaka *m*

**剛** 1429 [T] Takeshi *m*, Takashi, Tsuyoshi, Katashi, Kowashi. (GŌ, KŌ, yoshi, take, taka, kata, masa, hisa, tsuyo)
一 Gōichi *m*
二 Takaji *m*
太郎 Kōtarō *m*
志 Takeshi *s*; Gōshi *sp*
男 Takeo *m*
昴 Yoshitaka *m*
彦 Masahiko *m*
靖 Takayasu *m*
雄 Katao *m*
寛 Yoshihiro *m*
蔵 Gōzō *m*

**——11 T2——**

**眞** 1429A See 真 1228

**翁** 1430 [T] Okina *la*. (Ō, U, oki, okina, toshi, oi, hito)
助 Ōsuke *m*
満 Okinamaro *m*

**——11 T3——**

**巣** 1431 [T] (SŌ, JŌ, su)
山 Suyama *s*
内 Sunouchi *s*
永 Sunaga *s*
南 Sunami *p*
森 Sumori *s*

**奝** 1432 Akira *m*. (KŌ)

**奝** 1433 (CHŌ, taka)
然 Chōnen *mh*

**寁** 1434 Toshi *m*. (SHŌ, SAN, toshi)

**寀** 1435 Akira *m*, Sadaka. (SAI)

**寂** 1436 [T] (JAKU, SEKI, yasu, shizu, chika)
念 Jakunen *ml*
然 Jakunen *ml*
超 Jakuchō *ml*
蓮 Jakuren *ml*

**宴** 1437 [T] (EN, mori, yoshi, yasu)
行 Moriyuki *m*
曲 Enkyoku *l*
至 Morichika *m*

**宿** 1438 (SHUKU, SUKU, ie, sumi, yado, oru)
木 Yadorigi *l*
毛 Sukumo *sp*
尼 Sukuni *s*
利 Sukuri *s*
谷 Shukuya *s*, Shukutani
奈麿 Sukunamaro *m*
弥 Sukune *m*
南 Sukunami *s*
屋 Yadoya *s* ⌈*ml*
屋飯盛 Y. Meshimori
禰 Sukune *m*
禰麿 Sukunemaro *m*

**寅** 1439 [N] Tora *m*. (IN, tora, tomo, nobu, tsura, fusa)
二 Toraji *m*
二郎 Torajirō *m*
三郎 Torasaburō *m*
之助 Toranosuke *m*
太郎 Toratarō *m*
次 Toraji *m*
次郎 Torajirō *m*
吉 Torakichi *m*
甫 Toratoshi *m*
栄 Tomoyoshi *m*
直 Toranao *m*
彦 Torahiko *m*
造 Nobuzō *m*
輔 Torasuke *m*

**莊** 1440 See 荘 933

**菌** 1441 Kusabira *m*. (KIN)

**萃** 1442 Shigeru *m*. (SUI, ZUI, atsu)

**莠** 1443 Hagusa *m*. (SHŪ)

**菖** 1444 Ayame *f*. (SHŌ)
蒲 Shōbu *p*
蒲井 Ayamei *s*

**著** 1445 [T] Akira *m*. (CHO, CHAKU, aki, tsugu, tsugi, ki)
寿 Akihisa *m*
座 Kimase *s*

**菴** 1446 Iori *m*. (AN, i) ⌈nobe *s*
宜物部 Anginomono-
原 Ihara *s*

**菜** 1447 [T] (SAI, na)
生 Nanase *s*
穂子 Naoko *f-l*

**萠** 1448 Kizashi *m*. (BŌ, MŌ, me, moe, megumi, memi)
子 Megumiko *f*
枝 Memie *f*
葉 Moeba *f*

**菱** 1449 (RYŌ, hishi)
川 Hishikawa *s*
川師宣 H. Moronobu
刈 Hishikari *p* ⌊*ma*
木 Hishiki *s*
山 Hishiyama *s*
山修三 H. Shuzō *ml*
田 Hishida *s*
田春草 H. Shunsō *ma*
江 Hishie *f*
村 Hishimura *s*
谷 Hishitani *s*
苅 Hishikari *s*
沼 Hishinuma *s*
屋 Hishiya *s*

**菅** 1450 Suga *s*, Kan. (KAN, suga, suge)
[3]子 Sugako *f*
[4]井 Sugai *s*, Sugenoi
[5]永 Suganaga *m*
田 Sugada *s*
生 Sugō *s*, Sugafu
[7]沢 Sugasawa *s*
村 Sugamura *s*
谷 Sugaya *sp*; Sugatani *s*, Suganoya
[8]沼 Suganuma *s*

菌 萃 莠 菖 著 菴 菜 萠 菱 菅 ▼ 菊 峯 黄 菫 斎 勗 皃 曼 晏 皐 春 章 堂 常 ▲ 晝 帯 望 翌 祭 習 盛 留 笛 笥

波 Suganami *s*
[9]治 Sugaji *m*
彦 Sugahiko *m*
[10]宮 Sugamiya *s*
家文草 Kanke bunsō *l*
家万葉集 K. man'yōshū *l*
家後草 K. kōsō *l*
原 Sugawara *s*, Sugahara ⌈Fumitoki *ml*
原文時 Sugawara no
原伝授手習鑑 S. denju tenarai kagami *la*
原孝標 S. no Takasue *mh* ⌈Musume *fl*
原孝標女 S. no T. no
原道真 S. no Michizane *ml*
屋 Sugaya *s*
[11]浪 Suganami *s*
根 Sugane *m*
野 Sugano *s*, Sugeno, Kanno
[12]間 Sugama *s*
[13]雄 Sugao *m*
[16]緒 Sugao *s*
[19]瀬 Sugase *s*

菊 1451 [T] Kiku *s*. (KIKU, hi, aki)
[1]一郎 Kikuichirō *m*
[2]二郎 Kikujirō *m*
入 Kikuiru *s*
[3]川 Kikugawa *sp*
三郎 Kikusaburō *m*
之助 Kikunosuke *m*
千代 Kikuchiyo *f*
[4]水 Kikusui *p*
山 Kikuyama *s*
井 Kikui *s*
五郎 Kikugorō *m*
[5]永 Kikunaga *s*
本 Kikumoto *s*
四郎 Kikushirō *m*
田 Kikuda *s*
田一夫 K. Kazuo *ml*
[6]次郎 Kikujirō *m*
地 Kikuchi *s*
地庫郎 K. Kurarō *ml*
池 Kikuchi *sp*
池大麓 K. Dairoku *mh*
池知勇 K. Chiyū *ml*
池武光 K. Takemitsu *mh* ⌈*mh*
池武時 K. Taketoki
池剣 K. Ken *ml* ⌈*ml*
池寛 K. Kan / Hiroshi
池幽芳 K. Yūhō *ml*
名 Kikuna *s*
[7]沢 Kikuzawa *s*
村 Kikumura *s*
村到 K. Itaru *ml*
谷 Kikuya *s*, Kikutani
花の約 Kikuka no chi-
男 Kikuo *m* ⌊giri *l*
里 Kikuzato *s*
[8]苗 Kikunae *f*
[9]亭 Kikutei *s*
亭香水 K. Kōsui *ml*
栄 Kikuei *m*
岡 Kikuoka *s*
岡久利 K. Kuri *ml*
[10]原 Kikuhara *s*
屋 Kikuya *s*
屋太兵衛 K. Tahee *ml*
[11]野 Kikuno *s*
盛 Kikumori *s*
島 Kikushima *s*
[12]陽 Kikuyō *p*
鹿 Kikuka *p*
間 Kikuma *sp*
[13]雄 Kikuo *m*
[15]蔵 Kikuzō *m*
[17]慈童 Kiku Jidō *la*
[19]瀬 Kikuse *m*

## 11 T4

峯 1452 See 峰 1351
村 Minemura *s*
村国一 M. Kuniichi *ml*

黄 See 1499

菫 1453 Sumire *f*. (KIN, KON)

斎 1454 [T] Itsuki *sm*; Hitoshi *m*. (SAI, toki, itsu, yoshi, tada, kiyo, iwai, imi)
[3]川 Saikawa *s*
[4]木 Saiki *s*
[5]田 Saida *s*
[6]吉 Tokiyoshi *m*
名 Tadana *m*
[7]男 Itsuo *m*
[8]所 Saisho *s*
京 Saikyō *s*
[10]宮 Itsuki *m-f*; Saiki *s*
[11]部 Inbe *s*, Imibe, Monoibe ⌈nari *ml*
部広成 Inbe no Hiro-
[12]間 Saima *s*
鹿 Saika *s*
[18]藤 Saitō *s*
藤史 S. Fumi *ml*
藤茂吉 S. Mokichi *ml*
藤実 S. Makoto *mh*
藤昌三 S. Shōzō *ml*
藤勇 S. Takeshi *ml*
藤野の人 S. Nonohito *ml*
藤道三 S. Dōsan *mh*
藤緑雨 S. Ryokuu *ml*
藤瀏 S. Ryū *ml*

勗 1455 Tsutomu *m*. (KYOKU, KOKU)

皃 1456 Susumu *m*. (BOKU, MOKU)

曼 1457 (MAN, BAN, hiro)

晏 1458 (AN, yasu, haru, sada, oso)
子 Yasuko *f*
代 Yasuyo *f*
尚 Yasumasa *m*

## 11 T5

皐 1459 See 皋 1197

春 1460 (SHU, SHŌ, tsuki) ⌈shine
米 Tsukishine *s*, Tsui-

章 1461 [T] Akira *m*, Shō. (SHŌ, aki, aya, fumi, nori, taka, yuki, akira, fusa, toshi, ⌊ki)
三 Yukizō *m*
子 Akiko *f*, Ayako, Fumiko
夫 Fumio *m*, Fusao
女 Ayame *f*
太郎 Shōtarō *m*
代 Akiyo *f*
生 Ayao *m*
男 Takao *m*
甫 Norimi *m*
明 Takaaki *m*
信 Akinobu *m*, Yukinobu
風 Akikaze *m*
業 Fuminari *m*
憲 Akinori *m*

堂 1462 [T] (DŌ, taka)
本 Dōmoto *s*
正 Dōshō *s*
前 Dōmae *s*
場 Dōba *s*
正 Dōshō *s*
園 Dōzono *s*

常 1463 [T] Tsune *m*, Tokiwa, Hisashi. (JŌ, SHŌ, tsune, toki, toko, hisa, nobu, tsura) ⌈negawa
[3]川 Tsunekawa *s*, Tsu-
三郎 Tsunesaburō *m*
子 Tsuneko *f*, Hirako
[4]木 Tsunegi *s*
山 Tokoyama *s*, Tsuneyama
井 Tsunei *s*
夫 Tokio *m*
与 Tokoyo *s*
太 Tsuneta *m*
[5]北 Jōhoku *p*
石 Tokonami *s*
田 Tsuneda *s*, Tsuneta, Tokita
[6]次 Tsunetsugu *m*
次郎 Tsunejirō *m*
羽 Tokuha *s*
吉 Tsunekichi *m*
光 Tsunemitsu *s*
世 Tokoyo *s*
世田 Tokiyoda *s*
民 Tsunetami *m*
[7]伴 Tsunetomo *m*
作 Tsunesaku *m*
那 Tsunena *m*
男 Tokoo *m*
呂 Tokoro *p*
見 Tsunemi *s*
[8]明 Tokoakira *m*
孟 Tsunetomo *m*
尚 Tsunenao *m*
[9]治 Hisaharu *m*
昨 Tonomukashi *s*
松 Tsunematsu *s*
栄 Tsuneshige *m*
泉 Tsuneizumi *s*
岡 Tsuneoka *s*
彦 Tunehiko *m*
[10]夏 Tokonatsu *l*
造 Tsunezō *m*
[11]深 Tsunemi *s*
陸 Hitachi *ph*
陸太田 H. Ōta *p*

陸国 Hitachinokuni *ph* ⌈doki *l*
陸国風土記 H. no fu-
隆 Tsuneo *m*
[12]喜 Jōki *s* ⌈neaki
晨 Tsunetoki *m*, Tsu-
賀 Tsuneyoshi *sm*
[13]滑 Tokonabe *s*; Tokoname *p*
雄 Tsuneo *m*, Tokio
誠 Tsunenaga *m*
葉 Tokiwa *sp*
[15]澄 Tsunesumi *p*
盤 Tokiwa *p* ⌈*sp*
磐 Jōban *p*; Tokiwa
磐井 Tokiwai *s*
磐舎 Tokiwanoya *m*
磐津 Tokiwazu *sa*
磐津文字太夫 T. Moji-dayū *ma*
磐麿 Tokiwamaro *m*
[16]操 Tsunemochi *m*
憲 Tsunenori *m*
緑 Tokiwa *m*

——11 T6——

晝 1464 See 昼 983

帶 1465 See 带 1192

望 See 1777

翌 1466 [T] Akira *m*. (YOKU, akira)
檜 Asunaro *l*

祭 1467 [T] (SAI, matsuri)
文 Saimon *l*
原 Saihara *s*

習 1468 [T] (SHŪ, JŪ, shige, nara)
田 Shutta *s*
志野 Narashino *p*
宜 Suge *s*

盛 1469 [T] Mori *sm*; Sakari *m*, Shigeru. (SEI, JŌ, mori, shige, take)
[1]一郎 Seiichirō *m*
[2]人 Morindo *m*
[3]之進 Morinoshin *m*
子 Moriko *f*
[4]仁 Takehito *m*
[5]正 Morimasa *m*
[7]亨 Moriyuki *m*
至 Moriyoshi *m*
[8]迂 Morisumi *m*
枝 Morie *f*
舎 Moriie *m*
[9]治 Moriji *m*
郁 Morika *m*
岡 Morioka *sp*
[10]高 Moritaka *s*
[11]康 Moriyasu *m*
[12]達 Morishige *m*
勝 Morikatsu *m*
[13]雄 Morio *m*
[14]徳 Moritomi *m*
彰 Moriaki *m*
[15]徹 Morisumi *m*
諸 Moritsura *m*
[16]樹 Shigeki *m*

留 1470 [T] (RYŪ, RU, tome, hisa, to, tane)
一 Taneichi *m*
夫 Tomeo *m*
辺蘂 Rubeshibe *p*
主 Rusu *s*
次 Tomeji *m*
守 Rusu *s*
吉 Tomekichi *m*
束 Futsuka *s*
寿都 Rusutsu *p*
萌 Rumoi *p*

笛 1471 [T] (TEKI, fue)
之巻 Fue no maki *la*
子 Fueko *f*
木 Fueki *s*
田 Fueda *s*
吹 Usui *s*, Utō
吹峠 Usui *s*

笥 1472 (SHI, ke)

笠 1473 Ryū *s*, Kasa. (RYŪ, RITSU, kasa)
[4]元 Kasamoto *s*
井 Kasai *s*
木 Kasagi *s*
[6]合 Kasai *s*
寺 Kasadera *s*
[7]沙 Kasasa *p*
村 Kasamura *s*
利 Kasari *p*
谷 Kasaya *s*
尾 Kasao *s*
[8]金村 Kasa no Kanamura *ml* ⌈*ml*
[9]信太郎 Ryū Shintarō
松 Kasamatsu *sp*
亭 Ryūtei *s*
亭仙果 R. Senka *ml*
岡 Kasaoka *sp*
[10]倉 Kasakura *s*
家 Kasaie *s*
原 Kasahara *sp*
屋 Kasaya *s*
屋三勝二十五年忌 K. Sankatsu nijūgo-nenki *la*
[11]野 Kasano *s*
麻呂 Kasamaro *m*
島 Kasajima *s*
[12]森 Kasamori *s*
貫 Kasanuki *s*
間 Kasama *sp*
[14]置 Kasagi *sp*
[18]縫 Kasanui *s*
縫専助 K. Sensuke *ml*
[23]懸 Kasakake *p*

——11 T7——

娑 1474 (SHA, SA)
羅羅馬飼 Sararaumakai *s*

梁 1475 Takashi *m*; Ryō *sm*. (RYŌ, yana, yane, mune, hari) ⌈rikawa *s*
川 Yanagawa *sp*; Ha-
田 Yanada *s*
守 Yanamori *m*
島 Yanashima *s*
満 Yanamaro *m*
塵秘抄 Ryōjin hishō *l*
瀬 Yanase *s*

梨 1476 (RI, nashi)
子 Nashiko *f*
木 Nashinoki *s*
本 Nashimoto *s*, Nashinomoto ⌈*l*
本集 Nashinomotoshū
羽 Nashiba *s*
壺五人 Nashitsubo no gonin *ml*

曽 1477 See 曾 1794

胷 1477A See 胸 1347

晢 1478 Akira *m*. (SETSU, SECHI, akira)

曹 1479 [I] (SŌ, ZŌ, tomo, nobu)
丸 Tomomaru *m*
洞宗 Sōdōshū *h*

悊 1480 Satoshi *m*. (TETSU, aki)
麿 Akimaro *m*

悠 1481 [I] Hisashi *m*. (YŪ, YU, hisa)
一郎 Yuichirō *m*
夫 Hisao *m*

悉 1482 (SHITSU, SHICHI)
皆屋康吉 Shikkaiya Yasukichi *l*
悲 Shihi *s*

恕 1483 Hakaru *m*, Hiroshi, Hiromu, Tadashi, Shinobu, Yurusu; Yuki *f*. (JO, SHO, hiro, yuki, michi, yoshi, nori, moro, kuni)
子 Hiroko *f*, Michiko
夫 Yoshio *m*
郎 Norio *m*
連 Yoshitsura *m*
胤 Morotane *m*

悪 1483A [T] Aku *s*. (AKU)
人正機説 Akunin shōki setsu *h*
太郎 Akutarō *la*
坊 Akubō *la*

君 1484 (KUN, kimi)
子 Kimiko *f*

魚 1485 [T] (GYO, GO, na, uo, o, io)
井 Manai *s*, Mamai

智 晢 曹 蜇 悠 悉 恕 悪 焄 魚 ▼ 黒 專 麥 埜 梵 啓 埿 基 雫 雪 啚 眞 異 貧 黄 國 展 透 進 ▲ 逸 庶 庵 庸 麻 康 毬 逗 逕 逞

百美 Naomi *f*
吉 Sunae *s*
名 Uona *m*
住 Uozumi *s*
住折蘆 U. Setsuro *ml*
谷 Uotani *s*
返 Ogaeri *s*
沼 Uonuma *s*, Unuma
津 Uozu *p*
彦 Nahiko *m*
員 Iokazu *m*
屋 Sakanaya *s*
島 Uojima *p* ⌈*l*
鳥平家 Gyochō Heike
貫 Natsura *m*
養 Uokai *m*, Nakai

黒 1486 [T] (KOKU, kuro)
³川 Kurokawa *sp*
川真頼 K. Mayori *ml*
子 Kuroko *s*
⁴井 Kuroi *s*
木 Kuroki *sp*
女 Kurome *f*
山 Kuroyama *s*
⁵石 Kuroishi *p*
正 Kokushō *s*
田 Kuroda *s*
田竹城 Kurodatakagi *s*
田庄 Kurodashō *p*
田孝高 Kuroda Yoshitaka *mh*
田辰男 K. Tatsuo *ml*
田長政 K. Nagamasa *mh* ⌈*mh*
田清隆 K. Kiyotaka
田清輝 K. Seiki / Kiyoteru *ma* ⌈*ml*
田清綱 K. Kiyotsuna
⁶州 Kurosu *s*
羽 Kurowa *s*; Kuro-
江 Kuroe *s* ⌊bane *p*
舟 Kurofune *s*
米 Kuroyone *s*
⁷住 Kurozumi *s*
沢 Kurosawa *s*
坂 Kurosaka *s*
谷 Kurotani *s*
衣聖母 Kokui seibo *l*
尾 Kuroo *s*
⁸沼 Kuronuma *s*
河 Kurokawa *s*
河内 Kurokōchi *s*, Kuruōchi
板 Kuroita *s* ⌈ta
股 Kuroto *s*, Sunoma-
金 Kurogane *s*
⁹保根 Kurohone *p*
神 Kurokami *s*
松 Kuromatsu *s*
松内 Kuromatsunai *p*
前 Kurosaki *s*
岩 Kuroiwa *s*
岩重吾 K. Jūgo *ml*
岩涙香 K. Ruikō *mlh*
¹⁰柳 Kuroyanagi *s*, Kuroyagi ⌈Shōha *ml*
柳召波 Kuroyanagi
竜会 Kokuryūkai *h*
原 Kurobara *s*
¹¹姫 Kurohime *p*
船 Kurofune *s*
野 Kurono *s*
部 Kurobe *sp*
島 Kuroshima *s*
島伝治 K. Denji *ml*
¹²須 Kurosu *s*
崎 Kurosaki *sp*
¹³鳩 Kurohato *s*
滝 Kurotaki *p*
塚 Kurozuka *la*
葛原 Tsuzurahara *s*, Tsurahara
¹⁴蜴蜥 Kurotokage *l*
¹⁵潮 Kokuchō *l*
¹⁷檜 Kurohi *l*
¹⁹瀬 Kurose *sp*
²¹磯 Kuroiso *p*

——11 T8——

專 1487 See 専 973

麥 1488 See 麦 456

埜 1489 See 野 1398

梵 1490 (BON)
天国 Bontenkoku *l*
行品 Bongyōbon *l*
唄 Bonbai *l*

啓 1491 [T] Hiroshi *m*, Hiromu, Hiraki, Hiraku, Hajime, Akira. (KEI, KAI, hiro, hira, taka, nobu, nori, haru, yoshi, hi, satoshi)
三 Keizō *m*
之助 Keinosuke *m*
子 Satoshiko *f*
久 Hiraku *m*
介 Keisuke *m*
夫 Hiroo *m*
太郎 Keitarō *m*
市 Keiichi *m*
次 Keiji *m*
次郎 Keijirō *m*
彅 Keikō *s*
虎 Keikō *s*
喜 Hiroki *m*
貫 Hironuki *m*
徳 Harunori *m*
蔵 Keizō *m*

埿 1492 Hiji *s*. (DEI)
部 Hatsukashibe *s*

基 1493 [T] Motoi *m*, Motoe, Hajime, Hajimu. (KI, moto, nori)
三 Norizō *m*
山 Kiyama *p*
氏 Motouji *m*
次郎 Motojirō *m*
全 Mototomo *m*
吉 Motokichi *m*
延 Motonaga *m*
政 Motokazu *m*
栄 Motoyoshi *m*
俊 Mototoshi *ml*
祥 Motosachi *m*
要 Motome *m*
惟 Motokore *m*
流 Motoharu *m*
逸 Motohaya *m*
隆 Kiirun *p* "Keelung"
揚 Motonobu *m*
愛 Motonaru *m*
標 Motoeda *m*
範 Motonori *m*
礎 Motoki *m*

雫 1494 Shitoke *p*. (shizuku)
石 Shizukuishi *sp*

雪 1495 [T] Yuki *f-la*; Kiyomu *m*, Kiyomi, Sosogu. (SETSU, yuki, kiyo)
下 Yukinoshita *sp*; Yukishita *s*
中梅 Setchūbai *l*
月花 Setsugekka *l*
山 Yukiyama *s*
夫 Yukio *m* ⌈ezu *l*
夫人絵図 Yuki Fujin
女五枚羽子板 Yuki-onna gomai hagoita *la*
舟 Sesshū *ma*
吹 Fubuki *s* ⌈*ml*
村友梅 Sesson Yūbai
臣 Yukiomi *m*
門 Setsumon *l*
岡 Yukioka *s*
野 Yukino *s*
雄 Yukio *m*
解 Yukige *l*

——11 T9——

啚 See 1517

眞 1496 See 真 1228

異 1497 [T] (I, koto, yori)
国日記 Ikoku nikki *h*

貧 1498 [T] (HIN)
富論 Hinpuron *l*

黄 1499 [T] Katsumi *m*. (KŌ, Ō, ki)
川田 Kikawada *s*
地 Ōji *s*
河 Kōga *p* "Yellow R."
表紙 Kibyōshi *l*
楊 Tsuge *s*
楊夫 Tsugeo *m*

——11 F3——

國 1500 See 国 745

展 1501 [T] (TEN, nobu, hiro)
狂 Hiroke *f*
男 Nobuo *m*

透 1502 [T] Tōru *m*. (TŌ, suki, suku,
一 Tōichi *m* ⌈yuki)
谷 Tōkoku *ml*

進 1503 [T] Susumu *m*; Shin *sm*.

(SHIN, yuki, nobu, susu, su, michi)
三郎 Shinzaburō *m*
士 Nobukoto *m*
平 Shinpei *m*
行 Nobuyuki *m*
男 Yukio *m*
来 Suzuki *s*
実 Susumi *m*
秀 Yukihide *m*
美子 Sumiko *f*
馬 Susume *m*
藤 Shindō *s*
藤純孝 S. Junkō *ml*

逸 1504 [T] Suguru *m.* (ITSU, ICHI, haya, toshi, yasu, hatsu, masa)
人 Hayato *m*, Yasuto
好 Itsuyoshi *m*
見 Henmi *s*, Itsumi; Hatsumi *m*
見猶吉 H. Yūkichi *ml*
枝 Itsue *f*
彦 Hayahiko *m*
朗 Toshiaki *m*
暁 Itsuaki *m*
雄 Toshio *m*
勢 Hayanari *m*, Masanari

庶 1505 [T] (SHO, chika, moro, mori) ⌈aki
明 Chikaaki *m*, Moro-

庵 1506 Iori *m*; Io *s*, Iho. (AN, io)
主 Ionushi *l*
地 Iochi *s*
谷 Ioriya *s*, Iboriya
治 Aji *p*
原 Iohara *s*, Iorihara; Ihara *sp*
智 Anchi *s*
跡 Anseki *s*

庸 1507 [T] Isao *m*, Mochiu. (YŌ, YU, yasu, tsune, mochi, nobu, nori)
子 Tsuneko *f*
之助 Yōnosuke *m*
久 Yasuhisa *m*
夫 Tsuneo *m*
太郎 Tsunetarō *m*
公 Tsunetomo *m*
雄 Tsuneo *m*
嵩 Tsunetaka *m*

麻 1508 [T] (MA, BA, asa, o, nusa)
子 Asako *f*
布 Azabu *sp*
田 Asada *s*
田剛立 A. Gōryū *mh*
生 Asō *sp-la*; Asabu *s*, Oe
生久 Asō Hisashi *mh*
生義輝 A. Yoshiteru
男 Nusao *m* ⌊*ml*
呂 Maro *m* (cf. 麿 2786)
呂子 Maroko *mh*
見 Omi *s*
柄 Ogara *s*
原 Asahara *s*
賀 Asaka *s*
植 Oe *p*
殖 Oe *s*
殖生 Maio *s*
積 Omi *p*
績 Omi *s* ⌈noichi
績一 Omiichi *m*, Omi-

康 1509 [T] Yasushi *m*, Shizuka. (KŌ, yasu, michi, shizu, yoshi)
[2]二 Yasuji *m*
[3]三郎 Yasusaburō *m*
工 Yasuyoshi *m*
子 Yasuko *f*
[4]元 Kōgen 1256–57
井 Yasui *s*
弌 Michikazu *m*
[5]永 Kōei 1342–45
四方 Yasuyomo *m*
田 Yasuda *s*
平 Kōhei 1058–65
正 Kōshō 1455–57; Yasumasa *m*
[6]百 Yasuo *m*
光 Yasumitsu *m*
圭 Yasukado *m*
成 Yasunari *m*
[7]安 Kōan 1361–62; Shizuyasu *m*
男 Michio *m*, Yasuo
応 Kōō 1389–90
匡 Yasutada *m*
[8]和 Kōwa 1099–1104
命 Yasunobu *m*
昌 Yasumasa *m*
秀 Yasuhide *m*
国 Yasukuni *m*
[9]信 Yasunobu *m*
保 Kōhō 964–68; Yasumochi *m*
治 Kōji 1142–44; Yasuji *m*
政 Yasumasa *m*
秋 Yasutoki *m*
荘 Yasutaka *m*
哉 Yasuya *m*, Yasutoshi
[11]陛 Yasuyori *m*
隆 Yasutaka *m*
[12]晴 Yasuharu *m*
裕 Yasumichi *m*
敬 Yasunori *m*
景 Yasukazu *m*
[13]雄 Yasuo *m*
禎 Yasutsugu *m*
誠 Yasuzane *m*
[14]暦 Kōryaku 1379–81
[15]賛 Yasuyoshi *m*
[16]融 Yasutō *m*
[18]爵 Yasutaka *m*
麿 Yasumaro *m*
穣 Yasushige *m*

## 11 F4

毬 1510 (KYŪ, GU, mari)
子 Mariko *f*

逗 1511 (ZU, TO)
子 Zushi *p*

逕 1512 (KEI, KYŌ, michi)
江 Michie *f*

逞 1513 Takuma *m.* (TEI, toshi, yoshi, yuki)
之 Yoshiyuki *m*
治 Toshiji *m*

逍 1514 (SHŌ)
遊愚抄 Shōyū gushō *l*
遙 Shōyō *ml*

這 1515 (SHA, GEN, kore, chika, hau)
田 Hōta *s*, Hauta
季 Koresue *m*

逢 1516 Ai *f*; Au *s*. (HŌ, BU, ai, ō)
坂 Ōsaka *sph*
沢 Aizawa *s*
瀬 Ōse *p*

## 11 F5

啚 1517 (CHŌ, ka)

## 11 F6

斎 See 1454

處 1518 See 処 177

虚 1519 [T] (KYO)
子 Kyoshi *ml*
子俳話 K. haiwa *l*
栗 Minashiguri *l*

產 1520 [T] (SAN, SEN, ubu, tada, umu, musubi)
子 Tadako *f*
山 Ubuyama *p*
田 Saita *s*
婦木 Ubumeki *s*
賀 Ubuga *s*

## 11 F7

鳥 1521 [T] Tori *m.* (CHŌ, tori)
[2]入 Toriire *s*
[4]方 Torikata *s*
山 Toriyama *s*
井 Torii *s*
[5]本 Torimoto *s*
辺山心中 Toribeyama shinjū *la*
田 Torita *s*
[6]羽 Toba *smh-ma-p*
羽家の子供 T. -ke no kodomo *l*
光 Torimitsu *s*
[7]沢 Torisawa *s*
谷部 Toriyabe *s*, Toyabe
尾 Torio *s*
[8]取 Tottori *sp*
居 Torii *s*
居大路 Toriiōji *s*
居清信 Torii Kiyonobu *ma* ⌈*ma*
居清長 T. Kiyonaga

逞 逍 這 逢 冐 斎 處 虚 産 鳥 ▼ 島 彪 問 寄 商 鬼 粛 爽 雀 亀 順 ▲ 馮 博 偉 傳 偕 傍 備 孫 喧 喫

[9]神山 Tonamiyama *s*, Tonami
迫 Torioi *la*
迫舟 T.-bune *la*
[10]海 Torinoumi *s*, Torimi; Chōkai *p*
原 Torihara *s*
屋 Toriya *p*
栖 Tosu *p*
[11]野 Torino *s*
巣 Torisu *s*, Tosu
遊 Takanashi *s*
[13]塚 Torizuka *s*
喰 Torihami *s*
雄 Torio *m*
越 Torigoe *sp*
越信 T. Shin *ml*
[14]飼 Torikai *s*
[16]養 Torikai *s*

**島** 1522 [T] Shima *sm.* (TŌ, shima)
ヶ原 Shimagahara *p*
[2]人 Shimando *m*
[3]川 Shimakawa *s*
口 Shimaguchi *s*
[4]内 Shimauchi *s*
井 Shimai *s*
中 Shimanaka *s*
中雄作 S. Yūsaku *ml*
山 Shimayama *s*
木 Shimaki *s*, Shimagi
木赤彦 Shimagi Akahiko *ml*
木健作 Shimaki Kensaku *ml*
方 Shimakata *s*
[5]本 Shimamoto *sp*
田 Shimada *sp*
田三郎 S. Saburō *mh*
田青峰 S. Seihō *ml*
田清次郎 S. Seijirō *ml*
田謹二 S. Kinji *ml*
[6]地 Shimaji *s*, Shimachi
地黙雷 Shimaji Mokurai *mh*
吉 Shimakichi *s*
名 Shimana *s*
[7]沢 Shimazawa *s*
村 Shimamura *s*
村民蔵 S. Tamizō *ml*
村抱月 S. Hōgetsu *ml*
谷 Shimatani *s*, Shimadani
図 Shimazu *m*
尾 Shimao *s*
尾敏雄 S. Toshio *ml*
[8]牧 Shimamaki *p*
宗 Shimamune *s*
居 Shimai *s*, Shimasue
[9]津 Shimazu *sm*
津久光 S. Hisamitsu *mh*
津斉彬 S. Nariakira *mh*
津重豪 S. Shigehide *mh*
津家久 S. Iehisa *mh*
津貴久 S. Takahisa *mh*
津義久 S. Yoshihisa *mh*
津義弘 S. Yoshihiro *mh*
岡 Shimaoka *s*
廻戯聞書 Shimameguri uso no kikigaki *l*
[10]浦 Shimaura *s*
倉 Shimakura *s*
原 Shimabara *sp*
屋 Shimaya *s*
[11]峰 Shimamine *s*
根 Shimane *sp*
野 Shimano *s*
[12]崎 Shimazaki *s*
崎藤村 S. Tōson *ml*
森 Shimamori *s*
袋 Shimabukuro *s*
貫 Shimanuki *s*
[16]橋 Shimahashi *s*
薗 Shimazono *s*
[17]鵆月白浪 Shimachidori tsuki no shiranami *la*

——11 F8——

**彪** 1523 Takeshi *m*, Hyō, Tsuyoshi, Akira. (HYŌ, aya, tora, take)
夫 Ayao *m*, Takeo

**問** 1524 [T] (MON, BUN, tada, yo, toi, tou)
叶 Toga *s*
田 Toida *s*
注所 Monjūsho *s*
計 Toga *s*

**寄** 1525 [T] (KI, yori, yose)
子 Yoriko *f*
木造 Yosegi-zukuri *a*
生木 Yadorigi *l*
谷 Yoriya *s*
居 Yorii *p*
島 Yorishima *p*

**商** 1526 [T] (SHŌ, aki, atsu, hisa)
人世帯薬 Akindo setai-gusuri *l*
人軍配団 A. gunpaiuchiwa *l*
人家職訓 A. kashokun *l*
次 Akitsugu *m*
利 Atsutoshi *m*
長 Akiosa *s*

**鬼** 1527 [T] (KI, oni)
ヶ城 Onigajō *s*
の継子 Oni no mamako *la*
[1]一 Kiichi *sm*
一法眼 K. Hōgen *mh*
一法眼三略巻 K. H. sanryaku no maki *la*
[3]小島 Okikojima *s*
[4]斗生 Kitosei *m*
王 Oniō *s*
王丸 Oniōmaru *ma*
[5]石 Onishi *p*
瓦 Onigawara *la*
生田 Onyūda *s*
[7]作左 Onisakuza *m*
沢 Kizawa *s*, Onizawa
尾 Onio *s*
[8]武 Onitake *sm*
武蔵 Onimusashi *m*
[9]俣 Kimata *m*
界島 Kikaigashima *la*
[10]涙村 Kinadamura *l*
原 Kihara *s*
[11]島 Onijima *s*, Kijima
[12]啾啾 Kishūshū *l*
貫 Onitsura *ml*
無里 Kinasa *p*
鹿毛無佐志鐙 Onikage Musashi abumi *la*
[13]塚 Onizuka *s*
極 Onikime *s*
越 Onikoshi *s*
[14]窪 Onikubo *s*
[16]頭 Kitō *s*

——11 U——

**粛** 1528 [T] Susumu *m*, Kiyoshi. (SHUKU, toshi, tada, tari, masa, kata, kane, haya)

**爽** 1529 Akira *m.* (SŌ, sa, saya, sawa)
子 Sayako *f*, Sawako
生子 Saoko *f*

**雀** 1530 Sasagi *s.* (JAKU, su, sagi, sasagi)
右衛門 Jakuemon *m*
部 Sasagibe *s*, Sasaibe, Sasabe
鶴 Suzu *f*

**亀** 1531 [N] Kame *sf*; Hisashi *sm*; Nagashi *m*, Susumu, Kagamu. (KI, kame, hisa, ama)
さん Kame-san *l*
[1]一 Kameichi *m*
[2]二 Kameji *m*
[3]川 Kamegawa *s*
三郎 Kamesaburō *m*
之助 Kamenosuke *m*
万太 Kimata *m*
千代 Kamechiyo *m-f*
[4]山 Kameyama *sp*
五郎 Kamegorō *m*
夫 Hisao *m*
太郎 Kametarō *m*
井 Kamei *s*
井勝一郎 K. Katsuichirō *ml*
[5]史 Hisashi *m*
甲鶴 Kikkōzuru *l*
田 Kameda *sp*
本 Kamemoto *s*
丘 Kameoka *m*
[6]次郎 Kamejirō *m*
光 Kamemitsu *m*
吉 Kamekichi *m*
[7]沢 Kamezawa *s*
村 Kamemura *s*
谷 Kameya *s*, Kamegaya, Kametani
[8]卦川 Kikegawa *s*
[9]垣 Kamegaki *s*
弥太 Kameyata *m*
美 Kimi *f*
岡 Kameoka *sp*
[10]倉 Kamekura *s*
屋 Kameya *s*
造 Kamezō *m*
[11]島 Kameshima *s*
崎 Kamesaki *s*
[13]雄 Kameo *m*

——12 L1——

**順** 1532 [T] Shitagō *ml*; Jun *m*, Su-

nao, Hajime, Osamu, Yasushi, Kazu. (JUN, yoshi, masa, nobu, toshi, yuki, yori, aya, nori, su, ari, osa, kazu, shige, nao, michi, mitsu, mune, moto, yasu)
1一 Toshikazu *m*, Jun'ichi
2二 Junji *m*
3三 Junzō *m*, Toshizō
三郎 Junzaburō *m*
之 Nobuyuki *m*
子 Yoshiko *f*
5四郎 Junshirō *m*
正 Nobumasa *m*
6次郎 Junjirō *m*
耳 Junji *m*
吉 Junkichi *m*
7作 Junsaku *m*
助 Junsuke *m*
8若 Masayori *m*
良 Nobuyoshi *m*
9治 Junji *m*
長 Ayanaga *m*
美子 Sumiko *f*
彦 Yoshihiko *m*, Michihiko
10恵 Nobue *f*
通 Masamichi *m*
造 Junzō *m*
11胤 Aritane *m*
域 Norikuni *m*
康 Yoshimichi *m*
12皓 Yasuaki *m*
朝 Naotomo *m*
13雄 Norio *m*
路 Masamichi *m*
義 Mitsuyoshi *m*
14徳 Yukinori *m*
徳院 Juntokuin *mlh*

## 12 L2

**馮** 1533 (HYŌ, yori)
代 Yoriyo *m*

**博** 1534 [T] Hiroshi *m*, Hiromu, Tōru *m*. (HAKU, hiro, haka)
3之 Hiroyuki *m*
4介 Hirosuke *m*
文 Hirobumi *m*
太郎 Hirotarō *m*
6多 Hakata *p*
多小女郎波枕 H. kojorō namimakura *la*
7邦 Hirokuni *m*
彪 Hiroaki *m*
8林 Hiromoto *m*
英 Hirohide *m*
9音 Hiroto *m*
11麻 Hakama *m*
麻呂 Hakamaro *m*
進 Hironobu *m*
14徳 Hakatoko *m*
精 Hiroyoshi *m*
15蔵 Hirozō *m*
19瀬 Hakase *m*

**偉** 1535 [T] Isamu *m*, Ōi. (I, take, yori)
久 Takehisa *m*

**傅** 1536 (FU, suke, yoshi)
田 Suketada *m*
助 Yoshisuke *m*

**偕** 1537 (KAI, tomo)
一郎 Kaiichirō *m*
子 Tomoko *f*
宣 Tomonobu *m*

**傍** 1538 [T] (HŌ, BŌ, kata, soba)
士 Hōji *s*
木 Hōki *s*
島 Sobashima *s*
陽 Soehi *s*

**備** 1539 [T] Sonō *m*, Sonawaru. (BI, tomo, mitsu, nari, masa, yoshi, mina, nobu, naga)
子 Masako *f*, Minako
中 Bitchū *ph*
治 Tomoharu *m*
前 Bizen *sph*
後 Bingo *ph*
愛 Mitsuyoshi *m*

## 12 L3

**孫** 1540 [T] (SON, mago, hiko, tada, sane, hiro)
一 Magoichi *m*
一郎 Magoichirō *m*
三郎 Magosaburō *m*
右衛門 Magoemon *m*
主 Hikonushi *s*
次郎 Magojirō *m*
吉 Magokichi *m*
名人 Hikonahito *s*
作 Magosaku *m*
兵衛 Magobee *m*
姫式 Hikohimeshiki *l*
顕 Tadaaki *m*

**喧** 1541 (KEN, KAN, haru)
子 Haruko *f*

**喫** 1542 [T] (KITSU)
茶養生記 Kissa yōjōki *la*

**項** 1543 [T] (KŌ, GŌ, uji)
羽 Kō U *mh-l* "Hsiang Yu"
羽と劉邦 Kō U to Ryū Hō *la* "Hsiang Yu & Liu Fang"

**須** 1544 [N] Motomu *m*. (SU, SHU, matsu, mochi)
3川 Sugawa *s*
之内 Sunouchi *s*
子 Suko *s*
久毛 Sukumo *s*
4戸 Suto *s*
山 Suyama *s*
木 Suki *p*
5加 Suga *s*
永 Sunaga *s*
田 Suda *s*
立 Sudate *s*
玉 Sutama *p*
6合 Sugō *s*
7佐 Susa *sp*
佐木 Susaki *s*
坂 Suzaka *s*
沢 Suzawa *s*
貝 Sugai *s*
見 Sumi *s*
8波 Suwa *s*
知 Suchi *s*
受武良 Suzumura *s*
9長 Sunaga *s*
10釜 Sugama *s*
恵 Sue *p*
原 Subara *s*, Suwara
原屋 Suwaraya *s*
11黒 Suguro *s*
12須木 Suzuki *s*, Susuki
崎 Susaki *sp*
崎屋 Suzakiya *l*
賀 Suga *s*, Suka
賀川 Sukagawa *sp*
賀井 Sukai *s*
賀田 Sukada *s*
賀院 Sukai *s*
13細 Susai *s*
14郷 Sugō *s*
16磨 Suma *sp-l*
磨子 Sumako *f*
磨源氏 Suma Genji *la*
磨都源平躑躅 S. no miyako Genpei tsutsuji *la*
18藤 Sudō *s*
藤南翠 S. Nansui *ml*

**惶** 1545 (KŌ, Ō, kashiko)

**愔** 1546 (IN, AN, ON, yoshi)
子 Yoshiko *f*

**惺** 1547 Satoshi *m*. (SEI, SHŌ)
窩 Seika *ml*
窩文集 S. bunshū *l*

**接** 1548 [T] (SETSU, SHŌ, tsugu, tsugi, tsura, mochi)

**揆** 1549 Hakaru *m*. (KI, GI)

**揖** 1550 (SHŪ, ITSU, i, osa)
保 Ibo *p*
保川 Ibogawa *p*
斐 Ibi *sp*; Segai *s*
斐川 Ibigawa *p*

**揚** 1551 [T] Akira *m*; Age *s*. (YŌ, aki, nobu, age)
屋 Ageya *s*
牙児奇獄 Yonkeru kigoku *l*

**猪** 1552 See 猪 1306

**猩** 1553 (SHŌ)
猩 Shōjō *la*

**猨** 1554 (EN, sa)
山 Sayama *s*

惶 愔 惺 接 揆 揖 揚 猪 猩 猨 ▼ 猶 塚 堤 塔 塀 堺 埴 隆 陰 随 陶 隅 陽 徝 循 街 復 御 ▲ 湧 游 渚 湊 渙 測 湜 淳 淞 渤

**猶** 1555 [T] (YŪ, YU, nao, sane, yori)
子 Naoko *f*
吉 Naokichi *m*
耳 Ikaka *s*
林 Naobayashi
治郎 Naojirō *m*
原 Konohara *s*
朔 Naomoto *m*
崎 Naozaki *s*

**塚** 1556 See 塚 1844

**堤** 1557 [T] Tsutsumi *s.* (TEI, tsutsumi)
中納言 T. Chūnagon *l*

**塔** 1558 [T] (TŌ)
沢 Tonosawa *s*
原 Tonohara *s*

**塀** 1559 (HEI, kaki)
加塀 Hakai *s*
和 Kakiwa *s*, Haga

**堺** 1560 Sakai *sp.* (KAI, sakai)
沢 Sakaisa *s* ⌈*mlh*
利彦 Sakai Toshihiko
枯川 S. Kosen *ml*

**埴** 1561 (SHOKU, JIKI, hani, hai, ha)
生 Hanyū *s*, Habu
谷 Haniya *s*
谷雄高 H. Yutaka *ml*
科 Hanishina *p* ⌈ra
原 Haniwara *s*, Haiba-
盧新羅人 Haniioshiragibito *s*

**隆** 1562 See 隆 1313

**陰** 1563 [T] (IN, ON, kage)
山 Kageyama *s*
守 Kagemori *m*
陽道 On'yōdō / Onmyōdō *h*
獣 Injū *l*
翳礼讃 In'ei raisan *l*

**随** 1564 [T] (ZUI, SUI, yori, yuki, aya, michi)
分附 Nabusazuke *s*, Nabusa, Naburi
光 Yorimitsu *m*
時 Yoritoki *m*
朝 Zuichō *s*
資 Ayasuke *m*

**陶** 1565 [T] Sue *s.* (TŌ, sue, su, yoshi)
山 Sueyama *s*, Suyama
山務 Sueyama Tsuto-
東 Sudō *s* ⌊mu *ml*
帰 Tōki *s*
浪 Sunami *s*
部 Suebe *s*
晴賢 Sue Harukata *mh*
器 Suki *s*, Sue
器所 Sue *s*

**隅** 1566 (GŪ, sumi, fusa)
山 Sumiyama *s*
田 Sumida *sp*; Suda *s*
田川 Sumidagawa *la*
田川花御所染 S. hana no gosho-zome *la*
田春妓女容性 Sumida no haru geisha katagi *l*
田葉吉 S. Yōkichi *ml*
屋 Sumiya *s*

**陽** 1567 [T] Akira *m*, Kiyoshi; Yō *sm*; Minami *s.* (YŌ, aki, akira, ya, haru, kiyo, o, hi, oki, taka, naka)
一 Yōichi *m*
二 Yōji *m*
丹 Yoni *s*
太郎 Yōtarō *m*
平 Nobuhira *s*
吉 Hiyoshi *m*
治 Takanobu *m*
春子 Yasuko *f*
恵 Akiyoshi *m*
通 Kiyomichi *m*
康 Kiyoyasu *m*
疑 Yagi *s*

**徝** 1568 Susumu *m.* (I, CHOKU)

**循** 1569 [T] (JUN, SHUN, mitsu, yuki, yoshi)

**街** 1570 [T] Chimata *s.* (GAI)
風 Tsumuji *s*

**復** 1571 [T] Shigeru *m*, Sakae, Atsushi. (FUKU, mata, nao)
六 Mataroku *m*

**御** 1572 [T] (GO, GYO, mi, o, nori, mitsu, oki, oya)
[8]土田 Mitoda *s*
子 Miko *s* ⌈koidan
子左 Mikohidari *s*, Mi-
子神 Mikogami *s*
[4]井子 Miiko *f*
木 Miki *s*
木本 Mikimoto *s*
木本幸吉 M. Kōkichi
手 Mite *s* ⌊*mh*
手代 Miteshiro *s*
手洗 Mitarai *s*, Mita-
[5]代 Mishiro *s* ⌊rashi
代田 Miyoda *p*
代川 Miyokawa *s*
田鍬 Mitasuki *m*
立 Mitate *s*
主人 Miushi *mh*
正 Mimasa *s*
本 Mimoto *s*
[6]存商売物 Gozonji no shōbai-mono *l*
名 Mina *s*
舟 Mifune *m*
[7]杖 Mitsue *m-f-p*
坊 Gobō *p*
坂 Misaka *p*
伽草子 Otogizōshi *l*
伽婢子 Otogibōko *l*
安 Miyasu *m*
返事 Otsuhechi *s*
巫 Mikanagi *s*, Mikannagi
[8]炊 Mikashigi *s*
牧 Mimaki *sm*
供田 Gokuden *s*
使 Mitsukai *s*, Mitsuka
所 Gose *p*
所浦 Goshoura *p*
所桜堀河夜討 Goshozakura Horikawa youchi *la*
国詞活用抄 Mikuni kotoba katsuyōshō *l*
[9]垣の下草 Mikaki no shitakusa *l*
神本 Mikamoto *s*
松 Omatsu *f*
津 Mitsu *p*, Mito
法 Minori *l*
法川 Minorigawa *s*
荘 Mishō *p*
春 Miharu *s*
岳 Mitake *sp*; Otake *s*
前 Mimae *s*, Misaki
前山 Gozenyama *p*
前崎 Omaezaki *p*
風 Norikaze *m*
看 Oroshi *s*
[10]浜 Mihama *p*
酒 Miki *f*
酒本 Mikimoto *s*
息 Miiki *s*
家流 Oie-ryū *la*
室 Mimuro *s*; Omuro
座 Mimashi *s* ⌊*p*
[11]船 Mifune *sm-p*
野江 Onoe *f*
宿 Mishuku *s*, Mishiku, Tonoi; Onjuku *p*
曹子島わたり Onzōshi shimawatari *l*
堂七番歌合 Midō shichiban utaawase *l*
堂関白 M. Kanpaku *mh*
堂関白記 M. K. ki *l*
堂関白集 M. K. shū *l*
[12]崎 Misaki *s*
[13]摂勧進帳 Gohiiki kanjinchō *la*
溝 Mikawa *s*, Mikō
殿場 Gotenba *p*
園 Misono *sp*
園生 Misonō *s*
[14]稲 Mishine *m*
嵩 Mitake *p*
[15]霊谷 Mikuriya *s*
幡 Mihata *s*
郷 Migō *s*
調 Mitsugi *sp*
影池 Mikageike *s*, Minoike, Minoichi
器所 Gokiso *s*
幣 Mitehara *s*
裳濯 Mimosuso *la*
裳濯川歌合 M.-gawa utaawase *l*
蔵 Mikura *s*

蔵島 Mikurashima *p*
厩 Minmaya *s*
廚 Mikuriya *sp*
廚屋 Mikuriya *s*
16薬袋 Minai *s*
19簾納 Misuno *s*
21鬮 Mikuji *s*
24饗 Okai *s*

湧 1573 See 涌 1065

游 1574 Yutaka *m.* (YŪ, YU)

渚 1575 Nagisa *m-f.* (SHO)

湊 1576 Minato *sm.* (SŌ, SU)

渙 1577 Kiyoshi *m.* (KAN)

測 1578 [T] (SOKU, hiro)
江 Hiroe *f*

湜 1579 (SHOKU, JIKI, kiyo)
子 Kiyoko *f*

渟 1580 (TEI, nu, nuna)
足 Nutari *s*

淞 1581 (SHŌ, SU, matsu)
世 Matsuyo *f*

渤 1582 (BOTSU, fuka)
海 Fukami *s*; Bokkai *p*

港 1583 [T] Minato *m-f-p.* (KŌ, GU, minato, tsu)
元 Tsumoto *s*
北 Kōhoku *p*
次郎 Kōjirō *m*
崎 Minatozaki *s*

湖 1584 [T] Hiroshi *m.* (KO, GO)
月抄 Kogetsushō *l*
山 Koyama *s*
北 Kohoku *p*
西 Kosai *p*
出 Koide *s*
東 Kotō *p*
南 Konan *p*
畔手記 Kohan shuki *l*
陵 Koryō *p*
鯉鮒 Koryū *m*

温 1585 [T] Atsushi *m*, Yutaka, Nodoka, Sunao, Tadasu, Tsutsumu, Narō; Nukumi *s*, Nukui. (ON, UN, atsu, yoshi, yasu, haru, masa, naga, iro, mitsu)
子 Atsuko *f*
文 Atsufumi *m*
井 Nukui *s*
乎 Yoshika *m*
次郎 Masajirō *m*
圭 Yoshikiyo *m*
知 Nagatomo *m*
泉 Onsen *p*
美 Atsumi *p*
海 Atsumi *m-p*

渡 1586 [T] Wataru *sm*, Watari. (TO, watari, watara, tada)
之助 Watarinosuke *m*
井 Watarai *s*
辺 Watanabe *s*
辺一夫 W. Kazuo *ml*
辺水巴 W. Suiha *ml*
辺光風 W. Kōfū *ml*
辺崋山 W. Kazan *mlh*
辺順三 W. Junzō *ml*
辺黙禅 W. Mokuzen *ml*
辺霞亭 W. Katei *ml*
守武 Tomotake *s*
利 Watari *s*
会 Watarai *s*
里 Watari *s*
沼 Watanuma *s*
海 Tokai *s*
海谷 Watamiya *s*
部 Watanabe *s*
島 Oshima *p*
貫 Watanuki *s*
植 Tonoe *s*
瀬 Watarise *s*, Watarase, Watase

湯 1587 [T] Yu *s.* (TŌ, yu)
2人 Yue *s*
3川 Yukawa *sp*
川秀樹 Y. Hideki *mlh*
上 Yukami *s*
口 Yuguchi *s*
之谷 Yunotani *p*
4山 Yuyama *s*
5布院 Yufuin *p*
田 Yuda *sp*
生 Yue *s*
本 Yumoto *sp*
本喜作 Y. Kisaku *ml*
6次 Yutsugi *s*
江 Yue *s*
池 Yuchi *s*
地 Yuchi *s*
地孝 Y. Takashi *ml*
7沢 Yuzawa *sp*
村 Yumura *s*
谷 Yūya *s*
邑 Yumura *s*
来 Yugi *p*
坐 Yue *s*
8河 Yukawa *s*
河原 Yugawara *p*
9津上 Yuzukami *p*
浅 Yuasa *sp*
浅半月 Y. Hangetsu *ml*
浅芳子 Y. Yoshiko *fl*
前 Yunomae *p*
10浦 Yunoura *p*
原 Yubara *sp*
座 Yue *m*

## 12 L4

焼 1588 [T] (SHŌ, yaki, yai)
津 Yaizu *p*

禄 1589 [N] (ROKU, RYOKU, yoshi, tomi, sachi, toshi)
夫 Yoshio *m*
寿 Yoshitoshi *m*
郎 Rokurō *m*

斌 1590 Akira *m*, Takeshi, Sakan, Sakae, Sakashi, Hitoshi, Hajime, Susumu. (HIN, aya, yoshi, take, akira, aki, toshi)
人 Ayato *m*
夫 Ayao *m*, Yoshio
彦 Ayahiko *m*
雄 Takeo *m*
衡 Toshihide *m*

峻 1591 Takashi *m.* (SHUN, taka, toshi, mine, chika, michi)
次 Toshitsugu *m*
雄 Takao *m*

崎 1592 (KI, saki)
川 Sakikawa *s*
子 Sakiko *f*
戸 Sakito *p*
元 Sakimoto *s*
山 Sakiyama *s*
永 Sakie *f*
田 Sakita *s*
村 Sakimura *s*

晙 1593 Akira *m.* (SHUN)

暎 1594 Akira *m.* (EI, YŌ, teru, akira)
二 Teruji *m*
臣 Teruomi *m*

晩 1595 [T] (BAN, kure, kage)
重 Kageshige *m*
涼 Banryō *l*
稲 Okute *f*
穂 Kureo *m-f*, Kureho

暁 1596 [T] Akatsuki *m*, Akira, Satoru, Satoshi; Akebono *sp*; Akeno *s.* (GYŌ, toshi, aki, akira, ake, toki)
台 Gyōdai *ml*
春 Toshiharu *m*
烏 Akegarasu *s*
烏敏 A. Haya *ml*
雄 Akeo *m*
霞 Akatsuka *s*

晴 1597 [T] Kiyoshi *m*, Haruru. (SEI, JŌ, haru, teru, hare, nari)
子 Haruko *f*
丸 Harumaru *m*
山 Haruyama *s*
夫 Haruo *m*
比古 Haruhiko *m*
具 Harutomo *m*
季 Harusue *m*
枝 Harumaki *s*
彦 Teruhiko *m*

景 Harukage *m*
善 Hareyoshi *m*
輝 Haruteru *m*
綱 Harutsuna *m*
賢 Harutaka *m*

**姫** 1598 See 姫 1358

**娘** 1599 [T] (RŌ, ra)
道成寺 Musume Dōjōji *a*

**婉** 1600 Tao *f*. (EN, ON, shina, tsuya, tao)
子 Shinako *f*, Tsuyako

**婧** 1601 (SEI, SHŌ, tada)
子 Tadako *f*

**婇** 1602 (SAI, une)
女 Uneme *f*

**婦** 1603 [T] (FU, FŪ)
中 Fuchū *p*
系図 Onna keizu *l*
負 Nei *sp*

**琮** 1604 (SŌ, SU, mizu)

**琚** 1605 Tama *f*. (KYO, KO)

**琅** 1606 (RŌ, tama)
枝 Tamae *f*

**瑛** 1607 Akira *m*. (EI, YŌ, aki, akira, teru)
子 Akiko *f*
代 Teruyo *f*

**琢** 1608 [N] Migaku *m*. (TAKU, aya, taka)
之助 Takunosuke *m*
禅 Takayoshi *m*
磨 Takuma *m*

**斑** 1609 (HAN, madara)
目 Madarame *s*
猫 Madara neko *l*
鳩 Ikaruga *sp*; Ikarugamo *s*
鳩宮 Ikaruga-no-miya *ph*

**朖** 1610 See 朗 1394

**腆** 1611 Atsushi *m*. (TEN)

**脚** 1612 [T] (KYAKU, KAKU, ashi, shi)
身 Ashitsumi *s*
咋 Ashikui *s*
結抄 Ayuishō *l*

**勝** 1613 [T] Katsu *sm*, Suguru, Suguro; Kachi *s*, Masa, Suguri; Masaru *m*, Sugure. (SHŌ, katsu, masa, yoshi, tō, nori, kachi, masu)
1一 Katsuichi *m*
一郎 Katsuichirō *m*
2二 Katsuji *m*
又 Katsumata *s*
人 Katsundo *m*
3川 Katsukawa *s*
川春章 K. Shunshō *ma*
三郎 Katsusaburō *m*
久 Masahisa *m*
4元 Katsumoto *m*
及 Katsuchika *m*
山 Katsuyama *sp*
五郎 Katsugorō *m*
井 Katsui *s*
夫 Katsuo *m*
太郎 Katsutarō *m*
升 Katsuyuki *m*
木 Katsuki *s*
木原 Nodehara *s*
5以 Katsuyuki *m*
代豆米 Masayotsume *f*
北 Shōboku *p*
司 Katsushi *m*
矢 Katsuya *s*
目 Katsume *s*
田 Katsuta *sp*; Shōda *s*, Suguta
央 Shōō *p*
本 Katsumoto *sp*
本清一郎 K. Seiichirō *ml*
6任 Katsutō *m*
次 Katsuji *m*
次郎 Katsujirō *m*
行 Masayuki *m*
亦 Katsumata *s*
全 Katsutake *m*
多 Katta *s*
谷 Katsuya *s*
7伴 Yoshitomo *m*; Suguritomo *s*, Kashiwadenotomo
沢 Katsuzawa *s*
村 Katsumura *s*
安芳 Katsu Yasuyoshi *mh*
男 Katsuo *m*
尾 Katsuo *s*
呂 Katsuro *s*, Suguro
見 Katsumi *s*
臣 Katsutomi *m*, Katsumi, Kachion
寿 Katsuyoshi *m*
8河 Katsukawa *s*
沼 Katsunuma *sp*
奐 Masaru *m*
易 Katsuyasu *m*
承夫 Katsu Yoshio *ml*
9俣 Katsumata *s*
津子 Katsuko *f*
治 Katsuji *m*
畑 Katsuhata *s*
昶 Katsuaki *m*, Katsutō
郎 Katsurō *m*
美 Katsumi *m*
重 Katsushige *m*
10修 Katsunaga *m*
浦 Katsuura *sp*; Katsura *s*
海 Katsumi *m*
殷 Katsumasa *m*
倉 Katsukura *s*
家 Katsuie *m*
屋 Katsuya *s*
馬 Katsuma *m*
11峰 Katsumine *s*
峰晋風 K. Shinpū *ml*
野 Katsuno *s*
部 Kachibe *s*, Katsube
皐 Katsutaka *m*
庸 Katsunobu *m*
進 Katsuyuki *m*
島 Katsushima *s*
商 Katsuaki *m*
12暁 Katsutoki *m*
賀瀬 Katsugase *s*, Shōgase
敞 Katsuaki *m*
間 Katsuma *sm*
間田 Katsumata *s*
13経 Yoshinori *m*
愛 Katsusane *m*
14鳴 Katsunari *m*
摘 Katsumi *m*
豪 Katsutake *m*
15徴 Katsuyoshi *m*
権 Katsunori *m*
摩 Katsukiyo *m*
蔵 Katsuzō *m*
17謙 Katsukata *m*
騂 Masaka *m*
慈 Katsunari *m*
18観 Katsumi *m*
齢 Katsutoshi *m*
曠 Katsuhiro *m*
22鬘経 Shōmangyō *l*
鬘経義疏 S. gisho *l*

**梅** 1614 See 梅 1374

**棧** 1615 Kakehashi *s*. (SAN, ZEN)

**棣** 1616 (TEI, TAI, tomi)

**梯** 1617 Kake *s*, Kakehashi. (TEI, hashi)

**椚** 1618 Kunugi *s*. (kunugi)
田 Kunugita *s*

**椒** 1619 (SHŌ, ki)
芽 Kinome *s*

**棹** 1620 (TAKU, sao)
江 Saoe *f*

**棭** 1621 (EKI)
斎 Ekisai *mlh*

**楉** 1622 (JAKU, NYAKU, tada)
田 Shimotoda *s*

**棒** 1623 [T] (BŌ)
屋 Bōya *s*
縛 Bō-shibari *la*

**椀** 1624 (WAN, mari)

子 Mariko *s*
久末松山 Wankyū sue no Matsuyama *la*
屋 Wan'ya *s*

棚 1625 (HŌ, BYŌ, tana, suke)
木 Tanaki *s*
田 Tanada *s*
沢 Tanazawa *s*
村 Tanamura *s*
谷 Tanaya *s*
倉 Tanagura *sp*
橋 Tanahashi *s*
網 Tanaami *s*
瀬 Tanase *s*

椙 1626 (sugi, soma)
川 Sugikawa *s*
山 Sugiyama *s*, Somayama
平 Sugihira *s*
社 Suginomori *s*
原 Sugihara *s*, Suginohara

棟 1627 [I] Takashi *m*, Munagi. (TŌ, mune, taka, sake, mine)
一 Muneichi *m*
一郎 Tōichirō *m*
方 Munakata *s*
居 Munesue *s*, Munasue
治 Muneharu *m*
造 Tōzō *m*
梁 Munehari *m*

椋 1628 Muku *s*. (RYŌ, kura, muku)
人 Kurahito *s*
原 Mukuhara *s*
梨 Mukunashi *s*
椅 Kurahashi *s*
椅部 Kurahase *s*
鳩十 Muku Hatojū *ml*
橋部 Kurahashibe *s*

椎 1629 (SUI, TSUI, shii, tsuchi)
の木 Shiinoki *l*
木 Shiinoki *s*
田 Shiida *p*
本 Shiigamoto *l*
名 Shiina *s*
名麟三 S. Rinzō *ml*
谷 Shiiya *s*
貝 Shiikai *s*
津 Shiizu *s*
原 Shiihara *s*
野 Shiino *s*
葉 Shiiba *p*
園詠草 Shiizono eisō *l*
橋 Shiihashi *s*

## 12 L5

視 1630 See 視 1348

將 1631 See 将 1040

竦 1632 Takashi *m*. (SHŌ, SHU)

短 1633 [T] (TAN)
歌 Tanka *l*
歌草原 T. sōgen *l*
歌撰格 T. senkaku *l*

硯 1634 Suzuriya *s*. (KEN, GEN, suzuri)
友社 Ken'yūsha *l*

硬 1635 [T] Katashi *m*. (KŌ, GŌ, GYŌ, kata)

眸 1636 Hitomi *m*. (BŌ, MU)

眼 1637 [T] (GAN, GEN, me, makuwashi)
目 Sakka *s*
部 Manabe *s*

皖 1638 Akira *m*, Kiyoshi. (KAN, GAN, kiyo)
是 Kiyoyuki *m*

皓 1639 Akira *m*, Hikaru, Hiroshi. (KŌ, aki, teru, hiro, tsuku)
子 Teruko *f*, Hiroko

稀 1640 (KI, KE, mare)
音家 Kineya *s*
雄 Mareo *m*

程 1641 [T] (TEI, nori, hodo, take, mina)
ケ谷 Hodogaya *s*
田 Hodota *s*
島 Hodojima *s*
塚 Hodotsuka *s*

税 1642 [T] Osamu *m*, Mitsugi; Chikara *sm*. (ZEI, SEI, chikara)
田 Saita *s*
所 Saisho *s*, Zeisho
所敦子 S. Atsuko *fl*
部 Chikarabe *s*

袴 1643 (KO, KU, hakama)
田 Hakamada *s*
塚 Hakamazuka *s*

補 1644 [T] Tasuku *m*. (HO, FU, BU, sada, suke)
子 Sukeko *f*
沓 Hokutsu *s*
鬼 Hoki *s*

裕 1645 [T] Hiroshi *m*, Yutaka. (YŪ, hiro, michi, suke, yasu)
子 Hiroko *f*
久 Yasuhisa *m*
仁 Hirohito *m*
吉 Yūkichi *m*
志 Sukeyuki *m*
宏 Michihiro *m*
弥 Hirohisa *m*
輔 Yūsuke

## 12 L6

兟 See 1922

喆 1646 See 哲 1227

弱 1647 [T] (JAKU, yowa, yoro)
法師 Yoroboshi *la*

蛙 1648 Kawazu *m*. (A)
川 Agawa *s*

蛤 1649 (KŌ, ai)
良 Aira *s*

蛯 1650 (ebi, hiru)
子 Ebiko *s*, Ebisu
江 Ebie *s*
野 Hiruno *s*

## 12 L7

貯 1651 [T] Osamu *m*. (CHO, moru)

谺 1652 Kodama *m*. (KA, GE)

釉 1653 Tsuya *f*. (YŪ, YU)

酢 1654 (SO, SAKU, ZAKU, su)
屋 Suya *s*

匏 1655 (HŌ, BYŌ, hisago)
子 Hisagoko *f*

転 1656 [T] Utata *m*. (TEN, hiro)
身の頌 Tenshin no shō *l*
法輪 Teburi *s*
寝の記 Utatane no ki *l*

軽 1657 [T] Karu *f*. (KEI, KYŌ, karu)
井沢 Karuizawa *p*
米 Karumai *p*
見 Karumi *s*
我孫 Karuabiko *s*
馬 Karume *s*
部 Karube *s*
間 Karuma *s*
雷集 Keiraishū *l*

詔 1658 [T] (SHŌ, nori)

⿰言必 1659 See 謚 2637A

証 1660 [T] Akira *m*. (SHŌ, akashi, mi, tsuku)
子 Akashiko *f*

詅 1661 (REI, RYŌ, teru)
子 Teruko *f*

楉 棒 椀 ▼ 棚 椙 棟 椋 椎 視 將 竦 短 硯 硬 眸 眼 皖 皓 稀 程 税 袴 補 裕 兟 喆 弱 蛙 蛤 蛯 貯 谺 釉 酢 匏 転 軽 詔 ⿰言必 証 詅 ▲ 訶 評 詠

匏 転 軽 詔 認 証 詅 ▼ 訶 評 詠 詞 款 報 就 断 斯 期 朝 舒 鈞 鈊 鈔 鈇 欽 紝 級 紡 紐 紗 紋 納 敝 敢 敞 散 敦 敬 ▲ 都 彭 靭 剰 創 割 馭

**訶** 1662 (KA, uta)
子 Utako *f*

**評** 1663 [T] Hakaru *s*, Hakari, Kōri. (HYŌ, tada)
判記 Hyōbanki *l*

**詠** 1664 [T] Uta *f*; Nagame *s*. (EI, YŌ, uta, naga, kane, kanu)
歌一体 Eiga ittai *l*
歌大概 E. taigai *l*

**詞** 1665 [T] (SHI, JI, koto, fumi, nari, nori)
の玉緒 Kotoba no tama-no-o *l*
子 Kotoko *f*, Fumiko
花集 Shikashū *l*

——12 L8——

**款** 1666 [T] (KAN, masa, suke, tada, yuku, yoshi)

**報** 1667 [T] (HŌ, o, tsugu)

**就** 1668 [T] (SHŪ, JU, nari, yuki)
久 Narihisa *m*
高 Naritaka *m*
馴 Nariyoshi *m*

**断** 1669 [T] Takeshi *m*, Sadamu. (DAN, sada, tō)
腸亭日乗 Danchōtei nichijō *l*

**斯** 1670 (SHI, kore, tsuna, nori)
波 Shiba *s*, Shinami
波義将 Shiba Yoshimasa *mh*
真田 Shimada *s*
臘 Shirō *s*

**期** 1671 [T] (KI, GI, GO, sane, toki, toshi, nori)

**朝** 1672 [T] Hajime *m*. (CHŌ, asa, tomo, toki, sa, tsuto, kata, nori)
[8]川 Asakawa *s*
子 Asako *f*, Tokiko
[4]戸 Asabe *s*
井 Asai *s*
日 Asahi *sp*; Asuka *s*
日奈 Asahina *sl*; Asaina *s*
[5]比奈 Asahina *sl*
永 Tomonaga *sm*
永三十郎 T. Sanjūrō *ml*
田 Asada *s*
生 Asō *s*; Asami *f*
[6]地 Asaji *p*
印奈 Asaina s, Asahina
成 Tomohira *m*
米 Asako *s*
[7]吹 Asabuki *s*
臣 Ason *sm*, Asomi
来 Asako *sf-p*
夷 Asahina *s*, Asaina
夷巡島記 Asaina shimameguri *la*
夷名 Asahina *s*, Asaina, Asatsuna
河 Asakawa *s*
明 Asake *s*
枝 Asaeda *s*
忠 Asatada *m*
宗 Asamune *sm*
定 Tomosada *m*
阜苗 Sanae *f*
武 Tsutomu *m*
[9]治 Tomoharu *m*
則 Tokinori *m*
妻 Asazuma *s*
妻子午 Asazumakouma *s*
香 Asaka *s*
岡 Asaoka *s*
[10]家 Asaya *s*
倉 Asakura *sp*
倉文夫 A. Fumio *ma*
倉敏景 A. Toshikage *mh*
倉義景 A. Yoshikage *mh*
原 Asahara *sm*
[11]猟 Asakari *m*
野 Asano *s*
野群載 Chūya gunsai *l*
[12]陽 Tomoo *m*
棟 Asamune *m*
賀 Asaka *s*
象 Tomokata *m*
[13]嵐夕雨 Asaarashi yūsame *l*
[16]積 Asaka *s*
融 Asaakira *m*
[17]霞 Asaka *p*

**舒** 1673 Noburu *m*, Shizuka. (JO, SHO, nobu, yuki)
子 Nobuko *f*
光 Nobumitsu *m*
明 Jomei *mlh*

**鈞** 1674 Hitoshi *m*. (KIN)

**鈊** 1675 (SHIN, toshi)
子 Toshiko *f*

**鈔** 1676 Kiyoshi *m*. (SHŌ)
吾 Shōgo *m*

**鈇** 1677 (FU, ono)
子 Onoko *f*

**欽** 1678 [N] Makoto *m*, Hitoshi. (KIN, KON, yoshi, tada, koku)
一 Yoshikazu *m*
明 Kinmei *mh*

**紝** 1679 Kinu *f*. (JIN, NIN)

**級** 1680 [T] (KYŪ, shina)
子 Shinako *f*

**紡** 1681 [T] (BŌ, HŌ, tsumu)
子 Tsumuko *f*

**紐** 1682 (CHŪ, NYU, kumi)
子 Kumiko *f*
育 Nyūyōku *p* "New York"

**紗** 1683 Suzu *f*. (SA, SHA, tae)
子 Taeko *f*
抜大押 Sanukiōoshi *s*
綾子 Sayako *f*

**紋** 1684 [T] (MON, BUN, aya)
子 Ayako *f*
太郎 Montarō *m*
次郎 Monjirō *m*
別 Monbetsu *p*

**納** 1685 [T] Osamu *m*; Osame *s*, Iri. (TŌ, NA, NŌ, tomo, nori, iri)
米 Nōme *s*
谷 Naya *s*
村 Namura *s*
所 Nōso *s*, Naso
部 Iribe *s*
富 Nōtomi *s*, Iritomi, Itomi
寛 Norihiro *m*

**敝** 1686 (HEI, BEI, hisa)

**敢** 1687 [T] Isamu *m*, Isami; Ae *s*. (KAN, ae)
臣族岸 Aeomizokugishi *s*

**敞** 1688 Takashi *m*, Hiroshi, Akira. (SHŌ, taka, hiro, aki, hisa)
子 Hiroko *f*
夫 Takao *m*

**散** 1689 [T] (SAN, nobu)
木奇歌集 Sanboku kikashū *l*
吉 Sanuki *s*, Saki
楽 Sangaku *a*

**敦** 1690 [N] Atsushi *m*, Osamu, Tsutomu. (TON, atsu, tsuru, tai, nobu)
子 Atsuko *f*
仁 Atsukimi *m*
介 Taisuke *m*
井 Tsurui *s*
有 Atsuari *m*
成 Atsuhira *m*
男 Tsuruo *m*
固 Atsukata *m*
盛 Atsumori *m*
賀 Tsuruga *sp*
儀 Atsunori *m*

**敬** 1691 [T] Takashi *m*, Hiroshi, Satoshi. (KEI, KYŌ, taka, yuki, yoshi, hiro, nori, toshi, atsu, haya, aki, itsu, kata, uya)
[1]一 Keiichi *m*

2二 Keiji *m*
八 Keihachi *m*
七 Keishichi *m*
3三 Keizō *m*
三郎 Keizaburō *m*
4介 Keisuke *m*
止 Keishi *m*
天牧童 Keiten Bokudō *ml*
夫 Yukio *m*, Toshio
5礼 Noriyuki *m*
6次郎 Keijirō *m*
行 Yoshiyuki *m*
光 Yukimitsu *m*
吉 Keikichi *m*
8信 Hiroyoshi *m*
9治 Keiji *m*
栄 Yukinaga *m*
直 Hirotada *m*
12款 Keisuke *m*
道 Norimichi *m*
13雄 Itsuo *m*
義 Takayoshi *m*
愛 Yoshinari *m*
16親 Takachika *m*, Yoshichika

—12 L9—

都 1692 See 都 1419

彭 1693 Sakaki *s*. (HŌ, BYŌ, chika, michi, mori)
城 Sakaki *s*
祖 Hōso *l*

靭 1694 Yukei *s*. (JIN, NIN, yuki)
子 Yukiko *f*
負 Yukie *sm-p*; Yukei *s*
負輔 Yukienosuke *m*
連 Hokaru *s*
雄 Yukio *m*
猿 Utsubo-zaru *la*
編 Yukiami *s*

—12 L10—

剩 1695 See 剰 1426

創 1696 [T] Hajimu *m*. (SŌ, SHŌ)
生 Sōsei *l*

割 1696A [T] (KATSU, saki, wari)
田 Warita *s*

馭 1697 (GYO, GO, nori)
戎慨言 Karaosame no uretamigoto *l*

勁 1697A Tsuyoshi *m*. (KEI, KYŌ)

勤 1698 [T] Tsutomu *m*; Isoshi *sm*. (KIN, iso, toshi, nori)
二 Kinji *m*
子 Isoko *f*

勘 1699 [T] Sadamu *m*. (KAN, KON, nori, sada)
一 Kan'ichi *m*
十 Kanjū *m*
文 Noribumi *m*
平 Kanpei *m*
次郎 Kanjirō *m*
助 Kansuke *m*
治 Kanji *m*
馬 Kanma *m*
解人 Kageto *m*
解由 Kageyu *m*
解由小路 Kadenokōji *s*
蔵 Kanzō *m*

—12 T1—

啻 1700 (SHI, TEI, TAI, tada)
子 Tadako *f*

—12 T2—

奠 1701 (TEN, sada)
子 Sadako *f*

傘 1702 Karakasa *s*. (SAN, kasa)
火 Kasabi *l*

索 1703 [T] (SAKU, moto)
人 Mogiki *m*
羅下 Sakurabe *s*

—12 T3—

翕 1704 (KYŪ, atsu)
子 Atsuko *f*

尋 1705 [T] Hiroshi *m*. (JIN, hiro, chika, tsune, nori, hitsu, mitsu)
来津 Hirokitsu *s*, Shikitsu

奢 1706 (SHA, haru)
灞都 Sabato *l*

素 1707 Hajime *m*, Shiroshi, Sunao; So *s*. (SO, SU, moto, shiro)
人 Shirō *m*
川 Sugawa *s*
三 Shirozō *m*
木 Shiroki *s*, Shiraki
谷 Sodani *s*
身 Motomi *m*
性 Sosei *ml*
直 Sunao *l*
彦 Motohiko *m*
袍落 Suō otoshi *la*
堂 Sodō *ml*
履 Motobumi *m*
衛 Motomori *m*

壹 1708 See 壱 467

喜 1709 [T] Konomu *m*, Tanoshi. (KI, yoshi, nobu, hisa, haru, yuki)
1一 Kiichi *m*, Yoshikazu
一郎 Kiichirō *m*
2又 Yoshisuke *m*
八 Kihachi *m*
十郎 Kijūrō *m*
八郎 Kihachirō *m*
人 Yoshindo *m*
入 Kiire *sp*
七 Kishichi *m*
七郎 Kishichirō *m*
3三 Kisabu *m*
三二 Kisōji *m*
三八 Kisohachi *m*
三次 Kisanji *m*
三郎 Kisaburō *m*
三蔵 Kisazō *m*
子 Yoshiko *f*
久人 Kikuto *m*
久三 Kikuzō *m*
久大 Kikuo *m*
久太郎 Kikutarō *m*
久田 Kikuta *p*
久雄 Kikuo *m*
之助 Kinosuke *m*
4仁 Yoshihito *m*, Yoshito
六 Kiroku *m*
文 Yoshinobu *m*
太郎 Kitarō *m*
5平次 Kiheiji *m*
代 Kiyo *m*
代一 Kiyoichi *m*
代太 Kiyota *m*
代田 Kiyota *s*
代次 Kiyoji *m*
市 Kiichi *m*
正 Yoshitaka *m*
生子 Kioko *f*
田 Kida *s*
田川 Kitagawa *s*
田貞吉 Kida Sadakichi *mh*
6光 Nobuhiro *m*
早 Kihaya *s*, Kiso
世啓 Kiyohiro *m*
多 Kita *sp*; Yoshikazu *m*
多川 Kitagawa *s*
多川歌麿 K. Utamaro *ma*
多方 Kitakata *p*
多山 Kitayama *s*
多村 Kitamura *s*
多村久城 K. Hisamura *ml*
多見 Kitami *s*
多野 Kitano *s*
多島 Kitajima *s*
7作 Kisaku *m*
安 Kiyasu *s*
志 Kishi *s*
谷 Kitani *s*
谷六花 K. Rikka *ml*
8知郎 Kichirō *m*
茂別 Kimobetsu *p*
東 Yoshiharu *m*
9勇爾 Kiyoji *m*
美子 Kimiko *s*
界 Kikai *p*
哉 Yoshichika *m*
重郎 Kijūrō *m*
10郎 Yukio *m*
連川 Kitsuregawa *s*, Kiregawa; Kiretsugawa *p*
起 Yoshikazu *m*
11望 Yoshimi *m*
12堅 Nobukata *m*
13福 Nobutomi *m*
稔 Yoshitoshi *m*
雄 Yoshio *m*, Hisao, Nobukazu

普 奠 傘 索 翕 尋 奢 素 壹 喜 ▼ 寔 寍 甯 密 寒 富 萬 著 募 葎 葺 菘 萋 葵 葡 葭 葆 菰 韮 菟 ▲ 萱 董 萩 落 黄 森 嵒 崖 崔 暑

雲 Kiun *ml*
楽 Yoshimoto *m*
14徳郎 Kitokurō *m*
15撰式 Kisenshiki *l*
23鑑 Yoshinori *m*

寔 1710 Makoto *m.* (SHOKU, kore, sane, tada)
弘 Korehiro *m*

寍 1711 See 寧 2181

甯 1712 See 寧 2181

密 1713 Hisoka *m,* Takashi. (MITSU)
田 Mitsuda *s*

寒 1714 [T] Kan *s.* (KAN, samu, fuyu)
川 Samukawa *sp,* Sangawa ; Sōkawa *s*
川光太郎 Samukawa Kōtarō *ml*
川鼠骨 S. Sokotsu *ml*
山落木 Kanzan rakuboku *l*
吉 Kankichi *m*
河 Samukawa *s*
河江 Sagae *sp*
出 Kande *s*
風沢 Sōsa *s*
紅集 Kankōshū *l*
雷 Kanrai *l*

富 1715 [T] Tomi *sm-p* ; Tomeri *m,* Tomeru, Tomasu, Yutaka, Sakae, Mitsuru, Atsushi. (FŪ, FU, tomi, yoshi, hisa, to, toyo, atsu, fuku)
ノ沢麟太郎 Tominosawa Rintarō *ml*
3川 Tomikawa *s*
小路 Tominokōji *s*
子 Tomiko *f*
久 Tomihisa *m,* Yoshihisa
久山 Fukuyama *p*
久田 Fukuda *s*
士 Fuji *sp-l*
士川 Fujikawa *p*
士山 Fuji-san *p-la*
士太郎 Fujitarō *m*
士太鼓 Fuji-daiko *la*
士吉田 F. Yoshida *p*
士名 Fujina *s*
士見 Fujimi *p*
士谷 Fujitani *s* ⌈*ml*
士谷成章 F. Nariakira
士谷御杖 F. Mitsue *ml*
士浅間 Fuji Asama *l*
士弥 Fujiya *m*
士松 Fujimatsu *sla*
士宮 Fujimiya *p*
士根 Fujimoto *s*
士額男女繁山 Fujibitai Tsukuba no shigeyama *la*
4山 Toyama *sp,* Tomiyama
井 Tomii *s*
木 Tomiki *s*
太郎 Tomitarō *m*
5加 Tomika *p*
永 Tominaga *sm*
永太郎 T. Tarō *ml*
永仲基 T. Nakamoto *mh*
平 Tomihira *sm*
本 Tomimoto *s*
本豊前掾 T. Buzen-nojō *ma*
田 Tomita *s,* Tonda
田林 Tondabayashi *p*
田砕花 Tomita Saika *ml*
田常雄 T. Tsuneo *ml*
6次郎 Tomijirō *m*
江 Tomie *p*
合 Tomiai *p*
守 Tomimori *sm*
光 Yoshimitsu *m*
吉 Tomiyoshi *sm*
成 Tominari *s*
米 Tome *s*
7佐雄 Fusao *m*
坂 Tomisaka *s*
沢 Tomizawa *sp*
沢有為男 T. Uio *ml*
沢赤黄男 T. Kakio *ml*
谷 Tomiya *sp* ; Tomigaya *s*
安 Tomiyasu *sm*
安風生 T. Fūsei *ml*
男 Hisao *m*
尾 Tomio *s*
尾木 Tomioki *s*
里 Tomisato *p*
来 Tomiki *s*; Togi *sp*; Tomiku *m*
来田 Fukuta *p*
8所 Tomidokoro *s,* Todokoro
枝 Tomie *m*
取 Tottori *s*
良野 Furano *p*
9城 Tomiki *s*
津 Futtsu *sp*
松 Tomimatsu *s,* Tomatsu
則 Yoshinori *m*
勅 Tomitoki *m*
直 Tominao *m*
岡 Tomioka *sp*
岡恋山開 T. koi no yamabiraki *la*
岡鉄斎 T. Tessai *ma*
10海 Tonomi *s*
浦 Tomiura *p*
祚子 Fusako *f*
高 Tomitaka *s*
家 Fuke *s,* Tomiie
倉 Tomikura *s*
原 Tomihara *s*
11野 Tomino *s,* Tonno
島 Tomijima *s*
12崎 Tomizaki *s*
森 Tomimori *s*
賀見 Fukami *s*
13塚 Tomizuka *s*
強 Tomikatsu *m*
張 Tomihari *s*
雄 Tomio *m*
勢 Fuse *s*
14豪 Futoshi *m*
16樫 Tomigashi *s,* Togashi
樫政親 Togashi Masachika *mh*
総江 Fusae *f*

萬 1716 See 万 43

著 1717 See 著 1445

募 1718 Tsunoru *m.* (BO, MU)

葎 1719 Mugura *m.* (RITSU)

葺 1720 (SHŪ, fuki)
合 Fukiai *p*

菘 1721 Takashi *m.* (SŪ, SHŪ, SHU, suzuna)
子 Suzunako *f*

萋 1722 (SAI, SEI, shige)
子 Shigeko *f*

葵 1723 Aoi *sf* ; Mamoru *m.* (KI, GI)
上 Aoi no Ue *la*

葡 1724 (HO, BU)
葡牙 Porutogaru *p* "Portugal"

葭 1725 (KA, KE, yoshi)
子 Yoshiko *f*
江 Yoshie *m*
原 Yoshihara *s*
葉 Yoshiba *s*

葆 1726 Shigeru *m.* (HO, HŌ, shige, yasu)
光 Yasumitsu *m*
見 Shigemi *m*

菰 1727 (KO, komo, makomo)
田 Komoda *s,* Makomoda
野 Komono *s*

韮 1728 (KYŪ, nira, hisa)
山 Nirayama *p*
沢 Nirasawa *s*
青集 Kyūseishū *l*
塚 Niratsuka *s*
崎 Nirasaki *p*

菟 1729 (TO, u)
田主水部 Udamohitoribe *s*
田野 Udano *p* ⌈*fh*
名日処女 Unai Otome
玖波集 Tsukubashū *l*
狭 Usa *s*
野 Uno *s,* Unu
道 Uji *s*

萱 1730 Kaya *f.* (KEN, KAN, kaya, tada, masa)
生 Kayō *s*
沼 Kayanuma *s*
草 Wasuregusa *l*
草に寄す W. ni yosu *l*
野 Kayano *s*, Sugano
島 Kayashima *s*
場 Kayaba *s*
森 Kayamori *s*
間 Kayama *s*

董 1731 Tadashi *m*, Tadasu, Shigeru, Makoto. (TŌ, tada, shige, nao, masa, yoshi, nobu)
一郎 Tōichirō *m*
子 Shigeko *f*
枝 Tadae *f*
重 Masashige *m*
躬 Tadami *m*

萩 1732 Hagi *sf-p.* (SHŪ, SHU, hagi)
大名 Hagi daimyō *la*
元 Hagimoto *s*
井 Hagii *s*
生田 Hagyūda *s*
本 Hagimoto *s*
田 Hagita *s*
谷 Hagiya *s*
原 Hagiwara *sp*
原恭次郎 H. Kyōjirō *ml*
原朔太郎 H. Sakutarō *ml*
原蘿月 H. Ragetsu *ml*
野 Hagino *sf* *ml*
野由之 H. Yoshiyuki
島 Hagishima *s*
森 Hagimori *s*
雄 Hagio *s*

落 1733 [T] (RAKU, ochi)
合 Ochiai *sp* *ml*
合直文 O. Naobumi
実 Ochimi *m*
城 Rakujō *l*
首 Rakushu *l*
話 Otoshibanashi *l*
葉 Ochiba *l*
窪 Ochikubo *l*

—12 T4—

黃 1734 See 黄 1499

森 1735 [T] Mori *sp*; Shigeru *m.* (SHIN, mori)
¹一 Moriichi *m*
³川 Morikawa *s*
川許六 M. Kyoroku *ml*
口 Moriguchi *s*
久保 Morikubo *s*
下 Morishita *s*, Morimoto
下雨村 Morishita Uson *ml*
⁴元 Morimoto *s*
戸 Morito *s*
戸辰男 M. Tatsuo *mh*
木 Moriki *s*
井 Morii *s*
太郎 Moritarō *m*
山 Moriyama *sp*
山汀川 M. Teisen *ml*
山啓 M. Kei *ml*
内 Moriuchi *s*
⁵永 Morinaga *s*
田 Morita *sp*
田草平 M. Sōhei *ml*
田思軒 M. Shiken *ml*
田義郎 M. Girō *ml*
本 Morimoto *s*
本治吉 M. Jikichi *ml*
本厚吉 M. Kōkichi *ml*
本薫 M. Kaoru *ml*
⁶江 Morie *s*
竹 Moritake *s*
吉 Moriyoshi *p*
有礼 Mori Arinori *mh*
有正 M. Arimasa *ml*
⁷住 Morizumi *s*
沢 Morisawa *s*
村 Morimura *s*
谷 Moriya *s*, Moritani
志げ Mori Shige *ml*
男 Morio *m*
尾 Morio *s*
⁸沼 Morinuma *s*
於菟 Mori Oto *ml*
林 Moribayashi *s*
茉莉 Mori Mari *fl*
実 Morizane *s*
居 Morii *s*
⁹信 Morinobu *s*
津 Morizu *s*
垣 Morigaki *s*
松 Morimatsu *s*
岡 Morioka *s*
重 Morishige *sm*
¹⁰脇 Moriwaki *s*
脇一夫 M. Kazuo *ml*
原 Morihara *s*
屋 Moriya *s*
泉 Moriizumi *s*
¹¹野 Morino *s*
部 Moribe *s*
島 Morishima *s*
¹²崎 Morisaki *s*
¹³園 Morizono *s*
園天涙 M. Tenrui *ml*
¹⁴鼻 Moribana *s*
¹⁵槐南 Mori Kainan *ml*
蔵 Morizō *m*
¹⁶橋 Morihashi *s*
¹⁹瀬 Morise *s*
²¹羅 Shinra *s*
羅万象 S. Banshō *ml*
²³鷗外 Mori Ōgai *ml*

崟 1736 Takashi *sm.* (GIN, GON, taka)

崖 1737 Kishi *s.* (GAI)

崔 1738 Sai *s.* (SAI, ZE, chika, taka)
之 Chikayuki *m*

暑 1738A [T] (SHO, atsu, natsu)

晨 1739 (SHIN, JIN, toki, aki, toyo)
子 Akiko *f*
江 Tokie *f*

晶 1740 [T] Akira *m.* (SHŌ, aki, masa, teru)
子 Akiko *f*
江 Akie *f*
穫 Masae *f*

量 1741 [T] Hakaru *m*, Hakari. (RYŌ, kazu, sato, tomi)
子 Kazuko *f*
行 Kazuyuki *m*
原 Kazumoto *m*
輔 Kazusuke *m*
慰 Kazuyasu *m*

最 1742 Masaru *m*, Yutaka, Takashi, Kaname. (SAI, mo, yoshi, iro)
一 Yoshikazu *m*
一郎 Saiichirō *m*
上 Mogami *sp* *mh*
上徳内 M. Tokunai
中 Monaka *m*
吉 Saikichi *m*
所 Saisho *s*
信 Yoshinobu *m*
首 Saishu *s*
原 Mobara *s*
誉子 Moyoko *f*
澄 Saichō *ml*

—12 T5—

童 1743 [T] (DŌ, waka, warawa)
馬漫語 Dōba mango *l*
絵解万国噺 Osanaetoki bankoku-banashi *l*

登 1744 [T] Noboru *sm*, Nobori; Minoru *m.* (TŌ, TO, taka, nari, chika, tomo, mi, naru, tomi, nori)
³川 Kawanobori *s*
三郎 Tōsaburō *m*
之 Chikayuki *m*
子 Takako *f*, Nariko, Tomiko
⁴山 Toyama *s*
内 Touchi *s*
⁵代太郎 Toyotarō *m*
石 Toishi *s*
⁶吉 Nariyoshi *m*
米 Tome *sp*, Toyoma
⁷坂 Tosaka *s*, Noborizaka
別 Noboribetsu *p*
志 Toshi *f*
⁹治 Takaharu *m*
美 Noriyoshi *m*
¹⁰倉 Tokura *s*
¹¹盛 Tōmori *m*
康 Naruyasu *m*
¹³張 Tobari *s*
張竹風 T. Chikufū *ml*
¹⁴徳 Tomonori *m*
¹⁹藻野 Tomono *f*
²¹鶴 Tozu *f*

窈 1745 Fukashi *m.* (YŌ)

窓 1746 [T] Mado *m.* (SŌ, mado)

崔暑晨晶量最童登窈窓▼棠掌袈袋営覚買貫貴賀棗畫單巽象衆粟景答筏策第筆等▲筑笹番崇畨勞望琴集桼

棠 1747 (TŌ, DŌ)
陰比事 Tōin hiji *l*

掌 1748 [T] (SHŌ, naka)
編小説 Shōhen shōsetsu *l*

袈 1749 (KA, KE, kesa)
江 Kesae *f*
裟 Kesa *f*

袋 1750 [T] (TAI, DAI)
井 Fukuroi *p*
布 Tafu *s*
草紙 Fukuro sōshi *l*

営 1751 [T] (EI, YŌ, yoshi)
成 Yoshinari *m*
邦 Yoshikuni *m*
篤 Yoshiatsu *m*

覚 1752 [T] Satoru *m*, Satoshi, Tadashi, Akira. (KAKU, sato, tada, yoshi, aki, akira, sada)
三 Kakuzō *m*
王院 Kakuōin *s*
本 Kakumoto *s*
太郎 Kakutarō *m*
次郎 Kakujirō *m*
行 Satoki *m*
弘 Satohiro *m*
長 Yoshinaga *m*
張 Kakubari *s*
猷 Kakuyū *ma*

買 1753 [T] Mei *s*. (BAI)

貫 1754 [T] Tōru *m*, Tsura; Nuki *s*. (KAN, tsura, nuki)
一 Kan'ichi *m*
之 Tsurayuki *ml*
井 Nukii *s*, Nukui
太郎 Kantarō *m*
名 Nukina *s*
城 Kanjō *m*
洞 Kandō *s*
長 Tsuranaga *m*

貴 1755 [T] Takashi *m*. (KI, yoshi, taka, atsu, ate, take, muchi)
子 Takako *f*, Ateko
太郎 Kitarō *m*
布禰 Kifune *s*
司 Kishi *s*
司山治 K. Yamaji *ml*
田 Kita *s*
志 Kishi *s*
志子 Kishiko *f*
志川 Kishigawa *p*
臣 Takaomi *m*
孝 Yoshinori *m*
命 Takayoshi *m*
恒 Takatsune *m*
泉 Itsuki *s*
島 Kishima *s*
道 Yoshimichi *m*
暢 Takamitsu *m*

賀 1756 [T] Iwō *m*. (KA, GA, yoshi, nori, shige, masu)
[8]川 Kagawa *s*
川豊彦 K. Toyohiko *mlh*
子 Yoshiko *f*, Noriko
[5]永 Kaya *s*
古 Kako *s*
田 Kada *s*
[6]名生 Anō *p*
[7]沢 Kazawa *s*
来 Kaku *s*
[8]茂 Kamo *sp*; Hamochi *s*
茂真淵 K. no Mabuchi *mlh*
良 Kara *s*
良倶 Karoku *m*
[10]訓 Yoshinori *s*
屋 Kaya *s*
[11]浪 Kanuma *s*
島 Kashima *s*
[12]陽 Kaya *sm*; Kayō *p*
陽院水閣歌合 Kayanoin Suikaku utaawase *l*
陽豊年 Kaya no Toyotoshi *ml*
集 Kashū *s*

——12 T6——

棗 1757 (SŌ, natsume)
田 Natsumeda *s*

畫 1758 See 画 991

單 1759 See 単 919A

巽 1760 Tatsumi *m*. (SON, yuki, yoshi)

象 1761 [T] Kisa *f*. (ZŌ, SHŌ, kata, kisa, taka, nori)
引 Zōhiki *la*
雄 Kisao *m*
潟 Kisakata *p*

衆 1762 [T] (SHŪ, SHU, hiro, tomo, moro, mori)
二 Shūji *m*
妙集 Shūmyōshū *l*
樹 Minaki *s*, Morogi

粟 1763 Awa *s*. (ZOKU, SHOKU, awa)
凡 Awanoōshi *s*
山 Awayama *s*, Momiyama
生 Ao *s*, Awafu
生田 Aōda *s*
田 Awata *s*
田口 Awataguchi *sla*
田口吉光 A. Yoshimitsu *ma* ⌈hito *mh*
田真人 Awata no Ma-
米宮 Amenomiya *s*
竹 Awatake *s*
津 Awazu *s*
冠 Sakka *s*
屋 Awaya *s*
野 Awano *sp*
野原 Awanohara *s*
島浦 Awashimaura *p*
賀 Awaga *s* ⌈hara
飯原 Awaihara *s*, Ai-

景 1764 [T] Akira *m*. (KEI, KYŌ, kage, hiro)
[3]子 Hiroko *f*
[4]方 Kagemasa *m*
与 Kagetomo *m*
山 Kageyama *s*
山英子 K. Hideko *fh*
[5]正 Kagemasa *m*
[7]戒 Keikai *ml*
[8]明 Kageaki *m*
季 Kagesue *m*
奉 Kagetomo *m*
事 Keigoto *l*
[9]保 Kageyasu *m*
柄 Kagemoto *m*
祐 Kagesuke *m*
政 Kagemasa *m*
乗 Kagenori *m*
重 Kageshige *m*
[10]時 Kagetoki *m*
晋 Kagekuni *m*
[11]惇 Kageatsu *m*
清 Kagekiyo *m-la*
盛 Kagemori *m*
[12]勝 Kagekatsu *m*
欽 Kageyoshi *m*
[13]紹 Kagetsugu *m*
新 Kagechika *m*
[14]漸 Kagetsugu *m*
[16]樹 Kageki *m*
憲 Kagenori *m*

答 1765 [T] (TŌ, sato, toshi, tomi, tomo, nori) ⌈Tsubo
本 Taho *s*, Tsuho,

筏 1766 (BATSU, ikada)
井 Ikadai *s*
井嘉一 I. Kaichi *ml*

策 1767 [T] (SAKU, SHAKU, kazu, tsuka, mori)
三 Sakuzō *m*
之助 Sakunosuke *m*
太郎 Sakutarō *m*

第 1768 [T] (DAI, TEI, kuni, tsuki)
一作 Daiissaku *l*
六天 Dairokuten *l*
五郎 Daigorō *m*

筆 1769 [T] Funde *s*. (HITSU, fude)
一郎 Fudeichirō *m*
川 Fudekawa *s*
子 Fudeko *f*

等 1770 [T] Hitoshi *m*. (TŌ, tomo, toshi, shina, hitoshi, taka) ⌈ko, Hitoshiko
子 Tomoko *f*, Shina-

枝 Shinae *f*
等力 Todoroki *sp*
等木 Todoroki *s*
綱 Tomotsuna *m*, Toshitsuna

**筑** 1771 (TSUKU, CHIKU)
上 Chikujō *p*
井 Tsukui *s*
山 Tsukuyama *s*, Tsukiyama
邦 Chikuhō *p*
波 Tsukuba *sm-p*
波問答 T. mondō *l*
城 Chikujō *p*
前 Chikuzen *ph*
後 Chikugo *sp*
紫 Tsukushi *sph*; Chikushi *ph*
紫奥 T. no oku *l*
紫道記 T. dōki *l*
紫野 Chikushino *p*
穂 Chikuho *p*
摩 Chikuma *sp*
摩地 Tsukamachi *s*

**笹** 1772 Sasa *f*. (sasa)
[3]子 Sasako *sf*
川 Sasakawa *s*
川臨風 S. Rinpū *ml*
[4]山 Sasayama *s*
井 Sasai *s*
木 Sasaki *s*
[5]田 Sasada *s*
市 Sasaichi *m*
生 Sasō *s*
本 Sasamoto *s*
本寅 S. Tora *ml*
[7]沢 Sasazawa *s*
沢美明 S. Yoshiaki *ml*
沢左保 S. Saho *ml*
村 Sasamura *s*
谷 Sasaya *s*
尾 Sasao *s*
[9]沼 Sasanuma *s*
神 Sasagami *p*
栄 Sasae *f*
岡 Sasaoka *s*
[10]倉 Sasakura *s*
原 Sasawara *s*
屋 Sasaya *s*
[11]野 Sasano *sf*
部 Sasabe *s*
島 Sasashima *s*
[12]崎 Sasazaki *s*
森 Sasamori *s*
間 Sasama *s*
[13]淵 Sasabuchi *s*
淵友一 S. Tomoichi *ml*
[19]瀬 Sasase *s*

## 12 T7

**番** 1773 [T] Ban *s*, Tsugai. (BAN, HAN, tsugi, tsugu, tsura, fusa)
町皿屋敷 Banchō sarayashiki *la*
匠 Banshō *s*
匠谷 Banshōya *s*
匠谷英一 B. Eiichi *ml*
長 Bao *s*
場 Banba *s*
御 Hanmo *s*

**崇** 1774 [T] Takashi *m*. (SŪ, SU, SŌ, taka, kata, shi)
伝 Sūden *mh*
明 Kataakira *m*
神 Sujin *mh*
恵 Takae *f*
徳 Sutoku *mh*; Katanori *m*

**喬** 1775 Takashi *m*. (KYŌ, GYŌ, taka, nobu, tada, suke, moto)
木 Takagi *s*
言 Nobukoto *m*
求 Takamoto *m*
蔚 Takashige *m*
樹 Takaki *m*

## 12 T8

**勞** 1776 See 労 491A

**望** 1777 [T] Nozomu *m*. (BŌ, MŌ, mochi, mi)
月 Mochizuki *sp*
田 Mochida *s*
陀 Mōda *s*
東 Mōtō *m*
城 Mochiki *m*

**琴** 1778 [T] Koto *f*. (KIN, GON, koto)
二 Kotoji *m*
子 Kotoko *f*
田 Kotoda *s*
平 Kotohira *p*
丘 Kotooka *p*
南 Kotonami *p*
海 Kinkai *p*
浜 Kotohama *p*
後集 Kotojirishū *l*
歌譜 Kinkafu *l*

**集** 1779 [T] Tsudoi *m*. (SHŪ, JŪ, ai, chika, i)
田 Sokuta *s*
堂 Sudō *s*

**棐** 1780 Tasuku *m*. (HI, suke)

**斐** 1781 Ayaru *m*, Akira. (HI, aya, i, yoshi, naga)
川 Hikawa *p*
子 Ayako *f*
伊川 Hiigawa *p*
多 Hida *m*
邦 Yoshikuni *m*
後前 Higochika *m*
雄 Ayao *m*

**悲** 1782 [T] (HI)
田院 Hiden'in *p*

**惠** 1783 See 恵 1226

**惑** 1784 [T] (WAKU, KOKU, OKU, madoi)

**惣** 1785 [N] (SŌ, SU, fusa). See also 総 2662
一 Sōichi *m*
八 Sōhachi *l*
三郎 Sōsaburō *m*
之助 Sōnosuke *m*
太郎 Sōtarō *m*
助 Sōsuke *m*

**黑** 1786 See 黒 1486

**煮** 1787 [T] (SHA, ni)

**然** 1788 [T] (ZEN, NEN, shika, nari, nori)
良 Shikayoshi *m*

**無** 1789 [T] (MU, BU, nashi, na)
[2]二 Muni *m*, Arikazu
[3]三四 Musashi *m*
子 Nashiko *f*
[4]手右衛門 Muteemon *m*
[5]布施経 Fuse nai kyō *la*
市 Muichi *m*
[6]尽 Tsukuna *s*
名抄 Mumyōshō *l*
名草子 Mumyō-zōshi *l*
名秘抄 M.-hishō *l*
[7]住一円 Mujū Ichien *mlh*
花果 Ichijuku *l*
[8]明と愛染 Mumyō to aizen *la*
学祖元 Mugaku Sogen *mh*
[11]理之介 Murinosuke *m*
弦弓 Mugenkyū *l*
[12]着成恭 Muchaku Seikyō *ml*
[14]漏 Muro *s*

**晉** 1790 See 晋 1215

**晳** 1791 (SEKI, SHAKU, aki)
子 Akiko *f*

**普** 1792 [T] Hiroshi *m*, Susumu. (FU, kata, hiro, yuki)
川 Fukawa *s*
子 Hiroko *f*
代 Fudai *p*
春 Kataharu *m*
勧坐禅儀 Fukan zazengi *l*
賢 Fugen *l*

**智** 1793 [N] Satoru *m*, Satoshi, Tomo, Sakashi, Akira. (CHI, nori, tomo, sato, toshi, tomi, moto)
三郎 Tomosaburō *m*
子 Satoko *f*
仁 Tomohito *m*, Toshihito
月 Chigetsu *fl*
夫 Norio *m*
正 Chishō *mh*
津子 Chizuko *f*
泉子 Chiiko *f*
恵子 Chieko *f*

惑 惣 黒 煮 然 無 晉 晳 普 智 ▼ 曾 堯 堅 尊 奥 善 兜 厨 雁 属 犀 過 遍 遂 遅 ▲ 運 遊 達 道 逷 逹 奥 甦 趁 超

真 Chishin *mh*
寛 Tomohiro *m*
義 Tomonori *m*
準 Tomonori *m*
頭 Chizu *sp*
聡 Chisato *m*

**曾** 1794 Sō *s.* (sō, zō, so, katsu, tsune, nari, masu)
[3]川 Sogawa *s*
[4]方布 Sohō *s*
山 Soyama *s*
木 Soki *s*
丹 Sotan *ml*
丹後 Sotango *ml*
丹集 Sotanshū *l*
[5]布川 Sofukawa *s*
田 Soda *s*
[7]谷 Sodani *s*, Sogae
呂利 Sorori *s*
我 Soga *sl* ⌈*la*
我会稽山 S. Kaikeizan
我廼家 Soganoya *s*
我部 Sogabe *s*
[8]和 Sowa *s*
歩曾歩 Sofusofu *s*
良 Sora *ml*; Katsura *s*
[9]政 Katsumasa *m*
[10]宮 Somiya *s*
益 Tsunenori *m*
原 Sohara *s*
[11]根 Sone *s*
根田 Soneda *s*
根原 Sonehara *s*
根崎 Sonezaki *sp*
根崎心中 S. shinjū *la*
野 Sono *s*
野綾子 S. Ayako *fl*
[14]雌 Soshi *s*
爾 Soni *p*
[19]禰 Sone *s*
禰好忠 S. no Yoshitada *ml*

## 12 T9

**堯** 1795 Takashi *m.* (GYŌ, taka, nori, aki)
一 Akikazu *m*
文 Takafumi *m*
孝 Gyōkō *ml*
信 Takanobu *m*
治 Noriharu *m*
爾 Takaji *m*

**堅** 1796 [T] Katashi *m*, Tsuyoshi. (KEN, kata, kaki, taka, yoshi, mi)
太郎 Kentarō *m*
田 Katada *sp*
守 Yoshimori *m*
高 Katataka *m*
造 Kenzō *m*
魚 Katsuo *m*
磐 Kakiwa *m-f*
蔵 Kenzō *m*

**尊** 1797 Takashi *m.* (SON, taka)
子 Takako *f*
円 Son'en *mh*
礼 Takahiro *m*
氏 Takauji *m*
成 Takahira *m*
祀 Takatoshi *m*
孫 Takahiko *m*
関 Takayasu *m*
澄 Takazumi *m*
輝 Takateru *m*

**奥** 1798 [T] Oku *s.* (ō, oku, oki, fuka, sumi, uchi, mura)
の細道 Oku no hosomichi *l*
[3]川 Okugawa *s*
子 Okuko *f*
[4]戸 Okuto *s*, Okudo
中 Okunaka *s*
山 Okuyama *s*
井 Okui *s*
[5]代 Okudai *s*
尻 Okushiri *p*
平 Okudaira *s*
田 Okuda *s*
本 Okumoto *s*
[6]守 Okimori *m*
寺 Okudera *s*
多摩 Oku-tama *p*
[7]住 Okuzumi *s*
沢 Okuzawa *s*
村 Okumura *s*
村五百子 O. Ioko *fh*
谷 Okuya *s*
志 Fukashi *m*
兵衛 Okubee *m*
実 Sumizane *m*
[8]明方 Okumyōgata *p*
居 Okui *s*
[9]津 Okutsu *p*
秋 Okuaki *s*
泉 Okuizumi *s*
[10]脇 Okuwaki *s*
倉 Okugura *s*
宮 Okumiya *s*
原 Okuhara *s*
[11]野 Okuno *s* ⌈*ml*
野信太郎 O. Shintarō
野健男 O. Takeo *ml*
島 Okushima *s*
[12]崎 Okusaki *s*
富 Okutomi *s*, Okuto
貫 Okunuki *s*
道 Okumichi *m*
[13]隈 Okuzumi *s*
義抄 Ōgishō *l*
[18]藤 Okufuji *s*
麿 Okimaro *m*
[19]瀬 Okuse *s*

**善** 1799 [T] Yoshi *m*, Tadashi; Zen *s.* (ZEN, yoshi, taru, sa)
[1]一 Zen'ichi *m*, Yoshikazu
一郎 Zen'ichirō *m*
[2]七 Zenshichi *m*
十郎 Zenjūrō *m*
[3]三郎 Zenzaburō *m*
之 Yoshiyuki *m*
子 Yoshiko *f*
[4]仁 Taruhito *m*
方 Yoshikata *m*
太郎 Zentarō *m*
[5]四郎 Zenshirō *m*
[6]次郎 Zenjirō *m*
[7]作 Zensaku *m*
助 Zensuke *m*
兵衛 Zenbee *m*
[8]知 Utō *s*
知鳥 Utō *sla*
知鳥安方忠義伝 U. Yasukata chūgiden *l*
国 Yoshikuni *m*
[9]法寺 Zenbōji *s*
治郎 Zenjirō *m*
郎 Yoshirō *m*
界 Zegai *la*
直 Yoshinao *m*
重郎 Zenjūrō *m*
[10]通寺 Zentsūji *p*
[11]剛 Yoshikata *m*
[12]富 Yoshitomi *s*
堯 Yoshitaka *m*
道 Yoshimichi *sm*
[13]雄 Yoshio *m*
淵 Yoshibuchi *s*
[15]澄 Yoshizumi *sm*
導寺 Zendōji *p*
[16]隣 Yoshichika *m*
衛 Yoshie *m*
滋 Yoshishige *sm*
積 Yoshizumi *s*
[21]縄 Yoshitada *m*

## 12 T10

**兜** 1800 Kabuto *s.* (kabuto)
木 Kabutogi *s*
町 Kabutochō *p*
碁盤忠信 Hoshikabuto Goban Tadanobu *la*

## 12 F2

**厨** 1800A See 廚 2417

**雁** 1801 Taka *s.* (GAN, GEN, kari)
の寺 Gan no tera *l*
厂金 Gankarigane *la*
宇丸 Karyūmaru *m*
金 Karigane *m*
部 Karibe *s*
礫 Gan tsubute *l*

## 12 F3

**属** 1802 [T] Saka *s*, Sakka, Sakan. (ZOKU, tsura, masa, yasu)

**犀** 1803 (SAI, SEI, kata)
川 Saigawa *p*
星 Saisei *ml*
蔵 Saizō *m*

**過** 1804 [T] (KA)
去現在因果経 Kako genzai ingakyō *la*

**遍** 1805 [T] (HEN)
昭 Henjō *ml*
遍古 Bebeko *s*

**遂** 1806 [T] Togeru *m.* (SUI, katsu, naru, tsuku)
良 Katsuyoshi *m*
長 Katsunaga *m*

**遅** 1807 [T] (CHI, matsu)
栄 Matsue *m*

塚 Chizuka *s*
塚麗水 C. Reisui *ml*

運 1808 [T] Hakobu *m*. (UN, kazu, yuki, yasu)
子 Kazuko *f*
夫 Kazuo *m*
美 Kazumi *m*
雄 Kazuo *m*

遊 1809 [T] (YŪ, YU, yuki, naga)
子方言 Yūshi hōgen *l*
行上人 Yugyō Shōnin *ml*
行柳 Y. yanagi *la*
佐 Yusa *sp*
馬 Asuma *s*, Yūma

達 1810 [T] Itaru *m*, Tōru, Susumu, Satoru, Satoshi. (TATSU, michi, sato, yoshi, tō, shige, tada, tate, nobu, hiro, katsu)
²二 Tatsuji *m*
人 Tatsundo *m*
³三 Tatsuzō *m*
之助 Tatsunosuke *m*
之輔 Tatsunosuke *m*
⁴夫 Tatsuo *m*
⁶次郎 Tatsujirō *m*
吉 Tatsukichi *m*
⁷栄 Michie *f*
安 Michiyasu *m*, Satoyasu
夸 Tatsuya *m*
谷 Takeya *s*
谷窟 Takeya *s*, Tagaya
⁹治 Tatsuji *m*
¹⁰海 Tatsumi *m*
¹¹朗 Tōru *m*
¹²等 Tatto *m*, Tachito
道 Satomichi *m*
¹⁵賛 Tatsuji *m*
摩 Daruma *mh*

道 1811 [T] Osamu *m*, Michi, Osame, Wataru, Naoshi. (DŌ, michi, tsune, nori, yuki, yori, ji, chi, masa, tsuna, ne)
¹一 Michikazu *m*
²二 Dōni *mh*
力 Michiyoshi *m*
³川 Michikawa *s*
上 Michigami *s*
下 Michishita *s*
三 Michinao *m*
子 Michiko *f*
大 Michiō *m*
千代 Tsunachiyo *m*
也 Michinari *m*
⁴元 Dōgen *mlh*
山 Michiyama *s*
中膝栗毛 Dōchū hizakurige *l*
文 Michiaki *m*
夫 Michio *m*, Tsuneo
太郎 Michitarō *m*
⁵旧 Michifuru *m*
田 Ōchita *s*
生 Michitaka *m*
⁶行 Michiyuki *m-l*
守 Chimori *s*
芝 Michishiba *l*
吉 Michisachi *m*
有 Michiari *m*
因 Michiyoshi *m*
存 Michimasa *m*
成 Michinari *m*, Michishige
成寺 Dōjōji *p-la*
⁷別 Chiwaki *m*
助 Michisuke *m*
志 Dōshi *p*
芳 Michika *m*
⁸阿弥 Dōami *ml*
和留 Michiwaru *m*
明 Michiaki *sm*; Dōmyō *s*
明寺 Dōmyōji *p-la*
実 Michizane *m*
⁹昭 Dōshō *mh*
祖 Saido *s*, Funato
祖土 Saido *sp*
祖木 Sainoki *s*
祖尾 Sainoo *s*
長 Michinaga *m*
春 Dōshun *mlh*
香 Michika *m*
風 Michikaze *s*
¹⁰倫 Michitomo *m*
師 Michinoshi *s*
家 Dōke *s*
真 Michizane *m*
原 Dōgen *s*
通 Michitō *m*
¹¹隆 Michitaka *m*
理山 Ubeyama *s*
紀 Michitoshi *m*
¹²揚 Michiaki *m*
富 Michitomi *sm*
智 Dōchi *s*
善 Michitaru *m*
運 Michikazu *m*
¹³暁 Michitoshi *m*
雄 Michio *m*
雲 Michimo *m*
遠 Michitō *m*
¹⁴頓堀 Dōtonbori *p*
輔 Michisuke *m*
¹⁶幾 Michioki *m*
¹⁷綱 Michitsuna *m*
綱母 M. no Haha *fl*
¹⁹瀬 Dōnose *s*
鏡 Dōkyō *mh*
²⁰機 Michinori *m*

## 12 F4

毱 1812 (KIKU, GOKU, mari)
子 Mariko *f*

逵 1813 Tōru *m*. (KI, GI, katsu, michi, tsuji)
邑 Tsujimura *s*

## 12 F6

奥 See 1798

## 12 F7

甦 1814 (so)
生平 Sobuhei *m*

趁 1815 Shitagō *m*. (CHIN)

超 1816 [T] Koeru *m*, Koyuru, Tōru. (CHŌ, yuki, ki, tatsu, oki)
子 Yukiko *f*

## 12 F8

爲 1817 See 為 1005

筒 1818 [T] (TŌ, tsutsu)
井 Tsutsui *s*
居 Tsutsui *s*
賀 Tsuga *p*

閏 1819 (JUN, SHUN, uru)
三郎 Junzaburō *m*
子 Uruko *f*
江 Urue *f*

閑 1820 [T] (KAN, GEN, shizu, yasu, mori, nori, yori)
子 Shizuko *f*
吟集 Kanginshū *l*
居友 Kankyo no tomo *l*
院 Kan'in *s*
情末摘花 Kanjō suetsumuhana *l*
衛 Morie *m*; Shizue *f*

開 1821 [T] Hiraku *m*, Hiraki. (KAI, haru, hira, saku, haruki, hiraki)
目鈔 Kaimokushō *l*
田 Kaida *sp*; Kaiden *s*
成 Kaisei *p*
城 Haruki *m*
発 Kaihotsu *s*
高 Kaikō *s*
高健 K. Takeshi *ml*
帳利益札遊合 Kaichō riyaku fuda asobiawase *l*
聞 Kaimon *p*

間 1822 [T] Kan *s*, Hazama. (KAN, KEN, ma, chika, hashi)
²人 Hashūdo *s*, Hashiride, Manabe, Marehito, Maui
³下 Mashita *s*
⁴中 Manaka *s*
山 Mayama *s*
⁶世田 Maseda *s*
仲 Manaka *s*
守 Mamori *m*
⁸所 Madokoro *s*
⁹柄 Makara *s*
¹⁰宮 Mamiya *s*
宮林蔵 M. Rinzō *mh*
宮茂輔 M. Mosuke *ml*
庭 Maniwa *s*
¹¹野 Mano *s*, Aino
部 Manabe *s*, Mabe
部詮房 Manabe Akifusa *mh*
島 Majima *s*
島冬道 M. Fuyumichi *ml*
島琴山 M. Kinzan *ml*
¹²崎 Masaki *s*
¹³淵 Mabuchi *s*

奥 甦 趁 超 爲 筒 閏 閑 開 間 ▼ 鹿 鳰 鳩 傳 傑 傀 僧 傾 徑 喰 幌 猾 獅 摸 摂 愹 慎 階 隈 塘 堪 塚 塙 塩 ▲ 堀 滉 湾 滂 溢 溥 漠 漫 湛 渥

[17]鍋 Manabe *s*
[19]瀬 Mase *s*, Manase

### —12 U—

**鹿** 1823 [N] (ROKU, shika, ka, shishi)
の子餅 Kanokomochi *l*
の巻筆 Shika no makifude *l*
[2]人 Shikahito *m*
又 Shikamata *s*, Kanomata
[3]之助 Shikanosuke *m*
子木 Kanokogi *s*, Kakogi
子木孟郎 Kanokogi Takeshirō *ma*
[4]火屋 Kabiya *l*
文 Kaya *m*
山 Kayama *s*
内 Shikauchi *s*
毛 Kage *s*
[5]北 Kahoku *p*
央 Kaō *p*
田 Shikada *s*, Kada
目 Kanome *s*
本 Kamoto *p*
生 Shishifu *s*
[6]次郎 Shikajirō *m*
伏兎 Kabuto *s*, Kanbe, Ninbe
地 Kaji *s*
地亘 K. Wataru *ml*
吉 Shikakichi *m*
西 Rokusei *p*
[7]住 Kazumi *s*
村 Shikamura *s*
町 Shikamachi *p*
志村 Kashimura *s*
足 Shikatari *m*; Kanoashi *p*
児島 Kagoshima *sp*
児島寿蔵 K. Juzō *ml*
角 Kazuno *p*
[8]沼 Kanuma *sp*
股 Shikamata *s*
取 Katori *sm*
[9]持 Kamochi *s*
持雅澄 K. Masazumi *ml*
苑寺 Rokuonji *p*
背 Kase *s*
追 Shikaoi *p*
[10]浜 Shikahama *s*
討 Shishiuchi *s*
倉 Shikakura *s*
屋 Kanoya *p*
[11]部 Shikabe *p*
野 Shikano *sp*, Kano; Mino *s*
野武左衛門 S. Buzaemon *mla*
島 Kashima *sp*
島田 Kashimada *s*
島台 Kashimadai *p*
島紀行 Kashima kikō *l*
[12]間 Shikama *s*
[13]園 Shikazono *s*
[14]鳴集 Rokumeishū *l*
鳴館 Rokumeikan *phla*
窪 Shikakubo *s*
[19]瀬 Kanose *p*

### —13 L2—

**鳰** 1824 Nio *s.* (nio)
子 Nioko *f*

**鳩** 1825 (KYŪ, KU, hato, yasu)
ケ谷 Hatogaya *sp*; Hatogai *s*
子 Hatoko *f*
山 Hatoyama *sp*
山一郎 H. Ichirō *mh*
居 Hatoi *s*
彦 Yasuhiko *m*

**傳** 1826 See 伝 359

**傑** 1827 [T] Takeshi *m*, Masaru, Takashi. (KETSU)

**傀** 1828 (KAI)
儡子記 Kugutsu-mawashi no ki / Kairaishiki *l*

**僧** 1829 [T] (SŌ)
旻 Sōmin *mh*

**傾** 1830 [T] (KEI, KYŌ, katabu)
子 Katabuko *mh*
城反魂香 Keisei hangonkō *la*
城壬生大念仏 K. Mibu dainenbutsu *la*
城色三味線 K. irojamisen *l*
城阿波の鳴門 K. Awa no Naruto *la*
城無間鐘 K. muken no kane *la*

### —13 L3—

**徑** 1831 See 径 576

**喰** 1832 (hō, kui)
丸 Kuimaru *p*
代 Hōjiro *sp*

**幌** 1833 Akira *m.* (KŌ, horo)
加内 Horokanai *p*
延 Horonobe *p*
泉 Horoizumi *p*

**猾** 1834 (KATSU, KACHI, ukeshi)

**獅** 1835 (SHI)
子 Shishi *s*
子文六 S. Bunroku *ml*

**摸** 1836 (BAKU, MAKU, nori)

**摂** 1837 [T] Osamu *m.* (SETSU, SHŌ, kane, kanu)
津 Settsu *sph*
待 Settai *la*

**愹** 1838 Isamu *m.* (YŌ)

**慎** 1839 [T] Makoto *m.* (SHIN, JIN, chika, nori, yoshi, mitsu)
三 Shinzō *m*
之 Chikayuki *m*
之助 Shinnosuke *m*
太郎 Shintarō *m*
吉 Shinkichi *m*
英 Norihide *m*
治 Shinji *m*
科 Mashina *s*

**階** 1840 [T] (KAI, yori, hashi, tomo)
上 Hashikami *p*
土 Shinato *s*
戸 Shinato *s*, Shinando
見 Shinami *s*
藤 Kaitō *s*

**隈** 1841 Kuma *s.* (WAI, E, kuma)
川 Kumagawa *s*
子 Kumako *f*
元 Kumamoto *s*
本 Kumamoto *s*
部 Kumabe *s*
笹 Kumazasa *l*
鷹 Kumataka *s*

**塘** 1842 Tsutsumi *m.* (TŌ)

**堪** 1843 Tatae *s.* (KAN, TAN, tae)
子 Taeko *f*

**塚** 1844 (CHŌ, tsuka)
口 Tsukaguchi *s*
田 Tsukada *s*
本 Tsukamoto *s*
平 Tsukahira *s*
谷 Tsukatani *s*
脇 Tsukawaki *s*
原 Tsukahara *s*
原渋柿園 T. Jūshien *ml*
野 Tsukano *s*
崎 Tsukazaki *s*
越 Tsukagoe *s*
瀬 Tsukase *s*

**塙** 1845 Hanawa *sf-p*; Ban *s*, Han. (KŌ, KYŌ, hana)
田 Hanawada *s*
団右衛門 Ban / Hanawa Dan'emon *mh-l*
坂 Hanesaka *s*
保己一 Hanawa Hokinoichi *ml*

**塩** 1846 [T] Shio *m.* (EN, shio)
[2]入 Shioiri *s*, Shionoiri
[3]川 Shiokawa *sp*
[4]山 Shioyama *s*; Enzan *p*
井 Shioi *s*
井雨江 S. Ukō *ml*
月 Shiozuki *s*
[5]尻 Shiojiri *sp*
尻公明 S. Kōmei *m l*
田 Shioda *sp*
田良平 S. Ryōhei *ml*
[6]江 Shionoe *p*

[7]沢 Shiozawa *sp*
谷 Shioya *sp*; Shionoya *s*, En'ya, Shōya
谷鵜平 E. Uhei *ml*
見 Shiomi *s*
[8]冶 En'ya *s*
[9]津 Shiotsu *s*
[10]浜 Shiohama *s*
浦 Shioura *s*
脇 Shiowaki *s*
釜 Shiogama *p*
屋 Shioya *s*
原 Shiobara *sp*
[11]野 Shiono *s*
野入 Shionoiri *s*
野谷 Shionoya *s*
野義 Shionogi *s*
麻呂 Shiomaro *m*
島 Shiojima *s*
[12]崎 Shiozaki *s*
焼 Shioyaki *m*
[13]塚 Shiozuka *s*
路 Shioji *s*
[14]飽 Shiowaku *s*, Shiwato, Shia
[18]藤 Shiofuji *s*
[19]瀬 Shioze *s*

堀 1847 [I] Hori *s*. (KUTSU, hori)
ノ内 Horinouchi *s*
[3]川 Horikawa *s*
之内 Horinouchi *p*
口 Horiguchi *s*
口大学 H. Daigaku *ml*
[4]戸 Kutto *s*
中 Horinaka *s*
山 Horiyama *s*
井 Horii *s*
切 Horikiri *s*
内 Horiuchi *s*, Horinouchi
内通孝 Horiuchi Michitaka *ml*
木 Horiki *s*
木克三 H. Katsuzō *ml*
[5]北 Horikita *s*
永 Horinaga *s*
込 Horigome *s*
本 Horimoto *s*
田 Hotta *s*
田正俊 H. Masatoshi *mh*
田正睦 H. Masayoshi *mh*
田善衛 H. Yoshie *ml*
[6]江 Horie *sf*
池 Horiike *s*
西 Horinishi *s*
米 Horigome *s*, Horigome
[7]沢 Horizawa *s*
村 Horimura *s*
谷 Horiya *s*, Horinoya
尾 Horio *s*
[8]河 Horikawa *smh*
河院百首 H.-in hyakushu *l*
河院艶書合 H.-in kesōbumi awase *l*
金 Horikane *p*
[9]津 Horizu *s*
辰雄 Hori Tatsuo *ml*
岡 Horioka *s*
[10]家 Horiya *s*
屋 Horiya *s*
[11]野 Horino *s*
部 Horibe *s*
留 Horidome *s*
[12]場 Horiba *s*
[13]越 Horikoshi *s*
[18]藤 Horifuji *s*
[23]籠 Horikome *s*

滉 1848 Hiroshi *m*. (KŌ, hiro)

湾 1849 [T] Mizukuma *m*. (WAN)

滂 1850 Hiroshi *m*. (HŌ, awa)

溢 1851 (ITSU, ICHI, mitsu)

溥 1852 Hiroshi *m*. (HAKU, hiro)

漠 1853 [I] (BAKU, MAKU, hiro, tō)
男 Hiroo *m*

溭 1854 (SHOKU, JIKI, nami)
子 Namiko *f*

湛 1855 Tatae *m*. Tatō; Mizuki *s*. (TAN, DAN, kiyo, yasu)
子 Kiyoko *f*
慶 Tankei *ma*

渥 1856 Atsushi *m*. (AKU, atsu, hiku)
子 Atsuko *f*
見 Atsumi *s*
美 Atsumi *s*
美清太郎 A. Seitarō *ml*

滑 1857 [T] (KOTSU, KATSU, name, nameri)
川 Namekawa *sp*, Namerikawa
川道夫 Namekawa Michio *ml*
良 Satara *s*
稽本 Kokkeibon *l*
稽和合人 Kokkei wagōjin *l*

淵 1858 Fuchi *s*; Fukashi *m*. (EN, fuchi, hiro, nobu, suke, sue, nami, fuka)
川 Fuchigawa *s*
上 Fuchigami *s*
辺 Fuchibe *s*
本 Fuchimoto *s*
名 Fuchina *sm*
沢 Fuchizawa *s*
岡 Fuchioka *s*
野 Fuchino *s*
崎 Fuchizaki *s*

溝 1859 [I] (KŌ, KU, mizo)
川 Mizogawa *s*
上 Mizogami *s*
口 Mizoguchi *s*
口白羊 M. Hakuyō *ml*
井 Mizoi *s*
辺 Mizobe *p*
田 Mizota *s*
江 Mizoe *s*
呂木 Mizorogi *s*
杭 Mizogui *s*
畑 Mizohata *s*
部 Mizobe *s*
落 Mizoochi *s*
淵 Mizobuchi *s*
端 Mizohata *s*

漢 1860 [T] Aya *s*. (KAN, aya, kami, kuni, nara)
人 Ayando *s*
才伎 Ayanotebito *s*
主 Ayanushi *s*
字三音考 Kanji san'onkō *l*
城 Ayaki *s*
長 Ayanonaga *s*
書 Ayanofumi *s*; Kanjo *lh* "Han Shu"
部 Ayabe *s*

満 1861 [T] Mitsuru *m*. (MAN, BAN, mitsu, maro, masu, michi, ari)
[3]之進 Mitsunoshin *m*
子 Mitsuko *f*
[4]山 Mitsuyama *s*
王野 Mionoya *s*, Mitsuwano
夫 Mitsuo *m*
木 Maki *s*
太郎 Mantarō *m*
[5]田 Mitsuda *s*
生野 Mionoya *s*, Miinoya
[6]仲 Manjū *la*
[7]快 Mitsuyoshi *m*
谷 Mitsutani *s*
[8]和 Mitsuyoshi *m*
[9]岡 Mitsuoka *s*
[11]留 Mitsutome *s*
[12]納 Mitsunō *s*
喜 Maki *s*
董 Mitsuyoshi *m*
[15]範 Mitsunori *m*
[17]濃 Mannō *p*

滝 1862 [T] Taki *s*; Takeshi *m*. (RYŪ, RYŌ, RŌ, taki, yoshi)
ケ崎 Takigasaki *s*
[3]川 Takigawa *sp*
川幸辰 T. Yukitoki *ml*
三 Takizō *m*
上 Takigami *s*; Takinoue *p*
子 Takiko *f*
口 Takiguchi *s*
口入道 T. Nyūdō *l*
口武士 T. Takeshi *ml*
口修造 T. Shūzō *ml*
下 Takishita *s*
[4]山 Takiyama *s*
中 Takinaka *s*
太郎 Takitarō *m*
井 Takii *s*
井孝作 T. Kōsaku *ml*
内 Takiuchi *s*
[5]平 Takihira *s*
本 Takimoto *s*
田 Takita *s*
田樗陰 T. Choin *ml*
[7]沢 Takizawa *sp*
沢馬琴 T. Bakin *ml*

摂 愹 慎 階 隈 塘 堪 塚 塙 塩 ▼ 堀 滉 湾 滂 溢 溥 漠 溭 湛 渥 滑 淵 溝 漢 満 滝 ▲ 源 嵾 卿 頎 殖 媛 媋 腮 腹 瑍

漠 漫 湛 渥 滑 淵 溝 漢 満 滝 ▼ 源 嵃 卿 頎 殖 媛 媋 腮 腹 瑍 瑗 項 煜 煇 煥 煌 強 張 弾 暄 暖 暗 暉 禍 禅 ▲ 禎 福 楙 楸 椰 楓 椴 楪 椿 極

村 Takimura *s*
谷 Takiya *s*, Takidani
[8]波 Takinami *s*
[9]亭 Ryūtei *s*
亭鯉丈 R. Rijō *ml*
春一 Taki Haruichi *ml*
[10]浦 Takiura *s*
脇 Takiwaki *s*
原 Takihara *s*, Takiwara
[11]浪 Takinami *s*
根 Takine *p*
野 Takino *sp*
野川 Takinogawa *s*
島 Takishima *s*
[12]崎 Takizaki *s*
崎安之助 T. Yasunosuke *ml* ⌈ma
[13]廉太郎 Taki Rentarō
[18]藤 Takitō *s*
[19]瀬 Takise *s*

**源** 1863 [T] Minamoto *s*; Hajime *m*. (GEN, moto, yoshi)
をぢ Gen-oji *l*
[1]一 Gen'ichi *m*
一郎 Gen'ichirō *m*
[2]二 Genji *m*
八 Genhachi *m*
九郎 Genkurō *m*
[3]川 Minagawa *s*
三郎 Genzaburō *m*
之助 Gennosuke *m*
子 Motoko *f*
[4]内 Gennai *ml*
太 Genta *m*
太夫 Gendayū *la*
太郎 Gentarō *m*
[5]右衛門 Gen'emon *m*
四郎 Genshirō *m*
平盛衰記 Genpei seisuiki *l*
氏 Genji *sl-lm-h*
氏供養 G. kuyō *la*
氏物語 G. monogatari *l*
氏物語玉の小櫛 G. m. tama no ogushi *l*
氏鶏太 G. Keita *ml*
田 Genda *s*
[6]次郎 Genjirō *m*
行 Motoyuki *m*
行家 Minamoto no Yukiie *mh* ⌊ki *ml*
光行 M. no Mitsuyu-
吉 Genkichi *m*
[7]吾 Gengo *m*
助 Gensuke *m* ⌈ki *l*
[8]注余滴 Genchū yoteki
実朝 Minamoto no Sanetomo *mh*
空 Genkū *mlh*
[9]信 Genshin *mlh*
治 Genji *m*
政 Motomasa *m*
為朝 Minamoto no Tametomo *mh*
為義 M. no Tameyoshi *mh* ⌈ml
重之 M. no Shigeyuki
俊頼 M. no Toshiyori *ml* ⌈mh
高明 M. no Takaakira
通親 M. no Michichika *mh*
順 M. no Shitagō *ml*
[12]登 Motonori *m*
間 Motoma *s*
[13]満仲 Minamoto no Mitsunaka *mh*
経信 M. no Tsunenobu *ml*
経基 M. no Tsunemoto *mh* ⌈mh
義仲 M. no Yoshinaka
義家 M. no Yoshiie *mh* ⌈mo *mh*
義朝 M. no Yoshito-
義経 M. no Yoshitsune *mh* ⌈ka *mh*
義親 M. no Yoshichi-
[15]蔵 Genzō *m*
慶 Genkei *m*
[16]頼光 Minamoto no Yorimitsu *mh*
頼信 M. no Yorinobu *mh* ⌈mlh
頼政 M. no Yorimasa
頼家 M. no Yoriie *mh*
頼朝 M. no Yoritomo *mh* ⌈mh
頼義 M. no Yoriyoshi
範頼 M. no Noriyori *mh* ⌈ml
[18]顕兼 M. no Akikane

——13 L4——

**嵃** 1864 Takashi *m*. (GEN)

**卿** 1865 Akira *m*. (KYŌ, KEI, aki, nori)

**頎** 1866 (KI, GE, yoshi)
子 Yoshiko *f*

**殖** 1867 [T] Shigeru *m*. (SHOKU, JIKI, masu, ue, tane, nobu, naka, mochi, e)
子 Masuko *f*
月 Uetsuki *s*
田 Ueda *s*
栗 Ekuri *s*
穂 Nobuo *m*

**媛** 1868 Hime *f*. (EN, ON, hime)

**媋** 1869 (SHUN, haru)
子 Haruko *f*

**腮** 1870 (SAI, nina)
太郎 Ninatarō *m*

**腹** 1871 [T] (FUKU, hara)
目 Harami *s*
赤 Haraka *m*
巻 Haramaki *s*

**瑍** 1872 Akira *m*. (KAN, akira)

**瑗** 1873 (EN, mitsu, ni, tama, teru)

**項** 1874 (KYOKU, KOKU, tama)
子 Tamako *f*

**煜** 1874A Hikaru *m*. (IKU, OKU)

**煇** 1875 Atsushi *m*, Akira. (KI, teru, akira)
栄 Terue *f*

**煥** 1876 (KAN, aki, akira)
光 Akimitsu *m*

**煌** 1877 (KŌ, Ō, aki, teru)
子 Akiko *f*

**強** 1878 [T] Tsuyoshi *m*, Tsutomu. (KYŌ, GŌ, take, tsuyo, atsu, katsu, sune, kowa)
力伝 Gōrikiden *l*
哉 Kyōei *m*

**張** 1879 [T] Chō *sm*. (CHŌ, haru, tomo, hari, tsuyo)
本 Harimoto *s*
次 Harutsugu *m*
良 Chō Ryō *mh-la* "Chang Liang"
替 Harigae *s*
間 Harima *s*
幹 Hariki *m*
赫宙 Chō Kakuchū *ml*

**弾** 1880 [T] Dan *s*. (DAN, TAN, tada)
正 Danjō *mh*
正尹 D.-no-in *mh*
正忠 D.-no-jō *mh*
正疏 D.-no-sakan *mh*
正弼 D.-no-hitsu *mh*
男 Tadao *m*
間 Hazuma *s*

**暄** 1881 (KEN, KAN, nobu, atsu)

**暖** 1882 [T] (DAN, NAN, haru, atsu, yasu)
子 Haruko *f*

**暗** 1883 [T] Kura *s*, Kurai, Harai. (AN)
夜行路 An'ya kōro *l*

**暉** 1884 Akira *m*, Terasu; Teru *m-f*. (KI, teru, aki, akira)
三 Terumi *m*
児 Terunori *m*
昌 Akimasa *m*
峻 Teruoka *s*
衛 Terue *f*

**禍** 1885 [T] (KA, GA, maga)

**禅** 1886 [T] (SEN, ZEN, yoshi)
竹 Zenchiku *mla*

宗 Zenshū *h*
師曾我 Zenji Soga *la*

禎 1887 [N] Sadamu *m*, Tadashi. (TEI, yoshi, sada, tada, tomo, tsugu, sachi)
子 Sachiko *f*
次 Teiji *m*
次郎 Teijirō *m*
利 Yoshitoshi *m*
栄 Yoshie *f*
章 Sadaaki *m*

福 1888 [T] Fuku *s*. (FUKU, tomi, yoshi, sachi, saki, yo, taru, toshi, mura, moto)
の神 F. no kami *la*
[3]川 Fukugawa *s*
三郎 Fukusaburō *m*
巳 Yoshimi *m*
丸 Fukumaru *m*
子 Tomiko *f*, Yoshiko, Sakiko; Fukugo *s*
士 Fukushi *s*
士幸次郎 F. Kōjirō *ml*
[4]元 Fukumoto *s*
水 Fukumizu *s*
中 Fukunaka *s*
山 Fukuyama *sp*
王 Fukuō *s*
王寺 Fukuōji *s*
井 Fukui *sp*
太郎 Fukutarō *m*
与 Fukuyo *s*
[5]永 Fukunaga *s*
永武彦 F. Takehiko *ml*
生 Fussa *p*
本 Fukumoto *s*
本日南 F. Nichinan *mlh*
本和夫 F. Kazuo *ml*
田 Fukuda *sp*
田夕咲 F. Yūsaku *ml*
田正夫 F. Masao *ml*
田行誡 F. Gyōkai *ml*
田英子 F. Hideko *fh*
田恆存 F. Tsuneari *ml*
田栄一 F. Eiichi *ml*
田清人 F. Kiyoto *ml*
田部 Fukudabe *s*
田徳三 Fukuda Tokuzō *mlh*
田蓼汀 F. Ryōtei *ml*
[6]次郎 Fukujirō *m*
羽 Fukuba *s*
江 Fukue *sp*
地 Fukuchi *sp*
地桜痴 F. Ōchi *ml*
地源一郎 F. Gen'ichirō *mh*
光 Fukumitsu *sp*
当 Tonda *s*, Futagi
吉 Fukukichi *m*
朱 Fukusa *s*
西 Fukunishi *s*
[7]住 Fukuzumi *s*
村 Fukumura *s*
沢 Fukuzawa *s*
沢諭吉 F. Yukichi *ml*
谷 Fukuya *s*, Ukigai
男 Tomio *m*
見 Fukumi *s*
角 Fukuzumi *s*
[8]林寺 Fukurinji *s*
知 Fukuchi *s*
知山 Fukuchiyama *p*
[9]依 Fukuyori *s*
松 Fukumatsu *m*
草 Sakigusa *m*; Saigusa *s*
草部 Saigusabe *s*
長 Fukunaga *s*, Tominaga
栄 Fukuei *p*
岡 Fukuoka *sp*
岡孝弟 F. Takachika *mh*
[10]将 Fukumochi *m*, Tomimochi
浦 Fukuura *s*
家 Fukke *s*, Fuke
室 Fukumuro *s*
恵 Fukue *s*
原 Fukuhara *s*
原麟太郎 F. Rintarō *ml*
[11]掛 Fukukake *s*
野 Fukuno *sp*
部 Fukube *p*
翁自伝 Fukuō jiden *l*
留 Fukudome *s*
麻呂 Sakimaro *m*
島 Fukushima *sp*
[12]渡 Fukuwatari *p*
崎 Fukuzaki *sp*
禄壽 Fukurokuju *mh*
富 Fukutomi *sp*
富草子 F.-zōshi *l*
富長者 F. chōja *l*
富菁児 F. Seiji *ml*
喜田 Fukukita *s*
森 Fukumori *s*
智 Fukuchi *s*
間 Fukuma *p*
[13]雄 Fukuo *m*
督 Yoshimasa *m*
[18]麿 Sachimaro *m*
[19]瀬 Fukuse *s*

楙 1889 Shigeru *m*. (BŌ, MU, shige)

楸 1890 Hisagi *m*. (SHŪ, SHU)

椰 1891 (YA, yashi)
子 Yashiko *f*

楓 1892 (FŪ, FU, kaede)
麻呂 Kaedemaro *m*

椴 1893 (TAN, DAN, todo, kui)
木 Todoki *s*
法華 Todohokke *p*

楳 1894 (BŌ, MU, ume)
一 Umeichi *m*
川 Umekawa *s*
田 Umeda *s*

椿 1895 Tsubaki *f-p*. (CHIN, tsubaki, tsuba)
井 Tsubai *s*
本 Tsubakimoto *s*
峠 Tsubakitōge *p*
紅 Tsubani *s*, Tsubae
説弓張月 Chinsetsu yumiharizuki *l*

極 1896 [T] Kiwamu *m*, Kiwame. (KYOKU, GOKU, kiwa, naka, mune)
人 Kiwame *m*
子 Kiwako *f*
月晦 Hinashi *s*, Hizuname
馬 Kiwame *m*
楽六時讃 Gokuraku rokujisan *l*

楯 1897 Tate *s*, Tatenuki. (JUN, SHUN, tate, tachi)
叉 Tatenuki *s*
石 Tateishi *s*
臣 Tateomi *m*
岡 Tateoka *s*
衛 Tateyoshi *m*
縫 Tatenuki *s*

楊 1898 Yanagi *s*. (YŌ, yanagi, yagi, ya, yana, yanai)
井 Yagii *s*, Yanai
公 Yako *s*
枝 Yōji *s*
枳 Yaki *s*
胡 Yako *s*
柳 Yanaizu *s*
梅 Yamamomo *s*
貴 Yagi *s*
貴妃 Yō-kihi *fh-la* "Yang Kuei-fei"
廬原 Uzuhara *s*

楫 1899 (SHŪ, JŪ, kaji)
子 Kajiko *f*
江 Kajie *s*
取 Katori *s*, Kajitori
取魚彦 Katori Nahiko *ml*
野 Kajino *s*
斐 Segai *s*

楢 1900 (YŪ, YU, nara)
川 Narakawa *p*
下 Narage *s*
山節考 Narayama-bushikō *l*
井 Narai *s*
木 Naraki *s*
林 Narabayashi *s*
舎 Naranoya *m*
岡 Naraoka *s*
原 Narahara *s*, Narabara
菊 Naragiku *f*
崎 Narasaki *s*
葉 Naraha *sp*
園 Narazono *m*

楠 1901 [N] Kusunoki *sp*, Kusu. (NAN, kusu)
[3]川 Kusugawa *s*
久 Kusuku *s*
[4]元 Kusumoto *s*
太郎 Kusutarō *m*
山 Kusuyama *s*
山正雄 K. Masao *ml*
木 Kusunoki *s*, Kusuki
木正行 Kusunoki Masatsura *mh*

楓 椴 楳 椿 極 楯 楊 楫 楢 楠 ▼ 植 祺 晙 睦 靖 裲 裾 碑 碇 碓 雉 雄 雅 稗 稚 稠 稔 稜 ▲ 辞 辟 蛭 蜂 猇 解 群 路 跡 詳

木正成 K. Masashige *mh*
井 Kusui *s*
$^{5}$田 Kusuda *s*
本 Kusumoto *s*
本憲吉 K. Kenkichi *ml*
$^{6}$次 Kusuji *m*
$^{7}$男 Kusuo *m*
見 Kusumi *s*
$^{9}$美 Kusumi *s*
$^{10}$原 Kusubara *s*
$^{11}$後 Kusujiri *s*
$^{19}$瀬 Kusunose *s*
$^{21}$露 Kusu no tsuyu *l*

**植** 1902 [T] (SHOKU, JIKI, ue, tane, nao)
$^{4}$中 Uenaka *s*
山 Ueyama *s*
井 Uei *s*
月 Uetsuki *s*
木 Ueki *sp*
木枝盛 U. Emori *mlh*
$^{5}$田 Ueda *s*
田寿蔵 U. Juzō *ml*
本 Uemoto *s*
$^{6}$竹 Uetake *s*
$^{7}$村 Uemura *s*
村正久 U. Masahisa *mlh*
村諦 U. Tai *ml*
$^{9}$松 Uematsu *s*
松寿樹 U. Hisaki *ml*
草 Uekusa *s*
長 Tanenaga *m*
$^{10}$柳 Ueyanagi *s*
家 Taneie *m*
栗 Uekuri *s*
原 Uehara *s*
$^{11}$野 Ueno *s*
島 Uejima *s*
$^{12}$場 Ueba *s*

## 13 L5

**祺** 1903 (KI, GI, yoshi, yasu, sachi)
子 Yoshiko *f*, Yasuko, Sachiko
和 Yoshikata *m*

**晙** See 2110

**睦** 1904 [N] Mutsumi *m*, Chikashi, Atsushi, Makoto. (BOKU, MOKU, mutsu, chika, yoshi, toki, tomo, nobu, mu)
之 Tomoyuki *m*
子 Mutsuko *f*, Chikako
仁 Mutsuhito *m*
月 Mutsuki *f*
文 Mutsumi *f*
沢 Mutsuzawa *p*
玄 Chikaharu *m*
美 Mutsumi *f*
陸 Mutsumu *m*
道 Yoshimichi *m*
睦 Mutsumu *m*

**靖** 1905 [N] Yasushi *m*, Osamu, Hakaru, Kiyoshi. (SEI, JŌ, yasu, nobu, shizu)
三郎 Yasusaburō *m*
文 Yasuyuki *m*
夫 Shizuo *m*
彦 Yasuhiko *m*
胤 Nobutane *m*
章 Yasufumi *m*
道 Yasumichi *m*

**裲** 1906 (RYŌ)
襠 Uchikake *l*

**裾** 1907 (KYO, KO, suso)
巳 Susomi *f*
野 Susono *p*

**碑** 1908 Ishibumi *l*. (HI)

**碇** 1909 Ikari *s*. (TEI, CHŌ, ikari)
ケ関 Ikarigaseki *p*
之助 Ikarinosuke *m*
山 Ikariyama *s*
谷 Ikariya *s*
潜 Ikarikazuki *la*

**碓** 1910 (TAI, TE, usu)
川 Usugawa *s*
井 Usui *sp*
氷 Usui *sp*
男 Usuo *m*

**雉** 1911 (CHI, kiji, nobu, fusa)
本 Kijimoto *s*

**雄** 1912 [T] Takeshi *m*, Yū. (YŪ, o, take, katsu, kazu, taka, kata, nori, yoshi)
$^{1}$一 Yūichi *m*
一郎 Yūichirō *m*
$^{2}$二 Yūji *m*
二郎 Yūjirō *m*
人 Ondo *m*
力衛 Orie *m*
$^{3}$三郎 Yūsaburō *m*
之助 Yūnosuke *m*
$^{4}$太郎 Yūtarō *m*
$^{5}$比古 Kazuhiko *m*
只 Katsutada *m*
$^{6}$次 Yūji *m*
吉 Yūkichi *m*
早馬 Osame *m*
年 Katsuchika *m*
$^{7}$君 Ogimi *f*
物川 Omonogawa *p*
$^{8}$和 Yūwa *p*
幸 Yūkō *m*
昇 Takenori *m*
兎 Oto *m*
武 Ōmu *p*
$^{9}$祐 Yūsuke *m*
風 Okaze *m*
彦 Katsuhiko *m*
$^{10}$家 Oe *s*
$^{11}$略 Yūryaku *mh*
章 Takefumi *m*
$^{12}$勝 Okatsu *p*, Ogachi
$^{15}$端 Katsumasa *p*
踏 Yūtō *p*

**雅** 1913 [T] Masashi *m*, Masari, Miyabi, Tadashi, Hitoshi. (GA, masa, tsune, tada, nori, nari, moto)
$^{1}$一 Masaichi *m*, Masakazu
$^{2}$二 Masaji *m*
二郎 Tsunejirō *m*
人 Masando *m*
$^{3}$川 Tsunekawa *s*
川滉 T. Hiroshi *ml*
万 Masakazu *m*
子 Masako *f*
之助 Masanosuke *m*
$^{4}$太郎 Masatarō *m*
也 Tsuneya *m*
孔 Masamichi *m*
$^{5}$史 Masachika *m*
$^{6}$休 Masayasu *m*
宅 Masaie *m*
光 Tsuneteru *m*
$^{7}$言集覧 Gagen shūran *l*
充 Masamichi *m*
$^{8}$英 Norie *m*
事 Masakoto *m*
$^{9}$美 Masami *f*
$^{10}$訓 Masakuni *m*
郎 Masarō *m*
$^{11}$脩 Masaharu *m*
規 Masanori *m*
常 Masatsune *m*
庸 Masanobu *m*
$^{12}$富 Masatomi *m*
$^{13}$睦 Masanobu *m*
楽 Uta *m*
楽川 Utakawa *s*
楽介 Utanosuke *m*
$^{14}$嘉 Masayoshi *m*
$^{15}$儀 Masayoshi *m*
澄 Masazumi *m*
$^{16}$親 Masachika *m*
$^{17}$縁 Masayori *m*

**稗** See 2123

**稚** 1914 (CHI, waka, waku, nori)
子 Wakako *f*
内 Wakkanai *p*
女 Wakume *f*

**稠** 1915 Shigeru *m*, Shigeshi, Amane; Shige *f*. (CHŌ, shige)
尚 Shigehisa *m*

**稔** 1916 [N] Minoru *m-f*. (NEN, toshi, naru, nari)
足 Toshitari *m*
男 Toshio *m*
彦 Naruhiko *m*

**稜** 1917 (RYŌ, RŌ, izu, taka, taru)
人 Takato *m*
彦 Izuhiko *m*, Taruhiko
威 Itsue *s*
威子 Itsuko *f*
威言別 Itsu no kotowake *l*
威道別 Itsu no chiwake *l*
威雄 Itsuo *m*

## 13 L6

辞 1918 (JI, SHI, koto)

辟 1919 (HEKI, HYAKU, nori)
田 Hirata *s*
秦 Haihata *s*
槻 Hijitsuki *s*

蛭 1920 (SHITSU, hiru)
川 Hirukawa *sp*
可 Hiruka *s*
田 Hiruta *s*
河 Hirukawa *s*
間 Hiruma *s*

蜂 1921 Hachi *s.* (HŌ, hachi)
田 Hachida *s*
谷 Hachiya *s*
屋 Hachiya *s*
巣 Hachinosu *s*
須 Hachisu *s*
須賀 Hachisuka *s*

## 13 L7

兟 1922 Susumu *m.* (SHIN)

解 1923 [T] Satoru *m*; Toki *s.* (KAI, GE, toki, hiro, za)
子 Hiroko *f*
以 Zai *f*
礼 Kere *s*
体新書 Kaitai shinsho *lh*
良 Kera *s*
脱 Gedatsu *l*

群 1924 [T] (GUN, KUN, mura, tomo, mure, moto)
南 Gunnan *p*
書類従 Gunsho ruijū *l*
馬 Gunma *p*
蜂 Gunbō *l*
樹 Muraki *m*

路 1925 [T] Ōji *s.* (RO, michi, ji, nori, yuki)
久 Michihisa *m*
子 Michiko *f*
子工 Michinokoda *s*
通 Rotsū *ml*

跡 1926 [T] (SEKI, SHAKU, ato)
川 Togawa *s*
田 Atoda *s*
成 Atonari *m*
見 Atomi *s*, Tomi
部 Atobe *s*

詳 1927 [T] (SHŌ, zō, mitsu, tsuma)

詢 1928 Makoto *m.* (JUN, SHUN)

誂 1929 (CHŌ, atsurae)
染遠山麓子 Atsuraezome Tōyamaganoko *l*

詣 1930 (KEI, GEI, GAI, yuki)
見 Yukimi *m*

詫 1931 (TAKU)
間 Takuma *p*

試 1932 [T] (SHI, mochi)

詩 1933 [T] (SHI, uta)
之家 Shi no ie *l*
臣 Utaomi *m*
神 Shishin *l*
草社 Shisōsha *l*
風土 Shifūdo *l*
聖 Shisei *l*

詮 1934 Satoru *m*, Satoshi, Akira. (SEN, aki, toshi, nori, sato, haru, tomo, akira)
子 Akiko *f*
太郎 Sentarō *m*
允 Akisane *m*
実 Akimitsu *m*
茂 Akitō *m*
信 Akinobu *m*
兼 Akikane *m*

誠 1935 [T] Makoto *m-f*; Masashi *m*, Akira, Takashi. (SEI, JŌ, masa, yoshi, aki, akira, nobu, shige, sane, mi, kane, taka, sumi, tane, tomo, naga, nari, naru, nori, moto)
[1]一 Yoshikazu *m*
一郎 Seiichirō *m*
[2]二 Seiji *m*
二郎 Seijirō *m*
[3]三 Seizō *m*
三郎 Seizaburō *m*
子 Masako *f*
之 Taneyuki *m*
之助 Seinosuke *m*
[4]内 Nobumasa *m*
介 Seisuke *m*
文 Masafumi *m*
夫 Masao *m*
太郎 Seitarō *m*
[5]司 Seiji *m*
白 Masashi *m*
[6]次 Seiji *m*
次郎 Seijirō *m*
成 Takanari *m*
[7]佑 Kanesuke *m*
克 Shigekatsu *m*
[8]明 Nobuaki *m*
定 Akisada *m*
忠 Sanetada *m*
[9]治 Seiji *m*
弥 Shigehiro *m*
亮 Seisuke *m*
美 Saneyoshi *m*
[10]記 Motoki *m*
[11]康 Naruyasu *m*
[12]博 Yoshihiro *m*
道 Masamichi *m*
[13]寛 Shigehiro *m*
業 Nobuoki *m*

## 13 L8

瓺 1936 (CHŌ, DŌ, mika)
尻 Mikashiri *s*
玉 Mikatama *s*
取 Mikatori *s*

嗣 1937 [T] (SHI, JI, tsugi, tsugu, sane, hide)
夫 Tsuguo *m*
定 Tsugisada *m*
武 Tsugitake *m*
郎 Shirō *m*
頼 Tsuguyori *m*

幹 1938 [T] Miki *m*, Motoki, Tsuyoshi, Takashi. (KAN, miki, moto, ki, mi, yoshi, tsune, toshi, tomo, kara, eda, kuru, taru, masa, yomi, yori)
一郎 Kan'ichirō *m*
之助 Kannosuke *m*, Mikinosuke
太 Mikita *m*
示 Yoshimi *f*
次郎 Mikijirō *m*
直 Mikitada *m*
彦 Mikihiko *m*
郎 Motoo *m*
雄 Mikio *m*
嗣 Mototsugu *m*
興 Motooki *m*

鉤 1939 Magari *sm.* (KŌ, KU)

鈿 1940 (DEN, uzu)
女 Uzume *f*

鉦 1941 (SEI, SHŌ, kane)
次郎 Kanejirō *m*

鈺 1942 (GYOKU, GOKU, kane)
宣 Kaneyoshi *s*

鈍 1943 [T] (DON)
太郎 Dontarō *la*

鉛 1944 [T] Namari *s.* (EN, kana)
山 Kanayama *s*

鉢 1945 (HACHI, ho)
かづき Hachikazuki *l*
木 Hachinoki *la*

鉅 1946 Tsuyoshi *m*, Takeshi; Ōshika *sm*; Ōka *s.* (KYO, GO, ō, ōka, saza)
鹿 Ōka *s*, Sazaka

鈴 1947 [T] (REI, RYŌ, suzu, rin)
[3]川 Suzukawa *s*

幹 鉤 鈿 鉦 鈺 鈍 鉛 鉢 鉅 鈴 ▼ 鉄 紘 終 紬 組 紙 紺 紹 純 経 細 鼓 殿 献 猷 ▲ 飫 飯 新 馴 凱 勤 勣 勧 亂 亶

子 Suzuko *f*
[4]太郎 Reitarō *m*
木 Suzuki *s*
木三重吉 S. Miekichi *ml*
木大拙 S. Daisetsu *mh*
木文治 S. Bunji *mh*
木田 Suzukida *s*
木正三 Suzuki Shōsan *ml*
木弘恭 S. Hiroyasu *ml*
木花蓑 S. Hanamino *ml*
木虎雄 S. Torao *ml*
木信太郎 S. Shintarō *ml*
木春信 S. Harunobu *ma*
木泉三郎 S. Senzaburō *ml*
木梅太郎 S. Umetarō *mh*
木貫太郎 S. Kantarō *mh*
木善太郎 S. Zentarō *ml*
[5]田 Suzuta *s*
[6]江 Suzue *sf*
虫 Suzumushi *l*
[7]村 Suzumura *s*
[9]治郎 Rinjirō *m*
[10]屋 Suzuya *s*
[11]峰 Reihō *p*
野 Suzuno *s*
[12]賀 Suzuka *s*
鹿 Suzuka *sp*
鹿野風呂 S. Noburo *ml*
[13]雄 Suzuo *m*

鉄 1948 [T] Tetsu *sm*; Kurogane *s*; Magane *m*. (TETSU, kane, kimi, toshi)
一郎 Tetsuichirō *m*
二 Tetsuji *m*
三 Tetsuzō *m*
之助 Tetsunosuke *m*
工 Kanuchi *s*
夫 Kaneo *m*, Kimio
山 Tessan *s*
太郎 Tetsutarō *m*
平 Tetsuhei *m*, Teppei
次郎 Tetsujirō *m*
吉 Tetsukichi *m*
男 Tetsuo *m*
臣 Tetsuomi *m*
師 Kanuchi *s*
屋 Tetsuya *s*
馬 Tetsuma *m*
朗 Toshiaki *m*
輪 Kanawa *la*
蔵 Tetsuzō *m*

紘 1949 Hiroshi *m*. (KŌ, GYŌ, hiro)

終 1950 [T] (SHŪ, tsuki, nochi)
の栖 Tsui no sumika *l*

紬 1951 (CHŪ, tsumugi)
子 Tsumugiko *f*

組 1952 (SO, SHO, kumi, kumu)
子 Kumiko *f*

紙 1953 [T] Kami *s*. (SHI, kami)
子 Kamiko *f*
田 Kamida *s*
谷 Kamiya *s*
風船 Kamifūsen *la*
屋 Kamiya *s*

紺 1954 [T] (KON)
口 Konku *s*
村 Konmura *s*
谷 Kontani *s*
屋 Kon'ya *s*
野 Konno *s*
部 Konbe *s*

紹 1955 [T] (SHŌ, tsugu, tsugi, aki)
子 Tsugiko *f*
仁 Tsuguhito *m*
巴 Shōha *ml*
房 Akifusa *m*
念 Tsugumune *m*
美 Jōmi *s*
雄 Tsugio *m*

純 1956 [T] Atsushi *m*, Jun, Makoto, Kiyoshi, Sunao, Itaru. (JUN, yoshi, sumi, atsu, aya, ito, tsuna, tō)
一 Jun'ichi *m*
一郎 Jun'ichirō *m*
友 Sumitomo *m*
夫 Sumio *m*
正 Sumimasa *m*, Yoshimasa, Yoshitada
吉 Junkichi *m*
如 Tsunayuki *m*
孝 Sumitaka *m*
明 Yoshiaki *m*
信 Yoshinobu *m*
彦 Atsuhiko *m*, Sumihiko
郎 Ayao *m*
雄 Sumio *m*
義 Sumiyoshi *m*
資 Yoshisuke *m*
精 Sumikiyo *m*

経 1957 [T] Osamu *m*. (KEI, KYŌ, tsune, nori, fu, nobu, furu)
[4]介 Keisuke *m*
夫 Tsuneo *m*
[6]式 Tsunenori *m*
世秘策 Keisei hisaku *lh*
[8]明 Tsuneakira *m*, Noriaki
孟 Tsunemoto *m*
国集 Keikokushū *l*
[9]信 Tsunenobu *ml*
治 Tsuneharu *m*
則 Tsunetoki *m*
[10]家 Tsuneie *m*
[11]裕 Norihiro *m*
教 Tsunenori *m*
済 Tsunenari *m*
済要録 Keizai yōroku *lh*
済録 Keizairoku *lh*
[12]道 Tsunemichi *m*
[13]雅 Tsunetada *m*
幹 Tsunemoto *m*
義 Norishige *m*
[14]甄 Tsuneaki *m*
[15]慰 Tsuneyasu *m*
[16]綸 Tsuneo *m*
輝 Tsuneteru *m*
[18]顕 Tsuneaki *m*

細 1958 [T] Kuwashi *m*. (SAI, SEI, hoso)
[2]入 Hosoiri *p*
[3]川 Hosokawa *s*
川重賢 H. Shigekata *mh*
川勝元 H. Katsumoto *mh*
川幽斎 H. Yūsai *ml*
川頼之 H. Yoriyuki *mh*
[4]戸 Hosodo *s*
山 Hosoyama *s*
木 Hosoki *s*
井 Hosoi *s*
井和喜蔵 H. Wakizō *mlh*
井魚袋 H. Gyotai *ml*
内 Hosouchi *s*
[5]田 Hosoda *s*
田民樹 H. Tamiki *ml*
田源吉 H. Genkichi *ml*
矢 Hosoya *s*
[6]江 Hosoe *p*
合 Hosoai *s*
辻 Hosotsuji *s*
[7]沢 Hosozawa *s*
村 Hosomura *s*
谷 Hosoya *s*, Hosonoya
谷源二 Hosoya Genji *ml*
貝 Hosogai *s*
見 Hosomi *s*
[8]沼 Hosonuma *s*
[9]岡 Hosooka *s*
[10]倉 Hosokura *s*
屋 Hosoya *s*
[11]浪 Hosonami *s*
渓 Hosotani *s*
根 Hosone *s*
野 Hosono *s*
雪 Sasameyuki *l*
島 Hosojima *s*
萱 Hosokaya *s*
[13]淵 Hosobuchi *s*
堀 Hosobori *s*
越 Hosogoe *s*
越夏村 H. Kason *ml*

**———13 L9———**

鼓 1959 [T] Tsuzumi *s*. (KO)
常良 T. Tsuneyoshi *ml*

殿 1960 [T] Tonomori *s*. (DEN, tono, ato, sue)
木 Tonoki *s*
村 Tonomura *s*
来 Tonoki *s*
岡 Tonooka *s*
原 Tonohara *s*
塚 Tonozuka *s*

献 1961 [T] (KEN, KON, take)

猷 1962 (YŪ, YU, michi, yuki, nori, kazu)
子 Michiko *f*
太郎 Yūtarō *m*
彦 Michihiko *m*

飫 1963 (o, yo)
富 Ō *s*, Obu

飯 1964 [T] Ii *s*. (HAN, ii, meshi)
[3]川 Iigawa *s*
土用 Iitoyo *s*
久保 Iikubo *s* ⌈*p*
[4]山 Iiyama *sp*; Hanzan
井 Meshii *s*
[5]石 Iishi *p*
田 Iida *sp*; Handa *s*
田川 Iidagawa *p* ⌈*ml*
田年平 Iida Toshihira
田武郷 I. Takesato *ml*
田莫哀 I. Bakuai *ml*
田竜太 I. Ryūta *ml*
田蛇笏 I. Dakotsu *ml*
田屋 Iidaya *s*
田橋 Iidabashi *p*
[6]吉 Iiyoshi *s*
[7]坂 Iizaka *p*, Iisaka
沢 Iizawa *s*
沢匡 I. Tadasu *ml*
村 Iimura *s*
尾 Iio *s*, Inoo
[8]沼 Iinuma *s*
河 Iigawa *s*, Ikō
[9]垣 Iigaki *s*
南 Iinan *p*
泉 Iizumi *s*
岡 Iioka *sp*
[10]酒盃 Isahai *s*
高 Iitaka *sp*
倉 Iigura *s*
室 Iimuro *s*
浜 Iihama *s*
原 Iihara *s*
[11]浪 Iinami *s*, Iinuma
野 Iino *sp*
能 Hannō *p*
盛 Iimori *sp*; Meshimori *ml*
麻呂 Imaro *m*
島 Iijima *sp*
島正 I. Tadashi *ml*
[12]富 Iitomi *s*
笹 Iizasa *s*
森 Iimori *s*
[13]塚 Iizuka *sp*
塚友一郎 I. Tomoi- ⌊chirō *ml*
豊 Iide *p*
淵 Iibuchi *s*
[14]窪 Iikubo *s*
郷 Iigō *s*
[17]館 Iidate *p*
篠 Iizasa *s*, Iishino

新 1965 [T] Arata *sm*; Shin *m-p*; Hajime *m*, Susume, Akira; Atarashi *s*. (SHIN, nii, ara, chika, waka, yoshi, imaki, ima) ⌈kazu
[1]一 Shin'ichi *m*, Ara-
一郎 Shin'ichirō *m*
[2]十津川 Shin-totsugawa *p*
十郎 Shinjūrō *m*
八 Shinpachi *m*
七 Shinshichi *m*
[3]川 Arakawa *s*, Niikawa, Nikkawa; Shinkawa *p*
三郎 Shinzaburō *m*
万葉集 Shin-man'yōshū *l*
久保 Shinkubo *s*
千載集 Shin-senzaishū *l*
之允 Shinnojō *m*
之助 Shinnosuke *m*
[4]戸 Niinohe *s*
元 Niimoto *s*
今 Niima *s*
内 Shinnai *a* ⌈ma
山 Niiyama *s*, Araya-
太郎 Shintarō *m*
井 Arai *sp*
井田 Niida *s* ⌈*mlh*
井白石 Arai Hakuseki
井洸 A. Kō *ml*
井紀一 A. Kiichi *ml*
[5]比古 Chikahiko *m*
比恵 Imahie *s*
比叡 Imahie *s*
右衛門 Shin'emon *m*
生 Niibu *s*, Niifu, Niikura ⌈*l*
古文林 Shin-kobunrin
古今集 S.-kokinshū *l*
今集美濃家苞 S.-k. Mino no iezuto *l*
市 Shin'ichi *p*
平 Shinpei *m*
平家 Shin-heike *l*
田 Nitta *sp*
田目 Aratame *s*
田次郎 Nitta Jirō *ml*
田義貞 N. Yoshisada
田潤 N. Jun *ml* ⌊*mh*
[6]旭 Shin-asahi *p*
次郎 Shinjirō *m*
地 Shinchi *p*
行内 Shingyōji *s*
江 Arae *s*
合 Niiai *s*
吉 Shinkichi *m*
吉富 Shin-yoshitomi *p*
宅 Shintaku *s*
庄 Shinjō *sp*; Jinjō *p*
曲赫映姫 Shinkyoku Kaguyahime *la*
世帯 Arajotai *l*
名 Niina *s*
西蘭 Nyūjiirando *p* "New Zealand"
[7]体詩抄 Shintaishishō
沢 Shinsawa *s* ⌊*l*
村 Niimura *s*, Shinmura, Shimura
村出 Shinmura Izuru
助 Shinsuke *m* ⌊*ml*
利根 Shin-tone *p*
谷 Niitani *s*, Araya, Niiya, Shin'ya, Shintani
条 Shinjō *s*
花摘 Shin-hanatsumi *l*
尾 Arao *s*
里 Niisato *sp*
見 Niimi *sp*; Shinmi *s*, Shinomi, Niima
見正興 Shinmi Masaoki *mh*
[8]沼 Niinuma *s*
和 Shinwa *p*
和様 Shinwayō *a*
即物性 Shinsoku bussei *l* ⌈zaimon *l*
版歌祭文 Shinpan uta-
免 Shinmen *s*, Niimi
実 Niimi *s*
学 Niimanabi *l*
学異見 N. iken *l*
阜 Niifu *s* ⌈*s*
居 Arai *sp*, Nii; Niori
居格 Nii Itaru *ml*
居浜 Niihama *p*
国 Niikuni *s*
武道伝来記 Shin budō denraiki *l*
良 Shinra *s*
良貴 Shiragi *s*
[9]保 Shinbo *s*
拾遺集 Shin-shūishū *l*
城 Niiki *s*, Shinjō; Shinshiro *p*
垣 Niigaki *s*
津 Niitsu *p* ⌈*p*
治 Niihari *sp*; Niiharu
松 Niimatsu *s*
籾 Aramomi *s*
勅撰集 Shin-chokusenshū *l*
冠 Niikappu *p*
荘 Shinjō *s*
美 Niimi *s* ⌈*ml*
美南吉 N. Nankichi
音羽屋 Shintowaya *s*
妻 Niizuma *s*
発田 Shibata *sp*; Shiōda *s*
泉 Niizumi *s*
岡 Niioka *s* ⌈*l*
[10]俳話会 Shinhaiwakai
海 Shinkai *s* ⌈*ma*
海竹太郎 S. Taketarō
家 Niiya *s*, Araya, Shin'ya, Niinomi; Niie *m*
倉 Niikura *s*
宮 Shingū *sp*
畠 Niibata *s*
原 Niibara *s*
座 Shinza *p*
屋 Niiya *s*, Shin'ya
[11]後撰集 Shin-gosenshū *l* ⌈ishū *l*
後拾遺集 Shin-goshū-
得 Shintoku *p*
野 Niino *sp*
宿 Shinjuku *p*
著百種 Shincho hyakushu *l*
笠 Niigasa *m*
魚目 Shin'uonome *p*
島 Niijima *s*
島本 Niijimahon *p*
島栄治 Niijima Eiji *ml*
島襄 N. Jō *mlh*
島繁 N. Shigeru *ml*
[12]湊 Shinminato *p*
渡戸 Nitobe *s*, Niitobe
渡戸稲造 Nitobe Inazō *mlh* ⌈kajin *l*
粧之佳人 Shinsō no
納 Niiro *s*, Shiiro, Niira, Shiyū
富 Shintomi *p*
開 Shinkai *sp*
間 Shinma *s*, Niima
間進一 S. Shin'ichi *ml*
[13]堀 Shinbori *s*, Nippori, Niibori
漢 Imakinoaya *s*

漢人 Imakiayahito s, Imakinoayahito
葉集 Shin'yōshū *l*
楽 Niira *s*
14演芸 Shin'engei *l*
猿楽記 Shinsarugaku-
郷 Shingō *p* ⌊ki *l*
銅 Shindō *s*
関 Niizeki *s*
関良三 N. Ryōzō *ml*
15潟 Niigata *p*
撰字鏡 Shinsen jikyō *l*
撰姓氏録 S. shōjiroku *l*
撰朗詠集 S. rōeishū *l*
撰莵玖波集 S. Tsukubashū *l*
撰組 Shinsengumi *l*
撰髄脳 Shinsen zuinō *l*
穂 Niibo *p*
続古今集 Shin-zoku-kokinshū *l*
熊 Niikuma *m*
選組 Shinsengumi *l*
選組始末記 S. shimatsuki *l*
16興 Niioki *s*
17篠津 Shinshinotsu *p*
墾 Niihari *l*
18藤 Shindō *s*
19韻 Shin'in *l*
21鶴 Niitsuru *p*
羅 Shiragi / Shinra *ph* "Silla"
羅楽 Shiragi gaku *a*

## —13 L10—

**馴** 1966 (JUN, SHUN, nare, yoshi)

## —13 L11—

**凱** 1967 Tanoshi *m*. (GAI, yoshi, toki)
一 Tokiichi *m*
金 Yoshikane *m*
実 Yoshizane *m*
陣八島 Gaijin Yashima *la*

**勤** 1968 See 勤 1698

**勣** 1969 Iwao *m*. (SEKI, SHAKU)

**勧** 1970 Susumu *m*. (KAN, KEN, yuki)
学院 Kangakuin *ph*
進帳 Kanjinchō *la*
修寺 Kajūji *s* ⌈aku *l*
善懲悪 Kanzen chō-
善懲悪覗機関 K.c. nozoki karakuri *la*

## —13 L12—

**氶** 1971 Osamu *m*. (CHI)

## —13 T2—

**亶** 1972 Yutaka *m*. (TAN, SEN, tada, atsu)

**稟** 1973 Ukuru *m*. (RIN)

## —13 T3—

**嵒** 1974 Iwao *m*. (GAN)
雄 Iwao *m*

**義** 1975 [T] Tadashi *m*, Yoshi, Tsutomu. (GI, yoshi, nori, aki, shige, take, chika, michi, yori)
1一 Giichi *m*
3三 Yoshizō *m*
三郎 Yoshisaburō *m*, Gisaburō
子 Yoshiko *f*, Noriko
士 Takeo *m*
久 Yoshihisa *m*
之 Yoshiyuki *m*
之介 Yoshinosuke *m*
4心 Yoshimune *m*
元 Yoshiyuki *m*, Yoshinaga ⌈suke
介 Yoshisuke *m*, Gi-
友 Yoshitomo *m*
文 Yoshifumi *m*
止 Yoshitome *m*
五 Yoshikazu *m*
夫 Yoshio *m*
太 Yoshihiro *m*
太夫 Gidayū *ma-a*
太郎 Yoshitarō *m*
5比 Yoshichika *m*, Yoshihisa
礼 Yoshiakira *m*
令 Yoshiharu *m*
公 Yoshimasa *m*, Yoshihiro
処 Yoshisumi *m*
央 Yoshichika *m*
四郎 Gishirō *m*
正 Yoshimasa *m*, Yoshisada
6光 Yoshimitsu *m*, Yoshiteru, Yoshiaki
広 Yoshihiro *m*
7弘 Yoshihiro *m*
助 Yoshisuke *m*
利 Yoshimasa *m*
克 Yoshikatsu *m*
発 Yoshimichi *m*
男 Yoshio *m*
局 Yoshichika *m*
8明 Yoshiaki *m*
杵 Yoshiki *m*
知 Yoshitomo *m*
和 Yoshichika *m*, Yoshimasa, Yoshiyori
苗 Yoshitane *m*
忠 Noritada *m*
秀 Yoshihide *m*
居 Yoshisue *m*
武 Yoshitake *m*
尚 Yoshihisa *m*
国 Yoshikuni *m*
固 Yoshitaka *m*
良 Yoshio *m*, Norina-
9保 Yorio *m* ⌊ga
治 Yoshiharu *m*
昭 Yoshiaki *m*
珍 Yoshinori *m*
弥 Yoshimitsu *m*
柄 Yoshie *m*, Yoshitsuka
政 Yoshimasa *m*
故 Yoshimoto *m*
垣 Yoshitaka *m*
城 Yoshikuni *m*
則 Yoshinori *m*
勇 Yoshitoshi *m*, Yoshitake, Yoshio
美 Yoshitomi *m*
栄 Yoshitomo *m*
巻 Yoshimaki *m*, Yoshimaru
岡 Yoshioka *s*
建 Yoshitake *m*
彦 Yoshihiko *m*
門 Yoshikado *m*
貞 Yoshisada *m*
10将 Yoshimasa *m*
格 Yoshitada *m*
始 Yoshimoto *m*
修 Yoshinaga *m*
倫 Yoshitsugu *m*
祚 Yoshitoshi *m*
祇 Yoshimoto *m*
郎 Yoshirō *m*
高 Yoshitaka *m*, Yoshiue
員 Yoshikazu *m*
竜 Yoshitatsu *m*
恭 Yoshitada *m*
威 Yoshitoshi *m*
11清 Yoshikiyo *m*
深 Yoshitō *m*
隆 Yoshitaka *m*
胸 Yoshimune *m*
視 Yoshimi *m*
理 Yoshitada *m*, Yoshitoshi
規 Yoshinori *m*
務 Yoshikane *m*
朗 Yoshirō *m*
教 Yoshinori *m*
著 Yoshitsugu *m*
章 Yoshitaka *m* ⌈*ml*
堂周信 Gidō Shūshin
盛 Yoshimori *m*
留 Yoshito *m*
恕 Yoshikuni *m*
亀 Yoshihisa *m*
12備 Yoshinari *m*
陽 Yoshihi *m*
勝 Yoshikatsu *m*
晴 Yoshiharu *m*
朝 Yoshitomo *m*
温 Yoshiatsu *m*, Yoshiyasu
貴 Yoshiatsu *m*
登 Yoshitaka *m*
智 Yoshitoshi *m*
堅 Yoshikata *m*
量 Yoshikazu *m*
景 Yoshikage *m*
喬 Yoshitaka *m*
13植 Yoshitane *m*
雄 Yoshio *m*
詮 Yoshitoshi *m*, Yoshiakira
淵 Gien *mh*
満 Yoshimitsu *m*
経 Yoshitsune *m*
経千本桜 Y. senbon-zakura *la*
経新高館 Y. Shin Takadachi *l*
経記 Gikeiki *l*
意 Yoshimoto *m*
照 Yoshiteru *m*
蓁 Yoshishige *m*
舜 Yoshikiyo *m*
愛 Yoshichika *m*
14演 Gien *mh*

徳 Yoshinori *m*
弼 Yoshisuke *m*
旗 Yoshitaka *m*
暢 Yoshinaga *m*
種 Yoshitane *m*
輔 Yoshisuke *m*
韶 Yoshiaki *m*
数 Yoshikazu *m*
農 Yoshitami *m*
算 Yoshikazu *m*
15澄 Yoshizumi *m*
輝 Yoshiteru *m*
蕃 Yoshimori *m*
履 Yoshifumi *m*
調 Yoshishige *m*
銀 Yoshikane *m*
統 Yoshimune *m*
続 Yoshitsugu *m*
寮 Yoshiie *m*
質 Yoshitada *m*, Yoshimoto, Yoshikata
16積 Yoshisane *m*
綏 Yoshiyasu *m*
賢 Yoshinori *m*
興 Yoshioki *m*
17懐 Yoshichika *m*
謀 Yoshitsumu *m*
謙 Yoshinori *m*, Yoshikane
慈 Yoshishige *m*
18曜 Yoshiteru *m*
19鏡 Yoshikane *m*, Yoshiakira
23鑑 Yoshinori *m*

**寝** 1976 [T] (SHIN, ne)
屋川 Neyagawa *p*
覚 Nezame *l* ⌈*a*
殿造 Shinden-zukuri
園 Shin'en *l*

**寛** 1977 [T] Hiroshi *m*, Kan, Yutaka. (KAN, hiro, tomo, chika, tō, tomi, nori, hito, o, tora, nobu, mune, moto, yoshi, oki)
1一郎 Kan'ichirō *m*
2九郎 Kankurō *m*
人 Hirōto *m*, Hirondo
二郎 Kanjirō *m*
3三郎 Kanzaburō *m*
4仁 Kannin 1017–21; Tomohito *m*
元 Kangen 1243–47
文 Kanbun 1661–73
5永 Kan'ei 1624–44
永寺 Kan'eiji *p*
申 Hiromi *m*
正 Kanshō 1460–66
平 Kanpyō / Kanpei 889–98
6次 Kanji *m*
次郎 Kanjirō *m*
7弘 Kankō 1004–12
8和 Kanwa 985–87
延 Kan'en 1748–51
9保 Kanpō 1741–44
治 Kanji *m* 1087–94
祐 Tomimasa *m*
政 Kansei 1789–1801
政三奇人 K. no sankijin *mh*
政三博士 K. no sanhakase *mh*
哉 Kansuke *m*
10恵 Hiroyoshi *m*
造 Kanzō *m*
11剛 Hiroyoshi *m*
裕 Tomimasa *m*
12喜 Kangi 1229–32
14徳 Kantoku 1044–46
16憶 Kanzō *m*
篤 Tomoatsu *m*

**莖** 1978 See 茎 684

**墓** 1979 [T] Haka *s*, Hakamori. (BO, haka, tsuka)

**蒿** 1980 Yomogi *f*. (KŌ)

**蒸** 1981 [T] Tsumaki *m*. (JŌ, tsugu)

**蒨** 1982 Shigeru *m*. (SEN)

**蓉** 1983 (YŌ, YU, hasu)
身 Hasumi *f*

**蓁** 1984 Shigeru *m*. (SHIN, shige, hari)
原 Harihara *s*

**蓜** 1984A (HAI)
島 Haijima *s*

**蒔** 1985 (JI, SHI, maki)
子 Makiko *f*
田 Makita *s*

**蒜** 1986 (SAN, hiru)
田 Hiruta *s*
園 Hiruzono *m*

**茲** 1987 Shigeru *m*. (JI, shige, kore, tsuna)
俊 Koretoshi *m*
親 Korechika *m*

**蒼** 1988 Shigeru *m*. (SŌ, shige, ta)
生子 Tamiko *f*
穹 Sōkyū *l*
氓 Sōbō *l*

**幕** 1989 [T] (MAKU, BAKU)
内 Makuuchi *s*
田 Makuta *s*
別 Makubetsu *p*
谷 Makuya *s*
屋 Makuya *s*

**夢** 1990 [T] (MU, BŌ, yume)
助 Yumesuke *m*
応の鯉魚 Muō no rigyo *l*
前 Yumesaki *p*
浮橋 Yume no ukihashi *l* ⌈*mlh*
窓疎石 Musō Soseki

**葉** 1991 [T] (YŌ, ha, ba, nobu, tari, fusa)
山 Hayama *sp*
山嘉樹 H. Yoshiki *ml*
若 Hawaka *s*
室 Hamuro *s*
栗 Haguri *p*

**葦** 1992 (I, ashi)
名 Ashina *s*
谷 Ashiya *s*
室 Ashiya *s*
原 Ashiwara *s*
屋 Ashiya *s*
野 Ashino *s*
渡 Ashiwatari *s*
崎 Ashizaki *s*
敷 Ashiki *s*
繁 Ashishige *s*

**蒲** 1993 Gama *s*. (HO, BU, gama, kama)
刈 Kamagari *p*
田 Kabata *s*, Katsukida ⌈*p*
生 Gamō *sm-p*; Kamō
生君平 G. Kunpei *mh*
地 Kamachi *s*
江 Kamae *p*
坂 Hosaka *s*
沢 Kamasawa *s*
谷 Kamaya *s*
郡 Gamagōri *p*
原 Kanbara *sp*; Kamahara *s* ⌈ake *ml*
原有明 Kanbara Ari-

**葛** 1994 Kazura *s*, Kashii, Kuzō, Kasai, Fujii. (KATSU, kuzu, kado, kazu, sachi, fuji, tsura, katsura)
3上 Kazukami *s*
子 Sachiko *f*
4山 Kuzuyama *s*, Kadoyama, Katsurayama, Kazura, Kashio
井 Kadoi *s*, Fujii
井広成 F. Hironari *ml*
5目 Kuzume *s*
生 Kuzuo *s*; Kuzuu *p*
6西 Kasai *s*, Kassai
西善蔵 Kasai Zenzō
7谷 Kuzudani *s* ⌊*ml*
尾 Katsurao *p*
見 Katsumi *s*
巻 Kuzumaki *sp*; Kazumaki *s*
城 Kazuraki *sla*; Katsuragi *s*; Katsujō *m*
城天狗 Kazuraki ten-
岡 Kuzuoka *s* ⌊gu *l*
10原 Kuzuhara *s*, Katsurahara, Tsuzurahara
11根 Kuzune *m*
野 Kuzuno *s*; Kadono
盛 Kazumori *m* ⌊*sm*
12貫 Kasanuki *s*
14飾 Katsushika *sp*

馴 凱 勤 勣 勧 亂 亶 稟 嗇 義 ▼ 寝 寛 莖 墓 蒿 蒸 蒨 蓉 蓁 蓜 蒔 蒜 茲 蒼 幕 夢 葉 葦 蒲 葛 ▲ 歳 暑 暈 嵩 崧 嵐 當 發 蒙 累

飾北斎 K. Hokusai *ma*
[18]鎮 Fujitsune *m*

—13 T4—

歳 1995 [T] (SAI, SEI, toshi, tose, isa)
三 Toshizō *m*
久 Toshihisa *m*
男 Isao *m*
兼 Toshikane *m*

暑 1996 See 暑 1738 A

暈 1997 Higasa *s*. (UN)

嵓 1998 See 嵒 1974

崧 1999 Takashi *m*. (SHŪ, SHU)

嵐 2000 Arashi *sm*. (RAN)
山 Arashiyama *p-la*
雪 Ransetsu *ml*

—13 T5—

當 2001 See 当 282

發 2002 See 発 953

蒙 2003 (MŌ)
求和歌 Mōgyū waka *l*

累 2004 [T] Rui *f*. (RUI, taka)
教 Takako *f*

蜀 2005 (SHOKU, kuni)
山人 Shokusanjin *ml*

罪 2006 [T] (ZAI, tsumi)
山 Tsumiyama *s*

意 2007 [T] (I, oki, moto, nori, o, osa, mune, yoshi)
次 Okitsugu *m*
気陽 Ikiyō *m*
成 Motonari *m*
壱 Okikazu *m*
岐 Oki *s*
忠 Noritada *m*
美麿 Omimaro *m*
留 Okihisa *m*
舒 Motonobu *m*
富 Ō *s*
薩 Osato *s*

—13 T6—

跫 2008 (KYŌ)
音 Ashioto *la*

羨 2009 (SEN, ZEN, yoshi, nobu)
子 Yoshiko *f*

誉 2010 [T] Homare *m*, Homaru, Takashi. (YO, yoshi, taka, shige, nori, homu, hon, yasu, moto)
子 Yoshiko *f*
代 Takayo *f*
田 Honda *sm*; Konda *s*
次郎 Takajirō *m*
津 Honzu *s*
富 Takayoshi *m*
純 Shigesumi *m*
弼 Yoshisuke *m*

貰 2011 (SEI, morai)
聟 Morai-muko *la*

資 2012 [T] Tasuku *m*. (SHI, suke, toshi, yasu, yori, moto, tada, yoshi)
子 Sukeko *f*
公 Suketaka *m*
芝 Sukeshige *m*
吉 Motokichi *m*
忠 Suketada *m*
承 Sukekoto *m*
貞 Sukesada *m*
始 Sukemoto *m*
雄 Yasuo *m*
凱 Sukeyoshi *m*
徳 Sukekatsu *m*
弼 Toshisuke *m*
邁 Suketaka *m*

豊 2013 [T] Toyo *s*, Bun, Bunno; Yutaka *m-p*; Minoru *m*, Noboru, Hiroshi. (HŌ, BU, toyo, atsu, mori, hiro, to, yuta, kata, yoshi)
[1]一郎 Toyoichirō *m*
[3]川 Toyokawa *sp*
三久 Tomihisa *m*
三郎 Toyosaburō *m*
子 Atsuko *f*
口 Toyoguchi *s*
[4]水 Toyomizu *s*
仁 Yutahito *m*
中 Toyonaka *p*
日子 Toyohiko *m*
山 Toyoyama *p*
夫 Toyoo *m*
太 Toyota *m*
太郎 Toyotarō *m*
[5]北 Hōhoku *p*
永 Toyonaga *s*
四郎 Toyoshirō *m*
平 Toyohira *p*
玉 Toyotama *p*
本 Toyomoto *s*
丘 Toyooka *p*
田 Toyoda *sp*, Toyota
田三郎 Toyoda Saburō *ml*
田佐吉 T. Sakichi *mh*
[6]次 Toyoji *m*
竹 Toyotake *s*
行 Toyoyuki *m*
吉 Toyokichi *m*
広 Toyohiro *m*
名賀 Toyonaga *s*
[7]住 Toyozumi *s*
作 Toyosaku *m*
沢 Toyozawa *s*
村 Toyomura *s*
助 Toyosuke *m*
里 Toyosato *p*
臣 Toyotomi *s*
臣秀次 T. Hidetsugu *mh*
臣秀吉 T. Hideyoshi *mh*
[8]明 Toyoake *p*
昌 Toyomasa *m*
受 Toyuke *s*
国 Toyokuni *ma*
[9]信 Toyonobu *m*, Toyoshige
津 Toyotsu *p*
治 Toyoji *m*
治郎 Toyojirō *m*
松 Toyomatsu *p*
科 Toyoshina *p*
秋 Toyoaki *m*
前 Buzen *sph*
栄 Toyosaka *p*, Toyasaka
泉 Toyoizumi *s*
岡 Toyooka *sp*
彦 Toyohiko *m*
[10]俊 Toyotoshi *m*
浜 Toyohama *p*
浦 Toyoura *sp*; Toyora *s*
泰 Toyoyasu *m*
恵 Hiroyoshi *m*
恭 Toyoyuki *m*
原 Toyohara *s*; Toyomoto *m*
[11]頃 Toyokoro *p*
隆 Toyotaka *m*
後 Bungo *ph*
後国 Bungonokuni *ph*
後国風土記 B. no fudoki *l*
後高田 Bungo Takada *p*
根 Toyone *p*
野 Toyono *sp*
能 Toyono *p*
産 Toyotada *m*
島 Toshima *sp*; Toyoshima *s*, Teshima
島与志雄 Toyoshima Yoshio *ml*
[12]崎 Toyosaki *s*
富 Toyotomi *p*
答 Toyokazu *m*
道 Bundō *s*
間 Toyoma *s*
[13]階 Toyoshina *s*, Toshina
福 Toyofuku *s*
誠 Toyonori *m*
[14]郷 Toyosato *p*
[15]敷 Toyonobu *m*
穎 Toyokai *m*
熙 Toyoteru *m*
[16]綺 Toyohatori *s*
親 Yoshika *m*
橘 Toyokichi *m*
橋 Toyohashi *p*
[17]雍 Toyochika *m*
[18]饒 Bunyō *s*, Toyoyuta

筧 2014 Kakei *sm*, Kakehi. (KEN, GEN)

筠 2015 Take *m*. (KIN, take, taka)
彦 Takehiko *m*

筥 2016 Hako *s.* (KYO, hako, kiyo)
室 Kiyomuro *s*
崎 Hakozaki *s*

舜 2017 Hitoshi *m.* (SHUN, kiyo, toshi, mitsu, yoshi)
二 Toshiji *m*
子 Toshiko *f*
江 Yoshie *f*
世 Toshiyo *m*
治 Shunji *m*

愛 2018 [T] Chikashi *m*, Megumu. (AI, E, yoshi, chika, naru, sane, nari, aki, nori, hide, yori, tsune, yasu, aya, mashi)
一郎 Aiichirō *m*
川 Aikawa *sp*
三 Aizō *m*
子 Aiko *f*; Ayashi *s*, Mashiko
仁 Naruhito *m*
日抄 Aijisshō *l*
甲 Aikō *sp*; Aikawa *s*
民 Chikatami *m*, Narumi
多茂 Atamu *s*
多義 Aitagi *s*
作 Aisaku *m*
沢 Aizawa *s*
別 Aibetsu *p*
[8]知 Aichi *sp*, Echi
知川 Echigawa *p*
若 Aiwaka *s*
宕 Atago *sp*, Otagi
宕空也 A. Kūya *la*
[9]信 Chikanobu *m*
洲 Aisu *s*
発 Yoshichika *m*, Yoshishige, Chikanari, Naritoki
昶 Yoshiteru *m*
彦 Aihiko *m*, Yoshihiko
[10]郎 Yoshio *m*
[11]野 Aino *sp*
[12]曾 Aso *s*
智 Aichi *s*, Echi, Aechi
善 Yoriyoshi *m*
[13]媛 Ehime *p*
雄 Yoshio *m*, Yoshitaka
義 Akiyoshi *m*
[14]輔 Aisuke *m*
[15]勲 Yoshihiro *m*
[16]橘 Aikitsu *m*
親 Naruchika *m*
臧 Naritsugu *m*
[20]護若塒箱 Aigonowaka negurabako *la*

**—13 T7—**

粲 2019 Akira *m*, Yutaka, Tsubara. (SAN)

**—13 T8—**

會 2020 See 会 454

瑟 2020A (SHITSU, SHICHI, koto)
子 Kotoko *f*

禁 2021 [T] (KIN, shime)
秘抄 Kinpishō *lh*
野 Shimeno *s*

楚 2022 Shimoto *m*; Ubara *f.* (SO, SHO, taka)
子 Takako *f*
囚之詩 Soshū no shi *l*
満人 Somahito *ml*; Somando *m*

督 2023 [T] Tadasu *m*, Osamu, Susumu. (TOKU, tada, masa, yoshi, kami, kō, suke)
正 Tadamasa *m*
応 Yoshio *m*
章 Tadaaki *m*

業 2024 [T] Hajime *m.* (GYŌ, GŌ, nari, nobu, nori, oki, kazu, kuni, fusa)
子 Nariko *f*
尹 Naritada *m*
平 Narihira *m*
合 Nariai *s*
苦 Gōku *l*
景 Narikage *m*
繁 Norishige *m*

電 2025 [T] Inazuma *s.* (DEN)

雷 2026 [T] Ikazuchi *sm*; Azuma *m.* (RAI)
太 Raita *m*
太郎強悪 Ikazuchi Tarō gōaku *l*
電 Raiden *la*

雲 2027 [T] (UN, kumo, mo, yuku)
切 Kumokiri *s*
井 Kumoi *s*
井竜雄 K. Tatsuo *mh*
州往来 Unshū ōrai *l*
母 Unmo *l*
母谷 Ubagatani *s*
母集 Kirarashū *l*
谷 Kumodani *s*, Kumoya, Unkoku
出川 Kumodegawa *s*
林院 Unrin'in *sla*; Uriin *s*, Ujii
英 Kira *s*
津 Kumotsu *s*
飛 Unebi *s*
掃 Unara *s*
野 Unno *s*
雀 Hibari *s*
雀山 Hibariyama *la*
梯 Unade *s*

**—13 T9—**

牽 2028 (KEN, toki, toshi, kuru, hiki, hita)

楽 2029 [T] Tanoshi *m*; Raku *s.* (RAKU, GAKU, yoshi, moto, sasa)
水 Motomi *m*
平 Yoshihira *m*
成 Yoshinari *m*
世 Rase *s*, Nara
阿弥 Rakuami *la*
浪 Sasanami *s*, Gakurō
楽前 Sasanokuma *s*
楽熊 Sasanokuma *s*

聖 2030 [T] Satoshi *m*, Satoru, Akira, Takara; Kiyo *f.* (SEI, SHŌ, masa, sato, toshi, kiyo, hijiri)
三稜玻璃 Seisanryō hari *l*
子 Masako *f*
丸 Hijirimaru *mh*
夫 Masao *m*
明王 Seimei-ō *mh*
武 Shōmu *mh*
家族 Seikazoku *l*
勝 Masakatsu *m*
遊廓 Hijiri yūkaku *l*
徳太子 Shōtoku Taishi *mh*
徳太子伝暦 S. T. denryaku *l*
讃 Toshiakira *m*
籠 Seirō *p*

愗 2031 Tsutomu *m.* (BŌ, MO)

愚 2032 [T] (GU)
弟賢兄 Gutei kenkei *l*
問賢註 Gumon kenchū *l*
管抄 Gukanshō *l*

悳 2033 Isao *m*, Shin. (TOKU, nori, shin, yoshi)
吾 Shingo *m*
郎 Tokurō *m*
輝 Noriteru *m*

煦 2034 (KU, aki)

照 2035 [T] Terasu *m*, Terashi, Akira. (SHŌ, teru, akira, teri, aki, ari, toshi, nobu, mitsu)
子 Teruko *f*
千賀 Teruchika *m*
久 Teruhisa *m*
内 Teruuchi *s*
山 Teruyama *s*
井 Terui *s*
男 Teruo *m*
阿 Terukuma *m*
沼 Terunuma *m*
実 Teruzane *m*
映 Teruaki *m*
重 Terushige *m*
屋 Teruya *s*
峰 Terumine *s*
部 Terube *s*
道 Terumichi *m*
葉狂言 Teriha kyōgen *l*
煦 Teruaki *m*
幡 Teruhata *s*
憑 Teruyori *m*

牽楽聖慭愚悳煦照▼奨塣塗勢率準廉遠圓圍園逌遐虚載歯越麁僩僘僮僑僖僐催像猿徳▲喩鳴摘摺慊慬慥愷

—13 T10—

奨 2036 [T] Susumu *m*, Tsutomu. (SHŌ, SŌ)

塣 2037 Tōru *m*. (TEI)

塗 2038 [T] (TO, michi)
師谷 Nushitani ***s***

—13 T11—

勢 2039 [T] (SEI, nari)
田 Seta ***s***
多 Seta ***sp***
似 Sei ***f***
和 Seiwa ***p***
喜門 Sekito ***s***

率 2040 [T] (SOTSU, RITSU, yori, nori, isa)
川 Isakawa ***s***
道 Yorimichi ***m***

準 2041 [T] Hitoshi *m*, Narō. (JUN, SHUN, nori, toshi)
人 Norito ***m***
三郎 Junzaburō ***m***
之助 Junnosuke ***m***
策 Junsaku ***m***

—13 F3—

廉 2042 [T] Kiyoshi *m*, Sunao, Tadashi. (REN, kiyo, yasu, kado, suga, yuki, osa)
之 Kiyoshi ***m***
子 Kiyoko ***f***, Kadoko
次郎 Renjirō ***m***
吉 Renkichi ***m***
助 Rensuke ***m***
香 Kiyoka ***m***
屋 Kadoya ***s***
岡 Kadooka ***s***

遠 2043 [T] Tōshi *m*. (EN, ON, tō)
4山 Tōyama ***s***
井 Tōi ***s***
田 Enda ***s***, Onda ; Tōda ***sp***
矢 Tōya ***s***
6州 Enshū ***ma***
江 Tōtōmi ***ph***; Tōtsuōmi ***s***
地 Onchi ***s***
地輝武 O. Terutake ***ml***
7坂 Tōzaka ***s***
別 Enbetsu ***p***
9城 Onjō ***s***
11淡海 Tōtsuōmi ***s***
渓 Otani ***m***
峰 Tōmine ***s***
野 Tōno ***p***
12賀 Onga ***p***
軽 Engaru ***p***
賀川 Ongagawa ***p***
15敷 On'yū ***sp***
16隣集 Enrinshū ***l***
18藤 Endō ***s***
藤周作 E. Shūsaku ***ml***
藤慎吾 E. Shingo ***ml***

圓 2044 See 円 78

圍 2045 See 囲 501 A

園 2046 [T] Sono *s*. (EN, ON, sono)
人 Sonondo ***m***
三郎 Sonosaburō ***m***
井 Sonoi ***s***
木 Sonoki ***s***
山 Sonoyama ***s***
田 Sonoda ***s***
生 Sonō ***sf***
辺 Sonobe ***s***
池 Sonoike ***s***
池公致 S. Kin'yuki ***ml***
村 Sonomura ***s***
城寺 Onjōji ***p***
面 Sonomo ***m***
部 Sonobe ***sp***

—13 F4—

逌 2047 (TEI, yū)
爾 Yūji ***m***

遐 2048 Haruka *m*. (KA, GE, haru, tō)
子 Haruko ***f***
仁 Tōhito ***m***

—13 F6—

虚 2049 See 虛 1519

載 2050 [T] Koto *f*. (SAI, TAI, koto, nori, toshi)
仁 Kotohito ***m***
吉 Saikichi ***m***

—13 F7—

歯 2051 [T] (SHI, ha, kata, toshi)
朶尾 Shidao ***s***

越 2052 [T] Koshi *s*. (ETSU, OCHI, ECHI, o, koshi, koe)
ケ谷 Koshigaya ***s***
二 Koshiji ***m***
人 Etsujin ***ml***
川 Koshigawa ***s***, Echigawa, Erakawa
中 Etchū ***ph*** ; Koshinaka ***s***
水 Koshimizu ***s***
山 Koshiyama ***s***
石 Koshiishi ***s***, Uchishi
田 Koshida ***s***
生 Ogose ***sp*** ; Koshio ***s***, Koshifu
坂 Osaka ***s***
坂部 Osakabe ***s***
沢 Koshizawa ***s***
村 Koshimura ***s***
谷 Koshigaya ***p***
知 Ochi ***sp***
前 Echizen ***sph***
廼 Koshino ***p***
振 Otsufuru ***s***
後 Echigo ***ph***
後獅子 Echigo-jishi ***a***
後谷 Echigoya ***s***
野 Koshino ***s***
部 Koshibe ***s***
部禅尼 K. no Zenni ***fl***
部禅尼消息 K. no Z. shōsoku ***l***
智 Ochi ***s***, Echi
智越人 O. Etsujin ***ml***
智人 Ochibito ***s***
替 Koshigae ***s***
塚 Koshizuka ***s***, Koezuka
路 Koshiji ***p***

—13 U—

麁 2053 (SO, ara)
子 Arako ***s***
草 Arakusa ***l***
鹿火 Arakabi ***f***
蝦夷 Araemishi ***s***

—14 L2—

僩 2054 Hiroshi *m*, Takeshi, Yutaka. (KAN, KEN, hiro)

僘 2055 Hiroshi *m*. (SHŌ)

僮 2056 Kaburu *sm*. (DŌ)

僑 2957 Takashi *m*. (KYŌ, GYŌ, taka)

僖 2058 (KI, yoshi, yasu)
子 Yoshiko ***f***

僐 2059 (ZEN, SEN, yoshi)
子 Yoshiko ***f***

催 2060 [T] (SAI, SE, toki)
馬楽 Saibara ***l***
馬楽譜入文 S. fuiriaya ***l***

像 2061 [T] (ZŌ, SHŌ, kata, mi, nori, sue)
一 Zōichi ***m***
見 Katami ***m***

—14 L3—

猿 2062 Saru *m*. (EN, ON, saru, mashi, sa)
人 Sarundo ***m***
子 Mashiko ***s***, Masuko
山 Saruyama ***s***, Sayama
田 Saruta ***s***
払 Sarufutsu ***p***
投 Sanage ***p***
尾 Mashio ***s***
来川 Iwagawa ***s***
若 Saruwaka ***sa***
島 Sashima ***sp***
渡 Saruwatari ***s***, Sawatari, Ento
楽 Sarugaku ***la***
蓑 Sarumino ***l***
橋 Saruhashi ***s***

徳 2063 [T] Isao *m*, Atsushi, Megumu, Noboru, Tadashi.

(TOKU, nori, e, yasu, yoshi, toko, tomi, akira, atsu, ari, katsu, sato, nari, naru)
[1]一 Tokuichi *m*
[2]力 Tokuriki *s*
七 Tokushichi *m*
[3]川 Tokugawa *s*
川光圀 T. Mitsukuni *mh*
川吉宗 T. Yoshimune ⌈*mh*
川実紀 T. jikki *h*
川斉昭 T. Nariaki *mh*
川秀忠 T. Hidetada *mh*
川家光 T. Iemitsu *mh*
川家定 T. Iesada *mh*
川家茂 T. Iemochi *mh*
川家斉 T. Ienari *mh*
川家治 T. Ieharu *mh*
川家宣 T. Ienobu *mh*
川家重 T. Ieshige *mh*
川家康 T. Ieyasu *mh*
川家達 T. Iesato *mh*
川家慶 T. Ieyoshi *mh*
川家継 T. Ietsugu *mh*
川家綱 T. Ietsuna *mh*
川義直 T. Yoshinao *mh*
川慶喜 T. Yoshinobu/⌈Keiki *mh*
川頼房 T. Yorifusa *mh*
川頼宣 T. Yorinobu ⌈*mh*
川綱吉 T. Tsunayoshi *mh*
三 Tokuzō *m*
三郎 Tokusaburō *m*
大寺 Tokudaiji *s*
久 Tokuhisa *sm*
丸 Tokumaru *s*
之助 Tokunosuke *m*
之島 Tokunoshima *p*
子 Tokuko *f*
[4]山 Tokuyama *sp*
井 Tokui *s*
五郎 Tokugorō *m*
太古 Tokotako *m*
太郎 Tokutarō *m*
太理 Tokutari *m*
[5]永 Tokunaga *sm*
永直 T. Sunao *ml*
司 Tokushi *m*
本 Tokumoto *s*
包 Norikane *m*
田 Tokuda *s*
田秋声 T. Shūsei *ml*
田球一 T. Kyūichi *mh*
[6]次 Tokuji *m*, Noritsugu
次郎 Tokujirō *m*
地 Tokuji *p*
江 Tokue *s*
竹 Tokutake *s*
全 Norimasa *m*
光 Tokumitsu *s*
[7]仰 Noritaka *m*
沢 Tokusawa *s*
弘 Tokuhiro *sm*
村 Tokumura *s*
至 Yasuyuki *m*
見 Tokumi *s*
出 Tokude *s*
寿 Tokuju *m*
[8]和歌後万載集 Tokuwaka gomanzaishū *l*
若 Tokuwaka *s*
武 Tokutake *s*
[9]治 Tokuji 1306–08
治郎 Tokujirō *m*
松 Tokumatsu *m*
政 Tokumasa *s*
岡 Tokuoka *s*
重 Tokushige *s*
[10]海 Noriumi *m*
真 Norizane *m*
原 Tokuhara *s*
[11]野 Tokuno *s*
能 Tokunō *s*
宿 Tokushuku *s*
留 Tokutome *s*
島 Tokushima *sp*
[12]晴 Yoshiharu *m*
富 Tokutomi *s*
富蘇峰 T. Sohō *ml*
富蘆花 T. Roka *ml*
間 Tokuma *s*
[13]植 Tokuue *s*
楽 Tokura *s*
業 Norinari *m*
[14]増 Tokumasu *s*
[15]蔵 Tokuzō *m*

喩 2064 (YU, aki)
義 Akiyoshi *m*

鳴 2065 [T] (MEI, naki, nari, naru)
子 Naruko *p*
女 Nakime *f*
沢 Narusawa *p*
見 Narumi *s*
門 Naruto *sp*
門秘帖 N. hichō *l*
神 Narukami *la*
海 Narumi *s*
海仙吉 N. Senkichi *l*
海要吉 N. Yōkichi *ml*
雪 Meisetsu *ml*
島 Narushima *s*
瀬 Naruse *sp*

摘 2066 [T] (TEKI, tsumi)

摺 2067 (SHŌ, suri, su)
沢 Surizawa *s*
宜 Suge *s*

慊 2068 (KEN, mitsu, yasu)

慬 2069 (KIN, GON, nori)

慥 2070 Makoto *m*, Tashika. (SŌ, sada)

愷 2071 Yasushi *m*, Yutaka. (GAI, yasu, yoshi, hide, sue)
子 Yasuko *f*, Yoshiko
介 Hidesuke *m*
夫 Yasuo *m*

隑 2072 (GAI, yasu)
夫 Yasuo *m*

際 2073 [T] (SAI, SEI, kiwa)
子 Kiwako *f*

隠 2074 [T] Nabari *s*. (IN, ON, yasu, ⌊kage)
元 Ingen *mh*
地 Ochi *p*
岐 Oki *sph*
居 Kagei *s*
曾 Ozo *s*

塡 2075 Mitsu *f*. (TEN, sada, mitsu, masa)

境 2076 [T] Sakai *sm-p*; Sakae *p*. (KYŌ, KEI, sakai)
川 Sakaigawa *p*
長 Sakai *s*
野 Sakaino *s*
部 Sakaibe *s*
港 Sakaiminato *p*

増 2077 [T] (ZŌ, masu, mashi, ma, naga)
[3]川 Masukawa *s*
子 Masuko *sf*; Mashiko *s*
[4]山 Masuyama *s*
井 Masui *s*
毛 Mashike *p*
[5]永 Masunaga *s*
田 Masuda *sp*
田八風 M. Happū *ml*
本 Masumoto *s*
[6]次郎 Masujirō *m*
式 Masutsune *m*
[7]沢 Masuzawa *s*
村 Masumura *s*
尾 Masuo *s*
見 Masumi *s*
[8]阿弥 Zōami *ma*
[9]岡 Masuoka *s*
重 Masushige *m*
[11]野 Masuno *s*, Mashino, Koshino
基 Zōki *ml*
島 Masujima *s*
[12]喜 Masuki *s*
淵 Masubuchi *s*
勤 Masutoshi *m*
業 Masunari *m*
[15]穂 Masuho *sp*; Masuo *s*
蔵 Masuzō *m*
[18]燿 Masuteru *m*
[19]鏡 Masu kagami *l*

漢 2078 See 漢 1860

漥 2078A See 窪 2203

演 2079 [T] Hiroshi *m*. (EN, nobu, hiro)

滲 2080 Kiyoshi *m*. (RYŌ)

漸 2081 Susumu *m*, Susumi. (ZEN, tsugu)

漢 漥 演 滲 漸 ▼ 漣 漂 漱 漾 漁 漆 燁 媼 腰 曄 弼 旗 瑞 嵯 槭 椹 楷 様 槍 榲 槌 樺 模 榑 榊 榎 榛 颯 晙 暢 郷 頌 頔 頓 ▲ 碩 禎 福 祿 禔

**漣** 2082 (REN, nami)

**漂** 2083 [T] (HYŌ)
民宇三郎 Hyōmin Usaburō *l*

**漱** 2084 (SŌ)
石 Sōseki *ml*

**漾** 2085 (YŌ, nami)
子 Namiko *f*

**漁** 2086 [T] (GYO, RYŌ, suna, fuki)
田 Sunada *s*, Fukita

**漆** 2087 Urushi *s*, Nuri. (SHITSU, urushi, nuri, uru)
戸 Urushido *s*
山 Urishiyama *s*
畑 Urushibata *s*
原 Urushibara *s*
馬 Urushima *s*
部 Urushibe *s*, Nuribe, Nurube
島 Nurishima *s*
崎 Urushizaki *s*
葉 Uruha *s*
間 Uruma *s*, Urushima

——14 L4——

**燁** 2088 (YŌ, teru)
子 Teruko *f*

**媼** 2089 (Ō, UN, ON, baba)

**腰** 2090 [T] (YŌ, koshi)
川 Koshigawa *s*
祈 Koshiinori *l*
高 Koshitaka *s*
原 Koshihara *s*
塚 Koshizuka *s*
越 Koshigoe *s*

**曄** 2091 Akira *m*. (YŌ, aki, teru, akira)
子 Teruko *f*
道 Terumichi *s*

**弼** 2092 Tasuku *m*, Takashi, Tadashi. (HITSU, suke, nori, tane)
一 Sukeichi *m*
成 Sukenari *m*
基 Tanemoto *m*

**旗** 2093 [T] (KI, GI, hata, taka)
子 Hatako *f*
江 Hatae *f*
野 Hatano *s*
魚 Kigyo *l*

**瑞** 2094 [N] Tama *f*. (ZUI, SUI, tama, mizu)
夫 Tamao *m*, Mizuo
西 Suisu *p* "Switzerland"
枝 Mizue *f*
典 Suēden *p* "Sweden"
笑 Zuishō *ml*
浪 Mizunami *p*
渓周鳳 Zuikei Shūhō *mh*
穂 Mizuho *p*
樹 Tamaki *m*

**嵯** 2095 (SA)
峨 Saga *sp*
の屋御室 Saganoya Omuro *ml*

**槭** 2096 (I, hi)
田 Hida *s*

**椹** 2097 Sawaragi *s*, Magusa, Mizuki. (JIN, fushi)

**楷** 2098 (KAI, nori)
子 Noriko *f*

**様** 2099 [T] (YŌ, sama)
似 Samani *p*

**槍** 2100 (SŌ, SHŌ, hoko, utsu)
田 Utsuda *s*

**榲** 2101 (ON, OTSU, sugi)
子 Sugiko *f*
谷 Tsuchiya *s*
邨 Sugimura *m*

**槌** 2102 (TSUI, TAI, tsuchi)
五郎 Tsuchigorō *m*
田 Tsuchida *s*

**樺** 2103 (KA, kaba, kara)
山 Kabayama *s*
太 Karafuto *p*
沢 Kabasawa *s*
島 Kabashima *s*

**模** 2104 [T] (BO, MO, nori)
一 Norikazu *m*
子 Noriko *f*
作 Katahitsukuri *s*

**榑** 2105 Kure *s*. (FU, kure)
子 Kureko *f*
山 Kureyama *s*
林 Kurebayashi *s*
松 Kurematsu *s*
族部 Haarabe *s*

**榊** 2106 Sakaki *sm*. (sakaki)
山 Sakakiyama *s*
山潤 S. Jun *ml*
田 Sakakida *s*
谷 Sakakiya *s*
原 Sakakibara *s*
原美文 S. Yoshinobu *ml*

**榎** 2107 Enoki *s*. (KA, KE, e, enoki)
下 Enoshita *s*
土 Edo *s*
戸 Enokido *s*
木 Enoki *s*
田 Enokida *s*, Eda
本 Enomoto *s*
本武揚 E. Takeaki *mh*
波 Enami *s*
並 Enami *s*
並屋 Enamiya *s*
津 Inatsu *s*

**榛** 2108 (SHIN, JIN, hari, haru, hai, han)
名 Haruna *m-p*
沢 Hanzawa *s*
谷 Hangaya *s*, Hangae, Kangaya
東 Shintō *p*
松 Haimatsu *s*
原 Haibara *sp*; Hanbara
葉 Shinba *s*, Shin'yō, Shiba, Han'yō
葉英治 Shinba Eiji *ml*

——14 L5——

**颯** 2109 (SATSU)
波 Sappa *s*, Sawa

**晙** 2110 Taosa *m*. (SHUN)

**暢** 2111 [N] Noburu *m*, Itaru, Tōru, Mitsuru. (CHŌ, nobu, naga, masa, mitsu)
夫 Nobuo *m*
気眼鏡 Nonki megane *l*
籌 Nobukazu *m*

**郷** 2112 [T] Gō *s*; Akira *m*. (GŌ, KYŌ, sato, aki, akira, nori)
ノ浦 Gōnoura *p*
太郎 Gōtarō *m*
古 Gōko *s*
司 Gōshi *s*; Satoshi *m*
四 Satoshi *m*
田 Gōda *s*
甫 Gōho *m*
原 Gōhara *s*
野 Gōno *s*
間 Gōma *s*

**頌** 2113 (SHŌ, JU, tsugu, nobu, uta, oto, yomu)

**頔** 2114 (TEKI, yoshi)
雄 Yoshio *m*

**頓** 2115 (TON, haya)
所 Tonjo *s*
田 Tomita *s*
阿 Ton'a *ml*

宮 Tongu *s*, Hayami, Hamiya
原 Tonbara *p*

碩 2116 Mitsuru *m*, Yutaka. (SEKI, JAKU, hiro, michi, ō)
人 Ōto *m*
六 Sekiroku *m*
文 Hirofumi *m*
彦 Michihiko *m*
哉 Hiroya *m*

禎 2117 See 禎 1887

福 2118 See 福 1888

祿 2119 See 禄 1589

禔 2120 (SHI, TEI, DAI, yoshi, kore)

稱 2121 See 称 1118

稙 2122 (SHOKU, JIKI, tane, nara)
通 Tanemichi *m*

稗 2123 (HAI, hie, nen, suke)
子伝 Haishiden *l*
方 Hikata *s*
田 Hieda *s*
田阿礼 H. no Are *ml*
貫 Hienuki *p*

種 2124 [T] (SHU, SHŌ, tane, shige, kazu, fusa, kusa, osa)
一郎 Shuichirō *m*
子 Taneko *f*
子島 Tanegashima *sph*
子島時堯 T. Tokitaka
山 Taneyama *s* ⌊*mh*
市 Taneichi *p*
田 Taneda *s*, Oita
田山頭火 T. Santōka
任 Tanetada *m* ⌊*ml*
行 Taneyuki *s*
村 Tanemura *s*, Tanamura
材 Taneki *m*
実 Tanezane *m*
英 Tanehide *m*
治郎 Tanejirō *m*
美 Taneyoshi *m*
彦 Tanehiko *ml*
殷 Tanetomi *m*
森 Tanemori *s*
樹 Shigeki *m*, Tanetatsu
憲 Tanekazu *m*

稲 2125 [T] (TŌ, ina, ine, ne, shine)
[2]人 Inato *m*
[3]川 Inakawa *s*
子 Ineko *f*
[4]山 Inayama *s*
戸 Inato *s*
井 Inai *sp*
木 Inaki *s*
毛 Inage *s*
毛詛風 I. Sofū *ml*
[5]布 Inashiki *m*
田 Inada *s*
目 Iname *m*
用 Inamochi *m*
本 Inamoto *s*
生 Inō *s*, Inafu
生若水 Inō Jakusui *mh*
石 Inaishi *s*
辺 Inabe *s*
[6]次 Inatsugi *s*
羽忍海 Inabanooshinumi *s*
吉 Inayoshi *s*
舟 Inafune *f*
[7]沢 Inazawa *sp*
村 Inamura *s* ⌈*mlh*
村三伯 I. Sanpaku
足 Inetari *m*, Inatari
見 Inami *s*
[8]枝 Inae *p*
延 Inanobe *s*
武 Inabu *p*
[9]津 Inatsu *s*, Inazu
城 Inagi *sp*
垣 Inagaki *sp*
垣足穂 I. Taruho *ml*
垣達郎 I. Tatsurō *ml*
畑 Inabata *s*
美 Inami *p*
香 Inaka *m*
岡 Inaoka *s*
[10]原 Inahara *s*
庭 Inaniwa *p*
庭川連 I. Kawatsura *p*
造 Inazō *m*
荷 Inari *sfh*
[11]掛 Inakake *s*
野 Inano *s*
野辺 Inanobe *s*
野屋 Inenoya *s*
留 Inatome *s*
島 Inajima *s*
[12]場 Inaba *s*
崎 Inazaki *s*
富 Inatomi *s*
森 Inamori *s*
筑 Inatsuki *p*
[13]植 Inaue *s*
葉 Inaba *sm-p*
[14]増 Inamasu *s*
置 Inagi *sm*; Ishiki *s*
[15]敷 Inashiki *p*
熱病 Imochi *l*
熊 Inaguma *s*
[16]橋 Inahashi *s*

## 14 L6

號 2126 See 号 272

雑 2127 [T] Kusa *s*. (ZATSU, ZŌ, SŌ, kazu, tomo, kusa)
古 Sako *s*
田 Kusata *s*
供 Zakku *s*, Zakkube
岸 Saiga *s*
賀 Saiga *s*
楽 Shidara *s*
誹 Zappai *l*
談集 Zōdanshū *l*

蜻 2128 (SEI)
蛉 Kagerō *l*

蜷 2129 (KEN, GEN, nina, mina)
川 Ninagawa *s*

粹 2130 See 粋 1132

精 2131 [T] Sei *m*, Kiyoshi, Tadashi, Makoto, Masashi, Akira, Suguru, Kuwashi, Hitoshi, Tsutomu. (SEI, SHŌ, kiyo, aki, yoshi, tada, shige, sumi, akira, shira, mori)
一 Seiichi *m*
一郎 Seiichirō *m*
八郎 Seihachirō *m*
七郎 Seishichirō *m*
三 Seizō *m*
之 Akiyuki *m*
夫 Tadao *m*
太郎 Seitarō *m*
古 Akihisa *m*
吉 Seikichi *m*
孝 Kiyotaka *m*
彦 Kiyohiko *m*
華 Yoshiharu *m*; Seika *p* ⌈*l*
進魚類 Shōjin gyorui

## 14 L7

踊 2132 [T] Odori *s*. (YŌ, YU)

輔 2133 [N] Tasuku *m*, Tasuke. (HO, FU, suke)
子 Sukeko *f*
臣 Sukeomi *m*
治野 Fujino *s*

茲 2134 (JI, KEN, GEN, kore)
岡 Koreoka *s*
矩 Korenori *m*
原 Korehara *s*
都歌 Shizu-uta *l*
監 Korekane *m*

該 2135 [T] (GAI, kane, kata, mori, kanu)

語 2136 [T] Katari *s*, Katarai. (GO, tsugu, koto, katari, kata)

認 2137 [T] (NIN, moro)

誦 2138 (SHŌ, JU, sumi)

誡 2139 (KAI, E, masa)

誥 2140 (KŌ, KOKU, nori, tsugu)

誌 2141 [T] (SHI)
村 Shimura *s*

榎 榛 颯 暎 暢 郷 頌 頔 頓 ▼ 碩 禎 福 祿 禔 稱 稙 稗 種 稲 號 雑 蜻 蜷 粹 精 踊 輔 茲 該 語 認 誦 誡 誥 誌 ▲ 読 説 肆 静 絙 絖 絶 給 絢

玆 該 語 認 誦 誠 誥 誌 ▼ 読 説 肆 静 絚 絖 絶 給 絢 結 鉽 鉱 銚 銘 銓 鉞 銑 銅 銭 甄 輌 韶 飾 飽 戡 [illegible] 穀 数 歌 ▲ 駁 駅 鄙 彰 亂 裏 豪 參

読 2142 [T] (DOKU, TOKU, yomi, oto, yoshi)
人不知 Yomibito shirazu *l*
子 Yomiko *f*
本 Yomihon *l*

説 2143 [T] (SETSU, SECHI, ZEI, toki, koto, kane, nobu, hisa, tsugu, aki, kanu, toku)
子 Setsuko *f*
太郎 Tokitarō *m*
田 Tokida *s*, Setsuda
光 Kotomitsu *m*
成 Kanenari *m*
男 Nobuo *m*
実 Tokizane *m*
望 Kanemochi *m*

—14 L8—

肆 2144 (SHI, SHITSU, tada, chika, naga, yotsu)
矢 Yotsuya *s*

静 2145 [T] Shizuka *m-f*; Yasushi *m*; Shizu *f*. (SEI, JŌ, shizu, yasu, kiyo, yoshi, hide, tsugu, chika)
[1]一 Seiichi *m*
[3]子 Shizuko *f*
也 Shizuya *m*
[4]戸 Shizurie *s*
六 Jōroku *m*
内 Shizunai *p*
夫 Shizuo *m*
太郎 Seitarō *m*
[5]田 Shizuta *s*
平 Yoshihira *m*
[7]弘 Yasuhiro *m*
吾 Seigo *m*
[8]枝 Shizue *f*
英 Shizuhide *m*
[9]治 Seiji *m*
治男 Shizuo *m*
香 Shizuka *f*
岡 Shizuoka *p*
妻 Shizuma *s*
[10]修 Shizusane *m*, Kiyoyasu
宮 Seimiya *s*, Seiya
家 Shizuo *m*
馬 Shizume *m*
[12]間 Shizuma *s*
[13]雄 Shizuo *m*
[14]嘉 Yasuyoshi *m*
衡 Hidechika *m*
緒 Shizuo *f*

絚 2146 (KŌ, hae)

絖 2147 (KŌ, nume)
子 Numeko *f*

絶 2148 [T] (ZETSU, tau, tae)
海中津 Zekkai Chūshin *ml*

給 2149 [T] (KYŪ, tari, haru)
黎 Kiire *s*

絢 2150 (JUN, SHUN, aya)
子 Ayako *f*
彦 Ayahiko *m*

結 2151 [T] Hitoshi *m*. (KETSU, KECHI, yui, kata)
子 Yuiko *f*
知 Ketchi *s*
城 Yūki *sp*
城哀草果 Y. Aisōka *ml*
城健三 Y. Kenzō *ml*
城素明 Y. Somei *ma*
崎 Yūsaki *s*
解 Ketsuge *s*

鉽 2152 Kanae *m*. (SHIKI)

鉱 2153 [T] (KŌ, KYŌ, kane)
三郎 Kanesaburō *m*

銚 2154 (CHŌ)
子 Chōshi *p*

銘 2155 [T] (MEI, BEI, aki, kata, na)
長 Akinaga *m*

銓 2156 (SEN, nori)
総 Norifusa *m*

鉞 2157 (ETSU, OCHI, ono)
太郎 Etsutarō *m*
次郎 Onojirō *m*

銑 2158 [T] (SEN, sane)
十郎 Senjūrō *m*
三郎 Senzaburō *m*

銅 2159 [T] (DŌ, kane)
工 Tanuchi *s*
吉 Dōkichi *m*
直 Tobeta *s*
鑼 Dora *l*

銭 2160 [T] (SEN, zeni)
形 Zenigata *s*
形平次捕物控 Z. Heiji torimono hikae *l*
谷 Sen'ya *s*
屋 Zeniya *s*
亀沢 Zenikamezawa *p*
湯新話 Sentō shinwa *l*

—14 L9—

甄 2161 (KEN, aki)

輌 2162 (tomo)
子 Tomoko *f*
音 Tomoto *m*
掛 Tomokake *s*
絵 Tomoe *f*

韶 2163 Akira *m*. (SHŌ, JŌ, aki, tsugu, yoshi, teru, masa, tsuna, miharu, oto)
子 Akiko *f*, Tsuguko, Miharuko
仁 Tsunahito *m*
夫 Yoshio *m*
光 Akimitsu *m*

飾 2164 [T] Akira *m*. (SHOKU, SHIKI, yoshi)
磨 Shikama *p*

飽 2165 [T] Akira *m*. (HŌ, HYŌ, aki, aku)
田 Akita *p*
田女 Akutame *f*
託 Hōtaku *p*
浦 Akura *s*
海 Akumi *sp*
庭 Aiba *s*
間 Akuma *s*, Nukima

—14 L10—

戡 2166 (KAN, katsu)

[illegible] 2167 Takashi *m*. (SHŌ, taka)
子 Takako *f*

穀 2168 [T] Minoru *m*. (KOKU, yoshi, yori, kura)
谷 Kuratani *s*
定 Yoshisada *m*
美 Yoshimi *m*

数 2169 [T] (SŪ, SHU, SU, kazu, ya, nori, hira)
子 Kazuko *f*
千木 Yachiki *m*
太 Kazuta *m*
井 Kazui *s*
江 Kazue *s*
見 Kazumi *s*
奇伝 Sakkiden *l*
直 Kazunao *m*
原 Suwara *s*
珠屋 Juzuya *s*
馬 Kazuma *m*
馬助 Kazumanosuke *m*
野 Kazuno *s*
寄屋造 Sukiya-zukuri *a*
衞 Kazue *m*
藤 Sudō *s*
藤五城 S. Gojō *ml*

歌 2170 [T] (KA, uta)
[3]川 Utagawa *s*
川豊国 U. Toyokuni *ma*
子 Utako *f*
[5]代 Utashiro *s*
田 Utada *s*
占 Utaura *la*
[6]仙 Kasen *ml-fl*
行燈 Uta andon *l*
合 Utaawase *l*
合類聚 U. ruijū *l*
吉 Utakichi *m*
[7]沢 Utazawa *sl*
会 Utakai *l*

志内 Utashinai *p*
返 Utagaeshi *l*
8枕 Utamakura *l*; Katsuragi *s*
林樸樕 Karin bokusoku *l*
9津 Utatsu *p*
10病 Kahei *l*
11祭文 Utazaimon *l*
12登 Utanobori *p*
道小見 Kadō shōken *l*
13経標式 Kakyō hyōshiki *l*
意考 Kaikō *l*
15舞伎 Kabuki *la*
舞伎十八番 K. jūhachiban *la*
舞髄脳記 Kabu zuinōki *l*
18麿 Utamaro *ma*

騣 2171 (sō, toshi)
栄 Toshiyoshi *m*

駅 2172 [T] (EKI)
川 Ekisen *p*
家 Ekiya *p*

——14 L11——

鄙 2173 (HI, hina)
唄 Hinauta *m*

彰 2174 [T] Akira *m.* (SHŌ, SŌ, aki, akira, tada, teru)
子 Akiko *f*
仁 Akihito *m*
祐 Shōsuke *m*
逸 Akihaya *m*
義 Akiyoshi *m*

——14 L13——

亂 2175 See 乱 437

——14 T2——

裏 2176 [T] Ura *m.* (RI, ura)
辻 Uratsuji *s*
松 Uramatsu *s*
襟 Uraeri *m*

豪 2177 [T] Takeshi *m*, Toshi, Tsuyoshi. (GŌ, KŌ, toshi, hide, take, tsuyo, kata, katsu)
夫 Hideo *m*
雄 Tsuyoo *m*

——14 T3——

參 2178 See 参 978

鳶 2179 (EN, tobi)
沢 Tobizawa *m*

察 2180 [T] Akira *m.* (SATSU, SECHI, aki, miru, mi)

寧 2181 [T] Yasushi *m.* (NEI, yasu, shizu, sada)
子 Yasuko *f*
雄 Shizuo *m*
親 Yasuchika *m*

壽 2182 See 寿 539

壺 2183 (KO, KU, tsubo)
内 Tsubouchi *s*
井 Tsuboi *s*
井栄 T. Sakae *fl*
井繁治 T. Shigeji *ml*
田 Tsubota *s*
田花子 T. Hanako *fl*

嘉 2184 [N] Yoshimi *m.* (KA, KE, yoshi, hiro)
1一 Kaichi *m*
一郎 Kaichirō *m*
2十 Kajū *m*
3子 Yoshiko *f*
4元 Kagen 1303–06
六 Karoku *m*
山 Kayama *s*
5代 Kashiro *s*
永 Kaei 1848–54
右衛門 Kaemon *m*
市 Kaichi *m*
平 Kahei *m*
平治 Kaheiji *m*
6次郎 Kajirō *m*
吉 Kakitsu 1441–44; Kakichi *m*
7作 Kasaku *m*
村 Kamura *s*
村磯多 K. Isota *ml*
兵衛 Kahee *m*
応 Kaō 1169–71
寿 Kazu *m*
8明 Yoshiaki *m*
芽市 Kameichi *m*
幸 Yoshiyuki *m*
承 Kajō 1106–08
9保 Kahō 1094–96
昼 Yoshihiru *m*
10悦 Kaetsu *s*, Kan'itsu, Kaya
祥 Kashō 848–51
真 Yoshimasa *m*
造 Kazō *m*
11基 Yoshimoto *m*
島 Kashima *p*
隆 Yoshitaka *m*
12陽 Kaya *s*
禄 Karoku 1225–27
納 Kanō *s*
納治五郎 K. Jigorō *mh*
道 Yoshimichi *m*
13猷 Yoshinori *m*
禎 Katei 1235–38
14徳 Yoshinori *m*
瑞 Yoshimizu *m*
暦 Karyaku 1326–29
15穂 Kaho *p*
慶 Kakyō 1387–89
16衡 Yoshihira *m*
樹 Yoshiki *m*
18顕 Yoshiaki *m*
藤 Katō *s*
藤次 Katōji *m*
19瀬 Kase *s*
20織 Kaori *m*

蔟 2185 Atsumu *m.* (SOKU)

蔀 2186 Shitomi *sm.* (BU, HO)

蓴 2187 Nunawa *m.* (SHUN, JUN)

蔔 2188 Ōne *s.* (HOKU)

蓊 2189 Shigeru *m*, Shigeki, Sakae. (Ō, U, shige)

暮 2190 [T] (BO, kure)
田 Kureta *s*
地 Kurechi *s*
笛集 Botekishū *l*

蔚 2191 Shigeru *m.* (I, UTSU, UCHI, shige, masa, mochi)
彦 Shigehiko *m*

蔓 2192 (MAN, BAN, tsuru)
子 Tsuruko *f*

蓋 2193 Kinugasa *s.* (GAI, futa, kasa)
山 Mikasayama *s*
縫 Kasanui *s*

蓑 2194 Mino *s.* (SA, mino)
夫 Minoo *m*
田 Minota *s*
助 Minosuke *m*
和 Minowa *s*
輪 Minowa *s*
麿 Minomaro *m*, Minomaru

蓬 2195 (HŌ, yomogi)
田 Yomogita *p*
生 Yomogifu *l*
伍 Hōitsu *m*
莱 Hōrai *lp*
莱曲 H. no kyoku *l*

蔦 2196 [N] Tsuta *s.* (CHŌ, tsuta, tatsu)
子 Tatsuko *f*
夫 Tatsuo *m*
木 Tsutaki *s*
本 Tsutamoto *s*
沢 Tsutazawa *s*
松 Tsutamatsu *m*
屋 Tsutaya *s*
紅葉宇都谷峠 Tsuta momiji Utsunoya tōge *la*

蓮 2197 (REN, hasu, hachisu)
の露 Hachisu no tsuyu *l*
井 Hasui *s*
田 Hasuda *sp*
田善明 H. Zenmei *ml*
池 Hasuike *s*
光 Hasumitsu *m*
如 Rennyo *mh*

蔓 蓋 蓑 蓬 蔦 蓮 ▼ 嵗 睿 彙 盡 棄 窪 翠 農 鼻 嵩 絜 紫 箙 箣 管 算 箕 節 箇 裔 誓 榮 需 聚 肇 甃 竪 碧 暋 惡 慤 愿 蓼 ▲ 墨 與 置 鳳 厲 曆

見 Hasumi *s*
阿弥 Ren'ami *ma*
沼 Hasunuma *sp*
葉 Hachisuba *s*

**——14 T4——**

嵗 2198 Takashi *m.* (AI, WAI, E)

睿 2199 See 叡 2555

彙 2200 (I, shige)
逦 Shigechika *m*

**——14 T5——**

盡 2201 See 尽 290

棄 2202 [T] (KI, sute)
子 Suteko *f*

窪 2203 Kubo *s.* (A, kubo)
川 Kubokawa *sp*
川鶴次郎 K. Tsurujirō *ml*
山 Kuboyama *s*
井 Kuboi *s*
田 Kubota *s*
田空穂 K. Utsubo *ml*
田章一郎 K. Shōichirō *ml*
谷 Kuboya *s*
寺 Kubodera *s*
津 Kubotsu *s*
島 Kuboshima *s*

**——14 T6——**

翠 2204 Midori *sm-f*; Misu *s*; Akira *m.* (SUI, aki)
川 Midorigawa *s*
静 Akiyoshi *m*

農 2205 [T] (NŌ, atsu, tami, toki, taka, toyo, naru)
人 Atsuto *m*
雄 Tokio *m*

鼻 2206 [T] (BI, hana)
山人 Bisanjin *ml*
金剛 Hanakongō *ma*
豊後 Hanabungo *ml*

嵩 2207 Takashi *m*; Take *s*, Dake. (SŪ, SHŪ, taka, take)
山 Suseyama *s*
年 Takatoshi *m*

絜 2208 (KETSU, KECHI, kiyo, toyo)
行 Kiyoyuki *m*

紫 2209 [T] Murasaki *f.* (SHI, murasaki, mura)
子 Murako *f*
文要領 Shibun yōryō *l*
合 Yūda *s*
安 Murayasu *s*
式部 Murasaki Shikibu *fl*
式部家集 M.S. kashū *l*
波 Shiwa *p*
垣 Shigaki *s*
苑 Shion *l*
原 Murasakibara *s*
桃 Shitō *s*
野 Murasakino *s*
雲寺 Shiunji *p*
関 Shiseki *s*
藤 Shitō *s*
羅欄花 Araseitō *l*

箙 2210 Ebira *la.* (FUKU)

箣 2211 See 策 1767

管 2212 [T] Kan *s.* (KAN, suge, uchi)
恒 Sugetsune *m*
野 Kanno *s*

算 2213 [T] (SAN, kazu, tomo)
文 Kazufumi *m*
馬 Kazuma *m*
衛 Kazue *m*

箕 2214 (KI, mi, miru, mino)
川 Minokawa *s*
田 Mita *s*, Minota
勾 Minowa *s*
曲 Minoo *s*, Minowa
作 Mizukuri *s*
作麟祥 M. Rinshō *mh*
沢 Misawa *f*
尾 Minoo *s*
面 Minoo *sp*; Minomo *s*
浦 Minoura *s*
原 Minohara *s*
島 Minoshima *s*
郷 Minosato *p*
輪 Minowa *sp*

節 2215 [T] Setsu *m*, Takashi, Makoto, Misao. (SETSU, toki, yo, yoshi, sada, nori, o, fu, taka, take, fushi, hodo, misa, mine, tomo, moto)
子 Setsuko *f*, Sadako
分 Setsubun *la*
成 Tokinari *m*
男 Misao *m*, Hodoo
治 Setsuji *m*
美 Sadami *f*
美子 Fumiko *f*
用集 Setsuyōshū *l*
雄 Yoshio *m*, Norio
義 Noriyoshi *m*
蔵 Setsuzō *m*
繁 Takashige *m*

箇 2216 [O] (KO, KA, kazu, tomo)

**——14 T7——**

裔 2217 (EI, sue)
生 Sueo *m*

誓 2218 [T] Chikō *m.* (SEI, ZEI, chika)
夫 Chikao *m*
堂 Chikataka *m*
願寺 Seiganji *p–la*

**——14 T8——**

榮 2219 See 栄 969

需 2220 [T] Motome *m*; Machi *f.* (JU, mitsu, moto)

聚 2221 (SHŪ, JU, SHU, atsu, tsumu)
岩 Atsutaka *m*

肇 2222 [N] Hajime *m*, Hajimu, Tadashi. (CHŌ, hatsu, koto, tada)
子 Hatsuko *f*
四 Chōyo *m*
蔚 Tadamasa *m*

**——14 T9——**

甃 2223 (SHŪ, ishi)
の上 Ishi no ue *l*

竪 2224 Chiisago *s.* (JU, SHU, tate, tatsu, nao)
川 Tategawa *s*
山 Tateyama *s*
野 Tateno *s*
興 Tatsuoki *m*

碧 2225 Midori *m-f*; Kiyoshi *m*; Heki *l.* (HEKI, HYAKU, ao, tama)
川 Midorigawa *s*
玉集 Hekigyokushū *l*
南 Hekinan *p*
海 Aomi *m*; Hekikai *p*
梧桐 Hekigotō *ml*

**——14 T10——**

暋 2226 Tsutomu *m.* (MIN, BIN)

惡 2227 See 悪 1483 A

慤 2227A See 慤 2403

愿 2228 Sunao *m*, Makoto. (GEN, GAN, yoshi, nao)
一 Gen'ichi *m*
子 Naoko *f*
江 Yoshie *f*
治 Genji *m*
徳 Yoshinori *m*

**——14 T11——**

蓼 2229 Tade *s.* (RYŌ, RYŪ, tade)
太 Ryōta *m*
汀 Ryōtei *m*
沼 Tadenuma *s*

墨 2230 [T] Sumi *s.* (BOKU, MOKU, sumi)
之助 Suminosuke *m*
水十二夜 Bokusui jūniya *l*
汁一滴 Bokujū itteki *l*
田 Sumida *p*
江 Sumie *s*, Suminoe
俣 Sunomata *sp*
染桜 Sumizome-zakura *la*
塗 Suminuri *l*
塗女 S. onna *la*

—— 14 T12 ——

與 2231 See 与 101

—— 14 F2 ——

置 2232 [T] (CHI, oki, yasu, ki)
戸 Oketo *p*
始 Okisome *s*
塩 Ojio *s*
賜 Ototashi *s*

鳳 2233 Hō *s.* (HŌ, BU, taka)
平 Hōhei *m*
至 Fukeshi *sp*
来 Hōrai *p*

厲 2234 Takashi *m.* (REI, RAI)

暦 2235 [T] (RYAKU, REKI, toshi)
仁 Ryakunin 1238–39
応 Ryakuō 1338–42

—— 14 F3 ——

圖 2236 See 図 502

團 2237 See 団 310

匱 2238 Kanae *m.* (YOKU)

廓 2239 Akira *m.* (KAKU, hiro, akira)
髄 Hironaka *m*

適 2240 [T] Kanō *m.* (TEKI, masa, yuku, atsu)
子 Yukuko *f*
永 Masanaga *m*

—— 14 F4 ——

遣 2241 [T] (KEN)
唐船 Kentōsen *l*

—— 14 F6 ——

虞 2242 [O] Kari *s.* (GU, yasu, kari, suke, mochi)
人 Karihito *s*
臣 Yasuomi *m*

—— 14 F7 ——

趙 2243 Chō *s.* (CHŌ)

—— 14 F8 ——

聞 2244 [T] (BUN, MON, hiro)

関 2245 [T] Seki *sp*; Tōru *m.* (KAN, KEN, seki, mori, mi)
ケ原 Sekigahara *p*
2八州繋馬 Kanhasshū tsunagiuma *la*
3川 Sekikawa *sp*
口 Sekiguchi *s*
口次郎 S. Jirō *ml*
4戸 Sekido *s*
山 Sekiyama *s*
内 Sekiuchi *s*
水 Sekimizu *s*
中 Sekinaka *s*
5矢 Sekiya *s*
白 Kanpaku *h*
本 Sekimoto *s*
目 Sekime *s*
田 Sekida *s*
四郎 Sekishirō *m*
6江 Sekie *s*
羽 Kan-U *mh-l* "Kuan Yü"
寺 Sekidera *sp*
寺小町 S. Komachi *la*
西 Kansai *p*
7沢 Sekizawa *s*
村 Sekimura *s*
谷 Sekiya *s* ⌈*mh*
谷清景 S. Kiyokage
尾 Sekio *s*
孝和 Seki Takakazu
8和 Sekiwa *s* ⌊*mh*
取千両幟 Sekitori senryō-nobori *la*
金 Sekigane *p*
定 Morisada *m*
東 Kantō *p* ["Kwantung"]
良一 Seki Ryōichi *ml*
9城 Sekijō *p*
前 Sekisen *p*
岳 Sekioka *s*
岡 Sekioka *s*
10宮 Sekinomiya *p*
原 Sekihara *s*
原与市 S. Yoichi *la*
屋 Sekiya *sl*
11根 Sekine *s*
根弘 S. Hiroshi *ml*
野 Sekino *s*
宿 Sekiyado *p*
島 Sekijima *s*
12場 Sekiba *s*
崎 Sekizaki *s* ⌈*ml*
登久也 Seki Tokuya
13塚 Sekizuka *s*
雄 Sekio *m*
18藤 Sekifuji *s*

—— 14 F9 ——

鼎 2246 Kanae *sm-p.* (TEI, kane)

—— 14 F10 ——

歴 2247 [T] (REKI, RYAKU, tsune, furu, yuki)
程 Rekitei *l*

—— 14 U ——

肅 2248 See 粛 1528

黽 2249 Tsutomu *m.* (BŌ, MYŌ, BEN)

爾 2250 [N] Mitsuru *m*, Chikashi. (JI, NI, shika, chika)
也 Chikaya *m*
散南 Nisanamu *s*

幽 2251 [T] (YŪ)
玄 Yūgen *l*
斎 Yūsai *ml* ⌈ki *l*
斎翁聞書 Y.-ō kikiga-

—— 15 L2 ——

億 2252 [T] Hakaru *m.* (OKU, YAKU, IKU, yasu)

儁 2253 Masaru *m*, Toshi. (SHUN, toshi)

僻 2254 (HEKI, higa)
言調 Higagoto shirabe *l*

儀 2255 [T] Tadashi *m*, Nori, Kitaru. (GI, nori, yoshi)
一 Giichi *m*
一郎 Giichirō *m*
子 Noriko *f*, Yoshiko
任 Yoshitō *m*
作 Gisaku *m*
助 Gisuke *m*
兵衛 Gihee *m*
俄 Kega *s*
達 Norisato *m*
義 Noriyoshi *m*

—— 15 L3 ——

增 2256 See 増 2077

憘 2257 See 憙 2559

撰 2258 Eramu *m.* (SEN, SAN, nobu)
集抄 Senjūshō *l*

播 2259 (BAN, hiro, hari, kashi, suke)
本 Harimoto *s*
州 Banshū *p*; Hirokuni *m*
州平野 B. heiya *l*
磨 Harima *sph*
磨国 Harimanokuni *ph* ⌈doki *l*
磨国風土記 H. no fu-

幟 2260 (SHI, taka)
仁 Takahito *m*

幡 2261 (HAN, HON hata, man)

幟 幡 ▼ 德 徸 衝 徵 衜 澁 澔 潭 潯 溪 潛 潟 澗 潮 澄 潤 嵮 嫩 嶋 鴇 膝 暚 暤 暲 璉 瑤 璋 樣 楡 槿 樛 榧 槫 樅 樟 槻 槐 槇 標 樋 ▲ 槯 横

川 Hatagawa *s*
文 Hataaya *s*, Hatamu
井 Hatai *s*
太郎 Mantarō *m*
多 Hata *sp*
多幡美 Hatabami *s*
豆 Hazu *sp*
美 Hami *s*
彦 Hatahiko *m*
屋 Hataya *s*
掛 Hatakake *s*
野 Hatano *s*
鎌 Hatagama *s*

德 2262 See 徳 2063

徸 2263 (DŌ, yuki)

衝 2264 [T] (SHŌ, SHU, tsugi, michi, tsuku, mori)

徵 2265 [T] Akira *m*, Kiyoshi. (CHŌ, aki, yoshi, sumi, oto, miru)

衜 2266 See 道 1811

澁 2267 See 渋 1334

澔 2268 Yowa *f*. (KŌ, GŌ). See also 浩 1068

潭 2269 Hiroshi *m*. (TAN, DON)

潯 2270 Hiroshi *f*. (JIN, SHIN)

溪 2271 See 渓 1330 A

潛 2272 [T] Hisomu *m*. (SEN, ZEN, sumi)
枝 Sumie *f*

潟 2273 (SEKI, SHAKU, kata)
子 Katako *f*
東 Katahigashi *p*
保 Katanoho *s*

澗 2274 (KAN, KEN, tani, ma)
生 Tanio *m*
雄 Tanio *m*
潟 Magata *s*

潮 2275 [T] Ushio *m*. (CHŌ, shio)
田 Ushioda *s*
来 Itako *p*
音 Chōon *l*
崎 Shiozaki *s*
騒 Shiosai *l*

澄 2276 [T] Kiyoshi *m*, Sumeru, Kiyomu, Sumeri, Tōru; Sumi *f*. (CHŌ, sumi, kiyo, sumu)
川 Sumikawa *s*
子 Sumiko *f*
元 Sumimoto *m*
田 Sumida *s*
男 Sumio *m*
美子 Sumiko *f*

潤 2277 [T] Jun *m*, Uruu, Uruo, Hiroshi, Masaru, Sakae. (JUN, SHUN, uru, masu, mitsu, hiro)
一郎 Jun'ichirō *m*
夫 Masuo *m*
次郎 Junjirō *m*
身 Hiromi *m*
登 Masumi *m*
象 Mitsutaka *m*
瓢 Junpyō *m*

—15 L4—

嵮 2278 Tadashi *m*. (SAKU, JAKU)

嫩 2279 Futaba *f*. (DON, NON)

嶋 2279A See 島 1522

鴇 2280 Hō *s*. (HŌ, toki)
田 Tokida *s*, Tokita
根 Tōgane *s*
崎 Tokizaki *s*

膝 2281 (SHITSU, hiza)
栗毛 Hizakurige *l*

暚 2282 Akira *m*. (YŌ)

暤 2283 Akira *m*. (KŌ, GŌ, akira)

暲 2284 Akira *m*, Susumu *m*; Aki *f*. (SHŌ, aki)

璉 2285 (REN, teru, tsura)

瑤 2286 (YŌ, tama)
子 Tamako *f*

璋 2287 Akira *m*. (SHŌ, tama, aki, teru)
八 Shōhachi *m*
子 Tamako *f*
光 Akimitsu *m*
男 Tamao *m*
敏 Akitoshi *m*
悦 Teruyoshi *m*

樣 2288 See 様 2099

楡 2288A (YU, nire)
井 Nirei *s*
木 Nireki *s*

槿 2289 Asagao *l*. (KIN)
花戯書 Hachisu zaregaki *l*

樛 2290 (RYŌ, tsuga)
子 Tsugako *f*

榧 2291 (HI, kaya)
木 Kayaki *s*, Kayanoki

槫 2292 (TAN, SEN, kuruma)
林 Kurumabayashi *s*

樅 2293 (SHU, SHŌ, momi)
山 Momiyama *s*

樟 2294 (SHŌ, kusu)
子 Kusuko *f*
本 Kusumoto *s*

槻 2295 (KI, tsuki)
子 Tsukiko *f*
本 Tsukimoto *s*

槐 2296 (KAI, E, enji, enisu)
本 Enisunomoto *m*
郎 Enjirō *m*

槇 2297 Maki *s*. (SHIN, TEN, maki)
子 Makiko *f*
山 Sakakiyama *s*
太郎 Makitarō *m*
田 Makita *s*
本 Makimoto *s*
本楠郎 M. Kusurō *ml*
村 Makimura *s*
桂 Makibashira *s*
島 Makinoshima *s*

標 2298 [T] Kozue *m*, Meate; Shimeki *s*. (HYŌ, shibe, shime, sue, eda, shina, kata, taka, hide)
津 Shibetsu *p*
茶 Shibecha *p*
葉 Shiba *s*, Shimeha
継 Katatsugu *m*

樋 2299 (TŌ, TSU, hi)
口 Higuchi *s*, Hinokuchi
口一葉 Higuchi Ichiyō *fl*
口竜峡 H. Ryūkyō *ml*
川 Higawa *s*
山 Hiyama *s*
田 Hida *s*, Toida
爪 Hizume *s*
沼 Hinuma *s*
畑 Hibata *s*
前 Hinokuma *s*
泉 Toizumi *s*
浦 Hiura *s*
脇 Hiwaki *p*
野 Hino *s*
渡 Hiwatari *s*
熊 Higuma *s*

權 2300 [T] (GON, KEN, nori, yoshi)
一 Gon'ichi *m*
八 Gonpachi *m*
七 Gonshichi *m*
三 Gonzō *m*
大 Gondai *m*
士 Norio *m*
之允 Gennosuke *m*
左衛門 Gonzaemon *m*
田 Gonda *s*
正 Gonshō *s*
平 Gonbei *s*
四郎 Gonshirō *m*
助 Gonsuke *m*
兵衛 Gonbee *m*
治 Gonji *m*
現造 Gongen-zukuri *a*
瓶 Gonbei *s*
野 Gonno *s*
蔵 Gonzō *m*
藤 Gondō *s*

横 2301 [T] (Ō, yoko)
[3]川 Yokogawa *sp*; Yogawa *s*
[4]内 Yokouchi *s*
手 Yokote *sp*
井 Yokoi *s*
井小楠 Y. Shōnan *mh*
井也有 Y. Yayū *ml*
山 Yokoyama *s*
山大観 Y. Taikan *ma*
山白虹 Y. Hakukō *ml*
山有策 Y. Yūsaku *ml*
山健堂 Y. Kendō *ml*
山源之助 Y. Gennosuke *ml*
木 Yokoki *s*
[5]田 Yokota *sp*
矢 Yokoya *s*
[6]地 Yokochi *s*
江 Yokoe *s*
竹 Yokotake *s*
芝 Yokoshiba *p*
光 Yokomitsu *sm*
光利一 Y. Riichi *ml*
[7]沢 Yokozawa *s*
坂 Yokosaka *s*
村 Yokomura *s*
谷 Yokotani *s*, Yokoya
尾 Yokoo *s*
充 Yokomitsu *m*
[8]佩 Yokohagi *s*
知 Yokochi *s*
[9]松 Yokomatsu *s*
前 Yokomae *s*
[10]浜 Yokohama *sp*
倉 Yokokura *s*
屋 Yokoya *s*
[11]野 Yokono *s*
島 Yokoshima *sp*
[12]須賀 Yokosuka *sp*
曾根 Yokosone *s*
森 Yokomori *s*
道 Yokomichi *s*
[13]堀 Yokobori *s*
塚 Yokozuka *s*
溝 Yokomizo *s*
溝正史 Y. Seishi *ml*
張 Yokobari *s*
越 Yokogoshi *p*
[14]関 Yokozeki *s*
[16]橋 Yokobashi *s*
[19]瀬 Yokose *sp*
瀬夜雨 Y. Yau *ml*

—15 L5—

鄉 2302 See 郷 2112

緺 2303 Motoru *m*. (EI)

禕 2304 (I, yoshi)
健 Yoshitake *m*

確 2305 [T] Katashi *m*, Akira; Tashika *f*. (KAKU, kata, tai)
子 Katako *f*
悟 Taigo *m*

端 2306 [T] Hata *s*, Tan; Tadashi *m*, Tadasu, Hajime. (TAN, hashi, masa, tada, ha, hata, nao, moto)
子 Masako *f*
夫 Masao *m*, Tadao
守 Hamori *m*
居 Hashii *m*
連 Masatsura *m*
野 Tanno *p*
館 Hatadate *s*

稻 2307 See 稲 2125

穗 2308 [T] Minoru *m-f*. (SUI, ZUI, ho, o)
井 Hoi *s*
井田 Hoida *s*
阪 Hosaka *s*
坂 Hosaka *s*
別 Hobetsu *p*
谷 Hodani *s*
苅 Hogari *s*
波 Honami *s*
保 Hoshifu *s*
高 Hotaka *p*
瓮 Hohe *s*
集 Hoatsume *s*, Hozume
積 Hozumi *sm-p*
積忠 H. Kiyoshi *ml*
積陳重 H. Nobushige *mh*
稷 Hozumi *s*, Honomi

—15 L6—

糊 2309 (KO, GO, nori)

耦 2310 (GŪ, GŌ, GU, tomo)

聡 2311 [N] Satoshi *m*, Satoru, Akira; Toshi *f*. (SŌ, SU, aki, sato, toshi, sa, to, tomi, toki)
夫 Tomio *m*
敏 Satoshi *m*
善 Akiyoshi *m*
頼 Akiyori *m*

蝶 See 2495

蝮 2312 Tajihi *s*. (FUKU, BUKU)
壬 Tajihimibu *s*
壬部 Tajihibe *s*
椿 Hamatsubaki *s*

蝦 2313 (GA, ebi, emi)
夷 Ezo *h*; Emishi *m-h*
原 Ebihara *s*
蟆鉄拐 Gama tekkai *l*

—15 L7—

踏 2314 [T] (TŌ, fumi, fuma)
瀬 Fumase *p*

醇 2315 Atsushi *m*. (JUN, SHUN, atsu)

輪 2316 [T] (RIN, wa)
之内 Wanouchi *p*
田丸 Wadamaru *m*
座 Waza *s*
島 Wajima *sp*
賀月 Wakatsuki *s*
違 Wachigai *s*
蔵 Rinzō *l*

賜 2317 [T] Tamō *m*. (SHI, tama, masu)
子 Tamako *f*

賤 2318 Shizu *f*. (SEN, ZEN, shizu)
子 Shizuko *f*
夫 Shizuo *m*
香 Shizuka *f*
機 Shizuhata *l*
機帯 Shizuhataobi *a*

誕 2319 (TAN, DAN, nobu)

論 2320 [T] (RON, RIN, toki, nori)

誹 2321 (HI). (cf. 俳 1036)
風柳多留 Haifū yanagidaru *l*

誼 2322 (GI, yoshi, koto)
衡 Yoshihiro *m*

請 2323 [T] (SEI, SHIN, uke)
川 Ukegawa *s*
地 Ukeji *s*

諄 2324 Itaru *m*, Makoto. (JUN, atsu, sane, shige, tomo, nobu)
子 Atsuko *f*
太郎 Juntarō *m*

談 2325 [T] Katari *m*. (DAN, TAN, kata, kanu, kane)
林 Danrin *l*
林十百韻 D. toppyakuin *l*

諒 2326 Makoto *m*, Masa; Aki *f*.

賜 賎 誕 論 誹 誼 請 諄 談 諒 ▼ 諏 調 諸 絹 絃 絵 統 続 鉉 鋤 鋳 銕 鋒 鋪 銹 鉾 鋳 鋭 銀 餅 駙 駛 駒 ▲ 戯 毅 歓 歎 敵 敷 鄭 影 愈 雍

(RYŌ, aki, masa, asa)
一 Masakazu *m*
兄 Akie *m*

**諏** 2327 (SU, SHU)
佐 Susa *s*
訪 Suwa *sp*
訪部 Suwabe *s*
訪都 Suwa ichi *l*

**調** 2328 [T] Shirabe *s*; Mitsugi *sm*; Tsuki *sf*. (CHŌ, tsugu, tsugi, shige, tsuki)
川 Tsukinokawa *s*
子 Chōshi *s*
月 Tsukizuki *s*, Tsukazuki, Chikazuki
布 Chōfu *p*; Tetsukuri *s*, Tatsukuri
伎 Tsuki *s*
伏曾我 Chōbuku Soga *la*
使 Tsugitsukai *s*
所 Zusho *s*, Chōsho
所広郷 Z. Hirosato *mh*
興 Tsugioki *m*

**諸** 2329 [T] Moro *s*. (SHO, JO, SHA, moro, tsura, mori)
[3]川 Morokawa *s*
[4]井 Moroi *s*
木 Morogi *s*
木野 Morogino *s*
[5]田 Morota *s*
兄 Moroe *m*
立 Morotate *m*
[7]会 Moroai *m*
見里 Moromisato *s*
角 Morokado *s*
[9]垣 Morogaki *s*
姉 Moroe *f*
星 Moroboshi *s*
岡 Morooka *s*
[11]野 Morono *s*
魚 Morona *m*
[12]富 Morodomi *p*
遊 Moroyū *s*
道聴耳世間猿 Shodō kikimimi sekenzaru
[13]塚 Morotsuka *p* ⌊*l*
葛 Morokuzu *sm*
照 Moroteru *m*
[16]橋 Morohashi *s*
[18]藤 Morofuji *s*

——15 L8——

**絹** 2330 [T] Kinu *f*. (KEN, kinu, masa)
川 Kinugawa *s*
山 Kinuyama *s*
田 Kinuta *s*
谷 Kinutani *s*
香 Kinuka *f*

**絃** 2331 (GEN, KEN, tsuru, o, ito)
上 Genjō *la*
夫 Tsuruo *m*

**絵** 2332 [T] (KAI, e)
本曾我 Ehon Soga *l*
合 Eawase *la*
坂 Ezaka *s*
見 Emi *s*
面 Ezura *s*
巻物 Emaki-mono *la*
師草子 Eshi no sōshi *l*
馬 Ema *sla-a*
菱 Ebishi *s*
詞 Ekotoba *l*

**統** 2333 [T] Osamu *m-f*; Sumeru *m*, Tsuzuki; Moto *f*. (TŌ, mune, sumi, nori, kane, tsuna, tsune, osa)
一 Tsunekazu *m*, Tō-
仁 Osahito *m* ⌊ichi
秋 Sumiaki *m*
理 Munemasa *m*
雄 Kaneo *m*
間 Norisato *m*

**続** 2334 [T] Tsuzuki *s*; Tsuzuku *m-f*. (ZOKU, SHOKU, tsugi, tsugu, hide)
[3]千載集 Zoku senzaishū *l*
[4]木 Tsuzuki *s* ⌈gi *l*
日本紀 Shoku Nihon-
日本後紀 Zoku Nihon kōki *l*
[5]古今集 Z. kokinshū *l*
古事談 Z. kojidan *l*
本朝文粋 Z. honchō monzui *l*
[6]世継 Shoku yotsugi *l*
耳塵集 Zoku nijinshū *l*
[8]明鳥 Z. akegarasu *l*
[9]信 Tsuginobu *m*
拾遺集 Zoku shūishū *l*
草庵集 Z. sōanshū *l*
[10]浦島子伝 Z. Urashimago-no-den *l*
[11]後拾遺集 Z. goshūishū *l*
後撰集 Z. gosenshū *l*
[12]道中膝栗毛 Z. dōchū hizakurige *l*
[14]猿蓑 Z. sarumino *l*
[15]蔵 Tsugizō *m*

**鉉** 2335 (GEN, KEN, tsuru)
子 Tsuruko *f*

**鋤** 2336 (JO, SHO, suki)
柄 Sukie *s*, Sukigara

**鋳** 2337 Kazari *s*. (kazari)
谷 Kazariya *p*

**銕** 2338 (TETSU, kane)
胤 Kanetane *m*

**鋒** 2339 (HŌ, FU, hoko, saki)
子 Hokoko *f*

**鋪** 2340 Nobu *f*. (HO, FU, nobu, haru, shige, suke)
猪 Nobui *m*
綱 Nobutsuna *m*

**銹** 2341 (RI, toshi, sen)
之允 Sennojō *m*
子 Toshiko *f*
秋 Toshiaki *m*

**鉾** 2342 (BŌ, MU, hoko)
子 Hokoko *f*
久 Muku *s*
田 Hokoda *p*

**鋳** 2343 [T] (CHŪ, i)
方 Igata *s*
式 Ishiki *f*
谷 Itani *s*
銭司 Susenji *s*
銭部 Chūsenbu *s*

**鋭** 2344 [T] Toshi *m*, Satoki. (EI, toshi, toki)
太郎 Eitarō *m*
市 Eiichi *m*
清 Toshikiyo *m*
雄 Tokio *m*
憲 Toshikazu *m*

**銀** 2345 [T] Shirogane *m*. (GIN, GON, kane)
二郎 Ginjirō *m*
三郎 Ginzaburō *m*
之助 Ginnosuke *m*
太郎 Gintarō *m*
次郎 Ginjirō *m*
佐 Kanesuke *m*
杏 Ichō *s*
座 Ginza *p*
語録 Gingoroku *l*
閣寺 Ginkakuji *pha*
蔵 Ginzō *m*

——15 L9——

**餅** 2346 (HEI, mochi)
原 Mochihara *s*
屋 Mochiya *s*

——15 L10——

**駙** 2347 (FU, chika, tsuku, toshi)

**駛** 2348 (SHI, haya, toshi)
夫 Hayao *m*
馬 Hayama *m*
量 Toshikazu *m*

**駒** 2349 [N] (KU, koma)
[3]之助 Komanosuke *m*
[4]井 Komai *s*
木 Komagi *s*
木根 Komagine *s*
[5]代 Komayo *f*
込 Komagome *sp*
目 Komame *s*
田 Komada *s*
田信二 K. Shinji *ml*
[6]次郎 Komajirō *m*
吉 Komakichi *m*

[7]沢 Komazawa *s*
形 Komagata *s*
村 Komamura *s*
谷 Komaya *s*
[8]林 Komabayashi *s*
[10]宮 Komamiya *s*
[11]猪 Komai *f*
野 Komano *s*
[12]場 Komaba *sp*
崎 Komazaki *s*
[13]雄 Komao *m*
[14]槌 Komatsuchi *m*

—15 L11—

戯 2350 [T] (GI, GE)
作 Gesaku *l*
作三昧 G.-zanmai *l*

毅 2351 [N] Takeshi *m*, Tsuyoshi, Tsuyoki, Kowashi, Hatasu, Sadamu, Shinobu. (KI, GI, GE, take, tsuyo, mi, kata, taka, toshi, nori, yoshi)
彦 Takehiko *m*
陸 Kiroku *m*
雄 Takeo *m*

歓 2352 [T] (KAN, yoshi)
子 Yoshiko *f*

歎 2353 (TAN)
異抄 Tan'ishō *l*

敵 2354 [T] (TEKI, toshi)
討義女英 Katakiuchi gijo no hanabusa *l*

敷 2355 [T] (FU, nobu, shiki, hira)
田 Shikida *s*
地 Shikichi *s*
村 Shikimura *s*
見 Shikimi *s*
根 Shikine *s*
島 Shikishima *p*
智 Fuchi *s*

—15 L12—

鄭 2356 Tei *s.* (TEI)

影 2357 [T] (EI, YŌ, kage)
山 Kageyama *s* ⌈*ml*
山正治 K. Masaharu
光 Kagemitsu *m*

—15 T2—

愈 2358 Masaru *m*; Masu *f.* (YU, iyo, masu, yasu)
子 Iyoko *f*

雍 2359 (YŌ, YU, yasu, chika, kazu)
人 Kazuhito *m*
子 Yasuko *f*
仁 Yasuhito *m*
通 Chikamichi *m*

—15 T3—

賣 2360 See 売 466

臺 2361 See 台 276

實 2362 See 実 678

寢 2363 See 寝 1976

寮 2364 [T] (RYŌ, ie, tomo, matsu)

審 2365 [T] Akira *sm.* (SHIN, aki)

蔵 See 2424

甍 2366 Iraka *s.* (BŌ)

蕡 2367 Minoru *m*; Shige *f.* (FUN, BUN)

蔣 2368 (SHŌ, SŌ, komo) ⌈chi
池 Komoike *s*, Komo-

燕 2369 See 燕 2570

蔭 2370 (IN, ON, kage)
山 Kageyama *s*
見 Kagemi *m*

蕃 2371 Shigeru *m*, Shigeri. (BAN, shige, mitsu, mori, shiku, fusa)
良 Hara *s*, Hora
樹 Shigeki *m*

蕉 2372 (SHŌ)
門 Shōmon *l*
門頭陀 S. zuda *l*
堅稿 Shōkenkō *l*

蕪 2373 (BU, MU, kabura)
木 Kaburagi *s*
坂 Kaburasaka *s*
村 Buson *ml* ⌈shū *l*
村七部集 B. shichibu-
屋 Kaburaya *s*

—15 T4—

嵬 2374 Takashi *m*, Kewashi. (KAI)

—15 T5—

晶 2375 Akira *m.* (KYŌ, GYŌ)

裳 2376 (SHŌ, mo)
咋 Mokui *s*
原 Mobara *s*

賞 2377 [T] Takashi *m.* (SHŌ, taka, yoshi, suke, homu)
成 Yoshishige *sm*
善 Suketaru *m*
雅 Takamasa *m*

—15 T6—

器 2378 [T] (KI, kata)

鞏 2379 (KYŌ, KU, kata, yoshi)

節 2380 See 節 2215

箸 2381 Akira *m.* (CHO, hashi, aki,
尾 Hashio *s* ⌊tsuku)

篁 2382 Takamura *sm-l*; Takai *s*; Taka *f.* (KŌ, ō, taka)
雄 Takeo *m*

箱 2383 [T] (SHŌ, sō, hako)
山 Hakoyama *s*
田 Hakoda *s*
羽 Hakoba *s*
守 Hakomori *s*
根 Hakone *p*
崎 Hakozaki *s*

範 2384 [T] Susumu *m.* (HAN, nori)
一 Norikazu *m*
三 Hanzō *m*
子 Noriko *f*
夫 Norio *m*
平 Hanpei *m*
田 Hanta *s*
宗 Norimune *m*
規 Noritada *m*
頼 Noriyori *m*

—15 T7—

魯 2385 (RO)
文 Robun *ml*
迅 Ro Jin *ml* "Lu Hsün"
国 Rokoku *p* "Russia"

—15 T8—

墨 2386 See 墨 2230

瑩 2387 Akira *m*; Teru *f.* (EI, YŌ, teru, akira)

製 2388 [T] (SEI, nori)
保 Noriyasu *m*

黎 2389 (REI, RAI, tami)
子 Tamiko *f*
吉 Reikichi *m*

霊 2390 [T] (REI, RYŌ, tama, yoshi)
山 Ryōzen *p*; Yoshiyama *s*
田 Tamada *s*

範魯墨瑩製黎霊▼舞慧輦賛質賚箭監盤磐齊暫慤慰黙熟勲熱熙熊奬墅導幣履廣廚遵選遲▲遙趣魁蔵慶閭闇

異記 Reiiki *l*
亀 Reiki 715–17
鞍 Tamakura *s*

舞 2391 [T] (BU, MU, mai)
の木 Mai no hon *l*
台百箇条 Butai hyakkajō *l*
阪 Maisaka *p*
原 Maibara *sp*
姫 Maihime *l*
楽 Bugaku *a*
鶴 Maizuru *p*

慧 2392 Satoshi *m*, Satoru, Kei, Akira. (KEI, E, sato, akira)

輦 2393 (REN, nori)
止 Kurumado *s*

賛 2394 [T] Tasuku *m*, Akira. (SAN, yoshi, suke, ji)
子 Yoshiko *f*
雄 Yoshio *m*

質 2395 [T] Sunao *m*, Tadashi. (SHITSU, SHICHI, tada, moto, kata, mi, sada)

賚 2396 (RAI, tama, yori)
夫 Tamao *m*
四郎 Raishirō *m*

## 15 T9

箭 2397 (SEN, ya)
口 Yaguchi *s*, Yanokuchi
内 Yanai *s*
括 Yahazu *s*
野 Yano *s*
集 Yatsume *s*

監 2398 [T] Akira *m*. (KAN, KEN, mi, aki, kane, teru, tada)
物 Kenmotsu *sm*

盤 2399 [T] (BAN, HAN, maru, yasu)
吉 Bankichi *m*

磐 2400 Iwao *m*. (HAN, BAN, iwa)
一 Iwaichi *m*
子 Iwako *f*
太郎 Iwatarō *m*
田 Iwata *p*
余 Iware *s*
奈 Iwana *s*
城 Iwaki *p*
前 Iwamae *m*
恵 Iwae *m*
梨別 Iwanasuwake *s*
梯 Bandai *p*
瀬 Iwase *s*

## 15 T11

齊 2401 See 斉 701

暫 2402 [T] Shibaraku *la*. (ZAN)

慤 2403 Sunao *m*. (KAKU, yoshi, masa, nao)
麿 Yoshimaro *m*

慰 2404 [T] (I, yasu, nori)
子 Yasuko *f*

黙 2405 [T] (MOKU)
阿弥 Mokuami *ml*

熟 2406 [T] (JUKU)
田 Niita *s*
皮高麗 Oshikawakoma *s*
蝦夷 Nigiemishi *s*

勲 2407 [T] Tsutomu *m*, Isao. (KUN, isa, koto, hiro, iso)
夫 Isao *m*
光 Isamitsu *m*
男 Isao *m*

熱 2408 [T] (NETSU, atsu)
川 Atsukawa *s*, Niekawa
代 Atsuyo *f*
田 Atsuta *sp*
田祝部 Atsutahafuribe *s*
海 Atami *sp*
塩加納 Atsushiokanō *p*

熙 2409 Hiroshi *m*, Hiromu, Ki. (KI, I, hiro, sato, teru, oki, yoshi, nori)
子 Hiroko *f*, Teruko
永 Yoshinaga *m*
成 Norinari *m*
栄 Hirohide *m*
造 Hirozō *m*
景 Hirokage *m*

熊 2410 [N] Kuma *s*. (YŪ, kuma, kage)
[1]一 Kumaichi *m*
[3]川 Kumagawa *s*
三郎 Kumasaburō *m*
丸 Kumamaru *s*
[4]毛 Kumage *p*
井 Kumai *s*
井田 Kumaida *s*
木 Kumaki *s*
山 Kumayama *sp*
王丸 Kumaōmaru *m*
[5]代 Kumashiro *s*
切 Kumagiri *s*
石 Kumaishi *p*
田 Kumada *s*
本 Kumamoto *sp*
[6]次 Kumaji *m*
次郎 Kumajirō *m*
吉 Kumakichi *m*
庄 Kumanoshō *s*
耳 Yūji *s*
[7]沢 Kumazawa *s*
沢蕃山 K. Banzan *mh*
沢復六 K. Mataroku *ml*
阪 Kumasaka *s*
坂 Kumasaka *sla*
村 Kumamura *s*
谷 Kumagaya *sp*; Kumagai *s*, Kumagae
谷武雄 Kumagai Takeo *ml*
[8]取 Kumatori *p*
取谷 Hishiya *s*
[9]津 Kumazu *s*
岡 Kumaoka *s*
彦 Kumahiko *m*
[10]倉 Kumakura *s*
[11]野 Kumano *sp*; Yuya *fa-la*
野川 Kumanogawa *p*
野跡 Kumanoato *p*
埜御堂 Kumanomido *s*
猪 Kumai *f*
[12]崎 Kumasaki *s*
喜 Kumaki *m*
[13]雄 Kumao *m*
勢 Kumase *s*
[16]凝 Kumakori *m*
[17]懐 Kumazuki *s*
[24]襲 Kumaso *h*

## 15 T12

奬 2411 See 奨 2036

墅 2412 Motoi *m*. (SHŌ, SŌ)

導 2413 [T] (DŌ, michi, osa)
子 Michiko *f*

幣 2414 [T] Shide *m*. (HEI, BEI, nusa)
一 Nusakazu *m*
帛 Mitegura *s*
原 Shidehara *s*
原喜重郎 S. Kijūrō *mh*

## 15 F3

履 2415 [T] (RI, fumi)

廣 2416 See 広 316

廚 2417 (CHŪ, kuriya)
川 Kuriyagawa *s*
川白村 K. Hakuson *mh*

遵 2418 [T] Jun *m*. (JUN, SHUN, nobu, chika, yori, yuki)
子 Nobuko *f*

選 2419 [T] (SEN, SAN, kazu, nobu, yori, yoshi)
子 Yoriko *f*
子内親王 Senshi Naishinnō *fl*

## 15 F4

遲 2420 See 遅 1807

遙 2421 Haruka *m*. (YŌ, haru, tō, michi)

——15 F7——

趣 2422 [T] (SHU, toshi, koshi)
山 Koshiyama *s*

——15 F8——

魁 2423 Isao *m*, Isamu, Tsutomu; Sakigake *s*. (KAI, KE)

蔵 2424 [T] Kura *s*; Osamu *m*. (zō, sō, kura, tada, toshi, masa, yoshi)
人 Kurando *m*
下麿 Kurajimaro *m*
元 Kuramoto *s*
六 Kuraroku *m*
王 Zaō *p*
方 Kurakata *s*
太 Kurata *m*
田 Kurata *s*
本 Kuramoto *s*
主 Kuruji *s*
老 Kuraoi *m*
持 Kuramochi *s*
重 Kurashige *s*
原 Kurahara *s* ⌈*mh*
原伸二郎 K. Shinjirō
原惟人 K. Korehito *ml*
野 Kurano *s*
紀 Kuraki *m*

慶 2425 [T] Yoshi *m*; Iwai *s*. (KEI, KYŌ, yoshi, yasu, nori, chika, michi, iwai)
[3]三 Keizō *m*
三郎 Keizaburō *m*
子 Keiko *f*, Yoshiko
之 Yoshino *f*
之助 Keinosuke *m*
[4]夫 Yoshio *m*
太郎 Keitarō *m*
[5]四郎 Keishirō *m*
田 Iwaida *s*
[6]次郎 Keijirō *m*
光院 Keikōin *s*
吉 Keikichi *m*
[7]作 Keisaku *m*
利 Yasutoshi *m*
安 Keian 1648–52
応 Keiō 1865–68
応義塾 K. Gijuku *p*
[8]定 Yoshisada *m*
[9]長 Kyōchō/Keichō 1596–1615 ⌈han *l*
長勅版 Keichō chokuhan *l*
香 Yoshika *m*
[11]隆 Keiryū *m*
野 Keino *s*
[12]勝 Yoshikatsu *m*
喜 Yoshinobu *m*
[13]寛 Yoshitomo *m*
雲 Kyōun 704–08; Keiun *ml* 704–08
[15]蔵 Keizō *m*
[16]滋 Yoshishige *sm*
滋保胤 Y. no Yasutane *ml*

閭 2426 (RO, RYO, sato)

誾 2427 Tadashi *m*. (GIN, GON)

——15 F11——

摩 2428 [T] (MA, BA, kiyo, nazu)
耶夫人 Maya-bunin *fh*
理勢 Marise *m*
島 Mashima *s*
賀部 Makabe *s*
漏 Maro *m*

——15 F12——

塵 2429 (JIN)
芥集 Jinkaishū *lh*
溜 Hakidame *l*

——15 U——

鼠 2430 (so, nezumi)
小紋東君新形 Nezumi-komon haru no shingata *la*

——16 L2——

凝 2431 [T] Kōru *m*. (GYŌ, kori)

儒 2432 [T] (JU, NYU, haka, hito, michi, yasu, yoshi)

儔 2433 (CHŪ, tomo, toshi)

儇 2434 (KEN, toshi)
儀 Toshiyoshi *m*

儘 2435 (JIN, michi, mama)
田 Mamada *s*

——16 L3——

獨 2436 See 独 788

噓 2437 (KYO)
の果 Uso no mi *l*

壇 2438 [T] (DAN)
浦 Dannoura *ph*
浦兜軍記 D. kabuto gunki *la*

懌 2439 (EKI, YAKU, yoshi, tsugu)
子 Yoshiko *f*

憶 2440 [T] (OKU, zō)
良 Okura *ml*
頼 Okurai *s*

隨 2441 See 随 1564

險 2442 See 険 1308

隣 2443 [T] Chikashi *m*, Tonari. (RIN, chika, sato, tada, naga)
夫 Tadao *m*
信 Chikanobu *m*, Naganobu

擇 2444 See 択 404

擔 2445 See 担 581

擯 2446 Tasuku *m*. (RIN)

撿 2447 (KEN)
見川 Kemigawa *s*

操 2448 [T] Misao *m*; Ayatsuri *a*. (sō, misa, mochi, aya, sao, toru)
子 Misako *f*
加 Misaka *f*
浄瑠璃 Ayatsuri jōruri *la*

徵 2449 See 徴 2265

衡 2450 [T] Hitoshi, *m*, Mamoru. (KŌ, GYŌ, hira, hiro, chika, hide)
能 Hirayoshi *m*

徹 2451 [T] Tetsu *m*, Itaru, Tōru, Akira, Osamu, Hitoshi. (TETSU, michi, yuki, tō)
一 Tetsuichi *m*
二 Tetsuji *m*
三 Tetsuzō *m*
太郎 Tetsutarō *m*
志 Tetsushi *m*
郎 Tetsurō *m*
書記 Tesshoki *l*
蔵 Tetsuzō *m*

衛 2452 [T] Mamoru *m*, Mamori. (EI, E, mori, hiro, yoshi)
万 Moritaka *m*
士 Eshi *m*, Morito
士夫 Ejio *m*
守 Emori *m*
佐 Esuke *m*
好 Moriyoshi *m*
門 Emon *mh*
彦 Morihiko *m*
衛 Morimichi *m*
藤 Eitō *s*, Etō

澤 2453 See 沢 404

澈 2454 Kiyoshi *m*. (TETSU)

澯 2455 Kiyoshi *m*. (SAN)

澂 2456 See 澄 2276

濁 2457 [T] (DAKU, nigori)
川 Nigorikawa *sp*

澪 2458 Mio *f-l.* (REI, RYŌ, mio)
標 Miotsukushi *l*

澳 2459 Oki *s.* (Ō, oki)
門 Makao *p* "Macao"
野 Okino *m*
麿 Okimaro *m*

滋 2460 [T] Shigeru *m*, Shigeshi. (SHI, JI, shige, masu, asa, fusa)
子 Shigeko *f*
田 Shida *s*
生 Shigefu *s*
秀 Masuhide *m*
春 Shigeharu *m*
彦 Shigehiko *m*
野 Shigeno *sm*; Shino *s*
野貞主 Shigeno no Sadanushi *ml*
賀 Shiga *p*

## 16 L4

豫 2461 See 予 62

彈 2462 See 弾 1880

膳 2463 Kashiwade *sm*; Zen *s.* (ZEN, SEN, yoshi)
天 Kashiwade *s*
次 Yoshitsugu *m*
住 Zejū *s*
伴 Kashiwadenotomo *s*
所 Zeze *s*
清 Yoshikiyo *m*
部 Kashiwade *s*

燒 2464 See 焼 1588

熾 2465 (SHI, taru)
仁 Taruhito *m*

嶝 2466 Noboru *m.* (TŌ)

嶟 2467 Takashi *m.* (SON)

曉 2468 See 暁 1596

暾 2469 Hajime *m.* (TON)

曈 2470 (DŌ, aki)

璟 2471 (EI, YŌ, akira)

璞 2472 Makoto *m*; Tama *f.* (HAKU, tama)

璃 2473 (RI, aki)
子 Akiko *f*

嫗 2474 Baba *f.* (Ō, baba)

嫺 2475 (KAN, KEN, shizu)
子 Shizuko *f*

嬉 2476 (KI, yoshi)
子 Yoshiko *f*
野 Ureshino *p*

樴 2477 (SHIKI, SHOKU, kui)

橡 2478 Tsurubami *l.* (ZŌ, SHŌ, tochi)

橳 2478A (SHŌ, nude)
島 Nudejima *sp*

樵 2479 Kikori *m.* (SHŌ, JŌ, soma)
夫 Somao *m*

樗 2480 (CHO)
牛 Chogyū *ml*
良 Chora *ml*

橿 2481 (kashi, kashiwa)
田 Kashiwada *s*
山 Kashiyama *s*
村 Kashimura *s*
谷 Kashiwaya *s*
尾 Kashio *s*
原 Kashiwara *s*
野 Kashiwano *s*

樽 2482 Taru *s.* (SON, taru)
川 Tarukawa *s*
子 Taruko *f*
之助 Tarunosuke *m*
井 Tarui *s*
井藤吉 T. Tōkichi *mh*
本 Tarumoto *s*
沢 Tarusawa *s*
見 Tarumi *s*
味 Tarumi *s*

樹 2483 [T] Tatsuki *m*, Itsuki. (JU, SHU, tatsu, shige, ki, miki, mura, na)
一郎 Kiichirō *m*
人 Tatsundo *m*
子 Tatsuko *f*, Shigeko, Mikiko
下 Juge *s*
夫 Tatsuo *m*
次郎 Shigejirō *m*
海 Ki no umi *l*
胤 Muratane *m*

橘 2484 [N] Tachibana *sp.* (KITSU, KICHI)
[2]八衢 T. no Yachimata *ml*
[3]三千代 T. no Michiyo *fh*
川 Kikkawa *s*
[4]内 Kitsunai *s*
[5]田 Kitsuda *s*
永愷 Tachibana no Nagayasu *ml*
[6]守部 T. no Moribe *mh*
成季 T. no Narisue *ml*
[7]谷 Kitsuya *s*
[8]宗利 Tachibana Munetoshi *ml*
奈良麻呂 T. no Naramaro *mh*
糸重子 T. Itoeko *fla*
東世子 T. Toseko *fl*
[10]高 Kittaka *s*, Kitaka
屋 Tachibanaya *s*
[11]逸勢 Tachibana no Hayanari *ml*
[15]諸兄 T. no Moroe *mlh*

橋 2485 [T] Hashi *s.* (KYŌ, GYŌ, hashi, taka)
[3]川 Hashikawa *s*
川文三 H. Bunzō *ml*
口 Hashiguchi *s*
[4]元 Hashimoto *s*
井 Hashii *s*
爪 Hashizume *s*
山 Hashiyama *s*
[5]田 Hashida *s*
田東声 H. Tōsei *ml*
本 Hashimoto *sp*
本左内 H. Sanai *mh*
本多佳子 H. Takako *fl*
本宗吉 H. Sōkichi *mh*
本英吉 H. Eikichi *ml*
本雅邦 H. Gahō *ma*
本夢道 H. Mudō *ml*
本徳寿 H. Tokuju *ml*
本鶏二 H. Keiji *ml*
[6]弁慶 Hashi Benkei *la*
[7]作 Kurahone *s*
村 Hashimura *s*
谷 Hashitani *s*
[10]倉 Hashikura *s*
[11]姫 Hashihime *l*
野 Hashino *s*
部 Hashibe *s*, Hashinobe
[12]場 Hashiba *s*
[13]詰 Hashizume *s*

## 16 L5

磔 2486 (TAKU)
茂左衛門 Haritsuke Mozaemon *la*

魄 2487 (HAKU, ai)

魂 2488 [T] (KON, GON, tama, mitama, moto)

鴨 2489 Kamo *sm.* (Ō, kamo)
川 Kamogawa *p*
下 Kamoshita *s*
方 Kamogata *p*
井 Kamoi *s*
打 Kamouchi *s*, Kamoji
田 Kamoda *s*
池 Kamochi *s*
志田 Kamoshida *s*
足 Ichō *s*
長明 Kamo no Chōmei *ml*

島 Kamojima *p*
脚 Ichō *s*
継 Kamotsugu *m*

稹 2490 Shigeru *m.* (SHIN, TEN, DEN)

稽 2491 (KEI, KAI, toki, nori, yoshi)
子 Tokiko *f*

穏 2492 [T] Yasuki *m.* (ON, yasu, shizu, toshi)
子 Yasuko *f*, Shizuko
仁 Yasuhito *m*
香 Yasuka *m*
野 Ono *s*
雄 Toshio *m*
徳 Yasunori *m*

積 2493 [T] Tsumoru *m*, Seki. (SEKI, SHAKU, SHI, tsumu, kazu, tsumi, sane, katsu, mori, sa, atsu, mochi, tsune)
丹 Shakotan *p*
田 Tsumida *s*
正 Katsumasa *m*
成 Saneshige *m*
善 Kazuyoshi *m*, Moriyoshi, Atsuyoshi
雄 Morio *m* ⌈gumi
組 Tsubukumi *s*, Tsu-

穆 2494 Atsushi *m.* (BOKU, MOKU, kiyo, atsu, yoshi, yasu, mutsu, tō)
人 Mutsundo *m*
子 Kiyoko *f*, Atsuko
文 Yasufumi *m*
夫 Yoshio *m*
佐 Mukasa *s*
英 Kiyohide *m*
詔 Atsuyoshi *m*
留 Atsuyoshi *m*
凞 Kiyohiro *m*

## 16 L6

蝶 2495 [N] (CHŌ)
子 Chōko *f*

## 16 L7

辨 2496 See 弁 275

輯 2497 Atsumu *m.* (SHŪ, JŪ, mutsu)

睶 2498 Atsushi *m.* (SHUN)

輝 2499 [T] Akira *m*, Hikaru, Kagayaki. (KI, teru, akira)
子 Teruko *f*
久 Teruhiko *m*
元 Terumoto *m*
夫 Teruo *m*
北 Kihoku *p*
充 Terumichi *m*
和 Teruyasu *m*
承 Teruyoshi *m*
虎 Terutora *m*
政 Terumasa *m*
香 Teruka *f*
規 Teruchika *m*
智 Terutoshi *m*
雄 Teruo *m*
徳 Teruakira *m*
聴 Terutoshi *m*

醍 2500 (DAI)
醐 Daigo *smh-p*

醒 2501 Samuru *m*; Same *f.* (SEI, SHŌ)
井 Samegai *sp*
睡笑 Seisuishō *l*

頤 2502 Yasushi *m.* (I)

頰 2503 (KYŌ, tsura, ho)
垂 Hotaru *m*

頭 2504 [T] Akira *m.* (TŌ, ZU, aki, kami)
山 Tōyama *s*
山満 T. Mitsuru *mh*
本 Zumoto *s*

頴 2505 Isao *m*, Satoshi. (EI, YŌ, hide, kai, saka, toshi)
人 Sakahito *m*
川 Egawa *s*
才新誌 Eisai shinshi *l*
田 Kaita *p*
田島 Etajima *s* ⌈*ml*
田島一二郎 E. Ichijirō
則 Hidenori *m*
娃 Ei *sp*; Eno *s*
雄 Hideo *m*

頼 2506 [T] Rai *sm*; Tanomu *m*; Yoshi *f.* (RAI, yori, nori, yo, yoshi)
[3]三 Raizō *m*
三樹三郎 Rai Mikisaburō *mh*
[4]山陽 Rai San'yō *mh*
升 Yorinori *m*
[5]央 Yorihisa *m*
由 Yoriyuki *m*
[6]母木 Tanomogi *s*
行 Yoshiyuki *m*
旨 Yorimune *m*
全 Yorimitsu *m*
存 Yorinaga *m*
名 Yorina *m*
多 Yorimasa *m*
[7]位 Yoritaka *m*
里 Yori *f* ⌈naga
寿 Yorikazu *m*, Yori-
[8]明 Yorihiro *m*
知 Yorioki *m*
幸 Yoritaka *m*
芸 Yoriyoshi *m*
易 Yoriosa *m*
[9]信 Yorinobu *m*
則 Yorinori *m*, Yoritsune
宣 Yorinobu *m*
政 Yorimasa *m*
政家集 Y. kashū *l*
[10]倫 Yorimichi *m*
桓 Yoritake *m*
郡 Yorikuni *m*
恭 Yoritaka *m*
通 Yorimichi *ml*
殷 Yoritaka *m*
[11]救 Yorisuke *m*
恕 Yorihiro *m*
[12]朝 Yoritomo *m*
[13]慎 Yoriyoshi *m*
稔 Yoritoshi *m*
義 Yorichika *m*
筠 Yoritaka *m*
[14]郷 Yorinori *m*
説 Yorihisa *m*
戩 Yorikatsu *m*
寧 Yoriyasu *m*
熙 Yorioki *m*
[15]潤 Yorimitsu *m*
徸 Yoriyuki *m*
誼 Noriyoshi *m*
慶 Yorinori *m*
[16]錦 Yorikane *m*
[17]聴 Yoritoshi *m*
[18]職 Yorimoto *m*
襄 Rai Noboru *mh*
縄 Yoritsugu *m*

諸 2507 See 諸 2329

諺 2508 Takeshi *m.* (GEN, koto, ō)

謀 2509 [T] Hakaru *m.* (BŌ, MU, koto, nobu)

諭 2510 [T] Satoshi *m*, Satosu. (YU, sato, tsugu)
吉 Yukichi *m*

諢 2511 (KON, odoke)
話浮世風呂 Odokebanashi ukiyoburo *l*

諟 2512 (SHI, JI, TEI, TAI, aki, sane, tada)
子 Akiko *f*

諠 2513 (KEN, KAN, yoshi)
子 Yoshiko *f*

諫 2514 Isamu *m.* (KAN, KEN, isa, tada)
山 Isayama *s*
早 Isahaya *p*

諷 2515 (FŪ, yomu, oto) ⌊getsu *l*
詠十二月 Fūei jūnika-

諦 2516 Akira *m.* (TEI, TAI, aki, akira)
子 Akiko *f*
成 Teisei *m*
寛 Akihiro *m*

## 16 L8

靜 2517 See 静 2145

翰 2518 (KAN, fumi, naka, moto, oto, ha)
於 Fumio *m*

虣 2519 Takeshi *m.* (HŌ, BŌ)

錡 2520 Kanae *m.* (KI, GI)

錞 2521 (JUN, SHUN, TON, tomo)
彦 Tomohiko *m*

鋸 2522 (KYO)
南 Kyonan *p*

録 2523 [T] (ROKU, RYOKU, fumi, toshi)
之助 Rokunosuke *m*
子 Fumiko *f*
郎 Rokurō *m*

錫 2524 Tamō *m*, Atō; Suzu *f.* (SHAKU, SEKI, suzu, masu, yasu)
子 Suzuko *f*
枝 Suzue *f*
胤 Masutane *m*
類 Yasuyoshi *m*

錦 2525 [N] Nishiki *sp.* (KIN, KON, kane, nishiki)
一 Kin'ichi *m*
小路 Nishikikōji *s*
戸 Nishikido *sla*
文 Kanefumi *m*
木 Nishikigi *la*
古利 Nishikori *s*
古里 Nishikori *s*
光山 Kinkōzan *s*
民 Nishigorinotami *s*
吾 Kingo *m*
見 Nishikimi *s*
部 Nishikibe *s*, Nishigori
貫 Nishikini *s*
絵 Nishikie *a*
織 Nishigori *s*

絲 2526 (SHI, ito, yori, tae, tame)

練 2527 [T] (REN, neri)
木 Neriki *s*
馬 Nerima *p*

綜 2528 (SŌ, ZU, osa)
子 Osako *f*

綽 2529 Yutaka *m*; Hiro *f.* (SHAKU, nobu, hiro, yasu, yoshi, hi)
子 Nobuko *f*

綴 2530 Tsuzuki *s.* (TEI, TETSU, tsuzu)
喜 Tsuzuki *sp*; Tsuruhe

綉 2531 (SHŪ, SHU, hide)
子 Hideko *f*

綣 2532 (KEN, KAN, he, heso)
村 Hesomura *s*, Hemura, Henmura

綺 2533 Kanhatori *s*, Kanta. (KI, aya, kamuhata)
子 Ayako *f*
堂 Kidō *ml*
語抄 Kigoshō *l*

綏 2534 Yasushi *m.* (SUI, ZUI, yasu, masa, yoshi)
子 Yasuko *f*
枝 Yasue *f*
彦 Yasuhiko *m*
稔 Yasunari *m*

緑 2535 [T] Midori *m-f-p.* (RYOKU, ROKU, tsuka, tsuna, nori, midori)
川 Midorigawa *s*
太郎 Rokutarō *m*
舎 Midorinoya *m*
雨集 Ryokuushū *l*
野 Minano *s*
簔談 Ryokusadan *l*

網 2536 [T] Yosami *s.* (MŌ, ami, a)
干 Aboshi *s*
干屋 Aboshiya *s*
中 Aminaka *s*
代 Ajiro *s*
走 Abashiri *p*
谷 Amitani *s*
倉 Amikura *s*
野 Amino *sp*
野菊 A. Kiku *fl*
部 Yosamibe *s*

緒 2537 [T] (SHO, JO, SHA, o, tsugu)
川 Ogawa *p*
方 Ogata *sp*
方洪庵 O. Kōan *mh*
田 Oda *s*
形 Ogata *s*
明 Oake *s*
嗣 Otsugu *m*

綿 2538 [T] (MEN, BEN, wata, tsura, masa, masu, yasu)
内 Watauchi *s*
木 Wataki *s*
打 Watauchi *s*
引 Watabiki *s*
屋 Wataya *m*
野 Watano *s*
貫 Watanuki *s*
麿 Watamaro *m*

継 2539 [T] (KEI, KAI, tsugu, tsugi, tsune, hide)
人 Tsugihito *m*
之助 Tsugunosuke *m*
子 Tsuguko *f*
屯 Tsugutamuro *m*
男 Tsuguo *m*
述 Tsugunobu *m*
信 Tsugunobu *m*, Tsuginobu
路 Tsugiji *f*

維 2540 [T] Tsunagu *m*, Tamotsu. (I, YŌ, tsuna, kore, fusa, sumi, shige, tada, masa, yuki, suke)
子 Tsunako *f*, Koreko
大 Tsunahiro *m*
也納 Uiin *p* "Vienna"
氏美学 Ishi bigaku *l*
佐子 Isako *f*
男 Fusao *m*
叙 Korenobu *m*
哉 Shigeya *m*
重 Tsunashige *m*
彬 Koreaki *m*
盛 Koremori *m*
摩経 Yuimakyō *l*
摩経義疏 Y. gisho *l*
摩郷 Imasato *m*
織 Koreori *m*

綾 2541 [N] Aya *sp.* (RYŌ, aya)
人 Ayando *m*
川 Ayakawa *s*
小路 Ayanokōji *s*
上 Ayagami *p*
子 Ayako *f*
也 Aya *f*
夫 Ayao *m*
井 Ayai *s*
田 Ayada *s*
足 Ayatari *ml*
垣 Ayagaki *s*
郁 Ayaka *f*
南 Ryōnan *p*
部 Ayabe *sp*
鼓 Aya no tsuzumi *la*
歌 Ayauta *p*
蔵 Ayazō *m*
麿 Ayamaro *m*
瀬 Ayase *sp*

## 16 L9

餘 2541A See 余 448

鞘 2542 (SHŌ, saya)
子 Sayako *f*

鞍 2543 (AN, kura)
子 Kurako *f*
山 Anzan *p*
手 Kurate *p*
岡 Kuraoka *s*
馬 Kurama *p*
馬天狗 K. tengu *la*
馬出 K. ide *l*
馬参 K. mairi *la*
掛 Kurakake *s*
部 Kuratsukuribe *s*
貫 Kuranuki *s*
智 Kurachi *s*

親 2544 [T] Chikashi *m*, Yoshimi, Itaru. (SHIN, chika, mi, naru, moto, yori, miru, oya)
子 Chikako *f*

尹 Chikamasa *m*
行 Chikayuki *ml*
民 Chikahito *m*
孚 Chikasane *m*
男 Chikao *m*
房 Chikafusa *m*
保 Chikayasu *m*
松 Oyamatsu *s*
音 Motone *m*
従 Chikayori *m*
葆 Chikayasu *m*
賀 Chikayoshi *m*
善 Chikayoshi *m*
誠 Chikanobu *m*
廉 Chikayuki *m*
蔵 Chikatada *m*
鸞 Shinran *mh*

融 2545 [T] Tōru *m-la*; Nagashi *m*. (YŪ, YU, tō, suke, akira, aki, michi, yoshi)
成 Sukenari *m*

—16 L11—

鮒 2546 (FU, funa)
子田 Fushida *s*
主 Funanushi *m*

鮎 2547 (SEN, DEN, NEN, ayu)
川 Ayukawa *s*, Aikawa
川信夫 Ayukawa Nobuo *ml*
之助 Ayunosuke *m*
沢 Ayuzawa *s*
貝 Ayukai *s*
貝槐園 A. Kaien *ml*

—16 L12—

數 2548 See 数 2169

歎 2549 Takeshi *m*. (KŌ)

歖 2550 See 喜 2169

—16 L13—

鄰 2551 See 隣 2443

—16 L14—

勵 2552 See 励 430

勳 2553 See 勲 2407

劉 2554 Ryū *sm*, Mizuki; Mizuchi *m*. (RYŪ, RU, nobu)

叡 2555 Satoshi *m*, Akira, Tōru. (EI, sato, toshi, masa, tada, yoshi)
尊 Eison *mh*

—16 T2—

褒 2556 (HŌ, yoshi)
子 Yoshiko *f*

—16 T3—

菑 2557 Shigeru *m*. (JI)

養 2558 [T] Mamoru *m*. (YŌ, yasu, nobu, kai, yoshi, kiyo, osa, suke)
一 Yōichi *m*
二 Yōji *m*
父 Yabu *sp*; Kaifu *s*
田 Yōda *s*
仲 Nobunaka *m*
老 Yōrō *p-la* 717–24
老律令 Y. ritsuryō *l*
利 Yoshitoshi *m*
和 Yōwa 1181–82
秀 Yoshihide *m*
信 Osanobu *m*
長 Yasunaga *m*
蚕 Kogai *s*
根 Yasumoto *m*
道 Nobumichi *m*
徳 Yamato *s*

憙 2559 Yoshi *f*. (KI, yoshi, toshi)
子 Yoshiko *f*
彦 Yoshihiko *m*
雄 Toshio *m*

熹 2560 (KI, yoshi, toshi, hiro)
季 Hirosue *m*
郎 Toshirō *m*

寴 2561 See 親 2544

憲 2562 [T] Tadashi *m*, Tadasu, Ken, Toshi, Akira. (KEN, nori, toshi, kazu, sada)
一 Ken'ichi *m*
二郎 Kenjirō *m*
三 Kenzō *m*
夫 Sadao *m*
太 Kenta *m*
太郎 Kentarō *m*
正 Toshimasa *m*
次 Kenji *m*
作 Kensaku *m*
信 Toshinobu *m*
治 Kenji *m*
法十七条 Kenpō jūshichijō *l*
相 Norisuke *m*
宣 Kazunobu *m*
重 Norishige *m*
陰 Norikage *m*
欽 Noriyoshi *m*
福 Noriyoshi *m*
顕 Noriaki *m*
藤 Norifuji *m*

薊 2562A Azami *s*. (KEI, KAI, azami)

薆 2563 Kaoru *m*. (AI)

蕗 2564 Fukiawase *s*. (RO, fuki)
子 Fukiko *f*

薤 2565 (KAI, nira)
山 Nirayama *s*
露行 Kairokō *l*

蕨 2566 Warabi *sp*; Ketsu *s*. (KETSU)
桐軒 Warabi Tōken *ml*
真 Ketsu Shin *ml*
橿堂 Warabi Kyōdō *ml*

薫 2567 [T] Kaoru *m*, Tsutomu. (KUN, shige, hide, nio, yuki, kao, kuru, tada, nobu, hō, fusa, masa)
子 Shigeko *f*, Nioko
丸 Shigemaru *m*
兵 Kunpei *m*
明 Shigetoshi *m*
信 Hōshin *m*

薬 2568 [T] Kusuri *m*; Kusushi *sm*. (YAKU, kusu, kusuri)
子 Kusuko *f*
戸 Kusushie *s*
君 Kusuriko *fh*
師 Yakushi *s*
師山 Yakushiyama *s*
師寺 Yakushiji *sp*
師如来 Yakushi Nyorai *mh*
袋 Minae *s*, Minai, Irazu

薄 2569 [T] Susuki *s*; Itaru *m*. (HAKU, usu, susuki, susu)
井 Usui *s*
木 Susuki *s*
氷 Usurai *ml*
田 Susukida *s*
田泣菫 S. Kyūkin *ml*
尾屋 Susukioya *s*
葉 Usuba *s*
雲 Usugumo *m*

—16 T4—

燕 2570 Tsubame *p*. (EN, yasu, yoshi, naru, teru)
夫 Yasuo *m*

—16 T5—

冀 2571 Chikashi *m*. (KI, kuni)

鴛 2572 (EN, oshi)
海 Enkai *s*

窮 2573 [T] Kiwamu *s*. (KYŪ, KU, mi)
田 Kubota *s*
死 Kyūshi *l*

—16 T6—

篝 2574 Kagari *m*. (KŌ, KU)
火 Kagaribi *l*

築 2575 [T] (CHIKU, tsui, tsuki, tsuku)
山 Tsukiyama *s*
地 Tsukiji *p*; Tsuiji *sp*

薄 燕 冀 鴛 窮 篝 築 ▼ 篤 震 霓 賢 髯 整 憑 凞 學 壁 興 曆 歷 還 邊 遼 遜 邁 遲 盧 臧 磨 幾 齒 龜 優 隱 擦 壞 壕 ▲ 擬 懐 濱 澀 濬 濯 濠 澗

城 Tsuiki *s*, Tsuki
部 Tsukube *s*
館 Tsukidate *p*

篤 2576 [T] Atsushi *m.* (TOKU, atsu, sumi, shige)
子 Atsuko *f*
太郎 Tokutarō *m*
次郎 Tokujirō *m*
志郎 Tokushirō *m*
治 Tokuji *m*
珍 Atsuyoshi *m*
彦 Atsuhiko *m*
倉 Atsukura *m*
胤 Atsutane *ml*
栞 Atsusuke *m*

## 16 T8

震 2577 [T] Shin *m.* (SHIN, nari, naru, oto, nobu)

霓 2578 (GEI)
裳微吟 Geishō bigin *l*

## 16 T9

賢 2579 [T] Satoshi *m*, Satoru, Masaru, Suguru, Tadashi, Sakashi. (KEN, yoshi, masa, kata, sato, tada, masu, saka, taka, toshi, nori, yasu, yori, katsu)
[1]一郎 Ken'ichirō *m*
[3]三 Kenzō *m*, Katamitsu
子 Katako *f*, Satoko
之助 Kennosuke *m*
[4]木 Sakaki *m-l*
太郎 Kentarō *m*
[5]外集 Kengaishū *l*
礼 Yoshinori *m*
四郎 Kenshirō *m*
[6]次 Yoshitsugu *m*, Kenji
次郎 Kenjirō *m*
[7]作 Kensaku *m*
吾 Kengo *m*
[9]保 Yoshiyasu *m*
信 Yoshinobu *m*
治 Kenji *m*
祐 Masachi *m*
[10]俊 Masatoshi *m*; Kenshun *mh*
竜 Kenryū *m*
造 Kenzō *m*
[12]策 Kensaku *m*
[15]蔵 Kenzō *m*

## 16 T11

髯 2580 (ZEN, NEN, hige)
九郎 Higekurō *m*

整 2581 [T] Hitoshi *m*, Totonō, Osamu. (SEI, SHŌ, nari, masa, nobu, yoshi)
方 Masakata *m*
明 Nariaki *m*

## 16 T12

憑 2582 Atsushi *m.* (HYŌ, yori, mitsu)

凞 2583 See 熙 2409

## 16 T13

學 2584 See 学 719

壁 2585 [T] Kabe *s.* (HEKI, kabe)
谷 Kabeya *s*
草 Kabegusa *l*
屋 Kabeya *s*

## 16 T14

興 2586 [T] Sakan *m.* (KŌ, KYŌ, oki, ki, tomo, saki, fuka, fusa)
[2]人 Okindo *m*
[3]之 Tomoyuki *m*
丸 Okimaru *m*
[4]文 Okinori *m*
[5]右 Kōsuke *m*
正 Okimasa *m*
生 Okinari *m*
[6]次郎 Kōjirō *m*
世 Okiyo *s*
[8]国 Kōkoku 1340–46
[9]津 Okitsu *s*
直 Okinao *m*
風 Okikaze *m*
建 Okitatsu *m*
重 Okishige *m*
[10]除 Kōjo *p*
家 Okiie *m*
屋 Okiie *m*
[11]梠 Kōrogi *s*
根昇 Okinenobori *m*
野 Okino *s*
部 Okoppe *p*
[12]貫 Okitsura *m*
道 Okimichi *s*
[13]福寺 Kōfukuji *p*
禅護国論 Kōzen gokokuron *lh*
詩 Okiuta *m*
[14]増 Okinaga *m*
[15]統 Okimune *sm*
[16]膳 Kōzen *s*
[21]譲館 Kōjōkan *ph*

## 16 F2

曆 2587 See 暦 2235

歷 2587A See 歴 2247

## 16 F3

還 2588 [T] (KAN)
魂紙料 Sukikaeshi *l*

## 16 F4

邊 2589 See 辺 179

遼 2590 Haruka *m.* (RYŌ, tō)

遜 2591 Yuzuru *m.* (SON, yasu)
子 Yasuko *f*

邁 2592 Susumu *m*, Tsutomu. (MAI, BAI, taka, yuki, tō)

遲 2593 Noboru *m*, Susumu, Terasu. (SEN, take, nori, akira)
子 Takeko *f*
雄 Takeo *m*

## 16 F6

盧 2594 Iori *m*; Ro *s.* (RO, RYO, ie, yoshi)

## 16 F9

臧 2595 (ZŌ, SŌ, yoshi, tsugu, atsu)
子 Yoshiko *f*

## 16 F11

磨 2596 [N] Migaku *m*, Osamu. (MA, BA, kiyo, usu)
井 Usui *s*
谷 Usutani *s*
磋夫 Masao *m*
輔 Masuke *m*

## 16 F14

幾 2597 [T] Chikashi *m.* (KI, KE, iku, chika, oki, nori, fusa)
三郎 Ikusaburō *m*
之輔 Ikunosuke *m*
子 Ikuko *f*
太郎 Ikutarō *m*
田 Ikuta *s*
平 Ikuhei *m*
世 Ikuyo *s*
男麻呂 Kiomaro *m*
馬 Ikuma *m*

## 16 U

齒 2598 See 歯 2051

龜 2598A See 亀 1531

## 17 L2

優 2599 [T] Masaru *m*, Yutaka. (YŪ, U, masa, hiro, katsu)
美 Masami *m*
厳 Masayoshi *m*

## 17 L3

隱 2600 See 隠 2074

擦 2601 Akira *m.* (SATSU)

壞 2602 [T] Tsuchi *f.* (KAI, E)
島 Tsukureshima *s*, Eshima, Hotokorojima

壕 2603 Hori *s.* (GŌ, KŌ, hori)
越 Horikoshi *s*
越菜陽 H. Saiyō *ml*

懝 2604 (GI, sato, nori)

懐 2605 [T] Kitasu *m.* (KAI, E, kane, yasu, chika, mochi, taka, tsune, kanu)
之 Yasuyuki *m*
子 Kaneko *f*
月堂 Kaigetsudō *s*
世 Mochiyo *m*
成 Kanehira *m*
国 Mochikuni *m*
良 Kanenaga *m*
春 Yasuharu *m*
風藻 Kaifūsō *l*
通 Chikamichi *m*
徳堂 Kaitokudō *ph*

濱 2606 See 浜 1070

澀 2607 See 渋 1334

濬 2608 Fukashi *m.* (SHUN)

濯 2609 Arō *m.* (TAKU, JOKU)

濠 2610 Hori *s.* (GŌ)
洲 Gōshū *p* "Australia"

濶 2611 Hiroshi *m.* (KATSU, KACHI, hiro)
子 Hiroko *f*

濃 2612 [T] Atsushi *m*, Nō. (NŌ, JŌ, atsu)
子 Atsuko *f*

濤 2613 (TŌ, nami)
川 Namikawa *s*
子 Namiko *f*
五郎 Namigorō *m*

鴻 2614 Hiroshi *m*; Kō *s.* (KŌ, GU, hiro, toki)
山 Ōyama *s*
太郎 Kōtarō *m*
本 Kōnomoto *s*
田 Kōnota *s*
池 Kōnoike *s*
野 Kōno *s*
巣 Kōnosu *p*
臚館 Kōrokan *ph*

潔 2615 [T] Kiyoshi *m.* (KETSU, KECHI, kiyo, yoshi, yuki)
茂 Kiyomoto *m*
真 Kiyomi *m*
雄 Yoshio *m*
興 Kiyoki *m*
綱 Kiyotsuna *m*

## 17 L4

膽 2616 See 胆 845

曦 2617 See 曦 2914

璘 2618 Hikaru *m.* (RIN)

璐 2619 (RO, tama)
太郎 Tamatarō *m*

環 2620 [T] Tamaki *m-f.* (KAN, tama)
江 Tamae *f*
貫 Kannuki *s*

彊 2621 Tsutomu *m.* (KYŌ, GŌ, take, kowa)

橿 2622 Kashiwa *m.* (KYŌ, kashi, kashiwa)
原 Kashihara *p*, Kashiwara; Kashiwabara *s*

檀 2623 Dan *s*; Mayumi *m-f.* (DAN)
一雄 D. Kazuo *ml*
上 Danjō *s*
風 Danpū *la*
野 Danno *s*
越 Dan'otsu *m*

檜 2624 Hinoki *s.* (KAI, hi)
山 Hiyama *sp*
山田 Hiyamada *s*
坂 Hisaka *s*
枝岐 Hinoemata *p*
垣 Higaki *sla*
前 Hinokuma *s*
原 Hinohara *p*
隈 Hinokuma *s*
園 Hizono *s*

## 17 L5

穗 2625 See 穂 2308

矯 2626 Takeshi *m*, Isami. (KYŌ, tada)

禪 2627 See 禅 1886

禧 2628 Osamu *m*, Yoshi. (KI, yoshi, tomi, saki, toshi)
子 Yoshiko *f*, Sakiko

瞭 2629 Akira *m.* (RYŌ, aki)

瞳 2630 Akira *m*; Hitomi *f.* (DŌ)

## 17 L6

鴿 2631 (KŌ, hato)
巣江 Kozue *f*

糟 2632 (SŌ, kasu)
谷 Kasuya *s*

糠 2633 (KŌ, nuka, ara)
子 Nukako *f*
虫 Nukamushi *m*
信 Nukanobu *s*

聴 2634 [T] Akira *m.* (CHŌ, aki, toshi, yori)
子 Akiko *f*

聰 2635 See 聡 2311

## 17 L7

輕 2636 See 軽 1657

臻 2637 Itaru *m.* (SHIN)

謐 2637A Shizuka *m.* (HITSU, yasu)

謨 2638 Hakaru *m.* (BO, MO, koto, akira, nori, fumi)

諧 2639 Kanō *m.* (KAI, GAI, nari, yuki)

謎 2640 (MEI)
帯一寸徳兵衛 Nazo no obi chotto Tokubee *la*

諶 2641 Makoto *m.* (JIN, nobu, tsumu)
貞 Nobusada *m*

謡 2642 [T] Utai *la.* (YŌ)
曲 Yōkyoku *l*

謌 2643 (KA, uta)
郎 Utarō *m*

講 2644 [T] (KŌ, tsugu, nori, michi)
道館 Kōdōkan *p*
殿 Kōden *s*

謹 2645 [T] Susumu *m.* (KIN, KON, chika, mori, nori, nari)
一郎 Kin'ichirō *m*
之助 Kinnosuke *m*
治 Kinji *m*
度 Chikanori *m*

謙 2646 [T] Ken *m*, Yuzuru. (KEN, nori, kane, kata, yoshi, aki, shizu)
一 Ken'ichi *m*
二 Kenji *m*
二郎 Kenjirō *m*
十郎 Kenjūrō *m*
三 Kenzō *m*
三郎 Kenzaburō *m*
介 Kensuke *m*
夫 Shizuo *m*

謹 謙 ▼ 錄 鍬 鍾 鍋 鍛 鍵 縄 練 緒 綠 緾 緝 緩 緑 綱 総 龍 鞠 騂 駸 豁 瓢 鮪 鮮 鮭 鮫 戯 劍 羲 嬴 褰 舊 薿 藎 薗 藁 薦 薩 曇 翼 簀 ▲ 簑 篷

四郎 Kenshirō *m*
次 Kenji *m*
次郎 Kenjirō *m*
吉 Kenkichi *m*
和 Norikazu *m*
昌 Norimasa *m*
信 Kenshin *m*
治 Kenji *m*
亮 Yoshiaki *m*
雄 Yoshio *m*
輔 Kensuke *m*
蔵 Kenzō *m*

## 17 L8

**錄** 2647 See 録 2523

**鍬** 2648 (SHŪ, SHŌ, suki, kuwa)
形 Kuwagata *s*

**鍾** 2649 (SHŌ, SHU, atsu)
馗 Shō Ki *mh-la* "Chung K'uei"

**鍋** 2650 (KA, nabe)
八撥 Nabe yatsubachi ⌊*l*
井 Nabei *s*
太郎 Nabetarō *m*
田 Nabeta *s*
谷 Nabetani *s*, Nabeya
倉 Nabekura *s*
島 Nabeshima *s*
島閑叟 N. Kansō *mh*

**鍛** 2651 [T] Kitō *m*, Kitae; Kanuchi *s*, Katashi. (TAN, kaji, ka)
冶 Kaji *s*, Kanuchi
師 Kanuchi *s*

**鍵** 2652 Kagi *sl.* (KEN, GEN, kagi)
子 Kagiko *f*
山 Kagiyama *s*
太郎 Kentarō *m*
次郎 Kenjirō *m*
谷 Kagiya *s*
武 Kagitake *m*
富 Kagitomi *s*

**縄** 2653 See 繩 2955

**練** 2654 See 練 2527

**緒** 2655 See 緒 2537

**綠** 2656 See 緑 2535

**緾** 2657 See 纏 2988

**緝** 2658 Tsugu *f.* (SHŪ, tsugi, tsugu, masa)
子 Tsugiko *f*
煕 Tsugihiro *m*

**緩** 2659 [T] (KAN, yasu, hiro, nobu, ⌊fusa)
子 Hiroko *f*
稔 Yasunari *m*

**縁** 2660 [T] Heri *s.* (EN, yori, yuka, yasu, masa, mune, yo- ⌊shi)
子 Yukako *f*
外縁 Engaien *l*
信 Yorinobu *m*

**綱** 2661 [T] Tsuna *sm.* (KŌ, tsuna)
子 Tsunako *f*
川 Tsunagawa *s*
手 Tsunade *m*
野 Tsunano *s*
紀 Tsunanori *m*
島 Tsunajima *s*
島梁川 T. Ryōsen *ml*

**総** 2662 [T] Fusa *f*; Suburu *m.* (SŌ, SU, fusa, osa, sa, nobu, michi)
一郎 Sōichirō *m*
三郎 Sōzaburō *m*
太郎 Sōtarō *m*
生 Fusō *s*
社 Sōja *p*
角 Agemaki *l*
明 Fusaaki *m*
長 Fusanaga *m*
領 Sōryō *p*

## 17 L9

**龍** 2663 See 竜 1199

**鞠** 2664 (KIKU, KOKU, mari, tsugu, mitsu)
子 Mariko *f*
智 Kikuchi *s*
瀬 Marise *s*

## 17 L10

**騂** 2665 (SEI, SHŌ, ka)

**駸** 2666 Susumu *m.* (SHIN)

**豁** 2667 Hiroshi *m*, Hiraku, Tōru. (KATSU, hiro, akira, yuki)
夫 Hiroo *m*
通 Hiromichi *m*

## 17 L11

**瓢** 2668 (HYŌ, hisago)
郎 Hisagorō *m*

**鮪** 2669 Shibi *m.* (YŪ, U)

**鮮** 2670 [T] Akira *m.* (SEN, akira, asa)
田 Asada *s*

**鮭** 2671 (KEI, sake)
川 Sakegawa *p*
延 Sakenobe *s*

**鮫** 2672 (KŌ, KYŌ, same)
人 Kōjin *l*
川 Samegawa *sp*
造 Samezō *m*
島 Samejima *s*

## 17 L13

**戯** 2673 See 戲 2350

**劍** 2674 Osamu *m.* (REN, kazu, yoshi, osa)

## 17 T3

**羲** 2675 Tadashi *m.* (GI)

**嬴** 2676 (EI, YŌ, mitsu)

**褰** 2677 (KEN, to)
張 Tobari *s*

**舊** 2678 See 旧 119

**薿** 2679 Shigeru *m.* (GI)

**藎** 2680 Susumu *m.* (JIN, e)

**薗** 2681 Sono *f.* (EN, ON, sono)
八 Sonohachi *ma*
田 Sonoda *s*
部 Sonobe *s*

**藁** 2682 (KŌ, wara)
谷 Waraya *s*, Waragai
科 Warashina *s*
品 Warashina *s*
屋詠草 Waraya eisō *l*

**薦** 2683 [T] Komo *s.* (SEN, komo, shige, nobu)
口 Komoku *s*
田 Komoda *s*
河 Suruga *s*
集 Komozume *s*

**薩** 2684 (SATSU)
陀 Satta *s*
埵 Satta *s*, Sassui
摩 Satsuma *sph*
摩守 S. no Kami *la*
摩浄雲 S. Jōun *ma*

## 17 T4

**曇** 2685 [T] (DON)
徴 Donchō *mh*

## 17 T6

**翼** 2686 [T] Tsubasa *m*, Tasuku, Tamotsu. (YOKU, suke)

**簀** 2687 (SAKU, JAKU, su)

秦 Suhata *s*

簑 2688 See 蓑 2194

篷 2689 (HŌ, BU, toma)
子 Tomako *f*

築 2690 See 梁 1475

篠 2691 Sasa *s*, Shino. (SHŌ, shino, sasa)
ノ井 Shinonoi *p*
4山 Shinoyama *s*, Sasayama
井 Shinoi *s*
木 Shinogi *s*
5田 Shinoda *s*
田太郎 S. Tarō *ml*
田悌二郎 S. Teijirō *ml*
本 Shinomoto *s*
6江 Shinoe *f*
7沢 Shinozawa *s*
9俣 Shinomata *s*
岡 Shinooka *s*
10倉 Sasakura *s*
宮 Shinomiya *s*
栗 Sasaguri *p*
原 Shinohara *s*, Sasahara
原志都児 Shinohara Shizuji *ml*
原梵 S. Bon *ml*
原温亭 S. Ontei *ml*
原鳳作 S. Hōsaku *ml*
屋 Sasaya *s*
11野 Sasano *s*
笥 Sasaki *s*
12崎 Shinozaki *s*
13塚 Shinozuka *s*

—17 T8—

營 2692 See 営 1751

霞 2693 Kasumi *sm-f-p*. (KA, kasumi)
ケ関 Kasumigaseki *p*
翁 Kaoki *m*
間昼 Kamagaya *s*

霜 2694 [T] (SŌ, SHŌ, shimo)
子 Shimoko *f*
山 Shimoyama *s*
田 Shimoda *s*
村 Shimomura *s*
邨 Shimomura *s*
鳥 Shimotori *s*
越 Shimokoshi *s*

—17 T10—

覧 2695 [T] (RAN, mi, kata, tada, miru)

—17 T11—

聲 2696 See 声 465

髭 2697 (SHI, hige)
野 Higeno *s*

聳 2698 (SHŌ, SHU, taka)
子 Takako *f*

—17 T13—

懃 2699 Tsutomu *m*. (KIN, GON)

懋 2700 Tsutomu *m*, Shigeru, Susumi. (BŌ, MU, shige, masa, yoshi)

慈 2701 [T] Shigeru *m*. (JI, SHI, shige, chika, nari, yasu, yoshi)
子 Chikako *f*
円 Jien *ml*
光寺 Jikōji *s*
悲心鳥 Jihishinchō *l*
照寺 Jishōji *p*
鎮 Jichin *ml*

—17 T14—

墾 2702 [T] Tsutomu *m*, Hiraku; Araki *s*. (KON)
田 Konda *s*

—17 T15—

輿 2703 (YO, koshi)
水 Koshimizu *s*
石 Koshiishi *s*

—17 F3—

應 2704 See 応 509

膺 2705 Osamu *m*. (YŌ, ō)

—17 F5—

厳 2706 [T] Itsuki *m*, Ikashi, Gen. (GEN, GON, GAN, itsu, izu, yoshi, iwa, kane, taka, hiro, tsuyo, ikashi)
丸 Itsumaru *m*
子 Itsuko *f*, Izuko, Takako
水 Itsumi *m*
山 Izuyama *s*
木 Kyūragi *p*
太郎 Itsutarō *m*
戈 Ikashihoko *m*
比古 Izuhiko *m*
石 Ikashi *s*
平 Iwahei *m*
秀 Iwahide *m*
浄 Hirokiyo *m*
美 Izumi *s*
原 Izuhara *p*
島 Itsukushima *p*
穂 Izuho *m*

—17 F6—

戴 2707 Tai *s*. (TAI, DAI)
恩記 Daionki *l*

—17 F8—

闌 2708 Takeshi *m*. (RAN, take, suso)
更 Rankō *ml*

闇 2709 (AN, kura)
中政治家 Anchū seijika *l*

闊 2710 Hiroshi *m*. (KATSU, KACHI, hiro)
子 Hiroko *f*

—18 L3—

擴 2711 See 拡 799

攄 2712 Noburu *m*. (CHO)

濟 2713 See 済 1336

濹 2714 (BOKU)
東綺譚 Bokutō kidan *l*

—18 L4—

彌 2715 See 弥 832

嶸 2716 Takashi *m*. (EI, YŌ)

瓊 2717 Tama *f*. (KEI, GYŌ, SEN, ZEN, tama, ni, yoshi)
玖 Tamaki *f*
缶 Nibe *m*

嬬 2718 (JU, tsuma)
恋 Tsumagoi *p*

曙 2719 Akebono *sf*; Akira *m*. (SHO, JO, ake, akira)
覧 Akemi *m*

曜 2720 [T] Terasu *m*, Akira; Teru *f*. (YŌ, teru)
禧 Teruyoshi *m*

燿 2721 (YŌ, teru)
胤 Terutane *m*

櫂 2722 (TAKU, JAKU, kaji)
子 Kajiko *f*

檥 2723 (GAI, kaji)
媛 Kajihime *fh*

檮 2724 (TŌ, JU, yusu)
原 Yusuhara *p*

—18 L5—

禮 2725 See 礼 146

瞻 2726 (SEN, mi)

蟻 2727 Tadashi *m*. (GI)

穟 2728 Hiizuru *m*. (SUI, ZUI, hide, hina)

翼 簣 ▼ 簑 篷 簗 篠 營 霞 霜 覧 聲 髭 聳 懃 懋 慈 墾 輿 應 膺 厳 戴 闌 闇 闊 擴 攄 濟 濹 彌 嶸 瓊 嬬 曙 曜 燿 櫂 檥 檮 禮 瞻 蟻 穟 ▲ 穫 礎

檮 禮 瞻 蟻 穩 ▼ 穫 礎 磷 礒 蟬 職 謠 謹 轉 嬲 鵠 踰 韓 經 緣 緯 緘 縫 鎗 鎰 鎚 鎌 鎮 鞭 馥 顔 類 額 顕 歸 雜 難 館 騎 駿 ▲ 鯉 観 齢 勸 齋

**穫** 2729 [T] Minoru *m.* (KAKU, WAKU, e)

**礎** 2730 [T] (SO, SHO, ki)

**磷** 2731 Kiyoshi *m.* (RIN)

**礒** 2732 Iwao *m.* (GI, iso)
子 Isoko *f*
辺 Isobe *s*
田 Isoda *s*
野 Isono *s*
部 Isobe *s*
崎 Isozaki *s*

**—18 L6—**

**蟬** 2733 (SEN, ZEN, semi)
丸 Semimaru *m-la*

**職** 2734 [T] (SHOKU, SHIKI, moto, yori, tsune, yoshi)
仁 Yorihito *m*
男 Tsuneo *m*
直 Motonao *m*, Yorinao
俊 Yoshitoshi *m*
原抄 Shokugenshō *lh*
隆 Mototaka *m*

**—18 L7—**

**謠** 2735 See 謡 2642

**謹** 2736 See 謹 2645

**轉** 2737 See 転 1656

**嬲** 2738 Uwanari *l.* (JŌ, DŌ)

**鵠** 2739 (KOKU, GOKU, nori, tazu)
世 Tazuyo *m*

**踰** 2740 Koshi *s.* (YU, YŌ, koshi)
部 Koshibe *s*
部大炊 Koshibeōi *s*

**—18 L8—**

**韓** 2741 Kara *s.* (KAN, GEN, kara)
白水郎 Karaama *s*
国 Kankoku *p* "(Republic of) Korea"; Karakuni *mh*

**經** 2742 See 経 1975

**緣** 2743 See 縁 2660

**緯** 2744 [T] Tsukane *m.* (I)

**緘** 2745 (I)
藤 Itō *s*

**縫** 2746 (HŌ, BU, nui)
二 Nuiji *m*
川 Nuigawa *s*
子 Nuiko *f*
伴 Kinunuinotomo *s*

**鎗** 2747 (SŌ, SHŌ, yari)
田 Yarita *s*

**鎰** 2748 (ITSU, ICHI, kagi)
子 Kagiko *f*

**鎚** 2749 (TSUI, TAI, tsuchi)
之助 Tsuchinosuke *m*

**鎌** 2750 [N] (KEN, kama, kata, kane)
ヶ谷 Kamagaya *p*
太郎 Kamatarō *m*
田 Kamata *s*
形 Kamagata *s*
足 Kamatari *m*
治 Kenji *m*, Kamaji
倉 Kamakura *sp*
倉殿 K.-dono *mh*
倉幕府 K. bakufu *h*
原 Kamahara *s*
野 Kamano *s*
滝 Kamataki *s*
腹 Kamabara *la*
髭 Kamabige *la*

**鎮** 2751 [T] Shizumu *m*, Osamu, Shizumi, Shizume, Yasushi, Mamoru. (CHIN, shizu, yasu, shige, tsune, shin, masa, tane, naka)
一 Shin'ichi *m*
三 Chinzō *m*
目 Shizume *s*
次郎 Chinjirō *m*
休 Shigetane *m*
西 Chinzei *p*
吾 Masamichi *m*
男 Yasuo *m*, Shigeo
実 Shizusane *m*
治 Shizuharu *m*
重 Shigeatsu *m*
家 Shigeie *m*
馬 Shizuma *m*
漣 Shigenami *m*
静 Tsuneyasu *m*
衛 Yasumori *m*

**—18 L9—**

**鞭** 2752 (BEN, HEN, muchi)
子 Muchiko *f*

**馥** 2753 Kaoru *f.* (FUKU, BUKU)

**顔** 2754 [T] (GAN, kao)
師 Kaoshi *l*

**類** 2755 [T] (RUI, yoshi, tomo, nashi)
聚名義抄 Ruijū myōgishō *l*
聚国史 R. kokushi *l*

**額** 2756 [T] Nuka *s.* (GAKU, nuka)
川 Nukagawa *s*
戸 Kōto *s*
田 Nukada *sp*
田六福 N. Roppuku *ml*
田王 N. no Ōkimi *fl*
田部 Nukadabe *s*
賀 Nukaga *s*

**顕** 2757 [T] Akira *m.* (KEN, aki, akira, teru, taka)
[3]三 Kenzō *m*
子 Akiko *f*
[5]允 Akimasa *m*, Akikoto
[6]次 Takatsugu *m*
行 Akiyuki *m*
光 Akimitsu *m*
成 Kensei *m*
[7]如 Kennyo *mh*
孝 Akinori *m*
[8]注密勘 Kenchū mitsukan *l*
房 Akifusa *m*
[9]信 Akinobu *m*
治 Kenji *m*
昭 Kenshō *ml*
[10]時 Akitoki *m*
家 Akiie *m*
[11]能 Akiyoshi *m*
[12]達 Akitate *m*
智 Akinori *m*
[13]義 Akiyoshi *m*
[14]輔 Akisuke *ml*
彰 Akira *m*

**—18 L10—**

**歸** 2758 See 帰 1018

**雜** 2759 See 雑 2127

**難** 2760 [T] (NAN)
波 Naniwa *ph-la*; Nanba *s*
波土産 Naniwa miyage *l*
波田 Nanbata *s*
波江 Naniwae *s*
波鉦 Naniwa dora *l*
波鑑 N. kagami *la*

**館** 2761 [T] Tate *s*, Tachi, Yakata. (KAN, tate, tachi)
山 Tateyama *sp*
山一子 T. Kazuko *fl*
村 Tatemura *s*
林 Tatebayashi *sp*
岩 Tateiwa *p*
野 Tateno *s*, Tachino

**騎** 2762 [T] (KI, GI, nori)
西 Kisai *p*

**駿** 2763 Hayashi *m*, Hayao, Toshi, Takashi. (SHUN, toshi)

吉 Shunkichi *m*
男 Toshio *m*
河 Suruga *sph*
東 Suntō *p*

——18 L11——

鯉 2764 [N] (RI, koi)
三郎 Risaburō *m*
江 Koie *s*
吉 Koikichi *m*
沼 Koinuma *s*
登 Koito *s*
淵 Koibuchi *s*

観 2765 [T] Shimesu *m.* (KAN, mi, aki, maro, miru)
心寺 Kanshinji *p*
世 Kanze *s*
世元清 K. Motokiyo *mla*
世清次 K. Kiyotsugu *mla*
応 Kan'ō 1350–52
阿弥 Kan'ami *mla*
依 Akiyori *m*
音 Kannon *fh*
音寺 Kan'onji *p*
音岩 Kannon'iwa *l*
勒 Kanroku *mh*
潮楼 Kanchōrō *ml*

——18 L13——

齢 2766 [T] (REI, RYŌ, yo, toshi, naka)
子 Toshiko *p*

——18 L16——

勷 2767 Susumu *m.* (YŌ)

——18 T2——

齋 2768 See 斎 1454

襄 2769 Noboru *m.* (JŌ)
一 Jōichi *m*
夫 Jōfu *m*

——18 T3——

燾 2770 (JU, CHŪ, teru)
次 Teruji *m*

藩 2771 [T] (HAN)
翰譜 Hankanpu *lh*

藍 2772 Ai *s.* (RAN, ai)
川 Aikawa *s*
子 Aiko *f*
住 Aisumi *p*
沢 Aizawa *s*
谷 Aiya *s*
香 Aikyō *s*
染川 Aisomegawa *la*
原 Aibara *s*
野 Aino *s*

藤 2773 [N] Fuji *sfla*; Tō *s*; Katsura *m.* (TŌ, fuji, tsu, hisa)
ノ木 Fujinoki *s*
ケ谷 Fujigaya *s*
ケ崎 Fujigasaki *s*
[1]一 Tōichi *m*
一郎 Tōichirō *m*
[2]二郎 Tōjirō *m*
十郎 Tōjūrō *m*
[3]三郎 Tōzaburō *m*
川 Fujikawa *s*
川忠治 F. Chūji *ml*
下 Fujishita *s*, Toke
大路 Fujiōji *s*
丸 Fujimaru *s*
子 Fujiko *f*
[5]戸 Fujito *sla*; Fujiie *m*
元 Fujimoto *s*
中 Fujinaka *s*
山 Fujiyama *s*
木 Fujiki *s*
太 Tōta *m*
太郎 Tōtarō *m*
井 Fujii *s*
井右門 F. Umon *mh*
井浩祐 F. Kōyū *ma*
井真澄 F. Masumi *ml*
[5]永 Fujinaga *s*; Tōei *la*
代 Fujishiro *p*
右衛門 Tōemon *m*
市郎 Tōichirō *m*
生 Fujiu *s*
四郎 Tōshirō *m*
平 Fujidaira *s*
本 Fujimoto *s*
矢淵 Fujiyabuchi *s*
氏 Tōshi *s*
田 Fujita *sp* ⌈*mh*
田小四郎 F. Koshirō
田茂吉 F. Mokichi *ml*
田東湖 F. Tōko *mh*
田信勝 F. Nobukatsu *ml*
田幽谷 F. Yūkoku *mh*
[6]江 Fujie *s* ⌈chi *m*
吉 Fujiyoshi *s*; Tōki-
[7]作 Tōsaku *m*
坂 Fujisaka *s*
沢 Fujisawa *sp*
沢古実 F. Furumi *ml*
沢桓夫 F. Takeo *ml*
沢清造 F. Seizō *ml*
好 Fujiyoshi *s*
杜 Fujinomori *s*
村 Fujimura *s*; Tōson *ml*
村操 F. Misao *ml*
助 Tōsuke *m*
谷 Fujitani *s*, Fujiya, Fujigaya ⌈kashū *l*
谷和歌集 Fujigaya wa-
安 Fujiyasu *s*
尾 Fujio *s*
里 Fujisato *p*
寿丸 Fujijumaru *m*
[8]牧 Fujimaki *s*
門 Fujito *s*, Fujikado
波 Fujinami *s*
沼 Fujinuma *s*
林 Fujibayashi *s*
枝 Fujieda *sp*; Fujie *s*
枝静男 Fujieda Shizuo *ml* ⌈*ma*
若丸 Fujiwakamaru
居 Fujii *s*
居教恵 F. Kyōe *ml*
並 Fujinami *s*
[9]咲 Fujisaki *s*
津 Fujitsu *sp*
城 Fujishiro *s*
松 Fujimatsu *s*
栄 Tōei *la*
巻 Fujimaki *s*
岡 Fujioka *sp*
重 Fujishige *s*
[10]浦 Fujiura *s*
栩 Fujiu *s*
高 Fujitaka *s*
倉 Fujikura *s*
原 Fujiwara *sp*
原元命 F. no Motonaga *mh* ⌈to *mh*
原不比等 F. no Fuhi-
原冬嗣 F. no Fuyutsugu *mh*
原仲麻呂 F. no Nakamaro *mh*
原行成 F. no Yukinari / Kōzei *mlh*
原百川 F. no Momokawa *mh* ⌈*ml*
原宇合 F. no Umakai
原広嗣 F. no Hirotsugu *mh* ⌈ka *mh*
原成親 F. no Narichi-
原佐世 F. no Sukeyo *ml* ⌈*ml*
原明衡 F. no Akihira
原忠平 F. no Tadahira *mh* ⌈chi *ml*
原忠通 F. no Tadami-
原秀能 F. no Hidetō *ml* ⌈*mh*
原秀郷 F. no Hidesato
原秀衡 F. no Hidehira *mh*
原実方 F. no Sanekata *ml* ⌈ri *mh*
原実頼 F. no Saneyo-
原定 F. Sadamu *ml*
原定家 F. no Teika / Sadaie *ml*
原良房 F. no Yoshifusa *mh* ⌈ne *mla*
原信実 F. no Nobuza-
原信実朝臣集 F. no N. Ason shū *l*
原信頼 F. no Nobuyori *mh* ⌈*ml*
原為家 F. no Tameie
原浜成 F. no Hamanari *ml*
原時平 F. no Tokihira *mh* ⌈yasu *ml*
原倫寧 F. no Tomo-
原俊成 F. no Toshinari / Shunzei *mlh*
原高光 F. Takamitsu *ml* ⌈*fh*
原宮子 F. no Miyako
原泰衡 F. no Yasuhira *mh* ⌈nori *mh*
原通憲 F. no Michi-
原惺窩 F. Seika *ml*
原清衡 F. no Kiyohira *mh* ⌈da *mh*
原陳忠 F. no Nobuta-
原隆信 F. no Takanobu *ma* ⌈*mh*
原隆家 F. no Takaie
原隆能 F. no Takayoshi *ma*
原基俊 F. no Mototoshi *ml*

観 齢 勸 齋 襄 燾 藩 藍 藤 ▼ 嶷 嶽 嶺 蟲 叢 爵 齋 贄 璧 擧 雙 邇 麿 篶 簡 攄 衜 獺 瀏 瀞 瀬 鵬 曠 櫛 礪 疇 禰 ▲ 穏 穣 穠 蟻 螺 鐔 蹴 蹊 證

原基経 F. no Moto-
tsune *mh* ⌈ra *mh*
原基衡 F. no Motohi-
原道長 F. no Michi-
naga *mh*
原純友 F. no Sumito-
mo *mh* ⌈gu *mh*
原種継 F. no Tanetsu-
原審爾 F. Shinji *ml*
原頼長 F. no Yorina-
ga *mh* ⌈chi *mh*
原頼通 F. no Yorimi-
原頼嗣 F. no Yoritsu-
gu *mh* ⌈ne *mh*
原頼経 F. no Yoritsu-
[11]掛 Fujikake *s*
浪 Fujinami *s*
根 Fujine *s*
野 Fujino *sp*
野古白 F. Kohaku *ml*
堂 Tōdō *s*
島 Fujishima *sp*
島武二 F. Takeji *ma*
盛 Fujimori *s*
[12]崎 Fujisaki *sp*
袴 Fujibakama *l*
富 Fujitomi *s*
森 Fujimori *s*
森成吉 F. Seikichi *ml*
森朋夫 F. Tomoo *ml*
森淳三 F. Junzō *ml*
貫 Fujinuki *s*
間 Fujima *s*
[13]塚 Fujitsuka *s*
[14]裏葉 Fuji no uraba *l*
[16]橋 Fujihashi *sp*
[18]甕冊子 Tsuzurabumi
[19]瀬 Fujise *s* ⌊*l*
[21]縄 Fujinawa *s*
[23]懸 Fujikake *s*

**———18 T4———**

嶷 2774 Satoshi *m.* (GI, sato)

嶽 2775 (GAKU, take, taka)
夫 Takeo *m*

嶺 2776 Mine *s.* (REI, RYŌ, ne, mine)
子 Mineko *f*
田 Mineda *s*
岸 Minegishi *s*

**———18 T6———**

蟲 2777 See 虫 224

**———18 T8———**

叢 2778 Kusamura *s.* (SŌ, SU, mura)
人 Murato *m*

**———18 T9———**

爵 2779 [O] (SHAKU, SAKU, taka, kura)

**———18 T11———**

齋 2780 See 斎 1454

贄 2781 Nie *s.* (SHI, nie)
川 Niekawa *s*
田 Nieda *s*

**———18 T13———**

璧 2782 (HAKU, BYAKU, tama)
子 Tamako *f*

**———18 T14———**

擧 2783 See 挙 1207

**———18 T16———**

雙 2784 See 双 53

**———18 F4———**

邇 2785 Chikashi *m.* (JI, NI, chika, taka)
宗 Takamune *s*
摩 Nima *sp*; Niwa *s*
邇芸 Ninigi *m*

**———18 F11———**

麿 2786 [N] Maro *m.* (maro, maru). Also written as 麻呂
枝 Maroe *f*

**———18 F14———**

篶 2787 (EN, suzu)
子 Suzuko *m*

簡 2788 [T] Yasushi *m*, Akira. (KAN, KEN, hiro, fumi, akira)
子 Hiroko *f*, Fumiko
治 Kanji *m*
野 Kanno *s*

**———19 L3———**

攄 2789 Sometimes used for 據 2712, q.v.

衜 2790 Tadashi *m.* (DŌ). See also 道 1811

獺 2791 (DATSU)
祭 Dassai *l* ⌈haiwa *l*
祭書屋俳話 D. shooku

瀏 2792 Kiyoshi *m.* (RYŪ, kiyo)

瀞 2793 Kiyoshi *m.* (SEI, JŌ, kiyo)
子 Kiyoko *f*

瀬 2794 [T] Iwata *s.* (RAI, se)
[3]川 Segawa *s*
川如皐 S. Jokō *ml*
之口 Senokuchi *s*
下 Seshimo *s*, Seshita
口 Seguchi *s*
上 Segami *s*
[4]木 Seki *s*
戸 Seto *sp*
戸口 Setoguchi *s*
戸川 Setogawa *s*
戸山 Setoyama *s*
戸内 Setouchi *sp*
戸内晴美 S. Harumi
戸田 Setoda *p* ⌊*ml*
山 Seyama *s*
[5]左衛門 Sezaemon *m*
古 Seko *s*
田 Seta *p*
平 Sehei *m*
本 Semoto *s*
[6]在 Sezai *s*
名 Sena *s*
[7]村 Semura *s*
谷 Sedani *s*
兵衛 Sebee *m*
尾 Seo *s*, Senoo
見 Semi *s*
[8]沼 Senuma *s*
沼茂樹 S. Shigeki *ml*
沼夏葉 S. Kayō *fl*
河 Segawa *s*
[9]畑 Sebata *s*
[10]脇 Sewaki *s*
高 Setaka *p*
[11]浪 Senami *s*
峰 Semine *p*
能 Seno *s*
野 Seno *s*
野川 Senogawa *p*
島 Seshima *s*
[12]場 Seba *s*
崎 Sesaki *s*
棚 Setana *p*
賀 Sega *s*
間 Sema *s*
[15]端 Sebata *s*
[18]藤 Setō *s*

**———19 L4———**

鵬 2795 (HŌ, BU, tomo, yuki)
一 Tomoichi *m*

曠 2796 Hiroshi *m*, Akira. (KŌ, hiro,
野 Arano *l* ⌊akira)
詞 Hiroshi *m*

櫛 2797 (SHITSU, SHICHI, kushi, kiyo)
代 Kushiro *s*, Kujiro
引 Kushibiki *sp*
田 Kushida *s*
田民蔵 K. Tamizō *ml*
形 Kushigata *p*
原 Kushihara *s*
笥 Kushige *s*, Kushiji, Kushizu
淵 Kushibuchi *s*
橋 Kushibashi *s*

**———19 L5———**

礪 2798 (REI, to)
波 Tonami *p*

疇 2799 Hitoshi *m.* (CHŪ, une, tomo)
之丞 Unenojō *m*
彦 Unehiko *m*

禰 2800 (NE)
知風 Nechikaze *s*
宜田 Negita *s*
津 Nezu *s*
麻呂 Nemaro *m*
寝 Neshine *s*, Neshime
磋節 Misao *f*

穩 2801 See 穏 2492

穡 2802 [N] Minoru *m*, Yutaka, Osamu. (JŌ, NYŌ, shige)

穠 2803 Shigeru *m*, Atsushi. (JŌ, NYU, shige)
子 Shigeko *f*

——19 L6——

蟻 2804 (GI, ari)
川 Arikawa *s*
通 Aridōshi *la*

螺 2805 (RA, nishi)
木 Hōki *s*
田 Nishida *s*
江 Nishie *s*, Sazae
沢 Kaisawa *s*
良 Tsubura *s*

——19 L7——

罇 2805A Motai *s*. (SON)

蹴 2806 (SHŪ, SHUKU, ke)
速 Kehaya *m*

蹊 2807 (KEI, GAI, michi)
子 Michiko *f*

證 2808 See 証 1660

譓 2809 Satoshi *m*. (KEI, E)

識 2810 [T] (SHIKI, SHOKU, SHI, sato, tsune, nori)
子 Tsuneko *f*
仁 Satohito *m*

——19 L8——

總 2811 See 総 2662

繽 2812 Hiroshi *m*. (EN)

縮 2813 [T] (SHUKU, nao) ⌈*s*
見屯倉 Shijimimiyake

績 2814 [T] Isao *m*, Tsumugu. (SEKI, SHAKU, isa, sane, mitsu, nari, nori, mori)
子 Isako *f*

鏈 2815 Katashi *m*. (REN)

鏑 2816 (TEKI, kabura)
木 Kaburagi *s* ⌈*ma*
木清方 K. Kiyokata

鏡 2817 [T] Kagami *sf-p*; Akira *m*. (KYŌ, kane, kagami, toshi, aki, akira, mi)
山 Kagamiyama *s*
石 Kagamiishi *p*
花 Kyōka *ml*
男 Kagami otoko *la*
味 Kagami *s*
枝 Toshie *f*
野 Kagamino *p*
島 Kagashima *s*
湖 Kaneko *f*

鵺 2818 Nue *la*. (YA)

鵡 2819 (MU, BU)
川 Mukawa *p*

鶉 2820 (SHUN, JUN, uzura)
衣 Uzuragoromo *l*
尾 Uzurao *s*

鶏 2821 [T] (KEI, KAI)
冠 Kaede *s*, Kaide
冠井 Kaedei *s*, Kaede, Kaide, Tosakai
聟 Niwatori muko *la*
頭 Keitō *l*

鵜 2822 (TEI, TAI, u)
川 Ugawa *s*
木 Uki *s*
甘部 Ukaibe *s*
沢 Usawa *s*
取 Utō *s*
高 Utaka *s*
野 Uno *s*
祭 U no matsuri *la*
飼 Ukai *sla*
殿 Udono *sp*
養 Ukai *s*
瀞 Unotoro *s*

——19 L9——

馦 2823 Kaoru *m*. (KEN)

韻 2824 [T] (IN, oto)

——19 L10——

縣 2825 See 県 1252

髓 2826 [T] (ZUI, SUI, sune, naka)

顓 2827 Tadashi *m*. (SEN)

頸 2828 (KEI, kubi)
城 Kubiki *p*

——19 L11——

鯰 2829 (namazu)
田 Namazuda *s*

鯖 2830 Saba *m*. (SEI, SHŌ, saba)
江 Sabae *p*
麻呂 Sabamaro *m*

鯨 2831 [T] Kujira *m*. (GEI)
井 Kujirai *s*
伏 Isafushi *s* ⌈oka
岡 Kujiraoka *s*, Kuji-

鯛 2832 [N] (CHŌ, tai)
の味噌津 Tai no mi-
二 Taiji *m* ⌊sozu *l*

——19 L13——

艷 2833 [N] Tsuya *f*. (EN, tsuya, yoshi, ō, moro)
子 Tsuyako *s*
太 Tsuyata *m*
姿女舞衣 Hadesugata onnamaiginu *la*

——19 L17——

勸 2834 See 勧 1970

——19 T3——

藝 2835 See 芸 689

藏 2836 See 蔵 2424

藻 2837 (SŌ, mo)

藺 2838 (RIN, i)
牟田 Imuda *s*
都絵 Itsue *f*

蘭 2839 [N] (RAN)
学 Rangaku *lh* ⌈*lh*
学事始 R. kotohajime
奢待 Ranjatai *l*
越 Rankoshi *p*

藪 2840 Yabu *s*, Sō. (SŌ, SU, yabu)
下 Yabushita *s*
内 Yabuuchi *s*, Yabunouchi
中 Yabunaka *s*
本 Yabumoto *s*
田 Yabuta *s*
田義雄 Y. Yoshio *ml*
原 Yabuhara *s*, Yago-
野 Yabuno *s* ⌊hara
塚 Yabutsuka *s*
塚本 Yabuzukahon *p*
崎 Yabusaki *s*

蘇 2841 (SO, SU, haru, iki)
二 Haruji *m*
我 Soga *s*
我入鹿 S. no Iruka *mh*
我石川麻呂 S. no Ishikawamaro *mh*
我馬子 S. no Umako *mh* ⌈*mh*
我稲目 S. no Iname
我蝦夷 S. no Emishi
宗 Soga *s* ⌊*mh*

宜 Soga *s*
連 Soren *p* "U.S.S.R."
陽 Soyō *p*
提売 Soteme *f*

**蘆** 2842 (RO, RYO, ashi, yoshi)
川 Ashigawa *s*
刈 Ashikari *la*
辺 Ashibe *s*
田 Ashida *s*
名 Ashina *s*
沢 Ashizawa *s*
尾 Susukio *s*
荻集 Rotekishū *l*
原 Ashiwara *s*
屋 Ashiya *sp*
屋道満大内鑑 A. Dōman ōuchi kagami *la*
野 Ashino *s*
渡 Ashiwatari *s*
塚 Ashizuka *s*
葉 Ashiba *s*
敷 Ashiki *s*

——19 T6——

**羹** 2843 Atsumono *l*. (KŌ, atsu)
見 Atsumi *s*

**簾** 2844 (REN, sumi)
子 Sumiko *f*

**簸** 2845 (HA, hi)
川 Hikawa *p*
川上 Hinokawakami *l*
河上 Hinokawakami *l*
浦 Minoura *s*

——19 T8——

**霧** 2846 [T] (MU, BU, kiri)
島 Kirishima *p*

——19 T9——

**鶩** 2847 Tsutomu *m*. (MU, BU)

——19 T11——

**繁** 2848 [T] Shigeru *m*, Shigeshi. (HAN, shige, toshi, eda)
二 Shigeji *m*
三 Shigezō *m*
太郎 Shigetarō *m*
田 Shigeta *s*
氏 Shigeuji *m*
次 Toshiji *m*
吉 Shigekichi *m*
在家 Hanzaike *s*
栄 Shigetaka *m*
造 Shigezō *m*
野 Shigeno *s*
野天来 S. Tenrai *ml*
野話 Shigeshige yawa *l*
数 Toshikazu *m*
蔭 Shigekage *m*
蔵 Shigezō *m*
矯 Shigetada *m*

——19 T12——

**豐** 2849 See 豊 2013

**醫** 2850 See 医 743

**攀** 2851 Yoshi *s*. (HAN, hiku, yoshi, yori)

**贇** 2852 (IN, yoshi, un)
五郎 Ungorō *m*
夫 Yoshio *m*
雄 Yoshio *m*

——19 T13——

**蟹** 2853 Kani *s*. (KAI, GE, kani)
子丸 Kanikomaru *ml*
山伏 Kani yamabushi *la*
田 Kanita *p*
本 Kanimoto *s*
江 Kanie *sp*
守 Kanimori *m*
沢 Kanizawa *s*
谷 Kanitani *s*
島 Kanijima *s*

——19 T15——

**樂** 2854 See 楽 2029

——19 F3——

**廬** 2855 Iori *f*. (RO, RYO)

——19 F9——

**韙** 2856 (I, yoshi)

——19 F11——

**靡** 2857 Nabiku *m*. (HI)

**麴** 2858 Kōji *p*. (KIKU)
池 Kikuike *s*

——19 F14——

**畿** 2859 (KI, GE, chika)
内 Kinai *p*

——19 U——

**璽** 2860 [O] (JI, shirushi)

——20 L3——

**壞** 2861 See 壊 2603

**懷** 2862 See 懐 2605

**懽** 2863 (KAN, yoshi)
子 Yoshiko *f*

**瀧** 2864 See 滝 1862

**瀛** 2865 (EI, YŌ, oki)

**徽** 2866 (KI, yoshi)
子 Yoshiko *f*

——20 L4——

**騰** 2867 [T] Noboru *m*. (TŌ, kari)

**璣** 2868 Tamaki *m*. (KI, KE)

**機** 2869 [T] (KI, KE, nori, hata)
野 Inano *s*

——20 L6——

**蠣** 2870 (REI, RAI, kaki)
崎 Kakizaki *s*

——20 L7——

**釋** 2871 See 釈 1395

**辦** 2872 See 弁 275

**疆** 2873 Tsutomu *m*. (KYŌ, KŌ)

**轍** 2874 Wadachi *m*. (TETSU)

**譯** 2875 See 訳 1402

**議** 2876 [T] (GI, nori, taka)

**護** 2877 [T] Mamoru *m*. (GO, KO, mori, sane)
上 Gojō *s*
戸 Morito *m*
立 Moritatsu *m*
臣 Moriomi *m*
国 Morikuni *m*
良 Morinaga *m*
得久 Goeku *s*
躬 Morimi *m*
麗都留 Gomatsuru *s*

——20 L8——

**縷** 2878 (RŌ, RU, aya)
女 Ayame *f*
紅新草 Rukō shinsō *l*

**織** 2879 [T] Hatori *s*. (SHIKI, SHOKU, ori, oru, ri)
人 Orito *m*
之助 Orinosuke *m*
仁 Orihito *m*
戸 Orito *s*
井 Orii *s*
目 Orime *s*
本 Orimoto *s*
田 Oda *s*, Orita; Ota *p*
田正信 Oda Masanobu *ml*
田信長 O. Nobunaga *mh*
田純一郎 O. Jun'ichirō *ml*
田作之助 O. Sakunosuke *ml*
衣 Orie *f*
茂 Orimo *s*, Orishige
居 Orii *m*
畑 Orihata *s*
原 Orihara *s*
都 Ritsu *f*

部 Oribe *sm*; Hatori-be *s*
越 Orikoshi *s*
衛 Orie *m*

鐙 2880 (TŌ, abumi, abu)
屋 Abumiya *s*

鏘 2881 Takashi *m.* (SHŌ, sō, naru)

鐔 2882 (SHIN, JIN, tsuba)
屋 Tsubaya *s*

鐘 2883 [T] Atsumu *m.* (SHŌ, SHU, kane)
の音 Kane no ne *la*
巳 Kanemi *m*
子 Kaneko *f*
打 Kaneuchi *s*
江 Kanegae *s*
巻 Kanemaki *s*
崎 Kanezaki *s*

—20 L10—

韜 2884 (TŌ, yoshi)

韡 2885 (I, shige)
雄 Shigeo *m*

—20 L11—

鰕 2886 (KA, KE, ebi)
十郎 Ebijūrō *m*

鰍 2887 (SHŪ, kajika)
沢 Kajikazawa *p*

—20 L12—

雞 2887A See 鶏 2821

雛 2888 (SŪ, SU, JU, hina)
子 Hinako *f*
田 Hinada *s*
形 Hinagata *s*
屋 Hinaya *s*
亀 Hinaki *m*

離 2889 [T] Akira *m.* (RI, aki, tsura, akira)

—20 L13—

辭 2890 See 辞 1918

獻 2891 See 献 1961

斆 2892 See 学 719

寵 2893 Utsuku *f*, Utsukushi. (CHŌ, yoshi)

—20 T3—

蘭 2894 See 蘭 2839

藹 2895 Shigeru *m.* (AI)

繭 2896 (KEN, mayu)
子 Mayuko *f*

—20 T5—

竇 2897 Toku *s.* (TŌ, TOKU, ana)
田 Anata *s*

黨 2898 See 党 1191

羆 2899 Higuma *m.* (HI)
取谷 Hishiya *s*

—20 T6—

嚴 2900 See 厳 2706

籌 2901 (JU, CHŪ, kazu, koto)
三 Kazuzō *m*

—20 T8—

麗 2902 [T] (REI, RAI, yoshi, kazu, akira, tsugu, tsura, yori)
子 Reiko *f*, Yoshiko

麓 2903 Fumoto *m*; Hayama *s.* (ROKU)
草分 F. no kusawake *l*

—20 T11—

馨 2904 [N] Kaoru *sm.* (KEI, KYŌ, ka, yoshi, kiyo)
一 Keiichi *m*
邦 Yoshikuni *m*

—20 T12—

繁 2905 See 繁 2848

—20 T13—

贊 2906 See 賛 2394

覺 2907 See 覚 1952

—20 T15—

甕 2908 Motai *s.* (YŌ, YU, mika, kame)
川 Mikagawa *s*
子 Kameko *f*
男 Mikao *m*
麿 Mikamaro *m*

—20 T17—

龔 2909 Sunao *m.* (KYŌ, KU, nori, yoshi)

—20 F—

麪 2910 (MEN)
麭 Pan *l*

—21 L1—

攝 2911 See 摂 1837

權 2912 See 権 2300

爛 2913 Tadare *l.* (RAN)

曦 2914 Asahi *m.* (GI, teru, yoshi)
子 Teruko *f*
正 Yoshimasa *m*
章 Teruaki *m*

—21 L5—

穐 2915 (SHŪ, SHU, aki)
三 Akizō *m*

之助 Akinosuke *m*
山 Akiyama *s*
田 Akita *s*

礒 2916 [N] Iso *s.* (KI, KE, iso, shi)
[1]一 Isoichi *m*
[3]川 Isogawa *s*
子 Isoko *p*
上 Isogami *s*
[4]山 Isoyama *s*
[5]永 Isonaga *s*
辺 Isobe *s*
田 Isoda *s*
目 Isome *s*
[6]次 Isoji *m*
合 Isoai *s*
吉 Isokichi *m*
[7]村 Isomura *s*
谷 Isoya *s*, Isogaya, Isogai
足 Isotari *m*
貝 Isogai *s*
貝雲峰 I. Unbō *ml*
[8]林 Isobayashi *s*
[9]城 Shiki *p*
前 Isozaki *s*
[11]野 Isono *s*
部 Isobe *sp*
菜 Isona *f*
島 Isojima *s*
[13]雄 Isoo *m*
馴松 Sonare no matsu *l*

—21 L7—

辯 2917 See 弁 275

讓 2918 Yuzuru *m*, Yuzuri. (JŌ, NYŌ, masa, nori, yoshi, uya, semu)
吉 Jōkichi *m*
治 Jōji *m*
衛 Jōe *m*

耀 2919 Akira *m.* (YŌ, teru, aki)
男 Teruo *m*
星 Terutoshi *m*

—21 L8—

鐵 2920 See 鉄 1948

鐵 2921 See 鉄 1948

鐸 2922 (TAKU, DAKU, suzu, sute)
木 Suzuki *s*
木孝 S. Takashi *ml*
男 Suzuo *m*

繪 2923 See 絵 2332

繹 2924 (EKI, YAKU, tsugu, nobu, tsura, mitsu)

—21 L9—

饒 2925 Atsushi *m*, Yutaka, Ōshi. (JŌ, NYŌ, nigi, tomo, o)
石川 Oishikawa *s*
村 Nyōmura *s*

—21 L10—

鶴 2926 [N] Tsuru *s*. (KAKU, GAKU, tsuru, tsu, zu, tazu)
ケ島 Tsurugashima *p*
ノ門 Tsurunoto *m*
[1]一 Tsuruichi *m*
[2]八 Tsuruhachi *s*
八鶴次郎 T. Tsurujirō *l*
二郎 Tsurujirō *m*
[3]三 Tsuruzō *m*
三郎 Tsurusaburō *m*
川 Tsurukawa *s*
丸 Tsurumaru *s*
[5]四郎 Tazushirō *m*
本 Tsurumoto *s*
田 Tsuruta *sp*
田知也 T. Tomoya *ml*
[6]吉 Tsurukichi *m*
次郎 Tsurujirō *m*
[7]沢 Tsuruzawa *s*
谷 Tsuruya *s*
来 Tsurugi *p*
貝 Tsurugai *s*
見 Tsurumi *sp*
見祐輔 T. Yūsuke *ml*
[8]所 Tsurudo *m*
居 Tsurui *p*
[9]松 Tsurumatsu *m*
岡 Tsurugaoka *s*; Tsuruoka *sp*
[10]原 Tsuruhara *s*
造 Tsuruzō *m*
屋 Tsuruya *s*
屋南北 T. Nanboku *ml*
[11]峰 Tsurumine *s*
野 Tsuruno *s*
亀 Tsurukame *la*
[12]崎 Tsuruzaki *s*
賀 Tsuruga *s*
賀斎 Tsurugasai *m*
集 Tsurui *f*
間 Tsuruma *s*
[13]淵 Tsurubuchi *s*
雄 Tsuruo *m*
群 Tsurumura *m*
殿 Tsurudono *s*
[14]飼 Tsurukai *s*
[16]橋 Tsuruhashi *s*
[21]齢 Tsuyo *f*

—21 L11–17—

競 2927 [T] Kisō *m*, Kurabu; Kisoi *s*, Kioi. (KYŌ, KEI)

顥 2928 Akira *m*. (GŌ, KŌ)

顧 2929 [T] (KO, mi)
弥太 Koyata *m*

齡 2930 See 齢 2766

歡 2931 See 歓 2352

—21 T—

亹 2932 Tsutomu *m*. (BI)

藥 2933 See 薬 2568

蘊 2934 Osamu *m*. (ON, mori)

蘘 2935 (JŌ, myōga)
屋 Myōgaya *s*

巖 2936 [N] Iwao *m*, Iwai. (GAN, GEN, iwa, yoshi, o, mine, michi)
川 Iwakawa *s*
本 Iwamoto *s*
本善治 I. Zenji *ml*
村 Iwamura *s*
谷 Iwaya *s*
谷小波 I. Sazanami *ml*
垣 Iwagaki *s*
崎 Iwasaki *s*
雲 Iwakumo *s*

羅 2937 (RA, tsura)
山 Razan *mlh*
山文集 R. bunshū *lh*
生門 Rashōmon *l*
曳 Abiki *s*
臼 Rausu *p*
馬 Rōma *p* "Rome"

囂 2938 Shizuka *m*. (GŌ)

轟 2939 Todoroki *s*. (KŌ, GŌ)
木 Todoroki *s*

鶯 2940 (Ō, YŌ, uguisu)
沢 Uguisusawa *p*
谷 Uguisudani *p*

露 2941 [T] Akira *m*. (RO, tsuyu)
子 Tsuyuko *f*
久保 Tsuyukubo *s*
口 Tsuyuguchi *s*
五郎兵衛 Tsuyu no Gorobee *ml*
木 Tsuyuki *s*
団々 Tsuyudandan *l*
西亜 Roshia *p* "Russia"
伴 Rohan *ml*
国 Rokoku *p* "Russia"
香 Tsuyuka *f*
原 Tsuyuhara *sl*
崎 Tsuyusaki *s*

譽 2942 See 誉 2010

彝 2943 Tsune *m-f*. (I, tsune, tomo, nori)
雄 Tsuneo *m*

—21 F—

屬 2944 See 属 1802

—22 L—

囎 2945 (SO)
唹 Soo *sp*

灘 2946 Nada *p*. (NAN, nada)
崎 Nadasaki *p*

櫻 2947 See 桜 1373

聯 2948 Tsurane *m*. (REN, tsura)

讀 2949 See 読 2142

躋 2950 Noboru *m*. (SEI, SAI, nori)
造 Seizō *m*

鑄 2951 See 鋳 2343

鐶 2952 Tamaki *m*. (KAN)

鑓 2953 (yari)
水 Yarimizu *s*
田 Yarita *s*
田研一 Y. Ken'ichi *ml*

繡 2954 (SHŪ, SHU, SHŌ, nui)
子 Nuiko *f*

繩 2955 Nawa *s*. (JŌ, SHŌ, tada, tsuna, nawa, tsugu, nao, nori, tsune, masa)
子 Tadako *f*
田 Nawata *s*
主 Tadanushi *m*
直 Tadanao *m*
倉 Nawakura *s*
稚 Nawachi *s*
綯 Nawanai *l*

聽 2956 See 聴 2634

驍 2957 Takeshi *m*, Gyō, Suguru. (GYŌ, isa)
夫 Isao *m*

懿 2958 Atsushi *m*. (I, yoshi, atsu, hisa, nao)
子 Yoshiko *f*, Atsuko
修 Yoshinaga *m*

誉 Yoshishige *m*

——22 T——

繫 2959 (KEI, KAI, tsuna, tsugu)
子 Tsunako *f*

覽 2960 See 覧 2695

——22 F——

魔 2961 [T] (MA)
風恋風 Makaze koikaze *l*

——23 L3——

灑 2962 Kiyoshi *m.* (SAI, SE)

——23 L4——

櫟 2963 Kunugi *f.* (REKI, RYAKU, nobu, ichi, ichii)
子 Nobuko *f*, Ichiiko
木 Ichiki *s*
本 Ichinomoto *s*
津 Ichitsu *s*
原 Ichihara *s*, Kunugihara, Hirahara

——23 L5——

穰 2964 See 穣 2802

——23 L8——

續 2965 See 続 2334

纈 2966 (KŌ)
纈 Kōketsu *sa*; Kikutoji *s*, Kukuri, Hanabusa

鑛 2967 See 鉱 2153

鑑 2968 [T] Akira *m.* (KAN, GAN, aki, akira, kane, nori, shige, mi, miru, kata)
正 Akimasa *m*
次郎 Kanjirō *m*
任 Akitaka *m*
定 Shigesada *m*
重 Akishige *m*
真 Ganjin *mh*
連 Akitsura *m*
備 Akinobu *m*
載 Kanekoto *m*
種 Akitane *m*, Kanetane

——23 L10——

體 2969 See 体 358

髓 2970 See 髄 2826

驛 2971 See 駅 2172

髞 2972 Takashi *m.* (SŌ, taka)

——23 L11——

鬚 2973 (SHU, hige)
継 Higetsugu *m*

——23 L12——

鷄 2973A See 鶏 2821

鶺 2974 Rei *m.* (RYŌ)

鷗 2975 Kamome *f.* (Ō, U)
外 Ōgai *ml*

鷦 2976 Sasagi *s.* (SHŌ)
鷯 Sasagi *s*, Misosazai

——23 T——

籠 2977 (RŌ, ko, komori, kago)
太鼓 Rō taiko *la*
手田 Koteda *s*
沢 Kozawa *s*
谷 Komoriya *s*
祇王 Rō-Giō *la*
宮 Komiya *s*, Kagomiya
島 Kagoshima *s*

霽 2978 (SEI, SAI, haru, hare, nari, nori)
見 Harumi *m*
堅 Harukata *m*

鬘 2979 (MAN, BAN, tsura, katsura)

鷲 2980 Washi *s.* (SHŪ, JU, washi)
山 Washiyama *s*
田 Washida *s*
光 Washimitsu *m*
尾 Washio *s*, Washinoo
見 Washimi *s*, Sumi
津 Washizu *s*
栖 Washizu *s*
宮 Washimiya *p*
野 Washino *s*
巣 Washisu *s*
塚 Washizuka *s*
森 Washimori *s*
雄 Washio *m*
敷 Washishiki *p*
頭 Washinozu *s*

響 2981 [T] (KYŌ, KŌ, oto, hibiki)
山 Hibikiyama *s*
庭 Aiba *s*

鑒 2982 Akira *m.* (KAN, GAN, mi, nori)
江 Norie *f*

襲 2983 (SHŪ, JŪ, so, tsugi, yori)
津彦 Sotsuhiko *m*

懸 2984 [T] (KEN, GEN, kake, tō)
葵 Kakeaoi *l*

——24 L——

衢 2985 (GU, KU, chimata)

欑 2986 Shigeru *m.* (SAN, ZAN)

礫 2987 Sazai *m.* (REKI, RYAKU)

纒 2988 Matomu *m.* (TEN, maki)
向 Makimuku *s*

觀 2989 See 観 2765

——24 T——

巖 2990 See 巌 2936

巍 2991 Takashi *m.* (GI, taka)
八郎 Gihachirō *m*
洋 Takahiro *m*
則 Takanori *m*

靈 2992 See 霊 2390

鷺 2993 Sagi *sla.* (RO, sagi)
谷 Sagitani *s*
池 Saginoike *s*
坂 Sagisaka *s*
沼 Saginuma *s*
屋 Sagiya *s*
雄 Sagio *sm*

——24 F——

闗 2994 See 関 2245

鷹 2995 Takatori *s.* (YŌ, Ō, taka)
4木 Takagi *s*
5司 Takatsukasa *s*
主 Takanushi *m*
甘戸 Takakaibe *s*
6次郎 Takajirō *m*
羽 Takaba *s*
7阪 Takawaki *s*
谷 Takagai *s*
見 Takami *s*
8取 Takatori *sm*
9治 Takaji *m*
松 Takamatsu *s*
岡 Takaoka *p*
10栖 Takasu *p*
11清 Takakiyo *m*
野 Takano *s*
部屋 Takabeya *s*
巣 Takasu *s*; Takanosu *p*
島 Takashima *sp*
12森 Takamori *s*
15箸 Takahashi *s*
16穂 Takao *m*
嘴 Takahashi *s*
衛 Takae *m*
養戸 Takakaibe *s*
19諶 Takanobu *m*

欑 礫 纓 觀 巖 巍 靈 鷺 闞 鷹 ▼ 礹 龝 鑰 鰺 麟 顱 顯 鹽 靄 饗 廳 驢 驥 靉 籬 欝 變 讚 鱸 鱷 斷 矗 戀 纘 鑽 鸚 靏 灣 繼 麤 ▲

——25 L——

礹 2996 Iwao *m.* (GEN, GAN)

龝 2997 See 穐 2915

鑰 2998 (YAKU, kagi)
之助 Kaginosuke *m*

鰺 2999 (SŌ, aji)
ケ沢 Ajigasawa *p*
坂 Ajisaka *s*

麟 3000 (RIN)
也 Rin'ya *m*
蔵 Rinzō *m*

顱 3001 (RO, RU, hachi)
郎 Hachirō *m*

顯 3002 See 顕 2757

——25 T——

鹽 3003 See 塩 1846

靄 3004 (AI, moya)
子 Moyako *f*

饗 3005 (KYŌ, KŌ, ae, ai)
庭 Aeba *s*, Aiba ⌈*ml*
庭篁村 Aeba Kōson
場 Aeba *s*, Aiba

——25 F——

廳 3006 See 庁 174

——26 L——

驢 3007 (RO, RYO)
鞍橋 Roankyō *l*

驥 3008 Hayama *m*, Takeshi. (KI, toshi) ⌈zu
一 Kiichi *m*, Toshika-

靉 3009 (AI)
日 Aijitsu *l*

——26 T——

籬 3010 Magaki *s.* (RI, kaki)

欝 3011 Shigeru *m.* (UTSU, UCHI)

變 3012 See 変 970

——27 L——

讚 3013 Sarara *s.* (SAN, sasa)
井 Sai *s*, Sanui, Sanai
次郎 Sanjirō *m*
母 Sanomo *s*
岐 Sanuki *sph*
岐典侍日記 S. no Tenji nikki *l*

鱸 3014 Suzuki *s.* (RO, suzuki)
庖丁 Suzuki-bōchō *la*
庖丁青砥切味 S.-b. aoto no kireaji *l*

鱷 3015 (GAKU, wani)
川 Wanikawa *s*
石 Waniishi *s*
淵 Wanibuchi *s*

斷 3016 See 断 1669

——27 T——

矗 3017 (CHIKU, CHŪ, nobu, nao)
江 Naoe *f*
昶 Nobuteru *m*

戀 3018 See 恋 1223

——28 L——

纘 3019 Tsugu *m.* (SAN)

鑽 3020 (SAN, taka)
一 Takaichi *m*

——29 L——

鸚 3021 (Ō)
鵡小町 Ōmu Komachi *la*
鵡返文武二道 Ō.-gaeshi bunbu nidō *l*

靏 3022 (KAKU, tsuru)
雄 Tsuruo *m*

——30 L——

灣 3023 See 湾 1849

——31 L——

繼 3024 See 継 2539

——36 T——

麤 3025 (SO, ara)
郎 Arao *m*
鹿火 Arakabi *m*
鹿比 Arakabi *m*

# A COMPREHENSIVE INDEX OF JAPANESE NAMES

## Part II. From Readings to Characters

# A

A *l* 亜 525. (予 62, 足 461, 吾 491, 亜 525, 我 545, 阿 569, 蛙 1648, 窪 2203, 網 2536)
Aba *p* 阿波 569
Abaka *s* 阿墓
Abashiri *p* 網走 2536
Abe *s* 安部 472, 安閉, 阿倍 569, 阿部; *sp* 安倍 472, 阿閉 569
~ Chūzō *ml* 安部忠三 472 「人 569
Abehashihito *s* 阿閇間
Abe Ichizoku *l* 阿部一族 「472
~ Isoo *mlh* 安部磯雄
~ Jirō *ml* 阿部次郎 569
~ Kōbō *ml* 安部公房 472 「569
Abemaro *m* 阿閉麻呂
Abe Masahiro *mh* 阿部正弘
Abeno *p* 阿部野
Abe Nobuyuki *mh* 阿部信行
~ no Hirafu *mh* 阿倍比羅夫
Abenokadōdo *s* 阿閉門人
Abe no Nakamaro *mh* 阿倍仲麻呂
~ no Sadatō *mh* 安倍貞任 472 「晴明
~ no Seimei *mh* 安倍
~ no Yoritoki *mh* 安倍頼時
~ Shinnosuke *ml* 阿部真之助 569
~ Shizue *fl* 阿部静枝
~ Tomoji *ml* 阿部知二 「能成 472
~ Yoshishige *ml* 安倍
Abi *s* 阿比 569
Abiki *s* 羅曳 2937
Abiko *s* 安彦 472, 安孫子, 吾孫 491, 吾孫子, 我彦 545, 我孫, 阿比古 569, 阿珥古, 阿孫; *sp* 我孫子 545
Abo *s* 安保 472, 阿保 569
Aboshi *s* 網干 2536
Aboshiya *s* 網干屋
Abu *sp* 阿武 569. (虻 1134, 鐙 2880)
(abumi 鐙)
Abumiya *s* 鐙屋
(abura 油 593)
Aburadani *s* 油谷
Aburai *s* 油井
Aburakasu Yodogawa *l* 油糟淀川
Aburakawa *s* 油川
Aburanokōji *s* 油小路
Aburaya *s* 油屋
Abuta *p* 虻田 1134
Abutsuni *fl* 阿仏尼 569
Achi *p* 阿智
Achiba *s* 阿知波
Achiki *s* 安勅 472; *mh* 阿直岐 569
Achime no waza *l* 阿知女作法 「使主
Achi no Omi *mh* 阿知
Adachi *s* 足達 461, 安立 472, 阿達 569; *sp* 足立 461, 安達 472 「原
Adachigahara *la* 安達
Adachi Yasumori *mh* 安達泰盛
Adakai *s* 出雲郷 523
Adaki *s* 安宅 472
Ade *sp* 安諦
Adegawa *s* 阿出川 569
Adogawa *p* 安曇川 472
Adoki *s* 安勅
Ae *s* 安拝, 安閉, 敢 1687. (允 217, 肖 451, 敢 1687, 饗 3005)
Aeba *s* 饗庭, 饗場
~ Kōson *ml* 饗庭篁村
Aechi *s* 愛智 2018
Aeomizokugishi *s* 敢臣族岸 1687
Afuri *s* 泥障 594
Afurika *p* "Africa" 阿弗利加 569
Aga *sp* 英賀 693. (上 47)
Agano *s* 上野
Agari *s* 上利; *m* 東 771
Agata *s* 安形 472, 阿形 569; *sp* 英多 693, 県 1252. (県)
Agatai *m* 県居
Agatainukai *s* 県犬養
~ no Hitokami *ml* 県犬養人上
Agatamaro *m* 県麿
Agatamori *m* 県守
Agatanoatae *s* 県直
Agatanomiyatsuko *s* 県造
Agatanushi *s* 県主
Agatanushisakito *s* 県主前利
Agatsuma *p* 吾妻 491
Agawa *s* 吾河, 阿川 569, 蛙川 1648; *p* 吾川 491
~ Hiroyuki *ml* 阿川弘之 569
Age *s* 揚 1551; *p* 安芸 472. (上 47, 揚 1551, 挙 1207)
Agemaki *l* 総角 2662
Agematsu *sp* 上松 47
Agemo *p* 挙母 1207
Ageo *sp* 上尾 47
Ageta *s* 上田
Ageya *s* 揚屋 1551
Agi *s* 阿木 569
Ago *p* 阿児
Agō *s* 淡河 1340
Agoin *s* 安居院 472
(agu 称 1118)
Agui *s* 安食 472; *sml-p* 安居院; *p* 阿久比 569
Aguranabe *l* 安愚楽鍋 472
Aguri *sp* 余田 448
Ahira *p* 吾平 491
Ahiru *s* 阿比留 569, 畔蒜 1110
Aho *s* 安保 472, 英保 693, 神 853
Ai *s* 阿井 569, 阿比, 藍 2772; *f* 合 270, 逢 1516. (合 270, 会 454, 和 638, 相 868, 姶 1091, 埃 1294, 逢 1516, 蛤 1649, 集 1779, 愛 2018, 歳 2198, 餽 2487, 蔓 2563, 藍 2772, 藹 2895, 靄 3004, 饗 3005, 靉 3009)
Aiau *s* 相合 868
Aiba *s* 合葉 270, 相羽 868, 相庭, 相場, 相葉, 飽庭 2165, 響庭 2981, 饗庭 3005, 饗場
Aibara *s* 合原 270, 相原 868, 藍原 2772
Aibetsu *p* 愛別 2018
Aibuchi *s* 相淵 868
Aichi *s* 愛智 2018; *sp* 愛知
Aida *s* 会田 454, 相田 868; *p* 英田 693
Aiga *s* 合賀 270, 秋賀 878
Aigikoe *l* 相聞 868
Aigonowaka negurabako *la* 愛護若塒箱 2018
Aihara *s* 粟飯原 1763
Aihiko *m* 愛彦 2018
Aiho *p* 秋穂 878
Aiichirō *m* 愛一郎 2018
Aiiso *s* 相磯 868
Aijima *s* 相島
Aijisshō *l* 愛日抄 2018
Aijitsu *l* 靉日 3009
Aika *s* 秋鹿 878
Aikawa *s* 淡河 1340, 愛甲 2018, 愛若, 鮎川 2547, 藍川 2772; *sp* 合川 270, 相川 868, 愛川 ⌊2018
Aiki *s* 相木 868
Aikitsu *m* 愛橘 2018
Aiko *f* 相子 868, 愛子 2018, 藍子 2772
Aikō *sp* 愛甲 2018
Aikyō *s* 藍香 2772
Aimi *p* 会見 454
Aimono *s* 四十物 188
Aino *s* 姶罪 1091, 間野 1822, 藍野 2772; *sp* 愛野 2018
Ainoura *s* 相浦 868
Aioi *sp* 相生 「良 1091
Aira *s* 蛤良 1649; *sp* 姶
Aisaki *s* 相崎 868
Aisaku *m* 愛作 2018
Aiso *s* 相曾 868, 相磯

Aisō *s* 相宗
Aisogawa *s* 会會川 454
Aisomegawa *la* 藍染川 2772 「2018
Aisu *s* 会州 454, 愛州
Aisuke *m* 愛輔
Aisumi *p* 藍住 2772
Aita *s* 英多 693, 莫田 1175
Aitagi *s* 愛多義 2018
Aiuchi *s* 相内 868
Aiura *s* 相浦
Aiwaka *s* 愛若 2018
Aiya *s* 藍谷 2772
Aiyama *s* 相山 868
Aizawa *s* 会沢 454, 相沢 868, 逢沢 1516, 愛沢 2018, 藍沢 2772
~ Yasushi *mh* 会沢安 454
Aizō *m* 愛三 2018
Aizu *sph* 会津 454
~ Bange *p* 会津坂下
~ Takada *p* 会津高田
~ Yaichi *ml* 会津八一
Aji *p* 庵治 1506. (味 572, 鰺 2999) 「525
Ajia *p* "Asia" 亜細亜
Ajigasawa *p* 鰺ケ沢 2999
Ajikata *p* 味方 572
Ajikawa *s* 阿治川 569
Ajiki *s* 安勅 472, 安勅城, 安喰, 阿直 569, 味木 572; *sp* 安食 472
Ajima *s* 安島, 阿島 569
Ajimi *sp* 安心院 472
Ajimu *s* 安心院
Ajioka *s* 味岡 572
Ajiro *s* 足代 461, 網代 2536
Ajisaka *s* 鰺坂 2999
Ajisu *p* 阿知須 569
Ajito *m* 味戸 572
Aka *p* 赤 443. (丹 79, 赤 443, 明 623, 紅 1423, 赭 2498)
Akabane *s* 赤埴 443; *sp* 赤羽, 赤羽根
Akabashi *s* 赤橋
Akabayashi *s* 赤林
Akabira *p* 赤平
Akabori *sp* 赤堀
Akaboshi *s* 赤星
Akada *s* 赤田
Akadomari *p* 赤泊
Akae *m* 赤兄
Akaezo fūsetsukō *lh* 赤蝦夷風説考
Akagaki *s* 赤垣
Akagari *s* 胝 1082
Akagawa *s* 赤川 443
Akagi *s* 赤木; *sp* 赤城
~ Kakudō *ml* 赤木格堂 「介
~ Kensuke *ml* 赤木健
~ Kōhei *ml* 赤木桁平
Akagire *s* 胝 1082
Akahagi *s* 赤荻 443
Akahani *s* 赤土, 赤埴
Akahiko *m* 赤彦
Akahito *m* 赤人
Akaho *s* 赤穂
Akahon *l* 赤本
Akai *s* 赤井
Akaigawa *p* 赤井川
Akaike *sp* 赤池
Akaishi *s* 赤石
Akaiwa *s* 赤岩; *p* 赤磐
~ Sakae *ml* 赤岩栄
Akaji *s* 赤地
Akama *s* 赤間
Akamaro *m* 阿歌麿 569
Akamatsu *s* 赤松 443
~ Mitsusuke *mh* 赤松満祐 「則村
~ Norimura *mh* 赤松
Akami *s* 赤見
Akamine *s* 赤嶺
Akamizaka *s* 赤見坂
Akan *p* 阿寒 569
Akanabe *s* 茜部 928
Akanashi *s* 杠 418; *sm* 杜 423 「(茜 928)
Akane *s* 赤根 443, 赤禰.
Akaneya *s* 茜屋
Akano *s* 赤野443
Akanuma *s* 阿鹿沼 569
Akao *s* 赤尾 443
Akaogi *s* 赤荻
Akaoka *p* 赤岡
Akara *f* 紅良 1423
(akaru 明 623)
Akaru tae *l* 明る妙
Akasa *s* 赤佐 443 「坂
Akasaka *s* 赤阪; *sp* 赤
Akasaki *s* 赤崎; *p* 赤碕
Akashi *s* 赤司, 赤石; *sf-p-l* 明石 623; *m* 丹 79, 杲 712. (証 1660)
Akashiko *f* 証子
Akashina *p* 明科 623
Akashio *s* 赤塩 443
Akashita *s* 丹下 79
Akasu *s* 赤須 443
Akatsu *s* 赤津 「1596
Akatsuka *s* 赤塚, 暁霞
Akatsuki *m* 暁
Akawa *s* 淡河 1340
Akayama *s* 赤山 443
Akayu *p* 赤湯
Akaza *s* 赤座
Akazawa *s* 赤沢
Akaze *s* 赤畝 「部
Akazome *s* 赤染, 赤染
~ Emon *fl* 赤染衛門
Ake *m* 吾笥 491. (朱 341, 明 623, 南 912, 暁 1596, 曙 2719)
Akebayashi *s* 明林 623
Akebono *sf* 曙 2719; *sp* 暁 1596
Akechi *sp* 明智 623
~ Mitsuhide *mh* 明智光秀
Akeda *s* 明田
Akedagawa *s* 明田川
Akegarasu *s* 暁烏 1596; *l* 明烏 623
~ Haya *ml* 暁烏敏 1596
~ nochi no masayume *l* 明烏後正夢 623
Akeha *f* 朱華 341
Akehama *p* 明浜 623
Akeharu *m* 南晴 912
Akemi *m* 曙覧 2719; *f* 朱 341, 朱実
Akemiko *f* 明珠子 623
Akemine *s* 明峰
Akeno *s* 暁 1596; *p* 明野 623
Akeo *m* 暁雄 1596
Akera *s* 朱楽 341, 明浦 623, 明楽 「341
~ Kankō *ml* 朱楽菅公
Aketo *s* 明渡 623
Aki *s* 安吉 472; *sf-p* 安芸; *sp* 安岐; *f* 吾樹 491, 彬 1370, 暲 2284, 諒 2326. (了 9, 口 29, 士 41, 日 77, 文 86, 夫 104, 礼 146, 且 162, 右 171, 丙 198, 白 216, 壮 243, 印 260, 光 281, 旭 300, 在 314, 成 322, 西 336, 言 439, 亨 440, 彣 510, 見 518, 昉 619, 明 623, 知 636, 杲 712, 昌 715, 信 782, 洞 821, 炳 837, 映 840, 昭 841, 研 875, 秋 878, 亮 911, 表 914, 昴 943, 昱 944, 発 953, 昼 983, 昶 1004, 乗 1016, 倬 1027, 晄 1084, 晅 1085, 耿 1129, 食 1159, 晁 1188, 晃 1189, 晋 1215, 哲 1227, 淳 1337, 炫 1344, 晤 1353, 晧 1355, 彬 1370, 皎 1375, 朗 1394, 紀 1424, 著 1445, 菊 1451, 章 1461, 揭 1480, 商 1526, 揚 1551, 陽 1567, 斌 1590, 暁 1596, 瑛 1607, 皓 1639, 敞 1688, 敬 1691, 晨 1739, 晶 1740, 覚 1752, 晳 1791, 堯 1795, 卿 1865, 焕 1876, 煌 1877, 暉 1884, 詮 1934, 紹 1955, 義 1975, 愛 2018, 煦 2034, 照 2035, 喩 2064, 曄 2091, 郷 2112, 精 2131, 説 2143, 銘 2155, 甄 2161, 韶 2163, 飽 2165, 彰 2174, 察 2180, 翠 2204, 徴 2265, 暲 2284, 璋 2287, 聡 2311, 諒 2326, 審 2365, 箸 2381, 曈 2470, 璃 2473, 頭 2504, 諟 2512, 諦 2516, 融 2545, 瞭 2629, 聴 2634, 謙 2646, 顕 2757, 観 2765, 鏡 2817, 離 2889, 穐 2915, 耀 2919, 鑑 2968)
Akiba *s* 秋馬 878, 秋葉, 秋場; *sm* 秋庭
Akie *m* 諒兄 2326; *f* 秋江 878, 昶恵 1004, 晶江 1740
Akifusa *m* 昭房 841, 紹房 1955, 顕房 2757
Akigusa *s* 秋草 878
Akihaya *m* 彰逸 2174
Akihira *ml* 明衡 623
Akihiro *m* 哲浩 1227, 諦寛 2516 「古 2131
Akihisa *m* 著寿 1445, 精
Akihito *m* 彰仁 2174
Akiho *s* 秋保 878; *sm* 秋穂; *m* 空穂 723
Akiie *m* 顕家 2757
Akiji *m* 明治 623
Akika *m* 秋香 878
Akikane *m* 詮兼 1934
Akikata *m* 在賢 314
Akikaze *m* 章風 1461
Akikazu *m* 日一 77, 亮一 911, 堯一 1795

Akikiyo *m* 口人 29, 秋清 878
Akiko *f* 昌女 715, 秋子 878, 昱子 944, 耿子 1129, 章子 1461, 瑛子 1607, 晨子 1739, 晶子 1740, 晢子 1791, 煌子 1877, 詮子 1934, 韶子 2163, 彰子 2174, 璃子 2473, 諟子 2512, 諦子 2516, 聴子 2634, 顕子 2757
Akikoto *m* 顕允
Akikuni *m* 昭訓 841
Akima *s* 秋間 878
Akimaro *m* 晢麿 1480
Akimasa *m* 壮昌 243, 暉昌 1884, 顕允 2757, 鑑正 2968 「朗徹 1394
Akimichi *m* 亮道 911,
Akimitsu *m* 明光 623, 彬光 1370, 煥光 1876, 詮実 1934, 韶光 2163, 璋光 2287, 顕光 2757
Akimori *s* 秋森 878
Akimoto *s* 秋元, 秋本; *m* 紀元 1424
～ Fujio *ml* 秋元不死男 878 「代
～ Matsuyo *fl* 秋元松
Akina *s* 阿支奈 569, 阿祇奈 「銘長 2155
Akinaga *s* 秋永 878; *m*
Akinari *m* 秋成 878
Akindo setai-gusuri *l* 商人世帯薬 1526
～ gunpai uchiwa *l* 商人軍配団
～ kashoku kun *l* 商人家職訓
Akino *s* 秋野 878
Akinobu *m* 西暢 336, 昌信 715, 晅宣 1085, 章信 1461, 詮信 1934, 顕信 2757, 鑑備 2968
Akinori *m* 明軌 623, 晃昇 1189, 章憲 1461, 顕孝 2757, 顕智 「2915
Akinosuke *m* 穐之助
Akinoura *s* 荒浦 935
Aki no yonaga *l* 秋夜長 878
Akio *s* 秋尾, 秋保; *m* 了雄 9, 杲雄 712, 倬男 1027, 晁雄 1188, 晃夫 1189
Akioka *s* 秋岡 878
Akiosa *s* 商長 1526
Akiōshi *s* 安芸凡 472
Akira *s* 科良 877, 秋良 878, 箸 2381; *m* 了 9, 士 41, 丹 79, 壬 116, 公 156, 旦 162, 右 171, 央 182, 正 205, 正丹, 正朗, 白 216, 行 245, 卯 259, 全 271, 光 281, 旭 300, 在 314, 成 322, 名 346, 吟 369, 亨 440, 冏 512, 坦 574, 昉 619, 旺 620, 昕 621, 明 623, 的 635, 享 662, 命 671, 旻 710, 杲 712, 昌 715, 学 719, 良 767, 果 770, 東 771, 信 782, 信良, 洞 821, 玲 835, 映 840, 昭 841, 秋 878, 亮 911, 表 914, 昴 943, 発 953, 奐 979, 昼 983, 看 998, 昶 1004, 省 1013, 倬 1027, 晄 1084, 耿 1129, 晟 1187, 晁 1188, 晃 1189, 党 1191, 泰 1203, 哲 1227, 冐 1258, 晈 1355, 彬 1370, 皎 1375, 朗 1394, 奝 1432, 宷 1435, 著 1445, 章 1461, 翌 1466, 晢 1478, 啓 1491, 彪 1523, 爽 1529, 揚 1551, 陽 1567, 斌 1590, 晙 1593, 暎 1594, 暁 1596, 瑛 1607, 皖 1638, 皓 1639, 証 1660, 敞 1688, 晶 1740, 覚 1752, 景 1764, 斐 1781, 智 1793, 幌 1833, 卿 1865, 奐 1872, 煇 1875, 暉 1884, 詮 1934, 誠 1935, 新 1965, 粲 2019, 聖 2030, 照 2035, 暐 2091, 郷 2112, 精 2131, 韶 2163, 飾 2164, 飽 2165, 彰 2174, 察 2180, 翠 2204, 廓 2239, 徹 2265, 晧 2282, 皞 2283, 暲 2284, 璋 2287, 確 2305, 聡 2311, 審 2365, 皛 2375, 瑩 2387, 慧 2392, 賛 2394, 監 2398, 徹 2451, 輝 2499, 頭 2504, 諦 2516, 叡 2555, 憲 2562, 擦 2601, 瞭 2629, 曈 2630, 聴 2634, 鮮 2670, 曙 2719, 曜 2720, 顕 2757, 顕彰, 簡 2788, 曠 2796, 鏡 2817, 離 2889, 耀 2919, 顥 2928, 露 2941, 鑑 2968, 鑒 2982. (礼 146, 旦 162, 白 216, 旭 300, 存 313, 名 346, 言 439, 冏 512, 見 518, 侃 551, 昉 619, 旺 620, 明 623, 知 636, 英 693, 学 719, 述 748, 信 782, 映 840, 昭 841, 亮 911, 昱 944, 発 953, 奐 979, 昼 983, 祥 1074, 剣 1151, 高 1163, 晟 1187, 党 1191, 哲 1227, 威 1251, 冐 1258, 炫 1344, 晧 1355, 郎 1394, 章 1461, 翌 1466, 晢 1478, 陽 1567, 斌 1590, 暎 1594, 暁 1596, 瑛 1607, 覚 1752, 奐 1872, 煇 1875, 煥 1876, 暉 1884, 詮 1934, 誠 1935, 照 2035, 徳 2063, 暐 2091, 郷 2112, 精 2131, 飽 2165, 彰 2174, 廓 2239, 暉 2285, 璋 2287, 聡 2311, 瑩 2387, 慧 2392, 環 2471, 輝 2499, 諦 2516, 融 2545, 暹 2593, 讃 2638, 豁 2667, 鮮 2670, 曙 2719, 顕 2757, 観 2765, 簡 2788, 曠 2796, 鏡 2817, 離 2889, 麗 2902, 穐 2915, 鑑 2968)
Akirakeiko *fh* 明子 623
Akirashi *m* 明四
Akisachi *m* 明祥
Akisada *m* 誠定 1935
Akisane *m* 詮允 1934
Akishige *m* 鑑重 2968
Akishima *s* 秋島 878; *p* 昭島 841
Akishino *s* 秋篠 878
～ gesseishū *l* 秋篠月清集
Akisuke *ml* 顕輔 2757
Akita *s* 安木田 472, 穐田 2915; *sp* 秋田 878; *p* 秋多, 飽田 2165
Akitada *m* 言忠 439, 秋忠 878 「任 2968
Akitaka *m* 炫隆 1344, 鑑
Akita Minoru *ml* 秋田実 878
Akitane *m* 鑑種 2968
Akitani *s* 秋谷 878
Akitate *m* 顕達 2757
Akita Ujaku 秋田雨雀 878
Akiteru *m* 日照 77
Akitō *m* 詮茂 1934
Akitoki *s* 秋時 878; *m* 顕時 2757
Akitoshi *m* 璋敏 2287
Akitsu *m* 秋津 878; *p* 安芸津 472
Akitsugu *m* 口次 29, 見次 518, 商次 1526
Akitsumaro *m* 秋津麿 878
Akitsune *m* 明恒 623
Akitsura *m* 鑑連 2968
Akiuji *m* 明氏 623
Akiwa *s* 秋和 878
Akiya *s* 秋谷
Akiyama *s* 穐山 2915; *sp* 秋山 878
～ Kiyoshi *ml* 秋山清
～ Shūkōryō *ml* 秋山秋紅蓼 「1461
Akiyo *f* 昭四 841, 章代
Akiyori *m* 聡頼 2311, 観依 2765
Akiyoshi *sm* 秋吉 878; *m* 昭義 841, 表美 914, 陽恵 1567, 愛義 2018, 喩義 2064, 彰義 2174, 翠静 2204, 聡善 2311, 顕能 2757, 顕義
Akiyuki *m* 晧之 1355, 精之 2131, 顕行 2757
Akizane *m* 昭実 841
Akizato *s* 秋里 878
Akizawa *s* 秋沢
～ Shūji *ml* 秋沢修二
Akizō *m* 白三 216, 穐三 2915
Akizuki *s* 秋月 878
～ Keita *ml* 秋月桂太
Akō *s* 安香 472; *p* 赤穂 443 「569
Akogashima *s* 阿子島
Akogi *s* 阿古木; *la* 阿漕 「433
Akō rōshi *l* 赤穂浪士
Aku *s* 悪 1483A. (悪, 渥 1856, 飽 2165)
Akubi *s* 日外 77
Akubō *la* 悪坊 1483A
Akui *s* 阿久井 569
Akuin *s* 安居院 472
Akuma *s* 阿曲 569, 飽間
Akumi *sp* 飽海 ⌊2165
Akumo *s* 安曇 472

Akune *p* 阿久根 569
Akunin shōki setsu 悪人正機説 1483A
Akura *s* 飽浦 2165
Akusawa *s* 阿久沢 569
Akushima *s* 阿子島
(akuta 芥 475)
Akutagawa *sla* 芥川
~ Ryūnosuke *ml* 芥川竜之介
Akutame *f* 飽田女 2165
Akutarō *la* 悪太郎 1483A
Akutsu *s* 阿 569, 阿久津; *sp* 圷 240
~ Ōno *p* 圷大野
Akyū *p* 秋保 878
Ama *s* 天 93, 白水郎 216, 安間 472, 安摩, 阿万 569, 海 1071; *sp* 海部; *sp-la* 海士; *m* 安万 472; *la* 海人 1071. (天 93, 尼 175, 甘 207, 雨 759, 海 1071, 亀 1531)
Amabe *sp* 海部 1071
Amabiko *l* 天彦 93
Amabu *s* 海部 1071
Amada *sp* 天田 93
~ Guan *ml* 天田愚庵
Amadani *s* 天谷
Amadera *s* 天寺
Amafuji *s* 天藤
Amagai *s* 天貝
Amagasa *s* 天笠
Amagasaki *sp* 尼崎 175
Amagatarai *s* 天語 93
Amagatari *s* 天語, 海語 1071 「谷 759
Amagaya *s* 天谷 93, 雨
Amagi *sp* 天城 93; *p* 甘木 207
~ Yugashima *p* 天城湯ケ島 93
Amaha *sp* 天羽
Amahiko *s* 天孫; *m* 海人彦 1071
Amahyō *s* 天丙 93
Amai *s* 天井
Amaike *s* 天池
Amainu *sm* 天狗
Amainukai *s* 海犬養 1071
Amaka *s* 安幕 472, 安蟇
Amakai *s* 天海 93
Amakasu *s* 甘粕 207, 甘糟
Amakata *s* 天方 93
Amakawa *s* 天川
Amaki *s* 天木
Amako *s* 天児, 尼子 175
Amakuni *sm* 天国 93
Amakura *sm* 天座
Amakusa *splh* 天草
~ Shirō Tokisada *mh* 天草四郎時貞
Amami *s* 天見, 天海, 甘味 207
Amamiya *s* 天宮 93
Amamoto *s* 天本
Amana *s* 海士名 1071
Amanawa *s* 甘縄 207
Amane *s* 尼子 175; *m* 周 736, 稠 1915
Amani *s* 天児 93
Amanibe *s* 孔王部 58
Amanie *s* 孔王部
Amano *s* 天野 93, 甘濃 207
Amanō *s* 甘名宇
Amanohara *sm* 天原 93
Amanoinukai *s* 海犬甘 1071 「の刈藻
Amano karumo *l* 海人
Amanome *s* 天生目 93
Amanomiya *s* 天宮
Amano Teisuke *ml* 天野貞祐
~ Tōrin *ml* 天野桃隣
Amanoya *s* 天宅, 天谷, 天野谷, 天野屋
Amanuma *s* 天沼
Amari *s* 天利, 甘利 207, 余 448, 安幕 472
Amarume *sp* 余目 448
Amasaki *s* 尼崎 175
Amaterasu Ōmikami *fh* 天照大神 93
Amatsu *sp* 天津 「湊
~ Kominato *p* 天津小
Amaya *s* 天矢, 雨夜 759
Amayo no ki *l* 雨夜記
Amayuki *s* 天行 93
(ame 天, 雨 759)
Amegaya *s* 雨谷
Amejima *s* 小豆島 21
Amemiya *s* 雨宮 759
Amemori *s* 雨森
Amenomiya *s* 下米宮 46, 粟米宮 1763
Amenomori *s* 雨森 759
~ Hōshū *mh* 雨森芳洲
Amenouzume-no-mikoto *fh* 天鈿女命 93
Amerika *p* "America" 亜米利加 525
Ametani *s* 阿免谷 569
Ameyama *s* 雨山 759
Ami *s* 浴 1064; *p* 阿見 569. (浴 1064, 網 2536)
Amibe *s* 浴部 1064
Amida *mh* 阿弥陀 569
Amikura *s* 網倉 2536
Aminaka *s* 網中
Amino *sp* 網野
~ Kiku *fl* 網野菊
Amitani *s* 網谷
Amo *s* 安毛 472
Amō *s* 天生 93, 天羽
Amorigoto *l* 天降言
(an 行 245, 安 472, 按 1044, 莫 1175, 菴 1446, 晏 1458, 庵 1506, 愔 1546, 暗 1883, 鞍 2543, 闇 2709)
Ana *s* 穴太 158. (穴, 莫 1175, 竇 2897)
Anabuki *p* 穴吹 158
Anahara *s* 穴原
Anaho *s* 穴太, 莫太 1175, 莫保
Anahobe *s* 穴穂部 158
Anai *s* 穴井
Anaki *s* 安奈木 472
Anami *s* 阿南 569
Anamizu *sp* 穴水 158
Anan *p* 阿南 569
Anana *s* 阿那名
Anao *s* 孔王 58
Anashi *s* 穴磯 158
Anata *s* 穴田, 竇田 2897
Anato *s* 穴太 158; *m* 予何人 62
Anayama *s* 穴山 158
Anazawa *s* 穴沢
Anchi *s* 奄智 668, 庵智 1506 「治家 2709
Anchū seijika *l* 闇中政
Anda *s* 合田 270
Ando *p* 安堵 472 「藤
Andō *s* 安東, 安堂, 安
~ Hiroshige *ma* 安藤広重
~ Ichirō *ml* 安藤一郎
~ Nobumasa *mh* 安藤信正 「益
~ Shōeki *mh* 安藤昌
~ Tsuguo *ml* 安東次 ⌊男
(ane 姉 847)
Anegawa *sp* 姉川
Aneha *s* 姉歯
An'ei 1172–81 安永 472
Aneko *f* 姉子 847
Anenokōji *s* 姉小路
Anesaki *s* 姉崎
~ Chōfū *ml* 姉崎嘲風
Anetai *s* 姉帯
Anfu *s* 安富 472
Angen 1175–77 安元
Anginomononobe *s* 菴宜物部 1446 「569
Anhiru *s* 安蒜 472, 阿蛭
Ani *p* 阿仁. (兄 181)
Aniko *m* 兄子
Anjiki *s* 安喰 472, 安飾
Anjō *s* 安生, 安祥; *sp* 安城 「城家の兄弟
Anjōke no kyōdai *l* 安
Anjū *s* 安住
Ankokuji *p* 安国寺
Anma *s* 安間, 阿間 569
Anna 968–70 安和 472
Annaka *sp* 安中
Annan *p* 安南
Annen *s* 安念
Anno *s* 阿武 569, 阿武方, 阿野
Annō *s* 安納 472
Annotsu *s* 安濃津
Ano *s* 穴太 158, 阿野 569
Anō *sp* 穴生 158, 穴太, 安濃 472; *p* 賀名生 1756
Anouchi *s* 阿内 569
Anpachi *p* 安八 472
Anpo *s* 安保
Anpuku *s* 安福
Anraku *s* 安楽
Anrakuan sakuden *ml* 安楽庵策伝
Anryū *s* 安立
Ansei 1854–60 安政
Anseki *s* 庵跡 1506
Antei 1227–29 安貞 472
Antoku *mh* 安徳
Anu *s* 安努
Anwa 968–70 安和
An'ya kōro *l* 暗夜行路 1883
Anzai *s* 安在 472, 安西, 安斉; *sml* 安斎
~ Fuyue *ml* 安西冬衛
~ Ōkaishi *ml* 安斎桜磈子
Anzan *p* 鞍山 2543
Anzawa *s* 安沢 472
Anzō *s* 安蔵
(anzu 杏 487)
Anzukko *l* 杏っ子
Ao *s* 正月一日 205, 安居

472, 阿保 569, 粟生 1763. (青 700, 碧 2225)
Aō *s* 青生 700
Aochi *s* 青地
Aōda *s* 粟生田 1763
Aōdō Denzen *ma* 亜欧堂田善 525
Aoe *sf* 青江 700
～ Shunjirō *ml* 青江舜二郎
Aogai *s* 青貝
Aogaki *s* 青柿; *p-l* 青垣
Aogashima *p* 青ケ島
Aogi *s* 仰木 360
Aogu *m* 仰
Aohon *l* 青本 700
Aoi *s* 青井; *sf* 葵 1723
Aoike *s* 青池 700
Aoi no Ue *la* 葵の上 1723
Aojima *s* 青島 700, 青嶹
Aojishi *l* 青猪
Aoki *sp* 青木
～ Getto *ml* 青木月斗
～ Kensaku *ml* 青木健作 「陽
～ Kon'yō *mh* 青木昆
～ Shigeru *ma* 青木繁
～ Shūzō *mh* 青木周蔵
Aomi *m* 碧海 2225
Aōmi *s* 青梅 700
Aomori *sp* 青森
Aomugi *l* 青麦
Aonahata *s* 青名端
Aonao *s* 青女子
Aone *s* 青根; *l* 青嶺
Aoneko *l* 青猫
Aoni yoshi *l* 青丹よし
Aono *s* 青野 「吉
～ Suekichi *ml* 青野季
Aonuma *s* 青沼
Aooka *s* 青岡
Aoshiba *l* 青芝
Aoshika *s* 青鹿
Aosoi *s* 青襲
Aota *s* 青田
Aoto *s* 青戸, 青砥
Aoya *p* 青谷
Aoyagi *s* 青柳
～ Yūbi *ml* 青柳有美
～ Yutaka *ml* 青柳優
Aoyama *sp* 青山
～ Kason *ml* 青山霞村
～ Sugisaku *ml* 青山杉作
Ao-zukin *l* 青頭巾
Ara *s* 荒 935. (改 379, 荒 935, 新 1965, 麁 2053, 粿 2633, 麤 3025)
Arabia *p* "Arabia" 亜剌比亜 525
Arabuka *s* 荒深 935
Arae *s* 新江 1965
Araemishi *s* 麁蝦夷 2053
Aragaki *s* 荒垣 935
～ Hideo *ml* 荒垣秀雄
Arahata *s* 荒波多, 荒畑, 荒幡 「村
～ Kanson *mlh* 荒畑寒
Arai *s* 荒井, 荒居; *sp* 新井 1965, 新居
～ Hakuseki *mlh* 新井白石
～ Kiichi *ml* 新井紀一
～ Kō *ml* 新井洸
Arajotai *l* 新世帯
Araka *s* 荒賀 935
Arakabi *m* 麤鹿火 3025, 麤鹿比; *f* 麁鹿火 2053
Arakane *s* 荒金 935
Arakawa *s* 淡河 1340, 新川 1965; *sp* 荒川 935
Arakazu *m* 新一 1965
Arake *s* 有家 303
Araki *s* 安楽城 472, 荒木 935, 荒城, 新木 1965, 墾 2702; *m* 荒樹 935
Arakida *s* 荒木田
～ Moritake *ml* 荒木田守武
Araki Mataemon *mh-l* 荒木又右衛門
～ Sadao *mh* 荒木貞夫
～ Sōtarō *mh* 荒木宗太郎
～ Takashi *ml* 荒木巍
Arako *s* 麁子 2053
Arakusa *l* 麁草 「巻
Aramaki *s* 荒牧 935, 荒
Ara Masahito *ml* 荒正
Arami *s* 荒身 ⌊人
Aramimi *m* 荒耳
Aramori *s* 新籾 1965
Aramoto *s* 荒本 935
Aranami *s* 荒波
Arando *m* 荒人 「2796
Arano *s* 荒野; *l* 曠野
Arao *s* 荒生 935, 新尾 1965; *sp* 荒尾 935; *m* 荒男, 麤郎 3025
Araoka *s* 安良岡 472, 荒岡 935
Arara *s* 荒, 荒荒. (荒)
Araragi *s* 荒
Arasa *s* 有在 303
Arasawa *s* 安良沢 472, 荒沢 935
Arase *s* 荒瀬 「2209
Araseitō *l* 紫羅欄花
Arashi *sm* 嵐 2000
Arashima *s* 荒島 935
Arashiyama *p-la* 嵐山 2000
Arasuke *m* 荒助 935
Arata *s* 荒田; *sm* 新 1965
Aratae *s* 荒田殖 935
Aratai *s* 荒田井
Aratame *s* 新田目 1965
Aratani *s* 荒谷 935
Araya *s* 荒谷, 荒屋, 新谷 1965, 新屋
Arayama *s* 荒山 935, 新山 1965
Arazō *m* 荒三 935
Are *m* 阿礼 569. (似 350, 形 414, 肖 451)
(ari 也 23, 可 165, 生 214, 光 281, 有 303, 存 313, 在 314, 似 350, 作 362, 社 406, 茂 691, 盈 1200, 益 1201, 惟 1290, 得 1299, 現 1360, 順 1532, 満 1861, 照 2035, 徳 2063, 蟻 2804)
Ariake *sp* 有明 303; *m* 在明 314
Ariaketei *s* 在明亭
Ariaya *m* 有言 303
Arichi *s* 有地
Aridōshi *la* 蟻通 2804
Arie *s* 有江 303; *p* 有家
Arieda *m* 有条
Arifuji *m* 有藤
Arifuku *m* 有福
Ariga *s* 有我, 有賀
～ Nagao *ml* 有賀長雄
Arihara *s* 有原, 在原 314
～ no Narihira *ml* 在原業平
Arihira *m* 在衡
Arihōshi *s* 有法師 303
Arii *s* 有井
Ariie *m* 有家
Ariizumi *s* 有泉
Ariji *s* 有路
Arikata *m* 有象
Arikawa *s* 在川 314, 蟻川 2804; *sp* 有川 303
Arikazu *m* 有良, 無二 1789
Ariki *s* 有木 303
Ariko *f* 在子 314
Arikōrō *ma* 有幸郎 303
Arikoto *m* 有功
Arima *sp* 有馬 「晴信
～ Harunobu *mh* 有馬
～ no Ōji *mh* 有馬皇子
～ Shinshichi *mh* 有馬新七
Arimatsu *p* 有松
Arima Yorichika *ml* 有馬頼義
Arimichi *s* 有道
Arimitsu *sm* 有光
Arimochi *s* 有持
Arimori *s* 有森
Arimoto *s* 有元, 有本
～ Hōsui *ml* 有本芳水
Arimune *m* 有梁
Arimura *s* 有村; *m* 在村 314
Arino *s* 有野 303
Arinobu *sm* 在信 314
Arinori *m* 有格 303, 在経 314
Ario *s* 有尾 303
Ariō *s* 有王
Arioka *s* 有岡
Ariosa *m* 有容
Arisada *s* 在狭田 314
Arisaka *s* 有坂 303
Arisato *m* 有瀰
Arisawa *s* 有沢
Arishige *m* 可重 165
Arishima *s* 有島 303
～ Ikuma *mla* 有島生馬
～ Takeo *ml* 有島武郎
Ariso *s* 有磯
Arisugawa *s* 有栖川
～ -no-miya Taruhito *mh* 有栖川宮熾仁
Arisuke *m* 有允
Arita *s* 在田 314; *sp* 有田 303
Aritaka *m* 有尚
Aritake *s* 有竹
Aritaki *s* 有滝
Aritane *m* 順胤 1532
Aritomi *s* 有富 303
Aritomo *m* 有公
Ariwara *s* 有原, 在原 314 「原業平
～ no Narihira *ml* 在
Ariya *s* 有家 303; *m* 存 313, 在屋 314
Ariyama *s* 有山 303

Ariyoshi *sm* 有吉; *m* 有快, 有徽 「子
～ Sawako *fl* 有吉佐和
Arizono *s* 有園
Arō *m* 濯 2609
(aru 有 303, 存 313)
Aruga *s* 有賀 303
Arutaki *s* 阿留多岐 569
Arutakii *s* 阿留多岐怡
Aruzenchin *p* "Argentine" 亜爾然丁 525
Asa *s* 旦 162; *p* 安佐 472, 厚狭 985. (元 60, 旦 162, 亘 262, 夙 299, 旭 300, 昕 622, 浅 827, 晁 1188, 麻 1508, 朝 1672, 諒 2326, 滋 2460, 鮮 2670)
Asaakira *m* 朝融 1672
Asaarashi yūsame *l* 朝嵐夕雨
Asaba *s* 浅波 827, 浅場, 浅葉; *sp* 浅羽
Asabe *s* 朝戸 1672
Asabu *s* 麻生 1508
Asabuki *s* 朝吹 1672
Asada *s* 浅田 827, 麻田 1508, 朝田 1672, 鮮田 2670 「立 1508
～ Gōryū *mh* 麻田剛
Asae *s* 浅江 827
Asaeda *s* 朝枝 1672
Asagao *l* 槿 2289
Asahara *s* 浅原 827, 麻原 1508; *sm* 朝原 1672
～ Rokurō *ml* 浅原六朗 827
Asahi *sm-f-p* 旭 300; *sp* 朝日 1672; *m* 曦 2914. (旭 300)
Asahikawa *p* 旭川
Asahiko *m* 旭彦, 浅彦 827
Asahina *s* 朝印奈 1672, 朝夷, 朝夷名; *sl* 朝比奈, 朝日奈
Asai *s* 阿佐井 569, 朝井 1672; *sp* 浅井 827
～ Chū *ma* 浅井忠
～ Jūsaburō *ml* 浅井十三郎
Asaina *s* 朝日奈 1672, 朝印奈, 朝夷, 朝夷名
Asai Nagamasa *mh* 浅井長政 827
Asaina shimameguri *la* 朝夷巡島記 1672
Asai Ryōi *ml* 浅井了意 827
Asaji *m* 浅次; *p* 朝地 1672 「827
～ ga yado *l* 浅茅が宿
Asajirō *m* 浅次郎
Asaka *s* 阿尺 569, 阿積, 浅香 827, 浅賀, 麻賀 1508, 朝香 1672, 朝賀, 朝積; *sp* 安積 472; *p* 朝霞 1672
Asakari *m* 朝猟
Asaka Tanpaku *mh* 安積澹泊 472
Asakawa *s* 朝川 1672, 朝河; *sp* 浅川 827
Asake *s* 朝明 1672
Asaki *s* 浅木 827, 浅黄
Asako *s* 阿左古 569, 浅古827, 朝米 1672; *sf* 浅子827; *sf-p* 朝来 1672; *f* 夙子 299, 亜沙子 525, 昕子 622, 晁子 1188, 麻子 1508, 朝子 1672
Asakuchi *p* 浅口 827
Asakura *s* 浅倉; *sp* 朝倉 1672 「夫
～ Fumio *ma* 朝倉文
～ Toshikage *mh* 朝倉敏景 「義景
～ Yoshikage *mh* 朝倉
Asakusa *sp* 浅草 827
～ kurenaidan *l* 浅草紅団
～ no hi *l* 浅草の灯
Asama *sp* 浅間
Asamagatake omokage-zōshi *l* 浅間嶽面影草紙
Asamaki *s* 大西風 48
Asamaru *m* 阿沙丸 569
Asami *s* 安佐美 472, 阿佐美 569, 浅水 827, 浅見, 浅海; *f* 朝生 1672
～ Fukashi *ml* 浅見淵 827
～ Keisai *mh* 浅見絅斎
Asamune *sm* 朝宗 1672; *m* 朝棟
Asamura *s* 浅村 827
Asanae *s* 浅江
Asano *s* 浅野, 朝野 1672
～ Akira *ml* 浅野晃 827
～ Nagamasa *mh* 浅野長政
～ Rikyō *ml* 浅野梨郷
～ Sōichirō *mh* 浅野総一郎
Asanuma *s* 浅沼
Asao *s* 亘尾 262, 浅尾 827; *m* 旦夫 162
Asaoka *s* 浅岡 827, 朝岡 1672
Asari *s* 阿佐利 569, 浅利 827
Asashichi *m* 浅七
Asashina *p* 浅科
Asatada *m* 朝忠 1672
Asatsuna *s* 朝夷名
Asawa *s* 浅輪 827
Asaya *s* 朝家 1672
Asayama *s* 浅山 827
Asazuma *s* 朝妻 1672
Asazumakouma *s* 朝妻子午
(ashi 足 461, 芦 484, 脚 1612, 葦 1992, 蘆 2842)
Ashiato *l* 足迹 461
Ashiba *s* 足羽, 芦葉 484, 蘆葉 2842 「484
Ashibe *s* 蘆辺; *p* 芦辺
Ashibetsu *p* 芦別
Ashibi *l* 馬酔木 1257
Ashida *s* 茨田 932, 蘆田 2842; *sp* 芦田 484
～ Enosuke *ml* 芦田恵之助
～ Hitoshi *mh* 芦田均
Ashigara *p* 足柄 461
～ -kami *p* 足柄上
～ -shimo *p* 足柄下
Ashikaga *sp* 足利
～ Masatomo *mh* 足利政知 「持氏
～ Mochiuji *mh* 足利
～ Motouji *mh* 足利基氏 「氏
～ Shigeuji *mh* 足利成
～ Tadayoshi *mh* 足利直義 「氏
～ Takauji *mh* 足利尊
～ Yoshiaki *mh* 足利義昭 「義詮
～ Yoshiakira *mh* 足利
～ Yoshihisa *mh* 足利義尚 「義政
～ Yoshimasa *mh* 足利
～ Yoshimi *mh* 足利義視 「利義満
～ Yoshimitsu *mh* 足
～ Yoshimochi *mh* 足利義持 「義教
～ Yoshinori *mh* 足利
～ Yoshiteru *mh* 足利義輝
Ashikari *p-l* 芦刈 484; *la* 蘆刈 2842
Ashikawa *s* 蘆川; *sp* 芦川 484 「敷 2842
Ashiki *s* 葦敷 1992, 蘆
Ashikita *sp* 芦北 484
Ashikui *s* 脚咋 1612
Ashima *s* 余島 448
Ashimori *p* 足守 461
Ashina *s* 阿支奈 569, 葦名 1992, 蘆名 2842; *sp* 芦品 484
Ashino *s* 芦野, 葦野 1992, 蘆野 2842
Ashio *s* 足穂 461; *p* 足尾
～ Dōzan *ph* 足尾銅山
Ashioto *la* 跫音 2008
Ashiro *p* 安代 472
Ashishige *s* 葦繁 1992
Ashitsumi *s* 脚身 1612
Ashiwada *p* 足和田 461
Ashiwake obune *l* 排蘆小船 1317
Ashiwara *s* 芦原 484, 葦原 1992, 蘆原 2842
Ashiwatari *s* 葦波 1992, 蘆渡 2842
Ashiya *s* 芦谷 484, 葦谷 1992, 葦室, 葦屋; *sp* 蘆屋 2842; *p* 芦屋 484
～ Dōman ōuchi kagami *l* 蘆屋道満大内鑑 2842
Ashiyasu *p* 芦安 484
Ashiyoro *p* 足寄 461
Ashizaki *s* 葦崎 1992
Ashizawa *s* 芦沢 484, 蘆沢 2842
Ashizuka *s* 蘆塚
Aso *s* 阿曾 569, 愛曾 2018; *sp* 安蘇 472, 阿蘇 569
Asō *s* 阿相, 浅生 827, 朝生 1672; *sp-la* 麻生 1508
～ Hisashi *mh* 麻生久
Asōji *m* 阿三次 569
Asomi *sm* 朝臣 1672
Ason *sm* 朝臣
Asonuma *s* 阿曾沼 569
Asotani *s* 阿曾谷
Asō Yoshiteru *ml* 麻生義輝 1508
Asōzu *s* 浅水 827
Assabu *p* 厚沢部 985

Asshi *s* 合志 270
Asuka *s* 安宿 472, 朝日 1672; *sp* 飛鳥 1014; *p-l* 明日香 623
Asukabe *s* 飛鳥部 1014
Asukadera *p* 飛鳥寺
Asuka-gawa *la* 飛鳥川
Asukai *sp* 飛鳥井
~ Masachika *ml* 飛鳥井雅親 「井雅経
~ Masatsune *ml* 飛鳥
Asuka no Kiyomihara-no-miya *ph* 飛鳥清御原宮
~ no Kiyomihara ritsuryō *h* 飛鳥清御原律令 「助 461
Asuke *s* 阿介 569; *sp* 足
~ Soichi *ml* 足助素一
Asuma *s* 遊馬 1809
Asunaro *l* 翌檜 1466
Asuwa *sp* 足羽 461
Ata 阿田 569. (呰 972)
Atae *s* 直 988; *m* 与 101
Atago *sp* 愛宕 2018
~ Kūya *la* 愛宕空也
Atai *sm* 直 988
Ataka *s* 阿高 569; *sp-la* 安宅 472
Atake *s* 阿竹 569
Ataki *s* 安宅木 472
Atakumabito *s* 阿太肥人 569
Atame *f* 呰女 972
Atami *s* 阿多見 569; *sp* 熱海 2408
Atamu *s* 愛多茂 2018
Atano *s* 上遠野 47
Atarashi *s* 新 1965
Ataru *m* 中 75, 方 85, 任 ⌊235
Atato *s* 防夫 374
(ate 貴 1755)
Ateko *f* 貴子
Aterazawa *s* 左沢 169
Atetsu *p* 阿哲 569
Ato *s* 阿刀, 迹 1249. (与 101, 跡 1926, 殿 1960)
Atō *s* 阿藤 569; *m* 予 62, 与 101, 錫 2524; *p* 阿東 569
Atobe *s* 跡部 1926
Atoda *s* 跡田
Atōda *s* 阿刀田 569
Atogi *s* 安勅 472, 安勅城
Atoji *s* 阿閉 569
Atomi *s* 跡見 1926; *m* 与美 101
Atomiya *s* 後宮 1300
Atonari *m* 跡成 1926
Atsu *f* 府 740, 厚 985. (毛 117, 仍 123, 功 135, 石 172, 匹 187, 同 298, 団 310, 孜 378, 充 521, 孝 541, 即 648, 京 663, 宏 674, 忠 705, 昌 715, 阜 731, 府 740, 抵 797, 春 963, 厚 985, 重 1017, 配 1141, 衷 1190, 惇 1288, 陸 1312, 淳 1337, 萃 1442, 商 1526, 温 1585, 敦 1690, 敬 1691, 翕 1704, 富 1715, 暑 1738A, 貴 1755, 渥 1856, 強 1878, 暄 1881, 暖 1882, 純 1956, 亶 1972, 豊 2013, 徳 2063, 農 2205, 聚 2221, 適 2240, 醇 2315, 諄 2324, 熱 2408, 積 2493, 穆 2494, 篤 2576, 臧 2595, 濃 2612, 鍾 2649, 龔 2843, 懿 2958)
Atsuari *m* 敦有 1690
Atsufumi *m* 温文 1585
Atsugi *sp* 厚木 985
Atsuhiko *m* 純彦 1956, 篤彦 2576
Atsuhiro *m* 敦成 1690
Atsuike *s* 厚池 985
Atsuji *s* 阿閉 569
Atsukata *m* 敦固 1690
Atsukawa *s* 厚川 985, 熱川 2408
Atsukeshi *p* 厚岸 985
Atsukimi *m* 敦仁 1690
Atsuko *f* 孜子 378, 充子 521, 阜子 731, 配子 1141, 衷子 1190, 淳子 1337, 温子 1585, 敦子 1690, 翕子 1704, 渥子 1856, 豊子 2013, 諄子 2324, 穆子 2494, 篤子 2576, 濃子 2612, 懿子 2958
Atsukuni *m* 淳国 1337
Atsukura *m* 篤倉 2576
Atsuma *p* 厚真 985
Atsumaru *m* 兌 447
Atsumi *s* 阿都扇 569, 厚見 985, 渥見 1856, 渥美, 龔見 2843; *m* 厚生 985; *m-p* 温海 1585; *p* 温美 「郎 1856
~ Seitarō *ml* 渥美清太
Atsumo *s* 安曇 472, 厚母 985
Atsumono *l* 龔 2843
Atsumonozaki *l* 厚物咲 985
Atsumori *m* 敦盛 1690
Atsumu *m* 伍 229, 同 298, 侑 557, 専 973, 修 1038, 蔟 2185, 輯 2497, 鐘 2883
Atsunari *m* 厚生 985
Atsunobu *m* 惇信 1288
Atsunori *m* 淳教 1337, 敦儀 1690 「鬘
Atsura *m* 吾髪 491, 吾
(atsurae 誂 1929)
Atsuraezome tōyamaganoko *l* 誂染遠山麓子
Atsuryū *sp* 且来 192
Atsusa *s* 厚狭 985
Atsusanosuke *m* 厚狭之介
Atsushi *m* 忠 705, 専 973, 重 1017, 烝 1210, 惇 1288, 陸 1312, 淳 1337, 復 1571, 温 1585, 腆 1611, 敦 1690, 富 1715, 渥 1856, 煇 1875, 睦 1904, 純 1956, 徳 2063, 醇 2315, 穆 2494, 賰 2498, 篤 2576, 慿 2582, 濃 2612, 穠 2803, 饒 2925, 懿 2958; *m-f* 厚 985 「納 2408
Atsushiokanō *p* 熱塩加
Atsusuke *m* 篤棐 2576
Atsuta *sp* 熱田 2408; *p* 厚田 985
Atsutahafuribe *s* 熱田祝部 2408 「岩 2221
Atsutaka *m* 厚生 985, 聚
Atsutake *s* 厚誉 985
Atsutane *ml* 篤胤 2576
Atsuto *m* 農人 2205
Atsutomo *m* 厚比 985
Atsutoshi *m* 商利 1526
Atsuuji *m* 惇氏 1288
Atsuyasu *m* 同保 298
Atsuyo *f* 熱代 2408
Atsuyoshi *m* 積善 2493, 穆詔 2494, 穆韶, 篤珍 2576
Atsuyuki *m* 忠幸 705
Atsuzawa *s* 厚沢 985
Au *s* 逢 1516. (合 270, 会 454, 相 868)
Aumi *m* 相見
Awa *s* 粟 1763; *p* 安房 472, 阿波 569. (禾 220, 淡 1340, 粟 1763, 澇 1850)
Awachika *s* 淡近 1340
Awafu *s* 粟生 1763
Awaga *s* 粟賀
Awai *s* 淡相 1340
Awaihara *s* 粟飯原 1763
Awaji *m* 淡 1340; *m-p* 淡路
Awajiya *s* 淡屋
Awaka *s* 淡河
Awamaro *m* 淡理
Awano *s* 阿波野 569; *sp* 粟野 1763
Awanohara *s* 粟野原
Awa no Naruto *l* 阿波之鳴門 569
Awanoōshi *s* 粟凡 1763
Awano Seiho *ml* 阿波野青畝 569
Awara *p* 芦原 484
Awase *s* 淡瀬 1340
Awashi *s* 合志 270; *m* 淡 1340
Awashima *s* 淡島
~ Kangetsu *ml* 淡島寒月 「浦 1763
Awashimaura *p* 粟島
Awasō *s* 且来 162
Awata *s* 禾田 220, 粟田 1763
Awataguchi *sla* 粟田口
~ Yoshimitsu *ma* 粟田口吉光
Awatake *s* 粟竹
Awata no Mahito *mh* 粟田真人
Awatsu *s* 粟津
Awaya *s* 粟屋
Awayama *s* 粟山
Awazu *s* 粟津
Aya *s* 阿野 569, 漢 1860; *sf* 文 86; *sp* 安益 472, 綾 2541; *f* 綾也, 彩 1413. (礼 146, 朱 341, 技 381, 言 439, 肖 451, 英 693, 采 707, 奇 752, 郁 890, 恵 1226, 彧 1255, 理 1361, 彬 1370, 章 1461, 彪 1523, 順 1532, 随 1564, 斌 1590, 琢 1608, 紋 1684, 斐 1781, 漢 1860, 純 1956, 愛 2018, 絢 2150, 操 2448, 綺

2533, 綾 2541, 縷 2878)
Ayabe *s* 漢部 1860; *sp* 綾部 2541
Ayada *s* 綾田
Ayagaki *s* 綾垣
Ayagami *p* 綾上
Ayahiko *m* 文彦 86, 斌彦 1590, 絢彦 2150
Ayahiro *m* 恵寛 1226
Ayahito *m* 文仁 86, 恵仁 1226
Ayaho *s* 英保 693
Ayai *s* 綾井 2541
Ayaka *f* 綾郁
Ayakawa *s* 綾川
Ayaki *s* 漢城 1860
Ayako *f* 文子 86, 朱子 341, 采子 707, 彧子 1255, 章子 1461, 紋子 1684, 斐子 1781, 絢子 2150, 綺子 2533, 綾子 2541
Ayakoto *m* 文勲 86
Ayama *p* 阿山 569
Ayamaro *m* 綾麿 2541
Ayame *f* 菖 1444, 章女 1461, 縷女 2878
Ayamei *s* 菖蒲井 1444
Ayami *m* 文質 86
Ayanaga *m* 順長 1532
Ayanaka *m* 英尚 693
Ayando *s* 漢人 1860; *m* 綾人 2541
Ayanofumi *s* 漢書 1860
Ayanokōji *s* 綾小路 2541
Ayanonaga *s* 漢長 1860
Ayanori *m* 文規 86
Ayanotebito *s* 漢才伎 1860
Aya no tsuzumi *la* 綾鼓 2541
Ayanushi *s* 漢主 1860
Ayao *m* 郁夫 890, 彧雄 1255, 彬男 1370, 章生 1461, 彪夫 1523, 斌夫 1590, 斐雄 1781, 純郎 1956, 綾夫 2541
Ayaru *m* 斐 1781
Ayase *sp* 綾瀬 2541
Ayashi *s* 愛子 2018
Ayasuke *m* 随資 1564
Ayatari *ml* 綾足 2541
Ayato *m* 斌人 1590
Ayatoshi *m* 文聡 86
Ayatsuri *a* 操 2448
~ jōruri *la* 操浄瑠璃
Ayauta *p* 綾歌 2541
Ayayoshi *m* 文彬 86
Ayazō *m* 綾蔵 2541
(ayu 鮎 2547)
Ayuba *s* 阿由葉 569
Ayuishō *l* 脚結抄 1612
Ayukai *s* 鮎貝 2547
~ Kaien *ml* 鮎貝槐園
Ayukawa *s* 鮎川
~ Nobuo *ml* 鮎川信夫
Ayumaro *m* 年魚麿 342, 年麻呂
Ayumi *m* 歩 694
Ayune *f* 香魚音 961
Ayunosuke *m* 鮎之助
Ayuzawa *s* 鮎沢 2547
Aza *s* 此口 254
Azabu *sp* 麻布 1508
Azakami *s* 阿座上 569
Azami *s* 生明 214, 阿射弥 569, 薊 2562A. (薊)
Aze *s* 畔 1110, 畔蔵. (囿 990, 校 1096, 畔 1110, 畦 1381, 畤 1382)
Azebu *s* 安詮院 472
Azechi *s* 田寿地 189, 安土 472; *sfl-ph* 按察 1044; *mh* 按察使
Azegami *s* 畔上 1110
Azehiru *s* 畔蒜
Azekura *s* 畔蔵, 畦籠 1381, 畤籠 1382
~-zukuri *a* 校倉造 1096
Azemuro *s* 畤籠 1382
Azetaka *s* 畔高 1110
Azeyanagi *s* 畔柳
Azō *s* 安蔵 472
Azuchi *p* 安土
~ Momoyama *h* 安土桃山
Azuki *s* 小豆 21
Azukijima *s* 小豆島
Azukisawa *sp* 小豆沢
Azuma *s* 我妻 545; *sp* 吾妻 491; *sm-p* 東 771; *m* 雷 2026. (春 963)
~ asobi *l* 東遊 771
Azumabito *m* 東人
Azumai *s* 東井
Azumaji *s* 東道
Azuma kagami *lh* 吾妻鏡 491
Azumamaro *m* 春麿 963; *ml* 春満
Azuma mondō *l* 吾妻問答 491
Azumaro *m* 安頭麻呂 472
Azuma uta *l* 東歌 771
Azumaya *l* 東屋
Azumi *s* 安住 472, 安積, 阿墓 569, 阿曇; *sp* 安曇 472
~ Atsushi *ml* 安住敦
~ no Hirafu *mh* 阿曇比羅夫 569
Azumōdo *m* 東人 771
Azusa *m* 梓 1366. (梓)
~ miko *l* 梓神子
Azusagawa *p* 梓川
Azusawa *s* 小豆沢 21

# B

(ba 芭 473, 庭 1244, 馬 1257, 麻 1508, 葉 1991, 摩 2428, 磨 2596)
Baba *s* 馬場 1257, 嫗 2474. (媼 2089, 嫗 2474)
~ Kochō *ml* 馬場孤蝶
Babata *s* 馬喰田 1257
Baba Tatsuo *mh* 馬場辰猪
(bai 毎 444, 売 466, 貝 498, 枚 630, 妹 848, 倍 1025, 埋 1041, 唄 1045, 培 1291, 陪 1307, 梅 1374, 買 1753, 邁 2592)
Baigan *ml* 梅巌 1374
Baitei Kinga *ml* 梅亭金鵞
Bakan *ph* 馬関 1257
Bakeichō *l* 化銀杏 56
Bakemono Soga *l* 化物曾我
Bakin *ml* 馬琴 1257
(baku 麦 456, 莫 1175, 摸 1836, 漠 1853, 幕 1989)
Bakusui *ml* 麦水 456
Bamen *s* 馬面 1257
Ban *s* 伴 361, 坂 390, 番 1773, 塙 1845. (万 43, 卍 197, 伴 361, 坂 390, 曼 1457, 晩 1595, 番 1773, 満 1861, 蔓 2192, 播 2259, 蕃 2371, 盤 2399, 磐 2400, 鬘 2979)
Banba *s* 伴馬 361, 番場 1773
Banbayashi *s* 伴林 361
Banchō sarayashiki *la* 番町皿屋敷 1773
Banda *s* 伴田 361
Bandai *s* 万代 43; *p* 磐梯 2400
Bandaiya *s* 万代屋 43
Ban Dan'emon *mh-l* 塙団右衛門 1845
Bandō *s* 坂東 390, 板東 632
Bankichi *m* 磐吉 2399
Bannai *s* 坂内 390
Banno *s* 伴野 361, 坂野 390
Ban Nobumoto *mlh* 伴信友 361
Banpei *m* 伴平
Banroku *m* 万緑 43
Banryō *l* 晩涼 1595
Banshō *s* 番匠 1773
Banshōya *s* 番匠谷
~ Eiichi *ml* 番匠谷英一
Banshū *sp* 播州 2259
~ heiya *l* 播州平野
Banzai *s* 坂西 390
Bao *s* 番長 1773
Bashō *ml* 芭蕉 473
~ shichibushū *l* 芭蕉七部集
Basugi *s* 馬杉 1257
Batatsu *s* 馬達
Batō *p* 馬頭
(batsu 抜 384, 茇 681, 筏 1766)
(be 戸 59, 缶 543, 畔 1110, 部 1418)
Bebeko *s* 逼逼古 1805
Befu *sp* 別府 435
(bei 米 343, 明 623, 敝 1686, 銘 2155, 幣 2414)
Bekkai *p* 別海 435
Bekki *s* 別木, 別喜
Bekku *s* 別宮
Ben *s* 卞 84. (弁 275, 面 904, 勉 1263, 勔 1425, 眄 2249, 綿 2538, 鞭 2752)
Benchiyo *m* 弁千代 275
(beni 紅 1423)

Beniya *s* 紅谷
Benjirō *m* 弁治郎 275
Ben no Naishi *fl* 弁内侍
Benzō *s* 弁蔵; *m* 弁三
Beppu *sp* 別府 435
Berugii *p* "Belgium" 白耳義 216
Berurin *p* "Berlin" 伯林 363
Besshiyama *p* 別子山 435
Bessho *s* 別処, 別所
Betchaku *s* 別役
(betsu 別)
Betsugan wasan *l* 別願和讃
Betsui *s* 別井
Betsuyaku *s* 別役
Bettō *mh* 別当
(bi 未 210, 尾 505, 味 572, 咩 783, 弥 832, 美 923, 眉 997, 弭 1072, 毘 1195, 梶 1371, 備 1539, 鼻 2206, 亹 2932)
Bibai *p* 美唄 923
Bibuga *s* 弁官 275
Biei *p* 美瑛 923
Bifuka *p* 美深
Bihoro *p* 美幌
Bin *m* 敏 1409. (忞 702, 旻 710, 珉 1076, 岷 1080, 瓶 1388, 敏 1409, 暋 2226)
Bingo *ph* 備後 1539
Bin'ichi *m* 敏一 1409
Bisai *p* 尾西 505
Bisanjin *ml* 鼻山人 2206
Bisei *p* 美星 923
Bishamon *mh* 毘沙門 1195
Bitchū *ph* 備中 1539
Bitō *s* 尾藤 505
Bizen *sph* 備前 1539
(bo 母 326, 牡 407, 拇 798, 姥 1090, 募 1718, 墓 1979, 模 2104, 暮 2190, 謨 2638)
(bō 毛 117, 矛 150, 戊 208, 卯 259, 防 374, 坊 389, 牡 407, 牟 455, 朋 616, 房 658, 茅 690, 茂 691, 茆 926, 虻 1134, 畝 1142, 彪 1241, 萠 1448, 傍 1538, 棒 1623, 眸 1636, 紡 1681, 望 1777, 棋 1894, 夢 1990, 愁 2031, 罷 2249, 鉾 2342, 豊 2366, 謀 2509, 虢 2519, 懋 2700)
Bōfu *p* 防府 374
Bogoshū *l* 戊午集 208
Bōjō *s* 坊城 389
Bokkai *p* 渤海 1582
Boku *s* 朴 255. (卜 10, 木 109, 目 191, 朴 255, 牧 610, 昃 1456, 睦 1904, 墨 2230, 穆 2494, 濹 2714)
Bokujū itteki *l* 墨汁一滴 2230
Bokusui *ml* 牧水 610
～ jūniya *l* 墨水十二夜 2230
Bokutō kidan *l* 濹東綺譚 2714
Bokuyō *ml* 卜養 10
～ kyōkashū *l* 卜養狂歌集
Bomatsu *s* 母末 326
Bōmon *s* 坊門 389
(bon 凡 37, 梵 1490)
Bonbai *l* 梵唄
Bonchō *ml* 凡兆 37
Bongyōbon *l* 梵行品 1490
Bōno *s* 坊野 389
Bōnomoto *s* 坊本
Bōnotsu *p* 坊津
Bontenkoku *l* 梵天国 1490
Bō-shibari *la* 棒縛 1623
Boshi jojō *l* 母子叙情 326 「407
Botan-dōrō *l* 牡丹燈籠
Botekishū *l* 暮笛集 2190
(botsu 勃 896, 渤 1582)
Bōya *s* 棒屋 1623
(bu 二 4, 分 64, 无 92, 生 214, 歩 694, 奉 717, 武 751, 務 1377, 部 1418, 逢 1516, 補 1644, 葡 1724, 無 1789, 蒲 1993, 豊 2013, 蔀 2186, 鳳 2233, 蕪 2373, 舞 2391, 篷 2689, 縫 2746, 鵬 2795, 鵡 2819, 霧 2846, 鶩 2847)
Buaku *la* 武悪 751
Bubai *s* 分倍 64
Budō denraiki *l* 武道伝来記 751
Bue *s* 武衛
Bugaku *a* 舞楽 2391
Buhee *m* 武兵衛 751
Buhei *m* 武平
Bui *la* 浮標 1069
Buichi *m* 武一 751
Buke giri *l* 武家義理
Bukichi *m* 武吉
(buku 伏 234, 服 618, 蝮 2312, 馥 2753)
Buma *s* 武間 751
Bun *s* 豊 2013. (分 64, 文 86, 汾 397, 汶 398, 彣 510, 枌 624, 蚊 1135, 問 1524, 紋 1684, 聞 2244, 蕡 2367)
Bun'an 1444–49 文安 86
Bunbai *sp* 分倍 64
Bunbu nidō mangoku tōshi *l* 文武二道万石通 86
～ sazareishi *l* 文武さざれ石
Bunchū 1372–75 文中
Bundan mudabanashi *l* 文壇無駄話 「2013
Bundō *s* 分銅 64, 豊道
Bun'ei 1264–75 文永 86
Bungakukai *l* 文学界
Bungei ichiba *l* 文芸市場 「部
～ kurabu *l* 文芸倶楽
Bungo *m* 文吾; *ph* 豊後 2013
Bungonokuni *ph* 豊後国
～ no fudoki *l* 豊後国風土記
Bungorō *m* 文五郎 86
Bungo Takada *p* 豊後高田 2013
Bungyō *sp* 分校 64
Bun'ichi *m* 文一
Bunji *m* 文二, 文次, 1185–90 文治
Bunjirō *m* 文次郎, 文治郎
Bunka 1804–18 文化
～ shūreishū *l* 文華秀麗集
Bunki 1501～04 文亀
Bunkichi *m* 文吉
Bunkyō *p* 文京 「論
～ hifuron *l* 文京秘府
Bunkyū 1861–64 文久
Bunmei 1469–87 文明
Bunna 1352–56 文和
Bunno *s* 豊 2013 「86
Bunnosuke *m* 文之輔
Bun'ō 1260–61 文応
Bunpei *m* 文平
Bunpitsu ganshinshō *l* 文筆眼心抄
Bunpō 1317–19 文保
Bunro *m* 文呂
Bunrō *m* 文楼
Bunroku *m* 文六; 1592–96 文禄
Bunrokurō *m* 文六郎
Bunryaku 1234–35 文暦
Bunsei 1818–30 文政
Bunshichi *m* 文七
Bunshō 1466–67 文正
～ tattokuroku *l* 文章達徳録
～ zōshi *l* 文正草子
Bunsui *p* 分水 64
Bunsuke *m* 文輔 86
Buntarō *m* 文太郎
Buntō *l* 文党
Bunwa 1352–56 文和
Bun'ya *s* 文屋; *ma* 文弥
～ no Watamaro *mh* 文屋綿麻呂
～ no Yasuhide *ml* 文屋康秀
Bunyō *s* 豊饒 2013
Bunzaburō *m* 文三郎 86 「門
Bunzaemon *m* 文左衛
Bunzō *m* 文三, 文蔵
Buppōzō *l* 仏法僧 128
(buru 陣 1056)
Bushō retsuden *l* 武将列伝 751
Buson *ml* 蕪村 2373
～ shichibushū *l* 蕪村七部集
Busshi *la* 仏師 128
Bussokuseki no uta *l* 仏足石歌
Butai hyakkajō *l* 舞台百箇条 2391
(butsu 勿 110, 仏 128, 物 611)
Buzen *sph* 豊前 2013
Buzō *m* 武三 751
(byaku 白 216, 壁 2782)
Byakuchi 650–54 白雉 216
Byakuya *l* 白夜
(byō 平 203, 妙 614, 苗 685, 並 765, 病 1250, 棚 1625, 匏 1655, 彭 1693)
Byōshō rokushaku *l* 病牀六尺 1250

# C

(cha 茶 931)
Chadani *s* 茶谷
Chaki *s* 茶木
Chakkujaku *s* 大工廻 48
(chaku 拓 586, 著 1445)
Chatsubo *la* 茶壺 931
Chaya *p* 茶屋
(chi 一 3, 千 44, 市 195, 地 241, 池 251, 芡 286, 血 337, 知 636, 乳 657, 茅 690, 持 801, 治 825, 祐 852, 為 1005, 胝 1081, 值 1278, 致 1407, 智 1793, 遅 1807, 道 1811, 雉 1911, 稚 1914, 乳 1971, 置 2232)
Chiaki *s* 千秋 44, 千明
Chiba *s* 千馬; *sp* 千葉
Chibahara *s* 千葉原
Chiba Kameo *ml* 千葉亀雄 「明
～ Taneaki *ml* 千葉胤
Chibetto *p* "Tibet" 西蔵 336 「千引 44
Chibiki *s* 地引 241; *m*
Chibu *p* 知夫 636
Chiburi *s* 千夫 44, 千役, 知夫 636 「役湊 44
Chiburinominato *s* 千
Chibusa *m* 千英
(chichi 父 65, 秩 1119)
Chichibu *sp* 秩父
Chichii *s* 乳乳井 657
Chichio *m* 秩夫 1119
Chichioni *s* 父鬼 65
Chichiri *s* 知夫 636
Chichishiro *s* 茅代 690
Chichiwa *s* 千千和 44, 千千輪
Chichiyo *m* 父代 65
Chida *s* 地田 241
Chidori *sf* 千鳥 44
Chieda *m* 千枝
Chieko *f* 千栄子, 智恵子 1793
Chifuri *m* 千振 44
Chifuru *m* 千古
Chifuyu *m* 千冬
Chiga *s* 千賀
Chiganoura *p* 千賀浦
Chigara *s* 千柄
Chigasaki *s* 千ヶ崎; *p* 茅ヶ崎 690, 茅崎
Chigaura *s* 千賀浦 44
Chigaya *s* 千萱
Chigetsu *fl* 智月 1793
Chigira *s* 千明 44; *sp* 千木良
Chigiri *s* 千装
Chigiriki *l* 千切木
Chigiru *m* 契 980
Chigo *s* 児 497. (児)
Chigu *s* 地倶 241
Chigusa *s* 千草 44; *sp* 千種 「顕
～ Tadaaki *mh* 千種忠
Chihara *s* 千原
Chiharu *m* 千春
Chihaya *s* 千早, 千速, 千岩, 千破屋, 千屋, 千磐; *m* 千剣
～ Akasaka *p* 千早赤坂
Chihe *s* 乳戸 657
Chihiro *m* 千丈 44, 千仭, 千尋
Chiiko *f* 智泉子 1793
Chiikobe *s* 千子部 44
(chiisa 小 21)
Chiisabe *s* 千子部 44
Chiisagata *p* 小県 21
Chiisago *s* 小子, 竪 2224
Chiisakobe *s* 小子部 21, 千子部 44, 少子部 88
Chijiiwa *sp* 千千岩 44
Chijiwa *s* 千千和, 千千輪; *sp* 千千石
Chika *s* 近 506, 値賀 1278. (力 11, 九 16, 寸 34, 凡 37, 子 38, 元 60, 分 64, 内 81, 及 83, 比 135, 尼 175, 央 182, 史 183, 用 193, 允 217, 次 226, 年 342, 似 350, 判 434, 亨 440, 近 506, 局 514, 見 518, 考 540, 身 546, 味 572, 知 636, 和 638, 京 663, 実 678, 周 736, 俔 774, 信 782, 恒 809, 昵 839, 前 921, 発 953, 参 978, 直 988, 哉 1006, 浮 1069, 時 1086, 真 1228, 速 1237, 規 1349, 務 1377, 躬 1396, 寂 1436, 悠 1481, 庶 1505, 這 1515, 峻 1591, 彭 1693, 尋 1705, 崔 1738, 登 1744, 間 1822, 慎 1839, 睦 1904, 新 1965, 義 1975, 寛 1977, 愛 2018, 肆 2144, 静 2145, 誓 2218, 爾 2250, 尉 2347, 雍 2359, 遵 2418, 慶 2425, 隣 2443, 衡 2450, 親 2544, 幾 2597, 懐 2605, 謹 2645, 慈 2701, 邇 2785, 畿 2859)
Chikaaki *m* 周秋 736, 周亮, 庶明 1505
Chikada *s* 近田 506
Chikafusa *m* 親房 2544
Chikage *m* 千蔭 44
Chikagiku *m* 近菊 506
Chikaharu *m* 睦玄 1904
Chikahiko *m* 新比古 1965
Chikahito *m* 親民 2544
Chikai *m* 千頴 44
Chikakata *m* 近方 506
Chikaki *s* 近木
Chikakiri *m* 近霧
Chikako *f* 周子 736, 俔子 774, 務子 1377, 睦子 1904, 親子 2544, 慈子 2701
Chikama *s* 近間 506
Chikamasa *m* 親尹 2544
Chikamatsu *sml* 近松 506
～ Hanji *ml* 近松半二
～ Monzaemon *ml* 近松門左衛門
～ Shūkō *ml* 近松秋江
Chikami *s* 千頭 44; *m* 近神 506
Chikamichi *m* 周陸 736, 雍通 2359, 懐通 2605
Chikanari *m* 愛発 2018
Chikane *m* 近嶺 506
Chikanobu *m* 知信 636, 愛信 2018, 隣信 2443, 親誠 2544
Chikanori *m* 謹度 2645
Chikao *m* 次雄 226, 前雄 921, 真夫 1228, 誓夫 2218, 親男 2544
Chikaoka *s* 近岡 506
Chikara *sm* 税 1642; *m* 力 11, 力人, 千幹 44, 能 1397; *m-p* 主税 196. (税 1642)
Chikarabe *s* 税部
Chikarahito *s* 健人 1282
Chikaraishi *s* 力石 11
Chikasane *m* 親孚 2544
Chikashi *m* 九 16, 千樫 44, 史 183, 史侍, 近 506, 夾 534, 即 648, 周 736, 睦 1904, 愛 2018, 爾 2250, 隣 2443, 親 2544, 冀 2571, 幾 2597, 邇 2785
Chikashige *m* 周重 736
Chikata *m* 千方 44
Chikatada *m* 親蔵 2544
Chikataka *m* 周翰 736, 誓堂 2218
Chikatami *m* 愛民 2018
Chikatoshi *m* 近俊 506
Chikatsu *s* 千勝 44
Chikatsugu *m* 前次 921
Chikatsuōmi *s* 近淡海 506
Chikawa *m* 千川 44
Chikaya *m* 爾也 2250
Chikayama *s* 近山 506
Chikayasu *m* 親保 2544, 親葆
Chikayori *m* 親従
Chikayoshi *m* 親善, 親賀
Chikayuki *s* 見千 518; *m* 及行 83, 周之 736, 周恕, 崔之 1738, 登之 1744, 慎之 1839, 親廉 2544; *ml* 親行
Chikazaka *s* 近坂 506
Chikazawa *s* 近沢
Chikaze *m* 千風 44
Chikazuki *s* 調月 2328
Chikō *m* 矢 215, 誓 2218
Chiku *s* 知久 636; *p* 竺 729. (竹 247, 竺 729, 筑 1771, 築 2575, 矗 3017)
Chikubushima *p-la* 竹生島 247
Chikugo *sp* 筑後 1771
Chikuhakukai *l* 竹柏会 247
Chikuhei *m* 知久平 636
Chikuho *p* 筑穂 1771
Chikuhō *p* 筑邦
Chikujō *p* 筑上, 筑城
Chikuma *s* 千熊 44, 竹馬 247; *sp* 筑摩 1771; *p* 千曲 44 「千倉 44
Chikura *m* 竹良 247; *p*

Chikurinshō *l* 竹林抄
Chikusai *l* 竹斎 ⌊247
Chikushi *ph* 筑紫 1771
Chikushino *p* 筑紫野
Chikuzen *ph* 筑前
Chima *s* 知間 636
Chimata *s* 岐 599, 街 1570; *m* 千俣 44, 知又 636. (衢 2985)
Chime *s* 千綿 44
Chimori *s* 道守 1811
Chimura *s* 千村 44, 地村 241; *m* 千屯 44
Chimuro *m* 千室
Chin *s* 沈 399, 玢 604; *sm* 陳 1311. (沈 399, 玢 604, 枕 627, 珍 836, 陣 1056, 砧 1112, 陳 1311, 趁 1815, 椿 1895, 鎮 2751)
China *p* 知名 636
Chinami *m* 因 311
Chinda *s* 珍田 836
Chine *s* 茅根 690; *f* 千子 44
Chinen *s* 知念 636
Chinjirō *m* 鎮次郎 2751
Chino *s* 千野 44, 知野 636; *sp* 茅野 690
～ Masako *fl* 茅野雅子
Chinone *s* 茅根 「蕭々
Chino Shōshō *ml* 茅野
Chinseki *ml* 珍磧 836
Chinsetsu yumiharizuki *l* 椿説弓張月 1895
Chintō *p* "Tsingtao" 青島 700, 青隝
Chinu *s* 茅停 690, 茅渟, 珍 836
Chinuma *s* 血沼 337
Chinzei *p* 鎮西 2751
Chinzō *m* 鎮三
Chiori *m* 千織 44
Chippubetsu *p* 秩父別 1119
Chiran *p* 知覧 636
Chirei *l* 地霊 241
Chiryaku 1065–69 地暦
Chiryū *p* 知立 636
(chisa 苣 680)
Chisaka *s* 千坂 44
Chisako *f* 苣子 680
Chisakobe *s* 小口部 21, 小子部
Chisato *m* 智聡 1793
Chisawa *s* 千沢 44
Chise *s* 持是 801
Chishiki *s* 知識 636
Chishima *sp* "Kuriles" 千島 44
Chishin *mh* 智真 1793
Chishiro *s* 千代 44, 茅代 690
Chishō *mh* 智正 1793; 1177–81 治承 825
Chisono *f* 千苑 44
Chisuwa *s* 千須和
Chita *s* 千田, 知田 636; *p* 知多
Chitaru *m* 千足 44
Chitei no ki *l* 池亭記 251
Chitose *m-p* 千歳 44; *f* 千年生; *p* 千年
Chitōshū *l* 池塘集 251
(chitsu 秩 1119)
Chiwaki *s* 千脇 44, 血脇 337; *m* 千別 44, 道別 1811
Chiya *s* 千谷 44, 千屋
Chiyako *f* 千谷子
Chiya Michio *ml* 千谷道雄 「郎 337
Chiyarikurō *m* 血槍九
Chiyaritarō *m* 血槍太郎
Chiyo *sf* 千代 44
Chiyoda *sp* 千代田
Chiyodōji *m* 千代童子
Chiyogawa *sp* 千代川
Chiyojo *fl* 千代女
Chiyokura *s* 千代倉
Chiyoma *s* 千代間
Chiyomatsu *sm* 千代松
Chiyoni *fl* 千代尼
Chiyonō *m* 千代能
Chiyonosuke *m* 千代之助 「郎
Chiyosaburō *m* 千代三
Chiyoshi *f* 千麗
Chizu *sp* 智頭 1793
Chizue *f* 千鶴笑 44
Chizuka *s* 遅塚 1807
～ Reisui *ml* 遅塚麗水
Chizuko *f* 千鶴子 44, 智津子 1793
Chizura *s* 千装 44
(cho 除 1059, 猪 1306, 著 1445, 貯 1651, 箸 2381, 樗 2480, 攄 2713)
Chō *s* 趙 2243; *sm* 長 939, 重 1017, 晁 1188, 張 1879. (丁 8, 丈 36, 仗 127, 庁 174, 兆 244, 杖 422, 町 426, 条 457, 帖 563, 長 939, 岧 940, 迢 1000, 祧 1004, 重 1017, 姚 1088, 釘 1154, 晁 1188, 彫 1412, 釣 1416, 奝 1433, 嵒 1517, 鳥 1521, 朝 1672, 超 1816, 塚 1844, 張 1879, 碇 1909, 稠 1915, 誂 1929, 瓺 1936, 暢 2111, 銚 2154, 蔦 2196, 肇 2222, 趙 2243, 徵 2265, 潮 2275, 澄 2276, 調 2328, 澂 2456, 蝶 2495, 聴 2634, 鯛 2832, 寵 2893)
Chōan *ml* 長庵 939
Chōbee *m* 長兵衛
Chōboku *s* 長北
Chōbuku Soga *la* 調伏曾我 2328
Chōdō *s* 長藤 939
Chōfu *p* 調布 2328
Chōgen *mh* 重源 1017; 1028–37 長元 939
Chōgō *s* 長郷
Chōgorō *m* 長五郎
Chogyū *ml* 樗牛 2480
Chōhei *m* 長平 939
Chōhō *s* 999–1004 長保
Chōichi *m* 長一
Chōji *m* 1104–06 長治
Chōjikoku hyōryūki *l* 長耳国漂流記
Chōjirō *m* 長二郎, 長次郎
Chōjō 1132–35 長承
Chōjūrō *m* 長十郎
Chōka *l* 長歌
Chōkai *p* 鳥海 1521
Chō Kakuchū *ml* 張楮宙 1879
Chōkan 1163–65 長寛 939
Chōka senkaku *l* 長歌撰格
Chōko *f* 蝶子 2495
(choku 勅 898, 直 988, 陟 1309, 敕 1405, 稙 1568)
Chōkurō *m* 重九郎 1017
Chokusenshū *l* 勅撰集 898
Chokutei *s* 勅丁
Chōkyō 1487–89 長亨 939
Chōkyū 1040–44 長久
Chōmei *s* 長命; *ml* 長明
Chōnan *sp* 長南
Chōnen *mh* 奝然 1433
Chōno *s* 丁野 8
Chōnohanawa *s* 庁鼻和 174
Chōon *l* 潮音 2275
Chora *ml* 樗良 2480
Chōroku 1457–60 長禄 939 「暦
Chōryaku 1037–40 長
Chō Ryō *mh-la* "Chang Liang" 張良 1879 「流
Chōryū *ml* 長竜 939, 長
Chōsa *s* 帖佐 563
Chōsei *p* 長生 939
Chōshi *s* 丁子 8, 調子 2328; *p* 銚子 2154
Chōsho *s* 調所 2328
Chōshō 1132–35 長承 939 「藻
Chōshū eisō *l* 長秋詠
Chōsokabe *s* 長曾我部
～ Motochika *mh* 長曾我部元親
Chōtarō *m* 長太郎
Chōtoku 995–99 長徳
Chōwa 1012–70 長和
Chōya gunsai *l* 朝野群載 1672
Chōyo *m* 肇四 2222
Chōyō *sp* 長陽 939
Chōzaburō *m* 長三郎
Chōzō *m* 長蔵
Chū *sm* 中 75; *m* 忠 705. (中 75, 丑 99, 冲 225, 仲 227, 虫 324, 沖 400, 注 591, 宙 673, 忠 705, 柱 854, 茆 927, 昼 983, 衷 1190, 紐 1682, 紬 1951, 鋳 2343, 廚 2417, 儔 2433, 燾 2770, 疇 2799, 籌 2901, 矗 3017)
Chūbachi *s* 中鉢 75
Chūbee *m* 忠兵衛 705
Chūbei *p* "C. America" 中米 75
Chūgai keiiden *l* 中外経緯伝
Chūgan Engetsu *mlh* 中巌円月
Chūgo *s* 中後
Chūhei *m* 忠平 705
Chūichi *m* 忠一
Chūji *m* 忠志, 忠治

Chūjirō *m* 忠二郎, 忠次郎, 忠治郎
Chūjō *s* 中条 75; *mh* 中将
Chūka *p* 中和
Chūko zasshōshū *l* 中古雑唱集
Chūkyō *s* 中鏡
Chūma *s* 中馬, 中摩
Chūman *s* 中馬
Chūnagon *mh* 中納言
Chūnan *p* 仲南 227
Chūō *p* 中央 75
Chūrui *p* 忠類 705
Chūsaku *m* 忠作
Chūsenbu *s* 鋳銭部 2343
Chūshin *ml* 中津 75
Chūshingura *la* 忠臣蔵 705
Chūshin kogane no tanzaku *l* 忠臣金短冊
~ suikoden *l* 忠臣水滸伝
Chūsuke *m* 忠介
Chūta *m* 忠太
Chūtō *p* "Middle East" 中東 75
Chūya *m* 忠也 705
Chūzaburō *m* 忠三郎
Chūzō *m* 宙造 673, 忠三 705, 忠造, 忠蔵
Chūzu *p* 中主 75

# D

(da 打 136, 田 189, 兊 447, 朶 458, 陀 568, 妥 708, 柁 856)
Dai *s* 代 125. (乃 27, 大 48, 内 81, 太 105, 代 125, 台 276, 昊 482, 奈 696, 待 785, 耐 884, 苔 929, 岱 955, 薹 1170, 袋 1750, 第 1768, 禔 2120, 醍 2500, 戴 2707)
Daian *p* 大安 48
Daianji *p* 大安寺
~ hibun *l* 大安寺碑文
Daibosatsu tōge *l* 大菩薩峠
Daibuku *s* 大仏供
Daibutsu *a* 大仏
~ kuyō *la* 大仏供養
Daichō *s* 大長
Daichōwa *l* 大調和
Daidō *s* 大道, 台堂 276; 806–10 大同 48
Daidōji *sp* 大道寺
Daie *la* 大会
Daiei *p* 大栄; 1521–28 大永
Daigo *s* 大胡, 大後; *smh-p* 醍醐 2500; *p* 大子 48
Daigō *s* 大郷
Daigohō *s* 大悟法
~ Susumu *ml* 大悟法進
~ Toshio *ml* 大悟法利雄
Daigorō *m* 大五郎, 代五郎 125, 第五郎 1768
Daiguji *s* 大宮司 48
Daiho *s* 大甫
Daihō 701–04 大宝
Daihōji *sp* 大宝寺
Daiissaku *l* 第一作 1768
Daiji 1126–31 大治 48
Daijō *s* 大条
Daikaichi *s* 大河一
Daikichirō *m* 大吉郎
Daikō *s* 大幸
Daikoku *smh* 大黒
~ renga *la* 大黒連歌
Daikokuya *s* 大黒屋
Daiku *s* 大工
Daikuhara *s* 大工原
Daimaru *s* 大丸
Daimon *p* 大門
Daimonji *s* 大文字
Daimyō nagusami Soga *l* 大名曾我
Dainagon *mh* 大納言
~ Tameie shū *l* 大納言為家集
Daini *s* 大耳; *sm* 大弐
Dainichi *s* 大日
Daiō *p* 大王
Daionki *l* 戴恩記 2707
Dairikinosuke *m* 大力之助 48
Dairi shika awase *l* 内裏詩歌合 81
Dairokuten *l* 第六天 1768
Daisaiin *fl* 大斎院 48
~ goshū *l* 大斎院御集
Daisaku *m* 大作
Daisen *p* 大山
Daishirō *m* 大四郎
Daisuke *m* 大輔
Daita *p* 代田 125
Daitarō *m* 大太郎 48
Daitō *s* 大藤; *p* 大東
Daitoku *s* 大徳
Daitokuji *p* 大徳寺
Daiwa *p* 大和
Daiyō *s* 大用
Daiyū *p* 大雄
Daizaburō *m* 大三郎
Daizen *s* 大善; *sm* 大膳
Daizennosuke *s* 大善
Daizō *m* 大三亮
Dake *s* 嵩 2207
(daku 濁 2457, 鐸 2922)
Dan *s* 団 310, 弾 1880, 檀 2623. (旦 162, 団 310, 但 351, 男 495, 偒 772, 段 874, 断 1669, 湛 1855, 弾 1880, 暖 1882, 椴 1893, 誕 2319, 談 2325, 壇 2438, 檀 2623)
Danchōtei nichijō *l* 断腸亭日乗 1669
Dangomori *s* 団子森 310
Danjō *s* 檀上 2623; *mh* 弾正 1880
~ -no-hitsu *mh* 弾正弼
~ -no-in *mh* 弾正尹
~ -no-jō *m* 弾正忠
~ -no-sakan *mh* 弾正疏 2623
Dan Kazuo *ml* 檀一雄
Danno *s* 団野 310, 段野 874, 檀野 2623
Dannoura *ph* 壇浦 2438
~ kabuto gunki *la* 壇浦兜軍記
Dan'otsu *m* 檀越 2623
Danpei *m* 団平 310
Danpū *la* 檀風 2623
Danrin *l* 談林 2325
~ toppyakuin *l* 談林十百韻
Danroku *m* 団六 310
Dan Takuma *mh* 団琢磨
Darani *s* 陀羅尼 568
Daruma *mh* 達摩 1810
Dassai *l* 獺祭 2791
~ shooku haiwa *l* 獺祭書屋俳話
Date *sp* 伊達 237
~ kurabe Okuni Kabuki *la* 伊達競阿国戯場
~ Masamune *mh* 伊達政宗
~ Munenari *mh* 伊達宗城
~ Tokuo *ml* 伊達得夫
(datsu 獺 2791)
Dazai *s* 大宰 48, 太宰 105
Dazaifu *ph* 大宰府 48, 太宰府 105
Dazai no Gon-no-sotsu *mh* 大宰権師 48
~ Osamu *ml* 太宰治 105
~ Shundai *mh* 太宰春台
(de 手 118, 出 523, 勅 898)
Debuchi *s* 出淵 523
Degawa *s* 出川
Deguchi *s* 出口
~ Nao *fh* 出口直
~ Nobuyoshi *mh* 出口延佳
~ Wanisaburō *mh* 出口王仁三郎 1492)
Dei *s* 出井. (泥 594, 埿
Deie *s* 出家 523
Dejima *sp* 出島
Deki *s* 出来
Dekiboshi *m* 出来星
Dekimaru *m* 出来丸
Dekishima *s* 出来島
Deme *s* 出目
Demizu *s* 出水
Demizugawa *p* 出水川
Demura *s* 出村
Den *s* 田 189; *sm* 伝 359. (田 189, 佃 352, 伝 359, 拈 583, 鈿 1940, 殿 1960, 電 2025, 稹 2490, 鮎 2457)
Denbee *m* 伝兵衛 359
Denbei *m* 伝平
Denda *s* 伝田
Den'emon *m* 伝右衛門
Dengaku *a* 田楽 189
Dengorō *m* 伝五郎 359
Dengyō *mh* 伝教
Den'ichirō *m* 伝一郎
Denji *m* 伝次, 伝治
Denjirō *m* 伝二郎

Denmāku *p* "Denmark" 丁抹 8
Denpōrin *s* 伝法輪 359
Densaku *m* 伝作
Densuke *m* 伝助
Denzaburō *m* 伝三郎
Denzō *m* 伝蔵
Deon *s* 出温 523
Deshi *s* 勅市 898
Deshima *sp* 出島 523
Deshimaru *s* 弟子丸 764
Deura *s* 出浦 523
Deushi *s* 出牛
Dewa *s* 出庭; *ph* 出羽
Deyama *s* 出山
(do 土 42, 戸 59, 奴 256, 所 600, 努 728, 度 1009, 怒 1222)
(dō 同 298, 洞 821, 桐 1103, 堂 1462, 童 1743, 棠 1747, 道 1811, 瓺 1936, 僮 2056, 銅 2159, 衜 2263, 導 2413, 瞳 2470, 曈 2630, 鬫 2738, 衜 2790)
Dōami *ml* 道阿弥 1811
Dōba *s* 堂馬 1462
～ mango *l* 童馬漫語 1743
Dobashi *s* 土橋 42
Doburi *s* 井石 103
Dōchi *s* 道智 1811
Dōchū hizakurige *l* 道中膝栗毛
Dodo *s* 百百 265
Dōdo *sp* 百百
Dodoi *s* 百井
Dōgen *s* 道原 1811; *mlh* 道元
Dohi *s* 土肥 42
Dohibara *s* 土肥原
Dohō *ml* 土芳
Doi *s* 土井, 土肥; *sp* 土居
～ Bansui *ml* 土井晩翠
～ Kōchi *ml* 土居光知
Doitsu *p* "Germany" 独逸 788
Doiuchi *s* 土井内 42
Dojō *l* 土上
Dōjōji *p-la* 道成寺 1811
Dōke *s* 道家
Dōkichi *m* 銅吉 2159
Dokō *s* 土公 42
(doku 独 788, 読 2142)
Dokura *sm* 土蔵 42
Dōkyō *mh* 道鏡 1811
Dōmae *s* 堂前 1462
Domeki *s* 百目木 265, 百目鬼
Domon *s* 土門 42
Dōmoto *s* 堂本 1462
Dōmyō *s* 道明 1811
Dōmyōji *p-la* 道明寺
(don 邨 645, 盾 984, 鈍 1943, 潭 2269, 嫩 2279, 曇 2685)
Donari *p* 土成 42
Donburi *s* 井石 103, 丼 206
Donchō *mh* 曇徴 2685
Dōni *mh* 道二 1811
Dōnose *s* 道瀬
Dontarō *la* 鈍太郎 1943
Doppo *ml* 独歩 788
Doppogin *l* 独歩吟
Dora *ph* "Thailand?" 度羅 1009; *l* 銅鑼 2159
～ gaku *a* 度羅楽 1009
(doro 泥 594)
Doro ningyō *l* 泥人形
Doronosuke *m* 泥之助
Dōshi *p* 道志 1811
Dōshō *s* 堂正 1462; *mh* 道昭 1811
Dōshun *mlh* 道春
Dota *sp* 土田 42
Dote *s* 土手
Dōtonbori *p* 道頓堀 1811
Dōzono *s* 堂園 1462

# E

(e 也 23, 上 47, 兄 181, 丙 198, 江 252, 朴 255, 守 284, 朽 419, 会 454, 条 457, 朶 458, 衣 520, 亜 525, 恵 535, 杷 625, 枝 631, 苗 685, 依 780, 姉 847, 柯 855, 柄 862, 荏 930, 負 981, 廻 994, 重 1017, 家 1185, 笑 1209, 恵 1226, 座 1245, 烏 1256, 得 1299, 隈 1841, 殖 1867, 愛 2018, 徳 2063, 榎 2107, 誠 2139, 歳 2198, 槐 2296, 絵 2332, 慧 2392, 衛 2452, 壊 2602, 懐 2605, 蘁 2680, 穫 2729, 譓 2809)
Eawase *la* 絵合 2332
Ebara *s* 江原 252, 柄原 862, 荏原 930
～ Koyata *ml* 江原小弥太 252
Ebashi *s* 江橋
Ebata *s* 江畑, 江畠, 江端, 江幡
Ebayashi *s* 江林
Ebeotsu *p* 江別乙
Ebetsu *p* 江別
Ebi *s* 衣非 520, 衣斐, 海老 1071. (蛯 1650, 蝦 2313, 鰕 2886)
Ebie *s* 蛯江 1650
Ebihara *s* 海老原 1071, 蛯原 1650, 蝦原 2313
Ebijima *s* 海老島 1071
Ebijūrō *m* 鰕十郎 2886
Ebiko *s* 蛯子 1650
Ebina *s* 蛯名, 蝦名 2313; *sp* 海老名 1071
～ Danjō *mh* 海老名弾正
Ebine *s* 海老根
Ebira *la* 箙 2210
Ebisawa *s* 海老沢 1071, 蛯沢 1650
Ebishi *s* 絵菱 2332
Ebisu *s* 戎 321, 胡子 879, 蛯子 1650; *m* 毛人 117; *mh* 夷子 535. (戎 321, 夷 535)
～ Bishamon *mh-la* 夷毘沙門
～ Daikoku *mh-la* 夷大黒
Ebisugawa *s* 夷川
Ebitani *s* 蛯谷 1650
Ebizuka *s* 海老塚 1071
Eboshi *s* 烏帽子 1256
～-ori *la* 烏帽子折
Echi *s* 愛智 2018, 越智 2052; *sp* 愛知 2018. (悦 1054, 越 2052)
Echigawa *s* 越川; *p* 愛知川 2018
Echigo *sph* 越後 2052
～-jishi *a* 越後獅子
Echigoya *s* 越後谷
Echihata *s* 杜智秦 423, 依智秦 780
Echizen *sph* 越前 2052
Eda *s* 江田 252, 枝田 631, 英太 693, 榎田 2107. (兄 181, 材 420, 条 457, 朶 458, 枝 631, 柯 855, 柄 862, 捨 1324, 族 1343, 幹 1938, 標 2298, 繁 2848)
Edagawa *s* 枝川 631
Edaki *s* 枝木
Edako *f* 朶子 458
Edamatsu *s* 枝松 631
Edamoto *s* 枝元
Edayoshi *s* 枝吉
Edo *s* 榎土 2107; *sph* 江戸 252
～ bakufu *h* 江戸幕府
Edogawa *sp* 江戸川
～ Ranpo *ml* 江戸川乱歩
Edo meishoki *l* 江戸名所記
～ nagauta *a* 江戸長唄
～ sakusha burui *l* 江戸作者部類
～ sunago kichirei Soga *la* 江戸砂子慶曾我
～ umare uwaki no kabayaki *l* 江戸生艶気樺焼
Edoza *l* 江戸座
Egaki *s* 画 991
Egakibe *s* 画部
Egami *s* 江上 252
Egao *f* 笑顔 1209
Egara *s* 荏柄 930
Egarinai *s* 江刈内 252
Egashira *s* 江頭
Egawa *s* 江川, 穎川 2505
～ Tan'an *m* 江川坦庵
Egi *s* 江木 252
Egōshū *mh* 会合衆 454
Eguchi *sla* 江口 252
～ Kiyoshi *ml* 江口渙
～ Shin'ichi *ml* 江口榛一
Eguro *s* 江黒
Egusa *s* 江草
Ehado *s* 江波戸

Ehafuri *s* 衣祝 520
Ehana *s* 江花 252
Ehara *s* 家原 1185
Ehime *p* 愛媛 2018
Ehira *s* 江平 252 ⌈2332
Ehon Soga *l* 絵本曾我
Ei *s* 江井 252; *sp* 穎娃 2505. (永 149, 英 693, 映 840, 栄 969, 哉 1006, 盈 1200, 暎 1594, 瑛 1607, 詠 1664, 営 1751, 睿 2199, 裔 2217, 緆 2303, 鋭 2344, 影 2357, 瑩 2387, 衛 2452, 璟 2471, 穎 2505, 叡 2555, 贏 2676, 嶸 2716, 瀛 2865)
Eichō 1096–97 永長
Eien 987–89 永延
Eifuku Mon'in *fl* 永福門院
Eiga *l* 栄花 969
～ ittai *l* 詠歌一体 1664
～ taigai *l* 詠歌大概
Eigenji *p* 永源寺 149
Eigo *m* 英五 693
Eigorō *m* 英五郎, 栄五郎 969
Eihachirō *m* 栄八郎
Eiheiji *p* 永平寺 149
Eiho 1081–84 永保
Eiichi *m* 英一 693, 栄一 969, 鋭市 2344
Eiichirō *m* 英一郎 693, 栄一郎 969
Eiji *m* 英二 693, 栄司 969, 栄次; 1141–42 永治 149
Eijirō *m* 栄次郎 969
Eijō 1046–53 永承 149
Eikan 983–85 永観
Eikichi *m* 永吉, 英吉 693, 栄吉 969
Eikyō 1429–41 永享 149
Eikyū 1113–18 永久
Eiman 1165–66 永万
Einin 1293–99 永仁
Einosuke *m* 栄之助 969
Eiraku *s* 永楽 149
Eiroku 1558–70 永禄
Eiryaku 1160–61 永暦
Eisai *mh* 栄西 969
～ shinshi *l* 穎才新誌 2505
Eisaku *sm* 永作 149; *m* 英作 693, 栄作 969
Eishi *m* 英資 693
Eishirō *m* 栄四郎 969
Eishō 1504–21 永正 149

Eiso 989–90 永祚
Eison *mh* 叡尊 2555
Eisuke *m* 永孚 149, 栄介 969, 栄助
Eitarō *m* 永太郎 149, 英太郎 693, 栄太郎 969, 鋭太郎 2344
Eitetsu *m* 英喆 693
Eito *s* 永戸 149
Eitō *s* 衛藤 2452
Eitoku 1381–84 永徳 149
Eiwa 1375–79 永和
Eizaburō *m* 永三郎, 栄三郎 969
Eizō *m* 永造 149, 英三 693, 英造, 英蔵, 栄蔵
Ejima *s* 江島 252 ⌊969
～ Kiseki *ml* 江島其磧
Ejimaya *s* 江島屋
Ejio *m* 衛士夫 2452
Ejiputo *p* "Egypt" 埃及 1294
Ejiri *s* 江尻 252
Eka *s* 会加 454
Eki *s* 衣枳 520; *m* 益 1201. (亦 325, 役 368, 易 714, 益 1201, 訳 1402, 棭 1621, 駅 2172, 懌 2439, 繹 2924)
Ekiken *mh* 益軒 1201
Ekisai *mlh* 棭斎 1621
Ekisen *p* 駅川 2172
Ekiya *p* 駅家
Ekken *mh* 益軒 1201
Ekotoba *l* 絵詞 2332
Ekuni *s* 兄国 181
Ekurashi *m* 兄食下
Ekuri *s* 殖栗 1867
Ema *s* 江馬 252, 江間; *sla-a* 絵馬 2332
Emai *s* 円満井 78
Emaiza *a* 円満井座
Emaki-mono *la* 絵巻物 2332
Emaro *m* 兄麻呂 181
Ema Shōko *fl* 江間章子 252
～ Shū *ml* 江馬修
Emi *s* 絵見 2332; *sf* 恵美 1226; *sp* 江見 252. (笑 1209, 蝦 2313)
Emiko *f* 可笑子 165, 笑子 1209, 恵美子 1226, 得美子 1299
Emi no Oshikatsu *mh* 恵美押勝 1226

Emishi *m* 蝦夷 2313
Emi Suiin *ml* 江見水蔭 252
Emon *mh* 衛門 2452
Emori *s* 江守 252, 江森; *m* 衛守 2452
Emosaku *m* 右衛門作 171 ⌈862
Emoto *s* 江本 252, 柄本
Emukae *p* 江迎 252
Emura *s* 江村, 枝村 631
Emuro *s* 朴室 255
En *s* 役 368; *m* 延 739; *f* 恵武 1226. (円 78, 奄 668, 苑 682, 炎 697, 延 739, 衍 786, 兗 910, 宴 1437, 猨 1554, 婉 1600, 塩 1846, 淵 1858, 媛 1868, 瑗 1873, 鉛 1944, 遠 2043, 園 2046, 猿 2062, 演 2079, 鳶 2179, 燕 2570, 鴛 2572, 縁 2660, 薗 2681, 鵷 2787, 縯 2812, 艶 2833)
Ena *p* 恵那 1226
Enami *s* 永並 149, 江波 252, 江南, 江乗, 榎波 2107, 榎並 ⌈252
～ Bunzō *ml* 江南文三
Enamiya *s* 榎並屋 2107
Enari *s* 江成 252
Enatsu *s* 江夏
Enbetsu *p* 遠別 2043
Enbun 1356–61 延文
Enchi *s* 円地 78 ⌊739
～ Fumiko *fl* 円地文子
Enchin *mh* 円珍
Enchō 923–31 延長 739
Enchū *l* 炎昼 697
Enda *s* 遠田 2043
Endō *s* 遠藤
～ Shingo *ml* 遠藤慎吾
～ Shūsaku *ml* 遠藤周作
Engaien *l* 縁外縁 2660
Engaru *p* 遠軽 2043
Engen 1336–40 延元 739
Engetsu *ml* 円月 78
Engi 901–23 延喜 739
Engishiki *l* 延喜式
Engyō 1308–11 延慶
～ ryōkyō sochinjō *l* 延慶両卿訴陳状
(enisu 槐 2296)
Enisunomoto *m* 槐本
Eniwa *p* 恵庭 1226

(enji 槐 2296)
Enjirō *m* 延次郎 739, 槐郎 2296
Enjō *s* 円城 78, 円乗
Enjōji *s* 円城寺
Enkai *s* 鴛海 2572
Enkakuji *p* 円覚寺 78
～ shari *pa* 円覚寺舎利
Enkei 1308–11 延慶 739
Enkichi *m* 延吉
Enkyō 1744–48 延享
Enkyoku *l* 宴曲 1437
Enkyū 1069–74 延久 739
Enmon 1356–61 延文
Ennin *mh* 円仁 78
En-no-gyōja *mh-p-la* 役の行者 368 ⌈角
～ no Ozunu *mh* 役小
Eno *s* 江野 252, 穎娃 2505
En'ō 1239–40 延応 739
Enobe *s* 江部 252
Enoki *s* 榎 2107, 榎木
Enokida *s* 榎田
Enokido *s* 榎戸
Enokoshū *l* 犬子集 107
Enomoto *s* 榎本 2107
～ Takeaki *mh* 榎本武揚
Enoshima *p* 江ノ島 252; *la* 江野島, 江之島, 江島 ⌈産
～ miyage *l* 江之島土
Enoshita *s* 榎下 2107
Enpō 1673–81 延宝 739
Enrinshū *l* 遠隣集 2043
Enryaku 782–806 延暦 739
Enryakuji *p* 延暦寺
Enshōji *s* 円勝寺 78
Enshū *ma* 遠州 2043
Ento *s* 猿渡 2062
Entoku 1489–92 延徳 739
Enu *s* 余奴 448, 江沼 252
Enuma *s* 江野財; *sp* 江沼
En'ya *s* 塩谷 1846, 塩冶
～ Uhei *ml* 塩谷鵜平
Enzan *p* 塩山
Era *s* 江良 252, 恵良 1226
Erakawa *s* 越川 2052
Eramu *m* 択 382, 撰 2258
(eri 択 382, 衿 873)
Eriguchi *s* 江里口 252
Erikawa *s* 江利川

Eriko *f* 衿子 873
Erita *s* 択田 382
Esaka *s* 江坂 252
Esaku *m* 恵尺 1226
Esashi *p* 江刺 252, 江差, 枝幸 631
Eshi *m* 衛士 2452
Eshima *s* 壊島 2602
Eshi no sōshi *l* 絵師草子 2332
Eshin Sōzu *mh* 恵心僧都 1226
Eshinu *s* 吉野 278
Esuke *m* 衛佐 2452
Esumi *s* 江角 252
Etajima *s* 穎田島 2505; *p* 江田島 252
~ Ichijirō *ml* 穎田島一二郎 2505
Etake *s* 江竹 252
Etchū *ph* 越中 2052
Eten *s* 烏天 1256
Eto *s* 江渡 252
Etō *s* 江頭, 江藤, 恵藤 1226, 衛藤 2452
~ Jun *ml* 江藤淳 252
Etōko *f* 兄遠子 181
Etosaki *p* 江戸崎 252
Etō Shinpei *mh* 江藤新平
Etouchi *s* 荏戸内 930
(etsu 日 76, 悦 1054, 越 2052, 鉞 2157)
Etsuji *m* 悦次 1054
Etsujin *ml* 越人 2052
Etsujirō *m* 悦二郎 1054
Etsumokushō *l* 悦目抄
Etsune *s* 依常 780
Etsure *s* 江連 252
Etsutarō *m* 悦太郎 1054, 鉞太郎 2157
Etsuzō *m* 悦蔵 1054
Ezaka *s* 絵坂 2332
Ezaki *s* 江崎 252
Ezawa *s* 江沢
Ezo *h* 蝦夷 2313
Ezoe *s* 江副 252, 江添
Ezu *s* 江頭
Ezuka *s* 江塚
Ezumi *s* 江積
Ezura *s* 江面, 絵面 2332
Ezuriko *p* 江釣子 252

# F

(fu 二 4, 双 53, 父 65, 不 94, 夫 104, 付 126, 布 170, 生 214, 伏 234, 吹 370, 扶 383, 芙 474, 孚 483, 巫 524, 甫 533, 缶 543, 斧 659, 阜 731, 府 740, 封 884, 怤 954, 負 981, 風 986, 浦 1067, 浮 1069, 釜 1160, 峰 1351, 乾 1411, 傅 1536, 婦 1603, 補 1644, 鉄 1677, 富 1715, 普 1792, 楓 1892, 経 1957, 榑 2105, 輔 2133, 節 2215, 鋒 2339, 鋪 2340, 駙 2347, 敷 2355, 鮒 2546)
(fū 風 986, 婦 1603, 富 1715, 楓 1892, 諷 2515)
Fube *sp* 布部 170
Fubito *sm* 史 183; *m* 文儒 86
Fuboku wakashō *l* 夫木和歌抄 104
Fubuki *s* 雪吹 1495
Fuchi *s* 淵 1858, 敷智 2355
Fuchibe *s* 淵辺 1858
Fuchigami *s* 淵上
Fuchigawa *s* 淵川
Fuchimoto *s* 淵本
Fuchina *sm* 淵名
Fuchino *s* 淵野
Fuchioka *s* 淵岡
Fuchisō *l* 風知草 986
Fuchizaki *s* 淵崎 1858
Fuchizawa *s* 淵沢
Fuchū *p* 府中 740, 婦中 1603
Fuda *s* 布田 170. (札 145)
Fudaba *s* 札場
Fudai *p* 普代 1792
Fudako *f* 札子 145
(fude 筆 1769)
Fudeichirō *m* 筆一郎
Fudekawa *s* 筆川
Fudeko *f* 筆子
Fudō *mha-la* 不動 94
Fudōchō *l* 不同調
Fudoki *l* 風土記 986
~ itsubun *l* 風土記逸文
(fue 呂 459, 笛 1471)
Fueda *s* 笛田
Fuefuki *s* 布也布伎 170
Fūei jūnikagetsu *l* 諷詠十二月 2515
Fueki *s* 笛木 1471
~ ryūkō *l* 不易流行 94
Fueko *f* 不朽子, 笛子 1471
Fue no maki *la* 笛之巻
~ no shiratama *l* 不壊の白珠 94
Fugakudan hei *l* 巫学談弊 524
Fūgashū *l* 風雅集 986
Fugen *l* 普賢 1792
(fugu 寒 1714)
Fuhito *s* 二人 4; *m* 不比等 94
Fuishi *s* 武石 751
Fuji *sf-la* 藤 2773; *sp-l* 富士 1715. (葛 1994, 藤 2773) 「1715
~ Asama *l* 富士浅間
Fujibakama *l* 藤袴 2773
Fujibayashi *s* 藤林
Fujibitai Tsukuba no shigeyama *l* 富士額男女繁山 1715
Fuji daiko *la* 富士太鼓
Fujidaira *s* 藤平 2773
Fujie *s* 藤江, 藤枝
Fujieda *sp* 藤枝
~ Shizuo *ml* 藤枝静男
Fujigasaki *s* 藤ケ崎
Fujigaya *s* 藤ケ谷, 藤谷 「集
~ wakashū *l* 藤谷和歌
Fujihashi *p* 藤橋
Fujihira *s* 藤平
Fujii *s* 葛 1994, 葛井, 藤井 2773, 藤居
Fujiie *m* 藤戸
Fujii Hironari *ml* 葛井広成 1994 「2773
~ Kōyū *ma* 藤井浩祐
~ Kyōe *ml* 藤居教恵
~ Masumi *ml* 藤井真澄
~ Umon *mh* 藤井右門
Fujijumaru *m* 藤寿丸
Fujikado *s* 藤門
Fujikake *s* 藤掛, 藤懸
Fujikawa *s* 藤川; *p* 富士川 1715 「2773
~ Chūji *ml* 藤川忠治
Fujikazu *m* 二十冬 4
Fujiki *s* 藤木 2773
Fujiko *f* 藤子
Fujikura *s* 藤倉
Fujima *s* 藤間
Fujimaki *s* 藤牧, 藤巻
Fujimaru *s* 藤丸
Fujimatsu *s* 藤松; *sla* 富士松 1715
Fujimi *p* 富士見
Fujimiya *p* 富士宮
Fujimori *s* 藤盛 2773, 藤森
~ Junzō *ml* 藤森淳三
~ Seikichi *ml* 藤森成吉
~ Tomoo *ml* 藤森朋夫
Fujimoto *s* 富士根 1715, 藤元 2773, 藤本
Fujimura *s* 藤村
~ Misao *ml* 藤村操
Fujina *s* 富士名 1715
Fujinaga *s* 藤永 2773
Fujinaka *s* 藤中
Fujinami *s* 藤波, 藤並, 藤浪
Fujinawa *s* 藤縄
Fujine *s* 藤根
Fujino *s* 輔治野 2133; *sp* 藤野 2773
Fujinoki *s* 藤ノ木
Fujino Kohaku *ml* 藤野古白
Fujinomori *s* 藤杜
Fuji no uraba *l* 藤裏葉
Fujinuki *s* 藤貫
Fujinuma *s* 藤沼
Fujio *s* 藤生, 藤尾; *m* 不二夫 49, 不二雄
Fujiōji *s* 藤大路 2773
Fujioka *sp* 藤岡
Fujirō *m* 夫次郎 104
Fujisaka *s* 藤坂 2773
Fujisaki *s* 藤咲; *sp* 藤崎 「1715
Fujisan *p-la* 富士山
Fujisato *p* 藤里 2773
Fujisawa *sp* 藤沢 「実
~ Furumi *ml* 藤沢古

～ Seizō *ml* 藤沢清造
～ Takeo *ml* 藤沢桓夫
Fujise *s* 藤瀬
Fujishige *s* 藤重
Fujishima *sp* 藤島
～ Takeji *ma* 藤島武二
Fujishiro *s* 藤城; *p* 藤代
Fujishita *s* 藤下
Fujita *sp* 藤田
Fujitaka *s* 藤高
Fujita Koshirō *mh* 藤田小四郎
～ Mokichi *ml* 藤田茂吉
Fujitani *s* 富士谷 1715, 藤谷 2773
～ Mitsue *ml* 富士谷御杖 1715
～ Nariakira *ml* 富士谷成章
Fujita Nobukatsu *ml* 藤田信勝 2773
Fujitarō *m* 富士太郎 1715
Fujita Tōko *mh* 藤田東湖 2773
～ Yūkoku *mh* 藤田幽谷
Fujito *s* 藤門; *sla* 藤戸
Fujitomi *s* 藤富
Fujitsu *sp* 藤津
Fujitsuka *s* 藤塚
Fujitsune *m* 葛鎮 1994
Fujiu *s* 藤生 2773, 藤栩
Fujiura *s* 藤浦
Fujiwakamaru *ma* 藤若丸
Fujiwara *sp* 藤原
～ no Akihira *ml* 藤原明衡
～ no Fuhito *mh* 藤原不比等
～ no Fuyutsugu *mh* 藤原冬嗣
～ no Hamanari *ml* 藤原浜成
～ no Hidehira *mh* 藤原秀衡
～ no Hidesato *mh* 藤原秀郷
～ no Hidetō *ml* 藤原秀能
～ no Hirotsugu *mh* 藤原広嗣
～ no Kiyohira *mh* 藤原清衡
～ no Kōzei *ml* 藤原行成
～ no Michinaga *mh* 藤原道長
～ no Michinori *mh* 藤原通憲
～ no Miyako *fh* 藤原宮子
～ no Momokawa *mh* 藤原百川
～ no Motohira *mh* 藤原基衡
～ no Motonaga *mh* 藤原元命
～ no Mototoshi *ml* 藤原基俊
～ no Mototsune *mh* 藤原基経
～ no Nakamaro *mh* 藤原仲麻呂
～ no Narichika *mh* 藤原成親
～ no Nobutada *mh* 藤原陳忠
～ no Nobuyori *mh* 藤原信頼
～ no Nobuzane *mla* 藤原信実
～ ～ ～ Ason shū *l* 藤原信実朝臣集
～ no Sadaie *ml* 藤原定家
～ no Sanekata *ml* 藤原実方
～ no Saneyori *mh* 藤原実頼
～ no Shunzei *mlh* 藤原俊成
～ no Sukeyo *ml* 藤原佐世
～ no Sumitomo *mh* 藤原純友
～ no Tadahira *mh* 藤原忠平
～ no Tadamichi *ml* 藤原忠通
～ no Takaie *mh* 藤原隆家
～ no Takamitsu *ml* 藤原高光
～ no Takanobu *ma* 藤原隆信
～ no Takayoshi *ma* 藤原隆能
～ no Tameie *ml* 藤原為家
～ no Tanetsugu *mh* 藤原種継
～ no Teika *ml* 藤原定家
～ no Tokihira *mh* 藤原時平
～ no Tomoyasu *ml* 藤原倫寧
～ no Toshinari *mlh* 藤原俊成
～ no Umakai *ml* 藤原宇合
～ no Yasuhira *mh* 藤原泰衡
～ no Yorimichi *mh* 藤原頼通
～ no Yorinaga *mh* 藤原頼長
～ no Yoritsugu *mh* 藤原頼嗣
～ no Yoritsune *mh* 藤原頼経
～ no Yoshifusa *mh* 藤原良房
～ no Yukinari *mlh* 藤原行成
～ Sadamu *ml* 藤原定
～ Seika *ml* 藤原惺窩
～ Shinji *ml* 藤原審爾
Fujiya *s* 藤谷; *m* 富士弥 1715
Fujiyabuchi *s* 藤矢淵
Fujiyama *s* 藤山
Fujiyasu *s* 藤安
Fujiyoshi *s* 藤好, 藤吉
Fuji Yoshida *p* 富士吉田 1715
(fuka 老 334, 作 362, 玄 522, 武 751, 底 992, 甚 1267, 浚 1329, 深 1341, 渤 1582, 奥 1798, 淵 1858, 興 2586)
Fukabara *s* 深原 1341
Fukabori *s* 深堀
Fukada *sp* 深田
～ Kyūya *ml* 深田久弥
～ Yasukazu *ml* 深田康算
Fukae *s* 深栖; *sm-p* 深江
Fukagai *s* 深谷
Fukagawa *sp* 深川
Fukai *s* 深井, 深海
Fukaki *s* 深木
Fukakusa *s* 深草
Fukamachi *s* 深町
Fukamauchi *s* 深間内
Fukame *s* 深目
Fukami *s* 老見 334, 深水 1341, 深見, 深海, 渤海 1582, 富賀見 1715; *m* 深覧 1341
Fukamichi *m* 玄通 522
Fukamizo *s* 深溝 1341
Fukan zazengi *l* 普勧坐禅儀 1792
Fukano *s* 深野 1341
Fukao *s* 深尾; *m* 玄夫 522
～ Shōji no shuki *l* 深尾正治の手記 1341
～ Sumako *fl* 深尾須磨子
Fukasaku *s* 深作
Fukase *s* 深瀬
～ Motohiro *ml* 深瀬基寛
Fukashi *m* 沖 400, 玄 522, 洸 813, 浚 1329, 淑 1335, 深 1341, 窈 1745, 奥志 1798, 淵 1858, 濬 2608
Fukasu *s* 深洲 1341, 深栖, 深巣, 深淵
Fukatsu *s* 武律 751, 深津 1341
Fukaura *p* 深浦
Fukautsu *s* 深溝
Fukawa *s* 布川 170, 伏丸 234, 府川 740, 深和 1341, 普川 1792
Fukaya *sp* 深谷 1341
Fukayabu *m* 深養父
Fukayama *s* 深山
Fukayasu *p* 深安
Fukazaka *s* 深坂
Fukazawa *s* 深沢
～ Shichirō *ml* 深沢七郎
Fuke *s* 浮気 1069, 富家 1715, 福家 1888. (吹 370, 更 528)
Fukeda *s* 更田
Fukehi *s* 深日 1341
Fukei *s* 吹負 370
Fukeshi *s* 風至 986; *sp* 鳳至 2233
(fuki 吹 370, 葺 1720, 漁 2086, 蕗 2564)
Fukiage *sp* 吹上 370
Fukiai *p* 葺合 1720
Fukiawase *s* 蕗 2564
Fukii *s* 吹井 370
Fukiko *f* 蕗子 2564
Fukino *s* 吹野 370
Fūkin shirabe no hitofushi *l* 風琴調一節 986
Fukio *m* 吹雄 370
Fukita *s* 吹田, 漁田 2086
Fukiyama *s* 吹山 370
Fukke *s* 福家 1888
Fuku *s* 福. (伏 234, 吹 370, 服 618, 副 1428, 復 1571, 富 1715, 葺 1720, 腹 1871, 福 1888, 箙 2210, 蝮 2312, 馥 2753)
Fukuba *s* 福羽 1888
Fukube *p* 福部
Fukuchi *s* 福知, 福智; *sp* 福地
～ Gen'ichirō *mh* 福地源一郎
～ Ōchi *ml* 福地桜痴
Fukuchiyama *p* 福知山
Fukuda *s* 富久田 1715; *sp* 福田 1888
Fukudabe *s* 福田部
Fukuda Eiichi *ml* 福田栄一
～ Gyōkai *ml* 福田行誡

〜 Hideko *fh* 福田英子
〜 Kiyoto *ml* 福田清人
〜 Masao *ml* 福田正夫
〜 Ryōtei *ml* 福田蓼汀
〜 Tokuzō *mlh* 福田徳三 「存
〜 Tsuneari *ml* 福田恒
〜 Yūsaku *ml* 福田夕咲
Fukudome *s* 福留
Fukue *s* 福恵; *sp* 福江
Fukuei *p* 福栄
Fukugawa *s* 福川
Fukugo *s* 福子
Fukuhara *s* 福原
〜 Rintarō *ml* 福原麟太郎 「370
Fukui *sp* 福井; *m* 吹負
Fukujirō *m* 福次郎 1888
Fukukake *s* 福掛
Fukukichi *m* 福吉
Fukukita *s* 福喜田
Fukuma *p* 福間
Fukumaru *m* 福丸
Fukumatsu *m* 福松
Fukumi *s* 福見
Fukumitsu *sp* 福光
Fukumizu *s* 福水
Fukumochi *m* 福将
Fukumori *s* 福森
Fukumoto *s* 福元, 福本
〜 Kazuo *ml* 福本和夫
〜 Nichinan *mlh* 福本日南
Fukumura *s* 福村
Fukumuro *s* 福室
Fukunaga *s* 福永, 福長
〜 Takehiko *ml* 福永武彦
Fukunaka *s* 福中
Fukunishi *s* 福西
Fukuno *sp* 福野
Fuku no kami *la* 福の ⌊神
Fukuo *m* 福雄
Fukuō *s* 福王
Fukuōji *s* 福王寺
Fukuō jiden *l* 福翁自伝
Fukuoka *sp* 福岡
〜 Takachika *mh* 福岡孝弟
Fukura *s* 福浦
Fukurai *s* 福来
Fukurinji *s* 福林寺
Fukuroi *p* 袋井 1750
Fukurokuju *mh* 福禄壽 1888
Fukuroōmono *s* 負嚢者 981 「1750
Fukuro sōshi *l* 袋草紙
Fukuryū *l* 伏流 234
Fukusa *s* 福朱 1888
Fukusaburō *m* 福三郎
Fukuse *s* 福瀬
Fukushi *s* 福士 「郎
〜 Kōjirō *ml* 福士幸次
Fukushima *sp* 福島
Fukuta *p* 富来田 1715
Fukutarō *m* 福太郎 1888
Fukutomi *sp* 福富
〜 chōja *l* 福富長者
〜 Seiji *ml* 福富菁児
〜-zōshi *l* 福富草子
Fukuwatari *p* 福渡
Fukuya *s* 福谷
Fukuyama *sp* 福山; *p* 富久山 1715
Fukuyo *s* 福与 1888
Fukuyori *s* 福依
Fukuzaki *sp* 福崎
Fukuzawa *s* 福沢
〜 Yukichi *ml* 福沢諭吉
Fukuzumi *s* 福角, 福住
Fuma *s* 夫馬 104. (踏 2314)
Fumase *p* 踏瀬
Fumi *s* 文 86, 書 1216; *f* 二三 4, 二美, 文章 86, 生仁 214. (文 86, 史 183, 冊 190, 典 733, 良 767, 郁 890, 奎 913, 迪 1001, 記 1149, 書 1216, 章 1461, 詞 1665, 踏 2314, 履 2415, 翰 2518, 録 2523, 譜 2638, 簡 2788)
Fumiaki *m* 文士 86, 文明, 文炳, 文郷
Fumihiko *m* 文彦, 奎彦 913, 記彦 1149
Fumihiro *m* 文披 86
Fumihito *m* 不美人 94
Fumiho *m* 文秀 86
Fumii *f* 史伊 183
Fumiji *m* 二三次 4
Fumika *f* 文郁 86
Fumiko *f* 双美子 53, 文三子 86, 文子, 史子 183, 典子 733, 章子 1461, 詞子 1665, 節美子 2215, 録子 2523, 簡子 2788
Fumimaro *m* 文麿 86
Fumimasa *m* 文祇
Fumimochi *m* 書持 1216 「*m* 章業 1461
Fuminari *sm* 文成 86;
Fuminori *m* 文任 86
Fuminushi *m* 書主 1216
Fumio *m* 文夫 86, 文男, 文雄, 章夫 1461, 翰於 2518
Fumisato *m* 文郷 86
Fumishi *m* 文
Fumitada *m* 文質
Fumitaka *m* 文峰
Fumitoki *m* 文時
Fumiya *s* 文室
Fumiyo *f* 文代
Fumoto *m* 麓 2903
〜 no kusawake *l* 麓の草分
(fumu 枚 630, 書 1216)
(fun 分 64, 冊 190, 汾 397, 芬 477, 玢 604, 枌 624, 粉 1133, 書 1216, 賁 2367)
(funa 船 1391, 鮒 2546)
Funaba *s* 船場 1391
Funabashi *sp* 舟橋 339; *sp-la* 船橋 1391
〜 Nobukata *mh* 舟橋宣賢 339
〜 Seiichi *ml* 舟橋聖一
Funa-Benkei *la* 船弁慶 1391
Funada *s* 船田
Funado *s* 舟戸 339, 船戸 1391, 船渡
Funae *s* 船江
Funagata *p* 舟形 339
Funagi *s* 船木 1391
Funahiki *p* 船引
Funaho *p* 船穂
Funai *s* 舟井 339; *sp* 船井 1391
Funaki *s* 舟木 339
〜 Shigenobu *ml* 舟木重信
Funako *f* 船子 1391
Funakoshi *s* 舟越 339; *sp* 船越 1391
Funakura *s* 船倉
Funami *s* 舟見 339, 船見 1391
Funamizu *s* 船水
Funamoto *s* 舟本 339, 船本 1391
Funanami *s* 舟波 339
Funanushi *m* 鮒主 2546
Funaoka *s* 舟岡 339; *sp* 船岡 1391
Funasaka *s* 船坂
Funato *s* 岐 599, 道祖 1811
Funatobe *s* 船戸部 1391
Funatogawa *s* 船戸川
Funato-no-kami *mh* 岐神 599 「津 1391
Funatsu *s* 舟津 339, 船
Funayama *s* 舟山 339, 船山 1391
〜 Kaoru *ml* 船山馨
Funazaki *s* 船崎
Funde *s* 筆 1769
(fune 舟 339, 船 1391)
Funo *sp* 布野 170. (史 183)
Funobori *s* 五六 91
Fun'ya *s* 文室 86, 文屋
Funyū *s* 舟生 339, 船生 1391 「山人 986
Fūrai Sanjin *ml* 風来
Furano *p* 富良野 1715
Furansu *p* "France" 仏蘭西 128
Fūren *p* 風連 986
(furi 降 1058, 振 1320)
Furihata *s* 降旗 1058, 降幡 「髪 1320
Furiwakegami *l* 振分
Furu *sla* 布留 170. (旧 119, 古 154, 両 531, 昔 699, 雨 759, 故 880, 降 1058, 振 1320, 経 1957, 歴 2247)
Furuari *s* 古在 154
Furubayashi *s* 古林
Furubira *p* 古平
Furudate *s* 古館
Furudono *p* 古殿
Furue *s* 古江
Furugōri *s* 古郡
Furuhashi *s* 古橋
Furuhata *s* 古畑
Furuhito no Ōe *mh* 古人大兄 「井 119
Furui *s* 古井, 古居, 旧
Furuichi *s* 古市 154, 古 ⌊都
Furuike *s* 古池
Furuinosuke *m* 古猪之 ⌊助
Furujō *s* 古城
Furukawa *s* 古河, 布留川 170; *sp* 古川 154
〜 Kairai *ml* 古川魁蕾
Furuki *s* 古木
Furuko *f* 古子

Furukoshi *s* 古越
Furuku *s* 古来
Furumatsu *s* 古松
Furumi *s* 古見
Furumiya *s* 古宮
Furumori *s* 古森
Furumoto *s* 古本
Furumura *s* 古村
Furuno *s* 古野
Furuoya *s* 古尾谷
Furusaka *s* 古坂
Furusaki *s* 古崎
Furusato *s* 古里, 古郷
～ no hana *l* 故郷の花 880
Furusawa *s* 古沢 154
Furuse *s* 古瀬
Furushima *s* 古島
Furushō *s* 古庄, 古性, 古荘 ⌈1320
Furuta *s* 古田; *p* 振田
Furutani *s* 古谷 154
Furuteya *s* 古手屋
Furuuchi *s* 古内
Furuwatari *s* 古渡
Furuya *s* 古矢, 古谷, 古屋, 古家, 降矢 1058
～ Kayao *ml* 古家榧夫 154
Furuyama *s* 古山
Furuyasu *s* 古安
Furuya Tsunatake *ml* 古谷綱武 ⌈986
Fūryūbutsu *l* 風流仏
Fūryū mijinzō *l* 風流微塵蔵
～ odori *a* 風流踊
～ senbō *l* 風流懺法
～ Shidōken-den *l* 風流志道軒伝
～ Soga *l* 風流曾我
Fusa *f* 総 2662. (方 85, 旧 119, 処 177, 芝 289, 成 322, 芳 480, 角 547, 林 633, 房 658, 苓 687A, 英 693, 亮 911, 宣 919, 重 1017, 記 1149, 弦 1345, 寅 1439, 章 1461, 隅 1566, 番 1773, 惣 1785, 雉 1911, 葉 1991, 業 2024, 種 2124, 蕃 2371, 滋 2460, 維 2540, 薫 2567, 興 2586, 幾 2597, 緩 2659, 総 2662)
Fusaaki *m* 総明
Fusae *f* 富総江 1715
Fusagorō *m* 房五郎 658
Fusahito *m* 成仁 322
Fusajirō *m* 房次郎 658
Fusakichi *m* 房吉
Fusako *f* 成子 322, 房子 658, 富祚子 1715
Fusami *f* 亮美 911
Fusanaga *m* 総長 2662
Fusano *s* 房野 658
Fusanobu *m* 英延 693
Fusanosuke *m* 房之助 658
Fusao *m* 房雄, 章夫 1461, 富佐雄 1715, 維男 2540
Fusatarō *m* 房太郎 658
Fusatomi *m* 英美 693
Fusatoshi *m* 房俊 658
Fusatsune *m* 英経 693
Fusazō *m* 房造 658
Fuse *s* 布勢 170, 富勢 1715; *sp* 布施 170. (伏 234, 防 374)
Fuseda *s* 布施田 170
Fuseki *s* 武石 751
Fuse nai kyō *la* 無布施経 1789
Fuseshima *s* 伏島 234
Fuseya *s* 伏屋
Fushaku shinmyō *l* 不惜身命 94
Fushi *s* 風至 986. (伏 234, 槵 2097, 節 2215)
Fushida *s* 斛子田 2546
Fushihara *s* 不死原 94, 伏原 234
Fushijima *s* 伏島
Fushikata *s* 十代田 18
Fushiki *s* 伏木 234
Fushimi *sma-p* 伏見
Fushiyo *f* 伏代 ⌈383
Fusō 総生 2662; *p* 扶桑
～ ryakuki *l* 扶桑略記
Fusōshū *l* 扶桑集
Fussa *p* 福生 1888
Fusso *s* 弗措 330
(futa 二 4, 双 53, 両 531, 蓋 2193)
Futaba *sf* 二葉 4; *f* 嫩 2279; *p* 双葉 53
Futabashi *s* 二橋 4
Futabatei *s* 二葉亭
～ Shimei *ml* 二葉亭四迷
Futagami *s* 二上, 二神
Futagawa *s* 二川
Futagi *s* 福当 1888
Futai *s* 二井 4
Futaki *sm* 二木
Futaku *s* 二九
Futamata *s* 二俣
Futamatsu *s* 二松
Futami *sp* 二見; *m* 二王; *p* 双三 53, 双海
Futamoto *s* 二本 4
Futamura *s* 二村
Futaomote *s* 二面
Futara *s* 二荒 ⌈袴
Futari-bakama *la* 二人袴
～ daimyō *la* 二人大名
～ Shizuka *la* 二人静 (futatsu 二)
Futatsu chōchō kuruwa *la* 双蝶蝶曲輪 53
Futatsugi *s* 二木 4
Futatsui *p* 二ツ井
Futatsuyanagi *s* 二柳
Futawatari *s* 二渡
Futayama *s* 二山
Futayanagi *s* 二柳
Futo *s* 風斗 986. (人 14, 大 48, 太 105, 弟 764)
Futogimi *m* 人君 14
Futokubi *m* 太首 105
Futomi *m* 大三 48
Futoshi *m* 大, 太 105, 富豪 1715
Futoshige *m* 太茂 105
Futsu *sp* 布津 170. (仏 128, 弗 330, 祓 1125)
Futsuka *s* 留束 1470
Futto *sp* 古渡 154
Futtsu *sp* 富津 1715
Fuwa *s* 不羽 94, 不波; *sph-la* 不破
Fūyōshū *l* 風葉集 986
(fuyu 冬 161, 生 214, 那 416) ⌈161
Fuyu aozora *l* 冬青空
Fuyuhiko *m* 冬彦
Fuyuhikoshū *l* 冬彦集
Fuyuji *m* 冬二
Fuyuki *s* 冬木
Fuyuko *f* 那子 416
Fuyuo *m* 冬夫 161
Fuyutomi *m* 冬宝
Fuyutsugu *s* 冬嗣
Fuzakashi *s* 汗 248
Fuzan *p* "Pusan" 釜山 1160
Fūzoku monzen *l* 風俗文選 986

# G

(ga 瓦 201, 何 513, 我 545, 河 597, 芽 683, 画 991, 荷 1259, 峨 1350, 娥 1356, 賀 1756, 禍 1885, 雅 1913, 蝦 2313)
(gachi 活 819)
Gagen shūran *l* 雅言集覧 1913
Gahana *s* 辻葩 320
Gahiko *s* 我彦 545
(gai 乂 5, 外 139, 艾 159, 苅 479, 亥 519, 害 1181, 街 1570, 崖 1737, 詣 1930, 凱 1967, 愷 2071, 隑 2072, 該 2135, 蓋 2193, 諧 2639, 擬 2723, 蹊 2807)
Gaijin Yashima *la* 凱陣八島 1967
Gaishi *m* 外史 139
(gaku 学 719, 岳 956, 楽 2029, 額 2756, 嶽 2775, 斅 2892, 鶴 2926, 鰐 3015)
Gakuichi *m* 学一 719
Gakkan'in *ph* 学館院
Gakurō *s* 楽浪 2029
Gakusetsu kikkaibukuro *l* 学説乞丐袋 719
Gakushūin *p* 学習院
Gama *s* 蒲 1993
Gamagōri *p* 蒲郡
Gama tekkai *l* 蝦蟆鉄拐 2313
Gamō *sm-p* 蒲生 1993
～ Kunpei *mh* 蒲生君平
(gan 丸 40, 元 60, 含 453, 完 471, 妧 613, 垣 795,

岸 941, 岩 942, 悍 1051, 桓 1100, 莟 1172, 原 1231, 偐 1275, 紈 1421, 眼 1637, 睆 1638, 雁 1801, 嵒 1974, 愿 2228, 厳 2706, 顔 2754, 巌 2936, 鑑 2968, 鑒 2982, 礹 2996)
Gangyō 877–85 元慶 60
Ganji 1864–65 元治
Ganjin *mh* 鑑真 2968
Gankarigane *la* 雁厂金 1801
Ganmaku *m* 岩捲 942
Gan no tera *l* 雁の寺 1801
～ tsubute *l* 雁礫
Garakuta bunko *l* 我楽多文庫 545
Gasu *la* 炭塵 1186
(gatsu 月 80)
Gazan *s* 峨山 1350
(ge 乂 5, 下 46, 外 139, 牙 202, 茢 479, 芽 683, 夏 1161, 華 1266, 谺 1652, 頎 1866, 遐 2048, 戯 2350, 蟹 2853, 畿 2859)
Gedatsu *l* 解脱 1923
(gei 芸 689, 迎 746, 猊 1302, 詣 1930, 霓 2578, 鯨 2831)
Geiami *mla* 芸阿弥 689
Geihoku *p* 芸北
Geikan *l* 芸鑑
Geino *p* 芸濃
Geirinkanpo *l* 芸林間
Geisei *p* 芸西 ⌊歩
Geishō bigin *l* 霓裳微吟 2578
Gejō *s* 下条 46
Geki *sm* 外記 139. (逆 1235)
Gekiza *p* 外記座 139
Gekkyūden *la* 月宮殿 80
Gemyōbu *f* 外命婦 139
Gen *sm* 玄 522; *m* 元 60, 厳 2706. (元 60, 幻 261, 言439, 玄 522, 妍 612, 妧 613, 俔 774, 研 875, 彦 1007, 唁 1047, 拳 1206, 原 1231, 県 1252, 虔 1253, 偐 1275, 炫 1344, 弦 1345, 睅 1352, 現 1360, 這 1515, 硯 1634, 眼 1637, 雁 1801, 閑 1820, 源 1863, 筧 2014, 蜷 2129, 茲 2134, 愿 2228, 絃 2331, 鉉 2335, 戯 2350, 毅 2351, 諺 2508, 鍵 2652, 厳 2706, 韓 2741, 巌 2936, 懸 2984, 礹 2996)
Genbō *mh* 玄昉 522
Genboku to Chōei *la* 玄朴と長英
Genbuku Soga *la* 元服曾我 60
Genbun 1736–41 元文
Genchū 1384–92 元中
～ yoteki *l* 源注余滴 1863
Genda *s* 源田; *m* 源太
Gendayū *la* 源太夫
Gendō *ml* 玄洞 522
Gen'e *mh* 玄慧
Gen'ei *s* 現影 1360; 1118–20 元永 60
Gen'emon *m* 源右衛門 1863 ⌈522
Gengenshū *l* 玄玄集
Gengi *m* 源治 1863
Gengo *s* 玄御 522; *m* 源吾 1863
Gengyō 877–85 元慶 60
Genhachi *m* 源八 1863
Gen'ichi *m* 源一, 愿一 2228
Gen'ichirō *m* 玄一郎 522, 弦一郎 1345, 源一郎 1863 ⌈婆 1360
Geniyasaba *l* 現爾也娑
Genji *l-lm-h* 源氏 1863; *m* 源二, 愿治 2228; 1864–65 元治 60
～ Keita *ml* 源氏鶏太 1863
～ kuyō *la* 源氏供養
～ monogatari *l* 源氏物語
～ ～ tama no ogushi *l* 源氏物語玉の小櫛
Genjirō *m* 源次郎
Genjō *la* 玄上 522, 玄象, 絃上 2331
Genjūan no ki *l* 幻住庵記 261
Genkai *ma-p* 玄海 522
Genkaku sanbō *l* 玄鶴山房
Genkei *m* 元圭 60, 元啓, 元敬, 元経, 玄渓 522, 源慶 1863
Genki 1570–73 元亀 60
Genkichi *m* 源吉 1863
Genkō 1321–24 元亨 60; 1331–34 元弘
～ shakusho *lh* 元亨釈書
Genkū *ml* 玄空 522; *mlh* 源空 1863
Genkurō *m* 源九郎
Genkyū 1204–06 元久
Genmei *mh* 元明 ⌊60
Genna 1615–24 元和
Gennai *ml* 源内 1863
Gennin 1224–25 元仁 60
Gennosuke *m* 元之助, 源之助 1863, 権之允 2300
Gen'ō 1319–21 元応 60
Gen-oji *l* 源をぢ 1863
Genpei seisuiki *l* 源平盛衰記 ⌈禄 60
Genroku 1688–1704 元
～ chūshingura *la* 元禄忠臣蔵 ⌈暦
Genryaku 1184–85 元
Genshin *mlh* 源信 1863
Genshirō *m* 源四郎
Genshō *mh* 元正 60
Gensuke *m* 源助 1863
Gentarō *m* 玄太郎 522, 源太郎 1863 ⌈60
Gentoku 1329–31 元徳
Genwa 1615–24 元和
Gen'yōsha *h* 玄洋社 522
Genzaburō *m* 源三郎 1863 ⌈1360
Genzai nue *la* 現在鵺
～ shichimen *la* 現在七面 ⌈度
～ Tadanori *la* 現在忠
Genzō *m* 元三 60, 源蔵
Gero *p* 下呂 46 ⌊1863
Gesaku *l* 戯作 2350
～-zammai *l* 戯作三昧
Gesu *s* 下司 46
(getsu 月 80)
(gi 伎 232, 技 381, 岐 599, 枝 631, 宜 675, 芸 689, 其 734, 奇 752, 俟 1035, 祇 1127, 耆 1214, 翅 1248, 淇 1328, 揆 1549, 期 1671, 葵 1723, 逵 1813, 祺 1903, 義 1975, 旗 2093, 儀 2255, 誼 2322, 戯 2350, 毅 2351, 錡 2520, 擬 2604, 羲 2675, 嶷 2679, 蟻 2727, 礒 2732, 嶷 2774, 蟻 2804, 議 2876, 曦 2914, 巍 2991) ⌈1975
Gidayū *ma-a* 義太夫
Gidō Shūshin *ml* 義堂周信
Gien *mh* 義淵, 義演
Gifu *p* 岐阜 599
Gigaku *a* 伎楽 232
Gigeiten *l* 伎芸天
Gihachirō *m* 巍八郎 2991
Gihee *m* 儀兵衛 2255
Giichi *m* 義一 1975, 儀一 2255
Giichirō *m* 儀一郎
Gikeiki *l* 義経記 1975
(gin 吟 369, 崟 1736, 銀 2345, 誾 2427)
Ginan *p* 岐南 599
Gingoroku *l* 銀語録 2345 ⌈次郎
Ginjirō *m* 銀二郎, 銀
Ginkakuji *pha* 銀閣寺
Ginnosuke *m* 銀之助
Ginowa *s* 宜野湾 675
Gintarō *m* 銀太郎 2345
Ginza *p* 銀座
Ginzaburō *m* 銀三郎
Ginzō *m* 銀蔵
Giō *fa-la* 祇王 1127
Gion *sp* 祇園
Girisha *p* "Greece" 希臘 445
Gisaburō *m* 義三郎 1975
Gisaku *m* 儀作 2255
Gishirō *m* 義四郎 1975
Gisuke *m* 義介, 儀助
(gitsu 仡 131) ⌊2255
Go *sp* ["Wu"] 呉 735. (乂 49, 戸 59, 五 91, 牛 111, 午 112, 互 200, 乎 221, 伍 229, 冴 348, 吾 491, 昨 621, 苣 680, 呉 735, 狐 789, 胡 879, 悟 1053, 祜 1124, 後 1300, 晤 1353, 梧 1365, 魚 1485, 御 1572, 湖 1584, 期 1671, 馭 1697, 鉅 1946, 語 2136, 糊 2309, 護 2877)
Gō *s* 江 252, 郷 2112. (江 252, 合 270, 号 272, 仰 360, 昊 711, 匣 742, 恆 805, 恒 809, 洽 816, 降 1058, 浩 1068, 峆 1079, 航 1136, 皐 1197, 晧

1355, 剛 1429, 皐 1459, 項 1543, 硬 1635, 強 1878, 業 2024, 郷 2112, 豪 2177, 澔 2268, 皞 2283, 耦 2310, 壕 2603, 濠 2610, 彊 2621, 顥 2928, 囂 2938, 轟 2939)
Gobō *p* 御坊 1572
Gochō *s* 牛腸 111, 後町 1300
Gōda *s* 合田 270, 郷田 2112
Godai *s* 五大院 91, 五代, 五代院, 後醍院 1300; *m* 五大 91
Godaigo *mh* 後醍醐 1300
Godaiin *s* 後醍院
Godairiki koi no fūjime *l* 五代力恋緘 91
Godai Tomoatsu *mh* 五代友厚
Gōdanshō *l* 江談抄 252
Godō *s* 伍堂 229
Gōdo *p* 神戸 853
Goeku *s* 護得久 2877
Gofukakusa *mh* 後深草 1300
Gōhara *s* 郷原 2112
Gohensha *s* 五返舎 91
Gohiiki kanjinchō *la* 御摂勧進帳 1572
Gōho *m* 郷甫 2112
Gohoku *p* 吾北 491
Gohongi *s* 五本木 91
Goi *s* 五井
Goichi *m* 五一, 悟一 1053, 梧一 1365
Gōichi *m* 剛一 1429
Goichirō *m* 五一郎 91
Goino *s* 五位野
Goiya *s* 五井屋
Gojō *s* 護上 2877; *sp* 五条 91
Gojōme *p* 五城目
Goka *p* 五箇, 五霞
Gōka *s* 江香 252
Gokameyama *mh* 後亀山 1300
Gokami *s* 後上
Gokan *s* 五間 91, 後間 1300, 後閑
Gōkan *l* 合巻 270
Gokanjo *lh* "Hou-Han shu" 後漢書 1300
Gokase *p* 五ヶ瀬 91
Gokashō *p* 五個荘
Gōkawa *s* 合川 270
Goki *p* 五畿 91
Gokijō *s* 五鬼上
Gokiso *s* 五器所, 御器所 1572
Gokita *s* 五木田 91
Gokō *s* 後神 1300
Gōko *s* 郷古 2112
Gokoe *s* 牛糞 111
Gokomatsu *mh* 後小松 1300
Gokoso *s* 牛糞 111
(goku 玉 204, 局 514, 砡 1111, 琙 1812, 極 1896, 鈺 1942, 鵠 2739)
Gōku *l* 業苦 2024
Gokuden *s* 御供田 1572
Gokuraku rokujisan *l* 極楽六時讃 1896
Gokyū *s* 五弓 91
Gōma *s* 郷間 2112
Gomatsuru *s* 護麗都留 2877
Gomei *s* 五明 91
Gomi *s* 五味
Gomibuchi *s* 五味淵
Gomikawa *s* 五味川
～ Junpei *ml* 五味川純平
Gomi Yasusuke *ml* 五味康祐
～ Yasuyoshi *ml* 五味保義
Gomizunoo *mlh* 後水尾 1300
Gomurakami *mh* 後村上
Gomyō *s* 五明 91
(gon 心 49, 吟 369, 言 439, 芹 478, 唁 1047, 崟 1736, 琴 1778, 慬 2069, 権 2300, 銀 2345, 誾 2427, 魂 2488, 厳 2706)
Gonbee *m* 権兵衛 2300
Gonbei *s* 権平, 権瓶
Gonda *s* 権田
Gondai *m* 権大
Gondō *s* 権藤
Gongen-zukuri *a* 権現造
Gon'ichi *m* 権一
Gonji *m* 権治
Gonno *s* 権野
Gōno *s* 郷野 2112
Gonohe *sp* 五戸 91
Gonoi *s* 五井
Gōnosochi-shū *l* 江帥集 252
Gōnoura *p* 郷ノ浦 2112
Gonpachi *m* 権八 2300
Gonshichi *m* 権七
Gonshirō *m* 権四郎
Gonshō *s* 権正
Gonsuke *m* 権助
Gonzaemon *m* 権左衛門
Gonzō *m* 権三, 権蔵
Gorai *s* 五来 91, 牛来 111
(gori 心 49)
Gōrikiden *l* 強力伝 1878
Gorō *m* 五郎 91, 吾郎 491
Gorobee *m* 五郎兵衛 91
Goroemon *m* 五郎右衛門
Goryō *s* 五料
Goryōkaku kessho *la* 五稜郭血書
Goryōken Arubeshi *ml* 呉陵軒可有 735
Gosaga *mh* 後嵯峨 1300
Gosanjō *mh* 後三条
Gose *p* 御所 1572
Goseda *s* 五姓田 91
～ Hōryū *ma* 五姓田芳柳
Goseki *s* 五艘, 後関 1300
Gosen *p* 五泉 91
Gosenshū *l* 後撰集 1300
Gosha hōgo *l* 五車反故 91
Gōshi *s* 郷司 2112; *sp* 合志 270, 剛志 1429
Goshiki *p* 五色 91
Goshikizumi *l* 五色墨
Goshima *s* 五島
Goshirakawa *mlh* 後白河 1300
Goshogawara *p* 五所川原 91
Goshōtsukuri *s* 呉床作 735
Goshoura *p* 御所浦 1572
Gosho-zakura Horikawa youchi *la* 御所桜堀河夜討
Gōshū *p* "Australia" 濠洲 2610
Goshūishū *l* 後拾遺集 1300
Gosu *s* 呉須 735
Gosuke *s* 吾助 491; *m* 五介 91
Gōtarō *m* 郷太郎 2112
Gotenba *p* 御殿場 1572
Gotō *s* 五藤 91, 後藤 1300; *sp* 五島 91
Gōto *s* 合渡 270, 神門 853
Gotobain *mlh* 後鳥羽院 1300
～ Kunaikyō *fl* 後鳥羽院宮内卿
Gotō Chūgai *ml* 後藤宙外
Gotomi *s* 五富 91
Gotō Miyoko *fl* 五島美代子
～ Shigeru *ml* 五島茂
～ Shinpei *mh* 後藤新平 1300
～ Shōjirō *mh* 後藤象二郎
～ Sueo *ml* 後藤末雄
～ Yūjō *ma* 後藤祐乗
Gotōta *s* 後藤田
Gōtsu *s* 合津 270
Goyōzei *mh* 後陽成 1300
Gozan bungaku *l* 五山文学 91
Gozenyama *p* 御前山 1572
Gōzō *m* 剛蔵 1429
Gozonji no shōbaimono *l* 御存商売物 1572
Gōzu *p* 江津 252
(gu 共 292, 后 304, 求 537, 具 718, 呉 735, 俣 777, 虹 882, 球 1359, 紅 1423, 琙 1510, 港 1583, 愚 2032, 虞 2242, 耦 2310, 鴻 2614, 衢 2985)
(gū 宮 1184, 隅 1566, 耦 2310)
Gudai *s* 母台 326
Gujō *sp* 郡上 1146
Gukanshō *l* 愚管抄 2032
Gūke *s* 郡家 1146
Gūko *s* 郡戸
Gumon kenchū *l* 愚問賢註 2032
Gun *s* 郡 1146. (軍 906, 郡 1146, 群 1924)
Gunbō *l* 群蜂
Gunji *s* 軍子 906, 軍司, 軍地, 郡司 1146
Gunma *p* 群馬 1924
Gunnan *p* 群南
Gunpei *m* 軍平 906
Gunshirō *m* 軍四郎
Gunsho ruijū *l* 群書類従 1924
Guntō *s* 郡東 1146

Gusai *ml* 救済 1406
Gushi *s* 具志 718
Gutei kenkei *l* 愚弟賢兄 2032
Guze Kannon *a* 救世観音 1406
(gyaku 逆 1235)
(gyo 魚 1485, 御 1572, 馭 1697, 漁 2086)
Gyō *m* 驍 2957. (叶 132, 行 245, 刑 258, 仰 360, 形 414, 邢 415, 協 548, 幸 661, 茎 684, 迎 746, 俠 773, 挾 1043, 勍 1150, 硎 1384, 暁 1596, 硬 1635, 喬 1775, 堯 1795, 紘 1949, 業 2024, 僑 2057, 晶 2375, 凝 2431, 衡 2450, 橋 2485)
Gyōbu *s* 刑部 258, 形舞 414
Gyōbuzaemon *m* 刑部左衛門 258
Gyochō Heike *l* 魚鳥平家 1485
Gyōda *sp* 行田 245
Gyōdai *ml* 暁台 1596
Gyōki *mh* 行基 245
Gyōkō *ml* 堯孝 1795
(gyoku 玉 204, 珏 1111, 鈺 1942)
Gyokurin'en *l* 玉林宴 204
Gyokushinka *l* 玉簪花
Gyokutō *p* 玉東
Gyokuyōshū *l* 玉葉集
Gyōmei *s* 行明 245, 行命
Gyōmyo *s* 行明
Gyōson Daisōjō shū *l* 行尊大僧正集
Gyōtoku *s* 行徳
(gyū 及 83, 牛 111, 汲 403)
Gyūba *l* 牛馬 111

# H

(ha 巴 97, 吐 242, 羽 246, 芭 473, 波 596, 杷 625, 派 812, 春 963, 破 1113, 華 1266, 埴 1561, 葉 1991, 歯 2051, 端 2306, 翰 2518, 簸 2845)
Haarabe *s* 榑族部 2105
Haba *s* 羽場 246
Habara *s* 羽原
Habe *s* 羽部, 波部 596
Habikino *p* 羽曳野 246
Haboro *p* 羽幌
Habu *s* 七生 17, 羽生 246, 埴生 1561; *sp* 八生 19, 土生 42
Habuchi *s* 羽淵 246
Habuka *s* 羽深
Habuki *s* 羽吹
Habuku *m* 省 1013
Habuto *s* 羽太 246
Hachi *s* 蜂 1921. (八 19, 釟 1153, 蜂 1921, 鉢 1945, 顚 3001)
Hachida *s* 八太 19, 八田, 八多, 蜂田 1921
Hachidaishū *l* 八代集
Hachidō *s* 八道 19
Hachiemon *m* 八右衛門
Hachihonmatsu *p* 八本松
Hachiji *m* 八次
Hachijirō *m* 八次郎
Hachijō *s* 八条; *p* 八丈
Hachijōjima *p* 八丈島
Hachijūrō *m* 八十郎
Hachikai *p* 八開
Hachikazuki *l* 鉢かづき 1945
Hachiman *p* 八幡 19
~ -zukuri *a* 八幡造
Hachimangū *p* 八幡宮
Hachimantai *p* 八幡平
Hachimonjiya *sp* 八文字屋
~ Jishō *ml* 八文字屋自笑
~ Kiseki *ml* 八文字屋其磧
~ Kishō *ml* 八文字屋其笑
~ Zuishō *ml* 八文字屋瑞笑
Hachimori *sp* 八森
Hachinohe *sp* 八戸
Hachinoki *la* 鉢木 1945
Hachinosu *s* 蜂巣 1921
Hachiōji *p* 八王子 19
Hachirō *m* 八郎, 顚郎 3001
Hachiroemon *m* 八郎右衛門 19
Hachirogata *p* 八郎潟
Hachiryū *p* 八竜
Hachisaburō *m* 釟三郎 1153
Hachisō *m* 八左右 19
Hachisu *s* 蜂須 1921. (蓮 2197)
Hachisuba *s* 蓮葉
Hachisuka *s* 蜂須賀 1921
Hachisu no tsuyu *l* 蓮の露 2197
~ zaregaki *l* 槿花戯書 2289
Hachiuma *s* 八馬 19
Hachiya *s* 蜂谷 1921, 蜂屋; *m* 八箭 19
Hachiyama *s* 八山
Hadame *s* 甚目 1267
Hadano *p* 秦野 1202
Hadara *m* 豹 1140
Hadesugata onnamaiginu *la* 艶姿女舞衣 2833
(hae 蓑 1170, 絙 2146)
Hafuri *s* 祝部 851
Hafuribe *s* 祝部
Hafuriyama *s* 祝山
Haifū yanagidaru *l* 誹風柳多留 2321
Haga *s* 羽賀 246; *sp* 芳賀 480, 塀和 1559; *p* 波賀 596, 垪和 793
Hagai *s* 垪和
Haga Mayumi *ml* 芳賀檀 480
Hagata *p* 波方 596
Hagawa *s* 羽川 246
Haga Yaichi *ml* 芳賀矢一 480
Hagemi *s* 底 992
Hagemu *m* 働 55, 百 265
Hageta *s* 羽毛田 246
Hagi *sf-p* 萩 1732. (萩)
~ daimyō *la* 萩大名
Hagii *s* 萩井
Hagimori *s* 萩森
Hagimoto *s* 萩元, 萩本
Hagino *sf* 萩野
~ Yoshiyuki *ml* 萩野由之
Hagio *s* 萩雄
Hagishima *s* 萩島
Hagita *s* 萩田
Hagiwara *sp* 萩原
~ Kyōjirō *ml* 萩原恭次郎
~ Ragetsu *ml* 萩原蘿月
~ Sakutarō *ml* 萩原朔太郎
Hagiya *s* 萩谷
Hagizono *m* 芳宜園 480
Hagoromo *la* 羽衣 246
Hagura *s* 羽倉
Haguri *s* 羽栗, 羽黒; *p* 葉栗 1991
Haguro *sp* 羽黒 246
Hagusa *m* 莠 1443
Hagyū *s* 羽生 246
Hagyūda *s* 萩生田 1732
Hahakabe *s* 波波伯 596, 波波伯部, 波波泊, 波波泊部 666)
Hahaki *s* 伯岐 363. (帚
Hahakigi *l* 帚木
~ betchū *l* 帚木別註
(hai 灰 302, 坏 388, 貝 498, 拝 585, 背 957, 俳 1036, 配 1141, 排 1317, 埴 1561, 蓜 1984A, 榛 2108, 稗 2123)
Haibara *s* 埴原 1561; *sp* 榛原 2108
Haibun *l* 俳文 1036
Haifū Yanagidaru *l* 誹風柳多留 2321
Haigō *s* 拝郷 585
Haihata *s* 辟秦 1919
Haijima *s* 蓜島 1984A
Haijin Buson *l* 俳人蕪村 1036
Haikai *l* 俳諧
~ gozan *l* 俳諧御傘
~ jiin *l* 俳諧次韻
~ Mutamagawa *l* 俳諧武玉川
~ ōkukazu *l* 俳諧大句数
~ rengashō *l* 俳諧連歌抄
~ shichibushū *l* 俳諧七部集
Haikaitei kuraku *la* 俳諧亭句楽
Haikai uma no kuso *l* 俳諧馬の糞
Haiku *l* 俳句
Haimase *s* 波伊万世 596
Haimatsu *s* 榛松 2108
Haino *s* 灰野 302

~ Shōhei *ml* 灰野庄平
Hairi *s* 羽入 246
Haisei *l* 俳星 1036
Haishi *s* 羽石 246
Haishiden *l* 稗子伝 2123
Haito *s* 隼人 1230
Haji *s* 土師 42, 吐師 242
Hajika *s* 初鹿 427
Hajikano *sp* 初鹿野
Hajime *m* 一 3, 一馬, 土師萠 42, 大 48, 元 60, 弌 74, 丕 163, 本 212, 吉 278, 初 427, 児 497, 玄 522, 甫 533, 刱 605, 叔 649, 斧 659, 宗 679, 東 771, 祖 850, 祝 851, 首 920, 春 963, 哉 1006, 俶 1026, 始 1092, 原 1231, 朔 1393, 紀 1424, 啓 1491, 基 1493, 順 1532, 斌 1590, 朝 1672, 素 1707, 源 1863, 新 1965, 業 2024, 肇 2222, 端 2306, 暾 2469
Hajimu *m* 一 3, 元 60, 孟 667, 基 1493, 創 1696, 肇 2222
Hajin *ml* 巴人 97 ⌈42
Haji Seiji *ml* 土師清二
Hajitomi *la* 半蔀 213
Hajiyama *s* 八十八間 19
Haka *s* 墓 1979. (伯 363, 博 1534, 墓 1979, 儒 2432)
Hakai *s* 塀加塀 1559
Hakama *m* 博麻 1534. (袴 1643)
Hakamada *s* 袴田 1643
Hakamaro *m* 伯麻呂 363, 博麻呂 1534
Hakamazuka *s* 袴塚 1643
Hakamori *s* 墓 1979
Hakari *s* 評 1663; *m* 量 1741
Hakaru *m* 寸 34, 斗 71, 永 149, 平 203, 成 322, 図 502, 玄 522, 法 824, 計 895, 恕 1483, 揆 1549, 量 1741, 靖 1905, 億 2252, 謀 2509, 謨 2638
Hakase *m* 博瀬 1534
(hakashi 刀 12)
Hakashima *s* 八角島 19
Hakata *s* 伯 363; *sp* 伯太, 伯方; *p* 博多 1534
~ kojorō namimakura *la* 博多小女郎波枕
Hakatoko *m* 博徳
Haki *p* 杷木 625
Hakidame *l* 塵溜 2429
Hakii *s* 羽切井 246, 波木井 596, 破切居 1113
Hakkenden *l* 八犬伝 19
Hakkyoi *ml* "Po Chü-i" 白居易 216
Hako *s* 筥 2016. (函 1232, 筥 2016, 箱 2383)
Hakoba *s* 箱羽
Hakobu *m* 運 1808
Hakobune *l* 方舟 85
Hakoda *s* 箱田 2383
Hakodate *p* 函館 1232
Hakomori *s* 箱守 2383
Hakone *p* 箱根
Hakoyama *s* 箱山
Hakozaki *s* 筥崎 2016, 箱崎 2383
(haku 白 216, 伯 363, 佰 554, 狛 567, 泊 592, 迫 747, 陌 792, 柏 866, 粕 1390, 剝 1427, 博 1534, 溥 1852, 璞 2472, 魄 2487, 薄 2569, 璧 2782)
Hakuba *p* 白馬 216
Hakubakai *a* 白馬会
Hakuchi 650–54 白雉
Hakui *s* 羽喰 246; *sp* 羽咋
Hakujitsu *l* 白日 216
Haku Kyoi *ml* "Po Chü-i" 白居易
Hakuōshū *l* 白桜集
Haku Rakuten *ml-la* "Po Lo-tien" 白楽天
Hakuri *s* 余技 448
Hakuro *l* 白路 216
Hakurō *s* 白狼
Hakusan *p* 白山
Hakuseki *mlh* 白白
Hakusen *p* 伯仙 363
Hakushi monjū *l* 白氏文集 216
Hakushū *p* 白州
Hakusui *p* 白水
Hakuta *s* 白田; *p* 伯太 363 ⌈216
Hakuyōkyū *l* 白羊宮
Hama *s* 浜 1070. (浜)
Hamabe *s* 浜辺, 浜部
Hamada *sp* 浜田 ⌈介
~ Hirosuke *ml* 浜田広
Hamadaki *s* 浜高屋
Hamagawa *s* 浜川
Hamaguchi *s* 浜口
~ Osachi *ml* 浜口雄幸
Hamai *s* 浜井
Hamaji *s* 浜地
Hamajima *sp* 浜島
Hamakita *sp* 浜北
Hamako *f* 破魔子 1113
Hamamasu *p* 浜益 1070
Hamamatsu *sp* 浜松
~ Chūnagon *l* 浜松中納言
Hamamoto *s* 浜本
~ Hiroshi *ml* 浜本浩
Hamamura *s* 浜村
~ Yonezō *ml* 浜村米
Hamana *sp* 浜名 ⌊蔵
Hamanaka *sp* 浜中
Hamanari *m* 浜成
Hamanishi *s* 浜西
Hamano *s* 浜野
Hamanoike *s* 浜池
Hamao *s* 浜尾
Hamaoka *sp* 浜岡
Hamaomi *m* 浜臣
Hamasaka *p* 浜坂
Hamasaki *sp* 浜崎
~ Tamashima *p* 浜崎玉島
Hamatake *s* 浜高屋
Hamatani *s* 浜谷
Hamatonbetsu *p* 浜頓別 ⌈2312
Hamatsubaki *s* 蝮椿
Hamaya *s* 浜谷 1070, 浜屋 ⌈2261
Hami *s* 芳美 480, 幡美
Hamiya *s* 頓宮 2115
Hamochi *s* 賀茂 1756; *p* 羽茂 246
Hamori *m* 端守 2306
Hamoto *s* 羽 246, 羽咋, 羽茂
Hamura *p* 羽村 ⌈1991
Hamuro *s* 羽室, 葉室
Han *s* 塙 1845. (凡 27, 反 69, 氾 143, 半 213, 帆 239, 汎 249, 弁 275, 伴 361, 阪 375, 坂 390, 泛 395, 判 434, 板 632, 垣 795, 班 1075, 畔 1110, 般 1137, 斑 1609, 番 1773, 飯 1964, 榛 2108, 幡 2261, 範 2384, 盤 2399, 磐 2400, 藩 2771, 繁 2848, 攀 2851)
Hana *sf* 花 481. (芳 480, 花 481, 英 693, 胖 843, 班 1075, 華 1266, 塙 1845, 鼻 2206)
Hanabō *s* 花坊 481
Hanabungo *ml* 鼻豊後 2206
Hanabusa *s* 花房 481, 纐纈 2966; *sm-p* 英 693
~ Itchō *ma* 英一蝶
~ sōshi *l* 英草紙
Hana chiru sato *l* 花散里 481
Hanada *s* 花田
~ Hiroshi *ml* 花田比露思 ⌈輝
~ Kiyoteru *ml* 花田清
Hanae *f* 花枝, 花笑, 花
Hanagasa *s* 花笠 ⌊恵
Hanagasaki *s* 花ケ崎
Hanagata *s* 花形
Hanagatami *la* 花筐
Hanagi *s* 花木
Hanago *la* 花子
Hanagoyomi hasshōjin *l* 花暦八笑人
Hanai *s* 花井
Hanaizumi *p* 花泉
Hanaka *m* 花香
Hanakawa *s* 花川
Hanako *f* 花子, 春中子 963, 華子 1266 ⌈2206
Hanakongō *ma* 鼻金剛
Hanamaki *p* 花巻 481
Hanami *s* 土海 42, 花見 481
Hanamizu *s* 花水
Hanamori *m* 花守
Hanamoto *s* 花本
Hanamura *s* 花村
Hanamure *s* 花簇
Hanano *s* 花野
Hana no en *l* 花宴
Hanao *s* 花生
Hanaoka *s* 花岡, 華岡 1266 ⌈481
~ Kenji *ml* 花岡謙二
Hanari *s* 羽成 246
Hanasakajii *l* 花咲爺
Hanasato *s* 花里 ⌊481
(hanashi 咄 1046)
Hanashibon *l* 咄本
Hanashima *s* 花島 481
Hanatani *s* 花谷
Hanaue *s* 花上, 花植
Hanawa *sf-p* 塙 1845; *sp* 花輪 481

Hanawada *s* 塙田 1845
Hanawa Dan'emon *mh-l* 塙団右衛門
~ Hokinoichi *ml* 塙保己一
Hanaya *s* 花谷 481, 花家, 花屋 ; *p* 花矢
Hanayama *sp* 花山
Hanayanagi *s* 花柳
Hanayasu *s* 花安
Hanazaki *s* 花崎
Hanazakura oru shōshō *l* 花桜折る少将
Hanazawa *s* 花沢
Hanazono *sp* 花園
Hanazuka *s* 花塚
Hanba *s* 半場 213, 朱馬 341 「原 2108
Hanbara *s* 半原 213, 榛
Handa *s* 吐田 242, 見田 518, 飯田 1964 ; *sp* 半田 213
Handani *s* 半谷
Handa Ryōhei *ml* 半田良平 「義之
~ Yoshiyuki *ml* 半田
Handayū *ma* 半太夫
Handō *s* 半藤
Hane *s* 羽根 246. (羽)
Haneda *s* 羽根田, 判門田 434 ; *sp* 羽田 246
Haneguri *s* 羽栗
Hanekawa *s* 羽川
Hanemochi *s* 羽, 羽茂, 羽咋
Hanesaka *s* 塙坂 1845
Hangae *s* 榛谷 2108
Hangaya *s* 半谷 213, 榛谷 2108 「213
Hangetsushū *l* 半月集
Hani *s* 羽仁 246. (土 42, 赤 443, 埴 1561) 「246
~ Gorō *ml* 羽仁五郎
Haniioshiragibito *s* 埴盧新羅人 1561
Hanishi *sfl* 土師 42 ; *m* 土作
Hanishibe *s* 土師部
Hanishina *p* 埴科 1561
Haniwara *s* 埴原
Haniya *s* 埴谷
~ Yutaka *ml* 埴谷雄高
Hanji *m* 半治 213
Hanjo *la* 班女 1075
Hanjūshin *l* 半獣神 213
Hankanpu *lh* 藩翰譜 2771
Hankechi *l* 手巾 118
Hanma *s* 半間 213
Hanmo *s* 番御 1773
Hanmonten *p* "Panmunjon" 板門店 632
Hanningen *l* 半人間 213
Hanno *s* 半乃, 判乃 434
Hannō *p* 飯能 1964
Hannoura *p* 羽ノ浦 246
Hanoi *p* "Hanoi" 河内 597 「平 2384
Hanpei *m* 半平 213, 範
Hanpeida *m* 半平太 213
Hanshirō *m* 半四郎
Hanta *s* 範田 2384
Hantarō *m* 半太郎 213
Han'ya *s* 半谷, 垣谷 795 ; *m* 奇弥 752
Han'yō *s* 榛葉 2108
Hanyū *s* 土生 42, 丹生 79, 半布 213, 羽二生 246, 羽入, 羽丹生, 赤生 443, 波入 596, 埴入 1561 ; *sp* 羽生 246 ; *m* 赤 443 「213
Hanzaburō *m* 半三郎
Hanzaemon *m* 半左衛門
Hanzaike *s* 繁在家 2848
Hanzan *p* 飯山 1964
Hanzawa *s* 半沢 213, 榛沢 2108
Hanzō *m* 半造 213, 伴三 361, 範三 2384
Happō *s* 八方 19
Happōya *s* 八甫谷
Hara *s* 蕃良 2371 ; *sp* 原 1231. (原, 腹 1871)
~ Asao *fl* 原阿佐緒
Harada *s* 原田 ⌊1231
~ Hinjin *ml* 原田浜人
~ Magoshichirō *mh* 原田孫七郎
~ Minoru *ml* 原田実
~ Taneji *ml* 原田種茅
~ Yasuko *fl* 原田康子
~ Yoshito *ml* 原田義人 「舟
Hara Gesshū *ml* 原月
Haragi *s* 原木
Haraguchi *s* 原口
Harahashi *s* 原橋
Hara Hōitsuan *ml* 原抱一庵
Harai *s* 暗 1883. (祓 1125)
Haraigawa *s* 祓川
Haraji *s* 原地 1231
Haraka *m* 腹赤 1871
Harakawa *s* 原川 1231
Harako *sf* 原子
~ Kōhei *ml* 原子公平
Harakoshi *s* 原越
Haramaki *s* 腹巻 1871, 服巻 618
Harami *s* 腹目 1871 ; *m* 原見 1231. (孕 274)
Haramiishi *sp* 孕石 274
Haramura *s* 原村 1231
Harano *s* 原野
Haranofuefuki *s* 大角吹 48 「1231
Haranomachi *p* 原町
Hara Saburō *ml* 原三郎
~ Sekitei *ml* 原石鼎
Harashima *s* 原島
Hara Tamiki *ml* 原民喜
~ Tanzan *ml* 原坦山
Harayama *s* 原山
Harazaki *s* 原崎
Harazawa *s* 原沢
(hare 晴 1597, 霽 2978)
Hareyoshi *m* 晴善 1597
Hari *f* 針 1155. (針, 梁 1475, 張 1879, 蓁 1984, 榛 2108, 播 2259, 霽 2978)
Harigae *s* 張替 1879
Harigai *s* 針貝 1155
Harigane *s* 針金
Harigatani *s* 針ケ谷, 針谷
Harihara *s* 蓁原 1984
Harikawa *s* 梁川 1475
Hariki *m* 張幹 1879
Harima *s* 張間 ; *sph* 播磨 2259
Harimanokuni *ph* 播磨国
~ no fudoki *l* 播磨国風土記
Harimoto *s* 張本 1879, 播本 2259
Harishige *s* 針重 1155
Haritsuka *s* 針塚
Haritsuke Mozaemon *la* 礫茂左衛門 2486
Hariya *s* 針屋 1155
Haru *s* 施 831 ; *sf* 春 963 ; *f* 波留 596. (大 48, 元 60, 日 77, 内 81, 令 155, 立 194, 合 270, 全 271, 会 454, 花 481, 玄 522, 明 623, 知 636, 孟 667, 青 700, 良 767, 東 771, 怡 808, 治 825, 施 831, 弨 833, 珍 836, 昭 841, 美 923, 春 963, 栄 969, 迢 1000, 浩 1068, 時 1086, 始 1092, 華 1266, 脩 1281, 流 1332, 敏 1409, 晏 1458, 啓 1491, 喧 1541, 陽 1567, 温 1585, 晴 1597, 奢 1706, 喜 1709, 開 1821, 婼 1869, 張 1879, 暖 1882, 詮 1934, 遐 2048, 榛 2108, 給 2149, 鋪 2340, 遙 2421, 蘇 2841, 霽 2978) 「栄明 969
Haruaki *s* 春秋 963 ; *m*
Haruakira *m* 玄明 522, 治剣 825
Harubara *s* 春原 963
Haruchika *m* 明親 623, 春及 963, 春周, 春邇
Harue *s* 春殖 ; *m-f* 春枝 ; *m-p* 春江 ; *f* 春恵
Harueda *s* 春枝
Harufuji *s* 春藤
Haruhi *p* 春日
Haruhiko *m* 東彦 771, 春良 963, 春彦, 晴比古 1597
Haruhiro *m* 玄広 522
Haruhisa *m* 春久 963
Harui *s* 春井
Haruichi *m* 春一
Haruji *m* 春治, 春路, 蘇二 2841
Harujirō *m* 春次郎 963
Haruka *m* 遐 2048, 遙 2421, 遼 2590
Harukage *m* 晴景 1597
Harukata *s* 春遂 963 ; *m* 霽堅 2978
Harukawa *s* 春川 963
Haruki *s* 春木 ; *m* 開城 1821. (開)
Haruko *f* 全子 271, 玄子 522, 東子 771, 怡子 808, 治子 825, 美子 923, 春小 963, 春子, 迢子 1000, 喧子 1541, 晴子 1597, 婼子 1869, 暖子 1882, 遐子 2048
Harukuni *m* 治国 825
Harumaki *s* 晴枝 1597
Harumaru *m* 晴丸

Harumasa *m* 玄上 522, 春譲 963
Harumi *m* 治胤 825, 春泉 963, 春海, 霽見 2978
Harumichi *s* 春道 963
Harumitsu *m* 治三 825, 治通, 春光 963
Harumori *m* 治保 825
Harumoto *s* 春本 963
Haruna *s* 春名; *m* 春魚; *m-p* 榛名 2108
Harunaga *m* 治脩 825
Haruno *p* 春野 963
Harunobu *m* 春山; *ma* 春信
Harunori *m* 啓徳 1491
Harunosuke *m* 治之助 825
Haruo *m* 大夫 48, 孟雄 667, 春夫 963, 春生, 春雄, 晴夫 1597
Haruru *m* 晴 「治済
Harusada *m* 治貞 825,
Harusame *l* 春雨 963
Harushige *m* 美樹 923, 春重 963, 春樹, 春繁
Harushima *s* 春島
Harusue *m* 晴季 1597
Haruta *s* 治田 825, 春田 963
Harutaka *m* 晴賢 1597
Harutarō *m* 春太郎 963
Haruteru *m* 晴輝 1597
Haruto *m* 玄門 522, 治人 825, 春門 963
Harutomo *m* 晴具 1597
Harutsugedori *l* 春告鳥 963 「張次 1879
Harutsugu *m* 玄次 522,
Harutsuna *m* 流綱 1332, 晴綱 1597
Haruura *m* 玄上 522
Haruyama *s* 春山 963, 晴山 1597 「963
～ Yukio *ml* 春山行夫
Haruyasu *m* 敏保 1409
Haruyo *m* 春節 963
Haruyoshi *m* 内膳 81, 治祇 825, 昭良 841
Haruzumi *s* 春澄 963
Haruzō *m* 春三
Haryū *s* 針生 1155
～ Ichirō *ml* 針生一郎
Hasada *s* 羽佐田 246
Hasaki *p* 波崎 596
Hasama *s* 羽佐間 246; *sp* 挾間 1048; *p* 迫 747

Hasami *p* 波佐見 596
Hase *sp* 長谷 939; *p* 初瀬 427. (丈 36, 支 63)
～ Ken *ml* 長谷健 939
Haseba *s* 長谷場
Hasebe *s* 丈部 36, 走部 441, 長谷部 939
Hasebeji *s* 丈部路 36
Hasegawa *s* 長谷河 939; *sp* 長谷川 「銀作
～ Ginsaku *ml* 長谷川
～ Izumi *ml* 長谷川泉
～ Kanajo *fl* 長谷川かな女 「延
～ Kōen *ml* 長谷川幸
～ Minokichi *ml* 長谷川巳之吉
～ Nyozekan *ml* 長谷川如是閑
～ Reiyoshi *ml* 長谷川零余子 「雨
～ Shigure *fl* 長谷川時
～ Shin *ml* 長谷川伸
～ Shirō *ml* 長谷川四郎 「逝
～ Sosei *ml* 長谷川素
～ Tenkei *ml* 長谷川天渓 「等伯
～ Tōhaku *ma* 長谷川
Hasekura *s* 支倉 63
～ Tsunenaga *mh* 支倉常長
Hasemi *s* 長谷見 939
Haseo *m* 長雄
Hasetsuka *s* 丈 36
Hasetsukabe *s* 丈部, 杖部 422 「939
Haseyama *sp* 長谷山
Hashi *s* 橋 2485. (美 923, 梯 1617, 間 1822, 階 1840, 端 2306, 箸 2381, 橋 2485) 「場 2485
Hashiba *s* 羽柴 246, 橋
Hashibe *s* 橋部
Hashi Benkei *la* 橋弁
Hashida *s* 橋田 ⌊慶
Hashidate *s* 外立 139, 外出, 橋立 2485
Hashida Tōsei *ml* 橋田東声
Hashiguchi *s* 橋口
Hashihime *l* 橋姫
Hashii *s* 八信井 19, 橋井 2485; *m* 端居 2306
Hashikami *p* 階上 1840
Hashikawa *s* 橋川 2485
～ Bunzō *ml* 橋川文三

Hashikura *s* 橋倉
Hashima *sp* 羽島 246
Hashimoto *s* 橋元 2485; *sp* 橋本
～ Eikichi *ml* 橋本英吉
～ Gahō *ma* 橋本雅邦
～ Keiji *ml* 橋本鶏二
～ Mudō *ml* 橋本夢道
～ Sanai *mh* 橋本左内
～ Sōkichi *mh* 橋本宗吉 「子
～ Takako *fl* 橋本多佳
～ Tokuju *ml* 橋本徳寿
Hashimura *s* 橋村
Hashino *s* 橋野
Hashinobe *s* 橋部
Hashio *s* 箸尾 2381
(hashira 柱 854)
(hashiri 走 441) 「1822
Hashiride *s* 走出, 間人
Hashirii *s* 走井 441
Hashiro *s* 波白 596
Hashitani *s* 橋谷 2485
Hashiyama *s* 橋山
Hashizume *s* 橋爪, 橋詰
Hashūdo *s* 間人 1822
(hasu 芙 474, 蓉 1983, 蓮 2197)
Hasuda *sp* 蓮田 2197
～ Zenmei *ml* 蓮田善
Hasui *s* 蓮井 ⌊明
Hasuike *s* 蓮池
Hasumi *s* 荷見 1259, 蓮見 2197, 蓮実; *f* 蓉身 1983; *p* 羽須美 246
Hasumitsu *m* 蓮光 2197
Hasunuma *sp* 蓮沼
Hasuyo *f* 芙代 474
Hasuzono *s* 羽洲園 246
Hata *s* 羽太, 羽田, 伯 363, 波太 596, 波多, 畑 838, 畠 1198, 秦 1202, 端 2306; *sp* 八多 19, 波田 596, 幡多 2261. (果 770, 畑 838, 将 1040, 畠 1198, 秦 1202, 旗 2093, 幡 2261, 端 2306, 機 2869)
Hataaya *s* 幡文 2261
Hatabami *s* 幡多幡美
Hatada *s* 畑田 838
Hatadate *s* 端館 2306
Hatae *s* 波多江 596; *f* 旗江 2093
Hatagama *s* 幡鎌 2261

Hatagawa *s* 畑川 838, 秦川 1202, 幡川 2261
Hatahiko *m* 幡彦
Hatai *s* 羽田井 246, 畑井 838, 幡井 2261
Hataide *s* 秦井手 1202
Hatakake *s* 幡掛 2261
Hatakasu *s* 安口 472
(hatake 畠 1198)
Hatakeda *s* 畠田
Hatakeno *s* 畠野
Hatakeyama *s* 畠山
～ Masanaga *mh* 畠山政長 「重忠
～ Shigetada *mh* 畠山
～ Yoshinari *mh* 畠山義就 「子 2093
Hatako *f* 二十子 4, 旗
Hatakuchi *s* 安口 472
Hatakumi *s* 爪土 115
Hatamu *s* 幡文 2261
Hatanaka *s* 畑中 838, 畠中 1198
Hatano *s* 波田野 596, 波多野, 秦野 1202, 旗野 2093, 幡野 2261; *sp* 畑野 838 「治 596
～ Kanji *ml* 波多野完
Hatanosuke *ml* 将之助 1040
Hatasa *s* 畑佐 838
Hata Sahachirō *mh* 秦佐八郎 1202
Hatashi *m* 果之 770
Hatashō *p* 秦荘 1202
Hatasu *m* 果 770, 倮 1287, 毅 2351
Hatasumi *m* 秦誦 1202
Hata Toyokichi *ml* 秦豊吉 「2261
Hataya *s* 畑屋 838, 幡屋
Hatayama *s* 畑山 838
Hatayasu *s* 安口 472; *m* 果安 770
Hatayo *m* 二十世 4
(hato 鳩 1825, 鴿 2631)
Hatogai *s* 鳩貝 1825
Hatogaya *sp* 鳩ケ谷
Hatoi *s* 鳩居
Hatoko *f* 鳩子
Hatori *s* 羽鳥 246, 服 618, 服部, 織 2879
Hatoribe *s* 織部
Hatoyama *s* 八十八間 19; *sp* 鳩山 1825
～ Ichirō *mh* 鳩山一郎
(hatsu 八 19, 初 427, 泊

592, 発 953, 宋 1178, 逸 1504, 肇 2222)
Hatsuda s 八太 19, 八田, 八多, 初田 427
Hatsugai s 初谷
Hatsugarasu l 初鴉
Hatsugi m 羽衝 246
Hatsugiku f 初菊 427
Hatsujirō m 初次郎
Hatsuka s 羽束 246
Hatsukade s 廿日出 102
Hatsukaichi p 廿日市
Hatsukaiwa s 廿日岩
Hatsukano s 初鹿野 427
Hatsukashi s 羽束 246, 羽束志, 泥 594
Hatsukashibe s 泊橿部 592, 埿部 1492
Hatsuko f 初子 427, 肇子 2222
Hatsume m 初芽 427
Hatsumi s 初見; m 発身 953, 逸見 1504
Hatsune sl 初音 427
Hatsuo m 初偶
Hatsuoka s 初岡
Hatsuru m 果 770
Hatsuse sp 泊瀬 592; m 初瀬 427
Hatsushika s 初鹿
Hatsushima s 初島
Hatsutarō m 初太郎
Hatsuyama s 初山
Hatsuyuki la 初雪
Hatsuzawa s 初沢
Hatta s 八太 19, 八多, 初田 427, 弭田 1072; sp 八田 19
～ Motoo ml 八田元夫
～ Tomonori ml 八田知紀
Hattō p 八東
Hattori s 神服 853; sp 服部 618
～ Bushō ml 服部撫松
～ Dohō ml 服部土芳
～ Motoharu ml 服部躬治
～ Nankaku mh 服部南郭
～ Naoto ml 服部直人
～ Ransetsu ml 服部嵐雪
～ Tatsu ml 服部達
～ Yoshika ml 服部嘉香
(hau 這 1515)
Hauta s 這田
Hawai p "Hawaii" 布哇 170; p 羽合 246
Hawaka s 葉若 1991
Haya s 芳養 480; m 敏 1409. (早 295, 夙 299, 迅 307, 快 372, 剣 1151, 隼 1230, 速 1237, 捷 1323, 敏 1409, 逸 1504, 粛 1528, 敬 1691, 頓 2115, 駛 2348)
Hayaatsu m 快温 372
Hayabusa s 隼 1230
Hayafuji s 早藤 295
Hayafune s 早船
Hayahiko s 迅彦 307, 逸彦 1504
Hayakawa sp 早川 295
～ Ikutada ml 早川幾忠
Hayakita p 早来
Hayako f 早子, 隼子 1230
Hayakumo s 早雲 295
Hayama s 吐山 242, 羽山 246, 早馬 295, 麓 2903; sp 葉山 1991; m 駛馬 2348, 驥 3008
～ Yoshiki ml 葉山嘉樹 1991
Hayami s 早水 295, 早見, 早速, 頓宮 2115; sm 速 1237, 速水; sm-p 速見
Hayanari s 早生 295; m 逸勢 1504
Hayano s 早野 295
Hayao s 早尾; m 速雄 1237, 捷郎 1323, 駛夫 2348, 駿 2763
Hayasaka s 早坂 295
Hayase s 早瀬, 迅瀬 307
Hayashi s 林 633; m 隼 1230, 速 1237, 敏 1409, 駿 2763
Hayashibara s 林原 633
～ Raisei ml 林原来井
Hayashibe s 林部
Hayashida sp 林田
Hayashide s 林出
Hayashi Fumiko fl 林芙美子
～ Fusao ml 林房雄
～ Hisao ml 林久男
～ Jussai mh 林述斎
～ Keiko fl 林圭子
～ Kokei ml 林古渓
Hayashima sp 早島 295
Hayashi Mikaomi ml 林甕臣 633
～ Nobuatsu mh 林信篤
～ Razan mlh 林羅山
～ Senjūrō mh 林銑十郎
～ Shihei mh 林子平
～ Tatsuo ml 林達夫
Hayashiya s 林屋
Hayashi Yawara ml 林和
～ Yūzō mh 林有造
Hayashizaki s 林崎
Hayata s 早田 295, 隼太 1230
Hayatake s 早竹 295
Hayatarō m 隼太郎 1230
Hayato sm-p 隼人; m 勇人 908, 逸人 1504; m-f 速人 1237
Hayatō s 早藤 295
Hayatsu s 早津
Hayayuki m 隼之 1230
Hayazaki s 早崎 295
Hayuka s 羽床 246, 羽牀
Hazama s 谷 449, 迫間 747, 狭間 790, 廻間 994, 峡 1078, 間 1822
Hazawa s 羽沢 246
Hazu sp 幡豆 2261
Hazuma s 弭間 1072, 弾間 1880
Hazumi s 羽積 246; s 羽住 246; m (he 氏 223, 部 1418, 綣 2532)
(hebi 蛇 1387)
Hebiguchi s 蛇口
Hebizuka s 蛇塚
Hegi s 枌 624
Heguri s 平群; s 平栗 203; sp (hei 丙 198, 平 203, 兵 499, 並 765, 坪 793, 炳 837, 柄 862, 陛 1307, 瓶 1388, 塀 1559, 敝 1686, 餅 2346, 幣 2414)
Heian h 平安 203
Heiankyō ph 平安京
Heibee m 平兵衛
Heichū l 平中
Heiemon m 平右衛門
Heihachi m 平八
Heihachirō m 平八郎
Heiichi m 平一
Heiji m-l 1159–60 平治
Heijirō m 平次郎
Heijō p "Pyongyang" 平壌
Heijōkyō ph 平城京
Heike l-h 平家
～ nyogo no shima la 平家女護島
Heikichi m 平吉
Heikodama s 平児玉
Heikyoku la 平曲
Heima s 平右馬
Heinai m 平内
Heinosuke m 平之助
Heisaburō m 平三郎
Heishi s 平氏, 瓶子 1388
Heishirō m 丙子郎 198, 平四郎 203
Heisuke m 平助
Heita m 平太
Heitarō m 平太郎
Heitsuji s 比叡辻 137
Heiuma s 平右馬 203
Heiwa p 平和
Heizaemon m 平左衛門
Heizō m 平蔵
Heki s 戸来 59; sp 戸木, 日置 77; l 碧 2225. (辟 1919, 碧 2225, 僻 2254, 壁 2585)
Hekida s 日置田 77
Hekigotō ml 碧梧桐 2225
Hekigyokushū l 碧玉集
Hekikai p 碧海
Hekinan p 碧南
Hekobori s 背評 957, 脊許 1212
Hemeden l 変目伝 970
Hemura s 綣村 2532
Hen s 卞 84. (片 82, 辺 179, 変 970, 偏 1273, 遍 1805, 鞭 2752)
Henjō ml 遍昭 1805
Henmi s 辺見 179, 逸見 1504
～ Yūkichi ml 逸見猶吉
Henmura s 綣村 2532
Hentsū Karuizawa l 変通軽井茶話 970
Hera sp 平良 203
Herai s 戸来 59
Heri s 縁 2660
Hesaka s 部坂 1418
(heso 綣 2532)
Hesomura s 綣村
Heta p 戸田 59
Hetsuji s 戸次
Hetsutsu s 平秩 203
Hi s 氷 140. (一 3, 干 26, 火 52, 日 77, 比 137, 氷 140, 丕 163, 妃 411, 彼 578, 披 582, 肥 617, 飭

651, 昆 945, 卑 976, 負 981, 飛 1014, 秘 1117, 毘 1195, 俾 1279, 菊 1451, 啓 1491, 陽 1567, 棐 1780, 斐 1781, 悲 1782, 碑 1908, 槭 2096, 鄙 2173, 榧 2291, 樋 2299, 誹 2321, 綽 2529, 檜 2624, 篋 2845, 靡 2857, 羆 2899)
Hiasa *s* 日浅 77
Hiba *p* 比婆 137
Hibana *s* 日鼻 77
Hibara *s* 肥原 617
Hibari *s* 雲雀 2027
Hibariyama *la* 雲雀山
Hibata *s* 樋畑 2299
Hibi *s* 日弁 77, 日比
(hibiki 響 2981)
Hibikiyama *s* 響山
Hibino *s* 日比野 77
～ Shirō *ml* 日比野士朗
Hibiya *sp* 日比谷
Hichisō *p* 七宗 17
Hida *s* 比田 137, 肥田 617, 飛田 1014, 飛弾, 槭田 2096, 樋田 2299; *m* 斐多 1781; *ph* 飛騨 1014
Hidai *s* 比田井 137
Hidaka *sp* 日高 77
～ Rokurō *ml* 日高六郎
～ Tadaichi *ml* 日高只一
Hidaki *s* 肥田木 617
Hidano *s* 肥田野
Hidari Jingorō *ma* 左甚五郎 169
Hidase *s* 飛弾瀬 1014
Hide *s* 秀 726; *m* 禾 220; *f* 日出 77. (一 3, 之 24, 未 210, 次 226, 任 235, 成 322, 求 537, 寿 539, 幸 661, 英 693, 季 725, 秀 726, 東 771, 品 916, 昆 945, 栄 969, 俶 1026, 毘 1195, 淑 1335, 咄 1354, 彬 1370, 嗣 1937, 愛 2018, 愷 2071, 静 2145, 豪 2177, 標 2298, 続 2334, 衡 2450, 穎 2505, 綉 2531, 継 2539, 薫 2567, 穏 2728)
Hideaki *m* 英斌 693, 秀秋 726, 栄顕 969, 栄耀
Hidebumi *m* 秀文 726
Hidechika *m* 静衡 2145
Hidegorō *m* 英五郎 693
Hidehaya *m* 英早
Hidehiko *m* 英彦
Hidehiro *m* 英熙, 秀恕
Hidehisa *m* 秀能 726
Hideho *m* 秀伯
Hidei *m* 秀猪
Hideichi *m* 秀一
Hideji *m* 英二 693, 秀司 726, 秀次, 秀治
Hidejirō *m* 秀次郎
Hidekai *m* 秀穎 969
Hidekane *m* 秀宝, 栄懐
Hidekatsu *m* 秀一 726
Hidekazu *m* 栄一 969
Hideki *m* 秀来 726, 秀幹, 秀樹, 栄材 969
Hidekichi *m* 英吉 693, 秀吉 726
Hideko *f* 秀子, 昆子 945, 栄子 969, 綉子 2531
Hidekoto *m* 英肇 693
Hidemaro *m* 英麿
Hidemaru *m* 秀円 726
Hidemasu *m* 秀剰
Hidemata *m* 秀復
Hidematsu *m* 秀松
Hidemi *m* 英泉 693, 秀心 726, 秀実, 秀観
Hidemitsu *m* 秀光, 秀臣
Hidemochi *m* 秀用
Hidemori *m* 秀守
Hidemoto *m* 栄帰 969
Hidenaga *m* 英脩 693
Hidenaka *m* 秀央 726
Hidenami *m* 秀並
Hidenari *m* 秀成
Hiden'in *p* 悲田院 1782
Hidenobu *m* 秀延, 秀進, 毘信 1195
Hidenori *m* 一孝 3, 日出雄 77, 寿軌 539, 穎則 2505
Hideo *m* 日出男 77, 日出雄, 英夫 693, 英男, 英雄, 秀夫 726, 秀伯, 秀雄, 東雄 771, 咄夫 1354, 豪夫 2177, 穎雄 2505
Hideoki *m* 秀発 726
Hideomi *m* 秀臣
Hideru *m* 英 693 726
Hidesaburō *m* 秀三郎
Hidesada *m* 秀完
Hidesane *m* 秀実
Hidesato *m* 秀聖
Hideshi *m* 秀, 秀司
Hideshige *m* 英薫 693
Hideshima *s* 秀島 726
Hidesuke *m* 愷介 2071
Hidetada *m* 秀忠 726
Hidetaka *m* 英雄 693, 秀嶠 726
Hidetake *m* 秀武
Hidetame *m* 英為 693
Hidetarō *m* 英太郎, 秀太郎 726
Hideteru *m* 秀煌
Hidetō *mh* 秀能
Hidetomi *m* 秀禧
Hidetora *m* 秀虎
Hidetoshi *m* 英敏 693
Hidetsugu *m* 英二, 秀次 726, 秀世
Hidetsune *m* 英寿 693, 秀典 726
Hidetsurumaru *m* 日出鶴丸 77
Hideya *p* 日出谷
Hideyasu *m* 秀康 726
Hideyo *m* 秀世
Hideyori *m* 秀頼
Hideyoshi *m* 秀吉, 秀兆 秀幸 726
Hideyuki *m* 英征 693,
Hidezō *m* 秀三, 秀造
Hie *p* 日吉 77. (稗 2123)
Hieda *s* 稗田
～ no Are *ml* 稗田阿礼
Hieizan *p* 比叡山 137
Hie Jinja *p* 日吉神社 77
Hienuki *p* 稗貫 2123
Hiezu *p* 日吉津 77
Hifu *f* 一二 3
Hifumi *f* 一二三
Hifuno *f* 一二野
(higa 僻 2254)
Higagoto shirabe *l* 僻言調
Higaki *sla* 檜垣 2624
Higano *s* 日向野 77
Higan-sugi made *l* 彼岸過迄 578
Higasa *s* 暈 1997
Higashi *s* 干河岸 26; *sp* 東 771. (東)
Higashiango *s* 東安居
Higashi-asai *p* 東浅井
～ -awakura *p* 東粟倉
Higashibōjō *s* 東坊城
Higashi-chichibu *p* 東秩父
～ -chikuma *p* 東筑摩
Higashida *s* 東田
Higashidani *s* 東谷
Higashide *s* 東出
Higashidōri *p* 東通
Higashifushimi *s* 東伏見
Higashigawa *sp* 東川
Higashihara *s* 東原
Higashi-ibaraki *p* 東茨城
～ -ichiki *p* 東市来
～ -iwai *p* 東磐井
～ -iyayama *p* 東祖谷山
～ -izu *p* 東伊豆
～ -izumo *p* 東出雲
Higashijō *s* 東条
Higashi-kagura *p* 東神楽
～ -kamo *p* 東加茂
～ -kanbara *p* 東蒲原
～ -kasugai *p* 東春日井
Higashikata *s* 東方
Higashi-katsushika *p* 東葛飾
Higashiko *f* 東子
Higashi-kubiki *p* 東頸城
Higashikuni *s* 東久邇
～ Naruhiko *mh* 東久邇稔彦
Higashi-kunisaki *p* 東国東
～ -kushira *p* 東串良
～ -kutchan-kō *l* 東倶知安行
Higashikuze *s* 東久世
Higashima *s* 東島
Higashi-matsuura *p* 東松浦
～ -matsuyama *p* 東松山
～ -mokoto *p* 東藻琴
～ -morokata *p* 東諸県
Higashimura *s* 東村
Higashi-murayama *p* 東村山
～ -muro *p* 東牟婁
～ -nada *p* 東灘
Higashinari *s* 東生; *p* 東成
Higashi-naruse *p* 東成瀬
Higashine *p* 東根
Higashino *sp* 東野
Higashi-nose *p* 東能瀬
Higashio *s* 東尾
Higashi-okitama *p* 東置賜
Higashionna *s* 東恩納
Higashi-rishiri *p* 東利尻
Higashisanjō *s* 東三条

Higashi-sefuri *p* 東背振 「河
～ -shirakawa *p* 東白
～ -sonogi *p* 東彼杵
～ -sumiyoshi *p* 東住吉
～ -tagawa *p* 東田川
～ -takasu *p* 東鷹栖
～ -tonami *p* 東砺波
～ -tottori *p* 東鳥取
～ -tsugaru *p* 東津軽
～ -tsuno *p* 東津野
Higashiura *sp* 東浦
Higashi-usuki *p* 東臼杵
～ -uwa *p* 東宇和
Higashiyama *sp* 東山
～ -dono no sakura no iromaku *la* 東山殿花五彩幕 「東山梨
Higashi-yamanashi *p*
Higashiyama sakura sōshi *la* 東山桜荘子
Higashi-yatsushiro *p* 東八代 「川
～ -yodogawa *p* 東淀
Higashiyoka *p* 東与賀
Higashi-yoshino *p* 東吉野
～ yuri *p* 東由利
Higashizono *s* 東園
Higata *sp* 干潟 26
Higawa *s* 樋川 2299
(hige 髯 2580, 髭 2697, 鬚 2973) 「2580
Higekurō *m* 髯九郎
Higeno *s* 髭野 2697
Higeta *s* 日下田 77
Higetsugu *m* 鬚継 2973
Higo *s* 比護 137; *sph* 肥後 617 「1781
Higochika *m* 斐後前
Higuchi *s* 樋口 2299
～ Ichiyō *fl* 樋口一葉
～ Ryūkyō *ml* 樋口竜峡 「2899
Higuma *s* 樋熊; *m* 羆
Higurashi *s* 日夜 77, 日暮 「*l* 向日葵 312
Higuruma *s* 氷車 140;
Higusa *s* 日種 77
Higyō *l* 秘楽 1117
Hihara *s* 日原 77
Hiigawa *p* 斐伊川 1781
Hiiki *s* 日益 77
(hiiragi 柊 860)
Hiiro *s* 日色 77
Hiizu *m* 禾 220, 秀 726
Hiizuru *m* 穏 2728
Hiji *s* 埿 1492; *p* 日出 77. (一 3, 土 42, 肱 844)
Hijikata *s* 一方 3, 土方 42, 土形; *m* 土堅
～ Teiichi *ml* 土方定一
Hijikawa *p* 肱川 844
Hijiki *s* 飛鋪 1014
Hijimaro *m* 土麻呂 42
Hijinoya *s* 泥谷 594
(hijiri 聖 2030)
Hijirimaru *mh* 聖丸
Hijiri yūkaku *l* 聖遊廓
Hijitsuki *s* 辟槻 1919
Hijiwara *s* 土原 42
Hijiya *s* 日出谷 77, 泥谷 594
Hijiyama *s* 日出山 77
Hika *s* 比嘉 137, 俾加 1279
Hikaka *m* 日香蚊 77
Hikami *sp* 氷上 140
Hikari *sp* 光 281
Hikaru *m* 光, 炎 294, 玄 522, 晃 1189, 皓 1639, 煌 1874A, 輝 2499, 璘 2618
～ Genji *lm* 光源氏 281
Hikasa *s* 日笠 77
Hikata *s* 稗方 2123
Hikawa *sp* 氷川 140; *p* 斐川 1781, 簸川 2845
Hikawagishi *s* 干河岸 26
Hiketa *sp* 引田 144
Hiki *s* 日置 77; *sp* 比企 137. (引 144, 疋 166, 匹 187, 卒 732, 牽 2028)
Hikida *s* 比喜田 137, 引田 144, 疋檀 166, 匹田 187, 匹壇
Hikigawa *p* 日置川 77
Hikimi *p* 匹見 187
Hikino *s* 疋野 166
Hikita *s* 疋田, 匹他 187
Hikitani *s* 卒渓 732
Hikiwada *s* 疋和田 166
Hiki Yoshikazu *mh* 比企能員 137
Hiko *m* 彦 1007. (士 41, 久 45, 光 281, 位 354, 良 767, 彦 1007, 孫 1540)
Hikoaki *m* 彦昴 1007
Hikobe *s* 彦部
Hikoda *s* 彦田
Hikoe *m* 彦衛
Hikohimeshiki *l* 孫姫式 1540
Hikohyō *m* 彦兵 1007
Hikoichi *m* 彦一
Hikoishi *m* 彦石
Hikojirō *m* 彦次郎
Hikokubo *s* 彦久保
Hikokurō *m* 彦九郎
Hikoma *m* 彦馬
Hikomatsu *m* 彦松
Hikonahito *s* 孫名人 1540
Hikone *sp* 彦根 1007
Hikonushi *s* 孫主 1540
Hikosaburō *m* 彦三郎
Hikosaka *s* 彦坂 ⌊1007
Hikosuke *m* 彦助
Hikotada *m* 彦士
Hikotari *m* 士十 41
Hikoya *s* 彦家 1007
Hikozō *m* 彦三
(hiku 渥 1856, 攀 2851)
Hikuma *sp* 日前 77
Himatsuri *s* 日祀, 日奉
Hime *f* 媛 1868. (妃 411, 姫 1358, 媛 1868)
Himeda *s* 姫田 1358
Himedo *p* 姫戸
Himeji *p* 姫路
Himeko *f* 姫子; *fh* 卑弥呼 976
Himeno *s* 姫野 1358
Himeshima *sp* 姫島
Himetone *f* 命婦 671
Himi *p* 氷見 140
Himiko *fh* 卑弥呼 976
Himuka *m* 日向 77
Himuro *sla* 氷室 140
(hin 玢 604, 品 916, 浜 1070, 彬 1370, 貧 1498, 斌 1590)
(hina 夷 535, 鄙 2173, 穏 2728, 雛 2888)
Hinada *s* 日南田 77, 雛田 2888
Hinade *s* 火撫 52
Hinaga *s* 日永 77, 飛永 1014
Hinagata *s* 雛形 2888
Hinai *sp* 比内 137
Hinaka *s* 日中 77
Hinaki *m* 雛亀 2888
Hinako *s* 日名子 77; *f* 比勿子 137, 雛子 2888
Hinamaro *m* 夷麿 535
Hinameshi *mh* 日並知 77
Hinamori *sp* 夷守 535
Hinase *sp* 日生 77
Hinashi *s* 極月晦 1896
Hinata *s* 日南田 77; *sm-p* 日向
Hinatano *s* 日向野
Hinatsu *s* 日夏
～ Kōnosuke *ml* 日夏耿之介
Hinauta *m* 鄙唄 2173
Hinaya *s* 雛屋 2888
Hinazu *s* 火撫 52
Hine *s* 日根 77 「137
Hinekazura *s* 比尼縵
Hineno *s* 日根野 77
Hino *s* 火野 52, 樋野 2299; *sp* 日野 77
～ Ashihei *ml* 火野葦平 52
Hinode *p* 日ノ出 77
Hinodejima *l* 日の出島
Hinoe *m* 丙 198 「2624
Hinoemata *p* 檜枝岐
Hinohara *p* 檜原
Hinokage *p* 日之影 77
Hinokawakami *l* 簸川上 2845, 簸河上
Hinoki *s* 檜 2624
Hinokuchi *s* 樋口 2299
Hinokuma *s* 日前 77, 樋前 2299, 檜前 2624, 檜隈
Hinomizu *s* 日野水 77
Hinonishi *s* 日野西
Hinoshima *s* 日野島
Hino Sōjō *ml* 日野草城
～ Suketomo *mh* 日野資朝 「子
～ Tomiko *fh* 日野富
Hinpuron *l* 貧富論 1498
Hinuma *s* 日沼 77, 樋 ⌊沼 2299
Hio *s* 日尾 77
Hioki *s* 日沖; *sp* 日置
Hiomi *s* 一二三 3
Hira *s* 日和 77, 比良 137, 平 203. (永 149, 行 245, 旬 301, 成 322, 位 354, 均 387, 夷 535, 担 574, 披 582, 枚 630, 英 693, 勃 896, 迪 1001, 挙 1207, 救 1406, 啓 1491, 開 1821, 数 2169, 敷 2355, 衡 2450)
Hirabara *s* 平原 203
Hirabayashi *s* 平林
～ Hatsunosuke *ml* 平林初之助

~ Hyōgo *ml* 平林彪吾
Hirabe *s* 平部
Hiradaira *s* 平平
Hirade *s* 平手, 平出
Hirado *sp* 平戸
Hirafu *m* 比羅夫 137
Hirafuku *s* 平福 203
~ Hyakusui *mla* 平福百穂
Hiraga *sp* 平賀
~ Gennai *mlh* 平賀源内 「元義
~ Motoyoshi *ml* 平賀
(hiragi 柊 860)
Hiragiya *s* 柊屋
Hirahara *s* 櫟原 2963
Hirahata *s* 平畑 203
~ Seitō *ml* 平畑静塔
Hirai *s* 平井, 飛来 1014
~ Banson *ml* 平井晩村 203
Hiraide *s* 平井出, 平出
~ Shū *ml* 平出修
Hiraishi *s* 平石
Hiraiwa *s* 平岩, 平厳
Hiraizumi *sp* 平泉
Hiraka *sp* 平鹿; *m* 平瓮
Hirakata *s* 平方, 平形; *sp* 枚方 630
Hirakawa *sp* 平川 203
Hiraki *s* 平木, 平城; *m* 啓 1491, 開 1821. (開)
~ Hakusei *ml* 平木白星 203 「六
~ Niroku *ml* 平木二
Hirako *sf* 平子
Hirakō *s* 平光
Hiraku *m* 拓 586, 発 953, 通 1239, 啓 1491, 啓久, 開 1821, 豁 2667, 墾 2702
Hirakubo *s* 平久保 203
Hirakuni *s* 平郡
Hirakuri *s* 平栗
Hirakushi *s* 平櫛
Hirama *s* 平間
Hiramaro *m* 日良麿 77, 比良麿 137
Hiramatsu *s* 平松 203
Hirame *s* 平目
Hirami *s* 平見
Hiramine *s* 平峯
Hiramitsu *sm* 平光
Hiramori *sm* 平森; *m* 平林
Hiramoto *s* 平元, 平本
Hiranai *p* 平内
Hirano *s* 比良野 137, 平野 203, 枚野 630 「203
~ Banri *ml* 平野万里
~ Ken *ml* 平野謙
~ Kuniomi *mh* 平野国臣 「宣紀
~ Nobunori *ml* 平野
Hiranori *m* 平昇
Hiranuma *s* 平沼
~ Kiichirō *mh* 平沼騏一郎
Hirao *s* 平尾, 平保; *sp* 平生; *m* 平夫
Hiraoka *s* 平岡; *sp* 枚岡 630
Hiraomi *m* 夷臣 535
Hirasa *s* 平佐 203
Hirasaka *s* 平坂
Hirasawa *s* 平沢
~ Keishichi *ml* 平沢 ⌊計七
Hirase *s* 平瀬
Hirashima *s* 平島
Hirata *s* 辟田 1919; *sp* 平田 203, 枚田 630
~ Atsutane *ml* 平田篤胤 「三郎
~ Jisaburō *ml* 平田次
~ Tokuboku *ml* 平田 ⌊禿木
Hirate *s* 平手
Hirato *s* 平戸
Hiratomi *s* 平富
Hirato Renkichi *ml* 平戸廉吉
Hiratori *sp* 平取
Hiratsuka *sp* 平塚
~ Haruko *fh* 平塚明 ⌊子
Hirauchi *s* 平内
Hirawa *s* 平和
Hirawatari *s* 平渡
Hiraya *sp* 平谷
Hirayama *s* 平山
~ Rokō *ml* 平山蘆江
Hirayanagi *s* 平柳
Hirayoshi *s* 衡能 2450
Hirazumi *s* 平住 203
Hiro *s* 広 316; *m* 門 601; *f* 泱 589, 綽 2529. (口 29, 丈 36, 大 48, 戸 59, 丑 99, 太 105, 仮 122, 外 139, 氾 143, 礼 146, 公 156, 丕 163, 央 182, 四 188, 汎 249, 先 280, 光 281, 広 316, 泛 395, 汪 401, 弘 410, 助 431, 谷 449, 完 471, 芼 476, 玄 522, 坦 574, 披 582, 拓 586, 泱 589, 門 601, 明 623, 官 672, 宏 674, 宗 679, 昊 711, 衍 786, 拡 799, 拾 802, 恢 806, 洪 811, 洸 813, 洞 821, 洋 822, 弥 832, 胖 843, 祖 850, 郊 888, 勃 896, 宥 918, 栄 969, 厚 985, 彦 1007, 倶 1028, 浩 1068, 容 1182, 泰 1203, 野 1398, 郭 1417, 都 1419, 曼 1457, 恕 1483, 啓 1491, 展 1501, 博 1534, 孫 1540, 測 1578, 皖 1639, 裕 1645, 転 1656, 敞 1688, 敬 1691, 尋 1705, 衆 1762, 景 1764, 普 1792, 達 1810, 滉 1848, 溥 1852, 漠 1853, 淵 1858, 解 1923, 紘 1949, 寛 1977, 豊 2013, 倜 2054, 演 2079, 碩 2116, 嘉 2184, 廓 2239, 聞 2244, 播 2259, 潤 2277, 勲 2407, 熙 2409, 衡 2450, 衛 2452, 綽 2529, 熹 2560, 凞 2583, 優 2599, 濶 2611, 鴻 2614, 緩 2659, 豁 2667, 厳 2706, 闊 2710, 簡 2788, 曠 2796)
Hirō *s* 平生 203, 拾 802
Hiroaki *sm* 泰右 1203; *m* 弘亨 410, 弘明, 弘耿, 拓章 586, 野口 1398, 博彣 1534
Hirobe *s* 広部 316
Hirobumi *m* 弘記 410, 博文 1534
Hiroe *s* 広江 316; *f* 宏枝 674, 洸江 813, 測江 1578
Hirofumi *m* 碩文 2116
Hirohara *s* 広原 316
Hiroharu *m* 弘玄 410
Hirohashi *s* 広橋 316; *sm* 広端 「広鰭
Hirohata *s* 広畑, 広幡,
Hirohide *m* 汎秀 249, 博英 1534, 熙栄 2409
Hirohisa *m* 裕弥 1645
Hirohito *m* 礼云 146, 裕仁 1645 「広矛
Hirohoko *m* 広戈 316,
Hiroi *s* 広井; *sm* 広居
Hiroichi *m* 弘一 410
Hiroichirō *m* 広一郎 316, 弘一郎 410
Hiroie *m* 弘家
Hirojirō *m* 広次郎 316
Hirokage *m* 熙景 2409
Hirokami *p* 広神 316
Hirokata *m* 広斥, 弘毅 410
Hirokatsu *m* 門勝 601
Hirokawa *sp* 広川 316
Hiroke *f* 展狂 1501
Hiroki *s* 広木 316; *m* 啓喜 1491
Hirokichi *m* 広吉 316
Hirokitsu *s* 尋来津 1705
Hirokiyo *m* 弘精 410, 厳浄 2706
Hiroko *f* 大子 48, 氾子 143, 央子 182, 光子 281, 泛子 395, 汪子 401, 完子 471, 芼子 476, 拾子 802, 恢子 806, 宥子 918, 浩子 1068, 郭子 1417, 恕子 1483, 皓子 1639, 裕子 1645, 敞子 1688, 景子 1764, 普子 1792, 解子 1923, 熙子 2409, 凞子 2583, 濶子 2611, 緩子 2659, 闊子 2710, 簡子 2788
Hirokore *m* 広惟 316
Hirokuni *m* 広国, 博邦 1534, 播州 2259
Hiromatsu *s* 広松 316
Hirome *m* 広人, 弘 410, 弘馬
Hiromi *m* 広相 316, 弘視 410, 弘毅, 寛申 1977, 潤身 2277; *p* 広見 316
Hirōmi *sm* 広海, 浩洋 1068
Hiromichi *m* 丕道 163, 広通 316, 広道, 弘達 410, 豁通 2667
Hiromitsu *m* 弘光 410, 拡充 799
Hiromo *m* 光雲 281
Hiromori *m* 広守 316, 容盛 1182
Hiromoto *m* 広元 316, 博林 1534
Hiromu *m* 弘 410, 坦 574, 拡 799, 洋六 822, 恕 1483, 啓 1491, 博 1534, 熙 2409, 凞 2583
Hiromura *m* 弘邑 410
Hiromushi *m* 広虫 316
Hironaga *m* 広大

Hironaka *s* 広中, 弘中 410; *m* 廓髄 2239
Hironao *m* 大直 48, 広胖 316 「1977
Hirondo *m* 広人, 寛人
Hironiwa *sm* 広庭 316
Hirono *sp* 広野
Hironobu *m* 宏亘 674, 博進 1534
Hironori *m* 丑徳 99, 弘訓 410, 弘毅
Hironuki *m* 啓貫 1491
Hironuma *s* 広沼 316
Hiroo *m* 泱夫 589, 洋大 822, 啓夫 1491, 漢男 1853, 豁夫 2667; *m-p* 広尾 316 「410
Hirooka *s* 広岡, 弘岡
Hirosada *m* 弘涉
Hirosaki *s* 広崎 316; *p* 弘前 410
Hirosato *m* 大慧 48
Hirosawa *s* 広沢 316
Hirose *s* 弘瀬 410; *sp* 広瀬 316, 弘世 410
～ Tesshi *ml* 広瀬哲士 316
Hiroshi *m* 大 48, 仁 57, 氾 143, 礼 146, 央 182, 未 211, 汎 249, 光 281, 広 316, 広志, 汪 401, 弘 410, 弘矣, 完 471, 昊 482, 寿 539, 坦 574, 拓 586, 泱 589, 京 663, 宙 673, 宏 674, 昊 711, 周 736, 衍 786, 拡 799, 洪 811, 洸 813, 洽 816, 洋 822, 弥蔓 832, 厚 985, 浩 1068, 寛 1177, 容 1182, 泰 1203, 庬 1241, 恕 1483, 啓 1491, 博 1534, 湖 1584, 皓 1639, 裕 1645, 敞 1688, 敬 1691, 尋 1705, 普 1792, 滉 1848, 滂 1850, 溥 1852, 紘 1949, 寛 1977, 豊 2013, 僩 2054, 徹 2055, 演 2079, 潭 2269, 潤 2277, 熙 2409, 凞 2583, 瀾 2611, 鴻 2614, 豁 2667, 闊 2710, 曠 2796, 曠詞, 績 2812; *f* 潯 2270
Hiroshige *m* 礼重 146, 広城 316, 広滋; *ma* 広重
Hiroshima *sp* 広島
Hiroshina *s* 広階
Hirosue *m* 熹季 2560
Hirosuke *m* 大翼 48, 広介 316, 広助, 博介 1534
Hirota *s* 弘田 410; *sp* 広田 316; *m* 広太
Hirotada *m* 敬直 1691
Hirotae *m* 広市 316
Hirotake *m* 弘毅 410
Hirota Kōki *mh* 広田弘毅 316
Hirotani *s* 広谷
Hirotarō *m* 広太郎, 博太郎 1534
Hirota-sha utaawase *l* 広田社歌合 316
Hiroto *m* 宏富 674, 博音 1534
Hirōto *m* 寛人 1977
Hirotomo *m* 礼朝 146, 広曹 316, 広寛
Hirotsu *s* 広津
Hirotsugu *m* 太次 105, 広次 316, 弘調 410
Hirotsu Kazuo *ml* 広津和郎 316
～ Ryūrō *ml* 広津柳浪
Hirouji *m* 太氏 105
Hiroumi *sm* 広海 316, 浩洋 1068
Hirowake *m* 広弁 316
Hirowatari *s* 広渡
Hiroya *s* 広谷, 広屋; *m* 磧哉 2116
Hiroyama *s* 広山 316
Hiroyasu *m* 公靖 156, 広居 316
Hiroyoshi *m* 汎慶 249, 広楽 316, 弘達 410, 弘義, 弘廬, 官佳 672, 博精 1534, 敬佶 1691, 寛恵 1977, 寛剛, 豊恵 2013
Hiroyuki *m* 弘之 410, 浩運 1068, 博之 1534
Hirozō *m* 広蔵 316, 博蔵 1534, 熙造 2409
Hiru *s* 比留 137. (日 77, 昼 983, 蛯 1650, 蛭 1920, 蒜 1986)
Hirui *sp* 昼飯 983
Hiruka *s* 蛭可 1920
Hirukawa *s* 蛭河; *sp* 蛭川
Hiruma *s* 比留間 137, 昼間 983, 蛭間 1920
Hiruno *s* 蛯野 1650
Hiruta *s* 蛭田 1920, 蒜田 1986
Hiruzono *m* 蒜園
Hisa *s* 久 45, 必佐 120, 比佐 137. (九 16, 之 24, 久 45, 上 47, 文 86, 旧 119, 比 137, 引 144, 永 149, 古 154, 央 182, 平 203, 仙 228, 向 312, 玖 409, 芬 477, 寿 539, 往 579, 奄 668, 昔 699, 学 719, 尚 753, 良 767, 者 769, 恒 809, 弥 832, 胡 879, 故 880, 宣 919, 長 939, 栄 969, 契 980, 昶 1004, 修 1038, 桐 1103, 書 1216, 陳 1311, 能 1397, 剛 1429, 常 1463, 留 1470, 悠 1481, 商 1526, 亀 1531, 敝 1686, 敞 1688, 喜 1709, 富 1715, 韮 1728, 説 2143, 藤 2773, 懿 2958)
Hisaaki *m* 尚知 753
Hisabumi *m* 修文 1038
Hisachika *m* 久浮 45, 久慎 「879
Hisae *f* 央江 182, 胡江
Hisagi *m* 楸 1890
(hisago 匏 1655, 瓢 2668)
Hisagoko *f* 匏子 1655
Hisagorō *m* 瓢郎 2668
Hisaharu *m* 久明 45, 常治 1463 「彦 809
Hisahiko *m* 久寛 45, 恒
Hisai *p* 久居 45
Hisaichi *m* 寿一 539
Hisaichirō *m* 久一郎 45
Hisaita *s* 久板 「郎
～ Eijirō *ml* 久板栄二
Hisaji *m* 久次, 央二 182, 玖次 409
Hisajima *s* 久島 45
Hisaka *s* 日坂 77, 檜坂 2624
Hisakata *m* 久雄 45
Hisakatsu *m* 長克 939, 長亮
Hisakawa *s* 久川 45
Hisaki *s* 久木; *m* 寿樹 539
Hisako *f* 九子 16, 久子 45, 古子 154, 向子 312, 寿子 539, 弥子 832, 昆沙子 945, 常子 1463
Hisama *s* 久間 45
Hisamatsu *s* 久松
～ Sen'ichi *ml* 久松潜一
Hisamichi *m* 久進
Hisamitsu *sm* 久光
Hisamochi *m* 久採
Hisamoto *sm* 久本; *m* 久柄, 久順
Hisamune *sm* 久宗
Hisamura *s* 久村; *m* 久域 「久大
Hisanaga *s* 久永; *m*
Hisanao *m* 寿巨 539
Hisanari *m* 久容 45
Hisano *s* 久野
Hisanobu *m* 九申 16
Hisanohama *p* 久之浜 45 「徳 753
Hisanori *m* 寿準 539, 尚
Hisao *m* 久雄 45, 寿男 539, 寿雄, 恒夫 809, 宣夫 919, 昶夫 1004, 悠夫 1481, 亀夫 1531, 喜雄 1709, 富男 1715
Hisasato *s* 久郷 45
Hisashi *sm* 亀 1531; *m* 十 18, 久 45, 仁 57, 永 149, 央 182, 旡 279, 序 507, 寿 539, 尚 753, 恆 805, 恒 809, 弥 832, 長 939, 栄 969, 常 1463, 悠 1481, 亀史 1531
Hisata *s* 久田 45
Hisato *m* 久仁, 寿人 539, 長人 939
Hisatome *s* 久留 45
Hisatomi *sm* 久富
Hisatomo *m* 久作, 尚同 753
Hisatoshi *m* 久利 45, 久幹, 古寿 154
Hisatsugi *sm* 久継 45
Hisatsugu *m* 久次, 久接, 久語, 久静, 古子 154 「*m* 尚経 753
Hisatsune *sm* 久恒 45;
Hisatsura *m* 久連 45, 久葛
Hisaya *s* 久家; *m* 久弥
Hisayama *sp* 久山
Hisayasu *m* 久雍, 胡保 879
Hisayoshi *sm* 久吉 45; *m* 久宣, 久徴, 寿吉 539, 寿祺 「尚敬
Hisayuki *m* 尚志 753,
Hisaza *s* 久座 45
Hisazumi *s* 久住

(hishi 菱 1449)
Hishida s 菱田 「草
～ Shunsō ma 菱田春
Hishie f 菱江 「刈
Hishikari s 菱苅；p 菱
Hishikawa s 菱川
～ Moronobu ma 菱川師宣
Hishiki s 菱木
Hishima s 飛島 1014
Hishimura s 菱村 1449
Hishinuma s 菱沼
Hishitani s 菱谷
Hishiya s 日出谷 77, 菱屋 1449, 熊取谷 2410, 羆取谷 2899
Hishiyama s 菱山 1449
～ Shūzō ml 菱山修三
Hisoka m 密 1713
Hisomu m 比曾牟 137, 潜 2272
Hita s 飛鳴 1014；p 日田 77. (牽 2028)
Hitachi sp 日立 77；ph 常陸 1463 「国
Hitachinokuni ph 常陸
～ no fudoki l 常陸国風土記 「田
Hitachi Ōta p 常陸太
Hitaka m 氷高 140
Hitani s 日谷 77
Hitarashi s 日夜
Hito m 人 14, 比登 137, 比等. (一 3, 人 14, 士 41, 仁 57, 他 129, 云 147, 公 156, 史 183, 仙 228, 民 333, 兵 499, 侍 559, 即 648, 者 769, 客 917, 倫 1037, 翁 1430, 寛 1977, 儒 2432)
Hitō p "Philippines" 比島 137
Hitoe f 仁江 57
Hitokabegawa p 人首川 14
Hitokami m 人上
Hito ka oni ka l 人耶鬼耶
Hitoki m 一木 3
Hitokoe m 一声
Hitokure l 一塊
Hitomaro m 人丸 14, 人麻呂, 人麿
～ eigu l 人丸影供
Hitomaru s 一円 3
Hitomatsu s 一松
Hitomi s 一見, 人見 14；m 一視 3, 眸 1636；f 瞳 2630 「14
～ Tōmei ml 人見東明
Hitona m 人名
Hitoo s 人尾；m 仁雄
Hitora s 人羅 ⌊57
Hitori s 倭 1283
Hitorigoto l 独言 788
Hitoshi m 一 3, 人 14, 仁 57, 仁志, 匀 72, 文 86, 与 101, 平 203, 伍 229, 同 298, 旬 301, 均 387, 和 638, 斉 701, 恒 809, 倫 1037, 将 1040, 陸 1312, 斎 1454, 斌 1590, 鈞 1674, 欽 1678, 等 1770, 雅 1913, 舜 2017, 準 2041, 精 2131, 結 2151, 衡 2450, 徹 2451, 整 2581, 疇 2799. (等 1770)
Hitoshiko f 等子 「57
Hitosugi s 一杉 3, 仁杉
Hitotsubashi sp 一橋 3
Hitotsugi s 一木
Hitotsuyanagi s 一柳
Hitowa m 人磐 14
Hitoyoshi p 人吉
(hitsu 必 120, 匹 187, 尋 1705, 筆 1769, 弼 2092, 謐 2637A) 「210)
Hitsuji s 日辻 77. (未
Hitsujiko f 未子
Hiuke s 日生下 77
Hiun l 飛雲 1014
Hiura s 日浦 77, 樋浦 2299 「和 137
Hiwa s 上神 47；sp 比
Hiwada sp 日和田 77
Hiwaki p 樋脇 2299
Hiwasa sp 日和佐 77
Hiwatari s 樋渡 2299
(hiya 冷 349)
Hiyakawa s 冷川
Hiyama s 日山 77, 樋山 2299；sp 檜山 2624
Hiyamada s 檜山田
Hiyamuda s 冷牟田 349
Hiyoki s 日能 77
Hiyori s 日和
Hiyorimi m 日和見
Hiyoshi s 日新, 日義；sp 日吉；m 日英, 陽吉 1567
(hiza 膝 2281)
Hizakurige l 膝栗毛
Hizen ph 肥前 617
Hizennokuni ph 肥前国 「風土記
～ no fudoki l 肥前国
Hizono s 檜園 2624
Hizuka s 飛塚 1014
Hizume s 二十九日 4, 十二月晦日 18, 日詰 77, 極月晦 1896, 樋爪 2299
(ho 火 52, 布 170, 帆 239, 伯 363, 甫 533, 歩 694, 秀 726, 保 781, 浦 1067, 畝 1142, 部 1418, 補 1644, 葡 1724, 葆 1726, 蒲 1993, 輔 2133, 蔀 2186, 穂 2308, 鋪 2340, 頬 2503)
Hō s 鳳 2233, 鴇 2280. (方 85, 包 218, 邦 417, 苞 476, 芳 480, 抱 584, 放 606, 朋 616, 昉 619, 房 658, 宝 676, 苞 688, 奉 717, 保 781, 法 824, 祝 851, 封 885, 寀 1178, 捧 1318, 峰 1351, 逢 1516, 傍 1538, 棚 1625, 匏 1655, 報 1667, 紡 1681, 彭 1693, 葆 1726, 喰 1832, 滂 1850, 蜂 1921, 豊 2013, 飽 2165, 蓬 2195, 鳳 2233, 鴇 2280, 鋒 2339, 虣 2519, 褒 2556, 薫 2567, 篷 2689, 縫 2746, 鵬 2795)
Hōan s 法安 824；1120–24 保安 781
Hoashi s 帆足 239
～ Banri mh 帆足万里
Hoatsume s 穂集 2308
Hobara p 保原 781
Hobe s 凡部 37
Hobetsu p 穂別 2308
Hobo s 保母 781, 保保
Hōbutsushū l 宝物集 676
(hochi 祓 1125, 咄 1354)
Hochina s 保知名 781
Hoda s 保田 「2308
Hodani s 保谷, 穂谷
Hodate s 保立 781
(hodo 高 1163, 程 1641, 節 2215)
Hodogaya s 程ケ谷 1641；p 保土ケ谷 781
Hodojima s 程島 1641
Hodokosu m 忠 705, 施 831
Hodoo m 節男 2215
Hodota s 程田 1641
Hodotsuka s 程塚
Hōei 1704–11 宝永 676
Hōen 1135–41 保延 781
Hōga s 法元 824
Hogara m 朗 1394
Hogari s 穂苅 2308, 保刈 781
Hogawa s 保川
Hōgen l 1156–59 保元
Hōgetsu ml 抱月 584
Hogi s 言 439. (寿 539)
Hogura sm 秀倉 726
Hohe s 穂僉 2308
Hōhei m 鳳平 2233
Hōhoku p 豊北 2013
Hoi s 穂井 2308；p 宝飯
Hōichi m 宝一 ⌊676
Hoida s 穂井田 2308
Hōitsu m 蓬伍 2195
Hōji s 傍士 1538；1247–49 宝治 676
～ ninen hyakushu l 宝治二年百首
Hōjiro sp 喰代 1832
Hōjō s 宝性 676；sp 北条 138；p 方城 85
～ Akitoki mh 北条顕時 138 「606
Hōjōgawa la 放生川
Hōjō Hideji ml 北条秀司 138
Hōjōji sp 法城寺 824
Hōjōki l 方丈記 85
Hōjō Makoto ml 北条誠 138 「子
～ Masako fh 北条政
～ Masamura mh 北条政村 「元一
～ Motokazu ml 北条
～ Sanetoki mh 北条実時 「重時
～ Shigetoki mh 北条
～ Sōun mh 北条早雲
～ Takatoki mh 北条高時
～ Tamio ml 北条民雄
～ Tokifusa mh 北条時房 「時政
～ Tokimasa mh 北条
～ Tokimune mh 北条時宗 「時頼
～ Tokiyori mh 北条
～ Tokiyuki mh 北条時行 「政
～ Ujimasa mh 北条氏

~ Ujitsuna *mh* 北条氏綱 「康
~ Ujiyasu *mh* 北条氏
~ Yasutoki *mh* 北条泰時 「義時
~ Yoshitoki *mh* 北条
(hoka 外 139)
Hōka *s* 芳香 480
Hōkabe *s* 伯伯部 363, 波波伯 596, 波波伯部, 波波泊部 「139
Hokanosuke *m* 外之助
Hokaru *s* 靭連 1694
Hokasaburō *m* 外三郎 139
Hōkazō *la* 放下僧 606
Hokazono *s* 外園 139
Hokekyō *lh* 法華経 824
~ gisho *l* 法華経義琉
Hoki *s* 甫鬼 533, 保木 781, 啌 1047, 浦鬼 1067, 補鬼 1644
Hōki *s* 法貴 824, 傍木 1538, 螺木 2805; *ph* 伯伎 363, 伯耆; 770–80 宝亀 676
Hōkiichi *m* 保己一 781
Hōkiwara *s* 伯耆原 363
Hokiyama *s* 甫喜山 533
Hokkaidō *p* 北海道 138
Hokkeji *s* 法花寺 824
Hokkekyō *lh* 法華経
Hokkitsu *p* 北橘 138
(hoko 戈 108, 矛 150, 槍 2100, 鋒 2339, 鉾 2342)
Hokoda *p* 鉾田
Hokoko *f* 鋒子 2339, 鉾子 2342
Hokoo *m* 矛雄 150
(hoku 北 138, 副 1428, 葍 2188)
Hokubei *p* "N. America" 北米 138
Hokubō *p* 北房
Hokubu *p* 北部
Hokudan *s* 北淡
Hokugō *sp* 北郷
Hokura *s* 保倉 781
Hokurikudō *p* 北陸道
Hokuryū *p* 北竜 ⌊138
Hokusai *ma* 北斎
Hokusei *s* 北勢
Hokusen *p* "N. Korea" 北鮮
Hokushi *ml* 北枝
Hokutsu *s* 補沓 1644
Homa *s* 保間 781
Hōman *s* 宝満 676
Homare *m* 誉 2010
Homaru *m* 誉
Homi *s* 保見 781
Homiki *m* 秀幹 726
(homu 誉 2010, 賞 2377)
(hon 本 212, 品 916, 誉 2010, 幡 2261)
Honade *s* 火撫 52
Honai *p* 保内 781
Honake *s* 火撫 52
Honami *s* 穂波 2308
Hon'ami *s* 本阿弥 212
~ Kōetsu *ma* 本阿弥光悦
Honbetsu *p* 本別
Honchō *s* 本蝶
~ Kaikeizan *l* 本朝会稽山
~ monzui *l* 本朝文粋
~ mudaishi *l* 本朝無題詩 「十四孝
~ nijūshikō *l* 本朝二
~ ōin hiji *l* 本朝桜陰比事
~ shoseki mokuroku *l* 本朝書籍目録
~ reisō *l* 本朝麗藻
Honda *s* 本田, 本多; *sm* 誉田 2010 「212
~ Akira *ml* 本多顕彰
~ Kiyoji *ml* 本田喜代治 「太郎
~ Kōtarō *mh* 本多光
~ Shuchiku *ml* 本田種竹
~ Shūgo *ml* 本多秋五
~ Toshiaki *mh* 本多利
Hondo *sp* 本渡 ⌊明
Hondō *s* 本堂, 本道, 本
(hone 骨 1213) ⌊藤
Honekawa *la* 骨皮
Hōnen *mlh* 法然 824
Hongawa *sp* 本川 212
Hongō *s* 北郷 138, 本江 212; *sp* 本郷
Hongū *p* 本宮
Hon'iden *s* 本位田
Hon'inbō *sm* 本因坊
Honji *ph* 品治 916, 品遅
Honjibe *s* 品遅部
Honjo *s* 本所 212
Honjō *sp* 本庄, 本城, 本荘, 本匠 「男
~ Mutsuo *ml* 本庄陸
Honkawane *p* 本川根
Honkon *p* "Hongkong" 香港 961
Honma *s* 本間 212
~ Hisao *ml* 本間久雄
~ Yuiichi *ml* 本間唯
Honme *s* 本目 ⌊一
Honmoku *s* 本目, 本牧
Honmura *s* 本村
Honna *p* 本名
Honnō *sp* 本納
Honobe *s* 保延 781
Hōnoki *s* 朴木 255
Honomi *s* 穂樸 2308
(honoo 炎 697)
Honoo no hito *la* 炎の人 「239
Honosuke *m* 帆之助
Honsaki *s* 本咲 212
Honshuku *s* 本宿
Hon'ya *s* 千屋 44
Hon'yabakei *p* 本耶馬渓 212
Honzawa *s* 本沢
Honzu *s* 誉津 2010
Hooka *s* 保岡 781 「824
Hōōtaisetsu *l* 法王帝説
Hora *s* 蕃良 2371. (秀 726, 洞 821)
Horado *p* 洞戸
Horage *s* 洞下
Horaguchi *s* 洞口
Hōrai *s* 宝来 676; *p* 鳳来 2233; *lp* 蓬萊 2195
~ no kyoku *l* 蓬萊曲
Hōreki 1751–64 宝暦 676
Hori *s* 保利 781, 堀 1847, 壕 2603, 濠 2610. (彫 1412, 堀 1847, 壕 2603)
Hōri *s* 祝部 851
Horiba *s* 堀場 1847
Horibe *s* 堀部
Horidome *s* 堀留
Horie *sf* 堀江
Horifuji *s* 堀藤
Horigome *s* 堀込, 堀米
Horiguchi *s* 堀口
~ Daigaku *ml* 堀口大
Horii *s* 堀井 ⌊学
Horiike *s* 堀池
Horikane *p* 堀金
Horikawa *s* 堀川; *smh* 堀河
~ -in hyakushu *l* 堀河院百首
~-~ kesōbumi awase *l* 堀河院艶書合
Horiki *s* 本力 212, 堀木 1847
~ Katsuzō *ml* 堀木克
Horikiri *s* 堀切 ⌊三
Horikita *s* 堀北
Horikome *s* 堀籠
Horikoshi *s* 堀越, 壕越 2603
~ Saiyō *ml* 壕越菜陽
Horime *s* 堀米 1847
Horimonoya *s* 彫物屋 1412
Horimoto *s* 堀本 1847
Horimura *s* 堀村
Horinaga *s* 堀永
Horinaka *s* 堀中
Horinishi *s* 堀西
Horino *s* 堀野 「堀内
Horinouchi *s* 堀ノ内,
Horinoya *s* 堀谷
Horio *s* 堀尾
Horioka *s* 堀岡
Hori Tatsuo *ml* 堀辰雄
Horiuchi *s* 堀内
~ Michitaka *ml* 堀内通孝 「屋
Horiya *s* 堀谷, 堀家, 堀
Horiyama *s* 堀山
Horizawa *s* 堀沢
Horizu *s* 堀津
(horo 洞 821, 幌 1833)
Horoizumi *p* 幌泉
Horokanai *p* 幌加内
Horonobe *p* 幌延
Horouchi *s* 洞内 821
Hōryaku 1751–64 宝暦 676
Hōryūji *p* 法隆寺 824
Hosa *s* 保佐 781
Hosaka *s* 保坂, 蒲坂 1993, 穂阪 2308, 穂坂
Hōseidō Kisanji *ml* 朋誠堂喜三二 616
Hoshi *s* 保志 781, 星 946. (斗 70, 星 946, 参 978)
Hōshi *s* 法示 824
Hoshida *s* 星田 946
Hoshifu *s* 穂保 2308
Hoshii *s* 星井 946
Hoshijima *s* 星島
Hoshikabuto Goban Tadanobu *la* 兜碁盤忠信 1800
Hoshikawa *s* 星川 946
Hoshiko *f* 星子
Hoshikura *s* 星倉
Hōshin *m* 薫信 2567

Hoshina *s* 保科 781, 星名 946 「正之 781
~ Masayuki *mh* 保科
Hoshino *sp* 星野 946
~ Bakujin *ml* 星野麦人 「助
Hoshinosuke *m* 星之
Hoshino Tatsuko *fl* 星野立子 「知
~ Tenchi *ml* 星野天
Hoshi no uta *l* 星歌
Hoshio *m* 星郎
Hoshi otsu shūfū gojōgen *l* 星落秋風五丈原
Hoshito *s* 星戸
Hoshi Tōru *mh-la* 星
Hoshiya *s* 星谷 ⌊亨
Hoshi yadoru tsuyu no tamagiku *la* 星舎露玉菊
Hoshiyama *s* 星山
Hoshizawa *s* 星沢
Hōshō *s* 円満 78, 円満井, 宝正 676, 宝生
Hōshōdan *s* 円満団 78
Hōshuyama *p* 宝珠山
(hoso 細 1958) ⌊676
Hōso *l* 彭祖 1693
Hosoai *s* 細合 1958
Hosobori *s* 細堀
Hosobuchi *s* 細淵
Hosoda *s* 細田
~ Genkichi *ml* 細田源吉
~ Tamiki *ml* 細田民
Hosodo *s* 細戸 ⌊樹
Hosoe *p* 細江
Hosogai *s* 細貝
Hosogoe *s* 細越
~ Kason *ml* 細越夏村
Hosoi *s* 細井
~ Gyotai *ml* 細井魚袋
Hosoiri *p* 細入
Hosoi Wakizō *mlh* 細井和喜蔵
Hosojima *s* 細島
Hosokawa *s* 細川
~ Katsumoto *mh* 細川勝元 「重賢
~ Shigetaka *mh* 細川
~ Yoriyuki *mh* 細川頼之
~ Yūsai *ml* 細川幽斎
Hosokaya *s* 細萱
Hosoki *s* 細木
Hosokura *s* 細倉
Hosomi *s* 細見
Hosomura *s* 細村
Hosonami *s* 細浪
Hosone *s* 細根
Hosono *s* 細野
Hosonoya *s* 細谷
Hosonuma *s* 細沼
Hosooka *s* 細岡
Hosotani *s* 細渓
Hosotsuji *s* 細辻
Hosouchi *s* 細内
Hosoya *s* 細矢, 細谷, 細屋
~ Genji *ml* 細谷源二
Hosoyama *s* 細山
Hosozawa *s* 細沢
Hosshin wakashū *l* 発心和歌集 953
Hosshinshū *l* 発心集
(hosu 干 26)
Hōsui *m* 芳水 480
Hosuto *s* 法師人 824
Hota *s* 程田 1641
Hōta *s* 這田 1515
Hotaka *p* 穂高 2308
Hōtaku *p* 飽託 2165
Hotaru *m* 頬垂 2503
Hotchi *s* 発地 953, 発智
Hotei *sp* 布袋 170
Hoten *p* "Mukden" 奉天 717
Hotoda *s* 保土田 781, 保戸田
Hotogi *s* 仏木 128
Hotoke *f* 仏
~ no hara *la* 仏原
Hotokorojima *s* 壊島 2602 「676
Hōtoku 1449–52 宝徳
Hotori *sm* 辺 179
Hototogisu *l* 不如帰 94
~ kojō no rakugetsu *la* 沓手鳥孤城落月 698 「953, 咄 1354)
Hotsu *s* 保津 781. (発
Hotta *s* 発田 953, 堀田 1847 「正俊
~ Masatoshi *mh* 堀田
~ Masayoshi *mh* 堀田正睦
~ Yoshie *ml* 堀田善衛
Hoya *s* 梅干 1374
Hōya *p* 保谷 781
Hoyama *s* 帆山 239
Hōzawa *s* 杜沢 423
Hōzōin *s* 宝蔵院 676
(hozu 上 47, 末 211, 秀 726)
Hozue *sm-f-p* 上枝 47; *m-f* 秀枝 726; *f* 末枝 211 「秀真
Hozuma *s* 秀吉 726; *sm*
Hozume *s* 穂集 2308
Hozumi *s* 八月一日 19, 八月晦日, 八月朔日, 八朔, 秀積, 保津美 781, 保住, 保積, 穂穙 2308; *sm* 秀実 726; *sm-p* 穂積
~ Kiyoshi *ml* 穂積忠
~ Nobushige *mh* 穂積陳重 「宮 19
Hozumiya *s* 八月一日
Hozunomiya *s* 八月一日宮 「碧 2225)
(hyaku 百 265, 辟 1919,
Hyakugaku renkan *l* 百学連環 265
Hyakuhana *s* 百花
Hyakukien *l* 百鬼園
Hyakuman *la* 百万
Hyakunin isshu *l* 百人一首 「首燈
~ ~ akashi *l* 百人一
~ ~ kaikanshō *l* 百人一首改観抄
Hyakutake *s* 百武
Hyakutarō *m* 百太郎
Hyakuzō *m* 百三
Hyō *m* 彪 1523. (氷 140, 兵 499, 豹 1140, 評 1663, 漂 2083)
Hyōbanki *l* 評判記 1663
Hyōbu *m* 兵部 499
~ -kyō *l* 兵部卿
Hyōdō *s* 兵動, 兵頭, 兵
Hyōe *m-fl* 兵衛 ⌊藤
Hyōgo *p* 兵庫
Hyōgorō *m* 兵五郎
Hyōichi *m* 兵一
Hyōji *m* 兵治
Hyōkichi *m* 兵吉
Hyōmin Usaburō *l* 漂民宇三郎 2083
Hyōnosen *p* 豹山 1140
Hyōsaburō *m* 兵三郎
Hyōsu *s* 兵須 ⌊499
Hyōten *l* 氷点 140
Hyōtō *l* 氷島
Hyōzu *s* 兵主
Hyūga *p* 日向 77

# I

I *s* 胆 845, 猪 1306. (口 28, 已 31, 五 91, 井 103, 以 134, 丕 163, 生 214, 伊 237, 似 350, 位 354, 囲 501A, 亥 519, 衣 520, 夷 535, 炊 602, 矣 665, 居 737, 医 743, 依 780, 怡 808, 胆 845, 祝 851, 委 960, 泉 965, 為 1005, 倚 1033, 射 1144, 黄 1170, 威 1251, 倭 1283, 唯 1286, 惟 1290, 猗 1301, 猪 1306, 姨 1357, 姫 1358, 移 1378, 尉 1410, 菴 1446, 異 1497, 偉 1535, 揖 1550, 徝 1568, 集 1779, 斐 1781, 葦 1992, 意 2007, 械 2096, 蔚 2191, 彙 2200, 禕 2304, 鋳 2343, 慰 2404, 熙 2409, 頤 2502, 維 2540, 熈 2583, 緘 2745, 藺 2838, 韙 2856, 彝 2943, 懿 2958)
Iai *s* 井合 103
Iami *sp* 伊阿弥 237
Iba *s* 井波 103, 伊庭 237, 射場 1144
Ibana *s* 井花 103
Ibara *sp* 井原. (荆 899, 茨 932)
Ibaraki *sp* 茨木, 茨城
Ibarasawa *s* 茨沢; *p* 荆沢 899
Ibata *s* 茨田 932
Ibayashi *s* 伊林 237
Ibe *s* 井部 103, 伊部 237
Ibi *s* 衣斐 520; *sp* 揖斐 1550
Ibigawa *p* 揖斐川

Ibo *p* 揖保
Ibogawa *p* 揖保川
Iboriya *s* 庵谷 1506
Ibuka *s* 井深 103
Ibuki *sp* 伊吹 237
~ Takehiko *ml* 伊吹武彦
Iburi *s* 千夫 44; *p* 胆振 845
Ibuse *s* 井伏 103
~ Masuji *ml* 井伏鱒二
Ibusuki *sp* 指宿 800
Ichi *s* 市 195. (乙 2, 一 3, 弌 74, 市 195, 聿 332, 壱 467, 単 919A, 都 1419, 逸 1504, 溢 1851, 鎰 2748, 櫟 2963)
Ichiaku no suna *l* 一握の砂 3 「195
Ichiba *s* 一場; *sp* 市場
Ichibagase *s* 一番ケ瀬 3
Ichibashi *s* 市橋 195
Ichibee *m* 市兵衛
Ichiboku-zukuri *a* 一木造 3
Ichida *s* 市田 195
Ichigorō *m* 市五郎
Ichiguchi *s* 市口
Ichihara *s* 櫟原 2963; *sp* 市原 195
~ Toyota *ml* 市原豊田
Ichihasama *p* 一迫 3
Ichihashi *s* 市橋 195
Ichihii *s* 壱比韋 467
Ichiho *m* 一保 3
Ichii *s* 市井 195. (櫟 2963)
Ichiiko *f* 櫟子
Ichiji *m* 一治 3
Ichijiku *s* 九 16; *l* 無花果 1789
Ichijima *sp* 市島 195
~ Shunjō *ml* 市島春城 「果
Ichiji no hate *l* 市路の
Ichijō *s* 一条 3, 一城, 一乗 「良
~ Kanera *ml* 一条兼
~ Shigemi *ml* 一条重美
Ichikai *sp* 市貝 195
Ichikawa *s* 一川 3, 一河, 市河 195; *sp* 市川
~ Daimon *p* 市川大門 「十郎
~ Danjūrō *ma* 市川団
~ Fusae *fh* 市川房枝
~ Sadanji *ma* 市川左団次
~ Tameo *ml* 市川為雄
Ichike *s* 市毛
Ichiki *s* 一木 3, 市木 195, 市征, 櫟木 2963; *sp* 市来 195
Ichiko *s* 市古 「1378
Ichiku *s* 市来; *ml* 移竹
Ichikura *s* 一倉 3, 市倉 195
Ichimachida *s* 一町田 3
Ichimaru *m* 一丸, 市丸 195 「田
Ichimata *s* 一万 3, 一万
Ichimatsu *s* 一松
Ichimiya *p* 一宮
Ichimoji *s* 一文字
Ichimori *s* 一森 「郡
Ichimura *s* 市村 195, 市
Ichimuro *s* 一室 3
Ichindo *m* 市人 195
Ichinei Issan *mlh* 一寧一山 3 「有半
Ichinen yūhan *l* 一年
Ichino *s* 市野 195
Ichinohagima *s* 一風迫 3 「一風迫
Ichinohazama *s* 一迫,
Ichinohe *sp* 一戸
Ichinoi *s* 一井
Ichinokami *s* 市正 195
Ichinomiya *sp* 一宮 3; *p* 一の宮
Ichinomoto *s* 櫟本 2963
Ichinosawa *s* 市野沢 195
Ichinose *s* 一ノ瀬 3, 一之瀬, 一瀬, 市之瀬 195, 市瀬
Ichinoseki *p* 一関 3
Ichinotani *ph* 一谷
~ futaba gunki *la* 一谷嫩軍記
Ichi no tori *l* 一の酉
Ichio *s* 一尾; *m* 一大, 一生
Ichioka *s* 市岡 195
Ichirō *m* 一郎 3, 伊知郎 237 「壱体比
Ichirohi *s* 壱礼比 467,
Ichiroichi *m* 一郎一 3
Ichiryū *s* 一柳 「195
Ichisaburō *m* 市三郎
Ichisaka *s* 一坂 3
Ichisawa *s* 市沢 195
Ichise *s* 市瀬
Ichishi *s* 市師; *p* 一志 3
Ichisugi *s* 一杉
Ichisuke *m* 一資
Ichitani *s* 一谷
Ichitarō *m* 一太郎, 市太郎 195
Ichitsu *s* 櫟津 2963
Ichiu *p* 一宇 3
Ichiura *s* 市浦 195
Ichiyama *s* 一山, 市山 195
Ichiyanagi *s* 一柳 3
Ichiya shikasen *l* 一夜四歌仙
Ichiyō *fl* 一葉
Ichiyuki *s* 市征 195
Ichizaemon *m* 市左衛門 「195
Ichizō *m* 一三 3, 市蔵
Ichizuka *s* 市塚
Ichō *s* 銀杏 2345, 鴨足 2489, 鴨脚
Ida *s* 井田 103, 伊田 237, 猪田 1306
Idate *s* 伊達 237
Ide *s* 井代 103, 井出, 出 523, 射出 1144; *sp* 井手 103. (出 523)
Ideha *s* 出庭
Idehara *s* 出原
Idei *s* 出井, 出射
Idemitsu *s* 出光
Ideno *s* 出野
Ide no Akemi *ml* 井出曙覧 103
Ideta *s* 出田 523
Ide Takashi *ml* 出隆
Idewa *s* 出浦
Ido *s* 井戸 103
Ie *s* 伊江 237. (戸 59, 宅 283, 舎 721, 長 939, 室 1183, 宮 1184, 家 1185, 屋 1233, 捨 1324, 宿 1438, 寮 2364, 盧 2594)
Ieda *s* 家田 1185
Iedokoro *s* 家所
Iefune *m* 家船
Iehara *s* 家原
Ieiri *s* 家入
Iejima *sp* 家島
Iekado *m* 家門
Ieki *s* 家木, 家城
Ieko *f* 舎子 721, 屋子 1233
Iemasa *m* 家正 1185
Iemochi *m* 家茂
Iemura *s* 家村
Iemutsu *m* 捨六 1324
Ienaga *sm* 家永 1185; *m* 家良
~ Saburō *ml* 家永三郎
Ienaka *s* 家中
Ienari *m* 家斉
Ienobu *m* 家尹
Ienori *m* 宅命 283
Iesada *m* 家存 1185, 家
Iesaki *m* 家祥 └治
Iesato *m* 家達
Iesuke *m* 家介
Ietaka *ml* 家隆
Ieya *s* 家屋
Ieyasu *m* 家康
Ieyoshi *m* 舎栄 721
Iezaki *s* 家崎 1185
Ifuku *s* 伊福 237
Ifunaki *s* 伊舟城
Iga *sp* 伊賀
Igai *s* 猪飼 1306
Igaki *s* 井垣 103
Igarashi *sp* 五十嵐 91
Igari *s* 猪狩 1306
Igata *s* 井形 103, 伊形 237, 鋳方 2343
Igawa *s* 猪川 1306; *sp* 井川 103
Igazaki *s* 伊ケ崎 237
Igeta *s* 井下田 103, 井桁
Igimi *s* 五千里 91
Igu *s* 印具 260, 居具 737; *sp* 伊具 237 「1306
Iguchi *s* 井口 103, 猪口
Igui *s* 印具 260; *l* 居杭 737
Igumi *s* 井汲 103
Igumo *s* 井雲
Iguro *s* 井畔
Igusa *s* 少草 88, 井草 103, 伊草 237
Ihachi *m* 亥八 519
Ihara *s* 井原 103, 伊原 237, 井原 523, 猪原 1306, 菴原 1446; *p* 庵原 1506 「鶴 103
~ Saikaku *ml* 井原西
~ Seiseien *ml* 伊原青々園 237 「237
Ihashi *s* 井橋 103, 伊橋
Ihee *m* 伊兵衛, 射兵衛 └1144
Ihi *s* 伊比 237
Ihira *s* 井平 103
Iho *s* 伊保 237, 庵 1506
Ihoki *s* 伊福 237
Ii *s* 井伊 103, 伊井 237, 飯 1964. (飯)

Iibuchi *s* 飯淵
Iichirō *m* 猪一郎 1306
Iida *sp* 飯田 1964
～ Bakuai *ml* 飯田莫哀
Iidabashi *p* 飯田橋
Iida Dakotsu *ml* 飯田蛇笏
Iidagawa *p* 飯田川
Iida Ryūta *ml* 飯田竜太
～ Takesato *ml* 飯田武郷
Iidate *p* 飯館
Iida Toshihira *ml* 飯田年平
Iidaya *s* 飯田屋
Iide *p* 飯豊
Iigaki *s* 飯垣
Iigawa *s* 飯川, 飯河
Iigō *s* 飯郷
Iigura *s* 飯倉
Iihama *s* 飯浜
Iihara *s* 飯原
Iiho *s* 指弘 800
Iijima *sp* 飯島 1964
～ Tadashi *ml* 飯島正
Iikubo *s* 飯久保, 飯窪
Iimaro *m* 飯麻呂
Iimori *s* 飯森; *sp* 飯盛
Iimura *s* 飯村
Iimuro *s* 飯室
Iinami *s* 飯浪
Iinan *p* 飯南
Ii Naosuke *mh* 井伊直弼 103
Iiniwa *s* 五百盤 91
Iino *sp* 飯野 1964
Iinuma *s* 飯沼, 飯浪
Iio *s* 指保 800, 飯尾 1964
Iioka *sp* 飯岡
Iishi *s* 井石 103; *p* 飯石 1964
Iishino *s* 飯篠
Iishiro *s* 邑代 460
Ii Tairō no shi *la* 井伊大老の死 103
Iitaka *sp* 飯高 1964
Iitomi *s* 飯富
Iitoyo *s* 飯土用
Iiyama *sp* 飯山
Ii Yōhō *ma* 伊井蓉峰 237
Iiyoshi *s* 飯吉 1964
Iizaka *p* 飯坂
Iizasa *s* 飯笹, 飯篠
Iizawa *s* 飯沢
～ Tadasu *ml* 飯沢匡
Iizuka *sp* 飯塚
～ Tomoichirō *ml* 飯塚友一郎
Iizumi *s* 飯泉

Ijichi *s* 伊地知 237
Ijima *s* 井島 103
Ijimi *s* 一二三 3
Ijimino *sp* 五十公野 91
Ijimu *s* 伊自牟 237
Ijira *sp* 伊自良
Ijiri *s* 井尻 103
Ijūin *sp* 伊集院 237
Ijūrō *m* 伊十郎
Ika *sp* 伊香. (昭 841)
(ikada 筏 1766)
Ikadai *s* 筏井
～ Kaichi *ml* 筏井嘉一
Ikado *s* 井門 103
Ikaga *s* 伊何我 237, 伊宜我, 胆香瓦 845, 為歌可 1005
Ikagawa *s* 五十川 91
Ikago *s* 五十字, 伊香 237; *sp* 五十子 91
Ikahata *s* 五十畑, 五十幡
Ikaho *p* 伊香保 237
Ikai *s* 猪甘 1306, 猪飼, 猪養
Ikaiei *p* "Weihaiwei" 威海衛 1251
Ikaka *s* 猶耳 1555
Ikami *s* 伊神 237
Ikari *s* 五十里 91, 五十海, 井狩 103, 猪狩 1306, 碇 1909. (碇)
Ikarigaseki *p* 碇ケ関
Ikarikazuki *la* 碇潜
Ikarinosuke *s* 碇之助
Ikariya *s* 奴借屋 256, 碇谷 1909
Ikariyama *s* 碇山
Ikaruga *sp* 斑鳩 1609; *p* 何鹿 513
～ -no-miya *ph* 斑鳩宮 1609
Ikarugamo *l* 斑鳩
Ikashi *s* 厳石 2706; *m* 厳. (茂 691, 厳 2706)
Ikashihoko *m* 厳戈
Ikashiko *s* 五十子 91
Ikashimaro *m* 茂丸 691
Ikata *p* 伊方 237
Ikatsuji *s* 五十辻 91, 五辻
Ikawa *s* 五十河, 井川 103, 伊川 237
Ikazaki *sp* 五十崎 91
Ikazuchi *s* 五十土; *sm* 雷 2026
～ Tarō gōaku *l* 雷太郎強悪
Ike *s* 伊気 237, 池 251. (池, 活 819)
Ikeana *s* 池穴 251

Ikebe *s* 池辺, 池部
～ Yoshikata *ml* 池辺義象
Ikebuchi *s* 池淵
Ikebukuro *sp* 池袋
～ Kiyokaze *ml* 池袋清風
Ikeda *sp* 池田
～ Daigo *ml* 池田大伍
～ Katsumi *ml* 池田克巳
～ Kiyoshi *ml* 池田潔
Ikedo *s* 池戸
～ Mitsumasa *mh* 池田光政
Ikegai *s* 池貝
Ikegame *s* 生亀 214, 池亀 251
Ikegami *s* 池上, 池尻
Ikegata *s* 生形 214
Ikegawa *p* 池川 251
Ikegaya *s* 池谷
Ikeguchi *s* 池口
Ikehara *s* 池原
Ikehata *s* 池畑, 池端
Ikei *s* 池井, 活井 819
Ikejima *s* 池島 251
Ikejiri *s* 池尻, 池後
Ikeko *f* 池子
Ike Kōurō *ml* 池皐雨郎
Ikemachi *s* 池町
Ikematsu *s* 池松
Ikemori *s* 池森; *sm* 池守
Ikemoto *s* 池本
Ikemura *s* 池村
Ikenaga *s* 池永
Ikenishi *s* 池西
Ikeno *s* 池野
Ikenobe *s* 池辺
Ikenobō *s* 池坊
Ikenohata *s* 池之端
Ikenokoshi *s* 池越
Ikenoshiri *s* 池後
Ikenoshita *s* 池下
Ike no Taiga *ma* 池大雅
Ikenotani *s* 池野谷
Ikenouchi *s* 池内
～ Tomojirō *ml* 池内友次郎
Ikenoue *s* 池上
Ikenoya *s* 池ノ谷
Ikenushi *m* 池主
Ikeo *s* 池尾
Ikeru *m* 生 214
Ikesaki *s* 池崎 251
Ikeshita *s* 池下
Iketa *s* 井ケ田 103, 井下田, 井桁

Iketani *s* 池谷 251
～ Shinzaburō *ml* 池谷信三郎
Iketari *s* 池谷
Iketsu *s* 池津
Ikeuchi *s* 池内
Ikeura *s* 池浦
Ikeya *s* 池谷
Ikeyama *s* 池山
Ikezawa *s* 池沢
Ikezoe *s* 池添
Ikezumi *s* 生悦住 214
Iki *s* 井城 103, 木 109, 伊木 237, 伊吉, 伊岐, 猪木 1306; *sph* 壱岐 467. (生 214, 寿 539, 息 1224, 域 1290A, 蘇 2841)
Ikiko *f* 生子 214
Ikimatsu *s* 生松
～ Keizō *ml* 生松敬三
Ikimi *s* 五十公 91, 五十君
Ikina *p* 生名 214
Ikinari *s* 行形 245
Ikine *s* 生稲 214
Ikio *m* 五木雄 91, 寿夫 539
Ikito *s* 生戸 214
Ikitsuki *p* 生月
Ikiyō *m* 意気陽 2007
Ikkaku Sennin *la* 一角仙人 3
Ikkatai *s* 一方井
Ikkawa *s* 生川 214
Ikki *s* 一木 3
Ikku *sp* 一宮; *ml* 一九
Ikkyū *ml* 一休
～ Sōjun *ml* 一休宗純
Ikō *s* 伊香 237, 飯河 1964
Ikoku *s* 伊谷 237
～ nikki *h* 異国日記 1497
Ikoma *s* 井駒 103, 所古 600; *sp* 生駒 214
Iku *s* 一宮 3, 生 214; *f* 亥久 519. (生 214, 如 412, 杙 421, 活 819, 郁 890, 昱 944, 育 958, 彧 1255, 煜 1874A, 億 2252, 幾 2597)
Ikube *s* 生部 214
Ikuchi *s* 生池
Ikude *s* 生出
Ikuechi *s* 生越
Ikuha *s* 的 635
Ikuhabe *s* 的部
Ikuhei *m* 幾平 2597
Ikuhiko *m* 郁彦 890
Ikuhina *s* 生夷 214

Ikuhō Mon'in *fh* 郁芳門院 890
Ikui *s* 生井 214, 生夷
Ikuine *s* 生稲
Ikuji *s* 生地
Ikujirō *m* 郁次郎 890
Ikuko *f* 郁子, 幾子 2597
Ikuma *s* 井熊 103, 生馬 214, 生熊, 伊熊 237 ; *m* 幾馬 2597
Ikumi *s* 井汲 103
Ikumo *s* 芋毛 288
Ikunishi *s* 王宮西 90
Ikuno *sp* 生野 214
Ikunosuke *m* 幾之輔 2597
Ikuo *m* 郁夫 890, 郁良 ; 「*f* 生越 214
Ikura *s* 井倉 103, 伊倉 ⌊237
Ikure *s* 勇礼 908
Ikurō *m* 育郎 958
Ikurumi *s* 王壬 90, 王生 「2597
Ikusaburō *m* 幾三郎
Ikusaka *s* 生坂 214
Ikusaku *m* 育作 958
Ikusanokimi *s* 将軍 1040
Ikushi *s* 生石 214
Ikushien *mh* 郁子園 890
Ikushima *s* 生島 214, 生幾
Ikushino *s* 五十君野 91
Ikusue *s* 生末 214
Ikuta *s* 幾田 2597 ; *sp* 生田 214 「盛
～ Atsumori *la* 生田敦
～ Chōkō *ml* 生田長江
～ Chōsuke *ml* 生田蝶介
Ikutagawa *sla* 生田川
Ikutahara *p* 生田原
Ikuta Kizan *ml* 生田葵山 「819
Ikutama *s* 生玉, 活玉
Ikutamabe *s* 生玉部 214
Ikutarō *m* 昱太郎 944, 幾太郎 2597
Ikuta Shungetsu *ml* 生田春月 214
～ Yorozu *mh* 生田万
Ikutsu *s* 生津
Ikutsuki *s* 生月
Ikutsune *m* 如常 412
Ikuyo *s* 幾世 2597
Ikuyoshi *m* 昱禧 944
Ikuzawa *s* 生沢 214
Ikuze *s* 一宮善 3
Ima *s* 今 67, 伊馬 237 ; *f* 伊麻. (今 67, 未 210, 新 1965)
Imabari *sp* 今治 67
Imabayashi *s* 今林
Imabetsu *p* 今別
Imabori *s* 今堀
Imada *s* 今田
Imadate *sp* 今立
Imade *s* 今出
Imadegawa *s* 今出川
Imado *s* 今戸
～ shinjū *l* 今戸心中
Imae *s* 今江
Imaebisu *sm* 今毛人
Imaeda *s* 今枝
Imafu *s* 今府
Imafuji *s* 今藤
Imafuku *s* 今福
Imagane *sp* 今金
Imagawa *s* 今川
～ kana mokuroku *h* 今川仮名目録
～Ryōshun *mh* 今川了俊 「義元
～ Yoshimoto *mh* 今川
Imagire *s* 今切, 今給黎
Imagumano *sp* 今熊野
Imagunbai *s* 今韋倍
Ima Harube *ml* 伊馬春部 237
Imahashi *s* 今橋 67
Imahie *s* 新比恵 1965, 新比叡
Imai *s* 今井 67, 今居
Imaichi *p* 今市
Imaida *s* 今井田
Imai Fukujirō *ml* 今井福治郎 「楊
～ Hakuyō *ml* 今井白
～ Kuniko *fl* 今井邦子
Imaizumi *s* 今泉
Imajō *sp* 今庄
Ima kagami *l* 今鏡
Imakebito *m* 今毛人
Imaki *sm* 今城 ; *sfl* 今木. (新 1965)
Imakiayahito *s* 新漢人
Imakinoaya *s* 新漢
Imakinoayahito *s* 新漢人 「才伎 67
Imakinotebito *s* 今来
Imakita *s* 今北
Imako *f* 今子
Imakōji *s* 今小路
Imakure *s* 今給黎
Imamairi *s* 今良 ; *l* 今参
Imamatsuri *s* 今奉
Imamatsuribe *s* 今奉
Imamichi *s* 今道
Imamine *s* 今峰
Imamiya *s* 今宮
Imamoto *s* 今本
Imamura *s* 今村
Imanaka *s* 今中
Imanari *s* 今成
Imanishi *s* 今西
Imano *s* 今野
～ Kenzō *ml* 今野賢三
Imao *s* 今尾
Imaōji *s* 今大路
Imaoka *s* 今岡
Imari *sp* 伊万里 237
Imasaka *s* 今坂 67
Imasato *m* 維摩郷 2540
Imashi *m* 乃 27
Imashiro *s* 今城 67
(imasu 坐 542)
Imataka *s* 今鷹 67
Imatake *s* 今武
Imatarō *m* 今太郎
Imayō *l* 今様
～ heta dangi *l* 当世下手談義 282
～ Satsuma uta *la* 今様薩摩歌 67
Imayoshi *s* 今吉
Imazato *s* 今里
Imazawa *s* 今沢
Imazeki *s* 今関
Imazu *sp* 今津
Imazumi *s* 五十棲 91
(imi 忌 462, 斎 1454)
Imibe *s* 斎部 「462
Imikanuchi *s* 忌鉄師
Imiki *s* 伊美吉 237, 忌寸 462
Imizu *s* 井水 103, 伊弥頭 237 ; *p* 射水 1144
(imo 芋 288, 妹 848)
Imoarai *sp* 一口 3
Imobuchi *s* 芋淵 288
Imochi *l* 稲熱病 2125
Imoda *s* 芋田 288
Imoji *s* 出雲路 523 ; *l* 伊文字 237
Imokawa *s* 五百川 91, 芋川 288
Imoko *mh* 妹子 848
Imon *s* 巳汶 31 「853
Imonokubo *s* 神久保
Imori *s* 伊森 237
Imose *s* 芋瀬 288
Imoseyama onna teikin *la* 妹背山婦女庭訓 848
Imoseushi *p* 妹背牛
Imoto *s* 井本 103, 井元, 伊本 237
Imube *s* 斉部 701
Imuda *s* 藺牟田 2838
Imura *s* 井村 103, 猪村 1306
In *s* 尹 98. (匂 72, 尹 98, 引 144, 允 217, 印 260, 因 311, 音 962, 院 1055, 殷 1139, 員 1167, 胤 1269, 寅 1439, 愔 1546, 陰 1563, 隠 2074, 蔭 2370, 饗 2852)
Ina *s* 為名 1005, 為奈, 猪名 1306 ; *sp* 伊那 237, 伊奈 ; *p* 伊南. (稲 2125)
Inaba *s* 稲場 ; *sm-p* 稲葉 ; *ph* 因幡 311
Inabadō *l* 因幡堂
Inabanooshinumi *s* 稲羽忍海 2125
Inabata *s* 稲畑
Inabe *s* 猪名部 1306, 猪奈部, 稲辺 2125 ; *sp* 員弁 1167
Inabu *p* 稲武 2125
Inabuchi *s* 南淵 912
Inada *s* 生稲 214, 稲田 2125
Inadome *s* 稲留
Inae *p* 稲枝
Inafu *s* 稲生
Inafune *f* 稲舟
Inagaki *sp* 稲垣
～ Taruho *ml* 稲垣足穂 「郎
～ Tatsurō *ml* 稲垣達
Inagawa *s* 伊奈川 237, 稲川 2125 ; *p* 猪名川 1306
Inage *s* 稲毛 2125
～ Sofū *ml* 稲毛詛風
Inagi *sm* 稲置 ; *sp* 稲城
Inaguma *s* 稲熊
Inahara *s* 稲原
Inahashi *s* 稲橋
Inai *s* 井上 103 ; *sp* 稲井
Inaishi *s* 稲石 ⌊2125
Inajima *s* 稲島
Inaka *m* 稲香
Inakadate *p* 田舎館 189
Inaka Genji *l* 田舎源氏
Inakake *s* 稲掛 2125

Inaka shibai *l* 田舎芝居 189
Inakawa *s* 稲川 2125
Inaki *s* 印支 260, 因支 311, 稲木 2125
Inakibe *s* 印支部 260
Inamasu *s* 稲増 2125
Iname *m* 稲目
Inami *s* 伊波 237, 居波 737, 稲見 2125; *sp* 井波 103, 稲美 2125
Inamochi *s* 稲用
Inamori *s* 稲森
Inamoto *s* 稲本
Inamura *s* 稲村
~ Sanpaku *mlh* 稲村三伯
Inaniwa *p* 稲庭
~ Kawatsura *p* 稲庭川連
Inano *s* 稲野, 機野 2869
Inanobe *s* 稲延 2125, 稲野辺
Inaoka *s* 稲岡
Inari *sfh* 稲荷
Inasa *sp* 引佐 144
Inashiki *m* 稲布 2125; *p* 稲敷
Inashiro *s* 印代 260
Inatari *m* 稲足 2125
Inato *s* 稲戸; *m* 稲人
Inatome *s* 稲留
Inatomi *s* 稲富 2125
Inatsu *s* 榎津 2107, 稲津
Inatsugi *s* 稲次
Inatsuki *p* 稲筑
Inaue *s* 稲植 1306
Inawashiro *sp* 猪苗代
Inayama *s* 稲山 2125
Inayoshi *s* 稲吉
Inazaki *s* 稲崎
Inazawa *sp* 稲沢
Inazō *m* 稲造
Inazu *s* 稲津
Inazuma *s* 電 2025
Inba *s* 印幡 260; *p* 印旛
Inbe *s* 伊部 237, 印部 260, 忌部 462, 斉部 701, 斎部 1454
~ no Hironari *ml* 斎部広成
Inden *s* 位田 354
Indo *p* "India" 印度 260
Indō *s* 犬童 107, 印東 260, 印藤, 因藤 311
Ine *s* 亥子 519; *p* 伊根 237. (禾 220, 稲 2125)
In'ei raisan *l* 陰翳礼讃 1563
Ineko *f* 禾子 220, 祝年子 851, 稲子 2125
Inenoya *s* 稲野屋
Inenuki *s* 十時 18
Inetari *m* 稲足 2125
Ingen *mh* 隠元 2074
Iniwa *s* 五百盤 91
Injū *l* 陰獣 1563
Inmaki *s* 印牧 260
Innai *p* 院内 1055
Innami *sp* 印南 260
Innan *s* 印南
Innoshima *p* 因島 311
Innosō *s* 院相 1055
Innyaku *s* 印鑰 260
Ino *s* 井野 103, 伊農 237, 居野 737, 猪 1306, 猪野; *sp* 伊野 237
Inō *s* 伊能 237, 伊統, 稲生 2125. (猪 1306)
Inobe *s* 井野辺 103
Inoge *s* 猪野毛 1306
Inohana *s* 猪鼻
Inohara *s* 猪原
Inoie *s* 猪家 水 2125
Inō Jakusui *mh* 稲生若水
Inokashi *s* 猪橋 1306
Ino Kenji *ml* 猪野謙二
Inokichi *m* 伊之吉 237, 猪之吉 1306
Inoko *s* 猪子; *m* 豕 530
Inokoshi *s* 猪越 1306, 猪腰, 射越 1144
Inokuchi *s* 井野口 103, 猪口 1306, 猪野口; *sp* 井口 103
Inokuma *s* 猪隈 1306, 猪熊
Inoma *s* 猪間
Inomata *s* 猪又, 猪股, 猪俣
Inomo *s* 井面 103
Inomoto *s* 井本 1964
Inoo *s* 猪尾 1306, 飯尾
Inose *s* 猪瀬 1306
Inoshiri *s* 井尻 103, 井後
Inoshishi *s* 猪 1306
Inoshita *s* 井下 103
Inosuke *m* 伊之助 237
Inō Tadataka *mh* 伊能忠敬
Inotsuji *s* 射辻 1144
Inoue *s* 井上 103, 井於
~ Enryō *mh* 井上円了
~ Fumio *ml* 井上文雄
~ Harimanojō *ma* 井上播磨掾
~ Isamu *ml* 井上勇
~ Junnosuke *mh* 井上準之助
~ Kaoru *mh* 井上馨
~ Kōbun *ml* 井上康文
~ Kowashi *mh* 井上毅
~ Michiyasu *ml* 井上通泰
~ Mitsuharu *ml* 井上光晴
~ Nisshō *mh* 井上日召
~ Tetsujirō *mlh* 井上哲次郎
~ Tomoichirō *ml* 井上友一郎
~ Tsutomu *ml* 井上勤
~ Yasushi *ml* 井上靖
~ Yoshio *ml* 井上良雄
Inoyama *s* 猪山 1306
Inu *s* 犬 107. (犬, 狗 566)
Inubōmaru *m* 犬房丸
Inubuse *s* 犬伏 107
Inue *s* 犬江
Inugami *s* 犬神; *sp* 犬上
~ no Mitasuki *mh* 犬上御田鍬
Inugawa *s* 犬川
Inuhariko *l* 狗張子 566
Inui *s* 犬井 107, 乾 1411
Inukai *s* 犬甘 107, 犬養; *sp* 犬飼
~ Takeru *ml* 犬養健
~ Tsuyoshi *mh* 犬養毅
Inukake *s* 犬懸
Inumaru *s* 犬丸
Inumura *s* 犬村
Inusaka *s* 犬坂, 犬阪
Inuta *s* 犬田
Inutade *s* 紅草 1423
Inutagawa *m* 犬田川 107
Inuta Shigeru *ml* 犬田卯
Inu Tsukubashū *l* 犬筑波集
Inuyama *sp* 犬山
Inuyamabushi *la* 犬山伏
Inuzuka *s* 犬塚
Inuzuki *s* 狗月 566
Inzai *p* 印西 260
Io *s* 井尾 103, 伊尾 237, 庵 1506. (魚 1485, 庵 1506)
Iō *s* 井生 103
Iochi *s* 伊大知 237, 庵地 1506
Ioe *f* 五百枝 91
Iogi *s* 五百木
Iohara *s* 庵原 1506
Ioi *s* 五百井 91
Iōji *s* 伊大地 237, 伊大知 1306
Ioka *s* 井岡 103, 猪岡
Iokazu *m* 魚員 1485
Ioki *s* 五百木 91
Iokibe *s* 五百木部, 五百旗頭
Ioki Hyōtei *ml* 五百木瓢亭
Iokii *s* 五百木井
Ioko *f* 五百子
Iomi *s* 伊臣 237
Iono *s* 五百野 91, 医王野 743
Iōno *s* 伊王野 237
Ionushi *l* 庵主 1506
Iorai *s* 五百蔵 91
Iorei *s* 五百歳
Iori *m* 伊織 237, 菴 1446, 庵 1506, 廬 2594; *f* 廬 2855
Iorihara *s* 庵原 1506
Ioriya *s* 庵谷
Iorobi *s* 五百籠 91
Ioroi *s* 五百蔵, 五百籠
Iose *s* 五百瀬
Iōshima *p* 伊王島 237
Ioto *m* 五百人 91
Iozumi *s* 五十棲, 五百住, 五百棲
Ippei *m* 一平 3
Ippeisotsu no jūsatsu *l* 一兵卒の銃殺
Ippen Shōnin *ml* 一遍上人
~ ~ goroku *l* 一遍上人語録
Ippitsu *s* 一筆
Ippitsuan Kakō *ml* 一筆庵可候
Ippō *s* 一品
Ipponmatsu *p* 一本松
Ira *s* 伊良 237
Iraka *s* 甍 2366
Irako *s* 五十子 91, 五十郎, 伊良子 237
~ Suzushiro *ml* 伊良子清白
(iratsuko 郎 1145)
Iratsume *l* 以良都女 134
Irazu *s* 薬袋 2568
Irazumi *s* 五十棲 91, 五百棲
Irei *s* 伊礼 237
Iri *s* 射 1144, 納 1685. (入 15, 納 1685)
Iriai *s* 入交 15
Iribe *s* 納部 1685
Irie *s* 入江 15
Irigorō *m* 入五郎

Irihirose *p* 入広瀬
Iriki *sp* 入来
Irikiin *s* 入来院
Irikura *s* 入倉
Irimajiri *s* 入交
Irimazari *s* 紅白 1423
Irimaze *s* 入交 15
Irimoya-zukuri *a* 入母屋造
Irimura *s* 入村
Irino *s* 入野
Irita *s* 入田
Iritani *s* 入谷
Iritomi *s* 納富 1685
Iritono *s* 入戸野 15
Iritsuki *s* 入月
Iriuchijima *s* 入内島
Iriya *s* 入矢, 入屋
Iriyama *s* 入山
Irizawa *s* 入沢
(iro 色 345, 紅 1423, 温 1585, 最 1742)
Irobe *s* 色部 345
Iroha *l* 伊呂波 237
～ jiruishō *l* 伊呂波字類抄
Irokawa *s* 色川 345
Iroki *m* 色樹
Iroko *f* 色子
Iroku *m* 亥六 519
Ironushi *m* 色主 345
Irota *s* 色田
Irotake utazaimon-zoroe *l* 色竹歌祭文揃
Irozange *l* 色懺悔
(iru 入 15)
Iruka *m* 入鹿
Iruma *sp* 入間
Irumagawa *sl* 入間川
Irumano *s* 入間野
Iruru *m* 容 1182
Isa *sf-p* 伊佐 237. (佐 131, 功 135, 伊 237, 沙 392, 武 751, 砂 876, 軍 906, 勇 908, 歳 1995, 率 2040, 勲 2407, 諫 2514, 績 2814, 驍 2957)
Isaburō *m* 伊三郎 237
Isachi *f* 猪幸 1306
Isada *m* 居貞 737
Isafushi *s* 鯨伏 2831
Isagane *s* 砂金 876
Isagawa *s* 沙川 392
Isago *s* 伊金 237, 伊砂, 砂金 876; *m* 砂
Isagoda *s* 沙田 392
Isahai *s* 飯酒盃 1964
Isaharu *m* 威勇治 1251
Isahaya *p* 諫早 2514
Isaka *s* 井坂 103, 伊坂 237, 猪坂 1306
Isakawa *s* 五十川 91, 去来川 266, 砂川 876, 率川 2040 「子 2814
Isako *f* 維佐子 2540, 績
Isami *m* 一二三 3, 武命 751, 勇 908, 勇三, 敢 1687, 矯 2626
Isamitsu *m* 勲光 2407
Isamu *m* 力 11, 伊武 237, 亥三 519, 制 656, 武 751, 勇 908, 悍 1051, 浩 1068, 傈 1287, 猛 1305, 偉 1535, 敢 1687, 愹 1838, 魁 2423, 諫 2514
Isanaga *m* 功長 135
Isano *s* 伊佐野 237
Isao *sp* 有功 303; *m* 力 11, 十六 18, 佐夫 131, 功 135, 公 156, 亥勇夫 519, 軍雄 906, 勇 908, 勇広, 勇魚, 烈 1211, 庸 1507, 歳男 1995, 憲 2033, 徳 2063, 勲 2407, 勲夫, 勲男, 魁 2423, 穎 2505, 績 2814, 驍夫 2957; *f* 怡積弘 808
Isaoshi *m* 功 135
Isara *s* 馬工 1257
Isato *s* 井里 103
Isawa *s* 石禾 172; *sp* 石和; *p* 胆沢 845
Isayama *s* 不知山 94, 伊佐山 237, 勇山 908, 諫山 2514
～ no Fumitsugu *ml* 勇山文継 908
Isayoshi *m* 勇記
Ise *sp* 伊勢 237
Isechi *s* 伊瀬地, 伊瀬知
Iseda *s* 伊勢田
Ise-dayū shū *l* 伊勢大輔集
Isefū *l* 伊勢風
Isehara *p* 伊勢原
Iseho *s* 指保 800
Iseki *s* 井石 103, 井関, 伊関 237 「物語
Ise monogatari *l* 伊勢
～ ～ ketsugishō *l* 伊勢物語闕疑抄
Isen *p* 伊仙 「品遅部
Isenohonchibe *s* 伊勢
Iseri *s* 井芹 103
Isero *s* 指保 800
Ise Sōzui *mh* 伊勢宗瑞
Iseya *s* 伊勢屋 ⌊237
Isezaki *sp* 伊勢崎
Ishi *f* 石 172. (石, 研 875, 甃 2223)
Ishiai *s* 石合 172
Ishiba *s* 石場
Ishibai *s* 石灰
Ishibashi *s* 研橋 875; *sp* 石橋 172 「月
～ Ningetsu *ml* 石橋忍
～ Shian *ml* 石橋思案
～ Tatsunosuke *ml* 石橋辰之助
Ishibata *s* 石幡
Ishibe *sp* 石部 「2540
Ishi bigaku *l* 維氏美学
Ishibumi *l* 碑 1908
Ishida *s* 石田 172
～ Baigan *mh* 石田梅巌
～ Hakyō *ml* 石田波郷
～ Mitsunari *mh* 石田三成
Ishide *s* 石出, 石榑
Ishido *s* 石戸 「藤
Ishidō *s* 石堂, 石塔, 石
Ishidome *s* 石留
Ishidoriya *p* 石鳥谷
Ishidoshiro *s* 石徹白
Ishiga *s* 石賀
Ishigaki *s* 石垣
Ishigame *s* 石亀
Ishigami *s* 石神
Ishigane *s* 石金
Ishigaya *s* 石谷
Ishige *s* 石毛; *sp* 石下
Ishigeta *s* 石桁
Ishigōoka *s* 石郷岡
Ishiguro *s* 石黒
Ishihama *s* 石浜
～ Kinsaku *ml* 石浜金作
Ishihara *s* 石原 ⌊作
～ Atsushi *ml* 石原純
～ Shintarō *ml* 石原慎太郎 「束
～ Yatsuka *ml* 石原八
Ishii *s* 石居, 石射; *sp* 石井 「亭
～Hakutei *ma* 石井柏
～ Kikujirō *mh* 石井菊次郎 「子
～ Momoko *fl* 石井桃
～ Naozaburō *ml* 石井直三郎 「月
～ Rogetsu *ml* 石井露
～ Tsuruzō *ml* 石井鶴
Ishijima *s* 石島 ⌊三
Ishikage *m* 石陰
Ishikami *s* 石上
Ishikari *sp* 石狩
Ishikarigawa *l* 石狩川
Ishikawa *s* 石河; *sp* 石川 「川千代松
～ Chiyomatsu *mh* 石
～ Iwao *ml* 石川巌
～ Jōzan *ml* 石川丈山
～ Jun *ml* 石川淳
～ Keirō *ml* 石川桂郎
～ Kin'ichi *ml* 石川欣一 「雅望
～ Masamochi *ml* 石川
～ Rikinosuke *mh* 石川理紀之助
～ Sanshirō *mlh* 石川三四郎 「啄木
～ Takuboku *ml* 石川
～ Tatsuzō *ml* 石川達三 「助
～ Zensuke *ml* 石川善
Ishiki *s* 石来, 稲置 2125; *f* 鋳式 2343
Ishikina *fh* 石寸名 172
Ishikiri *s* 石切
Ishikizukuri *s* 石柷作
Ishiko *s* 石来, 石河; *f* 五四子 91
Ishikoshi *sp* 石越 172
Ishikura *s* 石倉
Ishikure *s* 石榑 「亦
～ Chimata *ml* 石榑千
Ishimaki *s* 石巻
Ishimaru *s* 石丸
Ishimatsu *s* 石松
Ishimi *s* 五十君 91
Ishimichi *s* 石道 172
Ishimitsu *s* 石光
Ishimoda *s* 石母田
～ Shō *ml* 石母田正
Ishimori *s* 石森
～ Nobuo *ml* 石森延男
Ishimoto *s* 石本
Ishimura *s* 石村
Ishinaga *sp* 石永
Ishini *s* 夷隅 535
Ishino *s* 石野 172
Ishinokami *s* 石上
Ishinomaki *p* 石巻
Ishinosuke *m* 石之助
Ishi no ue *l* 甃の上 2223
Ishio *s* 石尾 172
Ishiō *s* 石王
Ishioka *sp* 石岡

Ishioroshi *s* 石下
Ishira *s* 伊志良 237
Ishirai *s* 石占井 172, 石来
Ishirō *s* 伊四郎 237
Ishisaka *s* 石坂 172
～ Yōhei *ml* 石坂養平
～ Yōjirō *ml* 石坂洋次郎
Ishiseya *s* 石瀬屋
Ishisone *s* 石曾根
Ishitari *m* 石足
Ishitome *sp* 柘榴 864
Ishiuchi *s* 石内 172, 石摶
Ishiura *s* 石浦
Ishiwa *s* 石禾
Ishiwada *s* 石和田
Ishiwata *s* 石渡, 石綿
Ishiwatari *s* 石渡
Ishiyaku *s* 石躍
Ishiyama *sp* 石山
～ -dera engi emaki *ha* 石山寺縁起絵巻
～ Tetsurō *ml* 石山徹郎
Ishizaki *s* 石崎
Ishizawa *s* 石沢
Ishizu *s* 石津
Ishizuka *s* 石塚
～ Tomoji *ml* 石塚友二
Ishizukuri *s* 石作
Ishuichi *s* 以首一 134
Iso *s* 五十 91, 石 172, 伊蘇 237, 磯 2916. (石 172, 勤 1698, 勲 2407, 礒 2732, 磯 2916)
Isoai *s* 磯合
Isoarashi *s* 五十嵐 91
Isobata *s* 五十幡
Isobayashi *s* 磯林 2916
Isobe *s* 五十部 91, 石辺 172, 印部 260, 礒辺 2732, 礒部, 磯辺 2916; *sp* 磯部 2916
Isoda *s* 礒田 2732, 磯田 2916, 磯貝
Isogai *s* 印貝 260, 磯谷
～ Unbō *ml* 磯貝雲峰
Isogami *s* 磯上
Isogawa *s* 磯川
Isogaya *s* 磯谷
Isogimi *m-f* 五十君 91
Isohiko *m* 五十彦
Isoho *l* "Aesop" 伊曾保 237
Isoi *s* 五百井 91
Isoichi *m* 磯一 2916
Isoji *m* 磯次
Isōji *m* 伊三次 237
Isojima *s* 磯島 2916
Isokawa *s* 五十川 91
Isokichi *m* 磯吉 2916
Isoko *f* 勤子 1698, 礒子 2732; *p* 磯子 2916
Isoma *m* 五十馬 91
Isomae *s* 磯前 2916
Isome *s* 井染 103, 居初 737, 磯目 2916
Isomura *s* 磯村
Isona *f* 磯菜
Isonaga *s* 磯永 2916
Isono *s* 礒野 2732, 磯野
Isonokami *sp* 石上 172
～ Gen'ichirō *ml* 石上玄一郎
～ no Otomaro *ml* 石上乙麻呂
～ no Yakatsugu *ml* 石上宅嗣
～ sasamegoto *l* 石上私淑言
Isoo *m* 磯雄 2916
Isoroku *m* 五十六 91
Isoshi *s* 伊子志 237, 伊蘇志; *sm* 勤 1698; *m* 克 442
Isotari *m* 五十足 91, 石足 172, 磯足 2916
Isoya *s* 磯谷
Isoyama *s* 磯山
Isozaki *s* 礒崎 2732, 磯崎 2916
Isozumi *s* 五十棲 91
Issa *ml* 一茶 3
Issan *s* 一山
～ Ichinei *mlh* 一山一寧
Issei *m* 一生, 一清
Isshiki *sp* 一色
Isshin niga byakudō *la* 一心二河白道
Issō *s* 一噌
Issun-bōshi *l* 一寸法師
Isuka *s* 伊砂 237
Isuke *m* 伊助
Isumi *p* 夷隅 535
Isurugi *s* 岩動 942; *p* 石動 172
Isusaba *s* 五十集 91
Isuyama *s* 五十山
Isuzu *m-f* 五十鈴
Isuzugawa *s* 五十川
(ita 板 632)
Itabashi *sp* 板橋
Itabeoka *s* 板部岡
Itadori *p* 板取
Itagaki *s* 板垣
～ Naoko *fl* 板垣直子
～ Taisuke *mh* 板垣退助
～ Takaho *ml* 板垣鷹穂
Itahana *s* 板鼻
Itahara *s* 板原
Itai *s* 板井
Itaka *s* 伊高 237
Itako *s* 板荷 632; *p* 潮来 2275
Itakura *sp* 板倉 632
～ Katsushige *mh* 板倉勝重
～ Shigemasa *mh* 板倉重昌
Itami *sp* 伊丹 237
～ Mikihiko *ml* 伊丹三樹彦
Itamiya *s* 伊丹屋
Itamochi *s* 板茂 632
Itani *s* 井谷 103, 伊谷 237, 鋳谷 2343
Itano *p* 板野 632 237
Itari *p* "Italy" 伊太利
Itarō *m* 亥太郎 519
Itaru *m* 之 24, 及 83, 至 485, 効 653, 周 736, 到 901, 昶 1004, 格 1099, 造 1236, 致 1407, 達 1810, 純 1956, 暢 2111, 諄 2324, 徹 2451, 親 2544, 薄 2569, 臻 2637
Itasaka *s* 板坂 632
Itasawa *s* 板沢
Itasu *m* 致 1407
Itate *s* 迎達 746
Itatsu *s* 板津 632
Itaya *s* 板谷
Itayama *s* 板山
Itayanagi *p* 板柳
Itchū *ma* 一忠 3
Itchūbushi *la* 一中節
Iteya *s* 射屋 1144
Ito *s* 井門 103, 伊覩 237, 系 977; *p* 伊都 237. (文 86, 糸 720, 系 977, 弦 1345, 純 1956, 紘 2331, 絲 2526)
Itō *s* 井東 103, 井藤, 伊統 237, 伊藤, 忌町 462, 緘藤 2745; *sp* 伊東 237
Itoda *s* 井戸田 103; *sp* 糸田 720
Itode *m* 五十迹手 91
Itō Einosuke *ml* 伊藤永之介 237
Itoeko *f* 糸重子 720
Itoga *s* 糸賀
Itogawa *s* 井戸川 103, 糸川 720
Itō Genboku *mh* 伊東玄朴 237
～ Gessō *ml* 伊東月草
～ Gingetsu *ml* 伊藤銀月
～ Hakubun *mh* 伊藤博文
Itohara *s* 糸原 720
Itō Hirobumi *mh* 伊藤博文 237
～ Hitoshi *ml* 伊藤整
Itoi *s* 糸井 720
Itoigawa *p* 糸魚川
Itō Jakuchū *ma* 伊藤若中 237
Itoji *m* 糸治 720
Itō Jinsai *mhl* 伊藤仁斎 237
Itoko *f* 生都子 214, 糸子 720
Itokoku *ph* 伊都国 237
Itoku *s* 糸久 720
Itomi *s* 伊臣 237, 納富 1685
～ 代治 237
Itō Miyoji *mh* 伊東巳代治 237
Itonaga *s* 糸永 720
Itō Noe *fl* 伊藤野枝 237
Itonuki *p* 糸貫 720
Itoo *s* 糸尾
Itori *s* 井鳥 103
Itō Sachio *ml* 伊藤左千夫 237
～ Sei *ml* 伊藤整
～ Senzō *ml* 伊東専三
Itoshi *f* 糸之 720
Itoshima *p* 糸島
Itō Shinkichi *ml* 伊藤信吉 237
Itoshiro *sp* 石徹白 172
Itō Shizuo *ml* 伊東静雄 237
～ Shōu *ml* 伊藤松宇
～ Sukemasu *mh* 伊東祐益
Itotake shoshinshū *l* 糸竹初心集 720
Itō Tōgai *mh* 伊藤東涯 237
Itoya *s* 糸屋 720
Itoyama *s* 糸山
Itō Yoshio *ml* 伊藤嘉夫 237
Itozawa *s* 糸沢 720
Itōzu *s* 到津 901
Itsu *s* 伊津 237; *m* 胆津 845. (乙 2, 一 3, 弌 74, 五 91, 伍 229, 聿 332, 壱 467, 斎 1454, 逸 1504, 揖 1550, 敬 1691, 溢

1851, 厳 2706, 鎰 2748)
Itsuaki *m* 逸暁 1504
Itsubo *s* 井坪 103, 伊坪 237
Itsue *s* 稜威 1917; *f* 逸枝 1504, 藺都絵 2838
Itsukai *s* 猪使 1306
Itsukaichi *p* 五日市 91
Itsuki *s* 伊吹 237, 貴泉 1755; *sm* 斎 1454; *m* 五十槻 91, 済 1336, 樹 2483, 厳 2706; *m-f* 斎宮 1454; *p* 五木 91
Itsukizono *m* 五十槻園
Itsuko *f* 五子, 稜威子 1917, 厳子 2706
Itsukushima *p* 厳島
Itsumaru *m* 厳丸
Itsumatsu *s* 五松 91
Itsumi *s* 逸見 1504; *m* 五観 91, 厳水 2706
Itsu no chiwake *l* 稜威道別 1917
～ no kotowake *l* 稜威言別
Itsuo *m* 五雄 91, 伊都雄 237, 斎男 1454, 敬雄 1691, 稜威雄 1917
Itsutarō *m* 厳太郎 2706
Itsuwa *p* 五和 91
Itsuyoshi *m* 逸好 1504
Itto *s* 者度 769
Ittsuji *s* 五辻 91
Iuchi *s* 井内 103
Iura *s* 井浦
(iwa 石 172, 岩 942, 磐 2400, 厳 2706, 巌 2936)
Iwabe *s* 岩部 942
Iwabori *s* 岩堀
Iwabuchi *s* 岩淵
Iwadani *s* 岩渓
Iwadate *s* 岩立, 岩楯, 岩館
Iwade *sp* 岩出
Iwadeyama *p* 岩出山
Iwadō *s* 岩堂
Iwae *m* 磐恵 2400
Iwafuji *s* 岩藤 942
Iwafune *p* 岩舟; *p-la* 岩船
Iwagaki *s* 岩垣, 巌垣 2936
Iwagami *s* 岩上 942
～ Jun'ichi *ml* 岩上順一
Iwagawa *s* 猿来川 2062
Iwaguchi *s* 岩口 942
Iwahara *sp* 岩原
Iwahashi *s* 岩橋
Iwahei *m* 厳平 2706
Iwahide *m* 厳秀
Iwahisa *m* 岩亀 942
Iwai *s* 石井 172, 慶 2425; *sm* 祝 851; *sp* 岩井 942; *m* 巌 2936. (斎 1454, 慶 2425)
Iwaichi *m* 磐一 2400
Iwaida *s* 慶田 2425
Iwaide *s* 岩井出 942
Iwaizumi *p* 岩泉
Iwajirō *m* 岩次郎, 岩治郎
Iwakado *s* 岩門
Iwakami *s* 石上 172
Iwakata *s* 岩片 942
Iwakawa *s* 岩川, 巌川 2936
Iwaki *sp* 石城 172, 岩木 942, 岩城; *p* 磐城 2400
Iwakichi *m* 岩吉 942
Iwaki Juntarō *ml* 岩城準太郎
Iwakina *f* 石寸名 172
Iwakiri *s* 岩切 942
Iwaki Yukinori *ml* 岩城之徳
Iwako *f* 岩子, 磐子 2400
Iwakoshi *s* 岩越 942
Iwakubo *s* 岩窪
Iwakumo *s* 岩雲, 巌雲 2936
Iwakuni *sp* 岩国 942
Iwakura *sp* 岩倉
～ Masaji *ml* 岩倉政治
～ Tomomi *mh* 岩倉具視
Iwakuri *s* 岩郡
Iwama *sp* 岩間
Iwamae *m* 磐前 2400
Iwamasa *s* 岩政 942
Iwamatsu *s* 岩松
Iwami *s* 岩見; *sp* 石見 172; *p* 岩美 942
Iwaminojo-shiki *l* 石見女式 172
Iwamitsu *s* 岩満 942
Iwamizawa *p* 岩見沢
Iwamori *s* 岩森
Iwamoto *s* 岩元, 岩本, 巌本 2936
～ Zenji *ml* 巌本善治
Iwamura *s* 巌村; *sp* 岩村 942
Iwamurabe *s* 岩村部
Iwamuro *sp* 岩室
Iwana *s* 磐奈 2400
Iwanaga *s* 石野 172, 岩永 942
～ Yutaka *ml* 岩永胖
Iwanai *p* 岩内
Iwanami *s* 岩波, 岩浪, 岩陽
～ Shigeo *ml* 岩波茂雄
Iwanari *s* 岩成
Iwanasu *s* 石无 172
Iwanasuwake *s* 石生別, 磐梨別 2400
Iwane *sm* 岩根 942; *m* 五十羽 91, 石根 172
Iwano *s* 石野, 岩野 942
～ Hōmei *ml* 岩野泡鳴
Iwanokami *s* 石上 172
Iwanuma *sp* 岩沼 942
Iwao *s* 岩尾; *sm* 岩男; *m* 五八夫 91, 石雄 172, 岩 942, 勣 1969, 嵒 1974, 嵒雄, 磐 2400, 礒 2732, 巌 2936, 礹 2996
Iwaoka *s* 岩岡 942
Iwappara *p* 岩原
Iware *s* 石村 172, 磐余 2400
Iwarugi *s* 岩動 942
Iwasa *s* 岩佐, 岩浅
Iwasaburō *m* 岩三郎
Iwasaka *s* 岩坂
Iwasaki *s* 巌崎 2936; *sp* 岩崎 942
～ Yatarō *mh* 岩崎弥太郎
Iwasa Matabee *ma* 岩佐又兵衛
～ Tōichirō *ml* 岩佐東一郎
Iwasawa *s* 岩沢
Iwase *s* 石背 172, 磐瀬 2400; *sp* 岩瀬 942
～ Tadanari *mh* 岩瀬忠震
Iwashi *s* 石志 172
Iwashige *s* 岩重 942
Iwashiki *m* 石布 172
Iwashima *s* 岩島 942
Iwashimizu *sl* 石清水 172
Iwashiro *s* 石代; *p* 岩代 942
Iwashita *s* 岩下
～ Shunsaku *ml* 岩下俊作
Iwata *s* 岩田, 瀬 2794; *m* 岩太 942; *p* 磐田 2400
Iwatake *s* 岩竹 942
Iwataki *p* 岩滝
Iwatani *s* 岩谷
Iwatarō *m* 磐太郎 2400
Iwataru *s* 岩垂 942
Iwate *sp* 岩手
Iwato *s* 岩戸, 岩門
Iwatō *s* 岩藤
～ Yukio *ml* 岩藤雪夫
Iwatoko *m* 石床 172
Iwatsu *s* 岩津 942
Iwatsuka *s* 岩塚
Iwatsuki *s* 岩月, 岩附; *p* 岩槻
Iwatsukuri *s* 石作 172
Iwauchi *s* 石内, 岩内 942
Iwaura *s* 石占 172
Iwawaki *s* 岩脇 942
Iwaya *s* 岩谷, 岩屋, 巌谷 2936
～ Bakuai *ml* 岩谷莫哀 942
Iwayama *s* 岩山
Iwaya Sazanami *ml* 巌谷小波 2936
Iwazu katarazu *l* 不言不語 94
Iwazumi *m* 石積 172
Iwō *m* 祝 851, 賀 758
(iya 礼 146, 未 210, 弥 832, 珍 836)
Iya *s* 射屋 1144
Iyahito *m* 弥仁 832
Iyakōri *s* 弥郡
Iyama *s* 井山 103
Iyataka *m* 弥高 832
Iyayotsugi *l* 弥世継
Iyo *m* 以節 134; *m-p* 伊予 237; *f* 弥 832. (愈 2358)
Iyobe *s* 伊予部 237
Iyoda *s* 伊与田, 伊予田
Iyoko *f* 愈子 2358
Iyoku *s* 伊谷 237, 伊能
Iyo Mishima *p* 伊予三島
Iyori *s* 伊従
Izaki *s* 井崎 103, 伊崎 237
Izawa *s* 井沢 103, 伊沢 237, 伊雑
～ Shūji *mh* 伊沢修二
Izayoi *l* 十六夜 18
Izen *ml* 惟然 1290
Izō *m* 亥三 519
Izu *s* 出淵 523; *sp* 伊豆 237. (五 91, 何 513, 出 523, 泉 965, 稜 1917, 厳 2706)
Izubuchi *s* 伊豆淵, 出淵 523
Izuchiyomaru *m* 伊土代丸 237
Izue *f* 何恵 513
Izuha *s* 出羽 523
Izuhara *s* 伊原 237, 泉原 965; *p* 厳原 2706

Izuhiko *m* 稜彦 1917, 厳比古 2706
Izuho *m* 厳穂 「523
Izui *s* 井出井 103, 出井
Izuishi *s* 出石
Izuka *s* 井塚 103
Izuki *s* 伊月 237
Izuko *f* 厳子 2706
Izume *s* 猪爪 1306
Izumi *s* 厳美 2706; *sm-f-p* 泉 965; *sp* 出水 523, 和泉 638; *m* 五三 91, 井泉水 103, 出見 523. (泉 965)
Izumida *s* 泉田
Izumi-ga-jō *l* 和泉が城 638
Izumihara *s* 泉原 965
Izumikawa *s* 泉川
Izumi Kyōka *ml* 泉鏡花
Izumino *s* 五十公野 91
Izumi Ōtsu *p* 泉大津 965
~ Sano *p* 泉佐野
~ Shikibu *fl* 和泉式部 638
Izumitani *s* 泉谷
Izumitei *s* 泉亭
Izumiya *s* 泉谷, 泉屋
Izumiyama *s* 泉山
Izumizaki *sp* 泉崎
Izumizawa *s* 泉沢
Izumo *sp* 出雲 523
Izumonokuni *ph* 出雲国 「風土記
~ no fudoki *l* 出雲国
~ no miyatsuko no kamu yogoto *l* 出雲国造神賀詞
Izumo no Okuni *fa* 出雲阿国
Izumoto *s* 泉本 965
Izumozaki *p* 出雲崎 523
Izu Nagaoka *p* 伊豆長岡 237 「出野 523
Izuno *s* 伊津野, 伊野,
Izuru *m* 出 「出石 523
Izushi *s* 伊頭志 237; *sp*
Izushima *s* 伊豆島 237
Izuta *s* 伊豆田
Izutani *s* 泉谷 965
Izutsu *s* 伊秋 237, 伊秩; *sf-la* 井筒 103
Izutsuya *s* 井筒屋
Izuya *s* 伊豆屋 237
Izuyama *s* 伊豆山, 厳山 2706
Izuyo *f* 出世 523

# J

(ja 邪 642, 射 1144, 蛇 1387)
(jaku 夕 33, 汐 250, 宅 283, 択 382, 沢 404, 若 692, 柘 864, 席 1242, 寂 1436, 雀 1530, 楉 1622, 弱 1647, 碩 2116, 簀 2687, 櫂 2722)
Jakuchō *ml* 寂超 1436
Jakuemon *m* 雀右衛門 1530 「寂念
Jakunen *ml* 寂然 1436,
Jakuren *ml* 寂蓮
Jakushi *s* 若芝 692
Jasei no in *l* 蛇性の婬 1387
Jashūmon *l* 邪宗門 642
Jawa *p* "Java" 瓜哇 305
Jayanagi *l* 蛇柳 1387
(ji 二 4, 巳 30, 士 41, 下 46, 仕 124, 示 148, 尼 175, 氏 223, 次 226, 地 241, 而 264, 寺 268, 耳 331, 自 340, 似 350, 児 497, 侍 559, 祀 640, 兕 758, 事 768, 持 801, 治 825, 柿 867, 茨 932, 俟 1035, 除 1059, 視 1348, 時 1382, 詞 1665, 道 1811, 辞 1918, 路 1925, 嗣 1937, 蒔 1985, 慈 1987, 兹 2134, 爾 2250, 贊 2394, 滋 2460, 諟 2512, 齒 2557, 慈 2701, 邇 2785, 璽 2860)
Jian 1021–24 治安 825
Jibe *s* 児部 497
Jibiki *s* 地引 241, 地曳
Jibu *p* 治部 825
Jibutarō *m* 治部太郎
Jichin *ml* 慈鎮 2701
Jiemon *m* 治右衛門 825
Jien *ml* 慈円 2701
Jigemura *s* 寺家村 268
Jigokuhen *l* 地獄変 241
Jigorō *m* 治五郎 825
Jihara *s* 地原 241
Jihee *m* 治兵衛 825
Jihishinchō *l* 慈悲心鳥 2701
Jiichirō *m* 治一郎 825
Jijō 1178–81 *l* 治承
Jijū *sm* 侍従 559
Jiken *s* 自見 340
(jiki 直 988, 埴 1561, 湜 1579, 漫 1854, 殖 1867, 植 1902, 稙 2122)
Jikihara *s* 直原 988
Jikka *sp* 十和 18
Jikkinshō *l* 十訓抄
Jikkunshō *l* 十訓抄
Jikkyoku *m* 十旭
Jikōji *s* 慈光寺 2701
(jiku 宍 470, 竺 729)
Jimeishō *l* 自鳴鐘 340
Jimokuji *p* 甚目寺 1267
Jimyōin *s* 持明院 801
Jin *s* 陣 1056. (仁 57, 壬 116, 仭 122, 任 235, 尽 290, 迅 307, 忱 371, 臣 527, 辰 738, 神 853, 陣 1056, 訒 1147, 奏 1202, 甚 1267, 陳 1311, 紝 1679, 靭 1694, 尋 1705, 晨 1739, 慎 1839, 椹 2097, 榛 2108, 潯 2270, 塵 2429, 儘 2435, 諶 2641, 藎 2680, 鐔 2882)
Jinba *s* 神波 853
Jinbo *s* 神保
Jinbō *sp* 神保
Jinbo Kōtarō *ml* 神保光太郎
Jindō *s* 袖藤 1107
Jinen Koji *la* 自然居士 340
Jingo *m* 甚吾 1267
~-keiun 767–70 神護景雲 853
Jingorō *m* 甚五郎 1267
Jingū *s* 神宮 853; *fh* 神
Jingūji *s* 神宮寺 ⌊功
Jin'ichi *m* 甚一 1267
Jin'ichirō *m* 甚一郎
Jinjō *p* 新庄 1965
Jinkaishū *lh* 塵芥集 2429
Jinki 724–29 神亀 853
Jinkō *p* 信更 782
Jinmei *s* 神明 853
Jinmoku *s* 甚目 1267
Jinmu *mh* 神武 853
Jinnai *s* 陣内 1056
Jinnaka *s* 神中 853
Jinno *s* 神野, 陣野 1056
Jinnō shōtōki *l* 神皇正統記 853 「陳内 1311
Jinnouchi *s* 陣内 1056,
Jinō *s* 耳名宇 331
Jinseki *p* 神石 853
Jinshichi *m* 甚七 1267
Jintarō *m* 甚太郎
Jinushi *s* 地主 241
Jin'yomo *m* 甚与茂 1267
Jinzaburō *m* 甚三郎
Jinzai *s* 神在 853, 神西
~ Kiyoshi *ml* 神西清
Jippensha Ikku *ml* 十返舎一九 18
Jirō *m* 二郎 4, 二朗, 次郎 226, 侍郎 559, 治郎 825, 治朗 「門
Jiroemon *m* 治郎右衛
Jiromaru *m* 二郎丸 4
Jirozaemon *m* 次郎左衛門 226 「825
Jiryaku 1065–69 治暦
Jisaburō *m* 治三郎
Jisaku *m* 治策
Jisenseki *l* 二千石 4
Jishō *ml* 自笑 340; 1177–81 治承 825
Jishōji *p* 慈照寺 2701
Jisoji *s* 二十二 4
Jisuke *m* 治輔 825
Jiteiki *l* 耳底記 331
Jitō *flh* 持統 801
(jitsu 十 18, 日 77, 実 678, 昵 839)
Jitsukata *s* 実方 678
Jitsukawa *s* 実川
Jiunsai *ml* 而慍斎 264
Jizaimaru *s* 自在丸 340
Jizō-mai *la* 地蔵舞 241
Jo *s* 徐 1049. (女 114, 汝 394, 如 412, 助 431, 序 507, 叙 893, 徐 1049, 除

1059, 茹 1171, 恕 1483, 舒 1673, 諸 2329, 鋤 2336, 緒 2537, 曙 2719)
Jō *s* 城 796. (丈 36, 上 47, 仍 123, 仗 127, 召 152, 丞 296, 成 322, 状 365A, 杖 422, 劭 429, 条 457, 床 508, 帖 563, 邵 646, 定 677, 忠 705, 尚 753, 承 760, 城 796, 浄 823, 茸 925, 貞 982, 乗 1016, 祥 1074, 晟 1187, 渉 1331, 尉 1410, 剰 1426, 巣 1431, 常 1463, 盛 1469, 晴 1597, 靖 1905, 誠 1935, 蒸 1981, 静 2145, 韶 2163, 樵 2479, 濃 2612, 嬲 2738, 襄 2769, 瀞 2793, 穣 2802, 穠 2803, 譲 2918, 饒 2925, 嚢 2935, 縄 2955)
Jōan 1171–75 承安 760
Jōban *p* 常磐 1463
Jōben *ml* 浄弁 823
Jōbō *p* 上房 47
Jōbōji *p* 浄法寺 823
Jōchō *ma* 定朝 677
Jōdai *s* 上代 47
Jōdo sanbukyō *l* 浄土三部経 823
~ Shinshū *h* 浄土真宗
Jōdoshū *h* 浄土宗
Jōe *m* 譲衛 2918
Jōei 1232–33 貞永 982
Jōfu *m* 襄夫 2769
Jōgan 859–77 貞観 982
Jōge *p* 上下 47
Jōgen 1207–11 承元 760; 976–78 貞元 982
Jogo *s* 余語 448
Jōgū Shōtoku hōōtaisetsu *lh* 上宮聖徳法王帝説 47
Jōhana *p* 城端 796
Jōhei *m* 丈平 36; 931–38 承平 760
Jōhen *p* 城辺 796
Jōhō 1074–77 承保 760
Jōhoku *p* 常北 1463
Jōichi *m* 尉一 1410, 襄一 2769
Jōji *m* 譲治 2918; 1362–68 貞治 982
Jōjima *p* 城島 796
Jōjin *mh* 成尋 322
~ Ajari Haha no shū *l* 成尋阿闍梨母集
Jōjirō *m* 丈次郎 36
Jōkei *mh* 貞慶 982
Jokaisen kidan *l* 女誡扇綺譚 114
Jōki *s* 常喜 1463
Jōkichi *m* 浄吉 823, 譲吉 2918
Jokō *ml* 如皐 412
Jōkō *s* 上甲 47; *m* 浄鉱 823
(joku 濯 2609)
Jōkyō 1684–88 貞享 982
Jōkyū 1219–22 承久 760
Jomei *mlh* 舒明 1673
Jōmi *s* 紹美 1955
Jōnan *p* 城南 796
Jōno *s* 条野 457, 城野 796
~ Saigiku *ml* 条野採菊 457
Jōō 1652–55 承応 760; 1222–24 貞応 982
Joraishi *ml* 如儡子 412
Jōroku *m* 静六 2145
Jōruri *la* 浄瑠璃 823
Jōryaku 1077–88 承暦 760
Jō Samon *ml* 城左門 796
Josetsu *ma* 如拙 412
Jōsō *ml* 丈草 36
Jōtarō *m* 丈太郎, 条太郎 457
Jōtō *p* 上道 47, 城東 796
Jōtoku 1097–99 承徳 760
Jōuchi *s* 城内 796
Jōwa 834–48 承和 760; 1345–50 貞和 982
Jōyō *p* 上陽 47, 城陽 796
Jōzuka *s* 定塚 677
(ju 戍 328, 住 355, 充 521, 寿 539, 受 730, 重 1017, 従 1050, 袖 1107, 授 1315, 就 1668, 頌 2113, 誦 2138, 需 2220, 聚 2221, 竪 2224, 儒 2432, 樹 2483, 嬬 2718, 檮 2724, 燾 2770, 雛 2888, 籌 2901, 鷲 2980)
(jū 十 18, 廿 102, 戎 321, 住 355, 充 521, 拾 802, 柔 907, 重 1017, 従 1050, 習 1468, 集 1779, 楫 1899, 輯 2497)
Juei 1182–85 寿永 539
Jūemon *m* 十右衛門 18, 重右衛門 1017
Juge *s* 樹下 2483
Jūgorō *m* 重五郎 1017
Jūhei *m* 重平
Juichi *m* 寿一 539
Jūichiya *s* 十一谷 18
~ Gisaburō *ml* 十一谷義三郎
Jūji *s* 十字; *m* 十司, 重治 1017
Jūjirō *m* 重次郎
Jukichi *m* 寿吉 539
Jūkichi *m* 重吉 1017
(juku 熟 2406)
Jūmonji *p* 十文字 18
Jūmon saihishō *l* 十問最秘抄
Jun *m* 恂 807, 淳 1337, 順 1532, 純 1956, 遵 2418, 潤 2277. (旬 301, 侚 562, 恂 807, 洵 815, 盾 984, 准 1023, 隼 1230, 惇 1288, 淳 1337, 順 1532, 循 1569, 閏 1819, 楯 1897, 詢 1928, 純 1956, 馴 1966, 準 2041, 絢 2150, 蓴 2187, 潤 2277, 醇 2315, 諄 2324, 遵 2418, 錞 2521, 鶉 2820)
~ -Den jitsujitsuki *l* 旬殿実々記 301
Jun'ichi *m* 順一 1532, 純一 1956
Jun'ichirō *m* 淳一郎 1337, 純一郎 1956, 潤一郎 2277
Jūnidan sōshi *l* 十二段草子 18
Junji *m* 淳治 1337, 順二 1532, 順耳, 順治
Junjirō *m* 順次郎, 潤次郎 2277
Junkichi *m* 順吉 1532, 純吉 1956
Junnosuke *m* 淳之助 1337, 準之助 2041
Junpyō *m* 潤瓢 2277
Junsaku *m* 順作 1532, 準策 2041
Junshirō *m* 順四郎 1532
Junsuke *m* 順助
Juntarō *s* 諄太郎 2324
Juntokuin *mlh* 順徳院 1532
Junzaburō *m* 順三郎, 閏三郎 1819, 準三郎 2041
Junzō *m* 順三 1532, 順造
Jūō *p* 十王 18
Jurō *m* 寿郎 539
Jūrō *m* 十郎 18
Jusaburō *m* 寿三郎 539
Jūsandaishū *l* 十三代集 18
Jūsan'ya *l* 十三夜
Jūshiya *m* 十四屋
Jūshiyama *p* 十四山
Jūsuke *m* 重助 1017
Jūta *m* 十太 18
Jūtarō *m* 重太郎 1017
Jūtoku *m* 従徳 1050
(jutsu 朮 209, 述 748, 術 1298)
Juzuya *s* 数珠屋 2169

# K

Ka *s* 何 513. (一 3, 力 11, 下 46, 火 52, 化 56, 日 77, 戈 108, 加 121, 可 165, 甲 184, 禾 220, 乎 221, 仮 231, 圭 267, 瓜 305, 伽 357, 赤 443, 芬 477, 芳 480, 花 481, 何 513, 我 545, 佳 560, 呼 571, 河 597, 卦 647, 金 664, 庚 741, 果 770, 神 853, 柯 855, 科 877, 郁 890, 香 961, 迦 999, 哉 1006, 蚊 1135, 夏 1161, 家 1185, 哥 1193, 哿 1194, 荷 1259, 華 1266, 倮 1287, 椛 1363, 啓 1517, 谺 1652, 訶 1662, 葭 1725, 袈 1749, 賀 1756, 過 1804, 鹿 1823, 禍 1885, 遐 2048, 樺 2103, 榎 2107, 歌 2170, 嘉 2184, 箇 2216, 謌 2643, 鍋 2650, 鍜 2651, 騂 2665, 霞 2693, 鰕

2886, 馨 2904)
(kaba 椛 1363, 樺 2103)
Kabasan *p* 加波山 121
Kabasawa *s* 樺沢 2103
Kabashima *s* 樺島
Kabata *s* 下野 46, 加畑 121, 蒲田 1993
Kabayama *s* 加場山 121, 樺山 2103
(kabe 壁 2585)
Kabe *s* 加部 121; *sp* 可部 165, 壁 2585
Kabegusa *l* 壁草
Kabeya *s* 壁谷, 壁屋
Kabiya *l* 鹿火屋 1823
Kabocha *s* 加保茶 121
(kabu 冠 905)
Kabuki *s* 冠木; *la* 歌舞伎 2170
~ jūhachiban *la* 歌舞伎十八番 「鏑 2816)
(kabura 冠 905, 蕪 2373,
Kaburagi *s* 冠城 905, 蕪木 2373, 鏑木 2816
~ Kiyokata *ma* 鏑木清方
Kaburasaka *s* 蕪坂 2373
Kaburaya *s* 蕪屋
Kaburu *s* 禿 496; *sm* 僮 2056
Kabuto *s* 加太 121, 甲 184, 兜 1800, 鹿伏兎 1823. (兜 1800)
Kabutō *s* 甲藤 184
Kabutochō *p* 兜町 1800
Kabutogi *s* 兜木
Kabu zuinōki *l* 歌舞髄脳記 2170
Kachi *s* 加地 121, 可知 165, 勝 1613. (徒 1048, 捷 1323, 硈 1385, 勝 1613, 猾 1834, 潤 2611, 闊 2710)
Kachibe *s* 勝部 1613
Kachii *s* 加地井 121
Kachio *m* 捷男 1323
Kachion *m* 勝臣 1613
Kachō *s* 華頂 1266
Kachōen *l* 花鳥編 481
Kada *s* 加田 121, 荷 1259, 荷田, 賀田 1756, 鹿田 1823 「在満 1259
~ no Arimaro *ml* 荷田
~ no Azumamaro *ml* 荷田春満
Kadenokōji *s* 勘解由小路 1699
Kadensho *l* 花伝書 481
Kado *s* 加戸 121, 加登; *sp* 上 47; *m* 門 601. (上 47, 戸 59, 圭 267, 角 547, 門 601, 柯 855, 閂 1010, 矩 1108, 葛 1994, 廉 2042)
Kadobayashi *s* 門林 601
Kadobe *s* 門部
Kadode *s* 角出 547
Kadoguchi *s* 門口 601
Kadohari *s* 角張 547
Kadoi *s* 角井, 門井 601, 葛井 1994; *m* 門居 601
Kadokawa *s* 角川 547; *sp* 門川 601
Kadoko *f* 廉子 2042
Kadokuni *m* 角国 547
Kadokura *s* 門倉 601
Kadoma *s* 角間 547, 門馬 601; *sp* 門真
Kadomatsu *s* 門松
Kadomoto *s* 角本 547
Kadono *s* 上遠野 47, 角野 547, 門野 601; *m* 葛野 1994
Kadōno *s* 上遠野 47
Kadooka *s* 廉嵎 2042
Kadō shōken *l* 歌道小見 2170 「田 601
Kadota *s* 角田 547, 門
Kadotani *s* 角谷 547
Kadowaki *s* 門脇 601
Kadoya *s* 角屋 547, 門谷 601, 門屋, 廉屋 2042
Kadoyama *s* 角山 547, 葛山 1994
Kadoya Shichirōbee *mh* 角屋七郎兵衛 547
Kaede *s* 楓 1892, 鶏冠 2821, 鶏冠井
Kaedei *s* 鶏冠井
Kaedemaro *m* 楓麻呂 1892 「54 嘉永 2184
Kaei *l* 花影 481; 1848–
Kaemon *m* 嘉右衛門
(kaeri 帰 1018)
Kaeriyama *s* 帰山
Kaeruda *s* 入 15
Kaetsu *s* 嘉悦 2184
Kafu *p* "Washington" 華府 1266
Kafū *ml* 荷風 1259
Kaga *s* 加宜 121; *sp* 加賀. (利 436, 香 961)
Kagae *s* 加加江 121
Kagai *s* 利井 436
Kagami *s* 加加見 121, 加加美, 加賀美, 各牟 277, 利光 436, 神鑒 853, 鏡味 2817; *sf-p* 鏡; *sp* 各務 277, 香美 961; *p* 香我美. (鏡 2817)
Kagamigahara *sp* 各務原 277
Kagamihara *s* 各務原
Kagamiishi *p* 鏡石 2817
Kagamino *p* 鏡野
Kagami otoko *la* 鏡男
~ Shikō *ml* 各務支考 277 「2817
Kagamiyama *s* 鏡山
Kagamu *m* 亀 1531
Kaga no Chiyojo *fl* 加賀の千代女 121
Kagari *m* 篝 2574
Kagaribi *l* 篝火
Kagashima *s* 鏡島 2817
Kagatsume *s* 加加爪 121
Kagawa *s* 加川, 賀川 1756; *sp* 香川 961
~ Kageki *ml* 香川景樹 「景柄
~ Kagemoto *ml* 香川
~ Susumu *ml* 香川進
~ Toyohiko *mlh* 賀川豊彦 1756
Kagaya *s* 加賀谷 121
Kagayaki *m* 輝 2499
Kagayama *s* 加賀山 121
Kage *s* 鹿毛 1823. (杮 867, 陰 1563, 晩 1595, 景 1764, 隠 2074, 影 2357, 蔭 2370, 熊 2410)
Kageaki *m* 景明 1764
Kageatsu *m* 景惇
Kagechika *m* 景新
Kagei *s* 隠居 2074
Kagekatsu *m* 景勝 1764
Kageki *m* 景樹
Kagekiyo *m-la* 景清
Kagekuni *m* 景晋
Kagemasa *m* 景方, 景正, 景政
Kagemi *m* 蔭見 2370
Kagemitsu *m* 影光 2357
Kagemori *m* 陰守 1563, 景盛 1764
Kagemoto *m* 景柄
Kagen 1303–06 嘉元 2184 「景憲
Kagenori *m* 景乗 1764,
Kagerō *l* 蜻蛉 2128
Kageshige *m* 晩重 1595, 景重 1764
Kagesue *m* 景季
Kagesuke *m* 景祐
Kageto *m* 勘解人 1699
Kagetoki *m* 景時 1764
Kagetomo *m* 景与, 景奉
Kagetsu *la* 花月 481
Kagetsugu *m* 景漸 1764, 景紹 「紙 481
Kagetsu sōshi *l* 花月草
Kageyama *s* 陰山 1563, 景山 1764, 影山 2357, 蔭山 2370 「1764
~ Hideko *fh* 景山英子
~ Masaharu *ml* 影山正治 2357
Kageyasu *m* 景保 1764
Kageyoshi *m* 景欽
Kageyu *m* 勘解由 1699
Kagi *sl* 鍵 2652. (鍵, 鎰 2748, 鑰 2998)
Kagiko *f* 鍵子 2652, 鎰子 2748 「2998
Kaginosuke *m* 鑰之助
Kagitake *m* 鍵武 2652
Kagitomi *s* 鍵富
Kagiya *s* 鍵谷
Kagiyama *s* 鍵山
(kago 籠 2977)
Kagomiya *s* 籠宮
Kagoshima *s* 籠島; *sp* 鹿児島 1823
~ Juzō *ml* 鹿児島寿蔵
Kagu tsuchi *l* 迦具土 999
Kagura *p-a* 神楽 853
~ uta *l* 神楽歌
~ ~ fuiriaya *l* 神楽歌譜入文
Kaguyama *s* 香山 961
Kahee *m* 嘉兵衛 2184
Kahei *m* 嘉平; *l* 歌病 2170
Kaheiji *m* 嘉平治 2184
Kahi *s* 柯斐 855
Kaho *p* 嘉穂 2184
Kahō 1094–96 嘉保
Kahoku *p* 河北 597, 香北 961, 鹿北 1823
Kai *s* 柯斐 855; *sf-ph* 甲斐 184. (刈 50, 介 66, 夬 100, 甘 207, 价 236, 合 270, 灰 302, 回 309, 快 372, 改 379, 会 454, 芥 475, 苅 479, 貝 498,

戒 511, 卦 647, 恢 806, 柄 862, 計 895, 界 967, 廻 994, 海 1071, 皆 1196, 啓 1491, 偕 1537, 堺 1560, 開 1821, 傀 1828, 階 1840, 解 1923, 楷 2098, 誡 2139, 槐 2296, 絵 2332, 嵬 2374, 魁 2423, 稽 2491, 穎 2505, 継 2539, 養 2558, 薊 2562A, 薤 2565, 壊 2602, 懐 2605, 檜 2624, 諧 2639, 鶏 2821, 蟹 2853, 繫 2959)
Kaibara *s* 貝原 498, 海原 1071; *p* 柏原 866
~ Ekiken / Ekken *mh* 貝原益軒 498
Kaibe *s* 海辺 1071, 海部
Kaibo *s* 海保
Kaibu *sp* 海部
Kaichi *m* 佳一 560, 嘉一 2184, 嘉市
Kaichirō *m* 嘉一郎
Kaichōon *l* 海潮音 1071
Kaichō riyaku fuda asobi-awase *l* 開帳利益札遊合 1821
Kaida *s* 合田 270, 改田 379, 貝田 498, 戒田 511; *sp* 開田 1821 (see also Kaita)
Kaidan'in shitennō *a* 戒壇院四天王 511
Kaide *s* 鶏冠 2821, 鶏冠井
Kaiden *s* 開田 1821
Kaidō *s* 海道 1071, 海藤, 皆藤 1196
Kaidōki *l* 海道記 1071
Kaieda *s* 海江田
Kaifu *s* 養父 2558
Kaifūsō *l* 懐風藻 2605
Kaiga *s* 貝賀 498, 海賀 1071 ⌈2605
Kaigetsudō *a* 懐月堂
Kaigo *s* 海後 1071
Kaiho *s* 海保 ⌈法保
Kaihō *s* 海北, 海宝, 海
Kaihoku *s* 海北
Kaiho Seiryō *mh* 海保青陵
Kaihotsu *s* 開発 1821
Kaihō Yūshō *ma* 海北友松 1071
Kaii *s* 改井 379 ⌈1537
Kaiichirō *m* 偕一郎
Kaijima *s* 貝島 498
Kaijinmaru *l* 海神丸
Kaijū *s* 戒重 511 ⌊1071
Kaikawa *s* 貝川 498
Kaikei *ma* 快慶 372
Kaiko *f* 貝子 498, 佳似子 560
Kaikō *s* 開高 1821; *l* 海紅 1071, 歌意考 2170
Kaikoku heidan *h* 海国兵談 1071
Kaikō Takeshi *ml* 開高健 1821
Kaimokushō *l* 開目鈔
Kaimon *p* 開聞
Kainan *p* [" Hainan "] 海南 1071
Kaine *s* 甲斐根 184
Kaino *s* 戒野 511
Kainō *s* 戒能
Kainoshō *s* 甲斐庄 184
Kainuma *s* 貝沼 498, 海沼 1071
Kai-ōi *l* 貝おほひ 498
Kaion *ml* 海音 1071
Kaionji *s* 海音寺
~ Chōgorō *ml* 海音寺潮五郎 ⌈1828
Kairaishiki *l* 傀儡子記
Kairo *s* 海渡 1071
Kairokō *l* 薤露行 2565
Kaisawa *s* 螺沢 2805
Kaise *s* 貝瀬 498, 海瀬 1071
Kaisei *p* 開成 1821
Kaisō *p* 海草 1071
Kaita *sp* 海田; *p* 穎田 2505 (see also Kaida)
Kaitai shinsho *lh* 解体新書 1923 ⌈1071
Kaito *s* 垣外 795, 海渡
Kaitō *s* 垣内 795, 海東 1071, 階藤 1840
Kaitokudō *ph* 懐徳堂 2605 ⌈内松三 795
Kaitō Matsuzō *ml* 垣
Kai tsūshōkō *h* 華夷通商考 1266
Kaiya *s* 海谷 1071
Kaizaki *s* 海崎
Kaizō *m* 戒三 511
Kaizu *s* 貝津 498; *sp* 海津 1071 ⌈塚 498
Kaizuka *s* 海塚; *sp* 貝
Kaizumi *s* 海住 1071
Kaji *s* 加治 121, 梶 1371, 鹿地 1823, 鍛冶 2651; *sp* 可児 165. (柁 856, 梶 1371, 楫 1899, 鍛 2651, 櫂 2722, 檝 2723)
Kajie *s* 楫江 1899
Kajigaya *s* 梶ケ谷 1371
Kajihime *fh* 檝媛 2723
Kajii *s* 梶井 1371
~ Motojirō *ml* 梶井基 (kajika 鰍 2887) ⌊次郎
Kajikawa *s* 柁川 856, 梶川 1371; *sp* 加治川 121
Kajikazawa *p* 鰍沢 2887
Kajiki *s* 梶木 1371; *sp* 加治木 121
Kajiko *f* 楫子 1899, 櫂子 2722 ⌈間 1371
Kajima *s* 加島 121, 梶
Kajimoto *s* 梶本
Kajimura *s* 梶村
Kajin no kigū *l* 佳人之奇遇 560
Kajinari *m* 梶成 1371
Kajino *s* 梶野, 楫野 1899
Kajirō *m* 嘉次郎 2184
Kajishima *s* 梶島 1371
Kajita *s* 梶田
Kajitani *s* 梶谷
Kajitori *s* 楫取 1899
Kajitsuka *s* 梶塚 1371
Kajiura *s* 梶浦 ⌈正之
~ Masayuki *ml* 梶浦
Kajiwara *s* 梶原
~ Kagetoki *ml* 梶原景時 ⌈亘 1823
Kaji Wataru *ml* 鹿地
Kajiya *s* 加治屋 121, 梶谷 1371
Kajiyama *s* 梶山
Kajō 1106–08 嘉承
Kajū *m* 嘉十 ⌊2184
Kajūji *s* 勧修寺 1970
Kakaishō *l* 河海抄 597
Kakaji *p* 香香地 961
Kakan'ō *l* 花間鶯 481
Kake *s* 梯 1617; *sp* 加計 121. (掛 1321, 懸 2984)
Kakeaoi *l* 懸葵
Kakefuda *s* 掛札 1321
Kakegawa *p* 掛川
Kakehashi *s* 掛橋, 桟 1615, 梯 1617
Kakehi *s* 垣見 795; *sm* 筧 2014
Kakei *sm* 筧; *ml* 荷兮 1259; 1387–89 嘉慶 2184
Kakeya *p* 掛合 1321
Kaki *s* 垣 795. (垣, 柿 867, 塀 1559, 堅 1796, 蠣 2870, 籬 3010)
Kakiage *s* 書上 1216
Kakibe *s* 部曲 1418
Kakichi *m* 嘉吉 2184
Kakida *s* 垣田 795, 柿田 867
Kakiemon *s* 柿衛門
Kakigara *p* 牡蠣殻 407
Kakihana *s* 柿花 867
Kakihara *s* 柿原
Kakiko *f* 垣子 795
Kakimi *s* 垣見 ⌈867
Kakimoto *s* 垣本, 柿本
Kakinoki *p* 柿木
Kakinomoto *s* 柿本; *l* 柿の本 ⌈本人麻呂
~ no Hitomaro *ml* 柿
~ ~ ~ Ason kanmon *l* 柿本人麻呂朝臣勘
Kakinuma *s* 柿沼 ⌊文
Kakio *m* 赤黄男 443
Kakioka *s* 柿岡 867
Kakishima *s* 柿島
Kakisu *s* 柿栖
Kakito *s* 垣内 795
Kakitsu *s* 垣内, 嘉吉 2184
Kakitsubata *la* 杜若 423
Kakitsuda *s* 垣内田 795
Kakiuchi *s* 垣内, 柿内 867 ⌈*m-f* 堅磐 1796
Kakiwa *s* 塀和 1559;
Kakiyama *s* 柿山 867
Kaki yamabushi *la* 柿山伏 ⌈*p* 柿崎 867
Kakizaki *s* 蠣崎 2870;
Kakizawa *s* 柿沢
Kakizono *s* 柿園
Kako *s* 可児 165, 賀古 1756; *sp* 加古 121
Kakō *s* 口 28
Kakogawa *sp* 加古川 121, 狩小川 791
Kako genzai ingakyō *la* 過去現在因果経 1804
Kakogi *s* 鹿子木 1823
Kakotoshi *s* 神楽師 853, 神薬師
Kaku *s* 加来 121, 角 547, 賀来 1756; *m* 格 1099. (各 277, 角 547, 拡 799, 恪 803, 客 917, 革 937, 画 991, 格 1099, 郭

1417, 脚 1612, 覚 1752, 廓 2239, 確 2305, 慤 2403, 穫 2729, 鶴 2926, 靏 3022)
Kakubari *s* 覚張 1752
Kakuda *sp* 角田 547
～ Kōkōkaku *ml* 角田浩々歌客
Kakuichi *m* 角一
Kakujirō *m* 覚次郎 1752
Kakumi *s* 各務 277
Kakumoto *s* 覚本 1752
Kakumu *s* 各務 277
Kakunodate *p* 角館 547
Kakunōin *s* 覚王院 1752
Kakuoka *s* 角岡 547
Kakurai *s* 加倉井 121
～ Akio *ml* 加倉井秋を
Kakushin kurabu *l* 革新倶楽部 937
Kakutarō *m* 覚太郎 1752
Kakutō *p* 加久藤 121
Kakuya *s* 角谷 547, 角屋
Kakuyū *ma* 覚猷 1752
Kakuzō *m* 覚三
Kakyō 1387–89 嘉慶 2184 「2170
～ hyōshiki *l* 歌経標式
(kama 釜 1160, 蒲 1993, 鎌 2750) 「鎌腹
Kamabara *s* 鎌原; *la*
Kamabige *la* 鎌髭
Kamachi *s* 蒲地 1993
Kamae *s* 一尺八分 3; *p* 蒲江 1993
Kamagari *p* 蒲刈
Kamagata *s* 鎌形 2750
Kamagaya *s* 霞間昼 2693; *p* 鎌ケ谷 2750
Kamahara *s* 蒲原 1993, 鎌原 2750
Kamai *s* 釜井 1160
Kamaishi *p* 釜石
Kamaji *m* 鎌治 2750
Kamajirō *m* 庚午治郎 741, 釜次郎 1160
Kamakura *sp* 鎌倉 2750
～ bakufu *h* 鎌倉幕府
～ -dono *mh* 鎌倉殿
Kamano *s* 鎌野
Kamanoe *s* 一尺二寸 3
Kamaru *m* 可丸 165
Kamasawa *s* 蒲沢 1993
Kamata *s* 畑田 838, 釜田 1160, 鎌田 2750
Kamataki *s* 鎌滝
Kamatari *m* 鎌足
Kamatarō *m* 鎌太郎
Kamato *s* 門真 601
Kamatsuka *s* 一尺八寸 3, 一寸八分, 一寸六分 「谷 1993
Kamaya *s* 釜屋 1160, 蒲
Kamayachi *s* 釜范 1160, 釜范
Kamayatsu *s* 釜范
Kame *sf* 亀 1531. (瓶 1388, 亀1531, 甕 2908)
Kamechiyo *m-f* 亀千代 1531
Kameda *sp* 亀田
Kamegaki *s* 亀垣
Kamegawa *s* 亀川
Kamegaya *s* 亀谷
Kamegorō *m* 亀五郎
Kamei *s* 亀井
Kameichi *m* 亀一, 嘉芽市 2184
Kamei Katsuichirō *ml* 亀井勝一郎 1531
Kameji *m* 亀二
Kamejirō *m* 亀次郎
Kamekichi *m* 亀吉
Kameko *f* 甕子 2908
Kamekura *s* 亀倉 1531
Kamemitsu *m* 亀光
Kamemoto *s* 亀本
Kamemura *s* 亀村
Kamenosuke *m* 亀之 ⌊助
Kameo *m* 亀雄
Kameoka *sp* 亀岡; *m* 亀丘
Kamesaburō *m* 亀三郎
Kamesaki *s* 亀崎
Kame-san *l* 亀さん
Kameshima *s* 亀島
Kameshiri *s* 瓶尻 1388
Kametani *s* 亀谷 1531
Kametarō *m* 亀太郎
Kameya *s* 亀谷, 亀屋
Kameyama *sp* 亀山
Kameyata *m* 亀弥太
Kamezawa *s* 亀沢
Kamezō *m* 亀造
Kami *s* 上 47, 甘味 207, 神 853, 紙 1953; *sp* 加美 121, 可美 165; *p* 香美 961. (上 47, 天 93, 尹 98, 正 205, 甫 533, 昇 713, 神 853, 柄 862, 首 920, 省 1013, 称 1118, 宰 1180, 漢 1860, 紙 1953, 督 2023, 頭 2504)
Kamiagata *sp* 上県 47
Kamiakutsu *s* 上阿久津 「*sp* 神林 853
Kamibayashi *s* 上林;
Kamibe *s* 上部 47
Kamichi *s* 上地
Kamichika *s* 神近 853
～ Ichiko *flh* 神近市子
Kamida *s* 紙田 1953
Kamide *s* 上出 47
Kamifuji *s* 神藤 853
Kamifunao *s* 上舟尾 47
Kami-furano *p* 上富良野 「1953
Kamifūsen *la* 紙風船
Kamigaki *s* 神垣 853
Kamigata *sp* 上方 47
Kamigō *p* 上郷
Kamigōri *p* 上郡
Kami-gotō *p* 上五島
Kamiguchi *s* 上口
Kamigyō *p* 上京
Kami-hei *p* 上閉伊
Kamihira *s* 上平
Kamiichi *s* 上依知; *p* 上市 「丸
Kamiichimaru *m* 上一
Kami-ina *p* 上伊那
Kamiishi *s* 上石
Kami-ishizu *p* 上石津
Kamiiso *p* 上磯
Kamiita *p* 上板
Kamiizumi *s* 上泉; *p* 神泉 853 「秀信 47
～ Hidenobu *ml* 上泉
Kamijima *s* 上島, 神島 853 「貫 47
～ Onitsura *ml* 上島鬼
Kamijō *s* 上条
Kamijōzu *s* 上上手
Kamikanki *s* 上神吉
Kamikatsu *sp* 上勝
Kamikawa *s* 上河; *sp* 上川, 神川 853
Kami-kawachi *p* 上河内 47
Kamikawai *s* 上川井
Kamiki *s* 神木 853, 神吉, 神去
Kamikichi *s* 神吉
Kamikita *p* 上北 47
Kami-kitayama *p* 上北山 「紙子 1953
Kamiko *s* 神子 853; *f*
Kami-koani *p* 上小阿仁 47 「上高地
Kamikōchi *s* 上垣内; *p*
Kamikoso *s* 神社 853
Kamikubo *s* 上久保 47
Kami-kuishiki *p* 上九一色
Kamikuni *s* 神三郡 853
Kamikura *s* 上倉 47, 神蔵 853
Kamimagari *s* 上勾 47
Kamimaki *p* 上牧
Kami-mashiki *p* 上益城
～-matsura *p* 上松浦
Kamimatsuura *s* 上松浦
Kamimikawa *s* 上三川
Kamimine *sp* 上峰
Kami-minochi *p* 上水 ⌊内
Kamimizu *s* 上水
Kamimoku *p* 上牧
Kamimoto *s* 上本 47, 本 853 「神村 853
Kamimura *s* 上村 47,
Kaminaga *s* 神永, 神長
Kaminaka *s* 上中 47; *p* 上那賀 「*la* 神鳴
Kaminari *s* 神成 853;
Kami-niikawa *p* 上新川 47
Kaminishi *s* 上西
Kamino *s* 神野 853; *p* 上野 47
Kaminobu *s* 上信
Kaminoho *p* 上之保
Kaminokuni *p* 上ノ国
Kaminomiya *s* 上宮
Kaminoseki *p* 上関
Kaminukiimi *s* 上抜井見
Kaminuma *s* 上沼
Kaminuri *s* 神漆 853
Kamio *s* 神尾
Kamioka *s* 上岡 47; *sp* 神岡 853
Kamiri *s* 上利 47
Kamiryō *s* 上領
Kamisago *s* 上砂
Kami-saibara *p* 上斎原
Kamisaka *s* 上坂, 神坂 853
Kamisaku *s* 神作
Kamisato *s* 上郷 47; *sp* 上里
Kamise *s* 神瀬 853
Kami-shihi *p* 上志比 47
～-shihoro *p* 上士幌
Kamishiro *s* 上代

Kamisu *p* 神栖 853
Kami-sunagawa *p* 上砂川 47
～-taira *p* 上平
～-takai *p* 上高井
Kamitakara *p* 上宝
Kamitoko *s* 上床
Kami-tonda *p* 上富田
Kamitōno *s* 上遠野
Kamitsu *s* 神津 853
Kamitsuagata *s* 上県 47
Kami-tsue *p* 上津江
～-tsuga *p* 上都賀
Kamitsukasa *s* 上司
～ Shōken *ml* 上司小剣
Kamitsuke *s* 上毛
Kamitsukefu *s* 上毛布
Kamitsukenu *s* 上毛野
Kamitsuki *s* 上月
Kami-tsushima *p* 上対馬
Kamiuchi *s* 上有智
Kami-ukena *p* 上浮穴
Kamiura *sp* 上浦
Kamiutae *s* 神刑部 853
Kamiya *s* 上谷 47, 神谷 853, 神屋, 紙谷山 1953, 紙屋 「47
Kami-yahagi *p* 上矢作
Kamiyakko *s* 神奴 853
Kami-yaku *p* 上屋久 47
Kamiyama *s* 加美山 121; *sp* 上山 47, 神山 853 「田 47
Kami-yamada *p* 上山
Kamiyamasa *s* 上山佐
Kamiyama Shigeo *ml* 神山茂夫 853
Kamiyanagi *s* 上柳 47
Kamiyato *s* 神谷戸 853
Kamiyosami *s* 上網 47
Kamiyoshi *s* 神吉 853
Kami-yūbetsu *p* 上湧別 47 「沢 853
Kamizawa *s* 上沢, 神
Kamizumi *s* 神墨
Kamo *sm* 鴨 2489; *sp* 加茂 121, 賀茂 1756. (鴨 2489)
Kamō *p* 蒲生 1993
Kamochi *s* 加持 121, 鹿持 1823, 鴨池 2489
～ Masazumi *ml* 鹿持雅澄 1823
Kamoda *s* 鴨田 2489
Kamogata *p* 鴨方
Kamogawa *p* 加茂川 121, 鴨川 2489
Kamoi *s* 鴨井
Kamoji *s* 鴨打
Kamojima *p* 鴨島
Kamome *p* 鷗 2975
Kamo monogurui *la* 加茂物狂 121 「1319
Kamon *s* 加門; *sm* 掃部
Kamo no Chōmei *ml* 鴨長明 2489
～ no Mabuchi *mlh* 賀茂真淵 1756 「121
Kamonomiya *s* 加茂宮
Kamori *s* 掃守 1319; *m* 佳盛 560 「2489
Kamoshida *s* 鴨志田
Kamoshita *s* 鴨下
Kamoto *p* 鹿本 1823
Kamotsugu *m* 鴨継 2489
Kamouchi *s* 鴨打
(kamu 神 853)
Kamuenai *p* 神恵内
(kamuhata 綺 2532)
Kamura *s* 加村 121, 香村 961, 嘉村 2184
～ Isota *ml* 嘉村礒多
Kamuro *m* 禿 496. (禿)
Kamuroji *s* 禿氏
Kamuroya *s* 円谷 78
Kan *s* 冠 905, 菅 1450, 寒 1714, 管 2212; *m* 寛 1977. (干 26, 甘 207, 汗 248, 亘 262, 肝 408, 完 471, 串 516, 侃 551, 邯 643, 官 672, 垣 795, 神 853, 柑 858, 冠 905, 巻 975, 奐 979, 看 998, 咸 1003, 捍 1042, 悍 1051, 晅 1085, 桓 1100, 栞 1220, 函 1232, 睅 1352, 乾 1411, 菅 1450, 喧 1541, 渙 1577, 皖 1638, 款 1666, 敢 1687, 勘 1699, 寒 1714, 萓 1730, 貫 1754, 閑 1820, 間 1822, 堪 1843, 漢 1860, 換 1872, 煥 1876, 暄 1881, 幹 1938, 勧 1970, 寛 1977, 僴 2054, 戡 2166, 管 2212, 関 2245, 澗 2274, 歓 2352, 監 2398, 嫺 2475, 諠 2513, 諫 2514, 翰 2518, 綣 2532, 環 2620, 緩 2659, 韓 2741, 館 2761, 観 2765, 簡 2788, 懽 2863, 鐶 2952, 鑑 2968, 鑾 2982)
(kana 門 601, 金 664, 奏 951, 哉 1006, 鉛 1944)
Kanachi *s* 金持 664
Kanada *sp* 金田; *p* "Canada" 加奈陀 121
Kanadehon chūshingura *la* 仮名手本忠臣蔵 231
Kanadome *s* 京 663
Kanae *s* 金戸 664, 金江, 金重; *sm-p* 鼎 2246; *m* 香苗 961, 鉽 2152, 匱 2238, 錡 2520; *f* 佳秧 560
Kanagaki *s* 仮名垣 231, 神奈垣 853 「文 231
～ Robun *ml* 仮名垣魯
Kanagawa *p* 神奈川 853
Kanagi *p* 金木 664, 金
Kanahara *s* 金原 └城
Kanai *s* 金居; *sp* 金井; *m* 叶 132 「笑 664
～ Sanshō *ml* 金井三
Kanaji *s* 金出地, 金持
Kanaki *s* 十七夜 18
Kanako *f* 金中子 664, 神奈子 853, 奏子 951
Kanakubo *s* 金久保 664, 金窪 「倉 853
Kanakura *s* 金鞍, 神長
Kanakusuku *s* 金城 664
Kana majiri musume setsuyō *l* 仮名文章娘節用 231
Kanamari *s* 神余 853
Kanamaru *s* 金丸 664
Kaname *m* 中 75, 要 1218, 要人, 紀 1424, 最 1744; *f* 哉女 1006
Kan'ami *mla* 観阿弥 2765
Kanamori *s* 金森 664
Kanamura *s* 金村
Kanan *p* ["Honan"] 河南 597
Kanando *m* 要人 1218
Kana no motosue *l* 仮字本末 231
Kanaoka *s* 金岡 664
Kanari *s* 哿 1194; *m* 可也 165
Kanasagō *p* 金砂郷 664
Kanasana *s* 金鑽
Kanasasu *s* 金刺
Kanasugi *s* 金杉
Kanatsume *s* 金集
Kanawa *s* 金輪; *la* 鉄輪 1948
Kanawaka *m* 金若 664
Kanaya *s* 金谷; *sp* 金屋 「*sp* 金山 664
Kanayama *s* 鉛山 1944;
Kanayomi Hakkenden *l* 仮名読八犬伝 231
Kanazawa *sp* 金沢 664
～ Bunko *pl* 金沢文庫
～ Tanetomi *ml* 金沢種美 「231
Kana-zōshi *l* 仮名草子
Kanazu *sp* 金津 664
Kanba *s* 神庭 853
Kanbara *s* 神原; *sp* 蒲原 1993
～ Ariake *ml* 蒲原有明
～ Katsushige *ml* 神原克重 853
～ Tai *ml* 神原泰
Kanbashi *m* 芳 480
Kanbayashi *s* 上林 47
～ Akatsuki *ml* 上林暁
Kanbe *s* 神戸 853, 掃部 1319, 鹿伏兎 1823
Kanbun 1661–73 寛文 1977 「2765
Kanchōrō *ml* 観潮楼
Kanda *s* 刈田 50; *sp* 苅田 479, 神田 853
Kandabashi *sp* 神田橋
Kandachi *s* 神立
Kanda Takahira *mlh* 神田孝平
Kande *s* 寒出 1714
Kando *s* 神戸 853, 神奴, 神門
Kandō *s* 貫洞 1754
Kandori *s* 香取 961
Kane *s* 兼 1268; *m* 金 664, 矩 1108. (尺 96, 包 218, 印 260, 光 281, 金 664, 宝 676, 易 714, 具 718, 周 736, 侶 778, 封 885, 倚 1033, 矩 1108, 兼 1268, 務 1377, 粛 1528, 詠 1664, 撰 1837, 誠 1935, 鉦 1941, 鉦 1942, 鉄 1948, 該 2135, 説 2143, 鉱 2153, 銅 2159, 鼎 2246, 談 2325, 統 2333, 鋏 2338, 銀 2345, 監 2398, 錦 2525, 懐 2605, 謙 2646, 厳 2706,

鎌 2750, 鏡 2817, 鐘 2883, 鑑 2968)
Kaneai *m* 具集 718, 兼魄 1268 「兼離
Kaneaki *m* 兼日, 兼洞,
Kaneakira *m* 兼明
Kaneari *m* 兼在
Kanebayashi *s* 金林 664
Kanechika *m* 兼及 1268, 兼集 「田 1268
Kaneda *s* 金田 664, 兼
Kanedo *s* 金戸 664
Kaneeda *s* 金枝
Kanefumi *m* 錦文 2525
Kanefuru *m* 兼古 1268
Kanefusa *m* 兼房, 兼莫
Kanefushi *m* 兼節
Kanegae *s* 鐘江 2883
Kanegasaki *p* 金ケ崎 664
Kanehako *s* 金箱
Kaneharu *m* 兼花 1268, 兼青, 兼流
Kanehide *m* 包秀 218, 兼之 1268
Kanehiko *m* 庚子彦 741
Kanehira *s* 兼平 1268; *sm* 金平 664; *m* 周平 736, 兼衡 1268, 懐成 2605
Kanehiro *m* 兼大 1268, 兼戸, 兼外, 兼宏, 兼熙, 兼聞
Kanehisa *m* 兼古
Kanehito *m* 兼仁, 兼仙
Kan'ei *s* 金居 664; 1624–44 寛永 1977
Kaneida *s* 金井田 664, 金居田
Kaneie *m* 金宿, 兼宅 1268, 兼舎, 兼家, 兼屋
Kan'eiji *p* 寛永寺 1977
Kaneizumi *s* 金泉 664
Kanejirō *m* 鉦次郎 1941
Kanekane *m* 兼銅 1268
Kanekata *m* 兼像
Kanekawa *s* 金川 664
Kanekazu *m* 兼計 1268, 兼員
Kaneki *s* 金木 664
Kanekichi *m* 兼吉 1268
Kanekiyo *m* 兼心, 兼井, 兼玉, 兼白, 兼研
Kaneko *s* 我如古 545, 金子 664, 金古, 金児; *sf* 兼子 1268; *f* 包子 218, 周子 736, 封子 885, 懐子 2605, 鏡湖 2817, 鐘子 2883
～ Chikusui *ml* 金子筑水 664
～ Fukyū *ml* 金子不泣
～ Kentarō *mh* 金子堅太郎 「園
～ Kun'en *ml* 金子薫
～ Mitsuharu *ml* 金子光晴 「元臣
～ Motoomi *ml* 金子
Kanekoto *m* 兼籌 1268, 鑑载 2968
Kaneko Tōta *ml* 金子兜太 664
～ Yōbun *ml* 金子洋文
Kanekuni *m* 兼州 1268
Kanemachi *m* 兼待
Kanemaki *s* 印牧 260, 印巻, 金巻 664, 鐘巻 2883 「兼正 1268
Kanemasa *m* 金蔵 664,
Kanematsu *s* 兼松; *m* 甲峰松 184
Kanemi *m* 鐘巳 2883
Kanemichi *m* 金道 664, 兼陸 1268, 兼逵
Kanemitsu *sm* 金光 664; *m* 兼充 1268
Kanemochi *s* 金持; *m* 兼持, 説望 2143
Kanemori *sm* 金守 664, 金盛; *m* 兼杜 1268, 兼関, 兼護
Kanemoro *m* 兼師
Kanemoto *s* 金本 664, 兼本 1268; *m* 兼下, 兼太, 兼体, 兼源, 務本 1377
Kanemuma *m* 兼馬 1268
Kanemura *s* 兼村
Kan'en 1748–51 寛延 1977 「*m* 懐良 2605
Kanenaga *s* 金長 664;
Kanenami *m* 兼並 1268
Kanenari *s* 金成 664; *m* 兼入 1268, 兼生, 兼作, 兼得, 説成 2143
Kaneno *s* 金野 664
Kanenobu *m* 兼言 1268, 兼信, 兼施 「2883
Kane no ne *la* 鐘の音
Kanenori *m* 包教 218, 兼曲 1268, 兼廻, 兼教
Kaneo *s* 金生 664, 金尾; *m* 金雄, 庚子郎 741, 鉄夫 1948, 統雄 2333
Kaneoki *m* 兼奥 1268
Kaneoto *m* 兼乙
Kaneoya *s* 金親 664
Kanesaburō *m* 兼三郎 1268, 鉱三郎 2153
Kanesada *m* 兼員 1268
Kanesaka *s* 金坂 664, 兼坂 1268
Kanesaki *s* 金崎 664; *m* 兼前 1268
Kanesane *m* 兼実
Kanesawa *s* 金沢 664
Kaneshichi *m* 甲子七 184 「兼重 1268
Kaneshige *sm* 金重 664,
Kaneshiki *s* 金敷 664
Kaneshima *s* 金島
Kaneshiro *s* 金城
Kanesogi *s* 金曾木
Kanesuke *m* 兼相 1268, 兼輔, 誠佑 1935, 銀佐 2345
Kanesumi *m* 兼純 1268
Kanetada *m* 金田 664, 兼惟 1268
Kanetaka *s* 金高 664, 兼高 1268; *m* 包高 218, 兼上 1268, 兼山, 兼位, 兼伯, 兼孝, 兼梢, 兼敬, 兼崇; *ma* 包女 218, 兼女 1268
Kanetake *m* 兼武, 兼毅
Kanetane *m* 兼植, 銕胤 2338, 鑑種 2968
Kanetani *s* 金谷 664
Kanetari *m* 兼足 1268
Kanetarō *m* 兼太郎
Kaneto *s* 金鋳 664, 兼人 1268
Kanetō *s* 兼頭
Kanetoki *m* 兼辰, 兼刻
Kanetomi *m* 兼福
Kanetomo *m* 兼付, 兼公, 兼同, 兼伴, 兼知, 兼奉, 兼倫, 兼流, 兼備, 兼等
Kanetoshi *m* 包蔵 218
Kanetsu *s* 金津 664
Kanetsugu *m* 包次 218, 兼従 1268, 兼続
Kanetsuka *s* 金塚 664
Kanetsuna *s* 金綱
Kanetsune *sm* 兼常 1268; *m* 兼積
～ Kiyosuke *ml* 兼常清佐
Kanetsura *m* 兼列
Kaneuchi *s* 金内 664, 鐘打 2883 「兼氏
Kaneuji *s* 兼姓 1268; *m*
Kaneumi *s* 金海 664
Kaneura *m* 兼裏 1268
Kanewaka *m* 兼分, 兼若, 兼涌 「金山 664
Kaneyama *sp* 兼山; *p*
Kaneyasu *s* 金安, 金保; *sm* 兼安 1268; *m* 具慶 718
Kaneyo *m* 兼代 1268
Kaneyori *m* 兼仍, 兼自, 兼順
Kaneyoshi *s* 鈺宣 1942; *m* 包幸 218, 包是, 金甫 664, 兼令 1268, 兼伝, 兼宝, 兼香, 兼誼
Kaneyuka *m* 兼床
Kaneyuki *sm* 金行 664; *m* 周行 736
Kanezaki *s* 鐘崎 2883
Kanezane *m* 包真 218
Kanezashi *s* 金刺 664, 金指 「兼角
Kanezumi *m* 兼住 1268,
Kangakuin *ph* 勧学院 1970
Kangaya *s* 榛谷 2108
Kangen 1243–47 寛元 1977
Kangi *s* 神吉 853, 冠木 905, 冠城; 1229–32 寛喜 1977 「1820
Kanginshū *l* 閑吟集
Kango *m* 完吾 471
Kanhasshū tsunagiuma *la* 関八州繋馬 2245 「綺 2533
Kanhatori *s* 神服 853,
Kanhō *s* 神保 853
Kani *s* 蟹 2853; *sp* 可児 165. (掃 1319, 蟹 2853)
Kan'ichi *m* 勘一 1699, 貫一 1754
Kan'ichirō *m* 幹一郎 1938, 寛一郎 1977
Kanie *sp* 蟹江 2853
Kanijima *s* 蟹島 「丸
Kanikomaru *ml* 蟹子
Kanimori *s* 掃 1319, 掃守, 掃部; *m* 蟹守 2853
Kanimoto *s* 蟹本
Kan'in *s* 閑院 1820
Kanita *p* 蟹田 2853
Kanitani *s* 蟹谷

Kanitsu *s* 加悦 121, 嘉悦 2184 「山伏 2853
Kani yamabushi *la* 蟹
Kanizawa *s* 蟹沢
Kanja *s* 甘蔗 207
Kanji *m* 完二 471, 完治, 完爾, 勘治 1699, 寛次 1977, 簡治 2788; *m* 1078–94 寛治 1977
Kanjinchō *la* 勧進帳 1970
Kanjirō *m* 勘次郎 1699, 寛二郎 1977, 寛次郎, 鑑次郎 2968
Kanji san'onkō *l* 漢字三音考 1860 「漢書
Kanjo *lh* "Han shu"
Kanjō *m* 貫城 1754
~ suetsumuhana *l* 閑情末摘花 1820
Kanjū *m* 勘十 1699
Kanke bunsō *l* 菅家文草 1450
~ kōsō *l* 菅家後草
~ man'yōshū *l* 菅家万葉集
Kanki *sp* 神吉 853
Kankichi *m* 寒吉 1714
Kankō 1004–12 寛弘 1977
Kankoku *p* "(Republic of) Korea" 韓国 2741
Kankōshū *l* 寒紅集 1714
Kankurō *m* 寛九郎 1977
Kankyo no tomo *l* 閑居友 1820
Kanma *m* 勘馬 1699
Kanmaru *s* 神丸 853
Kanmichi *s* 上道 47
Kanmu *mh* 桓武 1100
~ Heishi *h* 桓武平氏
Kanmuri *s* 冠 905
~ Matsujirō *ml* 冠松次郎
Kannabe *p* 神辺 853
Kannabi *sp* 甘南備 207
Kannagi *s* 巫部 524
Kannami *s* 神波 853; *p* 函南 1232
Kannari *sp* 金成 664
Kannin 1017–21 寛仁 1977
Kanno *s* 神野 853, 菅野 1450, 管野 2212, 簡野 2788 「農; *m* 神生
Kannō *s* 神尾 853, 神
Kannon *fh* 観音 2765
Kannon'iwa *l* 観音岩
Kannosuke *m* 幹之助 1938
Kannuki *s* 環貫 2620
Kano *s* 加野 121, 狩野 791, 蚊野 1135; *sp* 鹿野 1823. (彼 578)
Kanō *s* 十七夜 18, 十七夜月, 加名生 121, 加能, 加納, 金太 664, 狩野 791, 嘉納 2184; *sm* 和 638; *m* 叶 132, 協 548, 適 2240, 諧 2639
Kan'ō 1350–52 観応 2765
Kanō Akatsuki *ml* 加納暁 121
Kanoashi *p* 鹿足 1823
Kanoe *f* 庚 741
Kanō Eitoku *ma* 狩野永徳 791
~ Hōgai *ma* 狩野芳崖
~ Jigorō *mh* 嘉納治五郎 2184
Kanokogi *s* 鹿子木 1823
~ Takeshirō *ma* 鹿子木孟郎 「子餅
Kanokomochi *l* 鹿の
Kanō Masanobu *ma* 狩野正信 791
Kanomata *s* 鹿又 1823
Kanome *s* 鹿目
Kanomi *s* 神麻績 853
Kanō Motonobu *ma* 狩野元信 791
Kan'onji *p* 観音寺 2765
Kanō Sakujirō *ml* 加能作次郎 121 「楽 791
~ Sanraku *ma* 狩野山
Kanose *p* 鹿瀬 1823
Kanosue *s* 彼末 578
Kanō Tan'yū *ma* 狩野探幽 791
Kanoto *m* 辛 493
Kanouchi *s* 加内 121, 叶内 132
Kanoya *p* 鹿屋 1823
Kanpaku *h* 関白 2245
Kanpei *m* 勘平 1699; 889–98 寛平 1977
Kanpō 1741–44 寛保
Kanpyō 889–98 寛平
Kanra *sp* 甘楽 207
Kanrai *l* 寒雷 1714
Kanrei *s* 神例 853
Kanroji *s* 甘露寺 207
Kanroku *mh* 観勒 2765
Kansai *p* 関西 2245
Kansaichi *s* 神私 853
Kansei 1789–1801 寛政 1977 「政三博士
~ no sanhakase *mh* 寛
~ no sankijin *mh* 寛政三奇人
Kansha *s* 神社 853
Kanshii *p* "Kwangsi" 広西 316
Kanshinji *p* 観心寺 2765
Kanshitsuzō *a* 乾漆像 1411 「1977
Kanshō 1460–66 寛正
Kansuke *m* 勘助 1699, 寛哉 1977
Kanta *s* 綺 2533
Kantan *la* 邯鄲 643
~ shokoku *l* 邯鄲諸国
Kantarō *m* 貫太郎 1754
Kanto *s* 完戸 471
Kantō *p* ["Kwantung"] 関東 2245
Kantoku 1044–46 寛徳 1977
Kanton *p* "Canton, Kwangtung" 広東 316
Katsukeno *s* 上毛野 47
Kantsukone *s* 神努 853
Kantsumichi *s* 上道 47
(kanu 光 281, 易 714, 周 736, 侶 778, 倚 1033, 兼 1268, 詠 1664, 摂 1837, 該 2135, 説 2143, 談 2325, 懐 2605)
Kan-U *mh-l* "Kuan Yü" 関羽 2245
Kanuchi *s* 金 664, 金作, 鉄工 1948, 鉄師, 鍛 2651, 鍛冶, 鍛師
Kanuma *s* 加沼 121, 賀浪 1756; *sp* 鹿沼 1823
Kanwa 985–87 寛和 1977 「1003
Kan'yōkyū *la* 咸陽宮
Kanzaburō *m* 寛三郎 1977 「神崎
Kanzaki *s* 神前 853; *sp*
~ Kiyoshi *ml* 神崎清
Kanzan rakuboku *l* 寒山落木 1714
Kanzawa *s* 神沢 853
Kanze *s* 観世 2765
~ Kiyotsugu *mla* 観世清次
~ Motokiyo *mla* 観世元清
Kanzen chōaku *l* 勧善懲悪 1970
~ ~ nozoki karakuri *la* 勧善懲悪覗機関
Kanzō *m* 勘蔵 1699, 寛造 1977, 寛憶
Kanzu *s* 上津 47
Kao *f* 娥 1356. (薫 2567, 顔 2754)
Kaō *p* 鹿央 1823; 1169–71 嘉応 2184
Kaoki *m* 霞群 2693
Ka Ōkin *mh* "Ho Ying-ch'in" 何応欽 513
Kaori *m* 嘉織 2184; *f* 加男利 121, 香居 961
Kaoru *m* 芬 477, 芳 480, 郁 890, 香織 961, 蔆 2563, 薫 2567, 馩 2823, 馨 2904; *m-f* 香 961; *f* 香保留, 馥 2753
Kaoshi *l* 顔師 2754
Kappa *l* 河童 597
Kappo *la* 合浦 270
Kara *s* 甘良 207, 賀良 1756, 韓 2741; *ph* "Kaya / Karak" 加羅 121, 伽羅 357; *l* 唐 1246. (辛 493, 柄 862, 唐 1246, 樺 2103, 韓 2741)
Karaama *s* 韓白水郎
Karafuto *p* 樺太 2103
Karaguri *s* 京 663
Karahashi *s* 唐橋 1246
Karahata *s* 唐端 「862
Karai *s* 加来 121, 柄井
~ Senryū *ml* 柄井川柳
Karakama *s* 唐鎌 1246
Karakane *s* 唐金
Karakasa *s* 傘 1702
Karakawa *s* 唐川 1246
Karaki *s* 神楽 853, 唐木 1246
Karakida *s* 唐木田
Karaki Junzō *ml* 唐木順三
Karakoromo *s* 唐衣
Karakuni *mh* 韓国 2741
Karakuwa *p* 唐桑 1246
Karamatsu *s* 唐松
Karamono *s* 唐物
Kara monogatari *l* 唐物語

Karaosame no uretamigoto *l* 馭戎慨言 1697
Karasaki *s* 唐崎 1246
Karasawa *s* 柄沢 862, 唐沢 1246
Karashima *sp* 辛島 493
Karasu *p* 香良州 963. (烏 1256)
Karasugane *l* 烏金
Karasuma *p* 烏丸
Karasumaro *m* 烏麿
Karasumaru *sp* 烏丸
～ Mitsuhiro *ml* 烏丸光広
Karasuyama *p* 烏山
Karatsu *sp* 唐津 1246
Karaushi *s* 唐牛
Karawatari *s* 唐渡
Kara-yō kenchiku *a* 唐様建築
(kare 枯 859) 「鏡 43
Kareedosukōpu *l* 万華
Kareki *s* 枯木 859
Kare-sansui *a* 枯山水
Kari *s* 虞 2242. (刈 50, 苅 479, 狩 791, 借 1032, 雁 1801, 虞 2242, 鵩 2867)
Karibe *s* 刈部 50, 苅部 479, 雁部 1801
Kaributo *p* 狩太 791
Karigane *m* 雁金 1801
Karihito *s* 虞人 2242
Karikomi *s* 刈込 50, 苅込 479 「樸樕 2170
Karin bokusoku *l* 歌林
Karino *s* 狩野 791
Karita *s* 刈田 50, 苅田 479 「呂
Karitamaro *m* 苅田麻
Karitamaru *m* 苅田丸
Karito *s* 狩戸 791
Kariwa *p* 刈羽 50
Kariya *s* 苅谷 479, 狩谷 791, 借屋 1032; *p* 刈谷 50 「斎 791
～ Ekisai *mlh* 狩谷棭
Kariyama *s* 苅山 479
Kariyone *s* 苅米
Karōdo *s* 唐人 1246
Karoku *m* 賀良倶 1756, 嘉六 2184; 1225–27 嘉禄 「軽 1657)
Karu *f* 軽 1657. (借 1032,
Karuabiko *s* 軽我孫
Karube *s* 軽部
Karuizawa *p* 軽井沢

Karukaya *s* 苅萱 479
～ Dōshin *lm* 苅萱道心
～ ～ Tsukushi no iezuto *la* 苅萱桑門筑紫轢
Karuma *s* 軽間 1657
Karumai *p* 軽米
Karume *s* 借馬 1032, 軽馬 1657
Karumi *s* 軽見
Karuta *s* 加留田 121
Karyaku 1326–29 嘉暦 2184 「1801
Karyūmaru *m* 雁宇丸
Kasa *s* 笠 1473; *sp* 加佐 121. (笠 1473, 傘 1702, 蓋 2193)
Kasabi *l* 傘火 1702
Kasadera *s* 笠寺 1473
Kasagi *s* 笠木; *p* 笠置
Kasahara *sp* 笠原
Kasai *s* 河西 597, 香西 961, 笠井 1473, 笠合, 葛 1994, 葛西; *sp* 加西 121
Kasaie *s* 笠家 1473
Kasai Zenzō *ml* 葛西善蔵 1994
Kasajima *s* 笠島 1473
Kasakake *p* 笠懸
Kasaku *m* 嘉作 2184
Kasakura *s* 笠倉 1473
Kasama *sp* 笠間
Kasamaro *m* 笠麻呂
Kasamatsu *s* 重松 1017; *sp* 笠松 1473
Kasamori *s* 笠森
Kasamoto *s* 笠元
Kasamura *s* 笠村
Kasano *s* 笠野
Kasa no Kanamura *ml* 笠金村
Kasanu *m* 重 1017
Kasanui *s* 笠縫 1473, 蓋縫 2193 「助 1473
～ Sensuke *ml* 笠縫専
Kasanuki *s* 笠貫, 葛貫
Kasao *s* 笠尾 1473 ⌊1994
Kasaoka *sp* 笠岡
Kasari *p* 笠利
Kasasa *p* 笠沙
Kasatsuji *s* 司辻 164
Kasaya *s* 笠谷 1473, 笠屋
～ Sankatsu nijūgonenki *la* 笠屋三勝二十五年忌

Kase *s* 加世 121, 加勢, 加瀬, 鹿背 1823, 嘉瀬 2184. (悴 1287A)
Kaseda *s* 悴田; *sp* 加世田 121
Kasei 1804–29 化政 56
Kasen *ml-fl* 歌仙 2170
Kasetani *s* 加瀬谷 121
Kasha *s* 我謝 545
Kashi *s* 白檮 216. (炊 602, 柏 866, 播 2259, 樫 2481, 橿 2622)
Kashiba *p* 香芝 961
Kashibara *s* 樫原 2481
(kashigi 炊 602)
Kashihara *sp* 柏原 866; *p* 橿原 2622 「184
Kashihiko *m* 甲子彦
Kashii *s* 柏井 866, 香椎 961, 葛 1994
(kashiko 惶 1545)
Kashima *s* 賀島 1756; *sp* 鹿島 1823; *p* 嘉島 2184 「1823
Kashimada *s* 鹿島田
Kashimadai *p* 鹿島台
Kashima kikō *l* 鹿島紀行
Kashimo *sp* 加子母 121
Kashimoto *s* 柏本 866
Kashimura *s* 鹿志村 1823, 樫村 2481
Kashino *s* 柏野 866
Kashio *s* 葛山 1994, 樫尾 2481; *m* 甲子男 184
Kashiro *s* 嘉代 2184
Kashirō *m* 甲子郎 184
Kashiwa *sm-p* 柏 866; *m* 橿 2622. (柏 866, 樫 2481, 橿 2622)
Kashiwabara *s* 橿原; *smh* 柏原 866
Kashiwabuchi *s* 柏淵
Kashiwada *s* 柏田, 樫田 2481
Kashiwade *s* 膳天 2463, 膳部; *sm* 膳
Kashiwadenotomo *s* 勝伴 1613, 膳 2463
Kashiwagi *sla* 柏木 866
Kashiwaguma *s* 柏熊
Kashiwakura *s* 柏倉
Kashiwamoto *s* 柏本
Kashiwamura *s* 柏村
Kashiwano *s* 樫野 2481
Kashiwara *s* 樫原; *p* 橿原 2622

Kashiwaya *s* 柏谷 866, 柏屋, 樫谷 2481
Kashiwazaki *p-la* 柏崎 866 「山 2481
Kashiyama *s* 柏山, 樫
Kasho *s* 家所 1185
Kashō 848–51 嘉祥 2184
Kashōki *l* 可笑記 165
Kashū *s* 加集 121, 賀集 1756; *p* "California" 加州 121 「961
Kasokabe *s* 香宗我部
Kasori *s* 加曾利 121
Kassai *s* 葛西 1994
Kasu *p* 加須 121. (春 963, 粕 1390, 糟 2632)
Kasube *s* 春部 963
Kasuga *s* 春; *sp* 春日
Kasugabe *sp* 春部, 春日部
Kasuga Gongen kenki *la* 春日権現験記
Kasugai *sp* 春日井; *p* 春日居 「竜神
Kasuga ryūjin *la* 春日
Kasugata *s* 春遂
Kasugawa *s* 粕川 1390
Kasuga-zukuri *a* 春日造 963
Kasukabe *s* 月下部 80
Kasumi *sm-f-p* 霞 2693; *p* 香住 961. (霞 2693)
Kasumigaseki *p* 霞ケ関
Kasuya *s* 加須屋 121, 粕谷 1390, 糟谷 2632; *p* 粕屋 1390
Kata *s* 片 82, 方 85, 加田 121. (一 3, 才 36, 片 82, 方 85, 戈 108, 功 135, 礼 146, 斥 167, 右 172, 允 217, 包 218, 交 293, 名 346, 似 350, 状 365A, 形 414, 声 465, 艮 529, 和 638, 効 653, 命 671, 周 736, 固 744, 良 767, 岩 942, 訒 1147, 容 1182, 姿 1217, 兼 1268, 陳 1311, 捧 1318, 済 1336, 剛 1429, 粛 1528, 傍 1538, 硬 1635, 朝 1672, 敬 1691, 象 1761, 崇 1774, 普 1792, 堅 1796, 犀 1803, 雄 1912, 豊 2013, 歯 2051, 像 2061, 該 2135, 語 2136, 結 2151, 銘 2155,

豪 2177, 潟 2273, 標 2298, 確 2305, 談 2325, 毅 2351, 器 2378, 鞏 2379, 質 2395, 賢 2579, 謙 2646, 覧 2695, 鎌 2750, 鑑 2968)
Kataakira *m* 崇明 1774
Katabā *s* 片羽 82
Katabami *s* 片波江, 方波羽 85
Katabe *s* 刑部 258
(katabu 傾 1830)
Katabuchi *s* 片淵 82
Katabuko *mh* 傾子 1830
Katada *s* 片田 82; *sp* 堅田 1796
Katae *s* 片江 82
Katagami *s* 片上
~ Noburu *ml* 片上伸
Katagiri *s* 片切, 片桐
~ Akinori *ml* 片桐顕智 「且元
~ Katsumoto *mh* 片桐
Katahara *s* 形原 414
Kataharu *m* 容大 1182, 普春 1792 「2273
Katahigashi *p* 潟東
Katahira *sp* 片平 82
Katahirata *s* 片平田
Katahiro *m* 容衆 1182
Katahito *m* 周仁 736
Katahitsukuri *s* 模作 2104
Kataka *s* 安宅 472
Katakai *s* 片貝 82
Katakiuchi gijo no hanabusa *l* 敵討義女英 2354
Katako *f* 潟子 2273, 確子 2305, 賢子 2579
Katakura *s* 片倉 82
Katamasa *m* 方正 85
Katami *s* 片見 82; *m* 像見 2061
Katamitsu *m* 陳光 1311, 賢三 2579
Katamori *m* 容保 1182
Katamu *m* 固 744
Katamura *s* 片村 82
Katana *m* 形名 414. (刀 12)
Katane *s* 片根 82
Kataniwa *s* 片庭
Katano *s* 片野; *sp* 交野 293
Katanobu *m* 容頌 1182
Katanoho *s* 潟保 2273
Katanori *m* 崇徳 1774
Katao *m* 剛雄 1429
Kataoka *s* 片岡 82
~ Kenkichi *mh* 片岡健吉
~ Teppei *ml* 片岡鉄兵
~ Yoshikazu *ml* 片岡良一
Kataoki *m* 容住 1182
Katarai *s* 語 2136
Katari *s* 語; *m* 談 2325. (語 2136)
Katase *s* 片瀬 82
Katashi *m* 介 66, 艮 529, 固 744, 重 1017, 硈 1385, 剛 1429, 硬 1635, 堅 1796, 確 2305, 鍛 2651, 鏈 2815
Katashina *sp* 片品 82
Katata *s* 片多
Katataka *m* 堅高 1796
Katatoki *m* 方言 85
Katatsugu *m* 標継 2298
Katauta niya mondō *l* 片歌二夜問答 82
Katayama *s* 片山, 形山 414, 固山 744 「82
~ Hiroko *fl* 片山広子
~ Koson *ml* 片山孤村
~ Sen *mh* 片山潜
~ Toshihiko *ml* 片山敏彦
Katayanagi *s* 片柳
Katayori *s* 片寄
Katei 1235–38 嘉禎 2184
Katō *s* 加頭 121, 加藤, 河東 597, 嘉藤 2184; *p* 加東 121
~-bushi *a* 河東節 597
~ Chikage *ml* 加藤千蔭 121 「鳥
~ Chōchō *ml* 加藤朝
~ Hiroyuki *mlh* 加藤弘之
Katōji *m* 嘉藤次 2184
Katō Kagemasa *ma* 加藤景正 121 「春
~ Kaishun *ml* 加藤介
~ Kazuo *ml* 加藤一夫
Katōki *s* 加藤木
Katō Kiyomasa *mh* 加藤清正 「将之
~ Masayuki *ml* 加藤
~ Michio *ml* 加藤道夫
Katori *s* 上句 47, 香 961, 楫取 1899; *sm* 鹿取 1823; *sp* 香取 961; *m* 可都里 165
~ Hozuma *mla* 香取秀真 961
~ Nahiko *ml* 楫取魚彦 1899
Katō Shūichi *ml* 加藤周一 121
~ Shūson *ml* 加藤楸邨
~ Takaaki *mh* 加藤高明
~ Takeo *ml* 加藤武雄
~ Tomosaburō *mh* 加藤友三郎
~ Tōri *ml* 加藤東籬
~ Totsudō *ml* 加藤咄堂
Katsu *sm* 勝 1613; *m* 克 442; *m-f* 捷 1323. (一3, 万 43, 弌 74, 功 135, 甲 184, 且 192, 包 218, 克 442, 坦 574, 和 638, 劼 652, 独 788, 活 819, 柿 867, 亮 911, 品 916, 桂 1102, 尅 1260, 勉 1263, 健 1282, 捷 1323, 硈 1385, 勝 1613, 割 1696A, 曾 1794, 遂 1806, 達 1810, 逵 1813, 猾 1834, 滑 1857, 強 1878, 雄 1912, 葛 1994, 徳 2063, 戡 2166, 豪 2177, 積 2493, 賢 2579, 優 2599, 潤 2611, 豁 2667, 闊 2710)
Katsuaki *m* 克明 442, 健晋 1282, 勝昶 1613, 勝商, 勝敞
Katsube *s* 勝部
Katsuchika *m* 勝及, 雄年 1912
Katsue *m* 克衛 442
Katsugase *s* 勝賀瀬 1613
Katsugorō *m* 勝五郎
Katsuharu *m* 弌春 74
Katsuhata *s* 勝畑 1613
Katsuhiko *m* 功彦 135, 克彦 442, 雄彦 1912
Katsuhiro *m* 勝曠 1613
Katsuhisa *m* 勝久
Katsuhito *m* 和仁 638
Katsui *s* 勝井 1613
Katsuichi *m* 勝一
Katsuichirō *m* 勝一郎
Katsuie *m* 勝家
Katsuji *m* 勝二, 勝次, 勝治
Katsujirō *m* 勝次郎
Katsujō *m* 葛城 1994
Katsukata *m* 勝謙 1613
Katsukawa *s* 勝川, 勝河 「春章
~ Shunshō *ma* 勝川
Katsuki *s* 香月 961, 勝木 1613; *m* 一月 3
Katsukida *s* 蒲田 1993
Katsukiyo *m* 勝摩 1613
Katsuko *f* 克子 442, 勝津子 1613
Katsukura *s* 勝倉
Katsuma *sm* 勝間; *m* 勝馬
Katsumasa *m* 勝殷, 曾政 1794, 雄端 1912, 積正 2493
Katsumata *s* 勝又 1613, 勝亦, 勝俣, 勝間田
Katsume *s* 加集 121, 勝目 1613
Katsumi *s* 香積 961, 勝見 1613, 葛見 1994; *sm* 克巳 442; *m* 且子 192, 克 442, 克三, 黄 1499, 勝臣 1613, 勝美, 勝海, 勝摘, 勝観
Katsumine *s* 勝峰
~ Shinpū *ml* 勝峰晋風
Katsumoto *sp* 勝本; *m* 且元 192, 勝元 1613
~ Seiichirō *ml* 勝本清一郎
Katsumura *s* 勝村
Katsunaga *m* 勝修, 遂長 1806
Katsunari *m* 勝鳴 1613, 勝慈
Katsundo *m* 勝人
Katsuno *s* 勝野
Katsunobu *m* 勝庸
Katsunori *m* 勝権
Katsunuma *sp* 勝沼
Katsuo *s* 勝尾; *m* 桂男 1102, 勝夫 1613, 勝男, 堅魚 1796
Katsura *s* 勝浦 1613, 曾良 1794; *sm-f-p* 桂 1102; *m* 藤 2773. (葛 1994, 鬘 2979)
Katsurada *s* 桂田 1102
Katsuragawa *s* 桂川
~ Hoshū *mh* 桂川甫周
Katsuragi *s* 葛城 1994, 歌枕 2170
Katsurahara *s* 葛原 1994

Katsurai *s* 桂井 1102
Katsura Kogorō *mh* 桂小五郎
Katsurano *s* 桂野
Katsurao *p* 葛尾 1994
Katsura Rikyū *pa* 桂離宮 1102
~ Tarō *mh* 桂太郎
Katsurayama *s* 桂山, 葛山 1994
Katsuro *s* 勝呂 1613
Katsurō *m* 勝郎
Katsusaburō *m* 勝三郎
Katsusada *m* 克禎 442
Katsusane *m* 勝愛 1613
Katsushi *m* 勝司
Katsushige *m* 勝重
Katsushika *sp* 葛飾 1994 「斎
~ Hokusai *ma* 葛飾北
Katsushima *s* 勝島 1613
Katsuta *sp* 勝田
Katsutada *m* 雄只 1912, 克惟 442
Katsutaka *m* 勝皐 1613, 勝全, 勝豪
Katsutarō *m* 克太郎 442, 勝太郎 1613
Katsutō *m* 勝任, 勝祁
Katsutoki *m* 勝暁
Katsutomi *m* 勝臣
Katsutoshi *m* 克捷 442, 勝齢 1613
Katsuura *sp* 勝浦
Katsuya *s* 勝矢, 勝谷, 勝屋
Katsuyama *sp* 勝山
Katsuyasu *m* 勝易
Katsu Yasuyoshi *mh* 勝安芳
Katsuyo *f* 捷世 1323
Katsuyoshi *m* 勝寿 1613, 勝徴, 遂良 1806
Katsu Yoshio *ml* 勝承夫 1613
Katsuyuki *m* 克之 442, 勝升 1613, 勝以, 勝進
Katsuzawa *s* 勝沢
Katsuzō *m* 克三 442, 勝蔵 1613 「50
Katta *s* 勝多; *sp* 刈田
Kattō *s* 甲藤 184
Kawa *s* 川 20. (汾 397, 河 597)
Kawaai *m* 川相 20
Kawaakari *l* 河明り 597
Kawaba *p* 川場 20
Kawabara *s* 川原, 河原 597
Kawabata *s* 川畑 20, 川幡, 川端, 川鰭, 河端 597, 河鰭 「20
~ Bōsha *ml* 川端茅舎
~ Chie *fl* 川端千枝
~ Gyokushō *ma* 川端玉章
~ Ryūshi *ma* 川端竜子
~ Yasunari *ml* 川端康成
Kawabe *s* 川部, 河部 597; *sp* 川辺 20, 河辺 597
Kawabuchi *s* 川淵 20
Kawachi *sp* 河内 597
Kawachihiji *s* 西垩 336
Kawachihijibe *s* 西垩部 「内長野 597
Kawachi Nagano *p* 河
Kawachinoayanofumi *s* 西漢文 336
Kawachinofumi *s* 西文
Kawachiya *l* 河内屋 597
Kawachi Yoshino *p* 河内芳野 「田 597
Kawada *s* 川田 20, 河
~ Jun *ml* 川田順 20
Kawadani *s* 川谷
Kawade *s* 川手, 河手 597, 河出
Kawado *s* 川戸 20
Kawaeda *s* 川枝
Kawafuku *s* 川副
Kawage *p* 河芸 597
Kawagishi *s* 川岸 20
Kawagoe *s* 河越 597; *sp* 川越 20 「川口 20
Kawaguchi *sp* 河口 597,
~ Ichirō *ml* 川口一郎
~-ko *p* 河口湖 597
~ Kō *ml* 川口浩 20
~ Matsutarō *ml* 川口松太郎
Kawaguna *s* 河郡名 597
Kawahara *s* 川原 20; *sp* 河原 597
Kawahashi *s* 川橋 20
Kawahigashi *sp* 河東 597 「碧悟桐
~ Hekigotō *ml* 河東
Kawahira *s* 川平 20
Kawahire *s* 河鰭 597
Kawahito *s* 川人 20
Kawai *s* 川合, 河井 597, 河居, 河相; *sm* 川相 20; *sp* 川井, 河合 597
~ Gyokudō *ma* 川合玉堂 20 「597
~ Sora *ml* 河合曾良
~ Suimei *ml* 河井酔茗
Kawaji *s* 川地 20, 川治, 川路, 河池 597, 河治, 河路 「尻 20
Kawajiri *s* 河尻; *sp* 川
~ Seitan *ml* 川尻清潭
Kawaji Ryūkō *ml* 川路柳虹 「聖謨
~ Toshiakira *mh* 川路
Kawakado *s* 川角
Kawakame *s* 川尻
Kawakami *s* 河上 597; *sp* 川上 20
~ Bizan *ml* 川上眉山
~ Hajime *mlh* 河上肇 597 「郎
~ Jōtarō *mh* 河上丈太
~ Otojirō *ma* 川上音二郎 20 「子
~ Sayoko *fl* 川上小夜
~ Tetsutarō *ml* 河上徹太郎 597
Kawakare *s* 川枯 20
Kawakatsu *s* 川勝
Kawakita *s* 川喜田, 川喜多, 汾陽 397, 河北 597, 河喜田; *sp* 川北 20
Kawako *f* 河子 597
Kawakubo *s* 川久保 20, 川窪, 河窪 597
Kawakuma *s* 河曲
Kawama *s* 河間
Kawamae *p* 川前 20
Kawamagari *s* 川勾, 河曲 597
Kawamata *s* 川又 20, 川跨, 河又 597, 河俣; *sp* 川俣 20
Kawamatsu *s* 川松
Kawami *s* 川見
Kawaminami *s* 汾陽 397, 河南 597; *p* 川南
Kawamo *s* 川面 ⌊20
Kawamori *s* 川森, 河盛 597 「蔵
~ Yoshizō *ml* 河盛好
Kawamoto *s* 川元 20, 河本 597; *sp* 川本 20
Kawamura *s* 川村, 河村 597 「20
~ Karyō *ml* 川村花菱
~ Zuiken *mh* 河村瑞軒 597, 河村瑞賢
Kawana *s* 川名 20, 河名 597, 河奈
Kawanabe *s* 川那辺 20, 川鍋, 河鍋 597; *p* 川辺 20
Kawanaka *s* 川中
Kawanakajima *p* 川中島
Kawanami *s* 川波, 川浪, 汾陽 397, 河南 597, 河浪 「根 20
Kawane *s* 河曲; *p* 川
Kawanishi *s* 河西 597; *sp* 川西 20 「597
Kawano *s* 川野, 河野
Kawanobe *s* 川辺 20, 川野辺
Kawanōbito *s* 川首
Kawanobori *s* 登川 1744
Kawanoe *p* 川之江 20
Kawanuma *p* 河沼 597
Kawaoi *s* 川生 20
Kawara *s* 甲良 184, 河原 597; *sp* 川原 20; *p* 香春 961. (瓦 201)
Kawarabayashi *s* 川原林 20, 瓦林 201, 河原林 597 「河原田 597
Kawarada *s* 川原田 20,
Kawaragi *s* 河原木
Kawarai *s* 川原井 20, 瓦井 201, 河原井 597
Kawara Tarō *l* 河原太郎
Kawaratsukurimarōdo *s* 甲作客 184
Kawarazaki *s* 河原崎 597
Kawarazuka *s* 河原塚
Kawaru *m* 更 528
Kawasaki *sp* 川崎 20, 河崎 597 「太郎 20
~ Chōtarō *ml* 川崎長
~ Togai *ml* 川崎杜外
Kawasakiya *s* 川崎舎
Kawasato *sp* 川里
Kawase *s* 川瀬, 河瀬 597 「川島 20
Kawashima *s* 河島; *sp*
~ Chūnosuke *ml* 川島忠之助
Kawashiro *s* 川城
Kawashita *s* 川下
Kawasugi *s* 河杉 597
~ Hatsuko *fl* 河杉初子

Kawasuke *m* 川相 20
Kawatake *s* 河竹 597
~ Mokuami *ml* 河竹黙阿弥 「繁俊
~ Shigetoshi *ml* 河竹
~ Shinshichi *ml* 河竹新七
Kawatana *p* 川棚 20
Kawatani *s* 川谷
Kawatei *s* 川廷
Kawato *s* 川東, 河東 597 「川内 20
Kawauchi *s* 河内; *sp*
Kawaue *p* 川上
Kawaura *s* 川浦; *p* 河浦 597
Kawawa *s* 川和 20, 河匂 597; *sp* 河曲
Kawayashiro *l* 河社
Kawazoe *s* 川添 20, 河副 597, 河添; *sp* 川副 20 「国基
~ Kunimoto *ml* 川副
Kawazu *s* 川津; *sp* 河津 597; *m* 蛙 1648
Kawazumi *s* 川角 20, 川隅, 川澄, 河角 597
Kawazura *s* 川面 20, 河面 597
Kaya *s* 加舎 121, 加屋, 仮谷 231, 茅 690, 賀永 1756, 賀屋, 嘉悦 2184, 嘉陽; *sm* 賀陽 1756; *sp* 加悦 121, 柏 866; *m* 鹿文 1823; *f* 萱 1730. (茅 690, 草 934, 萱 1730, 榧 2291)
Kayaba *s* 萱場 1730; *p* 茅場 690
Kayahara *s* 茅原
~ Kazan *ml* 茅原華山
Kayaki *s* 柏木 866, 榧木 2291
Kayako *f* 茅子 690
Kayama *s* 加山 121, 香山 961, 萱間 1730, 鹿山 1823, 嘉山 2184
Kayamori *s* 萱森 1730
Kayane *m* 茹 1171
Kayano *s* 茅野 690, 萱野 1730
Kayanoin shichishu utaawase *l* 高陽院七首歌合 1163
~ Suikaku utaawase *l* 賀陽院水閣歌合 1756
Kayanoki *s* 榧木 2291
Kaya no Toyotoshi *ml* 賀陽豊年 1756
Kayanuma *s* 萱沼 1730
Kayashima *s* 茅島 690, 萱島 1730 「1756
Kayō *s* 萱生; *p* 賀陽
Kayoi Komachi *la* 通小町 1239
Kayoko *f* 甲代子 184, 圭世子 267, 佳代子 560 「河精 597
Kayoshi *m* 可賀 165; *f*
(kaza 風 986)
Kazado *s* 風戸
Kazahana *l* 風花
Kazahaya *s* 風早
Kazakiku *s* 風吉
Kazakiri *s* 風吉
Kazama *s* 風間
Kazamaki *s* 風巻
~ Keijirō *ml* 風巻景次郎
Kazamaura *p* 風間浦
Kazamatsuri *s* 風祭
Kazami *s* 風見
Kazan *mlh* 花山 481
Kazan'in *s* 華山院 1266; *smlh* 花山院 481
~ Nagachika *ml* 花山院長親
Kazaoka *s* 風岡 986
Kazari *s* 錺 2337. (錺)
Kazariya *p* 錺谷
Kazawa *s* 賀沢 1756
(kaze 吹 370, 風 986)
Kazo *p* 加須 121
Kazō *m* 嘉造 2184
Kazu *s* 石 172; *m* 和 638, 順 1532, 嘉寿 2184. (一 3, 二 4, 九 16, 七 17, 十 18, 八 19, 三 22, 万 43, 千 44, 弌 74, 円 78, 五 91, 尹 98, 収 133, 冬 161, 司 164, 主 196, 牙 202, 年 342, 多 347, 利 436, 毎 444, 会 454, 壱 467, 応 509, 寿 539, 妍 612, 枚 630, 知 636, 和 638, 効 653, 宗 679, 沓 698, 良 767, 法 824, 政 881, 計 895, 品 916, 春 963, 参 978, 重 1017, 師 1130, 般 1137, 員 1167, 起 1262, 兼 1268, 胤 1269, 倭 1283, 教 1408, 紀 1424, 順 1532, 量 1741, 策 1767, 運 1808, 雄 1912, 猷 1962, 葛 1994, 業 2024, 種 2124, 雑 2127, 数 2169, 算 2213, 箇 2216, 雍 2359, 選 2419, 積 2493, 憲 2562, 斂 2674, 籌 2901, 麗 2902)
Kazuaki *m* 一西 3
Kazuchika *m* 一力, 和親 638
Kazue *s* 数江 2169; *m* 一衛 3, 万衛 43, 可寿丙 165, 主計 196, 数衛 2169, 算衛 2213; *f* 和家 638, 計 895
Kazufumi *m* 算文 2213
Kazufusa *m* 一英 3, 員種 1167 「16
Kazuhata *s* 九寸五分
Kazuhiko *m* 一位 3, 一彦, 雄比古 1912
Kazuhiro *m* 一口 3, 一敞, 一個
Kazuhisa *m* 一九
Kazuhito *m* 雍人 2359
Kazuho *m* 一秀 3
Kazui *s* 数井 2169
Kazuji *m* 一二 3
Kazukiyo *m* 一清
Kazuko *f* 一寿子, 二子 4, 千女 44, 弌子 74, 加寿子 121, 収子 133, 主子 196, 多子 347, 妍子 612, 和子 638, 効子 653, 計子 895, 紀子 1424, 量子 1741, 運子 1808, 数子 2169
Kazuma *m* 一馬 3, 万馬 43, 主馬 196, 計馬 895, 春馬 963, 員馬 1167, 数馬 1408, 数馬 2169, 算馬 2213
Kazumaki *s* 葛巻 1994
Kazumanosuke *m* 数馬助 2169
Kazumaru *m* 一丸 3
Kazumasa *m* 一予, 一政, 七妛 17, 三政 22, 和応 638, 参正 978
Kazumi *s* 鹿住 1823, 数見 2169; *m* 一省 3, 八三 19, 三角 22, 三省, 運美 1808
Kazumitsu *m* 三充 22
Kazumo *s* 一最 3
Ka-zumō *la* 蚊相樸 1135
Kazumori *m* 葛盛 1994
Kazumoto *m* 量原 1741
Kazunao *m* 司直 164, 数直 2169 「角 1823
Kazuno *s* 数野; *p* 鹿
Kazunobu *m* 和誠 638, 憲宣 2562
Kazunomiya *m* 一宮 3; *fh* 和宮 638
Kazunori *m* 千礼 44, 員規 1167
Kazuo *m* 一夫 3, 一生, 一男, 一音, 一雄, 九穂 16, 七雄 17, 五雄 91, 年雄 342, 寿乙 539, 和夫 638, 和男, 和郎, 法夫 824, 計夫 895, 参男 978, 胤雄 1269, 倭夫 1283, 運夫 1808, 運雄
Kazura *s* 葛 1994, 葛山
Kazuraki *sla* 葛城
~ tengu *l* 葛城天狗
Kazusa *sp* 加津佐 121; *ph* 上総 47 「貞 638
Kazusada *m* 一定 3, 和
Kazusane *m* 一仁 3
Kazushige *m* 一成, 一誠, 重量 1017
Kazushime *f* 一四明 3
Kazusuke *m* 二祐 4, 二裕, 量輔 1741
Kazuta *sm* 収多 133; *m* 数太 2169
Kazutada *m* 員維 1167
Kazutaka *m* 一啓 3, 和高 638
Kazutane *m* 一種 3
Kazuto *m* 和外 638
Kazutō *m* 一十 3
Kazutoki *m* 一睦
Kazutoshi *m* 一敬, 万年 43, 員恵 1167
Kazutoyo *m* 一豊 3
Kazutsugu *m* 胤継 1269
Kazutsura *m* 一貫 3
Kazuuji *m* 和氏 638
Kazuyasu *m* 和育, 員昆 1167, 量慰 1741
Kazuyori *m* 員従 1167
Kazuyoshi *m* 一布 3, 一成, 十吉 18, 万吉 43, 和幸 638, 和義, 積善 2493
Kazuyuki *m* 一以 3, 一到, 千之 44, 量行 1741
Kazuzō *m* 籌三 2901
(ke 化 56, 介 66, 夬 100,

毛 117, 加 121, 价 236, 圭 267, 灰 302, 気 319, 希 445, 芥 475, 花 481, 祉 608, 卦 647, 恢 806, 奎 913, 桂 1102, 食 1159, 家 1185, 掛 1321, 笥 1472, 稀 1640, 葭 1725, 袈 1749, 榎 2107, 嘉 2184, 魁 2423, 幾 2597, 蹴 2806, 璣 2868, 機 2869, 鰕 2886, 磯 2916)
Kebu *s* 癸生 952
Kebukawa *s* 癸生川
(kechi 夬 100, 血 337, 決 402, 結 2151, 絜 2208, 潔 2615)
Kedo *s* 毛戸 117
Kedōin *p* 祁答院 641
Kega *s* 儀俄 2255
Kegon *p-l* 華厳 1266
Kehaya *m* 蹴速 2806
Kei *s* 荊 899; *m* 慧 2392. (兄 181, 刑 258, 圭 267, 形 414, 邢 415, 冏 512, 径 576, 京 663, 茎 684, 計 895, 荊 899, 奎 913, 系 977, 契 980, 桂 1102, 勍 1150, 皆 1196, 恵 1226, 巠 1229, 渓 1330A, 畦 1381, 硎 1384, 啓 1491, 逕 1512, 軽 1657, 敬 1691, 勁 1697A, 景 1764, 傾 1830, 卿 1865, 経 1957, 境 2076, 慧 2392, 慶 2425, 稽 2491, 継 2539, 薊 2562A, 鮭 2671, 瓊 2717, 蹊 2807, 譓 2809, 鶏 2821, 頸 2828, 馨 2904, 競 2927, 繫 2959) 「2425
Keian 1648–52 慶安
~ Genju *ml* 桂庵玄樹 1102 「斑 663
Keibyō ippan *l* 京猫一
Keichō 1596–1615 慶長 2425 「版
~ chokuhan *l* 慶長勅
Keichū *mlh* 契沖 980
Keieishō *l* 形影抄 414
Keigo *m* 奎吾 913
Keigoto *l* 景事 1764
Keihachi *m* 敬八 1691
Keihoku *p* 京北 663
Keiichi *m* 啓市 1491, 敬一 1691, 馨一 2904
Keiji *m* 気司 319, 恵二 1226, 啓次 1491, 敬二 1691, 敬治
Keijirō *m* 啓次郎 1491, 敬次郎 1691, 慶次郎 2425 「663
Keijō *p* "Seoul" 京城
Keikai *ml* 景戒 1764
Keikichi *m* 桂吉 1102, 敬吉 1691, 慶吉 2425
Keikin *s* 契斤 980
Keiko *f* 慶子 2425
Keikō *s* 啓乕 1491, 啓虎; *m* 恵弘 1226
Keikōin *s* 慶光院 2425
Keikokushū *l* 経国集 1957
Keima *s* 刑馬 258
Keino *s* 慶野 2425
Keinosuke *m* 桂之助 1102, 啓之助 1491, 慶之助 2425
Keiō 1865–68 慶応
~ Gijuku *p* 慶応義塾
Keiraishū *l* 軽雷集 1657
Keiro *s* 卦婁 647
Keiryū *m* 慶隆 2425
Keisaku *m* 気作 319, 慶作 2425
Keisei Awa no Naruto *la* 傾城阿波の鳴門 1830
~ hangonkō *l* 傾城反魂香 「1957
~ hisaku *lh* 経世秘策
~ irojamisen *l* 傾城色三味線 1830
~ Mibu dainenbutsu *la* 傾城壬生大念仏
~ muken no kane *la* 傾城無間鐘
Keisen *p* 桂川 1102
Keishi *m* 敬止 1691
Keishichi *m* 敬七
Keishirō *m* 慶四郎 2425
Keisuke *m* 圭介 267, 計介 895, 恵介 1226, 啓介 1491, 敬介 1691, 敬款, 経介 1957
Keita *m* 圭太 267
Keitarō *m* 恵太郎 1226, 啓太郎 1491, 慶太郎 2425 「天牧童 1691
Keiten Bokudō *ml* 敬
Keitō *l* 鶏頭 2821
Keiun *ml* 704–08 慶雲 2425
Keizaburō *m* 圭三郎 267, 恵三郎 1226, 敬三郎 1691, 慶三郎 2425
Keizai yōroku *lh* 経済要録 1957
Keizairoku *lh* 経済録
Keizō *m* 圭三 267, 計三 895, 桂三 1102, 恵三 1226, 啓三 1491, 啓蔵, 敬三 1691, 慶三 2425, 慶蔵 「食満 1159
Kema *s* 毛馬 117; *sm-p*
Kemase *s* 気仙 319
Kemigawa *s* 検見川 2447
Kemori *s* 家守 1185
Ken *m* 健 1282, 憲 2562, 謙 2646. (犬 107, 見 518, 妍 612, 倪 774, 研 875, 巻 975, 建 995, 倦 1034, 涓 1061, 晅 1085, 剣 1151, 奉 1206, 県 1252, 虔 1253, 兼 1268, 健 1282, 険 1308, 炫 1344, 弦 1345, 現 1360, 乾 1411, 喧 1541, 硯 1634, 萱 1730, 堅 1796, 間 1822, 暄 1881, 献 1961, 勧 1970, 筧 2014, 牽 2028, 僩 2054, 慊 2068, 蜷 2129, 玆 2134, 甄 2161, 遣 2241, 関 2245, 澗 2274, 権 2300, 絹 2330, 絃 2331, 鉉 2335, 監 2398, 儇 2434, 検 2447, 嫺 2475, 諠 2513, 諫 2514, 綣 2532, 憲 2562, 賢 2579, 謙 2646, 鍵 2652, 褰 2677, 鎌 2750, 顕 2757, 簡 2788, 譴 2823, 繭 2896, 馨 2904, 懸 2984)
Kena *s* 毛穴 117
Kenbō *s* 兼房 1268
Kenbuchi *p* 剣淵 1151
Kenchō *l* 倦鳥 1034; 1249–56 建長 995
Kenchōji *p* 建長寺
Kenchū mitsukan *l* 顕注密勘 2757
Ken'ei 1206–07 建永 995 「2579
Kengaishū *l* 賢外集
Kengen 1302–03 乾元 1411 「吾 2579
Kengo *m* 健吾 1282, 賢
Ken'ichi *m* 研一 875, 兼一 1268, 健一 1282, 憲一 2562, 謙一 2646
Ken'ichirō *m* 健一郎 1282, 賢一郎 2579
Kenji *m* 研二 875, 兼二 1268, 健二 1282, 健次, 健治, 憲次 2562, 憲治, 賢次 2579, 賢治, 謙二 2646, 謙次, 謙治, 鎌治 2750, 顕治 2757; 1275–78 建治 995
Kenjirō *m* 健二郎 1282, 健次郎, 健治郎, 憲二郎 2562, 賢次郎 2579, 謙二郎 2646, 謙次郎, 鍵次郎 2652
Kenji shinshiki *l* 建治新式 995
Kenjō *s* 見城 518
Kenjūrō *m* 謙十郎 2646
Kenkichi *s* 巻吉 975; *m* 健吉 1282, 謙吉 2646
Kenkō *ml* 兼好 1268
Kenkyū 1190–99 建久 995
Kenmochi *s* 剣持 1151
Kenmoku *s* 見目 518
Kenmotsu *s* 剣持 1151; *sm* 監物 2398 「995
Kenmu 1334–38 建武
~ nenkanki *l* 建武年間記
Kennin 1201–04 建仁
Kenninji *p* 建仁寺
Kennosuke *m* 剣之助 1151, 賢之助 2579
Kennyo *mh* 顕如 2757
Kenouchi *s* 家内 1185
Kenpō 1213–19 建保 995 「七条 2562
~ jūshichijō *l* 憲法十
Kenrei Mon'in *fh* 建礼門院 995
~ ~ Ukyō-dayū shū *l* 建礼門院右京大夫集
Kenryaku 1211–13 建暦
Kenryū *m* 賢竜 2579
Kensaku *m* 健作 1282, 憲作 2562, 賢策 2579, 賢作
Kensei *m* 顕成 2757
Kenshirō *m* 賢四郎 2579, 謙四郎 2646
Kenshin *m* 謙信
Kenshō *ml* 顕昭 2757
Kenshun *mh* 賢俊 2579
Kensuke *m* 健介 1282,

健助, 謙介 2646, 謙輔
Kenta *m* 憲太 2562
Kentarō *m* 研太郎 875, 健太郎 1282, 堅太郎 1796, 憲太郎 2562, 賢太郎 2579, 鍵太郎 2652
Kentoku 1370–72 建徳 995
Kentōsen *l* 遣唐船 2241
Kenu *m* 毛野 117
Kenuki *la* 毛抜 「1634
Ken'yūsha *l* 硯友社
Kenzaburō *m* 健三郎 1282, 謙三郎 2646
Kenzan *ma* 乾山 1411
Kenzō *m* 健三 1282, 健蔵, 堅蔵 1796, 堅造, 憲三 2562, 賢三 2579, 賢造, 賢蔵, 謙三 2646, 謙蔵, 顕三 2757
Keo *f* 毛生 117
Kera *s* 解良 1923; *p* 介良 66
Kere *s* 解礼 1923
Kesa *f* 今朝 67, 袈裟 1749. (祇 1127, 袈 1749)
Kesae *f* 袈江
Kesakatsu *m* 祇勝 1127
Kesami *f* 今朝美 67
Kesema *s* 気仙 319
Kesen *p* 気仙
Kesennuma *p* 気仙沼
Ketchi *s* 結知 2151
Ketōin *s* 祈答院 609
Ketsu *s* 蕨 2566. (夬 100, 穴 158, 血 337, 決 402, 杰 695, 契 980, 挈 1204, 傑 1827, 結 2151, 絜 2208, 蕨 2566, 潔 2615)
Ketsuge *s* 結解 2151
Ketsu Shin *ml* 蕨真 2566
Keuke *s* 毛受 117
Kewashi *m* 嵬 2374
Keyamura *s* 毛谷村 117
Kezori *s* 毛剃
Kezuka *s* 毛塚
Ki *s* 紀 1424; *m* 熙 2409. (乙 2, 几 6, 己 32, 寸 34, 大 48, 支 63, 木 109, 示 148, 卉 151, 甲 184, 生 214, 伎 232, 行 245, 企 269, 旡 279, 危 318, 気 319, 技 381, 玖 409, 妃 411, 材 420, 杖 422, 希 445, 忌 462, 束 536, 来 538, 岐 599, 祈 609, 杵 629, 枝 631, 林 633, 私 637, 祁 641, 京 663, 宜 675, 芸 689, 季 725, 其 734, 奇 752, 城 796, 跂 872, 軌 892, 癸 952, 屎 989, 哉 1006, 帰 1018, 倚 1033, 俟 1035, 祇 1127, 記 1149, 耆 1214, 息 1224, 翅 1248, 起 1262, 埼 1292, 淇 1328, 規 1349, 姫 1358, 紀 1424, 著 1445, 章 1461, 基 1493, 黄 1499, 寄 1525, 鬼 1527, 亀 1531, 揆 1549, 崎 1592, 椒 1619, 稀 1640, 期 1671, 喜 1709, 葵 1723, 貴 1755, 逵 1813, 超 1816, 頎 1866, 煇 1875, 暉 1884, 祺 1903, 僖 2058, 旗 2093, 棄 2202, 箕 2214, 置 2232, 愭 2257, 槻 2295, 毅 2351, 器 2378, 熙 2409, 嬉 2476, 樹 2483, 輝 2499, 錡 2520, 綺 2533, 歆 2550, 憙 2559, 熹 2560, 冀 2571, 熈 2583, 興 2586, 幾 2597, 禧 2628, 磯 2730, 騎 2762, 畿 2859, 徽 2866, 璣 2868, 機 2869, 磯 2916, 驥 3008)
Kiami *mh* 其阿弥 734
Kiba *s* 木場 109
Kibata *s* 木畑, 木幡
Kibe *s* 木辺, 木部
Kibi *sm-p* 吉備 278
Kibihonji *s* 吉備品遅
Kibiiwanasuwake *s* 吉備石无別
Kibimaro *m* 吉備麻呂
Kibi no Makibi *mh* 吉備真備
Kibinoshō *s* 気比庄 319
Kibitsu no kama *l* 吉備津の釜 278
Kibo *s* 宜保 675
Kibuchi *s* 杵淵 629
Kibyōshi *l* 黄表紙 1499
(kichi 吉 278, 劼 652, 姞 1089, 橘 2484)
Kichibee *m* 吉兵衛 278
Kichiemon *m* 吉右衛門
Kichigorō *m* 吉五郎
Kichijirō *m* 吉次郎
Kichijōten *fh* 吉祥天
Kichijūrō *m* 吉十郎
Kichimo *s* 吉母
Kichinai *m* 吉内
Kichinosuke *m* 吉之助
Kichirō *m* 吉郎, 喜知郎 1709 「衛 278
Kichirobee *m* 吉郎兵
Kichisa *f* 吉三
Kichisaburō *m* 吉三郎
Kichise *s* 吉瀬
Kichishō *m* 吉省
Kichisuke *m* 吉助
Kichiya *m* 吉弥
Kichizaemon *m* 吉左衛門
Kichizō *m* 吉蔵, 吉造
Kida *s* 京田 663, 喜田 1709
Kidai *s* 希代 445
Kidamari *s* 木里 109
Kida Sadakichi *mh* 喜田貞吉 1709
Kidate *s* 木立 109
Kido *s* 木戸, 城戸 796, 帰度 1018 「堂 2533
Kidō *s* 木藤 109; *ml* 綺
Kido Kōichi *mh* 木戸幸一 109 「796
Kidokoro *s* 木所, 城所
Kidosaki *s* 城戸崎
Kido Takayoshi *mh* 木戸孝允 109 「1755
Kifune *s* 木船, 貴布禰
Kiga *s* 木賀 109, 気賀 319
Kigake *s* 生懸 214
Kigaki *m* 木垣 109
Kigasawa *s* 気賀沢 319
Kigawa *s* 木川 109
Kigi *s* 木木, 木々
Kigin *ml* 季吟 725
Kigisu *s* 来吹 538
Kigi Takatarō *ml* 木々高太郎 109
Kigo *s* 木子, 木戸
Kigoku *s* 京極 663
Kigokuya *s* 京極屋
Kigoshō *l* 綺語抄 2533
Kigura *s* 木倉 109
Kigurashi *s* 木暮
Kigyo *l* 旗魚 2093
Kihachi *m* 喜八 1709
Kihachirō *m* 喜八郎
Kihara *s* 木原 109, 鬼原 1527
Kihaya *s* 喜早 1709
Kiheiji *m* 喜平次
Kihira *s* 木平 109, 紀平
Kihō *p* 紀宝 ⌊1424
Kihoku *p* 輝北 2499
Kii *s* 杵肄 629, 城井 796, 紀 1424; *sp* 紀伊
Kiichi *s* 私市 637, 紀一 1424; *sm* 鬼一 1527; *m* 木一 109, 希一 445, 喜一 1709, 喜市, 驥一 3008 「1527
~ Hōgen *mh* 鬼一法眼
~ ~ sanryaku no maki *la* 鬼一法眼三略巻
Kiichirō *m* 喜一郎 1709, 樹一郎 2483
Kiiko *f* 妃生子 411
Kiire *s* 給黎 2149; *sp* 喜入 1709 「基隆 1493
Kiirun *p* "Keelung"
(kiji 雉 1911)
Kijima *s* 鬼島 1527
Kijimadaira *p* 木島平 109
Kijimoto *s* 雉本 1911
Kijō *sp* 木城 109
Kijūrō *m* 喜十郎 1709, 喜重郎
Kikai *p* 喜界 「島 1527
Kikaigashima *la* 鬼界
Kikaku *ml* 其角 734
Kikawada *s* 黄川田 1499
Kikegawa *s* 亀卦川 1531
Kiki kayō *l* 記紀歌謡 1149
Kikira *s* 奇奇羅 752
Kikkawa *s* 切河 51, 吉川 278, 橘川 2484
Kikkōzuru *l* 亀甲鶴 1531
Kikonai *p* 木古内 109
Kikori *m* 樵 2479
Kikoshi *s* 木越 109
Kiku *s* 企救 269, 規矩 1349, 菊 1451. (菊, 毱 1812, 鞠 2664, 麴 2858)
Kikubo *s* 京久保 663
Kikuchi *s* 木口 109, 菊地 1451, 鞠智 2664; *sp* 菊池 1451
~ Chiyū *ml* 菊池知勇
~ Dairoku *mh* 菊池大麓
~ Hiroshi *ml* 菊池寛
~ Kan *ml* 菊池寛
~ Ken *ml* 菊池剣
~ Kurarō *ml* 菊地庫郎

~ Takemitsu *mh* 菊池武光 「武時
~ Taketoki *mh* 菊池
Kikuchiyo *f* 菊千代
Kikuchi Yūhō *ml* 菊池幽芳
Kikuda *s* 菊田
~ Kazuo *ml* 菊田一夫
Kikuei *m* 菊栄
Kikugawa *sp* 菊川
Kikugorō *m* 菊五郎
Kikuhara *s* 菊原
Kikui *s* 菊井
Kikuichirō *m* 菊一郎
Kikuike *s* 麴池 2858
Kikuiri *s* 菊入
Kikuji *m* 規矩次 1349
Kiku Jidō *la* 菊慈童 1451 「二郎
Kikujirō *m* 菊次郎, 菊
Kikuka *p* 菊鹿 「約
~ no chigiri *l* 菊花の
Kikuma *sp* 菊間
Kikumaro *m* 奇久麿 752
Kikumori *s* 菊盛 1451
Kikumoto *s* 菊本
Kikumura *s* 菊村
~ Itaru *ml* 菊村到
Kikuna *s* 菊名
Kikunae *f* 菊苗
Kikunaga *s* 菊永
Kikuno *s* 菊野
Kikunosuke *m* 菊之助
Kikuo *m* 菊男, 菊雄, 喜久大 1709, 喜久雄
Kikuoka *s* 菊岡 1451
~ Kuri *ml* 菊岡久利
Kikusaburō *m* 菊三郎
Kikuse *m* 菊瀬
Kikushima *s* 菊島
Kikushirō *m* 菊四郎
Kikusui *p* 菊水
Kikuta *p* 喜久田 1709
Kikutake *s* 企救岳 269
Kikutani *s* 菊谷 1451
Kikutarō *m* 喜久太郎 1709
Kikutei *s* 菊亭 1451
~ Kōsui *ml* 菊亭香水
Kikuto *m* 喜久人 1709
Kikutoji *s* 纐纈 2966
Kikuya *s* 菊谷 1451, 菊屋 「衛
~ Tahee *ml* 菊屋太兵
Kikuyama *s* 菊山
Kikuyō *p* 菊陽
Kikuzato *s* 菊里
Kikuzawa *s* 菊沢
Kikuzō *m* 菊蔵, 喜久三 1709
Kima *s* 木間 109
Kimachi *s* 来河 538, 来海 「座 1445
Kimase *s* 木間瀬 109, 著
Kimasuya *s* 京升屋 663
Kimata *s* 木全 109, 木俣; *m* 鬼俣 1527, 亀万太 1531 「109
~ Osamu *ml* 木俣修
Kimi *s* 吉躬 278, 岐弥 599; *f* 公 156, 君美 515, 亀美 1531. (仁 57, 王 90, 公 156, 正 205, 江 252, 后 304, 君 515, 林 633, 宮 672, 侯 777, 竜 1199, 乾 1411, 焄 1484, 鉄 1948)
Kimiaki *m* 王朝 90
Kimibukuro *s* 君袋 515
Kimifusa *m* 公房 156
Kimihei *m* 乙未平 2, 公平 156
Kimihide *m* 公任
Kimihira *sm* 公平
Kimihiro *m* 仁礼 57, 正博 205
Kimihito *m* 君仁 515
Kimikazu *m* 公麗 156
Kimiko *s* 吉侯 278, 吉彦; *f* 公子 156, 后子 304, 君子 515, 侯子 777, 焄子 1484, 喜美子 1709
Kimikobe *s* 吉弥侯部 278 「公韶
Kimimasa *m* 公正 156,
Kimimori *s* 公森; *m* 竜盛 1199
Kiminobu *m* 君養 515
Kimio *m* 公男 156, 君雄 515, 侯雄 777, 乾雄 1411, 鉄夫 1948 「156
Kimisaburō *m* 公三郎
Kimisato *m* 公利
Kimishima *s* 君島 515
Kimita *p* 君田
Kimite *m* 君手
Kimitsu *p* 君津
Kimiwada *s* 君和田
Kimiyo *f* 仁世 57
Kimiyoshi *m* 公賢 156, 公饗, 君美 515
Kimizuka *s* 公塚 156, 君塚 515
(kimo 肝 408)
Kimobetsu *p* 喜茂別 1709 「本, 木許
Kimoto *s* 木元 109, 木
Kimotsuki *s* 肝付 408, 肝衡; *sp* 肝属
Kimu *s* 金 664. (仁 57, 林 633) 「664
~ Darusu *ml* 金達寿
Kimura *s* 木村 109, 木邨, 木邑
~ Akebono *fl* 木村曙
~ Hisashi *mh* 木村栄
~ Ki *ml* 木村毅
~ Motomori *ml* 木村素衛 「八
~ Shōhachi *ml* 木村荘
~ Shōshū *ml* 木村小舟
~ Sōta *ml* 木村艸太
~ Suteroku *ml* 木村捨録
~ Tomiko *fl* 木村富子
~ Yōtarō *ml* 木村鷹太郎
Kin *s* 金 664. (今 67, 匀 72, 公 156, 均 387, 谷 446, 芹 478, 近 506, 君 515, 欣 603, 昕 622, 金 664, 衿 873, 訓 1148, 訢 1400, 菌 1441, 菫 1453, 鈞 1674, 欽 1678, 勤 1698, 琴 1778, 筠 2015, 禁 2021, 懂 2069, 槿 2289, 錦 2525, 謹 2645)
Kinadamura *l* 鬼涙村 1527
Kinai *p* 畿内 2859
Kin'aki *m* 公顕 156
Kin'akira *m* 公述
Kinami *s* 木南 109
Kinasa *s* 鬼無里 1527
Kinase *s* 木名瀬 109
Kinashi *s* 木梨
Kinbara *s* 金原 664
~ Seigo *ml* 金原省吾
Kinchika *m* 公允 156
Kindaishien *l* 近代詩苑 506
Kindaichi *sp* 金田一 664
~ Kyōsuke *ml* 金田一京助
Kine *s* 杵 629, 杵杵. (杵)
Kinebuchi *s* 杵淵
Kineda *m* 公条 156
Kineji *m* 甲子児 184
Kinekobe *s* 吉弥侯部 278
Kinenfuchi *s* 祈念仏 609
Kinenomiya *s* 杵宮 629
Kineo *m* 甲子男 184, 杵男 629 「1640
Kineya *s* 杵屋, 稀音家
Kinezumi *s* 木鼠 109
Kinfusa *m* 公維 156
Kinga *ml* 金鵞 664
Kingo *sm* 金吾; *m* 錦吾 2525 「664
Kingyokushū *l* 金玉集
Kinharu *m* 公元 156
Kinhaya *m* 公敬
Kinhira *m* 公衡
Kin'ichi *m* 均一 387, 欣一 603, 錦一 2525
Kin'ichirō *m* 謹一郎 2645
Kin'isa *m* 公績 156
Kinishi *s* 木西 109
Kin'ito *m* 公純 156
Kinji *m* 勤二 1698, 謹治 2645
Kinjirō *m* 金二郎 664, 金次郎, 金治郎
Kinkafu *l* 琴歌譜 1778
Kinkai *p* 琴海
Kinkaishū *l* 金槐集 664
Kinkakuji *p-l* 金閣寺
Kinkatsu *m* 公勝 156, 公遂
Kinkin sensei eiga no yume *l* 金々先生草花夢 664
Kinkoto *m* 公説 156
Kinkōzan *s* 錦光山 2525
Kinmasa *m* 公尹 156, 公政
Kinmei *mh* 欽明 1678
Kinmi *m* 公誠 156
Kinmichi *m* 公総
Kinmochi *m* 公望
Kinmon *p* "Quemoy, Golden Gate" 金門 664 「五三桐
~ gosan no kiri *l* 金門
Kinmura *m* 公城 156
Kinna *m* 公名
Kinnao *m* 公正, 公直
Kinnaru *m* 公功, 公考, 公燕
Kinnen shokoku-banashi *l* 近年諸国咄 ⌊506
Kinno *s* 金野 664
Kinnosuke *m* 金之助, 謹之助 2645

Kino *s* 木野 109
Kinobe *s* 木目
Kinobori *s* 木登
Kinoe *sp* 木江; *f* 甲 184
Ki no Haseo *ml* 紀長谷雄 1424
~ no Kaion *ml* 紀海音
Kinokami *s* 城上 796
Kinokarakaji *s* 紀辛梶 1424
Kinokuniya *s* 紀伊国屋
~ Bunzaemon *mh* 紀伊国屋文左衛門
Kinokunizō *s* 紀国造
Kinome *s* 椒芽 1619
Kinomoto *sp* 木之本 109
Kinomura *s* 木野村
Kinoomi *s* 木使主
Kinookasakinokume *s* 城丘前来目 796
Kin'osa *m* 公正 156, 公修, 公長, 公脩, 公揖
Kinosakahito *s* 紀酒人 1424
Kinosaki *p* 城崎 796
Kinoshita *s* 木下 109
~ Chōshōshi *ml* 木下長嘯子
~ Jun'an *mh* 木下順庵
~ Junji *ml* 木下順二
~ Mokutarō *ml* 木下杢太郎
~ Naoe *ml* 木下尚江
~ Rigen *ml* 木下利玄
~ Tsunetarō *ml* 木下常太郎
~ Yūji *ml* 木下夕爾
Kinoshō *s* 木庄
Kinosuke *m* 甲之助 184, 喜之助 1709
Kinoto *p* 乙 2
Kin'oto *m* 公翰 156
Ki no Tokibumi *ml* 紀時文 1424
~ no Tomonori *ml* 紀友則
~ no Tsurayuki *ml* 紀貫之
Kinouchi *s* 木ノ内 109, 木之内, 木野内
Kinoue *s* 木上
Ki no umi *l* 樹海 2483
~ no Yoshimochi *ml* 紀淑望 1424
Kinpei *m* 均平 387, 金平 664
Kinpira *lm* 金平
~ Jōruri *a* 金平浄瑠璃
Kinpishō *lh* 禁秘抄 2021
Kinpō *p* 金峰 664
Kinrai fūtaishō *l* 近来風体抄 506
Kinro Gyōja *ml* 近路行者
Kinsada *m* 谷定 446
Kinsashū *l* 金沙集 664
Kinsatsu *la* 金札
Kinseisetsu bishōnen roku *l* 近世説美少年録 506
Kinshō *s* 金生 664
Kinsumi *m* 公宜 156
Kintada *m* 公董
Kintake *m* 公毅
Kintarō *m* 金太郎 664
Kintaru *m* 公健 156
Kinteru *m* 公栄
Kintō *m* 公勝; *ml* 公任; *p* "Near East" 近東 506
Kintomo *m* 公共 156
Kintsumu *m* 公恪, 公積
Kintsune *m* 公彝
Kinu *f* 紝 1679, 絹 2330. (衣 520, 帛 716, 侯 777, 表 914, 砧 1112, 紈 1421, 絹 2330)
Kinue *f* 衣江 520, 帛江 716
Kinugasa *s* 衣笠 520, 衣繖, 蓋 2193
Kinugawa *s* 衣川 520, 絹川 2330
Kinuka *f* 絹香
Kinuko *f* 表子 914, 砧子 1112, 紈子 1421
Kinunui *s* 工 39, 工造
Kinunuinotomo *s* 縫伴 2746
Kinuo *m* 侯雄 777
Kinushiri *s* 衣揩 520
Kinuta *s* 絹田 2330; *m-la* 砧 1112
Kinutani *s* 絹谷 2330
Kinuyama *s* 絹山
Kinuyo *f* 帛世 716
Kinuzuri *s* 衣揩 520
Kin'ya *m* 金矢 664
Kin'yori *m* 公資 156
Kin'yōshū *l* 金葉集 664
Kin'yuki *m* 公致 156
Kinzane *m* 公誠
Kinzō *m* 欣造 603, 金造 664, 金蔵
Kioi *s* 競 2927
Kioko *f* 喜生子 1709
Kiomaro *m* 幾雄麻呂 2597
Kira *s* 雲英 2027; *sp* 吉良 278. (晃 1189)
Kirarashū *l* 雲母集 2027
Kirayuki *m* 晃之 1189
(kire 切 51)
Kiregawa *s* 喜連川 1709
Kireto *p* 切戸 51
Kiretsugawa *p* 喜連川 1709
(kiri 切 51, 桐 1103, 梧 1365, 霧 2846)
Kiribayashi *s* 桐林 1103
Kiribuchi *s* 桐淵
Kirigaya *s* 桐ケ谷
Kirigayatsu *s* 桐谷
Kirihara *s* 桐原
Kiri hitoha *la* 桐一葉
Kiriike *s* 切池 51
Kiriishi *p* 切石
Kiriki *s* 桐木 1103
Kiriko *s* 切木 51; *f* 桐子 1103
Kirimaro *m* 桐麿
Kirimura *s* 桐村
Kirino *s* 桐野
Kirinoya *s* 桐ノ谷
Kirishima *s* 桐島; *p* 霧島 2846
Kirishitan bungaku *l* 吉利支丹文学 278
Kirita *s* 切田 51, 桐田 1103
Kiritake *s* 桐竹
Kiritani *s* 桐谷
Kiritsubo *l* 桐壺
Kiriya *s* 桐谷
Kiriyama *s* 切山 51, 桐山 1103
Kirizawa *s* 桐沢
Kirizuma-zukuri *a* 切妻造 51
Kiroko *s* 木呂子 109
Kiroku *m* 喜六 1709, 毅陸 2351
Kirokuda *la* 木六駄 109
Kiryū *sp* 桐生 1103
~ ori *a* 桐生織
Kisa *s* 私 637; *f* 象 1761; *p* 吉舎 278. (私 637, 象 1761)
Kisabu *m* 喜三 1709
Kisaburō *m* 喜三郎
Kisai *s* 私 637, 私市; *p* 騎西 2762
Kisaichi *s* 私 637; *sp* 私市
Kisakata *p* 象潟 1761
Kisaku *m* 喜作 1709
Kisanji *m* 喜三次
Kisanuki *s* 木佐貫 109
Kisao *m* 象雄 1761
Kisara *s* 木皿 109
Kisaragi *m* 更衣 528; *f* 如月 412
Kisarazu *p* 木更津 109
Kisawa *sp* 木沢
Kisazō *m* 喜三蔵 1709
Kise *s* 木瀬 109
Kisei *p* 紀勢 1424
Kiseki *ml* 其磧 734
Kisenshiki *l* 喜撰式 1709
Kishi *s* 吉士 278, 吉志, 来住 538, 岸 941, 喜志 1709, 崖 1737, 貴司 1755, 貴志. (研 875, 岸 941)
Kishiba *s* 木柴 109
Kishibe *s* 吉志部 278, 吉使部, 吉師部, 岸部 941
Kishichi *m* 喜七 1709
Kishichirō *m* 喜七郎
Kishida *s* 岸田 941
~ Ginkō *mlh* 岸田吟香
~ Kunio *ml* 岸田国士
~ Ryūsei *mla* 岸田劉生
~ Toshiko *fh* 岸田俊子
Kishigami *s* 岸上
Kishigawa *s* 岸川; *p* 貴志川 1755
Kishii *s* 岸井 941
Kishiko *f* 岸子, 貴志子 1755
Kishima *s* 木島 109, 城島 796, 貴島 1755; *p* 杵島 629
Kishimi *s* 木志見 109
Kishimoto *sp* 岸本 941
Kishimura *s* 岸村
Kishina *s* 岸名
Kishinami *s* 岸波
Kishino *s* 岸野, 城篠 796
Kishinoue *s* 岸上 941
Kishiōji *s* 岸大路
Kishiro *s* 木城 109
Kishishita *s* 岸下 941
Kishiwada *sp* 岸和田
Kishi Yamaji *ml* 貴司山治 1755
Kishizawa *s* 岸沢 941
Kishō *ml* 其笑 734
Kishū *s* 来位 538

Kishuku *p* 岐宿 599
Kishūshū *l* 鬼啾啾 1527
Kiso *s* 木曾 109, 木蘚, 危寸 318, 岐阻 599, 岐蘚, 喜早 1709; *sp* 木祖
Kisō *m* 競 2927 ⌊109
Kisogawa *p* 木曾川 109
Kisohachi *m* 喜三八
Kisoi *s* 競 2927 ⌊1709
Kisōji *m* 喜三二 1709
Kiso Koku *ml* 木蘚穀 109
Kisosaki *p* 木曾岬
Kiso Yoshinaka *mh* 木曾義仲 「生記 1542
Kissa yōjōki *la* 喫茶養
Kisshō *m* 吉祥 278
Kisu *s* 支主 63, 金須 664
Kisugi *s* 来生 538
Kisuki *p* 木次 109
Kita *s* 貴田 1755; *sp* 木田 109, 北 138, 喜多 1709. (北 138, 朔 1393)
～ -adachi *p* 北足立 138
～ -aiki *p* 北相木
～ -aizu *p* 北会津
～ -akita *p* 北秋田
～ -amabe *p* 北海部
～ -arima *p* 北有馬
～ -azumi *p* 北安曇
Kitabashiri *s* 北
Kitabatake *s* 北畠
～ Akiie *mh* 北畠顕家
～ Chikafusa *ml* 北畠親房
～ Yaho *ml* 北畠八穂
Kitabayashi *s* 北林
Kitabe *s* 北辺, 北部
Kitabō *s* 北坊
Kitabori *s* 北堀
Kitada *s* 北田
Kitadate *s* 北館
Kitada Usurai *ml* 北田薄氷
Kitade *s* 北出
Kitae *m* 鍛 2651; *f* 北枝 138
Kitafuji *s* 北藤
Kitagaitō *s* 北垣内
Kitagaki *s* 北垣
Kitagata *sp* 北方
Kitagawa *s* 木田川 109, 北河 138, 喜田川 1709, 喜多川; *sp* 北川 138
～ Fuyuhiko *ml* 北川冬彦
Kitagawara *s* 北河原
Kitagawa Utamaro *ma* 喜多川歌麿 1709
Kitagō *p* 北郷 138
Kitaguchi *s* 北口
Kita-gunma *p* 北群馬
Kitahama *s* 北浜
Kitahara *s* 北原 「秋
～ Hakushū *ml* 北原白
～ Takeo *ml* 北原武夫
Kitahashi *s* 北橋
Kitahata *s* 北畑; *p* 北波多
Kita-hiyama *p* 北檜山
Kitai *s* 北井, 北居
Kita-ibaraki *p* 北茨城
Kitaike *s* 北池
Kita Ikki *mh* 北一輝
Kitajima *s* 喜多島 1709; *sp* 北島 138
Kitajiro *s* 北代, 北白
Kitajō *p* 北条
Kitaka *s* 橘高 2484; *p* 気高 319
Kitakami *sp* 北上 138
Kita-kanbara *p* 北蒲原
Kitakata *s* 北方; *p* 喜多方 1709 「城 138
Kita-katsuragi *p* 北葛
～ -katsushika *p* 北葛飾
～ -kawabe *p* 北川辺
Kitakaze *s* 北風
Kitaki *s* 木滝 109
Kitakoga *s* 北古賀 138
Kitakōji *s* 北小路
Kita-koma *p* 北巨摩
Kitakubo *s* 北久保
Kita-kuwada *p* 北桑田
～ -kyūshū *p* 北九州
Kitamado *s* 北窓
Kitamatsu *s* 北松
Kita-matsuura *p* 北松浦 「*sp* 北見 138
Kitami *s* 喜多見 1709;
Kita-mimaki *p* 北御牧
Kitami Shihoko *fl* 北見志保子
Kita Morio *ml* 北杜夫
～ -morokata *p* 北諸県
Kitamoto *sp* 北本
Kitamuki *s* 北向
Kitamura *s* 北村, 北邑, 喜多村 1709
～ Hisamura *ml* 喜多村久城 「138
～ Hisao *ml* 北村寿夫
～ Kigin *ml* 北村季吟
～ Kihachi *ml* 北村喜八 「松
～ Komatsu *ml* 北村小
～ Tōkoku *ml* 北村透谷 「村山
Kita-murayama *p* 北
～ -muro *p* 北牟婁
Kitanaka *s* 北中
Kitani *s* 木谷 109, 喜谷 1709
～ Rikka *ml* 喜谷六花
Kitaniwa *s* 北上神 138
Kitano *s* 喜多野 1709; *sp* 北野 138
～ Tenjin engi *la* 北野天神縁起
Kitao *s* 北尾
Kitaō *s* 北綏
Kitaōji *s* 北大路
Kitaoka *s* 北岡
Kitarō *m* 朔郎 1393, 喜太郎 1709, 貴太郎 1755
Kitaru *m* 来 538, 儀 2255
Kita-saitama *p* 北埼玉 138
～ -saku *p* 北佐久
～ -shidara *p* 北設楽
～ -shigeyasu *p* 北茂安
Kitashimizu *s* 北清水
Kita-shiobara *p* 北塩原 「川
Kitashirakawa *sp* 北白
Kita-sōma *p* 北相馬
Kitasono *s* 北園
～ Katsue *ml* 北園克衛
Kitasu *m* 懐 2605 「138
Kita-takaki *p* 北高来
～ -tama *p* 北多摩
Kitatani *s* 北谷
Kita-tsugaru *p* 北津軽
Kitatsuji *s* 北辻
Kita-tsuru *p* 北都留
～ -uonuma *p* 北魚沼
Kitaura *sp* 北浦
Kita-uwa *p* 北宇和
Kitawaki *s* 北脇
Kitaya *s* 北屋
Kitayama *s* 喜多山 1709; *sp* 北山 138
Kitayasu *m* 北安
Kitazaki *s* 北崎 「里
Kitazato *s* 北郷; *sm* 北
～ Shibasaburō *mh* 北里柴三郎
Kitazawa *s* 北沢
Kitazoe *s* 北副, 北添
Kitazume *s* 北爪, 北詰
Kitazumi *s* 北住
～ Toshio *ml* 北住敏夫
Kitō *s* 紀藤 1424, 鬼頭 1527; *sp* 城東 796; *m* 鍛 2651; *ml* 几董 6; *p* 木頭 109
Kitōin *p* 祈禱院 690
Kitokurō *m* 喜徳郎 1709
Kitosei *m* 鬼斗生 1527
Kitsu *s* 吉津 278, 息津 1224. (吉 278, 佶 558, 劼 652, 姞 1089, 部 1418, 喫 1542, 橘 2484)
Kitsuda *s* 橘田
Kitsugi *m* 木接 109
Kitsugu *s* 木次, 来次 538
Kitsujisaki *s* 吉事崎 278
Kitsuke *s* 木付 109
Kitsuki *s* 城 796; *p* 杵築 629
Kitsunai *s* 橘内 2484
(kitsune 狐 789)
Kitsunegawa *s* 狐川
Kitsunekaji *m* 狐鍛冶
Kitsunezuka *sla* 狐塚
Kitsuregawa *s* 喜連川 1709
Kitsuya *s* 橘谷 2484
Kittaka *s* 橘高
Kiuchi *s* 木内 109
Kiun *ml* 喜雲 1709
Kiura *s* 木浦 109
Kiwa *p* 紀和 1424. (極 1896, 際 2073)
Kiwako *f* 極子 1896, 際子 2073
Kiwame *m* 格 1099, 極 1896, 極人, 極馬
Kiwamu *m* 究 492, 極 1896, 窮 2573
Kiya *s* 木屋 109
Kiyama *s* 木山, 帰山 1018; *p* 基山 1493
～ Shōhei *ml* 木山捷平 109 「助
Kiyanosuke *m* 木屋之
Kiyasu *s* 喜安 1709
Kiyo *m* 喜代; *f* 聖 2030. (于 25, 心 49, 井 103, 氷 140, 玉 204, 白 216, 汐 250, 圭 267, 冽 549, 妍 612, 刷 655, 青 700 斉 701, 洗 817, 洋 822, 浄 823, 神 853, 研 875, 政 881, 除 1059, 祓 1125,

粋1132, 健1282, 淑1335, 淳 1337, 清 1342, 斎 1454, 雪 1495, 陽 1567, 湜 1579, 皖 1638, 湛 1855, 宮 2016, 舜 2017, 聖 2030, 廉 2042, 精 2131, 静 2145, 絜 2208, 澄 2276, 摩 2428, 激 2456, 穆 2494, 養 2558, 磨 2596, 潔 2615, 瀏 2792, 瀞 2793, 櫛 2797, 馨 2904)
Kiyō *m* 清生 1342
Kiyoaki *m* 神見 853, 清見 1342
Kiyochika *m* 政周 881, 清親 1342
Kiyoe *s* 清江
Kiyofuji *s* 清藤
Kiyofusa *m* 清房
Kiyohara *s* 清原
～ Nobukata *mh* 清原宣賢　「原深養父
～ no Fukayabu *ml* 清
～ no Motosuke *ml* 清原元輔　「武則
～ Takenori *mh* 清原
Kiyoharu *m* 清玄, 清治, 清晏, 清温, 清張
Kiyohide *m* 清秀, 清品, 清豪, 穆英 2494
Kiyohiko *m* 清彦 1342, 精彦 2131
Kiyohiro *m* 喜世啓 1709, 淳浩 1337, 穆熙 2494　「*m* 清尚
Kiyohisa *sm* 清久 1342;
Kiyohito *m* 清人
Kiyoichi *m* 喜代一 1709
Kiyoie *sm* 清家 1342
Kiyoji *m* 喜代次 1709, 喜勇爾
Kiyojima *s* 清島 1342
Kiyoka *m* 清哉, 廉香 2042
Kiyokami *s* 浄上 823
Kiyokata *m* 清剛 1342, 清豪, 清方　「清川
Kiyokawa *s* 清河; *sp*
Kiyokazu *m* 清枚, 清種
Kiyoki *m* 潔興 2615
Kiyokimi *m* 清公 1342
Kiyoko *f* 冽子 549, 妍子 612, 淑子 1335, 清子 1342, 湜子 1579, 湛子 1855, 廉子 2042, 穆子 2494, 瀞子 2793

Kiyomasa *m* 清正 1342
Kiyomasu *m* 清倍
Kiyome *m* 清芽, 清馬
Kiyomi *sm* 清海; *sm-p* 清見; *m* 冽泉 549, 浄三 823, 清水 1342, 清身, 清深, 雪1495, 潔真 2615
Kiyomichi *m* 陽通 1567
Kiyomine *s* 清岑 1342
Kiyomitsu *m* 清満
Kiyomiya *s* 清宮
Kiyomizu *s* 清水
～ -dera *p* 清水寺
～ Seigen chikai no sakura *la* 清水清玄誓約桜
Kiyomori *m* 清盛
Kiyomoto *s* 清本, 清源; *sma* 清元; *m* 潔茂 2615　「2276
Kiyomu *m* 雪 1495, 澄
Kiyomune *m* 清心 1342
Kiyomura *s* 清村
Kiyomuro *s* 宮室 2016
Kiyonaga *s* 清永 1342; *m* 清長, 清修
Kiyonari *sm* 清成; *m* 清就
Kiyondo *m* 清人
Kiyone *p* 清音
Kiyoniwa *m* 浄庭 823
Kiyono *s* 清野 1342; *m* 浄野 823　「清信
Kiyonobu *m* 清宣 1342,
Kiyonori *m* 清庸, 清意, 清徳
Kiyonuka *s* 清額
Kiyoo *m* 于夫 25, 刷雄 655, 清夫 1342
Kiyooka *s* 浄岡 823, 清岡 1342　「息, 神意
Kiyooki *m* 神気 853, 神
Kiyosaki *m* 清先 1342
Kiyosato *p* 清里
Kiyose *s* 清湍; *sp* 清瀬
Kiyoshi *sm* 清; *m* 白 216, 圭 267, 冽 549, 明 623, 忠 705, 洌 810, 洋 司 822, 浄 823, 亮 911, 美 923, 泉 965, 浩 1068, 絜 1204, 健 1282, 淑 1335, 淳 1337, 清義 1342, 鈊 1414, 粛 1528, 陽 1567, 渙 1577, 晴 1597, 皖 1638, 鈔 1676, 靖 1905, 純 1956, 廉 2042,

廉之, 澪 2080, 精 2131, 静 2145, 絜 2208, 碧 2225, 徹 2265, 澄 2276, 澈 2454, 澡 2455, 激 2456, 潔 2615, 礴 2731, 瀏 2792, 瀞 2793, 灑 2962
Kiyoshina *s* 清科 1342
Kiyosu *p* 清洲; *ph* 清州
Kiyosuke *m* 圭資 267, 清左 1342; *ml* 清輔
Kiyosumi *s* 清須美, 清棲, 清澄
Kiyota *s* 清田, 喜代田 1709; *m* 喜代太
Kiyotada *m* 清格 1342
Kiyotaka *m* 清恪, 清隆, 清猛, 精孝 2131
Kiyotake *m* 清勇 1342, 清健; *p* 清武
Kiyotari *m* 清足
Kiyoteru *m* 清輝, 清曦
Kiyotsugu *m* 清次, 清従, 清貢, 清族
Kiyotsuna *m* 清綱, 潔綱 2615
Kiyoura *s* 清浦 1342
～ Keigo *mh* 清浦奎吾
Kiyowa *f* 清輪
Kiyoyama *s* 清山
Kiyoyasu *m* 清行, 清安, 陽康 1567, 静修 2145
Kiyoyuki *m* 氷行 140, 皖是 1638, 絜行 2208
Kiyozawa *sp* 清沢 1342
～ Manshi *ml* 清沢満
Kiyozuka *s* 清塚　⌊之
Kiyozumi *s* 清住
Kizaki *s* 木崎 109
Kizashi *m* 萠 1448
Kizawa *s* 鬼沢 1527
Kizu *sp* 木津 109
Kizuka *s* 木塚
Kizukuri *sp* 木造
Kizutani *s* 木津谷
Ko *s* 子 38. (小 21, 三 22, 己 32, 子 38, 戸 59, 木 109, 女 114, 古 154, 巨 199, 乎 221, 巧 238, 去 266, 号 272, 光 281, 冴 348, 汻 393, 夸 452, 児 497, 庯 500, 君 515, 来 538, 呼 571, 股 615, 居 737, 固 744, 虎 754, 狐 789, 枯 859, 胡 879, 故 880, 栩 1095, 祜 1124, 粉

1133, 挙 1207, 庫 1243, 皎 1375, 許 1403, 教 1408, 湖 1584, 琚 1605, 袴 1643, 菰 1727, 裾 1907, 鼓 1959, 壷 2183, 箇 2216, 糊 2309, 護 2877, 顧 2929, 籠 2977)
Kō *s* 宏 674, 胛 842, 浩 1068; *sm* 幸 661, 高 1163, 鴻 2614; *sp* 国府 745; *m* 耕 1131, 晃 1189. (口29, 工 39, 孔 58, 功 135, 公 156, 勾 168, 尻 176, 甲 184, 巧 238, 行 245, 江 252, 劥 253, 光 281, 交 293, 岕 294, 后 304, 向 312, 広 316, 亙 317, 仰 360, 狂 366, 攷 377, 攻 380, 弘 410, 好 413, 杠 418, 亨 440, 谷 446, 杏 487, 告 490, 匣 504, 更 528, 考 540, 孝 541, 佼 552, 侊 553, 狗 566, 効 653, 幸 661, 享 662, 宏 674, 茎 684, 肯 709, 昊 711, 杲 712, 庚 741, 匣 742, 候 777, 恰 804, 恆 805, 恒 809, 洪 811, 洸 813, 洽 816, 胛 842, 肱 844, 神 853, 虹 882, 郊 888, 荒 935, 昂 943, 香 961, 皇 964, 巷 974, 厚 985, 岡 987, 虓 1019, 候 1029, 降 1058, 浩 1068, 峆 1079, 脇 1083, 晄 1084, 校 1096, 耿 1129, 耕 1131, 航 1136, 高 1163, 貢 1166, 寇 1177, 晃 1189, 皋 1197, 庨 1240, 鬲 1258, 後 1300, 皓 1355, 栲 1364, 教 1408, 紅 1423, 剛 1429, 奝 1432, 皐 1459, 黄 1499, 康 1509, 項 1543, 惶 1545, 港 1583, 硬 1635, 皖 1639, 蛤 1649, 幌 1833, 塙 1845, 滉 1848, 溝 1859, 煌 1877, 鉤 1939, 紘 1949, 蒿 1980, 督 2023, 誥 2140, 緪 2146, 絖 2147, 鉱 2153, 豪 2177, 澔 2268, 暭 2283, 篁 2382, 衡 2450, 戴 2549, 篝 2574, 興 2586, 壕 2603, 鴻 2614, 鴿 2631, 糠 2633, 講 2644, 綱

2661, 鮫 2672, 虆 2682, 曠 2796, 虁 2843, 疆 2873, 顯 2928, 轟 2939, 纈 2966, 響 2981, 饗 3005)
Koakutsu s 小圷 21
Koami s 小網
Kōami ma 功阿弥 135
Kōan m 幸安 661; 1278–88 弘安 410; 1361–62 康安 1509
Koana s 小穴 21
~ Ryūichi ml 小穴隆一
Koane f 小姉
Koaze s 小畔, 小疇
Koazumabito m 小東人
Koba s 小場, 木庭 109, 木場, 児馬 497
Kobae s 小八重 21
Kobai s 小唄
Kōbai l 紅梅 1423
Kobanawa s 庁 174, 庁鼻
Kobari s 小張 21
Kobatake s 小畠
Kobayakawa s 小早川
~ Takakage mh 小早川隆景
Kobayashi s 小林, 古林 154
~ Hideo ml 小林英夫 21, 小林秀雄
~ Isamu ml 小林勇
~ Issa ml 小林一茶
~ Kiyochika ma 小林清親
~ Kokei ma 小林古径
~ Takiji ml 小林多喜二
~ Yoshio ml 小林愛雄
Kobe s 戸部 59
Kōbe s 兄部 181; p 神戸 853
Kōben mh 高弁 1163
Kobi p 子生 38
Kobinata sp 小日向 21
Kōbō Daishi ml 弘法大師 410
Kōboku l 幸木 661
Kobori s 小堀 21
~ Annu fl 小堀杏奴
~ Enshū ma 小堀遠州
~ Tomone / Tomoto ma 小堀鞆音
Kobotoke s 小仏
Kobuchi s 小淵
Kobuchizawa p 小淵沢
Kōbukō s 後部高 1300
Kobuna s 小鮒 21
Kobunai s 小船井
Kobune s 小船
Kobuse s 小布施
Kobushi l 辛夷 493
Kochi s 己智 32, 巨智 199, 東風 771. (胐 1346)
Kōchi s 高地 1163; sp 河内 597; p 甲地 184, 高知 1163
Kochibe s 巨知部 199
Kochie s 子地上 38
Kochigami s 子地上
Kochijimi s 小縮 21
Kōchinoaya s 西漢 336
Kōchinofumi s 西文
Kochiura s 東風浦 771
Kōchiyama s 河内山 597
Kōchiyo m 幸千代 661
Kochō la 胡蝶 879
Kōchō 1261–64 弘長 410
Kōda s 迎田 746, 神田 853, 香田 961, 鴻田 2614; sp 甲田 184, 幸田 661
~ Aya fl 幸田文
Kodachi s 古立 154
Kōdaiji p 高台寺 1163
Kodaira sp 小平 21, 古平 154
Kodaka s 小高 21, 小鷹
Kodaki s 小滝
Kodama s 小玉; sp 児玉 497; m 木魂 109, 谺 1652
~ Gentarō mh 児玉源太郎 497
~ Kagai ml 児玉花外
Kodamashū l 山響集 89
Kodanjō s 小弾正 21
Kōda Rohan ml 幸田露伴 661
Kodashima s 古田島 154
Kodate s 小立 21, 小館, 子建 38, 神館 853
Kōdayū mh 光太夫 281, 幸太夫 661
Kōden s 講殿 2644
Kodera s 小寺 21, 木寺 109, 古寺 154
~ Yūkichi ml 小寺融吉 21
Kōdera s 国分寺 745; p 香寺 961
Kōdo s 神戸 853, 神門, 郡戸 1146
Kōdō s 甲藤 184, 幸堂 661
Kōdōkan p 講道館 2644; ph 弘道館 410
Kodomari p 小泊 21
Kōdō Tokuchi ml 幸堂得知 661
Koe s 小江 21. (吟 369, 呼 571, 肥 617, 越 2052)
Koeda s 小枝 21, 条 457
Kōei 1342–45 康永 1509
Koeki l 古駅 154
Koemi f 小笑 21
Koeru m 超 1816
Kōetsu mla 光悦 281
Koezuka s 越塚 2052
Kōfu p 甲府 184, 江府 252
Kofuda s 国府田 745
Kofuji s 小藤 21
Kofukata s 国府方 745
Kōfukata s 甲府方 184
Kofuke s 小更 21
Kōfukuji p 興福寺 2586
Koga s 久我 45, 古閑 154, 空閑 723; sp 古河 154, 古賀
Kōga sp 甲賀 184; p "Yellow River" 黄河 1499
Koga Harue ma 古賀春江 154
Kogai s 養蚕 2558
Kogaku s 古岳 154
Kogane s 小金 21
Koganei sp 小金井
~ Kimiko fl 小金井喜美子
~ Yoshikiyo mh 小金井良精
Koganesawa s 小金沢
Kōga Saburō ml 甲賀三郎 184
Koga Seiri mh 古賀精里 154
Kogawa s 小川 21, 古川 154, 粉川 1133; p 粉河
Kogaya s 古雅屋 154
Kōge p 郡家 1146
Kogen s 古閑 154
Kōgen 1256–57 康元 1509
Kogetsushō l 湖月抄 1584
Kogi s 小木 21
Kogiku s 小菊
Kogiso s 小木曾
Kogitsune ma 小狐
Kogo s 故後 880
Kogō sf-la 小督 21
Kōgo s 向後 312
Kogoi s 小倉 21
Kogoma s 小駒
Kōgon mlh 光厳 281
Kogōri p 小郡 21
Kogorō m 小五郎
Kōgorō m 行五郎 245
Kogoshi s 小越 21
Kogo shūi l 古語拾遺 154
Kogota p 小牛田 21
Koguchi s 小口, 古口 154
Kogura s 小蔵 21
Kogurashi s 小暮
Kogure s 小暮, 木暮 109, 木檜
~ Masaji ml 小暮政治 21
Kogusagawa s 小草川
Kogushi s 小串
Kogusuri s 小薬
Kōgyoku fh 皇極 964
Kohama s 小浜 21
Kohan shuki l 湖畔手記 1584
Kohana s 小花 21
Kohanawa s 小華和, 小塙
Kohara s 小原
Kohari s 小針
Koharu s 小春
Kō Haruto ml 耕治人 1131
Kohase s 小長谷 21
Kohasebe s 小長谷, 小長谷部
Kohashi s 小橋
Kohata s 小畑, 小畠, 小幡, 小疇, 木幡 109
Kohayato m 小隼人 21
Kōhei m 公平 156, 孝平 541, 幸平 661, 宏平 674; 1058–65 康平 1509
Koheiji m 小平次 21, 小平治
Kohi s 許斐 1403
Kohinata sp 小日向 21
Kohira s 小平
Kohirumaki s 小比類巻
Kohitsu s 小櫃, 古筆 154
Kohiyama s 小檜山 21
Kōho s 皇甫 964
Kōhō 964–68 康保 1509
Kohoku p 湖北 1584
Kōhoku p 江北 252, 更北 528, 港北 1583
Koi s 己斐 32, 許斐 1403. (恋 1223, 鯉 2764)

Kōi *m* 公威 156; *f* 更衣 528
Koibikyaku Yamato ōrai *la* 恋飛脚大和往来 1223
Koibuchi *s* 鯉淵 2764
Koichi *s* 小市 21; *m* 小一
Kōichi *m* 功一 135, 行一 245, 光一 281, 孝一 541, 幸一 661, 耕一 1131
Koichibee *m* 小市兵衛
Koichijō *s* 小一条 ⌊21
Koichirō *m* 小一郎
Kōichirō *m* 幸一郎 661, 浩一郎 1068
Koide *s* 古井出 154, 湖出 1584; *sp* 小出 21
～ Tsubara *ml* 小出粲
Koido *s* 小井土, 小井
Koie *s* 鯉江 2764 ⌊戸
Koigoromo *l* 恋衣 1223
Koikawa *s* 恋川
～ Harumachi *ml* 恋川春町 ⌈154
Koike *s* 小池 21, 古池
～ Kenji *ml* 小池堅治 21
Koikichi *m* 鯉吉 2764
Koiku *s* 小生 21
Koi no omoni *la* 恋重荷 1223
Koinuma *s* 小井沼 21, 肥沼 617, 鯉沼 2764
Koi nyōbō somewake tazuna *la* 恋女房染分手綱 1223
Koishi *s* 小石 21
Koishikawa *sp* 小石川
Koishiwara *p* 小石原
Koishiyama *s* 小石山
Koiso *s* 小磯 ⌈昭
～ Kuniaki *mh* 小磯国
Koitabashi *s* 小板橋
Koito *s* 鯉登 2764; *p* 小
Koiwa *s* 小岩 ⌊糸 21
Koiwai *s* 小岩井, 小祝
Koizumi *s* 小泉, 古泉 154 ⌈樫
～ Chikashi *ml* 古泉千
～ Magane *ml* 小泉鉄 21
～ Shinzō *ml* 小泉信三
～ Tōzō *ml* 小泉苳三
～ Yakumo *ml* 小泉八
Koji *sm* 小路 ⌊雲
Kōji *s* 巧児 238; *m* 小祖父 21, 孝二 541, 孝次, 孝治, 厚二 985, 浩二 1068, 晃治 1189; *p* 麹 2858; *l* 柑子 858; 1555–58 弘治 410; 1142–44 康治 1509
Kojidan *l* 古事談 154
Kojihi *m* 古慈悲
Kojijū *fl* 小侍待 21
Kojika *s* 小鹿
Kojiki *l* 古事記 154
～ akashi *l* 古事記燈
～ -den *l* 古事記伝
Kojima *s* 古島; *sp* 小島 21, 児島 497
Kōjima *s* 幸島 661
Kojima Hōshi *ml* 小島法師 21 ⌈497
～ Iken *mh* 児島惟謙
～ Kikuo *ml* 児島喜久雄 ⌈二郎 21
～ Masajirō *ml* 小島政
～ Nobuo *ml* 小島信夫
～ Tokuya *ml* 小島徳弥
～ Tsutomu *ml* 小島勗
～ Usui *ml* 小島烏水
Kōjimoto *s* 柑本 858
Kōjin *l* 行人 245, 鮫人 2672
Kojiro *s* 小城 21
Kōjiro *sp* 神代 853
Kōjirō *m* 幸次郎 661, 幸治郎, 耕二郎 1131, 港次郎 1583, 興次郎 2586
Kōjiro Tanesuke *ml* 神代種亮 853
Kojō *s* 古城 154
Kōjo *p* 興除 2586
Kōjōkan *ph* 興譲館
Kōjo Kazunomiya *l* 皇女和の宮 964
Kojūrō *m* 小十郎 21
Kōka *s* 甲可 184, 江香 252; 1844–48 弘化 410
Kōkabe *s* 伯伯壁 363
Kokabuto *s* 小甲 21
Kokagami *l* 小鏡
Kokai *s* 小貝, 小海
Kōkai *m* 宏海 674
Kokaji *s* 小梶 21; *sla* 小鍛冶
Kokame *s* 小亀
Kokan *s* 古関 154, 虎関 754 ⌈錬
～ Shiren *mlh* 虎関師
Kokarume *s* 小軽馬 21
Kokashiwa *s* 小柏
Kokatsu *s* 小勝
Kōkazu *s* 神一 853
(koke 苔 929)
Kokedera *p* 苔寺
Kōken *fh* 孝謙 541
Koke no koromo *l* 苔の衣 929 ⌈第 252
Kōke shidai *l* 江家次
Kōketsu *s* 交告 293; *sa* 纐纈 2966 ⌈410
Kōki *m* 光亀 281, 弘毅
Kōkichi *m* 亨吉 440, 孝吉 541, 幸吉 661, 享吉 662, 厚吉 985
Kōkichirō *m* 幸吉郎 661
Kokiden *ph* 弘徽殿 410
Kokigawa *s* 小来川 21
Kokin *l* 古今 154
Kokinshū *l* 古今集
～ -chū *l* 古今集注
～ ryōdo kikigaki *l* 古今集両度聞書
Kokin waka rokujō *l* 古今和歌六帖
～ wakashū *l* 古今和歌集 ⌈集正義
～ ～ seigi *l* 古今和歌
Kokishi *s* 王 90
Kokishunpū *l* 古稀春風 154
Kōkitsu *m* 幸橘 661
Kokka hachiron *l* 国歌八論 745 ⌈論余言
～ ～ yogen *l* 国歌八
～ ～ shūi *l* 国歌八論拾遺 ⌈1857
Kokkeibon *l* 滑稽本
Kokkei wagōjin *l* 滑稽和合人 ⌈154. (九 16)
Koko *s* 子子 38, 古爾
Kōko *s* 江湖 252; *f* 孝子 541, 幸子 661
Kokoe *s* 小越 21
Kōkōhei *s* 光孝平 281
Kōkoku 1340–46 興国 2586
Kokomo *m* 甲許母 184
Kokon *s* 古今 154
～ bakashū *l* 故混馬鹿集 880 ⌈聞集 154
～ chomonjū *l* 古今著
～ hyakubaka *l* 古今百馬鹿
Kokonoe *f* 九重 16
(koku 旭 300, 曲 327, 克 442, 谷 449, 告 490, 国 745, 刻 900, 圀 1002, 尅 1260, 鵠 1455, 黒 1486, 欽 1678, 惑 1784, 項 1874, 誥 2140, 穀 2168, 鞠 2664, 鵠 2739)
Kokubo *s* 小久保 21, 国保 745
Kokubu *sp* 国分
Kokubun *s* 国分
～ Ichitarō *ml* 国分一太郎
Kokubunji *p* 国分寺
Kokubu Seigai *ml* 国分青厓
Kokuchi *s* 古口 154
Kokuchō *l* 黒潮 1486
Kokufu *sp* 国府 745
～ Saitō *ml* 国府犀東
Kokui seibo *l* 黒衣聖母 1486
Kokuma *s* 小熊 21
Kokumai *s* 国米 745
Kokuna *s* 谷那 449
Kokune *s* 古久根 154
Kokura *p* 小倉 21
Kokure *s* 小榑
Kōkuri *ph* "Koguryŏ" 高句麗 1163
Kokuro *s* 小黒 21
Kokuryō *s* 国領 745
Kokuryūkai *h* 黒竜会 1486
Kokusen'ya kassen *la* 国姓爺合戦 745
Kokushō *s* 国正, 黒正 1486
Kokuzawa *s* 古久沢 154
Kōkyō *l* 孝経 541
Koma *s* 小馬 21, 小間, 古満 154, 巨万 199; *sm* 狛 567; *sph* "Koguryŏ" 高麗 1163; *m* 洽馬 816. (狗 566, 狛 567, 駒 2349)
Kōma *s* 高麗 1163
Komaba *sp* 駒場 2349
Komabayashi *s* 駒林
Komachi *s-fl* 小町 21
Komachiya *s* 小町谷
Komada *s* 駒田 2349
～ Shinji *ml* 駒田信二
Komae *sp* 狛江 567
Koma gaku *a* 高麗楽 1163
Komagari *s* 小勾 21
Komagata *s* 駒形 2349
Komagi *s* 駒木

Komagine *s* 駒木根
Komagome *sp* 駒込
Komai *s* 小舞 21, 狛井 567, 駒井 2349; *f* 駒猪
Komajirō *m* 駒次郎
Komaki *s* 小巻 21; *sf-p* 小牧
~ Bochō *ml* 小牧暮潮
Komakichi *m* 駒吉 2349
Komaki Ōmi *ml* 小牧近江 21
Komame *s* 駒目 2349
Komamiya *s* 駒宮
Komamura *s* 駒村
Koman *f* 小万 21
Komano *s* 駒野 2349
Komanochiisakobe *s* 狛竪部 567
Koma no Myōbu shū *l* 小馬命婦集 21
Komanosuke *m* 駒之助 2349
Komao *m* 駒雄
Komaru *s* 小丸 21
Kōmaru *s* 幸丸 661
Komata *s* 小又 21, 小俣, 古俣 154
Kōmata *s* 府役 740
Komatsu *sp* 小松 21
Komatsubara *s* 小松原
Komatsuchi *m* 駒槌 2349 「狗月 566
Komatsuki *s* 小月 21,
Komatsu Kiyoshi *ml* 小松清 21 「麿 661
Kōmatsumaro *m* 幸松
Kōmatsumaru *m* 幸松丸 「村 21
Komatsumura *s* 小松
Komatsuno *s* 小松野
Komatsushima *p* 小松島
Komatsuya *s* 小松屋
Komatsuzaki *s* 小松崎
Komatsuzawa *s* 小松沢
Komaya *s* 駒谷 2349
Komayo *f* 駒代
Komazaki *s* 駒崎
Komazawa *s* 駒沢
(kome 込 178, 米 343)
Kōme *sp* 神目 853
Komechi *s* 古明池 154, 米持 343 「田 343
Komeda *s* 込田 178, 米
Komefu *s* 米生
Kōmei *mh* 孝明 541
Komemori *m* 米守 343
Kometani *s* 米谷
Komeya *s* 米屋
Komeyama *s* 込山 178
Komi *s* 小見 21. (込 178)
Kōmi *sp* 小海 21
Kominami *s* 小南
Kominato *s* 小湊
Komine *s* 小峰
Komisaki *s* 日榑崎 76
Komito *s* 小見戸 21
Komiya *s* 小宮, 古宮 154, 籠宮 2977
Komiyama *s* 小見山 21, 小宮山 「明敏
~ Akitoshi *ml* 小宮山
~ Tenkō *ml* 小宮山天香
Komiya Toyotaka *ml* 小宮豊隆
Komizo *s* 小溝
Komo *s* 薦 2683. (菰 1727, 蒋 2368, 薦 2683)
Komō *p* 小生 21
Kōmo *s* 河面 597, 幸母 661, 香母 961, 紅毛 1423
Komochi *s* 蒋池 2368; *p* 子持 38
Komoda *s* 小茂田 21, 菰田 1727, 薦田 2683
Komōdo *s* 狛人 567
Komōdono *s* 狛人野
Komoike *s* 蒋池 2368
Komoku *s* 薦口 2683
Komon *s* 己 32, 古門 154
Komonji *s* 小文次 21
Komono *s* 菰野 1727
Komori *s* 小守 21, 小森, 古森 154. (籠 2977)
Komoriya *s* 小森谷 21, 籠谷 2977
Komoro *p* 小諸 21
Kōmoto *s* 河本 597, 高本 1163
Komoya *s* 古谷 154
Komozume *s* 薦集 2683
Kōmuchi *s* 神鞭 853
Komukai *s* 小向 21
Komuki *s* 昆解 945
Komura *s* 小村 21, 古村 154 「村 961
Kōmura *s* 幸村 661, 香
Komuraji *m* 小連 21
Komura Jutarō *mh* 小村寿太郎 「154
Komuro *s* 小室, 古室
~ Kutsuzan *ml* 小室屈山 21 「夫
~ Shinobu *mh* 小室信
Kōmyō *fh* 光明 281
Kon *s* 今 67, 近 506, 金 664, 昆 945. (亅 1, 今 67, 近 506, 艮 529, 坤 573, 欣 603, 昕 622, 金 664, 柑 858, 衿 873, 昆 945, 建 995, 恨 1052, 根 1372, 訢 1400, 菫 1453, 欽 1678, 紺 1954, 献 1961, 魂 2488, 諢 2511, 錦 2525, 謹 2645, 墾
Kona *s* 小納 21 ⌊2702)
Konagai *s* 小永井; *p* 小長井
Konagaya *s* 小長谷
Kōnai *s* 巫部 524, 神南 853 「子半 38
Konaka *s* 小中 21; *m*
Konakagawa *s* 小中川 21
Konakamura *s* 小中村
~ Kiyonori *ml* 小中村清矩
Kōnami *s* 神波 853
Konan *p* 湖南 1584
Kōnan *p* 甲南 184, 江南 252, 香南 961
Kōnantei *s* 江南亭 252
Konbe *s* 紺部 1954
Konbu *s* 昆布 945
Konda *s* 小墾田 21, 根田 1372, 誉田 2010, 墾田 2702; *p* 今田 67
Kondō *s* 近藤 506, 根東 1372 「506
~ Azuma *ml* 近藤東
~ Jūzō *mh* 近藤重蔵
~ Keiichi *ml* 近藤経一 「忠義
~ Tadayoshi *ml* 近藤
~ Yoshiki *ml* 近藤芳樹 「美
~ Yoshimi *ml* 近藤芳
Koneko *s* 子子子 38
Kongi *s* 昆解 945
Kongō *s* 今剛 67, 金剛 664
Kongōbuji *p* 金剛峰寺
Kon Hidemi *ml* 今日出海 67
Konikishi *s* 王 90
Kōnin *mh* 光仁 281; 810–24 弘仁 410
Konishi *s* 小西 21
Kōnishi *s* 香西 961
Konishi Izen *ml* 小西惟然 21 「行長
~ Yukinaga *mh* 小西
Konisho *s* 古仁所 154
Konita *s* 小荷田 21
Konjaku *l* 今昔 67
Konjiki *s* 近喰 506
Konjin *s* 金神 664
Kon Kan'ichi *ml* 今官一 67
Konkō *p* 金光 「明経
Konkōmyōkyō *lh* 金光
Konku *s* 紺口 1954
Konma *s* 金万 664
Konman *s* 今万 67, 金万 664
Konme *s* 小梅 21
Konmura *s* 紺村 1954
Konno *s* 今野 67, 近野 506, 金野 664, 昆野 945, 紺野 1954
Kono *s* 小野 21, 向野 312; *f* 古埜 154. (此 254, 好 413) 「能 184
Konō *s* 古野生 154, 甲
Kōno *s* 甲能, 甲野, 幸野 661, 香野 961, 高野 1163, 鴻野 2614; *sp* 河野 597 「此枝 254
Konoe *sfl* 近衛 506; *f*
~ Fumimaro *mh* 近衛文麿
Konohana *p* 此花 254
Konohara *s* 猶原 1555
Kōno Hironaka *mh* 河野広中 597
Kōnoike *s* 鴻池 2614
Kōnojō *m* 孝之丞 541
Konokonbō *s* 兄部坊 181
Konomi *s* 己斐 32, 許斐 1403; *f* 此美 254
Kōno Michiari *mh* 河野通有 597
Konomo *m* 好母 413
Kō no Moronao *mh* 高師直 1163
Kōnomoto *s* 鴻本 2614
Konomu *m* 好 413, 喜 1709
Konoshima *s* 木島 109
Kōnoshima *s* 府島 740
Kōno Shingo *ml* 河野慎吾 597
Kōnosu *p* 鴻巣 2614
Konosuke *s* 此助 254

Kōnosuke *m* 孝之助 541, 孝之亮, 孝之輔, 幸之助 661, 耕之介 1131
Kōno Toshigama *mh* 河野敏鎌 597
Konoura *p* 金浦 664
Kōno Yoichi *ml* 河野与一 597 「春 664
Konparu *s* 今春 67, 金
~ Zenchiku *mla* 金春 ⌊禅竹
Konrin *s* 金輪
Konsen *s* 金仙
Kontani *s* 紺谷 1954
Kontō *s* 言同 439
Kon Tōkō *ml* 今東光
Kōnu *p* 甲奴 184 ⌊67
Konuki *s* 小貫 21
Konuma *s* 小沼 「38
Konusubito *la* 子盗人
Kon'ya *s* 紺屋 1954
Konze *s* 金勝 664
Kōō 1389–90 康応 1509
Koōgi *l* 小扇 21
Kōōmaru *m* 幸王丸 661
Kōra *s* 高良 1163; *sp* 甲良 184 「麗 1163
Kōrai *ph* "Koryŏ" 高
Korai fūtaishō *l* 古来風体抄 154
(kore 之 24, 以 134, 云 147, 穴 158, 右 171, 兄 181, 伊 237, 此 254, 聿 332, 自 340, 官 672, 実 678, 是 947, 時 1086, 惟 1290, 這 1515, 斯 1670, 寔 1710, 茲 1987, 禔 2120, 玆 2134, 維 2540)
Koreaki *m* 是洞 947, 是彰, 維彬 2540
Koreakira *m* 惟明 1290, 惟斌
Korebe *s* 伊部 237
Korechika *m* 伊周, 是分 947, 惟前 1290, 惟親, 惟幾, 茲親 1987
Koredo *s* 惟戸 1290
Koreeda *s* 是枝 947; *m* 惟条 1290
Korehara *s* 玆原 2134
Korehiro *m* 是太 947, 寔弘 1710
Korekane *m* 玆監 2134
Korekata *m* 是賢 947
Korekatsu *m* 之勝 24
Korekazu *m* 是一 947
Korekimi *m* 是公
Korekiyo *m* 是清
Koreko *f* 是子, 維子 2540
Koremasa *m* 以正 134
Koremitsu *m* 惟詳 1290
Koremori *m* 維盛 2540
Koremune *sm* 伊統 237, 惟宗 1290
Korenaga *s* 是永 947
Korenobu *m* 維叙 2540
Korenori *m* 是儀 947, 玆矩 2134
Koreoka *s* 玆岡
Koreoki *m* 維織 2540
Koresada *m* 之貞 24
Koreshige *m* 惟精 1290
Koresue *m* 這季 1515
Koretada *m* 伊尹 237, 惟忠 1290, 惟紀, 惟粛
Koretō *s* 惟任
Koretoki *m* 以言 134
Koretoshi *m* 茲俊 1987
Koretsuna *m* 自綱 340
Koretsune *sm* 是恒 947
Koreyasu *m* 惟雍 1290
Koreyoshi *m* 伊美 237, 惟精 1290
Korezawa *s* 是沢 947
Korezumi *s* 惟住 1290
(kori 凝 2431)
Kōri *s* 郡 1146, 高利 1163, 評 1663; *sp* 桑折 1162. (郡 1146)
Kōriba *s* 郡場
Kōriki *s* 高力 1163
Kōrin *ma* 光林 281
Kōrinomiyatsuko *s* 郡領 1146
Kōrioka *s* 郡岡
Kōri Torahiko *ml* 郡虎彦
Kōriyama *sp* 郡山
Kōro *s* 紅露 1423
Kōrō *s* 上郎 47
Kōrogi *s* 興梠 2586
Kōrokan *ph* 鴻臚館 2614 「974
Kōro katei *l* 巷路過程
Koromo *s* 来余 538, 来臨; *p* 挙母 1207
Koromogawa *p* 衣川
Kōru *m* 凝 2431 ⌊520
Kōryaku 1379–81 康暦 1509
Koryō *p* 湖陵 1584
Kōryō *p* 広綾 316
Koryū *m* 湖鯉鮒 1584
Kōryūji *p* 広隆寺 316
Kosa *s* 小佐 21
Kōsa *s* 匝嵯 308; *m* 幸佐 661; *p* 甲佐 184
Kosaburō *m* 小三郎 21
Kōsaburō 好三郎 413
Kosagawa *s* 小佐川 21
Kosai *p* 湖西 1584
Kōsai *s* 香西 961; *m* 孝哉 541; *p* 甲西 184
Kosaji *s* 小佐治 21
Kosaka *s* 小阪; *sp* 小坂
Kōsaka *s* 上坂 47, 上阪, 香坂 961, 高坂 1163, 高 ⌊阪
Kosaku *s* 小作 21
Kōsaku *m* 孝作 541, 耕作 1131
Kosaza *p* 小佐佐 21
Kose *s* 小瀬, 己西 32, 古瀬 154, 巨勢 199, 居勢 737, 許勢 1403
Kosebe *s* 許西部
Kōsei *p* 甲西 184
~ shinpen *lh* 厚生新編 985 「田 199
Kosekakeida *s* 巨勢槭
Kose no Kanaoka *ma* 巨勢金岡
Kosenokashiketa *s* 巨勢槭田
Kosensui *l* 枯山水 859
Koshi *s* 越 2052, 踰 2740; *sp* 古志 154; *l* 高志 1163. (越 2052, 腰 2090, 趣 2422, 輿 2703, 踰 2740)
Kōshi *s* 高志 1163; *mlh* "Confucius" 孔子 58
Koshiba *s* 小柴 21
Koshibe *s* 越部 2052, 踰部 2740 「尼 2052
~ no Zenni *fl* 越部禅
~ ~ ~ shōsoku *l* 越部禅尼消息 「2740
Koshibeōi *s* 踰部大炊
Koshichō *l* 古史徴 154
Koshida *s* 越田 2052
Koshifu *s* 越生
Koshigae *s* 越替
Koshigawa *s* 越川, 腰川 2090
Koshigaya *s* 越ケ谷 2052; *p* 越谷
Koshigoe *s* 腰越 2090
Koshihara *s* 腰原
Koshiinori *l* 腰祈
Koshiishi *s* 越石 2052, 輿石 2703 「越路
Koshiji *m* 越二 2052; *p*
Koshikibu no Naishi *fl* 小式部内侍 21
Kōshima *s* 府島 740
Kōshimibu *s* 高志壬生 1163
Koshimizu *s* 越水 2052, 輿水 2703; *p* 小清水
Koshimo *f* 小霜 ⌊21
Koshimura *s* 越村 2052
Kōshina *s* 神志郡 853
Koshinaka *s* 越中 2052
Koshino *s* 越野, 増野 2077; *sf* 小篠 21; *p* 越廼 2052
Koshinuma *s* 越沼
Koshio *s* 小塩 21, 越生 2052
Koshiro *s* 小代 21, 小城, 古城 154, 香代 961
Koshirō *m* 小四郎 21
Kōshirō *m* 甲子郎 184, 孝四郎 541, 幸四郎 661 「文 154
Koshi seibun *l* 古史成
Koshitaka *s* 腰高 2090
Koshitsū *lh* 古史通 154
Koshiyama *s* 小檜山 21, 越山 2052, 趣山 2422
Koshizawa *s* 越沢 2052
Koshizuka *s* 越塚, 腰塚 2090 「1509
Kōshō 1455–57 康正
Kōshoku *p* 更埴 528
~ gonin onna *l* 好色五人女 413
~ ichidai onna *l* 好色一代女 「男
~ ~ otoko *l* 好色一代
Kōshū *p* 甲州 184
~ Kajikazawa adauchi *l* 甲州鰍沢報讐
Koso *s* 社 406. (社)
Kosobe *s* 巨曾部 199, 社戸 406, 許曾部 1403
Kosode Soga *la* 小袖曾我 21
Kosoge *s* 社下 406
Kōsokabe *s* 香宗我部 961, 香曾我部
Kosone *s* 小曾根 21, 巨曾根 199
Kosu *s* 古衆 154
Kōsu *s* 神主 853
Kosuda *s* 小須田 21

Kosudo *p* 小須戸
Kosuge *s* 小管; *sp* 小菅
Kosugi *sf* 小杉
～ Hōan *ml* 小杉放庵
～ Tengai *ml* 小杉天外
～ Yoshi *ml* 小杉余子
Kōsuke *m* 浩佑 1068, 耕輔 1131, 興右 2586
Kosukegawa *s* 小助川
Kota *s* 古田 154 ⌊21
Kotachi *s* 小太刀 21, 神館 853
Kotado *s* 古田土 154
Kōtaikō *fh* 皇太后 964
Kotaira *s* 古平 154
Kotajima *s* 古田島
Kotake *sp* 小竹 21
Kōtake *s* 神武 853, 高武 1163
Kōtaki *s* 上滝 47
Kotakumi *s* 木工 109
Kotani *s* 小谷 21
Kōtani *s* 神足 853
Kōtari *s* 神足
Kotarō *m* 小太郎 21
Kōtarō *m* 光太郎 281, 広太郎 316, 孝太郎 541, 幸太郎 661, 耕太郎 1131, 剛太郎 1429, 鴻太郎 2614 ⌈小竜
Kotatsu *s* 小達 21; *m*
Koteda *s* 籠手田 2977
Kotegawa *s* 小手川 21
Kōtei *l* 皇帝 964
Kōtetsu *m* 光哲 281
Koto *f* 古止 154, 琴 1778, 載 2050; *l* 古都 154. (士 41, 功 135, 言 439, 孚 483, 服 618, 采 707, 承 760, 事 768, 信 782, 政 881, 思 966, 紀 1424, 異 1497, 詞 1665, 琴 1778, 辞 1918, 瑟 2020A, 載 2050, 語 2136, 説 2143, 肇 2222, 誼 2322, 勲 2407, 諺 2508, 謀 2509, 讃 2638, 籌 2901)
Kotō *s* 小藤 21, 古東 154, 古藤; *p* 湖東 1584
Kōto *s* 額戸 2756
Kōtō *s* 厚東 985; *m* 勾当 168; *p* 江東 252
Kotoba no tama-no-o *l* 詞の玉緒 1665
Kotobuki *m* 寿 539
Kotoda *s* 琴田 1778
Kotōda *s* 古藤田 154
Kotohama *p* 琴浜 1778
Kotohira *p* 琴平
Kotohito *m* 政仁 881, 載仁 2050
Kotoji *m* 琴二 1778
Kotojirishū *l* 琴後集
Kotōke *s* 小藤花 21
Kotoko *f* 功子 135, 采子 707, 詞子 1665, 琴子 1778, 瑟子 2020A
Kōtoku *s* 幸徳 661; *mh* 孝徳 541
Kōtokui *s* 幸徳井 661
Kōtokuin *p* 高徳院 1163
Kōtoku Shūsui *mlh* 幸徳秋水 661
Kotome *f* 小留 21
Kotomi *m* 言鑒 439
Kotomichi *m* 言道
Kotomitsu *m* 説光 2143
Kotonami *p* 琴南 1778
Kotondo *m* 言人 439
Kotonushi *m* 事主 768
Kotoo *m* 小人大 21
Kotooka *p* 琴丘 1778
Kotosuga *m* 士清 41
Kototsuna *m* 言綱 439
Kotoyamatonouchi *s* 別倭種 435
Kotoyasu *m* 功康 135
(kotsu 勿 110, 忽 704, 骨 1213, 朏 1346, 滑 1857)
Kotsubo *s* 小坪 21
Kotsuji *s* 小辻
Kōtsuke *ph* 上毛 47
Kōtsuki *s* 香月 961; *sp* 上月 47
Kōtsuma *s* 高妻 1163
Kotsumori *s* 告森 490
Kotsuna *s* 忽那 704
Kōtsura *sp* 上津浦 47
Kotsutsumi *s* 小堤 21
Kottai-san *l* 太夫さん 105
Kō U *mh-l* "Hsiang Yu" 項羽 1543
Kouchi *s* 小内 21
Kouda *s* 古宇田 154
Kouma *s* 小馬 21
～ no Myōbu shū *l* 小馬命婦集
Koume *s* 小梅
Koumi *s* 小海
Kōun *ma* 光雲 281; *ml* 耕雲 1131
Koura *s* 小浦 21
Koushi *s* 小牛
Kō U to Ryū Hō *la* "Hsiang Yu and Lin Fang" 項羽と劉邦 1543
(kowa 強 1878, 彊 2621)
Kōwa 1381–84 弘和 410; 1099–1104 康和 1509
Kowada *s* 小和田 21
Kōwaka *sla* 幸若 661
Kōwakamaru *ma* 幸若 ⌊丸
Kowaki *s* 小脇 21
Kowarawako *m* 小童子
Kowashi *m* 剛 1429, 毅 2351
Kowata *s* 木綿 109
Kowatari *s* 古渡 154
Koya *s* 小屋 21
Kōya *s* 甲谷 184, 荒野 935; *mh* 空也 723; *p* 高野 1163
Koyabu *s* 小籔 21
Koyadaira *sp* 木屋平 109
Koyagi *s* 小野木 21
Kōyagi *p* 香焼 961
Kōyaguchi *p* 高野口 1163
Kōya hijiri *l* 高野聖
Koyaizu *s* 小柳津 21, 小柳筒
Koyake *s* 小宅
Koyama *s* 小山, 古山 154, 児山 497, 湖山 1584
Kōyama *s* 甲山 184, 光山 281, 幸山 661, 神山 853; *p* 高山 1163
Koyama Itoko *fl* 小山いと子 21 ⌈一 497
～ Keiichi *ml* 児山敬
～ Kiyoshi *ml* 小山清 21 ⌈太郎
～ Shōtarō *ma* 小山正
～ Teiho *ml* 小山鼎浦
Koyamatsu *s* 小谷松
Koyama Yūshi *ml* 小山祐士
Kōya monogurui *la* 高野物狂 1163 ⌈21
Koyanagawa *s* 小梁川
Koyanagi *s* 小柳
Koyano *s* 小谷野, 古谷野 154, 児谷野 497
Kōya-san *p* 高野山 1163
Koyasu *s* 小安 21, 子安 38
Kōyasu *p* 高安 1163
～ inu *l* 高安犬
Koyata *s* 小谷田 21; *m* 小弥太, 顧弥太 2929
Koyatsu *s* 小谷津 21
Koyō *s* 小用
Kōyō *ml* 紅葉 1423; *p* 高陽 1163
Koyorogi *s* 小余綾 21
Koyu *p* 児湯 497
Koyuri *f* 小百合 21
Koyuru *m* 超 1816
Koza *p* 古座 154
Kōza *p* 高座 1163 ⌈21
Kozaemon *m* 小左衛門
Kozagawa *p* 古座川 154
Kozai *s* 古在
Kozakai *s* 小酒井 21, 小堺; *sp* 小坂井
～ Fuboku *ml* 小酒井
Kozaki *s* 小崎 ⌊不木
Kōzaki *p* 神崎 853
Kozaki Hiromichi *mh* 小崎弘道 21
Kozakura *s* 小桜
Kōzan *p* 甲山 184
Kozaru *s* 小猿 21
～ Shichinosuke *la* 小猿七之助
Kozasa *s* 小笹 ⌈2977
Kozawa *s* 小沢, 籠沢
Kōzei *s* 香西 961; *ml* 行成 245 ⌈154
Kozeki *s* 小関 21, 古関
Kōzen *s* 幸前 661, 興膳 2586 ⌈護国論
～ gokokuron *lh* 興禅
Kōzō *m* 弘造 410, 孝蔵 541, 幸三 661, 荒造 935, 厚三 985, 耕三 1131, 耕象, 耕蔵
Kozono *s* 小園 21
Kozu *s* 木津 109
Kōzu *s* 神津 853; *sp* 上津 47
Kozuchi *s* 小槌 21
Kōzuchi *sp* 上有智 47
Kozue *m* 表 914, 標 2298; *m-f* 梢 1362; *f* 鴿巣江 2631
Kōzui *m* 光瑞 281
Kozuka *s* 小塚 21, 肥塚 617, 狐塚 789
Kōzuke *ph* 上野 47
Kōzukenosakamoto *s* 上毛野坂本 ⌈造 109
Kozukuri *s* 火作 52, 木

Kōzuma *s* 上妻 47
Kōzumi *s* 神墨 853, 香栖 961 「853
Kōzushima *p* 神津島
Kozutsumi *s* 小堤 21
(ku 九 16, 口 29, 工 39, 久 45, 孔 58, 弓 95, 旧 119, 功 135, 古 154, 公 156, 勾 168, 丘 219, 休 233, 伯 363, 攻 380, 泞 393, 玖 409, 弘 410, 朽 419, 夸 452, 究 492, 庯 500, 来 538, 供 555, 狗 566, 股 615, 昫 621, 苦 687, 具 718, 虎 754, 洪 811, 枯 859, 故 880, 糺 903, 穹 948, 倶 1028, 候 1029, 栩 1095, 矩 1108, 貢 1166, 宮 1184, 恭 1205, 庫 1243, 赳 1261, 胸 1347, 躬 1396, 救 1406, 糾 1422, 袴 1643, 鳩 1825, 溝 1859, 鉤 1939, 煦 2034, 壺 2183, 駒 2349, 鞏 2379, 窮 2573, 篝 2574, 龔 2909)
(kū 空 723)
Kuami *s* 朽綱 419
Kuba *s* 久方 45; *sp* 久芳
(kubi 頸 2828)
Kubihiki *la* 首引 920
Kubiki *p* 頸城 2828
Kubo *s* 久保 45, 久芳, 公保 156, 窪 2203. (窪)
Kubō *s* 久芳 45; *m* 公方 156 「窪寺 2203
Kubodera *s* 久保寺 45,
Kuboi *s* 久保井 45, 窪井 2203
Kubo Inokichi *ml* 久保猪之吉 45
Kubokawa *s* 久保川; *sp* 窪川 2203
～ Tsurujirō *ml* 窪川鶴次郎
Kuboki *s* 久保木 45
Kubomura *s* 久保村
Kuboniwa *s* 久保庭
Kubono *s* 久保埜, 久保野
Kubo Sakae *ml* 久保栄
Kuboshima *s* 久保島, 窪島 2203
Kubota *s* 窪田, 窮田 2573; *sp* 久保田 45
～ Fujiko *fl* 久保田不二子
～ Hikosaku *ml* 久保田彦作
～ Mantarō *ml* 久保田万太郎 「田正文
～ Masafumi *ml* 久保
Kubotani *s* 久保谷
Kubota Shōichirō *ml* 窪田章一郎 2203
～ Utsubo *ml* 窪田空穂 「天随 45
Kubo Tenzui *ml* 久保
Kubotsu *s* 窪津 2203
Kubouchi *s* 久保内 45
Kuboya *s* 窪谷 2203
Kuboyama *s* 久保山 45, 窪山 2203 「り江 45
Kubo Yorie *fl* 久保よ
Kubunden *s* 口分田 29
Kubushiro *s* 久布白 45
Kubutsu *s* 九仏 16
(kuchi 朽 419)
Kuchiba *sp* 口羽 29
Kuchiki *s* 朽木 419
Kuchinotsu *p* 口ノ津 29
Kuchira *s* 久地楽 45
Kuchiwa *p* 口和 29
Kuchizusami *l* 口遊
Kuchūdo *m* 口人
(kuda 下 46)
Kudaka *s* 久高 45
Kudamatsu *sp* 下松 46
Kudan *p* 九段 16
Kudara *sph* "Paekche" 百済 265 「宿
Kudaraasuka *s* 百済安
Kudara gaku *a* 百済楽
～ Kannon *a* 百済観音
～ no Kawanari *ma* 百済河成
Kudaratebito *s* 百済伎
Kudō *s* 工藤 39 「助
～ Heisuke *mh* 工藤平
Kudomi *s* 工富
Kudoyama *p* 九度山 16
Kudō Yoshimi *ml* 工藤好美 39
Kuga *s* 久我 45, 空閑 723, 陸 1312; *sp* 久賀 45; *p* 玖珂 409. (陸 1312) 「1312
Kugai *s* 久貝 45, 陸井
Kuga Katsunan *mlh* 陸羯南
Kugata *s* 陸田
Kuge *s* 久下 45, 久家
Kugeshū *l* 空華集 723
Kugetsuka *s* 具下場 718, 具下塚
(kugi 釘 1154)
Kugimiya *s* 釘宮
Kugimoto *s* 釘本
Kugino *sp* 久木野 45
Kugisaki *s* 釘崎 1154
Kugiya *s* 釘屋
Kugō *sp* 久郷 45
Kuguno *sp* 久久野
Kugutsu-mawashi no ki *l* 傀儡子記 1832
Kugyō *mh* 公暁 156
Kuhara *s* 久原 45
Kuhei *m* 九平 16
Kui *m* 咋 570; *p* 久井 45. (杙 421, 咋 570, 喰 1832, 椴 1893, 橛 2477)
Kuichirō *m* 九一郎 16
Kuimaru *p* 喰丸 1832
Kuita *s* 咋田 570
Kuize *s* 杙瀬 421 「85
Kujakubune *l* 孔雀船
Kuji *s* 久茲 45; *p* 久慈
～ hongi *l* 旧事本紀 119
Kujima *s* 九島 16, 久島 45
Kujioka *s* 鯨岡 2831
Kujira *m* 鯨
Kujirai *s* 鯨井
Kujiraoka *s* 鯨岡
Kujiro *s* 櫛代 2797
Kujō *s* 九条 16, 郡上 1146 「兼実 16
～ Kanezane *mh* 九条
～ Takeko *fl* 九条武子
Kujū *p* 九重, 久住 45
Kujūkuri *p* 九十九里 16 「216
～ -no-hama *p* 白里浜
Kūkai *ml* 空海 723
Kuki *s* 九鬼 16; *sp* 久喜 45. (茎 684, 柊 860)
Kukiko *f* 茎子 684
Kukimura *s* 久木村 45
Kukisaki *s* 柊崎 860; *p* 茎崎 684 「造 16
Kuki Shūzō *ml* 九鬼周
Kukita *s* 久木田 45
Kukuri *s* 八十一鱗 19, 久久利 45, 纐纈 2966
Kuma *s* 久間 45, 肥 617, 隈 1841, 熊 2410; *sp* 久万 45; *p* 球磨 1359. (曲 327, 阿 569, 前 921, 隈 1841, 熊 2410)
Kumabe *s* 隈部 1841
Kumada *s* 阿田 569, 熊田 2410
Kumagae *s* 熊谷
Kumagai *s* 熊谷
～ Takeo *ml* 熊谷武雄
Kumagawa *s* 隈川 1841, 熊川 2410
Kumagaya *sp* 熊谷
Kumage *p* 熊毛
Kumagiri *s* 熊切
Kumahiko *m* 熊彦
Kumahito *s* 肥人 617
Kumai *s* 熊井 2410; *f* 熊猪
Kumaichi *m* 熊一
Kumaida *s* 熊井田
Kumaishi *p* 熊石
Kumaji *m* 熊次
Kumajirō *m* 熊次郎
Kumaki *s* 熊木; *m* 熊喜 「45, 熊吉 2410
Kumakichi *m* 久万吉
Kumako *f* 隈子 1841
Kumakori *m* 熊凝 2410
Kumakura *s* 熊倉
Kumamaru *s* 熊丸
Kumamoto *s* 隈元 1841, 隈本; *sp* 熊本 2410
Kumamura *s* 熊村
Kumanai *s* 毛馬内 117
Kumando *m* 久馬人 45
Kumano *sp* 熊野 2410
Kumanoato *p* 熊野跡
Kumanogawa *p* 熊野川 「堂
Kumanomido *s* 熊埜御
Kumanoshō *s* 熊庄
Kumao *m* 熊雄
Kumaoka *s* 熊岡
Kumaōmaru *m* 熊王丸
(kumari 分 64)
Kumasaburō *m* 熊三郎 2410 「熊坂
Kumasaka *s* 熊阪; *sla*
Kumasaki *s* 熊崎
Kumase *s* 熊勢
Kumashiro *s* 熊代; *sp* 神代 853, 神稲
Kumaso *h* 熊襲 2410
Kumata *s* 来熊田 538
Kumataka *s* 隈鷹 1841
Kumatori *p* 熊取 2410
Kumawakamaru *m* 阿王丸 569, 阿新丸
Kumayama *sp* 熊山 2410
Kumazasa *l* 隈笹 1841

Kumazawa *s* 熊沢 2410
～ Banzan *mh* 熊沢蕃山 「復六
～ Mataroku *ml* 熊沢
Kumazu *s* 熊津
Kumazuki *s* 熊懐
Kume *sm* 来目 538; *sp* 久米 45; *f* 久梅, 粂 915. (粂) 「粂田 915
Kumeda *s* 久米田 45,
Kumee *f* 粂枝
Kumegawa *s* 久米川 45, 粂川 915
Kume Keiichirō *ma* 久米桂一郎 45
Kumekichi *m* 粂吉 915
Kumeko *f* 久芽子 45, 粂子 915
Kume Kunitake *mh* 久米邦武 45
Kumema *m* 粂馬 915
Kume Masao *ml* 久米正雄 45
Kumenan *p* 久米南
Kumeno *sf* 粂野 915
Kumera *s* 苦桃 687
Kumezō *m* 久米蔵 45
(kumi 与 101, 伍 229, 汲 403, 絚 1682, 組 1952)
Kumida *s* 汲田 403
Kumihama *p* 久美浜 45
Kumiji *m* 汲事 403
Kumiko *f* 九三子 16, 伍子 229, 汲子 403, 絚子 1682, 組子 1952
Kuminoyama *p* 久御山 45
Kumio *m* 与雄 101
(kumo 雲 2027)
Kumoda *s* 口分田 29
Kumodani *s* 雲谷 2027
Kumode *s* 口分田 29
Kumodegawa *s* 雲出川 2027
Kumoi *s* 雲井 「雄
～ Tatsuo *mh* 雲井竜
Kumokiri *s* 雲切
Kumon *s* 公文 156, 公門
Kumo ni magō Ueno no hatsuhana *la* 天衣紛上野初花 93
Kumoto *s* 久下 45
Kumotsu *s* 雲津 2027
Kumoya *s* 雲谷
(kumu 組 1952)
Kumura *s* 久村 45

(kun 君 515, 郡 1146, 訓 1148, 焄 1484, 勲 2407, 薫 2567)
Kunai *m* 宮内 1184
Kunaikyō *fl* 宮内卿
Kunenbō *m* 九年坊 16
Kunezaki *s* 久根崎 45
Kuni *s* 久邇, 国 745; *sp* 六合 61, 恭仁 1205; *m* 邦 417. (乙 2, 一 3, 之 24, 州 224, 地 241, 邦 417, 邑 460, 宋 468, 明 623, 呉 735, 国 745, 弟 764, 城 796, 洲 820, 圀 1002, 郡 1146, 訓 1148, 晋 1215, 域 1290A, 都 1419, 恕 1483, 第 1768, 漢 1860, 蜀 2005, 業 2024, 冀 2571) 「昭
Kuniaki *m* 国明 745, 国
Kuniakira *m* 国顕
Kunida *s* 国田
Kunie *s* 国江; *f* 都江 1419 「枝 745
Kunieda *s* 邦枝 417, 国
～ Kanji *ml* 邦枝完二 417 「745
～ Shirō *ml* 国枝史郎
Kunifusa *m* 国維
Kunigo *s* 救仁郷 1406
Kunihara *s* 国原 745
Kuniharu *m* 都治 1419
Kunihashira *m* 国柱 745
Kunihide *m* 国日出
Kunihiko *m* 邦彦 417, 国彦 745 「国広
Kunihiro *s* 国弘; *sm*
Kunihisa *sm* 国久
Kunii *s* 国井
Kuniichi *m* 国一
Kuniie *sm* 国家
Kunijirō *m* 邦治郎 417
Kunijumaru *m* 国寿丸
Kunika *m* 国香 ⌊745
Kuikane *m* 邦鼎 417
Kunikata *sm* 国方 745
Kunikazu *m* 邦一 417, 国十 745, 国多, 国算
Kunikida *s* 国木田
～ Doppo *ml* 国木田独歩
Kunikiyo *m* 郡廉 1146
Kuniko *f* 地子 241, 邦子 417, 国子 745, 洲子 820, 訓子 1148 「1205
Kuni-kyō *ph* 恭仁京

Kunimagi *s* 国覓 745
Kunimaro *m* 国満
Kunimatsu *s* 邦松 417, 国松 745
Kunimi *m* 邦省 417; *f* 久似美 45; *p* 国見 745
Kunimitsu *s* 国光
Kunimori *m* 国守
Kunimoto *s* 国元, 国本
Kunimune *m* 国宗
Kuninaga *m* 邦寿 417
Kuninaka *sm* 国中 745
Kuninao *m* 邦尚 417
Kuninari *m* 邦尚
Kuninobu *m* 邦房
Kuninomikotomochi *s* 国宰 745 「45
Kuninomiya *s* 久邇宮
Kuni-no-miyako *ph* 久邇京
Kunio *m* 一雄 3, 九二夫 16, 邦雄 417, 国士
Kunioka *s* 国岡 ⌊745
Kuniomi *m* 国臣
Kunioshi *m* 国忍
Kunisa *s* 国佐 「貞
Kunisada *s* 国定 : *m* 国
～ Chūji *mh-l* 国定忠治 「東
Kunisaki *s* 国崎; *sp* 国
～ Mokutarō *ml* 国崎望久太郎
Kunisawa *s* 国沢
Kunishi *s* 国司
Kunishige *sm* 国重; *m* 国臣, 国蕃
Kunishima *s* 国島
Kunisuke *m* 邦輔 417
Kunitachi *p* 国立 745
Kunitaka *m* 州孝 224, 郡孝 1146
Kunitake *sm* 国武 745; *m* 邦矛 417
Kunitarō *m* 邦太郎, 明太郎 623, 国太郎 745
Kuniteru *m* 郡昭 1146
Kunito *s* 郡戸
Kunitō *s* 国藤 745
Kunitoki *m* 国祝
Kunitomi *sm-p* 国富
Kunitomo *sm* 邦友 417, 国友 745; *m* 国納, 国儔 「亜
Kunitsugu *m* 国壬, 国
Kunitsukasa *s* 国司
Kunitsuko *s* 国造
Kunitsukuri *s* 国造

Kuniuji *m* 邦氏 417, 国氏 745
Kuniya *s* 国谷
Kuniyasu *sm* 国保, 国安; *m* 国康
Kuniyori *m* 国頼
Kuniyoshi *sm* 国吉; *m* 州乂 224, 邦栄 417, 邦敬, 国芳 745, 国栄, 国賀 「王 417
Kuniyoshi-ō *mh* 邦彦
Kuniyuki *m* 国行 745, 圀順 1002
Kunizō *m* 邦造 417, 邦三, 国三 745, 国造, 国蔵 「1148
Kunneppu *p* 訓子府
Kuno *s* 九野 16, 久埜 45, 久野
Kunō *s* 久能, 久納
Kunohe *sp* 九戸 16
Kunoki *s* 久能木 45
Kunori *s* 九里 16
Kuno Toyohiko *ml* 久野豊彦 45
Kunpei *m* 君平 515, 薫兵 2567
Kuntani *s* 訓谷 1148
Kunugi *s* 功力 135, 功内, 椚 1618; *f* 櫟 2963. (椚 1618)
Kunugihara *s* 櫟原 2963
Kunugita *s* 椚田 1618
Kura *s* 内蔵 81, 暗 1883, 蔵 2424; *sm* 倉 1165; *f* 久良 45. (位 354, 坐 542, 放 606, 府 740, 冥 1158, 食 1159, 倉 1165, 庫 1243, 座 1245, 椋 1628, 穀 2168, 蔵 2424, 鞍 2543, 闇 2709, 爵 2779) 「1165
Kurabayashi *s* 倉林
Kurabe *s* 倉部
Kurabu *m* 競 2927
Kurabuchi *p* 倉淵 1165
Kurachi *s* 倉地, 倉知, 鞍智 2543
Kuragaki *s* 倉垣
Kuragami *s* 倉上
Kuragano *s* 倉賀野
Kuragata *s* 倉形
Kurahara *s* 蔵原 2424
～ Korehito *ml* 蔵原惟人 「二郎
～ Shinjirō *ml* 蔵原伸
Kurahase *s* 椋椅部 1628

Kurahashi *s* 椋橋; *sp* 倉橋 1165 「1628
Kurahashibe *s* 椋橋部
Kurahashimaro *m* 倉梯麿 1165
Kurahashi Yumiko *fl* 倉橋由美子
Kurahei *m* 倉平
Kurahiko *m* 倉彦
Kurahito *s* 椋人 1628
Kurahone *s* 橋作 2485
Kurai *s* 倉井 1165, 暗 1883
Kuraishi *sp* 倉石 1165
Kuraji *m* 内蔵司 81, 庫治 1243 「2424
Kurajimaro *m* 蔵下麿
Kurakake *s* 倉掛 1165, 鞍掛 2543
Kurakane *s* 倉金 1165
Kurakata *s* 倉方, 倉片, 倉形, 蔵方 2424
Kurakazu *s* 倉員 1165, 倉数
Kuraki *s* 久郎 45, 倉木 1165; *m* 蔵紀 2424
Kurakichi *m* 内蔵吉 81, 倉吉 1165, 庫吉 1243
Kurako *f* 鞍子 2543
Kuraku *s* 工楽 39
Kurama *s* 坐間 542; *p* 鞍馬 2543
~ ide *l* 鞍馬出
~ mairi *la* 鞍馬参
Kuramata *s* 倉又 1165
Kurama tengu *la* 鞍馬天狗 2543
Kuramatsu *m* 倉松 1165
Kurami *s* 倉見; *f* 倉美
Kuramitsu *s* 倉光
Kuramochi *s* 倉持, 蔵持 2424
Kuramoto *s* 倉本 1165, 蔵元 2424, 蔵本
Kuramu *s* 公使 156
Kuranaga *s* 倉永 1165
Kuranari *s* 倉成
Kurando *m* 蔵人 2424
Kuranishi *s* 倉西 1165
Kurano *s* 倉野, 蔵野 2424
Kuranosuke *m* 内蔵之助 81, 倉之助 1165, 庫之助 1243
Kuranuki *s* 鞍貫 2543
Kuraoi *m* 蔵老 2424

Kuraoka *s* 倉岡 1165, 鞍岡 2543
Kuraroku *m* 蔵六 2424
Kurasaki *s* 倉崎 1165
Kurasawa *s* 倉沢
Kurashige *s* 倉茂, 倉重, 倉繁, 蔵重 2424
Kurashiki *p* 倉敷 1165
Kurashima *s* 倉島
Kurashina *s* 倉品, 倉科
Kurata *s* 倉田, 蔵田 2424; *m* 内蔵太 81, 蔵太 2424 「三 1165
~ Hyakuzō *ml* 倉田百
Kuratake *p* 倉岳
Kurata Momozō *ml* 倉田百三 「2168
Kuratani *s* 倉谷, 穀谷
Kurate *p* 鞍手 2543
Kuratomi *s* 倉富 1165
Kuratsuji *s* 倉辻
Kuratsuka *s* 倉塚
Kuratsukuribe *s* 鞍部 2543
Kurauchi *s* 倉内 1165
Kuraya *s* 倉谷
Kurayama *s* 倉山
Kurayoshi *m-p* 倉吉
Kure *s* 伎楽 232, 榑 2105; *sp* 呉 735. (呉, 紅 1423, 晩 1595, 榑 2105, 暮 2190)
Kureaya *s* 呉漢
Kurebayashi *s* 紅林 1423, 榑林 2105
Kurechi *s* 暮地 2190
Kureha *sf-la* 呉服 735; *f* 呉葉; *p* 呉羽
Kurehara *s* 呉服
Kurehato *s* 呉服
Kurehatori *s* 呉服
Kureho *m-f* 晩穂 1595
Kureki *s* 真継 1228
Kureko *s* 久連木 45; *f* 呉子 735, 榑子 2105
Kurematsu *s* 久連松 45, 榑松 2105
Kuremoto *s* 呉本 735
Kurenai *s* 紅 1423
Kureo *m-f* 晩穂 1595
Kurese *s* 呉妹 735
Kure Shigeichi *ml* 呉茂一
Kureta *s* 暮田 2190
Kureyama *s* 榑山 2105
Kuri *s* 九里 16, 久利 45, 久里; *f* 栗 1219. (栗)

Kuribayashi *s* 栗林
~ Issekiro *ml* 栗林一石路 「原
Kurihara *s* 栗辰; *sp* 栗
~ Kiyoko *fl* 栗原潔子
Kurihashi *p* 栗橋
Kurii *s* 栗井
Kūriigashira no hyōjō *l* 苦力頭の表情 687
Kuriita *s* 栗板 1219
Kuriiwa *s* 栗岩
Kurikara *ph* 倶利加羅 1028 「1219
Kurikaradani *s* 栗殻谷
Kurikawa *s* 栗川
Kuriki *s* 栗木, 栗城
Kurikoma *p* 栗駒
Kurikuma *m* 栗隈
Kurimata *s* 栗又, 栗股
Kurimoto *s* 栗本; *p* 栗源
~ Joun *ml* 栗本鋤雲
Kurino *sp* 栗野
Kurinomoto *l* 栗の本
Kurio *s* 栗生
Kurioka *s* 栗岡
Kurisaki *s* 栗崎
Kurisawa *p* 栗沢
Kurise *s* 栗瀬
Kurishima *s* 栗島
Kurita *s* 栗田; *p* 栗太
Kuritani *s* 栗谷
Kuriya *s* 栗谷. (厨 2417)
Kuriyagawa *s* 厨川
~ Hakuson *ml* 厨川白村
Kuriyaki *l* 栗焼 1219
Kuriyama *sp* 栗山
~ Riichi *ml* 栗山理一
~ Senpō *mh* 栗山潜鋒
Kurizuka *s* 栗塚
(kuro 玄 522, 畔 1110, 黒 1486)
Kurō *m* 久郎 45
Kurobane *p* 黒羽 1486
Kurobara *s* 黒原
Kurobe *sp* 黒部
Kuroda *s* 畔田 1110, 黒田 1486 「清隆
~ Kiyotaka *mh* 黒田
~ Kiyoteru *ma* 黒田清輝 「清綱
~ Kiyotsuna *ml* 黒田
~ Nagamasa *mh* 黒田長政
~ Seiki *ma* 黒田清輝
Kurodashō *p* 黒田庄

Kurodatakagi *s* 黒田竹城 「田辰男
Kuroda Tatsuo *ml* 黒
~ Yoshitaka *mh* 黒田
Kuroe *s* 黒江 ⌊孝高
Kuroemon *m* 九郎右衛門 16 「黒船
Kurofune *s* 黒舟 1486,
Kurogane *s* 黒金, 鉄 1948
Kurohato *s* 黒鳩 1486
Kurohi *l* 黒檜
Kurohime *p* 黒姫
Kurohone *p* 黒保根
Kuroi *s* 黒井
Kuroishi *p* 黒石
Kuroiso *p* 黒磯
Kuroita *s* 黒板
Kuroiwa *s* 黒岩
~ Jūgo *ml* 黒岩重吾
~ Ruikō *mlh* 黒岩涙香 「玄上 522
Kurokami *s* 黒神; *m*
Kurokawa *s* 黒河 1486; *sp* 黒川 「頼
~ Mayori *ml* 黒川真
Kuroki *sp* 黒木
Kuroko *s* 黒子
Kurokōchi *s* 黒河内
Kuromasa *m* 玄理 522
Kuromatsu *s* 黒松 1486
Kuromatsunai *p* 黒松
Kurome *f* 黒女 ⌊内
Kūron *p* "Kowloon" 九竜 16
Kurono *s* 黒野 1486
Kuronuma *s* 黒沼
Kuroo *s* 黒尾
Kurosaka *s* 黒坂 「崎
Kurosaki *s* 黒前; *sp* 黒
Kurosawa *s* 黒沢
Kurose *sp* 黒瀬
Kuroshima *s* 黒島
~ Denji *ml* 黒島伝治
Kurosu *s* 黒州, 黒須
Kurotaki *p* 黒滝
Kurotani *s* 黒谷
Kuroto *s* 黒股
Kurotokage *l* 黒蜥蜴
Kuroue *s* 畔上 1110
Kurowa *s* 黒羽 1486
Kuroyagi *s* 畔柳 1110, 黒柳 1486
Kuroyama *s* 黒山
Kuroyanagi *s* 畔柳 1110, 黒柳 1486
~ Shōha *ml* 黒柳召波

Kuroyone *s* 黒米
Kurozuka *la* 黒塚
Kurozumi *s* 黒住
(kuru 車 532, 来 538, 栗 1219, 牽 2028, 薫 2567)
Kuruhara *sp* 来原 538
Kuruidako *l* 狂い凧 366
Kuruji *s* 蔵主 2424
Kuruma *s* 車 532, 車間, 栗間 1219. (車 532, 榑 2292)
Kurumabayashi *s* 榑林
Kurumada *s* 車田 532
Kurumado *s* 輦止 2393
Kurumasa *s* 来正 538
Kuruma-sō *la* 車僧 532
Kurumatani *s* 車谷
Kurume *p* 久留米 45
Kurumi *s* 来海 538, 来河; *sf* 胡桃 879
Kurumizawa *s* 晃沢 1188
Kuruōchi *s* 黒河内 1486
Kururino *s* 苦林野 687
Kurushima *s* 久留島 45, 来島 538
Kurusu *s* 来栖, 栗栖 1219, 栗椋 「郎 538
~ Saburō *mh* 来栖三
Kuryū *s* 栗生 1219
~Sumio *ml* 栗生純夫
Kusa *s* 雑 2127. (艸 598, 草 934, 種 2124, 雑 2127)
Kusaba *s* 草場 934
Kusabira *l* 菌 1441
Kusabuka *s* 草深 934
Kusachi *s* 草地
Kusagawa *s* 草川
Kusagaya *s* 草ケ谷
Kusahana *s* 日鼻 77
Kusaichi *s* 草井地 934
Kusajika *s* 草鹿
Kusajima *s* 草島
Kusaka *s* 久下 45, 久坂, 六月一日 61, 日下 77, 草 934, 草鹿
Kusakabe *s* 日下部 77, 草壁 934
Kusakada *s* 日下田 77
Kusakado *s* 草鹿砥 934
Kusaka Genzui *mh* 久坂玄瑞 45
Kusakago *l* 草籠 934
Kusakari *s* 草刈
Kusaki *s* 久崎 45
Kusama *s* 草間 934
Kusamura *s* 草村, 叢 2778 「星 934
~ Hokusei *ml* 草村北
Kusanagi *s* 日柳 77, 草薙 934; *sl* 草薙
Kusano *s* 草野
~ Shinpei *ml* 草野心平 「58
Kusanoya *m* 孔舎農家
Kusa senri *l* 艸千里 598
Kusata *s* 雑田 2127
Kusatsu *p* 草津 934
Kusayanagi *s* 日柳 77, 草柳 934
Kusa-zōshi *l* 草双紙
Kusazumi *s* 久積 45
Kusebe *s* 孔世部 58
Kusemai *la* 曲舞 327
Kusenoto *l* 九世戸 16
Kuseshishido *s* 国背宍人 745
Kushi *s* 久志 45. (串 516, 奇 752, 釧 1415, 櫛 2797)
Kushibara *p* 串原 516
Kushibashi *s* 櫛橋 2797
Kushibiki *sp* 櫛引
Kushibuchi *s* 櫛淵
Kushida *s* 串田 516, 櫛田 2797 「孫一 516
~ Magoichi *ml* 串田
~ Tamizō *ml* 櫛田民蔵 2797
Kushigata *p* 櫛形
Kushige *s* 櫛笥. (匣 742)
Kushihara *s* 櫛原 2797
Kushiji *s* 櫛笥
Kushikino *p* 串木野 516
Kushima *p* 串間
Kushimoto *s* 久志本 45; *p* 串本 516
Kushira *p* 串良
Kushiro *s* 久代 45, 釧 1415, 櫛代 2797; *p* 釧路 1415
Kushizu *s* 櫛笥 2797
Kushō *s* 公荘 156
(kuso 屎 989)
Kusō *s* 草生 934
Kusu *sp* 楠 1901; *p* 玖珠 409. (奇 752, 楠 1901, 樟 2294, 薬 2568)
Kusubara *s* 楠原 1901
Kusuda *s* 楠田
Kusugawa *s* 楠川
Kusui *s* 楠井
Kusuji *m* 楠次
Kusujiri *s* 楠後
Kusuki *s* 楠木
Kusuko *f* 樟子 2294, 薬子 2568
Kusuku *s* 楠久 1901
Kusumi *s* 久隅 45, 久須見, 久須美, 楠見 1901, 楠美
Kusumoto *s* 楠元, 楠本, 樟本 2294
~ Kenkichi *ml* 楠本憲吉 1901 「楠
Kusunoki *s* 楠木; *sp*
~ Masashige *mh* 楠木正成 「正行
~ Masatsura *mh* 楠木
Kusunose *s* 楠瀬
Kusu no tsuyu *l* 楠露
Kusuo *m* 奇男 752, 楠男 1901
Kusuri *m* 薬 2568. (薬)
Kusuriko *fh* 薬君
Kusushi *sm* 薬
Kusushie *s* 薬戸 「1901
Kusutarō *m* 楠太郎
Kusuyama *s* 楠山
~ Masao *ml* 楠山正雄
Kusuyata *m* 久寿弥太 45
Kutami *s* 朽網 419
Kutani *sp* 久谷 45
Kutchan *p* 倶知安 1028
Kutō *s* 苦桃 687
Kutsu *p* 圷 240. (委 960, 堀 1847)
Kutsū *s* 三方一新 22
Kutsukake *s* 沓掛 698
Kutsukamuri *l* 沓冠
Kutsuki *s* 工月 39; *sp* 朽木 419
Kutsumi *s* 久津見 45
Kutsuna *s* 忽那 704
Kutsuwa *s* 三方一新 22
Kutsuwame *s* 七寸五分 17
Kutsuwata *s* 七寸五分, 三方一方 22, 三方一所
Kutsuzawa *s* 沓沢 698
Kutto *s* 堀戸 1847
Kuwa *s* 桑 1162, 躬和 1396. (桑 1162, 鍬 2648)
Kuwabara *s* 桑原 1162
~ no Haraaka *ml* 桑原腹赤
~ Takeo *ml* 桑原武夫
Kuwabata *s* 桑波田, 桑畑
Kuwada *s* 桑田
Kuwadani *s* 桑谷
Kuwae *s* 桑江
Kuwagata *s* 鍬形 2648
Kuwajima *s* 桑島 1162
Kuwakado *s* 桑門
Kuwaki *s* 桑木
~ Gen'yoku *ml* 桑木厳翼
Kuwakinu *p* 桑絹
Kuwako *f* 桑子
Kuwamoto *s* 桑本
Kuwamura *s* 桑村
Kuwana *p* 桑名
Kuwano *s* 桑野
Kuwaoka *s* 桑岡
Kuwashi *m* 細 1958, 精 2131
Kuwaya *s* 桑屋 1162
Kuwayama *s* 桑山
Kuwazawa *s* 桑沢
Kūya *mh* 空也 723
Kuyama *s* 久山 45
Kuze *sp* 久世; *p* 久瀬
Kuzō *s* 葛 1994
Kuzu *s* 国巣 745; *sla* 国栖. (葛 1994)
Kuzudani *s* 葛谷
Kuzuhara *s* 葛原
Kuzukami *s* 葛上
Kuzumaki *sp* 葛巻
Kuzumaro *m* 訓儒麿 1148
Kuzume *s* 葛目 1994
Kuzumi *s* 久住 45
Kuzune *m* 葛根 1994
Kuzuno *s* 葛野
Kuzuo *s* 葛生
Kuzuoka *s* 葛岡
Kuzuu *p* 葛生
Kuzuyama *s* 葛山
(kya 伽 357)
(kyaku 恪 803, 客 917, 格 1099, 脚 1612)
Kyakusha hyōbanki *l* 客車評判記 917
Kyara *s* 伽羅 357
~ makura *l* 伽羅枕
(kyo 巨 199, 去 266, 苣 680, 居 737, 挙 1207, 許 1403, 虚 1519, 琚 1605, 裾 1907, 筥 2016, 嘘 2437, 鋸 2522)
Kyō *s* 杏 487, 京 663. (叶 132, 凶 173, 兄 181, 巧 238, 劥 253, 共 292, 狂 366, 亨 440, 杏 487, 匡

504, 冏 512, 更 528, 夾 534, 孝 541, 協 548, 佼 552, 供 555, 径 576, 劾 653, 享 662, 京 663, 庚 741, 侠 773, 狭 790, 郊 888, 荆 899, 香 961, 虓 1019, 倞 1024, 挟 1043, 峡 1078, 脇 1083, 校 1096, 耿 1129, 耕 1131, 剣 1152, 恭 1205, 巠 1229, 庨 1240, 咼 1258, 胸 1347, 皎 1375, 教 1408, 逕 1512, 軽 1657, 敬 1691, 勁 1697A, 景 1764, 喬 1775, 傾 1830, 墧 1845, 卿 1865, 強 1878, 鉅 1946, 経 1957, 跫 2008, 僑 2057, 境 2076, 郷 2112, 鉱 2153, 晶 2375, 翬 2379, 慶 2425, 橋 2485, 頰 2503, 興 2586, 彊 2621, 橿 2622, 矯 2626, 鮫 2672, 鏡 2817, 疆 2873, 馨 2904, 譻 2909, 競 2927, 響 2981, 饗 3005)

Kyōchō 1596–1615 慶長 2425

Kyōden *ml* 京伝 663

Kyōei *m* 強哉 1878

Kyōgase *p* 京ガ瀬 663

Kyōgen *la* 狂言 366

Kyōgoku *sp* 京極 663

～ Kiyō *ml* 京極杞陽

～ Tamekane *ml* 京極為兼

Kyōgokuya *s* 京極屋

Kyohakushū *l* 挙白集 1207

Kyōhei *m* 恭平 1205

Kyōhō 1716–36 享保 662

Kyōichi *m* 叶一 132

Kyōji *m* 恭二 1205

Kyōka *ml* 鏡花 2817; *l* 狂歌 366 「663

Kyōkanoko *l* 京鹿子

Kyōko *f* 今日子 67

(kyoku 旭 300, 曲 327, 局 514, 勗 1455, 頊 1874, 極 1896)

Kyōku *l* 狂句 366

Kyōkunzō nagamochi *l* 教訓雑長持 1408

Kyokusanjin *ml* 曲山人 327

Kyokushi *p* 旭志 300

Kyokusui *l* 曲水 327

～ -no-en waka *l* 曲水宴和歌 「亭馬琴

Kyokutei Bakin *ml* 曲

Kyonan *p* 鋸南 2522

Kyorai *ml* 去来 266

Kyōraishi *s* 教来石 1408

Kyoraishō *l* 去来抄 266

Kyoroku *ml* 許六 1403

Kyōroku 1528–32 享禄 662

Kyoshi *ml* 虚子 1519

～ haiwa *l* 虚子俳話

Kyōshirō *m* 匡四郎 504

Kyōsuke *s* 亨介 440; *m* 恭介 1205, 恭助, 恭輔

Kyōtarō *m* 恭太郎

Kyōto *p* 京都 663 「662

Kyōtoku 1452–55 享徳

Kyōto Tsuda Sanzō *l* 凶徒津田三蔵 173

Kyōun 704–08 慶雲 2425

Kyōunshū *l* 狂雲集 366

Kyōwa *p* 共和 292, 協和 548; 1801–04 享和 662

Kyō warabe *l* 京童 663

Kyōzō *m* 恭三 1205

Kyū *s* 皀 494, 邱 644. (九 16, 久 45, 及 83, 弓 95, 旧 119, 丘 219, 休 233, 臼 338, 汲 403, 玖 409, 朽 419, 究 492, 皀 494, 求 537, 泣 590, 邱 644, 糺 903, 穹 948, 宮 1184, 笈 1208, 赳 1261, 球 1359, 躬 1396, 救 1406, 糾 1422, 毬 1510, 級 1680, 翕 1704, 韮 1728, 鳩 1825, 給 2149, 窮 2573)

Kyūan 1145–51 久安 45

Kyūbee *m* 九兵衛 16, 久兵衛 45 「644

Kyū Eikan *ml* 邱永漢

Kyūga *m* 久我 45

Kyūgo *s* 久後

Kyūgorō *m* 久五郎

Kyūhei *m* 久平

Kyūji *m* 久次, 久治

Kyūjirō *m* 久次郎, 久治郎

Kyūju 1154–56 久寿

Kyūkaku *s* 皀郭 494

Kyūkichi *m* 久吉 45

Kyūkin shishū *l* 泣菫詩集 590

Kyūno *s* 及能 83

Kyūnosuke *m* 久之助 45

Kyūragi *p* 厳木 2706

Kyūrō *m* 久郎 45

Kyūryū *p* "Kowloon" 九竜 16

Kyūsaku *m* 久作

Kyūseishū *l* 韮青集 1728

Kyūshi *l* 窮死 2573

Kyūshichi *m* 久七 45

Kyūshirō *m* 久四郎

Kyūtarō *m* 久太郎

Kyūtoku *s* 久徳

Kyūzaburō *m* 久三郎

Kyūzō *m* 久蔵

# M

(ma 十 18, 午 112, 目 191, 末 211, 守 284, 曲 327, 実 678, 茉 682A, 直 988, 真 1228, 馬 1257, 麻 1508, 間 1822, 増 2077, 澗 2274, 摩 2428, 磨 2596, 魔 2961)

Mabata *s* 馬喰田 1257

Mabe *s* 間部 1822

Mabechi *m* 真淵 1228, 馬淵 1257

Mabi *p* 真備 1228

Mabuchi *s* 間淵 1822; *sm* 馬淵 1257; *mlh* 真淵 1228

Machi *s* 町 426; *f* 需 2220. (市 195, 町 426, 待 785, 俟 1035)

Machida *p* 町田 426

～ Kashō *ma* 町田嘉章

Machide *s* 町出

Machiguchi *s* 町口

Machihiko *m* 町彦

Machii *s* 町井

Machijima *s* 町島

Machijiri *s* 町尻

Machijiriko *f* 町尻子

Machiko *f* 町子, 俟子 1035; *f-l* 真知子 1228

Machimoto *s* 坊本 389

Machino *s* 町野 426

Machiyama *s* 町山

Machiyo *sf* 万千代 43

(madara 斑 1609)

Madarame *s* 斑目

Madara neko *l* 斑猫

Madenokōji *sp* 万里小路 43

～ Nobufusa *mh* 万里小路宣房 「窓 1746)

Mado *m* 窓 1746. (円 78,

(madoi 惑 1784)

Madoka *m* 円 78, 円力; *f* 団 310

Madokoro *s* 間所 1822

Mae *s* 前 921. (前)

Maebara *sp* 前原

Maebaru *p* 前原

Maebashi *sp* 前橋

Maebe *s* 前部

Maeda *s* 前田

～ Akira *ml* 前田晁

～ Fura *ml* 前田普羅

Maedagawa *s* 前田川

Maeda Gen'i *mh* 前田玄以

Maedakō *s* 前田河

～ Hiroichirō *ml* 前田河広一郎

Maeda Kōsetsu *ml* 前田香雪 「名

～ Masana *mh* 前田正

～ Ringai *ml* 前田林外

～ Seison *ma* 前田青邨

～ Shozan *ml* 前田曙山

～ Tetsunosuke *ml* 前田鉄之助 「家

～ Toshiie *mh* 前田利

～ Yūgure *ml* 前田夕暮

Maeguchi *s* 前口

Maegura *s* 前倉

Maeha *s* 前波

Maehata *s* 前畑

Maejima *s* 前島

～ Hisoka *mh* 前島密

Maekawa *s* 前川

~ Samio *ml* 前川佐美
Maeki *s* 前木 ⌊雄
Maemi *f* 真恵美 1228
Maemura *s* 前村 921
Maenaka *s* 前中
Maenami *s* 前波
Maeno *s* 前野
Maeoka *s* 前岡
Maesawa *sp* 前沢
Maetsue *p* 前津江
Maetsugimi *s* 大夫 48
Maeyama *s* 前山 921
Maezono *s* 前園 「船
Mafune *m* 真舟 1228, 真
~ Yutaka *ml* 真船豊
(maga 勾 168, 曲 327, 禍 1885) 「垣, 籬 3010
Magaki *s* 曲木 327, 曲
Magami *s* 真上 1228, 真神 「鉄 1948
Magane *m* 真金, 真鉄,
Magari *s* 勾 168; *sm* 鉤 1939. (勾 168, 曲 327)
Magaribuchi *s* 曲淵
Magariki *s* 曲木 「168
Magarinoyukei *s* 勾靫
Magarisawa *s* 曲沢 327
Magasaki *s* 真崎 1228
Magase *s* 曲瀬 327
Magata *s* 勾田 168, 曲田 327, 澗潟 2274
Magawa *s* 真川 1228
(mago 孫 1540)
Magobee *m* 孫兵衛
Magoemon *m* 孫右衛門
Magoichi *m* 孫一
Magoichirō *m* 孫一郎
Magojirō *m* 孫次郎
Magokichi *m* 孫吉
Magome *sp* 馬込 1257
Magosaburō *m* 孫三郎 1540
Magosaku *m* 孫作
Magoshi *s* 馬越 1257
Magumi *s* 馬入
Magusa *s* 椹 2097
Mahari *m* 真榛 1228
Mahashi *s* 真橋
Mahiro *m* 真大
Mahitobe *s* 真人部
Mahora *m* 真秀
(mai 米 343, 毎 444, 枚 630, 妹 848, 舞 2391, 邁 2592) 「*p* 米原 343
Maibara *sp* 舞原 2391;
Maida *s* 米田, 毎田 444
Maiden *s* 毎田
Maie *s* 真家 1228
Maigetsushō *l* 毎月抄 444
Maihime *l* 舞姫 2391
Mai no hon *l* 舞の本
Maio *s* 麻殖生 1508
Mairu *m* 参 978
Maisaka *p* 舞阪 2391
Maita *s* 牧田 610, 前田 921
Maitaka *s* 毎高 444
Maiya *s* 米谷 343
Maizumi *s* 真泉 1228
Maizuru *p* 舞鶴 2391
Majima *s* 馬島 1257, 間島 1822; *sm* 真島 1228
~ Fuyumichi *ml* 間島冬道
~ Kinzan *ml* 間島琴山
Makabe *s* 摩賀部 2428; *sp* 真壁 1228
Makado *sm* 真門
Makaji *m* 真梶, 真揖, 真楫
Makanda *s* 真神田
Makao *p* "Macao" 澳門 2459 「柄 1822
Makara *s* 真柄 1228, 間
Makashi *m* 任 235
Makata *s* 万刀 43, 真形 1228 「風 1228
Makaze *m* 直風 988, 真
~ koikaze *l* 魔風恋風 2961
Maki *s* 万木 43, 万喜, 真 1228, 真木, 馬来 1257, 満木 1861, 満喜, 槇 2297; *sp* 牧 610, 巻 975. (在 314, 牧 610, 巻 975, 真 1228, 蒔 1985, 槇 2297, 纏 2988)
Makibashira *s* 槇桂 2297; *l* 真木柱 1228
Makibi *m* 真備
Makida *s* 馬来田 1257
Makie *m* 牧衛 610
Makiginu *la* 巻絹 975
Makiguchi *s* 牧口 610, 巻口 975
Makihara *s* 牧原 610
Maki Itsuma *ml* 牧逸馬
Makiko *f* 巻子 975, 蒔子 1985, 槇子 2297
Makime *s* 万城目 43
Makimoto *s* 槇本 2297
~ Kusurō *ml* 槇本楠郎
Makimuku *s* 纒向 2988
Makimura *s* 牧村 610, 槇村 2297
Makinishi *s* 牧西 610
Makino *s* 牧野 「2297
Makinoshima *s* 槇島
Makino Shin'ichi *ml* 牧野信一 610
Makinosuke *m* 万紀之助 43
Makinu *s* 馬被 1257
Makio *m* 牧雄 610, 巻雄 975, 真喜雄 1228
Makioka *s* 牧岡 610; *p* 牧丘
Makishima *s* 巻島 975
Makita *s* 牧田 610, 巻田 975, 蒔田 1985, 槇田 2297
Makitarō *m* 槇太郎
Makito *s* 牧戸 610
Makiuchi *s* 牧内
Makiuta *l* 牧唄
Makiyama *s* 牧山
Makiyo *m* 真清 1228
Makizono *sp* 牧園 610
Makkari *p* 真狩 1228
Makome *s* 馬籠 1257
(makomo 菰 1727)
Makomoda *s* 菰田
Makoto *sm* 良 767, 真人 1228; *m* 一 3, 丹 79, 尹 98, 允 217, 任 235, 忱 371, 孚 483, 充 521, 卓 660, 命 671, 実 678, 周 736, 信 782, 恂 807, 洵 815, 亮 911, 真 1228, 真言, 真琴, 惇 1288, 淳 1337, 訢 1400, 欽 1678, 寔 1710, 董 1731, 慎 1839, 睦 1904, 詢 1928, 純 1956, 慥 2070, 精 2131, 節 2215, 愿 2228, 諄 2324, 諒 2326, 璞 2472, 諶 2641; *m-f* 誠 1935
Maku *s* 馬来 1257. (莫 1175, 摸 1836, 漠 1853, 幕 1989)
Makubetsu *p* 幕別
Makui *s* 莫位 1175
Makura *s* 枕 627. (枕)
~ Jidō *la* 枕慈童
~ monogurui *la* 枕物狂
~ no sōshi *l* 枕草子
Makurazaki *p* 枕崎
Makuro *m* 真畔 1228
Makuta *s* 幕田 1989; *m* 馬来田 1257
Makuuchi *s* 幕内 1989
Makuwa *s* 馬加 1257
Makuwari *s* 馬加
(makuwashi 眼 1637)
Makuya *s* 幕谷 1989, 幕屋
Makuzu *m* 真葛 1228
(mama 儘 2435)
Mamada *s* 真真田 1228, 儘田 2435 「井 1485
Mamai *s* 円満井 78, 魚
Mame *s* 馬目 1257. (豆
Mameda *s* 豆田 ⌊438)
Mamejima *s* 小豆島 21
Mamiya *s* 馬神屋 1257, 間宮 1822 「輔
~ Mosuke *ml* 間宮茂
~ Rinzō *mh* 間宮林蔵
Mamori *sm* 守 284; *m* 間守 1822, 衛 2452
Mamoru *sm-f* 守 284; *m* 士 41, 役 368, 坤 573, 保 781, 捍 1042, 葵 1723, 衡 2450, 衛 2452, 養 2558, 鎮 2751, 護 2877
Mamune *f* 真宗 1228
Mamura *s* 真村 「川
Mamurokawa *p* 真室
Mamushi *m* 真虫
(man 万 43, 卍 197, 曼 1457, 満 1861, 蔓 2192, 幡 2261, 鬘 2979)
Mana *s* 曲直 327. (真 1228)
Manabe *s* 曲直部 327, 真辺 1228, 真部, 真鍋, 眼部 1637, 間人 1822, 間部, 間鍋 「房
~ Akifusa *mh* 間部詮
Manabu *m* 仕 124, 学 719
Managare *s* 真流 1228
Manai *s* 魚井 1485
Manaka *s* 真中 1228, 間中 1822, 間仲; *m* 真心 1228 「真巳 1228
Manami *s* 万波 43; *m*
Manase *s* 曲直瀬 327, 間瀬 1822 「1228
Manatsuru *m-p* 真鶴
Manba *p* 万場 43
Manchiyo *m* 万千代

Manda *s* 万田, 茨田 932
Mandai *s* 万代 43
Mandaishū *l* 万代集
Mandokoro *sp-h* 政所
(mane 弥 832) 「881
Maneba *s* 万年場 43, 万年馬
Man'emon *m* 万右衛門
Man'en 1860–61 万延
Mangoku *s* 万石
Man'ichirō *m* 万一郎
Manita *s* 真仁田 1228
Man'itsu *m* 万逸 43
Maniwa *s* 間庭 1822; *p* 真庭 1228
Manji *m* 万司 43, 1658–61 万治; *l* 卍 197. (卍)
Manjirō *m* 万次郎 43, 万治郎 「197
Manji-rōjin *ml* 卍老人
Manjiya *s* 万字屋 43
Manjōme *s* 万城目, 万場目
Manju 1024–28 万寿
Manjū *la* 満仲 1861
Mannen *ml* 万年 43
Mannensō *l* 万年艸
Mannō *p* 満濃 1861
Mannosuke *m* 万之助 43 「真野 1228
Mano *s* 間野 1822; *sp*
Manomaro *m* 真野麿
Manomori *m* 真野守
Manpei *m* 万平 43
Mantarō *m* 満太郎 1861, 幡太郎 2261, 万太郎 43 「賀
Mantei Ōga *ml* 万亭応
Man'yō daishōki *l* 万葉代匠記 「名
Man'yōgana *l* 万葉仮
Man'yōkō *l* 万葉考
Man'yōshū *l* 万葉集
～ akashi *l* 万葉集燈
～ daishōki *l* 万葉集代匠記
～ kogi *l* 万葉集古義
～ shō *l* 万葉集抄
～ suminawa *l* 万葉集墨縄
～ tama no ogoto *l* 万葉集玉の小琴
Manzai kyōkashū *l* 万載狂歌集
Manzō *m* 万三, 万蔵
Mao *s* 万尾
Maoka *p* 真岡 1228
Maomi *m* 真臣
Marai *p* "Malay" 馬来 1257
(mare 少 88, 希 445, 椀 1624, 稀 1640)
Marehito *s* 間人 1822
Marendo *m* 希人 445
Mareo *m* 希男, 希雄, 稀雄 1640
Maresuke *m* 希典 445
Mareyo *f* 希世
Mari *f* 守理 284, 茉莉 682A. (丸 40, 毬 1510, 椀 1624, 毱 1812, 鞠 2664)
Maribe *s* 目鯉部 191
Marigaya *s* 万里谷 43
Mariko *sf* 丸子 40, 鞠子 2664; *f* 万里子 43, 茉理子 682A, 真利子 1228, 真理子, 毬子 1510, 椀子 1624, 毱子 1812 「摩理勢 2428
Marise *s* 鞠瀬 2664; *m*
Maro *m* 麻呂 1508, 摩漏 2428, 麿 2786. (丸 40, 理 1361, 満 1861, 観 2765, 麿 2786)
Marōdo *s* 客 917
Maroe *f* 麿枝 2786
Maroko *mh* 麻呂子 1508
Maru *m* 円 78; *f* 丸 40. (丸, 円 78, 団 310, 巻 975, 麿 2786)
Marubae *s* 丸碆 40
Marubashi *s* 丸橋
～ Chūya *mh* 丸橋忠弥
Marubayashi *s* 丸林
Maruchi *s* 丸地
Marufusa *m* 丸房
Marugame *sp* 丸亀
Maruhonmono *a* 院本物 1055
Marui *s* 丸井 40
Marukawa *s* 丸川
Maruki *s* 万木 43
Maruko *sf-p* 丸子 40
Marumaru chinbun *l* 団々珍聞 310 「目
Marume *s* 丸女 40, 丸
Marumo *s* 丸毛, 丸茂
Marumori *sp* 丸森
Marumoto *s* 丸本
Marunari *m* 丸作
Maruno *s* 丸野
Marunouchi *p* 丸之内
Maruo *s* 丸尾
Maruoka *sp* 丸岡
～ Akira *ml* 丸岡明
～ Katsura *ml* 丸岡桂
～ Kyūka *ml* 丸岡九華
Maruseppu *p* 丸瀬布
Marushima *s* 丸島
Maruta *s* 丸田, 円田 78
Marutani *s* 丸谷 40
Maruya *s* 丸谷, 丸屋
Maruyama *s* 円山 78; *sp* 丸山 40
～ Kaoru *ml* 丸山薫
～ Masao *ml* 丸山真男
～ Ōkyo *ma* 円山応挙 78 「40
～ Sakura *ml* 丸山作楽
～ Shizuka *ml* 丸山静
～ Yoshimasa *ml* 丸山芳良
Maryū *s* 真流 1228
Masa *s* 勝 1613; *m* 諒 2326; *f* 全 271, 柾 861. (上 47, 大 48, 仁 57, 元 60, 予 62, 斗 71, 内 81, 方 85, 少 88, 尹 98, 礼 146, 公 156, 巨 199, 正 205, 允 217, 壮 243, 全 271, 各 277, 当 282, 旬 301, 存 313, 庄 315, 成 322, 多 347, 均 387, 利 436, 牟 455, 完 471, 匡 504, 応 509, 甫 533, 求 537, 征 580, 和 638, 宜 675, 芸 689, 若 692, 斉 701, 昌 715, 尚 753, 信 782, 柾 861, 相 868, 政 881, 客 917, 荘 933, 長 939, 要 950, 栄 969, 直 988, 修 1038, 将 1040, 格 1099, 祇 1127, 殷 1139, 容 1182, 晟 1187, 毘 1195, 奏 1202, 真 1228, 連 1238, 俾 1279, 倭 1283, 済 1336, 理 1361, 祗 1380, 剛 1429, 逸 1504, 粛 1528, 順 1532, 備 1539, 温 1585, 勝 1613, 款 1666, 萱 1730, 董 1731, 晶 1740, 属 1802, 道 1811, 雅 1913, 誠 1935, 幹 1938, 督 2023, 聖 2030, 塡 2075, 暢 2111, 留 2163, 蔚 2191, 適 2240, 端 2306, 諒 2326, 絹 2330, 憖 2403, 蔵 2424, 綏 2534, 綿 2538, 維 2540, 叡 2555, 薫 2567, 賢 2579, 整 2581, 優 2599, 緝 2658, 縁 2660, 懋 2700, 鎮 2751, 譲 2918, 縄 2955)
Masaaki *m* 仁監 57, 公明 156, 正旭 205, 正明, 正昭, 正晃, 正章, 成亮 322, 昌亮 715, 政章 881, 政鑑
Masaakira *m* 正旭 205, 正侃, 正学, 正章, 正瞭, 政璟 881, 政鑑
Masaari *m* 正益 205
Masaatsu *m* 政醇 881
Masabayashi *s* 正林 205
Masachi *m* 賢祐 2579
Masachika *m* 正判 205, 正身, 正遵, 正隣, 正親, 求周 537, 政近 881, 政知, 政速, 将愛 1040, 雅史 1913, 雅親
Masachiyo *m* 晟千世 1187 「田 881
Masada *s* 正田 205, 政
Masae *f* 昌穫 715, 晶穫 1740
Masaeda *m* 正柯 205
Masaemon *m* 政右衛門 881
Masafumi *m* 正文 205, 正簡, 允文 217, 祇文 1127, 理文 1361, 祗文 1380, 誠文 1935
Masafusa *m* 方房 85; *ml* 匡房 504
Masagaki *s* 正垣 205
Masago *s* 砂子 876, 真砂 1228
Masagoda *s* 沙田 392
Masagorō *m* 政五郎 881
Masaharu *m* 正治 205, 正陽, 政鋪 881, 雅脩 1913 「政秀 881
Masahide *m* 昌英 715,
Masahime *f* 正妃 205
Masahiko *m* 正彦, 政彦 881, 剛彦 1429
Masahira *m* 正均 205, 匡衡 504, 政均 881
Masahiro *m* 仁敬 57, 正大 205, 正広, 正弘, 正洪, 正博, 壮宏 243, 全弘 271, 匡衛 504, 昌碩 715, 政弘 881, 政胖, 政優
Masahisa *m* 正久 205,

正寿, 政尚 881, 勝久 1613
Masahito *m* 正士 205, 政倫 881, 直人 988
Masai *s* 正井 205; *m* 政猪 881
Masaichi *m* 政一, 雅一 1913 「宅 1913
Masaie *m* 政家 881, 雅
Masaike *s* 政池 881
Masaji *m* 正路 205, 政次 881, 政治, 雅二 1913
Masajirō *m* 政二郎 881, 政次郎, 温次郎 1585
Masaka *s* 真坂 1228; *m* 正鹿 205, 勝辞 1613
Masakado *m* 将門 1040
～ -ki *l* 将門記
Masakaki *l* 真賢木 1228
Masakane *m* 正鉦 205
Masakata *m* 正容, 政礼 881, 整方 2581
Masakatsu *m* 正坦 205, 正勝, 相勝 868, 政優 881, 聖勝 2030
Masakazu *m* 正一 205, 正応, 允計 217, 庄五 315, 信一 782, 政一 881, 妥一 950, 栄量 969, 雅一 1913, 雅万, 諒一 2326
Masaki *s* 柾木 861, 政木 881, 真崎 1228, 間崎 1822; *sm* 正木 205; *sm-f-p* 真幸 1228; *m* 昌生 715, 柾 861, 真前 1228; *p* 松前 869
Masakichi *m* 政吉 881
Masakida *s* 真鋒田 1228
Masaki Fujokyū *ml* 正木不如丘 205
Masakiyo *m* 政青 881, 政清, 政養
Masako *f* 方子 85, 正子 205, 匡子 504, 応子 509, 柾子 861, 相子 868, 政子 881, 栄子 969, 真佐子 1228, 倭子 1283, 備子 1539, 雅子 1913, 誠子 1935, 聖子 2030, 端子 2306
Masakoto *m* 正言 205, 正辞, 雅事 1913
Masakuni *m* 政国 881, 雅訓 1913
Masami *m* 正巳 205, 正太, 正見, 正美, 正幹, 正監, 昌三 715, 雅美 1913, 優美 2599; *f* 真善美 1228
Masamichi *s* 尹通 98; *m* 正倫 205, 正道, 正路, 昌猷 715, 順通 1532, 順路, 雅孔 1913, 雅充, 誠道 1935, 鎮吾 2751
Masamine *m* 政峻 881
Masamitsu *m* 正三 205, 正肥, 正満, 全侊 271, 和光 638, 昌弘 715, 政光 881, 政苗, 政参, 栄光 969
Masamori *s* 正司 205; *m* 正訥, 当壮 282, 政森 881
Masamoro *m* 正師 205
Masamoto *m* 正甫, 正孟, 正修, 正倫, 存身 313, 昌服 715, 真元 1228
Masamune *sm* 正宗 205, 当宗 282; *m* 政宗 881
～ Hakuchō *ml* 正宗白鳥 205 「政叢 881
Masamura *sm* 正村; *m*
Masana *m* 正声 205, 正魚, 正銘 「永 2240
Masanaga *m* 正脩, 適
Masanami *m* 正甫 205
Masanao *m* 正修, 正直, 正躬, 正愸, 昌胖 715
Masanari *m* 正也 205, 正生, 正城, 正備, 正誠, 正整, 政令 881, 政苗, 政誠, 逸勢 1504
Masando *m* 正人 205, 和人 638, 雅人 1913
Masano *s* 真砂野 1228
Masanobu *s* 政脩 881, 政業; *m* 正孚 205, 正身, 正達, 正演, 正敷, 正震, 正諶, 応叙 509, 昌綽 715, 政応 881, 雅庸 1913, 雅睦; *ma* 正信 205
Masanoki *m* 政宇 881
Masanori *sm* 正詮 205; *m* 方升 85, 方舟, 巨範 199, 正礼 205, 正令, 正式, 正則, 正得, 正章, 正弼, 正徳, 正儀, 正憲, 正鵠, 匡徳 504, 応理 509, 昌倫 715, 昌後, 昌道, 政則 881, 政憲, 将応 1040, 祇賀 1127, 雅規 1913
Masanosuke *m* 征之助 580, 政之助 881, 政之輔, 雅之助 1913
Masao *m* 正夫 205, 正男, 正雄, 壮夫 243, 完雄 471, 征夫 580, 宜雄 675, 昌夫 715, 昌吉, 昌幸, 昌矣, 政男 881, 長男 939, 栄右 969, 真棹 1228, 真雄, 誠夫 1935, 聖夫 2030, 端夫 2306, 磨磋夫 2596 「881
Masaoichi *m* 政尾市
Masaoka *s* 正岡 205, 昌岡 715, 政岡 881
～ Shiki *ml* 正岡子規 205
Masaoki *m* 正沖, 正陽, 正奥, 当起 282, 政興 881
Masaomi *m* 正臣 205
Masaori *m* 正織
Masaoto *m* 正己
Masari *m* 俊 1039, 雅 1913
Masarō *m* 雅郎
Masaru *m* 大 48, 仂 55, 甲 184, 平 203, 正児 205, 多 347, 克 442, 卓 660, 杰 695, 昌 715, 果 770, 長 939, 俊 1039, 真猿 1228, 勉 1263, 健 1282, 捷 1323, 勝 1613, 勝矣, 最 1742, 傑 1827, 僑 2253, 潤 2277, 愈 2358, 賢 2579, 優 2599. (多 347)
Masaruko *f* 多子
Masashi *m* 一 3, 仁 57, 方 85, 礼 146, 正 205, 正士, 正史, 正師, 正矣, 匡 504, 昌 715, 政 881, 雅 1913, 誠 1935, 誠白, 精 2131
Masashige *m* 正成 205, 董重 1731
Masasoe *m* 方副 85
Masasue *m* 正季 205
Masasuke *m* 正方, 正良, 正毘, 政助 881, 政輔
Masasumi *m* 正誠 205
Masatada *m* 正祥, 正産, 正禎, 匡也 504, 昌貞 715, 政忠 881, 政殷, 政恭, 政賢
Masataka *m* 正太 205, 正孝, 正隆, 正殷, 正嶢, 正喬, 応隆 509, 昌喬 715, 政崇 881, 真敞 1228
Masatake *s* 正強; *m* 正剛, 正献, 正毅
Masatane *m* 昌植 715
Masatarō *m* 政太郎 881, 雅太郎 1913
Masatate *m* 正健 205, 昌健 715
Masateru *m* 公光 156, 正明 205, 正映, 正燾, 当英 282
Masato *sm* 正戸 205; *m* 正人, 正外, 正表, 政人 881, 真達 1228
Masatō *m* 正徹 205
Masatoki *m* 正兌, 正辰, 正論, 当時 282
Masatomi *sm* 正富 205; *m* 雅富 1913
～ Ōyō *ml* 正富汪洋 205
Masatomo *m* 正大, 正全, 正肥, 正侶, 正致, 正曹, 政和 881, 政知
Masatora *m* 正彪 205
Masatoshi *m* 正世, 正年, 正俊, 正敏, 正倫, 正福, 正準, 正鋭, 正毅, 昌耆 715, 政敏 881, 政暦, 賢俊 2579
Masatsuchi *m* 正鎚 205
Masatsugu *m* 正次, 正治, 正紀, 正頌, 応韶 509, 理倢 1361
Masatsuna *m* 正綱 205
Masatsune *m* 正恒, 正倫, 応道 509, 昌英 715, 政常 881, 真常 1228, 雅常 1913
Masatsura *m* 正行 205, 端連 2306
Masaura *m* 正占 205
Masaya *m* 正八, 正也, 正哉
Masayasu *m* 正保, 正恭, 存保 313, 昌康 715, 理泰 1361, 雅休 1913
Masayo *s* 当世 282
Masayori *m* 正因 205, 正倚, 正順, 正憑, 昌由 715, 政和 881, 順若 1532, 雅縁 1913

Masayoshi *s* 正好 205; *m* 大韙 48, 仁義 57, 正因 205, 正治, 正栄, 正睦, 正凱, 正義, 正愛, 正誼, 昌寿 715, 昌甫, 昌達, 昌蔵, 昌穆, 昌熹, 昌臧, 政容 881, 政順, 政悳, 政養, 政蘆, 雅儀 1913, 雅嘉, 優厳 2599 「豆米 1613
Masayotsume *f* 勝代
Masayuki *m* 正之 205, 正行, 正徹, 成之 322, 昌言 715, 昌邁, 政偏 881, 荘行 933, 将志 1040, 勝行 1613
Masazane *m* 正誠 205
Masazono *s* 真砂園 1228
Masazumi *s* 正住 205, 正泉; *m* 正純, 正澂, 雅澄 1913 ˪863)
Mase *s* 間瀬 1822. (柵
Maseda *s* 間世田 1822
Maseki *s* 柵木 863
(mashi 尚 753, 益 1201, 愛 2018, 猿 2062, 増 2077)
Mashiba *s* 真柴 1228
Mashida *p* 益田 1201
Mashike *p* 増毛 2077
Mashiki *p* 益城 1201
Mashiko *s* 愛子 2018, 猿子 2062, 増子 2077; *sp* 益子 1201
Mashikobe *s* 目色部 191
Mashima *s* 馬島 1257, 摩島 2428; *sm* 真島 1228
Mashimizu *s* 真清水
Mashimo *s* 直下 988, 真下 1228
~ Hisen *ml* 真下飛泉
Mashina *s* 慎科 1839
Mashino *s* 真志野 1228, 増野 2077
Mashio *s* 真塩 1228, 猿尾 2062; *m* 真潮 1228
Mashita *s* 真下, 間下
Mashitachi *m* 益立 1201
Mashizu *s* 益津, 益頭
Masu *m* 益; *f* 舛 367, 愈 2358. (丈 36, 斗 71, 太 105, 升 113, 加 121, 舛 367, 沢 404, 助 431, 坐 542, 枡 628, 和 638, 昌 715, 尚 753, 施 831, 弥 832, 祐 852, 松 869, 長 939, 負 981, 倍 1025, 党 1191, 益 1201, 真 1228, 勉 1263, 俾 1279, 培 1291, 済 1336, 桝 1368, 剰 1426, 副 1428, 勝 1613, 賀 1756, 曾 1794, 満 1861, 殖 1867, 増 2077, 潤 2277, 賜 2317, 愈 2358, 滋 2460, 錫 2524, 綿 2538, 賢 2579)
Masuaki *sm* 舛明 367
Masubuchi *s* 増淵 2077
Masuda *s* 升田 113, 舛田 367, 沙田 392, 桝田 1368; *sp* 益田 1201, 増田 2077
~ Happū *ml* 増田八風
~ Tokisada *mh* 益田時貞 1201
Masue *m* 益得
Masuga *m* 真清 1228
Masugami *s* 益頭 1201
Masugi *s* 真杉 1228, 馬杉 1257 「1228
~ Shizue *fl* 真杉静枝
Masuhide *m* 滋秀 2460
Masuhiro *m* 益広 1201
Masuhito *m* 益人
Masuho *sp* 増穂 2077; *m* 十寸穂 18
Masui *s* 益井 1201, 益位, 増井 2077; *m* 桝伊 1368 「倍一 1025
Masuichi *m* 昌一 715,
Masujima *s* 増島 2077
Masujirō *m* 益次郎 1201, 増次郎 2077
Masu kagami *l* 増鏡
Masukawa *s* 益川 1201, 増川 2077
Masuke *m* 磨輔 2596
Masuki *s* 一寸木 3, 益城 1201, 増喜 2077; *m* 益材 1201, 真透 1228, 真鋤
Masuko *s* 猿子 2062; *sf* 益子 1201, 増子 2077; *f* 十寸子 18, 万栖子 43, 枡子 628, 和子 638, 益寿子 1201, 培子 1291, 桝子 1368, 殖子 1867
Masumi *s* 十寸見 18, 馬澄 1257, 増見 2077; *m* 真清 1228, 真澄, 潤登 2277
Masumizu *s* 舛水 367
Masumoto *s* 升本 113, 舛本 367, 桝本 1368, 増本 2077
Masumura *s* 増村
Masunaga *s* 増永
Masunari *m* 増業
Masuno *s* 増野
Masunosuke *m* 万寿之助 43
Masuo *s* 増尾 2077, 増穂; *m* 丈夫 36, 倍夫 1025, 真男 1228, 済夫 1336, 潤夫 2277
Masuoka *s* 舛岡 367, 増岡 2077
Masura *m* 益荒 1201
Masusaburō *m* 益三郎
Masushige *m* 増重 2077
Masutane *m* 錫胤 2524
Masutani *s* 桝谷 1368
Masutarō *m* 益太郎 1201
Masuteru *m* 増燿 2077
Masuto *s* 益戸 1201
Masutomi *s* 益富; *m* 斗福 71
Masutomo *m* 益以 1201
Masutoshi *m* 増勤 2077
Masutsune *m* 増式
Masuya *s* 升屋 113; *m* 加也 121
Masuyama *s* 増山 2077
Masuyoshi *m* 加孔 121
Masuzawa *s* 増沢 2077
Masuzō *m* 倍造 1025, 益蔵 1201, 増蔵 2077
Masuzu *s* 益頭 1201; *m* 真鈴 1228
Mata *s* 股 615; *m* 定 677. (又 13, 也 23, 加 121, 全 271, 亦 325, 役 368, 完 471, 股 615, 俣 779, 派 812, 益 1201, 真 1228, 復 1571)
Matachi *m* 真楯 1228
Matahito *m* 全仁 271
Mataichirō *m* 又一郎 13
Matajirō *m* 又次郎
Mataka *s* 役賀 368
Mataki *m* 完 471
Matakichi *m* 又吉 13
Matako *f* 又子, 全子 271 「*p* 真玉
Matama *m* 真瑶 1228;
Matano *s* 又野 13, 亦野 325, 股野 615, 俣野 779
Matao *m* 又夫 13, 又郎, 亦雄 325
Mataroku *m* 復六 1571
Matasaburō *m* 又三郎 13
Matasaku *m* 又策
Matashi *m* 又司, 完 471
Matasuke *m* 亦助 325
Matatarō *s* 亦太郎
Matate *m* 真楯 1228
Matawara *s* 又原 13
Matayo *f* 俣代 779
Matazō *m* 又蔵 13
Matezawa *s* 馬刀沢 1257
(mato 的 635)
Matoba *s* 的場
Matoi *s* 的井
Matomu *m* 纒 2988
Matono *s* 真野 1228
Matoshi *m* 真記
Matoya *s* 的屋 635
Matsu *sf* 松 869. (末 211, 当 282, 茉 682A, 待 785, 松 869, 枩 938, 俟 1035, 須 1544, 淞 1581, 遅 1807, 寮 2364, 磐 2400)
Matsuba *s* 松葉 869
Matsubara *sp* 松原
~ Jizōson *ml* 松原地蔵尊
Matsubase *p* 松橋
Matsubaya *s* 松葉谷
Matsubayashi *s* 松林
Matsubushi *p* 松伏
Matsuchi *s* 待乳 785
Matsuda *s* 茨田 932; *sp* 松田 869
Matsudai *p* 松代
Matsudaira *sp* 松平
~ Katamori *mh* 松平容保 「信綱
~ Nobutsuna *mh* 松平
~ Sadanobu *mh* 松平定信 「康英
~ Yasuhide *mh* 松平
~ Yoshinaga *mh* 松平慶永 「*ml* 松田常憲
Matsuda Tsunenori
Matsudo *sp* 松戸
Matsue *s* 松会; *sf-p* 松江; *m* 遅栄 1807
Matsueda *s* 松枝 869
Matsue Ishū *ml* 松江維舟 「重頼
~ Shigeyori *ml* 松江
Matsufuji *s* 松藤
Matsugaki *s* 松垣
Matsugane *s* 松金
Matsugo no me *l* 末期の眼 211

Matsuhashi *s* 松橋 869
Matsuhisa *s* 松久
Matsui *s* 松井, 松居
Matsuichirō *m* 松一郎
Matsuida *p* 松井田
Matsui Joryū *ml* 松井如流
Matsuishi *s* 松石
Matsui Shōō *ml* 松居松翁 「磨子
~ Sumako *fa* 松井須
Matsuji *s* 松地 ; *m* 松次
Matsujirō *m* 松次郎
Matsuka *s* 松家
Matsukage *s* 松蔭 ; *m* 松影
Matsukata *s* 松方
~ Masayoshi *mh* 松方正義
Matsukawa *sp* 松川
~ saiban *l* 松川裁判
Matsukaze *sla* 松風
Matsuki *s* 松木
Matsukichi *s* 松吉
Matsuko *f* 松子, 俟子 1035
Matsukuchi *s* 松口 869
Matsukuma *s* 松隈
Matsukura *s* 松倉
~ Yonekichi *ml* 松倉米吉
Matsumae *sp* 松前
Matsumaru *s* 松丸
Matsumi *s* 松見
Matsumiya *s* 松宮
~ Kankotsu *ml* 松宮寒骨 「松盛
Matsumori *s* 松森 ; *m*
Matsumoto *sp* 松元, 松本
~ Masao *ml* 松本昌夫
~ Seichō *ml* 松本清張
Matsumura *s* 松村
~ Eiichi *ml* 松村英一
~ Goshun *ma* 松村呉春
~ Midori *ml* 松村緑
Matsumuro *s* 松室
Matsumushi *la* 松虫
Matsunae *sm* 松苗
Matsunaga *sp* 松永
~ Hisahide *mh* 松永久秀
~ Sekigo *ml* 松永尺五
~ Teitoku *ml* 松永貞徳
Matsunami *s* 松波, 松並, 松南, 松浪, 松濤
~ Sukeyuki *ml* 松波資之
Matsunawa *s* 松繩
Matsundo *m* 松人
Matsune *sm* 松根
~ Tōyōjō *ml* 松根東洋城
Matsuno *sp* 松野
Matsunobu *s* 松信
Matsu no ha *l* 松の葉, 松農波
Matsunoki *s* 松木
Matsunoo *sla* 松尾
Matsu no ochiba *l* 松の落葉
Matsunosuke *m* 松之助, 枩之助 938
Matsunoya *s* 松屋 869, 松廼家 「家露八
~ Rohachi *mh-l* 松廼
Matsunoyama *p* 松之山
Matsunuma *s* 松沼
Matsuo *s* 松保 ; *sp* 松尾 ; *m* 松巌
~ Bashō *ml* 松尾芭蕉
Matsuoka *sp* 松岡
~ Eikyū *ma* 松岡映丘
~ Kōson *ml* 松岡荒村
~ Teisō *ml* 松岡貞総
~ Yōsuke *mh* 松岡洋右
~ Yuzuru *ml* 松岡譲
Matsuoto *m* 松韻
Matsura *sp* 松浦
~ -no-miya *l* 松浦宮
(matsuri 祭 1467) 「869
Matsusaburō *m* 松三郎
Matsusaki *s* 全先 271
Matsuse *s* 松瀬 869
~ Seisei *ml* 松瀬青々
Matsushige *p* 松茂
Matsushima *sp* 松島
Matsushiro *p* 松代
Matsushirō *m* 松四郎
Matsushita *s* 松下
Matsusue *s* 松末
Matsusuke *m* 松介, 松助
Matsusumi *s* 松角
Matsutarō *m* 松太郎
Matsutō *sp* 松任
Matsuu *s* 松生
Matsuura *sp* 松浦
~ Hajime *ml* 松浦一
~ Tatsuo *ml* 松浦辰男
Matsuwaki *s* 松脇
Matsuya *s* 松谷, 松屋
Matsuyama *sp* 松山
~ kagami *la* 松山鏡
~ tengu *la* 松山天狗
Matsuyani *la* 松脂
Matsuyo *f* 淞世 1581
Matsuyoshi *s* 松義 869 ; *sm* 松吉 「松阪
Matsuzaka *s* 松坂 ; *sp*
Matsuzaki *s* 松前 ; *sp* 松崎 「民
~ Tenmin *ml* 松崎天
Matsuzawa *s* 松沢
Matsuzō *m* 松三
Matsuzono *s* 松園
Matsuzuka *s* 松塚
Matsuzumi *s* 松住
Matta *s* 全田 271
Matto *sp* 真人 1228
Mattō *sp* 松任 869
Maue *s* 馬上 1257
Maui *s* 間人 1822
Mawaki *s* 真脇 1228
Mawari *s* 廻 994. (回 309)
Mawarimichi *s* 回道
Mawashi *m* 真鷲 1228
Mawatari *s* 馬渡 1257
Maya-bunin *fh* 摩耶夫人 2428
Mayahara *s* 馬屋原 1257
Mayama *s* 真山 1228, 間山 1822 「1228
~ Seika *ml* 真山青果
(mayu 眉 997, 繭 2896)
Mayuko *f* 繭子
Mayumi *sm* 真弓 1228 ; *m-f* 檀 2623
Maze *p* 馬瀬 1257
Me *m* 目 191. (人 14, 女 114, 目 191, 売 466, 芽 683, 咩 783, 妻 959, 馬 1257, 梅 1374, 萠 1448, 眼 1637)
Meate *m* 標 2298
Mebuta *s* 女部田 114
Medemaru *s* 珍丸 836
Mega *s* 女鹿 114, 目賀 191, 妻我 959, 妻鹿, 馬鹿 1257
Megata *s* 目賀田 191
Megumi *m* 仁 57, 恩 1225, 恵 1226. (萠 1448)
Megumiko *f* 萠子
Megumu *m* 仁 57, 竜 1199, 恵 1226, 愛 2018, 徳 2063
Meguro *sp* 目黒 191
Mei *s* 買 1753. (名 346, 明 623, 命 671, 芽 683, 冥 1158, 鳴 2065, 銘 2155, 謎 2640)
Meido no hikyaku *l* 冥途の飛脚 1158
Meifu sansuie *l* 冥府山水図 「623
Meigetsuki *l* 明月記
Meiji *mh* 1868–1912 明治 「叛臣伝
~ hanshinden *l* 明治
Meiko *f* 芽子 683
Meikō ōrai *l* 明衡往来 623
Meikyō *s* 名鏡 346
Meio *s* 命尾 671 「623
Meiō 1492–1501 明応
Meireki 1655–58 明暦
Meisaburō *m* 明三郎
Meisetsu *ml* 鳴雪 2065
Meishoki *l* 名所記 346
Meitoku 1390–94 明徳 623
Meiwa *p* 1764–72 明和
Mekari *sla* 和布刈 638
Mekata *s* 目加田 191,
Meki *s* 米木 343 ⌊目堅
Memanbetsu *p* 女満別
(memi 萠 1448) ⌊114
Memie *f* 萠枝
Memuro *p* 芽室 683
(men 免 762, 面 904, 勔 1425, 綿 2538, 麵 2910)
Menda *p* 免田 762
Mendori *s* 免取, 妻鳥 959
Menishi *s* 面西 904
Menjo *s* 毛所 117, 毛受
Menjō *s* 毛受, 校条 1096
Menju *s* 毛受 117
Menma *s* 毛馬
Meno *s* 米野 343
Menrai *s* 面来 904
Menuki *s* 目貫 191
Menukiya *s* 目貫屋
Menuma *p* 妻沼 959
Meo *s* 命尾 671
Meonosuke *m* 女男之助 114 「哉 104
Meoto zenzai *l* 夫妻善
Mera *s* 布良 170, 目良 191, 米良 343 ; *sp* 女良 114

(meshi 召 152, 飯 1964)
Meshida *s* 召田 152
Meshii *s* 飯井 1964
Meshiko *s* 目包 191, 目色; *f* 召子 152
Meshikobe *s* 目色部 191
Meshimori *s* 飯盛 1964
Meshino *s* 女篠 114
(mesu 召 152, 速 1237)
Metabi *s* 米多比 343
Mete *s* 目代 191
Metoki *s* 目時
Metoku *s* 目徳
Meura *s* 和布浦 638
Mezaki *s* 目崎 191
Mezamashigusa *l* 目不酔草
Mezuki *s* 売豆紀 466
(mi 三 22, 巳 30, 子 38, 心 49, 水 54, 仁 57, 丹 79, 方 85, 文 86, 王 90, 太 105, 壬 116, 示 148, 史 183, 申 185, 目 191, 未 210, 生 214, 后 304, 耳 331, 民 333, 位 354, 体 358, 好 413, 形 414, 見 518, 充 521, 臣 527, 甫 533, 身 546, 角 547, 味 572, 命 671, 実 678, 固 744, 並 765, 良 767, 俱 774, 洋 822, 弥 832, 相 868, 美 923, 泉 965, 参 978, 看 998, 省 1013, 酒 1066, 海 1071, 珠 1077, 扇 1156, 皆 1196, 益 1201, 真 1228, 胤 1269, 深 1341, 視 1348, 現 1360, 躬 1396, 御 1572, 証 1660, 登 1744, 望 1777, 堅 1796, 誠 1935, 幹 1938, 像 2061, 察 2180, 箕 2214, 関 2245, 毅 2351, 質 2395, 監 2398, 親 2544, 躬 2573, 覧 2695, 瞻 2726, 観 2765, 鏡 2817, 顧 2929, 繡 2954, 鑑 2968, 鑒 2982)
Miasa *p* 美麻 923
Mibayashi *s* 三林 22
Mibe *s* 三部
Mibori *s* 三堀
Mibu *s* 丹生 79, 壬 116, 生 214, 生玉, 生部; *sp* 壬生 116
Mibube *s* 乳部 657
Mibuchi *s* 三淵 22
Mibuichi *s* 三分一
Mibukawa *s* 壬生川 116, 癸生川 952
Mibuko *f* 三二子 22
Mibu no Nii *ml* 壬生二位 116 「生忠岑
~ no Tadamine *ml* 壬
Mibunoya *s* 丹生谷 79
Michi *m* 岐 599, 道 1811; *f* 理 1361. (孔 58, 方 85, 礼 146, 田 189, 行 245, 交 293, 有 303, 成 322, 伯 363, 利 436, 亨 440, 兑 447, 芳 480, 至 485, 吾 491, 充 521, 孝 541, 径 576, 岐 599, 享 662, 命 671, 宙 673, 宝 676, 学 719, 典 733, 俗 776, 信 782, 待 785, 陌 792, 美 922, 長 939, 参 978, 迪 1001, 度 1009, 倫 1037, 修 1038, 訓 1148, 皆 1196, 盈 1200, 聖 1229, 途 1234, 通 1239, 術 1298, 陸 1312, 理 1361, 務 1377, 能 1397, 教 1408, 恕 1483, 進 1503, 康 1509, 逕 1512, 順 1532, 随 1564, 峻 1591, 裕 1645, 彰 1693, 達 1810, 道 1811, 逵 1813, 満 1861, 路 1925, 猷 1962, 義 1975, 塗 2038, 磧 2116, 衢 2264, 導 2413, 遙 2421, 慶 2425, 儒 2432, 儘 2435, 徹 2451, 講 2644, 総 2662, 蹊 2807, 巌 2936)
Michiaki *sm* 道明 1811; *m* 倫明 1037, 通晃 1239, 道文 1811, 道揚
Michiakira *m* 通亮 1239
Michiari *m* 道有 1811
Michie *f* 達栄 1810, 逕江 1512
Michieda *m* 通枝 1239
Michifuru *m* 道旧 1811
Michigami *s* 道上
Michiharu *m* 通陽 1239
Michihiko *m* 順彦 1532, 猷彦 1962, 碩彦 2116
Michihiro *m* 美弘 922, 通簡 1239, 裕宏 1645
Michihisa *m* 路久 1925
Michihito *m* 方仁 85
Michiichirō *m* 迪一郎 1001
Michika *m* 道芳 1811, 道香
Michikata *m* 田賢 189
Michikatsu *m* 通勝 1239
Michikawa *s* 道川 1811
Michikaze *s* 道風
Michikazu *m* 康弌 1509, 道一 1811, 道運
Michiko *f* 交子 293, 亨子 440, 径子 576, 宙子 673, 典子 733, 美智子 923, 聖子 1229, 途子 1234, 恕子 1483, 道子 1811, 路子 1925, 猷子 1962, 導子 2413, 蹊子 2807
Michimasa *m* 倫正 1037, 理正 1361, 道存 1811
Michimo *m* 道雲
Michimori *m* 田盛 189
Michinaga *m* 陸長 1312; *mlh* 道長 1811
Michinao *m* 道三
Michinari *m* 通済 1239, 道也 1811, 道成
Michinobu *m* 盈進 1200, 通同 1239 「1925
Michinokoda *s* 路子工
Michinori *m* 方寸 85, 通憲 1239, 道機 1811
Michinoshi *s* 道師
Michio *m* 三千男 22, 芳生 480, 学夫 719, 理夫 1361, 康男 1509, 道夫 1811, 道雄
Michiō *m* 道大
Michioki *m* 道幾
Michirō *m* 修郎 1038
Michisachi *m* 道吉 1811
Michisato *m* 迪恰 1001
Michishiba *l* 道芝 1811
Michishige *m* 道成
Michishita *s* 道下
Michisuke *m* 道助, 道輔
Michitada *m* 能達 1397
Michitaka *m* 伯孝 363, 命孝 671, 通任 1239, 通孝, 通敬, 道生 1811, 道隆
Michitake *m* 行虎 245, 通伯 1239
Michitarō *m* 美智太郎 923, 道太郎 1811
Michitaru *m* 道善
Michitatsu *m* 通武 1239
Michiteru *m* 参顕 978
Michitō *m* 道通 1811, 道遠
Michitoki *m* 通候 1239
Michitomi *sm* 道富 1811; *m* 通禧 1239
Michitomo *m* 至大 485, 盈比 1200, 通誠 1239, 道倫 1811
Michitose *f* 三千年 22
Michitoshi *m* 通俊 1239, 道紀 1811, 道暁
Michitoyo *m* 通富 1239
Michitsugu *m* 通次
Michitsumu *m* 通積
Michitsuna *m* 道綱 1811
~ no Haha *fl* 道綱母
Michitsune *m* 通久 1239
Michitsura *m* 通貫
Michiu *m* 通生 「1811
Michiwaru *m* 道和留
Michiya *m* 通也 1239
Michiyama *s* 道山 1811
Michiyasu *m* 通庸 1239, 通泰, 達安 1810
Michiyo *f* 三千代 22
Michiyoshi *m* 陸良 1312, 道力 1811, 道因
Michiyuki *m* 命之 671; *m-l* 道行 1811 「真
Michizane *m* 道実, 道
Michizō *m* 道三
Mida Nyorai wasan *l* 弥陀如来和讃 832
Midō Kanpaku *mh* 御堂関白 1572
~ ~ ki *l* 御堂関白記
~ ~ shū *l* 御堂関白集
Midori *sm-f* 翠 2204; *m-f* 碧 2225; *m-f-p* 緑 2535; *f* 深翠 1341; *p* 美土里 923. (緑 2535)
Midorigawa *s* 翠川 2204, 碧川 2225, 緑川 2535
Midorinoya *m* 緑舎
Midō shichiban utaawase *l* 御堂七番歌合 1572 「923
Mie *sp* 三重 22; *f* 美柯
Miekichi *m* 三重吉 22
Mieko *f* 巳栄子 30
Mierō *m* 三重郎 22
Miesagusa *s* 三枝
Mifune *s* 三船; *sm-p* 御船 1572; *m* 真船 1228, 御舟 1572
Migai *s* 三貝 22 「2596
Migaku *m* 琢 1608, 磨

Migashima s 三ケ島 22
~ Yoshiko fl 三ケ島葭子 「尻
Migashiri s 三尻, 三賀
Migata s 三ケ田, 見形 518
Migi m 右 171. (右)
Migita s 右田 「寅彦
~ Nobuhiko ml 右田
Migiwa m 汻 393, 淇 1328 ; f 汀 142
Migō s 御郷 1572
Migome s 見米 518
Miguma s 三熊 22
Migusa sm 三種
Mihama p 美浜 923, 御浜 1572
Mihara s 見原 518 ; sp 三原 22 ; p 美原 923
Miharu s 御春 1572 ; m 美波留 923 ; p 三春 22. (韶 2163)
Miharuko f 韶子
Mihashi s 三橋 22, 三觜
Mihashira m 真柱 1228
Mihata s 三畠 22, 御幡 1572
Mihaya s 水速 54
Mihira s 三平 22
Mihito m 実仁 678, 躬仁 1396
Miho s 三穂 22, 美浦 923 ; sp 三保 22 ; p 美保 923
Mihoko f 美帆子
Mihota sp 三穂田 22
Mii s 美乃 923 ; sf 三五 22 ; p 三井
Miida s 三井田
Miidera p-la 三井寺
Miike sp 三池
Miiki s 御息 1572
Miiko f 御井子
Miinoya s 満生野 1861
Miiraku p 三井楽 22
(mika 瓺 1936, 甕 2908)
(mikado 帝 971)
Mikagawa s 甕川 2908
Mikageike s 御影池 1572 「尻 1388
Mikajiri s 三賀尻 22, 瓶
Mikaki m 三嘉喜 22, 実柿 678
~ no shitakusa l 御垣の下草 1572
Mikamaro m 甕麿 2908
Mikame sp 三瓶 22
Mikami s 三上, 三守, 三神, 見上 518
~ Otokichi ml 三上於菟吉 22
Mikamo sp 美甘 923 ; p 三加茂 22 「1572
Mikamoto s 御神本
Mikan s 美甘 923
Mikanagi s 御巫 1572
Mikannagi s 御巫
Mikao m 甕男 2908
Mikari sm 三狩 22
Mikasa sp 三笠
Mikasayama s 蓋山 2193
Mikashigi s 御炊 1572
Mikashiri s 瓺尻 1936
Mikata sm-p 三方 22; p 美方 923
Mikatama s 瓺玉 1936
Mikatori s 瓺取
Mikawa s 参河 978, 御溝 1572 : sph 三河 22 ; p 三川, 三加和, 美川 923 「22
Mikawaguchi s 三河口
Mikazuki s 朏 1346 ; sp 三日月 22
Mike s 三毛, 三池, 三家, 美気 923, 食 1159. (食) 「麿 923
Mikeimaro m 美毛比
Miki s 参木 978, 御木 1572 ; sm 三樹 22 ; sp 三木 ; m 美樹 923, 造酒 1236, 幹 1938 ; f 御酒 1572. (幹 1938, 樹 2483)
Mikihiko m 幹彦 1938
Mikijirō m 美亀次郎 923, 幹次郎 1938
Miki Kiyoshi ml 三木清 22
Mikiko f 樹子 2483
Mikimoto s 御木本 1572, 御酒本
~ Kōkichi mh 御木本幸吉 「1938
Mikinosuke m 幹之助
Mikio m 三喜男 22, 三樹雄, 巳喜男 30, 酒喜男 1066, 幹雄 1938
Mikita s 和田 638 ; sm 和 ; m 幹太 1938
Mikitada m 幹直
Miki Takeji ml 三木竹二 22
Mikizō m 美喜蔵 923
Mikkouchi s 三河口 22
Miko s 御子 1572. (巫
Mikō s 御溝 1572 ⌊524)
Mikobe s 巫部 524
Mikogami s 神子上 853, 御子神 1572
Mikohidari s 御子左
Mikoidan s 御子左
Mikoshi s 三越 22
Mikoshima s 神子島 853
Mikoshiro s 皇子代 964
Mikoto f 命 671
Mikuji s 御鬮 1572
Mikuki s 美嚢 923
Mikuma s 見雲 518; sm 巳熊 30
Mikumari s 水分 54
Mikumo sp 三雲 22
Mikuni s 三九二 ; sp 三国
~ kotoba katsuyōshō l 御国詞活用抄 1572
Mikura s 三倉 22, 御蔵 1572 ; f 三九娘 22
Mikurashima p 御倉島 1572
Mikuriya s 御霊谷, 御厨屋 ; sp 御厨
Mikurube s 三廻部 22, 釈迦牟尼仏 1395
Mikusa s 三草 22
Mima sp 美馬 923 ; p 三間 22
Mimae s 御前 1572
Mimaki s 三牧 22 ; sm 御牧 1572
Mimana ph "Kaya / Karak" 任那 235
Mimasa s 御正 1572
Mimasaka ph 美作 923
Mimashi s 御座 1572
Mimasu s 三枡 22, 三増
Mimata p 三股
Mimatsu s 三松
(mimi 耳 331)
Mimichi m 水道 54
Mimijirō m 耳次郎 331
Mimi yōraku l 耳瓔珞
Mimore m 三守 22
Mimori s 三森 ; sm 三守 ; m 水守 54
Mimoru m 三守 22
Mimosuso la 御裳濯 1572 「裳濯川歌合
~ -gawa utaawase l 御
Mimoto s 御本
Mimune s 三統 22
Mimura s 三村, 味村 572 「室 1572
Mimuro s 三室 22, 御
Mimurodo s 三室戸 22
Min mh 旻 710. (民 333, 珉 1076, 岷 1080, 眠 1376, 敏 1409, 睯 2226)
Mina s 御名 1572. (水 54, 汎 249, 南 912, 咸 1003, 皆 1196, 備 1539, 程 1641, 蜷 2129)
Minabe s 三辺 22 ; p 南部 912
Minabegawa p 南部川
Minabuchi sp 南淵
~ no Shōan mh 南淵請安 「視秧 1348
Minae s 薬袋 2568 ; m
Minagawa s 南川 912, 皆川 1196, 源川 1863
Minahiko m 皆彦 1196
Minai s 御薬袋 1572, 薬袋 2568
Minaka s 皆河 1196
Minakami sp 水上 54
~ Takitarō ml 水上滝太郎
~ Tsutomu ml 水上勉
Minakata s 南方 912
Minaki s 皆木 1196, 衆樹 1762
Minakiri s 皆吉 1196
Minako f 水無子 54, 汎子 249, 咸子 1003, 備子 1539
Minakuchi sp 水口 54
Minamata s 派 812 ; p 水俣 54
Minami s 陽 1567 ; sp 南 912 ; p 美並 923. (南 912)
~ -aiki p 南相木
~ -aizu p 南会津
~ -akita p 南秋田
~ -amabe p 南海部
Minamiarai s 南荒
Minami-arima p 南有馬
~ -ashigara p 南足柄
~ -azumi p 南安曇
Minamichi m 水道 54
Minami-chita p 南知多 912
Minamida s 南田
Minamidani s 南谷
Minamide s 南出

Minami-furano *p* 南富良野
～ Hiroshi *ml* 南博
～ -horo *p* 南幌 「倉
Minamiiwakura *s* 南岩
Minami-izu *p* 南伊豆
Minamikata *p* 南方
Minami-katsuragi *p* 南葛城
Minamikawa *s* 南川
Minami-kawachi *p* 南河内
～ -kawara *p* 南河原
～ -kayabe *p* 南茅部
Minamiko *f* 南子
Minami-koizumi mura *l* 南小泉村
～ -koma *p* 南巨摩
～ -kushiyama *p* 南串山
～ -kuwata *p* 南桑田
～ -maki *p* 南牧
～ -matsuura *p* 南松浦
～ -minowa *p* 南箕輪
～ -murayama *p* 南村山
～ -muro *p* 南牟婁
Minaminagao *s* 南長尾
Minami-naka *p* 南那珂
～ -nasu *p* 南那須
～ -oguni *p* 南小国
Minamiōji *s* 南大路
Minami-okitama *p* 南置賜 「窪
Minamionikubo *s* 南鬼
Minami-saitama *p* 南埼玉
～ -saku *p* 南佐久
～ -shidara *p* 南設楽
～ -shinano *p* 南信濃
～ Shinji *ml* 南新二
～ -takaki *p* 南高来
～ -tama *p* 南多摩
～ -tane *p* 南種子
～ -tsugaru *p* 南津軽
～ -tsuru *p* 南都留
～ -uonuma *p* 南魚沼
Minamiura *s* 南浦
Minami-uwa *p* 南宇和
Minamiyama *s* 南山
Minami-yamashiro *p* 南山城
Minamizawa *s* 南沢
Minamochi *s* 弓納持 95
Minamoto *s* 源 1863
～ no Akikane *ml* 源顕兼
～ no Michichika *mh* 源通親
～ no Mitsunaka *mh* 源満仲 「光行
～ no Mitsuyuki *ml* 源
～ no Noriyori *mh* 源範頼 「実朝
～ no Sanetomo *mh* 源
～ no Shigeyuki *ml* 源重之
～ no Shitagō *ml* 源順
～ no Takaakira *mh* 源高明 「源為朝
～ no Tametomo *mh*
～ no Tameyoshi *mh* 源為義 「俊頼
～ no Toshiyori *ml* 源
～ no Tsunenobu *ml* 源経信 「源経基
～ no Tsunemoto *mh*
～ no Yoriie *mh* 源頼家 「頼政
～ no Yorimasa *mlh* 源
～ no Yorimitsu *mh* 源頼光 「頼信
～ no Yorinobu *mh* 源
～ no Yoritomo *mh* 源頼朝 「頼義
～ no Yoriyoshi *mh* 源
～ no Yoshichika *mh* 源義親 「家
～ no Yoshiie *mh* 源義
～ no Yoshinaka *mh* 源義仲 「源義朝
～ no Yoshitomo *mh*
～ no Yoshitsune *mh* 源義経 「家
～ no Yukiie *mh* 源行
Minamura *s* 南村 912
～ Baiken *mh* 南村梅軒
Minano *s* 緑野 2535; *p* 皆野 1196
Minao *m* 南雄 912
Minasato *s* 南里
Minase *sp-l* 水無瀬 54; *f* 美奈敵 923; *p* 皆瀬 1196 「吟 54
～ sangin *l* 水無瀬三
Minashiguri *l* 虚栗 1519
Minato *s* 水門 54; *sm* 湊 1576; *m-f-p* 港 1583. (港)
Minatozaki *s* 港崎
Minawa *s* 三縄 22
Minawashū *l* 水沫集 54, 美奈和集 923
Minayama *s* 皆山 1196
Minayoshi *s* 皆吉
～ Sōu *ml* 皆吉爽雨
Minazawa *s* 南沢 912
Minazuki-barae *la* 水無月祓 54
Minbu *m* 民部 333
Minchō *ma* 明兆 623
Mine *s* 三根 22, 嶺 2776; *sp* 峰 1351; *f* 壬子 116, 生子 214, 美泥 923; *p* 美禰. (峰 1351, 峯 1452, 峻 1591, 棟 1627, 節 2215, 嶺 2776, 巖 2936)
Mineda *s* 嶺田 2776
Minegishi *s* 峰岸 1351, 嶺岸 2776
Minehama *p* 峰浜 1351
Mineichirō *m* 峰一郎
Mineko *f* 峰子, 嶺子 2776
Minematsu *s* 峰松
Minemoto *s* 峰元, 峰本
Minemura *s* 峰村, 峯村 1452 「一
～ Kuniichi *ml* 峯村国
Mineo *sf* 峰尾 1351
Minesaburō *m* 峰三郎
Mineshige *m* 峰重
Mineshima *s* 峰島
Mineta *s* 峰田
Mineura *s* 峰浦
Mineyama *p* 峰山
Minezaki *s* 峰崎
Mingō nisso *l* 岷江入楚 1080
Minishū *l* 壬二集 116
Minmaya *s* 御厩 1572; *p* 三厩 22
Mino *s* 巳野 30, 美努 923, 鹿野 1823, 蓑 2194; *sp* 三野 22; *p* 美濃 923. (蓑 2194, 箕 2214, 簑 2688)
Minō *p* 美嚢 923
Minobe *s* 美濃部
Minobu *p-la* 身延 546
Minofū *l* 美濃風 923
Minohara *s* 箕原 2214
Minoichi *s* 御影池 1572
Minoike *s* 御影池
Mino Kamo *p* 美濃加茂 923
Minokawa *s* 箕川 2214
Minomaro *m* 蓑麿 2194
Minomaru *m* 蓑麿
Minomata *s* 三俣 22
Minomo *s* 箕面 2214
Minomura *s* 三野村 22
Minoo *s* 箕曲 2214, 箕尾; *sp* 箕面; *m* 蓑夫 2194
Minori *s* 一日宮 3; *m* 実程 678, 美律 923, 躬則 1396; *p* 美野里 923; *l* 御法 1572
Minorigawa *s* 御法川
Minoru *m* 升 113, 正法 205, 成 322, 年 342, 利 436, 酉 526, 実 678, 実宜, 季 725, 秀 726, 秋 878, 稔 1115, 宗 1178, 登 1744, 豊 2013, 穀 2168, 賁 2367, 稷 2729, 穰 2802; *m-f* 稔 1916, 穂 2308
Minosato *p* 箕郷 2214
Minoshima *s* 箕島
Minosuke *m* 美之助 923, 蓑助 2194 「2214
Minota *s* 蓑田, 箕田
Minoto *m* 汸 141
Minoura *s* 箕浦 2214, 簸浦 2845
Minowa *s* 美濃輪 923, 蓑和 2194, 蓑輪, 箕勾 2214, 箕曲; *sp* 箕輪
Minpei *m* 民平 333
Minu *m* 三野 22, 敏 1409
Minuki *s* 三幣 22
Minunounesu *s* 三野宇泥須
Minusa *s* 三幣
Minushi *s* 水主 54
Mio *s* 三尾 22, 三保; *sl* 水尾 54; *f-l* 澪 2458. (澪)
Mioka *s* 三岡 22
Mioki *s* 三尾木, 三保木
Miono *m* 美越乃 923
Mionoseki *p* 美保関
Mionoya *s* 三尾谷 22, 丹生屋 79, 満王野 1861, 満生野
Miori *m* 美織
Miotsukushi *l* 澪標 2458
Mioya *s* 三保屋 22
Mippō *s* 光法 281
Mirasaka *p* 三良坂 22
Miroku *mh* 弥勒 832
～ Bosatsu *mh* 弥勒菩薩
Miru *sp* 三入 22. (三, 子 38, 見 518, 実 678, 相

868, 看 998, 省 1013, 躬 1396, 察 2180, 箕 2214, 徵 2265, 親 2544, 覧 2695, 観 2765, 鑑 2968)
Miruko *f* 見子 518, 海松子 1071
(misa 節 2215, 操 2448)
Misaka *s* 三阪 22, 三坂; *f* 操加 2448; *p* 御坂 1572
Misaki *s* 見崎 518, 味酒 572, 御前 1572, 御崎; *sp* 三崎 22; *m-f-p* 岬 829 「操子 2448
Misako *f* 好佐子 413,
Misakubo *p* 水窪 54
Misao *m* 貞 982, 節 2215, 節男, 操 2448; *f* 禰磋節 2800 「参岡 518
Misaoka *s* 三参岡 22, 見
Misasa *p* 三朝 22
Misasagi *p* 美陵 923
Misasaki *s* 陵 1310
Misato *s* 三里 22; *sp* 三郷; *m* 参里 978; *m-p* 美郷 923; *p* 美里
Misawa *sp* 三沢 22; *f* 箕沢 2214
Mise *s* 三瀬 22
Miseki *s* 三関
Mishiba *s* 三柴
Mishiku *s* 御宿 1572
Mishima *s* 未至磨 210; *sp* 三島 22 「島通庸
~ Michitsune *mh* 三
~ Shōdō *ml* 三島章道
~ Sōsen *ml* 三島霜川
~ Yukio *ml* 三島由起夫
Mishina *s* 三品, 三科
~ Rinkei *ml* 三品藺渓
Mishine *m* 御稲 1572
Mishiro *s* 御代 「678
Mishō *p* 御荘; *l* 実生
Mishuku *s* 御宿 1572
(miso 衣 520)
Misono *sp* 御園 1572
Misonō *s* 御園生
Misosazai *s* 鷦鷯 2976
Misu *s* 三栖 22, 三須, 深栖 1341, 翠 2204
Misugi *s* 三杉 22; *p* 美杉 923
Misui *p* 三水 22
Misumi *s* 美棲 923; *sp* 三角 22, 三隅; *m* 水澄 54, 躬澄 1396
~ Kan *ml* 三角寛 22
Misumu *f* 生清 214
Misuna *s* 三砂 22
Misuno *s* 御簾納 1572
Mita *s* 三田 22, 美田 923, 箕田 2214
Mitagawa *p* 三田川
Mitaka *sp* 三鷹
Mitake *s* 三嶽; *sp* 三岳 22, 御岳 1572; *m* 真長 1228; *p* 御嵩 1572
Mitaki *s* 三滝 22
Mitama *s* 美玉 923; *sp* 三珠 22. (魂 2488)
Mitami *sm* 民 333
Mitaminoomi *s* 民使主
Mitamura *s* 三田村 22
~ Engyo *ml* 三田村鳶魚
Mitani *s* 三谷, 三渓
~ Akira *ml* 三谷昭
Mitarai *s* 御手洗 1572
Mitarashi *s* 御手洗
Mita Reijin *ml* 三田澪人 22
Mitasuki *m* 御田鍬 1572
Mitate *s* 御立; *m* 三干 22, 美楯 923
Mite *s* 御手 1572
Mitegura *s* 幣帛 2414
Mitehara *s* 御幣 1572
Miteshiro *s* 三手代 22, 御手代 1572
~ no Hitona *ml* 三手代人名 22
Mito *s* 三戸 33, 見戸 518; *p* 水戸 54, 美都 923, 御津 1572
Mitō *p* 美東 923
Mitobe *s* 三戸部 22, 水戸部 54
Mitoda *s* 御土田 1572
Mitoma *s* 三苫 22
Mitome *s* 三留, 見留 518
Mitomi *s* 三戸見 22, 見富 518; *sp* 三富 22
~ Kyūyō *ml* 三富朽葉
Mitori *s* 倭 1283
Mitoshi *m* 美淑 923
Mitoya *s* 三刀谷 22; *p* 三刀屋
Mitoyo *sp* 三豊
Mitsu *s* 三津, 美津 923; *f* 完 471, 塡 2075; *p* 御津 1572. (十 18, 三 22, 円 78, 内 81, 仭 122, 允 217, 屯 222, 全 271, 光 281, 尖 294, 広 316, 米 343, 汾 397, 弘 410, 足 461, 完 471, 図 502, 充 521, 臣 527, 侊 553, 肥 617, 明 623, 即 648, 実 678, 苗 685, 秀 726, 並 765, 弥 832, 映 840, 叙 893, 則 902, 美 923, 参 978, 看 998, 称 1118, 師 1130, 晃 1189, 盈 1200, 益 1201, 恭 1205, 通 1239, 順 1532, 備 1539, 循 1569, 御 1572, 温 1585, 尋 1705, 密 1713, 慎 1839, 溢 1851, 満 1861, 瑗 1873, 詳 1927, 舜 2017, 照 2035, 慊 2068, 塡 2075, 暢 2111, 需 2220, 潤 2277, 蕃 2371, 憑 2582, 鞠 2664, 嬴 2676, 績 2814)
Mitsuaki *m* 光明 281, 光秋, 光淳, 光彰, 充晤 521
Mitsubuchi *s* 三淵 22
Mitsuchi *s* 三土
Mitsuchika *m* 光慈 281
Mitsuda *s* 光田, 密田 1713, 満田 1861
Mitsue *m* 三衛 22, 光徳 281; *m-f-p* 御杖 1572; *f* 光榎 281
Mitsufuji *s* 光藤
Mitsugawa *s* 三津川 22
Mitsugi *s* 三津木; *sm* 三木, 調 2328; *sp* 御調 1572; *m* 租 1116, 税 1642; *m-f* 貢 1166
~ Shun'ei *ml* 三津木春影 22
Mitsuha *m* 三羽
Mitsuharu *m* 光施 281, 光春, 光栄, 光華
Mitsuhashi *s* 三觜 22, 三ツ橋; *sp* 三橋
~ Takajo *fl* 三橋鷹女
Mitsuhide *m* 光秀 281
Mitsuhiro *m* 光広, 光弘, 光熙, 充曼 521, 晃弘 1189
Mitsuhito *m* 秀仁 726
Mitsui *s* 三井 22, 光井
Mitsuie *m* 光屋 「281
Mitsui Kōshi *ml* 三井甲之 22
Mitsuishi *sp* 三石
Mitsuji *m* 光次 281, 光治
Mitsujirō *m* 光次郎
Mitsuka *s* 三塚 22, 御使 1572
Mitsukabi *p* 三ケ日 22
Mitsukai *s* 御使 1572
Mitsukaidō *p* 水海道 54
Mitsukata *m* 十銘 18
Mitsuke *s* 見付 518; *p* 見附
Mitsuki *m* 三鬼 22
Mitsuko *f* 三光子, 弘子 410, 充子 521, 即子 648, 盈子 1200, 満子 1861; *f-l* 光子 281
Mitsukoshi *s* 三越 22
Mitsukuni *m* 光圀 281
Mitsukuri *s* 深作 1341
Mitsuma *s* 三間 22; *sp* 三豬; *m* 三馬
Mitsumaki *s* 三巻
Mitsumasa *m* 光大 281, 光仁, 光予, 光少, 光正, 光政, 光暢
Mitsumasu *sm* 光増
Mitsumata *s* 三俣 22, 三豬
Mitsumi *s* 水満 54
Mitsumochi *m* 光庸 281
Mitsumori *s* 三森 22
Mitsumoto *s* 光本 281; *m* 三林 22
Mitsumura *s* 三村, 光寸 281, 光村
Mitsuna *m* 光多
Mitsunaga *sm* 光永; *m* 光寿, 光栄
Mitsunari *m* 三成 22, 全成 271 「恒 1396
Mitsune *m* 三子 22, 躬
Mitsuno *s* 光野 281; *f* 並之 765
Mitsunō *s* 満納 1861
Mitsunobu *m* 光悦 281, 充常 521 「満範 1861
Mitsunori *m* 光議 281,
Mitsunoshin *m* 満之進
Mitsuo *s* 三尾 22; *m* 三夫, 三丘, 三男, 三鶴夫, 光夫 281, 光雄, 満夫 1861 「岡 1861
Mitsuoka *s* 光岡 281, 満
Mitsuoki *m* 光宙 281, 光政
Mitsuru *m* 十 18, 仭 122,

光 281, 在 314, 充 521, 盈 1200, 躬弦 1396, 富 1715, 満 1861, 暢 2111, 碩 2116, 爾 2250
Mitsusato *m* 円郷 78
Mitsushi *m* 三通士 22, 晃司 1189
Mitsushige *m* 十重 18, 光成 281, 光鎮 「923
Mitsushima *p* 美津島
Mitsusuke *m* 光夫 281, 光佐, 光承, 光副, 光伝 「忠 832
Mitsutada *m* 光孚, 弥
Mitsutaka *m* 光子 281, 光教, 潤象 2277
Mitsutake *s* 光武 281; *m* 光威, 光彪
Mitsutaku *m* 光宅
Mitsutani *s* 満谷 1861
Mitsutarō *m* 光太郎 281
Mitsutome *s* 満留 1861
Mitsutomi *m* 光禄 281, 光棣
Mitsutomo *m* 光孚
Mitsutoshi *m* 光勤, 炎寿 294; *ml* 光俊 281
Mitsutoyo *m* 光豊
Mitsuwano *s* 満王野 1861 「17
Mitsuwata *s* 七七五分
Mitsuyama *s* 光山 281, 満山 1861; *la* 三山 22
Mitsuyanagi *s* 三柳
Mitsuyasu *m* 光和 281
Mitsuyori *m* 光遵, 光親
Mitsuyoshi *sm* 光吉; *m* 三厳 22, 三巖, 円喜 78, 盈良 1200, 順義 1532, 備愛 1539, 満快 1861, 満和, 満董
Mitsuyuki *sm* 光行 281; *m* 光享
Mitsuzane *m* 光孚
Mitsuzawa *s* 三津沢 22, 光沢 281
Mitsuze *p* 三瀬 22
Mitsuzō *m* 三三, 光造 281, 光蔵, 明三 623
Mitsuzuki *s* 七七五分
Mitto *s* 三戸 22 └17
Mittomo *m* 三全
Miuki *s* 三木
Miumaya *p* 三厩
Miura *sp* 三浦
~ Baien *mh* 三浦梅園
~ Moriharu *ml* 三浦守治 「門
~ Shumon *ml* 三浦朱
~ Yasumura *mh* 三浦泰村
Miushi *mh* 御主人 1572
Miwa *s* 神 853; *sp* 三和 22; *sp-la* 三輪; *p* 美和 923. (神 853)
Miwahakishi *s* 神掃石
Miwa Jusō *mh* 三輪寿壮 22
Miwakawa *s* 神河 853
Miwamakamuda *s* 神麻加牟陀
Miwata *s* 三輪田 22
Miwayoda *s* 神依田 853
Miya *s* 三矢 22, 三谷; *sp* 宮 1184; *f* 壬八 116. (宮 1184)
Miyabara *sp* 宮原
Miyabayashi *s* 宮林
Miyabe *s* 宮辺, 宮部
Miyabi *m* 雅 1913
Miyachi *sm* 宮地 1184
Miyadani *s* 宮谷
Miyadera *s* 宮寺
Miyadokoro *s* 宮所
Miyafuji *s* 宮藤
Miyagaki *s* 宮垣
Miyagawa *s* 三宅川 22, 水谷川 54; *sp* 宮川 1184 「城
Miyagi *s* 宮木; *sp* 宮
~ Ken'ichi *ml* 宮城謙一 「雄
~ Michio *ma* 宮城道
Miyaguchi *s* 宮口
Miyai *s* 宮井, 宮居
Miyairi *s* 宮入
Miyaishi *s* 宮石
Miyaji *s* 宮司, 宮地, 宮治, 宮首, 宮道, 宮路
~ Karoku *ml* 宮地嘉六
Miyajima *sp* 宮島
~ Shinzaburō *ml* 宮島新三郎
~ Sukeo *ml* 宮島資夫
Miyajino *s* 宮道之
Miyajiri *s* 宮後
Miyake *s* 三家, 屯倉 222; *sm-p* 三宅 22
Miyakegawa *s* 三宅川
Miyakejima *p* 三宅島
Miyake Kaho *ml* 三宅花圃
~ Kanran *mh* 三宅観瀾
~ Setsurei *ml* 三宅雪嶺 「太郎
~ Shūtarō *ml* 三宅周
Miyaki *p* 三養基
Miyakichi *m* 宮吉 1184
Miyakita *s* 宮北
Miyako *s* 宮処; *sm-f* 都 1419; *sf* 宮子 1184; *sp* 宮古; *p* 京都 663. (都 1419)
~ -dayū Itchū *ma* 都太夫一中
Miyakoji *s* 宮古路 1184; *p* 都路 1419
Miyakojima *p* 都島
Miyakonojō *p* 都城
Miyako no Yoshika *ml* 都良香 「宮腰
Miyakoshi *s* 宮越 1184,
Miyakubo *s* 宮久保; *sp* 宮窪
Miyama *s* 三山 22, 見山 518, 宮山 1184, 真山 1228, 深山 1341; *p* 美山 923, 海山 1071
Miyamae *s* 宮前 1184
Miyamaro *m* 宮麻呂
Miyamatsu *s* 宮松
Miyamichi *s* 宮道
Miyamori *s* 宮森; *sp* 宮守
Miyamoto *s* 宮元, 宮本
~ Kenji *ml* 宮本顕治
~ Musashi *ml* 宮本武蔵 「子
~ Yuriko *fl* 宮本百合
Miyamura *s* 宮村
Miyanabe *s* 宮辺
Miyanaga *s* 宮永, 宮長
Miyanaka *s* 宮中
Miyanari *s* 宮成
Miyane *s* 宮根
Miyanishi *s* 宮西
Miyano *s* 宮野
Miyanojō *p* 宮之城
Miyanoshō *s* 宮庄
Miyao *s* 宮尾
Miyaoka *s* 宮岡
Miyase *s* 宮瀬
Miyashige *s* 宮重
Miyashiro *s* 宮城, 都城 1419; *sp* 宮代 1184
Miyashita *s* 宮下
Miya Shōji *ml* 宮柊二
Miyasu *m* 御安 1572
Miyata *sp* 宮田 1184
Miyatake *s* 宮武 「々
~ Kankan *ml* 宮武寒
~ Tobone *ml* 宮武外
Miyato *s* 宮戸 └骨
Miyatsugu *m* 宮継
Miyauchi *sp* 宮内
~ Kan'ya *ml* 宮内寒弥
Miyauji *s* 宮氏
Miyawada *s* 宮和田
Miyawaki *s* 宮脇
Miyayama *s* 宮山
Miyazaka *s* 宮坂
Miyazaki *sp* 宮崎
~ Koshoshi *ml* 宮崎湖処子
~ Muryū *ml* 宮崎夢柳
~ Sanmai *ml* 宮崎三昧 「安貞
~ Yasusada *mh* 宮崎
Miyazato *s* 宮里
Miyazawa *s* 宮沢
~ Kenji *ml* 宮沢賢治
Miyazono *s* 宮園, 宮薗
Miyazu *sp* 宮津
Miyazuka *s* 宮塚
Miyo *f* 美代 923, 俟 1029
Miyoda *p* 御代田 1572
Miyoji *m* 巳代次 30, 巳代治 「御代川 1572
Miyokawa *s* 三代川 22,
Miyokichi *m* 三代吉 22
Miyoko *f* 巳生子 30, 美代子 923
Miyori *sp* 三依 22
Miyoshi *s* 三吉; *sp* 三次, 三好, 三芳, 三善; *m* 仁義 57; *f* 皆良 1196 「慶 22
~ Chōkei *mh* 三好長
~ Jūrō *ml* 三好十郎
~ no Kiyoyuki *mh* 三善清行 「善康信
~ no Yasunobu *mh* 三
~ no Yasutsura *mh* 三善康連 「洛
~ Shōraku *ml* 三好松
~ Tatsuji *ml* 三好達治
~ Toyoichirō *ml* 三好豊一郎
Miyoshino *s* 三芳野
Miyoshiya *s* 三吉野
Miyozō *m* 美代蔵 923
Miyuki *s* 三幣 22; *m* 幸 661; *f* 真幸 1228, 深雪 1341; *l* 行幸 245
Miyume *f* 美夢 923

Miza *s* 美座
(mizo 泉 965, 溝 1859)
Mizobe *s* 溝部; *p* 溝辺
Mizobuchi *s* 溝淵
Mizoe *s* 美添 923, 溝江 1859
Mizogami *s* 溝上
Mizogawa *s* 溝川
Mizoguchi *s* 水口 54, 溝口 1859 「羊
～ Hakuyō *ml* 溝口白
Mizogui *s* 溝杭
Mizohata *s* 溝畑, 溝端
Mizoi *s* 溝井
Mizoochi *s* 溝落
Mizorogi *s* 溝呂木
Mizota *s* 溝田
(mizu 水 54, 壬 116, 癸 952, 瑞 2094)
Mizuchi *m* 劉 2554
Mizue *s* 水江 54; *f* 水枝, 壬恵 116, 瑞枝 2094
Mizufuji *s* 水藤 54
Mizugaki *s* 水垣, 美図垣 923
Mizugame *l* 水甕 54
Mizugōri *s* 水郡
Mizuguchi *s* 水口
Mizuhara *s* 水原
～ Shūōshi *ml* 水原秋桜子
Mizuhashi *s* 水橋
Mizuhaya *s* 水早
Mizuho *m* 水穂; *p* 瑞穂 2094
Mizui *s* 水井 54
Mizuide *s* 水出
Mizukaga *s* 水利
Mizu kagami *l* 水鏡
Mizukake muko *la* 水掛聟
Mizukami *sp* 水上
Mizukawa *s* 水川
Mizuki *s* 水木, 湛 1855, 樋 2097; *sm* 劉 2554
～ Kyōta *ml* 水木京太 54
～ Yōko *fl* 水木洋子
Mizukoshi *s* 水越
Mizukuki *s* 水茎
Mizukuma *m* 湾 1849
Mizukuri *s* 箕作 2214
～ Rinshō *mh* 箕作麟祥
Mizuma *s* 水間 54
Mizumachi *s* 水町
～ Kyōko *fl* 水町京子
Mizumaki *sp* 水巻
Mizumi *s* 水見
Mizumō *s* 水毛生
Mizumori *s* 水守
～ Kamenosuke *ml* 水守亀之助
Mizumoto *s* 水元, 水本
Mizumura *s* 水村
Mizunami *p* 瑞浪 2094
Mizuneko *s* 水子 54
Mizuno *s* 水野 「徳
～ Hironori *ml* 水野広
Mizunoo *s* 水尾, 水越
Mizuno Senko *fl* 水野仙子 「忠邦
～ Tadakuni *mh* 水野
Mizunoya *s* 水谷, 水野谷 「川
Mizunoyagawa *s* 水谷
Mizuno Yōshū *ml* 水野葉舟
Mizunuma *s* 水沼
Mizuo *sp* 水尾; *m* 瑞夫 2094
Mizuochi *s* 水落 54
～ Roseki *ml* 水落露石
Mizuoka *s* 水岡
Mizusaki *s* 水崎
Mizusawa *sp* 水沢
Mizushi *s* 水志
Mizushima *s* 水島
Mizushina *s* 水品
Mizuta *s* 水田
Mizutame *s* 水溜
Mizutani *s* 水谷, 水渓
～ Futō *ml* 水谷不倒
Mizutanigawa *s* 水谷
Mizutari *s* 水足 └川
Mizutarō *m* 水太郎, 壬太郎 116
Mizuto *s* 水登 54
Mizutori *s* 水鳥
Mizutsu *s* 水津
Mizuya *s* 美図屋 923
(mo 母 326, 茂 691, 面 904, 姥 1090, 畝 1142, 最 1742, 雲 2027, 慫 2031, 模 2104, 裳 2376, 謨 2638, 藻 2837)
(mō 毛 117, 百 265, 芼 476, 孟 667, 盲 936, 庬 1241, 猛 1305, 萠 1448, 望 1777, 蒙 2003, 網 2536)
Mōanjō *l* 盲安抄 936
Mobara *s* 最原 1742, 裳原 2376; *p* 茂原 691
(mochi 才 35, 弋 108, 以 134, 四 188, 用 193, 平 203, 行 245, 有 303, 式 306, 住 355, 仰 360, 杖 422, 舎 453, 会 454, 往 579, 抱 584, 物 611, 卓 660, 茂 691, 或 750, 保 781, 持 801, 施 831, 倚 1033, 将 1040, 挟 1043, 時 1086, 荷 1259, 後 1300, 採 1314, 捧 1318, 庸 1507, 須 1544, 接 1548, 望 1777, 殖 1867, 試 1932, 蔚 2191, 廣 2242, 餅 2346, 操 2448, 積 2493, 懐 2605)
Mochida *s* 用田 193, 持田 801, 望田 1777
Mochigase *sp* 用瀬 193
Mōchigimi *s* 大夫 48
Mochihara *s* 餅原 2346
Mochihito *m* 以仁 134
～ -ō *mh* 以仁王
Mochiji *s* 持地 801
Mochiki *s* 持木; *m* 望城 1777
Mochikoto *m* 持言 801
Mochikuni *m* 懐国 2605
Mochimaru *s* 持丸 801
Mochinaga *s* 持永; *m* 以良 134, 持長 801
Mochinori *m* 以紀 134, 茂憲 691
Mochinose *s* 用瀬 193
Mochise *s* 用瀬
Mochiu *m* 庸 1507
Mochiya *s* 餅屋 2346
Mochiyo *m* 懐世 2605
Mochiyori *m* 用随 193
Mochiyoshi *m* 以悦 134, 用徳 193
Mochizuki *s* 十五月 18; *sp* 望月 1777
Mōda *s* 望陀
(modori 反 69)
Modoribashi *s* 反橋
(moe 萠 1448)
Moeba *f* 萠葉
Mogaki *s* 茂垣 691
Mogami *s* 茂上; *sp* 最上 1742 「内
～ Tokunai *mh* 最上徳
Mogi *s* 茂木 691
Mogiki *s* 十 18; *m* 索人 1703 「歌 2003
Mōgyū waka *l* 蒙求和
Mohara *m* 専 973
Mohei *m* 茂平 691
Mohira *s* 毛牧 117
Mohitori *s* 水取 54
Moji *s* 文司 86, 文字, 門地 601; *sp* 門司
Mojinoya *s* 文字屋 86
Mokawa *s* 門河 601
Mokichi *m* 茂吉 691
Moku *m* 杢 486. (木 109, 目 191, 杢 486, 牧 610, 鼂 1456, 睦 1904, 墨 2230, 黙 2405, 穆 2494)
Mokuami *m* 杢網 486; *ml* 黙阿弥 2405
Mokui *s* 裳咋 2376
Mokunoshin *m* 杢之進 486 「前心後 191
Mokuzen shingo *l* 目
(momi 籾 887, 紅 1423)
Momii *s* 籾井
Momiji *f* 紅葉 1423
～ -gari *la* 紅葉狩
～ no ga *l* 紅葉賀
Momiko *f* 紅子
Momiyama *s* 籾山 887, 粟山 1763, 樅山 2293
～ Shigetsu *ml* 籾山梓月 887
Momo *s* 桃 1104; *f* 佰 554. (百 265, 李 488, 桃 1104)
Momō *p* 桃生 「265
Momochiyo *f* 百千代
Momoda *s* 桃田 1104
Momoe *s* 百江 265
Momohara *s* 桃原 1104
Momoi *s* 百井 265, 桃井 1104
Momoishi *p* 百石 265
Momojima *s* 百島
Momoka *f* 桃香 1104
Momokawa *s* 百川 265, 桃川 1104
Momoke *s* 百毛 265
Momoki *s* 十 18, 百木 265, 桃木 1104; *m* 百鬼 265, 百喜
Momoko *f* 百百子, 李子 488, 桃子 1104
Momokubari *s* 桃配
Momomaro *m* 桃麻呂
Momomaru *m* 桃丸
Momonoi *s* 桃井 「詮
～ Naoakira *ml* 桃井直
Momose *s* 百瀬 265
Momo-sumomo *l* 桃李 1104
Momota *s* 百田 265

Momotani *s* 百渓, 桃谷 1104
Momotari *sm* 百足 265
Momotarō *m* 桃太郎 1104
~ -zamurai *l* 桃太郎侍
Momota Sōji *ml* 百田宗治 265 「度
Momoto *s* 百元 ; *m* 百
Momotsu *s* 百津
Momoya *s* 桃谷 1104
Momoyama *s* 百百山 265 ; *p* 桃山 1104
~ monogatari *l* 桃山譚
Momoyo *f-l* 百夜 265
Momozawa *s* 桃沢 1104
Momozono *s* 桃園
Momozuka *s* 桃束 265
Momura *s* 毛牧 117
Mon *l* 門 601. (文 86, 本 212, 汶 398, 彣 510, 門 601, 蚊 1135, 問 1524, 紋 1684, 聞 2244)
Monai *s* 毛内 117
Monaka *m* 最中 1742
Monbetsu *p* 門別 601, 紋別 1684 「田 601
Monden *s* 文伝 86, 門
Mondo *m* 主水 196
Mondori *s* 水取 54, 水撤
Moniwa *s* 茂庭 691
Monji *s* 門司 601
Monjirō *m* 門次郎, 紋次郎 1684 「殊
Monju *mh* 文珠 86, 文
Monjūsho *s* 問注所 1524
Monma *s* 門馬 601, 門真, 門間
Monmu *mh* 文武 86
Monna *s* 門奈 601
(mono 物 611)
Monobe *p* 物部
Monoe *s* 物江
Monogusa Tarō *l* 物草太郎
Monoibe *s* 斎部 1454
Monomo *m* 物面 611
Mononobe *s* 物部
~ no Moriya *mh* 物部守屋 「尾輿
~ no Okoshi *mh* 物部
Mononofu *s* 物部
Monoō *s* 物応
Monoshirō *m* 物四郎
Monshi *s* 汶斯 398
Montan *s* 汶旦

Montarō *m* 紋太郎 1684
Montoku *mh* 文徳 86
~ jitsuroku *l* 文徳実録
Monzen *p* 門前 601
(morai 貰 2011)
Morai-muko *la* 貰聟
(more 守 284)
Mori *s* 毛利 117, 守 284, 杜 423 ; *sm* 盛 1469 ; *sp* 森 1735. (戸 59, 収 133, 司 164, 主 196, 壮 243, 守 284, 戍 328, 名 346, 杜 423, 労 491A, 囲 501A, 命 671, 林 633, 典 733, 保 781, 狩 791, 捍 1042, 容 1182, 隆 1313, 彬 1370, 訥 1399, 執 1420, 宴 1437, 盛 1469, 庶 1505, 彭 1693, 森 1735, 衆 1762, 策 1767, 閑 1820, 豊 2013, 精 2131, 該 2135, 関 2245, 衝 2264, 諸 2329, 蕃 2371, 衛 2452, 積 2493, 謹 2645, 績 2814, 護 2877, 蘊 2934)
Mōri *s* 毛利 117
Moriaki *m* 司亮 164, 守韶 284, 盛彰 1469
Mori Arimasa *ml* 森有正 1735
~ Arinori *mh* 森有礼
Moribana *s* 森鼻
Moribayashi *s* 森林
Moribe *s* 森部 ; *sm* 守部 284
Morichika *m* 宴至 1437
Morie *s* 森江 1735 ; *m* 守衛 284, 閑衛 1820 ; *f* 盛枝 1469
Morigaki *s* 森垣 1735
Moriguchi *s* 森口 ; *sp* 守口 284
Morihara *s* 森原 1735
Morihashi *s* 森橋
Morihiko *m* 衛彦 2452
Morii *s* 森井 1735, 森居
Moriichi *m* 守一 284, 森一 1735
Moriie *m* 盛舎 1469
Moriizumi *s* 森泉 1735
Moriji *m* 盛治 1469
Morika *m* 盛郁
Mori Kainan *ml* 森槐南 1735
Morokatsu *m* 盛勝 1469

Morikawa *s* 守川 284, 森川 1735
~ Kyoroku *ml* 森川許
Moriki *s* 森木 └六
Moriko *f* 司子 164, 守子 284, 執子 1420, 盛子 1469
Morikubo *s* 森久保 1735
Morikuni *m* 護国 2877
Morima *m* 守真 284
Mori Mari *fl* 森茉莉 1735
Morimasa *m* 盛正 1469
Morimatsu *s* 森松 1735
Morime *f* 杜女 423
Morimi *m* 護躬 2877
Morimichi *m* 衛衝 2452
Morimitsu *m* 戍光 328 ; *ma* 守米 284
Morimoto *s* 守元 284, 守本, 森下 1735, 森元, 森本
~ Jikichi *ml* 森本治吉
~ Kaoru *ml* 森本薫
~ Kōkichi *ml* 森本厚吉 「利元就 117
Mōri Motonari *mh* 毛
Morimura *s* 守村 284, 森村 1735
Morinaga *s* 守永 284, 森永 1735 ; *m* 護良 2877
Morinaka *s* 守中 284
Morindo *m* 盛人 1469
Morino *s* 森野 1735
Morinobu *s* 森信 ; *m* 主信 196
Morinoshin *m* 盛之進 1469 「284
Morinosuke *m* 守之助
Morinuma *s* 森沼 1735
Morio *s* 守尾 284, 森尾 1735 ; *m* 守峰 284, 盛雄 1469, 森男 1735, 績雄 2493 「1735
Mori Ōgai *ml* 森鷗外
Morioka *s* 守岡 284, 森岡 1735 ; *sp* 盛岡 1469
Moriomi *m* 護臣 2877
Moriosa *m* 守脩 284
Mori Oto *ml* 森於菟 1735
Morisada *m* 関定 2245
Morisaki *s* 森崎 1735
Morisawa *s* 森沢
Morise *s* 森瀬
Morishige *sm* 森重 ; *m* 守重 284, 収茂 133, 盛達 1469 「1735
Mori Shige *ml* 森志げ
Morishima *s* 森島
Morishita *s* 森下
~ Uson *ml* 森下雨村
Morisuke *m* 守丞 284
Morisumi *m* 盛廷 1469, 盛徴 「森田 1735
Morita *s* 守田 284 ; *sp*
~ Girō *ml* 森田義郎
Moritaka *s* 盛高 1469 ; *m* 衛万 2452
Mōri Takachika *mh* 毛利敬親 117
Moritake *s* 森竹 1735 ; *sm* 守武 284 「1735
Moritani *s* 守谷, 森谷
Moritarō *m* 森太郎
Morita Shiken *ml* 森田思軒 「草平
Morita Sōhei *ml* 森田
Moritatsu *m* 護立 2877
Morite *m* 守手 284
Mōri Terumoto *mh* 毛利輝元 117
Morito *s* 守戸 284, 森戸 1735 ; *m* 守度 284, 杜人 423, 衛士 2452, 護戸 2877
Moritoki *m* 守晨 284
Moritomi *m* 盛徳 1469
Moritomo *m* 守彝 284
Moritoshi *m* 守利
Morito Tatsuo *mh* 森戸辰男 1735
Moritsugu *m* 林次 633
Moritsura *m* 盛諸 1469
Moriuchi *s* 森内 1735
Moriuji *m* 司氏 164
Moriwaki *s* 森脇 1735
~ Kazuo *ml* 森脇一夫
Moriya *s* 守矢 284, 守家, 森谷 1735, 森屋 ; *sm* 守屋 284 ; *sp* 守谷 ; *m* 守舎 「山 1735
Moriyama *sp* 守山, 森
~ Kei *ml* 森山啓
~ Teisen *ml* 森山汀川
Moriyasu *s* 守安 284, 保康 781 ; *m* 盛康 1469
Moriyoshi *m* 盛至, 衛好 2452, 積善 2493 ; *p* 森吉 1735
Moriyuki *m* 守道 284, 宴行 1437, 盛亨 1469
Morizane *s* 森実 1735

Morizō *m* 守三 284, 守蔵, 森蔵 1735
Morizono *s* 森園
～ Tenrui *ml* 森園天涙
Morizu *s* 森津
Morizumi *s* 森住
Moro *s* 毛呂 117, 茂呂 691, 師 1130, 諸 2329. (支 63, 与 101, 収 133, 壱 467, 両 531, 委 960, 専 973, 度 1009, 倶 1028, 修 1038, 旅 1073, 師 1130, 殷 1139, 恕 1483, 庶 1505, 衆 1762, 認 2137, 諸 2329, 艶 2833)
Morō *s* 毛籠 117
Moroai *m* 諸会 2329
Moroaki *m* 庶明 1505
Moroboshi *s* 諸星 2329
Morodomi *p* 諸富
Moroe *m* 諸兄; *f* 諸姉
Morofuji *s* 諸藤
Morogaki *s* 諸垣
Morogi *s* 衆樹 1762, 諸木 2329
Morogino *s* 諸木野
Morohashi *s* 諸橋
Moroi *s* 諸井
Moroie *m* 師宅 1130
Moroka *m* 師香
Morokado *s* 諸角 2329
Morokawa *s* 諸川
Moro Kiyoharu *ml* 毛呂清春 117
Morokoshi *sp* 唐土 1246
Morokuni *s* 唐土
Morokuzu *sm* 諸葛 2329
Moromisato *s* 諸見里
Morona *m* 諸魚
Morono *s* 諸野
Moronobu *ma* 師宣
Moroo *m* 師男 ⌊1130
Morooka *s* 師岡, 諸岡 2329 ⌈田 2329
Morota *s* 師田 1130, 諸
Morotake *m* 専尭 973
Morotane *m* 恕胤 1483
Morotaru *m* 師垂 1130
Morotate *m* 諸立 2329
Moroteru *m* 諸照
Morotsuka *p* 諸塚
Moroyama *sp* 毛呂山 117
Moroyū *s* 諸遊 2329
Morozumi *s* 両角 531
(moru 貯 1651)
Mosaku *m* 茂作 691
Mōshi *mlh* "Mencius" 孟子 667
Mosōji *m* 茂三治 691
Motai *s* 母台 326, 母袋, 茂田井 691, 罇 2805A, 甕 2908
Mōtai *s* 馬渡 1257
Mōtari *s* 馬渡
Motegi *s* 茂手木 691; *sp* 茂木
Moto *s* 元 60; *m* 茂登 691; *f* 統 2333. (一 3, 下 46, 大 48, 心 49, 元 60, 止 87, 太 105, 尤 106, 旧 119, 収 133, 司 164, 本 212, 企 269, 台 276, 代 297, 民 333, 体 358, 扶 383, 址 386, 如 412, 初 427, 牟 455, 芳 480, 甫 533, 求 537, 孝 541, 身 546, 性 564, 征 580, 妧 613, 服 618, 林 633, 的 635, 孟 667, 宗 679, 苞 688, 茂 691, 其 734, 府 740, 固 744, 東 771, 祖 850, 柄 862, 故 880, 泉 965, 帰 1018, 倫 1037, 修 1038, 始 1092, 株 1098, 租 1196, 祇 1127, 師 1130, 原 1231, 規 1349, 根 1372, 朔 1393, 躬 1396, 許 1403, 部 1418, 紀 1424, 基 1493, 順 1532, 索 1703, 素 1707, 喬 1775, 智 1793, 源 1863, 福 1888, 雅 1913, 群 1924, 誠 1935, 幹 1938, 寛 1977, 意 2007, 誉 2010, 資 2012, 楽 2029, 節 2215, 需 2220, 端 2306, 質 2395, 魂 2488, 翰 2518, 親 2544, 職 2734)
Mōtō *m* 望東 1777
Motoaki *m* 元知 60
Motoakira *m* 元昭
Motoari *m* 元有
Motoatsu *m* 帰厚 1018
Motobumi *m* 素履 1707
Motochika *m* 元京 60
Motoda *s* 元田
Motodo *s* 本戸 212
Motoe *s* 本江; *m* 基 1493; *f* 求枝 537
Motoeda *m* 基標 1493
Motofuji *s* 元藤 60
Motofumi *m* 止文 87
Motofusa *m* 大英 48
Motogi *s* 本儀 212
Motogorō *m* 元五郎 60
Motohara *s* 本原 212, 泉原 965
Motoharu *m* 一治 3, 元治 60, 元春, 元施, 躬治 1396, 基流 1493
Motohashi *s* 元橋 60, 本橋 212
Motohaya *m* 基逸 1493
Motohiko *m* 始彦 1092, 素彦 1707 ⌈達, 元簡
Motohiro *m* 元弘 60, 元
Motoi *s* 元井, 本井 212; *m* 基 1493, 璧 2412
Motoichi *m* 元一 60
Motoiki *s* 元生
Motoji *s* 泉 965, 泉二
Motojima *s* 元島 60, 本島 212
Motojirō *m* 元次郎 60, 基次郎 1493
Motoka *f* 妧香 613
Motokata *m* 本賢 212
Motokawa *s* 本川
Motokazu *m* 基政 1493
Motoki *s* 元木 60, 本木 212, 故木 880, 根木 1372; *m* 大樹 48, 本樹 212, 材 420, 求己 537, 基礎 1493, 誠記 1935, 幹 1938 ⌈資吉 2012
Motokichi *m* 基吉 1493,
Motoki Shōzō *mh* 本木昌造 212
Motoko *f* 尤子 106, 扶子 383, 址子 386, 牟子 455, 宗子 679, 苞子 688, 府子 740, 師子 1130, 許子 1403, 源子 1863
Motokore *m* 基惟 1493
Motokura *s* 本倉 212
Motoma *s* 源間 1863
Motomasa *m* 元正 60, 源政 1863
Motomatsu *s* 本松 212
Motome *m* 求馬 537, 基要 1493, 需 2220; *f* 求女 537
Motomezuka *la* 求塚
Motomi *m* 素身 1707, 楽水 2029
Motomichi *m* 祖道 850
Motomitsu *m* 元蕃 60, 紀光 1424
Motomiya *sp* 本宮 212
Motomori *s* 元森 60; *m* 素衛 1707
Motomu *m* 亘 262, 求 537, 要 1218, 須 1544
Motomura *s* 元村 60; *m* 祖村 850
Motonaga *m* 元久 60, 元祥, 基延 1493
Motonami *m* 原南 1231
Motonao *m* 司直 164, 職直 2734 ⌈成 2007
Motonari *m* 元就 60, 意
Motonaru *m* 基愛 1493
Motonashi *s* 本梨 212
Motone *m* 親音 2544
Motono *s* 本野 212; *sp* 本埜
Motonobu *m* 元信 60, 株修 1098, 基揚 1493, 意舒 2007
Motonori *m* 一徳 3, 企宣 269, 株徳 1098, 規矩 1349, 基範 1493, 源登 1863 ⌈60
Motonosuke *m* 元之助
Motoo *sm* 元尾, 本尾 212; *m* 元夫 60, 元雄, 如雄 412, 始男 1092, 幹郎 1938 ⌈岡 212
Motooka *s* 元岡 60, 本
Motooki *m* 元興 60, 幹興 1938
Motoomi *m* 元臣 60
Motoori *s* 本告 212, 本居 ⌈宣長
～ Norinaga *mlh* 本居
～ Toyokai *ml* 本居豊
Motora *s* 元良 60 ⌊穎
～ Yūjirō *ml* 元良勇次郎
Motori *s* 水 54, 水取
Motoribe *s* 水部
Motoru *m* 絹 2303 ⌈60
Motosaburō *m* 元三郎
Motosachi *m* 基祥 1493
Motosada *m* 元貞 60
Motoshi *m* 材 420
Motosu *p* 本巣 212
Motosugi *sm* 本杉
Motosuke *ml* 元輔 60
Mototada *m* 元忠, 元督
Mototaka *m* 職隆 2734
Mototarō *m* 元太郎 60
Mototeru *m* 元照
Mototomo *m* 基全 1493
Mototoshi *m* 元僑 60; *ml* 基俊 1493

Mototsugu *m* 幹嗣 1938
Mototsune *m* 元恒 60
Motouji *m* 基氏 1493
Motoya *s* 本谷 212
Motoyama *s* 元山 60; *sp* 本山 212
～ Tekishū *ml* 本山荻舟 「太泰 105
Motoyasu *m* 元予 60,
Motoyoshi *m* 下吉 46, *sm* 元吉 60; *sm-p* 本吉 212; *m* 元昌 60, 元源, 元義, 原南 1231, 基栄 1493
Motoyuki *m* 元運 60, 性之 564, 躬行 1396, 源行 1863
Motozaki *s* 元崎 60
Motozawa *s* 元沢, 本沢 212
Motozō *m* 元造 60
Motozu *s* 本津 212
Motozumi *m* 原澄 1231
(motsu 物 611)
(moya 靄 3004)
Moyako *f* 靄子
Moyoko *f* 最誉子 1742
Mozaemon *m* 茂左衛 └門 691
Mozai *s* 茂在
Mozu *s* 万代 43, 方代 85, 毛受 117
Mozuka *s* 毛塚
Mozume *s* 万代 43, 物集 611, 物集女
Mozumime *s* 物集女
(mu 六 61, 无 92, 矛 150, 牟 455, 身 546, 武 751, 陸 1312, 務 1377, 眸 1636, 募 1718, 無 1789, 楙 1889, 楳 1894, 睦 1904, 夢 1990, 鉾 2342, 蕪 2373, 舞 2391, 謀 2509, 懋 2700, 鵡 2819, 霧 2846, 鶩 2847)
Mubezono *s* 郁子園 890
Muchaku Seikyō *ml* 無着成恭 1789
(muchi 責 1755, 鞭 2752)
Muchiko *f* 鞭子
Muchimaro *m* 武智麿 751
Mugaku Sogen *mh* 無学祖元 1789 「312
Mugasa *s* 六笠 61, 向笠
Muge *s* 身毛 546, 武義 751; *p* 武芸
Mugebe *s* 武宜部
Mugenkyū *l* 無弦弓 1789
Mugetsu *s* 牟宜都 455, 牟義都, 身毛津 546
Mugi *sp* 牟岐 455; *p* 武儀 751. (麦 456)
Mugifu *s* 麦生
Mugijima *s* 麦島
Mugiko *f* 麦子
Mugikura *s* 麦倉
Mugura *m* 葎 1719
Mugyū *s* 麦生 456
Muichi *m* 無市 1789
Muika *p* 六日 61
Muikaichi *p* 六日市
Mujū Ichien *mlh* 無住一円 1789
(muka 向 312)
Mukada *s* 向田
Mukadaka *sp* 向高
Mukade *s* 百足 265
Mukadeya *s* 百足屋
Mukai *s* 向 312, 向井, 迎 746. (向 312)
Mukaibō *s* 向坊
Mukaihara *p* 向原
Mukaihigashi *p* 向東
Mukaijima *p* 向島
Mukai Kyorai *ml* 向井去来
Mukaiyama *s* 向山
Mukasa *s* 武笠 751, 穆佐 2494
(mukashi 昔 699)
Mukashigatari tanzenburo *l* 昔語丹前風呂
Mukashigome mangoku tōshi *la* 昔米万石通
Mukawa *sp* 武川 751; *p* 鵡川 2819
(muke 向 312)
(muki 向, 剝 1427)
Mukinosukune *m* 向宿弥 312 「1427
Mukitokoro *l* 剝野老
Mukō *m* 向 312; *p* 向日
Mukōbata *s* 向畑
Mukōda *s* 向田
Mukōyama *s* 向山
Muku *s* 牟庫 455, 椋 1628, 鉾久 2342. (椋 1628)
Mukuchi *s* 陸口 1312
Mukuhara *s* 椋原 1628
Muku Hatojū *ml* 椋鳩十
Mukunashi *s* 椋梨
Mukuruma *s* 六車 61
(muma 馬 1257)
Mumo *s* 武茂 751
Mumyō hishō *l* 無名秘抄 1789
Mumyōshō *l* 無名抄
Mumyō to aizen *l* 無明と愛染
～ -zōshi *l* 無名草子
Munagi *m* 棟 1627
Munahachi *m* 六七八 61
Munakata *s* 宗方 679, 宗形, 棟方 1627; *sp* 宗像 679
Munaoka *s* 宗岳, 宗岡
Munasue *s* 棟居 1627
(mune 心 49, 旨 263, 志 464, 兵 499, 念 670, 宗 679, 斉 701, 肯 709, 指 800, 胸 1347, 能 1397, 致 1407, 梁 1475, 順 1532, 棟 1627, 極 1896, 寛 1977, 意 2007, 統 2333, 縁 2660)
Muneaki *m* 宗礼 679
Muneari *m* 宗在
Munechika *sm* 宗近; *m* 宗子, 宗睦
Muneda *s* 宗田
Munee *m* 宗徳
Munehari *m* 棟梁 1627
Muneharu *m* 胸治 1347, 棟治 1627
Muhehide *m* 宗穎 679
Munehira *m* 宗均
Munehiro *m* 宗広
Muneichi *m* 棟一 1627
Muneisa *m* 宗功 679
Muneji *m* 宗二
Muneko *f* 宗子
Munekuni *m* 旨国 263
Munemasa *m* 統理 2333
Munemichi *m* 宗孝 679, 宗理 「光
Munemitsu *s* 宗弘, 宗
Munemoto *m* 宗翰
Munemura *s* 宗村
Munenaga *m* 宗寿, 宗良
Munenao *m* 宗直
Munenari *m* 宗城, 致也 1407
Munenobu *m* 宗衍 679
Munenori *m* 宗軌, 宗啓, 宗懂
Muneo *m* 宗雄, 武直夫 751 「宗岳
Muneoka *s* 宗岡 679,
Muneomi *m* 宗臣
Munesada *m* 宗判
Munesane *m* 宗城
Muneshige *m* 宗茂, 宗薫
Munesue *s* 棟居 1627
Muneta *s* 宗田 679
Munetada *m* 宗忠, 宗理
Munetaka *m* 宗敬, 宗享; *mh* 宗尊
Munetake *m* 旨武 263, 旨剛, 宗武 679
Munetomo *m* 宗友
Muneyana *m* 宗梁
Muneyasu *m* 宗那, 宗賢
Muneyori *m* 宗従
Muneyoshi *m* 宗至, 宗恵, 宗敬, 宗厳, 宗贇, 宗巌
Muneyuki *m* 宗于
Muni *m* 無二 1789
Muō no rigyo *l* 夢応の鯉魚 1990
Mura *sf* 村 424. (央 100, 屯 222, 村 424, 邑 460, 邨 645, 幸 661, 城 796, 祐 852, 單 906, 宣 919, 祚 1126, 県 1252, 堿 1290A, 奥 1798, 福 1888, 群 1924, 紫 2209, 樹 2483, 叢 2778)
Murabayashi *s* 村林 424
Murachi *s* 村地
Muragaki *s* 村垣
Muraguchi *s* 村口
Murahashi *s* 村橋
Murai *s* 村井, 邑井 460
Muraichi *m* 邑一
Murai Chōan *lm* 村井長庵 424
～ ～ takumi no yaregasa *la* 村井長庵巧破傘
～ Gensai *ml* 村井弦斎
Muraishi *s* 村石
Muraji *s* 村地, 村治; *sm* 連 1238. (連)
Murajiko *m* 連子
Murajima *s* 村島 424
Murajiyasu *m* 連陽春 1238
Murakage *m* 祚景 1126
Murakami *s* 邑上 460; *sp* 村上 424

~ Kijō *ml* 村上鬼城
~ Namiroku *ml* 村上浪六 「月
~ Seigetsu *ml* 村上霽
~ Senjō *mh* 村上専精
Murakawa *s* 村川
Murake *s* 村挙 「1924
Muraki *s* 村木；*m* 群樹
Murakishi *s* 村岸 424
Murako *s* 伯 363；*f* 紫子 2209
Murakoshi *s* 村越 424
Murakoso *s* 村社
Murakumo *s* 村雲
Murakuni *s* 村国
Muramatsu *sp* 村松
~ Masatoshi *ml* 村松正俊 「孝
~ Sadataka *ml* 村松定
~ Shōfū *ml* 村松梢風
~ Takeshi *ml* 村松剛
Muramoto *s* 村本
Muranaka *s* 村中
Muranishi *s* 村西
Murano *s* 村野
~ Jirō *ml* 村野次郎
~ Shirō *ml* 村野四郎
Muranushi *s* 村主
Murao *s* 村尾
Muraoka *s* 邨岡 645；*sp* 村岡 424
Murasaka *s* 村坂
Murasaki *f* 紫 2209.（紫）
Murasakibara *s* 紫原
Murasakino *s* 紫野
Murasaki Shikibu *fl* 紫式部 「集
~ ~ kashū *l* 紫式部家
Murasame *sf* 村雨 424
Murasawa *s* 村沢
Murase *s* 村瀬
Murasugi *s* 村杉
Murata *sp* 村田 「海
~ Harumi *ml* 村田春
~ Jukō *mh* 村田珠光
Murataka *s* 村高
Muratane *m* 樹胤 2483
Muratani *s* 村谷 424
Murata Seifū *mh* 村田清風
Murato *m* 叢人 2778
Muratoki *m* 村侯 424
Muratsubaki *s* 村椿
Muratsuka *s* 村塚
Muraura *s* 村浦
Murayama *sp* 村山
~ Kaita *ml* 村山槐多
~ Tomoyoshi *ml* 村山知義
Murayasu *s* 紫安 2209
Murazaki *s* 村崎 424
Mure *sp* 牟礼 455.（軍 906, 群 1924）
Murinosuke *m* 無理之介 1789
Muro *s* 室 1183, 無漏 1789；*p* 牟婁 455.（室 ⌊1183）
Murō *sp* 室生
Murobushi *s* 室伏
Muroe *f* 室枝
Muroga *s* 室賀
Murogimi *l* 室君
Murohara *s* 室原
Murohashi *s* 室橋
Muro hogi no kotoba *l* 室寿嗣
Muroi *s* 室井
Murokawa *s* 室川
Muroki *s* 室木
Murokoshi *s* 室越
Muro Kōshin *ml* 室伏高信
~ Kyūsō *mh* 室鳩巣
Muromachi *sph* 室町
~ jidai koutashū *l* 室町時代小歌集
Murone *p* 室根
Murooka *s* 室岡
Muroran *p* 室蘭
Murō Saisei *ml* 室生
Murota *s* 室田 ⌊犀星
Murotani *s* 室谷
Muroto *p* 室戸
Murouchi *s* 室内 「屋
Muroya *s* 室谷；*sm* 室
Muroyama *s* 室山
Murozaki *s* 室崎
Murozawa *s* 室沢
Murozumi *s* 室住, 室積
~ Soshun *ml* 室積徂春
Musa *s* 牟佐 455, 身狭 546, 武社 751, 武佐, 武射
Musashi *s* 八道 19, 无邪志 92；*sm-p* 武蔵 751；*sp* 胸刺 1347；*m* 身挾 546, 無三四 1789
Musashiabumi *s* 武蔵鐙 751
Musashino *sp-l* 武蔵野
Musha *s* 武者
Mushakōji *s* 武者小路
Mushanokōji *s* 武者小路 「路実篤
~ Saneatsu *ml* 武者小
(mushi 虫 324)
Mushifu *s* 虫生
Mushika *s* 虫鹿
Mushimaro *m* 虫麿
Mushi mezuru himegimi *l* 虫めづる姫君
Mushio *m* 虫雄
Mushiroda *s* 席田 1242
Mushōzu *sp* 武生水 751
Musoda *s* 六十田 61
Musō Soseki *mlh* 夢窓疎石 1990
Musotani *s* 六十谷 61
Musu *s* 人首 14
(musubi 産 1520)
Musukobeya *l* 冷子洞房 349 「成寺 1599
Musume Dōjōji *a* 娘道
Muta *s* 牟田 455
Mutaguchi *s* 牟田口
Mutai *s* 務台 1377
Mutaka *s* 六平 61
Muteemon *m* 無手右衛門 1789
(muto 人 14)
Mutō *s* 武東 751, 武藤
Mutobe *s* 六人部 61, 身人部 546, 身度部
Mutori *s* 六人 61, 身人 546
Mutsu *sp* 陸奥 1312；*f* 六 61.（陸 1312, 睦 1904, 穆 2494, 輯 2497）
Mutsubi *m* 昵 839
Mutsuga *s* 六鹿 61
Mutsuhara *s* 六原
Mutsuhito *m* 睦仁 1904
Mutsuki *m* 正月 205；*f* 睦月 1904 「睦子 1904
Mutsuko *f* 陸奥子 1312,
Mutsumi *m* 昵 839, 睦 1904；*f* 睦文, 睦美
Mutsumu *m* 睦陸, 睦睦
Mutsu Munemitsu *mh* 陸奥宗光 1312
Mutsundo *m* 穆人 2494
Mutsuo *sm* 六雄 61；*m* 陸雄 1312
Mutsuomi *m* 陸臣
Mutsura *p-la* 六浦 61
Mutsuro *s* 陸路 1312
Mutsutomi *m* 六富 61
Mutsuura *s* 六浦
Mutsu waki *l* 陸奥話記 1312
Mutsuzaki *s* 六崎 61
Mutsuzawa *p* 睦沢 1904
(myō 卯 259, 名 346, 妙 614, 明 623, 命 671, 苗 685, 茅 690, 茆 926, 冥 1158, 猫 1304, 溝 1859, 瞑 2249)
Myōami *ml* 明阿弥 623
Myōbu *f* 命婦 671
Myōchikurin-banashi shichihenjin *l* 妙竹林話七偏人 614
Myōchin *s* 明珍 623
Myōe *mlh* 明恵
~ Shōnin kashū *l* 明恵上人歌集
(myōga 蘘 2935)
Myōgaya *s* 蘘屋
Myōgi *p* 妙義 614
Myōji *s* 苗代 685
Myōjō *sp-l* 明星 623
Myōken *s* 妙見 614
Myōkō *p* 妙高
Myōmi *s* 妙見
Myōsai *sp* 名西 346
Myōtō *sp* 名東
Myōtogi *s* 夫婦木 104
Myūdo *s* 身人 546
Myūto *s* 身人
Myūtobe *s* 身人部

# N

(n 武 751)
(na 七 17, 己 32, 水 54, 中 75, 勿 110, 号 272, 名 346, 多 347, 汝 394, 那 416, 声 465, 来 538, 林 633, 和 638, 命 671, 奈 696, 阜 731, 南 912, 称 1118, 椰 1367, 菜 1447,

魚 1485, 納 1685, 無 1789, 銘 2155, 樹 2483)
Nabaki *s* 南白亀 912
Nabari *s* 隠 2074; *p* 名張 346, 奈判利 696
Nabatame *s* 生天目 214
(nabe 鍋 2650)
Nabei *s* 鍋井
Nabekura *s* 鍋倉
Nabeshima *s* 鍋島
～ Kansō *mh* 鍋島閑叟
Nabeta *s* 鍋田
Nabetani *s* 鍋谷
Nabetarō *m* 鍋太郎
Nabeya *s* 鍋谷 「八撥
Nabe yatsubachi *l* 鍋
Nabika *s* 並河 765
Nabiku *m* 靡 2857
Naburi *s* 随分 1564
Nabusa *s* 随分
Nabusazuke *s* 随分附
Nachi *s* 生池 214; *p* 那智 416 「浦
～ Katsuura *p* 那智勝
Nada *s* 洋 822; *p* 灘 2946. (灘)
Nadachi *p* 名立 346
Nadara *s* 柳楽 1105; *m* 南陀羅 912
Nadasaki *p* 灘崎 2946
Nadase *sp* 夏足 1161
Nademaro *m* 奈底麿 696
(nae 苗 685, 秧 1114)
Naemura *s* 苗村 685
Naeshiro *s* 苗代
Naetarō *m* 苗太郎
Naga *m* 永 149; *p* 名賀 346. (久 45, 大 48, 元 60, 永 149, 市 195, 存 313, 亨 440, 条 457, 呂 459, 廷 501, 酉 526, 寿 539, 孟 667, 命 671, 延 739, 良 767, 待 785, 長 939, 栄 969, 直 988, 度 1009, 修 1038, 祥 1074, 莘 1168, 脩 1281, 隆 1313, 流 1332, 備 1539, 温 1585, 詠 1664, 斐 1781, 遊 1809, 誠 1935, 増 2077, 暢 2111, 肆 2144, 隣 2443)
Nagaai *s* 長合 939
Nagaaki *m* 長卿
Nagaakira *m* 長昱, 長祥, 長晟, 長著
Nagaana *s* 長岫
Nagabuchi *s* 永淵 149
Nagabumi *m* 長文 939
Nagachika *m* 長孺
Nagadoro *s* 長土呂
Nagae *s* 永江 149, 長永 939, 長江 「藤 939
Nagafuji *s* 永藤 149, 長
Nagahama *s* 永浜 149; *p* 長浜 939 「原 939
Nagahara *s* 永原 149, 長
Nagaharu *m* 永詮 149
Nagahashi *s* 長橋 939
Nagahata *s* 永幡 149, 長畑 939
Nagahide *m* 長秀
Nagahiro *s* 長広; *m* 命啓 671, 長溥 939, 脩広 1281 「*m* 存久 313
Nagahisa *sm* 永久 149;
Nagahito *m* 良仁 767
Nagahori *s* 永堀 149, 長堀 939 「井 939
Nagai *s* 永井 149; *sp* 長
Nagaie *m* 大室 48, 永長 149 「風
Nagai Kafū *ml* 永井荷
Nagaike *s* 永池
Nagaishi *s* 永石
Nagai Tatsuo *ml* 永井竜男 「939
Nagaiwa *s* 永岩, 長岩
Nagaizumi *p* 長泉
Nagakage *m* 長景
Nagakai *s* 長合
Nagakata *m* 長方
Nagakatsu *m* 良勝 767
Nagakawa *s* 永川 149, 長川 939
Nagakazu *m* 長和, 長猷
Nagaki *s* 永木 149, 長岐 939; *m* 修 1038
Nagakiyo *m* 長淳 939
Nagako *f* 存子 313, 良子 767, 栄子 969
Nagakoto *m* 長勲 939
Nagakubo *s* 永久保 149, 長久保 939
Nagakuni *m* 大国 48
Nagakura *s* 永倉 149, 長倉 939
Nagakute *p* 長久手
Nagamasa *m* 寿昌 539
Nagamatsu *s* 永松 149, 長松 939
Nagame *s* 詠 1664
Nagami *s* 永見 149, 長見 939, 流水 1332
Nagamichi *m* 長礼 939, 長訓, 修道 1038
Nagamine *s* 永峰 149, 長岑 939, 長峰, 長嶺
Nagamitsu *sm* 永光 149; *m* 長光 939, 長贏
Nagamiya *s* 長宮
Nagamochi *s* 永用 149, 永持; *m* 永有, 長操 939
Nagamori *s* 永盛 149, 永森, 長森 939; *sm* 永守 149; *m* 長盛 939, 長衛
Nagamoto *s* 永元 149, 長本 939; *m* 長職
Nagamune *s* 長統
Nagamura *s* 永村 149, 長村 939; *m* 長郡, 長群
Naganari *m* 長生, 長育, 長記, 直成 988
Naganawa *s* 長縄 939
Nagane *s* 永根 149, 長根 939 「長野 939
Nagano *s* 永野 149; *sp*
Naganobu *m* 栄信 969, 隣信 2443 「939
Naganohara *p* 長野原
Naganori *m* 長徳, 長誥, 脩孝 1281
Naganuma *s* 永沼 149; *sp* 長沼 939
Nagao *sm* 永緒 149, 長雄 939; *sp* 長尾; *m* 酉雄 526 「長岡 939
Nagaoka *s* 永岡 149; *sp*
Nagao Kagetora *mh* 長尾景虎
Nagaoka Hantarō *mh* 長岡半太郎
～-kyō *ph* 長岡京
Nagaoki *m* 長生
Nagaosa *s* 永長 149
Nagara *sm* 長良 939; *sp* 長柄
Nagaragawa *p* 長柄川
(nagare 流 1332)
Nagareyama *p* 流山
Nagaru *m* 長流 939
Nagasa *sp* 長狭
Nagasachi *m* 永祜 149
Nagasaka *s* 永坂; *sp* 長坂 939
Nagasaki *sp* 長崎
～ Takasuke *mh* 長崎高資
Nagasako *s* 永廻 149
Nagasaku *s* 永作
Nagasane *m* 永孚
Nagasawa *s* 永沢, 長沢 939
～ Mitsu *ml* 長沢美津
Nagase *s* 永瀬 149, 長瀬 939 「149
～ Kiyoko *fl* 永瀬清子
Nagashi *m* 永, 寿 539, 良 767, 長 939, 修 1038, 亀 1531, 融 2545
Nagashige *m* 長成 939
Nagashima *s* 永島 149; *sp* 長島 939
Nagashio *s* 長塩
Nagasone *s* 長曾根, 長曾禰
Nagasu *s* 長沙; *p* 長洲
Nagasuna *s* 長沙, 長砂
Nagata *s* 永田 149; *sp* 長田 939
Nagatada *m* 長祇
Nagata Hideo *ml* 長田秀雄
Nagataka *m* 長挙
Nagatake *m* 長孟
Nagataki *s* 長滝, 永滝 149 「衣
Nagata Kōi *ml* 永田耕
～ Kōkichi *ml* 永田衡吉 「彦 939
～ Mikihiko *ml* 長田幹
Nagatani *s* 永谷 149, 長谷 939 「青嵐 149
Nagata Seiran *ml* 永田
～ Tetsuzan *mh* 永田鉄山
Nagateru *m* 長監 939
Nagato *s* 永戸 149, 長戸 939; *sp* 長門
Nagatochi *s* 永地 149
Nagatome *s* 永留
Nagatomi *s* 永富; *m* 修美 1038
Nagatomo *s* 永友 149, 長友 939; *m* 永侖 149, 温知 1585
Nagatori *s* 永鳥 149
Nagatoshi *m* 長和 939, 長翁, 長順, 長詮
Nagatsu *s* 長津
Nagatsugu *m* 長説
Nagatsuka *s* 永塚 149, 長束 939, 長塚 「家
～ Masaie *mh* 長束正
～ Takashi *ml* 長塚節

Nagatsuma *s* 永妻 149, 長妻 939
Nagatsuna *m* 長維
Nagatsune *m* 永則 149
Nagaura *s* 永浦
Nagauta *a* 長唄 939; *la* 長歌
Nagawa *s* 奈河 696; *sp* 名川 346; *p* 奈川 696
Nagaya *s* 長谷 939, 長屋
~ -ō *mh* 長屋王
Nagayama *s* 永山 149, 長山 939
Nagayasu *sm* 永安 149; *m* 永愷, 長康 939
Nagayo *sp* 長与
Nagayori *sm* 長縁
Nagayo Senzai *mh* 長与専斎
Nagayoshi *s* 永吉 149; *m* 永福, 長吉 939, 長幸, 長貴, 長幹
Nagayo Yoshirō *ml* 長与善郎
Nagayuki *m* 長之
Nagi *p* 奈義 696. (梛
Nagino *s* 梛野 ⌊1367)
Nagio *m* 梛男
Nagisa *m* 沚 391; *m-f* 渚 1575; *f* 汀 142
Nagiso *p* 南木曾 912
Nago *s* 名合 346
Nagoe *s* 名越
Nagokata *s* 名児形
Nagoshi *s* 名越, 浪越 1339
Nagoya *s* 名児耶 346, 名越, 名護屋; *sp* 名古屋 「雲 1074
Nagumo *s* 南雲 912, 祥
Nagura *s* 名倉 346, 那倉 416, 奈倉 696
Naguri *p* 名栗 346
Nagusa *s* 名種
Naha *p* 那覇 416
Nahata *s* 名畑 346
Nahiko *m* 魚彦 1485
(nai 乃 27, 内 81)
Naidaijin-ke utaawase *l* 内大臣家歌合
Naie *p* 奈井江 696
Naiji *fh* 内侍 81
Naiki *s* 内呉, 内木, 内貴, 奈癸 696; *sm* 内記
Naishi *fh* 内侍 ⌊81
Naitō *s* 内藤
~ Arō *ml* 内藤濯
~ Jōsō *ml* 内藤丈草
~ Konan *ml* 内藤湖南
~ Meisetsu *ml* 内藤鳴雪 「策
~ Shinsaku *ml* 内藤鋠
~ Tatsuo *ml* 内藤辰雄
~ Toten *ml* 内藤吐天
Naizen *mh* 内膳
Najima *s* 名島 346
Naka *s* 仲 227; *sp* 中 75, 那珂 416; *p* 那賀. (心 49, 水 54, 支 63, 中 75, 収 133, 央 182, 半 213, 仲 227, 弁 275, 沖 400, 判 434, 考 540, 尚 753, 参 978, 班 1075, 莫 1175, 務 1377, 掌 1748, 殖 1867, 極 1896, 翰 2518, 鎮 2751, 齢 2766)
Nakaaki *s* 八月十五日 19
Nakaakira *m* 仲聴 227
Nakaba *s* 央馬 182, 夏秋 1161; *sm* 央 182; *m* 中 75, 半 213
Nakabachi *s* 中鉢 75
Nakabara *sp* 中原
Nakabaru *p* 中原
Nakabayashi *s* 中林
Nakabe *s* 中部
Nakabori *s* 中堀
Nakadai *s* 中台, 中代
Nakadaira *s* 中平
Nakadate *s* 中楯, 中館
Nakade *s* 中出
Nakae *s* 中江 「兆民
~ Chōmin *mlh* 中江
Nakaegawa *s* 中江川
Nakae Tōju *mh* 中江藤樹
Nakafuji *s* 中藤 「野
Naka-furano *p* 中富良
Nakafuri *s* 中布利
Nakagaki *s* 中垣
Nakagami *s* 中上, 中神
Nakagamigawa *s* 中上
Nakagane *s* 中金 ⌊川
Nakagata *s* 中方
Nakagawa *s* 中河, 仲川 227; *sp* 中川 75; *p* 那珂川 416, 那賀川
~ Jun'an *mh* 中川淳庵 75 「一政
~ Kazumasa *ml* 中川
~ Kiun *ml* 中川喜雲
~ Mikiko *fl* 中川幹子
~ Sōen *ml* 中川宋淵
~ Yoichi *ml* 中河与一
Nakagiri *s* 中桐
~ Kakutarō *ml* 中桐確太郎 「中心 75
Nakago *s* 仲子 227; *m*
Nakagō *p* 中郷
Nakagoe *s* 中越
Nakagome *s* 中牛馬, 中込
Nakagōri *s* 中郡
Nakaguchi *s* 中口
Nakaguki *s* 中久木, 中久喜, 中茎
Nakagyō *p* 中京
Nakahama *s* 中浜
Nakahara *s* 中原, 仲原 227 「75
~ Ayako *fl* 中原綾子
~ Chūya *ml* 中原中也
~ no Chikanobu *mh* 中原親能
Nakahashi *s* 中橋
~ Kōkan *l* 中橋公館
~ Tokugorō *mh* 中橋徳五郎
Nakahata *s* 中畑
Naka-heji *p* 中辺路
Nakahigashi *s* 中東
Nakahira *s* 中平
Nakahiro *m* 仲都 227, 仲博
Nakai *s* 中居 75, 仲井 227; *sp* 中井 75; *m* 魚養 1485 「竹山 75
~ Chikuzan *mh* 中井
~ Katsuhiko *ml* 中井克比古
Nakaide *s* 中出
Nakaigawa *s* 中井川
Nakaishi *s* 中石
Naka-izu *p* 中伊豆
Nakaizumi *s* 中泉
Nakaji *s* 中道, 中路, 仲地 227; *m* 仲治
Nakajima *sp* 中島 75, 仲島 227
~ Airō *ml* 中島哀浪 75
~ Atsushi *ml* 中島敦
~ Kawatarō *ml* 中島河太郎
~ Kenzō *ml* 中島健蔵
~ Kotō *ml* 中島孤島
~ Nobuyuki *mh* 中島信行
~ Shōen *ml* 中島湘煙
~ Takeo *ml* 中島斌雄
~ Utako *fl* 中島歌子
Nakajirō *m* 仲二郎 227, 仲次郎
Nakajō *s* 仲条; *sp* 中条 75 「原
Naka-kanbara *p* 中蒲
~ Kansuke *ml* 中勘助
~-kawachi *p* 中河内
~-kawane *p* 中川根
Nakaki *m* 仲芸 227
Nakakiri *s* 中吉 75
Nakakita *s* 中北
Nakako *f* 仲子 227
Nakakōji *s* 中小路 75, 仲小路 227 「75
Naka-koma *p* 中巨摩
~-kubiki *p* 中頸城
Nakakura *s* 中倉
Nakakusa *s* 半草 213
Nakama *s* 中万 75, 仲間 227; *sp* 中間 75
Nakamachi *s* 中町
Nakamaki *s* 中牧
Nakamaro *sm* 仲麻呂 227, 仲麿
Nakamaru *s* 中丸 75, 仲丸 227 「俣 227
Nakamata *s* 中俣 75, 仲
Nakamatsu *s* 中松 75
Nakame *s* 中目
Nakamichi *s* 中路; *sp* 中道 「中上川
Nakamigawa *s* 中三川,
~ Hikojirō *mh* 中上川彦次郎
Nakamikado *s* 中御門
Naka-minato *p* 那珂湊 416 「227
Nakamitsu *m-la* 仲光
Nakamiya *s* 中宮 75
Nakamizo *s* 中溝
Nakamori *s* 中森
Nakamoto *s* 中本, 中元, 中許, 仲本 227
Nakamuda *s* 中牟田 75
Nakamura *s* 中邑, 仲村 227; *sp* 中村 75
~ Akika *ml* 中村秋香
~ Burafu *ml* 中村武羅夫 「折
~ Fusetsu *mla* 中村不
~ Hakuyō *ml* 中村白葉
~ Jihei *ml* 中村地平
~ Kasō *ml* 中村花痩
~ Kenkichi *ml* 中村憲吉 「蔵
~ Kichizō *ml* 中村吉

~ Kusatao *ml* 中村草田男 「正直
~ Masanao *mlh* 中村
~ Masatsune *ml* 中村正常 「夫
~ Mitsuo *ml* 中村光
~ Saburō *ml* 中村三郎
~ Seiko *ml* 中村星湖
~ Shin'ichirō *ml* 中村真一郎
~ Shōji *ml* 中村正爾
~ Shūka *ml* 中村柊花
~ Teijo *fl* 中村汀女
Nakamyō *s* 中名生
Nakanbō *s* 中坊
Nakane *s* 中根
Naka-niida *p* 中新田
~-niikawa *p* 中新川
Nakanishi *s* 中西, 仲西 227 「75
~ Baika *ml* 中西梅花
~ Godō *ml* 中西悟堂
~ Inosuke *ml* 中西伊之助
Nakaniwa *s* 中庭
Nakano *s* 中埜; *sp* 中野; *sm-p* 仲野 227
Nakanobō *s* 中坊 75
Nakanoin *s* 中院
Nakanojō *p* 中之条
Nakano Kaichi *ml* 中野嘉一
~ Kikuo *ml* 中野菊夫
Nakanokuchi *sp* 中之口 「目 227
Nakanome *s* 中目, 仲
Nakano Minoru *ml* 中野実 75
Naka no Ōe *mh* 中大兄
Nakano San'in *ml* 中野三允 「重治
~ Shigeharu *ml* 中野
Nakanoshima *sp* 中之島 「野逍遙
Nakano Shōyō *ml* 中
~ Yoshio *ml* 中野好夫
Nakanuma *s* 中沼
Nakao *s* 仲尾 227, 中尾
Nakaōji *s* 中大路 ⌊75
Nakaoka *s* 中岡
~ Shintarō *mh* 中岡慎太郎
Nakaoki *s* 中沖
Nakarai *s* 半井 213; *m* 半
~ Bokuyō *ml* 半井卜養
~ Tōsui *ml* 半井桃水
Nakasa *s* 仲佐 227
Nakasaka *s* 中坂 75
Naka-satsunai *p* 中札内
Nakase *s* 中瀬, 中世
Nakasen *p* 中仙
Nakashi *m* 仲 227
Nakashiba *s* 中柴 75
Naka-shibetsu *p* 中標津
Nakashiro *s* 中城
Nakashizu *s* 中静
Nakasone *s* 中曾根, 仲宗根 227
Nakasu *s* 中須 75
Nakasuga *s* 中須賀
Nakasugi *s* 中杉
Nakasuji *s* 中筋
Nakata *sp* 中田; *s* 仲田 227
Naka-tado *p* 仲多度
Nakata Kōji *ml* 中田耕治 75
Naka-tane *p* 中種子
Nakatani *s* 中谷, 仲谷 227 「75
~ Takao *ml* 中谷孝雄
Nakatarō *m* 仲太郎 227
Nakatomi *s* 中臣 75; *sp* 中富
~ no Kamatari *mh* 中臣鎌足
~ no Yakamori *ml* 中臣宅守 「詞
~ no yogoto *l* 中臣寿
Nakatomiue *s* 中臣表
Naka-tonbetsu *p* 中頓
~-tosa *p* 中土佐 ⌊別
Nakatoshi *m* 仲寿 227
Nakatsu *sp* 中津 75
Nakatsuagata *s* 中県
Nakatsubo *s* 中坪
Naka-tsue *p* 中津江
~-tsugaru *p* 中津軽
Nakatsugawa *sp* 中津川
Nakatsugi *sm* 中次
Nakatsuji *s* 中辻
Nakatsuka *s* 中塚
~ Ippekirō *ml* 中塚一碧楼
Nakatsukasa *sfl-p* 中務
~ no Naishi *fl-l* 中務内侍
Nakatsune *m* 中康
Nakauchi *s* 中内
~ Chōji *ml* 中内蝶二
Nakauonuma *p* 中魚沼
Nakaura *s* 中浦
Nakawaniko *s* 中丸子
Nakaya *s* 中谷, 中矢, 中屋, 仲谷 227
Nakayabu *s* 中藪 75
Nakayama *s* 仲山 227; *sp* 中山 75
~ Gishū *ml* 中山義秀
~ Shōzaburō *ml* 中山省三郎
Nakayasu *s* 仲安 227; *sm* 中安 75
Nakaya Ukichirō *ml* 中谷宇吉郎
Nakayoshi *s* 中吉
Nakazaki *s* 中崎
Nakazato *sp* 中里
~ Kaizan *ml* 中里介山 「子
~ Tsuneko *fl* 中里恒
Nakazawa *s* 中沢, 仲沢 227 「75
~ Dōni *mh* 中沢道二
~ Rinsen *ml* 中沢臨川
Nakazono *s* 中園, 中薗
Naki *s* 名木 346, 奈癸 696. (泣 590, 鳴 2065)
Nakiama *la* 泣尼 590
Nakime *f* 鳴女 2065
Nakinin *s* 今帰仁 67
Nakiri *s* 万鬼 43, 百鬼 265
Nakisaichi *s* 奈癸私 696
Nako *s* 名子 346, 奈古 696
Nakoso *p* 勿来 110
Nakui *s* 名久井 346
Nakusa *s* 名草
Nama *s* 南摩 912. (生 ⌊214)
Namae *s* 生江
Namaezawa *s* 生江沢
Namai *s* 生井
Namakawa *s* 生川
Namamugi *s* 生麦
Namase *s* 生瀬
Namatame *s* 生田目
Namatsu *s* 生津
(namazu 鯰 2829)
Namazuda *s* 鯰田
(name 行 245, 並 765, 滑 1857)
Namegata *sp* 行方 245
Namekawa *sp* 滑川 1857
~ Michio *ml* 滑川道 ⌊夫
(nameri 滑)
Namerikawa *s* 滑川
Nami *f* 波 596. (方 85, 比 137, 冊 190, 次 226, 行 245, 因 311, 甫 533, 波 596, 並 765, 洋 822, 南 912, 浪 1339, 湲 1854, 淵 1858, 漣 2082, 漾 2085, 濤 2613)
Namiai *sp* 浪合 1339
Namie *s* 波江 596, 浪江 1339; *f* 波重 596, 並枝 765; *f-p* 浪江 1339
Namifuji *m* 並藤 765
Namigorō *m* 濤五郎 2613
Namihei *m* 浪平 1339
Namihide *m* 浪秀
Namiino *s* 七三五野 17
Namikai *m* 浪貝 1339
Namikata *s* 行方 245
Namikawa *s* 行川, 並川 765, 並河, 浪川 1339, 濤川 2613
Namiki *s* 双木 53, 行木 245; *sm* 並木 765, 並樹
~ Gohei *ml* 並木五瓶
~ Senryū *ml* 並木千柳
~ Shōzō *ml* 並木正三
~ Sōsuke *ml* 並木宗輔
Namiko *f* 勿巳子 110, 浪子 1339, 湲子 1854, 漾子 2085, 濤子 2613
Namikuri *s* 並栗 765
Namino *s* 浪野 1339; *sp* 波野 596
Naminohira *s* 波平
Namio *m* 洋大 822, 浪雄 1339
Namioka *s* 並岡 765; *p* 浪岡 1339
Namisada *m* 浪貞
Namita *s* 列田 257
Namitsukimononobe *s* 相槻物部 868
Namiyoshi *m* 甫美 533
Namizaki *s* 名見崎 346, 名美崎
Namura *s* 名村, 苗村 685, 納村 1685
(nan 男 495, 南 912, 暖 1882, 楠 1901, 難 2760, 灘 2946)
(nana 七 17)
Nanae *f* 七重; *p* 七飯
Nanai *s* 七井
Nanakai *p* 七会
Nanakama *s* 七家

Nanakamado *s* 七加家, 七家
Nanako *f* 七子
Nanakura *s* 七坐
Nanakuro *s* 七坐
Nanami *s* 七見, 名波 346 「帝 17
Nananomikado *mh* 七
Nanao *m* 七夫, 七雄; *p* 七尾
Nanasato *s* 七里
Nanasawa *s* 七沢
Nanase *s* 菜生 1447; *f* 七瀬 17
Nanashige *m* 七十
Nanatsuka *p* 七塚
Nanatsumen *l* 七つ面
Nanaumi *s* 七海
Nanayama *p* 七山
Nanba *s* 南場 912, 難波 2760; *sp* 南波 912
Nanbara *s* 南原
~ Shigeru *ml* 南原繁
Nanbata *s* 難波田 2760
Nanbatei *s* 浪花停 1339
Nanbo *s* 南保 912
Nanboku *s* 南木; *ml* 南北
~ shinwa *l* 南北新話
Nanbu *sp* 南部
Nanbuchi *s* 南淵
Nanbu Shūtarō *ml* 南部修太郎
Nandan *p* 南淡
Nan'e *s* 南江
Nangai *p* 南外
Nangen *s* 南原
Nangō *s* 南合; *sp* 南郷
Nangoku *p* 南国
~ taiheiki *l* 南国太平
Nangū *s* 南宮 ㇄記
(nani 何 513, 奈 696)
Naniai *p* 七二会 17
Nanie *f* 七二恵
Nanimaru *m* 何丸 513
Naniwa *p* 浪速 1339; *ph-la* 難波 2760
~ dora *l* 難波鉦
Naniwae *s* 難波江
Naniwa kagami *la* 難波鑑
~ miyage *l* 難波土産
Nanjō *s* 南城 912; *sp* 南条 「雄
~ Bun'yū *mh* 南条文
~ Norio *ml* 南条範夫
Nankai *p* 南海
Nankaidō *p* 南海道
Nankan *p* 南関
Nanke *s* 南家 「南京
Nankin *p* "Nanking"
Nanko *s* 南湖
Nankō *p* 南光
Nanmoku *p* 南牧
Nannō *p* 南濃
Nanrei *ml* 南嶺
Nanri *s* 南里
Nansei *s* 南晴; *p* 南勢
Nansen *p* "S. Korea" 南鮮
Nansenshō Somahito *ml* 南杣笑楚満人
Nanshoku ōkagami *l* 男色大鑑 495
Nansō *p* 南総 912
~ Satomi hakkenden *l* 南総里見八犬伝
Nansōshū *l* 南窗集
Nantō *p* 南島
Nan'un *s* 南雲
Nan'yō *p* 南陽
Nao *f* 直 988. (三 22, 仍 123, 収 133, 巨 199, 正 205, 矢 215, 朴 255, 而 264, 有 303, 多 347, 作 362, 均 387, 如 412, 亨 440, 君 515, 侃 551, 実 678, 若 692, 斉 701, 尚 753, 胖 843, 直 988, 修 1038, 真 1228, 巠 1229, 通 1239, 庭 1244, 脩 1281, 躬 1396, 野 1398, 順 1532, 猶 1555, 復 1571, 董 1731, 植 1902, 竪 2224, 愿 2228, 端 2306, 慤 2403, 縮 2813, 縄 2955, 懿 2958, 矗 3017)
Naoaki *m* 直諒 988
Naoatsu *m* 直温, 直惇
Naobayashi *m* 猶林 1555 「毘霊 988
Naobi no mitama *l* 直
Naochika *m* 直哉
Naoe *s* 直江; *m* 直徳; *f* 矗江 3017
Naoetsu *p* 直江津 988
Naofusa *m* 正房 205
Naoharu *m* 直治 988, 直浩, 直温
Naohide *m* 直幸, 直秀
Naohiko *m* 直彦
Naohira *m* 直平
Naohiro *m* 直胖
Naohisa *m* 直旧, 直富
Naoi *s* 直井 「一 988
Naoichi *m* 尚一 753, 直
Naoiri *m-p* 直入
Naoji *m* 直治
Naojirō *m* 朴次郎 255, 直二郎 988, 直次郎, 直治郎, 猶治郎 1555
Naokai *m* 直養 988
Naokawa *p* 直川
Naokazu *m* 直計
Naoki *s* 直木; *m* 直, 直大, 直生
Naokichi *m* 直吉, 直橘, 猶吉 1555
Naoki Sanjūgo *ml* 直木三十五 988
Naokiyo *m* 直廉
Naoko *f* 七緒子 17, 直子 988, 巠子 1229, 猶子 1555, 愿子 2228; *f-l* 菜穂子 1447 「服 988
Naokoto *m* 尚服 753, 直
Naokuma *m* 直熊
Naoma *m* 直馬
Naomasa *m* 直方, 直政, 直諒
Naomi *m* 尚監 753, 直心 988, 直見, 直臣, 直幹; *f* 魚百美 1485
Naomichi *m* 直方 988, 直道
Naomitsu *m* 均光 387, 尚備 753, 直円 988, 直映, 直称
Naomochi *m* 直有
Naomoto *m* 直旧, 直故, 直躬, 猶朔 1555
Naomune *m* 尚志 753
Naomura *s* 直村 988
Naonatsu *m* 実夏 678
Naondo *m* 直人 988
Naonobu *m* 尚信 753, 直惟 988, 直養
Naonori *m* 尚士 753, 直法 988, 直憧, 直徳, 直彝
Naosaburō *m* 直三郎
Naosane *m* 直期
Naoshi *m* 癶 447, 尚 753, 良 769, 直 988, 道 1811; *p* 直島 988
Naoshirō *m* 直四郎
Naosuke *m* 侃左 551, 直助 988, 直亮
Naota *m* 直太
Naotada *m* 直縄
Naotaka *m* 尚隆 753, 直応 988, 直孝, 直桓
Naotake *m* 尚武 753
Naotarō *m* 直太郎 988
Naoteru *m* 直昭
Naoto *m* 直人, 直砥
Naotō *m* 直柔
Naotoki *m* 直候 「1532
Naotomo *m* 直交, 順朝
Naotoshi *m* 尚敏 753, 直知 988, 直俊, 直穎
Naotsune *m* 直識
Naotsura *m* 直陳
Naoya *m* 有也 303, 直矢 988
Naoyasu *m* 直静, 直愈
Naoyoshi *m* 尚順 753, 直亮 988, 直好, 直良, 直候, 直康, 直義, 直禔
Naoyuki *m* 公行 156, 如雪 412, 尚征 753, 直随 998
Naozaki *s* 猶崎 1555
Naozane *m* 尚実 753, 尚真
Naozō *m* 直三 988, 直蔵
Naozumi *m* 尚住 753
Nara *s* 楽世 2029; *sp* 奈良 696. (習 1468, 楢 1900, 稙 2122)
Narabara *s* 楢原 1900
Narabashi *s* 奈良橋 696
Narabayashi *s* 楢林 1900
Narabe *s* 奈良部 696
Narabu *m* 双 53, 並 765
Nara ehon *la* 奈良絵本 696
Narage *s* 楢下 1900
Naragiku *f* 楢菊
Naraha *sp* 楢葉
Narahara *s* 奈良原 696, 楢原 1900
Narai *s* 成相 322, 奈良井 696, 楢井 1900
Narakawa *p* 楢川
Naraki *s* 楢木
Narakochibe *s* 奈良己知部 696
Narama *s* 奈良間
Naramaro *m* 奈良麿
Nara mōde *la* 奈良詣
Naranoya *m* 楢舎 1900
Narao *p* 奈良尾 696
Naraoka *s* 奈良岡, 楢岡 1900

Narasaki *s* 奈良崎 696, 楢崎 1900 「1468
Narashino *p* 習志野
Naraya *s* 奈良屋 696
Narayamabushikō *l* 楢山節考 1900
Naraya Mozaemon *mh* 奈良屋茂左衛門 696
Narazono *m* 楢園 1900
(nare 馴 1966)
(nari 入 15, 也 23. 功 135, 礼 146, 令 155, 平 203, 本 212, 生 214, 有 303, 成 322, 位 354, 体 358, 作 362, 攷 377, 均 387, 形 414, 亨 440, 克 442, 足 461, 考 540, 孝 541, 性 564, 往 579, 効 653, 宜 675, 宗 679, 苗 685, 斉 701, 忠 705, 周 736, 尚 753, 城 796, 政 881, 柔 907, 発 953, 育 958, 音 962, 廻 994, 為 1005, 校 1096, 記 1149, 容 1182, 造 1236, 威 1251, 得 1299, 済 1336, 規 1349, 救 1406, 教 1408, 備 1539, 晴 1597, 詞 1665, 就 1668, 登 1744, 然 1788, 曾 1794, 雅 1913, 稔 1916, 誠 1935, 愛 2018, 業 2024, 勢 2039, 徳 2063, 鳴 2065, 震 2577, 整 2581, 諧 2639, 謹 2645, 慈 2701, 績 2814, 霽 2978)
Nariai *s* 成相 322, 業合 2024 「明 2581
Nariaki *m* 成彬 322, 整
Nariakira *m* 成煥 322, 斉彬 701
Narichika *m* 成親 322
Narihira *m* 業平 2024
Narihisa *m* 就久 1668
Narihito *m* 体仁 358
Nariie *m* 成家 322
Narikage *m* 業景 2024
Narikane *m* 成包 322
Narikazu *m* 成和, 得一 1299
Nariki *s* 成木 322
Nariko *f* 体子 358, 柔子 907, 済子 1336, 登子 1744, 業子 2024
Narimasa *m* 成允 322
Narimichi *m* 成蹊
Narimoto *s* 作本 362; *m* 成元 322
Narinaga *m* 成命
Narinobu *m* 斉脩 701
Narinohara *s* 形原 414
Nario *s* 成尾 322
Narioki *m* 斉典 701
Narisawa *m* 成沢 322
Narishige *m* 斉茲 701
Narita *sp* 成田 322
Naritada *m* 業尹 2024
Naritaka *m* 斉荘 701, 就高 1668
Naritake *m* 斉貴 701
Naritari *m* 斉粛
Naritō *m* 斉広
Naritoki *m* 愛発 2018
Naritomi *s* 成富 322
Naritsugu *m* 愛臧 2018
Naritsuka *s* 成塚 322
Naritsura *m* 成烈
Nariwa *p* 成羽
Nariyasu *m* 斉徳 701
Nariyoshi *m* 成嘉 322, 斉斎 701, 威儀 1251, 就馴 1668, 登吉 1744
Nariyuki *m* 成之 322
Narō *m* 俗 776, 温 1585, 準 2041
Naru *p* 奈留 696. (功 135, 平 203, 去 266, 成 322, 完 471, 考 540, 育 958, 済 1336, 登 1744, 遂 1806, 稔 1916, 誠 1935, 愛 2018, 徳 2063, 鳴 2065, 農 2205, 親 2544, 燕 2570, 震 2577, 鏘 2881) 「912
Narubeshi *l* 南留別志
Naruchika *m* 愛親 2018
Naruge *s* 成毛 322
Naruhiko *m* 稔彦 1916
Naruhito *m* 愛仁 2018
Narui *s* 成井 322
Narukami *la* 鳴神 2065
Narukawa *s* 生川 214, 成川 322
Naruko *f* 成子, 済子 1336; *p* 鳴子 2065
Narumi *s* 成海 322, 鳴見 2065, 鳴海; *sm* 成見 322; *m* 成実, 愛民 2018; *f* 完美 471
~ Senkichi *l* 鳴海仙吉 2065 「吉
~ Yōkichi *ml* 鳴海要
Narumo *s* 成尾 322
Narusawa *s* 成沢; *p* 鳴沢 2065
Naruse *s* 成瀬 322; *sp* 鳴瀬 2065 「322
~ Jinzō *mh* 成瀬仁蔵
~ Mukyoku *ml* 成瀬無極
Narushige *m* 平林 203
Narushima *s* 成島 322, 鳴島 2065 「北 322
~ Ryūhoku *ml* 成島柳
Naruto *sp* 鳴門 2065; *m* 成人 322
Narutō *p* 成東
Naruto hichō *l* 鳴門秘帖 2065
Naruya *s* 成谷 322
Naruyasu *m* 登康 1744, 誠康 1935
Nasa *s* 奈佐 696
Nasai *m* 那歳 416
Nasanu naka *l* 生さぬ仲 214
Nase *p* 名瀬 346
(nashi 梨 1476, 無 1789, 類 2755)
Nashiba *s* 梨羽 1476
Nashiko *f* 梨子, 無子 1789
Nashimoto *s* 梨本 1476
Nashinoki *s* 梨木
Nashinomoto *s* 梨本
~ -shū *l* 梨本集
Nashiro *m* 名代 346
Nashitsubo no gonin *ml* 梨壺五人 1476
Naso *s* 納所 1685
Nasu *s* 奈須 696; *sp* 那須 416
Nasukata *s* 行方 245
Nasumi *s* 直見 988
Nasuno *s* 那須野 416
Natari *m* 名垂 346, 名足
Natashō *p* 名田庄
Natori *s* 名, 名理, 名執; *sp* 名取; *m* 名鳥
Natorigawa *l* 名取川
Natorigusa Heike monogatari *l* 牡丹平家譚 407
(natsu 夏 1161, 暑 1738A)
Natsuaki *s* 夏秋 1161
Natsubana otome *l* 夏花少女
Natsuhana *l* 夏花
Natsui *s* 夏井
Natsuka *s* 長束 939
Natsuki *m* 夏樹 1161
Natsu kodachi *l* 夏木
Natsuma *s* 夏間 └立
Natsu-matsuri Naniwa kagami *l* 夏祭浪花鑑 「1757)
Natsume *s* 夏目. (棗
Natsumeda *s* 棗田
Natsume Seibi *ml* 夏目成美 1161
~ Sōseki *ml* 夏目漱石
Natsumi *s* 夏見
Natsuno *sm* 夏野
Natsura *m* 魚貫 1485
Natsuyama *s* 夏山 1161
~ Shigeki *ml* 夏山繁樹
Natsuyo *f* 七月代 17
Natta *s* 名田 346 「畝
Naune *s* 長久939; *sp* 長
Nawa *s* 那波 416, 縄 2955; *sp* 名和 346. (縄 2955)
Nawachi *s* 縄稚
Nawakura *s* 縄倉
Nawamura *s* 苗村 685
Nawa Nagatoshi *mh* 名和長年 346
Nawanai *l* 縄綯 2955
Nawata *s* 縄田
Naya *s* 納谷 1685
Nayoro *p* 名寄 346
Nayuki *s* 名雪
Nazo no obi chotto Tokubee *la* 謎帯一寸徳兵衛 2640
(nazu 摩 2428)
Nazuka *s* 名塚 346
Nazuku *m* 号 272; *m-f* 名 346
(ne 子 38, 兄 181, 泥 594, 音 962, 直 988, 値 1278, 峰 1351, 根 1372, 道 1811, 寝 1976, 稲 2125, 嶺 2776, 禰 2800)
Neba *p* 根羽 1372
Nebashi *s* 根橋
Nebiki no kadomatsu *la* 寿の門松 539
Nebukawa *s* 根府川 1372 「2800
Nechikaze *s* 禰知風
Neda *s* 根田 1372
Nedate *s* 根立
Negami *p* 根上
Negi *s* 唁 1047, 根木 1372
Negishi *s* 根岸

Negita *s* 禰宜田 2800
Negoro *sp* 根来 1372
Nei *s* 根井; *sp* 婦負 1603. (寍 1711, 甯 1712, 寧 2181)
Neichi *m* 子一 38
Neishi *s* 根石 1372
(neko 猫 1304)
Nekomaru *s* 猫丸
Nekomata *s* 猫又
Nekoshi *s* 子子子 38
Nekoya *s* 猫屋 1304
Nemaro *m* 根麻呂 1372, 禰麻呂 2800 「元
Nemoto *s* 根本 1372, 根
Nemugaki *s* 合歓垣 270
Nemuko *f* 合歓子
Nemura *s* 根村 1372
(nemuri 眠 1376) 「453
Nemurigusa *l* 含羞草
Nemuri Kyōshirō *m* 眠狂四郎 1376
Nemuro *p* 根室 1372
(nen 年 342, 拈 583, 念 670, 染 968, 然 1788, 稔 1916, 稗 2123, 鮎 2547, 髯 2580)
Nenaga *m* 根長 1372
Nenashigusa *l* 根南志具佐 「仏踊 670
Nenbutsu odori *a* 念
Nenge mishō *l* 拈華微笑 583
Nenjo *s* 毛所 117
Nenjū gyōji hishō *l* 年中行事秘抄 342
Nenoi *s* 根ノ井 1372, 根
Neo *sp* 根尾 ⌊井
(neri 練 2527)
Neriki *s* 練木
Nerima *p* 練馬
Neshime *s* 禰寝 2800
Neshine *s* 禰寝
Netami *s* 米多比 343
(netsu 熱 2408)
Netsuko *s* 根子 1372
Neyagawa *p* 寝屋川
Nezame *l* 寝覚 ⌊1976
Nezu *s* 根津 1372, 禰津 2800 「権現裏 1372
～ Gongen ura *l* 根津
(nezumi 鼠 2430)
Nezumi-komon haru no shingata *la* 鼠小紋東君新形
(ni 二 4, 仁 57, 丹 79, 尼 175, 而 264, 耳 331, 似 350, 煮 1787, 瑗 1873, 爾 2250, 瓊 2717, 邇 2785)
Nibe *m* 瓊缶 2717
Nibu *s* 内生 81, 玢 604; *sp* 丹生 79
(nichi 日 77, 昵 839)
Nichihara *p* 日原 77
Nichinan *p* 日南
Nichireki *l* 日暦
Nichiren *mlh* 日蓮
Nie *s* 贄 2781. (牲 830, 贄 2781)
Nieda *s* 贄田
Niekawa *s* 牲川 830, 熱川 2408, 贄川 2781
(niga 苦 687)
Nigame *s* 二瓶 4
Nigami *s* 仁神 57
Nigamomo *s* 苦桃 687
Nigao *s* 仁賀保 57
Nigatake *s* 苦竹 687
Nigauri *s* 苦瓜; *l* 茘支 924
(nigi 和 638, 饒 2925)
Nigiemishi *s* 熟蝦夷 2406
Nigita *s* 和田 638
Nigitama *l* 和霊
Nigitemaro *m* 和布麿
(nigori 濁 2457)
Nigorikawa *sp* 濁川
Nigume *s* 釈迦如来 1395 「仏
Nigurome *s* 釈迦牟尼
Nihachi *s* 仁八 57
Nihashi *s* 二橋 4
Nihei *s* 二瓶, 仁瓶 57; *m* 二平 4
Nihira *s* 仁平 57
Niho *s* 仁保
Nihon *p* 日本 77
～ gaishi *lh* 日本外史
Nihongi *l* 日本紀
Nihon horyoshi *l* 日本捕虜志
～ kōki *l* 日本後記
～-koku genzaisho mokuroku *l* 日本国見在書目録
Nihonmatsu *sp* 二本松 4
Nihon reiiki *l* 日本霊異記 77
～ ryōiki *l* 日本霊異記
～ sanmon opera *l* 日本三文オペラ
～ shoki *l* 日本書紀
Nii *s* 丹比 79; *sp* 新居 1965. (新)
Niiai *s* 新合
Niibara *s* 新原
Niibata *s* 新畠
Niibe *s* 二部 4
Niibo *p* 新穂 1965
Niibori *s* 新堀
Niibu *s* 新生
Niichirō *m* 仁一郎 57
Niida *s* 仁井田, 新井田
Niie *m* 新家 「1965
Niifu *s* 新生, 新阜
Niigaki *s* 新垣
Niigasa *m* 新笠
Niigata *p* 新潟
Niihama *p* 新居浜
Niihari *sp* 新治; *l* 新墾
Niiharu *p* 新治
Nii Itaru *ml* 新居格
Niijima *s* 新島
～ Eiji *ml* 新島栄治
Niijimahon *p* 新島本
Niijima Jō *mlh* 新島襄
～ Shigeru *ml* 新島繁
Niikappu *p* 新冠
Niikawa *s* 新川
Niiki *s* 新城
Niikuma *m* 新熊
Niikuni *s* 新国
Niikura *s* 新生, 新倉
Niima *s* 新今, 新見, 新間
Niimanabi *l* 新学
～ iken *l* 新学異見
Niimatsu *s* 新松
Niimi *s* 新免, 新美, 新実; *sp* 新見 「南吉
～ Namikichi *ml* 新美
Niimoto *s* 新元
Niimura *s* 新村
Niina *s* 新名
Niino *sp* 新野
Niinō *s* 新納
Niinohe *s* 新戸
Niinomi *s* 新家
Niinuma *s* 新沼
Niioka *s* 新岡
Niioki *s* 新興
Niira *s* 新納, 新楽
Niiri *s* 二杁 4
Niiro *s* 新納 1965
Niisato *sp* 新里
Niita *s* 熟田 2406
Niitani *s* 新谷 1965
Niitarō *m* 丹斐太郎 79
Niitobe *s* 新渡戸 1965
Niitsu *p* 新津
Niitsuru *p* 新鶴
Niiya *s* 新谷, 新家, 新
Niiyama *s* 新山 ⌊屋
Niizeki *s* 新関
～ Ryōzō *ml* 新関良三
Niizuma *s* 新妻
Niizumi *s* 新泉
Niji *p* 二上 4. (虹 882)
Nijiko *f* 虹子
Nijinshū *l* 耳塵集 331
Nijō *sp* 二条 4; *p* 二丈
～ Tameuji *ml* 二条為氏 「良基
～ Yoshimoto *ml* 二条
Nijūgogen *l* 二十五絃
Nijūhasshuku *l* 二十八宿 「一代集
Nijūichidaishū *l* 二十
Nikaho *p* 仁賀保 57
Nikaidō *s* 二階堂 4
Nikami *s* 二上, 直上 988
Niki *s* 仁木 57
～ Etsuko *fl* 仁木悦子
Nikkawa *s* 新川 1965
Nikki *s* 二木 4, 仁木 57
Nikkō *sp-l* 日光 77
(niku 宍 470)
Nikuni *s* 二国 4
Nikurōbe *s* 釈迦牟尼仏 1395
Nikurube *s* 釈迦如来, 釈迦牟尼仏
Nima *sp* 邇摩 2785
Nimi *s* 仁見 57 「57
Nimura *s* 二村 4, 仁村
Nin *s* 任 235. (仁 57, 壬 116, 仞 122, 任 235, 忍 463, 荏 930, 葱 1169, 紝 1679, 靭 1694, 認 2137)
(nina 腮 1870, 蜷 2129)
Ninagawa *s* 蜷川
Nin'an 1166–69 仁安 57
Ninatarō *m* 腮太郎 1870
Ninbe *s* 鹿伏兎 1823
Ninbyō 1151–54 仁平 57
Ninden *s* 任田 235
Ningenkyō *l* 人間経 14
Ninigi *m* 邇邇芸 2785
Ninin bikuni *l* 二人比丘尼 4
～ Giō *la* 二人祇王
Ninji 1240–43 仁治 57
Ninjōbon *l* 人情本 14
Ninju 851–54 仁寿 57
Ninna 885–89 仁和;

*ph* "Kaya / Karak" 任那 235
Ninnaji *sp* 仁和寺 57
Ninohe *sp* 二戸 4
Ninohira *s* 仁ノ平 57
Ninokami *s* 二神 4
Ninomatsu *s* 二松
Ninomiya *s* 二宮
～ Sontoku *mh* 二宮尊徳
Ninomura *s* 二村
Ninotani *s* 二谷
Ninoue *s* 仁上 57
Ninpei 1151–54 仁平
Ninshō *mh* 忍性 463
Nintoku *mh* 仁徳 57
Ninwa 885–89 仁和
Nio *s* 仁保, 丹尾 79, 鳰 1824; *sp* 仁尾 57. (匂 73, 匂 168, 鳰 1824, 薫 2567)
Niō *smh-la* 仁王 57; *sla* 二王 4. (匂 73)
Nioe *f* 匂枝
Nioi *s* 匂, 乳井 657
Niokata *s* 香芳 961
Nioko *f* 匂子 73, 丹穂子 79, 鳰子 1824, 薫子 2567
Niōnomiya *l* 匂宮 73
Niori *s* 新居 1965
Nippon *p* 日本 77
～ eitaigura *l* 日本永代蔵 「日暮里 77
Nippori *s* 新堀 1965; *p*
(nira 韮 1728, 薤 2565)
Nirasaki *p* 韮崎 1728
Nirasawa *s* 韮沢
Niratsuka *s* 韮塚
Nirayama *s* 仁羅山 57, 薤山 2565; *p* 韮山 1728
Nire *s* 仁礼 57. (枌 624, 楡 2288A)
Nirei *s* 楡井
Nireki *s* 楡木
Nirō *m* 仁郎 57
Niroku shinpō *l* 二六新報 4 「三郎 57
Nisaburō *m* 二三郎, 仁
Nisanamu *s* 爾散南 2250
(nise 似 350, 偐 1275)
Nise-e *a* 似絵 350
～ Murasaki inaka Genji *l* 偐紫田舎源氏 1275 「2805)
Nishi *sp* 西 336. (西, 螺
～-aizu *p* 西会津 336

～ Amane *mlh* 西周
Nishiara *s* 西新
Nishiari *s* 西有
Nishi-arie *p* 西有家
～-arita *p* 西有田
～-asai *p* 西浅井
～-awakura *p* 西粟倉
Nishibayashi *s* 西林
Nishibe *s* 西部
Nishi-biwajima *p* 西枇杷島
Nishibori *s* 西堀
Nishi-chikuma *p* 西筑摩 「西田 336
Nishida *s* 螺田 2805; *sp*
Nishidai *s* 西代
Nishida Kitarō *mlh* 西田幾多郎
Nishidate *s* 西館
Nishida Tenkō *ml* 西田天香
Nishide *s* 西出
Nishie *s* 螺江 2805
Nishigai *s* 西貝 336
Nishigaki *s* 西垣
Nishigami *s* 西上, 西神
Nishigata *s* 西潟
Nishigawara *s* 西河原
Nishigaya *s* 西ケ谷
Nishigō *p* 西郷
Nishigori *s* 米錦 343, 錦部 2525, 錦織
Nishigōri *s* 西郡 336
Nishigorinotami *s* 錦民 2525 「336
Nishi-gōshi *p* 西合志
Nishiguchi *s* 西口
Nishihara *sp* 西原
Nishiharu *p* 西春
Nishi-haruchika *p* 西春近
Nishihata *s* 西畑
Nishihijirikobe *s* 西泥部, 西埿部
Nishihira *s* 西平
Nishihiro *s* 西広
Nishii *s* 西井, 西居
Nishi-ibaraki *p* 西茨城
Nishiide *s* 西出
～ Chōfū *ml* 西出朝風
Nishiike *s* 西池
Nishiiri *s* 西入
Nishiitsuji *s* 西五辻
Nishi-iwai *p* 西磐井
～-iyayama *p* 西祖谷山
～-izu *p* 西伊豆
Nishijima *s* 西島

～ Bakunan *ml* 西島麦
Nishijin *p* 西陣 ⌊南
Nishikado *s* 西角
Nishi-kamo *p* 西加茂
～-kanbara *p* 西蒲原
～-kasugai *p* 西春日井
Nishikata *s* 西片, 西形; *p* 西方
Nishikatsu *s* 西勝
Nishi-katsura *p* 西桂
Nishikawa *s* 西河; *sp* 西川
～ Joken *mh* 西川如見
～ Kōjirō *ml* 西川光二郎
Nishiki *s* 丹敷 79, 西亀 336; *sp* 錦 2525; *p* 西木 336, 西紀. (錦 2525)
Nishikibe *s* 錦部
Nishikido *s* 西木戸 336; *sla* 錦戸 2525
Nishikie *a* 錦絵
Nishikigi *la* 錦木
Nishikikōji *s* 錦小路
Nishikimi *s* 錦見
Nishikini *s* 錦貫
Nishikori *s* 錦古利, 錦古里 「336
Nishi-kubiki *p* 西頸城
Nishikubo *s* 西久保
Nishi-kunisaki *p* 西国東
Nishikura *s* 西倉
Nishima *s* 西間
Nishimaki *s* 西牧, 西巻
Nishimatsu *s* 西松
Nishi-matsuura *p* 西松 ⌊浦
Nishime *sp* 西目
Nishimeya *p* 西目屋
Nishimiya *s* 西宮
Nishimonai *s* 西馬音内
Nishimori *s* 西森
Nishimorinai *s* 西大音
Nishi-morokata *p* 西諸県 「本
Nishimoto *s* 西元, 西
Nishimuda *s* 西牟田
Nishimune *s* 西宗
Nishimura *s* 西村, 西邨 「樹
～ Shigeki *mlh* 西村茂
～ Tenshū *ml* 西村天囚 「村山
Nishi-murayama *p* 西
Nishimura Yōkichi *ml* 西村陽吉
Nishi-muro *p* 西牟婁

Nishimuta *s* 西牟田
Nishina *s* 仁秋 57, 仁科, 西名 336
Nishinaka *s* 西中
Nishinari *sp* 西成
Nishi-nasuno *p* 西那須野 「科芳雄 57
Nishina Yoshio *mh* 仁
Nishine *p* 西根 336
Nishino *s* 西野
Nishinoiri *s* 西野入
Nishinokyō *sp* 西京
Nishinomiya *sp* 西宮
～ Tōchō *ml* 西宮藤朝
Nishinoomote *p* 西表
Nishinoshima *sp* 西島
Nishino Tatsukichi *ml* 西野辰吉
Nishinotoi *s* 西東院; *sp* 西洞院
Nishinotōin *sp* 西洞院
Nishinouchi *s* 西内
Nishinoya *s* 西谷
Nishio *s* 西保, 西面; *sp* 西尾 「大条
Nishiōeda *s* 西大枝, 西
Nishioida *s* 西大条
Nishiōji *s* 西大寺, 西大路
Nishioka *s* 西岡 「賜
Nishi-okitama *p* 西置
～-okoppe *p* 西興部
Nishiori *s* 西織
Nishi-sakurajima *p* 西桜島
～-senboku *p* 西仙北
～-shirakawa *p* 西白河
～-sonogi *p* 西彼杵
～-tagawa *p* 西田川
Nishitakatsuji *s* 西高辻
Nishi-tama *p* 西多摩
Nishitani *sp* 西谷
Nishi-tonami *p* 西礪波
～-tosa *p* 西土佐
～-tsugaru *p* 西津軽
Nishiuchi *s* 西内
Nishiumi *sp* 西海
Nishiura *s* 西浦
Nishi-usuki *p* 西臼杵
～-uwa *p* 西宇和
Nishiwaki *sp* 西脇
～ Junzaburō *ml* 西脇順三郎
Nishiya *s* 西谷
Nishiyama *sp* 西山
～ Hakuun *ml* 西山泊雲

～ Sōin *ml* 西山宗因
Nishi-yashiro *p* 西八代
～-yodogawa *p* 西淀川
Nishiyori *s* 西依
Nishi-yoshino *p* 西吉野 「辻
Nishiyotsutsuji *s* 西四
Nishiza *s* 西座
Nishizaka *s* 西坂
Nishizaki *s* 西崎
Nishizawa *s* 西沢
Nishizono *s* 西園
Nishizuka *s* 西塚
Nissai *s* 入西 15
Nisshin *s* 日進 77；*mh* 日親
Nisugi *s* 仁杉 57
Nita *s* 仁田；*p* 仁多
Nitadori *sp* 似鳥 350
Nitanai *sp* 似内
Nitawara *s* 仁田原 57
Nitō *s* 仁藤
Nitobe *s* 二藤部 4, 新渡戸 1965 「造
～ Inazō *mlh* 新渡戸稲
Nitoda *s* 仁戸田 57
Nitori *s* 似 350
Nitta *s* 仁田 57；*sp* 新田 1965
～ Jirō *ml* 新田次郎
～ Jun *ml* 新田潤
～ Yoshisada *mh* 新田
Nitto *s* 日戸 77 ⌊義貞
Nittō *s* 日東
Nittono *s* 入戸野 15
Niwa *s* 二葉 4, 土神 42, 上神 47, 丹波 79, 邇摩 2785；*sp* 丹羽 79.（庭
Niwabi *l* 庭燎 ⌊1244）
Niwa Fumio *ml* 丹羽文雄 79
Niwagoke *l* 庭苔 1244
Niwaji *s* 仁和寺 57
Niwaki *s* 庭木 1244
Niwano *s* 庭野
Niwata *s* 庭田
Niwatori muko *la* 鶏聟 2821
Niwayama *s* 庭山 1244
Niyodo *p* 仁淀 57
(no 之 24, 乃 27, 野 1398, 埜 1489)
Nō *la* 能 1397.（生 214, 能 1397, 納 1685, 農 2205, 濃 2612）
Nōami *ma* 能阿弥 1397
Nobata *s* 野畑 1398
Nobayashi *s* 野林
Nobe *s* 野辺, 野部
Nobehara *s* 延原 739
Nobeji *sp* 野辺地 1398
Nobeoka *p* 延岡 739
Nobeta *s* 野辺田 1398
Nobeyama *s* 延山 739
Nobi *l* 野火 1398
Nobiru *m* 伸 353
Nobori *s* 野堀 1398；*sm* 昇 713, 登 1744；*m* 升 113
Noboribetsu *p* 登別 1744 「曙夢 713
Nobori Shomu *ml* 昇
Noborizaka *s* 登坂 1744
Noboru *sm* 登；*m* 上 47, 升 113, 卉 151, 聿 332, 伸 353, 舛 367, 昇 713, 昂 943, 陞 1057, 陞 1307, 陟 1309, 昇 1352, 豊 2013, 徳 2063, 嶝 2466, 暹 2593, 襄 2769, 騰 2867, 躋 2950
Nobu *s* 延生 739；*m* 伸 353；*f* 乃武 27, 声 465, 鋪 2340；*p* 延 739.（一 3, 之 24, 円 78, 内 81, 文 86, 山 89, 尹 98, 与 101, 収 133, 引 144, 永 149, 布 170, 申 185, 正 205, 允 217, 休 233, 江 252, 列 257, 亘 262, 同 298, 存 313, 互 317, 聿 332, 伸 353, 伝 359, 別 435, 言 439, 孚 483, 序 507, 応 509, 更 528, 寿 539, 身 546, 彼 578, 所 600, 房 658, 命 671, 宜 675, 辰 738, 延 739, 述 748, 信 782, 衍 786, 恂 807, 恒 809, 洵 815, 治 825, 施 831, 政 881, 叙 893, 宣 919, 長 939, 発 953, 昶 1004, 度 1009, 禹 1015, 重 1017, 修 1038, 将 1040, 悦 1054, 訒 1147, 昆 1195, 書 1216, 席 1242, 翅 1248, 脩 1281, 惟 1290, 堆 1295, 陳 1311, 振 1320, 移 1378, 設 1401, 寅 1439, 常 1463, 曹 1479, 啓 1491, 展 1501, 進 1503, 庸 1507, 順 1532, 備 1539, 揚 1551, 舒 1673, 散 1689, 敦 1690, 喜 1709, 董 1731, 喬 1775, 達 1810, 淵 1858, 殖 1867, 暄 1881, 睦 1904, 靖 1905, 雄 1911, 誠 1935, 純 1956, 寛 1977, 葉 1991, 羡 2010, 業 2024, 照 2035, 演 2079, 暢 2111, 頌 2113, 説 2143, 播 2258, 誕 2319, 諄 2324, 鋪 2340, 敷 2355, 遵 2418, 選 2419, 謀 2509, 綽 2529, 劉 2554, 養 2558, 薫 2567, 震 2577, 整 2581, 諶 2641, 緩 2659, 総 2662, 薦 2683, 繹 2924, 櫟 2963, 矗 3017）
Nobuaki *m* 伸顕 353, 信映 782, 信秋, 信卿, 信徴, 信璋, 信顕, 宣明 919, 誠明 1935
Nobuakira *m* 信旭 782, 信陽 「篤
Nobuatsu *m* 信厚, 信
Nobuchika *m* 信親
Nobue *f* 信朶, 順恵 1532
Nobufumi *m* 信文 782
Nobuhara *s* 信原
Nobuharu *m* 信元, 信霽, 陳令 1311 「信愛
Nobuhide *m* 信秀 782,
Nobuhiko *m* 宜彦 675
Nobuhira *s* 陽平 1567；*m* 江平 252, 信枚 782, 叙衡 893
Nobuhiro *m* 円裕 78, 信弘 782, 信昊, 信淵, 喜光 1709
Nobuhisa *m* 信古 782, 悦久 1054
Nobuhito *m* 信民 782
Nobui *m* 鋪猪 2340
Nobuichi *m* 信一 782
Nobuie *m* 信舎, 宣家 919
Nobuji *m* 申二 185, 信二 782, 信治
Nobujirō *m* 伸次郎 353
Nobuka *m* 延香 739
Nobukado *m* 信圭 782
Nobukage *m* 信景
Nobukane *m* 信包
Nobukata *m* 信方, 信形, 信賢, 喜堅 1709
Nobukatsu *m* 信勝 782
Nobukazu *m* 信十, 信紀, 宣算 919, 喜雄 1709, 暢籌 2111
Nobuki *s* 信木 782
Nobukichi *m* 延吉 739
Nobukiyo *m* 信心 782, 信磬
Nobuko *f* 允子 217, 亘子 262, 存子 313, 聿子 332, 更子 528, 命子 671, 延子 739, 述子 748, 信子 782, 衍子 786, 恂子 807, 宣子 919, 禹子 1015, 陳子 1311, 舒子 1673, 遵子 2418, 綽子 2529, 櫟子 2963；*f-l* 伸子 353
Nobukoto *m* 信思 782, 進士 1503, 喬言 1775
Nobukuni *s* 信国 782
Nobukura *m* 信蔵
Nobumachi *m* 信市
Nobumasa *m* 延全 739, 信真 782, 宣順 919, 禹昌 1015, 順正 1532, 誠内 1935
Nobumasu *m* 信賢 782, 述史 748
Nobumichi *m* 信享 782, 信学, 信達, 養道 2558
Nobumitsu *m* 信光 782, 舒光 1673
Nobumori *m* 洵盛 815
Nobumoto *m* 信泉 782, 信意
Nobumune *m* 信意
Nobunaga *m* 信亨；*mh* 信長
Nobunaka *m* 養仲 2558
Nobunao *m* 述直 748
Nobunari *m* 惟規 1290
Nobunaru *m* 伸愛 353
Nobunori *m* 信意 782, 信誉, 信業, 信愛, 惟規 1290
Nobuo *m* 伸雄 353, 言夫 439, 信夫 782, 信尾, 信郎, 信雄, 宣力 919, 修男 1038, 脩夫 1281, 陳雄 1311, 展男 1501, 殖穂 1867, 暢夫 2111, 説男 2143
Nobuoka *s* 信岡 782
Nobuoki *m* 信発, 信恩, 誠業 1935
Noburu *m* 伸 353, 辰 738, 延 739, 述 748, 信 782, 宣 919, 直 988, 陳

1311, 舒 1673, 暢 2111, 攄 2713
Nobusada *m* 孚貞 483, 諶貞 2641
Nobusane *m* 延信 739, 信志 782, 信愛
Nobusato *m* 信睿
Nobusawa *s* 信沢
Nobushige *m* 信重, 信蕃 「資, 信輔
Nobusuke *m* 信介, 信
Nobusumi *m* 宣維 919
Nobutada *m* 信尹 782, 信忠, 宣一 919
Nobutaka *m* 布高 170, 信公 782, 信孝, 信阜, 信宝, 信高, 信堅, 信賢
Nobutake *m* 信兕
Nobutane *m* 脩胤 1281, 靖胤 1905
Nobutarō *m* 延太郎 739, 信太郎 782
Nobuteru *m* 昶光 1004, 矗昶 3017
Nobutō *m* 信任 782
Nobutoki *m* 延秋 739, 信祝 782
Nobutomi *m* 喜福 1709
Nobutomo *ml* 信友 782
Nobutsugu *m* 允承 217, 信次 782, 信伝, 信緝, 宣次 919
Nobutsuka *m* 信策 782
Nobutsuna *m* 信綱, 宣維 919, 鋪綱 2340
Nobutsune *m* 信恒 782, 信常
Nobutsura *m* 信享, 信頬, 信綿, 信離
Nobuwaka *m* 信稚
Nobuya *m* 信也
Nobuyasu *m* 信愷
Nobuyo *m* 信節
Nobuyori *m* 信凭, 信随, 信頼
Nobuyoshi *m* 与良 101, 伝義 359, 房喜 658, 辰由 738, 信可 782, 信好, 信良, 信弥, 信祝, 信美, 信雄, 信義, 信嘉, 信慶, 宣嘉 919, 順良 1532
Nobuyuki *m* 亘行 262, 延子 739, 信之 782, 信行, 信順, 進行 1503, 順之 1532

Nobuzane *ml* 信実 782
Nobuzō *m* 寅造 1439
Nochi *s* 野地 1398. (后 304, 後 1300, 終 1950)
Nochinari *m* 後生 1300
Noda *sp* 野田 1398
Nodagawa *p* 野田川
Nodani *s* 野谷
Node *s* 野出
Nodehara *s* 勝木原 1613
Nodera *s* 野寺 1398
Nodoka *m* 和 638, 温 ⌊1585
Noe *f* 乃枝 27
Noga *s* 野賀 1398
Nōgaku *la* 能楽 1397
Nogami *sp* 野上 1398
~ Toyoichirō *ml* 野上豊一郎 「子
~ Yaeko *fl* 野上弥生
Nōgata *sp* 直方 988
Nogawa *s* 能川 1397, 野川 1398
Nōge *s* 直下 988
Nogi *s* 乃木 27, 乗木 1016; *sp* 野木 1398; *p* 能義 1397. (禾 220)
Nogiko *f* 乃木子 27
Nogi Maresuke *mh* 乃木希典
Nogimaro *m* 禾麿 220
Nogiwa *s* 野際 1398
Noguchi *s* 野口 「世
~ Hideyo *mh* 野口英
~ Neisai *ml* 野口寧斎
~ Ujō *ml* 野口雨情
~ Yonejirō *ml* 野口米 ⌊次郎
Nohagi *s* 野萩
Nohara *s* 野原
Nohata *s* 野畑
Nohira *s* 野平
Noi *s* 野井
Noichi *p* 野市
Nōin *ml* 能因 1397
~ Hōshi shū *l* 能因法師集 「枕
~ utamakura *l* 能因歌
Noiri *s* 野扒 1398
Noishiki *s* 野一色
Noji *s* 野路
Nojima *s* 能島 1397, 野島 1398
Nojiri *sp* 野尻
Nojiriko *p* 野尻湖
Nojō *s* 野条
Nōka *s* 苗鹿 685
Nokari *m* 野雁 1398
Nokariya *s* 野苅家

(noki 宇 285, 除 1059, 退 1236A)
Nokiai *m* 宇合 285
Nokita *s* 野北 1398
Noma *s* 野馬野間
Nomaguchi *s* 野間口
Noma Hiroshi *ml* 野間宏
~ Seiji *ml* 野間清治
Nōme *s* 納米 1685
Nomi *s* 乃美 27, 能見 1397, 野見 1398, 野宝; *sp* 能美 1397. (呑 489)
Nomitsu *s* 野満 1398
Nomiya *s* 野宮
Nomiyama *s* 野見山
~ Asuka *ml* 野見山朱鳥
Nomiyoshi *m* 呑義 489
Nomizo *s* 野溝 1398
Nomizu *s* 野水
Nomori *la* 野守
Nomoto *s* 野元, 野本
Nomozaki *p* 野母崎
Nomura *s* 能村 1397; *sp* 野村 1398 「泊月
~ Hakugetsu *ml* 野村
~ Kichisaburō *mh* 野村吉三郎
~ Kodō *ml* 野村胡堂
~ Shurindō *ml* 野村朱鱗洞 「畔
~ Waihan *ml* 野村隈
~ Yoshiya *ml* 野村吉 ⌊哉
(non 嫩 2279)
Nonagase *s* 野長瀬 1398
Nonaka *s* 野中
Nonami *s* 野波
None *s* 野根
Nonki megane *l* 暢気眼鏡 2111
Nono *s* 乃野 27
Nōno *s* 南野 912
Nonoe *s* 野於 1398
Nonogaki *s* 野野垣
Nonoguchi *s* 野々口, 野野口 「圃
~ Ryūho *ml* 野々口立
Nonoichi *p* 野野市
Nonomiya *s* 野野宮; *sla* 野宮 「野野村
Nonomura *s* 野々村,
~ Ninsei *ma* 野々村仁清 「宗達
~ Sōtatsu *ma* 野々村
Nonoyama *s* 野野山
Nori *s* 告 490; *m* 儀 2255. (丁 8, 了 9, 寸 34, 工 39, 士 41, 土 42, 化 56, 仁 57, 父 65, 中 75, 日 76, 卞 84, 方 85, 文 86, 升 113, 代 125, 以 134, 功 135, 礼 146, 永 149, 令 155, 仙 228, 任 235, 行 245, 刑 258, 式 306, 成 322, 曲 327, 舟 339, 似 350, 位 354, 伝 359, 伯 363, 状 365A, 阩 373, 利 436, 言 439, 肖 451, 至 485, 児 497, 図 502, 応 509, 里 517, 玄 522, 甫 533, 考 540, 孝 541, 明 623, 知 636, 劾 653, 制 656, 命 671, 官 672, 実 678, 芸 689, 忠 705, 昇 713, 学 719, 典 733, 周 736, 述 748, 律 787, 法 824, 珍 836, 祖 850, 祝 851, 政 881, 軌 892, 則 902, 品 916, 宣 919, 発 953, 背 957, 度 1009, 乗 1016, 准 1023, 倫 1037, 修 1038, 悟 1053, 陞 1057, 格 1099, 矩 1108, 称 1118, 祇 1127, 師 1130, 訓 1148, 記 1149, 益 1201, 恭 1205, 書 1216, 哲 1227, 威 1251, 得 1299, 後 1300, 陛 1307, 険 1308, 陳 1311, 視 1348, 規 1349, 理 1361, 能 1397, 致 1407, 教 1408, 紀 1424, 剰 1426, 章 1461, 恕 1483, 啓 1491, 基 1493, 庸 1507, 順 1532, 御 1572, 勝 1613, 程 1641, 詔 1658, 詞 1665, 斯 1670, 期 1671, 朝 1672, 納 1685, 敬 1691, 馭 1697, 勤 1698, 勘 1699, 尋 1705, 登 1744, 賀 1756, 象 1761, 然 1788, 智 1793, 堯 1795, 道 1811, 摸 1836, 慎 1839, 卿 1865, 雄 1912, 雅 1913, 稚 1914, 詮 1934, 誠 1935, 経 1957, 献 1962, 義 1975, 寛 1977, 意 2007, 誉 2010, 愛 2018, 業 2024, 憲 2033, 率 2040, 準 2041, 載 2050, 像 2061, 徳 2063, 僅 2069, 弼 2092, 楷 2098, 模 2104,

郷 2112, 詁 2140, 銓 2156, 数 2169, 節 2215, 儀 2255, 権 2300, 糊 2309, 論 2320, 統 2333, 毅 2351, 範 2384, 製 2388, 鞏 2393, 慰 2404, 熙 2409, 慶 2425, 稽 2491, 頼 2506, 緑 2535, 憲 2562, 賢 2579, 暹 2593, 幾 2597, 擬 2604, 謨 2638, 講 2644, 謹 2645, 謙 2646, 鵠 2739, 騎 2762, 識 2810, 續 2814, 機 2869, 議 2876, 彝 2909, 讓 2918, 彝 2943, 躋 2950, 縄 2955, 鑑 2968, 霽 2978, 鑾 2982)
Noriaki *m* 伯明 363, 孝顕 541, 経明 1957, 憲顕 2562
Noriakira *m* 文信 86
Noribumi *m* 則録 902, 勘文 1699
Norichika *m* 哲哉 1227
Norie *m* 雅英 1913; *f* 倫枝 1037, 鑾江 2982
Norifuji *m* 憲藤 2562
Norifumi *m* 則文 902
Norifusa *m* 周房 736, 銓総 2156
Noriharu *m* 堯治 1795
Norihide *m* 軌秀 892, 慎英 1839 「則彦 902
Norihiko *m* 位彦 354,
Norihiro *m* 仙弘 228, 納寛 1685, 経裕 1957
Norihisa *m* 了久 9, 典寿 733, 記久 1149
Norikage *m* 憲陰 2562
Norikane *m* 代包 125, 則兼 902, 教兼 1408, 徳包 2063
Norikaze *m* 御風 1572
Norikazu *m* 乗寿 1016, 模一 2104, 範一 2384, 謙和 2646
Noriki *s* 法木 824
Norikiyo *m* 則清 902, 規清 1349
Noriko *f* 式子 306, 命子 671, 法子 824, 祝子 851, 准子 1023, 格子 1099, 祇子 1127, 教子 1408, 賀子 1756, 義子 1975, 楷子 2098, 模子 2104, 儀子 2255, 範子 2384
Norikuni *m* 教邦 1408, 順域 1532
Norimasa *m* 宜政 919, 度正 1009, 徳全 2063, 謙昌 2646
Norimi *m* 章甫 1461
Norimichi *m* 敬道 1691
Norimitsu *m* 知満 636, 則光 902, 紀光 1424, 敬光 1691
Norimochi *m* 教用 1408
Norimori *m* 乗蘊 1016
Norimoto *m* 礼本 146
Norimune *m* 則宗 902, 範宗 2384
Norinaga *m* 宣長 919, 義良 1975
Norinao *m* 礼直 146
Norinari *m* 徳業 2063, 熙成 2409
Norinobu *m* 教翅 1408
Norio *m* 功男 135, 典夫 733, 律夫 787, 則雄 902, 師男 1130, 恕郎 1483, 順雄 1532, 智夫 1793, 節雄 2215, 権士 2300, 範夫 2384
Norisada *m* 紀貞 1424
Norisane *m* 則心 902
Norisato *m* 宣諭 919, 儀達 2255, 統閭 2333
Norishige *m* 周重 736, 法茂 824, 則蕘 902, 紀成 1424, 経義 1957, 業繁 2024, 憲重 2562
Norishiro *m* 応代 509
Norisue *m* 孝季 541, 乗杉 1016
Norisuke *m* 憲相 2562
Noritada *m* 乗紀 1016, 義忠 1975, 意忠 2007, 範規 2384
Noritaka *m* 明幸 623, 教尚 1408, 徳仰 2063
Noritake *s* 乗竹 1016; *m* 則武 902
Noritane *m* 式胤 306
Noritarō *m* 祝太郎 851
Noriteru *m* 則耀 902, 惠輝 2033 「祝詞 851
Norito *m* 準人 2041; *l*
Noritoshi *m* 乗命 1016
Noritsugu *m* 矩次 1108, 徳次 2063 「1016
Noritsuhiko *m* 乗津彦
Noritsuke *m* 乗付
Noritsuna *m* 乗統
Noritsune *m* 宣経 919, 乗秩 1016, 訓常 1148, 規矩 1349
Noriumi *m* 徳海 2063
Noriyasu *m* 製保 2388
Noriyo *f* 至世 485
Noriyori *m* 阡尚 373, 得道 1299, 範頼 2384
Noriyoshi *m* 則瓊 902, 矩最 1108, 哲致 1227, 致美 1407, 登美 1744, 節義 2215, 儀義 2255, 頼誼 2506, 憲欽 2562, 憲福
Noriyuki *m* 言志 439, 則来 902, 矩随 1108, 記之 1149, 視之 1348, 敬礼 1691
Norizane *m* 徳真 2063
Norizō *m* 基三 1493
Noro *s* 野呂 1398
～ Genjō *mh* 野呂元丈
Noromatsu *s* 野呂松
(noru 宜 675) 「野栄
Nosaka *s* 野坂 1398; *p*
Nōsakusho *l* 能作書
Nosawa *s* 能沢 ⌊1397
Nose *s* 能世, 能瀬, 野瀬 1398; *sp* 能勢 1397
Nosedani *s* 野世渓 1398
Nosegawa *sp* 野迫川
Noshichiri *s* 野七里
Noshiro *s* 野城; *p* 能代 1397
Nōso *s* 納所 1685
Nōsu *s* 野生司 1398
Notari *m* 野足
Noto *s* 能任 1397; *p* 能都, 能登
Notogawa *p* 能登川
Notojima *p* 能登島
Notomi *s* 納富 1685
Notoya *s* 能登屋 1397
Notsu *sp* 野津 1398
Notsuhara *p* 野津原
Nou *s* 能生 1397
Nouchi *s* 野内 1398
Nowaki *l* 野分
Noya *s* 野矢
Noyama *s* 野山
Noyasu *s* 野安
Noyo *s* 野与
Noyori *s* 野与, 野依
Noyuri *f* 野百合
Nozaka *s* 野坂
Nozaki *s* 野崎
～ Sabun *ml* 野崎左文
Nozarashi kikō *l* 野晒紀行
Nozashi *s* 野条
Nozato *s* 野里
Nozawa *sp* 野沢
Nozoe *s* 野副
Nozoki *s* 及位 83, 莅戸 1174. (莅)
Nozokido *s* 莅戸
Nozomu *m* 望 1777
Nozu *s* 能津 1397, 野津
Nozue *s* 野末 ⌊1398
Nozuka *s* 野塚
(nu 奴 256, 沼 595, 怒 1222, 野 1398, 渟 1580)
Nuda *s* 奴田 256
Nudachi *s* 月出里 80
(nude 椦 2478A)
Nudejima *sp* 椦島
Nue *la* 鵺 2818
Nuekako *s* 水主 54
(nui 縫 2746, 繡 2954)
Nuigawa *s* 縫川 2746
Nuiji *m* 縫二
Nuiko *f* 縫子, 繡子 2954
Nuka *s* 奴可 256, 額 2756. (各 277, 糠 2633, 額 2756)
Nukada *sp* 額田
Nukadabe *s* 額田部
Nukada no Ōkimi *fl* 額田王 「六福
～ Roppuku *ml* 額田
Nukaga *s* 額賀
Nukagawa *s* 額川
Nukako *f* 糠子 2633
Nukamushi *m* 糠虫
Nukanobu *s* 糠信
Nukariya *s* 奴借屋 256, 忽滑谷 704, 怒借屋 1222
Nukaruya *s* 忽滑谷 704
Nukata *s* 各田 277
Nukatabe *s* 各田部
(nuke 抜 384)
Nukegara *l* 抜殼
Nuki *s* 札 145, 貫 1754. (抜 384, 枌 624, 貫 1754)
Nukii *s* 貫井
Nukike no Futokubi *ml* 抜気太首 384
Nukima *s* 飽間 2165
Nukina *s* 貫名 1754
Nukita *s* 枌田 624
Nukiyama *s* 抜山 384
Nukui *s* 温 1585, 温井, 貫井 1754

Nukumi *s* 温 1585
Numa *s* 沼 595, 沼間. (沼)
Numabatake *s* 沼畠
Numabe *s* 沼部
Numachi *s* 沼知
Numagami *s* 沼上
Numaguchi *s* 沼口
Numai *s* 沼井
Numajima *s* 沼島
Numajiri *s* 沼尻
Numako *f* 沼子
Numakuma *p* 沼隅
Numakura *s* 沼倉
Numamoto *s* 沼本
Numanami *s* 沼波, 沼浪
Numano *s* 沼野
Numao *s* 沼尾
Numasaki *s* 沼前
Numata *sp* 沼田
Numazaki *s* 沼崎
Numazawa *s* 沼沢
Numazu *sp* 沼津
(nume 絖 2147)
Numeko *f* 絖子
(nuna 渟 1580)
Nunami *s* 沼波 595
～ Keion *ml* 沼波瓊音
Nunawa *m* 蓴 2187
(nuno 布 170)
Nunoda *s* 布田
Nunogami *s* 布上
Nunokawa *s* 布川
Nunoko *f* 布子
Nunome *s* 布目
Nunomura *s* 布村
Nunose *s* 布忍
Nunoshi *s* 布忍, 布師
Nunoshita *s* 布師田
Nunoya *s* 布屋
Nuri *s* 泥 594, 漆 2087. (泥 594, 漆 2087)
Nuribe *s* 漆部
Nurihe *s* 泥戸 594
Nurishima *s* 漆島 2087
(nuru 沃 396)
Nurube *s* 漆部 2087
Nuruhi *s* 垂氷 761
Nurutō *s* 奴留湯 256
Nuruya *s* 怒留湯 1222
Nusa *s* 札 145. (麻 1508, 幣 2414)
Nusakazu *m* 幣一
Nusao *m* 麻男 1508
(nushi 主 196)
Nushida *s* 主田
Nushimori *m* 主守
Nushitani *s* 塗師谷 2038
Nutari *s* 沼垂 595, 渟足 1580
Nuttari *sp* 沼垂 595
(nyaku 若 692, 楉 1622)
Nyakuichi *l* 若市 692
(nyo 女 114, 汝 394, 如 412, 茹 1171)
(nyō 女 114, 仍 123, 茸 925, 穣 2802, 譲 2918, 饒 2925)
Nyogan *ml* 如願 412
～ Hōshi shū *l* 如願法師集
Nyoirin Kannon *fh* 如意輪観音
Nyōmura *s* 饒村 2925
Nyonin geijutsu *l* 女人芸術 114
(nyu 紐 1682, 儒 2432, 穠 2803)
Nyū *sp* 丹生 79. (入 15, 乳 657)
Nyūbe *s* 入部 15
Nyūgawa *p* 丹生川 79, 壬生川 116
Nyūhito *s* 丹人 79
Nyūi *s* 乳井 657
Nyūjiirando *p* "New Zealand" 新西蘭 1965
Nyūnoya *s* 入野屋 15
Nyūyōku *p* "New York" 紐育 1682
Nyūzen *sp* 入善 15

# O

O *s* 呼唹 571. (小 21, 凡 37, 士 41, 大 48, 日 76, 方 85, 少 88, 夫 104, 生 214, 丘 219, 乎 221, 壮 243, 百 265, 広 316, 男 495, 尾 505, 於 607, 房 658, 矣 665, 良 767, 偶 772, 保 781, 勇 908, 表 914, 音 962, 彦 1007, 即 1145, 家 1185, 烏 1256, 隆 1313, 済 1336, 弦 1345, 峰 1351, 魚 1485, 麻 1508, 陽 1567, 御 1572, 報 1667, 雄 1912, 飫 1963, 寛 1977, 意 2007, 越 2052, 節 2215, 穂 2308, 絃 2331, 緒 2537, 饒 2925, 巌 2936)
Ō *s* 大 48, 王 90, 太 105, 生 214, 多 347, 呼唹 571, 音太 962, 飫富 1963, 飯富 1964, 意富 2007. (凡 37, 王 90, 太 105, 功 135, 公 156, 央 182, 巨 199, 生 214, 多 347, 伯 363, 均 387, 汾 397, 汪 401, 弘 410, 邑 460, 応 509, 臣 527, 往 579, 押 587, 泱 589, 旺 620, 迋 749, 洪 811, 胖 843, 相 868, 皇 964, 姶 1091, 秧 1114, 淡 1340, 桜 1373, 朗 1394, 翁 1430, 黄 1499, 逢 1516, 惶 1545, 奥 1798, 煌 1877, 鉅 1946, 媼 2089, 碩 2116, 蓊 2189, 横 2301, 篁 2382, 澳 2459, 嫗 2474, 鴨 2489, 諺 2508, 膺 2705, 艶 2833, 鶯 2940, 鷗 2975, 鷹 2995, 鸚 3021)
Oake *s* 緒明 2537
Ōakinai hiru ga Kojima *la* 大商蛭小島 48
Ōaku *s* 大阿久
Oama *sp* 小天 21
Ōama *s* 大甘 48; *mh* 大海人; *f* 大海
Ōami *sp* 大網
～ Shirasato *p* 大網白里
Ōan 1368–75 応安 509
Oana *s* 小穴 21
Ōan shinshiki *l* 応安新式 509
Ōarai *p* 大洗 48
Ōaraki *s* 大荒木, 邑楽 460
Ōasa *s* 大麻 48; *sp* 大朝
Ōasha *p* 大麻
(oba 姨 1357)
Ōba *s* 大羽 48, 大庭, 大場, 大峡
Oba ga sake *la* 伯母ケ酒 363
Ōba Hakusuirō *ml* 大場白水郎 48
～ Kakō *ml* 大場柯公
Obama *s* 小汀 21; *p* 小浜 505
Obanazawa *p* 尾花沢
Obara *sp* 小原 21
Obase *s* 小場瀬
～ Takuzō *ml* 小場瀬卓三
Obasute *la* 伯母捨 363, 姨捨 1357
Obata *s* 小畑 21, 小墾田, 小畠, 小幡, 小籏, 尾畑 505; *p* 小俣 21
Obatake *s* 小畠
Ōbatake *sp* 大畠 48
Obayashi *s* 尾林 505
Ōbayashi *s* 大林 48
Obe *s* 凡部 37
Ōbe *s* 大辺 48, 太部 105, 生部 214
Obi *s* 小尾 21. (帯 1192)
Obihiro *p* 帯広
Obikane *s* 帯包, 帯金
Obikawa *s* 及川 83
Obiko *f* 帯子 1192
Obinata *s* 帯刀
Obira *p* 小平 21
Obito *sm* 首 920; *m* 丘人 219. (首 920)
Obitomaro *m* 首麿
Obitona *m* 首名
Obitsu *p* 小櫃 21
Obiya *s* 帯谷 1192
Obokata *s* 小保方 21
Obonai *s* 小保内
Ōbori *s* 大堀 48
Ōboshi *s* 大星
Obu *s* 飫富 1963
Ōbu *s* 大生 48; *p* 大府
Obuchi *s* 小淵 21
Ōbuchi *s* 大淵 48
Obuse *sp* 小布施 21
Obusuma *s* 男衾 495
Obuto *sm* 首 920
Ochi *s* 小知 21, 邑智 460, 租地 1116, 越智 2052; *sp* 越知; *p* 隠地 2074. (日 76, 落 1733, 越 2052, 鉞 2157)
Ōchi *sp* 大内 48, 大市;

*m* 邑珍 460; *p* 邑智, 相知 868
Ochiai *sp* 落合 1733
~ Naobumi *ml* 落合直文
Ochiba *la* 落葉
Ochibito *m* 乎知人 221, 越智人 2052
Ochiburui *s* 十二仏 18, 十二仙, 十二神, 十二神島 「越人 2052
Ochi Etsujin *ml* 越智
Ochigori *s* 月日 80
Ochikubo *l* 落窪 1733
Ochimi *m* 落実
Ōchita *s* 道田 1811
Ōchō 1311–12 応長 509
Ōchoku *mh* 王直 90
Oda *s* 尾田 505, 緒田 2537, 織田 2879; *sm* 於田 607; *sp* 小田 21
Ōdabira *s* 太平 105
Ōdachi *s* 大達 48, 大館
Odagaki *s* 小田垣 21
Odagawa *s* 小田川
Odagiri *s* 小田切, 小田桐 「雄
~ Hideo *ml* 小田切秀
Odai *s* 小田井, 尾台 505
Ōdai *p* 大台 48
Odaira *s* 小平 21
Ōdaira *s* 大平 48
Odajima *s* 小田島 21
Oda Jun'ichirō *ml* 織田純一郎 2879
Odaka *sp* 小高 21
Ōdaka *sp* 大高 48
Oda Kankei *ml* 小田観螢 21
Odaki *s* 小田木, 小田切, 小滝
Odakura *s* 小田倉
Oda Masanobu *ml* 織田正信 2879
Odamura *s* 小田村 21
Odanaka *s* 小田中
Odani *s* 男谷 495
Odano *s* 小田野 21
Oda Nobunaga *mh* 織田信長 2879
~ Sakunosuke *ml* 織田作之助
Odasuku *s* 小助 21
Oda Takeo *ml* 小田嶽夫 「*sp* 大館
Ōdate *s* 大立 48, 大達;
Odatori *s* 小田鳥 21
Odawara *sp* 小田原
Odera *s* 小寺, 尾寺 505
Ōdera *s* 大寺 48
Ōdō *s* 応堂 509
(odoke 諢 2511)
Odoke-banashi ukiyo-buro *l* 諢話浮世風呂
Odori *s* 踊 2132
Odoro *s* 行行林 245
Odorobayashi *p* 行行林
Oe *s* 小江 21, 麻生 1508, 麻殖, 雄家 1912; *p* 麻植 1508
Ōe *s* 大声 48; *sp* 大江
Ōeda *s* 大江田, 大条, 大枝
Ōei 1394–1428 応永 509
Ōe Kenzaburō *ml* 大江健三郎 48
Ōemaru *ml* 大江丸
Ōe Mitsuo *ml* 大江満雄 「江朝綱
~ no Asatsuna *ml* 大
~ no Hiromoto *mh* 大江広元 「江匡房
~ no Masafusa *ml* 大
~ Ryōtarō *ml* 大江良太郎
Ōeyama *la* 大江山
Ōfuji *s* 大藤
Ōfuke *s* 大更
Ōfunato *sp* 大船渡
Ōfusa *s* 大房
Ofuta *s* 竹蓋 247
Oga *p* 男鹿 495
Ōga *s* 大神 48, 大賀, 大鋸; *sp* 相賀 868
Ogachi *p* 雄勝 1912
Ōgai *s* 大貝 48, 大萱; *ml* 鷗外 2975
Ōgaito *s* 大垣 48
Ōgaki *sp* 大垣, 大柿
Ogami *s* 尾上 505
Ōgane *s* 大金 48, 大兼, 大鐘
Ogano *s* 小彼 21, 小賀野; *sp* 小鹿野
Ogara *s* 麻柄 1508
Ogasa *sp* 小笠 21
Ogasawara *sp* 小笠原
Ōgashira *s* 大頭 48
Ogata *s* 小方 21, 尾方 505, 尾形, 緒形 2537; *sp* 緒方
Ōgata *s* 大形 48, 生形 214; *p* 大方 48, 大潟
Ogata Kamenosuke *ml* 尾形亀之助 505
~ Kenzan *ma* 尾形乾山 「2537
~ Kōan *mh* 緒方洪庵
~ Kōrin *ma* 尾形光林 505
Ogawa *s* 小河 21, 尾川 505; *sp* 小川 21; *p* 緒川 2537 「21
~ Mimei *ml* 小川未明
Ogawara *s* 小河原
Ogaya *s* 大鋸屋 48
Ogi *s* 尾木 505; *sp* 小木 21, 小城, 荻 1176. (荻)
Ōgi *sp* 正親 205. (扇
Ōgiba *s* 扇迫 ⌊1156)
Ōgida *s* 扇田
Ogie *sf* 荻江 1176
Ōgigayatsu *s* 扇谷 1156
Ogiko *f* 荻子 1176
Ōgihata *s* 扇畑 1156
~ Tadao *ml* 扇畑忠雄
Ōgihazama *s* 扇迫
Ōgiku *s* 大菊 48
Ogikubo *s* 荻久保 1176; *p* 荻窪 「205
Ōgimachi *smh* 正親町
~ Kinkazu *ml* 正親町公和
Ogimi *f* 雄君 1912
Ōgimi *s* 大儀見 48
Ogimura *s* 荻村 1176
Ōgin *s* 往岸 579
Ogino *s* 荻野 1176
Oginuma *s* 荻沼
Ogishima *s* 荻島
Ōgishō *l* 奥義抄 1798
Ogiso *s* 小木曾 21
Ogisu *s* 荻須 1176
Ogita *s* 荻田
Ogiwara *s* 荻原
~ Seisensui *ml* 荻原井泉水 「重秀
~ Shigehide *mh* 荻原
Ogiya *s* 荻谷
Ōgiya *s* 扇谷 1156
Ogiyama *s* 荻山 1176
Ogō *s* 小江 21
Ōgo *s* 大湖 48; *sp* 大胡
Ōgoe *sp* 大越
Ogōri *p* 小郡 21
Ogose *sp* 越生 2052
Ogoshi *s* 生越 214
Ōgoshi *s* 大越 48, 大腰
Ōgosho *mh* 大御所
Oguchi *s* 小口 21
Ōguchi *sm-p* 大口 48
Oguma *sp* 小熊 21
~ Hideo *ml* 小熊秀雄
Oguni *sp* 小国
Ogura *s* 小倉, 巨椋 199; *sp* 小椋 21
~ hyakunin isshu *l* 小倉百人一首
Oguri *s* 小栗
Ōguri *s* 大栗 48 「葉 21
Oguri Fūyō *ml* 小栗風
~ Hangan *l* 小栗判官
Oguro *s* 小黒 「呂
Oguromaro *m* 小黒麻
Ogurusu *sp* 小栗栖
Ōgusa *s* 大日 48, 大草
Ogushi *s* 小串 21
Ogusu *s* 小楠 「1176
Ogyū *s* 大給 48, 荻生
~ Sorai *mlh* 荻生徂来
Ohama *s* 小浜 21
Ōhama *sp* 大浜 48
Ohana *s* 小花 21, 尾花 505 「21, 大原 48
Ohara *s* 尾原; *sp* 小原
Ōhara *sp* 大原 「幸
Ohara gokō *la* 大原御
Ōharai no kotoba go-shaku *l* 大祓詞後釈
Ōhara Tomie *fl* 大原富枝 「学
~ Yūgaku *mh* 大原幽
Ōhari *s* 大針
Oharida *s* 小治田 21, 小墾田 「治
Ōharu *s* 大春 48; *sp* 大
Ohasama *s* 小馬 21
Ōhasama *sp* 大迫 48
Ohase *s* 小谷 21, 小泊瀬, 小長, 小長谷
Ohasebe *s* 小長谷部
Ōhashi *s* 大橋 48
~ Junzō *mh* 大橋順蔵
~ Matsuhei *ml* 大橋松平
~ Otowa *ml* 大橋乙羽
Ōhata *s* 大畠; *sp* 大畑
Ohayashi *s* 小林 21
Ōhazama *s* 大峡 48
Ōhi *s* 大日; *m* 大火
Ōhibiki *s* 大響
Ōhigashi *sp* 大東
Ōhigata *s* 大日方
Ōhimatsuri *s* 大日奉
Ohinata *s* 小向田 21
Ōhinata *s* 大日方 48, 大日南

Ōhira *sm-p* 大平; *sp* 大衡
Ōhisa *p* 大久
Ōhisu *s* 大日子 48
Ōhito *s* 首 912; *sp* 大仁
Ohitsu *s* 小櫃 21
Ōhitsuji *s* 大羊 48
Oho *s* 於保 607
Ōho *s* 大保 48; *sp* 大穂
Ōhō 1161-63 応保 509
Ohoma *s* 小補摩 21
Ōhori *s* 大堀 48
Oi *m* 老 334; *l* 笈 1208. (大 48, 辺 179, 生 214, 老 334, 負 981, 追 993, 笈 1208, 猊 1302, 狼 1303, 翁 1430)
Ōi *s* 多 347, 於 607; *sm* 大炊 48; *sp* 大井; *m* 壬 116, 浩 1068, 偉 1535; *p* 大飯 48. (大)
Oiba *s* 染葉 968
Oibe *s* 及部 83
Ōichi *sm* 大市 48
Oida *s* 老田 334, 笈田 1208
Oide *s* 生出 214
Ōide *s* 大出 48
Oie *f* 老江 334
Ōie *s* 大家 48
Oie-ryū *la* 御家流 1572
Ōigawa *p* 大井川 48
Ōi Hiroshi *ml* 大井広
~ Hirosuke *ml* 大井広介
Oiji *s* 生地 214
Ōikaihitōmo *s* 大猪甘人面 48
Oikata *s* 大日方
Oikawa *s* 及川 83, 生川 214, 老川 334, 追川 993, 笈川 1208
Oike *s* 尾池 505
Ōike *s* 大池 48
Ōi Kentarō *mh* 大井憲太郎
Oikoshi *s* 生越 214
Oimaro *m* 老麻呂 334
Oimatsu *la* 老松
Oimi *s* 生実 214
Ōimikado *s* 大炊御門 48
Oinata *s* 小日向 21
Oine *m* 大兄 48
Oi no kobumi *l* 笈の小文 1208
Ōinomikado *s* 大炊御門 48
Oi no obumi *l* 笈の小文 1208
Ōinoue *s* 大井上 48
Oinuma *s* 生沼 214, 老沼 334, 笈沼 1208
Oisaka *s* 狼坂 1303
Oisaki *s* 生長 214
Oishi *sp* 生石
Ōishi *s* 生石, 大石 48
Ōishida *sp* 大石田
Ōishihashidate *s* 大石橋立 2925
Oishikawa *s* 鐃石川
Ōiso *sp* 大磯 48
Oiso no mori *l* 老蘇の森 334
Oita *s* 大江田 48, 種田 2124
Ōita *s* 大井田 48; *sp* 大分
Ōiwa *s* 大岩, 大磐
Oiwake *s* 辺分 179, 辺方; *p* 追分 993
Oiyake *s* 岡宅 987
Ōizumi *sp* 大泉 48
~ Kokuseki *ml* 大泉黒石
Ōji *s* 凡治 37, 大地 48, 大路, 黄地 1499; *m* 邑治 460; *p* 王寺 90
Ojigoro *sp* 小路頃 21
Ojika *sp* 小値賀
Ojima *sp* 尾島 505
Ojimi *s* 大慈弥 48
Ōjin *mh-p* 応神 509
Ojio *s* 置塩 2232
Ojiya *p* 小千谷 21
Ōjō Gokurakuin *p* 往生極楽院 579
~ yōshū *lh* 往生要集
Oka *s* 丘 219, 岡 987. (允 217, 丘 219, 邱 644, 阜 731, 坻 794, 効 888, 岳 956, 岡 987, 原 1231, 堆 1295, 陵 1310)
Ōka *s* 相可 868, 鉅 1946, 鉅鹿. (鉅)
Okabayashi *s* 岡林 987
Okabe *sp* 岡部
Okada *s* 岡田
~ Keisuke *mh* 岡田啓介
~ Saburō *ml* 岡田三郎
~ Saburōsuke *ma* 岡田三郎助
~ Yachiyo *fl* 岡田八千代
Oka-dayū *l* 岡太夫
Okade *s* 岡出
Okado *s* 小門 21, 岡戸 987, 高門 1163
Ōkado *s* 大門 48, 多門 347
Okado Katsuji *ml* 小門勝二 21
Okae *s* 小鴨
Okaemon *m* 岡右衛門 987
Okaeri *s* 魚返 1485
Oka Fumoto *ml* 岡麓
Okagaki *p* 岡垣 987
Okagami *s* 岡上
Ōkagami *l* 大鏡 48
Okagawa *s* 岡川 987
Okahara *s* 岡原
Okaharu *p* 岡原
Okahashi *s* 岡橋
Okahira *s* 岡平
Okai *s* 岡井, 御饗 1572
Okaji *s* 岡地 987; *m* 男梶 495
Okajima *s* 岡島 987
Okako *f* 丘子 219, 阜子 731, 坻子 794
Okakura *s* 岡倉 987
~ Tenshin *mla* 岡倉天心
Okamaro *m* 岡麿
Okamatsu *s* 岡松
Okami *s* 岡見
Ōkami *s* 大上 48, 大神. (狼 1303)
Ōkaminosuke *m* 狼之助
Okamiya *s* 岡宮 987
Okamoto *s* 岡元, 岡本
~ Bun'ya *ma* 岡本文弥
~ Daimu *ml* 岡本大無
~ Hekisansui *ml* 岡本癖三酔
~ Iwao *ml* 岡本巌
~ Jun *ml* 岡本潤
~ Kanoko *fl* 岡本かの子
~ Keigaku *ml* 岡本圭岳
~ Kidō *ml* 岡本綺堂
~ Kisen *ml* 岡本起泉
~ Reika *ml* 岡本霊華
~ Shōhin *ml* 岡本松浜
Okamura *s* 岳村 956, 岡村 987
~ Shikō *ml* 岡村柿紅
Okanaga *s* 岡永
Okanami *s* 岡波
Ōkanda *s* 大神田 48
Okane *s* 岡根 987; *f* 於金 607
Ōkane *s* 大神 48
Okanishi *s* 岡西 987
Okaniwa *s* 岡庭
Okano *s* 岡埜, 岡野
Okanobori *s* 岡上
Okanobu *s* 岡信
Okano Chijū *ml* 岡野知十
~ Naoshichirō *ml* 岡野直七郎
~ Takeo *ml* 岡野他家夫
Okanoue *s* 岡上
Okao *s* 岡尾
Oka Onitarō *ml* 岡鬼太郎
Okaseri *s* 岡芹
Okashiwa *s* 小柏 21
Ōkasuga *s* 大春日 48
Ōkata *s* 大嘉多
Okatani *s* 岡谷 987
Oka Tōri *ml* 岡橙里
Okatsu *p* 雄勝 1912
Okauchi *s* 岡内 987
Ōkawa *s* 凡河 37, 大河 48, 淡川 1340; *sp* 大川 48
Ōkawabata *l* 大川端
Ōkawachi *sp* 大河内
Okawado *s* 小川戸 21
Ōkawamoto *s* 大河本 48
Ōkawara *s* 大川原; *sp* 大河原
Ōkawa Shūmei *mh* 大川周明
Ōkawato *s* 大河戸
Okaya *sp* 岡谷 987
Okayake *s* 岡宅
Okayama *sp* 岡山
Okayasu *s* 岡安
Ōkayō *s* 大萱生 48
Okazaki *sp* 岡崎 987
Okazakikume *s* 丘前来目 219
Okazaki Masamune *ma* 岡崎正宗 987
~ Seiichirō *ml* 岡崎清一郎
~ Sessei *ma* 岡崎雪声
~ Yoshie *ml* 岡崎義恵
Okazawa *s* 岡沢
~ Hidetora *ml* 岡沢秀虎
Okaze *m* 雄風 1912
Okazoe *s* 岡添 987
Oke *m* 弘計 410. (姥 1090, 桶 1369)
Okeda *s* 桶田
Okegawa *p* 桶川
Okehazama *p* 桶狭間
Okera *m* 朮 209
Oketani *s* 桶谷 1369
Oketo *p* 置戸 2232
Oki *s* 小旧 21, 冲 225, 息 1224, 意岐 2007, 澳 2459; *sph* 隠岐 2074.

(云 147, 処 177, 生 214, 沖 225, 印 260, 気 319, 住 355, 沖 400, 宋 468, 知 636, 宙 673, 典 733, 居 737, 発 953, 息 1224, 恩 1225, 座 1245, 起 1262, 隆 1313, 設 1401, 致 1407, 翁 1430, 陽 1567, 御 1572, 奥 1798, 超 1816, 寛 1977, 意 2007, 業 2024, 置 2232, 熙 2409, 澳 2459, 興 2586, 幾 2597, 瀛 2865)
Ōki *s* 大城 48, 大喜, 仰木 360, 和宇慶 638 ; *sp* 大木 48
~ Atsuo *ml* 大木惇夫
Okibe *s* 刑部 258
Okida *s* 恩田 1225
Ōkida *sp* 大分 48
Okigaki *s* 沖垣 400
Ōkiguchi *s* 大木口 48
Okihajime *s* 並始 765
Okihara *s* 沖原 400
Okihisa *m* 意留 2007
Okiie *m* 興家 2586, 興屋
Okijima *s* 沖島 400
Okikata *m* 起賢 1262
Okikaze *m* 興風 2586
Okikazu *m* 意壱 2007
Okiko *f* 沖子 225
Okimaro *m* 奥麿 1798, 澳麿 2459
Okimaru *m* 興丸 2586
Okimasa *m* 興正 「美
Okimi *f* 沖海 400 ; *p* 沖
Okimichi *s* 興道 2586
Ōki Minoru *ml* 大木実 48
Okimori *m* 奥守 1798
Okimune *sm* 興統 2586
Okimura *s* 沖村 400
Okina *la* 翁 1430. (翁)
Okinaga *sp* 息長 1224 ; *m* 興増 2586
Okinamaro *m* 翁満 1430
Okinao *m* 興直 2586
Okinari *m* 興生
Okindo *m* 興人
Okinenobori *m* 興根昇
Okino *s* 沖野 400, 興野 2586 ; *m* 澳野 2459
~ Iwasaburō *ml* 沖野岩三郎 400
Okinori *m* 興文 2586
Ōkisaichi *s* 大私 48
Okisato *sp* 息郷 1224
Okishige *m* 興重 2586
Okisome *s* 置始 2232
Okisu *s* 乙須 2 「400
Okita *s* 小喜多 21, 沖田
Ōkita *s* 大分 48, 大北, 大喜多 「任
Ōki Takatō *mh* 大木喬
Okitatsu *m* 興建 2586
Okitsu *s* 沖津 400, 興津 2586
Okitsugu *m* 意次 2007
Okitsura *m* 興貫 2586
Okiuta *m* 興詩
Okiyama *s* 沖山 400
Okiyo *s* 興世 2586
Okkotsu *s* 乙骨 2
Oko *s* 右近 171, 尾古 505
Ōko *s* 大日子 48, 大古, 大胡, 大庫
Ōkobira *s* 大河平
Okōchi *s* 大河内
Ōkōchi *s* 大川内 ; *sp* 大河内
Okoe *s* 烏胡跛 1256
Ōkoma *s* 大狛 48
Okonogi *s* 小此木 21
Okoppe *p* 興部 2586
Okori *s* 発 953
Okoshi *s* 小越 21, 起 1262 ; *m* 尾輿 505
Okosu *m* 起 1262 ⌊221
Okototen *l* 乎古止点
Oku *s* 奥 1798 ; *p* 邑久 460. (或 750, 屋 1233, 惑 1784, 奥 1798, 煜 1874A, 億 2252, 憶 2440)
Ōku *sp* 大伯 48
Okuaki *s* 奥秋 1798
Okubee *m* 奥兵衛 「窪
Ōkubo *sp* 大久保 48, 大
~ Tadayasu *ml* 大久保忠保 「利謙
~ Toshiaki *ml* 大久保
~ Toshimichi *mh* 大久保利通 「尾口 505
Okuchi *s* 邑智 460 ; *sp*
Okuda *s* 奥田 1798
Okudai *s* 奥代
Okudaira *s* 奥平
Okudani *s* 奥谷
Okudera *s* 奥寺
Okudo *s* 奥戸
Okue *s* 小久江 21
Okufuji *s* 奥藤 1798
Okugawa *s* 奥川
Okugura *s* 奥倉
Okuhara *s* 奥原
Okui *s* 奥井, 奥居 ; *m* 少咋 88
Okuizumi *s* 奥泉 1798
Okuko *f* 奥子
Okuma *sp* 小熊 21
Ōkuma *s* 大隈 48 ; *sp* 大熊 「次郎
~ Chōjirō *ml* 大熊長
~ Kotomichi *ml* 大隈言道 「信行
~ Nobuyuki *ml* 大熊
~ Shigenobu *mh* 大隈重信
Ōkumebe *s* 大来目部
Okumichi *m* 奥道 1798
Okumiya *s* 奥宮
Okumoto *s* 奥本
Okumura *s* 奥村
~ Ioko *fh* 奥村五百子
Okumyōgata *p* 奥明方
Okunaka *s* 奥中
Okuni *fa* 阿国 569, 於国 607
Ōkuni *s* 大国 48
Okuni Kabuki *a* 於国歌舞伎 607
Ōkuninushi no Kami *mh* 大国主神
Ōkuni Takamasa *mh* 大国隆正
Okuno *s* 奥野 1798
Ōku no Himemiko *flh* 大伯皇女 48, 大来皇女 「の細道 1798
Oku no hosomichi *l* 奥
Okuno Shintarō *ml* 奥野信太郎
~ Takeo *ml* 奥野健男
Okunuki *s* 奥貫
Okura *m* 小内蔵 21 ; *ml* 憶良 2440 ; *f* 於庫 607
Ōkura *s* 大倉 48, 巨椋 199 ; *sp* 大蔵 48
Ōkuradani *s* 大暗谷
Okurai *s* 憶頼 2440
Ōkura Kihachirō *mh* 大倉喜八郎 48
~ Nagatsune *mh* 大蔵永常
~ Tōrō *ml* 大倉桃郎
Okurezaki haruna no umegaka *la* 後開榛名梅ケ香 1300
Ōkuro *s* 大黒 48
Okurume *s* 小車梅 21
Okusaki *s* 奥崎 1798
Okuse *s* 奥瀬
Ōkushi *s* 大串 48
Okushima *s* 奥島 1798
Okushiri *p* 奥尻
Okuso *fh* 小屎 21「1798
Oku-tama *p* 奥多摩
Okute *f* 晩稲 1595
Okuto *s* 奥戸 1798, 奥富
Okutomi *s* 奥富
Okutsu *p* 奥津
Ōkuwa *sp* 大桑 48
Okuwaki *s* 奥脇 1798
Okuya *s* 奥谷
Okuyama *s* 奥山
Okuzawa *s* 奥沢
Okuzumi *s* 奥住, 奥隈
Ōkyū *s* 大給 48
Ōma *sp* 大間
Ōmachi *sp* 大町
~ Keigetsu *ml* 大町桂 ⌊月
Ōmae *s* 大前
Omaezaki *p* 御前崎 1572
Ōmagari *sp* 大曲 48
Ōmakoto *s* 大允
Ōmama *p* 大間間
Omaro *m* 壮麻呂 243
Ōmasa *s* 大政 48
Omasama *s* 小間 21
Omata *s* 小俣
Ōmata *s* 大亦 48, 大股 ; *m* 大派
Omatsu *f* 御松 1572
Ōmatsu *s* 大松 48
Ōme *s* 大目 ; *sp* 青梅 700
Omegawa *s* 男女川 495
Omi *s* 小見 21, 尾見 505, 尾身, 臣 527, 麻見 1508, 麻績 ; *sm* 使主 556 ; *p* 麻積 1508. (老 334, 臣 527)
Ōmi *s* 大見 48, 大弥 ; *sm* 大洋, 淡海 1340 ; *sp* 大海 48 ; *sph* 近江 506 ; *p* 青海 700
~ agata *l* 近江県 506
Ōmibu *s* 大生 48
Ōmichi *s* 大道
Omie *f* 臣江 527
Omigawa *p* 小見川 21
Ōmi Genji senjin yakata *la* 近江源氏先陣館 506 「八幡
~ Hachiman *p* 近江
Ōmihara *s* 大海原 48
Omiichi *m* 麻績一 1508
Omimaro *m* 意美麿 2007

Ominako *f* 老名子 334
Ominameshi *la* 女郎花 114
Ōminato *sp* 大湊 48
~ Tanabe *p* 大湊田名部
Ōmine *s* 大峰, 大嶺
Omino *s* 小見野 21, 小見濃
Ōminoashitsumi *s* 近江脚身 506 「1508
Ominoichi *m* 麻績一
Ōmi no Mifune *ml* 淡海三船 1340
Omio *f* 臣乙 527
Ōmi Seijin *mh* 近江聖人 506
Ōmishima *p* 大三島 48
Ōmiwa *s* 大神, 大三輪
Ōmiwashimotoda *s* 大神楉田
Ōmiya *sp* 大宮
Omiyama *s* 小見山 21
Ōmizo *s* 大溝 48
(omo 面 904, 表 914)
Omodaka *s* 沢潟 404
Omoga *p* 面河 904
(omoi 思 966)
Omoigusa *l* 思草
Omokage *l* 於母影 607
Omokawa *s* 面川 904
Omoki *s* 面木
Ōmomo *s* 大桃 48
Omonogawa *p* 雄物川 1912
Ōmori *sp* 大森 48
~ Fusakichi *mh* 大森房吉 「郎
~ Gitarō *ml* 大森義太
Omoshi *m* 重 1017
Omote *s* 表 914
Omotegō *p* 表郷
Omoto *s* 尾本 505; *f* 万年青 43
Ōmoto *s* 大元 48, 大本
Ōmu *p* 雄武 1912
~ -gaeshi bunbu nidō *l* 鸚鵡返文武二道3021
~ Komachi *la* 鸚鵡小町
Omura *s* 尾村 505
Ōmura *sp* 大村 48
~ Masujirō *mh* 大村益次郎 「純忠
~ Sumitada *mh* 大村
Omuro *p* 御室 1572
Ōmuro *s* 大室 48

Ōmusamiyakenotabe *s* 大身狭屯倉田部
Ōmuta *p* 大牟田
(on 臣 527, 苑 682, 音 962, 恩 1225, 愔 1546, 陰 1563, 温 1585, 婉 1600, 媛 1868, 遠 2043, 園 2046, 猿 2062, 隠 2074, 媼 2089, 榲 2101, 蔭 2370, 穏 2492, 薗 2681, 蘊 2934)
Ona *s* 小名 21 「21
Ōna *s* 大魚 48; *sp* 小谷
Onabuchi *s* 小女淵
Onagawa *sp* 女川 114
Onai *s* 小内 21, 尾内 505
Onaka *s* 尾中
Ōnaka *s* 大中 48
Ōnakadō *s* 大中道
Ōnakagawa *s* 大中川
Ōnakatomi *s* 大中臣
~ no Yoshinobu *ml* 大中臣能宣
Onami *f* 男波 495
On'ami *ma* 音阿弥 962
Ōnami *s* 大波
Ōnari *s* 大成
Ōnawa *s* 大縄
Onaya *s* 女屋 114
Onba *s* 老馬 334
Onbetsu *p* 音別 962
Onchi *s* 恩地 1225, 恩智, 遠地 2043
~ Kōshirō *ml* 恩地孝四郎 1225 「武 2043
~ Terutake *ml* 遠地輝
Onda *s* 音田 962, 恩田 1225, 遠田 2043
Ondo *m* 音人 962, 雄人 1912; *p* 音戸 962
~ -no-seto *p* 音戸瀬戸
Ōne *s* 大根 48, 蔄 2188
Ōnejime *p* 大根占 48
Onga *p* 遠賀 2043
Ongagawa *p* 遠賀川
(oni 鬼 1527)
Onigajō *s* 鬼ケ城
Onigawara *la* 鬼瓦
Onijima *s* 鬼島
Oni-kage Musashi abumi *la* 鬼鹿毛無佐志鐙
Onikime *s* 鬼極
Onikojima *s* 鬼小島
Onikoshi *s* 鬼越
Onikubo *s* 鬼窪
Onimusashi *m* 鬼武蔵

Ōnin 1467–69 応仁 509
Oni no mamako *la* 鬼の継子 1527
Onio *s* 鬼尾
Oniō *s* 鬼王
Oniōmaru *ma* 鬼王丸
Onisakuza *m* 鬼作左
Onishi *p* 鬼石
Ōnishi *sp* 大西 48
~ Hajime *ml* 大西祝
~ Kyojin *ml* 大西巨人
~ Yoshinori *ml* 大西克礼
Onitake *sm* 鬼武 1527
Onitsura *ml* 鬼貫
Onizawa *s* 鬼沢
Onizuka *s* 鬼塚
Onjō *s* 遠城 2043
Onjōji *p* 園城寺 2046
Onjuku *p* 御宿 1572
Onma *s* 老馬 334
Onmyōdō *h* 陰陽道 1563 「学 114
Onna daigaku *lh* 女大
~-goroshi abura jigoku *la* 女殺油地獄
~ Kabuki *a* 女歌舞伎
~ keizu *l* 婦系図 1603
Onnoko *s* 臣 527
Ono *s* 小能 21, 尾野 505, 斧 659, 穏野 2492; *sp* 小野 21. (自 340, 斧 659, 鉄 1677, 鉞 2157)
Ōno *s* 太 105, 巨野 199; *sm* 多 347; *sp* 大野 48
Ono Azusa *mh* 小野梓 21
Ōnobu *sp* 大生 48
Ono Bushi *ml* 小野蕪子 21
Onoda *s* 斧田 659; *sp* 小野田 21 「寺 659
Onodera *s* 小野寺, 斧
Onoe *sp* 尾上 505; *f* 御野上 1572
~ Kikugorō *ma* 尾上菊五郎 505
~ Saishū *ml* 尾上柴舟
Onogami *p* 小野上 21
Ōnogi *s* 大野木 48
Onoguchi *s* 小野口 21
Onohara *s* 小野原
Ōnohara *p* 大野原 48
Onojima *s* 小野島 21
Onojirō *m* 鉞次郎 2157
Onokawa *s* 小野川 21
Onoki *s* 小野木

Ōnoki *s* 大米 48, 大軒, 大野木; *sp* 大仰
Onoko *f* 鉄子 1677
Onoma *m* 斧馬 659
Ōnomi *p* 大野見 48
Onomichi *p* 尾道 505
Onomura *s* 小野村 21, 尾村 505 「夫 48
Ōno Nobuo *ml* 大野誠
Ono no Dofū *mla* 小野道風 21 「妹子
~ no Imoko *mh* 小野
~ no Komachi *fl* 小野小町
~ no Michikaze *mla* 小野道風 「野篁
~ no Takamura *ml* 小
Onooka *s* 小野岡
Ōno Rinka *ml* 大野林火 48
Onose *s* 小野瀬 21
Ōno Shachiku *ml* 大野洒竹 48
Onosuke *m* 自助 340
Ono Tōzaburō *ml* 小野十三郎 21
Onouchi *s* 小野内
Onoyama *s* 小野山
Ō no Yasumaro *ml* 太安万侶 105
Onozaka *s* 小野坂
Onozaki *s* 小野崎
Onozato *s* 小野里
Onozawa *s* 小野沢
Onozuka *sp* 小野塚
Onsen *p* 温泉 1585
Onuki *s* 小貫 21
Ōnuki *s* 大貫 48
Onuma *s* 小沼 21
Ōnuma *sp* 大沼 48
On'yōdō *h* 陰陽道 1563
Onyū *sp* 遠敷 2043
Onyūda *s* 鬼生田 1527
Onzōshi shimawatari *l* 御曹子島わたり 1572
Ōoka *sp* 大岡 48; *p* 大丘
~ seidan *l* 大岡政談
~ Shōhei *ml* 大岡昇平
~ Tadasuke *mh* 大岡忠相
Ōosa *s* 大日佐 48
Ooyu *ml* 少老 88
Ōoyu *m* 巨老 199
Oppuri *s* 十二神 18
Ōra *p* 邑楽 460
Ōraimono *l* 往来物 579

Oranda *p* "Holland" 和蘭陀 638
Ori *s* 小里 21. (宅 283, 折 385, 居 737, 織 2879)
Ōri *s* 大利 48
Oribe *sm* 織部 2879
Orido *s* 下津 46
Orie *m* 雄力衛 1912, 織衛 2879; *f* 織衣
Origasa *s* 折笠 385
Origuchi *s* 折口
~ Shinobu *ml* 折口信夫 「2879
Orihara *s* 折原, 織原
Orihashi *s* 折橋 385
Orihata *s* 織畑 2879
Orihito *m* 織仁
Orii *s* 下井 46, 折井 385, 折居, 織井 2879; *m* 織居
Orikoshi *s* 織越
Orime *s* 織目
Orimo *s* 折茂 385, 織茂 2879 「本 2879
Orimoto *s* 折本 385, 織
Orinosuke *m* 織之助
Orishige *s* 織茂
Orishimo *s* 折下 385
Orita *s* 折田, 織田 2879
Oritaku shiba no ki *lh* 折焚く柴の記 385
Orito *s* 折戸, 織戸 2879; *m* 織人
Oriyama *s* 折山 385
Orochi *la* 大蛇 48
Oroshi *s* 下風 46, 下嵐, 御看 1572; *sp* 下石 46
Oroshiya *s* 下家
(oru 止 87, 処 177, 宿 1438, 織 2879)
Ōrui *s* 大類 48
Oryō *s* 小椋 21
Osa *s* 日佐 76; *sm* 長 939. (他 129, 仟 130, 正 205, 吏 329, 伯 363, 孟 667, 官 672, 易 714, 受 730, 政 881, 長 939, 修 1038, 容 1182, 脩 1281, 理 1361, 紀 1424, 順 1532, 揖 1550, 意 2007, 廉 2042, 種 2124, 統 2333, 導 2413, 綜 2528, 養 2558, 総 2662, 斂 2674)
Ōsa *sp* 大佐 48
Osabe *s* 刑部 258, 長部 939; *m* 他戸 129
Ōsachi *s* 大幸 48 「939
Osada *s* 他田 129, 長田
Osadahimatsuribe *s* 他田日奉部 129
Osada Shūtō *ml* 長田秋濤 939 「雄
~ Tsuneo *ml* 長田恒
Osade *s* 小佐手 21
Osafune *sp* 長船 939
~ Nagamitsu *ma* 長船長光
Osahito *m* 統仁 2333
Osaka *s* 刑 258, 刑坂, 忍坂 463, 尾坂 505, 越坂 2052; *sp* 小坂 21. (邢 415)
Ōsaka *s* 大幸 48; *sp* 大阪; *sph* 逢坂 1516; *ph* 大坂 48
Osakabe *s* 刑事 258, 邢部 415, 忍坂部 463, 忍壁, 長壁 939, 越坂部 2052; *smh-p* 刑部 258
Ōsakaya *s* 大坂屋 48
Ōsake *s* 大辟
Ōsaki *s* 大幸, 大辟; *sp* 大崎 「2528
Osako *f* 仟子 130, 綜子
Ōsako *s* 大迫 48
Ōsaku *s* 大作
Osama *s* 後拈 1300
Osamaro *m* 正麿 205, 乎佐麿 221
Osamaru *s* 長丸 939; *m* 尾佐丸 505
Osame *s* 納 1685; *m* 道 1811, 雄早馬 1912
Osami *m* 修身 1038
Osamu *m* 一 3, 乃 27, 士 41, 収 133, 司 164, 平 203, 艾 286, 成 322, 攻 380, 制 656, 京 663, 受 730, 医 743, 治 825, 秋 878, 倫 1037, 修 1038, 耕 1131, 宰 1180, 脩 1281, 埒 1293, 理 1361, 紀 1424, 順 1532, 税 1642, 貯 1651, 納 1685, 敦 1690, 道 1811, 摂 1837, 靖 1905, 経 1957, 氶 1971, 督 2023, 蔵 2424, 徹 2451, 整 2581, 靨 2596, 禧 2628, 斂 2674, 膺 2705, 鎮 2751, 穣 2802, 蘊 2934; *m-f* 乱 437, 統 2333
Osamune *m* 長宗 939
Osamura *s* 長村
Osanaetoki bankoku-banashi *l* 童絵解万国噺 1743
Osanaga *m* 受長 730
Osanai *s* 小山内 21, 小佐内; *sp* 長内 939
~ Kaoru *ml* 小山内薫
Osano *s* 小佐野 21
Osanobu *s* 養信 2558
Osao *m* 伯男 363, 修夫 1038 「48
Osaragi *s* 小仏 21, 大仏
~ Jirō *ml* 大仏次郎
Ōsaragi *s* 大仏
Osari *s* 長利 939
Osarizawa *p* 尾去沢 505
Ōsasagi *s* 大雀 48
Osasue *m* 紀季 1424
Osatake *s* 尾佐竹 505
~ Takeo *mlh* 尾佐竹猛
Osato *s* 意薩 2007
Ōsato *sp* 大里 48, 大郷
Osatomi *s* 長富 939
Osauru *m* 長潤
Ōsawa *s* 大沢 48; *sp* 大佐和
Ōsawano *sp* 大沢野
Ose *s* 小瀬 21, 尾瀬 505
Ōse *s* 大瀬 48, 役 368; *p* 逢瀬 1516
Ōseijitsu *s* 大晴日 48
Ose Keishi *ml* 尾瀬敬止 505 「505
Oseki *s* 小塞 21, 尾塞
Ōseko *s* 大世古 48, 大迫
Ōseto *p* 大瀬戸
Oshamanbe *p* 長万部 939
Oshi *s* 凡 37; *sp* 忍 463. (忍, 排 1317, 推 1322, 駕 2572)
Ōshi *s* 凡 37, 首 920; *sm* 多 347; *m* 大脚 48, 饒 2925. (印 260, 押 587)
Oshiage *s* 押上
Ōshiama *s* 凡海 37
Oshiba *s* 尾芝 505
Ōshiba *s* 大芝 48, 大柴
Oshida *s* 忍田 463, 押田 587
Oshie *m* 教 1408
Ōshihito *s* 凡人 37
Oshika *sm* 小鹿 21
Ōshika *sm* 鉅 1946; *sp* 大鹿 48
Oshikabe *s* 忍壁 463
Oshikane *s* 押鐘 587
Ōshika Taku *ml* 大鹿卓 48
Oshikawa *s* 押川 587, 推川 1322
Oshikawakoma *s* 熟皮高麗 2406
Oshikawa Shunrō *ml* 押川春浪 587
Oshiki *s* 押木
Oshikiri *s* 押切
Oshiko *s* 石戸 172, 石生
Ōshikōchi *s* 凡川内 37, 凡河内 「内躬恒
~ no Mitsune *ml* 凡河
Oshikōji *s* 押小路 587
Oshikubo *s* 押久保
Oshikuma *m* 忍熊 463
Oshima *s* 小島 21; *p* 渡島 1586 「大島
Ōshima *s* 大志摩 48; *sp*
Oshimabara *s* 小島原 21 「大島博光 48
Ōshima Hiromitsu *ml*
~ Joun *ma* 大島如雲
Oshimaya *s* 小島屋 21
Oshimi *s* 忍 463, 押見 587; *sp* 忍海 463
Oshimizu *p* 押水 587
Oshimodoshi *l* 押戻
Oshimoto *s* 押元, 押本
Oshimura *s* 押村
Oshina *s* 推名 1322
Oshino *s* 押野 587; *p* 忍野 463
Oshinomi *s* 忍海
Oshinoumi *s* 凡海 37, 忍海 463 「463
Oshinumi *s* 凡海 37, 忍
Oshio *s* 忍峡, 押尾 587; *sl* 小塩 21
Ōshio *s* 大塩 48
~ Heihachirō *mh* 大塩平八郎
Oshioyama *s* 小塩山 21
Oshiro *s* 忍路 463, 尾城 505
Ōshiro *s* 大代 48, 大城
Oshisuke *m* 忍助 463
Oshita *s* 尾下 505
Ōshita *s* 大下 48
Oshitani *s* 押谷 587
Oshitari *s* 忍足 463
Ōshita Udaru *ml* 大下宇陀児 48
Oshito *s* 石戸 172
Oshiyama *s* 押山 587
Oshizaki *s* 忍崎 463
Oshizumi *s* 印具 260
Oso *s* 於曾 607. (晏 1458)

Osō *s* 小添 21
Ōso *s* 大蘇 48
Osome Hisamatsu ukina no yomiuri *la* 於染久松色読販 607
Osone *s* 小曾根 21
Ōsone *s* 大曾根 48
Osono *s* 小園 21, 小薗
Ōsono *s* 大園 48
Osu *s* 小須 21
Ōsu *s* 大須 48; *m* 大為
Ōsuga *s* 大菅; *sp* 大須賀 「字
～ Otsuji *ml* 大須賀乙
Ōsuge *s* 大菅
Ōsugi *s* 大杉
～ Sakae *mlh* 大杉栄
Ōsuke *m* 翁助 1430, 応輔 509
Ōsuma *s* 大須磨 48
Osumi *s* 小住 21; *sm* 小角, 小隅
Ōsumi *s* 大 48, 大住, 大角; *sm-ph* 大隅; *sp*
Ota *p* 織田 2879 ⌊大隈
Ōta *s* 巨田 199, 応田 509, 負他 981; *sp* 大田 48, 太田 105
Otabe *s* 小田部 21
Ōtachihimibube *s* 大蝮壬部 48
Ōtachikara *s* 大田税
Ōtachime *s* 大音
Ōta Dōkan *mh* 太田道灌 105
Otae *s* 刑部 258
Ōtagaki *s* 大田垣 48, 太田垣 105 「蓮月 48
～ Rengetsu *ml* 大田
Ōtagawa *s* 大田川
Otagi *sp* 愛宕 2018
Ōtaguro *s* 大田黒 48, 太田黒 105
Ōta Gyokumei *ml* 太田玉茗
Otai *s* 小田井 21
Ōtajiro *s* 大田代 48
Otaka *s* 尾高 505
Ōtaka *s* 大高 48, 大鷹
Ōtakara *s* 大宝, 大財
Otake *s* 小竹 21, 尾竹 505, 御岳 1572
Ōtake *s* 大武 48, 大岳; *sp* 大竹
Otakeda *s* 小竹田 21
Ōtake Shinsuke *ml* 大竹新助 48

Ōtaki *sp* 大滝, 大多喜, 王滝 90 「村 105
Ōta Kōson *ml* 太田鴻
Otama *m* 男玉 495
Ōtama *p* 大玉 48
Ōtamaro *m* 太田麿 105
Ōtami *s* 大田見 48
Ōta Mizuho *ml* 太田水穂 105 「畝 48
Ōta Nanpo *ml* 大田南
Otani *s* 小谷 21, 尾谷 505, 丘谷 219; *m* 遠渓
Ōtani *s* 大谷 48 ⌊2043
～ Fujiko *fl* 大谷藤子
～ Gyōseki *ml* 大谷繞石 「仏
～ Kubutsu *ml* 大谷句
Otari *s* 忍足 463; *m* 少足 88, 男足 495; *p* 小
Otaru *p* 小樽 ⌊谷 21
Ōta Seikyū *ml* 太田青丘 105
Otate *m* 小楯 21
Ōtawa *s* 大多和 48
Ōtawara *sp* 大田原
Ōta Yōko *fl* 大田洋子
Ōte *sp* 大手
Oteko *f* 小手子 21
Ōteru *s* 大煇 48, 大輝
Ōte Takuji *ml* 大手拓次
Oto *m* 於菟 607, 雄兎 1912. (乙 2, 己 32, 吟 369, 呂 459, 声 465, 男 495, 呼 571, 弟 764, 律 787, 音 962, 頤 2113, 読 2142, 韶 2163, 徵 2265, 諷 2515, 翰 2518, 震 2577, 韻 2824, 響 2981)
Otō *s* 大豆 48
Ōto *s* 大多和, 大音, 首 920; *sm-p* 大戸 48; *m* 碩人 2116
Ōtō *sp* 大任 48; *p* 大塔
Otoba *s* 乙葉 2
Otobe *sp* 乙部
Otobone *s* 乙骨
Otodo *m* 大臣 48
Otofuke *p* 音更 962
Otogawa *s* 音川 「1572
Otogibōko *l* 御伽婢子
Otogizōshi *l* 御伽草子
Otogorō *m* 音五郎 962
Otoguro *s* 乙黒 2
Otohata *s* 乙幡
Otohiko *m* 乙彦, 弟彦
Otoine *m* 弟稲 ⌊764

Otoineppu *p* 音威子府
Otoji *m* 音治 ⌊962
Otojirō *m* 音次郎, 音治郎
Otokawa *s* 乙川 2
Otokichi *m* 乙吉, 音吉 962 「509
Ōtoku 1084–87 応徳
Otokuma *m* 乙熊 2
Otokuni *sp* 乙訓; *ml* 乙州
Otomaro *m* 弟麻呂 764
Otomatsu *m* 音松 962
Otome *s* 乙面 2; *f* 大十女 48, 弟女 764, 音女 962; *f-p* 乙女 2; *l* 少女 88
Ōtomi *s* 大富 48
Ōtomo *s* 大友, 大供, 王供 90; *sp* 大伴 48
～ no Kanamura *mh* 大伴金村
～ no Ōji *mh* 大友皇子
～ no Sakanoe no Iratsume *fl* 大伴坂上郎女
～ no Tabito *ml* 大伴旅人
～ no Yakamochi *ml* 大伴家持
～ Sōrin *mh* 大友宗麟
～ Yoshishige *mh* 大友義鎮
Otomuto *m* 音人 962
Otona *m* 老人 334, 老夫; *f* 乙魚 2, 音那
Otonashi *s* 音無 ⌊962
Otondo *m* 音人
Ōtone *sp* 大利根 48
Ōtoneribe *s* 大舎人部
Otonushi *m* 音主 962
Otoo *m* 乙男 2
Ōtori *s* 大鳥 48
Ōtoribe *s* 大舎人部
Ōtori-zukuri *a* 大鳥造
Ōtose *s* 大刀西
Ōtoshi *m* 大歳, 大蔵
Otoshibanashi *l* 落話 1733
Otosuke *m* 音輔 962
Ototashi *s* 置賜 2232
Ototsu *s* 乙津 2
Otowa *p* 音羽 962
Otowaya *s* 音羽屋
Otoya *m* 男也 495, 音弥 962
Otoyama *s* 音山

Ōtoyo *p* 大豊 48
Otozō *m* 音三 962
Ōtozumi *s* 大角集 48
Otsu *sp* 乙津 2. (乙, 榲 2101)
Ōtsu *sp* 大津 48
Ōtsubo *s* 大坪 「郎
～ Sōjirō *ml* 大坪草二
Otsuburui *s* 十二仏 18, 十二仙, 十二神, 十二神島
Ōtsuchi *sp* 大槌 48
Otsufuru *s* 越振 2052
Otsugae *sp* 乙亥正 2
Otsugu *m* 緒嗣 2537
Otsuhata *s* 乙幡 2
Otsuhechi *s* 御返事 1572
Ōtsui *s* 大角集 48
Otsuji *s* 尾辻 505
Ōtsuji *s* 大辻 48
Ōtsuka *s* 大束, 大塚
～ Kinnosuke *ml* 大塚金之助
～ Kōzan *ml* 大塚甲山
～ Kusuoko *fl* 大塚楠緒子
Otsukawa *s* 乙川 2
Ōtsuka Yasuji *ml* 大塚保治 48
Otsuki *s* 小槻 21
Ōtsuki *s* 大即 48, 大胐, 大槻, 大築; *sp* 大月
～ Gentaku *mh* 大槻玄沢
～ Joden *ml* 大槻如電
～ Kenji *ml* 大槻憲二
Ōtsu-kyō *ph* 大津京
Ōtsume *s* 大角集
Ōtsumi *s* 大津美
Otsunu *m* 小角 21
Otsurui *s* 十二神島 18
Ottachi *s* 乙竹 2
Ottake *s* 乙竹
Ouchi *s* 尾内 505
Ōuchi *s* 桜内 1373; *sp* 大内 48
～ Hyōe *ml* 大内兵衛
Ōuchiyama *sp* 大内山
Ōuchi Yoshitaka *mh* 大内義隆
Ōuda *p* 大宇陀
Ōue *s* 大上
Ouki *lh* 小右記 21
Ōumi *s* 大海 48
Ōunabara *s* 大海原
Ōura *sp* 大浦
Ōusu *m* 大碓

Ōwa *s* 大和, 大輪; 961–64 応和 509
Owada *s* 小和田 21
Ōwada *s* 大和田 48; *sp* 大輪田
~-no-tomari *ph* 大輪田泊
~ Tateki *ml* 大和田建樹
Ōwake *s* 大捌
Ōwaki *s* 大脇
Ōwaku *s* 大和久
Ōwani *sp* 大鰐
Owari *m* 巳 31; *ph* 尾張 505
Owase *p* 尾鷲
Ōwashi *s* 大鷲 48
Ōwata *sp* 大曲
(oya 祖 850, 御 1572, 親 2544)
Ōya *s* 大矢 48, 大宅, 大谷, 大家, 君家 515; *sp* 大屋 48
Oyabe *p* 小矢部 21
Ōyabu *s* 大藪 48
Ōyagi *s* 大八木, 大米, 大谷木, 大野木
Oyaizu *s* 小柳津 21, 小柳筒
Ōyaizu *s* 大柳津 48
Oyakai *s* 小屋貝 21
Oyake *s* 小宅, 尾宅 505
Ōyake *s* 大家 48, 大屋; *sp* 大宅
~ no Yotsugi *ml* 大宅世継
Ōyako *s* 大陽胡
Oyakodaka *l* 父子鷹 65
Ōyaku *s* 大宅 48
Oyama *s* 尾山 505, 鴻山 2614; *sp* 小山 21
Ōyama *sp* 大山 48
Oyamada *s* 小山田 21
Ōyamada *sp* 大山田 48
Ōyama dōchū kurige no shiriuma *l* 大山道中栗毛後駿足
~ Ikuo *mlh* 大山郁夫
~ Iwao *mh* 大山巌
~ Teiichi *ml* 大山定一
Oyama Tokujirō *ml* 尾山篤二郎 505
Oyamatsu *s* 親松 2544
Ōyamazaki *p* 大山崎 48
Oyanagi *s* 小柳 21
Ōyanagi *s* 大柳 48
Ōyano *sp* 大矢野
Ōyashima gakkai *l* 大八洲学会
Ōyashirō *l* 大社
Ōya Sōichi *ml* 大宅壮一
Oyayubi *s* 拇 798
Ōyazu *s* 大谷津 48
(oyo 及 83)
(oyobi 及)
Oyobibe *s* 及部
Ōyodo *sp* 大淀 48
Oyokawa *s* 及川 83
Ō Yōmei *mlh* "Wang Yang-ming" 王陽明 90
Ōyosami *s* 大網 48
Ōyoshi *s* 大吉; *m* 大義
(oyu 老 334)
Ōyu *s* 大湯 48
Ōyue *s* 大湯人, 大湯坐
Oyuka *s* 男壮 495
Ōyuke *s* 大湯座 48
Oyumi *s* 生実 214; *m* 小弓 21
Ozaki *s* 小崎, 尾崎 505
~ Hirotsugu *ml* 尾崎宏次
~ Hōsai *ml* 尾崎放哉
~ Kazuo *ml* 尾崎一雄
~ Kihachi *ml* 尾崎喜八
~ Kōko *fl* 尾崎孝子
~ Kōyō *ml* 尾崎紅葉
~ Shirō *ml* 尾崎士郎
~ Yukio *mh* 尾崎行雄
Ozaku *sp* 小作 21
Ozasa *s* 小笹, 小篠
Ōzasa *s* 大笹 48
Ozase *s* 小篠 21
Ozato *s* 尾里 505
Ōzatsuma *s* 大薩摩 48
Ozawa *s* 小沢 21, 男沢 495, 尾沢 505
~ Hekidō *ml* 小沢碧童 21
~ Kiyoshi *ml* 小沢清
~ Roan *ml* 小沢蘆庵
~ Seiji *ma* 小沢征爾
~ Takeji *ml* 小沢武二
Ozeki *s* 小関, 尾関 505
Ōzeki *s* 大関 48
Ozeki San'ei *mh* 小関三英 21
Ozo *s* 隠曾 2074
Ozono *s* 尾園 505
Ōzora *s* 大空 48
Ozu *s* 小豆 21, 小津, 面図 904
Ōzu *s* 大頭 48; *sp* 大洲
Ōzuru *s* 大鶴
Ozutsumi *s* 小堤 21

# P

Pan *l* 麵麭 2910
Pari *p* "Paris" 巴里 97, 巴理
Peipin *p* "Peiping" 北平 138
Pekin *p* "Peking" 北京
Perusha *p* "Persia" 波斯 596
Pippu *p* 比布 137
Pontochō *p* 先斗町 280
Porando *p* "Poland" 波蘭 596
Porutogaru *p* "Portugal" 葡萄牙 1724

# R

(ra 良 767, 荒 935, 浦 1067, 郎 1145, 娘 1599, 螺 2805, 羅 2937)
Rachi *s* 良知 767
Rai *s* 来 538; *sm* 頼 2506. (礼 146, 来 538, 徠 1297, 雷 2026, 厲 2234, 黎 2389, 賚 2396, 頼 2506, 瀬 2794, 蠣 2870, 麗 2902)
Raiden *la* 来殿 538, 雷電 2026
Raigō wasan *l* 来迎和讃 538
Raijō *s* 来城
Raiki *l* "Li Chi" 礼記 146
Rai Mikisaburō *mh* 頼三樹三郎 2506
~ Noboru *mh* 頼襄
~ San'yō *mh* 頼山陽
Raishirō *m* 賚四郎 2396
Raita *m* 雷太 2026
Raizō *m* 頼三 2506
Raku *s* 楽 2029. (洛 818, 落 1733, 楽 2029)
Rakuami *la* 楽阿弥
Rakujō *l* 落城 1733
Rakushu *l* 落首
Rakuyō *ph* ["Lo-yang"] 洛陽 818
~ dengakuki *l* 洛陽田楽記
~ meishoshū *l* 洛陽名所集
(ran 乱 437, 嵐 2000, 覧 2695, 闌 2708, 藍 2772, 蘭 2839, 爛 2913)
Rangaku *lh* 蘭学 2839
~ kotohajime *l* 蘭学事始
Ranjatai *l* 蘭奢待
Rankō *ml* 闌更 2708
Rankoshi *p* 蘭越 2839
Ransetsu *ml* 嵐雪 2000
Rasa *p* 良佐 767
Rase *s* 楽世 2029
Rashōmon *l* 羅生門 2937
Rausu *p* 羅臼
Razan *mlh* 羅山
~ bunshū *lh* 羅山文集
Rebun *p* 礼文 146
Rei *m* 鵜 2974. (礼 146, 令 155, 冷 349, 励 430, 剣 432, 伶 565, 苓 687A, 玲 834, 茘 924, 秴 1115, 詅 1661, 鈴 1947, 厲 2234, 黎 2389, 霊 2390, 澪 2458, 齢 2766, 嶺 2776, 礪 2798, 蠣 2870, 麗 2902)
Reigon Hōshi *ml* 礼厳法師 146

Reihō *p* 鈴峰 1947
Reihoku *p* 苓北 687A
Reiiki *l* 霊異記 2390
Reijirō *m* 礼次郎 146
Reiki 715–17 霊亀 2390
Reikichi *m* 礼吉 146, 黎吉 2389
Reiko *f* 麗子 2902
Reinosuke *m* 礼之助 146
Reisaku *m* 励作 430
Reisuke *m* 礼助 146, 礼弼
Reitarō *m* 鈴太郎 1947
Reizei *smh* 冷泉 349
～ Tamesuke *ml* 冷泉為相
Reizō *m* 令蔵 155
(reki 暦 2235, 歴 2247, 檪 2963, 礫 2987)
Rekitei *l* 歴程 2247
(ren 恋 1223, 連 1238, 廉 2042, 漣 2082, 蓮 2197, 璉 2285, 簾 2393, 練 2527, 斂 2674, 鏈 2815, 簾 2844, 聯 2948)
Ren'ami *ma* 蓮阿弥 2197
Renga *l* 連歌 1238
～ hikyōshū *l* 連歌比況集
～ honshiki *l* 連歌本式
～ nusubito *la* 連歌盗人 「抄
～ shihōshō *l* 連歌致宝
～ shinshiki *l* 連歌新式
～ ～ kon'an *l* 連歌新式今案
Ren'ichirō *m* 連一郎
Renjirō *m* 廉次郎 2042
Renkichi *m* 廉吉
Rennyo *mh* 蓮如 2197
Renri hishō *l* 連理秘抄 1238
Rensuke *m* 廉助 2042
Rentarō *m* 廉太郎
Renzō *m* 連三 1238
(retsu 列 257, 冽 549, 洌 810)
Ri *s* 李 488. (有 303, 吏 329, 利 436, 李 488, 里 517, 亥 519, 俐 775, 降 1058, 浰 1063, 莅 1174, 理 1361, 梨 1476, 裏 2176, 銕 2341, 履 2415, 璃 2473, 鯉 2764, 織 2879, 離 2889, 籬 3010)
Ribee *m* 利兵衛 436

Rifu *s* 利生 ; *sp* 利府
Riichi *m* 利一
Riichirō *m* 理一郎 1361
Rijin Shōgun *mh* 利仁将軍 436
Rikashū *l* 李花集 488
(riki 力 11, 仂 55, 屶 291)
Rikichi *m* 利吉 436
Rikimaru *s* 力丸 11
Rikisaburō *m* 利喜三郎 436
Rikitarō *m* 利喜太郎
Rikizō *m* 力三 11, 力造, 力蔵
Rikkokushi *l* 六国史 61
(riku 六 , 陸 1312)
Rikubetsu *p* 陸別
Rikuchū *ph* 陸中
Rikuda *s* 陸田
Rikuhara *s* 陸原
Rikukawa *s* 陸川
Rikurō *m* 陸郎
Rikuzen *ph* 陸前
～ Takada *p* 陸前高田
Rikyū *ma* 利休 436
Rin *s* 林 633 ; *f* 侖 669. (林 633, 侖 669, 倫 1037, 鈴 1947, 稟 1973, 輪 2316, 論 2320, 隣 2443, 撛 2446, 綸 2527, 璘 2618, 磷 2731, 藺 2838, 麟 3000)
Rinbayashi *s* 林林 633
Ringorō *m* 林五郎
Rin'ichi *m* 林一
Rinji *m* 林治
Rinjirō *m* 林次郎, 林治郎, 鈴治郎 1947
Rinkan *l* 林間 633
Rinkichi *m* 林吉
Rinoie *s* 李家 488
Rinoue *s* 理上 1361
Rinpei *m* 林平 633
Rinsenshū *l* 林泉集
Rinshirō *m* 林四郎
Rintarō *m* 倫太郎 1037
Rin'ya *m* 麟也 3000
Rin'yū gaku *a* 林邑楽 633
Rinzō *m* 林蔵, 麟蔵 3000 ; *l* 輪蔵 2316
Ririura *l* 理里有楽 1361
Ri Ryō *mh-l* "Li Ling" 李陵 488
Risaburō *m* 利三郎 436, 鯉三郎 2764
Risaku *m* 理作 1361

Rishiri *p* 利尻 436
Risshō ankokuron *l* 立正安国論 194
Risuke *m* 利助 436
Ritsu *s* 立 194 ; *f* 織都 2879. (立 194, 律 787, 栗 1219, 笠 1473, 葎 1719, 率 2040)
Rittō *p* 栗東 1219
Ro *s* 呂 459, 盧 2594. (呂 459, 芦 484, 良 767, 侶 778, 亮 911, 旅 1073, 路 1925, 魯 2385, 閭 2426, 蕗 2564, 盧 2594, 璐 2619, 蘆 2842, 廬 2855, 露 2941, 鷺 2993, 顱 3001, 驢 3007, 鱸 3014)
(rō 老 334, 良 767, 郎 1145, 狼 1303, 浪 1339, 朗 1394, 娘 1599, 琅 1606, 滝 1862, 稜 1917, 縷 2878, 籠 2977)
Roankyō *l* 驢鞍橋 3007
Rōben *mh* 良弁 767
Robun *ml* 魯文 2385
Rōei *l* 朗詠 1394
Rō-Giō *la* 籠祇王 2977
Rohan *ml* 露伴 2941
Ro Jin *ml* "Lu Hsün" 魯迅 2385
Rōka *ml* 浪花 1339
Rokkaku *s* 六角 61
Rokkasen *ml-fl* 六歌仙
Rokkasho *p* 六ケ所
Rokoku *p* "Russia" 魯国 2385, 露国 2941
Roku *s* 角 547. (六 61, 氻 141, 禄 1589, 鹿 1823, 録 2523, 緑 2535, 麓 2903)
Rokubee *m* 六兵衛 61
Rokubutsu *s* 六物
Rokugawa *s* 六川
Rokugō *p* 六郷
Rokuhara *sph* 六波羅
Rokuichirō *m* 六一郎
Rokuji *m* 六二
Roku Jizō *la* 六地蔵
Rokujō *sp* 六条
Rokumeikan *ph-la* 鹿鳴館 1823
Rokumeishū *l* 鹿鳴集
Rokumura *s* 六村 61
Rokuno *s* 六野
Rokunohe *p* 六戸
Rokunosuke *m* 録之助 2523
Rokuonji *p* 鹿苑寺 1823

Rokurō *m* 六郎 61, 禄郎 1589, 録郎 2523
Rokusei *p* 鹿西 1823
Rokushika *s* 六鹿 61
Rokusho *s* 六所
Rokutarō *m* 緑太郎 2535
Rokuzō *m* 六造 61
Rōma *p* "Rome" 羅馬 2937
Rōmusha *l* 老武者 334
(ron 侖 669, 倫 1037, 論 2320) 「倫敦 1037
Rondon *p* "London"
～-tō *l* 倫敦塔
Roren *l* 呂蓮 459
Rōshi *mlh* "Lao-tzu" 老子 334 「西亜 2941
Roshia *p* "Russia" 露
Rōsodō Eiki *ml* 老鼠堂永機 334 「2977
Rō taiko *l* 籠祇王太鼓
Rotekishū *l* 蘆荻集 2842
Rotsū *ml* 路通 1925
(ru 児 497, 流 1332, 留 1470, 劉 2554, 縷 2878, 顱 3001) 「1470
Rubeshibe *p* 留辺蘂
Rui *f* 累 2004. (涙 1062, 滝 1862, 累 2004, 類 2755) 「国史
Ruijū kokushi *l* 類聚
～ ～ myōgishō *l* 類聚国史名義抄
Ruikon *l* 涙痕 1062
Rukō shinsō *l* 縷紅新草 2878
Rumoi *p* 留萠 1470
Ruson *p* "Luzon" 呂宋 459
Rusu *s* 留主 1470, 留守
Rusutsu *p* 留寿都
(ryaku 暦 2235, 歴 2247, 檪 2963, 礫 2987)
Ryakunin 1238–39 暦仁 2235
Ryakuō 1338–42 暦応
(ryo 呂 459, 侶 778, 旅 1073, 閭 2426, 盧 2594, 蘆 2842, 廬 2855, 驢 3007)
Ryō *s* 竜 1199 ; *sm* 梁 1475 ; *m* 良 767. (了 9, 令 155, 立 194, 冷 349, 剣 432, 両 531, 怜 565, 苓 687A, 良 767, 玲 835, 亮 911, 凉 1020, 淩 1022, 倞 1024, 稌 1115,

竜 1199, 陵 1310, 涼 1330, 菱 1449, 梁 1475, 椋 1628, 諒 1661, 量 1741, 滝 1862, 禰 1906, 稜 1917, 鈴 1947, 漻 2080, 漁 2086, 蓼 2229, 樛 2290, 諒 2326, 寮 2364, 霊 2390, 澪 2458, 綾 2541, 遼 2590, 瞭 2629, 簗 2690, 齢 2766, 嶺 2776, 鵜 2974)
Ryōa *ml* 了阿 9
Ryōanji *p* 竜安寺 1199
Ryōgen *s* 竜見; *mh* 良源 767
Ryōgoku *p* 両国 531
Ryōhei *m* 良平 767, 亮平 911
Ryōichi *m* 良一 767, 亮一 911
Ryōitsu *m* 良逸 767
Ryōji *m* 良治, 亮二 911
Ryōjin hishō *l* 梁塵秘抄 1475
Ryojun *p* " Port Arthur " 旅順 1073
Ryōkami *p* 両神 531
Ryōkan *mh* 良観 767; *mlh* 良寛
Ryōkichi *m* 良吉, 亮吉 911 「虎 1199
Ryōko *f* 良子 767; *l* 竜
(ryoku 力 11, 仂 55, 劣 291, 禄 1589, 録 2523, 緑 2535)
Ryokusadan *l* 緑簑談
Ryokuushū *l* 緑雨集
Ryōnan *p* 綾南 2541
Ryōnin *mh* 良忍 767
Ryōnosuke *m* 良之助
Ryōsaku *m* 良作, 亮策 911
Ryōsen *s* 竜山 1199
Ryōshi *m* 良士 767
Ryōsuke *m* 良助, 良輔
Ryōta *m* 良太; *ml* 蓼太 2229 「亮太郎 911
Ryōtarō *m* 良太郎 767,
Ryōtei *m* 蓼汀 2229
Ryōtsu *p* 両津 531
Ryōunshū *l* 凌雲集 1022
Ryōzen *p* 霊山 2390
Ryōzō *m* 良三 767, 良造, 良蔵, 亮三 911
(ryu 竜 1199, 隆 1313)
Ryū *s* 竜 1199, 笠 1473; *m* 劉 2554. (立 194, 柳 1105, 竜 1199, 隆 1313, 流 1332, 粒 1389, 留 1470, 笠 1473, 滝 1862, 蓼 2229, 劉 2554, 瀏 2792)
Ryūdokai *l* 竜土会 1199
Ryūgadake *p* 竜ケ岳
Ryūgasaki *p* 竜ケ崎
Ryūge *s* 竜花
Ryūgen *s* 竜見
Ryūgo *m* 立五 194, 柳梧 1105
Ryūhei *m* 竜平 1199
Ryūhoku *p* 竜北
Ryūichi *m* 柳一 1105, 竜一 1199, 隆一 1313
Ryūichirō *m* 隆一郎
Ryūji *m* 隆二, 隆次
Ryūjin *p* 竜神 1199
Ryūkatei Tanekazu *ml* 柳下亭種員 1105
Ryūkichi *m* 竜吉 1199, 隆吉 1313
Ryūkyō shinshi *l* 柳橋新詩 1105
Ryūma *m* 竜馬 1199
Ryūnosuke *m* 竜之介
Ryūō *p* 竜王
Ryūsaku *m* 柳作 1105
Ryūsen *s* 竜泉 1199
Ryū Shintarō *ml* 笠信太郎 1473
Ryūtanji Yū *ml* 竜胆寺雄 1199
Ryūtarō *m* 柳太郎 1105, 竜太郎 1199, 隆太郎 1313
Ryūtatsu *mla* 隆達
Ryūtei *s* 柳亭 1105, 笠亭 1473, 滝亭 1862
～ Rijō *ml* 滝亭鯉丈
～ Senka *ml* 笠亭仙果 1473
～ Tanehiko *ml* 柳亭種彦 1105
Ryūyō *p* 竜洋 1199
Ryūzaki *s* 竜崎
Ryūzaburō *m* 竜三郎
Ryūzenkō *l* 竜涎香
Ryūzō *m* 竜蔵, 竜三, 隆三 1313, 隆造
Ryūzōji *s* 竜造寺 1199

# S

Sa *m* 左 169. (二 4, 小 21, 五 91, 左 169, 早 295, 作 362, 佐 365, 渉 392, 坐 542, 咲 784, 狭 790, 相 868, 砂 876, 勇 908, 茶 931, 底 992, 為 1005, 祚 1126, 差 1164, 座 1245, 娑 1474, 爽 1529, 猨 1554, 朝 1672, 紗 1683, 善 1799, 楽 2029, 猿 2062, 嵯 2095, 蓑 2194, 聡 2311, 積 2493, 総 2662, 簑 2668)
Saba *sp* 佐波 365; *m* 鯖 2830. (鯖)
Sabae *s* 鯖江
Sabamaro *m* 鯖麻呂
Sabanosuke *m* 左馬助
Sabase *s* 佐橋 365 ⌊169
Sabashi *s* 佐橋
Sabato *l* 奢瀾都 1706
(sabu 三 22, 珊 834, 総 2662, 簑 2688)
Sabuemon *m* 三甫右衛門 22
Saburi *s* 佐分 365, 佐分利
Saburō *m* 三郎 22, 珊朗 834 「22
Saburobee *m* 三郎兵衛
Saburōji *m* 三郎治
Saburosuke *m* 三郎助
Sachi *s* 佐代 365, 佐治; *f* 相智 868. (士 41, 吉 278, 征 580, 刷 655, 幸 661, 祐 852, 祥 1074, 祜 1124, 茁 1173, 禄 1589, 禎 1887, 福 1888, 祺 1903, 葛 1994)
Sachibumi *m* 幸文 661, 幸翰
Sachihiko *m* 祐彦 852
Sachihiro *m* 幸弘 661
Sachiko *f* 祜子 1124, 禎子 1887, 祺子 1903, 葛子 1994 「福磨 1888
Sachimaro *m* 士観 41,
Sachio *m* 征朗 580, 幸生 661, 幸男
Sachū *m* 左中 169
Sachūda *s* 左中太, 佐中太 365
Sada *s* 佐太, 貞 982; *p* 佐田 365. (夬 100, 必 120, 尼 175, 正 205, 弁 275, 存 313, 成 322, 自 340, 決 402, 判 434, 会 454, 完 471, 安 472, 帖 563, 制 656, 定 677, 信 782, 治 825, 貞 982, 員 1167, 真 1228, 渉 1331, 済 1336, 晏 1458, 補 1644, 断 1669, 勘 1699, 奠 1701, 覚 1752, 禎 1887, 愷 2070, 塡 2075, 寧 2181, 節 2215, 質 2395, 憲 2562)
Sadaaki *m* 夬夫 100, 夬介, 定敬 677, 貞著 982, 貞融, 禎章 1887
Sadaakira *m* 貞発 982
Sadaatsu *m* 定豊 677
Sadachika *m* 貞親 982
Sadae *m* 定条 677 「982
Sadafusa *m* 定房, 貞成
Sadagasaki *s* 三段崎 22
Sadaharu *m* 貞喜 982
Sadahisa *m* 貞央
Sadaichi *m* 定一 677
Sadaie *ml* 定家
Sadaisa *m* 定功
Sadajirō *m* 定次郎, 定治郎, 貞治郎 982
Sadaka *m* 貞馨, 宷 1435
Sadakage *m* 信景 782
Sadakami *m* 定省 677
Sadakane *m* 定兼, 貞懐 982 「方 982
Sadakata *s* 定方 677, 貞
Sadakatsu *m* 定豪 677
Sadaki *m* 貞機 982, 貞喜
Sadakichi *m* 定吉 677
Sadakiyo *m* 定静, 貞祓 982
Sadako *f* 弁子 275, 成子 322, 決子 402, 制子 656, 定子 677, 貞子 982, 奠子 1701, 節子 2215
Sadakoto *m* 定護 677
Sadakuni *m* 貞訓 982

Sadamasa *m* 定正 677
Sadamasu *m* 定加, 貞升 982
Sadamatsu *m* 貞松
Sadame *m* 定 677
Sadami *m* 貞仁 982; *f* 節美 2215
Sadamichi *m* 弁道 275
Sadamitsu *m* 真光 1228; *p* 貞光 982
Sadamizu *m* 定琮 677
Sadamochi *m* 貞行 982
Sadamori *m* 貞守, 貞盛
Sadamoto *m* 定宗 677, 貞固 982
Sadamu *m* 夬 100, 処 177, 成 322, 定 677, 莫 1175, 理 1361, 断 1669, 勘 1699, 禎 1887, 毅 2351
Sadamune *m* 貞宗 982
Sadanaga *m* 定祥 677
Sadanaminoya *ml* 泊洦舎 592
Sadanari *m* 定功 677, 貞作 982, 貞亨
Sadanji *ma* 左団次 169
Sadanobu *m* 定信 677, 貞啓 982
Sadanori *m* 必典 120, 完識 471, 定忠 677, 定順, 定敬, 定識, 貞利 982, 貞勝, 貞雅, 貞載, 貞範 ⌈677
Sadanosuke *m* 定之助
Sadao *m* 定夫, 貞夫 982, 貞朗, 貞雄, 憲夫 2562
Sadaoi *m* 貞老 982
Sadaoki *m* 貞意, 貞置
Sadashige *m* 定芝 677
Sadasue *m* 貞居 982
Sadasuke *m* 定助 677
Sadatae *m* 貞巧 982
Sadataka *m* 完孝 471
Sadatake *m* 定武 677, 貞丈 982, 貞長
Sadatō *m* 貞融
Sadatoki *m* 貞斎, 貞説
Sadatomo *m* 貞幹
Sadatoshi *m* 定後 677, 定逸, 貞才 982
Sadatsugu *m* 貞次
Sadatsura *m* 貞羅
Sadayasu *m* 定静 677
Sadayori *m* 定猗, 貞寄 982
Sadayoshi *m* 定剛 677, 定温, 貞允 982, 貞俶, 貞哲, 貞義, 貞謙, 貞懿, 真義 1228
Sadayuki *m* 貞敬 982, 真行 1228
Sadazumi *m* 貞隅 982
Sade *s* 佐代 365
Sadehiko *m* 狭手彦 790
Sado *s* 狭度; *sp* 佐渡 365
~-gitsune *la* 佐渡狐
Sadoshima *sp-l* 佐渡島
Sadowara *sp* 佐土原
Sadoyama *s* 佐渡山
(sae 冴 348, 朗 1394)
Saegusa *s* 三枝 22, 三枝松, 三枝部
Saeki *sp* 佐伯 365
~ Shōichi *ml* 佐伯彰一 ⌈1394
Saeko *f* 冴子 348, 朗子
Saga *s* 相賀 868, 嵯峨 2095; *sp* 佐賀 365. (相 868)
Sagae *sp* 寒河江 1714
Sagami *s* 佐上 365; *fl-p* 相模 868
Sagamihara *p* 相模原
Sagami-ko *p* 相模湖
Sagamu *s* 相武
Sagane *s* 相根 ⌈365
Saganoseki *p* 佐賀関
Saganoya Omuro *ml* 嵯峨の屋御室 2095
Sagara *s* 左柄 169; *sp* 相良 868
Sagaraku *s* 相楽
Sagawa *s* 狭川 790; *sp* 佐川 365
Sagi *sla* 鷺 2993. (勾 168, 包 218, 雀 1530, 鷺 2993)
Saginoike *s* 鷺池
Saginuma *s* 鷺沼
Sagio *sm* 鷺雄
Sagisaka *s* 勾坂 168, 包坂 218, 鷺坂 2993
Sagitani *s* 鷺谷
Sagiya *s* 鷺屋
Sago *s* 三五 22
Sagō *s* 佐郷 365
Sagoromo *l* 狭衣 790
Sagoshi *s* 砂越 876
Sahachi *m* 佐八 365
Sahanai *s* 佐羽内
Saho *s* 佐保
Sahota *s* 佐保田
Sai *s* 西 336, 崔 1738, 讃井 3013; *p* 佐井 365, (才 35, 在 314, 西 336, 材 420, 幸 661, 斉 701, 釆 707, 妻 959, 哉 1006, 栖 1101, 財 1143, 宰 1180, 柴 1221, 栽 1254, 埼 1292, 採 1314, 済 1336, 彩 1413, 寀 1435, 菜 1447, 斎 1454, 祭 1467, 婇 1602, 妻 1722, 崔 1738, 最 1742, 犀 1803, 腮 1870, 細 1958, 歳 1995, 載 2050, 催 2060, 際 2073, 躋 2950, 灑 2962, 霽 2978)
Saibara *l* 催馬楽 2060
~ fuiriaya *l* 催馬楽譜入文
Saichi *m* 佐一 365
Saichō *ml* 最澄 1742
Saida *s* 才田 35, 斉田 701, 座田 1245, 斎田 1454
Saidaiji *p* 西大寺 336
Saido *s* 道祖 1811; *sp* 道祖土
Saiga *s* 西賀 336, 斉賀 701, 雑岸 2127, 雑賀
Saigawa *s* 斉川 701, 斎川 1454; *p* 犀川 1803
Saigō *s* 斉郷 701; *p* 西郷 336 ⌈貢
Saigon *p* "Saigon" 西
Saigō Takamori *mh* 西郷隆盛 ⌈郷従道
~ Tsugumichi *mh* 西
Saigū *s* 斉宮 701
Saigusa *s* 七種 17, 福草 1888; *sm* 三枝 22
Saigusabe *s* 福草部 1888
Saigusa Hiroto *ml* 三枝博音 22 ⌈高
~ Yasutaka *ml* 三枝康
Saigyō *ml* 西行 336
~ -zakura *la* 西行桜
Saihaku *p* 西伯 ⌈1467
Saihara *s* 西原, 祭原
Saihōji *p* 西芳寺 336
Saiichirō *m* 才一郎 35, 最一郎 1742
Saiissho *s* 三分一所 22
Saijō *s* 西城 336; *sp* 西条
~ Yaso *ml* 西条八十
Saika *s* 斎鹿 1454
Saikachi *sm* 西海枝 336
Saikai *p* 西海
Saikaidō *p* 西海道
Saikaku *ml* 西鶴
~ okimiyage *l* 西鶴置土産
~ oritome *l* 西鶴織留
~ shokoku-banashi *l* 西鶴諸国咄
Saiki *s* 才木 35, 佐脇 365, 斉木 701, 斎木 1454, 斎宮; *sp* 佐伯 365
Saikichi *m* 斉吉 701, 最吉 1742, 載吉 2050
Saikō 854–57 斉衡 701
~ danshō *l* 西公談抄
Saikoku *sp* 西国 ⌊336
~ risshihen *l* 西国立志編
Saikyō *s* 斎京 1454
Saima *s* 斉間 701, 斎間 1454
Saimaro *m* 才麿 35
Saimei *fh* 斉明 701
Saimoku *s* 西牧 336
Saimon *l* 祭文 1467
Saimura *s* 斉村 701
Sainen *s* 西念 336
Saino *s* 釆野 707
Sainoki *s* 道祖木 1811
Sainoo *s* 道祖尾
Saionji *s* 西園寺 336
~ Kinmochi *mh* 西園寺公望
Saiō toppyakuin *l* 西翁十百韵
Sairaikyo *s* 西来居
Sairyūji *s* 西隆寺
Saisaburō *m* 幸三郎 661
Saisaka *s* 三郎坂 22
Saisei *ml* 犀星 1803
Saisho *s* 斎所 1454, 税所 1642, 最所 1742
~ Atsuko *fl* 税所敦子 1642
Saishu *s* 最首 1742
Saita *s* 産田 1520, 税田 1642; *p* 財田 1143
Saitama *p* 埼玉 1292
Saito *p* 西都 336
Saitō *s* 在藤 314, 西藤 336, 西東, 斉藤 701, 斎藤 1454
~ Dōsan *mh* 斎藤道三
~ Fumi *ml* 斎藤史
~ Makoto *mh* 斎藤実
~ Mokichi *ml* 斎藤茂吉 ⌈野の人
~ Nonohito *ml* 斎藤

~ Ryokuu *ml* 斎藤緑雨
~ Ryū *ml* 斎藤瀏
~ Sanki *ml* 西東三鬼 336 「1454
~ Shōzō *ml* 斎藤昌三
~ Takeshi *ml* 斎藤勇
Saizō *m* 犀蔵 1803
Saizōshū *l* 才蔵集 35
Saji *sp* 佐治 365
Sajie *m* 左治衛 169
Sajima *m* 左司馬
Sajinu *s* 佐自努 365
Saka *s* 久里 45, 争 344, 佐香 365, 酒 1066, 属 1802; *sp* 坂 390. (尺 96, 争 344, 阪 375, 坂 390, 昌 715, 栄 969, 酒 1066, 祥 1074, 逆 1235, 穎 2505, 賢 2579)
Sakaabe *s* 坂合部 390
Sakaba *s* 坂場, 酒葉 1066
Sakabashi *s* 佐下橋 365
Sakabe *s* 争戸 344, 阪部 375, 坂戸 390, 坂部, 酒部 1066
Sakachi *s* 坂乳 390
Sakade *s* 酒出 1066
Sakado *s* 尺度 96
Sakae *m* 光 281, 昌 715, 秀 726, 復 1571, 斌 1590, 富 1715, 蒼 2189, 潤 2277; *m-f-p* 栄 969; *f* 祥枝 1074; *p* 境 2076
Sakaedani *s* 栄谷 969
Sakagami *s* 阪上 375, 坂上 390
Sakagawa *s* 坂川, 酒川 1066
Sakaguchi *s* 阪口 375, 坂口 390
~ Ango *ml* 坂口安吾
Sakahito *m* 穎人 2505
Sakahogai *l* 酒ほがい 1066
Sakahogi *p* 坂祝 390
Sakahoko *l* 逆矛 1235
Sakai *s* 佐介 365, 阪井 375, 栄井 969, 酒人 1066, 酒井, 酒居, 逆井 1235, 境長 2076; *sm-p* 境; *sp* 坂井 390, 界 967, 堺 1560. (界 967, 堺 1560, 境 2076)
Sakaibe *s* 坂谷部 390, 境部 2076
Sakaida *s* 坂井田 390, 酒井田 1066
~ Kakiemon *ma* 酒井田柿右衛門
Sakaide *p* 坂井出 390
Sakaigawa *p* 境川 2076
Sakai Hiroji *ml* 酒井広治 1066 「一
~ Hōitsu *mla* 酒井抱
~ Kosen *ml* 堺枯川 1560 「良伎 375
~ Kuraki *ml* 阪井久
Sakaimaro *m* 界麿 967
Sakaiminato *p* 境港
Sakaino *p* 境野 ⌊2076
Sakairi *s* 坂入 390
Sakaisa *s* 堺沢 1560
Sakai Toshihiko *mlh* 堺利彦
Sakaizumi *s* 酒泉 1066
Sakaji *s* 酒介
Sakaki *s* 坂木 390, 坂寄, 彭 1693, 彭城; *sm* 榊 2106; *m* 栄木 969; *m-l* 賢木 2579; *p* 坂城 390. (榊 2106)
Sakakibara *s* 榊原
~ Yoshibumi *ml* 榊原美文
Sakakida *s* 榊田
Sakakita *p* 坂北 390
Sakakiya *s* 榊谷 2106
Sakakiyama *s* 榊山, 槙山 2297
~ Jun *ml* 榊山潤 2106
Sakakura *s* 坂倉 390
Sakama *s* 坂間 「1066
Sakamaki *s* 坂巻, 酒巻
Sakamaro *m* 酒麻呂
Sakami *s* 酒見
Sakamitsu *s* 酒看都
Sakamizu *s* 坂水 390
Sakamo *s* 坂茂
Sakamochi *s* 坂茂
Sakamoto *s* 阪本 375, 坂元 390, 坂茂, 酒本 1066; *sp* 坂本 390
~ Etsurō *ml* 阪本越郎 375 「蓮洞 390
~ Gurendō *ml* 坂本紅
~ Hiroshi *ml* 坂本浩
~ Ryōma *mh* 坂本竜馬
~ Setchō *ml* 坂本雪鳥
~ Shihōda *ml* 坂本四方太
Sakamuki *s* 酒向 1066
Sakamura *s* 坂村 390
Sakan *s* 目 191; *m* 史 183, 壮 243, 昌 715, 昶 1004, 斌 1590, 属 1802, 興 2586
Sakanai *s* 坂名井 390
Sakanashi *s* 坂梨
Sakanaya *s* 魚屋 1485
Sakane *s* 阪根 375
Sakanishi *s* 坂西 390
Sakaniwa *s* 阪庭 375
Sakano *s* 坂野 390
Sakanoe *s* 阪上 375, 坂上 390, 坂於, 酒上 1066
~ no Iratsume *fl* 坂上郎女 390
Sakanoshita *s* 坂ノ下
Sakanoue *s* 坂上
~ no Mochiki *ml* 坂上望城
~ no Tamuramaro *mh* 坂上田村麻呂
Sakanushi *s* 坂主
Sakao *s* 坂尾; *m* 坂雄, 栄夫 969
Sakara *s* 酒良 1066
Sakari *sp* 十八女 18; *m* 壮 243, 盛 1469
Sakaru *m* 戊 208
Sakashi *m* 斌 1590, 智 1793, 賢 2579
Sakashita *sp* 坂下 390
Sakata *s* 佐方 365, 阪田 375, 栄田 969, 逆田 1235; *sp* 坂田 390; *p* 酒田 1066 「谷 390
Sakatani *s* 阪谷 375, 坂
Sakata Tōjūrō *ma* 坂田藤十郎
Sakato *s* 酒人 1066; *sp* 坂戸 390
Sakatoko *s* 酒作 1066
Sakauchi *sp* 坂内 390
Sakaue *s* 坂上
Sakaushi *s* 坂牛
Sakawa *s* 酒向 1066; *sp* 酒匂
Sakawada *s* 佐川田 365
Sakaya *s* 昌谷 715
Sakayama *s* 栄山 969
Sakayori *s* 阪寄 375, 酒寄 1066, 酒依
Sakazaki *s* 坂崎 390, 昌崎 715 「390
~ Shiran *ml* 坂崎紫瀾
Sakazume *s* 坂爪, 坂詰
(sake 酒 1066, 鮭 2671)
Sakegawa *p* 鮭川
Sakenobe *s* 鮭延
Sakenokimi *m* 酒君 1066
Saki *s* 散吉 1689. (兄 181, 先 280, 早 295, 幸 661, 肯 709, 咲 784, 祖 850, 首 920, 前 921, 祥 1074, 崎 1592, 割 1696A, 福 1888, 鋒 2339, 興 2586, 禧 2628) 「吉 365
Sakichi *m* 左吉 169, 佐
Sakie *f* 崎永 1592
Sakigake *s* 魁 2423
Sakigawa *s* 崎川 1592
Sakigusa *m* 福草 1888
Sakihana *s* 咲花 784
Sakiko *f* 咲喜子 784, 前子 921, 崎子 1592, 福子 1888, 禧子 2628
Sakimaro *m* 福麻呂 1888
Sakimitsu *s* 先光 280; *m* 前光 921
Sakimori *m* 防人 374
Sakimoto *s* 咲本 784, 崎元 1592
Sakimura *s* 崎村
Sakio *m* 左吉雄 169, 幸男 661
Sakisaka *s* 向坂 312
Sakita *s* 崎田 1592
Sakitane *m* 幸殖 661
Sakito *s* 前刀 921; *p* 崎戸 1592
Sakitoyo *m* 前豊 921
Sakiyama *s* 崎山 1592
Sakka *s* 目 191, 眼目 1637, 粟冠 1763, 属 1802
Sakkiden *l* 数奇伝 2169
Sako *s* 佐古 365, 迫 747, 雑古 2127. (迫 747)
Sakō *s* 酒匂 1066, 酒勾, 酒向; *m* 佐綱 365, 荘 933, 栄 969
Sakoda *s* 迫田 747
Sako Jun'ichirō *ml* 佐古純一郎 365
Sakoma *s* 迫間 747
Sakomi *s* 迫水
Sakomizu *s* 迫水
Sakon *m-fl* 左近 169
Sakon'emon *m* 左近衛
Sakonji *s* 左近司 ⌊門
Saku *f* 咲 784; *p* 佐久 365. (尺 96, 冊 190, 作 362, 咋 570, 咲 784, 柵 863, 朔 1393, 酢 1654, 索

1703, 策 1767, 開 1821, 幘 2278, 簣 2687, 爵 2779) 「口 365
Sakuchi *s* 左口 169, 佐
Sakuda *s* 作田 362
Sakuhei *m* 作平
Sakuji *s* 左今次 169 ; *m* 作次 362
Sakuki *p* 作木
Sakuma *s* 作間 ; *sp* 佐久間 365 ; *m* 咲麻 784
~ Teiichi *mh* 佐久間貞一 365 「山
~ Zōzan *mh* 佐久間象
Sakumi *f* 咲美 784
Sakumo *s* 祥雲 1074
Sakumoto *s* 作本 362
Sakuna *s* 作名
Sakunami *s* 作並
Sakune *s* 作根
Sakunosuke *m* 作之助, 策之助 1767
Sakura *sm-f-p* 桜 1373 ; *sp* 佐倉 365 ; *m* 作楽 362. (桜 1373)
Sakuraba *s* 桜間, 桜庭
Sakurabayashi *s* 桜林
Sakurabe *s* 索羅下 1703
Sakurada *s* 桜田 1373
~ Jisuke *ml* 桜田治助
~ Momoe *ml* 桜田百衛
~ Sakō *ml* 桜田左交
Sakurado *sm* 作楽戸 362
Sakurae *p* 桜江 1373
Sakuragawa *sp-la* 桜川
Sakuragi *sp* 桜木
Sakurahime zenden akebono-zōshi *l* 桜姫全伝曙草紙
Sakurai *s* 柵頼 863, 柵瀬 ; *sp* 桜井 1373
~ Chūon *ml* 桜井忠温
~ Jōji *mh* 桜井錠二
~ no eki *l* 桜井駅
~ Tendan *ml* 桜井天壇
Sakurajima *sp-l* 桜島
Sakurako *f* 咲良子 784
Sakurama *s* 桜間 1373
Sakuramachi *s* 桜町
Sakuramoto *s* 桜本
Sakurane *s* 桜根
Sakuraoka *s* 桜岡
Sakura Sōgo *mh* 佐倉宗吾 365
Sakurauchi *s* 桜内 1373
Sakurayama *s* 桜山
Sakurazawa *s* 桜沢
Sakurazono *m* 作楽園 362
Sakusaburō *m* 作三郎
Sakutarō *m* 作太郎, 策太郎 1767
Sakutō *p* 作東 362
Sakuya *s* 作屋
Sakuyama *s* 作山, 佐久山 365 「三 1767
Sakuzō *m* 作造 362, 策
Sakyō *s* 佐京 365, 佐鏡 ; *sp* 左京 169 ; *m* 左脇
Sama *s* 佐満 365. (様
Samani *p* 様似 ⌊2099)
Samata *s* 佐俣 365
Same *f* 醒 2501. (雨 759, 鮫 2672)
Samegai *sp* 醒井 2501
Samegawa *sp* 鮫川 2672
Samejima *s* 鮫島
Samezō *m* 鮫造
Sami *s* 佐海 365, 佐味
Samon *m* 左門 169
Samonji *s* 左文字
Samori *m* 左衛
Samoto *s* 佐本 365
(samu 祥 1074, 寒 1714)
Samukawa *s* 寒河 ; *sp* 寒川
~ Kōtarō *ml* 寒川光太郎 「骨
~ Sokotsu *ml* 寒川鼠
Samumitsu *m* 祥光 1074
Samurō *m* 三郎 22
Samuru *m* 醒 2501
(san 三 22, 山 89, 杉 425, 珊 834, 参 978, 閂 1010, 寋 1434, 産 1520, 棧 1615, 散 1689, 傘 1702, 蒜 1986, 粲 2019, 算 2213, 潒 2455, 讃 3013, 纘 3019, 鑽 3020)
Sana *s* 佐奈 365. (真 1228)
Sanada *sp* 真田
Sanae *f* 早苗 295, 朝阜苗 1672 「助 295
Sanaenosuke *m* 早苗之
Sanage *p* 猿投 2062
Sanagōchi *p* 佐那河内
Sanagu *s* 佐奈宜 ⌊365
Sanai *s* 讃井 3013
Sanaka *s* 佐仲 365 「21
Sanami *s* 佐波 ; *f* 小波
San'ami *ma* 三阿弥 22
Sanao *m* 真男 1228
Sanba *ml* 三馬 22
Sanbasō *lam* 三番叟
Sanbe *s* 三瓶 「絵詞
Sanbō ekotoba *l* 三宝
Sanboku *p* 山北 89
~ kikashū *l* 散木奇歌集 1689
Sanbō myōgishō *l* 三宝名義抄 22
Sanbongi *p* 三本木
Sanbon no hashira *la* 三本柱 「類字抄
Sanbō ruijishō *l* 三宝
Sanbu *p* 山武 89
Sanbuichisho *s* 三分一所 22
Sanda *p* 三田 「実録
Sandai jitsuroku *l* 三代
Sandaishū *l* 三代集
Sandaya *s* 三田谷
Sane *m* 実 678. (人 14, 子 38, 心 49, 仁 57, 収 133, 以 134, 札 145, 平 203, 允 217, 守 284, 志 464, 壱 467, 孚 483, 実 678, 学 719, 尚 753, 良 767, 信 782, 城 796, 咸 1003, 修 1038, 真 1228, 脩 1281, 孫 1540, 猶 1555, 斯 1671, 寔 1710, 誠 1935, 嗣 1937, 愛 2018, 銑 2158, 撰 2258, 諄 2324, 賛 2394, 選 2419, 積 2493, 諟 2512, 績 2814, 護 2877, 櫕 2986)
Saneai *m* 実和 673
Saneaki *m* 実曈
Saneakira *m* 実英, 実麗, 信明 782 「実徳
Saneatsu *m* 実淳 678,
Saneaya *m* 実順 「近
Sanechika *m* 実用, 実
Saneeda *m* 実枝
Saneharu *m* 実栄
Sanehide *m* 実穎
Saneisa *m* 実勲
Sanekata *ml* 実方
Sanekatsu *m* 実逵
Saneko *f* 真子 1228
Sanekoto *m* 実孚 678
Sanemi *m* 実堅, 実誠
Sanemichi *m* 真行 1228
Sanemitsu *m* 実光 678
Sanemochi *m* 実庸
Sanemori *m* 信董 782, 信謹, 真森 1228
Sanenobu *m* 真信
Sanenori *m* 実政 678
Saneoka *m* 実岳
Saneosa *m* 実揖, 実総
Sanesato *m* 実利
Saneshige *m* 実受, 積成 2493
Sanetada *m* 誠忠 1935
Sanetaka *ml* 実隆 678
Sanetake *m* 真節 1228
Sanetaru *m* 実福 678
Sanetō *m* 実遠, 実勝
Sanetomi *m* 実美
Sanetomo *m* 実朝
Sanetoshi *m* 仁寿 57, 実敏 678
Sanetsumu *m* 実万
Saneyane *m* 実梁
Saneyasu *m* 人康 14, 実廉 678, 真庸 1228
Saneyo *m* 実世 678
Saneyori *m* 実頼
Saneyoshi *sm* 実吉 ; *m* 誠美 1935
Sanezato *m* 真郷 1228
Sanezumi *m* 真澄
Sangada *s* 三个田 22
Sangaiya *s* 三階屋
Sangaku *a* 散楽 1689
Sangawa *sp* 寒川 1714
Sange *s* 三下 22
Sango *s* 三五
Sangō *p* 三郷
Sangokushi engi *l* 三国志演義
Sangoku tsūran zusetsu *lh* 三国通覧図説
Sangō shiiki *l* 三教指
Sangū *s* 山宮 89 ⌊帰
~ Makoto *ml* 山宮允
Sangyō gisho *l* 三経義疏 22
Sangyokushū *l* 三玉集
Sanhan kikan sōshitsu *l* 三半規管喪失
San'indō *p* 山陰道 89
Sanji *m* 山治
Sanjirō *m* 讃次郎 3013
Sanjō *sp* 三条 22
Sanjōnishi *s* 三条西
~ Sanetaka *ml* 三条西実隆 「季和
~ Suetomo *ml* 三条西
Sanjō Sanetomi *mh* 三条実美
~ wasan *l* 三帖和讃
Sanjūrō *m* 三重郎

Sanjūrokuninshū *l* 三十六人集
Sanka chōchūka *l* 山家鳥虫歌 89 「記
~ kesshōki *l* 山窩血笑
Sankashū *l* 山家集
Sankichi *m* 三吉 22
Sankō *p* 三光; *l* 山行 89
Sankurō *m* 三九郎 22
Sanmi *m-fl* 三位 「局
~ no Tsubone *fl* 三位
Sanmonjiya *s* 三文字屋
Sanna *ml* 三和, 参和
Sannai *p* 山内 89 ⌊978
Sannan *p* 山南
Sannin-gatawa *la* 三人片輪 22
~ hōshi *l* 三人法師
~ Kichizō kuruwa no hatsukai *l* 三人吉三廓初買
Sanninzuma *l* 三人妻
Sannohe *sp* 三戸
Sannomiya *s* 三宮
Sannosuke *m* 三之助
Sano *sp* 佐野 365
Sanoharu *m* 佐之治
Sanokawa *s* 佐野川
Sano Manabu *ml* 佐野学
Sanomo *s* 讃母 3013
Sano Tsunetami *mh* 佐野常民 365
Sanpei *m* 三平 22
Sanpū *ml* 杉風 425
Sanrai *l* 三籟 22
Sanriku *p* 三陸
Sansai *s* 三梓
Sansaku *m* 三作
Sansei *m* 三省; *p* "Shansi" 山西 89
Sanshichi zenden Nanka no yume *l* 三七全伝南阿夢 22
Sanshirō *m-l* 三四郎
Sanshō *la* 三笑
~-dayū *l* 山椒大夫
~-~ gonin musume *l* 三荘太夫五人嬢 22
Sansui chōkan *a* 山水長巻 89
Sansuke *m* 三介 22
Santō *s* 山登 89, 山藤; *sp* ["Shantung"] 山東; *p* 三島 22
~ Kyōden *ml* 山東京伝 89
Sanuga *s* 佐怒賀 365
Sanui *s* 讃井 3013
Sanuki *s* 佐貫 365, 散吉 1689; *sph* 讃岐 3013
~ no Tenji nikki *l* 讃岐典侍日記
Sanukiōoshi *s* 紗抜大押 1683
Sanu no Chigami no Otome *fl* 狭野茅上娘子 790
Sanwa *sp* 三和 22
San'yō *p* 山陽 89
San'yōdō *p* 山陽道
San'yūtei *s* 三遊亭 22
~ Enchō *mla* 三遊亭円朝
Sanzōshi *l* 三冊子
Sao *s* 佐尾 365. (棹 1620, 操 2448)
Saoe *f* 棹江 1620
Saoko *f* 爽生子 1529
Saori *s* 佐分 365; *p* 佐織
Saotome *s* 五月女 91, 早乙女 295
Saoyama *la* 佐保山 365
Sappa *s* 颯波 2109
Sapporo *p* 札幌 145
Sara *s* 佐良 365. (更 528)
Sarabetsu *p* 更別
Sarara *s* 佐良 365, 讃 3013
Sararaumakai *s* 娑羅羅馬飼 1474 「更級
Sarashina *sp* 更科 528,
~ kikō *l* 更科紀行
~ nikki *l* 更級日記
Saroma *p* 佐呂間 365
Saru *m* 猿 2062. (申 185, 去 266, 除 1059, 猿 2062)
Sarufutsu *p* 猿払
Sarugaku *la* 申楽 185, 猿楽 2062
~ dangi *l* 申楽談儀 185
Saruhashi *s* 猿橋 2062
Sarumino *l* 猿蓑
Sarundo *m* 猿人
Saruta *s* 猿田
Saruwaka *sa* 猿若
Saruwatari *s* 猿渡
Saruyama *s* 猿山
Saruyo *f* 申代 185
Sasa *s* 百百 265, 篠 2691; *sp* 佐々, 佐佐 365; *f* 笹 1772. (小 21, 笹 1772, 楽 2029, 篠 2691, 讃 3013)
Sasabe *s* 佐佐部 365, 雀部 1530, 笹部 1772
Sasabuchi *s* 笹淵
~ Tomoichi *ml* 笹淵友一 「田 1772
Sasada *s* 佐佐田 365, 笹
Sasae *f* 小竹枝 21, 笹栄 1772
Sasagami *p* 笹神
Sasage *s* 捧 1318
Sasagi *s* 雀 1530, 鷦鷯 2976. (雀 1530)
Sasagibe *s* 雀部
Sasaguri *p* 篠栗 2691
Sasahara *s* 佐佐原 365, 笹原 1772, 篠原 2691
Sasai *s* 佐佐井 365, 笹井 1772
Sasaibe *s* 雀部 1530
Sasaichi *m* 笹市 1772
Sasakawa *s* 佐佐川 365, 笹川 1772
~ Rinpū *ml* 笹川臨風
Sasaki *s* 佐々木 365, 佐左木, 佐佐木, 笹木 1772, 篠笥 2691. (陵 1310)
Sasakibe *s* 陵戸, 陵辺
Sasaki Hirotsuna *ml* 佐々木弘綱 365
~ Kiichi *ml* 佐々木基一 「郎
~ Kojirō *l* 佐々木小次
~ Kuni *ml* 佐々木邦
~ Mitsuzō *ml* 佐々木味津三 「茂索
~ Mosaku *ml* 佐佐木
~ Nobutsuna *ml* 佐佐木信綱; *mh* 佐々木信綱
~ Takamaru *ml* 佐々木孝丸
~ Takatsuna *mh-la* 佐々木高綱 「俊郎
~ Toshirō *ml* 佐左木
Sasakiyama *s* 佐佐貴山, 狭狭城山 790
Sasako *sf* 笹子 1772
Sasakura *s* 佐佐倉 365, 笹倉 1772, 篠倉 2691
Sasama *s* 笹間 1772
Sasamegoto *l* 私語 637
Sasameyuki *l* 細雪 1958
Sasamori *s* 笹森 1772
Sasamoto *s* 笹本
~ Tora *ml* 笹本寅
Sasamura *s* 笹村
Sasanami *s* 楽浪 2029; *f* 小波 21
Sasano *s* 小狭野, 篠野 2691; *sf* 笹野 1772
Sasanokuma *s* 楽楽前 2029, 楽楽熊
Sasanuma *s* 笹沼 1772
Sasao *s* 笹尾
Sasaoka *s* 笹岡
Sasase *s* 笹瀬
Sasashima *s* 笹島
Sasau *s* 笹生
Sasawara *s* 笹原
Sasaya *s* 笹屋, 笹谷, 篠屋 2691
Sasayama *s* 笹山 1772; *sp* 篠山 2691
Sasazaki *s* 笹崎 1772
Sasazawa *s* 笹沢
~ Saho *ml* 笹沢左保
~ Yoshiaki *ml* 笹沢美明
Sase *s* 佐世 365, 佐瀬
Sasebo *p* 佐世保
Saseyama *p* 佐世山
(sashi 刺 654, 指 800, 挾 1043, 差 1164)
Sashibara *s* 指原 800
Sashichi *m* 佐七 365
Sashida *s* 指田 800
Sashidō *s* 小食堂 21
Sashiga *s* 刺賀 654
Sashigami *s* 差紙 1164
Sashijiku *s* 指宿 800
Sashima *sp* 猿島 2062
Sashō *s* 佐生 365, 佐粧
Sasō *s* 佐佐布, 佐佐生, 佐宗, 佐雙, 笹生 1772
Sasoku *s* 早速 295
Sassa *sp* 佐々 365, 佐佐
~ Narimasa *mh* 佐々成政 「雪
~ Seisetsu *ml* 佐々醒
Sassui *s* 薩埵 2684
(sasu 刺 654)
Sasuga *s* 流石 1332
Sasuke *s* 佐介 365
Sata *sp* 佐多. (究 492, 莫 1175) 「365
~ Ineko *fl* 佐多稲子
Satake *s* 早竹 295, 佐竹 365, 佐武
Satani *s* 佐谷
Satara *s* 滑良 1857
Satarō *m* 佐太郎 365
Sato *m* 悟 1053; *f* 佐都 365; *p* 里 517. (仁 57

公 156, 吏 329, 利 436, 邑 460, 里 517, 束 536, 怜 565, 知 636, 惢 703, 学 719, 俐 775, 郊 888, 巷 974, 彦 1007, 悟 1053, 郡 1146, 恵 1226, 哲 1227, 県 1252, 敏 1409, 都 1419, 量 1741, 覚 1752, 答 1765, 智 1793, 達 1810, 詮 1934, 聖 2030, 徳 2063, 郷 2112, 睿 2199, 聡 2311, 慧 2392, 熙 2409, 閭 2426, 隣 2443, 諭 2510, 叡 2555, 賢 2579, 凞 2583, 憬 2604, 巖 2774, 識 2810)
Satō s 佐藤 365; p 佐東
Satofumi m 学文 719
Satogawa s 里川 517
Satoharu sm 里春
Satō Haruo ml 佐藤春夫 365
Satohiro m 覚弘 1752
Satohito m 識仁 2810
Satō Ichiei ml 佐藤一英 365 「2344
Satoki m 覚行 1752, 鋭
Satoko f 里子 517, 怜子 565, 俐子 775, 郊子 888, 都子 1419, 智子 1793, 賢子 2579
Satō Kōroku ml 佐藤紅緑 365
Satomi s 里見 517; f 郊美 888; p 里美 517
Satomichi m 達道 1810
Satomi hakkenden l 里見八犬伝 517
~ Ton ml 里見弴
Satomura s 里村
~ Kinzō ml 里村欣三
~ Shōha ml 里村紹巴
Satō Naokata mh 佐藤直方 365
Satonobu m 知暢 636
Satō Nobuhiro mh 佐藤信淵 365
~ Norikiyo ml 佐藤義清 「1227
Satoo m 惢夫 703, 哲夫
Satori s 左部 169, 佐鳥 365; m 悟里 1053
Satoru m 了 9, 仏 128, 兌 447, 知 636, 学 719, 俠 773, 悟 1053, 哲 1227, 済 1336, 暁 1596, 覚 1752, 智 1793, 達 1810, 解 1923, 詮 1934, 聖 2030, 聡 2311, 慧 2392, 賢 2579, 斅 2892
Satō Satarō ml 佐藤佐太郎 365
Satoshi m 刣 432, 邑 460, 里 517, 怜 565, 知 636, 俊 1039, 悟 1053, 秩 1119, 恵 1226, 哲 1227, 捷 1323, 敏 1409, 敏之, 悊 1480, 惺 1547, 暁 1596, 喆 1646, 敬 1691, 覚 1752, 智 1793, 達 1810, 詮 1934, 聖 2030, 郷司 2112, 郷四, 睿 2199, 聡 2311, 聡敏, 慧 2392, 穎 2505, 諭 2510, 叡 2555, 賢 2579, 巖 2774, 譓 2809. (啓 1491)
Satoshiko f 啓子
Satoshō p 里庄 517
Satō Sōnosuke ml 佐藤惣之助 365
Satosu m 諭 2510
Satouchi s 里内 517
Satoyasu m 達安 1810
Satoyoshi s 里吉 517
Satō Yoshisuke ml 佐藤義亮 365
Satsu f 佐都. (札 145, 冊 190, 刷 655, 殺 1138, 茁 1173, 颯 2109, 察 2180, 擦 2601, 薩 2684)
Satsuka s 佐塚 365
Satsuki sm 五月 91; f 皐月 1197, 皐月 1459
Satsuma sph 薩摩 2684
~ Jōun ma 薩摩浄雲
~ no Kami la 薩摩守
Satta s 薩陀, 薩埵
Satte p 幸手 661
Sawa s 沢 404, 颯波 2109; sp 佐波 365. (沢 404, 兌 447, 爽 1529)
Sawabara s 沢原 404
Sawabatake s 沢畑, 沢畠
Sawabe s 沢辺, 沢部
Sawachi s 沢地
Sawada s 沢田; p 佐和田 365 「二郎 404
~ Shōjirō ma 沢田正
Sawae s 沢江
Sawaguchi s 沢口
Sawahashi s 沢橋
Sawai s 沢井
Sawajirō m 沢二郎
Sawaki s 佐脇 365, 沢木 404 「一
~ Kin'ichi ml 沢木欣
Sawako f 爽子 1529
Sawamata s 沢俣 404
Sawamoto s 沢本
Sawamura s 沢村
~ Koi ml 沢村胡夷
~ Tanosuke ma-l 沢村田之助
Sawanaka s 沢中
Sawano s 沢野
Sawa Nobuyoshi mh 沢宣嘉 「久雄
Sawano Hisao ml 沢野
Sawao s 沢尾
Sawara sp 早良 295, 佐原 365; p 砂原 876
Sawarabi l 早蕨 295
Sawaragi s 椹 2097
Sawashima s 沢島 404
Sawatari s 猿渡 2062
Sawato s 沢渡 404
Sawauchi s 佐羽内 365; sp 沢内 404
Sawaura s 沢浦
Sawaya s 沢屋, 沢谷
Sawayama s 沢山
Sawayanagi s 沢柳
~ Masatarō mh 沢柳政太郎
Sawazaki s 沢崎
Saya s 茶谷 931; sp 佐屋 365. (居 737, 爽 1529, 鞘 2542)
Sayako f 爽子 1529, 紗綾子 1683, 鞘子 2542
Sayama s 茶山 931, 猨山 1554, 猿山 2062; sm 佐山 365; sp 狭山 790; m 左也馬 169
Sayanagi s 佐柳 365
Sayo sp 佐用; f 小夜 21
Sayogoromo l 小夜衣
Sayuri f 小百合
(saza 鉅 1946)
Sazae f 螺江 2805
Sazai m 礫 2987
Sazaka s 鉅鹿 1946
Sazarashi s 九石 16
Sazawa s 佐沢 365
Saze s 佐善
Sazen m 左膳 169
Sazō m 佐三 365
Sazuku m 授 1315
(se 世 335, 施 831, 背 957, 畝 1142, 脊 1212, 催 2060, 瀬 2794, 灑 2962)
Seba s 洗馬 817, 瀬場 2794
Sebata s 瀬畑, 瀬端
Sebee m 瀬兵衛
(sechi 折 385, 晢 1478, 説 2143, 察 2180)
Sechibaru p 世知原 335
Sedani s 瀬谷 2794
Sefuri p 背振 957
Sega s 瀬賀 2794
Segai s 揖斐 1550, 楫斐 1899; sp 清和井 1342
Segami s 瀬上 2794
Segawa s 瀬川, 瀬河
~ Jokō ml 瀬川如皐
Seguchi s 瀬口
Sehei m 瀬平
Sei sm 清 1342; m 省 1013, 精 2131; f 勢似 2039. (井 103, 正 205, 生 214, 成 322, 世 335, 西 336, 声 465, 性 564, 征 580, 制 656, 青 700, 斉 701, 城 796, 浄 823, 牲 830, 姓 846, 政 881, 星 946, 妛 950, 妻 959, 呰 972, 省 1013, 凊 1021, 倩 1031, 栖 1101, 晟 1187, 済 1336, 清 1342, 盛 1469, 惺 1547, 晴 1597, 婧 1601, 税 1642, 萋 1722, 犀 1803, 靖 1905, 誠 1935, 鉦 1941, 細 1958, 歳 1995, 貰 2011, 聖 2030, 勢 2039, 際 2073, 蜻 2128, 精 2131, 静 2145, 誓 2218, 請 2323, 製 2388, 醒 2501, 整 2581, 騂 2665, 瀞 2793, 鯖 2830, 躋 2950, 霽 2978)
Seiashō l 井蛙抄 103
Seibee m 清兵衛 1342
~ to hyōtan l 清兵衛と瓢箪 「成美 322
Seibi m 正美 205; ml
Seibu p 西部 336
Seichū m 正中 205
Seidan matsu no shirabe l 清談松の調 1342 「l 清談峰初花
~-mine no hatsuhana
Seiemon m 清右衛門
Seifū m 清風 「2218
Seiganji p-la 誓願寺

Seige *s* 清家 1342
Seigen *s* 西願 336; *l* 青玄 700
Seigenji *s* 生源寺 214
Seigo *s* 生子; *m* 省吾 1013, 静吾 2145
Seigō *m* 正剛 205
Seihachirō *m* 精八郎
Seihi *p* 西彼 336 ⌊2131
Seiichi *m* 清一 1342, 精一 2131, 静一 2145
Seiichirō *m* 成一郎 322, 清一郎 1342, 盛一郎 1469, 誠一郎 1935, 精一郎 2131
Seiiki *p-lh* 西域 336
Seiji *m* 政司 881, 済治 1336, 清二 1342, 清治, 誠二 1935, 誠司, 誠次, 誠治, 静治 2145
Seijirō *m* 清次郎 1342, 誠二郎 1935, 誠次郎
Seiji yōryaku *l* 政事要略 881
Seijiyu kōshaku *l* 清治湯講釈 1342
Seiju *m* 正寿 205
Seika *s* 清家 1342; *ml* 惺窩 1547; *p* 精華 2131
~ bunshū *l* 惺窩文集 1547
Seikanji *s* 清閑寺 1342
Seika no ichi *l* 青果の市 700
Seikazoku *l* 聖家族 2030
Seiken *m* 清見 1342
Seiki *m* 正記 205
Seikichi *m* 精吉 2131
Seikinha *l* 星菫派 946
Seiko *m* 清湖 1342
Seima *m* 清馬
Seimeiō *mh* 聖明王 2030
Seimiya *s* 清宮 1342, 静宮 2145
Seinaiji *p* 清内路 1342
Seinen *m* 正年 205, 成年 322
Seino *s* 清野 1342
Seinosuke *m* 清之助, 誠之助 1935
Seiōbo *fh-la* "Hsi-wang-mu" 西王母
Seirō *p* 聖籠 2030 ⌊336
Seisa *m* 清砂 1342
Seisaburō *m* 誠三郎 1935
Seisaku *m* 清作 1342
Seisanryō hari *l* 聖三稜玻璃 2030
Seishichi *m* 清七 1342
Seishichirō *m* 精七郎 2131
Seishirō *m* 征四郎 580, 清四郎 1342 ⌈納言
Sei Shōnagon *fl* 清少
Seisuishō *l* 醒睡笑 2501
Seisuke *m* 誠介 1935, 誠亮 ⌈1342
Seita *s* 背板 957, 清田
Seitan *p* 西淡 336
Seitarō *m* 清太郎 1342, 誠太郎 1935, 精太郎 2131, 静太郎 2145
Seitō *s* 清藤 1342; *m* 正菫 205; *p* "Tsingtao" 青島 700, 青嶹; *l* 青鞜
Seiwa *mh-p* 清和 1342; *p* 勢和 2039 ⌈2145
Seiya *s* 清家 1342, 静宮
Seiyama *s* 清山 1342
Seiyō dōchū hizakurige *l* 西洋道中膝栗毛 336
Seizaburō *m* 清三郎 1342, 誠三郎 1935
Seizō *m* 省三 1013, 清蔵 1342, 誠三 1935, 精三 2131, 躋造 2950
Seken mune-zan'yō *l* 世間胸算用 335
~ musuko katagi *l* 世間息子気質
~ musume katagi *l* 世間娘容気
~ tedai katagi *l* 世間手代気質
~ tekake katagi *l* 世間妾気質
Seki *s* 尺 96, 石 172, 世木 335, 関 2245, 瀬木 2794; *m* 積 2493. (夕 33, 尺 96, 斥 167, 石 172, 汐 250, 赤 443, 刺 654, 昔 699, 岩 942, 脊 1212, 席 1242, 迹 1249, 釈 1395, 寂 1436, 晢 1791, 跡 1926, 勣 1969, 碩 2116, 関 2245, 潟 2273, 積 2493, 錫 2524, 績 2814)
Sekiba *s* 関場 2245
Sekida *s* 関田
Sekidera *s* 関寺
~ Komachi *la* 関寺小町 ⌈96
Sekido *s* 関戸; *l* 尺土
Sekie *s* 尺采, 関江 2245
Sekifuji *s* 関藤
Sekigahara *p* 関ヶ原
Sekigane *p* 関金
Sekiguchi *s* 関口
~ Jirō *ml* 関口次郎
Sekihara *s* 関原
~ Yoichi *la* 関原与市
Sekijima *s* 関島
Sekijō *sm* 赤城 443; *p* 関城 2245
Sekikawa *sp* 関川
Sekime *s* 関目
Sekimizu *s* 関水
Sekimoto *s* 関本
Sekimura *s* 関村
Sekinaka *s* 関中
Sekine *s* 関根
~ Hiroshi *ml* 関根弘
Sekino *s* 関野
Sekinomiya *p* 関宮
Sekio *s* 関尾, 関岳, 関岡; *m* 関雄
Sekiroku *m* 碩六 2116
Seki Ryōichi *ml* 関良一 2245 ⌈942
Sekisaburō *m* 岩三郎
Sekisen *p* 関前 2245
Sekishirō *m* 関四郎
Seki Takakazu *mh* 関孝和 ⌈集 172
Sekitei kushū *l* 石鼎句
Sekito *s* 勢喜門 2039
Seki Tokuya *ml* 関登久也 2245
Sekitori senryō-nobori *la* 関取千両幟
Sekiuchi *s* 関内
Sekiwa *s* 関和 ⌈関屋
Sekiya *s* 関矢, 関谷; *sl*
Sekiyado *p* 関宿
Sekiya Kiyokage *mh* 関谷清景
Sekiyama *s* 関山
Sekizaki *s* 関崎
Sekizawa *s* 関沢
Sekizuka *s* 関塚
Seko *s* 世古 335, 瀬古
Sema *s* 瀬間 ⌊2794
Semi *s* 瀬見. (蟬 2733)
Semimaru *m-la* 蟬丸
Semine *p* 瀬峰 2794
Semoto *s* 瀬本
(semu 譲 2918)
Semura *s* 瀬村 2794
Sen *s* 千 44, 泉 965; *sm* 宣 919. (川 20, 山 89, 仟 130, 占 153, 仙 228, 亘 262, 全 271, 先 280, 芊 287, 舛 367, 担 581, 苫 686, 洗 817, 浅 827, 宣 919, 前 921, 茜 928, 泉 965, 染 968, 専 973, 閂 1010, 省 1013, 扇 1156, 晋 1215, 偂 1274, 船 1391, 釧 1415, 産 1520, 禅 1886, 詮 1934, 亶 1972, 蒨 1982, 羨 2009, 僊 2059, 銓 2156, 銑 2158, 銭 2160, 撰 2258, 潜 2272, 榑 2292, 賤 2318, 銅 2341, 箭 2397, 選 2419, 膳 2463, 鮎 2547, 暹 2593, 鮮 2670, 薦 2683, 瓊 2717, 瞻 2726, 蟬 2733, 顓 2827)
Sena *s* 肖奈 451, 瀬名
Senami *s* 瀬浪 ⌊2794
Senba *s* 千羽 44, 千波, 千場, 仙波 228, 洗場 817
Senbazuru *l* 千羽鶴 44
Senboku *p* 仙北 228, 泉北 965
Senbon *s* 千本 44
Senbonmatsu *s* 千本松
Senchō *p* 千丁
Senda *s* 千田, 仙田 228, 全田 271
Sendai *s* 千代 44; *sp* 仙台 228; *p* 川内 20
Sendo *s* 仙渡 228
Sendō *s* 仙道
Senga *s* 千賀 44
Sengawa *s* 千川
Senge *s* 千家 ⌈元麿
~ Motomaro *ml* 千家
Sengohyakuban uta-awase *l* 千五百番歌合 ⌈228
Sengoku *s* 千石, 仙石
Senhata *p* 千畑 44
Sen'ichirō *m* 専一郎 973
Senja *s* 神社 853 ⌈973
Senji *m* 宣治 919, 専治
Senjimon *l* 千字文 44
Senjirō *m* 仙次郎 228
Senjō *s* 千装 44
Senju *fa-la* 千手
Senjū *s* 千住
Senjuin *s* 千手院

Senjūrō *m* 銑十郎 2158
Senjūshō *l* 撰集抄 2258
Senka *ml* 仙果 228
Senkaku *ml* 仙覚
Senmaya *p* 千厩 44
Senmyō *l* 宣命 919
Senna *s* 仙名 228
Sennami *s* 仙波 ⌈965
Sennan *p* 仙南, 泉南
Senno *s* 千野 44
Sennojō *m* 釧之允 2341
Sen no Rikyū *ma* 千利休 44 ⌈973
Sennosuke *m* 専之助
Seno *s* 瀬能 2794, 瀬野
Senogawa *p* 瀬野川
Senokuchi *s* 瀬之口
Senoo *s* 瀬尾; *sp* 妹尾
Senryū *l* 川柳 20 ⌊848
Senryūtei *s* 千柳亭 44
Senshi *m* 千之
～ Naishinnō *fl* 選子内親王 2419
Senshirō *m* 仙四郎 228
Senshū *s* 千秋 44
Senshu waka *l* 千首和
Sensui *s* 泉水 965 ⌊歌
Sentarō *m* 千太郎 44, 仙太郎 228, 専太郎 973, 詮太郎 1934
Sentō *s* 千頭 44
～ hyakuban utaawase *l* 仙洞百番歌合 228
Sentomaru *m* 千任丸 44
Sentō shinwa *l* 銭湯新話 2160
Senuma *s* 瀬沼 2794
～ Kayō *fl* 瀬沼夏葉
～ Shigeki *ml* 瀬沼茂樹
Sen'ya *s* 銭谷 2160; *m* 千也 44, 千弥 ⌈2158
Senzaburō *m* 銑三郎
Senzai *lam* 千歳 44
Senzaishū *l* 千載集
Senzaki *s* 千崎, 先崎
Senzoku *s* 千足 44 ⌊280
Senzu *s* 仙頭 228
Seo *s* 妹尾 848, 瀬尾 2794
Sera *s* 世良 335, 西羅 336; *sp* 世羅 335
Seranishi *p* 世羅西
Serata *s* 世良田
(seri 芹 478, 迫 747)
Serikawa *s* 芹川 478
Serikoshi *s* 芹草越
Serino *s* 芹野
Serita *s* 芹田, 迫田 747
～ Hōsha *ml* 芹田鳳車
Serizawa *s* 芹沢 ⌊478
～ Kōjirō *ml* 芹沢光治
Seryū *s* 芹生 ⌈良
Sesaki *s* 瀬崎 2794
Seshima *s* 妹島 848, 瀬島 2794
Seshimo *s* 瀬下
Seshita *s* 瀬下
Sesonji *s* 世尊寺 335
Sesshōseki *la* 殺生石 1138
Sesshū *ma* 雪舟 1495
Sesson Yūbai *ml* 雪村友梅
Seta *s* 世田 335, 勢田 2039; *sp* 勢多; *p* 瀬田 2794
Setagaya *p* 世田谷 335
Setaka *p* 瀬高 2794
Setana *p* 瀬棚
Setchūbai *l* 雪中梅 1495
Seto *sp* 瀬戸 2794
Setō *s* 瀬藤
Setoda *p* 瀬戸田
Setogawa *s* 瀬戸川
Setoguchi *s* 瀬戸口
Setouchi *p* 瀬戸内
～ Harumi *ml* 瀬戸内晴美
Setoyama *s* 瀬戸山
Setsu *m* 節 2215. (切 51, 折 385, 殺 1138, 茁 1173, 設 1401, 晢 1478, 雪 1495, 接 1548, 摂 1837, 説 2143, 節 2215)
Setsubun *la* 節分
Setsuda *s* 説田 2143
Setsugekka *l* 雪月花 1495
Setsuji *m* 節治 2215
Setsuko *f* 茁子 1173, 説子 2143, 節子 2215
Setsumon *l* 雪門 1495
Setsuya *s* 世津谷 335
Setsuyōshū *l* 節用集
Setsuzō *m* 節蔵 ⌊2215
Settai *la* 摂待 1837
Settsu *sph* 摂津
Sewaki *s* 瀬脇 2794
Seya *s* 世谷 335, 瀬谷 2794 ⌈瀬山 2794
Seyama *s* 世家真 335,
Sezaemon *m* 瀬左衛門
Sezai *s* 瀬在
Sha *s* 車 532. (沙 392, 社 406, 車 532, 舎 721, 者 769, 酒 814, 柘 864, 砂 876, 射 1144, 捨 1324, 斜 1392, 娑 1474, 紗 1683, 奢 1706, 煮 1787)
Shakkō *l* 赤光 443
Shakkyō *la* 石橋 172
Shakotan *p* 積丹 2493
(shaku 尺 96, 斥 167, 石 172, 赤 443, 昨 570, 昔 699, 借 1032, 迹 1249, 釈 1395, 這 1515, 策 1767, 晳 1791, 跡 1926, 勣 1969, 潟 2273, 諸 2329, 積 2493, 錫 2524, 綽 2529, 緒 2537, 爵 2779, 績 2814) ⌈空 1395
Shaku Chōkū *ml* 釈迢
Shakudo *s* 赤土 443
Shakudō *s* 赤藤
Shakunage *l* 石楠 172
Shaku Nihongi *l* 釈日本紀 1395
Shakuzuru *sma* 赤鶴 443 ⌈hai" 上海 47
Shanhai *p-l* "Shang-
Shaō *ml* "Shakespeare" 沙翁 392
Sharebon *l* 洒落本 814
Shari *p* 斜里 1392; *la* 舎利 721
～ santan *l* 舎利讃歎
Shariki *p* 車力 532
Shasekishū *l* 沙石集 392
Shatani *s* 車谷 532
Shatei *l* 舎弟 721
Shazensō *l* 車前草 532
(shi 之 24, 巳 30, 子 38, 士 41, 下 46, 支 63, 止 87, 仕 124, 示 148, 只 157, 司 164, 石 172, 史 183, 四 188, 市 195, 矢 215, 白 216, 氏 223, 次 226, 此 254, 旨 263, 芝 289, 西 336, 自 340, 似 350, 孜 378, 址 386, 沚 391, 志 464, 至 485, 豕 530, 使 556, 侍 559, 似 561, 泗 588, 祉 608, 枝 631, 知 636, 私 637, 祀 640, 刺 654, 糸 720, 事 768, 指 800, 施 831, 姉 847, 柿 867, 茨 932, 是 947, 思 966, 皆 972, 屎 989, 咫 996, 俟 1035, 胝 1082, 時 1086, 始 1092, 祇 1127, 師 1130, 者 1214, 姿 1217, 柴 1221, 翅 1248, 視 1348, 移 1378, 祇 1380, 畤 1382, 砥 1386, 笥 1472, 脚 1612, 詞 1665, 斯 1670, 晉 1700, 崇 1774, 獅 1835, 辞 1918, 試 1932, 詩 1933, 嗣 1937, 紙 1953, 蒔 1985, 資 2012, 歯 2051, 禔 2120, 誌 2141, 肆 2144, 紫 2209, 幟 2260, 賜 2317, 滋 2460, 熾 2465, 積 2493, 諟 2512, 絲 2526, 髭 2697, 慈 2701, 贄 2781, 識 2810, 磯 2916)
Shia *s* 塩飽 1846
Shiba *s* 司馬 164, 志波 464, 柴 1221, 斯波 1670, 榛葉 2108, 標葉 2298; *sp* 芝 289. (芝, 柴 1221)
Shibafu *s* 芝生 289
Shiba Fukio *ml* 芝不器男
Shibagaki *s* 芝垣
Shibahana *s* 庁鼻 174
Shibahara *s* 芝原 289, 柴原 1221
Shibahashi *s* 柴橋
Shibai *s* 柴井
Shibakawa *sp* 芝川 289
Shibaki *s* 芝木
Shibakin *m* 芝金
Shibaki Yoshiko *fl* 芝木好子
Shibako *f* 柴子 1221
Shibakōji *s* 芝小路 289
Shiba Kōkan *ma* 司馬江漢 164
Shibama *s* 芝間 289
Shibamiya *s* 柴宮 1221
Shibamoto *s* 芝本 289, 柴本 1221
Shibamura *s* 芝村 289
Shibanai *s* 柴内 1221
Shibano *s* 芝野 289, 柴野 1221 ⌈山
～ Ritsuzan *mh* 柴野栗
Shibanuma *s* 柴沼
Shibaoka *s* 柴岡
Shibaraku *la* 暫 2402
Shiba Ryōtarō *ml* 司馬遼太郎 164 ⌈1221
Shibasaburō *s* 柴三郎
Shiba Sen *mlh* "Ssu-ma Ch'ien" 司馬遷 164

Shibata *s* 芝田 289; *sp* 柴田 1221, 新発田 1965
Shiba Tachito *mh* 司馬達等 164
Shibata Hakuyōjo *fl* 柴田白葉女 1221 「家
～ Katsuie *mh* 柴田勝
～ Kyūō *mh* 柴田鳩翁
～ Renzaburō *ml* 柴田錬三郎
～ Tenma *ml* 柴田天馬
Shiba Tatto *mh* 司馬達等 164
Shibata Zeshin *ma* 柴田是真 1221
Shibatei *s* 芝亭 289
Shibatsuji *s* 芝辻
Shibaya *s* 芝屋
Shibayama *s* 柴山 1221; *sp* 芝山 289
Shiba Yoshimasa *mh* 斯波義将 1670
Shibazaki *s* 芝崎 289, 柴崎 1221
(shibe 標 2298)
Shibecha *p* 標茶
Shiberia *p* "Siberia" 西伯利亜 336
Shibetsu *p* 士別 41, 標津 2298 「2669
Shibi *s* 志斐 464; *m* 鮪
Shibōta *s* 柴生田 1221
～ Minoru *ml* 柴生田稔 「1334)
Shibu *s* 四分 188. (渋
Shibue *s* 渋江, 渋谷
～ Chūsai *mh-l* 渋江抽斎
Shibuemon *m* 渋右衛 ⌊門
Shibui *s* 渋井
Shibukawa *s* 渋河; *sp* 渋川
～ Genji *ml* 渋川玄耳
～ Gyō *ml* 渋川驍
～ Shunkai *mh* 渋川春 ⌊海
Shibuki *s* 渋木
Shibun yōryō *l* 紫文要領 2209
Shibushi *p* 志布志 464
Shibuta *s* 志富田
Shibutani *s* 渋谷 1334
Shibuya *sp* 渋谷
～ Sadasuke *ml* 渋谷定輔
Shibuzawa *s* 渋沢
～ Eiichi *mh* 渋沢栄一
Shichi *s* 志知 464. (七 17, 室 1183, 時 1382, 悉 1481, 悉 2020A, 質 2395, 櫛 2797)
Shichichin *s* 七珍 17
Shichida *s* 七田
Shichifuku *s* 七福
Shichigahama *p* 七ケ浜 「宿
Shichigashuku *p* 七ケ
Shichiike *s* 志地池 464
Shichijō *s* 七条 17; *p* 七城 「落
Shichiki-ochi *la* 七騎
Shichiku shoshinshū *l* 糸竹初心集 720
Shichinohe *sp* 七戸 17
Shichiri *s* 七里
Shichirō *m* 七郎
Shichirobei *m* 七郎平
Shichiroku *m* 七六
Shichitarō *m* 七太郎
Shichiyō *l* 七曜
Shichizaemon *m* 七左衛門
Shida *s* 正田 205, 信田 782, 思 966, 滋田 2460; *sp* 志田 464, 信太 782; *p* 志太 464
Shidachi *s* 志立
Shidami *s* 志段, 志談
Shidan *s* 志談
Shidao *s* 歯朶尾 2051
Shidara *s* 雑楽 2127; *sp* 設楽 1401
Shida Sokin *ml* 志田素琴 464 「2414
Shidate *s* 志立; *m* 幣
Shida Yaba *ml* 志田野坡 464
Shidehara *s* 幣原 2414
～ Kijūrō *mh* 幣原喜重 ⌊郎
Shido *p* 志度 464
Shidō *s* 志道
Shidori *s* 委文 960
Shifūdo *l* 詩風土 1933
Shiga *sp* 四賀 188; *sp-la* 志賀 464; *p* 滋賀 2460
Shigaki *s* 紫垣 2209
Shiga Kiyoshi *mh* 志賀潔 464 「子 188
～ Mitsuko *fl* 四賀光
～ Naoya *ml* 志賀直哉 464 「穴太
Shiganoanaho *s* 志賀
Shigaraki *sp* 信楽 782
Shiga Shigetaka *mlh* 志賀重昂 464
Shige *s* 志毛; *m* 重 1017; *f* 臣 527, 苞 688, 稠 1915, 賁 2367. (十 18, 子 38, 方 85, 木 109, 以 134, 兄 181, 戊 208, 包 218, 列 257, 卯 259, 苄 287, 芝 289, 成 322, 枝 631, 林 633, 茂 691, 受 730, 兕 758, 信 782, 城 796, 茆 926, 茀 927, 草 934, 発 953, 栄 969, 咸 1003, 為 1005, 乗 1016, 重 1017, 従 1050, 殷 1139, 華 1168, 挙 1207, 柴 1221, 恵 1226, 甚 1267, 猗 1301, 隆 1313, 習 1468, 盛 1469, 順 1532, 婁 1722, 葆 1726, 董 1731, 賀 1756, 達 1810, 楙 1889, 稠 1915, 誠 1935, 義 1975, 蓁 1984, 茲 1987, 蒼 1988, 誉 2000, 誉 2010, 種 2124, 精 2131, 蓊 2189, 蔚 2191, 彙 2200, 諄 2324, 調 2328, 鋪 2340, 駛 2348, 蕃 2371, 滋 2460, 樹 2483, 維 2540, 薫 2567, 篤 2576, 薦 2683, 懋 2700, 慈 2701, 鎮 2751, 穣 2802, 穠 2803, 繁 2848, 韡 2885, 鑑 2968)
Shigeaki *m* 以昭 134, 茂明 691, 重陽 1017
Shigeatsu *m* 重厚, 鎮重 2751
Shigeaya *m* 成章 322
Shigechika *m* 重近 1017, 重隣, 重親, 彙邇 2200
Shigeeda *s* 重枝 1017
Shigefu *s* 滋生 2460
Shigehara *s* 茂原 691, 重原 1017
Shigeharu *m* 滋春 2460
Shigehide *m* 茂秀 691, 重栄 1017
Shigehiko *m* 枝彦 631, 栄彦 969, 重彦 1017, 蔚彦 2191, 滋彦 2460
Shigehiro *m* 重溥 1017, 重鴻, 誠弥 1935, 誠寛
Shigehisa *sm* 重久 1017; *m* 重旧, 稠尚 1915
(shigei 茂 691)
Shigeie *m* 重舎 1017, 鎮家 2751
Shigeiko *f* 茂子 691
Shigeji *s* 重地 1017; *m* 茂二 691, 重次 1017, 繁二 2848
Shigejirō *m* 樹次郎 2483
Shigekado *m* 卯外 259, 重廉 1017
Shigekage *m* 繁蔭 2848
Shigekane *m* 重鎌 1017
Shigekata *m* 重容
Shigekatsu *m* 重功, 誠克 1935 「従尹 1050
Shigekazu *m* 重一 1017,
Shigeki *m* 茂樹 691, 茆樹 926, 栄樹 969, 重喜 1017, 重樹, 盛樹 1469, 種樹 2124, 蓊 2189, 蕃樹 2371 「繁吉 2848
Shigekichi *m* 茂橘 691,
Shigekiyo *m* 木喜代 109
Shigeko *f* 子子 38, 苄子 287, 成子 322, 茂子 691, 茀子 927, 栄子 969, 婁子 1722, 董子 1731, 滋子 2460, 樹子 2483, 薫子 2567, 穠子 2803
Shigekore *m* 重茲 1017
Shigemaru *m* 薫丸 2567
Shigemasa *m* 茂済 691, 重昌 1017, 重政
Shigematsu *s* 重松
Shigemi *s* 重見; *m* 成相 322, 成実, 茂 691, 竜 1199, 葆見 1726
Shigemichi *m* 成達 322, 重迪 1017, 重理, 重教, 重道 「*m* 成允 322
Shigemitsu *sm* 重光;
Shigemori *s* 重森 1017; *sm-p* 重盛
Shigemoto *sm* 重元, 重本; *m* 茂苞 691, 重太 1017 「重村 1017
Shigemura *s* 茂村 691,
Shigenami *m* 鎮漣 2751
Shigenao *m* 重直 1017, 挙直 1207
Shigenari *m* 重成 1017, 重然 「1139
Shigene *m* 重音, 殷根
Shigeno *s* 茂野 691, 重野 1017, 繁野 2848; *sm* 滋野 2460
Shigenobu *sm-p* 重信 1017; *m* 戊申 208, 重靖 1017
Shigeno no Sadanushi *ml* 滋野貞主 2460

Shigenori *m* 茂徳 691, 重訓 1017, 重格, 重恭, 重威, 重険, 重徳
Shigenosuke *m* 恵之輔 1226 「野天来 2848
Shigeno Tenrai *ml* 繁
Shigeo *s* 木尾 109; *m* 方雄 85, 茂雄 691, 重雄 1017, 猗夫 1301, 鎮男 2751, 韡雄 2885
Shigeoka *s* 重岡 1017; *m* 茂岳 691
Shigeomi *m* 重臣 1017
Shigeoyu *m* 重老
Shigeri *m* 茂亥 691, 蕃 2371
Shigeru *m* 子 38, 仟 130, 申 185, 戊 208, 卯 259, 芊 287, 成 322, 林 633, 苞 688, 茂 691, 秀 726, 垂 761, 茷 927, 栄 969, 重 1017, 萃 1442, 盛 1469, 復 1571, 葆 1726, 董 1731, 森 1735, 殖 1867, 楙 1889, 稠 1915, 蒨 1982, 蓁 1984, 茲 1987, 蒼 1988, 蓊 2189, 蔚 2191, 蕃 2371, 滋 2460, 積 2490, 繇 2557, 蕤 2679, 懋 2700, 慈 2701, 穠 2803, 繁 2848, 藹 2895, 櫁 2986, 欝 3011
Shigesada *m* 鑑定 2968
Shigesane *m* 重仁 1017
Shigesato *m* 重里, 重巍
Shigeshi *m* 重, 彬 1370, 稠 1915, 滋 2460, 繁 2848
Shigeshige yawa *l* 繁野話
Shigesu *s* 重栖 1017
Shigesue *sm* 重末
Shigesumi *m* 誉純 2010
Shigeta *s* 茂田 691, 重田 1017, 繁田 2848; *m* 茂太 691
Shigetada *m* 木忠 109, 重忠 1017, 繁嬬 2848
Shigetaka *m* 重昂 1017, 重威, 重隆, 繁栄 2848
Shigetame *m* 林為 633
Shigetane *m* 鎮休 2751
Shigetarō *m* 茂太郎 691, 繁太郎 2848
Shigetatsu *m* 茂樹 691
Shigeteru *m* 林昱 633, 重光 1017, 重凞
Shigeto *m* 重任
Shigetō *m* 重遠
Shigetomi *s* 重富; *m* 重宝, 重盛
Shigetoshi *m* 重要, 重憲, 薫明 2567
Shigetsugu *m* 茂語 691, 重次 1017
Shigetsura *m* 重行
Shigeuji *m* 茂氏 691, 繁氏 2848 「哉 2540
Shigeya *m* 重哉 1017, 維
Shigeyama *s* 茂山 691, 重山 1017
Shigeyo *m* 重帯, 重齢
Shigeyoshi *m* 成節 322, 重憙 1017
Shigeyuki *m* 茂幸 691, 茂薫, 重幸 1017, 重進, 重恭; *ml* 重之
Shigezō *m* 繁三 2848, 繁造, 繁蔵
Shigi *s* 信貴 782
~ -san *p* 信貴山
Shigō *m* 至剛 485
Shigura *s* 志倉 464
Shigure *m-f* 時雨 1086
Shigureko *f* 時雨子
Shigure no kotatsu *l* 時雨の炬燵
Shihi *s* 悉悲 1482
Shihida *s* 志比陀 464
Shihonmatsu *s* 四本松 188
Shihoro *p* 士幌 41
Shii *s* 志比 464. (椎 1629)
Shiiba *p* 椎葉
Shiida *p* 椎田
Shiigamoto *l* 椎本
Shiihara *s* 椎原
Shiihashi *s* 椎橋
Shiikai *s* 椎貝
Shiina *s* 椎名
~ Rinzō *ml* 椎名麟三
Shiino *s* 椎野 「木
Shiinoki *s* 椎木; *l* 椎の
Shiinshū *l* 柿蔭集 867
Shiiro *s* 新納 1965
Shiiya *s* 椎谷 1629
Shiizono eisō *l* 椎園詠
Shiizu *s* 椎津 ⌊草
Shiji *s* 志道 464
Shijiki *s* 志自岐
Shijima *s* 四十方 188
Shijimimiyake *s* 縮見屯倉 2813 「464
Shijimimura *s* 志深村
Shijō *sp* 四条 188
Shijōnawate *p* 四条畷
Shijōnomiya *s* 四条宮
~ Shimotsuke-shū *l* 四条宮下野集
Shijōritsu *l* 至上律 485
(shika 而 264, 然 1788, 爾 2250, 鹿 1823)
Shikabe *p* 鹿部
Shikada *s* 鹿田 「485
Shikadōsho *l* 至花道書
Shikago *p* " Chicago " 市俄古 195
Shikahama *s* 鹿浜 1823
Shikahito *m* 鹿人
Shikajirō *m* 鹿次郎
Shikakichi *m* 鹿吉
Shikakubo *s* 鹿窪
Shikakura *s* 鹿倉
Shikama *s* 四釜 188, 志鎌 464, 鹿間 1823; *p* 色麻 345, 飾磨 2164
Shikamachi *p* 鹿町 1823
Shikamata *s* 鹿又, 鹿股
Shikamura *s* 鹿村
Shikano *sp* 鹿野
~ Buzaemon *mla* 鹿野武左衛門
Shikanohe *s* 志我閉 464
Shika no makifude *l* 鹿の巻筆 1823
Shikanosuke *m* 鹿之助
Shikaoi *p* 鹿追
Shikashū *l* 私家集 637, 詞花集 1665
Shikata *s* 四方 188; *sp* 志方 464 「多咄 637
Shikatabanashi *l* 私可
Shikatari *m* 鹿足 1823
Shikatsu *p* 師勝 1130
Shikauchi *s* 鹿内 1823
Shikayoshi *m* 然良 1788
Shikazono *s* 鹿園 1823
Shiki *s* 志紀 464, 志岐; *ml* 子規 38; *p* 磯城 2916. (及 83, 布 170, 式 306, 色 345, 食 1159, 鉽 2152, 飾 2164, 敷 2355, 檝 2477, 職 2734, 識 2810, 織 2879)
Shikiba *s* 式場 306
~ Ryūzaburō *ml* 式場隆三郎
Shikibu *mh-fh* 式部
Shikibuchi *sm* 及淵 83
Shikichi *s* 敷地 2355
Shikida *s* 敷田
Shikimi *s* 敷見
Shikimori *s* 式守 306
Shikimura *s* 敷村 2355
Shikinokami *s* 城上 796
Shikinokazura *s* 城縵
Shikine *s* 敷根 2355
Shikinobu *m* 及淵 83
Shikionron *l* 色音論 345
Shikishima *p* 敷島 2355
Shikishi Naishinnō *fl* 式子内親王 306
Shikitei Sanba *ml* 式亭三馬
Shikitsu *s* 尋来津 1706
Shikkaiya Yasukichi *l* 悉皆屋康吉 1482
Shikkō *s* 執行 1420
(shiko 色 345)
Shikō *ml* 支考 63
Shikofuchi *m* 色布知 345 「1332, 蓄 2371)
(shiku 布 170, 芝 289, 流
Shikyō *l* 四鏡 188
Shikyū *s* 四至内
Shima *s* 志馬 464, 志磨; *sm* 島 1522; *sm-p* 志摩 464. (島 1522)
Shimabara *sp* 島原
Shimabukuro *s* 島袋
Shimachi *s* 島地
Shima chidori tsuki no shiranami *la* 島衛月白浪
Shimada *s* 四真田 188, 斯真田 1670; *sp* 島田 1522
~ Kinji *ml* 島田謹二
Shimadani *s* 島谷
Shimada Saburō *mh* 島田三郎
~ Seihō *ml* 島田青峰
~ Seijirō *ml* 島田清次郎
Shimagahara *p* 島ケ原
Shimagi *s* 島木 「彦
~ Akahiko *ml* 島木赤
Shimaguchi *s* 島口
Shimahashi *s* 島橋
Shimai *s* 島井, 島居
Shimaji *s* 島地 「雷
~ Mokurai *mh* 島地黙
Shimakata *s* 島方
Shimakawa *s* 島川
Shimaki *s* 島木
Shimakichi *s* 島吉
Shimaki Kensaku *ml* 島木健作

Shimakura *s* 島倉
Shimamaki *p* 島牧
Shimameguri uso no kikigaki *l* 島廻戯聞書
Shimamine *s* 島峰
Shimamori *s* 島森
Shimamoto *sp* 島本
Shimamune *s* 島宗
Shimamura *s* 島村
～ Hōgetsu *ml* 島村抱月 「蔵
～ Tamizō *ml* 島村民
Shimana *s* 島名
Shimanaka *s* 島中
～ Yūsaku *ml* 島中雄作
Shimando *m* 島人
Shimane *sp* 島根
Shimano *s* 島野
Shimanuki *s* 島貫
Shimao *s* 島尾
Shimaoka *s* 島岡
Shimao Toshio *ml* 島尾敏雄
Shimasue *s* 島居
Shimatani *s* 島谷
Shimauchi *s* 島内
Shimaura *s* 島浦
Shimaya *s* 島屋
Shimayama *s* 島山
Shimazaki *s* 島崎
～ Tōson *ml* 島崎藤村
Shimazawa *s* 島沢
Shimazono *s* 島薗
Shimazu *sm* 島津; *m* 島図 「久光
～ Hisamitsu *mh* 島津
～ Iehisa *mh* 島津家久
～ Nariakira *mh* 島津斉彬 「重豪
～ Shigehide *mh* 島津
～ Takahisa *mh* 島津貴久 「義弘
～ Yoshihiro *mh* 島津
～ Yoshihisa *mh* 島津義久
Shime *sm-f-p* 七五三 17; *f* 示 148; *p* 志免 464. (ノ 7, ト 10, 示 148, 占 153, 禁 2021, 標 2298) 「葉 2298
Shimeha *s* 染羽 968, 標
Shimeharu *m* ノ治 7
Shimei *ml* 四明 188, 四迷 「七五三懸
Shimekake *s* 七五三 17,
Shimeki *s* 標 2298
Shimekichi *m* 占吉 153
Shimeko *f* ノ子 7, 七五三子 17
Shimeno *s* 禁野 2021
Shimeo *m* 注連雄 591
Shimesu *m* 示 148, 告 490, 宣 919, 観 2765
Shimesuke *m* 七五三介 17
Shimeta *s* ト田 10 「153
Shimetarō *m* 占太郎
Shimeuchi *s* 注連内 591
Shimizu *s* 志水 464; *sp* 清水 1342
～ Chiyo *fl* 清水千代
Shimizudani *s* 清水谷
Shimizu Hamaomi *ml* 清水浜臣
～ Ikutarō *ml* 清水幾太郎 「基吉
～ Motoyoshi *ml* 清水
～ Shin *ml* 清水信
Shimo *sp* 下 46. (霜 2694)
Shimo-agata *p* 下県 46
Shimoaki *s* 下秋
Shimoakutsu *sp* 下圷, 下阿久津
Shimobara *s* 下原
Shimobe *sp* 下部
Shimoburi *s* 下振
Shimochi *s* 下地
Shimoda *s* 霜田 2694; *sp* 下田 46
Shimodaira *s* 下平
Shimodake *s* 下竹
Shimodani *s* 下谷
Shimodate *p* 下館
Shimoda Utako *flh* 下田歌子
Shimoe *s* 下江
Shimoeda *s* 下枝
Shimofunao *s* 下舟尾, 下船尾
Shimofusa *ph* 下総
Shimogasa *s* 下笠
Shimoge *p* 下毛
Shimogō *sp* 下郷
Shimoguchi *s* 下口
Shimogura *s* 下倉, 下蔵
Shimogyō *p* 下京
Shimo-hei *p* 下閉伊
Shimohi *s* 下冰
Shimoi *s* 下井
Shimoichi *sp* 下市
Shimoide *s* 下出
Shimo-ina *p* 下伊那
Shimojima *s* 下島
Shimojō *sp* 下条
Shimo-kamagari *p* 下蒲刈
Shimokata *s* 下方
Shimokawa *s* 下河; *sp* 下川
Shimo-kita *p* 下北
～-kitayama *p* 下北山
Shimoko *f* 霜子 2694
Shimokōbe *s* 下河辺 46
～ Chōryū *ml* 下河辺長流
Shimokōchi *s* 下河内
Shimokoshi *s* 霜越 2694
Shimo-koshiki *p* 下甑
Shimoma *s* 下間 ⌊46
Shimo-mashiki *p* 下益城
Shimomichi *s* 下道
Shimo-minochi *p* 下水内
Shimomoto *s* 下元
Shimomura *s* 下村, 霜邨 2694, 霜村 「46
～ Chiaki *ml* 下村千秋
～ Kainan *ml* 下村海南
～ Kanzan *ma* 下村観山
～ Kojin *ml* 下村湖人
Shimonaka *s* 下中
～ Yasaburō *ml* 下中弥三郎
Shimoni *s* 下耳
Shimo-nida *p* 下仁田
～-niikawa *p* 下新川
Shimono *s* 下野
Shimonobu *s* 下生
Shimonoseki *p* 下関
Shimooka *s* 下岡
～ Renjō *mh* 下岡蓮杖
Shimori *s* 志茂 464
Shimōsa *s* 下日佐 46, 下訳語; *ph* 下総
Shimosaka *s* 下阪; *sm* 下坂
Shimosato *s* 下里, 下郷
Shimose *s* 下瀬
Shimoseko *s* 下世古
Shimose Masachika *mh* 下瀬雅允
Shimosone *s* 下曾根
Shimo-suwa *p* 下諏訪
～ -takai *p* 下高井
Shimoto *s* 下斗; *m* 楚 2022
Shimotoda *s* 楉田 1622
Shimotomai *s* 下斗米 46
Shimotome *s* 下斗女
Shimotori *s* 下鳥, 霜鳥 2694
Shimotsu *sp* 下津 46
Shimo-tsuga *p* 下都賀
Shimotsuke *sfl-ph* 下野 「野
Shimotsukeno *s* 下毛
Shimotsukenu *s* 下毛野 「*s* 下毛野俯見
Shimotsukenufushimi
Shimotsuma *s* 下間; *sp* 下妻
Shimotsumi *s* 下道
Shimotsumichi *s* 下道
Shimotsumiwa *s* 下神
Shimotsure *s* 下連
Shimotsuunakami *s* 下菟上
Shimoya *s* 下谷
Shimoyama *s* 霜山 2694; *sp* 下山 46 「田
Shimo-yamada *p* 下山
Shimoyamasa *s* 下山佐
Shimozawa *s* 子母沢 38, 下沢 46
～ Kan *ml* 子母沢寛 38
Shimukappu *p* 占冠 153
Shimura *s* 志村 464, 新村 1965, 誌村 2141
Shin *sm* 申 185, 伸 353, 信 782, 神 853, 進 1503; *m* 晋 1215, 真 1228, 悳 2033, 震 2577; *m-p* 新 1965. (三 22, 心 49, 只 157, 申 185, 伸 353, 忱 371, 辛 493, 臣 527, 身 546, 辰 738, 信 782, 津 826, 神 853, 参 978, 針 1155, 莘 1168, 奏 1202, 晋 1215, 真 1228, 甚 1267, 振 1320, 深 1341, 清 1342, 梓 1366, 進 1503, 鈊 1675, 森 1735, 晨 1739, 慎 1839, 兟 1922, 新 1965, 寝 1976, 蓁 1984, 悳 2033, 榛 2108, 誌 2141, 潯 2270, 槇 2297, 請 2323, 審 2365, 槇 2490, 親 2544, 震 2577, 臻, 2637, 駸 2666, 鎮 2751, 鐔 2882)
Shina *s* 志那 464; *p* "China" 支那 63. (芥 475, 科 877, 品 916, 倫

1037, 差 1164, 姿 1217, 婉 1600, 級 1680, 等 1770, 階 1840, 標 2298)
Shinada *s* 品田 916
Shinae *f* 等枝 1770
Shinagawa *sp* 品川 916
~ Yajirō *mh* 品川弥二郎
Shinakichi *m* 品吉
Shinako *f* 科子 877, 品子 916, 姿子 1217, 婉子 1600, 級子 1680, 等子 1770
Shinami *s* 志波 464, 斯波 1670, 階見 1840
Shinando *s* 階戸
Shinano *s* 信乃 782; *sp* 信濃; *l* 科野 877
Shin-asahi *p* 新旭 1965
Shinata *m* 西南北 336
Shinato *s* 階土 1840, 階戸
Shinba *s* 榛葉 2108
~ Eiji *ml* 榛葉英治
Shinbai *l* 真奪 1228
Shinbo *s* 新保 1965
Shinbori *s* 新堀
Shin budō denraiki *l* 新武道伝来記
Shinchi *p* 新地
Shincho hyakushu *l* 新著百種 「勅撰集
Shin-chokusenshū *l* 新
Shinden-zukuri *a* 寝殿造 1976
Shindō *s* 神藤 853, 真道 1228, 真藤, 進藤 1503, 新銅 1965, 新藤
~ Junkō *ml* 進藤純孝 (shine 稲 2125) ⌊1503
Shin'emon *m* 新右衛門 1965
Shin'en *l* 寝園 1976
Shin'engei *l* 新演芸 1965
Shingaku hayazome kusa *la* 心学早染草 49
Shingapōru *p* "Singapore" 星港 946
Shingo *m* 信吾 782, 真吾 1228, 悳吾 2033
Shingō *p* 神郷 853, 新郷 1965 「1228
Shingonshū *h* 真言宗
Shingorō *m* 真五郎
Shin-gosenshū *l* 新後撰集 1965
~ -goshūishū *l* 新後拾遺集 「宮 1965
Shingū *sp* 神宮 853, 新
Shingyōji *s* 新行内
Shinhaiwakai *l* 新俳話会 「摘
Shin-hanatsumi *l* 新花
~-Heike *l* 新平家
Shin'ichi *m* 真一 1228, 新一 1965, 鎮一 2751; *p* 新市 1965
Shin'ichirō *m* 信一郎 782, 真一郎 1228, 新一郎 1965
Shin'in *l* 新韻
Shinji *sp* 宍道 470; *m* 信二 782, 信次, 信治, 慎治 1839
~ hifumiden *l* 神字日文伝 853
Shinjirō *m* 晋次郎 1215, 信治郎 782, 新次郎 1965
Shinjō *s* 新荘, 新城, 新条; *sp* 新庄
Shinjuan kakochō *l* 真珠庵過去帳 1228
Shinjū futatsu haraobi *la* 心中二つ腹帯 49
~ kasane-izutsu *la* 心中重井筒
Shinjuku *p* 新宿 1965
Shinjūrō *m* 新十郎
Shinjū ten no Amijima *la* 心中天網島 49
~ yoigōshin *la* 心中宵庚申
Shinkai *s* 真貝 1228, 新海 1965; *sp* 新開
~ Taketarō *ma* 新海竹太郎
Shinkan *ml* 真観 1228
Shinkawa *p* 新川 1965
Shinkei *ml* 心敬 49
~ kasanegafuchi *l* 真景累ケ淵 1228
Shinki *m* 信毅 782
Shinkichi *m* 真吉 1228, 慎吉 1839, 新吉 1965
Shin-kobunrin *l* 新古文林 「集
~-kokinshū *l* 新古今
~-~ Mino no iezuto *l* 新古今集美濃家苞
Shinkubo *s* 新久保
Shinkyoku Kaguyahime *la* 新曲赫映姫
Shinkyokushō *l* 真曲抄 1228
Shinma *s* 新間 1965
Shin-man'yōshū *l* 新万葉集
Shinma Shin'ichi *ml* 新間進一
Shinmeichōkō *l* 神名帳考 853 「明造
Shinmei-zukuri *a* 神
Shinmen *s* 新免 1965
Shinmi *s* 新見 「興
~ Masaoki *mh* 新見正
Shinminato *p* 新湊
Shinmura *s* 新村
~ Izuru *ml* 新村出
Shinnai *la* 新内
Shinnen *m* 真稗 1228
Shinno *s* 信乃 782
Shinnojō *m* 新之允 1965
Shinnosuke *m* 信之介 782, 慎之助 1839, 新之助 1965
Shinnotō *s* 秦党 1202
Shinnyo *mh-la* 真如 1228
Shino *s* 志野 464, 滋野 2460, 篠 2691; *lm* 信乃 782. (忍 463, 信 782, 神 853, 姿 1217, 要 1218, 篠 2691) 「782
Shinō *s* 小竹 21, 信乃
Shinobe *s* 信部
Shinobu *sm-p* 信夫; *m* 仁 57, 忍夫 463, 恕 1483, 毅 2351; *m-f* 忍 463; *f* 訒 1147, 葸 1169
Shinobugaoka *s* 忍岡 463 「曆 853
Shinobumaro *m* 神符
Shinobunoya *ml* 志濃夫廼舎 464
Shinoda *s* 小竹田 21, 信田 782, 信濃田, 笹田 1773, 篠田 2691; *sp* 信太 782 「2691
~ Tarō *ml* 篠田太郎
~ Teijirō *ml* 篠田悌二郎
Shinoe *f* 篠江
Shinogi *s* 篠木
Shinogu *m* 凌 1022
Shinohara *s* 篠原 2691
~ Bon *ml* 篠原梵
~ Hōsaku *ml* 篠原鳳作
~ Ontei *ml* 篠原温亭
~ Shizuji *ml* 篠原志都児
Shinohe *sp* 四戸 188
Shinoi *s* 篠井 2691
Shi no ie *l* 詩之家 1933
Shinomata *s* 信俣 782, 篠俣 2691
Shinomi *s* 新見 1965
Shinomiya *s* 四宮 188, 篠宮 2691
Shinomoto *s* 篠本
Shinonoi *p* 篠ノ井
Shinooka *s* 篠岡
Shinoyama *s* 篠山
Shinozaki *s* 篠崎
Shinozawa *s* 篠沢
Shinozuka *s* 篠塚
Shinpachi *m* 新八 1965
Shinpan utazaimon *l* 新版歌祭文
Shinpei *m* 真平 1228, 進平 1503, 新平 1965
Shinra *s* 森羅 1735, 新良 1965; *ph* "Silla" 新羅 「象 1735
~ Banshō *ml* 森羅万
Shinran *mh* 親鸞 2544
Shinrei Yaguchi-no-watashi *l* 神霊矢口渡 853 「1228
Shinrokurō *m* 真六郎
Shinsarugaku-ki *l* 新猿楽記 1965
Shinsawa *s* 新沢
Shinsei *p* 真正 1228
Shinsengumi *l* 新撰組 1965, 新選組
~ shimatsuki *l* 新選組始末記 「鏡
Shinsen jikyō *l* 新撰字
~ rōeishū *l* 新撰朗詠集 「氏録
~ shōjiroku *l* 新撰姓
~ Tsukubashū *l* 新撰菟玖波集
Shin-senzaishū *l* 新千載集 「髄脳
Shinsen zuinō *l* 新撰
Shinshi *s* 進士 1503
Shinshichi *m* 新七 1965
Shinshinotsu *p* 新篠津
Shinshiro *p* 新城
Shinshirō *m* 信四郎 782
Shinshū *p* 信州
Shin-shūishū *l* 新拾遺集 1965
Shinshū Kawanakaji-

ma kassen *l* 信州川中島合戦 782
～ Shin *p* 信州新
Shinsoku bussei *l* 新即物性 1965
Shinsō no kajin *l* 新粧之佳人
Shinsuke *m* 新助
Shinta *s* 信田 782; *m* 信太 「抄 1965
Shintaishishō *l* 新体詩
Shintaku *s* 新宅
Shintani *s* 新谷
Shintarō *m* 信太郎 782, 慎太郎 1839, 新太郎 1965
Shintō *p* 榛東 2108
Shin-tone *p* 新利根 1965
Shintoku *ml* 信徳 782; *p* 新得 1965
Shintomi *p* 新富
Shintōshū *l* 神道集 853
Shintō taii *l* 神道大意
Shin-totsukawa *p* 新十津川 1965 「屋
Shintowaya *s* 新音羽
Shinu *s* 小竹 21 「1965
Shin'uonome *p* 新魚目
Shinuta *s* 小竹田 21
Shinwa *p* 新和 1965
Shinwayō *a* 新和様
Shin'ya *s* 新谷, 新屋, 新家; *m* 信也 782, 真也 1228
Shin'yō *s* 榛葉 2108
Shin-yoshitomi *p* 新吉富 1965
Shin'yōshū *l* 新葉集
Shinza *p* 新座
Shinzaburō *m* 進三郎 1503, 新三郎 1965
Shinzō *m* 信三 782, 真三 1228, 慎三 1839
Shin-zokukokinshū *l* 新続古今集 1965
Shio *m* 塩 1846; *f* 志保 464; *p* 志雄. (入 15, 汐 250, 塩 1846, 潮 2275)
Shioaki *m* 汐明 250
Shiobara *sp* 塩原 1846
Shioda *s* 四方田 188; *sp* 塩田 1846
Shiōda *s* 新発田 1965
Shioda Ryōhei *ml* 塩田良平 1846
Shiofuji *s* 塩藤
Shiogama *p* 塩釜
Shiohama *s* 塩浜
Shioi *s* 塩井
Shioiri *s* 塩入
Shioi Ukō *ml* 塩井雨江
Shioji *s* 塩路; *m* 四方治 188
Shiojima *s* 塩島 1846
Shiojiri *sp* 塩尻
～ Kōmei *ml* 塩尻公明
Shiomaro *m* 塩麻呂
Shiomi *s* 汐見 250, 塩見 1846; *f* 汐美 250
Shion *s* 施恩 831; *l* 紫苑 2209 「入野 15
Shiono *s* 塩野 1846; *sp*
Shionoe *p* 塩江 1846
Shionogi *s* 塩野義
Shionoha *p* 入之波 15
Shionoiri *s* 塩入 1846, 塩野入
Shionokawa *sp* 塩川
Shionoya *s* 塩谷, 塩野
Shiori *f* 栞 1220 ⌊谷
Shiosai *l* 潮騒 2275
Shiotsu *s* 塩津 1846
Shioura *s* 塩浦
Shiowaki *s* 塩脇
Shiowaku *s* 塩飽
Shioya *s* 塩屋; *sp* 塩谷
Shioyaki *m* 塩焼
Shioyama *s* 塩山
Shiozaki *s* 汐崎 250, 塩崎 1846, 潮崎 2275
Shiozawa *sp* 塩沢 1846
Shioze *s* 塩瀬
Shiozuka *s* 塩塚
Shiozuki *s* 塩月
Shippō *p-a* 七宝 17
(shira 白 216, 精 2131)
Shirabe *s* 調 2328
Shirabyōshi *fa-a* 白拍子 216
Shirae *s* 白江, 白柄
Shirafuji *s* 白藤
Shiragaki *p* 信楽 782
Shiragi *s* 新良貴 1965; *ph* "Silla" 新羅
～ gaku *a* 新羅楽
Shiragikukai *l* 白菊会 216
Shirahae *l* 白南風
Shirahama *sp* 白浜
Shirahata *s* 白畑, 白幡, 白旗
Shirahato *l* 白鳩
Shirahige *la* 白鬚
Shirai *s* 白井, 白猪
～ Kenzaburō *ml* 白井健三郎
～ Kyōji *ml* 白井喬二
Shiraishi *s* 白石
～ Jitsuzō *ml* 白石実三
Shiraiwa *s* 白岩
Shirakaba *l* 白樺
Shirakami *s* 白上, 白神
Shirakawa *smh-p* 白河; *sp* 白川
～ Atsushi *ml* 白川渥
～ kikō *l* 白河紀行
Shiraki *s* 素木 1707; *sp* 白木 216
Shirako *p* 白子
Shirakoshi *s* 白輿
Shirakura *s* 白倉
Shiramatsu *s* 白松
Shiramine *sp-l* 白峰
Shiramizu *s* 白水
Shiranami *s* 白浪
Shirane *sp* 白根
Shirani *s* 白土, 白仁
Shiranui *s* 白縫; *p* 不知火 94
Shiranuka *p* 白糠 216
Shirao *s* 白尾; *m* 白雄
Shiraogawa *s* 白男川
Shiraoi *p* 白老
Shiraoka *sp* 白岡
Shirasaka *s* 白坂
Shirasaki *s* 白崎
Shirasawa *sp* 白沢
Shirase *s* 白瀬
Shirashima *s* 白島
Shirasu *s* 白洲, 白須
Shirasugi *s* 白杉
Shirasuna *s* 白砂
Shirataka *sp* 白鷹
Shirataki *sp* 白滝
Shiratama *l* 白珠
Shirato *s* 白土, 白戸
Shiratori *sp* 白鳥
Shiratsu *s* 白津
Shiratsuka *s* 白柄, 白塚
Shiratsuki *s* 白築
Shiraya *s* 白谷
Shirayama *s* 白山
Shirayanagi *s* 白柳
～ Shūko *ml* 白柳秀湖
Shiren *mlh* 師錬 1130
(shiri 尻 176, 知 636, 後 1300)
Shiribeshi *p* 後志
Shirikake *s* 尻掛 176
Shirikishinai *p* 尻岸内
Shiritaka *s* 尻高
Shiritsuki *s* 後月 1300
Shiriuchi *p* 知内 636
Shiro *sm-f* 城 796; *m-f* 白 216. (太 105, 代 125, 白 216, 城 796, 背 956, 素 1707)
Shirō *s* 斯朧 1670; *m* 士郎 41, 四郎 188, 素人 1707, 嗣郎 1937; *ml* 士朗 41 「*m* 銀 2345
Shirogane *sm* 白金 216;
Shiroguchi *s* 城口 796
Shiroi *p* 白井 216
Shiroishi *p* 白石
Shirokawa *p* 城川 796
Shiroki *s* 白木, 素木 1707
Shiroko *f* 白子 216
Shirokura *s* 城倉 796
Shiromoto *s* 城本
Shiromukuge *l* 白木槿
Shirone *p* 白根 ⌊216
Shironushi *l* 代主 125
Shiroo *m* 四亮夫 188
Shirosaki *s* 城崎 796
Shirose *s* 白勢 216
Shiroshi *m* 白, 素 1707
Shiroshita *s* 城下 796
Shirota *s* 代田 125, 白田 216, 城田 796
Shirotori *sp* 白鳥 216
～ Seigo *ml* 白鳥省吾
Shirotsuka *s* 城塚 796
Shirouchi *s* 城内
Shiroyama *sp* 城山
Shirozō *m* 素三 1707
Shirōzu *sp* 白水 216
(shiru 印 260, 知 636, 訓 1148)
(shirushi 璽 2860)
Shirusu *m* 志 464, 記 1149, 紀 1424
Shisa *s* 志佐 464
Shisei *l* 詩聖 1933
Shiseki *s* 始関 1092, 紫関 2209 「四川 188
Shisen *p* "Szechwan"
Shisenshū *l* 私撰集 637
Shishi *s* 師子 1130, 獅子 1835. (宍 470, 完 471, 害 1181, 猊 1302, 猪 1306, 鹿 1823) 「神廻 853
Shishiba *s* 四柴 188, 神
Shishi Bunroku *ml* 獅子文六 1835
Shishido *s* 宍人 470, 宍戸, 完戸 471

Shishifu *s* 鹿生 1823
Shishiguri *s* 宍栗 470
Shishigusa *s* 完草 471
Shishihito *s* 害人 1181
Shishihitobe *s* 害人部
Shishiji *s* 志道 464, 完道 471
Shishikai *sp* 宍甘 470
Shishikō *s* 宍甘
Shishikui *p* 宍喰
Shishikura *s* 宍倉, 猊倉 1302
Shishikusa *s* 宍草 470
Shishima *s* 上上島 47
Shishin *l* 詩神 1933
Shishio *m* 宍夫 470
Shishiuchi *s* 四至内 188, 鹿討 1823
Shishizawa *s* 宍粟 470
Shishoku *l* 私燭 637
Shishūdo *s* 宍人 470
Shisō *p* 宍粟
Shisōsha *l* 詩草社 1933
Shisui *p* 泗水 588, 酒酒井 1066 「坤 573)
Shita *s* 信田 782. (下 46,
Shitada *p* 下田 46
Shitagō *m* 趁 1815; *ml* 順 1532
Shitakusa *l* 下草 46
Shitaya *s* 下谷 「188
Shitennō *smh* 四天王
Shitennōji *p* 四天王寺
Shitō *s* 市東 195, 志藤 464, 紫桃 2209, 紫藤
Shitoke *p* 雫 1494
Shitokitsuki *s* 米餅搗 343 「485
Shitoku 1384–87 至徳
Shitomi *sm* 蔀 2186
Shitori *s* 完利 471, 従者 1050, 後 1300; *sm* 倭 1283, 倭文; *sp* 白堤 216 「後部 1300
Shitoribe *s* 従者部 1050,
(shitsu 七 17, 室 1183, 後 1300, 執 1420, 悉 1482, 蛭 1920, 悪 2020A, 漆 2087, 肆 2144, 膝 2281, 質 2395, 櫛 2797)
Shitsuki *s* 志筑 464; *m* 後城 1300; *p* 後月
~ Tadao *mh* 志筑忠雄 464
Shitsumi *s* 七美 17
Shittaka *s* 尻高 176
Shiuchi *s* 四十住 188, 四至内, 吹智 370, 志内 464
Shiunji *p* 紫雲寺 2209
Shiura *sp* 市浦 195
Shiwa *s* 志波 464; *p* 志和, 紫波 2209 「464
Shiwahime *p* 志波姫
Shiwasuta *s* 十二月一日 18, 十二月田
Shiwato *s* 塩飽 1846
Shiyū *s* 新納 1965
Shizawa *s* 志沢 464; *sp* 宍粟 470
Shizu *s* 志津 464; *sf* 倭 1283, 倭文; *f* 静 2145, 賤 2318. (玄 522, 浄 823, 倭 1283, 後 1300, 寂 1436, 康 1509, 閑 1820, 靖 1905, 静 2145, 寧 2181, 賤 2318, 嫺 2475, 穏 2492, 謙 2646, 鎮 2751)
Shizue *f* 倭江 1283, 閑衛 1820, 静枝 2145
Shizugawa *p* 志津川 464
Shizuharu *m* 鎮治 2751
Shizuhata *s* 志豆機 464; *l* 賤機 2318
Shizuhataobi *a* 賤機帯
Shizuhide *m* 静英 2145
Shizuhiko *m* 倭彦 1283
Shizuka *m* 玄 522, 担 574, 康 1509, 舒 1673, 謐 2637A, 嚣 2938; *m-f* 静 2145; *f* 静香, 賤香 2318 「*sp* 後川
Shizukawa *s* 後河 1300;
Shizuki *f* 志豆紀 464
Shizuko *f* 倭文子 1283, 閑子 1820, 静子 2145, 賤子 2318, 嫺子 2475, 穏子 2492 「1494)
Shizuku *s* 志筑 464. (雫
Shizukuishi *sp* 雫石
Shizuma *s* 四十方 188, 静妻 2145, 静間; *m* 志津摩 464, 志津磨, 志頭磨, 鎮馬 2751
Shizume *s* 鎮目; *m* 静馬 2145, 鎮 2751
Shizumi *m* 鎮
Shizumu *m* 鎮
Shizunai *p* 静内 2145
Shizuno *s* 志津野 464
Shizuo *m* 浄夫 823, 倭夫 1283, 靖夫 1905, 静夫 2145, 静治男, 静家, 静雄, 寧雄 2181, 賤夫 2318, 謙夫 2646; *f* 静緒 2145
Shizuoka *p* 静岡
Shizuri *s* 志津梨 464
Shizurie *s* 静戸 2145
Shizusane *m* 静修, 鎮実 2751
Shizuta *s* 静田 2145
Shizu-uta *l* 玆都歌 2134
Shizuya *m* 静也 2145
Shizuyasu *m* 康安 1509
(sho 処 177, 且 192, 初 427, 助 431, 序 507, 所 600, 杵 629, 徐 1049, 書 1216, 庶 1505, 渚 1575, 暑 1738A, 組 1952, 楚 2022, 諸 2329, 鋤 2336, 曙 2719, 礎 2730)
Shō *s* 荘 933; *m* 正 205, 章 1461; *mh-fl* 少輔 88; *p* 庄 315. (小 21, 少 88, 井 103, 升 113, 召 152, 正 205, 生 214, 壮 243, 丞 296, 庄 315, 阡 373, 劭 429, 肖 451, 声 465, 匠 503, 床 508, 性 564, 征 580, 沼 595, 拗 605, 邵 646, 青 700, 昇 713, 昌 715, 尚 753, 承 760, 牲 830, 弨 833, 昭 841, 姓 846, 相 868, 松 869, 政 881, 荘 933, 岺 938, 星 946, 省 1013, 乗 1016, 凊 1021, 倢 1030, 倩 1031, 将 1040, 従 1050, 陞 1057, 祥 1074, 称 1118, 釗 1152, 釟 1153, 倉 1165, 宵 1179, 笑 1209, 烝 1210, 唱 1284, 埩 1293, 渉 1331, 清 1342, 梢 1362, 鈔 1414, 剰 1426, 寁 1434, 菖 1444, 春 1460, 章 1461, 常 1462, 恕 1483, 逍 1514, 商 1526, 惺 1547, 接 1548, 猩 1553, 淞 1581, 焼 1588, 婧 1601, 勝 1613, 椒 1619, 竦 1632, 詔 1658, 証 1660, 舒 1673, 鈔 1676, 敞 1688, 創 1696, 晶 1740, 掌 1748, 象 1761, 摂 1837, 詳 1927, 鉦 1941, 紹 1955, 聖 2030, 照 2035, 奨 2036, 傚 2055, 像 2061, 摺 2068, 槍 2100, 頌 2113, 種 2124, 精 2131, 誦 2138, 韶 2163, 韴 2167, 彰 2174, 衝 2264, 暲 2284, 璋 2287, 樅 2293, 樟 2294, 蒋 2368, 蕉 2372, 裳 2376, 賞 2377, 箱 2383, 璧 2412, 橡 2478, 檞 2478A, 樵 2479, 醒 2501, 緒 2537, 鞘 2542, 整 2581, 摺 2607, 鍬 2648, 鍾 2649, 騂 2665, 篠 2691, 霜 2694, 聳 2698, 鎗 2747, 鯖 2830, 鏘 2881, 鐘 2883, 繡 2954, 縄 2955, 鶚 2976)
Shō-Ajia *p* "Asia Minor" 小亜細亜 21
Shōami *s* 正阿弥 205
Shōan 1171–75 承安 760; 1299–1302 正安 205 「庄原 315
Shōbara *s* 荘原 933; *sp*
Shōbayashi *s* 庄林
Shōbee *m* 庄兵衛
Shōboku *p* 勝北 1613
Shōbu *p* 菖蒲 1444
Shōbuke *s* 正部家 205
Shōchiku *a* 松竹 869
Shōchō 1428–29 正長 205
Shōchū 1324–26 正中
Shōda *s* 正田, 庄田 315, 勝田 1613
Shōdai *s* 小代 21
Shodō kikimimi sekenzaru *l* 諸道聴耳世間猿 2329
Shōgaki *s* 正墻 205
Shōgase *s* 勝賀瀬 1613
Shōgawa *sp* 庄川 315
Shōge *s* 正化 205
Shōgen *s* 正玄; 1207–11 承元 760; 1259–60 正元 205
Shōgenji *s* 生源寺 214
Shōgo *m* 正五 205, 正吾, 鈔吾 1676
Shōgorō *m* 正五郎 205, 正午郎, 正吾郎
Shōha *ml* 召波 152, 紹巴 1955 「璋八 2287
Shōhachi *m* 正八 205,
Shōhaku *ml* 肖柏 451
Shōhara *s* 庄原 315
Shōhata *s* 正白田 205

Shōhei *m* 昇平 713; 931–38 承平 760; 1346–70 正平 205

Shōhen shōsetsu *l* 掌編小説 1748

Shōhi *s* 松扉 869

Shōhō 1074–77 承保 760; 1644–48 正保 205

Shōhōgenzō *l* 正法眼蔵

Shōichi *m* 正一, 正市, 昇一 713, 省市 1013

Shōji *s* 小路 21, 庄司 315, 名氏 346, 東海林 771, 荘司 933; *m* 正二 205, 正治, 昌司 715, 昌次

Shōjimura *s* 東海村 771

Shōjin gyorui *l* 精進魚類 2131

Shōjirō *m* 正二郎 205, 正次郎, 昇次郎 713, 釟次郎 1153

Shōjō *la* 猩猩 1553

Shōju *m* 松寿 869

Shōjumaru *m* 松寿丸

Shōka 1257–59 正嘉 205

Shōkan *m* 将監 1040

Shōkawa *p* 荘川 933

Shōkei 1332–33 正慶 205 「憲皇太后 841

Shōken Kōtaigō *flh* 昭

Shōkenkō *l* 蕉堅稿 2372

Shoki *l* 書紀 1216

Shō Ki *mh-la* "Chung K'uei" 鍾馗 2649

Shōkichi *s* 将吉 1040; *m* 正吉 205, 昌吉 715

Shōko *f* 宵子 1179

Shōkō *ml* 正広 205

(shoku 式 306, 色 345, 束 536, 俗 776, 食 1159, 埴 1561, 湜 1579, 寔 1710, 粟 1763, 溭 1854, 殖 1867, 植 1902, 蜀 2005, 稙 2122, 飾 2164, 続 2334, 織 2477, 職 2734, 識 2810, 織 2879)

Shokugenshō *lh* 職原抄 2734

Shōkuma *m* 正熊 205

Shō Kun *fh-la* "Chao Chün" 昭君 841

Shoku Nihongi *l* 続日本紀 2334

Shokusanjin *ml* 蜀山人 2005

Shoku yotsugi *l* 続世継 2334

Shōkyū 1219–22 承久 760 「1613

Shōmangyō *l* 勝鬘経

～ gisho *l* 勝鬘経義疏

Shōmei *m* 正明 205

Shōmon *l* 蕉門 2372

Shōmonki *l* 将門記 1040

Shōmon zuda *l* 蕉門頭陀 2372

Shōmu *mh* 聖武 2030

Shōmura *s* 荘村 933

Shōnagon *mh-fh* 少納言 88 「庄内 315

Shōnai *s* 荘内 933; *sp*

Shōnan *p* 沼南 595

Shōnen *m* 松年 869

Shōnenkō *l* 少年行 88

Shōni *mh* 少弐

Shōno *s* 正野 205, 生野 214, 庄野 315

Shōnō *s* 正能 205

Shōno Junzō *ml* 庄野潤三 315

Shonzui Gorō-tayū *ma* 祥瑞五郎太夫 1074

Shōō *p* 勝央 1613; 1288–93 正応 205; 1652–55 承応 760

Shōrai *l* 松籟 869

Shōraku *ml* 松洛

Shōriki *s* 正力 205

Shōryaku 990–95 正暦; 1077–81 承暦 760

Shōryōshū *l* 性霊集 564

Shōsaku *m* 昌作 715

Shosanbetsu *p* 初山別 427 「説神髄 21

Shōsetsu shinzui *l* 小

Shōshi *s* 庄子 315

Shoshine *s* 所神根 600

Shōshin'in *s* 正真院 205

Shōshō *mh-fh* 少将 88

Shōsōin *pa* 正倉院 205

Shōsuke *m* 正助, 昌介 715, 省輔 1013, 彰祐 2174 「205

Shōta *m* 小太 21, 正太

Shōtai 898–901 昌泰 715

Shōta no uma *l* 正太の馬 205

Shōtarō *m* 正太郎, 庄太郎 315, 章太郎 1461

Shōtei Kinsui *ml* 松亭金水 869

Shōtenchi *l* 小天地 21

Shōtetsu *ml* 正徹 205

Shōto *m* 小太 21

Shōtoku *fh* 称徳 1118; 1097–99 承徳 760; 1711–16 正徳 205

～ Taishi *mh* 聖徳太子 2030 「太子伝暦

～ ～ denryaku *l* 聖徳

Shōwa *p* 庄和 315, 1926– 昭和 841; 834–48 承和 760; 1312–17 正和 205 「1846

Shōya *s* 昌谷 715, 塩谷

Shōyama *s* 庄山 315

Shōyō *ml* 逍遙 1514

Shōyū gushō *l* 逍遊愚抄

Shōyūki *lh* 小右記 21

Shōzaburō *m* 正三郎 205, 庄三郎 315, 省三郎 1013

Shōzō *m* 正三 205, 正造, 正蔵, 庄蔵 315, 省三 1013, 省蔵, 祥三 1074

Shōzon *la* 正尊 205

Shōzu *s* 生水 214; *p* 小豆 21

Shu *s* 朱 341. (手 118, 収 133, 主 196, 州 224, 守 284, 舟 339, 朱 341, 注 591, 取 650, 周 739, 狩 791, 祝 851, 柊 860, 秋 878, 首 920, 柔 938, 修 1038, 酒 1066, 珠 1077, 株 1098, 脩 1281, 執 1420, 春 1460, 須 1544, 竦 1632, 菘 1721, 萩 1732, 衆 1762, 楸 1890, 菘 1999, 種 2124, 数 2169, 聚 2221, 竪 2224, 樅 2293, 諏 2327, 趣 2422, 樹 2483, 綉 2531, 鍾 2649, 聳 2698, 鐘 2883, 穐 2915, 繡 2954, 鬚 2973)

Shū *s* 周 736; *m* 秀 726, 修 1038. (十 18, 収 133, 主 196, 州 224, 戊 328, 舟 339, 充 521, 寿 539, 宗 679, 秀 726, 受 730, 周 736, 拾 802, 洲 820, 祝 851, 柊 860, 秋 878, 修 1038, 袖 1107, 脩 1281, 授 1315, 渋 1334, 執 1420, 莠 1443, 習 1468, 揖 1550, 就 1668, 葺 1720, 菘 1721, 萩 1732, 衆 1762, 集 1779, 楸 1890, 楫 1899, 終 1950, 崧 1999, 嵩 2207, 聚 2221, 甃 2223, 衝 2264, 輯 2497, 綉 2531, 鍬 2648, 緝 2658, 蹴 2806, 鰍 2887, 穐 2915, 繡 2954, 鷲 2980, 襲 2983)

Shūchi *p* 周知 736

Shuchō *s* 朱鳥 341

Shūchūshō *l* 袖中抄 1107

Shūda *s* 周田 736

Shudai *s* 首代 920

Shudō *s* 首藤

Shugyō *s* 執行 1420

Shūhō *p* 秋芳 878

Shuichi *m* 主一 196, 珠一 1077 「一 1038

Shūichi *m* 周一 736, 修

Shuichirō *m* 種一郎 2124 「802

Shūi gusō *l* 拾遺愚草

～ hyakuban utaawase *l* 拾遺百番歌合

Shūishū *l* 拾遺集

Shūji *m* 修二 1038, 衆二 1762

Shūjirō *m* 周次郎 736

Shūkashō *l* 拾菓抄 802

Shūkashū *l* 拾菓集

Shūkichi *m* 修吉 1038

(shuku 夙 299, 叔 649, 祝 851, 俶 1026, 淑 1335, 宿 1438, 粛 1528, 蹴 2806, 縮 2813) 「傘 726

Shūku karakasa *l* 秀句

Shukunami *s* 宿南 1438

Shukutani *s* 宿谷

Shukuya *s* 宿谷; *m* 夙夜 299

Shume *m* 主馬 196

Shumon *l* 朱門 341

Shūmyōshū *l* 衆妙集 1762

(shun 舛 367, 侚 562, 恂 807, 洵 815, 春 963, 盾 984, 准 1023, 俊 1039, 隼 1230, 倄 1277, 惇 1288, 浚 1329, 淳 1337, 循 1569, 峻 1593, 閏 1819, 婥 1869, 楯 1897, 詢 1928, 馴 1966, 舜 2017, 準 2041, 睃 2110, 絢 2150, 蓴 2187, 儁 2253, 潤 2277, 醇 2315, 遵

2418, 瞕 2498, 錞 2521, 濬 2608, 駿 2763, 鶉 2820)
Shunbara *s* 春原 963
Shundei *l* 春泥
Shundō *s* 春藤
Shun'e *ml* 俊恵 1039
Shun'ei *la* 春栄 963
Shungo *m* 俊吾 1039
Shunji *m* 舜治 2017
Shunjō *mh* 俊芿 1039
Shunkan *mh-la* 俊寛
Shunkichi *m* 俊吉, 駿吉 2763 ⌈963
Shunkinshō *l* 春琴抄
Shunnichi *s* 春日
Shun'oku Myōha *mh* 春屋妙葩
Shunpei *m* 俊平 1039
Shunpū bateikyoku *l* 春風馬堤曲 963
Shunrai *ml* 俊頼 1039
Shunrokurō *m* 俊六郎
Shunsaku *m* 俊作
Shunshoku eitai dango *l* 春色英対暖語 963
~ megumi no hana *l* 春色恵之花
~ tatsumi no sono *la* 春色辰巳園
~ umegoyomi *l* 春色梅児誉美
~ ume mibune *l* 春色梅美婦禰
Shunsuke *m* 俊助 1039
Shuntarō *m* 俊太郎
Shuntō *l* 春燈 963
Shunzei *ml* 俊成 1039
~ -kyō no Musume no shū *l* 俊成卿女集
~ Tadanori *la* 俊成忠
Shunzō *m* 俊蔵 ⌊度
Shuri *m* 修理 1038
Shurinosuke *m* 修理亮
Shūron *l* 宗論 679
Shūsaku *m* 周作 736
Shūseikai *l* 秋声会 878
Shushi *mlh* "Chu-tzu" 朱子 341
Shushigaku *h* 朱子学
Shu Shunsui *mh* 朱舜水
Shūsō *p* 周桑 736
Shusse Kagekiyo *la* 出世景清 523
Shūsuirei *la* 秋水嶺 878
Shūtarō *m* 周太郎 736
Shuten dōji *l* 酒顚童子 1066 ⌈920
Shutō *s* 守藤 284, 首藤
Shūtō *s* 周藤 736; *sp* 周東 ⌈述 748, 帥 883)
(shutsu 朮 209, 出 523,
Shutta *s* 習田 1468
Shuzen *m* 主膳 196
Shuzenji *p* 修善寺 1038; *la* 修禅寺
Shūzō *m* 秀三 726, 周三 736, 周蔵, 修三 1038, 修造
Shuzui *s* 守随 284
So *s* 素 1707. (十 18, 三 22, 処 177, 且 192, 初 427, 衣 520, 徂 577, 征 580, 所 600, 祖 850, 租 1116, 祚 1126, 酢 1654, 素 1707, 曾 1794, 甦 1814, 組 1952, 楚 2022, 麁 2053, 鼠 2430, 礎 2730, 蘇 2841, 噌 2945, 襲 2983)
Sō *s* 宋 468, 宗 679, 曾 1794, 藪 2840; *m* 荘 933. (三 22, 双 53, 爪 115, 壮 243, 早 295, 匝 308, 庄 315, 争 344, 走 441, 宋 468, 艸 598, 捌 605, 帚 666, 宗 679, 相 868, 荘 933, 草 934, 奏 951, 将 1040, 桑 1162, 倉 1165, 造 1236, 埩 1293, 掃 1319, 巣 1431, 曹 1479, 爽 1529, 湊 1576, 琮 1604, 創 1696, 窓 1746, 棗 1757, 崇 1774, 惣 1785, 曾 1794, 僧 1829, 蒼 1988, 奨 2036, 慥 2070, 潄 2084, 槍 2100, 雑 2127, 駁 2171, 彰 2174, 聡 2311, 蔣 2368, 箱 2383, 塑 2412, 蔵 2424, 操 2448, 綜 2528, 臓 2595, 糟 2632, 総 2662, 霜 2694, 鎗 2747, 叢 2778, 藻 2837, 藪 2840, 鏘 2881, 譟 2972, 鰺 2999, 鱻 3025)
Sōami *ma* 宗阿弥 679, 相阿弥
Sōanshū *l* 草庵集 934
(soba 傍 1538)
Sōba *s* 相馬 868
Sobae *l* 日照雨 77
Sobagai *s* 祖母井 850
Sobashima *s* 傍島 1538
Sōbetsu *p* 壮瞥 243
Sōbō *l* 蒼氓 1988
Sobue *sp* 祖父江 850
Sobuhei *m* 甦生平 1814
Sōbun *m* 宗文 679
Sochi *mh* 帥 883. (帥)
Sochinomiya Atsumichi *mh* 帥宮敦道
Sōchō *ml* 宗長 679
Soda *s* 曾田 1794
Sōda *s* 左右田 169, 早田 295, 宗田 679
~ Kiichirō *ml* 左右田喜一郎 169 ⌈谷 1794
Sodani *s* 素谷 1707, 曾
Sode *f* 袖 1107. (袖)
Sodegaura *p* 袖ケ浦
Sodeka *f* 袖香
Sodeko *f* 袖子
Sodeoka *s* 袖岡
Sodeshima *s* 袖島
Sodeura *s* 袖浦
Sodeyama *s* 袖山
Sodezaki *s* 袖崎
Sodō *ml* 素堂 1707
Sōdōshū *h* 曹洞宗 1479
(soe 添 1338, 副 1428)
Soeda *s* 副田; *sp* 添田
Soehi *s* 傍陽 1538 ⌊1338
Soejima *s* 副島 1428
~ Taneomi *mh* 副島種臣
Soekami *p* 添上 1338
Soeko *f* 添子
Soemu *m* 副武 1428
Soeno *s* 添野 1338
Soenomitsue *s* 添御杖
Sō Fukan *ml* 宗不旱 679
Sofukawa *s* 曾布川 1794
Sofusofu *s* 曾歩曾歩
Soga *s* 我何 545, 宗岳 679, 宗岡, 蘇我 2841, 蘇宗, 蘇宜; *sl* 曾我
Sōga *s* 相賀 868 ⌊1794
Sogabe *s* 曾我部 1794
Sogae *s* 曾谷
Soga Kaikeizan *la* 曾我会稽山
Sogame *s* 十亀 18
Soga no Emishi *mh* 蘇我蝦夷 2841
~ no Iname *mh* 蘇我稲目 ⌈鹿
~ no Iruka *mh* 蘇我入
~ no Ishikawamaro *mh* 蘇我石川麻呂
~ no Umako *mh* 蘇我馬子 ⌈1794
Soganoya *s* 曾我廼家
Sogawa *s* 曾川
(soge 枌 624)
Sogetani *s* 枌谷
Sōgi *s* 三木 22; *ml* 宗祇 679
~ shūen no ki *l* 宗祇終焉記 ⌈河
Sogō *s* 十川 18, 十合, 十
Sōgō *s* 小郷 21, 草郷 934
Sōhachi *l* 惣八 1785
Sohara *s* 曾原 1794
Sōhei *m* 宗平 679
Sohō *s* 曾方布 1794
Sōhō *mh* 宗彭 679
Sōi *s* 早尾 295 ⌈1785
Sōichi *m* 壮一 243, 惣一
Sōichirō *m* 総一郎 2662
Sōin *ml* 宗因 679
Soizumi *s* 祖泉 850
Sōja *p* 総社 2662
Soji *s* 南界 912
Sōji *s* 荘司 933; *m* 三二 22, 宗志 679
Sōjirō *m* 宗治郎
Sōjū *m* 荘十 933
Sōjun *ml* 宗純 679
Sōka *s* 草可 934; *p* 草加; *l* 早歌 295
Sōkan *ml* 宗鑑 679
Sōkawa *s* 寒川 1714
Soke *s* 村挙 424
Soki *s* 家宜 1185, 曾木 1794 ⌈578
Sōki *s* 佐脇 365, 彼杵
Sōkichi *m* 宗吉 679
Sōkō *p* "San Francisco" 桑港 1162
Sōkonshū *l* 草根集 934
(soku 足 461, 束 536, 即 648, 則 902, 息 1224, 速 1237, 族 1343, 測 1578, 蔟 2185)
Sokuta *s* 集田 1779
Sōkyū *l* 蒼穹 1988
Soma *s* 杣 626. (杣, 相 1626, 樵 2479)
Sōma *s* 宗右馬 679; *sp* 相馬 868
Somada *s* 杣田 626
Somagi *s* 杣木
Sōma Gyofū *ml* 相馬御風 868 ⌈2022
Somahito *ml* 楚満人

Somako *f* 杣子 626
Sōma Kokkō *ml* 相馬黒光 868 「2022
Somando *m* 楚満人
Somao *m* 樵夫 2479
Sōma Taizō *ml* 相馬泰三 868
Sōmatō *l* 走馬燈 441
Sōmatsu *m* 左右松 169
Somayama *s* 杣山 626, 椙山 1626
(some 染 968)
Someemon *m* 染右衛
Somei *s* 染井 ⌊門
Somekawa *s* 染川
Someko *f* 染子
Somemiya *s* 染宮
Somemura *s* 染村
Someno *s* 染野
Sometani *s* 染谷
Someya *s* 染谷, 染屋
~ Susumu *ml* 染谷進
Somezaki *s* 染崎
~ Nobufusa *ml* 染崎延房
Sōmin *mh* 僧旻 1829
Somiya *s* 曾宮 1794
Sōmiya *s* 宗宮 679
Sōmokuchūgyo *l* 艸木虫魚 598
Sōmon *l* 相聞 868
Sōmura *s* 宗村 679
(son 寸 34, 存 313, 村 424, 邨 645, 孫 1540, 巽 1760, 尊 1797, 嶟 2467, 樽 2482, 遜 2591, 鐏 2805A)
Sōnai *p* 荘内 933
Sonare no matsu *l* 磯馴松 2916
Sonawaru *m* 備 1539
Sone *s* 曾根 1794, 曾禰
Soneda *s* 曾根田
Sonehara *s* 曾根原
Son'en *mh* 尊円 1797
Sone no Yoshitada *ml* 曾禰好忠 1794
Sonezaki *sp* 曾根崎
~ shinjū *la* 曾根崎心
Soni *p* 曾爾 ⌊中
Sono *s* 曾野, 園 2046; *f* 薗 2681. (彼 578, 苑 682, 其 734, 囿 990, 園 2046, 薗 2681)
Sonō *sf* 園生 2046; *m* 弁 275, 備 1539
Sono Ayako *fl* 曾野綾子 1794
Sonobe *s* 苑部 682, 園辺 2046, 薗部 2681; *sp* 園部 2046
Sonoda *s* 其田 734, 園田 2046, 薗田 2681
Sonohachi *ma* 薗八
Sonoi *s* 園井 2046
Sonoike *s* 園池 「致
~ Kin'yuki *ml* 園池公
Sonoji *m* 其二 734
Sonoki *s* 彼杵 578, 園木 2046
Sonokichi *m* 其吉 734
Sonomo *m* 其母, 園面 2046
Sonomura *s* 園村
Sonondo *m* 園人
Sono omokage *l* 其面影 734
Sonosaburō *m* 園三郎 2046 「1785
Sōnosuke *m* 惣之助
Sonoyama *s* 園山 2046
Sono yukari hina no omokage *l* 其由縁鄙廼俤 734
~ yukikage *l* 其雪影
Soo *sp* 噌唹 2945
Sora *ml* 曾良 1794. (天 93, 空 723)
Sōra *s* 早良 295, 相楽 868 「空知
Sorachi *s* 空地 723; *p*
Sorai *mlh* 徂徠 577
Sōraku *sp* 相楽 868
Sora ni muraboshi *l* 天仁群星 93 「浪
~ utsu nami *l* 天うつ
Soren *p* "U.S.S.R." 蘇連 2841
(sori 反 69)
Sorimachi *sp* 反町
Sorita *s* 反田
(soro 候 1029)
Sorobee *m* 候兵衛
Sorori *s* 曾呂利 1794
Sōryō *p* 総領 2662
Sōsa *s* 寒風沢 1714; *sp* 匝嵯 308
Sōsaburō *m* 惣三郎 1785
Sosei *ml* 素性 1707
Sōsei *l* 創生 1696
Sōseki *ml* 漱石 2084
Soshi *s* 祖師 850, 曾雌 1794
Sōshi-arai Komachi *la* 草子洗小町 934
Soshiro *s* 十代 18
Soshiroda *s* 十代田
Sōshun *ml* 宗春 679
Soshū no shi *l* 楚囚之詩 2022
Sōso *s* 宗素 679
Sosogu *m* 雪 1495
Sōsuke *m* 惣助 1785
Sotan *ml* 曾丹 1794
Sotango *ml* 曾丹後
Sotanshū *l* 曾丹集
Sōtarō *m* 惣太郎 1785, 総太郎 2662
Sōtatsu *ma* 宗達 679
Soteme *f* 蘇提亮 2841
(soto 外 139)
Sotoba Komachi *la* 卒都婆小町 732, 卒塔婆小町
Sotogawa *s* 外川 139
Sotoji *m* 外治
Sotojirō *m* 外次郎
Sotome *p* 外海
Sōtome *s* 五月女 91; *sp* 早乙女 295
Sotomi *s* 外海 139
Sotomura *s* 外村
~ Shirō *ml* 外村史郎
Sotoo *m* 外雄
Sotoyama *s* 外山
Sotsu *f* 帥 883. (卒 732, 帥 883, 率 2040)
Sotsuhiko *m* 襲津彦 2983
Sowa *s* 曾和 1794
Soya *s* 征矢 580
Sōya *p* 宗谷 679
Soyagimi *s* 十八公 18
Soyagin *s* 十八公
Soyako *f* 征矢子 580
Soyama *s* 曾山 1794
Soyano *s* 征矢野 580
(soyo 勇 908)
Soyō *p* 蘇陽 2841
Soyota *s* 副田 1428
Sōzaburō *m* 総三郎 2662
Sōzei *ml* 宗砌 679
Sōzen *s* 宗前
Sōzō *m* 宗三
(su 司 164, 主 196, 守 284, 朱 341, 沙 392, 宋 468, 洲 820, 春 963, 為 1005, 栖 1101, 巣 1431, 進 1503, 雀 1530, 順 1532, 須 1544, 陶 1565, 湊 1576, 淞 1581, 琮 1604, 酢 1654, 素 1707, 崇 1774, 惣 1785, 摺 2067, 数 2169, 聡 2311, 諏 2327, 総 2662, 簀 2687, 叢 2778, 藪 2840, 蘇 2841, 雛 2888)
(sū 菘 1721, 崇 1774, 数 2169, 嵩 2207, 雛 2888)
Subara *s* 須原 1544
(sube 皇 964)
Suburu *m* 総 2262
Suchi *s* 須知 1544
Suchō *s* 朱鳥 341
Suda *s* 須田 1544, 隅田 1566
Sudate *s* 須立 1544
Sūden *mh* 崇伝 1774
Sudō *s* 寿藤 539, 首藤 920, 須藤 1544, 陶東 1565, 集堂 1779, 数藤 2169
~ Gojō *ml* 数藤五城
Sudoko *s* 寿床 539
Sudō Nansui *ml* 須藤南翠 1544
Sue *s* 陶 1565, 陶器, 陶器所; *p* 須恵 1544. (与 101, 末 211, 形 414, 村 424, 肖 451, 尾 505, 君 515, 季 725, 秀 726, 居 737, 淑 1335, 梢 1362, 副 1428, 陶 1565, 淵 1858, 殿 1960, 像 2061, 愷 2071, 裔 2217, 標 2298)
Sueba *s* 季羽 725
Suebe *s* 陶部 1565
Sueda *s* 末田 211
Suēden *p* "Sweden" 瑞典 2094
Sueharu *m* 季良 725
Sue Harukata *mh* 陶晴賢 1565
Suehide *m* 末昆 211, 季彬 725 「弘
Suehiro *sm* 末広 211, 末
~ -gari *la* 末広狩
~ Tetchō *ml* 末広鉄腸
Suehogi *m* 末寿
Sueie *s* 季家 725
Sueishi *s* 居石 737
Suekane *sm* 末包 211, 末兼
Suekawa *s* 末川
Sueki *s* 末木; *m* 末喜
Suekichi *m* 末吉, 尾吉 505, 季吉 725

Sueko *f* 末子 211, 尾子 505, 季子 725
Suekuma *m* 季熊
Suematsu *s* 末松 211
～ Kenchō *ml* 末松謙澄
Suemitsu *m* 末盈
Suemori *s* 末森
Suemoto *sm* 末元
Suemura *s* 末村
Suenaga *sm* 末永
Suenobu *sm* 末延; *m* 季誕 725
Sueo *m* 末雄 211, 季雄 725, 裔生 2217
Sueoka *s* 末岡 211
Sueoki *m* 季興 725
Suesada *m* 末貞 211
Sueshige *m* 季茲 725
Suetaka *s* 尾高 505; *sm* 末高 211; *m* 季宝 725, 季鳳, 副隆 1428
Suetake *sm* 末武 211
Suetomo *m* 末耦
Suetsugu *sm* 末次; *m* 季次 725
～ Heizō *mh* 末次平蔵 211 「花
Suetsumuhana *l* 末摘
Suetsune *sm* 末常
Sueyama *s* 陶山 1565
～ Tsutomu *ml* 陶山務
Sueyoshi *sm* 末次 211; *sm-p* 末吉; *m* 末彦, 季備 725, 季巌
～ Magozaemon *mh* 末吉孫左衛門 211
Suezō *m* 末蔵
Sufu *s* 周布 736, 周敷
Suga *s* 菅 1450, 須加 1544, 須賀; *sf* 清 1342, (苞 688, 清 1342, 菅 1450, 廉 2042)
Sugada *s* 菅田 1450
Sugafu *s* 菅生
Sugahara *s* 菅原
Sugahiko *m* 菅彦
Sugai *s* 西水 526, 菅井 1450, 須貝 1544
Sugaji *m* 菅治 1450
Sugako *f* 苞子 688, 菅子 1450 「1544
Sugama *s* 菅間, 須釜
Sugamiya *s* 菅宮 1450
Sugamura *s* 菅村
Suganami *s* 菅波, 菅浪
Sugane *m* 菅根
Sugano *s* 菅野, 萓野 1730
Suganoya *s* 菅谷 1450
Suganuma *s* 菅沼
Sugao *s* 菅緒; *m* 清夫 1342, 菅雄 1450
Sugaomi *m* 清臣 1342
Sugasawa *s* 菅沢 1450
Sugase *s* 菅瀬
Sugatani *s* 菅谷
Sugata Sanshirō *l* 姿三四郎 1217
Sugawa *s* 須川 1544, 素川 1707
Sugawara *s* 菅原 1450
～ denju tenarai kagami *la* 菅原伝授手習鑑 「原文時
～ no Fumitoki *ml* 菅
～ no Michizane *ml* 菅原道真 「孝標
～ no Takasue *ml* 菅原
～ ～ ～ no Musume *ml* 菅原孝標女
Sugaya *s* 菅屋; *sp* 菅谷
Suge *s* 習宜 1468, 摺宜 2067. (菅 1450, 管 2212)
Sugenaga *m* 菅永 1450
Sugeno *s* 菅野
Sugenoi *s* 菅井
Sugetsune *m* 管恒 2212
Sugi *s* 杉 425. (杉, 椙 1626, 榲 2101)
Sugibayashi *s* 杉林 425
Sugie *sf* 杉江
Sugifu *s* 杉生
Sugihara *s* 杉原, 椙原 1626 「平 1626
Sugihira *s* 杉平 425, 椙
Sugii *s* 杉井 425 「1626
Sugikawa *s* 杉川, 椙川
Sugiki *s* 杉木 425
Sugiko *f* 榲子 2101
Sugimori *s* 杉森 425
～ Hisahide *ml* 杉森久英 「郎
～ Kōjirō *ml* 杉森孝次
Sugimoto *s* 杉本
Sugimura *s* 杉村; *m* 榲邨 2101 「人冠 425
～ Sojinkan *ml* 杉村楚
Suginaka *s* 杉中
Suginami *p* 杉並
Sugino *s* 杉野
Suginohara *s* 椙原 1626
Suginome *s* 杉妻 425
Suginomori *s* 椙社 1626
Sugioka *s* 杉岡 425
Sugisaka *s* 杉坂
Sugisaki *s* 杉崎
Sugisawa *s* 杉沢
Sugishima *s* 杉島
Sugishita *s* 杉下
Sugita *s* 杉田 「白
～ Genpaku *ml* 杉田玄
～ Hisajo *fl* 杉田久女
Sugitani *s* 杉谷, 杉渓
Sugitate *s* 杉立
Sugita Tsuruko *fl* 杉田鶴子
Sugito *p* 杉戸
Sugiuchi *s* 杉内
Sugiura *s* 杉浦
～ Jūgō *mlh* 杉浦重剛
～ Minpei *ml* 杉浦明平 「重剛
～ Shigetaka *mlh* 杉浦
～ Suiko *fl* 杉浦翠子
Sugiwaka *s* 杉若
Sugiya *s* 杉谷 「1626
Sugiyama *s* 杉山, 椙山
～ Hizennojō *ma* 杉山肥前掾 425 「助
～ Heisuke *ml* 杉山平
～ Hideki *ml* 杉山英樹
～ Sanpū *ml* 杉山杉風
～ Tangonojō *ma* 杉山丹後掾
Sugō *s* 菅生 1450, 須合 1544, 須郷
(sugu 直 988)
Sugunari *m* 直成
Suguo *m* 直雄
Sugure *m* 勝 1613
Suguri *s* 村士 424, 村主, 勝 1613
Suguritomo *s* 勝伴
Suguro *s* 須黒 1544, 勝呂 1613; *sm* 勝
Suguru *sm* 勝; *m* 克 442, 英 693, 俊 1039, 捷 1323, 逸 1504, 精 2131, 賢 2579, 驍 2957
Suguta *s* 直田 988, 勝田 1613 「963, 栖原 1101
Suhara *s* 寿原 539, 春原
Suhata *s* 簀秦 2687
(sui 水 54, 吹 370, 出 523, 炊 602, 垂 761, 帥 883, 粋 1132, 推 1322, 萃 1442, 随 1564, 椎 1629, 遂 1806, 瑞 2094, 翠 2204, 穂 2308, 綏 2534, 穟 2728, 髄 2826)
Suia ganmoku *l* 水蛙眼目 54
Suibara *p* 水原
Suichō kōkei *l* 粋町甲閨 1132
Suifu *p* 水府 54 「帖
Suiha kuchō *l* 水巴句
Suikazura *l* 忍冬 463
Suiko *fh* 推古 1322
Suimei *l* 水明 54
Suinō *s* 出納 523
Suisōki *l* 水荘記 54
Suisu *p* "Switzerland" 瑞西 2094
Suita *s* 吹 370; *sp* 吹田
～ Junsuke *ml* 吹田順
Suitō *s* 出納 523 「助
Suitsu *s* 水津 54
Sujime *m* 文 86
Sujin *mh* 崇神 1774
Suka *s* 須賀 1544
Sukada *s* 須賀田
Sukagawa *sp* 須賀川
Sukai *s* 須賀井, 須賀院
Suke *m* 介 66. (又 13, 介 66, 友 70, 方 85, 夫 104, 左 169, 右 171, 允 217, 丞 296, 戎 321, 伴 361, 佑 364, 佐 365, 扶 383, 如 412, 助 431, 甫 533, 制 656, 芸 689, 昌 715, 典 733, 延 739, 承 760, 良 767, 祐 852, 相 868, 亮 911, 宥 918, 育 958, 為 1005, 哉 1006, 耿 1129, 高 1163, 差 1164, 毘 1195, 席 1242, 翅 1248, 脩 1281, 涼 1330, 理 1361, 救 1406, 副 1428, 傅 1536, 棚 1625, 棟 1627, 補 1644, 裕 1645, 款 1666, 崇 1774, 棐 1780, 淵 1858, 資 2012, 督 2033, 弼 2092, 稗 2123, 輔 2133, 虞 2242, 播 2259, 鋪 2340, 賞 2377, 賛 2394, 維 2540, 融 2545, 養 2558, 翼 2686) 「相近 868
Sukechika *m* 助参 431,
Sukefuyu *m* 甫冬 533
Sukegawa *s* 介川 66, 助川 431
Sukehide *m* 助暎
Sukehiko *m* 祐彦 852
Sukehiro *m* 右弘 171, 助弘 431, 祐泰 852

Sukehisa *m* 伴久 361
Sukeichi *m* 如意地 412, 助市 431, 弼一 2092
Sukekatsu *m* 資徳 2012
Sukekazu *m* 助千 431
Sukeko *f* 補子 1644, 資子 2012, 輔子 2133
Sukekoto *m* 資承 2012
Sukekuni *m* 祐邦 852
Sukemasa *m* 助当 431
Sukemasu *m* 祐殖 852
Sukematsu *s* 助松 431
Sukemichi *m* 助有, 助盈
Sukemori *m* 助林
Sukemoto *m* 資始 2012
Sukena *m* 助名 431
Sukenaka *m* 右仲 171
Sukenari *m* 介成 66, 弼成 2092, 融成 2545
Sukenobu *m* 允信 217, 扶信 383, 祐命 852
Sukenori *m* 祐方, 祐慶
Sukeoki *m* 佐興 365
Sukeomi *m* 輔臣 2133
Sukeroku *la* 助六 431
Sukesada *m* 佑貞 364, 資貞 2012
Sukeshige *m* 資芝
Suketada *m* 佐忠 365, 典田 733, 傳田 1536, 資忠 2012
Suketaka *m* 佐理 365, 祐丘 852, 資公 2012, 資邁 「431
Suketakaya *s* 助高屋
Suketake *m* 佐武 365
Suketane *m* 助種 431
Suketarō *s* 助太郎, 祐太郎 852
Suketaru *m* 賞善 2377
Suketō *m* 左任 169
Suketomo *m* 祐相 852, 涼朝 1330 「助賢 431
Suketoshi *m* 介寿 66,
Suketsugi *m* 佐世 365
Suketsugu *m* 助受 431
Sukeya *s* 佐谷 365
Sukeyama *p* 佑山 364
Sukeyasu *m* 祐靖 852, 副安 1428
Sukeyoshi *m* 助休 431, 資凱 2012
Sukeyuki *m* 祐之 852, 裕志 1645 「門 431
Sukezaemon *m* 助左衛
Sukezumi *m* 亮澄 911
Suki *s* 寸喜 34, 陶器 1565; *p* 周吉 736, 須木 1544. (伜 356, 透 1502, 鋤 2336, 鍬 2648)
Sukie *s* 鋤柄 2336
Sukigara *s* 鋤柄
Sukikaeshi *l* 還魂紙料 2588 「屋造 2169
Sukiya-zukuri *a* 数寄
Suko *s* 須子 1544
Sukoppei *m* 周滑平 736
Suku *s* 珠洲 1077. (少 88, 奇 752, 宿 1438, 透 1502)
Sukumo *s* 須久毛 1544; *sp* 宿毛 1438 「88)
Sukuna *s* 足奈 461. (少
Sukunamaro *m* 少麻呂, 宿奈麿 1438
Sukune *s* 足尼 461; *m* 宿弥 1438, 宿禰
Sukunemaro *m* 宿禰麿
Sukuni *s* 宿尼
Sukuri *s* 宿利
Suma *s* 寿摩 539; *sp-l* 須磨 1544
~ Genji *la* 須磨源氏
Sumako *f* 寿増子 539, 須磨子 1544
Sumami *s* 周参見 736
Suma no miyako Genpei tsutsuji *la* 須磨都源平躑躅 1544
(sumera 皇 964)
Sumeragi *s* 皇 「2276
Sumeri *s* 清 1342; *m* 澄
Sumeru *m* 澄, 統 2333
Sumi *s* 住 355, 角 547, 炭 1186, 須見 1544, 墨 2230, 鷲見 2980; *f* 澄 2276. (了 9, 処 177, 有 303, 在 314, 住 355, 伜 356, 好 413, 邑 460, 究 492, 角 547, 宜 675, 迂 749, 宣 919, 栖 1101, 炭 1186, 恭 1205, 淑 1335, 済 1336, 清 1342, 紀 1424, 宿 1438, 隅 1566, 奥 1798, 純 1956, 精 2131, 誦 2138, 墨 2230, 徴 2265, 潜 2272, 澄 2276, 統 2333, 澂 2456, 維 2540, 篤 2576, 簾 2844)
Sumiaki *m* 統秋 2333
Sumichiyo *f* 栖千代 1101
Sumida *s* 角田 547, 澄田 2276; *sp* 隅田 1566; *p* 墨田 2230
~ Chikurei *ml* 角田竹令 547
Sumidagawa *la* 角田川, 隅田川 1566
~ hana no goshozome *la* 隅田川花御所染
Sumida no haru geisha katagi *l* 隅田春妓女容性
Sumidawara *l* 炭俵 1186
Sumida Yōkichi *ml* 隅田葉吉 1566
Sumie *s* 墨江 2230; *f* 了江 9, 潜枝 2272
Sumihide *m* 住英 355
Sumihiko *m* 純彦 1956
Sumii *s* 住井 355 「2276
Sumikawa *s* 住川, 澄川
Sumikiyo *m* 純精 1956
Sumiko *f* 淑子 1335, 済子 1336, 進美子 1503, 順美子 1532, 澄子 2276, 澄美子, 簾子 2844
Sumikura *s* 角倉 547
Sumimaro *m* 角麿
Sumimasa *m* 純正 1956
Sumimoto *m* 澄元 2276
Suminami *s* 角南 547
Sumino *s* 住野 355, 角野 547
Suminoe *s* 住江 355, 住吉, 墨江 2230
Suminokura *s* 角倉 547
~ Ryōi *mh* 角倉了以
Suminosuke *s* 墨之助 2230 「住道
Suminoto *s* 住跡 355,
Suminuri *l* 墨塗 2230
S. onna *la* 墨塗女
Sumio *m* 住雄 355, 清雄 1342, 純夫 1956, 純雄, 澄男 2276
Sumire *f* 菫 1453
Sumita *sp* 住田 355
Sumi Taigi *ml* 炭太祇 1186
Sumitaka *m* 純孝 1956
Sumitani *s* 住谷 355
Sumitomo *s* 住友; *m* 純友 1956
Sumiya *s* 角谷 547, 角屋, 隅屋 1566
Sumiyama *s* 住山 355, 隅山 1566
Sumiyō *p* 住用 355
Sumiyoshi *sp-l* 住吉; *m* 純義 1956 「355
~ Gukei *ma* 住吉具慶
~ mōde *la* 住吉詣
~ -zukuri *a* 住吉造
Sumizane *m* 奥実 1798
Sumizome-zakura *la* 墨染桜 2230
(sumomo 李 488)
Sumomogi *s* 李木
Sumon *p* 守門 284
Sumori *s* 巣森 1431
Sumoto *p* 洲本 820, 栖本 1101 「澂 2456)
(sumu 清 1342, 澄 2276,
Sumuji *s* 住道 355
(sun 寸 34, 邨 645)
(suna 沙 392, 砂 876, 淳 1337, 漁 2086)
Sunada *s* 砂田 876, 漁田 2086
Sunadoi *s* 砂土居 876
Sunae *s* 魚吉 1485
~ shibari *l* 砂絵呪縛 876
Sunaga *s* 砂賀, 巣永 1431, 須永 1544, 須長
Sunagashi *s* 洲流 820
Sunagawa *l* 沙川 392; *sp* 砂川 876
Sunago *s* 砂金
Sunaji *s* 砂治
Sunako *s* 砂子
Sunami *s* 陶浪 1565; *sp* 角南 547; *p* 巣南 1431
Sunamura *s* 砂村 876
Sunanaga *s* 砂永
Sunao *m* 朴 255, 侃 551, 忠 705, 政 881, 是 947, 直 988, 惇 1288, 淳 1337, 淳夫, 順 1532, 温 1585, 素 1707, 純 1956, 廉 2042, 愿 2228, 質 2395, 愨 2403, 彝 2909; *l* 素直 1707
Sunaoshi *s* 砂押 876
Sunayama *s* 砂山
Sunazuka *s* 砂塚
Sundo *l* 寸土 34
(sune 強 1878, 髄 2826)
Sunohara *s* 春原 963
Sunomata *s* 洲股 820, 黒股 1486; *sp* 墨俣
Sunori *s* 苔 929 ⌊2230
Sunouchi *s* 洲内 820, 巣内 1431, 須之内 1544
Suntō *p* 駿東 2763

Suō *sph* 周防 736
～ otoshi *l* 素袍落 1707
Supein *p* "Spain" 西班牙 336
(suri 摺 2067)
Surizawa *s* 摺沢
Suruga *s* 珠流河 1077, 珠琉河, 薦河 2683; *sph* 駿河 2763
Susa *s* 諏佐 2327; *sp* 須佐 1544
Susai *s* 周西 736, 酒西 1066, 須細 1544
Susaki *s* 朱雀 341, 寿崎 539, 洲崎 820, 須佐木 1544; *sp* 須崎
Susami *sp* 周参見 736
Suseki *s* 栖関 1101
Susenji *s* 鋳銭司 2343
Suseyama *s* 嵩山 2207
(suso 裾 1907, 襴 2708)
Susogo *s* 下農 46, 下濃
Susomi *f* 裾巳 1907
Susono *p* 裾野
(susu 進 1503, 薄 2569)
Susuki *s* 須須木 1544, 薄 2569, 薄木. (薄)
Susukida *s* 薄田
～ Kyūkin *ml* 薄田泣菫
Susukio *s* 蘆尾 2842
Susukioya *s* 薄尾屋 2569
Susume *m* 進馬 1503
Susumi *s* 晋 1215; *m* 進実 1503, 漸 2081, 懋 2700
Susumu *m* 亅 1, 一 3, 二 4, 万 43, 上 47, 収 133, 生 214, 先 280, 丞 296, 存 313, 年 342, 亨 440, 旨 450, 侑 557, 効 653, 享 662, 歩 694, 昇 713, 延 739, 軍 906, 前 921, 羑 922, 迪 1001, 将 1040, 陞 1057, 貢 1166, 皋 1197, 益 1201, 烝 1210, 晋 1215, 函 1232, 偂 1274, 敏 1409, 乾 1411, 皃 1456, 阜 1459, 進 1503, 粛 1528, 亀 1531, 徝 1568, 斌 1590, 普 1792, 達 1810, 犹 1922, 新 1965, 勧 1970, 督 2023, 奨 2036, 漸 2081, 暲 2284, 範 2384, 邁 2592, 遲 2593, 謹 2645, 駸 2666, 藎 2680, 勸 2767
Sutama *p* 須玉 1544
Sute *f* 捨 1324. (捨, 棄 2202, 鐸 2922)
Sutegiku *f* 捨菊 1324
Suteji *m* 捨二
Sutejirō *m* 捨次郎
Sutekichi *m* 捨吉
Suteko *f* 棄子 2202
Sutenabe *f* 捨鍋 1324
Sutezō *m* 捨造
Suto *s* 須戸 1544
Sutoku *mh* 崇徳 1774
Suttsu *p* 寿都 539
Suu *sp* 周布 736
Suwa *s* 須波 1544; *sp* 諏訪 2327
Suwabe *s* 諏訪部
Suwa ichi *l* 諏訪都
Suwara *s* 須原 1544, 数原 2169
Suwaraya *s* 須原屋 1544
Suya *s* 酢屋 1654
Suyama *s* 巣山 1431, 須山 1544, 陶山 1565
Suzaka *s* 須坂 1544
Suzakiya *l* 須崎屋
Suzaku *mh* 朱雀 341
Suzawa *s* 須沢 1544
Suzu *f* 寿津 539, 珠鶴 1077, 雀鶴 1530, 紗 1683, 錫 2524; *p* 珠洲 1077. (表 914, 宰 1180, 錫 2524, 鴛 2787, 鐸 2922)
Suzue *sf* 鈴江 1947; *f* 錫枝 2524
Suzui *s* 酒酒井 1066
Suzuka *s* 鈴賀 1947; *sp* 鈴鹿
～ Noburo *ml* 鈴鹿野風呂
Suzukawa *s* 鈴川
Suzuki *s* 寿寿木 539, 進来 1503, 須須木 1544, 鈴木 1947, 鐸木 2922, 鱸 3014. (鱸)
～ -bōchō *la* 鱸庖丁
～-～ aoto no kireaji *l* 鱸庖丁青砥切味
～ Bunji *mh* 鈴木文治 1947
Suzukida *s* 鈴木田
Suzuki Daisetsu *ml* 鈴木大拙
～ Hanamino *ml* 鈴木花蓑
～ Harunobu *ma* 鈴木春信 「恭
～ Hiroyasu *ml* 鈴木弘
～ Kantarō *mh* 鈴木貫太郎 「重吉
～ Miekichi *ml* 鈴木三
～ Senzaburō *ml* 鈴木泉三郎 「太郎
～ Shintarō *ml* 鈴木信
～ Shōsan *ml* 鈴木正三
～ Takashi *ml* 鐸木孝 2922 「1947
～ Torao *ml* 鈴木虎雄
～ Umetarō *mh* 鈴木梅太郎 「太郎
～ Zentarō *ml* 鈴木善
Suzuko *f* 春秋子 963, 宰子 1180, 鈴子 1947, 錫子 2524, 鴛子 2787
Suzumura *s* 須受武良 1544, 鈴村 1947
Suzumushi *l* 鈴虫
(suzuna 菘 1721)
Suzunako *f* 菘子
Suzuno *s* 鈴野 1947
Suzuo *m* 鈴雄, 鐸男 ⌊2922
(suzuri 硯 1634)
Suzuriya *s* 硯
Suzushi *m* 冷 349, 凉 1020, 凊 1021
Suzuta *s* 鈴田 1947
Suzuya *s* 鈴屋

# T

(ta 太 105, 手 118, 他 129, 北 138, 夻 160, 田 189, 多 347, 朶 458, 妥 708, 柁 856, 咫 996, 為 1005, 碓 1910, 蒼 1988)
Tabashi *s* 田橋 189
Tabata *s* 田畑, 田端, 田幡, 多畑 347, 多端
～ Shūichirō *ml* 田畑修一郎 189
Tabayama *sp* 丹波山 79
Tabayashi *s* 田林 189
Tabe *s* 田部, 多部 347
Tabei *s* 田部井 189
(tabi 旅 1073)
Tabigawa *s* 旅川
Tabiko *f* 旅子
Tabira *p* 田平 189
Tabito *m* 旅人 1073; *p* 田人 189
Tabuchi *s* 田淵
Tabusa *s* 田総 「布施
Tabuse *s* 田伏; *sp* 田
Tachi *s* 田地, 田知, 立 194, 城 796, 館 2761. (刀 12, 立 194, 楯 1897, 館 2761)
Tachiarai *p* 太刀洗 105
Tachibai *la* 太刀奪
Tachibana *s* 田知花 189; *sp* 立花 194, 橘 2484
～ Hokushi *ml* 立花北枝 194
～ Itoeko *fla* 橘糸重子 2484 「利
～ Munetoshi *ml* 橘宗
～ no Hayanari *ml* 橘逸勢 「三千代
～ no Michiyo *fh* 橘
～ no Moribe *mh* 橘守部 「兄
～ no Moroe *mlh* 橘諸
～ no Nagayasu *ml* 橘永愷 「奈良麻呂
～ no Naramaro *mh* 橘
～ no Narisue *ml* 橘成季
～ no Yachimata *ml* 橘八衢
～ Toseko *fl* 橘東世子
Tachibanaya *s* 橘屋
Tachida *s* 立田 194
Tachigi *s* 立木
Tachigori *s* 日日 77
Tachihaki *s* 刀佩 12
Tachihara *s* 立原 194
～ Michizō *ml* 立原道造
Tachii *sp* 丹比 79
Tachiiri *s* 立入 194
Tachiishi *s* 立石
Tachiiwa *s* 立岩
Tachijima *s* 立島

Tachika *s* 田近 189
Tachikawa *s* 太刀川 105, 立河 194; *sp* 立川
~ bunko *l* 立川文庫
Tachimatsu *s* 立松
Tachimi *s* 立見
Tachimori *s* 日月 77
Tachino *s* 立野 194, 館野 2761
Tachishiro *s* 帯壬 1192
Tachito *m* 達等 1810
Tachiya *s* 太刀屋 105
Tachiyama *s* 立山 194
Tachizawa *s* 立沢
Tachū *m* 太仲 105, 多仲 347
Tada *s* 田田 189, 多田 347, 多多, 唯 1286. (一 3, 九 16, 三 22, 也 23, 子 38, 工 39, 士 41, 土 42, 孔 58, 中 75, 内 81, 止 87, 尹 98, 公 156, 只 157, 疋 166, 尼 175, 兄 181, 由 186, 田 189, 正 205, 矢 215, 允 217, 仕 235, 伊 237, 地 241, 江 252, 旬 301, 但 351, 伸 353, 位 354, 伝 359, 均 387, 孚 483, 廷 501, 匡 504, 良 529, 考 540, 身 546, 侃 551, 佶 558, 帖 563, 妙 614, 即 648, 斉 701, 忠 705, 周 736, 信 782, 政 881, 訂 894, 糺 903, 品 916, 単 919A, 帝 971, 貞 982, 直 988, 度 1009, 徒 1048, 祥 1074, 格 1099, 粋 1132, 殷 1139, 宰 1180, 衷 1190, 恭 1205, 真 1228, 唯 1286, 惟 1290, 陟 1309, 渉 1331, 済 1336, 規 1349, 理 1361, 祇 1380, 敕 1405, 糾 1422, 紀 1424, 斎 1454, 産 1520, 問 1524, 粛 1528, 孫 1540, 渡 1586, 婧 1601, 楷 1622, 評 1663, 款 1666, 欽 1678, 晉 1700, 寔 1710, 萱 1730, 董 1731, 覚 1752, 喬 1775, 達 1810, 弾 1880, 禎 1887, 雅 1913, 亶 1972, 資 2012, 督 2023, 精 2131, 肆 2144, 彰 2174, 肇 2222, 蓼 2229, 端 2306, 質 2395, 監 2398, 蔵 2424, 隣 2443, 諟 2512, 諫 2514, 維 2540, 叡 2555, 薫 2567, 賢 2579, 矯 2626, 覧 2695, 纒 2955)
Tadaaki *m* 忠丙 705, 忠秋, 忠発, 忠義, 糾明 1422, 孫顕 1540, 督章 2023
Tadaakira *m* 忠存 705, 忠亮, 忠哲, 忠威
Tadaari *m* 忠徳
Tadaatsu *m* 忠淳, 忠敬, 忠強, 忠篤
Tadachika *m* 忠見, 忠直, 忠親 「1731
Tadae *m* 忠藎; *f* 董枝
Tada Fuji *ml* 多田不二 347 「格文 1099
Tadafumi *m* 忠文 705,
Tadafusa *m* 忠総 705
Tadahachi *m* 只八 157
Tadaharu *m* 忠珍 705, 忠晴 「忠彦 705
Tadahiko *m* 正彦 205,
Tadahira *m* 三成 22, 忠平 705, 忠挙, 忠啓
Tadahiro *m* 忠洪, 忠嘉
Tadahisa *m* 忠寿, 忠敝
Tadahito *m* 正仁 205
Tadai *s* 唯井 1286
Tadaichi *m* 唯一, 惟一 1290 「道 988
Tadaji *m* 忠二 705, 直
Tadakane *m* 忠鼎 705
Tadakata *m* 忠良, 忠敬, 忠器
Tadakatsu *m* 九万 16, 忠勝 705, 唯一 1286
Tadakazu *m* 伊一 237, 忠沓 705, 忠籌, 唯一 1286
Tadaki *s* 只木 157; *sp* 但木 351; *ml* 中興 75
Tadakiyo *m* 忠舜 705
Tadako *f* 伸子 353, 忠子 705, 渉子 1331, 産子 1520, 婧子 1601, 晉子 1700, 纒子 2955
Tadakumo *m* 忠雲 705
Tadakuni *m* 忠邦, 忠郡 「*m* 忠位 705
Tadakura *s* 直椋 988;
Tadamasa *m* 正政 205, 忠当 705, 忠匡, 忠将, 忠祗, 忠済, 忠粛, 忠順, 忠款, 督正 2023, 肇蔚 2222
Tadamatsu *m* 尹松 98
Tadami *s* 忠見 705, 忠相; *sp* 只見 157; *m* 忠侃 705, 董躬 1731
Tadamichi *m* 忠宝 705, 忠恕, 度道 1009; *ml* 忠通 705
Tadamichishū *l* 田多民治集 189
Tadamine *ml* 忠岑 705
Tadamitsu *m* 忠光, 忠苗, 忠実, 忠瑗, 宰光 1180 「忠持
Tadamochi *m* 忠用 705,
Tadamori *m* 三守 22, 忠豊 705
Tadamoto *m* 忠大, 忠民, 忠幹
Tadamune *sm* 忠宗
Tadamura *s* 忠村
Tadana *m* 斎名 1454
Tadanai *s* 忠内 705
Tadanaka *m* 忠考, 忠翰 「纒直 2955
Tadanao *m* 忠直, 忠懿,
~ -kyō gyōjōki *l* 忠直卿行状記 705
Tada Nanrei *ml* 多田南嶺 347 「忠震
Tadanari *m* 忠礼 705,
Tadanaru *m* 忠愛
Tadando *m* 唯人 1286
Tadani *s* 田谷 189
Tadano *s* 只野 157
Tadanobu *m* 斉信 701, 忠言 705, 忠述, 忠信
Tada no Jijii *ml* 多田爺 347
Tadanori *m* 匡徳 504, 忠位 705, 忠学, 忠度, 忠怒, 忠悳, 唯糊 1286
Tadanushi *m* 纒主 2955
Tadao *m* 但夫 351, 忠夫 705, 忠郎, 忠雄, 直夫 988, 唯男 1286, 唯雄, 糾夫 1422, 紀男 1424, 弾男 1880, 精夫 2131, 端夫 2306, 隣夫 2443
Tadaoka *p* 忠岡 705
Tadaoki *m* 忠居, 忠意, 忠興, 直気 988
Tadaon *m* 忠臣 705
Tadaosa *m* 忠順
Tadare *l* 爛 2913
Tadasaki *m* 忠鋒 705
Tadasato *m* 忠学, 忠彦
Tadashi *m* 子ゝ 38, 仁 57, 中 75, 方 85, 尹 98, 公 156, 且 162, 正 205, 匡 504, 冽 549, 侃 551, 佶 558, 征 580, 斉 701, 忠 705, 延 739, 律 787, 政 881, 糺 903, 尭 910, 荘 933, 是 947, 貞 982, 直 988, 将 1040, 格 1099, 矩 1108, 砡 1111, 衷 1190, 恭 1205, 真 1228, 淳 1337, 規 1349, 理 1361, 糾 1422, 紀 1424, 恕 1483, 董 1731, 覚 1752, 善 1799, 禎 1887, 雅 1913, 義 1975, 廉 2042, 徳 2063, 弼 2092, 精 2131, 肇 2222, 儀 2255, 賾 2278, 端 2306, 質 2395, 闇 2427, 憲 2562, 賢 2579, 羲 2675, 讜 2727, 衢 2790, 顳 2827
Tadashige *m* 尹鎮 98, 忠重 705, 忠恵, 忠稠
Tadashirō *m* 匡四郎 504
Tadasono *m* 忠圉 705
Tadasu *m* 正 205, 忱 271, 孜 378, 匡 504, 征 580, 忠 705, 律 787, 治 825, 政 881, 訂 894, 糺 903, 貞 982, 直 988, 迪 1001, 格 1099, 矩 1108, 規 1349, 理 1361, 糾 1422, 温 1585, 董 1731, 督 2023, 端 2306, 憲 2562
Tadasue *m* 政孝 881
Tadasuke *m* 允亮 217, 忠賛 705, 忠翼, 敕介 1405 「忠篤
Tadasumi *m* 忠恭 705,
Tadatae *m* 忠克
Tadataka *m* 忠升, 忠位, 忠挙, 忠脩, 忠揚, 忠敞
Tadatake *m* 忠宝
Tadatami *m* 糺民 903
Tadateru *m* 忠英 705, 忠晃, 忠韶, 忠顕, 忠熹, 忠耀
Tadato *m* 忠人
Tadatō *m* 忠寛
Tadatoki *m* 忠言, 忠刻, 忠節
Tadatomo *m* 忠和, 忠宝, 忠倫, 周知 736
Tadatoshi *m* 孔敏 58, 忠勇 705, 忠俊, 忠要,

忠惇, 忠粛, 忠順, 忠禄, 惟俊 1290
Tadatsugu *m* 但次 351, 伝次 359, 忠次 705, 忠告
Tadatsune *m* 忠常
Tadatsuyo *m* 忠強
Tadayasu *m* 忠安, 忠容, 忠昆, 忠烈, 忠恭, 忠能, 忠裕, 忠廉, 忠養, 格安 1099
Tadayo *s* 直世 988
Tadayori *m* 忠和 705, 忠移, 忠順, 忠馮
Tadayoshi *m* 忠与, 忠休, 忠宴, 忠義, 忠候, 忠禄, 忠禎, 忠誠, 忠愛, 忠穀, 貞幹 982, 直義 988
Tada Yūkei *ml* 多田裕計 347
Tadayuki *m* 由行 186, 忠至 705, 忠敏, 忠恕, 忠進, 忠徹, 忠鵬
Tadazane *m* 忠似
Tade *s* 蓼 2229
Tadenuma *s* 蓼沼
Tadera *s* 田寺 189
Tado *s* 田戸, 多戸 347; *p* 多度
Tadokoro *s* 田所 189
Tadoshi *p* 多度志 347
Tadotsu *sp* 多度津
Tae *s* 田使 189; *m* 当 282; *f* 妙 614. (才 35, 布 170, 任 235, 巧 238, 当 282, 克 442, 妙 614, 紗 1683, 堪 1843, 絶 2148, 絲 2526)
Taeko *f* 任子 235, 紗子 1683, 堪子 1843
Taema *sla* 当麻 282
Taemi *s* 妙美 614
Taemitsu *m* 才光 35, 妙光 614
Tafu *s* 袋布 1750
Taga *s* 田賀 189; *sp* 多賀 347
Tagai *s* 互 200
Tagajō *p* 多賀城 347
Tagami *s* 多上; *sp* 田上 189 「之上 129
Taga minoue *l* 他我身
Tagashira *s* 田頭 189
Tagata *s* 田形; *sp* 田方
Tagawa *s* 田河, 多川 347; *sp* 田川 189
Tagaya *s* 多賀谷 347, 達谷窟 1810
Tagayasu *m* 耕 1131
Tage *s* 田下 189
Tagi *s* 多芸 347
Tagima *s* 当麻 282
Tagimahonjibe *s* 当麻品遅部
Tago *s* 田子 189
Taguchi *s* 田口 「汀
~ Kikutei *ml* 田口掬
~ Ukichi *mlh* 田口卯
Tagura *s* 田倉 ⌊吉
Tagusari *s* 日鎖 77, 田鎖 189
Taguwa *s* 田桑
Tahara *p* 田原
Tahee *m* 太兵衛 105, 多兵衛 347
Tahika *s* 田光 189
Tahira *sp* 田平
Taho *s* 答本 1765
Tai *s* 田井 189, 戴 2707; *p* "Thailand" 泰 1203. (大 48, 太 105, 代 125, 夳 160, 台 276, 当 282, 体 358, 対 405, 兌 447, 旲 482, 待 785, 耐 884, 苔 929, 岱 955, 帝 971, 帯 1192, 泰 1203, 退 1236A, 堆 1295, 砥 1386, 棣 1616, 敦 1690, 晉 1700, 袋 1750, 碓 1910, 載 2050, 槌 2102, 確 2305, 諟 2512, 諦 2516, 戴 2707, 鎚 2749, 鵜 2822, 鯛 2832)
Taichi *m* 太一 105, 太市, 多一 347
Taichirō *m* 太一郎 105
Taiei *p* 大栄 48
Taigi *ml* 太祇 105
Taigo *m* 確悟 2305
Taihei *p* 大平 48
Taiheiki *l* 太平記 105
Taihei shōjō *la* 大瓶猩猩 48
Taihō 701–04 大宝
Taihoku *p* "Taipei" 台北 276
Taiji *m* 泰二 1203, 泰治, 鯛二 2832; *p* 太地 105
Taijirō *m* 泰次郎 1203, 退二郎 1236A
Taika 645–50 大化 48
Taikan *ma* 大観 「276
Taiki *p* 大樹; *l* 台記
Taikichi *m* 泰吉 1203
Taiko *s* 大胡 48
Taikōki *l* 太閤記 105
Taikoku *p* "Thailand" 泰国 1203
Taiko no oto chiyū no sanryaku *la* 太鼓音智勇三略 105
Taikyoshū *l* 太虚集
Taikyū *p* "Taegu" 大邱 48 「当麻 282
Taima *s* 対間 405; *sp*
Taimei *p* 岱明 955
Tai no misozu *l* 鯛の味噌津 2832
Taira *s* 平良 203; *sp* 平; *m* 水 54, 坦 574, 泰良 1203. (平 203)
Tairadate *p* 平館
Tairai *s* 平子, 平井
Tairako *f* 平子
Tairaku *s* 平久
Taira no Kiyomori *mh-l* 平清盛
~ no Koremori *mh* 平維盛 「平将門
~ no Masakado *mh-l*
~ no Masako *fh* 平政子 「正盛
~ no Masamori *mh* 平
~ no Munemori *mh* 平宗盛 「度繁
~ no Norishige *mh* 平
~ no Sadabumi *mh* 平定文, 平貞文
~ no Sadamori *mh* 平貞盛 「重盛
~ no Shigemori *mh* 平
~ no Tadamori *mh* 平忠盛 「平忠常
~ no Tadatsune *mh*
~ no Takamochi *mh* 平高望 「子
~ no Tokuko *fh* 平徳
~ no Yasuyori *ml* 平康頼
Tairo *ml* 大魯 48
Taisaku *m* 泰作 1203
Taisei *p* 大成 48
Taisha *p* 大社
~ -zukuri *a* 大社造
Taishi *p* 太子 105
Taishin *p* 大信 48
Taishiya *s* 太子屋 105
Taishō *mh-p* 1912–26 大正 48
Taisuke *m* 大衛, 泰甫 1203, 退助 1236A, 敦介 1690
Taiten *l* 大典 48
Taitō *p* 台東 276
Taiwa *p* 大和 48
Taiwan *p* "Taiwan" 台湾 276
Taiyō *p* 大洋 48
Taizanbukun *la* 泰山府君 1203
Taizō *m* 岱三 955, 泰三 1203, 退蔵 1236A
Taji *s* 丹比 79, 田地 189, 田路
Tajihi *s* 丹治 79, 丹治比, 丹墀, 多治 347, 多治比, 蝮 2312
Tajihibe *s* 蝮壬部
Tajika *s* 田鹿 189
Tajima *s* 田嶼, 多島 347; *sp* 田島 189; *ph* 但馬 351 「189
~ Shōji *ml* 田島象二
Tajimi *sp* 多治見 347; *m* 但見 351
Tajimibu *s* 蝮壬 2312
Tajinko-mura *l* 多甚古村 347
Tajino *s* 但野 351
Tajiri *s* 多尻 347; *sp* 田
Tajitsu *s* 田実 ⌊尻 189
Tajō busshin *l* 多情仏心 347
Taka *s* 高 1163, 雁 1801; *f* 天 93, 篁 2382; *p* 多可 347. (乙 2, 子 38, 万 43, 上 47, 及 33, 方 85, 山 89, 王 90, 太 105, 升 113, 女 114, 比 137, 古 154, 公 156, 右 171, 立 194, 平 203, 正 205, 生 214, 丘 219, 任 235, 行 245, 竹 247, 宇 285, 共 292, 位 354, 仰 360, 伯 363, 社 406, 好 413, 肖 451, 孚 483, 廷 501, 応 509, 考 540, 孝 541, 邵 646, 卓 660, 幸 661, 享 662, 官 672, 宜 675, 宝 676, 茂 691, 学 719, 空 723, 阜 731, 卒 732, 固 744, 尚 753, 良 767, 垣 795, 恪 803, 珍 836, 荘 933, 岧 940, 岩 942, 昂 943, 穹 948, 岳 956, 香 961, 栄 969, 専 973, 飛 1014, 旅 1073, 桓 1100, 殷

1139, 財 1143, 高 1163, 宮 1184, 皋 1197, 恭 1205, 挙 1207, 姿 1217, 威 1251, 堆 1295, 猛 1306, 険 1308, 陟 1309, 陵 1310, 隆 1313, 捧 1318, 渉 1331, 峰 1351, 理 1361, 梢 1362, 能 1397, 教 1408, 剛 1429, 喬 1433, 阜 1459, 章 1461, 堂 1462, 啓 1491, 揚 1551, 陽 1567, 峻 1591, 琢 1608, 棟 1627, 敞 1688, 敬 1691, 崟 1736, 崔 1738, 登 1744, 貴 1755, 象 1761, 等 1770, 崇 1774, 喬 1775, 堯 1795, 堅 1796, 尊 1797, 雄 1912, 稜 1917, 誠 1935, 累 2004, 誉 2010, 筠 2015, 楚 2022, 僑 2057, 旗 2093, 鄗 2167, 農 2205, 嵩 2207, 節 2215, 鳳 2233, 幟 2260, 標 2298, 毅 2351, 賞 2377, 篁 2382, 橋 2485, 翰 2518, 賢 2570, 邁 2592, 懐 2605, 聳 2698, 厳 2706, 顕 2757, 嶽 2775, 爵 2779, 邇 2785, 議 2876, 巍 2972, 巍 2991, 鷹 2995, 鑽 3020)

Takaaki *m* 公明 156, 孝顕 541, 高明 1163, 高聴, 隆研 1313, 章明 1461

Takaari *m* 隆生 1313

Takaaya *m* 高琢 1163

Takaba *s* 高場, 高羽, 鷹羽 2995

Takabatake *s* 高畠 1163

～ Motoyuki *mlh* 高畠素之 「泉

～ Ransen *ml* 高畠藍

Takabayashi *s* 高林

Takabe *s* 高部

Takabeya *s* 鷹部屋 2995

Takabori *s* 高堀 1163

Takabumi *m* 尚文 753

Takachi *s* 高市 1163

Takachiho *s* 高千穏

Takachika *m* 孝弟 541, 高悠 1163, 挙周 1207, 敬親 1691

Takachio *s* 高知尾 1163

Takada *sp* 高田

Takadachi *l* 高館

Takada Hanbō *ml* 高田半峰 「厚

～ Hiroatsu *ml* 高田博

～ Mizuho *ml* 高田瑞穂 「浪吉

～ Namikichi *ml* 高田

Takadani *s* 高谷

Takadanobaba *p* 高田馬場

Takadaya *s* 高田屋

～ Kahee *mh* 高田屋嘉兵衛

Takadera *s* 高寺

Takado *s* 高戸

Takae *m* 鷹衛 2995; *f* 崇恵 1774

Takaeda *m* 高朶 1163

Takafuji *s* 高藤

Takafumi *m* 堯文 1795

Takagai *s* 鷹谷 2995

Takagaki *s* 高垣 1163

Takagami *s* 高上

Takagawa *s* 高川

Takagi *s* 竹城 247, 高城 1163, 都木 1419, 喬木 1775, 鷹木 2995; *sp* 高木 1163; *p* 高来

～ Kazuo *ml* 高木一夫

Takagishi *s* 高岸 「卓

Takagi Taku *ml* 高木

～ Teiji *mh* 高木貞治

Takagiwa *s* 高際

Takaguchi *s* 高口

Takaha *s* 高羽 「萩

Takahagi *s* 高萩; *p* 高

Takahama *sp* 高浜

～ Kyoshi *ml* 高浜虚子

～ Toshio *ml* 高浜年尾

Takahara *sp* 高原

Takaharu *m* 登治 1744

Takahase *s* 高長谷 1163

Takahashi *s* 高階, 高橋, 鷹箸 2995, 鷹嘴; *sp* 高梁 1163

～ Gorō *ml* 高橋五郎

～ Kageyasu *mh* 高橋景保 「巳

～ Kazumi *ml* 高橋和

～ Korekiyo *mh* 高橋是清 「高橋虫麻呂

～ no Mushimaro *ml*

～ Oden yasha monogatari *l* 高橋阿伝夜叉譚 「新吉

～ Shinkichi *ml* 高橋

～ Teiji *ml* 高橋禎二

～ ujibumi *l* 高橋氏文

～ Yoshitaka *ml* 高橋義孝

～ Yūichi *ma* 高橋由一

Takahata *s* 高畑, 高幡; *sp* 高畠

Takahei *s* 高幣

Takahide *m* 隆成 1313, 隆英

Takahiko *m* 孝孫 541, 恭彦 1205, 尊孫 1797

Takahira *s* 孝平 541, 高平 1163, 高比良; *m* 香平 961, 隆平 1313, 尊成 1797

Takahiro *s* 高広 1163; *m* 任弘 235, 高弘 1163, 隆玄 1313, 尊礼 1797, 巍洋 2991

Takahisa *sm* 高久 1163; *m* 高弥, 隆良 1313

Takahito *m* 幟仁 2260

Takahoko *s* 高鉾 1163

Takai *s* 高井, 篁 2382. (高 1163)

Takaichi *sp* 高市; *m* 殷一 1139, 鑽一 3020

Takaiko *f* 高子 1163

Takaishi *p* 高石

Takaito *m* 隆純 1313

Takaiwa *s* 高岩 1163

Takaji *s* 高地; *m* 珍次 836, 高次 1163, 剛二 1429, 堯爾 1795, 鷹治 2995

Takajirō *m* 高次郎 1163, 誉次郎 2010, 鷹次郎 2995

Takajō *p* 高城 1163

Takakado *m* 高門

Takakage *m* 孝景 541, 高陰 1163

Takakaibe *s* 鷹甘戸 2995, 鷹養戸 「高鎌

Takakata *m* 高謙 1163,

Takakatsu *m* 高柿

Takakazu *m* 高品, 隆師 1313

Takaki *s* 高境 1163; *sp* 高木; *m* 喬樹 1775

Takakiyo *m* 孝潔 541, 高精 1163, 高潔, 鷹清 2995

Takako *f* 任子 235, 邵子 646, 荘子 933, 穹子 948, 殷子 1139, 高子 1163, 登子 1744, 貴子 1755, 尊子 1797, 累教 2004, 楚子 2022, 鄗子 2167, 聳子 2698, 厳子 2706

Takaku *s* 高久 1163

Takakuni *ml* 隆国 1313

Takakura *s* 高倉 1163, 高座

Takakuraji *m* 高倉下

Takakusa *s* 高草

Takakusagi *s* 高草木

Takakusu *s* 高楠

～ Junjirō *mh* 高楠順次郎

Takakuwa *s* 高桑, 高鍬

～ Sumio *ml* 高桑純夫

Takama *s* 高天, 高間

Takamado *s* 高円

Takamaro *s* 高円; *m* 孚麿 483

Takamasa *m* 荘政 933, 隆正 1313, 隆道, 隆督, 賞雅 2377

Takamasu *m* 隆賢 1313

Takamatsu *s* 鷹松 2995; *sp* 高松 1163 「2995

Takami *s* 高見, 鷹見

Takamichi *s* 高道 1163; *m* 孝道 541, 隆術 1313, 隆彭 「順 1163

Takami Jun *ml* 高見

Takamiki *m* 孝幹 541

Takamine *s* 高峰 1163, 高嶺 「吉

～ Jōkichi *mh* 高峰譲

Takamitsu *m* 香光 961, 隆光 1313, 貴暢 1755; *ml* 高光 1163

Takamiya *sp* 高宮

Takamizawa *s* 高見沢

Takamizu *s* 高水

Takamochi *m* 高或

Takamori *s* 鷹森 2995; *sp* 高森 1163; *m* 隆盛 1313

Takamoto *s* 高本 1163; *m* 上基 47, 卓幹 660, 喬求 1775

Takamuko *s* 高向 1163

～ no Kuromaro *mh* 高向玄理

Takamuku *s* 高向

Takamune *s* 邇宗 2785; *m* 右宗 171

Takamura *sm-l* 篁 2382; *sp* 高村 1163 「郎

～ Kōtarō *ml* 高村光太

~ Kōun *ma* 高村光雲
Takamure *s* 高群
~ Itsue *fl* 高群逸枝
Takana *m* 隆声 1313
Takanabe *p* 高鍋 1163
Takanaga *m* 良長 767, 高修 1163, 隆孟 1313
Takanaka *s* 高中 1163 ; *m* 高翰, 高仲
Takanami *s* 高波, 高浪
Takanao *m* 高植, 隆董 1313
Takanari *m* 誠成 1935
Takanaru *m* 高遂 1163, 隆考 1313
Takanashi *s* 小鳥遊 21, 少鳥遊 88, 高梨 1163, 鳥遊 1521
Takanawa *s* 高輪 1163
Takane *sp* 高根 ; *m* 孝嶺 541
Takanezawa *p* 高根沢 1163 「1163
Takani *s* 竹仁 247, 高荷
Takanishi *s* 高西
Takano *s* 高濃, 鷹野 2995 ; *sp* 高野 1163
Takanobu *m* 孝順 541, 高順 1163, 高信, 高矗, 隆信 1313, 隆業, 陽治 1567, 堯信 1795, 鷹諶 2995
Takano Chōei *mh* 高野長英 1163 「太郎
~ Fusatarō *mh* 高野房
Takanori *m* 比徳 137, 孝章 541, 孝詮, 岳周 956, 高刑 1163, 高矩, 高寛, 高徳, 陟章 1309, 隆律 1313, 隆慰, 巍則 2991
Takanose *s* 高野瀬 1163
Takanosu *p* 鷹巣 2995
Takano Sujū *ml* 高野素十 1163
Takanuka *s* 高額
Takanuma *s* 高沼
Takanushi *m* 鷹主 2995
Takao *sm* 高雄 1163 ; *sp* 高尾 ; *m* 太雄 105, 宇夫 285, 孝雄 541, 幸夫 661, 隆夫 1313, 章男 1461, 峻雄 1591, 敞夫 1688, 鷹穂 2995
Takaoka *s* 高丘 1163 ; *smh* 高岳 ; *sp* 高岡 ; *p* 鷹岡 2995
Takaoki *s* 高沖 1163 ; *m* 隆興 1313 「1163
~ Yōzō *ml* 高沖陽造
Takaomi *m* 貴臣 1755
Takaono *p* 高尾野 1163
Takaosa *m* 高孟, 高修, 隆意 1313
Takao senjimon *l* 高尾船字文 1163
Takara *sm-f* 財 1143; *m* 聖 2030 ; *m-f* 宝 676
Takarabe *sp* 財部 1143
~ Takeshi *mh* 財部彪
Takarada *s* 宝田 676
Takaragi *s* 高良城 1163
Takarai *s* 宝井 676
~ Kikaku *ml* 宝井其角
Takaramoto *s* 宝本
Takara no tsuchi *la* 宝の槌
Takarao *s* 荆尾 899
Takarayama *s* 宝山 676
Takarazuka *p-a* 宝塚
Takasabu *s* 高三 1163
~ Ryūtatsu *mla* 高三隆達
Takasachi *m* 隆祐 1313
Takasago *p-la* 高砂
Takasai *s* 高斎 ⌊1163
Takasaka *s* 高阪, 高坂
Takasaki *sp* 高崎
~ Masahide *ml* 高崎正秀 「正風
~ Masakaze *ml* 高崎
Takasame *s* 高境
Takasato *m* 高達 1163, 高聡, 高嶷, 隆量 1313; *p* 高郷 1163 「兇
Takasawa *s* 高沢 ; *m* 高
Takase *sp* 高瀬
Takasebune *l* 高瀬舟
Takase Bun'en *ml* 高瀬文淵
Takashi *s* 高志, 高師 ; *sm* 隆 1313, 崟 1736 ; *m* 上 47, 大 48, 山 89, 天 93, 立 194, 丘 219, 仙 228, 任 235, 岦 291, 凸 323, 位 354, 充 521, 孝 541, 卓 660, 京 663, 宝 676, 宗 679, 旻 710, 杲 712, 尚 753, 恰 804, 郁 890, 亭 909, 荘 933, 昻 943, 穹 948, 岳 956, 俊 1039, 峆 1079, 殷之 1139, 高 1163, 皋 1197, 恭 1205, 拳 1206, 庨 1240, 陸 1312, 隆崇 1313, 峰 1351, 剛 1429, 梁 1475, 峻 1591, 棟 1627, 竦 1632, 敞 1688, 敬 1691, 密 1713, 嵇 1721, 最 1742, 貴 1755, 崇 1774, 喬 1775, 堯 1795, 尊 1797, 傑 1827, 嵺 1864, 誠 1935, 幹 1938, 崧 1999, 誉 2010, 僑 2057, 弼 2092, 蔚 2167, 崴 2198, 嵩 2207, 節 2215, 厲 2234, 嵬 2374, 賞 2377, 嶒 2467, 嶸 2716, 駿 2763, 鏘 2881, 巍 2972, 巍 2991
Takashiba *s* 高柴 1163
Takashige *m* 卓成 660, 高栄 1163, 喬蔚 1775, 節繁 2215
Takashika *s* 高鹿 1163
Takashima *sp* 高島, 鷹島 2995 「帆 1163
~ Shūhan *mh* 高島秋
Takashime *s* 尚目 753
Takashimizu *p* 高清水 1163
Takashina *s* 高階, 高品, 高科 ; *m* 高芥, 高標 「積善
~ no Sekizen *ml* 高階
Takashino *s* 高篠
Takashio *s* 高塩
~ Haizan *ml* 高塩背山
Takashiro *s* 高城 ; *m* 孝太 541
Takashita *s* 高下 1163
Takasō *s* 高左右
Takasu *s* 高洲, 高須, 鷹巣 2995 ; *p* 鷹栖
~ Baikei *ml* 高須梅渓 1163
Takasue *m* 隆季 1313 ; *m-f* 孝標 541 「女
~ no Musume *fl* 孝標
Takasugi *s* 高杉 1163
~ Ichirō *ml* 高杉一郎
~ Shinsaku *mh* 高杉晋作
Takasuka *s* 高須賀
Takasumi *m* 高維, 隆精 1313
Takata *sp* 高田 1163
~ Chōi *ml* 高田蝶衣
Takatada *m* 高亶
Takatama *s* 高玉
Takatarō *m* 高太郎
Takata Tamotsu *ml* 高田保 「尊輝 1797
Takateru *m* 隆璉 1313,
Takato *s* 稜人 1917 ; *m* 隆門 1313
Takatō *s* 高任 1163, 高頭, 高藤 ; *sp* 高遠 ; *m* 高邁, 隆任 1313, 隆遠
Takatoki *m* 孝時 541, 孝節, 高時 1163
Takatome *m* 孝徠 541
Takatomi *sp* 高富 1163 ; *m* 隆吉 1313
Takatomo *m* 公張 156, 孝友 541, 孝儔, 隆文 1313, 隆備
Takatori *s* 高鳥 1163; 鷹 2995 ; *sm* 鷹取 ; *sp* 高取 1163
Takatoshi *m* 乙叡 2, 孚俊 483, 宝寿 676, 学俊 719, 高峻 1163, 隆平 1313, 隆俊, 隆章, 尊祀 1797, 嵩年 2207 「津
Takatsu *s* 高畠 1163, 高
Takatsuchi *s* 高土
Takatsugu *m* 孝次 541, 高緒 1163, 隆韶 1313, 顕次 2757
Takatsuji *s* 高辻 1163
Takatsuka *s* 高塚
Takatsukasa *s* 高司, 鷹司 2995
Takatsuki *s* 高築 1163 ; *p* 高月, 高規
Takatsuma *s* 高妻
Takatsumu *m* 隆聚 1313
Takatsuna *m* 乙綱 2
Takatsune *m* 好経 413, 昻式 943, 貴恒 1755
Takauchi *s* 高内 1163
Takauji *m* 尊氏 1797
Takaura *s* 高浦 1163
Takauta *m* 隆謌 1313
Takawaki *s* 鷹阪 2995
Takawashi *p* 高鷲 1163
Takaya *s* 高宅, 高谷 ; *sp* 高屋
~ Sōshū *ml* 高屋窓秋
Takayabu *m* 高藪
Takayama *sp* 高山
~ Chogyū *ml* 高山樗牛 「彦九郎
~ Hikokurō *mh* 高山
~ Sōzei *ml* 高山宗砌

~ Tsuyoshi *ml* 高山毅
Takayanagi *s* 高揚; *sp* 高柳 「重信
~ Shigenobu *ml* 高柳
Takayasu *sm* 高安; *m* 孝綽 541, 高慶 1163, 隆定 1313, 隆抵, 隆育, 捧泰 1318, 剛靖 1429, 尊閑 1797
~ Gekkō *ml* 高安月郊 1163 「世
~ Kuniyo *ml* 高安国
Takayo *f* 誉代 2010
Takayori *m* 孝因 541, 高聴 1163
Takayoshi *m* 万穀 43, 公誉 156, 孝昌 541, 孝允, 孝恭, 孝義, 高泰 1163, 高陳, 高斌, 高潔, 恭慶 1205, 隆孝 1313, 隆衷, 隆禧, 琢禅 1608, 敬義 1691, 貴命 1755, 誉富 2010
Takayu *s* 高楡 1163
Takayuki *m* 尚之 753, 高行 1163, 高猷, 宮行 1184
Takaze *p* 高瀬 1163
Takazō *m* 邵蔵 646
Takazumi *m* 尊澄 1797
Take *s* 多気 347, 嵩 2207; *m* 筠 2015; *f* 壮 243, 竹 247, 武 751. (丈 36, 矛 150, 壮 243, 竹 247, 全 271, 広 316, 伯 363, 兵 499, 孟 667, 宝 676, 学 719, 武 751, 虎 754, 兕 758, 勇 908, 茸 925, 長 939, 岳 956, 建 995, 咫 996, 桓 1100, 高 1163, 烈 1211, 威 1251, 赳 1261, 健 1282, 猛 1305, 剛 1429, 盛 1469, 彪 1523, 偉 1535, 斌 1590, 程 1641, 貴 1755, 強 1878, 雄 1912, 献 1961, 義 1975, 筠 2015, 豪 2177, 嵩 2207, 節 2215, 毅 2351, 暹 2593, 彊 2621, 闌 2708, 嶽 2775)
Takeaki *m* 建顕 995
Takeba *s* 竹葉 247
Takebana *s* 竹花
Takebayashi *s* 竹林, 武林 751
Takebe *s* 竹部 247, 武部 751; *sp* 建部 995
~ no Ayatari *ml* 建部綾足
Takebu *s* 竹生 247
Takebuchi *s* 竹淵
Takechi *s* 竹知, 武内 751, 武市, 武知, 武智, 高市 1163; *m* 威知 1251 「麻呂 1163
Takechimaro *m* 高市
Takechi no Kurohito *ml* 高市黒人
~ Tetsuji *ml* 武智鉄二 751 「1100
Takechiyo *f* 桓千代
Takechi Zuizan *mh* 武市瑞山 751
Takeda *s* 健田 1282; *sp* 竹田 247, 武田 751
~ Gyōtenshi *ml* 武田仰天子 「247
~ Izumo *ml* 竹田出雲
~ Katsuyori *mh* 武田勝頼 751 「出雲 247
~ Koizumo *ml* 竹田小
~ Kōrai *ml* 武田交来 751 「雲斎
~ Kōunsai *mh* 武田耕
~ Ōtō *ml* 武田鶯塘
~ Rintarō *ml* 武田麟太郎 「玄
~ Shingen *mh* 武田信
~ Taijun *ml* 武田泰淳
Takee *s* 武江
Takefu *s* 武藤; *sp* 武生
Takefumi *m* 雄章 1912
Takegaki *s* 竹垣 247
Takegami *s* 竹上
Takegawa *s* 竹川, 武川 751
Takegorō *m* 竹五郎 247
Takeguchi *s* 竹口
Takegura *s* 竹倉
Takeguraya *s* 竹倉屋
Takehana *s* 竹鼻
Takehara *s* 武原 751; *sp* 竹原 247
Takehashi *s* 竹橋
Takehazama *s* 竹迫
Takehiko *m* 武彦 751, 健彦 1282, 筠彦 2015, 毅彦 2351
Takehira *s* 竹平 247
Takehiro *m* 武丕 751; *ma* 広啓 316
Takehisa *s* 竹久 247; *sm* 武久 751; *m* 偉久 1535
~ Yumeji *ml* 竹久夢二 247 「盛仁 1469
Takehito *m* 威仁 1251,
Takei *s* 竹井 247, 竹居, 武井 751, 武居; *m* 猛猪 1305
Takeichi *s* 竹市 247, 武市 751, 高市 1163
Takeiri *s* 竹入 247
Takeishi *s* 竹石, 武石 751 「昭夫
Takei Teruo *ml* 武井
Takeji *m* 竹治 247, 武二 751, 武次, 武治, 茸次 925
Takejirō *m* 竹二郎 247, 竹次郎, 武次郎 751
Takeka *m* 武香
Takekatsu *m* 全勝 271, 武甲 751
Takekawa *sl* 竹河 247
Takeki *m* 武幹 751, 虎 754, 赳城 1261, 健樹 1282, 猛 1305
Takeko *f* 武子 751, 威子 1251, 暹子 2593
Takekoshi *s* 竹越 247, 竹腰
~ Sansa *ml* 竹越三叉
~ Yosaburō *mh* 竹越与三郎
Takekuma *s* 武隈 751
Takekuni *m* 武第
Takema *s* 万千野 43, 竹万 247
Takemae *s* 竹前
Takemaro *m* 建麿 995
Takemasa *s* 竹政 247; *m* 武済 751, 武正, 武政, 猛昌 1305
Takemata *s* 竹俣 247
Takematsu *s* 竹松; *m* 武松 751
Takemi *s* 竹見 247; *m* 丈巳 36, 兵視 499, 武命 751, 猛省 1305
Takemitsu *s* 竹光 247; *sm* 武光 751
Takemiya *s* 竹宮 247, 武宮 751, 健軍 1282
Takemo *s* 竹門 247
Takemori *s* 竹森, 武森 751; *m* 岳守 956
Takemoto *s* 竹元 247, 竹本, 武本 751; *sm* 武元 「太夫 247
~ Gidayū *ma* 竹本義
Takemune *m* 長宗 939
Takemura *s* 竹村 247, 武村 751 「247
~ Toshio *ml* 竹村俊郎
Takenaga *s* 竹永, 武永 751 「武中 751
Takenaka *s* 竹中 247,
~ Iku *ml* 竹中郁 247
~ Kyūshichi *ml* 武永久七
Takendo *m* 武人 751
Takeno *s* 竹 247, 武野 751; *sp* 竹野 247
Takenobō *s* 竹坊 247
Takenobu *s* 武信 751; *m* 武修, 武整 「紹鷗
Takeno Jōō *mh* 武野
Takenori *m* 全徳 271, 孟伯 667, 武則 751, 武能, 雄昇 1912
Take no satouta *l* 竹の里歌 247
Takenoshita *s* 竹下, 竹之下 「751
Takenosuke *m* 武之助
Takenouchi *s* 竹ノ内 247, 竹内, 竹之内, 武内 751 「久一 247
~ Hisakazu *ma* 竹内
~ Masashi *ml* 竹内仁
~ Shikibu *mh* 竹内式部
Takenoya *sm* 竹屋
Take no yuki *la* 竹雪
Takenuki *s* 竹貫
Takeo *s* 竹尾; *sm* 竹雄; *sm-p* 武雄 751; *m* 壮夫 243, 全雄 271, 武夫 751, 武生, 武男, 岳男 956, 桓夫 1100, 烈男 1211, 赳夫 1261, 健夫 1282, 猛 1305, 猛雄, 剛男 1429, 彪夫 1523, 斌雄 1590, 義士 1975, 毅雄 2351, 暹雄 2593, 嶽夫 2775
~ Chūkichi *ml* 竹尾忠吉 247 「751
Takeoka *s* 竹岡, 武岡
Takeru *sm* 建 995; *m* 武 751, 威 1251, 健 1282, 健児, 猛 1305
Takerube *s* 武部 751, 建部 995 「751
Takesaburō *m* 武三郎
Takesada *m* 武定
Takesaki *s* 竹前 247

Takesato *m* 武郷 751
Takeshi *s* 武子, 剛志 1429; *sm* 武士 751; *sp* 武石; *m* 大 48, 壮 243, 孟 667, 英 693, 武 751, 武志, 虎 754, 洸 813, 勇 908, 長 939, 建 995, 虓 1019, 桓 1100, 烈 1211, 威 1251, 威士, 馬 1257, 赳 1261, 健 1282, 猛 1305, 乾 1411, 剛 1429, 彪 1523, 斌 1590, 断 1669, 傑 1827, 雄 1912, 鉅 1946, 倜 2054, 豪 2177, 毅 2351, 諺 2508, 虢 2519, 戡 2549, 矯 2626, 闌 2708, 驍 2957, 驥 3008. (孟 667)
Takeshiba *s* 竹柴 247
～ Kisui *ml* 竹柴其水
Takeshige *s* 武重 751; *m* 武林 「想庵
～ Musōan *ml* 武林無
Takeshima *s* 竹島 247, 武島 751 「羽衣
～ Hagoromo *ml* 武島
Takeshirō *s* 孟郎 667; *m* 武四郎 751
Takeshita *s* 竹下 247, 竹志田, 武下 751
Takeso *s* 武曾
Takesu *s* 竹州 247
Takesue *s* 武末 751
Takesuke *m* 竹介 247, 烈資 1211
Taketa *s* 建桁 995
Taketaba *s* 竹束 247, 竹
Taketani *s* 竹谷 ⌊廻
Taketarō *m* 武太郎 751
Taketo *m* 丈人 36
Taketomi *s* 竹富 247, 武富 751; *m* 武臣
Taketomo *s* 竹友 247
～ Sōfū *ml* 竹友藻風
Taketora *m* 桓虎 1100
Taketori *l* 竹取 247
Taketoshi *m* 兵俊 499, 武紀 751, 武敏, 武駿
Taketoyo *p* 武豊
Taketsu *s* 竹津 247, 武津 751 「辻 751
Taketsuji *s* 竹辻 247, 武
Takeuchi *s* 竹内 247, 武内 751 「勝太郎 247
～ Katsutarō *ml* 竹内
～ Seihō *ma* 竹内栖鳳
～ Toshio *ml* 竹内敏雄
～ Yoshimi *ml* 竹内好
Takewaka *s* 竹若
Takewaki *s* 竹脇
Takeya *s* 竹谷, 竹家, 竹屋, 武谷 751, 達谷 1810, 達谷窟
Takeyama *s* 竹山 247, 武山 751
～ Hideko *fl* 武山英子
～ Michio *ml* 竹山道雄 247
Takeyasu *sm* 武安 751; *m* 武要, 勇逸 908, 健康 1282
Takeyoshi *m* 孟芳 667, 孟懿, 武芳 751
Takeyuki *m* 武之, 武幸
Takezaki *s* 竹崎 247
～ Suenaga *mh* 竹崎季長 「751
Takezawa *s* 竹沢, 武沢
Takezō *m* 竹三 247, 竹蔵, 武蔵 751
Takezoe *s* 竹添 247
Takezono *s* 竹園
Takezuka *s* 竹塚
Taki *s* 多木 347, 多記, 多喜, 滝 1862; *sp* 多気 347, 多紀; *p* 多伎, 高城 1163. (滝 1862)
Takichi *m* 太吉 105
Takidani *s* 滝谷 1862
Takigami *s* 滝上
Takigasaki *s* 滝ケ崎
Takigawa *s* 多岐川 347; *sp* 滝川 1862
～ Kyō *ml* 多岐川恭 347
～ Yukitoki *mh* 滝川幸辰 1862
Takiguchi *s* 滝口
～ Nyūdō *l* 滝口入道
～ Shūzō *ml* 滝口修造
～ Takeshi *ml* 滝口武 ⌊士
Takihara *s* 滝原
Taki Haruichi *ml* 滝春一
Takihira *s* 滝平
Takii *s* 滝井 「作
～ Kōsaku *ml* 滝井孝
Takiji *m* 多喜二 347
Takiko *f* 滝子 1862
Takima *m* 多喜磨 347
Takimoto *s* 滝本 1862
Takimura *s* 滝村
Takinaka *s* 滝中
Takinami *s* 滝波, 滝浪
Takine *p* 滝根
Takino *sp* 滝野
Takinogawa *s* 滝野川
Takinoue *p* 滝上
Takio *m* 多喜男 347
Taki Rentarō *ma* 滝廉太郎 1862
Takise *s* 滝瀬
Takishima *s* 滝島
Takishita *s* 滝下
Takita *s* 田北 189, 滝田 1862
～ Choin *ml* 滝田樗陰
Takitarō *m* 滝太郎
Takitō *s* 滝藤
Takiuchi *s* 滝内
Takiura *s* 滝浦
Takiwaki *s* 滝脇
Takiwara *s* 滝原
Takiya *s* 滝谷
Takiyama *s* 滝山
Takizaki *s* 滝崎
～ Yasunosuke *ml* 滝崎安之助
Takizawa *s* 多喜沢 347; *sp* 滝沢 1862
～ Bakin *ml* 滝沢馬琴
Takizō *m* 多喜蔵 347, 滝三 1862
Tako *s* 大児 48, 多子 347, 多胡, 多湖; *p* 多古
Takō *s* 竹生 247 「古
Taku *s* 宅 283; *sp* 多久 347; *m* 卓 660. (干 26, 宅 283, 択 382, 沢 404, 拓 586, 卓 660, 倬 1027, 託 1147A, 啄 1285, 梼 1364, 琢 1608, 棹 1620, 詫 1931, 磔 2486, 濯 2609, 櫂 2722, 鐸 2922)
Takuan *mh* 沢庵 404
Takubo *s* 田久保 189, 田窳, 田窪
Takuboku *ml* 啄木 1285
Takuichi *m* 卓一 660
Takuji *m* 啄二 1285, 啄治
Takujun *s* 卓淳 660
Takukichi *m* 卓吉
Takuma *s* 田熊 189, 宅間 283, 宅磨, 宅麿, 託摩 1147A; *sp* 託麻; *m* 琢磨 1608, 逞 1513; *p* 詫間 1931
～ no Tamenari *ma* 宅磨為成 283
Takumi *s* 工匠 39, 任美 235; *sm* 工 39, 巧 238; *m* 内匠 81, 木工 109, 匠 503 「1608
Takunosuke *m* 琢之助
Takuo *m* 干雄 26, 卓雄
Takura *s* 宅 283 ⌊660
Takurō *m* 卓郎 660
Takusagawa *s* 田草川 189 「660
Takushirō *m* 卓四郎
Takuya *m* 卓哉
Takuzō *m* 卓造, 卓蔵
Tama *s* 多磨 347; *ma* 玉 204; *f* 珉 1076, 珠 1077, 琚 1605, 瑞 2094, 璞 2472, 瓊 2717; *p* 多摩 347. (玉 204, 圭 267, 玖 409, 玲 835, 珠 1077, 球 1359, 琅 1606, 瑗 1873, 琠 1874, 瑞 2094, 碧 2225, 瑤 2286, 璋 2287, 賜 2317, 霊 2390, 賚 2396, 璞 2472, 魂 2488, 璐 2619, 環 2620, 瓊 2717, 璧 2782)
Tamaari *m* 玉有 204
Tamaburu *m* 玉陣
Tamachi *sp* 田町 189
Tamada *s* 玉田 204, 霊田 2390
Tamae *sf* 玉江 204; *f* 玲枝 835, 球恵 1359, 琅枝 1606, 環江 2620
Tamagaki *m* 玉垣 204
Tamagami *s* 玉上
Tamagawa *sp* 田万川 189; *sp-l* 玉川 204
Tamagoe *s* 玉越
Tamahahaki *l* 玉箒子
Tamaho *p* 玉穂
Tamai *s* 玉井
Tamaji *m* 球二 1359
Tamakage *s* 玉楮 204
Tamakaji *s* 玉楮
Tamakatsuma *l* 玉勝間 「玉鬘
Tamakazura *la* 玉葛,
Tamaki *s* 田巻 189, 田牧, 玉木 204, 玉置; *sp* 玉城; *m* 手纏 118, 玉樹 204, 玖城 409, 珠璣 1077, 釧 1415, 瑞樹 2094, 璣 2868, 鐶 2952; *m-f* 環 2620; *f* 珠輝 1077, 瓊玖 2717
Tamakichi *m* 玉吉 204
Tamako *f* 玉子, 球子 1359, 琠子 1874, 賜子

2317, 瑤子 2286, 璋子 2287, 璧子 2782
Tamakoshi *s* 玉腰 204
Tamakura *s* 靈鞍 2390
Tamakushige *l* 玉櫛笥 204 「玉匣両浦嶼
～ futari Urashima *la*
Tamamatsu *sl* 玉松
～ Misao *mh* 玉松操
Tamami *f* 圭美 267
Tamamizu *s* 玉水 204
Tamamo *l* 玉藻
Tamamoshū *l* 玉藻集
Tamamoto *s* 玉本
Tamamura *sp* 玉村
Tamamushi *sl* 玉虫
～ no zushi *a* 玉虫厨子 「汝
Tamana *sp* 玉名；*m* 玉
Tamano *s* 玉乃；*sp* 玉野
Tama no i *la* 玉井
Tama no ogoto *l* 玉の小琴 「櫛
～ no ogushi *l* 玉の小
Tamanosuke *m* 玉之助
Tamanoura *p* 玉ノ浦
Tamanoya *s* 玉舎
Tamanyū *sp* 玉生
Tamao *m* 玉緒, 圭雄 267, 瑞夫 2094, 璋男 2287, 賚夫 2396
Tamaoka *sp* 玉岡 204
Tamaoki *s* 玉置
Tamaoya *s* 玉祖
Tamari *s* 玉利；*sp* 玉里
Tamaru *s* 田丸 189
Tamashima *sp* 玉島 204
Tamashimayama *s* 玉島山
Tamashiro *s* 玉代
Tamatarō *m* 璐太郎 2619
Tamate *s* 玉手 204
Tamaya *s* 玉谷；*sp* 玉屋
Tamayama *sp* 玉山
Tamayu *p* 玉湯
Tamazaki *s* 玉崎
Tamazawa *s* 玉沢
Tamazō *m* 玉造
Tamazukuri *s* 玉作；*p* 玉造
Tame *s* 多目 347, 多米. (為 1005, 絲 2526)
Tameatsu *m* 為適 1005
Tamechika *m* 為恭, 為寛
Tamegai *s* 為我井
Tamehisa *m* 為栄
Tameie *ml* 為家
Tamekane *m* 為兼
～ wakashō *l* 為兼和歌抄
Tamekichi *m* 為吉
Tamekiyo *m* 為浄
Tameko *f* 為子
Tamemasa *m* 為理
Tamemori *m* 為守
Tamemoto *m* 為紀
Tamenaga *sm* 為永
～ Shunsui *ml* 為永春水
Tamenao *m* 為修
Tamenaru *m* 為遂
Tamenobu *m* 為暄
Tamenori *m* 為実
Tamenosuke *m* 為之介
Tameo *m* 為生
Tamesaburō *m* 為三郎
Tamesada *m* 為定, 為貞
Tamesaki *m* 為兄
Tameshige *m* 為隆
Tamesuke *m* 為介, 為理；*ml* 為相
Tametaka *m* 為学
Tametarō *m* 為太郎
Tametari *m* 為善
Tametomo *m* 為禎
Tametsugu *m* 為知
Tameuji *ml* 為氏 「逸
Tameyasu *m* 為恭, 為
Tameyori *m* 為居
Tameyoshi *m* 為栄, 為貴, 為義
Tameyuki *m* 為是
Tamezō *m* 為造
Tami *sf* 民 333；*m* 為示 1005. (人 14, 民 333, 珉 1076, 彩 1413, 農 2205, 黎 2389)
Tamichi *s* 田路 189
Tamie *m* 民衛 333
Tamigata *s* 民形
Tamihiko *m* 民彦
Tamiko *f* 珉子 1076, 蒼生子 1988, 黎子 2389
Tamine *sp* 段嶺 874
Taminosuke *m* 民之助 333
Tamio *m* 人雄 14
Tamisuke *m* 民輔 333
Tamitaka *m* 民陟
Tamiya *s* 田宮 189, 民谷 333 「彦 189
～ Torahiko *ml* 田宮虎
Tamiyo *f* 彩世 1413
Tamō *s* 玉生 204；*m* 賜 2317, 錫 2524 「189
Tamokami *sp* 田母神
Tamon *s* 田麦, 多門 347；*m* 多聞 「189
Tamonmata *s* 田麦俣
Tamono *s* 田母野
Tamoto *s* 田本
Tamotsu *m* 支 63, 方 85, 任 235, 全 271, 有 303, 存 313, 扶 383, 完 471, 寿 539, 侅 773, 保 781, 将 1040, 惟 1290, 維 2540, 翼 2686
Tamura *s* 太村 105；*sp* 田村 189
Tamurako *f* 田村子
Tamura Ryūichi *ml* 田村隆一
～ Shōgyo *ml* 田村松魚 「郎
～ Taijirō *ml* 田村泰次
～ Toshiko *fl* 田村俊子
Tamuro *m* 屯 222. (屯)
Tamuromaro *m* 屯麿
Tamuronoosa *s* 部将 1418
Tan *s* 丹 79, 旦 162, 端 2306. (反 69, 丹 79, 旦 162, 井 206, 団 310, 但 351, 坦 574, 担 581, 胆 845, 段 874, 単 919A, 炭 1186, 探 1316, 淡 1340, 短 1633, 堪 1843, 湛 1855, 弾 1880, 椴 1893, 亶 1972, 潭 2269, 榑 2292, 端 2306, 誕 2319, 談 2325, 歎 2353, 鍛 2651) 「1625)
Tana *s* 多名 347. (棚
Tanaami *s* 田名網 189, 棚網 1625
Tanabata *s* 七夕 17
Tanabe *s* 一富士 3, 田名部 189, 田部, 多部 347；*sp* 田辺 189
～ Hajime *ml* 田辺元
～ Jūji *ml* 田部重治
～ no Sakimaro *ml* 田辺福麻呂
Tanada *s* 棚田 1625
Tanaga *s* 田永 189
Tanagura *sp* 棚倉 1625
Tanahashi *s* 棚橋
Tanaka *s* 田中 189, 田仲 「夫
～ Chikao *ml* 田中千禾
Tanakadate *s* 田中館
～ Aikitsu *mh* 田中館愛橘 「中冬二
Tanaka Fuyuji *ml* 田
～ Giichi *mh* 田中義一
～ Hidemitsu *ml* 田中英光
～ Jun *ml* 田中純
～ Katsumi *ml* 田中克已 「勝助
～ Katsusuke *mh* 田中
～ Kōtarō *ml* 田中貢太郎
Tanakamaru *s* 田中丸
Tanaka Ōdō *ml* 田中王堂
～ Ōjō *ml* 田中王城
～ Shōzō *mh* 田中正造
～ Sumie *fl* 田中澄江
～ Yasutaka *ml* 田中保隆
Tanaki *s* 棚木 1625
Tanami *s* 田波 189, 田南
Tanamiki *s* 田並木
Tanami Mishiro *ml* 田波御白
Tanamura *s* 田那村, 棚村 1625, 種村 2124
Tanase *s* 棚瀬 1625
Tanashi *sp* 田無 189
Tanasuenotebito *s* 手末才伎 118
Tanaya *s* 棚谷 1625
Tanazawa *s* 棚沢
Tanba *sp* 丹羽 79, 丹波
Tanbara *p* 丹原
Tanbase *s* 丹波瀬
Tanba Yosaku matsu yo no komurobushi *la* 丹波与作待夜の小室節
Tanbo *s* 反保 69, 丹保 79, 田保 189, 多武保
Tanbu *s* 丹生 79 ⌊347
Tanda *s* 丹田
Tandai *l* 探題 1316
Tandaishōshin-roku *l* 胆大小心録 845
Tane *s* 多褹 347. (子 38, 休 233, 任 235, 孚 483, 物 611, 苗 685, 栽 1254, 甚 1267, 胤 1269, 留

1470, 殖 1867, 植 1902, 誠 1935, 弼 2092, 稙 2122, 種 2124, 鎮 2751)
Taneda *s* 種田 2124
～ Santōka *ml* 種田山頭火 「島
Tanegashima *sph* 種子
～ Tokitaka *mh* 種子島時堯
Tanehide *m* 種英
Tanehiko *ml* 種彦
Taneichi *m* 留一 1470; *p* 種市 2124
Taneie *m* 植家 1902
Tanejirō *m* 種治郎
Tanekazu *m* 種憲
Taneki *m* 種材
Taneko *f* 孚子 483, 種子 2124
Tanemasa *m* 栽正 1254
Tanemichi *m* 稙通 2122
Tanemori *s* 種森 2124
Tanemoto *m* 弼基 2092
Tanemura *s* 種村 2124
Tanenaga *m* 植長 1902
Tanenobu *m* 胤信 1269
Taneo *m* 胤勇
Tanesachi *m* 胤禄
Tanesada *m* 胤貞
Tanesuke *m* 胤昌
Tanetada *m* 種任 2124
Tanetatsu *m* 種樹
Tanetomi *m* 種殷
Taneyama *s* 種山
Taneyoshi *m* 胤禄 1269, 種美 2124
Taneyuki *m* 誠之 1935, 種行 2124
Tanezane *m* 種実
Tange *s* 丹下 79
～ Sazen *lm* 丹下左膳
Tango *s* 丹呉; *sp* 丹後
Tani *s* 田荷 189, 谷 449, 渓 1330A. (谷 449, 足 461, 渓 1330A, 莱 1991, 澗 2274)
Taniai *s* 谷合 449
Tanibe *s* 谷部 「晁
Tani Bunchō *ma* 谷文
Tanida *s* 谷田
Tanide *s* 谷出
Tanifuji *s* 谷藤
Tanigae *s* 谷谷
Tanigaki *s* 谷垣
Tanigami *s* 谷上
Tanigishi *s* 谷岸
Tanigawa *s* 谷川, 谷河
Tanigaya *s* 谷谷
Tanigorō *m* 谷五郎
Taniguchi *s* 谷口
Tanigumi *p* 谷汲
Tanihara *s* 谷原
Tanihata *s* 谷畑
Tanihira *s* 谷平
Tanii *s* 谷井
Tani Jichū *mh* 谷時中
～ Kanae *ml* 谷鼎
～ Kaoru *ml* 谷馨
～ Kattō *ml* 谷活東
Tanikawa *s* 谷川, 谷河
～ Shuntarō *ml* 谷川俊太郎 「三
～ Tetsuzō *ml* 谷川徹
Tanikō *la* 谷行
Tanimori *s* 谷森
Tanimoto *s* 谷元, 谷本
Tanimura *s* 谷村
Taninaga *s* 谷永
Taninaka *s* 渓中 1330A
Tanino *s* 谷野 449
Tanio *m* 澗生 2274, 澗雄
Tanioka *s* 谷岡 449
Tanishima *s* 谷島
Tan'ishō *l* 歎異抄 2353
Tanitaka *s* 谷高 449
Tani Tateki *mh* 谷干
Taniuchi *s* 谷内 └城
Taniwa *s* 丹波 79
Taniwaki *s* 谷脇 449
Taniyama *sp* 谷山
Tanizaki *s* 谷崎
～ Jun'ichirō *ml* 谷崎潤一郎
～ Seiji *ml* 谷崎精二
Tanizawa *s* 谷沢
Tanizō *m* 谷蔵
Tanizu *s* 谷津
Tanji *s* 丹治 79
Tanjihi *s* 丹治比
Tanjirō *m* 丹次郎
Tanjo *s* 丹所
Tanka *l* 短歌 1633
～ senkaku *l* 短歌撰格
～ sōgen *l* 短歌草原
Tankei *ma* 湛慶 1855
Tankodama *s* 丹児玉 79
Tannai *s* 丹内, 谷内 449
Tannami *s* 丹南 79
Tannan *sp* 丹南
Tanno *s* 丹野; *p* 端野 2306
Tannomiya *s* 炭宮 1186
Tannori *s* 淡輪 1340
Tannowa *s* 淡輪
Tano *sp* 多野 347; *p* 田野 189
Tanō *s* 多納 347
Tanobe *s* 田野辺 189, 田野部
Tanobori *s* 田登 「347
Tanoemon *m* 多之衛門
Tanoguchi *s* 田野口 189
Tanohata *p* 田野畑
Tanoi *s* 田野井
Tanokami *s* 田母神
Tanokimi *s* 田公
Tanokuchi *s* 田口
Tanokura *s* 田野倉
Tanomo *s* 田母; *m* 田面 「2506
Tanomogi *s* 頼母木
Tanomu *m* 頼
Tanomura *s* 田能村 189, 田野村
～ Chikuden *mh* 田能村竹田
Tanoshi *m* 予 62, 喜 1709, 凱 1967, 楽 2029
Tanoshita *s* 田下 189
Tanosuke *m* 田之助
Tanouchi *s* 田内
Tanoue *s* 田上
Tanoura *p* 田浦
Tanrokubon *l* 丹緑本 79 「東 351
Tantō *s* 田頭 189; *p* 但
Tanuchi *s* 銅工 2159
Tanuma *sp* 田沼 189
～ Okitomo *mh* 田沼意知 「意次
～ Okitsugu *mh* 田沼
Tanushi *m* 田主
Tanushimaru *p* 田主丸
Tanzan *s* 丹山 79
Tanzawa *s* 丹沢
Tao *s* 田尾 189; *f* 婉 1600. (姚 1088, 婉 1600)
Taoda *s* 峠田 1081
Taoka *s* 田岡 189
～ Reiun *ml* 田岡嶺雲
Taoko *f* 姚子 1088
Taosa *m* 晙 2110
Tara *p* 太良 105
Taragi *p* 多良木 347
Taraku *s* 太楽 105
Tarami *s* 任美 235; *p* 多良見 347
Tarao *s* 多羅尾
(tarashi 足 461, 帯 1192)
Tarashiko *s* 帯士, 帯王; *f* 帯子
(tare 垂 761)
Taree *f* 垂枝
(tari 十 18, 足 461, 垂 761, 粛 1528, 給 2148)
Tarihi *s* 垂氷 761
Tariho *m* 足穂 461, 垂穂 761
Tarimaro *m* 垂麿
Tario *m* 多利男 347
Tarō *m* 太郎 105; *p* 田老 189
Tarobei *m* 太郎平 105
Tarōdachi *s* 太郎館
Tarōdate *s* 太郎館
Taroichi *m* 太郎一
Tarosaburō *m* 太郎三郎
Taru *s* 樽 2482. (立 194, 垂 761, 神 853, 健 1282, 善 1799, 福 1888, 稜 1917, 熾 2465, 樽 2482)
Taruhiko *m* 稜彦 1917
Taruhito *m* 善仁 1799, 熾仁 2465
Taruho *m* 足穂 461
Tarui *s* 樽井 2482; *sp* 垂井 761 「吉 2482
～ Tōkichi *mh* 樽井藤
Tarukawa *s* 樽川
Taruko *f* 樽子
Tarumi *s* 樽見, 樽味; *sp* 垂水 761
Tarumizu *p* 垂水
Tarumoto *s* 樽本 2482
Taruno *s* 足 461 「2482
Tarunosuke *m* 樽之助
Taruo *m* 神郎 853
Tarusawa *s* 樽沢 2482
Tasaka *s* 田阪 189, 田坂
Tase *s* 多勢 347
Tashika *m* 慥 2070; *f* 確 2305
Tashiro *sp* 田代 189
Tashita *s* 田下
Tasoko *p* 田底
Tasuke *m* 太介 105, 多助 347, 輔 2133
Tasuki *s* 手繦 118
Tasuku *m* 又 13, 介 66, 比 137, 右 171, 多助 347, 多須久, 佑 364, 佐 365, 助 431, 匡 504, 祐 852, 相 868, 将 1040, 救 1406, 補 1644, 棐 1780, 資 2012, 弼 2092, 輔

2133, 賛 2394, 攆 2446, 翼 2686
Tatae *s* 堪 1843; *m* 湛 1855 「多羅
Tatara *s* 多多良 347, 多
Tatari *s* 田又利 189
Tatasu *s* 河合 597
Tate *s* 立 194, 楯 1897, 館 2761. (干 26, 立 194, [illegible] 872, 盾 984, 建 995, 健 1282, 達 1810, 楯 1897, 竪 2224, 館 2761)
Tatebatake *s* 建畠 995
Tatebayashi *s* 立林 194; *sp* 館林 2761
Tatebe *s* 建部 995
Tateda *s* 立田 194
Tategawa *s* 立川, 立河, 竪川 2224
Tatehara *s* 立原 194
Tateiri *s* 立入
Tateishi *s* 立石, 建石 995, 楯石 1897
Tateiwa *s* 立岩 194; *p* 館岩 2761
Tatejima *s* 立島 194
Tatekawa *s* 建川 995
Tateki *sp* 干城 26; *m* 建城 995, 建樹
Tateko *f* [illegible]子 872
Tatema *s* 立馬 194
Tatematsu *s* 立松
Tatemi *s* 立見
Tatemichi *m* 建通 995
Tatemura *s* 館村 2761
Tateno *s* 立野 194, 建野 995, 竪野 2224, 館野 2761
Tatenomi *m* 楯臣 1897
Tateno Nobuyuki *ml* 立野信之 194
Tatenuki *s* 楯 1897, 楯叉, 楯縫
Tateo *m* 干雄 26, 立夫 194, 盾夫 984 「岡 1897
Tateoka *s* 立岡 194, 楯
Tateshi *s* 殺陣師 1138
Tateshina *sp* 立科 194
Tatewaki *s* 立脇; *sm* 帯刀 1192
Tateyama *s* 竪山 2224; *sp* 立山 194, 館山 2761
~ Kazuko *fl* 館山一子
Tateyoshi *m* 楯衛 1897
Tateyuku *s* 日立 77
Tatezawa *s* 立沢 194
Tatō *m* 湛 1855

Tatomi *sp* 田富 189
Tatsu *s* 竜 1199; *m* 立 194, 辰 738; *f* 起 1262. (立 194, 幸 661, 辰 738, 武 751, 建 995, 竜 1199, 挙 1207, 起 1262, 健 1282, 達 1810, 超 1816, 蔦 2196, 竪 2224, 樹 2483)
Tatsuaki *m* 立誠 194
Tatsue *s* 辰江 738
Tatsugō *p* 竜郷 1199
Tatsugorō *m* 辰五郎 738
Tatsuhara *s* 立原 194
Tatsuhebi *s* 竜蛇 1199
Tatsui *s* 辰井 738, 竜居 1199; *m* 辰猪 738
Tatsuichi *s* 辰市
Tatsuji *m* 辰治, 達二 1810, 達治, 達賛
Tatsujirō *m* 辰次郎 738, 達次郎 1810
Tatsuka *s* 立家 194
Tatsukai *s* 田令 189
Tatsukawa *s* 立川 194
Tatsuke *s* 田附 189
Tatsuki *s* 田付, 辰木 738, 竜木 1199; *m* 樹 2483
Tatsukichi *m* 達吉 1810
Tatsuko *f* 立子 194, 蔦子 2196, 樹子 2483; *p* 田子 189
Tatsukuri *s* 調布 2328
Tatsuma *sm* 辰馬 738; *m* 辰午, 竜馬 1199
Tatsumaro *m* 竜麻呂
Tatsumi *s* 立見 194, 辰巳 738; *m* 立身 194, 竜水 1199, 竜海, 巽 1760, 達海 1810
~ fugen *l* 辰巳婦言 738
Tatsunaga *m* 立暢 194
Tatsunami *s* 立波
Tatsundo *m* 達人 1810, 樹人 2483
Tatsuno *s* 立野 194; *sp* 辰野 738, 竜野 1199
Tatsunokuchi *p* 辰口 738
Tatsunosuke *m* 辰之助, 達之助 1810, 達之輔 「野隆 738
Tatsuno Yutaka *ml* 辰
Tatsuo *m* 辰男, 辰良, 辰男, 辰雄, 竜雄 1199, 挙雄 1207, 健夫 1282, 達夫 1810, 蔦夫 2196, 樹夫 2483
Tatsuō *ma* 竜王 1199
Tatsuoka *s* 辰岡 738, 竜岡 1199 「2224
Tatsuoki *m* 竜起, 竪興
Tatsurō *m* 辰郎 738
Tatsuru *m* 立 194, 建 995 「189
Tatsuruhama *p* 田鶴浜
Tatsusaburō *m* 辰三郎 738, 竜三郎 1199
Tatsushirō *m* 辰四郎 738 「竜田 1199
Tatsuta *sp* 立田 194; *la*
Tatsutane *m* 竜種
Tatsutarō *m* 辰太郎 738
Tatsuuma *s* 辰馬
Tatsuya *m* 辰弥, 達夸 1810
Tatsuyama *sp* 竜山 1199
Tatsuzawa *s* 立沢 194, 竜沢 1199
Tatsuzō *m* 達三 1810
Tatta *s* 立田 194
Tatto *m* 達等 1810
(tau 絶 2148) 「347
Tauchi *s* 田内 189, 多内
Tauko *f* 太生子 105
Taura *s* 田浦 189, 多浦 347
Tawada *s* 多和田
Tawara *s* 田原 189, 俵 1280. (俵)
Tawaragi *s* 俵木 「189
Tawaramoto *p* 田原本
Tawaraya *s* 田原屋, 俵屋 1280, 俵谷
Tawarayama *s* 俵山
Tawaraya Sōtatsu *ma* 俵屋宗達
Taya *s* 田谷 189, 田屋
Tayama *s* 田山
~ Katai *ml* 田山花袋
Tayasu *s* 田安 「宗武
~ Munetake *ml* 田安
Tayori *m* 伻 356
(tayu 妙 614)
Tayui *s* 田結 189 「105
Tazaemon *m* 太左衛門
Tazaki *s* 田崎 189
Tazawa *s* 田沢
Tazawako *p* 田沢湖
Tazei *s* 田制
Tazoe *s* 田添
(tazu 鴇 2739, 鶴 2926)

Tazushirō *m* 鶴四郎
Tazuyo *m* 鴇世 2739
Te *s* 手 118. (手, 弖 202, 勅 898)
Teburi *s* 伝法輪 359, 転法輪 1656
Tedate *m* 術 1298
Tega *s* 手賀 118
Tegara *s* 手柄
Tegarayama *s* 手柄山
Tegawa *s* 手川
Tegoshi *s* 手越
Tehata *s* 弖秦 202
Tehito *s* 才伎 35, 工匠 39
Tei *s* 丁 8, 鄭 2356; *m* 貞 982. (丁 8, 汀 142, 氐 297, 体 358, 廷 501, 定 677, 弟 764, 抵 797, 訂 894, 勅 898, 亭 909, 帝 971, 貞 982, 底 991, 釘 1154, 蔕 1170, 庭 1244, 停 1272, 偵 1276, 悌 1289, 砥 1386, 逞 1513, 堤 1557, 渟 1580, 棣 1616, 梯 1617, 程 1641, 霆 1700, 第 1768, 禎 1887, 碇 1909, 碓 1910, [illegible] 2037, 遉 2047, 禔 2120, 鼎 2246, 鄭 2356, 諟 2512, 諦 2516, 綴 2530, 鵜 2822) 「市
Teiichi *m* 貞一 982, 貞
Teiichirō *m* 貞一郎
Teiji *m* 貞二, 貞次, 貞治, 偵次 1276, 悌次 1289, 禎次 1887
Teijirō *m* 貞二郎 982, 貞次郎, 貞治郎, 悌二郎 1289, 禎次郎 1887
Teijō *m* 定条 677
Teika *ml* 定家
Teikichi *m* 定吉, 貞吉 982, 悌吉 1289 「1244
Teikin ōrai *l* 庭訓往来
Teine *p* 手稲 118 「982
Teinosuke *m* 貞之助
Teiriki *m* 帝力 971
Teisaburō *m* 貞三郎 982, 悌三郎 1289
Teisei *m* 諦成 2516
Teisuke *m* 定輔 677
Teitoku *ml* 貞徳 982
Teizō *m* 貞三, 貞造, 悌三 1289
Tejina *s* 手品 118
(teki 的 635, 迪 1001, 荻

1176, 笛 1471, 摘 2066, 頌 2114, 適 2240, 敵 2354, 鏑 2816)
Tekura *s* 言語同断 439
Tekurada *s* 言語同断
(ten 天 93, 苫 686, 典 733, 淀 1333, 添 1338, 展 1501, 腆 1611, 転 1656, 奠 1701, 塡 2075, 槇 2297, 稹 2490, 纏 2988)
Ten'an 857–59 天安
Tenarai *l* 手習 118
Tenashi *s* 手結 「93
Tenbun 1532–55 天文
Tenbyō 729–49 天平
Tenchi *mhl* 天智
～ ujō *l* 天地有情
Tenchō 824–34 天長
Tendai *h* 天台
～ daishi wasan *l* 天台大師和讃
Tendō *p* 天童 「天永
Ten'ei *p* 天栄; 1110–13
Ten'en 973–76 天延
Tengai *s* 手播 118
Tengen 978–83 天元 93
Tengi 1053–58 天喜
Tengyō 938–47 天慶
Tenioha *l* 手爾乎葉 118
Tenji 1124–26 天治 93
Tenjiku *sp* 天竺
～ Tokubee ikokubanashi *la* 天竺徳兵衛韓噺
～-yō *a* 天竺様 「林
Tenjin bayashi *s* 天神
Tenjō 1131–32 天承
Tenju 1375–81 天授
Tenkai *smh* 天海
Tenkawa *p* 天川
Tenko *la* 天鼓
Tenkō *l* 天香
Tenkyū *s* 天休
Tenmabayashi *p* 天間林
Tenmangū *p* 天満宮
～ natane no gokū *la* 天満宮菜種御供
Tenmei *s* 1781–89 天明
Tenmon 1532–55 天文
Tenmu *mlh* 天武
Tenmyō *s* 天命
Tenna 1681–84 天和
Tennin 1108–10 天仁
Tennō *p* 天王
Tennōji *p* 天王寺
Ten no yūgao *l* 天の夕顔 93
Ten'ō 781–82 天応
Tenpō 1830–44 天保
Tenpuku 1233–34 天福
Tenpyō 729–49 天平
～-hōji 757–65 天平宝字 「神護
～-jingo 765–67 天平
～-kanpō 749 天平感宝
～-shōhō 749–57 天平
Tenri *p* 天理 ⌊勝宝
Tenrō *l* 天狼
Tenroku 970–73 天禄
Tenryaku 947–57 天暦
Tenryū *p* 天竜
Tenryūji *p* 天竜寺
Tenshin *p* "Tientsin" 天津 「1656
～ no shō *l* 転身の頌
Tenshō 1131–32 天承 93; 1573–92 天正
Tensui *p* 天水
Tensuishō *l* 天水抄
Tentoku 957–61 天徳
～ utaawase *l* 天徳歌合
Tentsuchi *m* 伝槌 359
Tenwa 1681–84 天和 93
Ten'yō 1144–45 天養
Teppei *m* 鉄平 1948
Tera *s* 亘良 202, 氐良 297. (寺 268)
Terabayashi *s* 寺林
Terabe *s* 寺部
Terada *s* 寺田
Teradani *s* 寺谷
Terada Torahiko *ml* 寺田寅彦
～ Tōru *ml* 寺田透
Terado *s* 寺戸
Teradomari *p* 寺泊
Teragaki *s* 寺垣
Teraguchi *s* 寺口
Terahara *s* 寺原
Terai *sp* 寺井
Terajima *s* 寺島
～ Munenori *mh* 寺島宗則
Terakado *s* 寺門
Terakawa *s* 寺川
Teraki *s* 寺木
Terakoya *la-h* 寺小屋
Terakubo *s* 寺久保
Terakura *s* 寺倉
Teramachi *s* 寺町
Teramatsu *s* 寺松
Terami *s* 寺見
Teramoto *s* 寺本
Teramura *s* 寺村
Teranishi *s* 寺西
Terano *s* 寺野
Terao *s* 寺尾
～ Hisashi *mh* 寺尾寿
Teraoka *s* 寺岡
Terasaka *s* 寺坂
Terase *s* 寺瀬 「2035
Terashi *s* 寺師; *m* 照
Terashita *s* 寺下 268
Terasu *m* 暉 1884, 照 2035, 暹 2593, 曜 2720
Terato *s* 寺戸 268
Terauchi *s* 寺内
Terawaki *s* 寺脇
Terayama *s* 寺山
Terazaki *s* 寺崎
～ Hiroshi *ml* 寺崎浩
～ Kōgyō *ma* 寺崎広
Terazawa *s* 寺沢 ⌊業
(teri 照 2035) 「狂言
Teriha kyōgen *l* 照葉
Teru *m* 光 281; *m-f* 暉 1884; *f* 瑩子 2387, 曜 2720. (央 182, 光 281, 旭 300, 侊 553, 明 623, 英 693, 凭 727, 映 840, 昭 841, 栄 969, 昶 1004, 晟 1187, 晃 1189, 昆 1195, 暎 1594, 晴 1597, 瑛 1607, 晥 1639, 詥 1661, 晶 1740, 瑗 1873, 煇 1875, 煌 1877, 暉 1884, 照 2035, 燁 2088, 暐 2091, 韶 2163, 彰 2174, 璉 2285, 璋 2287, 瑩 2387, 監 2398, 熙 2409, 輝 2499, 燕 2570, 曜 2720, 燿 2721, 顕 2757, 熹 2770, 曦 2914, 耀 2919)
Teruaki *m* 光揚 281, 照映 2035, 照煦, 曦章 2914
Teruakira *m* 輝徳 2499
Teruatsu *m* 栄同 969
Terube *s* 照部 2035
Teruchika *m* 照千賀, 輝規 2499
Terue *f* 煇栄 1875, 暉衛 1884
Terufusa *m* 昭英 841
Teruhata *s* 照幡 2035
Teruhide *m* 英薫 693
Teruhiko *m* 光彦 281, 昶彦 1004, 晴彦 1597, 輝久 2499
Teruhisa *m* 光久 281, 照久 2035 「623
Terui *s* 照井; *m* 明居
Teruji *m* 暎二 1594, 熹次 2770
Teruka *f* 輝香 2499
Teruko *f* 央子 182, 明子 623, 映子 840, 晟子 1187, 皓子 1639, 詥子 1661, 照子 2035, 燁子 2088, 暐子 2091, 熙子 2409, 輝子 2499, 曦子 2914
Terukuma *m* 照阿 2035
Terumasa *m* 輝政 2499
Terumi *m* 暉三 1884; *f* 英真 693
Terumichi *s* 暐道 2091; *m* 照道 2035, 輝充 2499
Terumine *s* 照峰 2035
Terumoto *m* 輝元 2499
Teruni *m* 光瑗 281
Terunobu *m* 旭信 300
Terunori *m* 暉児 1884
Terunuma *s* 照沼 2035
Teruo *m* 央夫 182, 光均 281, 侊男 553, 晃央 1189, 照男 2035, 輝夫 2499, 輝雄, 耀男 2919
Teruoka *s* 暉峻 1884
Teruomi *m* 暎臣 1594
Terusato *m* 光熙 281
Terushige *m* 英薫 693, 照重 2035
Terutane *m* 燿胤 2721
Terutora *m* 輝虎 2499
Terutoshi *m* 晃年 1189, 輝智 2499, 輝聴, 耀星 2919
Terutsugu *m* 昆次 1195
Teruuchi *s* 照内 2035
Teruya *s* 照屋
Teruyama *s* 照山
Teruyasu *m* 輝和 2499
Teruyo *f* 瑛代 1607
Teruyori *m* 照憑 2035
Teruyoshi *m* 璋悦 2287, 輝承 2499, 曜禧 2720
Teruyuki *m* 英通 693, 昭之 841
Teruzane *m* 照実 2035
Teshigawara *s* 勅使河原 898; *sp* 勅使川原
Teshikaga *p* 弟子屈 764

Teshima *s* 手島 118, 豊島 2013 「118
～ Toan *mh* 手島堵庵
Teshio *p* 天塩 93
Teshiro *s* 手白 118
Teshirogi *s* 手代木
Tessan *s* 鉄山 1948
Tessei *p* 哲西 1227
Tesshoki *l* 徹書記 2451
Tetora *m* 手刀良 118
Tetsu *sm* 鉄 1948; *m* 徹 2451; *m-f* 哲 1227, 喆 1646. (哲 1227, 悊 1480, 喆 1646, 鉄 1948, 銕 2338, 徹 2451, 澈 2454, 綴 2530, 轍 2874)
Tetsuhei *m* 鉄平 1948
Tetsuichi *m* 徹一 2451
Tetsuichirō *m* 哲一郎 1227, 鉄一郎 1948
Tetsuji *m* 哲二 1227, 鉄二 1948, 徹二 2451
Tetsujirō *m* 哲次郎 1227, 鉄次郎 1948
Tetsukichi *m* 鉄吉
Tetsukuri *s* 調布 2328
Tetsuma *m* 鉄馬 1948
Tetsunosuke *m* 鉄之助
Tetsuo *m* 哲夫 1227, 鉄男 1948
Tetsuomi *m* 鉄臣
Tetsurō *m* 哲郎 1227, 徹郎 2451
Tetsushi *m* 哲史 1227, 徹志 2451 「1227
Tetsushirō *m* 哲四郎
Tetsutarō *m* 哲太郎, 鉄太郎 1948, 徹太郎 2451
Tetsuya *s* 鉄屋 1948
Tetsuzō *m* 哲造 1227, 哲三, 鉄三 1948, 鉄蔵, 徹三 2451, 徹蔵
Tetta *p* 哲多 1227
Teura *s* 土浦 42
Tezuka *s* 手束 118, 手塚
～ Tomio *ml* 手塚富雄
(to 乙 2, 刀 12, 人 14, 十 18, 士 41, 土 42, 仁 57, 戸 59, 斗 71, 止 87, 太 105, 外 139, 任 235, 吐 242, 百 265, 年 342, 杜 423, 利 436, 図 502, 門 601, 兎 763, 表 914, 音 962, 徒 1048, 途 1234, 迹 1249, 砥 1386, 敏 1409, 都 1419, 留 1470, 渡 1586, 富 1715, 菟 1729, 登 1744, 豊 2013, 聡 2311, 褰 2677, 礪 2798)
Tō *s* 東 771, 藤 2773. (刀 12, 十 18, 永 149, 冬 161, 允 217, 任 235, 当 282, 有 303, 在 314, 広 316, 豆 438, 忍 463, 玄 522, 更 528, 妙 614, 卓 660, 茂 691, 沓 698, 延 739, 迫 747, 東 771, 拾 802, 洽 816, 治 825, 耐 884, 到 901, 柔 907, 迢 1000, 昶 1004, 桐 1103, 桃 1104, 党 1191, 竜 1199, 途 1234, 速 1237, 通 1239, 唐 1246, 県 1252, 甚 1267, 深 1341, 桶 1369, 能 1397, 野 1398, 透 1502, 逗 1511, 島 1522, 塔 1558, 陶 1565, 湯 1587, 勝 1613, 棟 1627, 断 1669, 納 1685, 董 1731, 登 1744, 棠 1747, 答 1765, 等 1770, 達 1810, 筒 1818, 塘 1842, 漠 1853, 純 1956, 寛 1977, 塗 2038, 遠 2043, 遐 2048, 稲 2125, 樋 2299, 踏 2314, 統 2333, 遙 2421, 徹 2451, 嶝 2466, 穆 2494, 頭 2504, 融 2545, 遼 2590, 邁 2592, 濤 2613, 檮 2724, 藤 2773, 謄 2867, 鐙 2880, 韜 2884, 竇 2897, 懸 2984)
Toaki *s* 十秋 18 「1521
Toba *smh-ma-p* 鳥羽
～-ke no kodomo *l* 鳥羽家の子供
Tobari *s* 戸張 59, 登張 1744, 褰張 2677
～ Chikufū *ml* 登張竹風 1744
Tobata *sp* 戸畑 59
Tobe *s* 土部 42, 戸部 59, 戸辺; *smh-fh* 戸畔; *p* 砥部 1386
Tobeta *s* 銅直 2159
Tōbetsu *p* 当別 282
Tobi *p* 外山 139. (飛 1014, 鳶 2179)
Tobikoe *l* 飛越 1014
Tobikumo *l* 飛雲
Tobinaga *s* 飛永
Tobishi *s* 飛志
Tobishima *p* 飛島
Tobita *s* 飛田 「千句
Tobiume senku *l* 飛梅
Tobiyama *s* 飛山
Tobi-za *a* 外山座 139
Tobizawa *m* 鳶沢 2179
Tōboku *la* 東北 771
Tōbō-saku *ml-la* "Tung-fang Shuo" 東方朔
Tōbu *p* 東部 771
Toburi *s* 井 206
(tochi 栃 865, 杤 1095, 橡 2478)
Tōchi *s* 十市 18
Tochigi *s* 杤木 1095; *p* 栃木 865
Tochihara *s* 栃原
Tochii *s* 東地井 771
Tochiko *f* 栃子 865
Tochimoto *s* 栃本
Tochinai *s* 栃内
Tochio *m* 十一夫 18; *p* 栃尾 865
Tochiuchi *s* 栃内
Tochiya *s* 栃谷
Tochizawa *s* 栃沢
Toda *s* 吐田 242; *sp* 戸田 59 「田 2043
Tōda *s* 任田 235; *sp* 遠
Tō-daiwajō tōseiden *l* 唐大和尚東征伝 1246
Todaka *s* 戸高 59
Toda Kindō *ml* 戸田欽堂
～ Mosui *ml* 戸田茂睡
Todani *s* 戸谷, 外谷 139
(todo 椴 1893)
Tōdō *s* 藤堂 2773
Todohiko *m* 百十彦 265
Todohokke *p* 椴法華
Todoki *s* 椴木 ⌊1893
Todokoro *s* 戸所 59, 外 139, 外所, 外処, 都所 1419, 富所 1715
Todomu *m* 乙 2, 止 87, 停 1272
Todoroki *s* 八十八騎 19, 等等木 1770, 轟 2939, 轟木; *sp* 等等力 1770 「87
Todoromi *p* 止止呂美
Toeda *s* 戸枝 59
Tōei *p* 東栄 771; *la* 藤永 2773, 藤栄
Tōemon *m* 藤右衛門
Tōfusa *m* 延房 739
Toga *s* 化間 56, 門叶 601, 砥鹿 1386, 都賀 1419, 問叶 1524, 問計; *p* 利賀 436. (栂 1097)
Togaeri *s* 十返 18
～ Hajime *ml* 十返肇
Togai *s* 栂井 1097
Togakushi *p* 戸隠 59
Togama *m* 敏鎌 1409
Togami *s* 戸上 59, 砥上 1386
Tōgane *s* 鴇根 2280; *sp* 東金 771 「士
Tōgan Koji *la* 東岸居
Togano *s* 栂野 1097
Toganō *s* 戸叶 59
Togari *s* 戸苅, 戸鹿里, 利苅 436
Togasaka *s* 栂坂 1097
Togasaki *s* 戸賀崎 59, 戸ヶ崎
Togashi *s* 富樫 1717
～ Masachika *mh* 富樫政親
Togawa *s* 十川 18, 十河, 戸川 59, 外川 139, 刑苅 258, 砥川 1386, 跡川 1926 「骨 59
～ Shūkotsu *ml* 戸川秋
～ Yukio *ml* 戸川幸夫
～ Zanka *ml* 戸川残花
Tōge *s* 峠 1081. (峠)
Tōgenshū *l* 桃源集 1104
Togeri *m* 遂 1806
Tōge Sankichi *ml* 峠三吉 1081
Togezawa *s* 斗ケ沢 71
Togi *s* 研 875; *sp* 富来 1715. (炊 602, 研 875)
Tōgi *s* 東儀 771
Togikawa *s* 研川 875
Togitsu *p* 時津 1086
Togō *s* 十川 18, 都甲 1419 「郷 771
Tōgō *s* 十合 18; *sp* 東
Togōchi *p* 戸河内 59
Tōgō Heihachirō *mh* 東郷平八郎 771
(togu 炊 602)
Tōgū *s* 東宮 771
Toguchi *s* 戸口 59
Togura *sp* 戸倉
Tōhachi *m* 十八 18
Tōhaku *p* 東伯 771; *l* 冬柏 161 「1246
Tōhara *s* 東原 771, 唐原
Tōhei *m* 東平 771

Tohimi *m* 十一三 18
Tōhito *m* 遐仁 2048
Tōhoku *p* 東北 771
Toi *sp* 戸井 59; *p* 土肥 42. (問 1524)
Tōi *s* 遠井 2043
Toichi *s* 十市 18
Tōichi *m* 東一 771, 統一 2333, 透一 1502, 藤一 2773
Tōichirō *m* 東一郎 771, 棟一郎 1627, 董一郎 1731, 藤一郎 2773, 藤市郎
Toida *s* 戸井田 59, 問田 1524, 樋田 2299
Toide *sp* 戸出 59
Toike *s* 外池 139 「771
Tōin *s* 洞院 821; *p* 東員
Tōinhiji *l* 棠陰比事 1747
Toishi *s* 戸石 59, 登石 1744 「771
Toita *s* 戸板 59, 東池田
~ Yasuji *ml* 戸板康二 59 「2299
Toizumi *s* 戸泉, 樋泉
Toji *s* 都治 1419; *f* 刀自 12
Tōji *s* 田路 189, 東司 771, 東地; *p* 東児
Tojiko *f* 刀自子 12
Tōjima *s* 東島 771
Tojime *f* 刀自咩 12
Tojiri *s* 十二里 18
Tōjirō *m* 藤二郎 2773
Tōjō *sp* 東条 771, 東城; *p* 東庄
~ Hideki *mh* 東条英
Tōju *s* 東樹 ⌊機
Tōjūrō *m* 藤十郎 2773
Tokachi *p* 十勝 18
Tōkachō *l* 冬花帳 161
Tokai *s* 渡海 1586
Tōkai *sp* 東海 771
Tōkaidō *p* 東海道
Tōkaidōchū hizakurige *l* 東海道中膝栗毛
Tōkaidō meishoki *l* 東海道名所記
~ Yotsuya kaidan *la* 東海道四谷怪談
Tōkai ichiōshū *l* 東海一漚集
~ Sanshi *ml* 東海散士
Tōkamachi *p* 十日町 18
Tōkan kikō *l* 東関紀行 771

Tokanō *s* 戸叶 59
Tokari *s* 戸刈
Toke *s* 東家 771, 藤下 2773; *p* 土気 42
Toki *s* 十時 18, 北向 138, 兆向 244, 硎 1384, 解 1923; *sp* 土岐 42. (示 148, 可 165, 兆 244, 旬 301, 迅 307, 世 335, 言 439, 発 447, 怜 565, 林 633, 宗 679, 昔 699, 斉 701, 季 725, 其 734, 辰 738, 国 745, 侯 777, 信 782, 祝 851, 秋 878, 勅 898, 刻 900, 則 902, 発 953, 春 963, 候 1029, 時 1086, 訓 1148, 隆 1313, 朗 1394, 釈 1395, 敕 1405, 斎 1454, 常 1463, 暁 1596, 期 1671, 朝 1672, 晨 1739, 睦 1904, 解 1923, 凱 1967, 牽 2028, 催 2060, 像 2061, 説 2143, 農 2205, 節 2215, 鴇 2280, 聡 2311, 論 2320, 鋭 2344, 稽 2491, 鴻 2614)
Tōki *s* 陶帰 1565
Tokiari *s* 時存 1086
Tokichi *m* 都吉 1419
Tōkichi *m* 藤吉 2773
Tokida *s* 時田 1086, 説田 2143, 鴇田 2280
Tokie *f* 旬江 301, 晨江 1739
Tokieda *s* 時枝 1086
~ Motoki *ml* 時枝誠記
Tokifuri *m* 時雨
Tokigawa *s* 時川; *p* 都幾川 1419
Tokihara *s* 時原 1086
Tokihiko *m* 季彦 725
Tokihiro *sm* 時広 1086; *m* 言泰 439
Tokiichi *m* 凱一 1967
Tokijirō *m* 時次郎 1086
Tokiko *f* 旬子 301, 勅子 898, 時子 1086, 朝子 1672, 稽子 2491
Takikoto *m* 時言 1086
Tokikuni *m* 刻国 900
Tokimune *m* 時宗 1086
Tokina *m* 斉名 701, 時名 1086 「時華 1086
Tokinaga *m* 世良 335,
Tokinao *m* 時直
Tokinari *m* 節成 2215

Tokino *m* 祝乃 851
Tokinori *m* 朝則 1672
Tokio *m* 迅男 307, 言緒 439, 辰夫 738, 祝雄 851, 秋生 878, 勅夫 898, 時雄 1086, 常夫 1463, 常雄, 農雄 2205, 鋭雄 2344
Tokioka *s* 時岡 1086
Tokiomi *m* 宗臣 679
Tokisaburō *m* 時三郎 1086
Tokisada *m* 春定 963
Tokisato *m* 言知 439
Tokishige *sm* 時重 1086; *m* 可薫 165, 時懋 1086
Tokishika *m* 辰爾 738
Tokita *s* 常田 1463, 鴇田 2280
Tokitada *m* 時忠 1086
Tokitaka *m* 国隆 745
Tokitarō *m* 説太郎 2143
Tokitatsu *m* 言辰 439
Tokitō *s* 時任 1086
Tokitomo *s* 時友
Tokitoshi *m* 時敏
Tokitsugu *m* 季次 725
Tokitsumu *m* 時万 1086
Tokitsuna *m* 時綱
Tokiwa *sp* 常磐 1463, 常葉; *m* 松 869, 常 1463, 常緑; *p* 常盤
Tokiwai *s* 常磐井
Tokiwamaro *m* 常磐麿
Tokiwanoya *m* 常磐舎
Tokiwazu *sa* 常磐津
~ Moji-dayū *ma* 常磐津文字太夫
Tokiyama *s* 時山 1086
Tokiyasu *m* 時休
Tokiyoda *s* 常世田 1463
Tokiyori *m* 兆頼 244
Tokiyoshi *m* 辰吉 738, 時敬 1086, 斎吉 1454
Tokiyuki *m* 示元 148, 時于 1086
Tokizaki *s* 鴇崎 2280
Tokizane *sm* 時実 1086; *m* 説実 2143
Tokizawa *s* 時沢 1086
Toki Zenmaro *ml* 土岐善麿 42
Tokizō *m* 時蔵 1086, 訓三 1148
Toko *s* 土庫 42. (床 508, 常 1463, 徳 2063)
Tokō *s* 都甲 1419

Tokoakira *m* 常明 1463
Tokoi *s* 床井 508
Tokoku *ml* 杜国 423
Tōkoku *ml* 透谷 1502
Tokonabe *s* 常滑 1463
Tokoname *p* 常滑
Tokonami *s* 床次 508, 床波, 常石 1463
~ Takejirō *ml* 床次竹二郎 508
Tokonatsu *l* 常夏 1463
Tokonori *m* 外交官 139
Tokoo *m* 常男 1463
Tokoro *s* 戸頃 59, 野老 1398; *sm* 所 600; *p* 常呂 1463. (処 177)
Tokoronosuke *m* 処之助 「1398
Tokoroyama *s* 野老山
Tokorozawa *p* 所沢 600
Tokotako *m* 徳太古 2063
Tokoyama *s* 常山 1463
Tokoyo *s* 常与, 常世
Tokozumi *s* 往住 579
Toku *s* 得純 1299, 竇 2897. (列 257, 禿 496, 更 528, 得 1299, 督 2023, 悳 2033, 徳 2063, 説 2143, 読 2142, 篤 2576, 竇 2897)
Tokuda *s* 徳田 2063
Tokudaiji *s* 徳大寺
Tokuda Kyūichi *mh* 徳田球一
~ Shūsei *ml* 徳田秋声
Tokude *s* 徳出
Tokue *s* 得江 1299, 得重, 徳江 2063
Tokugawa *s* 徳川
~ Hidetada *mh* 徳川秀忠
~ Ieharu *mh* 徳川家治
~ Iemitsu *mh* 徳川家光 「茂
~ Iemochi *mh* 徳川家
~ Ienari *mh* 徳川家斉
~ Ienobu *mh* 徳川家宣
~ Iesada *mh* 徳川家定
~ Iesato *mh* 徳川家達
~ Ieshige *mh* 徳川家重 「継
~ Ietsugu *mh* 徳川家
~ Ietsuna *mh* 徳川家綱
~ Ieyasu *mh* 徳川家康

～ Ieyoshi *mh* 徳川家慶
～ jikki *h* 徳川実紀
～ Keiki *mh* 徳川慶喜
～ Mitsukuni *mh* 徳川光圀 「昭
～ Nariaki *mh* 徳川斉
～ Tsunayoshi *mh* 徳川綱吉 「房
～ Yorifusa *mh* 徳川頼
～ Yorinobu *mh* 徳川頼宣 「川吉宗
～ Yoshimune *mh* 徳
～ Yoshinao *mh* 徳川義直 「慶喜
～ Yoshinobu *mh* 徳川
Tokugorō *m* 徳五郎
Tokuha *s* 常羽 1463
Tokuhara *s* 徳原 2063
Tokuhira *sm* 得平 1299
Tokuhiro *sm* 徳弘 2063
Tokuhisa *sm* 徳久
Tokui *s* 徳井
Tokuichi *m* 徳一
Tokuji *s* 得地 1299; *m* 徳次 2063, 篤治 2576; *p* 徳地 2063; 1306–08 徳治
Tokujirō *m* 徳次郎, 徳治郎, 篤次郎 2576
Tokuju *m* 徳寿 2063
Tokuko *f* 徳子
Tokuma *m* 得馬 1299, 徳間 2063
Tokumaru *s* 徳丸
Tokumasa *s* 徳政
Tokumasu *s* 徳増
Tokumatsu *m* 徳松
Tokumi *s* 戸汲 59, 徳見 2063
Tokumitsu *s* 徳光
Tokumoto *s* 徳本
Tokumura *s* 徳村
Tokunaga *sm* 徳永
～ Sunao *ml* 徳永直
Tokuno *s* 徳野
Tokunō *s* 徳能; *sl* 得能 1299 「島 2063
Tokunoshima *p* 徳之
Tokunosuke *m* 徳之助
Tokuoka *s* 徳岡
Tokura *s* 土倉 42, 都倉 1419, 登倉 1744, 徳楽 2063
Tokuriki *s* 徳力
Tokurō *m* 悳郎 2033
Tokusa *sla* 木賊 109
Tokusaburō *m* 得三郎 1299, 徳三郎 2063
Tokushi *s* 禿氏 496; *m* 徳司 2063
Tokushichi *m* 徳七
Tokushige *s* 徳重
Tokushima *sp* 徳島
Tokushirō *m* 得四郎 1299, 篤志郎 2576
Tokushuku *s* 徳宿 2063
Tokutake *s* 徳竹, 徳武
Tokutari *m* 徳太理
Tokutarō *m* 徳太郎, 篤太郎 2576
Tokutome *s* 徳留 2063
Tokutomi *s* 徳富
～ Roka *ml* 徳富蘆花
～ Sohō *ml* 徳富蘇峰
Tokutsune *sm* 得恒 1299
Tokuue *s* 徳植 2063
Tokuwaka *s* 徳若
～ gomanzaishū *l* 徳和歌後万載集
Tokuyama *sp* 徳山
Tokuzawa *s* 徳沢
Tokuzō *m* 得三 1299, 徳三 2063, 徳蔵
Tōkyō *p* 東京 771
(toma 苫 686, 篷 2689)
Tōma *s* 十摩 18, 東万 771, 当間 282, 当摩, 藤間 2773; *sm* 東馬 771; *sp* 当麻 282 「686
Tomabechi *sp* 苫米地
Tomada *sp* 苫田
Tōmai *sp* 玉米 204
Tomako *f* 篷子 2689
Tomakomai *p* 苫小牧 686
Tomamae *p* 苫前
Tomari *sp* 泊 592
Tomaru *s* 外丸 139, 都丸 1419; *m* 戸丸 59, 止 87
Tomasu *m* 富 1715
Tomatsu *s* 戸松 59, 外松 139, 富松 1715
Tōmatsu *s* 東松 771
Tomatsuri *s* 戸祭 59
Tome *s* 富米 1715; *sp* 登米 1744. (止 87, 末 211, 姥 1090, 徠 1297, 留 ⌊1470)
Tomeji *m* 留次
Tomekichi *m* 留吉
Tomeko *f* 止子 87, 姥子 1090
Tomemaru *m* 末満留 211
Tomeo *m* 留夫 1470
Tomeri *m* 富 1715
Tomeru *m* 富
Tomi *s* 迹見 1249, 跡見 1926; *m-p* 富 1715. (十 18, 多 347, 臣 527, 祉 608, 肥 617, 私 637, 幸 661, 宝 676, 美 923, 殷 1139, 倖 1277, 禄 1589, 棟 1616, 富 1715, 暈 1741, 登 1744, 答 1765, 智 1793, 福 1888, 寛 1977, 徳 2063, 聡 2311, 禧 2628)
Tomiai *p* 富合 1715
Tomichika *f* 十九 18
Tomidokoro *s* 富所 1715
Tomie *f* 富枝; *p* 富江
Tomigashi *s* 富樫
Tomigaya *s* 富谷
Tomihara *s* 富原
Tomihari *s* 富張
Tomihide *m* 多栄 347
Tomihira *sm* 富平 1715
Tomihisa *m* 富久, 豊三久 2013
Tomii *s* 富井 1715
Tomiie *s* 富家
Tomijima *s* 富島
Tomijirō *m* 富次郎
Tomika *m* 十三日 18; *p* 富加 1715
Tomikatsu *m* 富強
Tomikawa *s* 富川
Tomiki *s* 富木, 富城; *sp* 富来
Tomiko *f* 倖子 1277, 富子 1715, 登子 1744, 福子 1888
Tomiku *m* 富来 1715
Tomikura *s* 富倉
Tomimasa *m* 寛祐 1977, 寛裕
Tomimatsu *s* 富松 1715
Tomimochi *m* 富将
Tomimori *s* 富森; *sm* 富守
Tomimoto *s* 富本
～ Buzennojō *ma* 富本豊前掾
Tominaga *s* 福長 1888; *sm* 富永 1715
～ Nakamoto *mh* 富永仲基
～ Tarō *ml* 富永太郎
Tominao *m* 臣直 527, 富直 1715
Tominari *s* 富成
Tōmine *s* 遠峰 2043
Tomino *s* 富野 1715
Tominokōji *s* 富小路
Tominosawa *s* 富ノ沢
～ Rintarō *ml* 富ノ沢麟太郎
Tomio *s* 富尾; *m* 乙未生 2, 外美雄 139, 宝男 676, 美雄 923, 富雄 1715, 福男 1888, 聡夫 2311
Tomioka *sp* 富岡 1715
～ koi no yamabiraki *la* 富岡恋山開
～ Tessai *ma* 富岡鉄斎
Tomioki *s* 富尾木
Tomisaka *s* 富坂
Tomisato *p* 富里
Tomita *s* 富田, 頓田 2115
Tomitaka *s* 富高 1715
Tomitarō *m* 富太郎
Tomita Saika *ml* 富田砕花 「雄
～ Tsuneo *ml* 富田常
Tomitoki *m* 富勅
Tomiura *p* 富浦
Tomiya *sp* 富谷
Tomiyama *s* 外宮山 139; *sp* 富山 1715
Tomiyasu *sm* 富安
～ Fūsei *ml* 富安風生
Tomiyoshi *sm* 富吉
Tomizaki *s* 富崎
Tomizawa *sp* 富沢
～ Kakio *ml* 富沢赤黄男
～ Uio *ml* 富沢有為男
Tomizu *s* 戸水 59
Tomizuka *s* 富塚 1715
Tomo *s* 伴 361; *m* 智 1793. (丈 36, 大 48, 友 70, 文 86, 止 87, 巴 97, 与 101, 戈 108, 付 126, 以 134, 比 137, 云 147, 公 156, 匹 187, 价 236, 全 271, 共 292, 交 293, 同 298, 有 303, 伴 361, 作 362, 伯 363, 那 416, 言 439, 呂 459, 孚 483, 供 555, 朋 616, 肥 617, 知 636, 和 638, 幸 661, 孟 667, 侖 669, 宝 676, 奉 717, 具 718, 述 748, 侶 778, 相 868, 委 960,

栄 969, 倶 1028, 倫 1037, 徒 1048, 始 1092, 郡 1146, 党 1191, 毘 1195, 皆 1196, 兼 1268, 偏 1273, 悌 1289, 流 1332, 致 1407, 寅 1439, 曹 1479, 偕 1537, 備 1539, 朝 1672, 納 1685, 登 1744, 衆 1762, 答 1765, 等 1770, 智 1793, 階 1840, 張 1879, 禎 1887, 睦 1904, 群 1924, 詮 1934, 幹 1938, 寛 1977, 雑 2127, 鞆 2162, 算 2213, 節 2215, 箇 2216, 耦 2310, 諄 2324, 寮 2364, 儔 2433, 錞 2521, 興 2586, 篷 2689, 類 2755, 鵬 2795, 疇 2799, 鐃 2925, 彜 2943)

Tomō *m* 兎毛 763

Tomoaki *m* 知晄 636, 知哲

Tomoatsu *m* 寛篤 1977

Tomoaya *m* 朋礼 616

Tomobayashi *s* 伴林 361 「部 70

Tomobe *s* 伴部; *sp* 友

Tomochi *p* 砥用 1386

Tomoda *s* 友田 70, 苫田 686

Tomoe *s* 友江 70; *m-f* 巴 97; *f* 友枝 70, 巴絵 97, 鞆絵 2162

Tomoeda *s* 友枝 70

Tomoeyama *s* 巴山 97

Tomohachi *m* 朋八 616

Tomoharu *m* 倫治 1037, 備治 1539, 朝治 1672

Tomohaya *m* 知速 636

Tomohiko *m* 倫彦 1037, 錞彦 2521

Tomohira *m* 友平 70, 朝成 1672

Tomohiro *sm* 友博 70; *m* 知淵 636, 致寛 1407, 智寛 1793 「呂久 459

Tomohisa *m* 有久 303,

Tomohito *m* 兼仁 1268, 智仁 1793, 寛仁 1977

Tomo-hōshi *ma* 友法師 70

Tomoichi *m* 鵬一 2795

Tomoji *m* 友二 70, 友治

Tomojirō *m* 友次郎

Tomokake *s* 鞆掛 2162

Tomokata *m* 朝象 1672

Tomokazu *m* 公一 156, 知二 636

Tomoki *s* 友木 70; *m* 朋来 616

Tomokichi *m* 友吉 70

Tomokiyo *m* 友精, 与清 101

Tomoko *f* 大子 48, 价子 236, 伯子 363, 那子 416, 供子 555, 朋子 616, 和子 638, 述子 748, 委子 960, 倫子 1037, 偕子 1537, 等子 1770, 鞆子 2162

Tomokuni *m* 具国 718

Tomomaru *m* 曹丸 1479

Tomomasa *m* 共昌 292, 奉政 717

Tomomatsu *s* 友松 70

Tomomi *m* 具視 718, 具瞻

Tomomichi *m* 友随 70

Tomomitsu *s* 友光; *m* 戈光 108, 朋満 616

Tōmon *s* 東門 771

Tomonaga *s* 友永 70; *sm* 朝永 1672 「十郎

~ Sanjūrō *ml* 朝永三

Tomonai *s* 伴 361

Tomonao *m* 寅直 1439

Tomonari *sm* 友成 70; *m* 友礼

Tomonaru *m* 供愛 555

Tomono *s* 友野 70, 伴野 361; *f* 登藻野 1744

Tomonobu *m* 伴信 361, 知一 636, 具選 718, 流宣 1332, 偕宣 1537

Tomonori *m* 友則 70, 登徳 1744, 智義 1793, 智準 「介 70

Tomonosuke *m* 友之

Tomo no Yoshio *mh* 伴善男 361

Tomoo *m* 知雄 636, 悌夫 1289, 朝陽 1672

Tomooka *s* 友岡 70

Tomori *m* 外守 139, 外衛

Tōmori *m* 登盛 1744

Tomosaburō *m* 友三郎 70, 知三郎 636, 智三郎 1793

Tomosachi *m* 共福 292

Tomosada *m* 朝定 1672

Tomoshi *m* 倶志 1028

Tomoshige *m* 共重 292

Tomoshirō *m* 友四郎 70, 知四郎 636

Tomotada *m* 有忠 303, 知十 636, 知止

Tomotaka *m* 与敬 101

Tomotake *s* 渡守武 1586; *m* 知健 636, 知強

Tomoto *m* 鞆音 2162

Tomotō *m* 知速 636

Tōmoto *s* 東本 771

Tomotsuna *m* 等綱 1770

Tomotsune *sm* 友常 70; *m* 知常 636

Tomouji *m* 具氏 718

Tomoya *m* 友哉 70, 知也 636

Tomoyama *s* 友山 70

Tomoyasu *sm* 友安; *m* 友悌, 知養 636

Tomoyo *m* 知福

Tomoyoshi *m* 友修 70, 知洗 636, 知義, 奉表 717, 寅栄 1439

Tomoyuki *m* 以之 134, 知至 636, 奉文 717, 睦之 1904, 興之 2586

Tomozawa *s* 友沢 70

Tomozō *m* 友三, 知三 636 「村 139

Tomura *s* 戸村 59, 外

Tomuro *s* 戸室 59

(ton 丼 206, 屯 222, 呑 489, 邨 645, 盾 984, 敦 1690, 頓 2115, 暾 2469, 錞 2521)

Ton'a *ml* 頓阿 2115

Tonami *s* 戸波 59, 戸浪, 外波 139, 鳥神山 1521; *p* 礪波 2798 「1521

Tonamiyama *s* 鳥神山

Tonan *m* 図南 502; *p* 都南 1419

Tonara *s* 戸奈良 59

Tonari *m* 兎也 763, 隣 2443

Tonbara *p* 頓原 2115

Tonda *s* 富田 1715, 福当 1888 「林 1715

Tondabayashi *p* 富田

Tone *s* 刀禰 12; *sp* 刀根, 利根 436. (舎 721)

Tonedachi *s* 刀根館 12

Tonegawa *s* 舎川 721; *sp* 利根川 436

Toneko *f* 外禰子 139, 利根子 436

Toneri *sm-p* 舎人 721

Toneriko *l* 秦皮 1202

Toneri Shinnō *mlh* 舎人親王 721

Tongu *s* 頓宮 2115

Tonizō *m* 十二蔵 18

Tonjo *s* 頓所 2115

Tonmon *s* 水主 54

Tonno *s* 富野 1715

(tono 外 139, 殿 1960)

Tonō *m* 唱 1284

Tōno *s* 東野 771; *p* 遠野 2043

Tonoe *s* 渡植 1586; *f* 外栄 139, 外恵

Tonohara *s* 塔原 1558, 殿原 1960

Tonoi *s* 御宿 1572

Tonoki *s* 殿木 1960, 殿来 「1715

Tonomi *s* 止美 87, 富海

Tōnomine *sph* 多武峰 347 「将

~ Shōshō *l* 多武峰少

Tonomo *sm-p* 主殿 196

Tonomori *s* 殿 1960

Tonomukashi *s* 常昨 1463 「殿村 1960

Tonomura *s* 外村 139,

~ Shigeru *ml* 外村繁 139 「岡 1960

Tonooka *s* 外野岡, 殿

Tonosawa *s* 塔沢 1558

Tonoshō *p* 土庄 42

Tō no Tsuneyori *ml* 東常縁 771

Tonoura *s* 外浦 139

Tonozuka *s* 殿塚 1960

Tooka *s* 外岡 139

Tora *m* 寅 1439; *f* 虎 754; *ph* "Thailand?" 度羅 1009. (玄 522, 艮 529, 虎 754, 寅 1439, 彪 1523, 寛 1977)

Toraakira *m* 虎明 754

Tora gaku *a* 度羅楽 1009

Toragorō *m* 虎五郎 754

Torahiko *m* 虎彦, 寅彦 1439

Torahime *p* 虎姫 754

Toraichirō *m* 虎一郎

Tōrai Sanna *ml* 唐来三和 1246

Toraiwa *s* 虎岩 754

Toraji *m* 虎児, 虎治, 寅二 1439, 寅次

Torajirō *m* 虎次郎 754,

寅二郎 1439, 寅次郎
Torakichi *m* 寅吉
Torakiyo *m* 虎清 754
Toranosuke *m* 虎之介, 虎之助, 寅之助 1439
Torao *s* 虎尾 754; *m* 艮雄 529, 虎雄 754
Toraōmaru *ma* 虎王丸
Torarokurō *m* 虎六郎
Torasaburō *m* 虎三郎, 寅三郎 1439
Torasuke *m* 寅輔
Torata *m* 虎太 754
Toratarō *m* 虎太郎, 寅太郎 1439
Toratoshi *m* 寅甫
Toraya *s* 虎谷 754, 虎屋
Torazawa *ma* 虎沢
Tōreki *l* 冬暦 161
Tori *s* 刀利 12; *m* 鳥 1521. (伻 356, 酉 526, 取 650, 鳥 1521) 「里
Tōri *s* 東籬 771; *sm* 東
Toribeyama shinjū *la* 鳥辺山心中 1521
Torigoe *sp* 鳥越
~ Shin *ml* 鳥越信
Torihami *s* 鳥喰
Torihara *s* 鳥原
Torii *s* 酉井 526, 鳥井 1521, 鳥居
~ Kiyonaga *ma* 鳥居清長 「清信
~ Kiyonobu *ma* 鳥居
Toriiōji *s* 鳥居大路
Toriire *s* 鳥入
Torikai *s* 鳥養, 鳥飼
Torikata *s* 鳥方
Toriko *f* 酉子 526
Torimi *s* 鳥海 1521
Torimitsu *s* 鳥光
Torimoto *s* 鳥本
Tōrin *ml* 桃隣 1104
Torino *s* 鳥野 1521
Torinoumi *s* 鳥海
Torio *s* 鳥尾; *m* 酉夫 526, 鳥雄 1521
Torioi *la* 鳥追
~ -bune *la* 鳥追舟
Torioto *m* 酉乙 526
Tōri Sannin *ml* 東里山人 771
Torisawa *s* 鳥沢 1521
Torisu *s* 鳥巣
Torita *s* 鳥田
Torite *p* 取手 650
Toriumi *s* 鳥海 1521
Toriya *p* 鳥屋
Toriyabe *s* 鳥谷部
Toriyama *s* 鳥山
Torizō *m* 酉三 526
Torizuka *s* 鳥塚 1521
Toroshi *sp* 取石 650
(toru 取, 執 1420, 操 2448)
Tōru *m* 公 156, 冲 225, 互 317, 利 436, 亨 440, 発 447, 明 623, 阜 731, 亮 911, 昶 1004, 涓 1061, 竜 1199, 泰 1203, 通 1239, 済 1336, 透 1502, 博 1534, 貫 1754, 達 1810, 達朗, 逵 1813, 超 1816, 塁 2037, 暢 2111, 関 2245, 澄 2276, 徹 2451, 叡 2555, 豁 2667; *m-la* 融 2545
Toruko *p* "Turkey" 土耳古 42
Tōryū *s* 東流 771
Tosa *s* 北向 138; *sph* 土佐 42
Tosabō *mh* 土佐房
Tōsaburō *m* 冬三郎 161, 登三郎 1744 「1744
Tosaka *s* 戸坂 59, 登坂
~ Jun *ml* 戸坂潤 59
Tosakai *s* 鶏冠井 2821
Tosaki *s* 戸前 59, 戸崎
Tōsaku *m* 藤作 2773
Tosa Mitsunaga *ma* 土佐光長 42
~ Mitsunobu *mh* 土佐光信 「起
~ Mitsuoki *ma* 土佐光
Tōsandō *p* 東山道 771
Tosa nikki *l* 土佐日記 42 「記燈
~ ~ akashi *l* 土佐日
Tosao *f* 都操 1419
Tosa Shimizu *p* 土佐清水 42
Tosayama *p* 土佐山
Tosa Yamada *p* 土佐山田 「歳 1995)
Tose *s* 刀西 12. (年 342,
Tōseikatsusha *l* 党生活者 1191
Tōsen *la* 唐船 1246
Tōsha *s* 当舎 282
Toshi *m* 利 436, 洌 1063, 敏 1409, 寔 1434, 逵 2043, 豪 2177, 儁 2253, 鋭 2344, 駿 2763; *f* 登志 1744, 聡 2311, 憲 2562. (才 35, 子 38, 牛 111, 代 125, 冬 161, 平 203, 夙 299, 迅 307, 老 334, 世 335, 年 342, 利 436, 言 439, 亨 440, 甫 533, 寿 539, 考 540, 攸 561, 佝 562, 明 623, 和 638, 祀 640, 命 671, 宗 679, 英 693, 斉 701, 季 725, 信 782, 施 831, 秋 878, 勇 908, 星 946, 系 977, 哉 1006, 倫 1037, 俊 1039, 洌 1063, 校 1096, 祚 1126, 記 1149, 剣 1152, 莫 1175, 烝 1210, 耆 1214, 要 1218, 恵 1226, 隼 1230, 威 1251, 健 1282, 惇 1288, 振 1320, 捷 1323, 淑 1335, 淳 1337, 理 1361, 敏 1409, 紀 1424, 翁 1430, 寔 1434, 章 1461, 逸 1504, 逞 1513, 粛 1528, 順 1532, 禄 1589, 斌 1590, 峻 1591, 暁 1596, 期 1671, 鈊 1675, 敬 1691, 勤 1698, 答 1765, 等 1770, 智 1793, 福 1888, 稔 1916, 詮 1934, 幹 1938, 鉄 1948, 歳 1995, 資 2012, 舜 2017, 牽 2028, 聖 2030, 照 2035, 準 2041, 載 2050, 歯 2051, 駁 2171, 豪 2177, 暦 2235, 儁 2253, 憘 2257, 聡 2311, 銅 2341, 鋭 2344, 駙 2347, 駛 2348, 毅 2351, 敵 2354, 趣 2422, 蔵 2424, 儔 2433, 儇 2434, 穏 2492, 穎 2505, 録 2523, 叡 2555, 憙 2559, 熹 2560, 憲 2562, 賢 2579, 禧 2628, 聴 2634, 駿 2763, 齢 2766, 鏡 2817, 繁 2848, 驥 3008)
Tōshi *s* 藤氏 2773
Toshiaki *m* 利精 436, 利謙, 敏明 1409, 逸朗 1504, 鉄朗 1948, 銅秋 2341
Toshiakira *m* 利見 436, 利豁, 敏昉 1409, 聖譲 2030
Toshiatsu *m* 利同 436
Toshiaya *m* 利彪, 俊章 1039
Toshi bunshū *l* 都氏文集 1419
Toshichika *m* 利恭 436, 利彰 「信田
Toshida *s* 土志田 42, 土
Toshie *f* 鏡枝 2817
Toshifumi *m* 明文 623, 紀文 1424
Toshifusa *m* 捷房 1323
Toshiharu *m* 年美 342, 利鋪 436, 暁春 1596
Toshihide *m* 寿幸 539, 斌衡 1590
Toshihiko *m* 利彦 436, 俊彦 1039, 敏彦 1409
Toshihira *m* 利行 436, 俊位 1039, 俊迪
Toshihiro *m* 冬弘 161, 亨弘 440
Toshihisa *m* 利剛 436, 俊久 1039, 俊寿, 紀久 1424, 歳久 1995
Toshihito *m* 利寛 436, 智仁 1793
Toshihogi *m* 利寿 436
Toshiie *m* 利家
Toshiji *m* 理二 1361, 逞治 1513, 舜二 2017, 繁次 2848
Toshika *m* 利皚 436
Toshikami *m* 利上
Toshikane *m* 利周, 歳兼 1995
Toshikata *m* 利声 436, 利器, 利賢, 利謙
Toshikatsu *m* 利雄, 敏功 1409, 敏且
Toshikawa *s* 利川 436
Toshikazu *m* 利和, 紀三 1424, 敏般 1409, 順一 1532, 鋭憲 2344, 駛量 2348, 繁数 2848, 驥一 3008 「鋭清 2344
Toshikiyo *m* 寿瀏 539,
Toshiko *f* 夙子 299, 年子 342, 利子 436, 甫子 533, 佝子 562, 祀子 640, 季子 725, 俊子 1039, 淑子 1335, 敏子 1409, 鈊子 1675, 舜子 2017, 銅子 2341, 齢子 2766
Toshikoto *m* 利功 436
Toshima *s* 戸島 59, 外島 139, 敏馬 1409; *sp* 豊島 2013; *p* 十島 18, 利島 436
Toshimaru *m* 俊丸 1039

Toshimasa *m* 利理 436, 俊懋 1039, 憲正 2562
Toshimasu *m* 利太 436
Toshimatsu *m* 寿松 539
Toshime *m* 俊馬 1039
Toshimi *m* 利見 436
Toshimichi *m* 平道 203, 利通 436
Toshimitsu *sm* 利光; *m* 英光 693
Toshimochi *m* 利以 436
Toshimori *m* 俊豊 1039
Toshimoto *m* 利初 436, 利躬, 俊基 1039
Toshimune *m* 俊順
Toshina *s* 豊階 2013
Toshinaga *m* 代長 125, 寿 539, 寿命, 俊久 1039, 者長 1214
Toshinaka *m* 利極 436
Toshinao *m* 利亨
Toshinari *m* 利克, 利為; *ml* 俊成 1039
～ no Musume *fl* 俊成女
Toshinaru *m* 俊親
Toshinobu *m* 勇宜 908, 俊信 1039, 俊将, 憲信 2562
Toshinori *m* 利制 436, 利謙, 寿修 539, 寿格, 和徳 638, 俊程 1039, 要範 1218
Toshio *s* 淑郎 1335; *m* 子男 38, 年魚 342, 利夫 436, 利雄, 佽男 561, 祀夫 640, 斉雄 701, 季雄 725, 勇夫 908, 俊士 1039, 俊夫, 俊雄, 健郎 1282, 敏男 1409, 敏郎, 逸雄 1504, 敬夫 1691, 稔男 1916, 穏雄 2492, 憙雄 2559, 駿男 2763
Toshioki *m* 夙興 299
Toshirō *m* 俊郎 1039, 惇郎 1288, 敏四郎 1409, 敏郎, 憙郎 2560
Tōshirō *m* 藤四郎 2773
Toshiroda *s* 十代田 18
Toshisada *m* 利定 436, 俊完 1039
Toshisane *m* 俊信
Toshishizu *m* 俊玄
To Shishun *mlh-l* "Tu Tzu-ch'un" 杜子春 423
Toshisuke *m* 年助 342, 資弼 2012
Toshitada *m* 利済 436, 利理, 俊政 1039
Toshitaka *m* 利誉 436, 淳高 1337
Toshitake *m* 俊雄 1039, 振武 1320
Toshitane *m* 利物 436
Toshitari *m* 稔足 1916
Toshitarō *m* 寿太郎 539
Toshitatsu *m* 年立 342
Toshito *m-f* 寿人 539
Toshitora *m* 利彪 436
Toshitsugu *m* 俊次 1039, 峻次 1591
Toshitsuna *m* 言綱 439, 寿縄 539, 等綱 1770
Toshitsune *m* 利幹 436
Toshitsura *m* 利位, 敏行 1409
Toshiwaza *m* 敏事
Toshiya *m* 俊弥 1039
Toshiyasu *m* 世安 335, 利考 436, 浰杢 1063
Toshiyo *m* 舜世 2017
Toshiyori *ml* 俊頼 1039
～ kudenshū *l* 俊頼口伝集 「無名抄
～ mumyōshō *l* 俊頼
～ zuinō *l* 俊頼髄脳
Toshiyoshi *m* 利和 436, 利可, 利美, 利温, 利徽, 俊義 1039, 俊賢, 俊懋, 駁栄 2171, 假儀 2434
Toshiyuki *m* 利行 436, 利通, 利随, 和孝 638, 敏行 1409
Toshizō *m* 利三 436, 順三 1532, 歳三 1995
Tōshūsai Sharaku *ma* 東洲斎写楽 771
Tōson *ml* 藤村 2773
Tosshin *s* 取石 650
Tosu *s* 鳥巣 1521; *p* 鳥栖
Tosuho *m* 十寸穂 18
Tōsuke *m* 藤助 2773
Tōta *m* 藤太
Tōtarō *m* 藤太郎
Tote *s* 栩 1095
Tōteru *m* 延光 739
(toto 十 18)
Totoki *s* 十木, 十時
Tōtōmi *ph* 遠江 2043
Totonō *m* 整 2581
Totori *s* 十鳥 18
Totsu *s* 戸津 59. (凸 323, 突 722, 咄 1046, 訥 1399)
Totsuka *s* 十束 18, 計束 895; *sp* 戸塚 59
Totsukawa *p* 十津川 18
Totsukuri *s* 土作 42
Tōtsuna *m* 玄綱 522
Tōtsuōmi *s* 遠江 2043, 遠淡海 「鳥取 1521
Tottori *s* 富取 1715; *sp*
(tou 問 1524) 「内 1744
Touchi *s* 土有知 42, 登
Tōwa *s* 唐和 1246; *p* 十和 18, 東和 771
Towada *sp* 十和田 18
～ Misao *ml* 十和田操
Towako *f* 永久子 149, 永遠子 「語 94
Towazu-gatari *l* 不問
Toya *s* 戸矢 59, 戸谷, 戸屋, 外谷 139
Tōya *s* 遠矢 2043; *p* 洞爺 821
Toyabe *s* 鳥谷部 1521
Toyama *s* 戸山 59, 外山 139, 登山 1744; *sp* 富山 1715
Tōyama *s* 当山 282, 東山 771, 遠山 2043, 頭山 2504
Toyama Chūzan *ml* 外山ゝ山 139
～ Masakazu *ml* 外山正一 「頭山満 2504
Tōyama Mitsuru *mh*
Toyama Usaburō *ml* 外山卯三郎 139
Toyasaka *p* 豊栄 2013
Toyo *s* 豊. (仁 57, 茂 691, 富 1715, 晨 1739, 豊 2013, 農 2205, 絜 2208)
Tōyō *p* 東洋 771, 東陽
Toyoake *p* 豊明 2013
Toyoaki *m* 豊秋
Toyochika *m* 豊雍
Toyoda *sp* 豊田
～ Saburō *ml* 豊田三郎
～ Sakichi *mh* 豊田佐 ∟吉
Toyofuku *s* 豊福
Toyoguchi *s* 豊口
Toyohama *p* 豊浜
Toyohara *s* 豊原
Toyohashi *p* 豊橋
Toyohatori *s* 豊綺
Toyohiko *m* 豊日子, 豊 ∟彦
Toyohira *p* 豊平
Toyohiro *m* 豊広
Toyohito *m* 茂仁 691
Toyoichirō *m* 豊一郎 2013
Toyoizumi *s* 豊泉
Toyoji *m* 豊次, 豊治
Toyojirō *m* 豊治郎
Toyoka *s* 十四日 18
Toyōka *s* 十八日
Toyokai *m* 豊穎 2013
Toyokawa *sp* 豊川
Toyokazu *m* 豊策
Toyokichi *m* 豊吉, 豊橘
Toyokoro *p* 豊頃
Toyokuni *ma* 豊国
Toyoma *s* 豊間; *sp* 登米 1744
Toyomasa *m* 豊昌 2013
Toyomatsu *p* 豊松
Toyomizu *s* 豊水
Toyomoto *s* 豊本; *m* 豊原
Toyomura *s* 豊村
Toyonaga *s* 豊永, 豊名賀
Toyonaka *p* 豊中
Toyone *p* 豊根
Toyono *sp* 豊野; *p* 豊能 「敷
Toyonobu *m* 豊信, 豊
Toyonori *m* 豊誠
Toyoo *m* 豊夫
Toyooka *sp* 豊岡; *p* 豊 ∟丘
Toyora *s* 豊浦
Toyosaburō *m* 豊三郎
Toyosaka *p* 豊栄
Toyosaki *s* 豊崎
Toyosaku *m* 豊作
Toyosato *p* 豊里, 豊郷
Toyoshige *m* 豊信
Toyoshima *s* 豊島; *sp* 十余島 18
～ Yoshio *ml* 豊島与志雄 2013 「豊科
Toyoshina *s* 豊階; *p*
Toyoshirō *m* 豊四郎
Toyosuke *m* 豊助
Toyota *s* 十代田 18; *sp* 豊田 2013; *m* 豊太
Toyotada *m* 豊産
Toyotaka *m* 豊隆
Toyotake *s* 豊竹
Toyotama *p* 豊玉
Toyotarō *m* 登代太郎 1744, 豊太郎 2013
Toyoteru *m* 豊煕

Toyotomi *s* 豊臣;*p* 豊富 「秀次
~ Hidetsugu *mh* 豊臣
~ Hideyoshi *mh* 豊臣秀吉
Toyotoshi *m* 豊俊
Toyotsu *p* 豊津
Toyoura *sp* 豊浦
Toyoyama *p* 豊山
Toyoyasu *m* 豊泰
Toyoyuki *m* 豊行, 豊恭
Toyoyuta *s* 豊饒
Toyozawa *s* 豊沢
Toyozumi *s* 豊住
Toyuke *s* 豊受
Tōzaburō *m* 藤三郎 2773
Tōzaka *s* 遠坂 2043
Tozaki *s* 土崎 42, 戸崎 59, 外崎 139
Tozakida *s* 土崎田 42
Tozawa *sp* 戸沢 59
Tōzō *m* 棟造 1627
Tozu *f* 登鶴 1744
Tsu *p* 津 826
(tsu 津, 桶 1369, 都 1419, 港 1583, 樋 2299, 藤 2773, 鶴 2926)
(tsū 通 1239)
(tsuba 椿 1895, 鐔 2882)
Tsubae *s* 椿紅 1895
Tsubai *s* 椿井
Tsubaki *f-p* 椿. (椿)
Tsubakimoto *s* 椿本
Tsubakitōge *p* 椿峠
Tsubame *f* 乙鳥 2; *p* 燕 2570
Tsubani *s* 椿紅 1895
Tsubara *m* 粲 2019
Tsubasa *m* 翼 2686
Tsubata *p* 津幡 826
Tsubaya *s* 鐔屋 2882
Tsube *s* 津辺 826
Tsubetsu *p* 津別
Tsubo *s* 答本 1765. (坪 575, 壺 2183)
Tsubogami *s* 坪上 575
Tsubohira *m* 坪平
Tsuboi *s* 坪井, 壺井 2183
~ Sakae *fl* 壺井栄
~ Shigeji *ml* 壺井繁治
~ Shōgorō *mh* 坪井正五郎 575
Tsubokawa *s* 坪川
Tsuboki *s* 坪木
Tsubokura *s* 坪倉
Tsubomi *s* 四月一日 188; *f* 莟 1172
Tsubone *f* 局 514
Tsubono *s* 坪野 575
~ Tekkyū *ml* 坪野哲久 「2183
Tsubota *s* 坪田, 壺田
~ Hanako *fl* 壺田花子
~ Jōji *ml* 坪田譲治 575
Tsubouchi *s* 坪内, 壺内 2183 「575
~ Shikō *ml* 坪内士行
~ Shōyō *ml* 坪内逍遙
Tsuboya *s* 坪谷
Tsuboyama *s* 坪山
(tsubu 粒 1389)
Tsubuki *s* 津吹 826
Tsubuku *s* 津布久
Tsubukumi *s* 積組 2493
Tsubura *s* 粒良 1389, 螺良 2805; *sm* 円 78
Tsuburai *s* 円井, 隆来 1313
Tsuburaya *s* 円谷 78
Tsuchi *f* 壌 2602. (土 42, 地 241, 盈 1200, 椎 1629, 槌 2102, 鎚 2749)
Tsuchida *s* 土田 42, 槌田 2102 「村 42
~ Kyōson *ml* 土田杏
~ Kōhei *ml* 土田耕平
Tsuchido *s* 土戸
Tsuchie *s* 土江
Tsuchigami *s* 土上
Tsuchigo *s* 土御
Tsuchigorō *m* 槌五郎 2102 「42
Tsuchigumo *la* 土蜘蛛
Tsuchigura *s* 土蔵
Tsuchiguruma *la* 土車
Tsuchihashi *s* 土橋
Tsuchii *s* 土井
Tsuchikado *s* 土門
Tsuchikawa *s* 土川
Tsuchiko *s* 土子
Tsuchikura *s* 土倉
Tsuchimi *s* 土水
Tsuchimikado *mh* 土御門
Tsuchimochi *s* 土持
Tsuchimoto *s* 土本
Tsuchimura *s* 土村
Tsuchino *s* 土野
Tsuchinosuke *m* 鎚之助 2749
Tsuchito *m* 土人 42
Tsuchitsukuri *m* 土作
Tsuchiura *sp* 土浦
Tsuchiya *s* 土谷, 土屋, 槌谷 2102
~ Bunmei *ml* 土屋文明 42 「雨
~ Chikuu *ml* 土屋竹
Tsuchiyama *sp* 土山
Tsuchizawa *s* 土沢
Tsuda *p* 津田 826
Tsudaka *p* 津高
Tsudake *s* 都竹 1419
Tsuda Mamichi *ml* 津田真道 826
~ Seifū *ml* 津田青風
~ Sōkichi *mlh* 津田左右吉
~ Umeko *fh* 津田梅子
Tsudo *s* 津戸
Tsudoi *m* 集 1779
Tsudome *s* 津留 826
Tsue *sp* 津江. (杖 422)
Tsuebe *s* 杖部
Tsūen *la* 通円 1239
Tsuga *sp* 都賀 1419; *p* 筒賀 1818. (樛 2290)
Tsugai *s* 番 1773
Tsugako *f* 樛子 2290
Tsugami *s* 津上 826
Tsugane *s* 津金
Tsugao *m* 都賀夫 1419
Tsugaru *sp-l* 津軽 826
Tsuga Teishō *ml* 都賀庭鐘 1419
Tsugawa *sp* 津川 826
Tsuge *s* 津下, 柘植 864, 黄楊 1499; *sp* 柘 864; *p* 都祁 1419. (告 490)
Tsugegaki *s* 柘垣 864
Tsugemori *s* 告森 490
Tsūgen sōmagaki *l* 通言総籬 1239
Tsugeo *m* 黄楊夫 1499
Tsugi *m* 二 4. (乙 2, 二 4, 月 80, 次 226, 存 313, 世 335, 亜 525, 承 760, 弟 764, 良 767, 系 977, 速 1237, 連 1238, 胤 1269, 族 1343, 副 1428, 著 1445, 接 1548, 番 1773, 嗣 1937, 紹 1955, 衝 2264, 調 2328, 続 2334, 継 2539, 緝 2658, 襲 2983)
Tsugihiro *m* 緝熙 2658
Tsugihito *m* 継人 2539
Tsugiji *f* 継路
Tsugikaze *ma* 亜風 525
Tsugiko *f* 亜子, 紹子 1955, 緝子 2658
Tsugimitsu *m* 次光 226
Tsuginobu *m* 二葉 4, 次信 226, 続信 2334, 継信 2539
Tsugio *m* 乙男 2, 二男 4, 次雄 226, 存男 313, 亜夫 525, 紹雄 1955
Tsugioki *m* 調興 2328
Tsugisada *m* 嗣定 1937
Tsugishige *m* 世茂 335
Tsugisho *s* 杤折 419
Tsugita *s* 次田 226
Tsugitake *m* 嗣武 1937
Tsugitsukai *s* 調使 2328
Tsugiyoshi *m* 次義 226, 世吉 335
Tsugizō *m* 続蔵 2334
Tsugu *m* 纘 3019; *f* 緝 2658; *p* 津具 826. (二 4, 子 38, 壬 116, 次 226, 世 335, 伝 359, 告 490, 序 507, 亜 525, 知 636, 受 730, 庚 741, 承 760, 倢 1030, 倫 1037, 従 1050, 貢 1166, 胤 1269, 族 1343, 晧 1355, 訳 1402, 紀 1424, 著 1445, 接 1548, 報 1667, 番 1773, 禎 1887, 嗣 1937, 紹 1955, 蒸 1981, 漸 2081, 頌 2113, 語 2136, 誥 2140, 説 2143, 静 2145, 韶 2163, 調 2328, 続 2334, 懌 2439, 論 2510, 緒 2537, 継 2539, 臧 2595, 講 2644, 緝 2658, 鞠 2664, 麗 2902, 繹 2924, 繩 2955, 繋 2959)
Tsuguoki *m* 晧章 1355
Tsuguakira *m* 承昭 760
Tsuguchika *m* 亜周 525
Tsuguhiko *m* 亜彦
Tsuguhito *m* 世仁 335, 紹仁 1955 「359
Tsugujirō *m* 伝二郎
Tsuguko *f* 韶子 2163, 継子 2539
Tsugumi *s* 積組 2493
Tsugumichi *m* 従道 1050
Tsugumitsu *m* 承叙 760
Tsugumo *s* 白 216
Tsugumune *m* 紹念 1955

Tsugunobu *m* 継述 2539, 継信
Tsugunori *m* 世徳 335, 従矩 1050
Tsugunosuke *m* 継之助 2539 「男 2539
Tsuguo *m* 嗣夫 1937, 継
Tsugutamuro *m* 継屯
Tsuguyori *m* 嗣頼 1937
Tsuguyoshi *m* 世誠 335
Tsuhara *s* 津原 826
Tsuho *s* 答本 1765
Tsui *s* 津井 826. (追 993, 堆 1295, 椎 1629, 槌 2102, 築 2575, 鎚 2749)
Tsuihiji *s* 六十里 61
Tsuiji *sp* 築地 2575
Tsuiki *s* 立木 194, 築城 2575 「栖 1950
Tsui no sumika *l* 終の
Tsuishine *s* 舂米 1460
Tsuishu *sm* 堆朱 1295
Tsuishuya *s* 堆朱屋
Tsuji *s* 十字 18, 辻 320, 都路 1419. (辻 320, 逵 1813) 「320
Tsuji basha *l* 辻馬車
Tsujibashi *s* 辻橋
Tsujihara *s* 辻原
Tsujii *s* 辻井
Tsuji Jun *ml* 辻潤
Tsujikawa *s* 辻川
Tsujiko *f* 辻子
Tsujimoto *s* 辻元, 辻本
Tsujimura *s* 辻村, 逵邑 1813
Tsujino *s* 辻野 320
Tsujioka *s* 辻岡
Tsujisawa *s* 辻沢
Tsujita *s* 辻田
Tsujiuchi *s* 辻内
(tsuka 束 536, 柄 862, 恭 1205, 策 1767, 塚 1844, 墓 1979, 緑 2535)
Tsukada *s* 束田 536, 塚田 1844
Tsukae *m* 恭兄 1205
Tsukagoe *s* 塚越 1844
Tsukaguchi *s* 塚口
Tsukahara *s* 束原 536, 塚原 1844
Tsukahira *s* 塚平
～ Jūshien *ml* 塚平渋柿園
Tsukaihatashite nibu kyōgen *l* 尽用二分狂言 290
Tsukamachi *s* 筑摩地 1771
Tsukamoto *s* 塚本 1844
Tsukane *m* 束 536, 束稲, 緯 2744
Tsukano *s* 塚野 1844
Tsukanu *m* 束 536
Tsukasa *s* 政 881; *m* 工 39, 士 41, 元 60, 仕 124, 仟 130, 司 164, 主 196, 任 235, 吏 329, 佰 554, 典 733, 良 767, 長 939, 師 1130, 宰 1180
Tsukasagi *s* 司城 164
Tsukase *s* 塚瀬 1844
Tsukatani *s* 塚谷
Tsukawaki *s* 塚脇
Tsukazaki *s* 塚崎
Tsukazuki *s* 調月 2328
(tsuke 付 126)
Tsukechi *p* 付知
Tsuki *s* 大月 48, 調伎 2328, 築城 2575; *m* 月 80; *f* 都生 1419, 調 2328. (坏 388, 舂 1460, 第 1768, 終 1950, 槻 2295, 調 2328, 築 2575)
Tsukida *s* 月田 80
Tsukidate *sp* 月館; *p* 築館 2575
Tsukigase *s* 月瀬 80
Tsukigata *sp* 月形, 月潟
Tsukihiko *m* 月彦
Tsukii *s* 月井
Tsukiji *p* 築地 2575
Tsukiko *f* 槻子 2295
Tsukikusa *l* 月草 80
Tsukimaro *m* 月満
Tsukimori *s* 月森
Tsukimoto *s* 月本, 槻本 2295
Tsukimura *s* 月村 80
Tsukinao *s* 月直
Tsukinoe *m* 月野柄
Tsukinokawa *s* 調川 2328
Tsukinowa *s* 月輪 80
Tsukioka *s* 月岡
Tsukisaranoki *s* 都岐沙羅柵 1419
Tsukise *sp* 月瀬 80
Tsukishima *s* 月島
Tsukishine *s* 舂米 1460
Tsukitate *p* 月館 80
Tsukitsukuri *s* 坏作 388
Tsukiyama *s* 筑山 1771, 築山 2575
Tsukiyasu *s* 月安 80
Tsukiyono *p* 月夜野
Tsukiyoshi *m* 月良
Tsukizaki *s* 月崎
Tsukizuki *s* 調月 2328
Tsukō *m* 仕 124, 伻 356, 孝 541
Tsuku *s* 即 648, 柘 864. (突 722, 柘 864, 委 960, 皖 1639, 証 1660, 筑 1771, 遂 1806, 衝 2264, 附 2347, 箸 2381, 築 2575) 「1771
Tsukuba *sm-p* 筑波
～ mondō *l* 筑波問答
Tsukubashū *l* 菟玖波集 1729
Tsukube *s* 築部 2575
Tsukubo *p* 都窪 1419
Tsukubōsen *l* 突棒船 722
Tsukuda *sm* 佃 352
Tsukude *p* 作手 362
Tsukui *s* 筑井 1771; *sp* 津久井 826
Tsukumi *p* 津久見
Tsukumo *sm-f-p* 九十九 16
Tsukuna *s* 無尽 1789
Tsukureshima *s* 壊島 ⌊2602
(tsukuri 作 362)
Tsukuru *m* 作
Tsukushi *s* 竹志 247, 竺志 729; *sph* 筑紫 1771
～ dōki *l* 筑紫道記
～ no oku *l* 筑紫奥
Tsukuyama *s* 筑山
Tsuma *f* 津摩 826; *p* 都万 1419. (妻 959, 孀 2718)
Tsumagari *s* 津曲 826
Tsumagi *s* 妻木 959
Tsumago *s* 妻籠
Tsumagoi *p* 嬬恋 2718
Tsumagoiyuki *la* 妻恋行 959 「1981
Tsumaki *s* 妻木; *m* 蒸
Tsumako *f* 妻子 959
Tsumatakumi *s* 爪工 115
Tsumatani *s* 妻谷 959
(tsume 爪 115)
Tsumeiro no ame *l* 爪色の雨
Tsumetakumi *s* 爪工
(tsumi 租 1116, 祇 1127, 罪 2006, 摘 2066, 積 2493)
Tsumida *s* 積田
Tsumie *s* 柘植 864
Tsumiyama *s* 罪山 2006
Tsumoi *s* 千万億 44
Tsumori *s* 津守 826, 都守 1419
Tsumoru *s* 千万億 44, 百千万億 265; *m* 万 43, 積 2493
Tsumoto *s* 津本 826, 港元 1583
(tsumu 万 43, 恪 803, 紡 1681, 聚 2221, 積 2493, 諶 2641)
(tsumugi 紬 1951)
Tsumugiko *f* 紬子
Tsumugu *m* 績 2814
Tsumuji *s* 街風 1570
Tsumuko *f* 紡子 1681
Tsumura *s* 津村 826
～ Hideo *ml* 津村秀夫
～ Nobuo *ml* 津村信夫
Tsumuraya *s* 円谷 78
Tsuna *sm* 綱 2661; *p* 津名 826. (之 24, 卓 660, 是 947, 倬 1027, 紀 1424, 斯 1670, 道 1811, 純 1956, 茲 1987, 詔 2163, 統 2333, 緑 2535, 維 2540, 綱 2661, 纒 2955, 繫 2959) 「1811
Tsunachiyo *m* 道千代
Tsunade *m* 綱手 2661
Tsunagawa *s* 綱川
Tsunagi *p* 津奈木 826
Tsunagu *m* 維 2540
Tsunahiro *m* 維大
Tsunahito *m* 詔仁 2163
Tsunajima *s* 綱島 2661
～ Ryōsen *ml* 綱島梁川
Tsunako *f* 維子 2540, 綱子 2661, 繫子 2959
Tsunami *s* 都並 1419
Tsunan *p* 津南 826
Tsunano *s* 綱野 2661
Tsunanori *m* 綱紀
Tsunao *m* 紀雄 1424
Tsunashige *m* 維重 2540
Tsunayuki *m* 純如 1956
Tsune *m* 恒 809, 法 824, 常 1463; *m-f* 彝 2943. (凡 37, 久 45, 方 85, 比 137, 永 149, 平 203, 式

306, 村 424, 毎 444, 序 507, 玄 522, 寿 539, 実 678, 英 693, 昔 699, 典 733, 恒 809, 法 824, 治 825, 則 902, 長 939, 倫 1037, 矩 1108, 秩 1119, 盈 1200, 常 1463, 庸 1507, 尋 1705, 曾 1794, 道 1811, 雅 1913, 幹 1938, 経 1957, 愛 2018, 歴 2247, 統 2333, 積 2493, 継 2539, 懐 2605, 職 2734, 鎮 2751, 識 2810, 彝 2943, 縄 2955)

Tsuneaki *m* 典明 733, 常晨 1463, 経甄 1957, 経顕 「経明 1957

Tsuneakira *m* 恒明 809,

Tsuneari *m* 恒存 809

Tsuneda *s* 常田 1463

Tsuneeda *m* 恒柯 809

Tsunegawa *s* 恒川, 恒河, 常川 1463

Tsunegi *s* 常木

Tsuneharu *m* 玄治 522, 経治 1957

Tsunehei *m* 恒平 809

Tunehiko *m* 常彦 1463

Tunehisa *m* 常久

Tsunei *s* 常井

Tsuneie *m* 経家 1957

Tsuneizumi *s* 常泉 1463

Tsuneji *m* 毎治 444

Tsunejirō *m* 恒二郎 809, 恒次郎, 矩次郎 1108, 常次郎 1463, 雅二郎 1913 「倫方 1037

Tsunekata *m* 恒堅 809,

Tsunekatsu *m* 序克 507

Tsunekawa *s* 常川 1463, 雅川 1913

~ Hiroshi *ml* 雅川滉

Tsunekazu *m* 長一 939, 統一 2333

Tsuneki *s* 常木 1463

Tsunekichi *m* 恒吉 809, 常吉 1463

Tsunekiyo *m* 恒清 809

Tsuneko *f* 凡子 37, 典子 733, 恒子 809, 常子 1463, 庸子 1507, 識子 2810

Tsunemaro *m* 則麿 902

Tsunematsu *s* 恒松 809, 常松 1463

Tsunemi *s* 常見, 常深; *m* 恒心 809

Tsunemichi *s* 経道 1957

Tsunemitsu *m* 序光 507, 常光 1463

Tsunemochi *m* 常操

Tsunemoto *m* 恒心 809, 経孟 1957, 経幹

Tsunena *m* 常那 1463

Tsunenaga *sm* 恒良 809; *m* 常誠 1463

Tsunenao *m* 常尚

Tsunenari *m* 経済 1957

Tsunenobu *ml* 経信

Tsunenori *m* 常憲 1463, 曾益 1794, 経式 1957, 経教

Tsuneo *m* 凡夫 37, 恒夫 809, 恒雄, 矩夫 1108, 秩夫 1119, 道夫 1811, 常隆 1463, 常雄, 庸夫 1507, 庸雄, 経夫 1957, 経綸, 職男 2734, 彝雄 2943

Tsuneoka *s* 常岡 1463

Tsunesaburō *m* 常三郎

Tsunesada *m* 恒貞 809

Tsunesaku *m* 常作 1463

Tsuneshichi *m* 恒七 809

Tsuneshige *m* 常栄 1463

Tsunesue *m* 長季 939

Tsunesumi *p* 常澄 1463

Tsuneta *s* 常田; *m* 恒太 809, 常太 1463

Tsunetada *m* 経雅 1957

Tsunetaka *m* 庸嵩 1507

Tsunetami *m* 常民 1463

Tsunetarō *m* 恒太郎 809, 庸太郎 1507

Tsuneteru *m* 雅光 1913, 経輝 1957 「人 444

Tsuneto *m* 凡人 37, 毎

Tsunetō *s* 恒藤 809

Tsunetoki *m* 常晨 1463, 経則 1957

Tsunetomi *s* 恒富 809

Tsunetomo *m* 常伴 1463, 常孟, 庸公 1507

Tsunetoshi *m* 典暁 733

Tsunetsugu *m* 常次 1463

Tsuneya *s* 恒屋 809; *m* 平也 203, 雅也 1913

Tsuneyama *s* 常山 1463

Tsuneyasu *m* 毎保 444, 経慰 1957, 鎮静 2751

Tsuneyoshi *sm* 恒吉 809, 常賀 1463; *m* 恒徳 809

Tsuneyuki *m* 恒之, 恒幸

Tsunezō *m* 平生三 203, 恒三 809, 常造 1463

Tsuno *s* 角 547, 津野 826, 都努 1419; *sp* 都濃. (角 547)

Tsunoda *s* 角田

Tsunoi *s* 角井, 都野井 1419 「826

Tsunomiya *s* 津ノ宮

Tsunomura *s* 角村 547

Tsunoo *s* 角尾

Tsunoori *s* 角折

Tsunoru *m* 募 1718

Tsunowa *s* 角和 547

Tsunu *s* 角. (角)

Tsunuga *s* 角鹿; *ph* 角我 「宿禰

Tsununosukune *m* 角

Tsura *s* 連 1238; *m* 貫 1754. (正 205, 行 245, 列 257, 位 354, 役 368, 享 662, 定 677, 忠 705, 面 904, 宣 919, 系 977, 貞 982, 倩 1031, 陣 1056, 班 1075, 般 1137, 茄 1171, 烈 1211, 連 1238, 偏 1273, 陳 1311, 寅 1439, 常 1463, 接 1548, 貫 1754, 番 1773, 属 1802, 葛 1994, 璉 2285, 諸 2329, 頬 2503, 綿 2538, 離 2889, 麗 2902, 繹 2934, 羅 2937, 聯 2948, 鬘 2979)

Tsurahara *s* 黒葛原 1486

Tsurahide *m* 連英 1238

Tsuraki *m* 列樹 257

Tsurako *f* 列子, 連子 1238

Tsuranaga *m* 貫長 1754

Tsurane *m* 聯 2948

Tsurayuki *m* 面幸 904; *ml* 貫之 1754

Tsureyama *s* 連山 1238

Tsurezuregusa *l* 徒然草 1048

(tsuri 釣 1416)

Tsuribune *s* 釣船

Tsurigitsune *la* 釣狐

Tsuru *s* 津留 826, 鶴 2926; *sp* 都留 1419. (弦 1345, 釣 1416, 敦 1690, 蔓 2192, 絃 2331, 鉉 2335, 鶴 2926, 靍 3022)

Tsurubami *l* 橡 2478

Tsurubuchi *s* 鶴淵 2926

Tsurudo *m* 鶴所

Tsurudono *s* 鶴殿

Tsuruga *s* 鶴賀; *sp* 敦賀 1690

Tsurugaoka *s* 鶴岡 2926

Tsurugasai *m* 鶴賀斎

Tsurugashima *p* 鶴ケ島 「1151)

Tsurugi *p* 鶴来. (剣

Tsuruhachi *s* 鶴八 2926

~ Tsurujirō *l* 鶴八鶴次郎

Tsuruhara *s* 鶴原

Tsuruhashi *s* 鶴橋

Tsuruhe *s* 綴喜 2530

Tsuruheiji *s* 二十里 4

Tsuruhiko *m* 弦彦 1345, 弦孫

Tsurui *s* 敦井 1690; *f* 鶴集 2926; *p* 鶴居

Tsuruichi *m* 鶴一

Tsurujirō *m* 鶴二郎

Tsurukai *s* 鶴貝, 鶴飼

Tsurukame *la* 鶴亀

Tsurukawa *s* 鶴川

Tsuruki *s* 弦木 1345

Tsurukichi *m* 鶴吉 2926

Tsuruko *f* 釣子 1416, 蔓子 2192, 鉉子 2335

Tsuruma *s* 鶴間 2926

Tsurumaki *s* 弦巻 1345, 鶴巻 2926

Tsurumaru *s* 水流丸 54, 鶴丸 2926

Tsurumatsu *m* 鶴松

Tsurumi *sp* 鶴見

Tsurumine *s* 鶴峰

Tsurumi Yūsuke *ml* 鶴見祐輔

Tsurumoto *s* 鶴本

Tsurumura *m* 鶴群

Tsuruno *s* 鶴野

Tsurunoto *m* 鶴ノ門

Tsuruo *m* 弦男 1345, 敦男 1690, 絃夫 2331, 鶴雄 2926, 靍雄 3022

Tsuruoka *sp* 鶴岡 2926

Tsurusaburō *m* 鶴三郎

Tsurushi *s* 九十九院 16, 四十九員 188, 四十四院

Tsuruta *sp* 鶴田 2926

~ Tomoya *ml* 鶴田知也

Tsuruya *s* 鶴屋, 鶴谷

～ Nanboku *ml* 鶴谷南北
Tsuruzaki *s* 鶴崎
Tsuruzawa *s* 鶴沢
Tsuruzō *m* 鶴三, 鶴造
Tsusaka *s* 津阪 826
Tsushi *s* 桶師 1369
Tsushima *sp* 対馬 405, 津島 826 「405
～ Kanji *ml* 対島完治
Tsushita *s* 津下 826
Tsuta *s* 蔦 2196. (伝 359, 蔦 2196)
Tsutae *m* 伝 359
Tsutahiko *m* 伝彦
Tsutaki *s* 蔦木 2196
Tsutamatsu *m* 蔦松
Tsuta momiji Utsunoya tōge *la* 蔦紅葉宇都谷峠
Tsutamoto *s* 蔦本
Tsutaya *s* 蔦屋
Tsutazawa *s* 蔦沢
Tsuto *s* 都刀 1419. (夙 299, 朝 1672)
Tsutō *m* 伝 359
Tsutomi *s* 都富 1419
Tsutomu *m* 力 11, 工 39, 仂 55, 功 135, 司 164, 伝 359, 孜 377, 孜 378, 励 430, 劼 652, 孟 667, 忞 702, 努 728, 事 768, 恪 803, 勉 1008, 格 1099, 耕 1131, 剣 1151, 釗 1152, 拳 1206, 勉 1263, 務 1377, 敏 1409, 乾 1411, 勔 1425, 勗 1455, 朝武 1672, 敦 1690, 勤 1698, 強 1878, 義 1975, 慗 2031, 奨 2036, 精 2131, 督 2226, 黽 2249, 勲 2407, 魁 2423, 薫 2567, 邁 2592, 彊 2621, 懃 2699, 懋 2700, 墾 2702, 騖 2847, 疆 2873, 疊 2932; *f* 劭 429
Tsutori *s* 都鳥 1419
(tsutsu 土 42, 廿 102)
Tsutsui *s* 筒井 1818, 筒居
Tsutsumi *s* 堤 1557; *m* 土巳 42, 塘 1842. (提 1557) 「言
～ Chūnagon *l* 堤中納
Tsutsumu *m* 温 1585
Tsutsuyama *s* 廿山 102
Tsuuchi *s* 津打 826
～ Jihee *ml* 津打治兵衛
Tsuwano *p* 津和野
Tsuya *s* 津谷; *f* 釉 1653, 艶 2833. (婉 1600, 艶 2833) 「艶子 2833
Tsuyako *f* 婉子 1600,
Tsuyama *sp* 津山 826
Tsuyata *m* 艶太 2833
Tsuyazaki *s* 津屋崎 826
Tsuyo *f* 鶴齢 2926. (烈 1211, 威 1251, 健 1282, 務 1377, 剛 1429, 強 1878, 張 1879, 豪 2177, 毅 2351, 厳 2706)
Tsuyoki *m* 毅 2351
Tsuyoo *m* 豪雄 2177
Tsuyoshi *m* 丁 8, 劤 253, 侃 551, 勅 651, 耐 884, 倞 1024, 勍 1150, 勉 1008, 健 1282, 健志, 剛 1429, 彪 1523, 勁 1697A, 堅 1796, 強 1878, 幹 1938, 鉅 1946, 豪 2177, 毅 2351 「(露 2941)
Tsuyu *s* 栗花落 1219.
Tsuyudandan *l* 露団々
Tsuyuguchi *s* 露口
Tsuyuhara *sl* 露原
Tsuyuhiji *s* 二十五里 4
Tsuyuka *f* 露香 2941
Tsuyuki *s* 露木
Tsuyuko *f* 露子
Tsuyu kosode mukashi hachijō *la* 梅雨小袖昔八丈 1374
Tsuyukubo *s* 露久保 2941
Tsuyu no Gorobee *ml* 露五郎兵衛
Tsuyuo *m* 栗花生 1219
Tsuyuri *s* 栗花落
Tsuyusaki *s* 露崎 2941
Tsuzaki *s* 津崎 826, 都崎 1419
Tsuzu *s* 通津 1239. (廿 102, 綴 2530)
Tsuzuki *s* 都筑 1419, 都築, 続 2334, 続木, 綴 2530; *sp* 綴喜; *m* 胤 1269, 統 2333 「1419
～ Shōgo *ml* 都築省吾
Tsuzuku *m-f* 続 2334
Tsuzumi *s* 都住 1419, 鼓 1959; *sf* 都都美 1419
～ Tsuneyoshi *ml* 鼓常良 1959
Tsuzume *s* 津爪 826
Tsuzura *s* 廿楽 102
Tsuzurabumi *l* 藤簍冊子 2773
Tsuzurahara *s* 黒葛原 1486, 葛原 1994
Tsuzuya *s* 廿屋 102

# U

(u 又 13, 于 25, 友 70, 打 136, 右 171, 生 214, 羽 246, 卯 259, 宇 285, 芋 288, 有 303, 佑 364, 兎 544, 侑 557, 於 607, 雨 759, 兎 763, 祐 852, 宥 918, 囿 990, 禹 1015, 栩 1095, 烏 1256, 得 1299, 翁 1430, 菀 1729, 蓊 2189, 優 2599, 鮪 2669, 鵜 2822, 鷗 2975)
(uba 姥 1090)
Ubagae *s* 祖母江 850
Ubagai *s* 祖母井
Ubagatani 雲母谷 2027
Ubaguchi *sp* 右左口 171
Ubai *s* 祖母井 850
Ubakai *s* 右馬飼 171
Ubara *f* 楚 2022, 茨 932
Ubaraki *s* 茨木
Ubari *s* 牛尿 111
Ubayaki *s* 姥沢 1090
Ube *p* 宇部 285
Ubeyama *s* 道理山 1811
(ubu 生 214, 幼 428, 産
Ubuga *s* 産賀 ⌊1520)
Ubukata *s* 生方 214, 生形, 幼方 428
～ Tatsue *fl* 生方たつゑ 214 「郎
～ Toshirō *ml* 生方敏
Ubumeki *s* 産婦木 1520
Ubuuchi *s* 生内 214
Ubuyama *p* 産山 1520
Uchi *p* 宇智 285. (中 75, 内 81, 打 136, 尉 1410, 奥 1798, 蔚 2191, 管 2212, 鬱 3011)
Uchibori *s* 内堀 81
Uchida *s* 内田, 打宅 136; *sp* 打田
～ Ginzō *mh* 内田銀蔵 81 「百閒
～ Hyakken *ml* 内田
～ Kōsai *mh* 内田康哉
～ Roan *ml* 内田魯庵
～ Senzan *ml* 内田沾山
Uchigaki *s* 内垣
Uchigasaki *s* 内ケ崎
Uchigikishū *l* 打聞集 136
Uchigō *sp* 内郷 81
Uchihara *sp* 内原
Uchiichi *s* 打越 136
Uchiike *s* 内池 81
Uchijima *s* 内島
Uchikake *l* 裲襠 1906
Uchikata *s* 内方 81
Uchikawa *s* 内川
Uchiki *s* 内木, 内樹, 打木 136
Uchiko *sp* 内子 81; *f* 有智子 303
Uchikoga *s* 内古閑 81
Uchikoshi *s* 打越 136
Uchikura *s* 内蔵 81; *sm* 内倉
Uchimaro *m* 内麿
Uchimaru *sm* 内丸
Uchimoto *s* 内本
Uchimura *s* 内村
～ Kanzō *ml* 内村鑑三
～ Naoya *ml* 内村直也
Uchinada *p* 内灘
Uchino *s* 内野, 海野 1071 「81
Uchinokura *s* 内野倉
Uchinuma *s* 内沼
Uchisaki *m* 内前
Uchisato *sm* 内郷
Uchishi *s* 越石 2052
Uchishika *s* 内芝 81
Uchito mōde *la* 内外詣
Uchiume *s* 内梅
Uchiumi *sp* 内海
Uchiura *sp* 内浦
Uchiya *s* 打矢 136

Uchiyama *s* 中山 75, 内山 81
~ Kanzō *ml* 内山完造
Uchizaki *s* 内崎
Uda *s* 打宅 136, 宇田 285, 兎太 763, 雨田 759; *smh* 宇多 285; *sp* 宇陀
Udagawa *s* 宇田川, 宇多川 「文海
~ Bunkai *ml* 宇田川
~ Genshin *mh* 宇田川玄真 「玄随
~ Genzui *mh* 宇田川
~ Yōan *mh* 宇田川榕
Udaka *s* 宇高 ⌊庵
Udamohitoribe *s* 菟田主水部 1729
Udano *p* 菟田野
Udanosakabe *s* 宇陀酒部 285
Uda Reiu *ml* 宇田零雨
Udaru *m* 宇陀児
Ude *s* 右手 171
Udeshi *s* 打越 136
Udo *s* 有渡 303
Udō *s* 右働 171, 右遠, 有動 303, 有働
Udono *sp* 鵜殿 2822
Ue *s* 於 607, 表 914; *sp* 上 47. (高 1163, 殖 1867,
Ueba *s* 植場 ⌊植 1902)
Uechi *s* 上地 47
Ueda *s* 殖田 1867, 植田 1902; *sp* 上田 47
~ Akinari *ml* 上田秋成
~ Bin *ml* 上田敏
~ Boku *ml* 上田穆
~ Hideo *ml* 上田英夫
~ Hiroshi *ml* 上田広
~ Juzō *ml* 植田寿蔵 1902
~ Kazutoshi *ml* 上田万年 47 「年
~ Mannen *ml* 上田万
~ Susumu *ml* 上田進
Uedōno *s* 上遠野
Uegaki *s* 上垣
Uehara *s* 上原, 植原 1902 「作 47
~ Yūsaku *mh* 上原勇
Uehata *s* 上畠
Uehira *s* 上平
Uei *s* 植井 1902 「1902
Uejima *s* 上島 47, 植島
Uekawa *s* 上川 47
Ueki *s* 上木; *sp* 植木 1902 「盛
~ Emori *mlh* 植木枝
Uekura *s* 上倉 47
Uekuri *s* 植栗 1902
Uekusa *s* 植草
Uematsu *s* 植松; *sp* 上松 47 「1902
~ Hisaki *ml* 植松寿樹
Uemi *s* 上見 47
Uemon *m* 右衛門 171
Uemonjō *m* 右衛門尉
Uemori *s* 上森 47
Uemoto *s* 上本, 植本 1902 「村 1902
Uemura *s* 上村 47, 植
~ Masahisa *mlh* 植村正久 「47
~ Shōen *fa* 上村松園
~ Tai *ml* 植村諦 1902
Uenaka *s* 上中 47, 植中 1902
Uenishi *s* 上西 47
Ueno *s* 上埜, 植野 1902; *sp* 上野 47
Uenohara *sp* 上野原
Ueno Takeo *ml* 上野壮夫
Uenoyama *s* 上野山
Uenuma *s* 上沼
Ueoka *s* 上岡
Ueru *m* 栽 1254
Uesaka *s* 上坂 47
Uesaki *s* 上崎
Uesugi *s* 上杉
~ Harumori *mh* 上杉治憲 「景勝
~ Kagekatsu *mh* 上杉
~ Kenshin *mh* 上杉謙信 「憲政
~ Norimasa *mh* 上杉
~ Norizane *mh* 上杉憲実 「重房
~ Shigefusa *mh* 上杉
~ Shinkichi *mh* 上杉慎吉 「憲
~ Ujinori *mh* 上杉氏
Uetake *s* 上竹, 植竹 1902
Uetani *s* 上谷 47
Uetsuka *s* 上塚
Uetsuki *s* 殖月 1867, 植月 1902 「山 1902
Ueyama *s* 上山 47, 植
Ueyanagi *s* 上柳 47, 植柳 1902
Uezawa *s* 上沢 47
Uezono *s* 上園
Uga *s* 宇賀 285
Ugaki *s* 宇垣 「一成
~ Kazushige *mh* 宇垣
Ugawa *s* 宇川, 鵜川 2822
Ugaya *s* 烏賀陽 1256
Ugayo *s* 烏賀陽
Ugetsu *l* 雨月 759
Ugo *p* 羽後 246
Ugō *s* 宇郷 285
Ugoshi *s* 打越 136
(uguisu 鶯 2940)
Uguisudani *p* 鶯谷
Uguisusawa *p* 鶯沢
Uhara *s* 兎原 763
Uhashi *s* 宇橋 285
Uheiji *m* 宇平治
Ui *s* 宇井
Uichi *m* 右一 171, 卯一 259, 宇一 285
Uiin *p* "Vienna" 維也納 2540
Uio *m* 有為男 303
Uirō *s* 陳外郎 1311
Uirōuri *la* 外郎売 139
Uiyamabumi *l* 初山踏 427
Uji *s* 菟道 1729; *sp* 宇治 285. (氏 223, 姓 846, 桓 1100, 項 1543)
Ujiaki *m* 氏暐 223
Ujiakira *m* 氏昉 「171
Ujie *s* 氏家; *m* 右治衛
Ujifune *m* 氏舟 223
Ujigawa *s* 宇治川 285
Ujihara *s* 氏原 223
Ujihiro *m* 氏宥
Ujihisa *m* 氏懿
Ujii *s* 雲林院 2027
Ujiie *sp* 氏家 223
~ Makoto *ml* 氏家信
Uji jūjō *l* 宇治十帖 285
Ujika *s* 宇自可
Ujikane *m* 氏鉄 223
Ujikimi *m* 氏公
Ujikiyo *m* 氏養
Ujima *m* 右司馬 171
Ujimasa *m* 氏政 223, 氏
Ujimune *m* 氏心 ⌊賢
Ujimura *s* 宇知村 285
Ujindo *m* 氏人 223
Ujinori *m* 氏中, 氏命
Ujisato *m* 氏郷, 氏識
Uji shūi *l* 宇治拾遺 285
Ujisuke *m* 氏如 223
Ujita *s* 氏田, 宇治田 285
Ujitaka *m* 氏共 223
Ujitake *m* 氏錡
Uji Tawara *p* 宇治田原 285
Ujiya *s* 氏家 223
Ujiyasu *m* 氏綏
Ujiyoshi *m* 氏彦, 氏燕
Ukagami *s* 宇賀神 285
Ukai *s* 鵜養 2822; *sla* 鵜飼
Ukaibe *s* 鵜甘部
Ukaji *s* 宇梶 285
Ukan *p* 有漢 303
Ukanume *s* 宇漢迷 285
Ukawa *s* 右川 171
(uke 受 730, 承 760, 食 1159, 請 2323)
Ukegawa *s* 受川 730, 請川 2323
Ukeji *s* 請地
Uken *p* 宇検 285
Ukena *s* 浮穴 1069, 浮名
(ukeshi 猾 1834)
Uki *s* 卯木 259, 宇木 285, 鵜木 2822. (浮 1069)
Ukichi *m* 右橘 171, 卯吉 259
Ukifune *la* 浮舟 1069
Ukigai *s* 浮貝, 福谷 1888
Ukiha *p* 浮羽 1069
Ukishima *s* 浮島
Ukita *s* 宇喜田 285, 宇喜多, 浮田 1069
~ Hideie *mh* 宇喜多秀家 285, 浮田秀家 1069 「和民
~ Kazutami *ml* 浮田
Ukiyo-buro *l* 浮世風呂
~ dōchū hizakurige *l* 浮世道中膝栗毛
~-doko *l* 浮世床
~-e *a* 浮世絵
~ oyaji katagi *l* 浮世親仁形気
~-zōshi *l* 浮世草子
Ukō *fl* 羽紅 246
Ukon *sm-f* 右近
Ukon'emon *m* 右近右衛門 「730)
Uku *sp* 宇久 285. (受
Ukuru *m* 稟 1973
Ukuso *s* 牛九十 111, 牛
Ukyō *p* 右京 171 ⌊糞
Uma *s* 有漢 303, 馬 1257; *p* 宇摩 285. (午 112, 宇 285, 味 572, 肥 617, 美 923, 馬 1257)
Umagoe *s* 馬越

Umahito *m* 肥人 617
Umaji *p* 馬路 1257
Umajirō *m* 馬次郎
Umakai *s* 右馬飼 171; *m* 宇合 285, 馬養 1257
Umako *f* 馬子
Umamikui *s* 馬工, 馬御織 「171
Umanosuke *m* 右馬允
Umaru *m* 生 214
Umasaka *s* 味尺 572
Umasake *s* 味淳, 味酒
Umashi *m* 可怜 165, 美 923, 美石. (味 572, 美 923)
Umashima *s* 馬島 1257
Umashine *m* 美稲 923; *ml* 味稲 572 「171
Umashirō *m* 右馬四郎
Umasugi *s* 馬杉 1257
Umasuke *m* 午介 112
Umayahara *s* 馬屋原 1257
Ume *sla* 梅 1374; *p* 宇目 285. (埋 1041, 梅 1374, 楳 1894)
Umebachi *s* 梅鉢 1374
Umebayashi *s* 梅林
Umebori *s* 梅暮里
Umeboshi *s* 梅干
Umechi *s* 梅地
Umeda *s* 楳田 1894; *sp* 梅田 1374
~ Haruo *ml* 梅田晴夫
~ Unpin *mh* 梅田雲浜
Umedo *s* 梅戸 「枝
Umegae *s* 梅香家; *l* 梅
Umegami *s* 梅上
Umegashima *p* 梅ケ島
Umegawa *s* 梅川
Umegoyomi *l* 梅暦
Umehara *s* 梅原
~ Hokumei *ml* 梅原北明 「竜三郎
~ Ryūsaburō *ma* 梅原
Umeichi *m* 楳一 1894
Umeji *s* 梅地 1374
Umejima *s* 梅島
Umekawa *s* 楳川 1894
Ume Kenjirō *mh* 梅謙次郎 1374
Umeki *s* 梅木
Umekichi *m* 梅吉
Umekita *s* 梅北
Umeko *f* 梅子
Umekōji *s* 梅小路
Umemiya *s* 梅宮

Umemori *s* 梅森
Umemoto *s* 梅本
~ Katsumi *ml* 梅本克巳
Umemura *s* 梅村
Umene *s* 梅根
Umeno *s* 梅野
Umenokōji *s* 梅小路
Umenoto *s* 梅門
Umenuma *s* 梅沼
Umeo *m* 梅男, 梅雄
Umeoka *sf* 梅岡
Umeshirō *m* 梅四郎
Umetada *s* 梅多田, 梅忠; *sm* 埋忠 1041
Umetani *s* 梅谷 1374, 梅渓
Umetarō *m* 梅太郎
Umetsubo *f* 梅壺
Umetsuji *s* 梅辻
Umeura *s* 梅浦
Umewaka *s* 梅若
Umeya *s* 梅屋
Umeyama *s* 梅山
Umezaki *s* 梅崎
~ Haruo *ml* 梅崎春生
Umezawa *s* 梅沢
Umezono *sm* 梅園
Umezu *s* 梅津
Umi *p* 宇美 285. (洋 822, 海 1071)
Umida *sp* 海田
Umieda *s* 海江田
Umihei *m* 海平
Umiki *m* 美樹 923
Umimatsu *s* 海松 1071
Uminoya *s* 海ノ屋
Umio *m* 海雄
Umon *m* 右門 171
~ torimonochō *l* 右門捕物帖
Umori *m* 右衛
(umu 産 1520)
(un 云 147, 呼 571, 芸 689, 温 1585, 敬 1691, 運 1808, 雲 2027, 媼 2089, 饂 2852)
Una *s* 烏那 1256. (海 1071, 畳 1997)
Unabara *s* 海原 1071
Unade *s* 雲梯 2027
Unagami *s* 海上 1071
~ Tanehira *ml* 海上胤平 「日処女 1729
Unai Otome *fh* 菟名
Unara *s* 雲掃 2027
Unazuki *p* 宇奈月 285

Une *s* 宇根, 畝 1142. (采 707, 畝 1142, 畦 1381, 婇 1602, 疇 2799)
Unebe *s* 畝米 1142
Unebi *s* 畝尾, 畝傍, 雲飛 2027 「1142
Unebiyama *p* 畝傍山
Unehiko *m* 疇彦 2799
Uneko *f* 畝子 1142
Uneme *sf-p* 采女 707; *f* 婇女 1602
Unemori *s* 畦森 1381
Unenojō *m* 疇之丞 2799
Uneo *s* 畝尾 1142; *m* 采男 707
Unesu *s* 宇泥須 285
Ungorō *m* 饂五郎 2852
Uni *s* 有弐 303
Unkoku *s* 雲谷 2027
Unmo *l* 雲母
Unno *s* 海野 1071, 雲野 2027 「1071
Unnokuchi *s* 海野口
Uno *s* 菟野 1729, 鵜野 2822; *sp* 宇野 285
Un'ō *ma* 呼翁 571
Unobe *s* 宇野辺 285
Uno Chiyo *fl* 宇野千代
Unoke *p* 宇ノ気
Unokichi *m* 宇之吉
Uno Kōji *ml* 宇野浩二
U no matsuri *la* 鵜祭 2822 「夫 285
Uno Nobuo *ml* 宇野信
Unoshima *s* 宇島
Unosuke *m* 卯之助 259
Unotoro *s* 鵜瀞 2822
Unozawa *s* 宇野沢 285
Unrin'in *sla* 雲林院 2027
Unshū ōrai *l* 雲州往来
Untei *plh* 芸亭 689
Unu *s* 菟野 1729
Unuma *s* 魚沼 1485
(uo 魚)
Uojima *p* 魚島
Uokai *m* 魚養
Uona *m* 魚名
Uonuma *s* 魚沼
Uotani *s* 魚谷
Uozu *p* 魚津
Uozumi *s* 魚住 「蘆
~ Setsuro *ml* 魚住折
Ura *s* 浦 1067; *m* 裏 2176. (卜 10, 上 47, 占 153, 浦 1067, 裏 2176)
Urabe *s* 卜部 10, 占部 153, 浦辺 1067, 浦部
~ Kanetomo *ml* 卜部兼倶 10
Uraeri *m* 裏襟 2176
Uragami *s* 浦上 1067
Uragare *l* 末枯 211
Uraguchi *s* 浦口 1067
Urahoro *p* 浦幌
Urai *s* 浦井 「河
Urakawa *s* 浦川; *p* 浦
Urakawara *p* 浦川原
Uraki *s* 浦木
Urako *f* 上子 47
Uramatsu *s* 浦松 1067, 裏松 2176 「介 1052
Urami no Suke *l* 恨の
Uramoto *s* 浦本 1067
Urana *s* 浦名
Urano *s* 浦野
Uraoka *s* 浦岡
Urasaki *s* 浦崎
Urasawa *s* 浦沢
Urase *s* 浦瀬
Urashima *s* 浦島
~-go no den *l* 浦島子
Urata *s* 浦田 ⌊伝
Uratani *s* 浦谷
Uratsuji *s* 裏辻 2176
Urausu *p* 浦臼 1067
Urawa *p* 浦和
Uraya *s* 浦谷
Urayama *s* 浦山
Urayasu *p* 浦安
Ureshino *p* 嬉野 2476
(uri 瓜 305, 売 466)
Urihari *s* 六月一日 61
Uriin *s* 雲林院 2027
Uri nusubito *la* 瓜盗
Urita *s* 瓜田 ⌊人 305
Uritani *s* 瓜谷
Uriwari *s* 瓜破
Urizane *m* 瓜実
Urizura *p* 瓜連
Uru *s* 宇留 285. (閏 1819, 漆 2087, 潤 2277)
Urue *m* 閏江 1819
Urugi *p* 売木 466
Uruha *s* 漆葉 2087
Uruko *f* 閏子 1819
Uruma *s* 漆間 2087
Uruno *s* 宇留野 285
Uruo *m* 潤 2277
Uruppu *p* 得撫 1299
Urushi *s* 漆 2087. (漆)
Urushibara *s* 漆原
Urushibata *s* 漆畑
Urushibe *s* 漆部

Urushido *s* 漆戸
Urushima *s* 漆馬, 漆間
Urishiyama *s* 漆山
Urushizaki *s* 漆崎
Uruu *m* 潤 2277
Uryū *s* 瓜生 305; *p* 雨竜 759 「305
～ Tadao *ml* 瓜生忠夫
Usa *s* 菟狭 1729; *sp* 宇佐 285; *f* 兎 763
Usaburō *m* 卯三郎 259, 宇三郎 285
Usagawa *s* 宇佐川
Usami *s* 宇佐見, 宇佐美; *m* 右左視 171
Usawa *s* 宇沢 285, 鵜沢 2822 「沈 399, 艮 529)
(ushi 孔 58, 丑 99, 牛 111,
Ushiama *s* 牛尼 111
Ushiba *s* 牛場
Ushibori *p* 牛堀
Ushibuka *p* 牛深
Ushida *s* 牛田
Ushie *f* 得志恵 1299
Ushigase *s* 牛ケ瀬 111
Ushigoe *s* 牛越
Ushigome *s* 牛込
Ushiji *m* 丑二 99
Ushijima *s* 牛島 111
Ushijirō *m* 丑次郎 99
Ushikai *m* 牛甘 111, 牛養 「宇鋪
Ushiki *s* 牛木, 宇敷 285,
Ushiku *s* 宇宿; *p* 牛久 111 「窪
Ushikubo *s* 牛久保, 牛
Ushikusa *s* 牛草
Ushima *s* 牛田
Ushimado *p* 牛窓
Ushimaro *s* 牛円; *m* 牛麿
Ushimaru *m* 牛丸
Ushio *s* 牛尾; *m* 潮 2275
Ushioda *s* 潮田
Ushioku *s* 牛奥 111
(ushiro 後 1300)
Ushirogu *s* 後
Ushiroku *s* 後宮
Ushiromiya *s* 後宮
Ushitarō *m* 有志太郎 303
Ushiyama *s* 牛山 111
Ushizawa *s* 牛沢
Ushizu *p* 牛津
Ushizuka *s* 牛塚
Ushū *m* 牛生 「2437
Uso no mi *l* 嘘の果
(usu 臼 338, 碓 1910, 薄 2569, 磨 2596)
Usuba *s* 薄葉 2569
Usuda *s* 薄田; *sp* 臼田 338
～ Arō *ml* 臼田亜浪
Usugawa *s* 碓川 1910
Usugumo *l* 薄雲 2569
Usui *s* 臼井 338, 臼射, 笛吹 1471, 笛吹峠, 薄井 2569, 磨井 2596; *sp* 碓井 1910, 碓氷
～ Taiyoku *ml* 臼井大翼 「見
～ Yoshimi *ml* 臼井吉
Usuki *sp* 臼杵
Usukine *s* 臼杵
Usukura *s* 臼倉
Usuo *m* 碓男 1910
Usurai *ml* 薄氷 2569
Usutani *s* 磨谷 2596
Uta *m* 雅楽 1913; *f* 詠 1664. (唄 1045, 哥 1193, 唱 1283, 訶 1662, 詠 1664, 詩 1933, 頌 2113, 歌 2170, 謌 2643)
～ andon *l* 歌行燈 2170
Utaawase *l* 歌合
～ ruijū *l* 歌合類聚
Utada *s* 歌田
Utagaeshi *l* 歌返
Utagawa *s* 歌川
～ Toyokuni *ma* 歌川豊国
Utai *la* 謡 2642
Utaka *s* 鵜高 2822
Utakai *l* 歌会 2170
Utakane *s* 一二三 3
Utakawa *s* 雅楽川 1913
Utakichi *m* 歌吉 2170
Utako *f* 唄子 1045, 哥子 1193, 訶子 1662, 歌子 2170
Utamakura *l* 歌枕
Utamaro *m* 宇多麻呂 285; *ma* 歌麿 2170
Utanobori *p* 歌登
Utanosuke *m* 雅楽介 1913
Utaomi *m* 詩臣 1933
Utarō *m* 謌郎 2643
Utashinai *p* 歌志内 2170
Utashiro *s* 歌代
Utata *m* 転 1656
Utatane *s* 一二三 3
～ no ki *l* 転寝の記 1656
Utatsu *p* 歌津 2170
Utaura *la* 歌占
Utazaimon *l* 歌祭文
Utazawa *l* 歌沢
Utazu *p* 宇多津 285
Uteichi *s* 打越 136
Utena *s* 台 276
Uto *s* 宇都 285; *p* 宇土
Utō *s* 宇藤, 笛吹 1471, 善知 1799, 鵜取 2822; *sla* 善知鳥 1799
～ Yasukata chūgiden *l* 善知鳥安方忠義伝
Utsu *s* 宇津 285, 宇都. (内 81, 打 136, 全 271, 尉 1410, 槍 2100, 蔚 2191, 欝 3011)
Utsubo *l* 宇津保 285
～-zaru *l* 靭猿 1694
Utsubusa *s* 内房 81
Utsuda *s* 槍田 2100
Utsuhi *s* 日内 77
Utsuho *l* 宇津保 285
Utsuki *s* 宇津木, 宇都木
Utsuku *f* 寵 2893
Utsukushi *f* 寵
Utsumaro *m* 内麿 81
Utsumi *s* 打見 136; *sp* 内海 81 「杖
～ Getsujō *ml* 内海月
Utsunari *m* 全成 271
Utsuno *s* 宇津野 285, 宇都野
～ Ken *ml* 宇都野研
Utsunomiya *s* 宇津宮; *sp* 宇都宮
Utsunoura *sp* 内之浦 81
Utsusemi *l* 空蟬 723
Uwa *p* 宇和 285. (上 47, 表 914)
Uwabu *s* 上符 47
Uwagawa *s* 宇和川 285
Uwahira *s* 上平 47
Uwaho *s* 上保
Uwajima *p* 宇和島 285
Uwakata *s* 上方 47
Uwanari *l* 嫐 2738
Uwano *s* 宇和野 285
Uwaumi *p* 宇和海
Uwazumi *s* 上住 47
(uya 礼 146, 恭 1205, 敬 1691, 譲 2918)
Uyako *f* 恭子 1205
Uyama *s* 宇山 285
Uzen *m* 右膳 171; *ph* 羽前 246
(uzu 太 105, 珍 836, 埋 1041, 鈿 1940)
Uzuhara *s* 楊盧原 1898
Uzuhashi *s* 埋橋 1041, 堆橋 1295
Uzuhiko *m* 珍彦 836
Uzuki *s* 卯月 259
Uzumagawa *p-l* 巴波川 97 「宇豆麿 285
Uzumaro *m* 珍麿 836,
Uzumasa *sp* 太秦 105
Uzume *f* 鈿女 1940
(uzura 鶉 2820)
Uzuragoromo *l* 鶉衣
Uzurao *s* 鶉尾
Uzushige *m* 太重 105

Wa *m* 和 638. (八 19, 王 90, 禾 220, 瓜 305, 吾 491, 和 638, 倭 1283, 輪 2316)
Waabe *s* 和安部 638
Wachi *s* 和地, 和智; *p* 和知
Wachigai *s* 輪違 2316
Wada *sp* 和田 638 「2874
Wadachi *s* 和達; *m* 轍
Wada Eisaku *ma* 和田英作 638
Wadagaki *s* 和田垣
Wada kassen onna-maizuru *la* 和田合戦女舞鶴
Wadaki *s* 和田木
Wadamaru *m* 輪田丸 2316 「山蘭 638
Wada Sanran *ml* 和田

~ Sanzō *ma* 和田三造
Wadatsu *s* 和田津
Wada Tsutō *ml* 和田伝
Wadayama *p* 和田山
Wada Yoshie *mh* 和田芳恵 「義盛
~ Yoshimori *mh* 和田
Wadō 708–15 和銅
Wadomari *p* 和泊
Waga *p* 和賀. (吾 491, 我 545)
Wagae *f* 吾枝 491
Wagatsuma *s* 我妻 545
Wagimo *l* 吾妹 491
Wagō *s* 吾河, 和合 638;
Waguri *s* 和栗 ⌊*p* 和郷
Wahei *m* 和平
(wai 隈 1841, 嵗 2198)
Waichi *m* 和一 638, 倭市 1283
Waichirō *m* 和一郎 638
Waida *s* 和井田
Wainai *s* 和井内
~ Sadayuki *mh* 和井内貞行
Wajima *sp* 輪島 2316
Waka *l* 和歌 638. (分 64, 王 90, 弁 275, 幼 428, 若 692, 涌 1065, 童 1743, 稚 1914, 新 1965)
Wakabayashi *s* 若林 692
~ Kyōsai *mh* 若林強 ⌊斎
Wakabe *s* 若部
Wakada *s* 若田
Waka dairinshō *l* 和歌題林抄 638 「蒙抄
~ dōmōshō *l* 和歌童
Wakae *s* 若江 692
Wakafuji *s* 若藤
Wakagi *s* 若木
Wakaguri *s* 若栗
Wakahara *s* 若原
Wakahime *f* 若比売
Wakaho *p* 若穂
Wakai *s* 和賀井 638, 若井 692 「若色 692
Wakairo *s* 十八女 18,
Wakaiso *s* 十八女 18
Wakaizumi *s* 若泉 692
Wakaki *s* 若癸
Wakako *f* 若子, 稚子 1914 「品 638
Waka kuhon *l* 和歌九
Wakakusa *p* 若草 692
Wakamaro *m* 若麻呂
Wakamatsu *sp* 若松
~ Shizuko *fl* 若松賤子
Wakameda *s* 若目田
Wakamei *s* 若命
Wakami *s* 若見
Wakamikoto *s* 若命
Wakamiya *sp* 若宮
Wakamizu *sm* 若水
Wakamori *s* 若森
Wakamurasaki *l* 若紫
Wakana *sf-la* 若菜
Wakan rōeishū *l* 和漢朗詠集 638
Wakao *s* 若尾 692
Wakaomi *s* 若麻績
Wakasa *s* 若竿; *sph* 若狭; *p* 若桜
Wakasagi *m* 若雀 「部
Wakasakurabe *s* 若桜
Waka sakusha burui *l* 和歌作者部類 638
Wakashima *s* 若島 692
Wakashiro *s* 若代
Wakasugi *s* 若杉
~ Kei *ml* 若杉慧
Wakatai jisshu *l* 和歌体十種 638
Wakatake *s* 若竹 692
Wakatarashi *s* 若帯
Waka teikin *l* 和歌庭訓 638
Wakatsu *m* 八 19
Wakatsuka *s* 若塚 692
Wakatsuki *s* 和歌月 638, 若月 692, 若槻, 輪賀月 2316 「次郎 692
~ Reijirō *mh* 若槻礼
Wakawa *s* 吾河 491
Wakayama *s* 若山 692; *p* 和歌山 638
~ Bokusui *ml* 若山牧水 692 「子
~ Kishiko *fl* 若山喜志
Wakayanagi *p* 若柳
Wakayue *s* 若湯座
Wakazono *s* 若園
Wake *sp* 和気 638. (分 64, 別 435, 訳 1402)
Wakebe *s* 分部 64
Wakehi *s* 訳樋 1402
Wake no Hiromushi *fh* 和気広虫 638
~ no Kiyomaro *mh* 和気清麻呂
Wakese *s* 分瀬 64
Waki *s* 和気 638; *sp* 和木; *sf-p* 脇 1083. (別 435, 涌 1065, 脇 1083)
Wakida *s* 脇田
Wakiko *f* 涌子 1065
Wakimoto *s* 脇本 1083
Wakino *s* 脇野
Wakinosawa *p* 脇野沢
Wakiya *s* 脇谷, 脇屋
Wakiyama *s* 脇山
Wakizaka *s* 脇坂
Wakizawa *s* 脇沢
Wakkanai *p* 稚内 1914
Wakō *s* 和光 638, 若生 692
Waku *s* 和久 638. (別 435, 若 692, 或 750, 涌 1065, 惑 1784, 稚 1914, 穫 2729)
Wakuda *s* 涌田 1065
Wakui *s* 和久井 638, 涌井 1065
Waku i *l* 涌井
Wakuko *f* 若子 692, 涌子 1065 「女 1914
Wakume *f* 若売 692, 稚
Wakumizu *s* 或水 750
Wakuraba *l* 老葉 334
Wakushima *s* 涌島 1065
Wakuta *s* 和久田 638
Wakutomo *s* 和久兎毛
Wakuya *p* 涌谷 1065
Wamyō ruijūshō *l* 倭名類聚鈔 1283
Wamyōshō *l* 和名抄 638
(wan 椀 1624, 湾 1849)
Wanami *s* 和波 638
Wani *s* 丸 40, 丸邇, 和爾 638, 和邇; *m* 和仁; *mh* 王仁 90. (赤 443, 鰐 3015)
Wanibe *s* 丸部 40, 和珥部 638, 和邇部
Wanibuchi *s* 鰐淵 3015
Waniishi *s* 鰐石
Wanikawa *s* 鰐川
Wankyū sue no Matsuyama *la* 椀久末松山 1624
Wanona-no-kuni *ph* 倭奴国 1283 「2316
Wanouchi *p* 輪之内
Wan'ya *s* 椀屋 1624
Wara *p* 和良 638. (藁 2682)
Warabi *sp* 蕨 2566
~ Kyōdō *ml* 蕨橿堂
~ Tōken *ml* 蕨桐軒
Waragai *s* 藁谷 2682
Warashina *s* 藁品, 藁科
Waraya *s* 藁谷
~ eisō *l* 藁屋詠草
(ware 余 448, 吾 491)
(wari 割 1696A)
Warita *s* 割田
Wasa *s* 和佐 638
Wasaburō *m* 和三郎
Wasada *sp* 早田 295
Wasaji *s* 和佐二 638
Wasaki *s* 和崎
Wasaku *m* 和作
Wasan *l* 和讃 「稲
Wase *s* 早苗 295; *f* 早
Waseda *p* 早稲田
Waseki *s* 上関 47
Washi *s* 鷲 2980. (鷲)
Washichi *m* 和七 638
Washida *s* 鷲田 2980
Washima *p* 和島 638
Washimi *s* 鷲見 2980
Washimitsu *m* 鷲光
Washimiya *p* 鷲宮
Washimori *s* 鷲森
Washino *s* 鷲野
Washinoo *s* 鷲尾
Washinozu *s* 鷲頭
Washio *s* 鷲尾; *m* 鷲雄
Washishiki *p* 鷲敷
Washisu *s* 鷲巣
Washiyama *s* 鷲山
Washizu *s* 鷲津, 鷲栖
Washizuka *s* 鷲塚
Wassamu *p* 和寒 638
Wasuke *m* 和介
Wasuregusa *l* 萱草 1730
~ ni yosu *l* 萱草に寄す 「2538)
(wata 日 76, 済 1336, 綿
Watabe *s* 渡部 1586
Watabiki *s* 綿引 2538
Wataki *s* 綿木
Watakushi *s* 下家 46
Watamaro *m* 綿麿 2538
Watamiya *s* 渡海谷 1586
Watamori *m* 和多守 638
Watanabe *s* 和田鍋, 渡辺 1586, 渡部
~ Junzō *ml* 渡辺順三
~ Katei *ml* 渡辺霞亭
~ Kazan *mlh* 渡辺崋山
~ Kazuo *ml* 渡辺一夫
~ Kōfū *ml* 渡辺光風
~ Mokuzen *ml* 渡辺黙禅
~ Suiha *ml* 渡辺水巴
Watano *s* 綿野 2538
Watanu *s* 四月一日 188

Watanuki *s* 四月, 四月一日, 四月朔日, 更衣 528, 渡貫 1586, 綿貫 2538
Watanuma *s* 渡沼 1586
(watara 度 1009, 渡 1586)
Watarae *s* 度会
Watarai *s* 下家 46, 渡井 1586, 渡会; *sp* 度会 1009
Watarase *s* 渡瀬
Watari *s* 日理 76, 亘理 317, 渡里 1586, 渡利; *sm* 亘 262, 亙 317, 渡 1586; *sp* 亘理 262; *m* 弥 832, 渉 1331, 済 1336. (渡 1586)
Watarinosuke *m* 渡之助
Watarise *s* 渡瀬
Wataru *sm* 亘 262, 亙 317, 渡 1586; *m* 和 638, 和多留, 和樽, 恆 805, 恒 809, 弥 832, 度 1009, 航 1136, 渉 1331, 済 1336, 移 1378, 道 1811
Watase *s* 渡瀬 1586
Watasu *sm* 亙 317; *m* 済 1336
Watatsumi *s* 海祇 1071
Watauchi *s* 綿内 2538, 綿打
Wataya *m* 綿屋
Watayō *s* 済陽 1336
Watsuji *s* 和辻 638
～ Tetsurō *ml* 和辻哲郎
Watsuka *p* 和束
Wauke *s* 和宇慶
Waza *s* 輪座 2316. (技 381, 事 768)
Wazayoshi *m* 技美 381
Waze *s* 吾全 491

# Y

(ya 八 19, 也 23, 文 86, 矢 215, 谷 449, 夸 452, 邪 642, 舎 721, 夜 766, 弥 832, 耶 889, 哉 1006, 室 1183, 家 1185, 屋 1233, 移 1378, 野 1398, 埜 1489, 陽 1567, 椰 1891, 楊 1898, 数 2169, 箭 2397, 鵺 2818)
Yaba *s* 八羽 19; *ml* 野坡 1398
Yabakei *p* 耶馬渓 889
Yabase *s* 八橋 19; *sp* 矢橋 215
Yabashi *s* 矢橋
Yabe *s* 八戸 19, 野部 1398; *sp* 矢部 215, 養父 2558
Yabu *s* 八生 19, 藪 2840. (藪)
Yabuhara *s* 藪原
Yabuki *sp* 矢吹 215
Yabumoto *s* 藪本 2840
Yabunaka *s* 藪中
Yabuno *s* 藪野
Yabunouchi *s* 藪内
Yabusaki *s* 八武崎 19, 藪崎 2840
Yabushita *s* 藪下
Yabuta *s* 藪田
～ Yoshio *ml* 藪田義雄
Yabutsuka *s* 藪塚
Yabuuchi *s* 藪内
Yabuzukahon *p* 藪塚本
Yachi *s* 谷内 449, 谷地
Yachida *s* 谷内田, 谷地田
Yachige *s* 八下 19
Yachiho *p* 八千穂
Yachiki *m* 数千木 2169
Yachimata *m* 八衢 19; *p* 八街
Yachiyo *p* 八千代
Yada *s* 矢田 215
Yadanji *m* 弥団次 832
Yada Sōun *ml* 矢田挿雲 215
～ Tsuseko *fl* 矢田津世子
(yado 宿 1438)
Yadome *s* 矢留 215
Yadori *m* 茇 681
Yadorigi *l* 宿木 1438, 寄生木 1525
Yadoru *m* 次 226, 茇 681, 舎 721
Yadoya *s* 宿屋 1438
～ Meshimori *ml* 宿屋飯盛
Yae *s* 八戸 19; *f* 八重
Yaegaki *s* 八重垣
Yaegashi *s* 八重樫
Yaegushi *s* 八重櫛
Yaekichi *m* 八重吉
Yaeko *f* 八重子
Yaesu *p* 八重洲
Yaeta *s* 八重田, 八重田; *m* 弥栄太 832
Yaeyama *s* 八相山 19
Yaezawa *s* 八重沢
Yagaki *s* 家垣 1185
Yagami *s* 矢上 215
Yagasaki *s* 矢ケ崎
Yageta *s* 八下田 19
Yagi *s* 矢木 215, 家城 1185, 家喜, 陽疑 1567, 楊貴 1898; *sp* 八木 19. (柳 1105, 楊 1898)
Yagihara *s* 八木原 19
Yagihashi *s* 八木橋
Yagi Hideji *mh* 八木秀次
Yagii *s* 楊井 1898
Yagi Jūkichi *ml* 八木重吉 19
Yagimoto *s* 柳元 1105, 柳本
Yaginuma *s* 八木沼 19, 柳沼 1105
Yagioka *s* 八木岡 19
Yagira *s* 柳楽 1105
Yagi Ryūichirō *ml* 八木隆一郎 19
Yagisawa *s* 八木沢
Yagishima *s* 柳島 1105
Yagishita *s* 八木下 19, 柳下 1105
Yagita *s* 八木田 19
Yagiyashi *s* 八木八四
Yagi Yoshinori *ml* 八木義徳
Yago *s* 八子, 矢後 215
Yagō *s* 矢郷
Yagohara *s* 藪原 2840
Yaguchi *s* 矢口 215, 谷口 449, 箭口 2397
Yagura *s* 矢倉 215
Yaguri *m* 舎 721
Yaguwa *s* 八鍬 19
Yagyū *sp* 柳生 1105
～ bugeichō *l* 柳生武芸帖
Yahaba *p* 矢巾 215
Yahachi *m* 弥八 832
Yahagi *s* 矢 215, 矢萩; *sp* 矢作, 矢矧
Yahana *s* 矢花
Yahanraku *la* 夜半楽 766
Yahata *sp* 八幡 19
Yahazu *s* 箭括 2397; *m* 抜 384
Yahee *m* 弥兵衛 832
Yahiko *p* 弥彦
Yahiro *s* 八尋 19
Yai *s* 谷井 449. (焼 1588)
Yaichi *m* 矢一 215, 弥一 832, 弥市
Yaichirō *m* 弥一郎, 弥市郎
Yaishi *s* 弥石
Yaita *sp* 矢板 215
Yaizu *p* 焼津 1588
Yaji *s* 矢地 215, 谷治 449
Yajirō *m* 弥二郎 832
Yaka *s* 家 1185. (宅 283, 家 1185)
Yakabe *s* 宅部 283
Yakabu *s* 八国生 19
Yakage *p* 矢掛 215
Yakahito *m* 家仁 1185
Yakame *s* 家亀
Yakami *s* 八神 19
Yakamochi *ml* 家持 1185
Yakamori *ml* 宅守 283
Yakara *m* 族 1343
Yakata *s* 八角島 19, 館 2761
Yakatoji *fh* 宅刀自 283
Yakatsugu *m* 宅嗣
Yakawa *s* 益甲 1201
(yake 宅 283, 家 1185)
Yakehitobe *s* 家人部
Yakeshi *s* 八祐 19
Yaki *s* 楊枳 1898. (焼 1588)
Yakichi *m* 弥吉 832
Yako *s* 八居 19, 楊公 1898, 楊胡
Yakō *s* 八国生 19, 矢向 215
Yakobu *s* 八国分 19, 八国生, 八国府
Yakoda *s* 谷古田 449
Yakou *s* 谷古宇
Yaku *p* 屋久 1233. (厄 68, 亦 325, 役 368, 易 714, 益 1201, 訳 1402, 懌 2439, 薬 2568, 繹 2924, 鑰 2998)
Yakū *s* 八国生 19
Yakumi *s* 厄巳 68
Yakumo *m-p-l* 八雲 19

～ mishō *l* 八雲御抄
Yakuno *p* 夜久野 766
Yakunugi *s* 八椚 19
Yakusha kuchi-jami-sen *l* 役者口三味線 368
～ rongo *l* 役者論語
Yakushi *s* 薬師 2568
Yakushiji *sp* 薬師寺
Yakushi Nyorai *mh* 薬師如来
Yakushiyama *s* 薬師山
Yakuta *m* 弥久太 832
Yakutarō *m* 弥久太郎
Yakutomi *s* 八九十三 19 ⌊889. (山 89)
Yama *s* 山 89; *p* 耶麻
Yama-arashi *l* 山嵐
Yamaba *s* 山羽, 山葉
Yamabara *s* 山原
Yamabata *s* 山幡
Yamabe *s* 山家; *sp* 山辺, 山部 ⌈赤人
～ no Akahito *ml* 山部
Yamabiki *s* 山引
Yamabiko *s* 山彦
Yamabito *m* 仙 228
Yamada *sp* 山田 89
～ Bimyō *ml* 山田美妙
～ Haseki *ml* 山田葩夕
Yamadaka *s* 山高
Yamada Kōsaku *ma* 山田耕筰 ⌈長政
～ Nagamasa *mh* 山田
Yamadani *s* 山谷
Yamada Seizaburō *ml* 山田清三郎
Yamadera *s* 山寺
Yamae *s* 山家; *p* 山江
Yamafuji *s* 山藤
Yamaga *s* 山我, 山家, 山賀; *sp* 山鹿, 山香
Yamagai *sp* 山谷
Yamaga Sokō *mh* 山鹿素行
Yamagata *s* 山片, 山肩; *sp* 山方, 山形, 山県
～ Aritomo *mh* 山県有朋
～ Bantō *mh* 山片蟠桃
～ Daini *mh* 山県大弐
Yamagishi *s* 山岸
～ Gaishi *ml* 山岸外史
～ Kayō *ml* 山岸荷葉
Yamagiwa *s* 山際, 山極
Yamagō *s* 山郷
Yamagoe *s* 山越
Yamaguchi *sp* 山口
～ Hatsujo *fl* 山口波津女 ⌈吉
～ Mokichi *ml* 山口茂
～ Seishi *ml* 山口誓子
～ Seison *ml* 山口青邨
Yamahata *s* 山畑
Yamahime *l* 山姫
Yamahira *s* 山平
Yamai *s* 山井
Yamairi *s* 山入
Yamaishi *s* 山石
Yamaji *s* 山地, 山道, 山路
～ Aizan *ml* 山路愛山
Yamakado *s* 山角, 山門
Yamakage *s* 山影, 山蔭
Yamakami *s* 山上
Yamakawa *s* 山河; *sp* 山川
～ Hitoshi *mh* 山川均
～ Kikue *flh* 山川菊栄
～ Tomiko *fl* 山川登美子 ⌈89
Yamaki *s* 八巻 19, 山木
Yamakita *sp* 山北
Yamakoshi *s* 山腰; *p* 山古志
Yamakubo *s* 山久保
Yamakuni *sp* 山国
Yamakura *s* 山倉
Yamamasu *s* 山桝
Yamamichi *s* 山道
Yamamiya *s* 山宮
Yamamomo *s* 楊梅 1898
Yamamori *s* 山森 89; *sm* 山守 ⌈本
Yamamoto *sp* 山元, 山
～ Gonnohyōe *mh* 山本権兵衛
～ Hōsui *ma* 山本芳翠
～ Kazuo *ml* 山本和夫
～ Kenkichi *ml* 山本健吉 ⌈正秀
～ Masahide *ml* 山本
～ Sanehiko *ml* 山本実彦
～ Senji *mh* 山本宣治
～ Shūgorō *ml* 山本周五郎
～ Shūji *ml* 山本修二
～ Shunkyo *ma* 山元春挙
～ Tarō *ml* 山本太郎
～ Tatsuo *mh* 山本達雄 ⌈友一
～ Tomoichi *ml* 山本
～ Tosanojō *ma* 山本土佐掾 ⌈星雄
～ Toseiyū *ml* 山元都
～ Yūzō *ml* 山本有三
Yamamura *s* 山村, 山邑
～ Bochō *ml* 山村暮鳥
～ Fusaji *ml* 山村房次
Yamamuro *s* 山室
～ Gunpei *mh* 山室軍平
～ Shizuka *ml* 山室静
Yamana *s* 山名
～ Mochitoyo *ml* 山名持豊 ⌈清
～ Ujikiyo *mh* 山名氏
Yamanaka *sp* 山中
～ Minetarō *ml* 山中峰太郎
Yamanari *s* 山成
Yamanashi *s* 月見里 80; *sp* 山梨 89
Yamanba *la* 山姥
Yamane *s* 山根
Yamaneko *s* 山猫
Yamanishi *p* 山西
Yamano *s* 山野
Yamanobe *s* 山野辺; *sp* 山辺
Yamanoe *s* 山上, 山於
～ no Okura *ml* 山上憶良 ⌈口
Yamanoguchi *sp* 山之
～ Baku *ml* 山之口貘
Yamanoi *s* 山井, 山野井
Yamanokami *s* 山上
Yamanoshiro *s* 山之城
Yamanouchi *s* 山之内; *sp* 山内; *p* 山ノ内
～ Toyoshige *mh* 山内豊信
～ Yoshio *ml* 山内義雄
Yamanoue *s* 山上
Yamao *s* 山尾
Yamaoka *sp* 山岡
～ Genrin *ml* 山岡元隣
～ Sōhachi *ml* 山岡荘八 ⌈鉄太郎
～ Tetsutarō *mh* 山岡
Yamaryō *s* 山領
Yamasa *sp* 山佐
Yamasaka *s* 山坂
Yamasaki *sp* 山前
Yamase *s* 山勢, 山瀬
Yamasendai *s* 山千代
Yamashima *s* 山島
Yamashina *s* 山科, 山階
Yamashiro *sp* 山代; *sph* 山背, 山脊, 山城
Yamashirobe *s* 山背部, 山脊部 ⌈山背大兄
Yamashiro no Ōe *mh*
Yamashiroya *s* 山城屋
Yamashita *s* 山下
～ Mutsu *ml* 山下陸奥
～ Hidenosuke *ml* 山下秀之助
Yamasu *s* 山須
Yamata *s* 矢股 215
Yamatai-koku *ph* 邪馬台国 642
Yamate *sp* 山手 89
～ Kiichirō *ml* 山手樹一郎
Yamato *s* 大養徳 48, 日本 77, 山戸 89, 山登, 和徳 638, 高市 1163, 養徳 2558; *sm* 和 638, 倭 1283; *sp* 大和 48, 大倭, 山門 89, 山都. (倭 1283)
～-e *a* 大和絵 48, 倭絵 1283 ⌈師
Yamatokanuchi *s* 倭鍛
Yamato Kōriyama *p* 大和郡山 48
Yamatoku *s* 山徳 89
Yamatomaro *m* 倭麻呂 1283 ⌈771
Yamatonoaya *s* 東漢
Yamatonofumi *s* 東文
Yamato shi uruwashi *l* 大和し美し 48
～ Takada *p* 大和高田
Yamatoya *s* 和屋 638
Yamatsumi *s* 山祇 89
Yamatsuri *p* 矢祭 215
Yamauba *la* 山姥 89
Yamauchi *s* 山打; *sp* 山内
Yamaura *s* 山浦
Yamawaki *s* 山脇
～ Shintoku *ml* 山脇信徳
～ Tōyō *mh* 山脇東洋
Yamaya *s* 山谷, 山家, 山屋 ⌈橋
Yamayakawa *s* 山谷加
Yamayoshi *s* 山吉
Yamaza *s* 山座
Yamazaki *sp* 山崎
～ Ansai *mh* 山崎闇斎

~ Shikō *ml* 山崎紫紅
~ Sōkan *ml* 山崎宗鑑
~ Toshio *ml* 山崎敏夫
~ Toyoko *fl* 山崎豊子
~ Yoshibee nebiki no kadomatsu *la* 山崎与次兵衛寿の門松
Yamazakurato *m* 山桜
Yamazato *s* 山里 ⌊戸
Yamazawa *s* 山沢
Yamazoe *sp* 山添
Yamazumi *s* 山住, 山角, 山澄
Yame *sp* 八女 19
Yamichi *s* 八道
Yamori *s* 矢守 215
Yamoto *p* 矢本
Yamura *s* 八村 19, 矢村
Yamuro *s* 矢袋 ⌊215
Yana *p* 八名 19. (柵 863, 柳 1105, 梁 1475, 楊 1898, 簗 2690)
Yanabe *s* 矢鍋 215
Yanabori *s* 柳堀 1105
Yanada *s* 梁田 1475, 簗田 2690
Yanadani *sp* 柳谷 1105
Yanaga *s* 弥永 832
Yanagawa *s* 柳河 1105; *sp* 柳川, 梁川 1475
~ Shun'yō *ml* 柳川春葉 1105 ⌈三
~ Shunzō *ml* 柳河春
Yanagi *s* 柳, 楊 1898. (柳 1105, 楊 1898)
Yanagida *sp* 柳田 1105
Yanagidaru *l* 柳樽, 柳多留
Yanagihara *s* 柳原
~ Byakuren *fl* 柳原白蓮 ⌈堂
~ Kyokudō *ml* 柳原極
Yanagimachi *s* 柳町
Yanagimoto *s* 柳元, 柳本 ⌈柳宗悦
Yanagi Muneyoshi *ml*
Yanagisawa *s* 柳沢
~ Ken *ml* 柳沢健
~ Yoshiyasu *mh* 柳沢吉保
Yanagishita *s* 柳下
Yanagita *s* 柳田
~ Kunio *ml* 柳田国男
~ Izumi *ml* 柳田泉
Yanagiuchi *s* 柳内
Yanagiya *s* 柳谷, 柳屋
Yanagizono *sm* 柳園
Yanagura *s* 柳倉
Yanahara *p* 柵原 863
Yanahashi *s* 柳橋 1105
Yanai *s* 谷内 449, 楊井 1898, 箭内 2397; *sp* 柳井 1105. (柳, 楊 1898)
Yanaihara *s* 矢内原 215
~ Tadao *ml* 矢内原忠雄 ⌈柳津 1105
Yanaizu *s* 楊柳 1898; *p*
Yanaka *s* 谷中 449
Yanamaro *m* 梁満 1475
Yanamori *m* 梁守
Yanase *s* 柳瀬 1105, 梁瀬 1475, 簗瀬 2690
Yanashima *s* 梁島 1475
Yanayama *s* 柳山 1105
Yanbe *s* 山家 89
Yane *s* 矢根 215. (梁 1475)
Yano *s* 矢乃 215, 谷野 449, 箭野 2397; *sp* 矢野 215
Yanō *s* 家納 1185
Yanobe *s* 矢延 215
Yano Hōjin *ml* 矢野峰人
Yanokuchi *s* 箭口 2397
Yano Ryūkei *ml* 矢野竜渓 215
Yanoshima *s* 矢野島
Yanosuke *m* 弥之助 832
Yanuma *s* 矢沼 215
Yao *sp-l* 八尾 19
Yaoita *s* 矢尾板 215
Yaoko *f* 八百子 19
Yaori *m* 八百里
Yaotome *l* 八少女
Yaotsu *p* 八百津
Yaoya *s* 八百屋
~ O-Shichi *la* 八百屋お七
Yaozaka *s* 矢尾坂 215
(yari 鎗 2747, 鑓 2953)
Yarimizu *s* 鑓水
Yarita *s* 鎗田 2747, 鑓田 2953 ⌈一
~ Ken'ichi *ml* 鑓田研
Yarō mushi *l* 野郎虫 1398
Yasabu *m* 弥三 832
Yasaburō *m* 弥三郎
Yasada *s* 矢定 215
Yasaka *sp* 八坂 19; *m* 八尺; *p* 弥栄 832
Yasaki *m* 弥幸
Yasakichi *m* 弥三吉
Yasato *p* 八郷 19
Yase *s* 屋瀬 1233
Yasetsukabe *s* 八丈部 ⌊19
(yashi 椰 1891)
Yashiki *s* 屋敷 1233
Yashiko *f* 椰子 1891
Yashima *s* 谷島 449, 家島 1185; *sp* 矢島 215; *sp-la* 八島 19; *la* 屋島 1233
Yashimoda *s* 谷下田 449
Yashio *p* 八潮 19
Yashiro *s* 八代, 矢代 215, 屋代 1233; *p* 社 406
~ Tōson *ml* 矢代東村 215
~ Yukio *s* 矢代幸雄
Yashita *s* 矢下
Yaso *m* 八十 19
Yasogawa *s* 八十川
Yasoji *m* 弥三次 832
Yasonami *s* 八並 19
Yasose *s* 八十瀬
Yasoshima *s* 八十島
Yasu *s* 八州, 矢集 215, 連 1238; *sm* 安 472; *sp* 夜須 766; *f* 坦 574, 息 1224; *p* 野洲 1398. (几 6, 又 13, 子 38, 予 62, 方 85, 文 86, 叶 132, 艾 159, 夳 160, 処 177, 休 233, 伏 234, 行 245, 全 271, 存 313, 快 372, 那 416, 安 472, 考 540, 協 548, 侃 551, 和 638, 宜 675, 定 677, 妥 708, 易 714, 居 737, 庚 741, 夜 766, 保 781, 抵 797, 弥 832, 柔 907, 昆 945, 育 958, 彦 1007, 倍 1025, 修 1038, 徐 1049, 弭 1072, 祥 1074, 耕 1131, 容 1182, 毘 1195, 泰 1203, 恭 1205, 烈 1211, 要 1218, 恵 1226, 連 1238, 席 1242, 甚 1267, 倶 1279, 健 1282, 倭 1283, 悌 1289, 術 1298, 得 1299, 済 1336, 祗 1380, 能 1397, 救 1406, 尉 1410, 寂 1436, 宴 1437, 晏 1458, 逸 1504, 庸 1507, 康 1509, 順 1532, 温 1585, 裕 1645, 寧 1711, 甯 1712, 葆 1726, 属 1802, 運 1808, 閑 1820, 鳩 1825, 湛 1855, 暖 1882, 祺 1903, 靖 1905, 誉 2010, 資 2012, 愛 2018, 廉 2042, 僖 2058, 徳 2063, 慊 2068, 愷 2071, 隑 2072, 隠 2074, 静 2145, 寧 2181, 置 2232, 虞 2242, 億 2252, 愈 2358, 雍 2359, 盤 2399, 慰 2404, 慶 2425, 儒 2432, 穏 2492, 穆 2494, 錫 2524, 綽 2529, 綏 2534, 綿 2538, 養 2558, 燕 2570, 賢 2579, 遜 2591, 懐 2605, 謐 2637A, 緩 2659, 縁 2660, 慈 2701, 鎮 2751) ⌈明, 順皓 1532
Yasuaki *m* 安旦 472, 安
Yasuakira *m* 安旦 472
Yasuba *s* 安場
Yasuchika *m* 安至, 安親, 寧親 2181
Yasuda *s* 安寿田 472, 保田 781, 家寿多 1185, 家須多, 康田 1509; *sp* 安田 472
~ Ayao *ml* 安田章生
~ Seifū *ml* 安田青風
~ Yojūrō *ml* 保田与重郎 781 ⌈靭彦 472
~ Yukihiko *ma* 安田
Yasue *s* 安江; *f* 安英, 妥江 708, 徐江 1049, 綏枝 2534
Yasufuku *s* 安福 472
Yasufumi *m* 靖章 1905, 穆文 2494 ⌈472
Yasufuruichi *p* 安古市
Yasugi *s* 八杉 19, 安木 472; *p* 安来
~ Sadatoshi *ml* 八杉貞利 19
Yasugorō *m* 安五郎 472
Yasuhara *s* 安原
Yasuharu *m* 安治, 泰敏 1203, 康晴 1509, 懐春 2605
Yasuhide *m* 育英 958, 康秀 1509
Yasuhiko *m* 快彦 372, 安彦 472, 泰彦 1203, 恭彦 1205, 鳩彦 1825, 靖彦 1905, 綏彦 2534
Yasuhira *m* 泰平 1203
Yasuhiro *m* 泰啓, 静弘 2145
Yasuhisa *m* 保栄 781,

庸久 1507, 裕久 1645
Yasuhito *m* 雍仁 2359, 穏仁 2492
Yasui *s* 谷井 449, 安井 472, 安居, 保井 781, 康井 1509; *ml* 野水 1398
Yasuichi *m* 保一 781
Yasuichirō *m* 安一郎 472
Yasui Santetsu *mh* 保井算哲 781
～ Sōtarō *ma* 安井曾太郎 472
Yasuji *m* 保二 781, 保治, 康二 1509, 康治
Yasujirō *m* 安次郎 472, 安治郎, 定二郎 677, 易二郎 714, 易次郎, 保次郎 781
Yasujo *f* 尉女 1410
Yasuka *m* 穏香 2492
Yasukabe *s* 安福 472
Yasukado *m* 康圭 1509
Yasukae *s* 安福 472
Yasukata *m* 保鞏 781, 保固, 泰賢 1203
Yasukawa *s* 安川 472, 保川 781
Yasukazu *m* 保選, 育一 958, 康景 1509
Yasuke *m* 弥助 832; *p* 八祐 19
Yasuki *m* 穏 2492
Yasukichi *m* 安吉 472, 保吉 781
Yasukiyo *m* 安王 472, 保浄 781, 泰舜 1203
Yasuko *f* 几子 6, 予子 62, 休子 233, 存子 313, 安子 472, 柔子 907, 昆子 945, 育子 958, 徐子 1049, 耕子 1131, 尉功 1410, 晏子 1458, 康子 1509, 陽春子 1567, 寍子 1711, 甯子 1712, 祺子 1903, 愷子 2071, 寧子 2181, 雍子 2359, 慰子 2404, 穏子 2492, 綏子 2534, 遜子 2591; *m* 彦三 1007
Yasukōchi *s* 安河内 472
Yasukuni *m* 安都, 康国 1509
「保馬 781
Yasuma *s* 安間 472; *m*
Yasumaro *m* 康麿 1509
Yasumasa *m* 安正 472, 安礼, 安誠, 安誠, 和正 638, 保昌 781, 保誠, 泰賢 1203, 晏尚 1458, 康正 1509, 康政, 康昌
Yasumatsu *s* 安松 472
Yasumi *s* 八住 19, 八角, 八隅, 安宅 472, 安見; *m* 八洲民 19
Yasumichi *m* 恵教 1226, 康裕 1509, 靖道 1905
Yasumi Toshio *ml* 八住利雄 19
Yasumitsu *sm* 安光 472, 安満; *m* 全光 271, 能光 1397, 康光 1509, 葆光 1726
Yasumo *s* 安雲 472
Yasumochi *m* 康保 1509
Yasumori *m* 安容 472, 鎮衛 2751
Yasumoro *m* 安認 472
Yasumoto *s* 安元, 安本; *m* 養根 2558
Yasumu *m* 休 233
Yasumura *s* 安村 472; *m* 安邑
Yasumuro *s* 安室
Yasunaga *sm* 安永; *m* 養長 2558
「協中 548
Yasunaka *s* 安中 472; *m*
Yasunari *sm* 安成 472; *m* 泰業 1203, 悌成 1289, 康成 1509, 綏稔 2534, 綏稔 2659
～ Jirō *ml* 安成二郎 472
～ Sadao *ml* 安成貞雄
Yasuno *s* 安野
Yasunobu *m* 泰舒 1203, 康命 1509, 康信
Yasunochi *m* 安後 472
Yasunori *m* 八州仙 19, 安典 472, 安憲, 容度 1182, 泰経 1203, 泰令, 恭行 1205, 康敬 1509, 穏徳 2492
Yasunosuke *m* 安之助 472, 保之助 781
Yasuo *m* 又郎 13, 子生 38, 安彦 472, 安雄, 倍男 1025, 耕雄 1131, 恭雄 1205, 甚夫 1267, 康百 1509, 康男, 康雄, 資雄 2012, 愷夫 2071, 隑夫 2072, 燕夫 2570, 鎮男 2751
Yasuoka *s* 安岡 472; *p* 泰阜 1203
「太郎 472
～ Shōtarō *ml* 安岡章
Yasuoki *m* 安居
Yasuomi *m* 保臣 781, 虞臣 2242
Yasuori *m* 安宅 472
Yasura *m* 野州良 1398
Yasuraoka *s* 安良岡 472
Yasusaburō *m* 安三郎, 康三郎 1509, 靖三郎 1905
「安貞, 安補
Yasusada *m* 安定 472,
Yasushi *m* 也寸志 23, 仁 57, 予 62, 艾 159, 休 233, 存 313, 安 472, 寿 539, 坦 574, 欣 603, 和 638, 易 714, 保 781, 泰 1203, 恭 1205, 悌 1289, 術 1298, 康 1509, 順 1532, 靖 1905, 愷 2071, 寧 2181, 頤 2502, 綏 2534, 鎮 2751, 簡 2788
Yasushige *m* 安殷 472, 安順, 安繁, 康穣 1509
Yasushima *s* 安島 472
Yasushiro *m* 泰代 1203
Yasuta *m* 術太 1298
Yasutada *m* 安但 472, 保忠 781, 康匡 1509
Yasutaka *s* 保高 781; *m* 安王 472, 安崇, 保孝 781, 保考, 康荘 1509, 康隆, 康爵
「蔵 781
～ Tokuzō *ml* 保高徳
Yasutake *s* 安武 472; *m* 保健 781
Yasutani *s* 安谷 472
Yasutari *sm* 安足
Yasutarō *m* 安太郎, 保太郎 781
Yasuto *m* 逸人 1504
Yasutō *m* 又玄 13, 康融 1509
「康秋 1509
Yasutoki *m* 済時 1336,
Yasutomi *sp* 安富 472; *m* 泰祉 1203
Yasutoshi *m* 保恵 781, 泰儔 1203, 康哉 1509, 慶利 2425
Yasutsugu *m* 安族 472, 安繹, 祥次 1074, 康禎 1509
Yasutsune *m* 泰経 1203
Yasuura *p* 安浦 472
Yasuya *m* 康哉 1509
Yasuyo *s* 安代 472; *f* 倭代 1283, 晏代 1458
Yasuyomo *m* 康四方 1509
Yasuyori *m* 康陛
Yasuyoshi *m* 安喜 472, 安歓, 和義 638, 宜慶 675, 保義 781, 泰義 1203, 康工 1509, 康賛, 静嘉 2145, 錫類 2524
Yasuyuki *m* 快之 372, 靖文 1905, 徳至 2063, 懐之 2605
Yasuzaemon *m* 安左衛門 472
Yasuzane *m* 康誠 1509
Yasuzawa *s* 安沢 472
Yasuzō *m* 倭蔵 1283
Yasuzuka *p* 安塚 472
Yasuzumi *s* 安住; *m* 安究, 安純
「449
Yata *s* 八田 19; *sp* 谷田
Yatabe *sp* 矢田部 215, 谷田部 449
Yatabori *s* 矢田堀 215
Yatagai *s* 八谷 19, 谷田貝 449
Yatagawa *s* 谷田川
Yatako *f* 八咫子 19
Yatarō *m* 矢太郎 215, 弥太郎 832
Yato *s* 谷戸 449
Yatō *s* 矢当 215, 矢頭
Yatomi *s* 矢富, 家富 1185, 屋富 1233; *p* 弥富 832
Yatori *s* 矢渡利 215
Yatose *f* 八年 19
Yatsu *s* 八都, 谷 449; *sp* 谷津. (八 19, 谷 449)
Yatsuchi *s* 矢土 215
Yatsuda *s* 谷津田 449
Yatsue *s* 山谷 89
Yatsugai *s* 谷貝 449
Yatsugaya *s* 谷谷
Yatsugi *s* 矢次 215; *m* 弥続 832
Yatsuhashi *s* 八ツ橋 19; *sp* 八橋
Yatsui *s* 谷井 449
Yatsuka *s* 八塚 19, 八握; *sm-p* 八束
Yatsukawa *s* 谷川 449
Yatsume *s* 矢集 215, 箭集 2397
Yatsumi *f* 八美 19
Yatsunami *s* 八並
Yatsuo *f* 八峰; *p* 八尾
Yatsurugi *s* 八剣
Yatsushiro *sp* 八代
Yatsuya *s* 谷谷 449

Yauchi *s* 矢内 215
Yauma *s* 八馬 19
Yawa *f* 柔 907
Yawahara *p* 谷和原 449
Yawaki *m* 和気 638
Yawara *m* 矢原 215, 和 638 「八幡 19
Yawata *sp* 矢幡 215; *p*
Yawatahama *p* 八幡浜
Yawata no mae *l* 八幡
Yaya *m* 八谷 ⌊前
Yayoi *sp-h* 弥生 832
Yayoshi *m* 弥吉
Yayū *ml* 也有 23
Yazaki *m* 矢崎 215
~ Dan *ml* 矢崎弾
~ Saganoya *ml* 矢崎 嵯峨の屋 「義盛
~ Yoshimori *ml* 矢崎
Yazama *s* 矢間
Yazato *s* 八里 19
Yazawa *s* 矢沢 215, 谷沢 449 「三 832
Yazō *s* 野三 1398; *m* 弥
Yazu *sp* 矢頭 215; *p* 八頭 19
Yazukuri *s* 矢作 215
(yo 予 62, 与 101, 代 125, 四 188, 伃 230, 吉 278, 聿 332, 世 335, 余 448, 服 618, 命 671, 昌 715, 夜 766, 俗 776, 依 780, 勇 908, 美 923, 帯 1192, 淑 1335, 問 1524, 福 1888, 飫 1963, 誉 2010, 節 2215, 頼 2506, 輿 2703, 齢 2766)
Yō *sm* 陽 1567. (丁 8, 永 149, 央 182, 用 193, 生 214, 羊 273, 孕 274, 幼 428, 和 638, 英 693, 洋 822, 映 840, 栄 969, 容 1182, 盈 1200, 要 1218, 庸 1507, 揚 1551, 陽 1567, 暎 1594, 瑛 1607, 詠 1664, 窈 1745, 営 1751, 熔 1838, 楊 1898, 蓉 1983, 葉 1991, 瀁 2085, 燁 2088, 腰 2090, 様 2099, 踊 2132, 瑤 2282, 瑶 2286, 影 2357, 雍 2359, 瑩 2387, 遙 2421, 璟 2471, 穎 2505, 維 2540, 養 2558, 謡 2642, 贏 2676, 膺 2705, 嶸 2716, 曜 2720, 燿 2721, 踰 2740, 瀛 2865, 甕 2908, 耀 2919, 鷲 2940, 鷹 2995)
(yobo 丁 8)
Yobono *s* 丁野
Yoboro *s* 丁
Yoboroko *sm* 丁子
Yoborono *s* 丁野
(yobu 召 152, 呼 571)
Yobuko *p* 呼子
Yoda *s* 与田 101, 余田 448, 養田 2558; *sp* 依田 780
~ Gakkai *ml* 依田学海
~ Jun'ichi *ml* 与田準一 101 「780
~ Shūho *ml* 依田秋圃
Yodo *p* 淀 1333. (淀)
Yōdo *s* 用土 193
Yodoe *p* 淀江 1333
Yodogawa *p-l* 淀川
~ aburakasu *l* 淀川油糟
Yodogimi *fh* 淀君
Yodono *s* 淀野
~ Ryūzō *ml* 淀野隆三
Yodoya *s* 淀屋
~ Tatsugorō *mh* 淀屋辰五郎
Yogawa *s* 横川 2301
Yogo *s* 余語 448; *p* 余
Yogō *s* 余郷 ⌊呉
Yogorō *m* 与五郎 101
Yogoroku *m* 四五六 188
Yogoto *l* 寿詞 539
Yogura *s* 与食 101
Yohito *m* 淑人 1335
Yohomi *s* 衣箱 520
(yoi 宵 1179)
Yoichi *m* 与一 101, 与市, 余一 448; *p* 余市
Yōichi *m* 陽一 1567, 養一 2558
Yoichiemon *m* 与一右衛門 101
Yoichirō *m* 与一郎
Yoinara *s* 四十八朝 188, 四十八願
Yoita *sp* 与板 101
Yōji *s* 楊枝 1898; *m* 陽二 1567, 養二 2558
Yōjirō *m* 羊治郎 273, 洋次郎 822
Yōka *p* 八鹿 19
Yōkaichi *p* 八日市
Yōkaichiba *p* 八日市場
Yōkan *mh* 永観 149
Yokata *s* 四方 188
Yokawa *s* 余川 448; *p* 吉川 278
(yoke 除 1059)
Yokemura *s* 除村
~ Yoshitarō *ml* 除村吉太郎
Yoki *m* 与喜 101. (除 1059, 移 1378, 能 1397)
Yokichirō *m* 与吉郎 101
Yokie *m* 能恵 1397
Yō-kihi *fh-la* "Yang Kuei-fei" 楊貴妃 1898 「琴菊 659
Yoki koto o kiku *l* 斧
Yokimura *s* 除村 1059
Yokitsume *s* 米集 343
Yokka *s* 四日 188
Yokkaichi *p* 四日市
(yoko 横 2301)
Yōko *f* 洋子 822
Yokobari *s* 横張 2301
Yokobashi *s* 横橋
Yokobori *s* 横堀
Yokochi *s* 横地, 横知
Yokoe *s* 横江
Yokogawa *sp* 横川
Yokogoshi *p* 横越
Yokohagi *s* 横佩
Yokohama *sp* 横浜
Yokoi *s* 横井 「楠
~ Shōnan *mh* 横井小
~ Yayū *ml* 横井也有
Yokoki *s* 横木
Yokokura *s* 横倉
Yokomae *s* 横前
Yokomatsu *s* 横松
Yokomichi *s* 横道
Yokomitsu *sm* 横光; *m* 横充
~ Riichi *ml* 横光利一
Yokomizo *s* 横溝
~ Seishi *ml* 横溝正史
Yokomori *s* 横森
Yokomura *s* 横村
Yokono *s* 横野
Yokoo *s* 横尾
Yokosaka *s* 横坂
Yokose *sp* 横瀬
~ Yau *ml* 横瀬夜雨
Yokoshiba *p* 横芝
Yokoshima *sp* 横島
Yokosone *s* 横曾根
Yokosuka *sp* 横須賀
Yokota *sp* 横田
Yokotake *s* 横竹
Yokotani *s* 横谷
Yokote *sp* 横手
Yokotomi *s* 与牛富 101
Yokouchi *s* 横内 2301
Yokoya *s* 横矢, 横谷, 横屋
Yokoyama *s* 横山
~ Gennosuke *ml* 横山源之助 「虹
~ Hakukō *ml* 横山白
~ Kendō *ml* 横山健堂
~ Taikan *ma* 横山大観
~ Yūsaku *ml* 横山有策
Yokozawa *s* 横沢
Yokozeki *s* 横関
Yokozuka *s* 横塚
(yoku 可 165, 沃 396, 杙 421, 昱 944, 浴 1064, 翌 1466, 匽 2238, 億 2252, 翼 2686)
Yokuya *l* 沃野 396
Yōkyoku *l* 謡曲 2642
Yomaze *s* 夜交 766
Yomi *l* 冥府 1158. (幹 1938, 読 2142)
Yomibito shirazu *l* 読人不知
Yomihon *l* 読本
Yomiko *f* 読子
Yomizu *m* 好津 413
Yomo *sf* 四方 188
Yomoda *s* 四方田
Yomoe *f* 四方恵
Yomogi *f* 蒿 1980. (蓬 2195)
Yomogifu *l* 蓬生
Yomogita *p* 蓬田
Yomoichi *m* 与望都 101
Yomoko *f* 四方子 188
Yomo no Akara *ml* 四方赤良
Yomoo *m* 四方男
Yomosa *s* 右衛門佐 171
Yomoshigoemon *m* 四方四五右衛門 188
(yomu 頌 2113, 諷 2515)
Yonaga *s* 依永 780
Yonago *p* 米子 343
Yonai *s* 米内 「光政
~ Mitsumasa *mh* 米内
Yonaiyama *s* 米内山
Yonayama *s* 米山, 米
Yone *s* 米. (米) ⌊内山
Yonebashi *s* 米橋
Yonebayashi *s* 米林
Yoneda *s* 米田
~ Yūrō *ml* 米田雄郎
Yonehara *s* 米原

Yonei *s* 米井
Yoneichi *s* 米市
Yonejima *s* 米島
Yonejirō *m* 米次郎
Yonekawa *s* 米川
～ Masao *ml* 米川正夫
Yonekichi *m* 米吉
Yonekizu *s* 米津
Yoneko *f* 米子 「窪
Yonekubo *s* 米久保, 米
Yonekura *s* 米倉
Yonemaru *s* 米丸
Yonematsu *m* 米松
Yonemitsu *s* 米光
Yonemochi *s* 米持
Yonemoto *s* 米元, 米本
Yonemura *s* 米村
Yoneno *s* 米野
Yoneoka *s* 米岡
Yonesato *s* 米里
Yonetani *s* 米谷
Yonetarō *m* 米太郎
Yonetsu *s* 米津
Yoneya *s* 米谷
Yoneyama *sp* 米山
Yonezaki *s* 米崎
Yonezawa *sp* 米沢
～ Junko *fl* 米沢順子
Yonezō *m* 米造, 米蔵
Yoni *s* 陽丹 1567
Yonkeru kigoku *l* 揚牙児奇獄 1551
Yono *sp* 与野 101
Yōno *s* 丁野 8
Yo no nezame *l* 夜の禰覚 766
Yōnosuke *m* 洋之助 822, 庸之助 1507
Yonōzu *p* 米水津 343
Yonushi *s* 四主 188
Yora *s* 与良 101
Yori *f* 頼里 2506. (之 24, 方 85, 无 92, 仍 123, 仗 127, 可 165, 由 186, 屯 222, 因 311, 自 340, 形 414, 利 436, 和 638, 即 648, 若 692, 凭 727, 典 733, 居 737, 奇 752, 尚 753, 依 780, 保 781, 亮 911, 為 1005, 帰 1018, 倚 1033, 従 1050, 時 1086, 株 1098, 託 1147A, 席 1242, 猗 1301, 陛 1307, 移 1378, 異 1497, 寄 1525, 順 1532, 馮 1533, 偉 1535, 猶 1555, 随 1564, 道 1811, 閑 1820, 階 1840, 幹 1938, 義 1975, 資 2012, 愛 2018, 率 2040, 穀 2168, 賚 2396, 遵 2418, 選 2419, 頼 2506, 絲 2526, 親 2544, 賢 2579, 憑 2582, 聴 2634, 縁 2660, 職 2734, 攀 2851, 麗 2902, 襲 2983)
Yoriakira *m* 自明 340
Yoriatsu *m* 仍敦 123
Yorichika *m* 頼義 2506
Yorifuji *s* 依藤 780
Yorihata *m* 仗幡 127
Yorihiro *m* 頼明 2506, 頼恕
Yorihisa *m* 仍久 123, 頼央 2506, 頼説
Yorihito *m* 職仁 2734
Yorii *p* 寄居 1525
Yorikane *m* 頼錦 2506
Yorikatsu *m* 頼戡
Yorikazu *m* 頼寿
Yoriko *f* 因子 311, 倚子 1033, 寄子 1525, 選子 2419
Yorikoto *m* 時言 1086
Yorikuni *m* 自国 340, 頼郡 2506
Yorimasa *m* 従正 1050, 頼多 2506, 頼政
～ kashū *l* 頼政家集
Yorimichi *m* 依徹 780, 率道 2040, 頼倫 2506; *ml* 頼通
Yorimitsu *s* 依光 780; *m* 帰光 1018, 随光 1564, 頼全 2506, 頼潤
Yorimoto *m* 頼職
Yorimune *m* 頼旨
Yorina *m* 頼名
Yorinaga *m* 頼存, 頼寿
Yorinao *m* 職直 2734
Yorinobu *m* 依信 780, 頼宣 2506, 頼信, 縁信 2660
Yorinori *m* 頼升 2506, 頼則, 頼郷, 頼慶
Yorio *m* 亮夫 911, 倚男 1033, 義保 1975
Yorioka *s* 依岡 780
Yorioki *m* 頼知 2506, 頼
Yoriosa *m* 頼易 ⌊熙
Yorishima *p* 寄島 1525
Yorisuke *m* 頼救 2506
Yorita *s* 依田 780
Yoritaka *m* 頼位 2506, 頼幸, 頼殷, 頼恭, 頼筠
Yoritake *m* 頼桓
Yoritoki *m* 随時 1564
Yoritomo *m* 頼朝 2506
Yoritoshi *m* 頼稔, 頼聡
Yoritsugu *m* 頼纒
Yoritsune *m* 頼則
Yoriuji *m* 依氏 780
Yoriya *s* 寄谷 1525
Yoriyasu *m* 頼寧 2506
Yoriyo *m* 馮代 1533
Yoriyoshi *m* 愛善 2018, 頼芸 2506, 頼慎
Yoriyuki *m* 和志 638, 頼由 2506, 頼僮
(yoro 弱 1647)
Yorō *s* 丁 8
Yōro *s* 丁 「2558
Yōrō *p-la* 717–24 養老
Yoroboshi *la* 弱法師 1647
Yorogi *sp* 余綾 448
Yoroi *s* 甲 184
Yōroko *s* 一字 3, 丁子 8, 丁字
Yoron *p* 与論 101
Yōrō ritsuryō *l* 養老律令 2558
Yoroshi *m* 宜 675
Yorozu *m* 万 43
～ chōhō *l* 万朝報
Yorozuya *s* 万屋
Yorozuyo *f* 万代
(yoru 万, 仗 127, 因 311, 凭 727, 夜 766)
Yoruka *f* 因香 311
Yoruki *s* 万木 43
Yorumune *m* 夜宗 766
Yosa *sp* 与謝 101
Yosaburō *m* 与三郎
Yosa Buson *ml* 与謝蕪村
Yosami *s* 衣羅 520, 依網 780, 網 2536; *sp* 依羅 780
Yosamibe *s* 網部 2536
Yosano *s* 与謝野 101
～ Akiko *fl* 与謝野晶子
～ Hiroshi *ml* 与謝野寛 「厳
～ Reigon *ml* 与謝野礼
～ Tekkan *ml* 与謝野鉄幹
Yosara *s* 依羅 780
Yosashichi *m* 与三七
(yose 寄 1525) ⌊101
Yosegi-zukuri *a* 寄木造
Yoshi *s* 攀 2851; *m* 与志 101, 芳 480, 佳 560, 夜詩 766, 悌 1289, 淑 1335, 彬 1370, 善 1799, 義 1975, 慶 2425, 禧 2628; *m-f* 与之 101; *f* 四四 188, 頼 2506, 懿 2559. (乂 5, 力 11, 之 24, 工 39, 仁 57, 孔 58, 元 60, 介 66, 中 75, 文 86, 与 101, 女 114, 壬 116, 礼 146, 召 152, 令 155, 艾 159, 可 165, 布 170, 兄 181, 由 186, 平 203, 正 205, 甘 207, 允 217, 伃 230, 休 233, 任 235, 价 236, 伊 237, 巧 238, 兆 244, 旨 263, 圭 267, 合 270, 吉 278, 因 311, 成 322, 住 355, 伝 359, 佐 365, 狂 366, 快 372, 攻 380, 如 412, 好 413, 利 436, 克 442, 芳 480, 芦 484, 至 485, 彣 510, 君 515, 甫 533, 寿 539, 考 540, 孝 541, 身 546, 佼 552, 佶 558, 佳 560, 往 579, 欣 603, 祉 608, 妍 612, 妙 614, 明 623, 林 633, 和 638, 叔 649, 幸 661, 命 671, 宜 675, 宝 676, 芸 689, 若 692, 英 693, 斉 701, 昌 715, 奉 717, 秀 726, 凭 727, 典 733, 辰 738, 尚 753, 承 760, 良 767, 侯 777, 持 801, 洗 817, 治 825, 弥 832, 珍 836, 祝 851, 祐 852, 到 901, 亮 911, 南 912, 表 914, 宣 919, 美 923, 是 947, 忒 954, 香 961, 栄 969, 為 1005, 彦 1007, 省 1013, 俶 1026, 候 1029, 倩 1031, 修 1038, 俊 1039, 悦 1054, 祥 1074, 時 1086, 姞 1089, 桂 1102, 称 1118, 記 1149, 容 1182, 衷 1190, 賀 1194, 泰 1203, 恭 1205, 烈 1211, 恵 1226, 哲 1227, 悌 1289, 惟 1290, 陳 1311, 淑 1335, 済 1336, 淳 1337, 理 1361, 彬 1370, 祗 1380, 能 1397, 訢 1400, 致 1407,

紀 1424, 剛 1429, 宴 1437, 斎 1454, 恕 1483, 康 1509, 逞 1513, 順 1532, 偉 1535, 傅 1536, 備 1539, 愔 1546, 陶 1565, 循 1569, 温 1585, 禄 1589, 斌 1590, 勝 1613, 款 1666, 欽 1678, 敬 1691, 喜 1709, 富 1715, 葭 1725, 董 1731, 最 1742, 営 1751, 覚 1752, 貴 1755, 賀 1756, 巽 1760, 斐 1781, 堅 1796, 善 1799, 達 1810, 慎 1839, 滝 1862, 源 1863, 頎 1866, 暉 1884, 禎 1887, 福 1888, 祺 1903, 睦 1904, 雄 1912, 誠 1935, 幹 1938, 純 1956, 新 1965, 馴 1966, 凱 1967, 義 1975, 寛 1977, 意 2007, 羨 2009, 誉 2010, 資 2012, 豊 2013, 舜 2017, 愛 2018, 督 2023, 楽 2029, 照 2035, 僖 2058, 僐 2059, 徳 2063, 愷 2071, 頔 2114, 禔 2120, 精 2131, 読 2142, 静 2145, 韶 2163, 飾 2164, 穀 2168, 嘉 2184, 節 2215, 愿 2228, 儀 2255, 憘 2257, 徴 2265, 権 2300, 禕 2304, 誼 2322, 毅 2351, 歓 2352, 賞 2377, 鞏 2379, 霊 2390, 賛 2394, 嫯 2403, 熙 2409, 選 2419, 蔵 2424, 慶 2425, 儒 2432, 懌 2439, 衛 2452, 膳 2463, 嬉 2476, 稽 2491, 穆 2494, 頼 2506, 諠 2513, 緯 2529, 綏 2534, 融 2545, 歆 2550, 叡 2555, 褒 2556, 養 2558, 憙 2559, 熹 2560, 燕 2570, 賢 2579, 整 2581, 盧 2594, 臧 2595, 潔 2615, 禧 2628, 謙 2646, 縁 2660, 歛 2674, 懋 2700, 慈 2701, 厳 2706, 瓊 2717, 職 2734, 類 2755, 艶 2833, 蘆 2842, 攀 2851, 賚 2852, 韙 2856, 懽 2863, 徽 2866, 韜 2884, 寵 2893, 麗 2902, 馨 2904, 羴 2909, 曦 2914, 譲 2918, 巌 2936, 懿 2958)

Yoshiaki *m* 可朗 165, 由章 186, 允明 217, 好暁 413, 美章 923, 美誠, 是洞 947, 純明 1956, 「義光 1975, 義明, 義昭, 義韶, 嘉明 2184, 嘉顕, 謙亮 2646

Yoshiakira *m* 仁詮 57, 克知 442, 義礼 1975, 義詮, 義鏡

Yoshiari *m* 能有 1397

Yoshiatsu *m* 吉鍾 278, 良敬 767, 営篤 1751, 義温 1975, 義貴

Yoshiba *s* 与芝 101, 吉羽 278, 吉葉, 吉場, 葭葉 1725

Yoshibayashi *s* 芳林 480

Yoshibuchi *s* 善淵 1799

Yoshibumi *m* 仁文 57

Yoshichi *m* 与七 101

Yoshichika *m* 吉亨 278, 芳幾 480, 祥哉 1074, 敬親 1691, 喜哉 1709, 善隣 1799, 義比 1975, 義央, 義局, 義和, 義愛, 義懐, 豊親 2013, 愛発 2018 「101

Yoshichirō *m* 与七郎

Yoshida *s* 由田 186, 佳田 560 ; *sp* 吉田 278

~ Genjirō *ml* 吉田絃二郎

~ Issui *ml* 吉田一穂

~ Kanetomo *mh* 吉田兼俱 「一

~ Ken'ichi *ml* 吉田健

~ Kōyū *mh* 吉田光由

~ Masatoshi *ml* 吉田正俊 「定房

~ Sadafusa *mh* 吉田

~ Seiichi *ml* 吉田精一

~ Shigeru *mh* 吉田茂

~ Shintō *mh* 吉田神道

~ Shōin *mh* 吉田松陰

~ Tōyō *ml* 吉田冬葉

Yoshidome *s* 吉留

Yoshie *s* 吉江 ; *m* 葭江 1725, 善衛 1799, 義柄 1975 ; *f* 吉柯 278, 好重 413, 省江 1013, 恵江 1226, 惟恵 1290, 彬江 1370, 禎栄 1887, 舜江 2017, 愿江 2228

~ Takamatsu *ml* 吉江喬松 278

Yoshifuji *s* 吉藤

Yoshifumi *m* 典文 733, 恵文 1226, 義文 1975, 義履 「尚古 753

Yoshifuru *m* 宜振 675,

Yoshifusa *m* 良房 767

Yoshiga *s* 吉賀 278

Yoshigaki *s* 吉垣

Yoshihama *s* 吉浜

Yoshihara *s* 葭原 1725

Yoshiharu *m* 与治 101, 好日 413, 利治 436, 美珍 923, 喜東 1709, 義令 1975, 義治, 義晴, 徳晴 2063, 精華 2131

Yoshihashi *s* 吉橋 278

Yoshihi *m* 義陽 1975

Yoshihide *m* 圭秀 267, 吉英 278, 欣秀 603, 淳秀 1337, 義秀 1975, 養秀 2558

Yoshihiko *m* 吉彦 278, 賀彦 1194, 順彦 1532, 義彦 1975, 愛彦 2018, 憙彦 2559

Yoshihira *sm* 吉平 278 ; *m* 楽平 2029, 静平 2145, 嘉衡 2184

Yoshihiro *s* 吉広 278, 吉弘 ; *m* 休広 233, 圭弘 267, 至弘 485, 昌裕 715, 良栄 767, 珍弘 836, 美宏 923, 是太 947, 恵弘 1226, 恵敬, 剛寛 1429, 誠博 1935, 義太 1975, 義公, 義広, 義弘, 愛勲 2018, 誼衡 2322

Yoshihiru *m* 嘉昼 2184

Yoshihisa *m* 好古 413, 芳久 480, 幸久 661, 美久 923, 栄喜 969, 富久 1715, 義久 1975, 義比, 義尚, 義亀

Yoshihito *m* 壬士 116, 宜仁 675, 栄仁 969, 喜仁 1709 「芳井 480

Yoshii *sp* 吉井 278 ; *p*

Yoshiichi *m* 芳市

Yoshiie *m* 吉宿 278, 義寮 1975 「勇 278

Yoshii Isamu *ml* 吉井

Yoshiike *s* 吉池

Yoshiizumi *s* 吉泉

Yoshijima *s* 吉島

Yoshijirō *m* 吉次郎, 芳次郎 480

Yoshika *s* 吉鹿 278 ; *m* 良馨 767, 是香 947, 温乎 1585, 慶香 2425

Yoshikado *m* 義門 1975

Yoshikage *m* 美蔭 923, 義景 1975

Yoshikai *s* 吉開 278

Yoshikane *s* 吉兼 ; *m* 凱金 1967, 義務 1975, 義銀, 義謙, 義鏡

Yoshikata *m* 吉固 278, 善方 1799, 善剛, 祺和 1903, 義堅 1975, 義質

Yoshikatsu *m* 義克, 義勝, 慶勝 2425

Yoshikawa *s* 吉河 278, 芳川 480 ; *sp* 吉川 278

~ Eiji *ml* 吉川英治

~ Kōjirō *ml* 吉川幸次郎 「惟足

~ Koretaru *mh* 吉川

Yoshikazu *m* 孔一 58, 由三 186, 休弌 233, 好一 413, 和三 638, 英一 693, 良知 767, 祥三 1074, 能運 1397, 欽一 1678, 喜一 1709, 喜多, 喜起, 最一 1742, 善一 1799, 誠一 1935, 義五 1975, 義員, 義量, 義数, 義算

Yoshiki *s* 吉木 278, 吉鋪, 吉識 ; *m* 可樹 165, 吉樹 278, 芳樹 480, 祥樹 1074, 義杵 1975, 嘉樹 2184 ; *p* 吉城 278, 吉敷 「101

Yoshikichi *m* 与四吉

Yoshikiyo *s* 吉清 278 ; *m* 吉廉, 温圭 1585, 義清 1975, 義舜, 膳清 2463

Yoshiko *f* 令子 155, 可子 165, 伃子 230, 休子 233, 伊子 237, 吉子 278, 吉孜子, 快子 372, 好子 413, 芳子 480, 佳子 560, 欣子 603, 妍子 612, 良子 767, 良志子, 美子 923, 是子 947, 忯子 954, 俶子 1026, 祥子 1074, 姞子 1089, 淑子 1335, 順子 1532, 愔子 1546, 喜子 1709, 葭子 1725, 賀子 1756, 善子 1799, 頎子 1866, 福子 1888, 祺子 1903, 義子

1975, 羡子 2009, 誉子 2010, 倍子 2058, 僐子 2059, 愷子 2071, 嘉子 2184, 儀子 2255, 歓子 2352, 賛子 2394, 慶子 2425, 懌子 2439, 嬉子 2476, 誼子 2513, 褒子 2556, 憙子 2559, 臧子 2595, 禧子 2628, 懽子 2863, 徽子 2866, 麗子 2902, 懿子 2958

Yoshikoshi *s* 吉越 278

Yoshikoto *m* 為功 1005

Yoshikuni *s* 吉国 278; *m* 吉邑, 誉邦 1751, 斐邦 1781, 善国 1799, 義国 1975, 義城, 義恕, 馨邦 2904

Yoshikura *s* 吉倉 278

Yoshima *s* 与島 101, 吉島 278; *p* 好間 413

Yoshimachi *s* 吉町 278

Yoshimaki *m* 義巻 1975

Yoshimaro *m* 懿麿 2403

Yoshimaru *sm* 吉丸 278; *m* 義巻 1975

Yoshimasa *m* 昌正 715, 彦正 1007, 福督 1888, 純正 1956, 義公 1975, 義正, 義利, 義和, 義政, 義将, 嘉真 2184, 曦正 2914

Yoshimasu *s* 吉益 278

Yoshimatsu *sp* 吉松

Yoshime *f* 烈女 1211

Yoshimi *s* 吉身 278, 吉海, 好見 413, 芦見 484, 妙見 614, 妙美, 美 923; *sp* 吉見 278; *m* 由美 186, 好 413, 叔省 649, 俶躬 1026, 修 1038, 悦耳 1054, 喜望 1709, 福巳 1888, 義視 1975, 穀美 2168, 嘉 2184, 親 2544; *f* 交 293, 好示 413, 幹示 1938

Yoshimichi *sm* 善道 1799; *m* 中行 75, 由路 186, 吉達 278, 吉義, 順康 1532, 貴道 1755, 睦道 1904, 義発 1975, 嘉道 2184

Yoshimine *s* 吉峯 278, 良岑 767; *m* 正節 205

~ no Harutoshi *ml* 良岑玄利 767 「安世

~ no Yasuyo *ml* 良岑

Yoshimitsu *s* 吉光 278, 吉満; *m* 栄光 969, 泰光 1203, 富光 1715, 義光 1975, 義弥; *mh* 義満; *ma* 女光 114

Yoshimizu *s* 吉水 278; *m* 嘉瑞 2184 「1335

Yoshimochi *m* 淑望

Yoshimori *s* 吉森 278; *m* 堅守 1796, 義盛 1975, 義蕃

Yoshimoto *s* 吉元 278, 吉本, 義始 1975; *m* 之元 24, 攻質 380, 好祖 413, 良太 767, 良基, 喜楽 1709, 義故 1975, 義祇, 義質, 義意, 嘉基 2184 「明 278

~ Ryūmei *ml* 吉本隆

Yoshimune *sm* 令宗 155; *m* 令家, 吉宗 278, 義心 1975, 義胸, 義統

Yoshimura *s* 吉村 278, 芳村 480; *m* 良邑 767

~ Tetsutarō *ml* 吉村鉄太郎 278 「寅太郎

~ Toratarō *mh* 吉村

Yoshina *s* 芳名 480

Yoshinaga *sm* 好永 413; *sm-p* 吉永 278; *m* 吉呂, 吉修, 欣永 603, 宝栄 676, 奉永 717, 覚長 1752, 義元 1975, 義修, 義暢, 熙永 2409, 懿修 2958 「*sm* 吉仲

Yoshinaka *s* 吉中 278;

Yoshinao *m* 善直 1799

Yoshinari *sm* 吉成 278; *m* 兆生 244, 好造 413, 幸得 661, 良成 767, 良業, 淑成 1335, 敬愛 1691, 誉成 1751, 義備 1975, 楽成 2029

Yoshindo *m* 喜人 1709

Yoshine *m* 仁道 57, 美稲 923

Yoshino *s* 良野 767; *sp* 吉野 278; *m* 芳野 480; *f* 慶之 2425 「278

~ Hideo *ml* 吉野秀雄

~ Gajō *ml* 吉野臥城

~ Sakuzō *mlh* 吉野作造 「衛門

~ Saemon *ml* 吉野左

~ Shizuka *la* 吉野静

~ Shōji *ml* 吉野鉦二

~ shūi *l* 吉野拾遺

~ Tennin *la* 吉野天人

Yoshinobu *m* 仁信 57, 令寿 155, 吉寅 278, 克修 442, 甫信 533, 致陳 1407, 喜文 1709, 最信 1742, 純信 1956, 慶喜 2425, 賢信 2579; *ml* 能宣 1397

Yoshinori *s* 賀訓 1756; *m* 由後 186, 吉甫 278, 吉品, 佐伝 365, 好玄 413, 好孝, 好義, 克礼 442, 芳徳 480, 良能 767, 珍頼 836, 美仁 923, 美撰, 勝経 1613, 喜鑑 1709, 富則 1715, 貴孝 1755, 義珍 1975, 義則, 義規, 義教, 義徳, 義賢, 義謙, 義鑑, 嘉猷 2184, 嘉徳, 愿徳 2228, 賢礼 2579

Yoshinosuke *m* 義之介 1975 「278

Yoshinotani *p* 吉野谷

Yoshinuma *s* 吉沼

Yoshio *s* 吉尾; *m* 元雄 60, 壬夫 116, 由夫 186, 伊男 237, 吉士 278, 吉雄, 快雄 372, 余四男 448, 芳夫 480, 芳男, 芳雄, 和夫 638, 宜雄 675, 秀郎 726, 尚男 753, 良士 767, 良夫, 良男, 良雄, 祐夫 852, 宜雄 919, 美男 923, 美臣, 栄夫 969, 俶男 1026, 俊夫 1039, 祥男 1074, 桂夫 1102, 能雄 1397, 紀男 1424, 恕夫 1483, 禄夫 1589, 斌夫 1590, 喜雄 1709, 善雄 1799, 義夫 1975, 義男, 義良, 義勇, 義雄, 愛郎 2018, 愛雄, 督応 2023, 皞雄 2114, 留夫 2163, 節雄 2215, 賛雄 2394, 慶夫 2425, 穆夫 2494, 潔雄 2615, 謙雄 2646, 贇夫 2852, 贇雄

Yoshioka *s* 義岡 1975; *sp* 吉岡 278; *m* 淑允 1335 「寺洞 278

~ Zenjidō *ml* 吉岡禅

Yoshioki *m* 義興 1975

Yoshioko *f* 吉報子 278

Yoshira *m* 克郎 442

Yoshirō *m* 由郎 186, 克郎 442, 芳郎 480, 佳郎 560, 倩郎 1031, 善郎 1799, 義郎 1975, 義朗

Yoshisaburō *m* 由三郎 186, 芳三郎 480, 義三郎 1975

Yoshisada *m* 義正, 義貞, 穀定 2168, 慶定 2425

Yoshisane *m* 義積 1975

Yoshisato *m* 能達 1397

Yoshishige *sm* 善滋 1799, 慶滋 2425; *m* 任重 235, 至鎮 485, 良茂 767, 珍重 836, 義蓁 1975, 義調, 義慈, 愛発 2018, 賞成 2377, 懿誉 2958

~ no Yasutane *ml* 慶滋保胤 2425

Yoshishirō *m* 狂四郎 366

Yoshisue *m* 倩孝 1031, 義居 1975

Yoshisuke *m* 由扶 186, 吉相 278, 傅助 1536, 喜又 1709, 純資 1956, 義介 1975, 義助, 義弼, 義輔, 誉弼 2010

Yoshisumi *m* 良澄 767, 義処 1975

Yoshitada *m* 伊賢 237, 吉品 278, 吉祗, 快彰 372, 好忠 413, 好問, 宝忠 676, 良地 767, 致公 1407, 善縄 1799, 純正 1956, 義格 1975, 義恭, 義理, 義質

Yoshitaka *s* 吉高 278; *m* 可官 165, 由恭 186, 成立 322, 克孝 442, 芳喬 480, 孝高 541, 宜孝 675, 宜剛, 美峻 923, 惟高 1290, 剛昴 1429, 喜正 1709, 善尭 1799, 義固 1975, 義垣, 義高, 義隆, 義章, 義旗, 義登, 義喬, 愛雄 2018, 嘉隆 2184

Yoshitake *s* 吉竹 278, 吉武; *m* 芳武 480, 佳丈 560, 義武 1975, 義勇, 義建, 禕健 2304

Yoshitami *m* 義農 1975

Yoshitane *m* 義苗, 義植, 義種

Yoshitani *s* 吉谷 278

Yoshitarō *m* 芳太郎 480, 義太郎 1975
Yoshitatsu *m* 義竜
Yoshiteru *m* 義光, 義照, 義輝, 義曜, 愛昶 2018
Yoshito *m* 吉人 278, 吉人, 芳人 480, 喜仁 1709, 義留 1975
Yoshitō *m* 吉十 278, 良任 767, 義深 1975, 儀任 2255; *f* 佳妙 560
Yoshitoki *m* 由言 186, 吉鴻 278
Yoshitome *m* 義止 1975
Yoshitomi *sp* 吉富 278; *m* 好美 413, 孝福 541, 善富 1799, 義美 1975
Yoshitomo *m* 吉偕 278, 良知 767, 勝伴 1613, 義友 1975, 義知, 義朝, 義栄, 慶寛 2425
Yoshitori *s* 好鳥 413
Yoshitoshi *s* 吉利 278; *m* 禄寿 1589, 喜稔 1709, 禎利 1887, 義勇 1975, 義祚, 義威, 義理, 義智, 義詮, 養利 2558, 職俊 2734
Yoshitsugu *m* 良世 767, 良蒸, 典次 733, 栄胤 969, 義倫 1975, 義著, 義続, 賢次 2579, 膳次 2463
Yoshitsuka *m* 義柄 1975
Yoshitsumu *m* 美積 923, 義諶 1975
Yoshitsune *m* 良経 767; *mh* 義経 1975
~ senbonzakura *la* 義経千本桜
~ Shin Takadachi *l* 義経新高館
Yoshitsura *m* 恕連 1483
Yoshiue *s* 吉植 278; *m* 義高 1975 「亮 278
~ Shōryō *ml* 吉植庄
Yoshiumi *p* 吉海
Yoshiura *s* 吉浦
Yoshiwa *p* 吉和
Yoshiwara *sp* 吉原
~ suzume *a* 吉原雀
Yoshiya *s* 吉屋
~ Nobuko *fl* 吉屋信子
Yoshiyama *s* 吉山, 霊山 2390
Yoshiyasu *m* 伊定 237, 良祺 767, 義温 1975, 義綏, 賢保 2579
Yoshiyori *m* 吉倚 278, 義和 1975
Yoshiyuki *s* 吉行 278; *m* 由之 186, 吉之 278, 如行 412, 好就 413, 利敬 436, 修之 1038, 時之 1086, 致行 1407, 逞之 1513, 敬行 1691, 善之 1799, 義之 1975, 義元, 嘉幸 2184, 頼行 2506 「淳之介 278
~ Junnosuke *ml* 吉行
Yoshizaka *s* 吉阪
Yoshizaki *s* 吉崎
~-bō *ph* 吉崎坊
Yoshizane *m* 凱実 1967
Yoshizawa *s* 吉沢 278, 吉臭, 芳沢 480
~ Yoshinori *ml* 吉沢義則 278
Yoshizō *m* 由蔵 186, 芳蔵 480, 義三 1975
Yoshizu *m* 美静 923
Yoshizuka *s* 吉塚 278
Yoshizumi *s* 吉住, 妙泉 614, 善積 1799; *sm* 善澄; *m* 好純 413, 義澄 1975
Yosōji *m* 与三次 101
Yosomatsu *m* 与三松
Yosomiya *s* 四十宮 188
Yosonara *s* 四十八朝
Yosoo *m* 与曾房 101
Yōsuke *m* 洋右 822
Yosuma *s* 四十方 188
Yosumi *s* 与住 101, 四十住 188
Yosuyama *s* 五十山 91
Yōtarō *m* 陽太郎 1567
Yoto *s* 与等 101
Yotoshi *s* 吉年 278, 吉利
(yotsu 四 188, 肆 2144)
Yotsuami *m* 四綱 188
Yotsugane *sp* 四纒
Yotsugi *s* 世継 335
~ Soga *la* 世継曾我
Yotsukaidō *p* 四街道 188
Yotsukura *p* 四倉
Yotsumoto *s* 四元, 四本
Yotsunoya *s* 乗 1016
Yotsuse *s* 四瀬 188
Yotsutsuji *s* 四辻
~ Yoshinari *ml* 四辻善哉
Yotsuya *s* 四屋, 四家, 肆矢 2144; *sp* 四谷 188
~ kaidan *l* 四谷怪談
Yotto *s* 者度 769
Youchi Soga *la* 夜計曾我 766
Yowa *f* 澔 2268. (弱 1647) 「2558
Yōwa 1181–82 養和
Yowai *m* 秴 1115
Yowa nasake ukina no yokogushi *l* 与話情浮名横櫛 101
~ no nezame *l* 夜半の寝覚 766 「代々木
Yoyogi *s* 代代木 125; *sp*
Yōyōshadan *l* 洋々社談 822
Yoyoshi *l* 世吉 335
Yōzaburō *m* 要三郎 1218 「101
Yozaemon *m* 与左衛門
Yoza ichiryū *a* 四座一流 188
~ yakusha mokuroku *l* 四座役者目録
Yōzō *m* 要造 1218, 要蔵
Yu *s* 湯 1587. (夕 33, 水 54, 弓 95, 由 186, 用 193, 酉 526, 油 593, 柚 857, 羑 922, 容 1182, 悠 1481, 庸 1507, 猶 1555, 游 1574, 湯 1587, 釉 1653, 遊 1809, 楢 1900, 猷 1962, 蓉 1983, 楡 2288A, 愈 2358, 雍 2359, 諭 2510, 融 2545, 踰 2740, 甕 2908)
Yū *s* 由 186; *sp* 由宇; *m* 雄 1912. (又 13, 夕 33, 友 70, 右 171, 由 186, 有 303, 佑 364, 邑 460, 酉 526, 侑 557, 祐 852, 柚 857, 勇 908, 宥 918, 羑 922, 囿 990, 涌 1065, 悠 1481, 猶 1555, 游 1574, 裕 1645, 釉 1653, 遊 1809, 楢 1900, 雄 1912, 猷 1962, 逌 2047, 喩 2064, 踊 2132, 幽 2251, 熊 2410, 融 2545, 優 2599, 鮪 2669)
Yuami *s* 浴 1064. (浴)
Yuamibe *s* 浴部
Yuasa *sp* 湯浅 1587
~ Hangetsu *ml* 湯浅半月
~ Yoshiko *fl* 湯浅芳子
Yuba *s* 弓場 95
Yūbai *ml* 友梅 70
Yubara *s* 由原 186, 油原 593; *sp* 湯原 1587
Yūbari *p* 夕張 33
Yūbetsu *p* 涌別 1065
(yubi 指 800)
Yubisui *s* 指吸
Yubisuku *s* 指宿
Yubu *s* 由布 186
Yuchi *s* 湯池 1587, 湯地
~ Takashi *ml* 湯地孝
Yuda *s* 油田 593; *sp* 湯田 1587
Yūda *s* 紫合 2209
Yue *s* 湯人 1587, 湯生, 湯江, 湯坐; *m* 湯座
Yufuin *p* 湯布院
Yūgao *lf-la* 夕顔 33
Yugawa *s* 油川 593
Yugawara *p* 湯河原 1587
Yugaya *s* 由茅 186
Yuge *s* 弓 95; *sp* 弓削
Yūgen *l* 幽玄 2251
Yugeta *s* 弓削田 95
Yugi *p* 湯来 1587
Yūgiri *lf-fl* 夕霧 33
Yuguchi *s* 湯口 1587
Yūgure ikashū *l* 夕暮遺歌集 33
Yugyō Shōnin *ml* 遊行上人 1809
~ yanagi *la* 遊行柳
Yuhama *s* 由浜 186
Yui *s* 由井, 油井 593, 油比; *sp* 由比 186. (唯 1286, 惟 1290, 結 2151)
Yuichi *m* 由一 186
Yūichi *m* 勇一 908, 雄一 1912 「雄一郎 1912
Yūichirō *m* 悠一郎 1481,
Yuiko *f* 結子 2151
Yuimakyō *l* 維摩経 2540
~ gisho *l* 維摩経義疏
Yuishinbōshū *l* 唯心房集 1286 「正雪 186
Yui Shōsetsu *mh* 由井
Yūji *s* 熊耳 2410; *m* 勇児 908, 雄二 1912, 雄次, 逌爾 2047
Yūjirō *m* 勇治郎 908, 雄二郎 1912

Yūjōbō *s* 祐乗坊 852
(yuka 床 508, 縁 2660)
Yukako *f* 縁子
Yukami *s* 湯上 1587
Yukari *m* 因 311
～ no fujinami *l* 所縁の藤波 600 「梅 186
～ no ume *l* 由佳里の
Yukawa *s* 湯河 1587; *sp* 湯川 「樹
～ Hideki *mlh* 湯川秀
Yukei *s* 靭 1694, 靭負
Yuki *s* 由木 186, 由起, 幸 661; *f* 恕 1483; *f-la* 雪 1495; *p* 由岐 186, 油木 593. (之 24, 于 25, 千 44, 元 60, 介 66, 文 86, 五 91, 升 113, 以 134, 礼 146, 公 156, 由 186, 行 245, 而 264, 先 280, 氏 297, 役 368, 如 412, 判 434, 亨 440, 走 441, 肖 451, 足 461, 志 464, 至 485, 来 538, 孝 541, 侑 557, 往 579, 征 580, 門 601, 放 606, 服 618, 幸 661, 享 662, 迂 749, 抵 797, 政 881, 到 901, 是 947, 為 1005, 将 1040, 徐 1049, 浴 1064, 時 1086, 恭 1205, 晋 1215, 通 1239, 起 1262, 偏 1273, 致 1407, 教 1408, 敏 1409, 章 1461, 恕 1483, 雪 1495, 透 1502, 進 1503, 逞 1513, 順 1532, 随 1564, 循 1569, 就 1668, 舒 1673, 敬 1691, 靭 1694, 喜 1709, 普 1792, 運 1808, 遊 1809, 道 1811, 超 1816, 詣 1930, 猷 1962, 勧 1970, 廉 2042, 歴 2247, 徸 2263, 遵 2418, 徹 2451, 維 2540, 薫 2567, 邁 2592, 潔 2615, 諧 2639, 豁 2667, 鵬 2795)
Yūki *s* 涌喜 1065; *sp* 結城 2151 「果
～ Aisōka *ml* 結城哀草
Yukiami *s* 靭編 1694
Yukichi *m* 諭吉 2510
Yūkichi *m* 祐吉 852, 勇吉 908, 裕吉 1645, 雄吉 1912 「以親 134
Yukichika *m* 千寸 44,
Yukida *s* 行田 245
Yukie *sm-p* 靭負 1694; *f* 亨江 440, 志依 464, 幸守 661, 幸枝, 容甲枝 1182 「1694
Yukienosuke *m* 靭負輔
Yuki Fujin ezu *l* 雪夫人絵図 1495
Yukigawa *s* 行川 245
Yukige *l* 雪解 1495
Yukihara *s* 直原 988
Yukihide *m* 進秀 1503
Yukihira *m* 行平 245
Yukihisa *m* 以久 134, 行芬 245
Yukiho *m* 征帆 580
Yukikage *m* 幸景 661
Yukikane *m* 幸謙
Yukikazu *m* 恭一 1205
Yūki Kenzō *ml* 結城健三 2151
Yukiki *m* 往来 579
Yukikiyo *m* 行心 245
Yukiko *f* 夕起子 33, 夕輝子, 至子 485, 幸子 661, 靭子 1694, 超子 1816 「晋匡 1215
Yukimasa *m* 以修 134,
Yukimatsu *m* 幸松 661
Yukimi *m* 詣見 1930
Yukimichi *m* 之通 24, 如道 412
Yukimitsu *m* 恭光 1205, 敬光 1691
Yukimoto *m* 幸民 661
Yukinaga *s* 浴永 1064; *m* 敬栄 1691
Yukinari *m* 行成 245, 行造, 教成 1408
Yukino *s* 雪野 1495
Yukinobu *m* 之布 24, 行信 245, 如信 412, 章信 1461
Yukinori *m* 行則 245, 順徳 1532 「1495
Yukinoshita *sp* 雪下
Yukio *s* 由木尾 186; *m* 由紀夫, 行夫 245, 行雄, 志雄 464, 往雄 579, 幸男, 幸雄 661, 雪夫 1495, 雪雄, 進男 1503, 敬夫 1691, 靭雄 1694, 喜郎 1709
Yukioka *s* 雪岡 1495
Yukiomi *m* 雪臣
Yuki-onna gomai hagoita *l* 雪夫人女五枚羽子板
Yukisaki *m* 行先 245
Yukishita *s* 雪下 1495
Yūki Somei *ma* 結城素明 2151
Yukitada *m* 行忠 245
Yukitaka *m* 之剛 24, 公孝 156, 幸専 661, 幸高
Yukitake *s* 行武 245
Yukitame *m* 行為
Yukitari *m* 幸足 661
Yukitō *m* 志純 464
Yukitoki *m* 幸辰 661
Yukitomo *m* 志朝 464
Yukitoshi *m* 行歳 245, 征捷 580, 幸年 661
Yukiyama *s* 行山 245, 雪山 1495
Yukiyasu *m* 幸健 661
Yukiyo *m-f* 幸世
Yukiyoshi *m* 行欣 245, 幸宜 661
Yukizawa *s* 行沢 245
Yukizō *m* 章三 1461
Yūko *f* 木綿子 109
Yūkō *m* 雄幸 1912
(yuku 水 54, 徂 577, 征 580, 許 1403, 款 1666, 巽 1760, 路 1725, 雲 2027, 適 2240)
Yukuhashi *p* 行橋 245
Yukuko *f* 徂子 577, 適子 2240 「夫 580
Yukuo *m* 行郎 245, 征
Yūma *s* 遊馬 1809
Yume no ukihashi *l* 夢浮橋 1990
Yumesaki *p* 夢前
Yumesuke *m* 夢助
Yumi *s* 由美 186. (弓 95, 弨 833) 「95
Yumiharizuki *l* 弓張月
Yumiko *f* 弓子
Yumimaro *m* 弓麿
Yumino *s* 弓野
Yumita *s* 弓田 「幡
Yumi Yawata *la* 弓矢
Yumoto *sp* 湯本 1587
～ Kisaku *ml* 湯本喜作
Yumura *s* 湯村, 湯邑
Yunamochi *s* 弓納持 95
Yuni *sp* 由仁 186
Yūnoki *s* 柚木 857
Yunomae *p* 湯前 1587
Yūnosuke *m* 勇之助 908, 雄之助 1912
Yunotani *p* 湯之谷 1587
Yunoura *p* 湯浦
Yura *sp* 由良 186
Yuranosuke *m* 由良之助 「利 186
Yuri *sf* 百合 265; *sp* 由
Yurigorō *m* 百合五郎 265
Yuri Kimimasa *mh* 由利公正 186
Yuriko *f* 由里子, 百合子 265 「助 186
Yurinosuke *m* 由利之
Yuriwaka Daijin *l* 百合若大臣 265
Yūroku *m* 祐六 852
(yuru 万 43)
Yurugi *s* 余綾 448
Yuruki *s* 万木 43
Yurusu *m* 恕 1483
Yūryaku *mh* 雄略 1912
Yusa *sp* 遊佐 1809
Yūsaburō *m* 勇三郎 908, 雄三郎 1912
Yūsai *ml* 幽斎 2251
～-ō kikigaki *l* 幽斎翁聞書
Yūsaki *s* 結崎 2151
Yūsaku *m* 勇作 908
Yūshi hōgen *l* 遊子方言 1809
Yūshō *ma* 友松 70
(yusu 檮 2724)
Yusuhara *p* 檮原
Yūsuke *m* 雄祐 1912, 裕輔 1645
Yusumi *s* 五百姓 91
(yusuru 万 43)
Yusurugi *s* 万木, 石動山 172 「2013)
(yuta 支 63, 茂 691, 豊
Yutahito *m* 茂仁 691, 豊仁 2013
Yutaka *m* 大 48, 完 471, 坦 574, 担 581, 肥 617, 胖 843, 浩 1068, 泰 1203, 隆 1313, 游 1574, 温 1585, 裕 1645, 富 1715, 最 1742, 亶 1972, 寛 1977, 粲 2019, 僩 2054, 愷 2071, 碩 2116, 綽 2529, 優 2599, 穣 2802, 饒 2925; *m-p* 豊 2013
Yutani *s* 油谷 593
Yūtarō *m* 祐太郎 852, 勇太郎 808, 雄太郎 1912, 猷太郎 1962
Yūtō *p* 雄踏 1912

Yutsugi *s* 湯次 1587
Yutsuki *f* 弓槻 95
Yūtsukuri *s* 作木綿 362
Yūwa *p* 雄和 1912
Yuya *s* 油屋 593, 建陽 995; *sp* 油谷 593; *fa-la* 湯谷 1587, 熊野 2410
Yuyama *s* 湯山 1587
Yuyū *s* 唯有 1286
Yuza *s* 由座 186
Yuzawa *sp* 湯沢 1587
Yūzen *l* 祐喜 852
～ -zome *a* 友禅染 70
Yūzō *m* 有三 303, 酉三 526, 勇三 908, 勇蔵
(yuzu 柚 857)
Yuzuhara *s* 由原 186, 柚原 857 「1587
Yuzukami *p* 湯津上
Yuzuki *s* 柚木 857; *m* 弓月 95
～ no Kimi *mh* 弓月君
Yuzuri *m* 譲 2918. (杠 418) 「杜 423
Yuzuriha *s* 杠, 杠葉; *sp*
Yuzuru *m* 弓弦 95, 由豆流 186, 遜 2591, 謙 2646, 譲 2918

# Z

(za 坐 542, 座 1245, 解 1923)
Zada *s* 座田 1245
Zai *f* 解以 1923. (才 35, 在 314, 材 420, 財 1143, 罪 2006)
Zaitsu *s* 財津 1143
Zakame *s* 座亀 1245
Zakku *s* 雑供 2127
Zakkube *s* 雑供戸
Zakōji *s* 座光寺 1245
(zaku 酢 1654)
Zama *p* 座間 1245
(zan 暫 2402, 欑 2986)
Zanboa *l* 朱欒 341
Zaō *p* 蔵王 2424
Zappai *l* 雑誹 2127
(zatsu 雑) 「1738)
(ze 是 947, 柴 1221, 崔
Zeami *mla* 世阿弥 335
Zeeroku bushidō *l* 上方武士道 47
Zegai *la* 是我意 947, 是界, 善界 1799
(zei 税 1642, 説 2143, 誓 2218)
Zeisho *s* 税所 1642
Zejū *s* 膳住 2463
Zekkai Chūshin *ml* 絶海中津 2148
Zen *s* 善 1799, 膳 2463. (全 271, 担 581, 浅 827, 前 921, 泉 964, 染 968, 棧 1615, 然 1788, 善 1799, 禅 1886, 僐 2059, 漸 2081, 潜 2272, 賤 2318, 膳 2463, 髯 2580, 瓊 2717, 蟬 2733)
Zenbee *m* 善兵衛 1799
Zenbōji *s* 善法寺
Zenchiku *mla* 禅竹 1886
Zendōji *p* 善導寺 1799
(zeni 銭 2160)
Zen'ichi *m* 善一 1799
Zen'ichirō *m* 善一郎
Zenigata *s* 銭形 2160
～ Heiji torimono hikae *l* 銭形平次捕物控 「沢
Zenikamezawa *p* 銭亀
Zeniya *s* 銭屋
Zenjirō *m* 善次郎 1799, 善治郎
Zenji Soga *la* 禅師曾我 1886
Zenjūrō *m* 善十郎 1799, 善重郎
Zensaburō *m* 善三郎
Zensaku *m* 善作
Zenshichi *m* 善七
Zenshirō *m* 善四郎
Zenshū *h* 禅宗 1886
Zensuke *m* 善助 1799
Zentarō *m* 善太郎
Zentei *s* 全亭 271
Zentsūji *p* 善通寺 1799
(zetsu 絶 2148)
Zeze *s* 膳所 2463
(zo 助 431, 徂 577, 祚 1126)
(zō 三 22, 匠 503, 造 1236, 曹 1479, 象 1761, 曾 1794, 像 2061, 増 2077, 雑 2127, 憶 2440, 橡 2478, 贓 2595)
Zōami *ma* 増阿弥 2077
Zōdanshū *l* 雑談集 2127
Zōhiki *l* 象引 1761
Zōichi *m* 像一 2061
Zōji *m* 造次 1236
Zōki *ml* 増基 2077.
(zoku 俗 776, 族 1343, 粟 1763, 属 1802, 続 2334)
Zoku akegarasu *l* 続明烏
～ dōchū hizakurige *l* 続道中膝栗毛
～ gosenshū *l* 続後選集 「遺集
～ goshūishū *l* 続後拾
～ honchō monzui *l* 続本朝文粋
～ kojidan *l* 続古事談
～ kokinshū *l* 続古今集
～ Nihon kōki *l* 続日本後記
～ nijinshū *l* 続耳塵集
～ sarumino *l* 続猿蓑
～ senzaishū *l* 続千載集
～ shintō taii *l* 俗神道大意 776
～ shūishū *l* 続拾遺集 2334
～ sōanshū *l* 続草庵集
～ Urashimago-no-den *l* 続浦島子伝
(zon 存 313)
(zu 不 94, 豆 438, 図 502, 治 825, 津 826, 逗 1511, 頭 2504, 綜 2528, 鶴 2926)
(zui 垂 761, 萃 1442, 随 1564, 瑞 2094, 穂 2308, 穏 2728)
Zuichō *s* 随朝 1564
Zuikei Shūhō *ml* 瑞渓周鳳 2094
Zuishō *ml* 瑞笑
Zuku *m* 木菟 109
(zumi 泉 965)
Zumoto *s* 頭本 2504
Zundo *s* 百度 265
Zushi *s* 図師 502; *p* 逗子 1511
Zusho *s* 調所 2328
～ Hirosato *mh* 調所広郷

# APPENDICES

# Appendix 1

## NAME CHARACTERS ARRANGED BY RADICALS

The following list contains all the characters given in Part I as initial characters, including the variant forms and the old forms of *tōyō kanji,* arranged in the traditional way according to their radicals and additional strokes. The classification in Nelson's *The Modern Reader's Japanese-English Character Dictionary* has been followed for the characters given there, and that in Ueda's *Daijiten* for other characters.

The numbers to the left of the characters indicate the number of strokes in them apart from the radical elements; and those to the right, the numbers under which the characters are listed in Part I of the index.

### RAD. 1

| Strokes | Character | No. |
|---|---|---|
| | 一 | 3 |
| 1 | 丁 | 8 |
| 2 | 三 | 22 |
| | 于 | 25 |
| | 万 | 43 |
| | 下 | 46 |
| | 与 | 101 |
| 3 | 五 | 91 |
| | 天 | 93 |
| | 不 | 94 |
| | 丑 | 99 |
| | 互 | 200 |
| 4 | 丕 | 163 |
| | 可 | 165 |
| | 且 | 192 |
| | 丙 | 198 |
| | 平 | 203 |
| | 正 | 205 |
| | 丞 | 296 |
| | 民 | 333 |
| 5 | 亘 | 262 |
| | 百 | 265 |
| | 亙 | 317 |
| | 両 | 531 |
| 6 | 呑 | 489 |
| | 吾 | 491 |
| | 巫 | 524 |
| | 亜 | 525 |
| | 更 | 528 |
| 7 | 武 | 751 |
| | 兩 | 755 |
| | 東 | 771 |
| | 画 | 991 |
| | 函 | 1232 |
| 8 | 昼 | 983 |
| 9 | 夏 | 1161 |
| | 哥 | 1193 |
| | 晋 | 1215 |
| 10 | 悪 | 1483A |
| 11 | 甦 | 1814 |
| 13 | 爾 | 2250 |
| 18 | 璽 | 2860 |

### RAD. 2

| Strokes | Character | No. |
|---|---|---|
| | 丨 | 1 |
| 2 | 也 | 23 |
| 3 | 中 | 75 |
| | 内 | 81 |
| | 卍 | 197 |
| 4 | 旧 | 119 |
| | 弁 | 151 |
| | 央 | 182 |
| | 史 | 183 |
| | 甲 | 184 |
| | 申 | 185 |
| | 由 | 186 |
| | 冊 | 190 |
| | 本 | 212 |
| | 凸 | 323 |
| | 世 | 335 |
| | 出 | 523 |
| 5 | 州 | 224 |
| | 印 | 260 |
| | 向 | 312 |
| | 曲 | 327 |
| 7 | 串 | 516 |
| | 果 | 770 |
| | 表 | 914 |
| 8 | 帥 | 883 |
| | 衷 | 1190 |
| | 甚 | 1267 |
| | 幽 | 2251 |
| 9 | 師 | 1130 |
| | 剛 | 1429 |
| 10 | 粛 | 1528 |
| 11 | 棗 | 1757 |
| 12 | 肅 | 2248 |
| 13 | 暢 | 2111 |
| 15 | 鴨 | 2489 |

### RAD. 3

| Strokes | Character | No. |
|---|---|---|
| 1 | 乂 | 5 |
| 3 | 尤 | 106 |
| 4 | 必 | 120 |
| | 氷 | 140 |
| | 永 | 149 |
| | 半 | 213 |
| 6 | 甫 | 533 |
| | 求 | 537 |
| 8 | 単 | 919A |
| | 為 | 1005 |
| 10 | 巢 | 1431 |
| | 梵 | 1490 |
| 12 | 業 | 2024 |
| 17 | 叢 | 2778 |

### RAD. 4

| Strokes | Character | No. |
|---|---|---|
| 1 | 〆 | 7 |
| | 九 | 16 |
| | 乃 | 27 |
| 2 | 丈 | 36 |
| | 丸 | 40 |
| | 千 | 44 |
| | 久 | 45 |
| | 及 | 83 |
| 3 | 丹 | 79 |
| | 少 | 88 |
| | 尹 | 98 |
| | 井 | 103 |
| | 夫 | 104 |
| | 午 | 112 |
| | 升 | 113 |
| 4 | 斥 | 167 |
| | 丼 | 206 |
| | 未 | 210 |
| | 末 | 211 |
| | 包 | 218 |
| | 丘 | 219 |
| | 乎 | 221 |
| | 弗 | 330 |
| 5 | 后 | 304 |
| | 危 | 318 |
| | 吏 | 329 |
| | 朱 | 341 |
| | 年 | 342 |
| | 争 | 344 |
| | 夷 | 535 |
| 6 | 励 | 430 |
| | 兵 | 499 |
| | 乕 | 500 |
| | 夾 | 534 |
| | 束 | 536 |
| | 来 | 538 |
| | 寿 | 539 |
| | 兎 | 544 |
| | 我 | 545 |
| | 承 | 760 |
| | 系 | 977 |
| 7 | 刷 | 655 |
| | 奉 | 717 |
| | 垂 | 761 |
| | 兔 | 763 |
| 8 | 卑 | 976 |
| | 盾 | 984 |
| | 咫 | 996 |
| | 眉 | 997 |
| | 看 | 998 |
| | 省 | 1013 |
| | 乗 | 1016 |
| | 重 | 1017 |
| | 胤 | 1269 |
| 9 | 殷 | 1139 |
| | 烏 | 1256 |
| | 勉 | 1263 |
| | 乘 | 1265 |
| | 島 | 1522 |
| 10 | 尉 | 1410 |
| | 彫 | 1412 |
| | 爽 | 1529 |
| | 兜 | 1800 |
| 11 | 喬 | 1775 |
| | 奥 | 1798 |
| 12 | 辟 | 1919 |
| | 殿 | 1960 |
| 14 | 戲 | 2350 |
| 15 | 縣 | 2825 |
| 16 | 巌 | 2706 |

### RAD. 5

| Strokes | Character | No. |
|---|---|---|
| | 乙 | 2 |
| 1 | 七 | 17 |
| 3 | 巴 | 97 |
| | 屯 | 222 |
| 7 | 乳 | 657 |
| 10 | 乿 | 1971 |
| 13 | 亂 | 2175 |

### RAD. 6

| Strokes | Character | No. |
|---|---|---|
| 1 | 了 | 9 |
| 2 | 才 | 35 |
| 3 | 予 | 62 |
| 7 | 事 | 768 |

### RAD. 7

| Strokes | Character | No. |
|---|---|---|
| | 二 | 4 |
| 2 | 元 | 60 |
| | 云 | 147 |
| 6 | 亞 | 1264 |
| 10 | 亶 | 1700 |

### RAD. 8

| Strokes | Character | No. |
|---|---|---|
| 1 | 之 | 24 |
| 2 | 六 | 61 |
| 3 | 市 | 195 |
| | 主 | 196 |
| 4 | 交 | 293 |
| | 亦 | 325 |
| | 亥 | 519 |
| | 充 | 521 |
| 5 | 亨 | 440 |
| 6 | 享 | 662 |
| | 京 | 663 |
| | 卒 | 732 |
| | 夜 | 766 |
| | 盲 | 936 |
| | 育 | 958 |
| 7 | 亭 | 909 |
| | 亮 | 910 |

# Appendix 2

# LIST OF RADICALS

The following is the traditional listing of the 214 radicals and radical numbers, arranged according to stroke count. Numbers in parentheses indicate variant forms as noted by Nelson.

| | | | | | | | | | | | | |
|---|---|---|---|---|---|---|---|---|---|---|---|---|
| **1** | 一 | 一 | 丨 | 丨 | 丶 | 丿 | 丿 | 一 | 乙 | 乚 | 乚 | 亅 |
| | 1 | (1) | 2 | (2) | 3 | 4 | (4) | (4) | 5 | (5) | (5) | 6 |
| **2** | 二 | 二 | 亠 | 亠 | 人 | 亻 | 𠆢 | 儿 | 入 | 入 | 八 | 八 |
| | 7 | (7) | 8 | (8) | 9 | (9) | (9) | 10 | 11 | (11) | 12 | (12) |
| 丷 | 冂 | 冂 | 冂 | 冂 | 冖 | 冫 | 几 | 几 | 凵 | 刀 | 刂 | 力 |
| (12) | 13 | (13) | (13) | (13) | 14 | 15 | 16 | (16) | 17 | 18 | (18) | 19 |
| 勹 | 匕 | 匕 | 匚 | 匚 | 匸 | 十 | 十 | 十 | 卜 | 卜 | 卜 | 卩 |
| 20 | 21 | (21) | 22 | (22) | 23 | 24 | (24) | (24) | 25 | (25) | (25) | 26 |
| 㔾 | 厂 | 厶 | 又 | 又 | 辶 | 阝 | 阝 | | | | | |
| (26) | 27 | 28 | 29 | (29) | (162) | (163) | (170) | | | | | |
| **3** | 口 | 囗 | 土 | 士 | 土 | 士 | 夂 | 夊 | 夂 | 夊 | 夕 | 大 |
| | 30 | 31 | 32 | (32) | (32) | 33 | 34 | (34) | (34) | 35 | 36 | 37 |
| 大 | 女 | 子 | 宀 | 寸 | 小 | ⺌ | 尢 | 尸 | 屮 | 屮 | 山 | 川 |
| (37) | 38 | 39 | 40 | 41 | 42 | (42) | 43 | 44 | 45 | (45) | 46 | 47 |
| 巛 | 工 | 己 | 已 | 巳 | 巾 | 干 | 幺 | 广 | 廴 | 廾 | 廾 | 弋 |
| (47) | 48 | 49 | (49) | (49) | 50 | 51 | 52 | 53 | 54 | 55 | (55) | 56 |
| 弓 | 彐 | 彐 | 彑 | 彡 | 彳 | 忄 | 扌 | 氵 | 丬 | 犭 | 艹 | 辶 |
| 57 | 58 | (58) | (58) | 59 | 60 | (61) | (64) | (85) | (90) | (94) | (140) | (162) |
| **4** | 心 | ⺗ | 忄 | 戈 | 戈 | 戶 | 户 | 手 | 手 | 扌 | 支 | 支 |
| | 61 | (61) | (61) | 62 | (62) | 63 | (63) | 64 | (64) | (64) | 65 | (65) |
| 攴 | 攵 | 文 | 斗 | 斤 | 方 | 无 | 旡 | 日 | 曰 | 月 | 木 | 欠 |
| 66 | (66) | 67 | 68 | 69 | 70 | 71 | (71) | 72 | 73 | 74 | 75 | 76 |
| 止 | 歹 | 歹 | 殳 | 毌 | 母 | 比 | 毛 | 毛 | 氏 | 气 | 水 | 氵 |
| 77 | 78 | (78) | 79 | 80 | (80) | 81 | 82 | (82) | 83 | 84 | 85 | (85) |
| 氺 | 火 | 灬 | 爪 | 爪 | 爫 | 爫 | 父 | 爻 | 爻 | 爿 | 丬 | 片 |
| (85) | 86 | (86) | 87 | (87) | (87) | (87) | 88 | 89 | (89) | 90 | (90) | 91 |
| 牙 | 牛 | 牜 | 犬 | 王 | 王 | 𤴓 | 礻 | 内 | 耂 | 月 | 月 | 艹 |
| 92 | 93 | (93) | 94 | (96) | (96) | (103) | (113) | (114) | (125) | (130) | (130) | (140) |

| 5 | 无 (71) | 旡 (71) | 母 (80) | 比 (81) | 氺 (85) | 牙 (92) | 玄 95 | 玉 96 | 王 (96) | 𤣩 (96) | 瓜 97 | 瓦 98 |
|---|---|---|---|---|---|---|---|---|---|---|---|---|
| 甘 99 | 生 100 | 用 101 | 田 102 | 疋 103 | 𤴔 (103) | 疒 104 | 癶 105 | 白 106 | 皮 107 | 皿 108 | 目 109 | 矛 110 |
| 矢 111 | 石 112 | 示 113 | 礻 (113) | 禸 114 | 禾 115 | 穴 116 | 穴 (116) | 立 117 | 立 (117) | 罒 (122) | 艮 (138) | 衤 (145) |
| 6 | 竹 113 | ⺮ (118) | 米 119 | 糸 120 | 缶 121 | 网 122 | 罒 (122) | 羊 123 | ⺶ (123) | ⺷ (123) | 羽 124 | 羽 (124) |
| 老 125 | 耂 (125) | 而 126 | 耒 127 | 耒 (127) | 耳 128 | 耳 (128) | 聿 129 | ⺻ (129) | 肉 130 | 肉 (130) | 月 (130) | 月 (130) |
| 臣 131 | 自 132 | 至 133 | 臼 134 | 舌 135 | 舛 136 | 舟 137 | 舟 (137) | 艮 138 | 艮 (138) | 色 139 | 艸 140 | 艹 (140) |
| 艹 (140) | 虍 141 | 虫 142 | 血 143 | 血 (143) | 行 144 | 衣 145 | 衤 (145) | 西 146 | 襾 (146) | 覀 (146) | 豕 (152) | 𧾷 (157) |
| 7 | 臣 (131) | 舛 (136) | 見 147 | 角 148 | 言 149 | 谷 150 | 豆 151 | 豕 152 | 豸 (153) | 貝 154 | 赤 155 | 走 156 |
| 足 157 | 身 158 | 車 159 | 辛 160 | 辰 161 | 辰 (161) | 辵 162 | 邑 163 | 酉 164 | 釆 165 | 里 166 | 镸 (168) | 麦 (199) |
| 8 | 金 167 | 長 168 | 镸 (168) | 門 169 | 阜 170 | 隶 171 | 隹 172 | 雨 173 | 青 174 | 靑 (174) | 非 175 | 斉 (210) |
| 9 | 面 176 | 革 177 | 韭 179 | 音 180 | 頁 181 | 風 182 | 飛 183 | 食 184 | 飠 (184) | 食 (184) | 首 185 | 香 186 |
| 10 | 韋 (178) | 馬 187 | 骨 188 | 高 189 | 髟 190 | 鬥 191 | 鬯 192 | 鬲 193 | 鬼 194 | 鬼 (194) | 竜 (212) | 竜 (212) |
| 11 | 髙 (189) | 魚 195 | 鳥 196 | 鹵 197 | 鹿 198 | 鹿 (198) | 麥 199 | 麻 200 | 麻 (200) | 黄 (201) | 黒 (203) | 亀 (213) |
| 12 | 黃 201 | 黄 (201) | 黍 202 | 黑 203 | 黒 (203) | 黹 204 | 黽 (205) | 鼎 (206) | 歯 (211) | | | |
| 13-14 | 黽 205 | 鼎 206 | 鼓 207 | 鼔 (207) | 鼠 208 | 鼠 (208) | 鼔 (207) | 鼻 209 | 鼻 (209) | 齊 210 | 斉 (210) | |
| 15-17 | 齒 211 | 齒 (211) | 龍 212 | 竜 (212) | 竜 (212) | 龜 213 | 亀 (213) | 龠 214 | | | | |

The "weathermark" identifies this book as having been designed and produced at the Tokyo offices of John Weatherhill, Inc. Typography and book design by Meredith Weatherby. Composed and printed by Kenkyusha, Tokyo. Bound at the Okamoto Binderies, Tokyo. The type face used is Monotype Imprint, with Chinese characters in hand-set Mincho and display matter in hand-set Futura.